I0814026

"Reading the New Testament, intentionally, through one's ethnic point of view (African American, Asian American, Hispanic, or Native American) does not violate an objective, traditional reading of Scripture. Rather, reading the Bible in and out of one's location exposes the bias of the (formerly so-called) 'objective' reading as a Euro-white reading and, at the same time, offers to the traditional readings fresh perspectives. Over and over. I thought the essays were worth the price of this book, but I was wrong. The commentaries interact with the essays in a manner that makes this book a required desk companion for anyone who wants to hear all the Word of God has to offer. A must-have for all Bible teachers and pastors."

Scot McKnight, author of *The Second Testament: A New Translation* and Julius R. Mantey Chair of New Testament at Northern Seminary

"In my own theological education, I was pressured to suppress my ethnic perspective and experiences, to conform to some sort of disembodied neutrality. Since then I have come to learn that my background, culture, and reading lens can actually enhance my ability to understand Scripture. I am thrilled to recommend *The New Testament in Color* because this 'library-in-a-book' reflects the beautiful mosaic of a many-colored hermeneutic. I wish someone had handed this book to me twenty-five years ago, and I hope many will read it now."

Nijay Gupta, professor of New Testament at Northern Seminary and author of *Tell Her Story: How Women Led, Taught, and Ministered in the Early Church*

"Rooted in a confessional commitment to the trustworthiness of Scripture, this book draws together a diverse group of theologically minded scholars. Together they explore the multiple interpretive possibilities that emerge when Christians read across and within racial and ethnic difference. Here the promise is that God's Word will be more faithfully understood when the colorful tapestry of God's creation of multiple cultures and peoples is embraced. In these ways, this book joins a vital chorus of minoritized biblical scholars who invite readers to ponder the Bible and its readers in rich multiplicity."

Eric Barreto, Weyerhaeuser Associate Professor of New Testament at Princeton Theological Seminary

"While it is not uncommon to encounter socially located interpretations grounded in a hermeneutic of suspicion, this work speaks from one of trust in the biblical text and a commitment to the central tenets of the Christian faith. It also moves beyond theories about these interpretations (although it does provide those discussions) to commentary on every New Testament book. This volume is a constructive contribution to debates about fundamental matters of interpretation from an impressive set of scholars of diverse ethnicities."

M. Daniel Carroll R. (Rodas), Scripture Press Ministries Professor of Biblical Studies and Pedagogy, Wheaton College

"The contributors of *The New Testament in Color* are experts not only in the biblical subject matter but also in identifying and sharing the gifts their social location brings to the hermeneutical task. The scope of this one-volume commentary provides a nearly kaleidoscopic vision of richly varied perspectives together with solid exegesis of the texts. The editors and authors have done the church and academy a great service, shaping a resource that promises to be a boon for seminary reading lists, a go-to in church and university libraries, and a must-have on every pastor's desk."

Kara Lyons-Pardue, professor of New Testament, Point Loma Nazarene University

"The American evangelical church has desperately needed this book, *The New Testament in Color*. For those of us who value the power and authority of God's Word while aware of the diverse experiences and realities that shape our own culturally unique stories, we have longed for this book. This text reminds us that God is a transcendent God who speaks through a transcendent source, but that God is also God with us, immanent in the Word and also in our lives."

Soong-Chan Rah, Robert B. Munger Professor of Evangelism at Fuller Theological Seminary and author of *The Next Evangelicalism*

"McCaulley, Ok, Padilla, Peeler, and the volume's contributors have broken new ground with *The New Testament in Color*. Its essays and commentary, written by scholars of the New Testament from across racial, ethnic, and gender identities, emerge from critical, socially located methods and insights that are also informed by the writers' ecclesial perspectives and experiences. The result is an important one-volume commentary on the New Testament that speaks from and reaches out to both academic and ecclesial communities."

Mary Foskett, Wake Forest Kahle Professor of religious studies and John Thomas Albritton Fellow at Wake Forest University

"*The New Testament in Color* is a book I long hoped would eventually be written and is in many ways overdue. The editors have done a superb job of gathering scholars from diverse ethnic backgrounds who interpret the biblical text adeptly using the familiar critical tools of exegesis, and who also demonstrate how reading from their particular social location provides theological insight germane to all of God's people. They show how the New Testament addresses a range of issues important to today's readers, including topics of restorative justice, immigration and hospitality, racial bias and violence, the priority of families and ecclesial communities, and so much more. Not to be missed are the excellent introductory essays, which trace the ethnic histories of peoples of color and their practice of reading the Bible with a hermeneutic of trust. Exegetically precise, theologically orthodox, and prophetically challenging, this book—in a word—preaches!"

Max J. Lee, Paul W. Brandel Professor of biblical studies at North Park Theological Seminary, Chicago, Illinois

"*The New Testament in Color* is informative, prophetic, reflective, and inspiring. The authors, drawn from a variety of ethnic backgrounds, are self-aware of their social location and write with a hermeneutic of trust in Scripture. This volume makes an extraordinary contribution to New Testament studies and sets the standard for future commentaries."

Lynn H. Cohick, distinguished professor of New Testament and director of Houston Theological Seminary, Houston Christian University

"This is the book I've been searching for throughout my teaching career. There is academic excellence here, coupled with a prophetic call to hear God's Word through the rich diversity of the authors' cultural, ethnic, and racial perspectives and wisdom. There is pastoral sensitivity to the varied experiences of readers, from the emotional and psychological toll of racialized oppression to the exhortation to humility directed toward White Christians (like me). Professors, students, and all participants in the body of Christ will find *The New Testament in Color* to be a valuable, instructive, and challenging resource for understanding the Bible, the church, and Christian discipleship."

Caryn A. Reeder, professor of New Testament at Westmont College

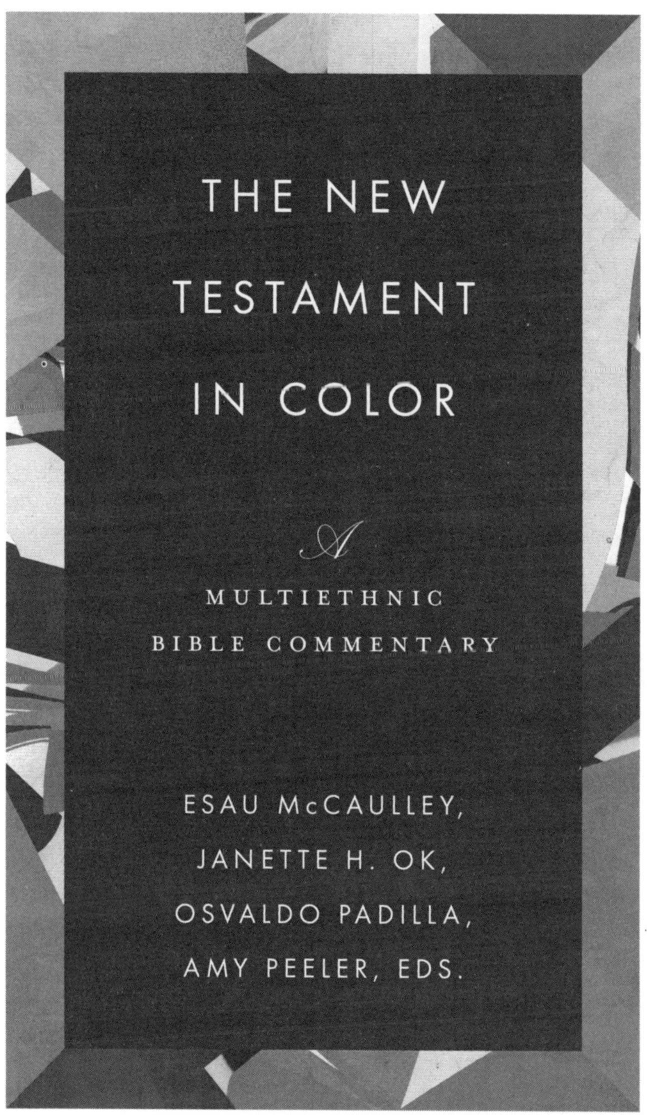

An imprint of InterVarsity Press
Downers Grove, Illinois

InterVarsity Press
P.O. Box 1400 | Downers Grove, IL 60515-1426
ivpress.com | email@ivpress.com

InterVarsity Press® is the publishing division of InterVarsity Christian Fellowship/USA®. For more information, visit intervarsity.org.

Cover design: David Fassett
Interior design: Daniel van Loon

ISBN 978-0-8308-1409-1 (print) | ISBN 978-0-8308-1829-7 (digital)

Printed in the United States of America ♾

Library of Congress Cataloging-in-Publication Data

Names: McCaulley, Esau, editor. | Ok, Janette H., editor. | Padilla, Osvaldo, editor. | Peeler, Amy L. B., editor.
Title: The New Testament in color : a multiethnic Bible commentary / Esau McCaulley, Janette H. Ok, Osvaldo Padilla, Amy Peeler, eds.
Description: Downers Grove, IL : IVP Academic, [2024] | Includes bibliographical references and index.
Identifiers: LCCN 2024004896 (print) | LCCN 2024004897 (ebook) | ISBN 9780830814091 (print) | ISBN 9780830818297 (digital)
Subjects: LCSH: Bible. New Testament–Commentaries. | BISAC: RELIGION / Biblical Commentary / New Testament / General | RELIGION / Biblical Studies / New Testament / General
Classification: LCC BS2341.52 .N495 2024 (print) | LCC BS2341.52 (ebook) | DDC 225.7–dc23/eng/20240227
LC record available at https://lccn.loc.gov/2024004896
LC ebook record available at https://lccn.loc.gov/2024004897

31 30 29 28 27 26 25 24 | 13 12 11 10 9 8 7 6 5 4 3 2

To our students and colleagues

at Beeson Divinity School, Fuller Theological Seminary,

and Wheaton College. We are grateful for your support

and pray that this book is a blessing to you!

CONTENTS

ACKNOWLEDGMENTS

Together, the volume editors would like to collectively thank IVP, who worked to bring this project to completion, including Anna Gissing for supporting the vision of the book and Rachel Hastings for all her hard work in getting it across the finish line.

Esau: I want to thank the coeditors: Amy, Osvaldo, and Janette for the unwavering diligence.

Janette: Thank you, Esau McCaulley, for initiating this project and inviting me to join the editorial team. It was an honor to work with you, Amy Peeler, and Osvaldo Padilla. Thanks to Phil King for helping me review manuscripts at the earliest stages. I am grateful for the Johnston-Barsotti Family Fellowship, which allowed me to complete this project during my sabbatical leave. Lastly, I am indebted to our contributors for making *The New Testament in Color* a rich, nuanced, and insightful gift to the church and all who read it.

Osvaldo: Thank you to my students at Beeson Divinity School, who have shown great enthusiasm for this project. May it be a blessing to you just as you bless my life daily. And a special thanks to Amy, Esau, and Janette, who have taught me a lot during this process.

Amy: Thank you to Esau McCaulley for inviting me into this project, and Janette Ok and Osvaldo Padilla for excellent conversations. I have learned so much from your work and from working with you. I am also grateful to the Center for Pastor Theologians who allowed me to explore the meaning of participating in this project at their Confronting Racial Injustice Conference.

INTRODUCTION

Esau D. McCaulley

I was sitting in a coffee shop, books taking up too much space on the tiny table in front of me, bemoaning the lack of attention the academy paid to the Black church and the distinctive interpretative habits of African American church leaders and scholars. My time in religious higher education had signaled in ways large and small its belief that the tradition that shaped me had little to say to the rest of the world. The important ideas and trends arose in Europe or White North American spaces.

Black Christians were deemed theologically simplistic or dangerous. I longed for people to know the tradition as I experienced it: life giving, spiritually robust, and intellectually stimulating. We had wrestled with God and found our way toward faith in the context of anti-Black racism often perpetuated by other Christians. I wanted to make that story and the fruits of our labor known. I still do.

While I sipped my coffee, I was struck by an idea that served as the genesis for this book. I often complained about White scholars neglecting African American voices, but I knew little about Asian American biblical interpretation, its theological and historical developments, and the gifts it offered to the body of Christ. The same was true regarding Latino/a interpretation and the Bible-reading habits of First Nations and Indigenous peoples.

In some ways, I was a hypocrite. I wanted people to attend to the contributions of my community without being similarly invested in others. I needed to spend less time complaining and more time listening. The *New Testament in Color: A Multiethnic Commentary on the New Testament* began with that insight. It was a hope that we might come together across ethnic difference and create something beautiful.

I wondered, "What fruit might come from the various ethnic groups sharing space in North America working together to produce a commentary?" What did I need to learn from my brothers and sisters in Christ beyond the Black-White binary that shaped my imagination in the American South?

It was natural that my lament was directed to where the power resides in the academy. In 2019, the Society of Biblical Literature, the largest body of biblical scholars in the world, did a study of its membership. That study showed that 86 percent (2,732 of 3,159) of its members who described themselves as college or university faculty were of European or Caucasian descent.[1]

Given the demographics of the United States (and the world), it is more than fair to say that we experience a disproportionate White or European dominance of biblical studies. If God gives his Spirit without measure

[1]Society of Biblical Literature, "2019 SBL Membership Data," January 2019, www.sbl-site.org/assets/pdfs/sblMemberProfile2019.pdf.

and equips the entire body of Christ to read and interpret the Bible, then it is a tragedy when the whole body of Christ is not engaged in the process of reading, interpreting, and applying these texts. No one part of the body has the right to speak for the whole. We need each other.

Does a lack of ethnic diversity matter? Isn't biblical interpretation simply a matter of translating verbs and nouns, linking together ideas as they come together into sentences, paragraphs, narratives, or letters? I was told that the only thing we needed to be good interpreters was proper understanding of the historical context alongside requisite grammatical, text-critical, and linguistic expertise.

I do not want to push any of those important and vital skills aside. All the contributors in this volume labored hard to gain the aforementioned tools of the scholarly trade. It is precisely because I believe that biblical texts are God's inspired Word to his people that we must do our very best to read them well and carefully.

But here is the rub. It matters that we have diverse representation in the process of biblical interpretation because it is always *ourselves* as persons with our experiences, biases, gifts, and liabilities that we bring to the text. We are not disembodied spirits with no histories or cultures. We are not exegetical machines; we are interpreting persons.

We come from somewhere, and that somewhere has left its mark whether we acknowledge it or not. When one culture dominates the discourse, we are closing ourselves off from what the Holy Spirit is saying among other cultures. Socially located interpretation, when rooted in a trust in God's Word, is a gift from particular cultures to the whole church. Socially located interpretation reflects a trust that none of our experiences were wasted, that all of who we are is useful to God.

Our cultures are not something we are called to set aside in the Bible-reading process because our cultures and ethnicities have their origins in God (Eph 3:14-15). Every culture and ethnicity, because it was created by people made in the image of God, contains within it both evidence of its divine origins (Gen 1:27-28) and elements of the fall (Gen 3).

Stated differently, there are no perfect cultures. Every culture and people is challenged and made into the best version of itself through an encounter with the living God. Our cultures are restless until they find their rest in their Creator. None of them are left unchanged. God's word to persons *and* cultures is always yes *and* no. He offers us all repentance for things that have gone astray and lauds our struggles toward the good, the true, and the beautiful.

Socially located biblical interpretation is nothing less than the record of the Spirit's work through scriptural engagement among the different ethnicities and cultures of the world. Unfortunately, too often the sanctification of culture has been confused with the *Westernization* of culture. That lie has done tremendous damage to the church. God's transfiguring work is not done in comparison with the West. Ethnicities do not become more holy as they approach likeness to Europe but to God.

That attempt of each culture and group to find themselves as they struggle to examine their lives and culture in light of the word of God is instructive not just for them; it is instructive to the whole body of Christ. We can, through listening to the voices of others, see the ways in which our own location has at times hindered out ability to read the text well. What we are aiming for, then, is mutual edification.

To give this resource as best a chance at success as possible, I invited three other editors from different social locations to help with the project: Janette Ok, Osvaldo Padilla, and Amy Peeler. I (Esau) served as the general editor of the project. We tried, through our work together, to model the kind of crosscultural cooperation that is a foretaste of the kingdom of God (Rev 7:9). I am grateful for their expertise and patience. I am a better reader of the Scriptures for having known them. Any remaining flaws in this project are a result of my failures, not theirs.

We tried to gather a cross section of contributors with a particular focus on North American ethnic minorities. Because this is a project about the whole body of Christ, there are scholars of majority culture (White North Americans) in the volume as well. For the most part, for reasons of scope, we did not include many international voices. We believe that there are many important other volumes and projects that are calling attention to the testimony of the Majority World. We laud and support their efforts.

In gathering the varied contributors to this volume, we asked them to bring the entirety of themselves to the process of reading and interpreting the New Testament. They are not speaking for an entire culture, but they are from some place. That place informs the kinds of questions they ask and the ways in which they apply biblical texts. Even with a focus on North America, we could not include every single culture and ethnicity, but we have tried to include as many as we could gather. Omissions are not due to malice but the inherent limitations of space. We ask for your goodwill in any lack in that regard.

Due to the varied ways in which Scripture has been used to justify indefensible things such as colonialization, slavery, and the studied disdain for non-Western cultures, much socially located biblical interpretation has been rooted in a hermeneutics of suspicion in the effort to resist those evils.

We believe that it is right to push back on the misuse of Scripture to justify evil, but we also believe that socially located biblical interpretation can engage in a hermeneutics of *trust* wherein we recognize that the God we encounter in biblical texts is in the end a friend, not an enemy. The editors wanted to honor the fact that the ecclesial communities from which we come found liberation and spiritual transformation through reading with the text, not against it. Some might consider this naivete. I disagree. I consider it hard-won wisdom.

In our notes of invitation to the contributors, we (the editors) stated that this posture of trust would be a distinctive in the project. We told them that we as editors began with a starting point of affirming "the central tenants of the Christian faith as found in texts such as the Apostles' and Nicene Creeds. Furthermore, we agree that Scripture is God's word to us that functions as the final guide for Christian faith and practice." Evoking Nicaea does not mean that we are privileging Western culture as defining Christianity for the world. Instead, it is an affirmation that God was at work among Christians of the past to tell us things that are true and good. We hope in the generations to come that, despite our compromises and failures, Christians will find some lasting value in our theological contributions. There are no pristine histories.

In other words, we do not assume that our cultures stand over the texts, but through the interaction of person, text, history, and culture, truths that others might miss shine out all the more brilliantly. The chorus can create a beauty the soloist cannot.

We have structured the book in such a way that we've included a series of articles related to ethnic identity and biblical interpretation at the beginning that will help orient the reader to the subsequent commentaries. It is helpful to engage with these first. We've also included various articles related to socially located biblical interpretation throughout the book. You will find that these enhance the reading of the commentaries, as they provide helpful insights on topics related to social and ethnic location in biblical interpretation.

In the pages that follow, we are not assuming that everyone agrees with every exegetical decision or application. Socially located biblical interpretation is not a panacea that cures all exegetical ills. Universal agreement is too high a bar for any book.

We are not asking for a paternalistic nodding of the head with all our conclusions, as if our work simply adds flavor to "real" scholarship and therefore should not be challenged. In the end, the fruit will be seen in the ways we help churchgoers, Bible study leaders, and students read the text more faithfully. Like any group of writers committed to serving the body of Christ, we welcome pushback given in good faith. Our goal is not to replace one form of hegemony with another or to close the conversation around these texts across cultures. We desire a shared pursuit to discover the mind of Christ and his purposes for his people.

Nonetheless, we do believe that these entries will indeed do what all good commentaries endeavor to accomplish: send the reader back to the text with fresh questions, answers, and a sense of wonder at the ways in which the ancient word remains ever new, challenging and inspiring us to follow our King and Lord more faithfully.

AFRICAN AMERICAN BIBLICAL INTERPRETATION

Esau D. McCaulley

What does it mean to speak of African American biblical interpretation? To refer to African American biblical interpretation does not suggest that the mere fact of black skin gives one a special insight into the meaning of biblical texts, nor does it suggest that all African Americans come to similar conclusions about biblical passages. To speak of African American biblical interpretation gets at the collision of two realities that cannot be denied. First, there is the God who created all things and desires a relationship with the varied peoples of the world. This God reveals himself and his character through the sacred Scriptures. To read these texts and to attempt to understand them is part of what it means to be a disciple of Jesus.

But we do not come to these texts as disembodied or disinterested minds. This leads us to a second reality. We have a host of experiences, questions, hopes, dreams, and traumas that we bring to the Bible-reading process. As much as we might try to picture it otherwise, biblical interpretation is not just a science. It is an art. The art of biblical interpretation implies an artist, a person, not a machine, doing the interpretation. To refer to African *American* biblical interpretation, then, refers to the ways in which living in America as a Black woman or man influences the kinds of questions, hopes, and traumas we bring to the Bible. In other words, it is not that our skin color causes us to interpret the Bible in a certain way. That would be putting the cart before the horse. Instead, our skin color has influenced the way in which American society has viewed, stereotyped, and distorted the image of God in us. Our process of Bible reading, then, has been a means of recovering what was taken from us. It has been and is an exercise in hope.

The Black experience is not uniform. It is as diverse as that of any other group of people. But there are patterns, questions that recur, and ways of dealing with those questions that fall into clusters or traditions. African American biblical interpretation, then, refers to the ongoing process of Black Christians attempting to make sense of the Black experience in the United States through the analysis of biblical texts.

These experiences do not create meanings of biblical texts, but they may allow us insight into implications of passages that others might not notice because they do not consider them. What I have in mind is Black biblical interpretations as motivated readings, not distorted ones. For example, African Americans were told that they were less than fully human. This caused us to come to the text with a heightened need to construct a biblical anthropology that took ethnicity seriously. Since most Christians of European descent never had to defend their full humanity through biblical texts against other Christians, then they might not be as apt to notice the ways in which the Bible addresses this topic.

Because the Black experience is at bottom a human experience, not every aspect of Black biblical interpretation will be unique. African Americans, like all Christians, desire a relationship with God. We reflect on issues of sin and repentance, of sanctification and salvation, of faith, hope, and love. The Black experience, precisely because it is a human one, connects at places with the wider Christian tradition of trying to make sense of what it means to follow God in a broken world.

African American biblical interpretation is one way of speaking about bringing the entirety of who we are to the Scripture-reading process, but what keeps it from spinning off into an exercise in making these texts say what we want them to say? The answer to this question is a confidence in the God who reveals himself through the Scriptures. We are able to bring our questions, experiences, hopes, and dreams to the Bible. But the Scriptures as God's word to us for our good are able to answer us back and redirect, refine, or clarify our questions. African American Christians, then, offer the results of their labors to understand God and live as disciples of Christ to the wider body in the hope that together we might discern God's purposes for us in the world.[1] Therefore, like any other portion of the body of Christ, African American Christians need the rest of the communion of saints across time and culture to be complete. To assert the value of African American biblical interpretation is to insist on our place in God's kingdom. It is not a demand for a solo performance; it is to join the chorus of cultures singing praises and offering laments to God.

African American biblical interpretation does not just describe a philosophy. It refers to a history and a community that lives in the aftermath of that history. What I refer to as the Black *ecclesial* tradition is the living community of faith that has wrestled with the struggles and joys of being Black and Christian in North America.[2] It is a storehouse of wisdom found in the sermons, testimonies, narratives, and confessional statements of Black churches and individuals. I compare it to the early centuries of Christianity, when the church fathers and mothers struggled to make sense of all the ways in which the gospel threw the Greco-Roman world they knew into chaos. These early debates and the method of solving them set the trajectory for what Christianity became. Christianity, then, was influenced by the culture into which it moved and breathed. In the same way, the Black ecclesial tradition in North America came into being at a certain point in history with certain pressing questions that influenced its ethos, issues, and concerns. What is that history, and how did it affect Black ecclesial interpretation?

African American biblical interpretation began as a counter to the distorted form of Christianity that many enslavers tried to pass along to the enslaved. For example, African people were told that they descended from Ham and for that reason were cursed to eternal slavery.[3] Black believers also had to deal with a religious, philosophical, scientific, and political consensus on Black ontological inferiority.[4] For enslaved and freed Blacks, slavery was not simply a moral issue; it was a legal

[1]Esau McCaulley, *Reading While Black: African American Biblical Interpretation as an Exercise in Hope* (Downers Grove, IL: IVP Academic, 2020), 22.

[2]McCaulley, *Reading While Black*, 4-5.

[3]Lisa M. Bowens, *African American Readings of Paul: Reception, Resistance, and Transformation* (Grand Rapids, MI: Eerdmans, 2020), 50-52.

[4]Delores S. Williams, *Sisters in the Wilderness: The Challenge of Womanist God-Talk* (Maryknoll, NY: Orbis Books, 1993), 75-95.

reality. Therefore, one of the first questions Black converts to Christianity had to answer was, What does the God I now serve have to say about the sufferings of the enslaved and disinherited? Many early African believers in the United States concluded that God desired their freedom. This is seen in the theological tracts and personal works they composed that opposed slavery.[5]

For this reason, Black biblical interpretation has often had an eye toward the social or political ramifications of biblical texts. The exodus narrative, for many, was not just a description of what God did in the past; it revealed the kind of God we serve and his posture toward those oppressed by society. One way to describe this concern with the implications of biblical passages on lived experiences is *social location*. That is to say, one key element of Black biblical interpretation is its focus on the questions arising out of the Black community, and the pressing questions in those foundational years were slavery and White supremacy.

A second key habit we see in this early era of Black biblical interpretation is a decidedly *doctrinal* and *canonical* emphasis. If the oppression of Black people was rooted in a false doctrine of persons, then the Black response was to correct that doctrine. For example, Lemuel Haynes used Acts 17:26 to argue for the essential equality of people of African descent in 1776:

> It hath pleased god to make of one Blood all nations of men, for to dwell upon the face of the Earth. Acts 17, 26. And as all are of one Species, so there are the same Laws, and aspiring principles placed in all nations; and the Effect that these Laws will produce, are Similar to Each other. Consequently we may suppose, that what is precious to one man, is precious to another, and what is irksom, or intolarable to one man, is so to another, consider'd in a Law of Nature. Therefore we may reasonably Conclude, that Liberty is Equally as pre[c]ious to a Black man, as it is to a white one, and Bondage Equally as intollarable to the one as it is to the other. . . . Not the Least precept, or practise, in the Scriptures, that constitutes a Black man a Slave, any more than a white one.[6]

Notice here his reference to Scripture as a corrective to the heretical anthropology that deemed blackness inferior to whiteness. We could also highlight arguments against slavery based on God's character. According to James Pennington, God's own character, what God is in himself, spoke against slavery.[7]

When I refer to African American Bible reading as canonical, I have in mind the habits of finding doctrinal applications from unexpected texts. Most opponents wanted to argue for slavery on either the basis of a few Pauline passages or distorted interpretations of the curse of Ham. Rather than simply provide counterinterpretations of those passages, African Americans brought the whole of the Christian witness into play on contested matters. For example, when a group of slaves petitioned to the House of Representatives of Massachusetts, they argued that the shape of the Christian life, including its teaching on marriage, family, and Christian community, made slavery untenable:

[5]See the moving letter of James Pennington to his former enslaver in Pennington, *The Fugitive Blacksmith; or, Events in the History of James W. C. Pennington, Pastor of a Presbyterian Church, New York, Formerly a Slave in the State of Maryland, United States*, 2nd ed. (London: Charles Gilpin, 1849), 79-84.

[6]Ruth Bogin, "'Liberty Further Extended': A 1776 Antislavery Manuscript by Lemuel Haynes," *The William and Mary Quarterly* 40 (1983): 85-105.

[7]James W. C. Pennington, *Two Years Absence or a Farewell Sermon* (Hartford, CT: H. G. Well, 1845), 23-24.

> Our lives are embittered to us. . . . By our deplorable situation we are rendered incapable of shewing our obedience to Almighty God. How can a slave perform the duties of husband to a wife or a parent to his child? How can a husband leave master to work and cleave to his wife? How can the wife submit themselves to their husbands in all things? How can the child obey their parents in all things? There is a great number of us sencear . . . members of the Church of Christ. How can the master and the slave be said to fulfill the command, "Live in Love let brotherly love contuner [continue] and abound Beare ye one anothers Bordens"? How can the master be said to Bear my Borden when he Bears me down with they Have [heavy] changes of slavery and operson against my will and how can we fulfill oure part of duty to him whilst in this condition as we cannot searve our God as we ought in this situation.[8]

Pennington makes a similar appeal to the wider witness of the Scriptures against slavery in his own works.[9] This habit of canonical and theological interpretation was needed because African converts were being told that one particular passage or two of the Bible supported a whole system of abuse. Rather than agreeing to fight on the ground determined by their oppressors, they opened the whole vista of the Scriptures to declare God's goodness and his will for their freedom. As Emerson Powery and Rodney Sadler note, this is not about the rejection of biblical authority. It was a rejection of distorted readings that sanctioned evil: "The formerly enslaved were critical interpreters of the biblical texts, not because they questioned the literal interpretation of the passage, but because they challenged the dominant cultural (and popular) paradigm of appropriation associated with the interpretive tradition of a biblical reading."[10] Canonical and theological readings of Scripture, then, were a defense against White supremacy, but also in keeping with the best habits of Bible reading throughout the history of the church.

If Black interpreters found in the Bible a God who countered the lies told them by slave masters, they also found more than affirmation. They also discovered challenges to be changed by an encounter with God. I want to highlight two examples of this dynamic. First, there is the aforementioned prominence of Acts 17:26 in Black Christian circles. It does not merely assert Black equality with people of European descent; it also gives Black Christians a picture of the church as a community that is united across racial lines when the experience of slavery might have led them toward separatism. For example, in 1856 the African Methodist Episcopal church adopted as its motto, "God Our Father, Christ Our Redeemer, Man Our Brother." Even though the denomination was founded due to the unchristian conduct of majority-White churches, its encounter with the Scriptures led its people to see the possibly of the church as one human family.[11] Second, there is the undoubted emphasis across the literature on the

---

[8]Cited in Allen Dwight Callahan, *The Talking Book: African Americans and the Bible* (New Haven, CT: Yale University Press, 2006), 35.

[9]Pennington, *Two Years Absence*, 27. See also the canonical arguments of Jarena Lee and Zilpha Elaw to justify their call to preach as recounted in Bowens, *African American Readings of Paul*, 73-96.

[10]Emerson B. Powery and Rodney S. Sadler Jr., *The Genesis of Liberation: Biblical Interpretation in the Antebellum Narratives of the Enslaved* (Louisville, KY: Westminster John Knox, 2016), 21.

[11]On the founding of the African Methodist Episcopal Church, see *The Doctrines and Discipline of the African Methodist Episcopal Church* (Philadelphia: Richard Allen and Jacob Tapsico, 1817), 3. Later the African Methodist Episcopal Church adopted the more gender-inclusive and expansive, "God Our Father, Christ Our Redeemer, the Holy Spirit Our Comforter, Humankind Our Family."

joy that Black believers found in their relationship with God. Yes, they desired freedom, but their actual relationship with Jesus was important. For example, consider the depiction of Charlotte Brooks's conversion as told in Octavia Rogers's important work highlighting the evils of slavery more broadly.

> Did any of the black people on his place believe in the teachings of their master?
>
> No, my child; none of us listened to him about singing and praying. I tell you we used to have some good times together praying and singing. He did not want us to pray, but we would have our little prayer-meeting anyhow. Sometimes when we met to hold our meetings we would put a big wash-tub full of water in the middle of the floor to catch the sound of our voices when we sung. When we all sung we would march around and shake each other's hands, and we would sing easy and low, so marster could not hear us. O, how happy I used to be in those meetings, although I was a slave! I thank the Lord Aunt Jane Lee lived by me. She helped me to make my peace with the Lord. O, the day I was converted! It seemed to me it was a paradise here below! It looked like I wanted nothing any more. Jesus was so sweet to my soul! Aunt Jane used to sing, "Jesus! the name that charms our fears." That hymn just suited my case. Sometimes I felt like preaching myself. It seemed I wanted to ask every body if they loved Jesus when I first got converted.[12]

Jesus made a difference in Charlotte's lived experience in a way that does not downplay her desire for liberation. Fervent testimony to the evils of injustice and to a relationship with God stand out a legacies of early Black encounters with the God of the Bible.

Early Black biblical interpretation displayed two further features. One is patience, and the other is a dual apologetic arising from interaction with Black and White critiques of the Scriptures. There is no need to provide documented evidence of Black patience with the Bible. The fact of Black Christianity itself shows this reality. The mere act of early Black inquirers in North America opening the Bible that was used to justify their oppression to discover the truth for themselves was an act of faith. Black Bible reading in the United States has at its origin a tremendous act of rebellion and patience.

But what do I mean about the dual apologetic? Early Black Bible readers had to counter lies coming from White Christians, such as the Ham myth that doomed African peoples to slavery.[13] But they also had to argue for the relevancy of Christianity to the concerns of African peoples. This required them to walk that fine line between criticizing White Christian churches and leaving space for Christianity itself. Christianity had to be a source of resistance. Consider the words of Leonard Black on the role that faith played in his decision to escape: "When God had opened my eyes, I grew very uneasy reflecting upon the condition of my brothers, who were enjoying their liberty in a land of freedom. I wanted also to be free. I resolved to be free. I made up my mind to runaway. . . . I then started for Boston. Then, as now, God alone was my only hope."[14] The apologetic of the direct relevance of Christianity to the Black desire for liberation helped

[12]Octavia V. Rogers Albert, *The house of bondage or Charlotte Brooks and other slaves original and life-like, as they appeared in their old plantation and city slave life; together with pen-pictures of the peculiar institution, with sights and insights into their new relations as freedmen, freemen, and citizens* (New York: Hunt and Eaton, 1890), 12.

[13]Frederick Douglass, *Narrative of the Life of Frederick Douglass, an American Slave* (Boston: Anti-slavery Office, 1845), 4.

[14]Leonard Black, *The Life and Sufferings of Leonard Black: A Fugitive from Slavery* (New Bedford, MA: Benjamin Lindsey, 1847), 22, 28.

counter the White Christian claims that God willed Black slavery.

What emerged out of this confluence of themes that resulted from the Black encounter with Scripture, and where were they housed? In Black churches, particularly Black Baptist, Methodist, and Pentecostal churches (although the presence of Black Reformed Christians cannot be denied). These churches, including the African Methodist Episcopal Church (A.M.E.), the Christian Methodist Episcopal Church (C.M.E.), the Church of God in Christ (C.O.G.I.C.), The National Baptist Church (N.B.C.), the National Baptist Church, USA (N.B.C. USA), and the Progressive Baptist Church (P.B.C,) are the fruit of Black encounter with the Bible. Their confessions—which on the whole emphasize the things Christians have always believed about God, including historic Christology and trinitarian theology as well as (Protestant) soteriology—are important testimonies to what Black people believed about God. But it is also true that in comparison to White-majority churches, Black Christians were more attuned to the political and social implications of Christian teaching as it related to freedom, equality, and justice.

This social concern moved along a spectrum. Some early Black Christian encounters with the Bible led to a form of quietism in which a heavy emphasis was placed on personal moral formation.[15] Others saw in those same biblical texts a call for the creation of a just society.

Eventually, African Americans did obtain more access to positions in higher education, and the Black ecclesial tradition of Bible reading entered the academy. The fount of this tradition in many respects was James Cone, whose thought also influenced early Black biblical scholars such as Charles Copher and Cain Hope Felder. They did important work on Black presence in the Bible, classism, racism, and the family.[16] But the heart of their work was not merely academic. They picked up on the emphasis on social location that emerged in the early Black ecclesial tradition. Highlighting Black presence in the Bible and other pressing issues in Black church spaces was their attempt to answer the questions Black believers had been wrestling with from the beginning. Furthermore, even though I disagree with some of Cone's conclusions, he was attempting to bring his understanding of Black faith into conversations with secular accounts of Black power.[17]

The twists and turns in the diffuse nature of the academy are too extensive to depict here.[18] There are a few trends worthy of note. First was the increased analysis of Black cultural and religious sources as dialogue partners with biblical ideas. Scholars began to see that the proper place to begin Black theological reflection was not simply to counter

[15]See the helpful and nuanced discussion of Jupiter Hammon, one early author often critiqued for emphasizing personal morality over social transformation, in Bowens, *African American Readings of Paul*, 22-49. See also my struggles with this issue in McCaulley, *Reading While Black*, 170-71.

[16]Cain Hope Felder, *Troubling Biblical Waters: Race, Class, and Family* (Maryknoll, NY: Orbis Books, 1989); Felder, "Race, Racism, and the Biblical Narratives," in *Stony the Road We Trod: African American Biblical Interpretation*, ed. Cain Hope Felder (Minneapolis: Augsburg Fortress, 1991), 127-45; Charles B. Copher, "The Black Presence in the Old Testament," in Felder, *Stony the Road*, 146-64. See also his anthology in Copher, *Black Biblical Studies: Biblical and Theological Issues on the Black Presence in the Bible* (Chicago: Black Light Fellowship, 1993).

[17]James Cone, *A Black Theology of Liberation*, 40th anniversary ed. (New York: Orbis Books, 1970). See another attempt in a different key in J. Doetis Roberts, *Liberation and Reconciliation: A Black Theology* (Louisville, KY: Westminster John Knox, 1971).

[18]See also Mitzi Smith, *Insights from African American Interpretation* (Minneapolis: Fortress, 2017), 1-76; Allen Dwight Callahan, *The Talking Book: African Americans and the Bible* (New Haven, CT: Yale University Press, 2006); Vincent Wimbush, "The Bible and African Americans: An Outline of an Interpretive History," in Felder, *Stony the Road*, 81-97.

White theological scholarship. Instead, one had to begin with Black Christians making sense out of God themselves. This work of making sense of God was not limited to explicitly theological resources. It included Black depictions of religion in secular works of art.[19] I have attempted to reflect that trend by highlighting the testimonies of early Black believers themselves.

Second, the most prominent development in African American biblical interpretation has been womanism. The nomenclature comes from Alice Walker, "who used the term to refer to a form of feminism that explicitly links issues of race to an appreciation of the abilities of and advocacy for the rights of Black women."[20] In the field of biblical studies, it has come to represent claiming the freedom of Black women to bring their whole selves to the exegetical project. Noted scholar Raquel St. Clair, quoting Koala Jones-Warsaw, describes womanism as "discover[ing] the significance and validity of the biblical text for Black women who today experience the 'tridimensional reality' of racism, sexism, and classism."[21]

The nature and scope of womanist biblical studies continues to be debated.[22] Some Black women identify as womanists; others work under the banner of feminism, and some adopt both. Some Black women do their scholarship apart from an explicit label. Whatever name Black women use, their contribution to the exegetical enterprise has been there from the beginning of Black reflection on God. It is necessary for the healthy function of the church and the academy.

Black Bible reading is not one thing. It is as diverse as the Black culture out of which it arises. Nonetheless, the strand I call home has developed habits and ways of being that I have described as "Black ecclesial interpretation." This way of Bible reading, rooted in profound trust in God and his word, has helped Black believers survive against seemingly impossible odds. Elements of this tradition are carried on in Black academic analysis of the Bible, but there are also places in which formal Black biblical interpretation charted its own course. The two are not strangers; they are members of the same family that exist sometimes in dynamic tension. The Black academy has posed hard questions to the church, and the church has responded in kind. This healthy tension is the key to helping Christians live their lives faithfully before God and humanity.

---

[19]See Williams, *Sisters in the Wilderness*, 32-51.

[20]McCaulley, *Reading While Black*, 180-81.

[21]Raquel St. Clair, "Womanist Biblical Interpretation," in *True to Our Native Land: An African American New Testament Commentary*, ed. Brian K. Blount, Cain Hope Felder, Clarice J. Martin, and Emerson B. Powery (Minneapolis: Fortress, 2007), 54.

[22]See Nyasha Junior, *An Introduction to Womanist Biblical Interpretation* (Louisville, KY: Westminster John Knox, 2015).

ASIAN AMERICAN BIBLICAL INTERPRETATION

Janette H. Ok

INTRODUCTION

What is Asian American biblical interpretation? To begin answering this question, it is necessary to ask, Who is Asian American? What does it mean to be Asian American? Addressing these questions is critical for the faith formation of Asian American Christians and the body of Christ as a whole because the histories, contexts, and identities of Asian American interpreters of Scripture matter theologically.

As a seminary student and moderator of the Asian American student group on campus, I invited an ethnic studies professor to speak for an event focusing on Asian American identity and ministry. I had read his book on the contemporary Asian American experience and found myself profoundly illuminated and affected by his concise overview of Asian American history. Learning more about the Chinese Exclusion Act of 1882 (the first significant US law to restrict any form of immigration to the United States), the inhumane treatment of Asian immigrants detained at Angel Island, the incarceration of Japanese Americans during World War II, and the racially motivated assault of Vincent Chin that led to his death in 1982 helped me understand my own political, coalitional, racialized, and faith identity as an Asian American. This scholar graciously declined the invitation, suggesting that a person with more theological background would be a better fit. Years later, I still wonder whether he was right. Is Christian faith and theology not rooted in history, experience, and particularity?

Theology is rooted in the particular—a peculiar beginning with "the God of Abraham, Isaac, and Jacob," who delivered Israel from slavery in Egypt, and who delivered humanity by raising Jesus from the dead. Even the concept of redemption cannot be understood apart from Yahweh's relationship with Israel and the sociocultural realities of ancient Israelite society. Israelite tribal society understood redemption as the means through which a lost family member was restored within the kinship circle through the act of a patriarch, as in the story of Boaz and Ruth.[1] Yahweh presents himself in Scripture metaphorically as the patriarch of a clan who announces his intention to redeem his lost family members, which he does by sending his eldest son and heir, Jesus Christ, "to give his life a ransom for many" (Mt 20:28).[2]

God's covenantal and incarnational nature as God in Christ is revealed in particularity and contextuality. Jesus Christ, God's eternal son, came in the flesh and in the fullness of our humanity for the work of redemption through his life, death, and resurrection. Jesus

[1]Sandra L. Richter, *The Epic of Eden: A Christian Entry into the Old Testament* (Downers Grove, IL: InterVarsity Press, 2008), 40-42.

[2]Richter, *Epic of Eden*, 45.

came among "with particulars," which includes his maleness, Jewishness, social location in first-century Palestine, and embodied historical concreteness.[3] God's work of redemption is culturally and ethnically specific and socially located, as well as universal and cosmic in scope.

Thus, in reconciling Asian Americans to God, Jesus redeems our cultural, sociopolitical, and ethnoracial identities.[4] This is why Daniel D. Lee argues that attempting to understand what it means to be Asian American is crucial for embracing the gospel for Asian Americans and articulating the gospel as Asian Americans: that is, "the task of defining Asian American identity is not preparation for theology, but is itself the theological work."[5] This chapter attempts to define Asian American identity and Asian American biblical interpretation as a theological and hermeneutical endeavor vital to the faith life of Asian American Christians.

ASIAN AMERICAN IDENTITY

Asian American identity is complex, diverse, and heterogeneous. The term includes a vast plurality of ethnic and cultural identities that trace their ancestral roots to the Asian continent, including East and Southeast Asia, the Indian subcontinent, and the Pacific Islands.[6] This complex diversity is also reflected in how people of Asian descent describe their own identity. Views of identity among Asian American immigrants, then, are often tied to the amount of time they spend in the United States. Asian immigrants who arrived in the past ten years are more likely to describe themselves based on their ethnic identity (e.g., Cambodian or Filipino) than those who have lived in the United States for more than two decades. They are also less likely than Asian immigrants who have arrived more than twenty years ago to think of themselves as typical Americans.[7]

That said, ethnic self-understanding cannot be easily separated from each subgroup's encounters with colonialism in Asia, and changing US immigration and settlement policies.[8] Despite their plurality and diversity, immigrants and migrants to the United States of Asian descent share experiences of racial discrimination, inequality, and exclusion from full participation in American life based on their race. These experiences, along with the

[3]Beth Felker Jones, *Practicing Christian Doctrine: An Introduction to Thinking and Living Theologically* (Grand Rapids, MI: Baker Academic, 2014), 137.

[4]Daniel D. Lee, *Doing Asian American Theology: A Contextual Framework for Faith and Practice* (Downers Grove, IL: IVP Academic, 2022), 37.

[5]Lee, *Doing Asian American Theology*, 57.

[6]Since 1997, the US Census Bureau has classified a person of the Asian race as "having origins in any of the original peoples of the Far East, Southeast Asia, or the Indian subcontinent including, for example, Cambodia, China, India, Japan, Korea, Malaysia, Pakistan, the Philippine Islands, Thailand, and Vietnam." See "About the Topic of Race," United States Census Bureau, March 1, 2022, www.census.gov/topics/population/race/about.html#:~:text=Asian%20%E2%80%93%20A%20person%20having%20origins,Islands%2C%20Thailand%2C%20and%20Vietnam. There are some countries situated in western Asia that also understand themselves as belonging to other geographical regions or continents, such as the Middle East (e.g., Iran and Kuwait) and Europe (e.g., Georgia and Armenia). However, that significant immigrant populations from Asia have come to the US from the eastern, Southeast, and south Asian regions is another reason why Asians from what is commonly referred to as west Asia are not usually described in the US as being Asian American. See P. Mimi Niles et al., "Honoring Asian Diversity by Collecting Asian Subpopulation Data in Health Research," *Res Nurs Health* 43, no. 3 (June 2022): 265-69.

[7]Neil G. Ruiz et al., "Diverse Cultures and Shared Experiences Shape Asian American Identities," Pew Research Center, May 8, 2023, www.pewresearch.org/race-ethnicity/2023/05/08/diverse-cultures-and-shared-experiences-shape-asian-american-identities/.

[8]See Tamara C. Ho, "The Complex Heterogeneity of Asian American Identity," in *T&T Clark Handbook of Asian American Biblical Hermeneutics*, ed. Uriah Y. Kim and Seung Ai Yang (London: T&T Clark, 2019), 17-26.

galvanizing success of racial and ethnic alliances, such as the Black Power and American Indian Movement, led two University of California, Berkeley student activists, Yuji Ichioka and Emma Gee, to conceptualize and coin the term "Asian American" in 1968.[9] Rather than accept how non–Asian Americans would label and lump together people of Asian descent as "Orientals," a term rife with colonizing and racist overtones, Ichioka and Gee sought to rally behind a banner of their own making and forge a critical mass to fight for greater equality. "Asian American" thus emerged in the late 1960s as a political, social, pan-Asian, coalitional identity anchored in the common desire to fight for greater racial and structural equality and justice in the United States.

In the late 1960s and '70s, Asian American identity focused on East Asian American experiences, that is, the experiences of Chinese, Japanese, and Korean Americans. Filipino Americans also played an integral role in early Asian American activism, forging alliances with Blacks, Latinos, and Native Americans. The term expanded in the 1970s and '80s to include Southeast Asian refugees from Vietnam, Cambodia, and Laos, including the Hmong people (who are an ethnic group without a nation or state). In more recent decades, "Asian American" has encompassed people of South Asian, Indian, and Pakistani descent. Most recently, efforts have been made to add Pacific Islanders and Native Hawaiians under the rubric of Asian American.[10] The various acronyms used to refer to Asian Americans reveal the evolving and contested status of the term, including APA (Asian Pacific American), ANA (Asian North American), Asian American Pacific Islander (AAPI), AANHPI (Asian American Native Hawaiian Pacific Islander), and APIDA (Asian Pacific Islander Desi American).[11] The identifier "Asian American" thus serves as an umbrella term that anchors a diversity of ethnic groups and rallies them in the common pursuit of justice and equality. Simultaneously, the label does not adequately convey the irreducible diversity among people of Asian descent living in the United States and their varying histories of education, immigration, acculturation, racialization, inclusion, exclusion, and multicultural relationality.

It is important to look at Asian migration to the United States through the lens of US imperialism, militarism, and territoriality in Asia. For example, after the Spanish-American War in 1889, many of the Pacific Islands were made into US colonies as the result of imperial wars, as in the case of Samoa, the Mariana Islands, and Guam, which remain US territories to this day. In this same year, the United States illegally annexed the Kingdom of Hawai'i, which later became the state of Hawai'i. After Spain's defeat in the Spanish-American War in 1889, the Philippine-American War broke out (1899–1902), resulting in the annexation of the Philippines by the United States. In 1975, nearly 130,000 Southeast Asian refugees migrated to

[9]Ichioka and Gee named the organization they started in their living room the Asian American Political Alliance, which is thought to be the first occurrence of the moniker *Asian American*. The Asian American Political Alliance sparked the rise of a political movement that unified Americans previously divided by their Asian ethnicity and joined forces with African American, Chicano, and Native American groups.

[10]Melissa Borja, interview by Eve Gerber, "The Best Books on Asian American History," *Five Books*, n.d., https://fivebooks.com/best-books/asian-american-history-melissa-borja/.

[11]E.g., not all Asian Americans agree on the benefits of including Native Hawaiian and Pacific Islanders under the rubric of Asian Pacific American or Asian Pacific Islander, since the experiences of Native Hawaiian Pacific Islander people have more in common with those of urban Native American people, and Native Hawaiian Pacific Islander people face more significant health and socioeconomic disparities than white Americans and Asian Americans. See Naomi Ishisaka, "Why It's Time to Retire the Term 'Asian Pacific Islander,'" *The Seattle Times*, November 30, 2020.

the United States after the fall of Saigon, which marked the end of the Vietnam War.

The impact of US imperialism and militarism on the idea of what it means to be a US citizen or American can also be seen within its borders.[12] When Japan attacked Pearl Harbor, deep-seated anti-Asian xenophobic policies and sentiments made it possible for the US government to legally incarcerate 120,000 Japanese immigrants, nearly two-thirds of them native-born American citizens, because they posed a supposed threat to national security.[13] Long before World War II, Asian Americans were considered racially unassimilable and were affected by immigration laws and restrictions that curbed their rights.[14] Thus, migration to the United States must also be seen through the lens of xenophobia.

Because the histories, contexts, and identities of Asian American interpreters of Scripture matter theologically, Lee offers a helpful hermeneutical rubric which he calls the "Asian American quadrilateral." The Asian American quadrilateral helps one gain a critical awareness of how the contextual themes of (1) Asian heritage, (2) migration experience, (3) American culture, and (4) racialization intersect and affect diverse Asian American identities and experiences.[15] These four elements inform and affect the other, while also interacting with other social categories such as religion, gender, class, sexual orientation, and age. The Asian American quadrilateral provides a distinctive framework for Asian Americans to talk about Asian American identity.

ASIAN AMERICAN BIBLICAL INTERPRETATION

What, then, does it mean to engage in Asian American biblical interpretation, and who gets to engage in it? Tat-siong Benny Liew rightly cautions that the very question of "'who' and/or 'what'" runs the risk of being exclusionary and essentialist, and attempts to delimit and define will inevitably be challenged and contested.[16]

That said, it is important to distinguish between biblical interpretation produced by Asian Americans from Asian American biblical interpretation.[17] One does not engage in Asian American biblical interpretation simply by being Asian American, just as one does not engage in feminist or womanist interpretation by virtue of being a woman. Rather, Asian American biblical interpretation explicitly and intentionally approaches biblical texts not only by means of exegesis but also through diverse and overlapping Asian American experiences and histories. It uses an interpretive framework of Asian heritage, migration experience, American culture, and racialization to generate further conversation and insights about the meaning and/or impacts of biblical texts. It engages in interdisciplinary research

[12]Nami Kim and Wonhee Anne Joh, "Introduction," in *Feminist Praxis Against U.S. Militarism*, ed. Nami Kim and Wonhee Anne Joh (Lanham, MD: Lexington Books, 2020), 10.

[13]By contrast, the US did not deem German Americans or Italian Americans a threat to national security, even though Germany and Italy fought with Japan against the US and its allies in the war. Amar Batra poignantly writes, "In 1942, America chose to define being American as being not Japanese." See Batra, "Have Things Gotten Better? Reflecting on the Japanese-American Internment," *The Daily Campus*, February 20, 2018, https://dailycampus.com/2018/02/20/2018-2-20-have-things-gotten-better-reflecting-on-the-japanese-american-internment/.

[14]Erika Lee, *America for Americans: A History of Xenophobia in the United States* (New York: Basic Books, 2019), 184-85.

[15]Lee, *Doing Asian American Theology*, 57.

[16]Tat-siong Benny Liew, *What Is Asian American Biblical Hermeneutics? Reading the New Testament* (Honolulu: University of Hawai'i Press, 2008), 4.

[17]Wongi Park, "Korean American Biblical Interpretation," in *The Oxford Handbook of the Bible in Korea*, ed. Won W. Lee (Oxford: Oxford University Press, 2022), 327.

that interacts closely with Asian American studies and often includes theological, postcolonial, ideological, liberationist, and intersectional approaches to reading the Bible.[18] Asian American biblical interpretation is committed to reading with, for, and about those who have been minoritized due to their Asian identity, while also offering them critique. It proposes a way forward toward greater justice and equality for Asian Americans.

From a confessional perspective, Asian American biblical interpretation has the potential to do what I describe above in response to the concrete needs and gifts of Asian American Christians in ways that both reflect the complexities of Asian American Christian identity and approach the Bible as Scripture. By Scripture, I mean how God actively speaks to us through the Bible, which witnesses to God's faithfulness to God's people over the ages and reveals the ways God is present and active in our world. Scripture guides, exhorts, rebukes, nourishes, empowers, shapes, and transforms the church. However, while Scripture is primary and foundational for understanding the will and character of God, the meaning behind it is not self-evident. That is, we rely on the Holy Spirit for revelation, and we interpret Scripture using reason through the lenses of tradition and experience. Contextual biblical interpretation is thus critically important for understanding Scripture.

Ecclesially oriented Asian American biblical interpretation is potentially one of its strongest contributions because such interpretations remain "on the ground," while also being rooted in sociohistorical and theological contexts of the biblical texts.[19] It uses theory and interdisciplinary and intersectional ways of engaging texts that are not divorced from Asian American lived experience. It pushes against the normativity and centrality of dominant White, patriarchal, colonial, and Christian nationalistic ways of being and reading. With such perspectives in place, the unique vision, concerns, and challenges of Asian American Christians will remain marginalized as cultural and foreign tokens within churches, seminaries and universities, and the guilds of biblical studies, as well as among Christians in the United States at large. When done in connection with the church and Asian American Christians of various stripes, including those who identify as evangelicals, Asian American biblical interpretation gives voice to the rich traditions of resistance, liberation, community, and spirituality that have nourished and sustained Asian American ecclesial and parachurch communities.[20] It has the potential to form Asian American students, ministers, and readers to develop greater capacities to think theologically and interpret the Bible critically as they consider and respond to the ways the gospel relates to their lives.

Asian American biblical interpretation stands in solidarity with other communities of color in the fight for racial justice, while seeking the interests of their own ethnic

[18]By *ideological*, I mean an approach that considers how the biblical texts and biblical interpreters may reflect and support certain ideologies, positionalities, and oppressive expressions of power.

[19]Pascal D. Bazzell uses the phrase "ecclesial-oriented" in his book *Urban Ecclesiology: Gospel of Mark,* Familia Dei *and a Filipino Community Facing Homelessness* (London: T&T Clark, 2018).

[20]See Meena Venkataramanan, "Asian Americans Are Changing the Face of Evangelicalism," *The Washington Post*, May 5, 2023, www.washingtonpost.com/nation/2023/05/03/asian-american-evangelicals/?pwapi_token=eyJ0eXAiOiJKV1QiLCJhbGciOiJIUzI1NiJ9.eyJzdWJpZCI6IjQ0NDM4NzciLCJyZWFzb24iOiJnaWZ0IiwibmJmIjoxNjg0MTIzMjAwLCJpc3MiOiJzdWJzY3JpcHRpb25zIiwiZXhwIjoxNjg1NDE5MTk5LCJpYXQiOjE2ODQxMjMyMDAsImp0aSI6ImE4MzAwZmFkLTZjYmItNGVlOC04YTQ2LTI4ZDU4NzU2NjEzOCIsInVybCI6Imh0dHBzOi8vd3d3Lndhc2hpbmd0b25wb3N0LmNvbS9uYXRpb24vMjAyMy8wNS8wMy9hc2lhbi1hbWVyaWNhbi1ldmFuZ2VsaWNhbHMvIn0.tzBy5T6yQqybPha1kDARMKdvG8n_TrZswzxF0jZsZho.

groups and the broader collective interests of Asian Americans. It takes on the critical hermeneutical task of helping Christian leaders, ministers, preachers, and teachers bridge today's issues and problems with the world of the Bible and its readers while forming disciples of Christ.

To engage in Asian American biblical interpretation is to bear public witness to the ways Asian Americans understand and live out the gospel and God's concern for justice for all who are marginalized and oppressed.[21] Asian American biblical interpretation ultimately concerns itself with the flourishing of humanity and the world, with a particular focus on people and communities who have "ethnic and/or affective ties to both sides of the Pacific" and whose sense of identity "exceeds the limits of national borders and narrow understandings of political territoriality and citizenship."[22]

EXAMPLES AND TRAJECTORIES FOR ASIAN AMERICAN BIBLICAL INTERPRETATION

Asian American identity remains diverse and heterogeneous. Likewise, the academic fields of Asian American studies and biblical studies are methodologically diverse and heterogeneous. Asian American biblical interpretation reflects this "multiplicity and multivocality" and cannot be reduced to a single approach, method, or project.[23] Rather, Asian American biblical interpretation has the potential to birth and equip new interpreters and interpreting communities to take seriously the contextuality of God and their identities as Asian American people of God.

Among the Asian American biblical interpretation scholarship produced over the past three decades, Chloe Sun discerns common themes revolving around "the issues and intersections of identity, race, gender, class, liberation, and how one's social location shapes the ways in which one interprets scripture."[24] Asian American biblical interpretation scholarship also tends to emphasize collective possibilities and the concerns of diverse ethnic groups, as evident in edited volumes, such as *The Bible in Asian America*, edited by Tat-siong Benny Liew and Gale A. Yee; *Ways of Being, Ways of Reading*, edited by Mary F. Foskett and Jeffrey Kah-Jin Kuan; *T&T Clark Handbook of Asian American Biblical Hermeneutics*, edited by Uriah Y. Kim and Seung Ai Yang; and "Special Issue: Asian American Biblical Criticism" for the journal *The Bible and Critical Theory*, edited by Jin Young Choi and Wong Park.[25] Liew's *What Is Asian American Biblical Hermeneutics: Reading the New Testament* is the first single-authored monograph of its kind to demonstrate Asian American biblical interpretation's multifaceted possibilities without attempting to narrowly define or explain it.[26] Gale Yee's *Towards an Asian American Biblical Hermeneutics: An Intersectional Anthology*

---

[21]Lee, *Doing Asian American Theology*, 73.

[22]Ho, "Complex Heterogeneity of Asian American Identity," 19.

[23]Chloe Sun, "Recent Research on Asian and Asian American Hermeneutics Related to the Hebrew Bible," *CurBR* 17, no. 3 (2019): 239.

[24]Sun, "Recent Research on Asian and Asian American Hermeneutics," 238.

[25]Tat-siong Benny Liew and Gale A. Yee, eds., *The Bible in Asian America* (Atlanta: Society of Biblical Literature, 2002); Mary F. Foskett and Jeffrey Kah-Jin Kuan, eds., *Ways of Being, Ways of Reading: Asian American Biblical Interpretation* (St. Louis: Chalice, 2006); Kim and Yang, *T&T Clark Handbook of Asian American Biblical Hermeneutics*; Jin Young Choi and Wongi Park, eds., "Special Issue: Asian American Biblical Criticism," *The Bible and Critical Theory* 16, no. 1 (2020). See SueJeanne Koh, "Asian American Christian Theology: Topographies, Trajectories, and Possibilities," *Religion Compass* 14, no. 10 (October 2020): 1-14.

[26]See Liew, *What Is Asian American Biblical Hermeneutics*.

presents a collection of essays in which she reads biblical texts through "an Asian American lens" in ways that interweave historical-critical, feminist, and intersectional analysis with Asian American studies and autobiography.[27] These groundbreaking volumes have charted the path for Asian American biblical interpretation and reflect the diverse spectrum of contexts, approaches/methods, and textual analyses reflected in Asian American biblical interpretation.

For example, in "Always Ethnic, Never 'American': Reading 1 Peter Through the Lens of the 'Perpetual Foreigner' Stereotype," I address the role of ethnic identity in the formation of Christian identity in 1 Peter and for Asian Americans.[28] Engaging research from the social sciences in my interpretation of 1 Peter, I explore the psychological impact of the stereotype of the perpetual foreigner imposed on Asian Americans. I consider how the stereotype's negative impact sheds light on, nuances, and even complicates the strategy I see the author of 1 Peter making in the letter to address his readers' social estrangement from the dominant culture. I argue that the author in effect encourages his addressees to see themselves as perpetual foreigners to build a stronger sense of Christian collective identity and internal group solidarity among believers, who are already at home in the dominant culture. However, I caution that 1 Peter's strategy must be appropriated with a double vision for Christian Asian Americans, who already experience the perpetual foreigner stereotype by virtue of their ethnic identities.

More personal and ecclesially oriented perspectives appear in *Mirrored Reflections: Reframing Biblical Characters*, edited by Young Lee Hertig and Chloe Sun. For example, Sun reflects on the challenges and intersection of gender, ethnicity, and social location in her essay "Bathsheba Transformed: From Silence to Voice."[29] Employing speech analysis, she traces the speech and character development of Bathsheba from 2 Samuel to 1 Kings to demonstrate how Bathsheba transforms from being like a passive, silent lamb without a voice to an assertive, resourceful woman who navigates the patriarchal structures with a sense of agency. Sun finds a role model in Bathsheba as she connects her own experience as an Asian American woman leader who had not used her voice as a change agent with that of Bathsheba, who found a balance between softness and toughness, between silence and speech.

A recent study titled "Asian American Emerging Adults and Theological Education" identified the importance of recognizing the diversity and complexity of Asian American identities to reduce the sense of erasure and marginalization felt especially by students of Southeast Asian and South Asian descent.[30] While there are some pan-Asian themes that resonate broadly, a one-size-fits-all approach to engaging in Asian American theology or biblical interpretation overlooks the complex and heterogeneous nature of Asian American identity and misconstrues that the Asian American community is ethnically and ecumenically diverse. Efforts are needed for greater inclusion of South and Southeast Asian American and Pacific

[27]Gale A. Yee, *Towards an Asian American Biblical Hermeneutics: An Intersectional Anthology* (Eugene, OR: Cascade, 2021).

[28]Janette H. Ok, "Always Ethnic, Never 'American': Reading 1 Peter Through the Lens of the 'Perpetual Foreigner' Stereotype," in Kim and Yang, *T&T Clark Handbook of Asian American Biblical Hermeneutics*, 417-26.

[29]Chloe Sun, "Bathsheba Transformed: From Silence to Voice," in *Mirrored Reflections: Reframing Biblical Characters*, ed. Young Lee Hertig and Chloe Sun (Eugene, OR: Wipf & Stock, 2010), 30-42.

[30]Daniel D. Lee, Steven Argue, Diana Kim, and Jason Chu, "Asian American Emerging Adults and Theological Education Findings and Recommendations," unpublished study from the Center for Asian American Theology and Ministry at Fuller Seminary, September 2020.

Islander Christian perspectives in Asian American biblical interpretation, along with perspectives of transnational adoptees, and multiracial and LGBTQIA+ identities.

An example of South Asian American biblical interpretation can be seen in Haley Gabrielle's article "DesiCrit in New Testament Interpretation: Paul's Ambiguous Identity in Acts." Gabrielle analyzes the book of Acts through a dimension of critical race theory called DesiCrit and demonstrates how Acts represents Paul's religious, national, and geographical identities as ambiguous and malleable, and compares his identities with the racial ambiguity and malleability of South Asian Americans. Attending to how both Paul and South Asian Americans leverage and constrain aspects of their identities to serve different ends, Gabrielle makes a connection between the ways Asian Americans are racialized and how their ambiguous racialization must be understood in light of "racial hierarchy rooted in anti-blackness."[31]

Mary F. Foskett reads John 4 from the perspective of an Asian American adoptee in "Navigating Networks: An Asian American Reading of the Samaritan Woman." She explains how Asian American adoptees face questions not only concerning the legitimacy of their national, racial, and ethnic identities but also about their familial and birth identities: *Where are you from? What are you? Whose are you?* Considering the ways adoptees navigate multiple networks that are not necessarily at odds with one another, Foskett reads the Samaritan woman in terms of the woman's manifold and complex networks (i.e., the references to places, human and nonhuman actors, ethnicity and gender, things) and within the frame of hospitality. Just as preexisting and new networks can coexist for Asian American adoptees, so the old and new networks and role of host and guest can coexist in the text: "Without relinquishing who they have been, both the Samaritan woman and Jesus are changed by who each other is."[32]

To See and Be Seen: Reading the New Testament As Asian Americans forthcoming book from Baker Academic written by myself and Jordan Ryan, offers New Testament interpretation from a distinctly Asian American perspective for and from the Asian American church. As an ecclesially oriented coauthored book, it engages in dialogical interchange between two Asian American New Testament scholars—a Filipino American male and a Korean American female. Ryan and I write from different ethnic traditions and institutional, ecclesial, and geographical contexts, taking seriously the particularities, complexities, and heterogeneity of their distinct Asian American identities while holding to the conviction that we share enough in common to offer integrated theological readings of New Testament themes and texts.

The examples above reveal the fact that Asian American biblical interpretation is an ethnically, ecumenically, and methodologically diverse phenomenon that resists exhaustive definition, even as it seeks to define itself.[33] It is a dynamic approach to reading the Bible that sees Christian faith as the motivation to embrace one's ethnic and racial identities and histories and "do justice and to love kindness and

---

[31]Haley Gabrielle, "DesiCrit in New Testament Interpretation: Paul's Ambiguous Identity in Acts," *The Bible and Critical Theory* 16, no. 1 (2020): 19-40, here 36.

[32]Mary F. Foskett, "Navigating Networks: An Asian American Reading of the Samaritan Woman," in *Reading Biblical Texts Together: Pursuing Minoritized Biblical Criticism*, ed. Tat-siong Benny Liew and Fernando F. Segovia (Atlanta: SBL Press, 2022), 293-307, here 305.

[33]See Koh, "Asian American Christian Theology," 2.

to walk humbly with our God" (Mic 6:8, NRSV adapted).[34] It has activist, coalitional, panethnic, and cross-racial roots in the pursuit of equal rights and justice for Asian Americans and other minoritized groups in the United States. It finds its grounding in the understanding that particularity and contextuality matter to God, and rejects the ideology of colorblindness. As Asian American biblical interpretation takes up more discursive space within academic circles and formative space within churches, it must continue to make room for minoritized voices within Asian America and Asian American Christianity and invest actively in cross-racial solidarity. In doing so, Asian American biblical interpretation reflects the complex, diverse, and heterogeneous identities and histories of individuals and communities who matter to God and who expand what it means to be the people of God.

[34]For examples of Asian American Christian churches, communities, and organizations in the late 1960s and early 1970s that "integrated their religious and racial identities and fused their faith with their social activism," see Jane Hong, "The Asian American Movement and the Church," *Journal of Asian American Studies* 24, no. 1 (February 2022): 63-94.

HISPANIC BIBLICAL INTERPRETATION

Osvaldo Padilla

INTRODUCTION

The goal of this essay is to explore the Hispanic habits of biblical interpretation in the United States. To attempt even a sketch of biblical interpretation in Latin America itself would be impossible in the amount of space provided for this essay. In any case, I lack the necessary breadth and expertise to provide an analysis of how the Bible is being interpreted in countries such as Ecuador, Venezuela, Cuba, and so on. This essay is thus about Hispanic biblical interpretation in the *United States.* As the readers may already know, even restricting this investigation to the United States is becoming extremely complex in light of the great diversity of Hispanics in the United States.

With this essay I seek simultaneously to introduce readers to the basics of Hispanic biblical interpretation and to ask critical questions of current practice and future possibilities. This latter aspect will be developed at the end of the essay.

In the introductory or basics of this chapter I will ask the following questions: What is Hispanic biblical interpretation? How is Hispanic biblical interpretation done (method)? Along the way I will provide examples to illustrate Hispanic biblical interpretation. In the second, more critical part of the chapter, I ask the following questions: What does it mean to be biblical in Hispanic biblical interpretation? How is the relationship between the Bible and ethnicity conceived in Hispanic biblical interpretation? What may be some of the future concerns of Hispanic biblical interpretation?

THE BASICS OF HISPANIC BIBLICAL INTERPRETATION

Before going any further, I must address a question of terminology: What is the proper term to use in speaking of the approach to Scripture described in this chapter? Both in the title and in the paragraphs above I use the term *Hispanic* biblical interpretation. Friends from other cultures, in an attempt to be respectful to my ethnicity, often ask me what term they should use. My answer tends to be that either *Hispanic* or *Latino/a* is acceptable in showing courtesy to the variegated group of people who engage in this type of interpretation. Throughout this essay I will use the term *Hispanic.* Why? First, and in an autobiographic pulling of the curtain, I confess to prefer *Hispanic* because this is the term I first learned when my family moved to the United States when I was thirteen years old. My friends who came from the same continent called each other and me *Hispanic.* Using the term gave a sense of solidarity to a shy boy from the Dominican Republic who had emigrated to a foreign land in which, as the late Cuban artist Celica Cruz sang, "people speak different / the sun on the skin does not feel the same."[1] So, it is likely that one of the reasons I

---

[1]In Spanish: "Se habla diferente/no se siente igual el sol."

prefer Hispanic is nostalgia! However, nostalgia is not part of the accepted academic apparatus, so I must provide other reasons.[2]

The term *Hispanic* stems from the fact that, with few exceptions, all nations in the Caribbean, Central America, and South America were colonized by Spain (España). It is from the English translation of the name of this country that the term *Hispanic* is derived. And since the language that unites these peoples (both in Latin America and the US) comes from Spain (although some parts of Spain do not speak Spanish but Catalán), *Hispanic* seemed a logical label.

There are, however, at least three problems with the use of *Hispanic*. First, to the extent that this label is based on the fact that Latin Americans who emigrated to the United States spoke as their first language Spanish, the word *Hispanic* as a designation could work. Nevertheless, while the first generation spoke and speaks Spanish, this is often not the case with successive generations. For example, many second-generation Hispanics only (or mostly) speak English. This phenomenon occurs among many ethnic minorities, where speaking the majority language is often a way of fitting in. Second-generation Hispanics, therefore, if they use Spanish at all, usually employ the language in its spoken form. Furthermore, their vocabulary tends to be limited, and properly written Spanish (i.e., orthography and syntax) is often altogether absent. I have had the strange experience of meeting Garcias and Padillas in different parts of the United States and starting a conversation in Spanish only to be told, "Sorry, I don't speak Spanish." In some states where there are three or four generations of Latin American families, the Spanish language is a thing of the past. This is not a criticism of the consecutive generations of Hispanics in the United States. We all have to find a way to function in a new culture, and sometimes we are so focused on the new language that the old language is forgotten. In many ways, mastering the new language is a matter of survival.

The second problem with the use of *Hispanic* relates to ideology. In short, if we use the term *Hispanic*, the argument goes, we are identifying primarily with the European (Spain) aspect of our ethnicity to the exclusion of our Native American and African roots, which are just as (if not more) formative of who we are as a people. Related to this is the question: Why use a term that highlights the identity of colonizers who brutalized our people and land, in some cases wiping out entire races?[3]

The third problem with the use of *Hispanic* is that this is a term that was imposed by the American Census Bureau in the 1970s. The term *Hispanic*, therefore, did away (perhaps unintentionally so) with the variety of Hispanics in the United States. People from Cuba to Chile were all lumped into one category: Hispanic. It is not unreasonable, therefore, to ask: Why use a term that flattens out our wonderful diversity?

For these and other reasons, a sector of scholarship suggests that we use the term "Latino/a biblical interpretation" to describe the approach to Scripture being shaped by the peoples of the Caribbean, Central, and South America residing in the United States. One of the advantages of using *Latino/a* is its inclusivity. By adding the letter *a* after the forward

[2]For what follows, see the helpful work of Miguel A. de La Torre and Edwin David Aponte, *Introducing Latino/a Theologies* (Maryknoll, NY: Orbis Books, 2001), 15-28.

[3]For example, many Spanish colonizers so abused the Native Americans of the Dominican Republic (the Taínos) that none remain today. See "Yale University Genocide Studies Program," https://gsp.yale.edu/case-studies/colonial-genocides-project/hispaniola (accessed June 15, 2023).

slash, a letter the Spanish language "regularly" (I put "regularly" in quotation marks because grammar actually is full of exceptions to the rule [*regula*!]) uses for feminine substantives, it is signaled that women are equal partners in the endeavor we call biblical interpretation. This is particularly important in our Latin American culture, where a certain species of machismo has been dominant in certain (not all!) nations of Latin America.[4] Thus, *Latino/a* is an attempt to shout loud and clear that it is not the gender of persons that qualifies them for ministry but rather the empowerment of the Holy Spirit. Christian women are just as empowered as men by the Holy Spirit.

However, just as there are problems with the use of *Hispanic*, so also there are problems with the use of *Latino/a*. First, *Latino/a* is just as European-derived as *Hispanic* is: the shift is simply from Spain to the language of Rome. Second, *Latino/a* is a neologism that even for native Spanish-speakers is difficult to pronounce. Consequently, it is aesthetically unpleasing and clumsy, likely because of the forward slash and the fact that *oa* is not a diphthong, so the flow of pronunciation is interrupted.

To conclude on the issue of proper naming, it is probably better to give ourselves the freedom to use both terms. Perhaps we should look to Ludwig Wittgenstein by focusing on what *Hispanic* or *Latino/a* actually *does* rather than worrying too much about names.[5] Paying attention to what Hispanic interpretation does may bring more clarity than attempting to discover a perfect label. So, I move on to describe what Hispanic or Latino/a biblical interpretation actually is and what it attempts to accomplish.

Defining Hispanic biblical interpretation turns out to be just as (if not more) contested as finding the correct label for it.[6] Here, one's fundamental theological and/or philosophical commitments play a large part. I will come back to this shortly. For now, to put it bluntly, there is no one single, authoritative definition of Hispanic biblical interpretation. In fact, some may say that not having a single definition is *itself* part of its ethos. There are many reasons for a lack of consensus as to what constitutes Hispanic biblical interpretation. First, there are theological differences among Hispanics in the United States. This is especially so as the Hispanic population has continued to grow very fast over the last few decades. Hispanics have grown from approximately 9.6 million in the 1970s to approximately 62.1 million by 2020.[7] This explosive growth is not just a matter of biological reproduction of Hispanics who live in the United States; much of the growth is also the result of Hispanics entering the United States for the first time, whether documented or undocumented. Hispanics who have lived for some generations in the United States are then mixed with those Hispanics who continually enter the country. The result is a mélange of different expressions of Christianity (not to mention Hispanics who belong to other

[4] I use the phrase "a certain species of machismo" deliberately. The abuse of women perpetuated by machismo exists in every culture, although its manifestations are different. For example, the radical forms of complementarianism present in some sections of North American evangelicalism are, to my mind, simply different variations of the machismo ethos.

[5] Wittgenstein (1889-1951) was one of the most important philosophers of our era, particularly in philosophy of language. For Wittgenstein, what matters in the understanding of a concept is not some metaphysical grasping of that concept but how it is used in a particular community. At the risk of simplification, Wittgenstein might say that when we decide how to use a concept in a community, *that* is precisely its meaning; there is no need to go deeper.

[6] For some of the challenges, see Benjamín Valentín, ed., *New Horizons in Hispanic/Latino(a) Theology* (Cleveland: Pilgrim, 2003). For the challenges from a more Roman Catholic perspective, see Néstor Medina, *Mestizaje: (Re)mapping Race, Culture, and Faith in Latina/o Catholicism* (Maryknoll, NY: Orbis Books, 2009).

[7] See the important statistics compiled by the Pew Research Center, "Hispanic Americans' Trust in and Engagement with Science," June 14, 2022, www.pewresearch.org/science/2022/06/14/a-brief-statistical-portrait-of-u-s-hispanics/.

religions or to none at all). Roman Catholicism continues to be the primary form of Christianity among Hispanics in the United States. However, it is declining, from 67 percent of adult Hispanics identifying as Roman Catholic in 2010 to 43 percent in 2022.[8]

Second, that Spanish is not an official language in the United States minimizes the capacity of—for lack of a better term—branding. So, for example, there is no Hispanic version of Lifeway, where the same Bibles (often with commentaries), theological books, children's books, Sunday school material, and so on can be printed in Spanish and easily found in stores anywhere from Texas to Massachusetts. This results in fragmentation. What tends to happen, especially in our internet era, is that different Hispanics search for preachers and teachers who communicate in Spanish. These teachers themselves represent a spectrum from evangelical fundamentalists to evangelical Calvinists and much in between. Third, Hispanics come from a different continent, not one country. Different Protestant missions evangelized Latin America, with the result that those who emigrate to the United States belong to different denominations.[9]

In light of the complexity of Christianity among Hispanics in the United States sketched above, it is difficult to provide a simple handbook or a how-to for Hispanic biblical interpretation. Instead of a handbook, we should think of Hispanic biblical interpretation as a group of interpretational tendencies that act more like a *grammar* to help us engage Scripture. Hispanic biblical interpretation is a diverse way of thinking about the Bible that is glued together by certain ideas and reflexes that are broadly shared by Hispanic believers. While the cogency of this approach is primarily articulated in the academy, it stems just as much from the *pueblo*, the *people* of different churches in the United States.

Although somewhat dated in light of the torrent of published material on Hispanic theology that is constantly emerging, Justo González's book *Santa Biblia* continues to shape Hispanic biblical interpretation.[10] The basic insight underlying this book, to which I will return shortly and which I also share, is that the Bible is never read from nowhere but always from somewhere. It would not be an exaggeration to say that acceptance of this insight serves as the foundation of this entire volume. This insight (not original to González) constitutes a break with some of the fundamental ideals of the Enlightenment, especially the type of raw objectivism, which, while producing great advancements in the sciences (e.g., physics), was not adequate for the study of theology, at least in the extreme forms of objectivism or scientific positivism. Scientific positivism works with an idea of reality in which there is a clean break between the object being studied (say, the moon) and the subject doing the study (the physicist). This positivism argued that there was such a thing as "the view from nowhere."[11] The subject observes an object with such purity that nothing gets in the way that could distort the nature of the object. In time (the nineteenth century), theology, in an attempt to follow the natural sciences and

[8]See Pew Research Center, "Among U.S. Latinos, Catholicism Continues to Decline but Is Still the Largest Faith," April 13, 2023, www.pewresearch.org/religion/2023/04/13/among-u-s-latinos-catholicism-continues-to-decline-but-is-still-the-largest-faith/#:~:text=U.S.%2Dborn%20Latinos%20are%20s.less,been%20relatively%20stable%20since%202010. Interestingly, among young Hispanics born in the US, 49 percent claim no religious affiliation as of 2020.

[9]See the work of Justo González, *Mañana: Christian Theology from a Hispanic Perspective* (Nashville: Abingdon, 1990); Pablo Deiros, *Protestantismo en América Latina: Ayer, Hoy y Mañana* (Nashville: Editorial Caribe, 1997).

[10]Justo González, *Santa Biblia: The Bible Through Hispanic Eyes* (Nashville: Abingdon, 1996).

[11]This is the title of the influential book by Thomas Nagel: *The View from Nowhere* (Oxford: Oxford University Press, 1986).

also justify its place in the university (especially in Germany), adopted a form of positivism, with F. C. Baur and the Tübingen school perhaps being the best examples.[12]

How would a belief in scientific positivism affect the reading of the Bible and the act of theologizing? The answers are numerous. It would mean that one could not bring any presuppositions (especially of the theological type) to the biblical text because if one did, then one could distort what the text really meant. Therefore, one's belief in, say, the Trinity, would have to be suspended while one studied the Bible. It would mean that one's religious experience, say, one's conversion, would be meaningless in attempting to understand the Bible. It would mean that one could not rely on the help of the Holy Spirit to make the biblical text come alive in the present. The positivist would say that such belief in the Holy Spirit may actually cloud one's judgment. What else would this way of approaching the Bible and theology mean? It would mean that the only people capable of providing a scientific understanding of the Bible would be those who had been trained in the university and had acquired the necessary critical methods that the academy had agreed could be employed in exegesis.

During the earlier decades of the United States, this positivist, Enlightenment-based, and actually ideological (not objective) approach to Scripture and theology did not permit people of color to study theology, did not permit women to study theology, did not permit minorities to study theology and gain a professional degree. One was not allowed (or, if done, one was not taken seriously) to import into the reading of the Bible one's suffering either as a race or as an individual, or one's experiences of poverty in helping to better to illuminate the life of Jesus, or one's motherhood in helping to better understand God's care for his children. All these experiences and more were viewed as detractions to serious study of theology. The conclusion of this ideology was that the theological seminaries and divinity schools of earlier decades in the United States were populated primarily by men of European descent.

It took suffering, protests, sacrifices, and—I would argue—the work of God's Spirit to bring these academic fortresses to the ground in order to be rebuilt in ways that truly honored God and the humans made in his image. In other cases, orthodox Christians founded their own institutions where Scripture could truly be studied Christianly. However, it is sad that many of these orthodox or conservative seminaries are committing the same mistakes of the past when they do not permit women to study the entire curriculum or when they do not create welcoming spaces for minorities. It is also sad when Christians return to some of these elite institutions and become as ideological as the predecessors. While I am in no way against Christians studying at elite universities and divinity schools (this position would actually be a mark of fundamentalism), there must be awareness of the particular challenges that may be present.

In short, then, minority biblical studies celebrates our diversity, ecclesial commitments, and ethnic-sociohistorical locations (of the present and the past). Such studies view these realities as strengths and not weaknesses, as crucial in making us who we are, as vital in the formation of our character in Christ. Hispanic biblical interpretation represents one of these minority biblical approaches to Scripture and theology.

[12]See the work of Johannes Zachhuber, *Theology as Science in Nineteenth Century Germany: From F. C. Baur to Ernst Troeltsch* (Oxford: Oxford University Press, 2013), 21-22, 26, 51, 61, 101. He calls this positivism "neo-rationalist" (22).

I return to González's *Santa Biblia* briefly to sketch what it means to read the Bible in Spanish.

1. Marginality. For González, Hispanic Protestants experience marginality in at least two ways. First, we may experience marginality from other Hispanics, sometimes, sadly, from Roman Catholic Hispanics. This situation is better now than when González wrote in 1996. However, it is still a sad experience that reminds us of the eschatological not-yet of our existence. The second way in which we experience marginality is due to our race and/or accent. In some parts of the United States this is very troublesome, as "normal" is defined in a particular way that excludes those who look or speak differently. González reminds us, however, that marginality was also the experience of the early Christians. First Peter is a book where the author turns marginality on its head. He explains our "dual reality" when he speaks of our condition as exiles and foreigners (1 Pet 1:1; 2:11), and yet we are at the same time God's elect (1 Pet 1:1), for whom God has prepared an inheritance that will never know corruption or perishing (1 Pet 1:3-9). Precisely because we have followed Christ in this path of marginality, one day we will receive "the crown of glory that never fades away" (1 Pet 5:4; in contrast to the crowns given to athletic victors, which, made of ivy or celery leaves, eventually faded). This dual reality of exile and belonginess makes 1 Peter similar to apocalyptic literature in that the reality on earth cannot be compared with the glorious reality awaiting us in heaven.[13]

2. Poverty. Although many Hispanics have prospered economically in the United States, many (if not most) live at levels of poverty or near-poverty. This is particularly the case with undocumented Hispanics. The experience of poverty gives us a lens to pay closer attention to characters in the Bible who were poor. González calls our attention to the famous passages of the Acts of the Apostles where the author speaks of the unity of the early Christians (Acts 2:44-45; 4:32-35).[14] These early communities were viewed as outstanding precisely because none among them had any need that was not met. Some scholars in the United States may fear that these passages push for communism. But that is because many of them have never experienced poverty and the place the church plays in this scenario. I well remember, as a young Christian in South Florida, how our small and poor church always found a way to help a recently exiled family from Colombia to pay the monthly rent.

3. Mestizaje *and* mulatez. The term *mestizo* is used of the offspring of Spanish and Natives. This mixed offspring was often viewed deprecatingly because they were not "pure" Spaniards. The term *mulatto* refers to the offspring of parents from African slaves and white Spaniards. Like mestizo, to be called *mulatto* used to be a pejorative. *Mulatez* is very common in the Caribbean. My mother is *mulatta*, while my father is of European descent. This mixture has always been my reality. In the Dominican Republic (where I was born), this mixture is normal. Under the brutal dictatorship of Rafael Leonidas Trujillo from the 1930s until his assassination in 1961, the concept of racial purity returned. Trujillo (himself mixed) attempted to make treaties with the dictator of Spain, Franco, in order to bring more white Spaniards

---

[13]On this motif of "dual reality," see Reinhard Feldmeier, *The First Letter of Peter*, trans. Peter Davis (Waco, TX: Baylor University Press, 2008). For a similar understanding of 1 Peter, see more recently Gerald Wagner and François Vouga, *Der erste Brief des Petrus* (Tübingen: Mohr Siebeck, 2020). From an Asian American perspective, see the work of Janette Ok, *Constructing Ethnic Identity in 1 Peter: Who You Are No Longer* (London: T&T Clark, 2021).

[14]Gonzalez, *Santa Biblia*, 66-68.

to the Dominican Republic. Trujillo desired to *blanquear la raza* ("make white the race"), because he believed that Mulattos were lazy and a shame to the nation. Although in some parts of the United States there has been some progress against this despicable racial purism, there is still a long road ahead. One of the gifts that the Hispanic church, especially those churches where there is high attendance of Caribbean Hispanics, can give the population of the United States is visual in nature. We desire that those who view mixed marriages and children as something weird would look at us. We have been living as a mixed race for centuries—and the result has been culturally enriching, not shameful.

4. Exiles and aliens. I covered some of this material under the rubric of marginality. Therefore, I will concentrate on the fifth and last aspect of Hispanic biblical interpretation.

5. Solidarity. One of the primary goals of Hispanic Christianity in the United States is solidarity. Many of us call each other *familia* (family) because of our oneness in Christ. Coming at the biblical text from this reality helps us understand why Paul was heartbroken and angry with the Corinthians because of their chronic divisions (1 Corinthians). We understand that we are brothers and sisters in the church. This understanding of solidarity also leads to seek and grant forgiveness quickly when one has been offended in the church. The seriousness with which we take solidarity, often in the family, has given us eyes to see why Jesus and the New Testament authors so often call us to "love one another."

These five traits, which are constantly being developed and deepened in Hispanic theology, serve as a grammar for Hispanic biblical interpretation. When reading the Scriptures or exploring a theological expression, many of us look for this grammar. When this grammar is present, we know we are moving in the right direction as students and teachers of Scripture. And it is possible that it can serve as a model for others.

THE FUTURE OF HISPANIC BIBLICAL INTERPRETATION: THEOLOGY OR ANTHROPOLOGY?

Although Hispanic biblical interpretation has developed well (but far from perfect), we must ask what some potential pitfalls may lie before us. My interaction with Hispanic biblical interpretation occurs through attending church (mainly evangelical and many times as a guest), attending academic societies, and reading books on the subject. The impressions I note below stem from these contexts. Although the issues that face Hispanic biblical interpretation are many, I have, for the sake of space and clarity, put them as either-or. This inevitably leads to simplification; but my comments are just a way to start the conversation. I will state the matter bluntly at the moment and flesh it out below. The question I wrestle with is the following: what is and will be the relationship between Scripture and Hispanic biblical interpretation?

Unfortunately, and especially in the context of churches, there are times when it seems to me that the study of the Bible becomes an end in itself. That is, the impression is given that our *raison d'être* is to study the Bible, pray, and encourage each other for evangelism, which is our task for the rest of the week. On the one hand, I am delighted that we are doing these things, which are central to what makes the church the church. On the other hand, there is often a lack of marrying the study of Scripture to the needs of the culture. This is unfortunate, because one of the defining factors of Hispanic biblical interpretation is that the practical and the theoretical are supposed to happen simultaneously. That is, we take pride in an approach to Scripture that is, to employ a slogan that is almost worn out, not *binary*. We critique Enlightenment-based biblical approaches because they tended to go into the metaphysical side without sufficient attempt to *practice* the Bible in our respective communities. And yet, we are often repeating the same mistake. Thus, a *vacío* (gap) exists when Hispanic biblical interpretation does not become involved in social and political matters that can help the Hispanic population in concrete areas such as medical improvement in the care of migrant workers, more humane immigrant laws, and unfair incarcerations, to give some examples. Often, there is a belief among some of us that involvement in political movements for the betterment of our people is not "biblical," that it may be a sign of liberalism creeping into our *iglesias evangélicas*.

On the other hand, when engaging in Hispanic biblical interpretation at the level of the academy, one often encounters a study of Scripture that is not theological. That is, if one understands theology as ultimately a meeting with the living God in the context of a people who seek to worship and know this God on the basis of Scripture and the traditions of the church, there is little that is actually theological. What one often discovers is a hunger to know more about our particular race. Of course, this is a good thing, especially for those of us who are trying to forge an identity in a new land. Nevertheless, *anthro*pology cannot be engaged at the cost of *theo*logy. In doing Hispanic biblical interpretation, we seek to understand our cultures with as much precision as possible. This includes studying the past of our native countries. In studying the far past of our peoples, we often encounter practices that seem questionable in light of Scripture. Some scholars are calling for "complete authenticity," which often means going beyond Scripture and the creedal statements of the church. At times it is argued that some of the narratives of our oldest ancestors are as authoritative as Scripture. This is anthropology in the name of theology. To be sure, there is much that we can learn from our pre-Columbian ancestors that can be integrated into our Christian existence. However, precisely because we are Christians, we must hold fast to the reality (a *faith* reality) that, as theologian T. F. Torrance used to say, "There is no God behind the back of Jesus Christ."[15] It is in Jesus Christ that we meet God, the one God who is Father, Son, and Holy Spirit.

[15]T. F. Torrance, *The Christian Doctrine of God: One Being Three Persons* (London: A&C Black, 1996), 243-44.

TURTLE ISLAND BIBLICAL INTERPRETATION

T. Christopher Hoklotubbe (Choctaw) and
H. Daniel Zacharias (Cree-Anishinaabe)

Very soon after Christopher Columbus was found lost on the shores of Turtle Island (now also called North America), Indigenous peoples of these lands had encounters with the Scriptures that were from the outset entangled in the colonial project.[1] Like much missionary effort past and present, the Scriptures were mediated by missionaries—ones who were socially and culturally bound to their own languages, histories, and cultural practices. As Indigenous followers of Jesus today seek to interpret the Bible for themselves and their communities, readers recognize that this is an act of intercultural interpretation and dialogue. Numerous patterns and emphases within Indigenous North American interpretation can be discerned, but foundational to it all is the attempt to read the Bible as Creator has made us. We seek to engage the Bible in and through our shared worldviews, lifeways, lands, experiences, histories, traditions, and struggles in order both to give due dignity to our heritage and to follow Jesus in the ways Creator has made us. Both of us, as men of mixed Indigenous and settler descent and as ones trained in the field of biblical studies, have undertaken an ongoing work that seeks to sketch out the ways in which Indigenous peoples of North America read the Scriptures, with the present essay a contribution to our evolving thoughts on the issue. We do so with deep awareness of and appreciation for many Indigenous theologians and practitioners who have gone on before us and shaped our thinking, as well as the robust communities of Indigenous followers of Jesus that we participate in and learn from, particularly NAIITS: An Indigenous Learning Community (formerly the North American Institute for Indigenous Theological Studies).

CORE ASSUMPTION

As is the case for many ethnic groups, there is a spectrum of belief and practice within the Christian community. Many Indigenous peoples in North America do not have discernibly different approaches to the scriptural text from the wider church, and often tend toward a more conservative reading, in large part due to the theology of the missionaries. Our attempt here to sketch a Turtle Island hermeneutics seeks to describe what defines the unique approach to the Christian Scriptures by those Indigenous folks who have sought to practice and/or align with their cultural heritage and therefore seek to decolonize their Christian discipleship. In our readings and encounters with Indigenous authors of

[1]Numerous thoughts from this chapter originate from T. Christopher Hoklotubbe, "Native American Interpretation of the Bible," in *Oxford Encyclopedias of the Bible: Digital Collection* (Oxford: Oxford University Press, 2022), www.oxfordreference.com/display/10.1093/acref/9780197669402.001.0001/acref-9780197669402-e-70.

this persuasion, several trends are consistent and will be described below. But foundational to all of them, in one form or another, is the core assumption that Creator God of Israel who revealed Godself to the Israelite patriarchs and matriarchs had not simply ignored the Indigenous Peoples of North America until the European colonizers arrived with the Bible-infused empire called Christendom.[2] Rather, Creator has always been present with us. Creator's fingerprints are imprinted on our stories, ceremonies, lands, worldviews, and lifeways as Indigenous Peoples.

In a seminal article on Indigenous interpretations of Scripture, Episcopal Bishop Steven Charleston (Choctaw) encourages Indigenous Christians to compare the Old Testament and its account of the Israelite people's history, teachings, and covenant with Creator Yahweh with their own histories, traditional teachings, ancestral laws, and covenants with Creator.[3] The Indigenous nations of Turtle Island have within their oral and written traditions the history, traditional teachings, ancestral laws, and covenant with Creator as well—our Original Instructions. According to Charleston, these ancestral stories, traditions, and ceremonial rites are Original Instructions given to each Indigenous nation. Indigenous Christians do not need to reject or relegate their traditions in order to accept the Old Testament as Scripture. Indigenous Christians can appreciate how the Old Testament explains Creator's unique dealings with a particular tribe and nation, which culminated in the coming of the Christ, Creator with Us (Emmanuel), for all the world. The Old Testament then enters a sacred circle of wisdom that shapes the Indigenous Christian—held as unique and sacred in its own particular way—alongside our own traditions. Native theologians therefore must discern how their own stories, rituals, and lifeways—the Native covenant—can both *inform* and *be informed* by their interpretation of the Christian Scriptures in order to empower, inspire, and guide Indigenous lives. With the prophet Amos (Amos 9:7), Indigenous peoples recognize that Creator has had a relationship with us long before European colonization. We were not godless heathen savages in empty and unused lands. Turtle Island hermeneutics will forever reject the doctrine of discovery and *terra nullius*.

INDIGENOUS INTERPRETIVE FRAMEWORKS

Turtle Island hermeneutics reads biblical narratives according to frameworks and categories that align with and arise from their heritage and lands. The field of biblical studies has increasingly recognized the foundational importance that one's social location plays in how one interprets Scripture. For example, Cuban American Fernando Segovia traces his own developmental stages of the personal voice, categorizing the process as (1) suppression of the personal voice, (2) irruption of the personal voice, and (3) entrenchment of the personal voice.[4] Similarly, Indigenous readers of Scripture do not seek a disconnected objectivity as they encounter Scripture. Indeed, even if this could be achieved, it would not be desired, as we are individuals grounded in and formed by human communities, which themselves are grounded and reliant on the wider community of creation. Turtle Island hermeneutics expressly does not seek

[2]See also, Randy Woodley, *Living in Color: Embracing God's Passion for Ethnic Diversity* (Downers Grove, IL: InterVarsity Press, 2001), 80-83.

[3]Steven Charleston, "The Old Testament of Native America," in *Lift Every Voice: Constructing Christian Theologies from the Underside*, ed. Susan Brooks Thistlethwaite and Mary Potter Engel (Maryknoll, NY: Orbis Books, 1990), 69-81.

[4]Fernando F. Segovia, *Decolonizing Biblical Studies: A View from the Margins* (Maryknoll, NY: Orbis, 2000), 145-56.

objectivity, nor is the goal a universal frame of reference. Because of the core assumption outlined above, Turtle Island hermeneutics recognizes the goodness within our cultural heritage. We belong to our families, we belong to our communities, and we belong to the land. These circles of relationship form the individual and inform our encounter with the scriptural text.

Indigenous interpretations of Scripture can often draw attention to previously underappreciated or unnoticed elements within the text, or resignify the meaning of technical terms or narrative elements and figures according to categories and frameworks familiar to our Indigenous experiences and heritage. For example, both the ministries and teachings of John the Baptist and Jesus can be appreciated in a new light when considered in conversation with the figure of the Trickster, popular among Indigenous stories. Tricksters often transgress cultural boundaries that encourage us to reflect on the meaning and function of our socially constructed conventions surrounding propriety, purity, and morality.[5] This description sounds a lot like what both John and Jesus are up to in the Gospels.[6]

Steven Charleston reads Matthew's account of Jesus' experience in the wilderness in terms of the Native experience of vision quests, something further explicated in the Matthew commentary in the present book. Although the precise protocols of vision quests vary across tribes, those undertaking such a quest often begin with a period of prayer and purification. Then their endurance and spirit are tested, which invites self-reflection, a spirit of humility, lamentation, and a recognition of their own vulnerability and need for Creator. A person may even receive a powerful vision that reveals something about their identity, their character, or what role they are to serve in their community—such transformative visions are "good medicine" or divine blessings.[7] Jesus undertakes his own vision quests. After Jesus is purified through his baptism, he sets off to the wilderness to fast and focus on prayer (Mt 4:2). At the end of his forty days of prayer and fasting, Jesus encounters the tempter, who tries to persuade Jesus to misuse his spiritual power for self-serving ends.[8] Here sin is understood as primarily relational rather than judicial, an imbalance in the shalom that God desires. Shalom, or the Harmony Way, is seen by scholars such as Randy Woodley (Keetoowah) as the Original Instructions to humankind.[9] For Terry LeBlanc (Mi'kmaq/Acadian), this restoration to harmony, the "restoration of right relationship and right relatedness," is also foundational for any Indigenous explorations of eschatology.[10]

---

[5]Clara Sue Kidwell, Homer Noley, George E. Tinker, and Jace Weaver, *A Native American Theology* (Maryknoll, NY: Orbis Books, 2001), 113-25.

[6]Steven Charleston, *The Four Vision Quests of Jesus* (New York: Morehouse, 2015), 56-64.

[7]Charleston, *Four Vision Quests*, 10-22, 51.

[8]For some Native American theologians, the concept of a devil who embodies pure evil as the apocalyptic enemy of Creator does not align with how they understand what evil entails. Some Indigenous readers have interpreted the devil as a literary personification of what constitutes evil and sin from an Indigenous perspective, namely, the actualization of our self-serving and destructive desires and actions that upsets the ideal balance and harmony with all of our kin—which includes humans, creatures, and creation itself. See Lisa A. Dellinger, "Sin—Ambiguity and Complexity and the Sin of Not Conforming," in *Coming Full Circle: Constructing Native Christian Theology*, ed. Steven Charleston and Elaine A. Robinson (Minneapolis: Fortress, 2015), 124-25, 127.

[9]See Randy S. Woodley, "The Harmony Way: Integrating Indigenous Values Within Native North American Theology and Mission" (PhD diss., Asbury Theological Seminary, 2010); Woodley, *Shalom and the Community of Creation: An Indigenous Vision*, Prophetic Christianity (Grand Rapids, MI: Eerdmans, 2012).

[10]Terry LeBlanc, "Toward an Indigenous Eschatology: Caution, Circle Ahead," in *Indigenous People and the Christian Faith: A New Way Forward*, ed. William H. U. Anderson and Charles Muskego (Wilmington, DE: Vernon, 2020), 238.

The above discussion highlights the relational framework in which the Scriptures are encountered by Indigenous readers, as relationship is a vital component to most Indigenous worldviews. One component of this relational framework is the conception of kinship. While kinship in the Christian community is basic to ecclesiology, Indigenous worldviews extend kinship to the entire community of creation. Within this community, humanity is not seen as hierarchically superior to any other of our creational kin.[11] Rather, Indigenous Peoples conceive of themselves as those who rely on the gifts of mother earth and on the gifts of service and sacrifice provided to us by the rest of the community of creation.[12] For Indigenous peoples, our personal and communal identities include the land, which inevitably affects how we relate to the world and subsequently read the Word.[13] The land and creation are among our first teachers and vehicles for Creator's revelation.

With this in mind, when we read Jesus' vision quest in the wilderness, do we consider what Jesus may have learned from Creation as he observed the plants, animals, terrain, sky, and stars? Is it possible that many of Jesus' parables and teachings about the birds of the air, the flowers of the field, and the mustard seed arose from his contemplation and observation of nature? For Charleston, Jesus' visions of the stones, the sky, and the mountaintop underscore the long-standing Indigenous conviction that we interexist and are interdependent with all our relations, which include nonhuman *persons*—even stones that Jesus is tempted to turn to bread. Rocks and stones are among our oldest relatives, and according to Charleston, they embody the oneness of God. In the narrative, the stones help Jesus regain his spiritual balance by recognizing his oneness and solidarity with his people and Creator.[14]

An Indigenous interpretation of the New Testament gives special attention to how it depicts creation. Mother earth, we notice in Romans 8:18-25, is described as suffering alongside us, groaning in labor pain, as we wait for our mutual redemption when Christ returns. Creation, in solidarity with us, longs to be set free from our mutual enslavement to death and for our coming glorification and adoption as the offspring of Creator. In Revelation 16:5-7, the waters are described as being represented by a spirit or angel who recognizes the justice of Creator in a manner that resonates with the spirituality and personhood that many Indigenous peoples ascribe to their waterways. Moreover, an Indigenous interpretation may appreciate how in Revelation 22:1-2 the tree of life has been restored in a cyclical fashion familiar to Indigenous sensibilities. The tree's leaves are good medicine that promises to address and heal the trauma our nations suffered, including cultural and physical genocide experienced among our children in residential school systems run by churches and governments. And in the face of polluted waterways and lakes, our ears cannot help but hear the declaration of the *Očhéthi Šakówiŋ* ("The Seven Council Fires," later called the Sioux Nation) that *Mní Wičóni*, or "water is life." We hold close to heart the work of water protectors when we envision the waters of life that flow from the throne of God through the middle of the city.[15]

---

[11]On this matter, Indigenous worldviews align with the biblical worldview as well. See Richard Bauckham, *Living with Other Creatures: Green Exegesis and Theology* (Waco, TX: Baylor University Press, 2011), chaps. 1–2.

[12]See H. Daniel Zacharias, "The Land Takes Care of Us: Recovering Creator's Relational Design," in *The Land: Majority World and Minoritized Theologies of Land*, ed. K. K. Yeo and Gene L. Green (Eugene, OR: Cascade, 2020), 69-97.

[13]See Ray Aldred, "The Land, Treaty, and Spirituality: Communal Identity Inclusive of Land," *Journal of NAIITS* 18 (2019): 1-17.

[14]Charleston, *Four Vision Quests*, 106.

[15]Barbara Rossing, "Waters Cry Out: Water Protectors, Watershed Justice, and the Voice of the Waters," in *Decolonizing Ecotheology*, ed. Susanah Mendoza and George Zachariah (Eugene, OR: Pickwick, 2022), 39-57.

WRESTLING WITH SCRIPTURE: ON CANAANITES, COWBOYS, AND INDIANS

Because of the relational framework and core assumptions discussed above, Turtle Island hermeneutics holds Scripture as a site to wrestle with the existential question of how one can be authentically Indigenous while also identifying with an institutional religion that was complicit with the physical and cultural genocide of their ancestors and lifeways.

As an example of this, the exodus narrative, with its themes of liberation, journey through the wilderness, and the inheritance and conquest of a promised land, is a rich, yet troubling story. Many Native readers encountering the exodus story cannot help but recall their own tribes' experiences of being displaced from their ancestral land by Christian settlers who thought the land was "promised" to them by some divine right, articulated in both the Doctrine of Discovery or Manifest Destiny. For example, Exodus 13:19 describes the Israelites as carrying the bones of their patriarch Joseph out of Egypt. For Charleston, this image brings to mind the many Choctaws, about 10 percent of whom were Christians themselves, who carried the bones of their ancestors along the Trail of Tears from Mississippi to Oklahoma.[16] Reading Exodus with a Turtle Island hermeneutic provides an opportunity to share stories often unknown or underappreciated by Western Euro-Americans. If we read Scripture in order to make sense of our own histories and lives, the question stands out, Whose stories are we telling? Reflecting on the tragic trauma of the Long Walk helps us to tell true stories about the past of how modern North American nations, with their the economic growth and expansion, were built on a foundation of broken treaties and the dispossession of Indigenous peoples from their lands. And yet, we hold out that Creator walked with us.

Although the exodus story has been essential to both African American and Latino/a liberation theologians, Robert Allen Warrior (Osage) has critically asked where Native Americans should see themselves in this narrative. Warrior argues that the story of Canaanites, the Indigenous Peoples of the Promised Land, whom the Israelites sought to conquer and whose land they claimed, poignantly resonates with the North American Indigenous experience. The God of Israel both liberates and conquers, Warrior warns. While biblical scholars may continue to debate over the extent to which the book of Joshua depicts a historical or idealized story of conquest and whether the Canaanites simply merged with the Israelites, the story of the destruction and dispossession of Indigenous peoples of the Promised Land remains palpable (Ex 23:23-33). Such stories informed the imagination and sermons of Puritan ministers, including Cotton Mather, who portrayed White colonists as "the chosen people" who had a divine claim on American soil, and Indigenous peoples as disposable and despicable Amalekites and Canaanites.[17] "America's self-image as a 'chosen people,'" Warrior contends, "has provided the rhetoric to mystify domination."[18]

In response to Warrior's take on the Canaanites, William Baldridge (Cherokee) points to the Gospel story of the Canaanite woman. In Matthew 15:21-26, a Canaanite woman asks

[16]Charleston, *Four Vision Quests*, 97.

[17]See, for example, Cotton Mather's sermon titled "Souldiers counselled and comforted. A discourse delivered unto some part of the forces engaged in the just war of New-England against the northern & eastern Indians," September 1, 1689.

[18]Robert Alan Warrior, "Canaanites, Cowboys, and Indians: Deliverance, Conquest, and Liberation Theology Today," in *Native and Christian: Indigenous Voices on Religious Identity in the United States and Canada*, ed. James Treat (New York: Routledge, 1996), 99.

Jesus to help her daughter, who is tormented by a demon. Despite the fact that Jesus denies her request because she is not a lost sheep of Israel but a dog (Mt 15:24-26), the woman boldly advocates for her daughter. Then, in a miraculous moment, according to Baldridge, "the son of the god of Canaanite oppression repents," and the daughter is healed.[19] For James Treat (Muscogee/Cherokee), Jesus is made to recognize the Canaanite woman's story and faith—a faith that was written beyond the pages of the story of Israel.[20] So, Baldridge concludes, if the Canaanite woman can change Jesus' mind, so too can Native Americans "change the very heart of God" and "his chosen people," resulting in healing, harmony, and reconciliation.

THE CROSS, CEREMONY, AND SACRED STORIES

Traditional Indigenous ceremonies and stories are also brought into conversation with Scripture and embraced in the lives of Indigenous followers of Jesus. In this regard, one of the most important individuals in the Native church was the late Richard Twiss (Lakota).[21] Twiss, along with many others who originally composed the NAIITS community, tirelessly and patiently argued for a seat at the theological table within Christianity, particularly within evangelical spaces. The earliest battles were fought in regard to Indigenous cultural ceremonies and practices as being valid forms of Christian discipleship and devotion.[22] Casey Church (Potawatomi) incorporates biblical passages into his ceremonies and sees alignments between the practice of smudging (the burning of herbs, including sage, sweet grass, cedar, and tobacco as an incense) and the ancient Hebrew practice of burning incense over the ark of the covenant (e.g., Ex 30:1-6, 34-36; Lk 1:8-10).[23] George E. "Tink" Tinker (Osage) reads the passion narrative in light of how Indigenous traditionalists understand what suffering on behalf of others accomplishes in the context of purification ceremonies such as the Sun Dance and the sweat lodge.[24] The experience of discomfort or pain in the context of such ceremonies and rituals is intended to help realign and sustain the harmony or balance of sacred energy within the cosmos and to reinforce prayers made to Creator. Vicarious suffering within Indigenous ceremonial contexts by no means functions to placate the anger of a wrathful god, overcome any sense of some original sin, or reconcile humanity with God. So, for some Native Americans, Jesus' suffering at the cross is *not* about what God *needs* in order to forgive, but the ultimate display of Creator's love for us and the tragic culmination of humanity being out of balance and out of line with the Original Instructions of Creator. As Jace Weaver puts it: when Jesus was murdered, God wept but then laughed at the folly

[19]William Baldridge, "Native American Theology: A Biblical Basis," in Treat, *Native and Christian*, 101.

[20]James Treat, "The Canaanite Problem," *Daughters of Sarah: The Magazine for Christian Feminists* 20 (1994): 24.

[21]See Richard Twiss, *One Church, Many Tribes: Following Jesus the Way God Made You* (Minneapolis: Chosen, 2000); Twiss, *Rescuing the Gospel from the Cowboys: A Native American Expression of the Jesus Way* (Downers Grove, IL: InterVarsity Press, 2015).

[22]In addition to the previously cited works by Twiss, numerous essays in the *Journal of NAIITS* wrestle with this issue. See, for example, the inaugural essay of the journal: Richard Twiss, Terry LeBlanc, and Adrian Jacobs, "Culture, Christian Faith and Error," *Journal of NAIITS* 1 (2003): 5-35.

[23]Casey Church, *Holy Smoke: The Contextual Use of Native American Ritual and Ceremony* (Cleveland, TN: Cherohala, 2017), 89-90.

[24]Kidwell et al., *Native American Theology*, 62-65, 79-83. Damian Costello, a Black Elk scholar, also states, "The cottonwood tree and the Sun Dance are linked to the cross in the Black Elk tradition." See Costello, "Black Elk Speaks," *Journal of NAIITS* 4 (2006): 46.

of humanity (Ps 2) and resurrected Jesus in vindication of his life and teachings.[25] Some Lakota Christians even refer to Jesus as the ideal Sun Dancer, whose suffering restores balance to our world.

The sacred story of the life-giving death of Christ resonates with an ancient Indigenous story, versions of which have been told across North America, namely, the story of Corn Mother. Tinker once challenged Christians to consider the possibility that Christ, as God's eternal and pervasive Logos or communication of "creativity and healing or salvation to human beings," actually inspired our ancestral stories, such as that of Corn Mother.[26] While Corn Mother stories may vary, each tale tells of a divine woman who willingly accepts her death so that her people might live. In one Penobscot retelling, the First Mother, compelled by the cries of her starving children, instructs her husband to kill her and to drag her body across the fields so that her flesh, blood, and bones might mix with the soil. Months later, corn begins to grow. In a word reminiscent of the Christian Eucharist, the First Man tells his people: "Remember and take good care of First Mother's flesh, because it is goodness become substance. . . . She has given her life so that you might live."[27] Similar to Jesus' sacrifice, Corn Mother's sacrifice invites people to gather around the table, recognize their shared kinship, and offer gratitude for the gifts of the Corn Mother. Corn Mother may even be a manifestation of the preexistent Christ/Logos. Of course, there are other stories of self-sacrifice within Indigenous traditions, including the Cherokee story shared by Woodley about the service and self-sacrifice of Grandmother Turtle, who died in her quest to retrieve mud from the bottom of the sea that would prove essential for creating the land mass we call Turtle Island (North America).[28]

Patty Krawec (Anishinaabe) poetically brings together an Anishinaabe story with the Gospel of Matthew as she reflects on what reconciliation might look like between Native Americans and missionaries in light of many of the tragic stories that are coming to light about church-run Indian residential schools. After describing Herod's slaughter of Israelite children, the Gospel of Matthew recalls the prophet Jeremiah's lament (Jer 31:15), "A voice was heard in Ramah, wailing and loud lamentation, Rachel weeping for her children; she refused to be consoled, because they are no more" (Mt 2:18). In the Anishinaabe story about how humans overhunted the deer, despite their ancient promise to take care of one another, the deer, like Rachel, refuse to be comforted and leave humans without a reliable source of meat. Native people too, Krawec states, can refuse to be comforted in light of stories of (sexual) abuse, forced labor, and cultural genocide that occurred at some boarding schools. Just as Herod slaughtered Israelite children because he felt his authority was threatened, so too did the Christian kingdom harm Indigenous children.

But what does sincere repentance and reconciliation look like? In her Anishinaabe story, the people set aside a season to reflect on their role in breaking a harmonious relationship with the deer and take full responsibility for their harm, eventually reconciling with the

[25]Jace Weaver, *That the People Might Live: Native American Literatures and Native American Community* (New York: Oxford University Press, 1997), 182n172.

[26]Kidwell et al., *Native American Theology*, 76-83.

[27]Richard Erdoes and Alfonso Ortiz, *American Indian Myths and Legends*, Pantheon Fairy Tale & Folklore Library (New York: Pantheon Books, 1984), 13.

[28]Woodley, *Shalom*, 144-47.

deer. So, Krawec holds out hope for reconciliation and peace. Policies can change, sovereignty can be respected, land can be restored.[29] A Turtle Island hermeneutic envisions a more comprehensive picture of how Creator has been revealed to Indigenous peoples in their ancestral ceremonies and sacred stories.

CONTRIBUTIONS

There is no singular Native American reading of Scripture, but some of these interpretive trends briefly sketched above certainly represent Turtle Island hermeneutics as we have broadly conceived it. Turtle Island hermeneutics, as its name implies, roots us not only to our social locations but to our communities and landscapes. This is approached in different ways by current Indigenous theologians. A representative of a more pan-Indigenous experience is the new English paraphrase called the First Nations Version, in which Terry Wildman sought to create a translation of the New Testament that would appeal to a broad range of Indigenous peoples who only encounter the Scriptures in the English language.[30] Alternatively, grassroots theologians such as Marcus Briggs-Cloud (Muscogee/Maskoke, son of the Wind Clan) advocate moving away from pan-Indigenous theological interpretations in favor of more localized theologies and readings of Scripture that attend to the cosmologies, ceremonies, and ideologies of a particular Indigenous community, rooted in a given land.[31]

Herein lies the promise and peril of our Turtle Island hermeneutics proposal. While Indigenous interpreters seek to reassert the dignity and wisdom of their ancestral stories and customs, Native Americans disagree with each other on how to reconcile perceived contradictions between Indigenous and biblical conceptions of creation, divinity, sacrifice, sin, and salvation. If Creator has manifested Godself to both Indigenous North Americans and Israelites, then which revelation "corrects" or supersedes the other? Should we imagine the Great Spirit/Mystery as essentially personal or as an impersonal power, as is the case with some Lakota understandings of *Wakan tanka*? Could we read Corn Mother's message of the interconnectedness of creation as inspired by Christ/Logos and even as a helpful corrective to interpretations of Genesis 1:28, which endorses the domination of creation—an ideology complicit with our deforestation and scarring of the earth in order to extract its resources at unsustainable rates? There may be no simple or universally satisfying answer to these questions. Yet, there are two things that are important for non-Indigenous Christians to recognize.

First, because Indigenous peoples do not tend to place people or things in hierarchies, the aforementioned "contradictions" are not nearly as distressing as they are for Western, Euro-American Christians. We can and do affirm Jesus as Lord, even as we see that Jesus needed to be confronted with his own people's complicated history of colonization and genocide (Mt 15:21-26)—our Christology is big enough to hold these things together.

Second, as Indigenous peoples reassert their personhood and proudly reclaim their cultural heritage, the working out of these questions is ours to discern in community. Questions of

[29]Patty Krawec, "Refusing to Be Comforted: What Rachel's Lament Teaches Us About the Work of Repairing Relationships," *Sojourners*, December 20, 2021, https://sojo.net/articles/refusing-be-comforted-krawec.

[30]Terry M. Wildman, ed., *First Nations Version: An Indigenous Translation of the New Testament* (Downers Grove, IL: InterVarsity Press, 2021).

[31]Marcus Briggs-Cloud, "Creation—The New Creation: A Maskoke Postcolonial Perspective," in Charleston and Robinson, *Coming Full Circle*, 89-118.

"contradictions," the dialectic between the Scriptures and our traditions, and the use/adaptation of our traditional ceremonies in our Christian discipleship all belong with Indigenous followers of Jesus specifically. We knew Creator then, and we follow Christ the Creator-made-flesh now. Indigenous North American interpretations of the Bible remain fertile ground for life-affirming theology, the power of which lies in their ability to reclaim and sustain traditions threatened by cultural extinction and to energize adherents through their poetic and constructive juxtaposition of Indigenous ceremonies, experiences, and sacred stories with biblical narratives and theological concepts.

SELECTED BIBLIOGRAPHY

Aldred, Ray. "The Land, Treaty, and Spirituality: Communal Identity Inclusive of Land." *Journal of NAIITS* 18 (2019): 1-17.

Baldridge, William. "Native American Theology: A Biblical Basis." In *Native and Christian: Indigenous Voices on Religious Identity in the United States and Canada*, edited by James Treat, 100-101. New York: Routledge, 1996.

Bauckham, Richard. *Living with Other Creatures: Green Exegesis and Theology*. Waco, TX: Baylor University Press, 2011.

Briggs-Cloud, Marcus. "Creation—The New Creation: A Maskoke Postcolonial Perspective." In *Coming Full Circle: Constructing Native Christian Theology*, edited by Steven Charleston and Elaine A. Robinson, 89-118. Minneapolis: Fortress, 2015.

Charleston, Steven. *The Four Vision Quests of Jesus*. New York: Morehouse, 2015.

———. "The Old Testament of Native America." In *Lift Every Voice: Constructing Christian Theologies from the Underside*, edited by Susan Brooks Thistlethwaite and Mary Potter Engel, 69-81. Maryknoll, NY: Orbis Books, 1990.

Charleston, Steven, and Elaine A. Robinson, eds. *Coming Full Circle: Constructing Native Christian Theology*. Minneapolis: Fortress, 2015.

Church, Casey. *Holy Smoke: The Contextual Use of Native American Ritual and Ceremony*. Cleveland, TN: Cherohala, 2017.

Costello, Damien. "Black Elk Speaks." *Journal of NAIITS* 4 (2006): 29-56.

Dellinger, Lisa A. "Sin—Ambiguity and Complexity and the Sin of Not Conforming." In *Coming Full Circle: Constructing Native Christian Theology*, edited by Steven Charleston and Elaine A. Robinson, 119-32. Minneapolis: Fortress, 2015.

Erdoes, Richard, and Alfonso Ortiz. *American Indian Myths and Legends*. Pantheon Fairy Tale & Folklore Library. New York: Pantheon Books, 1984.

Hoklotubbe, T. Christopher. "A Native American Interpretation of the Bible." In *Oxford Encyclopedias of the Bible: Digital Collection*. Oxford: Oxford University Press, 2022. www.oxfordreference.com/display/10.1093/acref/9780197669402.001.0001/acref-9780197669402-e-70.

Kidwell, Clara Sue, Homer Noley, George E. Tinker, and Jace Weaver. *A Native American Theology*. Maryknoll, NY: Orbis Books, 2001.

Krawec, Patty. "Refusing to Be Comforted: What Rachel's Lament Teaches Us About the Work of Repairing Relationships." *Sojourners*, December 20, 2021. https://sojo.net/articles/refusing-be-comforted-krawec.

LeBlanc, Terry. "Toward an Indigenous Eschatology: Caution, Circle Ahead." In *Indigenous People and the Christian Faith: A New Way Forward*, edited by William H. U. Anderson and Charles Muskego, 229-46. Wilmington, DE: Vernon, 2020.

Rossing, Barbara. "Waters Cry Out: Water Protectors, Watershed Justice, and the Voice of the Waters." In *Decolonizing Ecotheology: Indigenous and Subaltern Challenges*, edited by Susanah Lily L. Mendoza and George Zachariah, 39-57. Eugene, OR: Pickwick, 2022.

Segovia, Fernando F. *Decolonizing Biblical Studies: A View from the Margins*. Maryknoll, NY: Orbis, 2000.

Treat, James. "The Canaanite Problem." *Daughters of Sarah: The Magazine for Christian Feminists* 20 (1994): 20-24.

———, ed. *Native and Christian: Indigenous Voices on Religious Identity in the United States and Canada*. New York: Routledge, 1996.

Twiss, Richard. *One Church, Many Tribes: Following Jesus the Way God Made You*. Minneapolis: Chosen, 2000.

———. *Rescuing the Gospel from the Cowboys: A Native American Expression of the Jesus Way*. Downers Grove, IL: InterVarsity Press, 2015.

Twiss, Richard, Terry LeBlanc, and Adrian Jacobs. "Culture, Christian Faith and Error." *Journal of NAIITS* 1 (2003): 5-35.

Warrior, Robert Alan. "Canaanites, Cowboys, and Indians: Deliverance, Conquest, and Liberation Theology Today." In *Native and Christian: Indigenous Voices on Religious Identity in the United States and Canada*, edited by James Treat, 93-104. New York: Routledge, 1996.

Weaver, Jace. "A Biblical Paradigm for Native Liberation." In *Native and Christian: Indigenous Voices on Religious Identity in the United States and Canada*, edited by James Treat, 103-4. New York: Routledge, 1996.

———. *That the People Might Live: Native American Literatures and Native American Community*. New York: Oxford University Press, 1997.

Woodley, Randy S. "The Harmony Way: Integrating Indigenous Values Within Native North American Theology and Mission." PhD diss., Asbury Theological Seminary, 2010.

———. *Living in Color: Embracing God's Passion for Ethnic Diversity*. Downers Grove, IL: InterVarsity Press, 2001.

———. *Shalom and the Community of Creation: An Indigenous Vision*. Prophetic Christianity. Grand Rapids, MI: Eerdmans, 2012.

Zacharias, H. Daniel. "The Land Takes Care of Us: Recovering Creator's Relational Design." In *The Land: Majority World and Minoritized Theologies of Land*, edited by K. K. Yeo and Gene L. Green, 69-97. Eugene, OR: Cascade, 2020.

MAJORITY-CULTURE BIBLICAL INTERPRETATION

READING WHILE WHITE

Michael J. Gorman

The subtitle of this essay borrows from the phrase "driving while Black" and from the title of Esau McCaulley's important book, *Reading While Black*.[1] I allude to this book both apologetically, for displaying my lack of originality, and unapologetically, for suggesting its significance. But this essay is not simply about reading the Bible while *White* as others read while *Black*. It is about reading the Bible within some variation of White culture and privilege (as Christians of European heritage), while also desiring to be informed and shaped by other Christians, in the same North American macro-context, who read through the lens of various other colors, cultures, and particular contexts.

Like many others involved in this project, I have always been moved by the scriptural visions of the church in Acts and Revelation. As one of my students said while preaching on Pentecost Sunday in the immediate, raw wake of George Floyd's murder, "Today is Pentecost, the feast of antiracism."[2] Something similar could be said about the vision of the church triumphant in Revelation 7—a vision of antiracism:

> After this I looked, and there was a great multitude that no one could count, from every nation, from all tribes and peoples and languages, standing before the throne and before the Lamb, robed in white, with palm branches in their hands. They cried out in a loud voice, saying, "Salvation belongs to our God who is seated on the throne and to the Lamb!" (Rev 7:9-10)

These verses have often been seen—rightly—as a reminder that the mission of God encompasses the whole world and that the faithful who have been redeemed by the Lamb do come, and always will come, from all corners of the world. This text has therefore—again rightly—reinforced the global mission of the church.

Unfortunately, however, for many Christians, especially White North American Christians, this vision of the church as a global body has not yielded two other corollary conclusions. First, it has not caused us to attend sufficiently to the various nations, tribes, peoples, and languages within our own geographical and political borders that comprise an essential part of that global body. Second, the vision has seldom inspired us to appreciate the hermeneutical (interpretive) principles that arise from this vision. In short, these principles may be summarized in the phrase "contextual exegesis," or

[1]Esau McCaulley, *Reading While Black: African American Biblical Interpretation as an Exercise in Hope* (Downers Grove, IL: IVP Academic, 2020).

[2]Sunday homily by the Rev. Evan Ponton, then a Roman Catholic deacon, now a priest. George Floyd was an African American man detained and killed by Minneapolis police on May 25, 2020. Pentecost Sunday was May 31.

"contextual interpretation." That is, various people—and peoples—read and hear Scripture in differing contexts and thus with diverse interests, perspectives, and insights that are lacking in others.[3] These ways of engaging the text, therefore, constitute an amazing gift to the church as a whole and to White Christians in particular. Unfortunately, this is a gift that has not always been acknowledged as such, much less received and celebrated.

Here I propose that reading while White is a discipline with at least four basic elements: repentance, humility, unity, and communion (deep friendship). Along the way, I include some concrete steps to move those of us of White European heritage from *ignoring* minority voices to *hearing* such voices to *engaging* one another's voices. The goal of this essay is to reflect biblically, theologically, and practically about the reading of Scripture by Christians of European descent in the context of a multiethnic North America and multiethnic body of Christ. That is, it is about *reading while White but after whiteness*—the domination of white culture in North America and in the churches of North America on the basis of a belief in the supremacy of White people.[4]

REPENTANCE

For a long time in North America, biblical interpretation has been dominated by White people (especially men) of European descent. This does not mean that White men have read the Bible more, or more faithfully, than others but that their ways of reading and their interpretations have dominated the church—and the academy too. There are many reasons for this, not least that for a long time the greatest number of preachers were White men, and it is still the case that the greatest percentage of biblical scholars are White males.

For some people, this is simply a case of "It is what it is," or at least "It was what it was." Or a case of ignorance—"I did not know" or "No one told me" that I should listen to others or that there were different kinds of voices. But I want to suggest, along with many others, that this description of the situation is neither historically nor theologically accurate. In the Christian tradition we often speak of sin in terms of acts of *commission* and acts of *omission*. There is no doubt that both have been operative in the way the White majority has ignored or suppressed the interpretive contexts and contributions of others. This suggestion is not intended to make White people feel guilty about being White, but as Scripture tells us time and again, human beings—even those who are among the people of God—have an amazing capacity for self-centeredness and self-deception that blinds them to God, to truth, and to others.

Biblical interpretation is a Christian practice, a spiritual discipline. It does not take place in

[3]See further Michael J. Gorman, *Elements of Biblical Exegesis: A Basic Guide for Students and Ministers* (Grand Rapids, MI: Baker Academic, 2020), e.g., 17-18, 22-23, 71-72, 174-75.

[4]On whiteness, see, e.g., Willie James Jennings, "Can White People Be Saved? Reflections on the Relationship of Missions and Whiteness," in *Can "White" People Be Saved? Triangulating Race, Theology, and Mission*, ed. Love L. Sechrest, Johnny Ramírez-Johnson, and Amos Yong (Downers Grove, IL: IVP Academic, 2018), 27-43. Jennings speaks of Christianity and whiteness as a "fusion," as "two mutual interpenetrating realities" (28). Whiteness is not about a particular group of people per se but about a "deformed formation toward [human] maturity" (29), or goal for human life together, that actually destroys (34). In the New World, he says, "there was the White body—the civilized, honorable, and beautiful prototype—and the non-White body, most centrally the Black body—the uncivilized, primitive, dangerous, and ugly body" (38). Such attitudes have persisted about White and non-White bodies (Black, Brown, etc.). "Whiteness," argues Jennings, feels normal and natural" because "it is woven into how we imagine moving toward maturity"(40), and this malformation has often been "baptized" as "the blessing of God" (41). We can only break the fusion of whiteness and Christianity by "resisting its vision of maturity" (43) and offering an alternative.

a vacuum but both expresses and shapes our identity. Moreover, that identity is not just a matter of individual choice; we are all part of a body with a cultural context and a cultural history. Regarding context, two editors of the book *Can "White" People Be Saved?* claim, "Fear of living in a radically multiethnic country [or, I would add, church] is strong enough to drive members of the body of Christ to embrace profoundly un-Christian behaviors and actors."[5] As for cultural history, James Cone points this out in very strong (but appropriate), oft-quoted imagery: "Until we can see the cross and the lynching tree together, until we can identify Christ with a 'recrucified' black body hanging from a lynching tree, there can be no genuine understanding of Christian identity in America, and no deliverance from the brutal legacy of slavery and white supremacy."[6] We could, and should, also add other images to this one, since—sadly—Christians (or at least people bearing that name) have also treated Native Americans, Latinx immigrants, and others in parallel ways, often with allegedly biblical justification.[7]

Therefore, rather than denying that there is a problem, the Christian perspective prods us to say, "We have made mistakes and we are ready to change—to repent." For many of us, this repentance will entail a gradual but fairly radical conversion of our Christian worldview and hence of the practices that emerge from it and shape it, including biblical interpretation. According to N. T. Wright, a worldview is not something we look *at* but something we look *through*. "Worldviews," he writes, "are like spectacles [eyeglasses]; normally you take them for granted, and you only think about them when they are broken, dirty or out of focus."[8] This repentance will therefore also include asking the Lord to enable us to see more truly and clearly—both the Lord himself and our fellow interpreters. Repentance and worldview transformation clear the way for hearing and then engaging the other.

HUMILITY AND UNITY IN DIVERSITY

Repentance is an act of humility. But humility is not only an initial requirement for reading while White; it is perhaps the single greatest need. In his letter to the early believers in Philippi, Paul exhorts the church to practice Christlike humility as the fundamental requirement of Christian community, or *koinōnia*:

> If then there is any comfort in Christ, any consolation from love, any partnership [*koinōnia*] in the Spirit, any tender affection and sympathy, make my joy complete: be of the same mind, having the same love, being in full accord and of one mind. Do nothing from selfish ambition or empty conceit, but in humility regard others as better than yourselves. Let each of you look not to your own interests but to the interests of others. (Phil 2:1-4)

Interestingly, this passage could be misread to imply the opposite of my claim—that is, that Paul wants us all to think alike, to "be of the same mind" (Phil 2:2). But groupthink is not Paul's desire. The "same mind" he is describing

---

[5]Love L. Sechrest and Johnny Ramírez-Johnson, "Introduction: Race and Missiology in Glocal Perspective," in Sechrest, Ramírez-Johnson, and Yong, *Can "White" People Be Saved?*, 7.

[6]James H. Cone, *The Cross and the Lynching Tree* (Maryknoll, NY: Orbis, 2011), xv. See also Sechrest and Ramírez-Johnson: "Religious ideology has been central to the maintenance and origins of racialization and whiteness embedded in the European project inasmuch as gradations in skin pigmentation coincide with religious, geographical, and cultural divisions that segment the world into colonizers and the colonized" ("Introduction," 9-10).

[7]This history is well documented; see, e.g., many of the essays in Sechrest, Ramírez-Johnson, and Yong, *Can "White" People Be Saved?*

[8]N. T. Wright, *Paul and the Faithfulness of God* (Minneapolis: Fortress, 2013), 28.

is the mind of Christ, described in the following poetic verses:

> Let the same mind be in you that was in Christ Jesus,
>   who, though he existed in the form of God,
>   did not regard equality with God
>   as something to be grasped,
>   but emptied himself,
>   taking the form of a slave,
>   assuming human likeness.
>   And being found in appearance as a human,
>   he humbled himself
>   and became obedient to the point of death—
>   even death on a cross. (Phil 2:5-8)[9]

The mind of Christ—the way of Christ, the "one mind" of Christ—is not about sameness but about humble self-emptying that leads to honoring, appreciating, and loving the other, looking out for others' interests even as others look out for you. This is revolutionary—a revolution of love, as Dennis Edwards says: "laying aside privilege in service to others."[10] Many theological interpreters of racism identify privilege as "the critical resource mediated in racist societies."[11] It is therefore a privilege, a grace, to lay aside White privilege as we read Scripture together.

Paradoxically, there can be no unity without otherness, without diversity, as Paul makes clear in 1 Corinthians 12: "For just as the body is one and has many members, and all the members of the body, though many, are one body, so it is with Christ" (1 Cor 12:12).

To think about all of this in terms of biblical interpretation, two key principles emerge. First, Christian humility requires us to empty ourselves of the misguided notion that I, or we, know all or know best. We need to acknowledge and welcome others and their perspectives. When Paul says, "There is no longer Jew or Greek; there is no longer slave or free; there is no longer male and female; for all of you are one in Christ Jesus" (Gal 3:28), he does not mean that ethnic, socioeconomic, and gender distinctives disappear but that they are transcended. Yet they are only transcended when they persist. The same is true for biblical interpretation. Jews and Gentiles do not read Scripture in exactly the same way, but each benefits from the other. So too with slaves and free persons, and with men and women.

Honoring others' perspectives enriches my/our own perspective(s) so that true Christian community can exist. We benefit from scriptural readings that allow us to empty ourselves of false or limited assumptions about the Bible in order to understand and embody it more faithfully, both individually and corporately. In other words, diversity in scriptural interpretation contributes to a more faithful and functioning Christian community.

THE GOAL: COMMUNION (DEEP FRIENDSHIP IN CHRIST)

In his many publications about the theological interpretation of Scripture, Stephen Fowl often says that the goal of scriptural interpretation is greater love for God and neighbor. This understanding derives from Augustine's maxim that legitimate scriptural interpretation is that which fosters such "double love." Although both Augustine and Fowl would say that these two loves are fundamentally inseparable, it will be helpful to draw on the notion of friendship

---

[9]Philippians 2:5 is saying something like, "Let the Spirit shape you into the way of thinking and acting I have just described because you all [the Greek is a plural "you"] are in Christ together, and I am about to tell you what Christ did."

[10]Dennis R. Edwards," The Revolution Will Not Be Videoed," *Christianity Today*, May 29, 2020; www.christianitytoday.com/ct/2020/may-web-only/dennis-edwards-george-floyd-revolution-will-not-be-videoed.html?fbclid=IwAR3mcgS1XLjH8myn8SHr_qiThxDlPUtp6ncM4VXLv09Y5UNV0B9bZgZlqts.

[11]Sechrest and Ramírez-Johnson, "Introduction," 11.

in Christ—another way of understanding Christian community—to expand on this interpretive goal.

In his book *Friends in Christ: Paths to a New Understanding of the Church*, Brother John of Taizé—the ecumenical community of brothers north of Lyon, France—draws on both Scripture and various Christian writings about friendship to work toward a contemporary theology of friendship. He begins by describing Jesus as a friend of sinners and tax collectors, demonstrating that "divine love becomes real essentially in the endeavor to *make friends*." Jesus' ministry "reveals the face of a God passionately concerned with turning enemies into friends." We therefore are "called to *make friends* and to *be friends*." Moreover, friendship is something that must be cultivated, and to grow in friendship requires the transformation of our hearts.[12]

Brother John summarizes the thesis of his book as follows: "The clearest expression of the Christian faith, as the *offer in progress of a universal communion of fellowship in God*, is a worldwide network of friends, who are at the same time friends of God by being friends of Christ." It is God who has taken the initiative in establishing this fellowship/friendship, but we must take advantage of the means to deepen it: "through word and sacrament"—meditating on Scripture and participating in the Eucharist (the Lord's Supper), communion. But Brother John adds to these "classical means" what he calls "the sacrament of the brother," for "friendship with God is deepened and expressed in the love we shower on one another, particularly the neediest."[13]

"My brother or sister," Brother John writes in reflecting on 1 John, "is thus the visible and efficacious sign—the sacrament—of God's invisible presence."[14] When we receive other Christians in a sacramental way, we are actually receiving Christ (who lives in those others), as we do when we receive Scripture and holy Communion.[15] In the case of White Christians, it is not only that we need to acknowledge and practice the sacrament of the brother or sister who is not White but also that we must be willing to receive that human sacrament as a gift, for in many ways we are "the neediest" to whom Brother John refers.

Finally, Brother John—writing from his particular context and lifelong experience of promoting Christian friendship across traditions—says, "As far as possible, we need to live as if the church were already a worldwide network of friends not limited to those of the same denominational allegiance."[16] If we substitute words such as *ethnicity*, *race*, and *culture* for "denominational allegiance," then we have in this sentence the promise of multiethnic Christian friendship. And of course nothing global can ever occur until it begins in our own backyard. This friendship, this sibling sacramentality, can be nurtured by the practice of reading in communion—of attending to the gifts of shared goals mixed with distinct histories and contexts.[17]

---

[12]Brother John of Taizé, *Friends in Christ: Paths to a New Understanding of the Church* (Maryknoll, NY: Orbis, 2012), 88-91, emphases original. See further Willie James Jennings, *The Christian Imagination: Theology and the Origins of Race* (New Haven, CT: Yale University Press, 2010), who speaks of the "diseased social imagination" that keeps us from developing deep intimacy (e.g., 6-10, 250-88).

[13]Brother John of Taizé, *Friends in Christ*, 118, 126.

[14]Brother John of Taizé, *Friends in Christ*, 27.

[15]Another important scriptural basis for this conviction is of course Mt 25:31-46. We might add to that parable the question (and its implicit response), "Lord, when was it that we did not hear you interpreting Scripture?"

[16]Brother John of Taizé, *Friends in Christ*, 156.

[17]For a classic work on this topic, see Stephen E. Fowl and L. Gregory Jones, *Reading in Communion: Scripture and Ethics in Christian Life* (Grand Rapids, MI: Eerdmans, 1991).

In other words, deep friendship or communion only happens when we go beyond *hearing* others to *receiving* others, even as they receive us. Reading in communion with others does not mean the suppression of our own voice but rather the mutuality of giving and receiving that happens in true friendship, true *koinōnia*. That is, the discipline of reading while White with others who are not White is not at all about rivalry.

RETURNING TO REVELATION

I suggested at the start of this essay that Revelation 7 is one of the primary theological foundations for reading the Bible in multiethnic communion. Astute readers of Revelation will note, however, that this grand apocalyptic vision is not primarily about the church on earth or about biblical interpretation within that church. The vision is probably meant to signify the one, holy, catholic (universal), and suffering but finally triumphant church: the church that has patiently, faithfully endured. The people "from every nation, from all tribes and peoples and languages" (Rev 7:9), have lasted through the great temptation to capitulate in the face of evil and oppression. They have remained devoted to God and the Lamb, and they are forever shepherded by the Lamb who shed his blood on their behalf:

> Then one of the elders addressed me, saying, "Who are these, robed in white, and where have they come from?" I said to him, "Sir, you are the one who knows." Then he said to me, "These are they who have come out of the great ordeal; they have washed their robes and made them white in the blood of the Lamb.
>
> For this reason they are before the throne
> of God
> and worship him day and night within
> his temple,
> and the one who is seated on the throne
> will shelter them.
> They will hunger no more and thirst
> no more;
> the sun will not strike them,
> nor any scorching heat,
> for the Lamb at the center of the throne will
> be their shepherd,
> and he will guide them to springs of the
> water of life,
> and God will wipe away every tear from
> their eyes." (Rev 7:13-17)

But although this is a picture of the church triumphant, it is also an image of the church on earth inasmuch as the church is, both factually and aspirationally, one, holy, catholic, suffering, and (eventually) triumphant. The church everywhere on earth worships the same God, benefits from the same shed blood, longs for the same springs of life, and follows—or at least attempts to follow—the same crucified and resurrected Lamb-Lord wherever he goes (see Rev 14:4). In fact, this last reference comes from a similar vision of the church, a reprise of Revelation 7 in Revelation 14, that describes the multiethnic, faithful followers of the Lamb as those who have resisted the unholy trinity of dragon (Satan), beast, and prophet described in Revelation 12–13.

Nowhere in Revelation 7 or Revelation 14 does John the Seer say that the multiethnic people of God has survived by reading Scripture together. Yet scriptural allusions and images permeate Revelation. Moreover, we learn in the messages to the seven churches of Asia Minor (modern western Turkey) in Revelation 2–3 what sustains and challenges the churches, individually and together: it is the voice of the Spirit, which is synonymous with the voice of Jesus.[18] We know this because it is *Jesus* who speaks to the seven churches and

[18]These messages are often called letters, but they are more like prophetic oracles or pastoral admonitions.

tells John to write to each of their "angels" (that is how each message begins), and it is *Jesus* who concludes each message by saying, "Let anyone who has an ear listen to what *the Spirit* is saying to the churches" (emphasis added; see Rev 2:7, 11, 17, 29; 3:6, 13, 22).

The last word in that call to listen to the Spirit by listening to Jesus is critical: *churches*, plural; the words addressed to each individual church are actually intended for all seven churches. Whatever their separate civic and cultural identities, whatever their distinct as well as their shared histories, they are called to somehow hear the words of Jesus and discern the Spirit's message together. What Jesus says to and through the church at Ephesus, for example, needs to be heard in the other six churches. If we wish to follow the Lamb—and not the culture of the unholy trinity that manifests itself in (among other things) the notion of White supremacy, we need to hear Scripture read from diverse perspectives. The unity and faithfulness of the churches, and the church, depend on listening to Jesus speaking through multiple contexts. Otherwise, the book of Revelation could have had—indeed, should have had—just one message, not seven.

Those seven messages are found in a document destined to become Christian Scripture. And since the number seven signifies completeness, we can be quite sure that John (and Jesus!) intends for the network of churches in Asia Minor to be in communication and communion, centered on this soon-to-be scriptural text, with other early Christian communities that were even more diverse. For instance, communities of Jewish believers in Jerusalem or Rome needed to be in dialogue with Gentile believers in Corinth or Ephesus. In other words, the book of Revelation urges its hearers and readers to engage in something akin to multiethnic Bible reading if they want to remain faithful disciples—if they want the church to be the church.

It is therefore not a stretch to say that, for us today, multiethnic Bible reading in communion is essential to our own faithful discipleship and to the church being the church—a network of friends that extends our friendship, and God's, to others—in our time and place.

SOME PRACTICAL CONSIDERATIONS

If we acknowledge the importance of Christian communion as mutual gift-giving and gift-receiving in the form of persons and their interpretive perspectives, how do we begin to achieve that sort of deep friendship?[19]

The first thing to say is that we need to celebrate the God-given diversity in the church and acknowledge that reading from different contexts does not mean—or at least should not mean—a revision of the gospel or a compromise about orthodox Christian belief and practice. As the late Native American Richard Twiss said in his book *Rescuing the Gospel from Cowboys*, Western-shaped people wrongly fear protecting the Bible from "a kind of imagined 'Indigenous cultural invasion.'"[20] This fear, he rightly argues, is grounded in the mistaken notion that standard Western/White American readings of Scripture and expressions of faith are somehow unaffected by White culture and are objectively true. It is a gift for White readers of Scripture to be liberated from that dangerous error. Faithful reading of Scripture means that our cultural practices and the interpretations they have generated need to be reexamined and sometimes reshaped or even

[19]It is beyond the scope of this essay to address the difficult questions surrounding multiethnic churches—as theologically appropriate and desirable as they may be.

[20]Richard Twiss, *Rescuing the Gospel from the Cowboys: A Native American Expression of the Jesus Way* (Downers Grove, IL: InterVarsity Press, 2015), 36.

jettisoned. Christians from other contexts and perspectives may therefore make us better and more faithful interpreters.

Second, we need more resources like this commentary, and they need to be distributed and used widely in the church.[21]

Third, we need to find ways of cultivating multiethnic reading in communion. If this sort of practice is in fact a sacramental activity, a receiving of others and thus of Christ, then we must use our individual and corporate imaginations in order to make such experiences happen—within churches, between churches, within denominations, in parachurch ministries, and in other settings.

Finally, we need to dream—to imagine "a church that bears witness to the exponential creativity and profound pluriformity of a united church" because "the power of God in Christ is sufficient for creating unity out of dissension and brokenness."[22] We should be inspired toward repentance, humility, unity, and communion by this prayerful benediction from Ephesians (Eph 3:20-21), a letter about reconciliation and diverse unity in Christ: "Now to him who by the power at work within us is able to accomplish abundantly far more than all we can ask or imagine, to him be glory in the church and in Christ Jesus to all generations, forever and ever. Amen."

[21]Chapters on how Scripture is read by African American, Latinx, and Asian American interpreters may be found in Michael J. Gorman, *Scripture and Its Interpretation: A Global, Ecumenical Introduction to the Bible* (Grand Rapids, MI: Baker Academic, 2017).

[22]Sechrest and Ramírez-Johnson, "Introduction," 16.

GOSPEL OF MATTHEW

H. Daniel Zacharias

INTRODUCTION

Authorship. The Gospel of Matthew is anonymous, though early evidence consistently attributes the work to Matthew the disciple of Jesus. The earliest evidence of this attribution is the title itself, which was very early.[1] That the author used Mark as a source (including the story of his own call in Mt 9:9-13; see also Mk 2:13-17) has caused many commentators to suggest an anonymous Jewish believer as the author, though others have suggested a Gentile believer.[2] Still others continue to hold to traditional attribution. Craig Evans, for example, notes, "There is nothing in the life of the early church that compelled it to select the apostle Matthew" when more significant candidates were available.[3]

Dating. The dating of Matthew is based primarily on the relative dating of Mark (often dated to 65–70 CE) as well as the destruction of the temple in 70 CE. Most commentators date Matthew to after 70 CE, usually within the '80s or 90s.[4] Several commentators in the last few decades have argued for a pre-70 CE date for Matthew.[5] This necessitates an earlier date for Mark, and recourse is often made to the work of John A. T. Robinson and more recently Jonathan Bernier.[6] Besides the inconclusive arguments for dating Matthew based on more developed theology, the lack of internal indicators concerning the temple's destruction in Matthew is an important point in favor of an early dating. In particular, Matthew 17:24–27 and its approval of the temple tax can be read as a strong indicator of a pre-70 CE date, as after the destruction of the temple, the temple tax was still collected, but the Romans shifted the tax to the temple of Jupiter Capitolinus in Rome (Josephus, *J.W.* 7.6.6 §218; Dio Cassius, *Roman History* 65.7; Suetonius, *Domitinanus* 12). While deciding on the date of Matthew does not significantly influence its interpretation, there are good arguments for

[1]Martin Hengel, *The Four Gospels and the One Gospel of Jesus Christ: An Investigation of the Collection and Origin of the Canonical Gospels* (Harrisburg, PA: Trinity Press International, 2000), 48-53; Ulrich Luz, *Matthew 1–7*, trans. James E. Crouch, Hermeneia 61A (Minneapolis: Augsburg, 2007), 59. David Turner has suggested that the title is original to the text. See David L. Turner, *Matthew*, Baker Exegetical Commentary on the New Testament (Grand Rapids, MI: Baker, 2008), 11. See also Eusebius's quotation of Papias in *Hist. eccl.* 3.39.16.

[2]See, for a list of commentators who take these positions, W. D. Davies and Dale C. Allison, *Matthew 1–7*, International Critical Commentary 1 (New York: T&T Clark, 1988), 10-11.

[3]Craig A. Evans, *Matthew*, New Cambridge Bible Commentary (New York: Cambridge University Press, 2011), 4. Donald Hagner suggests that the disciple Matthew is indeed the source of significant portions of the Gospel, even if not the final author. See Donald A. Hagner, *Matthew*, 2 vols., Word Biblical Commentary 33A-B (Dallas: Word Books, 1993), lxxvii.

[4]Luz, *Matthew 1–7*, 58-59.

[5]The most recent being Evans, *Matthew*.

[6]John A. T. Robinson, *Redating the New Testament* (Philadelphia: Westminster, 1976); Jonathan Bernier, *Rethinking the Dates of the New Testament: The Evidence for Early Composition* (Grand Rapids, MI: Baker Academic, 2022). On an earlier date for Mark, see James G. Crossley, *The Date of Mark's Gospel: Insight from the Law in Earliest Christianity* (New York: T&T Clark, 2004).

both a pre- and post-70 CE dating. Matthew was written in the window of 60–95 CE.

Provenance. Determining the specific location and circumstances leading to the composition of Matthew is more difficult, and there are varying opinions among scholars. The Matthean emphasis on Torah and Jesus as the fulfillment and embodiment of Torah have led commentators to see the audience as Torah-observant Jews who had accepted Jesus as Messiah. There has also been the suggestion that this audience was undergoing pressure, if not outright hostility, from the Jewish community around them. Possible evidence of this is the castigation of the religious leaders in Matthew 23 and especially the teachings of Jesus that discuss persecution, particularly the statement in Matthew 10:17 that "they will hand you over to councils and flog you in their synagogues." But the level of the original audience's connection with Judaism remains debated.

My social location. I approach this commentary as an Indigenous man, shaped by a variety of communities and relationships, as we all are. Jesus too was an Indigenous man, connected to the land of his ancestors, shaped by the history of his people, and formed by the sacred texts and religious rituals of his heritage. Jesus and his earliest followers were connected to their lands and communities but were also under Roman imperial power. This is not unlike many Indigenous communities today who now work through postcolonial experiences or are still in the midst of decolonizing processes even as colonial powers govern their lands and communities. The Evangelist, too, was one who was embedded in a community, bringing forth, shaping, and re-actualizing the stories and teachings of Jesus for his community and the broader Christian community. Like Indigenous elders and storytellers, Matthew was a (re)storyteller; taking Mark, he added, edited, and expanded on this sacred tradition about the resurrected one. Indigenous peoples also rely on the telling and retelling of stories, applying and making them contextually relevant for their audience as they seek to pass on a cultural tradition to shape a community. While scholars continue to debate Matthew and his community's relationship with the Jewish community and Christian community, I suspect the community sought faithfulness to their Jewish traditions while also embracing this new multiethnic messianic community around the resurrected one. If this is the case, Indigenous followers of Jesus share similar circumstances with the Evangelist and his community. We too seek to honor—and in many cases reclaim—the heritage of our ancestors as followers of Christ. This at times places us into conflict or tension with our Indigenous communities, but perhaps more often places us in conflict and tension with our church communities.

In reading and commenting on Matthew, I seek to be faithful to the communicative intentions of Jesus, to the intentions of the Evangelist for his community, and in hopes that the life and teachings of Jesus transmitted in this Gospel might be encountered in fresh ways as it is encountered by Indigenous peoples. For Indigenous peoples of the world, our social location is not simply about the human circles that we belong to but the wider community of creation, of which we are but one part—a community that encompasses all flora and fauna, the landscapes, the waterways, the soil and the skies, the birds and the bugs, and the unseen spiritual world, often simply called "the spirit world" by Indigenous peoples. This interconnected life-web is formative in Indigenous worldviews, and I daresay that it is formative in the worldviews of Jesus and his earliest followers as well.[7]

ROOTS AND LOCATION (MATTHEW 1:1-25)

Beginnings matter to Indigenous peoples. Who is present at the beginning? Where is the person rooted? What are the relationships present at the outset? The first verse of Matthew opens with an incipit, an introductory statement that seems to introduce not only the most immediate section but the Gospel more broadly. The incipit introduces the new work of God in Christ, but does so by deliberately circling back to the beginning of creation and drawing to mind the Jewish creation story. No meaningful cultural work can be done apart from a people's creation stories, as they hold wisdom that helps the people to make sense of the land, the world, themselves, and the relationships they are a part of. This is true of the stories of Glooscap in the lands of Mi'kma'ki, the stories of Bunjil in the Wurundjeri lands now called Australia, or the Diné story of First Man and First Woman.[8] For Indigenous followers of Jesus, the Hebrew creation stories are also stories that shape and teach us, as they are the unique stories that shaped Christ and his people, and they help to reveal Creator's purposes in creation and so begin the grand story of God that culminates in the coming of the Savior. Because of the importance of creation stories, Matthew begins with recourse back to the Hebrew creation stories.

Most English translations do not do justice to the first two words of Matthew, *Biblos geneseōs*, which deliberately draws to mind Genesis 2:4 and the book of Genesis more broadly.[9] This new work of God through Christ, this new creation, is done in the context of creation, as this opening "evokes the story of God's creative and sovereign purposes for the whole world as the initial context for hearing the story of Jesus."[10] This literary invocation of creation sets the stage for the life of Christ that will unfold in the narrative. This circle back to creation will be noted again later in the birth narrative and is also present elsewhere in the New Testament (see Rev 22:2).

The titles applied to Jesus in the first verse anticipate ongoing themes throughout the Gospel about the identity of Jesus as the promised Messiah. This first verse not only provides a literary introduction but makes a strong claim within the Roman imperial context of Matthew's first audience, likely in Antioch. Jesus is the one "who contests and relativizes Rome's claim to sovereignty and divine agency and who offers a vision for a different social experience that enacts God's purposes."[11] This echo back to Genesis 2:4 also places the birth of Jesus into the family tree of all of creation. Genesis 2:4 functions as the close of the seven-days-of-creation story and bridges into the second creation story. The Hebrew word *toledot*, often translated as "account" or "genealogies," is used frequently in genealogies (Gen 5:1; 6:9; 10:1; etc.). This

[7]For more on the hermeneutical approach employed in this work, and as a helpful background to my theology around enculturation, please see the article titled "Turtle Island Biblical Interpretation" by myself and Christopher Hoklotubbe in the present volume.

[8]Silas Tertius Rand, *Legends of the Micmacs*, Wellesley Philological Publications (Cambridge, MA: Longmans, Green, 1894); Sam Wark, "Bunji the Eagle," June 2, 2014, video, 4:09, https://vimeo.com/97185996; Paul Zolbrod, *Diné Bahane': The Navajo Creation Story* (Albuquerque: University of New Mexico Press, 1987).

[9]Dale C. Allison, "Matthew's First Two Words," in *Studies in Matthew: Interpretation Past and Present* (Grand Rapids, MI: Baker, 2006), 157-62.

[10]Warren Carter, "Matthew and the Gentiles: Individual Conversion and/or Systemic Transformation?," *JSNT* 26 (2004): 262.

[11]Warren Carter, "Matthaean Christology in Roman Imperial Key: Matthew 1:1," in *The Gospel of Matthew in Its Roman Imperial Context*, ed. John K. Riches and David C. Sim, JSNTSup 276 (New York: T&T Clark, 2005), 143.

Hebrew word invokes kinship relations, and its first usage brings humanity into the family tree of the entire heavens and the earth.[12] That Matthew invokes this in his opening words reminds the reader that the Christ comes forth not only from his human ancestry but from all of creation. Christ is connected as an embodied person to all of creation, and his work of restoration and reconciliation is for all of creation (Jn 3:16; Col 1:15-20).[13]

The prologue as a whole focuses on the pedigree of Jesus and the circumstances surrounding his birth. The genealogy establishes Jesus' lineage as a Davidic descendant (Mt 1:1-17) and is laid out in a structured form of three sets of fourteen generations (Mt 1:17), although a quick tally reveals that Matthew was evidently counting creatively in order to highlight David.[14] Notable also in the genealogy are the annotations accompanying numerous names, which serve to highlight several parts of Israel's history and to include women in the genealogical story, highlighting "righteous Gentiles" in the family line of Jesus, who were often of marginal socioeconomic status.[15] This unique aspect of Matthew's genealogy bears significance for many Indigenous peoples today who have a mixture of Indigenous and non-Indigenous ancestry, sometimes over a number of generations. Jesus too had a multiethnic heritage through his family line, one that is proudly on display in Matthew's genealogy: "Hybridity is not denied and racial purity is not asserted."[16] As the genealogy and wider prologue sends the reader into the narrative, a literary device called the primacy effect conditions readers to identify themes that will play out. The genealogy prepares readers to see strong Davidic themes, themes of exile, of land and creation, and connections to women and Gentiles.

While modern Western readers today may be puzzled by Matthew's opening his book with a list of names, culture at the time of Jesus and many Indigenous cultures today see one's identity "not [as] a matter of achievement but of relationship."[17] The culmination of the stories of his ancestors will call forth Jesus and help to determine his life, vision, and calling, and each name in the genealogy invokes the stories of that ancestor's life. I am reminded, for instance, of Māori recitation of one's *whakapapa* (genealogical account).[18] Depending on the occasion, one's whakapapa may be extensive or shortened, and may encompass territories, landscapes, status, and kinship (with the entirety of creation), locating oneself within and as part of a created order. In the recitation of a whakapapa, the individual may make explicit points built on the elements of the whakapapa they are choosing to recite, the implications of which may be discerned by the hearers and may also be directly addressed in the following exchanges. Whakapapa's

[12]H. Daniel Zacharias, "The Land Takes Care of Us: Recovering Creator's Relational Design," in *The Land: Majority World and Minoritized Theologies of Land*, ed. K. K. Yeo and Gene L. Green (Eugene, OR: Cascade, 2020), 78-80.

[13]See Elizabeth A. Johnson, *Creation and the Cross: The Mercy of God for a Planet in Peril* (Maryknoll, NY: Orbis Books, 2018).

[14]H. Daniel Zacharias, *Matthew's Presentation of the Son of David: Davidic Tradition and Typology in the Gospel of Matthew* (London: T&T Clark, 2017), 40-52.

[15]Jason B. Hood, *The Messiah, His Brothers, and the Nations (Matthew 1.1-17)*, LNTS 441 (London: T&T Clark, 2011); Warren Carter, *Matthew and the Margins: A Socio-political and Religious Reading*, JSNTSup 204 (Sheffield: Sheffield Academic Press, 2003), 59-60.

[16]Mitzi J. Smith and Yung Suk Kim, *Toward Decentering the New Testament: A Reintroduction* (Eugene, OR: Cascade Books, 2018), 111.

[17]George T. Montague, *Companion God: A Cross-cultural Commentary on the Gospel of Matthew*, rev. ed. (New York: Paulist Press, 2010), 18.

[18]See Nēpia Mahuika, "A Brief History of Whakapapa: Māori Approaches to Genealogy," *Genealogy* 3 (2019): 1-13.

recitation can also serve to bring forth women's voices and other voices that may otherwise be forgotten or silenced.[19] While modern readers of Matthew may quibble over which names are chosen or excluded, and the differences between Matthew's and Luke's genealogies, these problems were not in the mind of the Evangelist, and learning from the Māori can help to read with fresh eyes. Matthew has made deliberate choices in the genealogy, even including something relatively unique among biblical genealogies—an event. In addition to the highlighting of the deportation to Babylon (Mt 1:11-12), Matthew's annotations to the genealogy (Mt 1:2-3, 5-6, 11, 16) serve to recall with greater focus significant events and relationships within Christ's family line.[20]

Among other things, the genealogy also highlights Jesus' familial connection to the land of Israel. Matthew does this by beginning the genealogy with Abraham, the one who first receives the promise of a land, of offspring, and of a responsibility to the world. Many modern readers do not connect themselves to the wider stories of their family tree, much less how they have been created and shaped by and because of the previous generations and the lands of their ancestors. This genealogy at the outset of Matthew sets before the reader the relational location out of which Jesus is born and from which he has been created and is being called forth. The genealogy establishes for the discerning reader that Jesus is created by this genealogical account and bound to the responsibilities of his future by this past as Matthew has told it. His own whakapapa is what has brought him forth and sends him out to his mission to end the trappings of exile under Roman imperial domination, to bring holistic healing to hurting peoples, and to establish this new yet ongoing work of the multiethnic messianic community.

The Evangelist next narrates the story of Jesus' birth by Mary through the Holy Spirit. The primary character of this first narrative section is Joseph, as he is a son of David (Mt 1:20), and his actions will decide whether Jesus and his mother will remain in his family line, as during this time betrothal already bound the individuals together as husband and wife.[21] Joseph is characterized as a righteous man whose actions are of primary importance for Jesus, highlighting once again the importance of ancestors and relationships for the shaping of Christ's character. Joseph is visited by an angel in a dream and is told to keep his wife because her pregnancy is from God.

The corporate nature of Christ's ministry is on display as Matthew shares the vision given to Jesus' adoptive father, one that will shape the life of Christ—to "save his people from their sins" (Mt 1:21). This formative vision from the unseen realm—the spirit world—expressing Matthew's soteriological vision, should not be massaged solely into a moral, individualistic reading. Jesus' ministry will be directed first to his people as a whole, not simply to individuals. "His people" has been established in the genealogy as the nation of Israel, including Gentiles such as Rahab and Ruth who have been enfolded into Israel as kin. As the narrative unfolds, it is also revealed that "his people" are those who follow his teachings (Mt 12:48-50; 28:10). His people require healing and wholeness not simply at the individual level but also from their collective transgressions and collective oppressions, from "their sins."

[19]Beverley Moana Hall-Smith, "Whakapapa (Genealogy), a Hermeneutical Framework for Reading Biblical Texts: A Māori Woman Encounters Rape and Violence in Judges 19–21" (PhD diss., Flinders University, 2017), 9.

[20]For a detailed study of the annotations in Matthew's genealogy, see Hood, *Messiah, His Brothers*.

[21]Zacharias, *Matthew's Presentation*, 56-57.

Warren Carter notes how political, social, and economic sins have already been invoked in the genealogy, as each name carries with it the stories from Scripture and tradition. The reality of Roman imperial oppression was keenly understood by the first audience in the Roman Empire, and the name of Jesus "commissions the yet-unborn baby."[22]

The Evangelist uses the first of many Old Testament quotations to indicate that the life of Jesus is in fulfillment of Israel's Scriptures. The nature of fulfillment is varied within Matthew's Gospel, at times indicating a direct fulfillment of predictive prophecy and at other times indicating a typological or thematic fulfillment. In modern society, shaped as it is by the printing press, readers can often find it difficult to reconcile themselves with the New Testament author's freestyle usage of the Scriptures, in which verses from disparate voices may be compounded together or oracles from Hebrew prophets may be read seemingly out of context. But like the oral cultures of Indigenous peoples that still survive today, stories and oral traditions are both sturdy and adaptive to situations. Oral stories are a living tradition that shapes the people who tell the story and the people who hear it, reminding them that even new works of God in the world follow the patterns of the past in similar and different ways.

INFANCY NARRATIVE (MATTHEW 2:1-23)

The continuation of Matthew's prologue moves forward chronologically by about two years, narrating the visit of the magi from the East who search for the one born king of the Jews. The magi's entrance into Jerusalem introduces the first antagonist, Herod the Great, who along with the rest of Jerusalem is troubled by the news of the arrival of the Christ. The magi are guided by the star to the residence in Bethlehem where Jesus and his mother are. This star is likely a celestial or angelic figure doing its work to help welcome Creator into the world.[23] The magi present Jesus with gifts and worship him, after which they are warned to avoid Herod. This passage is a clash of kings, as Jesus has already been presented as the rightful heir of King David (Mt 1:6, 16), and Herod is identified as the king several times in this passage (Mt 2:1-3, 9). The next time there is a concentration of usage for the title "king" is in reference to Jesus, spoken in mockery and contempt (Mt 27:11, 29, 37, 42).

The genealogy has prepared the reader for righteous Gentiles to be part of the unfolding messianic story, and in this case these Eastern magi represent the exemplary character: "Matthew forces his audience to identify with the pagan Magi rather than with Herod or Jerusalem's religious elite."[24] While the ministry of Jesus certainly focuses on Israel (Mt 9:36; 10:6; 15:24), the early hostility of the Jerusalem leadership and the surprising obedience and worship of Gentiles foreshadows the life and ministry of Jesus and his later followers as ones who will conflict with the powerful while drawing in those seen to be outsiders. This composite character of non-Jewish worshipers served to remind Matthew's readers of God's interaction with those outside Israel (e.g., Amos 9:7). But this is not simply a matter of learning through general revelation. What the magi identified in their cultural and religious practices pointed them to the Messiah and compelled them to act. Their worship is accepted, not reviled. Their stories are respected, not denigrated. And their gifts are received,

---

[22]Warren Carter, *Matthew and Empire: Initial Explorations* (Harrisburg, PA: Trinity Press International, 2001), 69.

[23]Dale C. Allison, *Studies in Matthew: Interpretation Past and Present* (Grand Rapids, MI: Baker, 2006), 17-42.

[24]Craig S. Keener, *The Gospel Of Matthew: A Socio-rhetorical Commentary* (Grand Rapids, MI: Eerdmans, 2009), 97-98.

not rejected. This story challenges the hegemonies of culture and worship for the church today, reminding us that the first acts of worship directed to Jesus were ones that would not have been allowed or accepted in the Jerusalem temple or local synagogue, in the same ways that Indigenous expressions of worship are often not allowed in modern church spaces. It also reminds the reader that "God will reveal himself wherever people are looking for him."[25]

Because the first two words of the gospel have drawn to mind Genesis, the reader is prepared for allusions to the stories of creation. Just prior to this section, Matthew tells us that Joseph "did not know" his wife (Mt 1:25 NKJV), which may be echoing "Adam knew Eve his wife" (Gen 4:1 NKJV). The magi are then introduced as coming "from the East" (Mt 2:1), echoing the description of Eden "in the east" (Gen 2:8). Finally, as the magi present the gifts of gold, frankincense, and myrrh, readers are perhaps reminded of Eden once again, as gold is present (Gen 2:11) as well as bdellium (Gen 2:12), an aromatic resin similar to myrrh. These are gifts from the earth, first given by Creator, now presented back to him.

This second half of Matthew's prologue is also significant for the concentration of Old Testament quotations (the first occurring in Mt 1:23). The birth and circumstances of Jesus' early life fulfill the trajectory of the Scriptures. Matthew's usage of the Scriptures indicates the flexibility and interactivity of early traditions with present circumstances and seeks to further entrench Jesus' life into the traditions of his people. Regarding Matthew's use of the Hebrew Scriptures, Graham Stanton states: "The OT is woven into the warp and woof of this gospel; the evangelist uses Scripture to underline some of his most prominent and distinctive theological concerns."[26] With the concentration of Old Testament quotations in the prologue, Matthew presents Jesus as God with us (Mt 1:23), as the promised Davidic king (Mt 1:23; 2:6, 23), and as the embodiment of Israel coming through the exile (Mt 2:15, 18). In the invocation of these Scriptures, Matthew betrays deep awareness of wider contexts of the prophets he quotes and of wider themes in the Old Testament.[27]

The chapter also introduces the reader to key places in Matthew's geographic landscape. In a profound mark of reversal, Jerusalem is now the place of antagonism toward Christ, and Egypt is the refuge. After this time of migration, Jesus and his family will settle in Galilee. That Jesus and his parents were refugees for a time ought to shape current modern perspectives. As Joe Kapolyo writes, "Jesus honoured all those who suffer homelessness on account of war, famine, persecution or some other disaster."[28] This geographic juxtaposition between Jerusalem and Galilee will continue through the narrative, as Matthew's Jesus will spend his time primarily in Galilee and will not enter Jerusalem until his final week. This early story not only foreshadows the crucifixion but places the Judean seat of power against the Christ. Jesus' ministry will take place in the shadow of the empire and will avoid the capital that first rejected him. The corruption of the Roman leadership is most fully on display in the slaughter of the innocent in Bethlehem for the maintaining of power. Whether it be the Pharaoh in Moses' day (Ex 1) or modern

[25]Joe Kapolyo, "Matthew," in *Africa Bible Commentary*, ed. Tokunboh Adeyemo (Grand Rapids, MI: Zondervan, 2006), 1136.

[26]Graham N. Stanton, *A Gospel for a New People: Studies in Matthew* (London: T&T Clark, 1992), 346.

[27]On this topic, see Nicholas G. Piotrowski, *Matthew's New David at the End of Exile: A Socio-rhetorical Study of Scriptural Quotations*, NovTSup 170 (Boston: Brill, 2016).

[28]Kapolyo, "Matthew," 1138.

colonial governments' enforcement of Indian residential schools, which forcibly removed children from their families and communities in order to "get rid of the Indian problem," the maintaining of power will often target the children of the marginalized.[29]

Numerous times through the prologue, the spirit world interacts directly with the vulnerable family of Jesus. This is most evident in the concentration of dreams (Mt 1:20; 2:12-13, 19, 22). Dreams are ways of knowing and a point of encounter with the spirit world. In the Old Testament and many Indigenous worldviews, dreams are seen as places of divine encounter (Num 12:6; Joel 2:28). That Joseph is the primary dreamer raises his status as someone highly attuned to the spirit world and the will of Creator.[30] At the close of this section, Joseph, the primary character in Matthew 1, returns to the story, with the angel having instructed him to flee for safety to Egypt until the death of Herod (Mt 2:13), then instructing him once more to return to "the land of Israel" (Mt 2:20). Jesus and his family cannot live out the rest of their days in Egypt, though the angel does not simply instruct Joseph to "return home." The land is also in need of redemption and healing, thus requiring the presence of the Christ, and so it is the land that calls him to return. The wisdom and history of a people resides in their landscapes as chronology collapses into geography. The genealogy has set forth the location in which Jesus is summoned to be, the place of promise, of kingdom, and of rebellion and exile. It is only in this land that the Christ can enact shalom.

JOHN THE BAPTIZER AND JESUS' BAPTISM (MATTHEW 3:1-17)

All four Gospels are consistent in prefacing Jesus' ministry with the ministry of John the Baptizer around the Jordan. This extended section on John highlights his popularity as a holy man and prophet. It also serves to ground Jesus into the line of the prophets, as the message of Jesus will echo John's words (Mt 4:17; 12:34; 23:33). There is much that is innovative and unique in the life and teachings of Jesus, but this section reminds us that Jesus also stands in continuity with his ancestral prophetic traditions and honors the teaching of his mentor.[31]

John is intensely critical of the religious leaders who come to him, warning them that they cannot rely on their Abrahamic descent. His message clearly indicates an apocalyptic judgment on all people, and he says that the awaited Messiah will soon arrive. Amid the masses coming to John, Jesus also approaches John for baptism. Although John is resistant initially, he relents and baptizes Jesus. Jesus also makes it clear that being baptized by John is an appropriate ceremony for him to undergo to bring himself into solidarity with John's renewal movement. Scholars recognize the importance of John's location in connecting back to Israel's story as Israel crossed the Jordan into the Promised Land (Josh 3:1–4:24). It is important to recognize here the Indigenous reading of the conquest narrative. Colonized peoples often read these narratives from the perspective of the invaded people and wrestle with the implications of this for today. This is particularly because language of the conquest from the biblical

[29]Duncan Campbell Scott ran the Canadian residential schools and mandated their attendance in 1920. This statement can be found at National Archives of Canada, Record Group 10, vol. 6810, file 470-2-3, vol. 7, 55 (L-3) and 63 (N-3).

[30]The presentation of Joseph in Matthew also highlights his righteous character. On this, see Philip F. Esler, "The Righteousness of Joseph: Interpreting Matt 1.18-25 in Light of Judean Legal Papyri," *NTS* 68 (2022): 326-43.

[31]For an extensive discussion on John as the mentor of Jesus, see John P. Meier, *Mentor, Message, and Miracles*, A Marginal Jew: Rethinking the Historical Jesus 2 (New York: Anchor Bible, 1994).

narrative was used during colonization, with language such as "Chosen People" for the European settlers and "Canaanites" for the Indigenous peoples.[32] John's location and Jesus' baptism connect Jesus not only to the story of his people but also to the land of his people. In Walter Brueggemann's words, land is a "primary category of faith." He states:

> Place is space that has historical meanings, where some things have happened that are now remembered and that provide continuity and identity across generations. Place is space in which important words have been spoken that have established identity, defined vocation, and envisioned destiny. Place is space in which vows have been exchanged, promises have been made, and demands have been issued. . . . Rootedness, in community and in a geographical land, is a conscious choice to be bound to the story of a place, be shaped and molded by it, and to be active in its upkeep. To delight in its beauty and suffer along with it, in sickness and in health. It is a covenant.[33]

Indigenous folks well understand the primal connection with one's ancestral landscapes. This is not simply a matter of loving the outdoors but rather of belonging to a place such that one's identity is inclusive of the land.[34] A communal identity inclusive of the land is often hard for settlers and colonial peoples to understand, due in part to the brevity of their time, historically speaking, within particular landscapes. But for Indigenous peoples, including Jesus, the land of one's people holds memories, and the Jordan River along with the twelve erected stones (Josh 4:8-9; Mt 3:9) continued to testify in Jesus' day. For Indigenous folks today, it is ceremonies that remind communities and individuals of their ongoing relationship to a land, to a place, and to a people. For Jesus, it would not have sufficed to be submersed in any water—it was this land and these waters to which he belonged and so had to be where the ceremony of baptism occurred. In doing so, he embodied the story of Israel, who also passed through the waters of the Red Sea before spending forty years in the wilderness.

After his baptism, the heavens open, God speaks from the heavens, and the Spirit descends on Jesus in the form of a dove. This triune presence at the baptism scene will later correspond to the commission to go out and baptize in the name of the Father, Son, and Spirit (Mt 28:19). The words that come from the heavens also affirm the divine sonship of Jesus, a theme that will continue through Matthew. Significant, too, is the theophanic manifestation of the Holy Spirit in a physical, if temporary, manifestation in dove form.[35] The Holy Spirit is first encountered as wind in Genesis 1:2, God is encountered as fire by Moses (Ex 3:1-14), and Jesus states that he is living water (Jn 7:37-44). In the Scriptures, not only is creation a location of divine encounter, but divine encounter occurs *in*, *through*, and *as* creation.[36] Many traditional Indigenous peoples have a worldview characterized by animacy, holding to creation as sacred and infused with divine presence and agency. This perspective of agency in

---

[32]See Robert Alan Warrior, "Canaanites, Cowboys, and Indians: Deliverance, Conquest, and Liberation Theology Today," in *Native and Christian: Indigenous Voices on Religious Identity in the United States and Canada*, ed. James Treat (New York: Routledge, 1996), 93-104.

[33]Walter Brueggemann, *The Land: Place as Gift, Promise, and Challenge in Biblical Faith*, 2nd ed., Overtures to Biblical Theology (Minneapolis: Fortress, 2002), 4.

[34]See Ray Aldred, "The Land, Treaty, and Spirituality: Communal Identity Inclusive of Land," *Journal of NAIITS* 18 (2019): 1-17.

[35]Although the physical nature of the Holy Spirit in Dove form is clear in Matthew, Luke makes it the most explicit in Lk 3:22.

[36]On the issue of Indigenous Christian animacy, see Mark I. Wallace, *Finding God in the Singing River: Christianity, Spirit, Nature* (Minneapolis: Fortress, 2005); Mark I. Wallace, *When God Was a Bird: Christianity, Animism, and the Re-enchantment*

nonhuman creation is also expressed in the Hebrew Scriptures, with Psalm 148 being a prime example.[37] That Matthew and the other synoptic authors portray the Holy Spirit enfleshed/enfeathered in other-than-human form ought to at least soften Western Christian perspective on differing worldviews, which are often labeled as animist or panentheist.[38]

TEMPTATION AND COMMISSION (MATTHEW 4:1-25)

The temptation in the wilderness is the second episode of preparation before Jesus' public ministry, a symbolic reenactment of Israel's time in the wilderness. This episode continues to bridge the divide between the realms of reality, physical and spiritual. The vision and voice of God as well as the enfeathered Holy Spirit at the baptism are now followed by Jesus' trial in the wilderness, where he will encounter the demonic power and at the end will be attended by angels.

This story is strongly reminiscent of the practice of some First Nations of a vision quest. While the practice varies from nation to nation, vision quests are still practiced by some Indigenous nations today, and Vine Deloria states that vision quests seems to have been a nearly universal practice among Indigenous nations prior to colonization.[39] They involve fasting, prayer, and an extended period of solitude in the wilderness. It is often a rite of passage from childhood to manhood but also practiced by those in the midst of life transitions or for times of spiritual renewal. Vision quests will sometimes have the seeker led by an elder to the place of the quest, which is often a demanding and even hostile environment.[40]

It should not be missed that it is the enfeathered Spirit, Dove, who leads Jesus to his vision quest—Jesus is led along by a bird. In Jesus' case, he faithfully follows Dove as she leads him to the badlands of Israel for his trial.[41] There is no mention of Dove's departure. In some vision quest practices today, the seeker is given a wide berth by the elder who aids them, as they must rely on themselves and any help the spirit world provides during this time of solitude. But the elder will remain within close enough range to provide aid if need be. The Spirit never departed from Christ, and perhaps the manifested Spirit remained perched close by throughout this time of trial.

Three temptations are narrated: a challenge to Jesus to use his divine power to satiate his hunger after his forty days of fasting, a challenge to jump from a high point and rely on God's promise of safety, and a challenge to worship Satan in order to receive the kingdoms of the world. These final words reveal that the

---

of the World, Groundworks: Ecological Issues in Philosophy and Theology (New York: Fordham University Press, 2018).

[37]On this, see Terence E. Fretheim, *God and World in the Old Testament: A Relational Theology of Creation* (Nashville: Abingdon, 2010), chap. 8.

[38]While animism as a label and concept has a long and troubled history, some modern scholars seek to refine and renew its usage. See, for example, Mari Joerstad, *The Hebrew Bible and Environmental Ethics: Humans, Non-humans, and the Living Landscape* (Cambridge: Cambridge University Press, 2019), chap. 2. Panentheism, as the Greek roots of the word imply ("all-in-God"), holds that all that exists is contained within and by God's ultimate power but that God is simultaneously separate from and greater than all that exists. For more on panentheism, see John W. Cooper, *Panentheism, the Other God of the Philosophers: From Plato to the Present* (Grand Rapids, MI: Baker Academic, 2006).

[39]Vine Deloria Jr. states that vision quests "seems to have been nearly universal" in the First Nations of North America. See Deloria, *The World We Used to Live In: Remembering the Powers of the Medicine Men* (Golden, CO: Fulcrum, 2006), xxiv.

[40]Steven Charleston, *The Four Vision Quests of Jesus* (New York: Morehouse, 2015), 102-3.

[41]I use "she" for the Holy Spirit here deliberately. While it is important to recognize that God is not gendered, both male and female express his image (Gen 1:27). Yet, gendered language and gendered metaphors, both male and female, are used for God in the Scriptures, with male language and metaphors being dominant. Yet, the word for the Spirit in Hebrew, *ruah*, is grammatically feminine, as is dove (*peristera*) in Matthew.

empires of the world, namely Rome, are under the power of the Evil One.[42] Jesus responds to all of these temptations with Scripture, quoting from Deuteronomy. This narrative continues to enact an Israel typology (see Deut 8:2). Jesus' quotations from Scripture are all drawn from Deuteronomy (Deut 8:3; 6:16, 13), which was narrated as the final teachings of Moses just prior to exiting the wilderness to enter the land of promise. The story of Israel shows their failure to honor the covenant, while this episode shows that Jesus is the faithful embodiment of Israel and its mission.

The vision quest is seen as liminal space in which the seeker interacts directly with the spirit world, both helpful and harmful spirits. This melding of the physical and spiritual world began at the baptism, with the heavens opening up (Mt 3:16), and continues through into the vision quest. Deloria notes how vision quests are sometimes referred to as dreaming, and often the recounting of one's dream/vision quest blurs the lines between visionary experience and physical experience.[43] This is similar to the recounting of Jesus' temptation, with a blurring of the lines between the visionary and the physical. Part of the work of a vision quest is to solidify one's sacred calling in life, expand one's knowledge, and receive power from Creator.[44] Like many Indigenous seekers, Jesus' vision quest propels him forward into his sacred duties.

Matthew 4:17 signals the beginning of Jesus' public ministry, with Jesus preaching the same message as John (Mt 3:2). Matthew 4:17 is also an important narrative turn, as the same phrase "from that time Jesus began to . . ." is used later, in Matthew 16:21. Together these verses bookend Jesus' public ministry in Galilee, with Matthew 16:21 turning the narrative focus toward Jerusalem and passion week. After the first act of public preaching, Jesus calls his first four disciples in two very similar stories that follow the same fourfold pattern.[45] All four men are fishermen from around the Sea of Galilee who are called by Jesus, and they then leave their jobs and begin to follow him. The first disciples are men of the lake, experiencing the difficulties of a colonial economy. Jesus' choice to move to Capernaum is a signal that the good news will issue not from the areas of imperial power, such as Tiberias or Sepphoris, nor from Jerusalem: "Jesus is located among the marginal, with the rural peasants not the urban wealthy, with the ruled not the rulers, with the powerless and exploited not the powerful."[46] So far in the Gospel there has been relatively little of Jesus' ministry narrated, and so the summary (Mt 4:23-25) intends to frame the ministry, which will be narrated in the following chapters.

One final exegetical issue that arises from both this section and the previous section of Matthew is a unique Matthean phrase, "kingdom of the heavens" (Mt 3:2; 4:17 [my translation]), which is the foundational proclamation of both John and Jesus. While it is still frequent in scholarship to state that "heavens" is a circumlocution in Matthew to avoid the use of "God" (understandable given the synoptic parallels), Jonathan Pennington convincingly argues that this is not simply a stand-in but reveals Matthew's symbolic universe, indicating the contrasting duality of heaven and earth.[47] Matthew's unusual usage

---

[42]Carter, *Matthew and Empire*, 102.
[43]Deloria, *World We Used to Live In*, 1.
[44]Deloria, *World We Used to Live In*, 2.
[45]Davies and Allison, *Matthew*, 392-93.
[46]Carter, *Matthew and Empire*, 103.
[47]Jonathan T. Pennington, *Heaven and Earth in the Gospel of Matthew*, NovTSup 126 (Boston: Brill, 2007).

of "heavens" when speaking of the kingdom of the Father (e.g., Mt 5:16) has been understood as a reference to God's invisible realm.[48] Yet, while we cannot discount the contrasting dualism of heaven and earth in early Jewish literature and within Matthew, it seems that Matthew's opening narratives, particularly the baptism, have prepared the reader to see that Creator's power and presence is already in both the spiritual (the invisible heaven) and physical realm (the visible heaven).[49] At the scene of his baptism, Creator has presented himself as being both in his heavenly realm, as the voice that speaks from the clouds, and incarnate as Dove, who comes down from the physical heaven.[50] Matthew's unique "kingdom of the heavens" signals not simply God's invisible realm but the totality of the physical and spiritual realms over which he is the creator and sustainer, and in both realms he is intimately active. The message of John, as well as the first words of proclamation from Jesus, is built on this reality of Creator's relationship to both the heavenly realm and the physical realm, and it is the basis on which we petition God in prayer (Mt 6:9).

SERMON ON THE MOUNT (MATTHEW 5:1–7:29)

The Sermon on the Mount commences by establishing the sermon's setting as well as audience. Jesus has for a period of time been ministering throughout the region (Mt 4:23-25). His reputation as a healer and holy man is established as Jesus indiscriminately gives of himself to the people who are in need. As the Gospel of Matthew features five large discourses, it is important to see first how Jesus has established himself as a wisdom keeper worthy of being listened to.[51] He has the pedigree of a king. His birth stands in opposition to the imperial powers. He has identified with John's renewal movement and gone on his vision quest, and in doing so identifies with and takes on himself the stories of his people. Following this, he has freely given of his power of healing. These stories establish him as a wisdom keeper, someone who will be sought out for his teaching. While Jesus' teaching is guidance toward human flourishing, it is not tyrannical or dictatorial.[52] His teaching is something that someone chooses to embrace, a teaching for those who have already made the choice to follow him (Mt 4:19).

It comes as no surprise to those familiar with the Jewish Scriptures that Jesus ascends a mountain to give this great teaching as his ancestor Moses had done, and it is no surprise to Indigenous peoples either. "Mountains are sites of spiritual power in Native tradition. They are signposts to the presence of God. . . . Mountains are spirit-filled."[53]

The sermon begins with the Beatitudes, a series of nine statements that all begin with the adjective *blessed*. The Beatitudes are descriptions of a state of being, not a promise of

[48]Pennington, *Heaven and Earth*, 340.

[49]Pennington, *Heaven and Earth*, 333, states, "Heaven and earth do not represent two original, opposing forces in the world, but biblically are seen as organically related realms all under the rule of God."

[50]The Greek *ouranos* is used for both the invisible realm of God and the sky. See "οὐρανός," in *Greek-English Lexicon of the New Testament and Other Early Christian Literature*, ed. Walter Bauer, William F. Arndt, F. Wilbur Gingrich, and Frederick W. Danker, 2nd ed. (Chicago: University of Chicago Press, 1979), 737-38.

[51]Wisdom Keepers, or Knowledge Keepers, are people within Indigenous communities who are recognized for their role in knowing and passing on cultural and spiritual knowledge for the community, often especially focused on teaching the younger generations.

[52]See Jonathan T. Pennington, *The Sermon on the Mount and Human Flourishing: A Theological Commentary* (Grand Rapids, MI: Baker Academic, 2017).

[53]Charleston, *Four Vision Quests*, 109.

blessing. Each of these descriptions of a blessed state has different results, describing "the way of being in the world that will result in their true and full flourishing now and in the age to come."[54] This beginning of the sermon points once again to the character of the speaker—Jesus is a walking beatitude, and by beginning the sermon in this way, the hearers are reminded that the speaker exemplifies his own words and so is not only trustworthy but also worthy of emulation. It is also a reminder that blessing can paradoxically be found in the reality of suffering: "Coping with suffering gives meaning to life—it is what gives us our strength."[55] The beatitudes spoken by Christ make it clear that following his ways marks out a community that is fundamentally at odds with Roman society, driven by the ideals of empire. The idea that the poor and downtrodden were blessed "would have been incomprehensible to Greek and Roman aristocrats."[56]

For some modern Indigenous readers of the text, the language of law conjures up colonial laws that oppressed Indigenous peoples and were weaponized to enforce their subjugation and dispossession of ancestral lands, or may bring to mind the trotting out of the "rule of law" whenever Indigenous peoples protest treaty violations. This is foreign to Jesus' mind as he speaks about the ongoing validity of the Mosaic law (Mt 5:17-20) but does highlight the ongoing importance of thinking about how Scriptures should be translated in modern vernacular.

Jesus moves to discuss the three righteous practices of charitable giving, prayer, and fasting. All three of these practices include a recurring theme of avoiding an attitude of hypocrisy and avoiding the practice of these things in order to be seen and praised by others. Jesus no doubt teaches in reaction to what he sees as false piety within both his own people and those outside Israel (Mt 6:1-2, 5, 7, 16). These holy habits are also characteristic of many Indigenous communities, though they are manifested in different ways. Giveaways are a common practice, whereby the person being honored in a gathering is the giver, not the receiver. This is a formalized method of giving done in public gatherings, but the quiet giving of money or items is also the ethos of many Indigenous communities.[57] Prayers accompany any communal ceremony and gathering of the people, whether it be for celebration, discussion, or mourning. Prayers are understood not simply as words spoken to Creator but also in communal events such as the dancing of one's prayers. Richard Twiss states: "When I'm dancing in the pow-wow, every step is a prayer: I dance my prayers for the people. Sometimes I imagine my prayers, I fantasize my prayers; they're not always audible. Sometimes my prayers are expressed in artistic ways."[58] Fasting likewise is a common practice, most often an individual practice: "We learn the value of water when we fast three or four days on the mountain, in the forest or in some other sacred place. . . . Our purpose in

[54]Pennington, *Sermon on the Mount*, 144.

[55]Bear Heart, *The Wind Is My Mother: The Life and Teachings of a Native American Shaman* (New York: Berkley, 1998), 137-38.

[56]James S. Jeffers, *The Greco-Roman World of The New Testament Era: Exploring the Background of Early Christianity* (Downers Grove, IL: InterVarsity Press, 1999), 189.

[57]See Randy S. Woodley, *Shalom and the Community of Creation: An Indigenous Vision*, Prophetic Christianity (Grand Rapids, MI: Eerdmans, 2012), 156.

[58]Kate Rae Davis and Richard Twiss, "Dancing Prayers: An Interview with Richard Twiss," *The Other Journal: An Intersection of Theology & Culture* 21 (2012), www.theotherjournal.com/2012/12/10/dancing-prayers-an-interview-with-richard-twiss/. For further discussion on dancing as prayer, see Richard Twiss, *One Church, Many Tribes: Following Jesus the Way God Made You* (Minneapolis: Chosen, 2000), 159-62; Wendy L. Peterson, "A Gifting of Sweetgrass: The Reclamation of Culture Movement and *NAIITS: An Indigenous Learning Community*" (PhD diss., Asbury Theological Seminary, 2018), 180-81.

fasting is to create harmony in the world and within ourselves."[59] Fasting was also frequently performed as part of a vision quest, or in general as an individual sought a vision.[60] Fasting functioned in similar ways in early Judaism, with its temporary suspense of communal gathering and its representation of piety in prayer (2 Sam 12:16) or preparation to receive a divine revelation (Dan 9:3; 10:2-3).[61]

The middle section of the sermon serves to reinforce the previous teachings but does so by way of lessons from life and creation. The creation as a place for revelation is understood in Christianity, reinforced by passages such as Psalm 19:1 and Romans 1:19-20. Indigenous communities, too, seek wisdom, teachings, and guidance from the community of creation of which they are a part. Jesus himself already established the sacred nature of heaven and earth earlier in the sermon (Mt 5:34-35). All creation is sacred, originating from and being animated by Creator (Col 1:15-20), and "the Earth is the first and primary medium of God's self-revelation."[62] Within this understanding, Jesus points to lessons from life and nature, showing us that possessions can deteriorate or be stolen, that one's eyes can determine one's life and internal workings, that money can corrupt, and that the beauty of flowers and bounty of nature to feed the birds remind us of Creator's care.[63] These are not mere analogies or illustrations—categories often used to relegate or subordinate a teaching to the "more literal sense." Jesus here points to creation as places and events that literally hold the lesson within themselves.

The close of the sermon challenges disciples to put into practice what has been taught. Following Jesus on the narrow path involves more than right thinking or proper doctrine but rather behaviors and attitudes that put on display the golden rule of Matthew 7:12. Despite the hardships that may come in life, despite those who may try to lead one astray, disciples must continue to strive to be bearers of good fruit and live like wise builders. Walking this good red road will ensure that we know and are known by the Lord on the last day (Mt 7:21-23).[64] In the closing examples of the sermon, the focus on the outworking deeds of a disciple is paramount in God's eyes.

HEALING MINISTRY (MATTHEW 8:1–9:38)

Matthew offered a summary statement of Jesus' work of healing prior to the sermon (Mt 4:23-25), and this extended section on healings will also include a summary statement near the beginning (Mt 8:16) and at its conclusion (Mt 9:35-36). These repeated narrative summaries make it clear that the healings, exorcisms, and other encounters as told by Matthew are a mere sampling of Jesus' work. The indiscriminate attitude of Jesus shines through in the series of events through this section, where Jesus not only gracefully encounters the outsiders and the outcasts but

---

[59]John S. Hascall, "The Sacred Circle: Native American Liturgy," in Treat, *Native and Christian*, 181.

[60]Bradford Keeney, *Shamanic Christianity: The Direct Experience of Mystical Communion* (Rochester, VT: Destiny Books, 2006), 46-47.

[61]In intertestamental Judaism fasting increasingly became a mark of an ascetic life. See John Muddiman, "Fasting," in *Anchor Bible Dictionary*, ed. David Noel Freedman (New York: Doubleday, 1992), 2:774.

[62]Wali Fejo, "The Voice of the Earth: An Indigenous Reading of Genesis 9," in *Earth Story in Genesis*, ed. Norman C. Habel and Shirley Wurst, The Earth Bible 2 (New York: Sheffield Academic Press, 2000), 141.

[63]Woodley notes how Indigenous concepts of redistribution run directly counter to Western capitalism and individualism (*Shalom*, 151-52).

[64]The "good red road" is a term used by some First Nations communities to refer to the spiritual work of living an ethical life of balance in harmony with Creator. See, for example, Samuel I. Mniyo, Robert Goodvoice, and Dan Beveridge, *The Red Road and Other Narratives of the Dakota Sioux* (Lincoln: University of Nebraska Press, 2020).

even the Roman oppressors and the oppressive kin within the communities.

Comparison of Jesus to the Indigenous medicine woman/man provides a helpful interpretive window. While the modern Western conception of medicine tends to be primarily mechanistic and physical, the medicine woman/man attended to both the physical and spiritual in the recognition that sickness was a complex mix of both disease (physical) and illness (psychological/psycho-spiritual) and so required both holistic diagnosis and adaptive approaches for the healing process.[65] Medicine women/men were sought out for advice, as they were acknowledged as wisdom keepers, those with a curious mind that delved deeply into the mysteries of life.[66] The medicine woman/man in the Cree tradition was understood as someone who could foresee things (see Mt 24–25).[67] The medicine woman/man, like Jesus, was seen as appointed to tasks by the spirit world and considered to be on call for the requests of the people, something Matthew similarly intimates in his summary statements of Jesus' ministry of healing.[68] The medicine woman/man was appointed to their task by Creator and recognized by the community. They did not typically advertise themselves (see Mt 9:30) but rather were known by word of mouth in their communities. The medicine woman/man recognizes that healing does not come from them but rather from Creator, and recognizes the importance of the patient's own part in the healing, both in diligently working toward wellness and in a trust in the medicines provided.[69] In the same way, we see the faith of those who seek out Jesus as an important part of the healing process (Mt 8:2; 9:29; see also Mt 13:58).

The holistic role of the medicine woman/man is instructive as we look at Jesus' healing ministry. Modern readers of Matthew see this narrative portion as moving back and forth between physical encounters of healing and spiritual encounters of exorcism, interspersed with teaching and dialogue. This bifurcation of the material and immaterial is more at home in modernity, with its foundations on Western dualism. In all of these cases through Matthew 8–9, Jesus the medicine man is giving medicine. The holistic medicine of physical healings of leprosy, paralysis, blindness, fever, death, and hemorrhaging brings about whole-life changes for those who were previously socially stigmatized and living at the margins of society. The faith of the centurion is turned into powerful spiritual medicine for Jesus' countrymen as he displays a faith they do not have. Jesus offers bitter medicines to those who seek to be disciples but are not willing to offer the necessary life sacrifices. And Jesus dispenses the medicine of acceptance to a tax collector named Matthew and in so doing brings Matthew out of the imperial system that was oppressing him and his fellow Israelites. In

---

[65]For a relatively recent analysis of one Indigenous nation's perspective on sickness, see David C. Posthumus, "Transmitting Sacred Knowledge: Aspects of Historical and Contemporary Oglala Lakota Belief and Ritual" (PhD diss., Indiana University, 2015), chap. 3. This understanding of sickness on a spectrum of disease and illness is why Indigenous peoples today can often readily embrace and make use of modern medicine while also embracing traditional medicines and practices—modern medicine with its mechanistic framing is imbalanced in its focus solely being on the physical components of illness. But in those cases where sickness is more on the side of disease than illness, modern medicine is used on the journey to well-being.

[66]Lee Irwin, *The Dream Seekers: Native American Visionary Traditions of the Great Plains* (Norman: University of Oklahoma Press, 1996), 160.

[67]Byron Apetagon, *Norway House Anthology: Stories of the Elders* (Winnipeg: Frontier School Division, 1991), 1:28.

[68]Deloria, *World We Used to Live In*, 13.

[69]Heart, *Wind Is My Mother*, 88-89.

all of these examples, whether the ailments are physical, spiritual, psychological, social, or a mixture of ailment and spiritual oppression (e.g., Mt 17:15-18), Jesus provides the medicines needed to restore shalom to the individual for the good of the individual and the community. Similarly,

> In our Native American way, medicine is not just a bunch of herbs or the training a physician receives. It's helping people attain that which is good in life. If you can point them in a new direction, saying this is the path, this is the way to go, that's a form of healing. When you give a lifting hand and make someone feel better for it, you've given that person medicine.[70]

Another indicator of Christ's generosity is his statement in Matthew 8:20 (author translation), "Foxes have dens and birds have nests, but the Son of Man has no place to lay his head." While this is sometimes read through a lens of voluntary poverty, akin to later church ascetic practices, this statement may in fact indicate the spirit of generosity that pervaded Christ's life. "The way Indigenous communities provide that is through the experience of generosity. We expect generosity, and we provide opportunities for generosity. We have ceremonies of generosity in feasts, potlatches, and giveaways."[71] The generosity of Indigenous leaders in Canadian Indigenous communities of the Northwest was the reason for the ban on the potlatch in 1884 by the Canadian government, as it was antithetical to a capitalist ethic of accumulation—the adoption of which was considered to be an important component of "civilizing" the "savages." This practice of wealth redistribution was often exemplified by the chief and other materially rich members of the community. In these communities, material lack by a leader was a strong sign of virtue and abundant generosity.[72] Up to this point in Matthew's Gospel, Jesus has been generous in his sharing of wisdom, teaching, and medicines. In light of Matthew 8:20, Jesus may also have been generous with his material possessions.

The medicine woman/man was also one recognized as having great power by virtue of their wisdom and their divine appointment. Two stories within this narrative section highlight in a unique way Jesus' power. The first is the encounter with the Roman centurion (Mt 8:5-13). The centurion not only represents the imperial and colonial power but as a high-ranking officer controls the might and power of Rome. Yet, his encounter with Jesus acknowledges the powerlessness of the state over human sickness. The centurion's address of Jesus as Lord is surprising, expressing his subordination to Jesus and his own powerlessness, and by extension a power Rome also lacks—Caesar is not a lord who can enact shalom and restore balance to a broken life.[73]

This unique power of Jesus is also manifested in the calming of the storm (Mt 8:23-27). This power to calm the storm comes by way of his relationship to the creation. This is evident in his direct address to the natural forces. The irony of the Christ speaking directly with natural forces while Indigenous peoples are often denigrated as animists should not be missed: "A classic Greek (Western) world view would say that any Native who believes a tree could talk would be involved in animism, spiritism, and/or pantheism, though Jesus spoke

---

[70]Heart, *Wind Is My Mother*, 117.

[71]Martin Brokenleg, "Circles of Courage," *Journal of NAIITS* 18 (2020): 4.

[72]Woodley, *Shalom*, 155.

[73]Dorothy Jean Weaver, "'Thus You Will Know Them by Their Fruits': The Roman Characters of the Gospel of Matthew," in Riches and Sim, *Gospel of Matthew*, 115-16.

directly to the winds and the waves and they 'heard' Him and actually obeyed."[74]

COMMISSIONING OF THE DISCIPLES (MATTHEW 10:1-42)

As the concentrated section of miracle stories concludes, the compassion of Jesus for his people is clear, as is the need. Jesus continues his proclamation and work of healing (Mt 9:35), but he also recognizes the oppression that the people face: "Jesus sees people who are oppressed, downtrodden, beat-up, and crushed. The historical and literary contexts indicate Rome and the religious elite as those who inflict social, economic, political, and religious abuse with misrule."[75] The language of sheep without a shepherd likely focuses the critique on the current religious leadership, with echoes drawing back to the critique of Israel's leadership in Ezekiel 34.[76] What is needed is new leadership for a renewed community, and this is what Jesus asks his disciples to pray for, workers for the harvest.

Immediately following this, Jesus commissions the Twelve to this work—the request for prayer being as much about seeking God's will as it is preparing their hearts and minds for the reality that they will be a part of the answer to their own prayer. Only some of the disciples have been encountered so far in the narrative, and the number twelve clearly signals a reconstituted Israel. The Jewish renewal movement begun by John now extends into the work of Jesus' disciples as they are sent out and told to focus in the first instance on Israel, as God chose Abraham and his descendants to receive his blessing and for them in turn to be a blessing to the nations (Gen 12:1-3). Yet even with the charge to avoid Gentiles and Samaritans (Mt 10:5-6), the disciples will yet be a witness to Gentiles (Mt 10:18), and the context of his directive is already couched within a narrative opening that highlighted righteous Gentiles in the genealogy, the magi of the birth narrative, and the faith of the Roman centurion. Within this narrative setting and with the framework of Jesus as medicine man, Jesus' directive to go only to Israel is because it is Israel who is in need of medicine (see Mt 9:12) and strength to live into their divine role.

Jesus knows not only that there is much work to be done but that this renewal movement will encounter fierce resistance by the current leadership. Jesus uses animal metaphors in Matthew 10:16 to help the disciples understand the situation. In being sent out as new shepherds, they are at the same time like sheep going in among wolves. He advises them to take the lesson of the snake and be shrewd but also morally upright and innocent like doves. He also then calls their attention to God's care for even the smallest of his creatures (Mt 10:29-31), a reminder to his human listeners of their common creatureliness and creational kinship. This mention of doves in Matthew 10:16 is a callback to the active incarnate presence of the Holy Spirit, and indeed Jesus tells his disciples that in the midst of trials, the Spirit will be with them (Mt 10:20), just as the Spirit was with Jesus in his trial.

---

[74]Richard Twiss, Terry LeBlanc, and Adrian Jacobs, "Culture, Christian Faith and Error," *Journal of NAIITS* 1 (2003): 13.

[75]Carter, *Matthew and the Margins*, 230.

[76]On this see Wayne S. Baxter, "Healing and the 'Son of David': Matthew's Warrant," *NovT* 48 (2006): 36-50; Carter, *Matthew and Empire*, 117-18. I use the designation "current religious leadership" here and throughout the commentary, particularly in the Mt 23 section, deliberately. History attests to the evils of antisemitism prevalent through much of church history, and in many cases verses from Matthew were used in support of antisemitism. But it is an egregious error to read Jesus' critique of the current leaders of his day as a blanket condemnation of Judaism and all Jewish people.

RISING OPPOSITION AND REJECTION (MATTHEW 11:1–12:50)

While opposition has been present from early on in the narrative (Mt 2:1-12, 16-18; 8:34; 9:3-5, 11-13, 34), this narrative section of Matthew's Gospel presents rising opposition and tensions between Jesus and many others. The first of these comes from a seemingly unlikely source. John the Baptizer has held a prominent position so far in the narrative, making questioning from John all the more confusing for some readers. A North American Indigenous lens on John the Baptizer at this point in the narrative may provide additional insight. Specifically, John seems to be playing the role of a sacred clown.[77] This designation today is unappealing due to modern clowns and their role to make us laugh with colorful wigs, balloon animals, and floppy shoes. But sacred clowns in some Indigenous cultures played an important role in their communities. The clown in some traditions was closer to modern clowns today, appearing during communal ceremonies and acting provocatively and outrageously. These clowns sought to delight and remind everyone not to take themselves too seriously.[78] Another type of clown in other Indigenous cultures, however, was more of a visionary, someone who also acted contrary to what was expected and made statements or asked questions designed to shock.[79] The work of this type of clown was to disorient and be a contrary presence to remind the people of the dualities of life.[80]

The model of sacred clown certainly fits John the Baptist. In readers' first encounter with John, his unusual dress and diet are highlighted, as is his unique practice of baptism and fiery preaching, against even the seemingly most religious people in his nation, calling them snakes. But John does not reserve his critique for only the Jewish leaders; he also makes uncomfortable the crowds who come to him, telling them that their lineage to Abraham is not enough and that the stones could be better children. Steven Charleston writes, "Like a sacred clown, he is a reminder that the power of the sacred can either sweep away the status quo or birth a new reality."[81]

As John enters the story again, he acts once more in a shocking way, joining the narrative at a seemingly high point and introducing chaos as a sacred clown. Jesus has given a masterful body of teaching and has exhibited abundant grace as he doles out his medicines to all who come to him, after which he commissions even more healers to go among the sick of his nation and offer healing. Whereas previously John acknowledged the worthiness of Jesus (Mt 3:14), now he has questions. The sacred clown indicates that not all is as it seems, and indeed this section of the Gospel narrates the rise in opposition to Jesus as the story begins to point toward the passion. John forewarned of a Messiah who would baptize by fire, and yet Jesus has been a graceful healing shepherd. Charleston writes, "In Native theology, John's role is to paint the

[77]In this discussion I rely heavily on Charleston, *Four Vision Quests*, 78-91.

[78]This type of clown is discussed in Randy S. Woodley, "The Harmony Way: Integrating Indigenous Values Within Native North American Theology and Mission" (PhD diss., Asbury Theological Seminary, 2010), 204.

[79]Charleston notes that the more visionary clowns come from the plains tradition, the *heyoka* (*Four Vision Quests*, 80-81). Many trickster figures in Indigenous stories fulfill the role of the clown in that they "are allowed to ask questions and act in ways in which we are not" ("Harmony Way," 204).

[80]Keeney states: "The sacred clowns and tricksters of other cultures set no limits on how they enact the contraries of life. At a joyous situation they will cry and at a sad situation they will laugh. In the stretching of those contraries, greater truths and possibilities for transformation are more likely to enter the scene" (*Shamanic Christianity*, 166).

[81]Charleston, *Four Vision Quests*, 83.

background so the figure in the foreground may stand out even more clearly. This is the work of the *heyoka* [sacred clown] in traditional Native society."[82]

As this sacred clown reminds readers of existing dualities, it is significant to note that Jesus both affirms his own work as that which is expected of the Messiah (Mt 11:4-5) and goes on to prophetically denounce the towns that have not repented (Mt 11:20-24), which at least partially aligns with John's first expectations.[83] In other words, the sacred clown has sparked a reminder of the duality of Christ's messianic work. Judgment and grace exist simultaneously; healing and reproach are intertwined realities. As this episode focused on John closes, Jesus compares himself once again with his forerunner—they are both excluded and condemned. Like sacred clowns, they live contrary to expectations. Jesus then closes by comparing himself with personified Wisdom from the Hebrew Scriptures, perhaps surprising readers in another way. Amy-Jill Levine writes, "Jesus assumes Wisdom's roles: mediating knowledge, demonstrating intimacy with the Deity, providing comfort. Readers may choose to see Jesus as thereby embodying the feminine presence of the Divine, or co-opting it."[84]

Within these episodes of rising tensions between John and Jesus, between Jesus and the local towns, and between Jesus and the religious leadership on the issue of Sabbath, Jesus makes several statements that further indicate the nature of the community he seeks to create around himself. Jesus offers a prayer to the Father, indicating not only his close relationship as the unique Son but also that those who have gathered around him have been appointed and have received a revelation from Creator. Later in this section, Jesus' close relationship with the Spirit is also highlighted (Mt 12:25-32). Those who have received this wisdom are not the powerful or the elite but the humble and the marginalized, identified as infants. This characterization aligns with scriptural tradition (Dan 1:4; Ps 19:7; 116:6; 119:130) but also works with the kinship language that Jesus has invoked in calling God Father, language he earlier instructed the disciples to use in prayer (Mt 6:9).

With this language of kinship in place, Jesus then moves to speak of rest from burdens and taking up his yoke (Mt 11:28-30). Warren Carter argues convincingly that Jesus' words are an imperial critique: "Most, whether rural or urban, lived around the poverty level, barely subsisting on a daily basis and lacking any surplus for either a safety margin or as a basis for improved production. For most, it is a world marked by desperate striving to meet the demands of empire."[85] The rest that Jesus offers by being yoked with him speaks to the social, economic, and spiritual burdens his followers are experiencing. As Jesus presents an alternative way of living, held together through kinship bonds and striving toward the shalom of God's ways, he also offers his intimate presence with all in the community. The typical translation of the yoke being "easy" is an unfortunate one in modern vernacular and inadequate to what Jesus is stating. The noun *chrēstos* can mean "good" as in best suited for a purpose, "good" in a moral sense, "kind" to denote a loving manner, or "suitable" pertaining to the ease of something.

[82]Charleston, *Four Vision Quests*, 83.

[83]On Jesus' response and messianic expectations, see my discussion in Zacharias, *Matthew's Presentation*, 94-95.

[84]Amy-Jill Levine, "Matthew," in *Women's Bible Commentary*, ed. Carol A. Newsom, Sharon H. Ringe, and Jacqueline E. Lapsley (Louisville, KY: Westminster John Knox, 2012), 472. Amy Peeler's work on the incarnation also shows how Jesus embraces the male and the female, stating that "there is an unparalleled inclusivity precisely in this process of the incarnation." See Peeler, *Women and the Gender of God* (Grand Rapids, MI: Eerdmans, 2022), 136.

[85]Carter, *Matthew and Empire*, 114.

This new community, like every community, carries with it roles and responsibilities for its members. But the burden will not be carried for a despotic Caesar but in service to all. It is a good yoke with a reasonable burden that invites us to strive not for our chief but alongside him.[86] The kinship bonds of this new community are reinforced at the close of this section, when Jesus points to the spiritual ties among him, his followers, and their mutual Father in the heavens.

TEACHING IN STORIES (MATTHEW 13:1-58)

This next extended discourse, the third of five major discourses in Matthew, happens the same day (Mt 13:1) as Jesus' kinship descriptions of the community. This highlights an oscillation back and forth between this new Jesus-centered kinship community and the crowds who are eager to listen to him. As this parable discourse continues, the first portion is for both the crowds and the disciples, but beginning at Matthew 13:36, Jesus speaks only to the disciples. The other Gospel authors spread Jesus' parables throughout his ministry, but Matthew has gathered most of the parables into this section, consisting of eight parables. Unlike the previous two discourses (Mt 5:3–8:1; 10:5–11:1), this one is punctuated with some dialogue with the disciples along with narrator insertions as well. Two parables receive explanations (Mt 13:18-23, 36-43), and Jesus answers the disciples' question of why he teaches in parables.

Significant is the note of the setting for this time of teaching, outside a building and beside a lake (Mt 13:1). Jesus preferred being out on the land to teach rather than in the synagogues (see Mt 5:1). This preference shows itself also in the horticultural components of his parables and teachings. Jesus chose spaces for ministry not simply for practicality or aesthetic but because he believed that place mattered—that the land and waters of his peoples had something to teach them. This land-based pedagogy is also an important component of Indigenous self-determination and decolonization today. Because colonization was at its core about dispossessing Indigenous peoples of their lands, decolonizing and education work hard to reconnect peoples to their ancestral lands.[87] Important also is the recognition that Indigenous peoples, in seeking self-determination and cultural reclamation, bind up their communal identities with their lands.[88]

Jesus has recognized the lack of leadership and the needs of his people so far in this narrative (see Mt 10:6). A reconstitution of his people will of necessity include their deep connection to their land and waters. It is from these lands and waters that lessons will arise and form into parables, from which Jesus will instruct them in the reality of God's sovereignty—the kingdom of the heavens. The lands and waters are also a flashpoint for this learning, as it is where Roman imperial oppression is keenly felt. The calling of the fishermen to be his first disciples (Mt 4:18-22), and now a place beside the lake to teach about the kingdom, signal a challenge to imperial oppression and an exhortation for his followers to reassert themselves as a people who belong to a land and are bound up in responsibilities to that place.[89]

---

[86]Carter, *Matthew and Empire*, 125-26.

[87]See Dawn Zinga and Sandra Styres, "Pedagogy of the Land: Tensions, Challenges, and Contradictions," *First Nations Perspectives* 4 (2011): 59-83.

[88]See Ray Aldred, "An Alternative Starting Place for an Indigenous Theology" (PhD diss., Toronto School of Theology, 2020), particularly chaps. 2-3.

[89]For a description of the oppressive economics and imperial control over the fisheries and resources of the land in Jesus' day, see Kenneth C. Hanson, "The Galilean Fishing Economy and the Jesus Tradition," *Biblical Theology Bulletin* 27 (1997): 99-111.

From this setting out on the land, the stories arise, are spoken forth, and are encountered by the hearers. Modern teaching and preaching practice often moves in a linear fashion from concept to illustration. This type of thinking causes modern readers to see the parables as illustrations of concepts, functioning like sermon illustrations to hammer home one of the three sermon points. Indigenous practices of storytelling are much less linear and resist purely propositional understandings. Indigenous stories, as well as ancient storytelling practices such as the parables, arose from historical circumstances, from the observation of nature, and from the stories of peoples. Teachings were then drawn from the stories, rather than the stories being told to encapsulate a concept. Jesus, like modern Indigenous storytellers, is "grounded in the very same processes that have brought meaning to the lives of our Ancestors: multidimensionality, repetition, abstraction, metaphor, and multiple sites of perception. In short, a multilayered conversation whose meaning shifts through time."[90]

The dynamic nature of storytelling, evident in both the Scriptures and First Nations traditions, ought to help readers embrace the robust nature of story and caution against the modern tendency to freeze stories into one prescribed meaning. Stories and traditions within oral cultures, such as Jesus' world and many First Nations cultures, demonstrate contextual adaptability as well as mechanisms that honor the communicative intent of the story or teaching. In much the same way, Indigenous Christians today seek to honor the communicative intent of the scriptural author as well as to engage in the dynamic and relational process of relevant scriptural interpretation and application.

In their retelling, these stories serve to reiterate old teachings and to speak in new ways to new situations, such that the past is always speaking to and shaping the present. Jesus calls his hearers to a new way of thinking that dynamically interacts with the past (Mt 13:52). This is a fluid and interactive process, with the listener being key. Like modern Indigenous storytelling, Jesus' parables "involve the active participation of the listener in the reckoning of their meaning and to a degree beyond what is typical for more straightforward forms of speech. If for no other reason than this variable of listener participation, it can be argued that the parables are intrinsically polyvalent, bearing multiple senses and resisting a singular determinate meaning."[91]

As mentioned earlier, Jesus' discourse is briefly interrupted at times, with a question from the disciples and then explanations for two of the parables. Parable explanations are not otherwise common in the Gospels, and despite Matthew's clustering of the parables into this discourse, it is made clear in Matthew 13:34 that parables were used often in Jesus' teaching to the crowds. Jesus spent time through his ministry doing and saying things his disciples and the crowds did not always understand, and only occasionally did the disciples seek an explanation. The swift desire for clarity and explanation is a hallmark of the Western mind but does not always fit in an experiential learning process, nor with a mode of teaching like parables that may be polyvalent in meaning.

An example of this clash between observing and pondering versus questions to achieve

[90]Leanne Betasamosake Simpson, *As We Have Always Done: Indigenous Freedom Through Radical Resistance* (Minneapolis: University of Minnesota Press, 2017), 205-6.

[91]G. P. Anderson, "Parables," in *Dictionary of Jesus and the Gospels*, ed. Joel B. Green, Jeannine Brown, and Nicholas Perrin (Downers Grove, IL: InterVarsity Press, 1992), 662.

clarity is evident in non-Indigenous experiences with Indigenous cultural expressions. Randy Woodley notes, "I was taught by elders to observe closely when a task was being done and not to ask questions."[92] This did not mean that questions were not pondered, and he notes that often the questions were later answered through repetition, pondering, or prayer.[93] This contrasted with his later experience as a teacher: "When I first began leading Sweat [lodge ceremonies] and non-Indians asked these question, I usually answered them even though I felt uneasy about it."[94] Woodley later realized that to experience the ceremony authentically, non-Indigenous folks needed to be instructed to refrain from asking questions immediately before and immediately after. This is a way of teaching that is at home in Indigenous cultures today—a process of observance, pondering, repetition, and occasionally explanation that comes after a delay of time.

This way of teaching is also present in Jesus' ministry. The Western mind does not always sit easily with mystery, pondering, and openness to wait for a forthcoming answer. Yet, Matthew makes it clear that this was one of the teaching methods of Jesus. Jesus was perfectly comfortable with letting questions linger, risking confusion on the part of the hearer, trusting that in Creator's timing an answer may come to the hearer, or recognizing that the polyvalence of meanings inherent in the parables would arise as circumstances drew them forth.

THE FATE OF JOHN THE BAPTIZER (MATTHEW 14:1-12)

This passage temporarily moves its focus from Jesus to focus on Herod the tetrarch and the circumstances of his beheading John the Baptizer. The narrative moves backward, beginning with Herod's response to a report about Jesus and his belief that Jesus is John who has returned from the dead. In his role as prophet, John did not shy away from speaking truth to power, criticizing Herod for marrying Herodias, his brother's wife. This was enough for Herod to imprison John. At his birthday celebration, Herodias's daughter dances for Herod, and Herod brashly promises to give her anything she asks for. Herodias tells her to ask for John's head, which Herod reluctantly gives. The account closes with John's disciples burying John's body and leaving to tell Jesus. The passage serves to build on the prophetic motif indicated most recently in Matthew 13:57 regarding the fate of prophets. While later Jesus will give several passion predictions (Mt 16:21-23; 17:22-23; 20:17-19), the fate of prophets and the fate of the Messiah's forerunner already serves as a narrative foreshadowing of Christ's fate.

Another important component of this story, which also aligns with the prophetic motif and foreshadowing of Christ's path, is the clash between the empire and this renewal movement. Jesus' words and actions have confronted the oppressive and immoral Roman system and will continue to do so, and John has done the same. Warren Carter states, "Matthew's account, while assuming some historical basis,

[92]Woodley, *Shalom*, 98.

[93]Indigenous peoples do not share all aspects of meaning, significance, and symbolism in their particular ceremonies and cultural practices, nor do they openly share all of their cultural stories freely. Several factors go into this, including the past colonial scrutiny of their practices, Christian judgmentalism, and lack of an established relationship with the hearer. The most important reason, though, is that these items are communally held knowledge, are tied to peoples and places, and are embodied in and learned through experiences. When stories or explanations are shared, especially in written form, the sharing is often selective, and the author has the earned respect and authority of their people to share these details.

[94]Woodley, *Shalom*, 99.

reinforces three pastoral-theological dynamics for its audience: the politically powerful resist God's empire; unbelief is expressed in hostility and violence; God's empire requires faithfulness even to death."[95]

A somewhat neglected component of this story is the grounds for John's condemnation of Herod Antipas and his marriage to Herodias. Herod and his half brother Herod Philip's wife Herodias (she was their niece through another half brother) fell in love while each was married to another, with both divorcing their spouses and then marrying each other. While readers with a Judeo-Christian heritage see this as immoral (just as John and Jesus did), adultery, divorce, and remarriage in the upper class of the Roman Empire was common.[96] Jesus has already spoken out against the lax Jewish divorce practices of his day, calling them to the vision presented in the creation story (Mt 5:32; 19:9; see Gen 2:24). That John so forcefully denounced Herod and Herodias shows his alignment with Jesus on this issue. A further component of the condemnation was likely the Levitical incest laws (Lev 18; 20), which Matthew likely signals by providing the shared ancestral name "Herod." Herod Antipas and Herodias clearly understood themselves as not being under any particular law beyond Roman law, and yet John held them to the teachings of his people enshrined in the Mosaic law. Tribal laws are bound to both communities and the land in which they reside. Herod the Great (Antipas's father) was an Idumean (termed a "half-Jew" by Josephus, *Ant.* 14.403), and Antipas's mother was Malthace, a Samaritan woman. Herodias's grandparents were Herod the Great and Mariamne; she was part of the Jewish Hasmonean family line. That John condemned Herod Antipas and Herodias based on the laws of his people speaks toward his expectation that they ought to have honored the Mosaic law, as it was the traditions that governed their Jewish and Samaritan ancestors, and governed the lands in which they resided and ruled over. John and Jesus did not see the Roman colonial laws as superseding the tribal laws of their people. Indigenous peoples today also give deference to their ancestral laws in spaces of overlapping sovereignties, something that has often had severe consequences from oppressive colonial powers.

THE MANY ARE FED (MATTHEW 14:13-36)

Jesus receives the news of John's death and attempts to withdraw to be by himself, likely for a time of mourning. When the crowds hear where he is heading, they are ready to meet him, and predictably Jesus has compassion on the crowds and heals those who are sick. The day draws to a close and they are in a remote place, so the disciples suggest that the crowds be dismissed to find food. Jesus instead orchestrates the feeding of this large group of people. Immediately afterward, Jesus forcefully sends the disciples away so he can dismiss the crowds. After the crowds depart, Jesus spends time by himself to pray into the night, the reason for his withdrawing in the first place. The disciples are far from shore on turbulent waters, and Jesus comes out to them, walking on the sea. The disciples are terrified, believing he is a ghost. Jesus speaks to them, and Peter asks Jesus to call him out on the water. Jesus does so, and Peter also walks on the water. The winds frighten Peter, and he begins to sink and calls out for Jesus to save him. Jesus takes Peter's

[95]Carter, *Matthew and the Margins*, 301.

[96]See Craig S. Keener, "Adultery, Divorce," in *Dictionary of New Testament Background*, ed. Craig A. Evans and Stanley E. Porter (Downers Grove, IL: InterVarsity Press, 2000), 7-8.

hand and rebukes his doubt. When they get into the boat, the wind stops. The disciples in the boat worship Jesus and confess him as the Son of God, recognizing his unique relationship and authority over the creation.

Several components in the telling of the feeding story may suggest what Ched Myers argues in regard to the synoptic parallel in Mark, namely that this should not be read strictly as a miracle story but as a dramatic socioeconomic reordering of relationship among those gathered.[97] I would also add that in addition to a socioeconomic reordering, there is a re-membering of the crowds to the community of creation of which they are a part, and in this understanding there is a foresight displayed on the part of Jesus—a recognition of what might be. The first component is the focus placed on the location of the story. Matthew twice informs the reader of the location as the wilderness (Mt 14:13, 15). If this story were approached apart from the wider narrative context, the inclination may be to understand the location as a desolate wasteland. But the wilderness has already been an important place in Matthew's narrative. The wild is a place where God's ways are being made known (Mt 3:3), where Jesus went through his vision quest (Mt 4:1-11), and the last location where the incarnate Spirit, the Dove, was in the story. It also connects Jesus and the crowds to John the Baptizer, as this was the land he resided in (Mt 3:1; 11:7)—and, importantly, it was this land that sustained John with food (Mt 3:4).

When the problem is presented to Jesus by the disciples, so is their solution: "Send the crowds away so they may go into the villages and buy food for themselves" (Mt 14:15). For the disciples, the only solution is to partake of the local economy, entangled as it is with the reality of Roman imperialism. Jesus has a better solution, and that is to remain in the very place that has sustained others in the past—like John in Matthew 3:4 and like their ancestors in Exodus 16. His challenge is to seek solutions within the community itself; they have the assets they need. In commenting on the parallel story in Mark, Myers states, "The only 'miracle' here is the triumph of the economics of sharing within a community of consumption over against the economics of autonomous consumption in the anonymous marketplace."[98] I would amend this thought to acknowledge the land within this framing—they are a community of consumption but also find themselves within a community of creation and within a landscape that provides for all those who move on the earth (Gen 1:12, 29-30). Creator's economics of sharing encompasses the reciprocity humanity has with the land, which takes care of them.

One final component suggests seeing this event as a reordering and re-membering event: that women and children are also part of the many gathered.[99] The modern mind may be predisposed to reading this note in terms of the (numerical) quantity of the crowd when instead it may be a signal of the quality of those mentioned. Later in the narrative,

[97]Ched Myers, *Binding the Strong Man: A Political Reading of Mark's Story of Jesus*, 20th anniversary ed. (Maryknoll, NY: Orbis Books, 2008), 205-10.

[98]Myers, *Binding the Strong Man*, 206. For the problematic bifurcation between the natural and supernatural, see the discussion in Craig S. Keener, *Miracles: The Credibility of the New Testament Accounts* (Grand Rapids, MI: Baker, 2011), especially chaps. 4-6.

[99]It has been noted how often this story, and the similar story in Mt 15, continues to ignore the presence of women and children by its continual reference as the "feeding of the five thousand." Jamie Clark-Soles rightly suggests that if we are going to continue to focus on the numerical quantity at all, it should be labeled "the feeding of the thirty-five thousand." See Jaime Clark-Soles, *Women in the Bible* (Louisville, KY: Westminster John Knox, 2020), 26, 188.

Matthew states, "Many women were also there, looking on from a distance; they had followed Jesus from Galilee, ministering to him" (Mt 27:55-56). The indication in this verse is that women performed a sacred role for Jesus, and he could not have continued his work without their vital support. Children, too, will become an important example to model the faith Christ expects of his disciples (Mt 19:13-15), and it is not insignificant that John the Evangelist provides in the parallel story the detail that the loaves and fish were provided by a young boy (Jn 6:9).

Rather than merely adding to the number of those present, the mention of the women and children may also be pointing to the means of satisfying this need for satiation—the whole community, inclusive of the land and looking to those that the wider society has deemed lesser and lacking agency. With this inclusive view of community, oppressed communities recognize the assets they already possess and can even work toward something like food sovereignty. Colonial and imperial oppression, compounded as it is today by capitalist economies of extraction, attempts to convince its subjects of their reliance on the global free-market economy for their needs and to tell them what their desires are. The imperially imposed economy attempts to persuade all citizens that it is only through them that satisfaction can occur. A turn to the entire community subverts this notion and opens eyes and hearts to different realities that protest oppressive economics by means of internal assets and contentment. This is by all accounts a miraculous feat that Jesus has performed, but rather than the laws of nature having been subverted, it is the imperial laws.

ADDRESSING TRADITIONS (MATTHEW 15:1-20)

In this passage Jesus is questioned by religious leaders about the lack of ceremonial washing on the part of his disciples. Jesus takes the opportunity to rebuke them for following their traditions, which ends up leading them to break the commands of God. Jesus then explains to the crowd what truly defiles a person. The disciples question Jesus about his strong rebuke of the Pharisees and then ask for an explanation concerning his teaching on defilement. As Jesus verbally spars with the Pharisees, it is clear that he holds to a relational ethic that supersedes a legalistic framework: "If we examine Jesus' rebukes and correctives of the Pharisees, he consistently directs their legal interpretations toward actions that restore relationship."[100] As with Jesus' teachings on divorce (Mt 5:31-32; 19:3-9), laws from within the Mosaic law or new laws arising from later tradition should not trump striving for harmony in relationships. Jesus takes the opportunity of this encounter to critique a way in which a legalistic ethic has trumped relationships, in this case the relationship between children and parents and the responsibility of caring within those relationships.

Jesus' teaching finds strong resonance with Indigenous ways of knowing. Specifically, Jesus' explanation to his disciples shows his focus on the heart as the source from which ills and disharmony in one's life arises, and conversely the heart is the place where knowledge and wisdom truly sit within the individual.

> First Nations communities understand that this learning in the heart can happen only through experience. It is experience that teaches a person's spirit. First Nations trust only the learning that has been learned

[100]Terry LeBlanc, "Toward an Indigenous Eschatology: Caution, Circle Ahead," in *Indigenous People and the Christian Faith: A New Way Forward*, ed. William H. U. Anderson and Charles Muskego (Wilmington, DE: Vernon, 2020), 238.

> experientially; book learning is suspect among all First Nations since it can credential without any of the living experience of the dynamics the latter kind of learning claims to know. . . . Heart thinking is not emotional nor is it irrational. It makes use of emotion along with cognition and deep intuition.[101]

It is important to note that Jesus is not necessarily condemning Jewish ritual purification practices and ceremonies. Indeed, these things were part of Jewish culture, and as a traditional Jewish man Jesus no doubt partook in his cultural practices. Christ's critique, echoing Isaiah the prophet (Mt 15:7-9), is that the ritual practices have taken on a life of their own, rather than arising from the heart of an individual. The Jewish practices of washing one's hands or eating particular foods were embodied rituals and cultural practices that were meant to signify the posture of one's heart and life before Creator in the community in which one was a part. The moment these practices became a rule by which others must measure up or be judged, the practice became disconnected from the posture of the heart. Jesus is not advocating a disembodied faith where ritual practices and ceremonies are unnecessary (a common modern Protestant way of reading), but rather warns his followers that these rituals can become rote motions rather than sincere expressions arising from one's heart. This reflects Indigenous ways of knowing, where ceremony and ritual work in a continuous circle from heart to hand, mutually reinforcing each other and solidifying one's understanding and emotions. Jesus' words here are not so much an indictment as a diagnosis—his Pharisee opponents have become dis-integrated, with their hearts disconnected from their cultural practices. Jesus' challenge is not to dismiss these cultural practices but to live and act in integrated ways rather than hypocritical ways, as hypocrisy is the dis-integration between one's heart and one's hands.

ENCOUNTER WITH THE CANAANITE WOMAN (MATTHEW 15:21-39)

As seen before in the narrative, Jesus intentionally took time to withdraw from more public spaces, in this case with his disciples. However, his popular reputation as a medicine man is far and wide, and his responsibility to that role ultimately means little time for rest. Jesus goes to the region of Tyre and Sidon, the coastline of the Mediterranean Sea and the farthest place that Jesus travels according to the Gospel author, over 75 kilometers from the Sea of Galilee as the crow flies. Even this far away from Galilee and Judea, Jesus does not escape recognition as the Son of David (Mt 15:22). While modern readers may only hear particular place names, the mention of Tyre and Sidon would have evoked stories and histories for early readers, as land is a storied place that holds the memories of peoples and communities. If Jesus had simply sought a stroll on the coast, there was a road leading directly west to a city called Acco. The specificity of this travel, a withdrawing from the familiar lands of his people, to these named cities is intentional on Jesus' part.

These were ancient cities, with Sidon in particular being an ancient coastal city of commerce (mentioned in Gen 10:19; 49:13). Jesus has entered in Gentile territory, a region filled with tensions between ethnic groups and political groups. Jewish historian Josephus also indicates that there were tensions and fights in these areas during this time (*J.W.* 2.478; *Ag. Ap.* 1.70). The place Jews of

[101]Martin Brokenleg, "Church—*Wocekiye Okolakiciye*: A Lakota Experience of the Church," in *Coming Full Circle: Constructing Native Christian Theology*, ed. Steven Charleston and Elaine A. Robinson (Minneapolis: Fortress, 2015), 140, 145.

Jesus' day possibly sought to avoid is where Jesus confidently walks. Current realities and histories need to be faced in order to walk in Creator's ways, and Jesus exemplifies this good road. To make it clear that the history of this place is in mind, Matthew specifically identifies the woman who approaches Jesus in Matthew 15:22 as a Canaanite, another reminder of the history of this place. Jesus here invokes the complicated histories and current realities in those lands, because nothing good comes from erasing or ignoring the past. Tyre and Sidon had contributed materials in the past for Israel and its building projects (2 Sam 5:11; 1 Kings 5:6) but also contributed to the idolatry of Israel, particularly under Solomon (1 Kings 11:33). The story of the Israelite conquest is also brought to the fore, the reality of Israel dispossessing the Canaanites at God's command and assigning this particular land as the allotment for the tribe of Asher (Josh 19:31-34). This land held the stories of dispossession, "a gift at the expense of the Canaanites."[102] Jesus, even while speaking and acting against the Roman colonial oppression of his day, nonetheless reminds himself and his followers that they too belong to complicated stories of dispossession.[103]

Within this complex historical milieu the Canaanite woman approaches Jesus, resulting in a surprising exchange—surprising because Christ's response seems uncharacteristic based on what has already unfolded in the narrative so far. Jesus ignores the woman's pleas in Matthew 15:23, stating that his work is only for Israel in Matthew 15:24, and calls her a dog in Matthew 15:26. Jesus is using a standard insult of the time, and it is given an ethnic framing. There are a number of hermeneutical approaches to this episode, yielding important insights that are well summarized by Jaime Clark-Soles.[104] Jesus here says something shocking, out of character and unfitting to the narrative world of Matthew—ultimately for the benefit of all involved, including even himself. After all, inclusion of the Gentiles in the Messiah's story has already been well-established in the early chapters with the magi, and Matthew has already indicated that righteous Gentile women are in Christ's own lineage (Mt 1:1-14). To truly speak ill of this woman because she is a Gentile would be to speak against some of his own ancestors.

The episode also challenges the disciples with regard to their ethnocentricity, challenges the woman to exhibit faith and endurance, and challenges the faithful reader in the present—is our Christology expansive enough to embrace Christ's "clowning" around, and even a Christ who can be sassed and corrected by a woman? Might we "see the woman as another Rahab or Ruth: she recognizes her salvation is with Israel's representative, yet she retains her Canaanite identification; she proves more faithful than insiders (the spies in Jericho; the disciples); and she does what she must to save her family"?[105] This courageous determination and faithfulness further connects Christ's work with the nations and will lead into another feeding miracle, this time with indication that this crowd is predominantly non-Jewish (Mt 15:31; see Mk 7:31).

---

[102]Carter, *Matthew and the Margins*, 322.

[103]For more on Indigenous readings of the conquest narrative, see note above.

[104]For a review of these approaches, see Clark-Soles, *Women in the Bible*, chap. 1. See also the excellent womanist perspective on this passage in Mitzi J. Smith, *Womanist Sass and Talk Back: Social (In)Justice, Intersectionality, and Biblical Interpretation* (Eugene, OR: Cascade Books, 2018), chap. 2.

[105]Levine, "Matthew," 474.

YOU ARE THE CHRIST (MATTHEW 16:1-28)

The conflict with the religious leadership continues, with the Pharisees and Sadducees last having been together in the wilderness with John (Mt 3:7). It seems likely that this group of leaders is from Jerusalem specifically, as Matthew indicated that an earlier group of religious leaders came from Jerusalem (Mt 15:1), and after this episode the Sadducees and Pharisees will continue to be in conflict with Jesus when in Judea and Jerusalem in the forthcoming chapters. Jewish historian Josephus also says that Sadducees enjoyed the "confidence of the wealthy" (*Ant.* 13.293-298), and wealth was more concentrated in the urban centers. These two groups were different from each other in terms of theology and had disputes in matters of Jewish purity.[106] Despite these differences, "they were willing to work together against their common enemy. As demonstrated in politics throughout history, 'my enemy's enemy can be my friend.'"[107] The makeup of this cadre of religious leaders is important for understanding the dynamics at play in this passage. A community can handle a renegade, but a renegade may be deemed a danger if they are not ultimately willing to acknowledge the community's leadership and so cannot be contained. With this internal dynamic, this group comes to ask Jesus for a sign from heaven.

In the narrative so far, Jesus has begun to cultivate a new community that challenges the empire, offers new moral and ethical constructs, and commissions new leadership characterized by service aimed toward Christ's shalom vision. While Rome was the ultimate imperial and colonial power, colonial realities often bring about a ruling group within the oppressed people, those who participate in and collude with the imperial power, oppressing their own community or members within it. Some within this Jewish governing elite continue to challenge Jesus, and a portion of this group will ultimately work to orchestrate his crucifixion. The last time Jesus was tested in this manner was by the devil in the wilderness (Mt 16:1; see Mt 4:1). The unfortunate history of antisemitism in Christianity may lead modern readers to antisemitic tropes that equate the Jewish leadership with the devil. But this is the second time the religious leaders have asked for a sign (Mt 12:38), and Jesus has clearly indicated his perspective on the current Jewish leadership by calling and sending out new leaders for Israel (Mt 10:5). Yet, Jesus is not forsaking his people or his traditions, and his nation lives in the reality of both colonial oppression and the current Jewish leadership—Jesus is participating in the community even as he critiques and subverts it. This work of temptation "concerns not Jesus' indisputable ability to do signs, but his allegiance. Does he perform their will or God's?"[108]

Jesus, like John before him, stands outside the established authority as a prophet of God and points only to the sign of the prophet Jonah, a foreshadowing of his coming death, burial, and resurrection. In his response to the religious leaders, Jesus recognizes their ability to discern the signs from creation, and yet they cannot interpret the signs of the current moment. Jesus here is pointing back to his ministry so far, in which good medicine has been poured out on those who need it, a renewed community has been established, and

[106]For a summary of these issues, see Gary G. Porton, "Sadducees," in Evans and Porter, *Dictionary of New Testament Background*, 1050-52.

[107]Samson L. Uytanlet and Kiem-Kiok Kwa, *Matthew: A Pastoral and Contextual Commentary*, Asia Bible Commentary Series (Carlisle, UK: Langham Global Library, 2017), 172.

[108]Carter, *Matthew and the Margins*, 330.

the Messiah walks among them. Jesus, the medicine man, diagnoses the issue. They are not able to interpret the plain signs in front of them, because they are ultimately unfaithful to God ("adulterous" in Mt 16:4) in their given roles as the shepherds of Israel, and just as the Evil One sought to pull Christ's allegiance away, so too are they evil.

Just as good medicine can spread throughout a community, so too can bad medicine. Jesus warns his followers not to be persuaded by those within their nation, that small cadre of religious leaders who are ultimately wed to the colonial powers, as Jesus reminds them of the simple lesson that a little yeast can work itself through a whole group. These leaders have already clashed with Jesus on significant issues of forgiveness, healing, hospitality, Sabbath, food laws, and new traditions. Their test seeks to tame Jesus and bring him under their authority, but Jesus stands above and beyond them as the Messiah, the authoritative interpreter and revealer of Creator's will for all peoples. Jesus reminds his disciples of the wilderness feedings, examples of communities functioning outside the established colonial economies in a new sharing economy that produced an excess. Will Christ's disciples recognize that this movement is for Israel and all of the nations? This is answered in the next pericope, a hinge point in the Gospel (Mt 16:21).

Jesus again travels far from traditional Jewish spaces, this time to Caesarea Philippi. As observed in earlier portions of the narrative, the locations Jesus chooses provide vital context for what is said and done. Caesarea Philippi held a shrine for the pagan god Pan and also highlighted the imperial realities of this land in both its name and with a marble temple in honor of Augustus Caesar (Josephus, *Ant.* 15.364). This place also stood near Mount Hermon, the tallest mountain in Israel and the marker of the northeastern boundary. The waters of Mount Hermon came forth in a spring at Caesarea Philippi, one of two springs that fed the Jordan River, the lifeblood of the land of Israel. Here Jesus brings his disciples to finally ask the question—"Who do you say that I am?" (Mt 16:15). This location speaks. It speaks of imperial oppression. It speaks of past failures of the covenant people. It speaks of the worship of false gods that oppress. But it also speaks of life—the gift of water that flows indiscriminately to sustain the land, the animals, and the people. It also stands as a natural geographic border between nations.

Here Peter, speaking on behalf of the disciples, declares that Jesus is "the Messiah, the Son of the living God" (Mt 16:16). This declaration is itself a special revelation directly from Creator (Mt 16:17), and it reveals that Christ's work, like the waters of Mount Hermon, will spread indiscriminately. He is not only the Jewish Messiah but also the "Son of the living God." This living God is the giver and sustainer of all life, human and nonhuman, and extends beyond this natural geographic border and toward all nations. This new confessing community that will form around Jesus will be governed by a shalom vision for all of creation and will contend with the oppressive powers and with death itself (Mt 16:18). But the oppressive powers will not prevail so long as the cruciform life of Jesus continues to be the model for the disciple. The challenge to contend for power and authority will be ever present, but Creator's way is one of self-giving and self-sacrificial love. The call is to continually take up one's cross and follow (Mt 16:24).

ALIGNING WITH THE CHRIST (MATTHEW 17:1-27)

Jesus and his disciples are still in the region of Caesarea Philippi, and he leads his inner group of disciples, Peter, James, and John, up a high mountain, likely one of the peaks of Mount Hermon. Six days prior, Jesus stated that "the Son of Man is to come . . . in the glory of his Father," and "there are some standing here who will not taste death before they see the Son of Man coming in his kingdom" (Mt 16:27-28). This vision quest up the mountain is now especially for the inner group of disciples. They have confessed Jesus as the Christ, and Jesus has begun to explain to them his path, which will include suffering and death (Mt 16:21, 25). Now it is important for these first followers of Jesus, those who will be elders and knowledge keepers in this new multiethnic people of God, to understand that the way of suffering and service is not antithetical to Creator's way of beauty and spirit. On the mountain, Jesus is transfigured before them, and two of Christ's ancestors visit him to encourage him for his upcoming sacred work. Visions are an essential component of some Indigenous spiritualities, providing a glimpse of the interconnectedness of all things, including the spiritual and physical world, and showing a person their place and role in the future as presented in the vision.[109]

Peter's mistake, laudable as it was, was to preserve the vision rather than understanding its forward-pointing nature. Peter sought to keep the encounter going by erecting tents for Jesus, Moses, and Elijah. The voice of God cuts off Peter's misguided interruption and brings the focus back to what this vision quest seeks to show Peter and the disciples—that Jesus in his life and teachings must be listened to. The same one who stands fully in the spiritual and physical realm is the same one who has made it clear that he must suffer and die and be raised from the dead (Mt 17:9). With the visionary experience fresh in their mind, Jesus then goes on to help them see with fresh eyes those things that have already been going on in their midst. They have been expecting Elijah to come in dramatic fashion, not unlike what they just experienced and were trying to prolong. Jesus instead tells them to look again at what has already unfolded—it was John the Baptizer who fulfilled the role of the coming Elijah. And just as the new Elijah was killed by the imperial power, so too will the Son of Man be killed (Mt 11:11-12). The vision quest has reoriented their vision, helping the disciples to view past events and peoples from Creator's perspective. The baptizing prophet and locust eater was the Elijah to come (Mal 3:1; Mt 11:10), preparing the way. Jesus is Creator's son, the promised Messiah. The shalom kingdom promised is not modeled on colonial power and leadership but in self-sacrificial love and service for others. And life will triumph over death. The disciples no longer attempt to rebuke Jesus over his teaching (Mt 16:22-23) but now properly respond to suffering with lament and grief. This lament will be further compounded in the forthcoming narrative as it is revealed that the delivering over of Jesus will come from within their midst (Mt 10:4; 20:18; 26:2, 15-16, 21, 23-25, 46).

At the close of this chapter, Jesus and his disciples return to their home base in Capernaum, where Peter is asked whether they pay the temple tax.[110] A short but important exchange then takes place between Peter and Jesus on the shores of the Sea of Galilee. Warren Carter suggests a reading of this exchange between Peter and Jesus that is compelling.[111] While commentators have seen Christ's words

---

[109]For one famous example and some accompanying analysis, see the discussion on Black Elk's vision in Damian Costello, *Black Elk: Colonialism and Lakota Catholicism* (Maryknoll, NY: Orbis Books, 2005).

[110]This particular section of text is relevant for the dating of Matthew. See the introduction to this chapter.

[111]See Carter, *Matthew and Empire*, 133-43.

as a short allegory or parable of sorts, equating the kings and their children ultimately to God and his children, Carter suggests that there is no short parable here. Jesus indicates foresight by speaking to Peter about the exchange Peter just had (Mt 17:25). Jesus' question indicates that in the Roman imperial economy, taxes are levied against the subjects and not against the ruling oppressive class. This certainly is an oppression, but Jesus will change it to an act of defiance. If the oppressive ruling class is exempt from taxes, then to not pay the tax is to seek to belong to that group. If not paying taxes is a social marker of the imperial oppressive class, Jesus will have none of it. He and his disciples will pay the tax and thus align with the oppressed masses in an act of solidarity and defiance. In so doing, Jesus and his disciples will not "offend" them by claiming solidarity with the ruling class.

There is yet a further component to this story. In order to pay the current tax request, Jesus instructs Peter to go catch a fish, in which a coin covering the tax for both of them can be paid. As with Matthew 17:25, Jesus here shows the gift of foresight. All fishermen know that fish go after shiny and colorful items; this is the basis of the fishing-lure industry. Jesus with his divine knowledge knows that the first fish Peter will catch will have a coin in its mouth, one that had been dropped by someone in the past and grabbed by the fish. But this particular miracle may be saying more. Jesus' earliest disciples were fishermen who participated in local fishing economies. They were sustained by the Sea of Galilee and what it provided. Just as Indigenous nations are often self-referential with respect to their main sources of food and sustenance (salmon people, people of the buffalo, etc.), so too were Jesus and his followers identified with the fish that sustained them.[112] This enduring legacy has continued, such that the "Jesus fish" symbol came to be used very early on, millennia before the modern bumper sticker. The *ichthys* symbol should serve today as not only a fitting acronym of the person of Christ but a reminder that he was an Indigenous man who identified with the land and the community of creation that sustained him and his earliest followers—they were people of the lake and relied on the fish of the lake.[113] The skills learned on the lake were an asset that was brought into their kingdom work as Jesus called them to be fishers of people (Mt 4:19). And it is now the fish that provide what is needed for this subversive act of solidarity and defiance. The fish, the nonhuman community of creation, is also on the side of the marginalized and oppressed. The lake and its fish inhabitants partner with these acts of defiance. The community of creation also aligns itself against the oppressive powers. Even the fish will participate in the paying of taxes if it means demarcating themselves from the ruling class who are aimed at oppression and resource extraction.[114]

This creaturely act of solidarity ought to spurn Christ-followers, attuned to the lands that sustain them, to reciprocal deeds of solidarity and partnership to the wider community of creation of which we are a part. Like in the primordial story of Cain and Abel, "the earth itself is in solidarity with the victim of violence," in this case the brutal taxation

[112]See, e.g., Tony Westman, Shelah Reljic, and Peter Jones, "Salmon People" (2015), www.nfb.ca/film/salmon_people/; Liz Bryan, *The Buffalo People: Prehistoric Archaeology on the Canadian Plains* (Edmonton: University of Alberta Press, 1991).

[113]The Greek word for fish, *ichthys*, became an acronym of Greek words identifying Christ: Jesus (*Iēsous*), Christ (*Christos*), God (*theos*), Son (*huios*), and Savior (*sōtēr*).

[114]The restriction of hunting grounds, suppression of treaty hunting rights, and continual battles over fishing rights continue to the present in many countries. See, for example, the documentary on the Burnt Church conflict of 2000, Alanis Obomsawin, *Is the Crown at War with Us?*, 2002, www.nfb.ca/film/is_the_crown_at_war_with_us/.

practices of Rome.[115] This exchange was a reminder for Peter and is a reminder for the reader today of the gifts provided by Creator and creation. Peter and his community had relied for their whole lives on the fish of the lake, and now in addition to the continuous self-giving comes another gift from the fish. Gifts invoke relationships of reciprocity and remind humanity once more of our reliance on creation and accompanying responsibilities—"When we rely deeply on other lives, there is urgency to protect them."[116]

KINGDOM ETHOS (MATTHEW 18:1-35)

Jesus begins the fourth extended discourse in the Gospel, sometimes called the church discourse or community discourse. Whereas a large portion of the previous parable discourse was directed to the crowds, Jesus again addresses only his disciples here, as he did in the Sermon on the Mount. The discourse is both instruction and parable, focusing on the ethos that should govern this new community. The initial question from the disciples, "Who is greatest in the kingdom of the heavens?" (Mt 18:1, my translation), sets the stage for Christ's shalom teachings, which serve to reorient his followers toward communal wellness. The disciples have understandably been shaped by the wider culture around them, which stresses power within a social hierarchy, something present in many societies and exemplified by Rome and its forebears. Even Christ's own metaphorical usage of *kingdom* to describe Creator's good road was and is prone to this hierarchical understanding of community. Kings, after all, have lieutenants, governors, and servants. Randy Woodley suggests "community of creation" as an alternative metaphor that connects with both biblical and Indigenous perspectives.[117] Other theologians have suggested *kindom* to emphasize the relationship and cohesive community envisioned in Christ's teachings.[118]

Regardless of which metaphor is used or emphasized today, the teachings of Jesus in this section of Matthew radically reshape the metaphor of kingdom and challenge disciples expressly *not* to strive for upward mobility. All of Jesus' parables and teachings about the kingdom dismantle the logic of empire and fundamentally redefine the metaphor and concept. There is no chain of command, no hierarchical roles as such. There is the king, and there are those in his kingdom, whom he has called family (Mt 12:46-50). Those in his kingdom do not sit within a hierarchy relative to the king and one another—it is a circle with Christ at the center, not a pyramid with Christ at the top. Jesus (as well as Matthew) also does this type of redefining of a core concept with "Son of David."[119] Jesus and the Evangelist go back to their traditions preserved in the Hebrew Scriptures in order to bring the people back to the foundational teachings of their people and their Creator, as we all become

[115]Ched Myers and Elaine Enns, *Ambassadors of Reconciliation*, vol. 1, *New Testament Reflections on Restorative Justice and Peacemaking* (Maryknoll, NY: Orbis Books, 2009), 63.

[116]Robin Wall Kimmerer, *Braiding Sweetgrass: Indigenous Wisdom, Scientific Knowledge and the Teachings of Plants* (Minneapolis: Milkweed Editions, 2013), 177. On the modern understanding of "pure gift" as one in which no reciprocity is involved or expected, John Barclay's discussion and taxonomy of gift is helpful. See Barclay, *Paul and the Gift* (Grand Rapids, MI: Eerdmans, 2015), particularly chap. 1.

[117]Woodley, *Shalom*, 39-40.

[118]This term has been suggested primarily by feminist commentators, though it is certainly at home in Indigenous ways of understanding. Its usage in Indigenous circles would emphasize the kinship within all of creation. See Elaine M. Wainwright, "A Transformative Struggle Towards the Divine Dream: An Ecofeminist Reading of Matthew 11," in *Readings from the Perspective of Earth*, ed. Norman C. Habel, The Earth Bible 1 (Sheffield: Sheffield Academic Press, 2000), 167-69.

[119]On this, see Zacharias, *Matthew's Presentation*, particularly 148-51.

susceptible to hegemonic drift.[120] Hegemonic drift is that desire to move from relationships of mutuality and communal flourishing to relationships of hierarchy, where certain commodities are controlled by those at the apex and flourishing is restricted at the top. In these types of societies, which modern capitalism and colonized countries exemplify, the preferences of those at the top become the measure for the rest. In the Hebrew Scriptures, this desire to be like other nations that concentrated power in the elites of society is consistently spoken against. For example, the Jewish king was to be a brother and was not to accumulate wealth (Deut 17:14-20). This teaching, along with the whole of the instructions present in the Mosaic law, functioned to set Israel apart as a community governed by shalom with Creator, with creation, and with one another.

In this context Jesus spends the entirety of this discourse to address the hegemonic drift, redefining what God's kingdom is to be like, and ends the teaching by offering a story that warns his disciples of the consequences of not addressing the drift. He begins by responding to this query of who is greatest. In response, Christ brings a child into the disciples' midst. This is no small or quaint act; it is a radical wake-up call to reject the empirical understanding of a hierarchical kingdom, as children sat near the bottom of the social hierarchy in Roman society. In this display of a child, representing also those who are *like* children, Jesus exemplifies the vulnerable person and calls his followers to "practice solidarity downward."[121] This teaching calls for an upending of the social hierarchy such that those at the bottom become the exemplars of faith and good living.

Not only is Jesus serious about upholding those on the margins as exemplars, but next he sternly warns his disciples not to participate in the systems that oppress those on the margins, using hyperbolic language of dismemberment. While readers may recoil at the harsh language of self-mutilation, the context of the teaching is a communal one. In the Greco-Roman world, it was common to speak of the body as an analogy of the state (e.g., Seneca, *Epistulae morales* 95.52), and the apostle Paul also uses the analogy of the body to describe the church (Rom 12:3-8; 1 Cor 12:12-27). The charge here is both radical and expansive, as the Roman Empire was upheld by slavery, dispossession, brutality, and heavy taxation. Those who enforced these measures were those at the top of the social hierarchy, and many aspired to move upward. Jesus makes it clear that this aspiration is antithetical to the kingdom he proclaims and calls his followers to cut themselves off from oppressive systems: "The combination of defining the human as a social being and denying any hierarchical systems, and a recognition of humans as a part of the greater whole, leads to a complete ethical system."[122] This is a radical teaching that is increasingly complicated, and all the more necessary, in the modern world of global capitalism and (neo)colonization—Christians in affluent nations must reconcile the fact that we participate in the oppression of others for our benefits and standards of life, and we must continue to ask ourselves what we need to cut off. Ched Myers and Elaine Enns write, "The

---

[120]I was introduced to this concept by Dr. Mark Rose. Mark is traditionally linked to the Gunditjmara Nation of Western Victoria.

[121]Myers and Enns, *Ambassadors of Reconciliation* 1:59.

[122]Brian Yazzie Burkhart, "What Coyote and Thales Can Teach Us: An Outline of American Indian Epistemology," in *American Indian Thought: Philosophical Essays*, ed. Anne Waters (Malden, MA: Wiley-Blackwell, 2004), 26.

church should take great care not to reproduce the pathologies of an oppressive society!"[123]

Jesus once again speaks of children and those like them, sternly warning his disciples that priority of both value and protection is held by Creator himself and reinforced by powerful spiritual beings—the angels of the presence.[124] Creator himself gives priority to those on the margins, and to mess with those on the margins is to mess with the likes of the angels Michael and Gabriel. To both reinforce this teaching about the marginalized and transition to the final section of teaching, Jesus tells the now-popular and frequently sentimentalized parable of the lost sheep. The parable speaks of God as shepherd, a metaphor for God in the Hebrew Scriptures (see Ezek 34). The contemporary reading (and singing) of this story as God's pursuit of the sinner for salvation does not precisely capture the parable's teaching in the context of this discourse. Jesus has just made it clear that it is the marginalized, those like children, who are under the protection of Creator and his powerful angels—it is these ones who are the ninety-nine. The stray sheep is the one who is far off from God's presence and God's ways. The previous verses have made it clear that those who are far off are the oppressors, the very ones whom empire upholds as exemplars at the top of the social hierarchy. Myers and Enns write, "This parable, as the structural center of the whole teaching, thus signals a subtle but crucial transition in Jesus' restorative logic. Not only are those who are 'scandalized' the moral center of the community; the *offender*, too, as an errant member, must be 'found' and restored."[125]

The parable of the lost sheep, then, is not about an individual's salvation as much as it is about an individual's restoration to both Creator and the community that they have harmed. This parable transitions into the section that has, most unfortunately, been labeled as pertaining to church discipline. This is a Western reading based on a legalistic and punitive ethic, but it is about reconciliation, not church discipline. How does the community of faith work to bring back the wandering sheep into the fold of kinship when harm has been done? What is missing in modern punitive readings of this passage is that the parable indicates that the offender is *both* responsible and vulnerable, and that the offender's transgression brings disharmony to the collective whole, with a collective responsibility toward restoration.[126] The resulting instruction is for the community to participate in a process chosen and guided by the victim. It is the victim who is addressed (Mt 18:15), and it is the victim who decides whether they have been rightly and truly heard (Mt 18:16-17). This process engages the community specifically for reconciliation between the parties and restoration of the offender.[127] This type of communal restoration practice was (and is) also common among some Indigenous nations with the practice of sentencing circles. At the

[123]Myers and Enns, *Ambassadors of Reconciliation* 1:60.

[124]For more on the significance of angels of the presence, see C. L. Seow, "Face פנים," in *Dictionary of Deities and Demons in the Bible*, ed. Karel van der Toorn, Bob Becking, and Pieter W. van der Horst, 2nd rev. ed. (Grand Rapid, MI: Eerdmans, 1999), 322-25.

[125]Myers and Enns, *Ambassadors of Reconciliation* 1:63, emphasis original.

[126]Myers and Enns, *Ambassadors of Reconciliation* 1:63. The authors also note that this is not to overemphasize sympathy for the perpetrator, as one of the foundational stories from Genesis indicates that the land stands on the side of the victims of violence as it did for Abel (Gen 4:10). On the issue of the individual and collective identity, see Terry LeBlanc and Jeanine LeBlanc, "Liberation: Self and Community in Relationship," in *Evangelical Theologies of Liberation and Justice*, ed. Mae Elise Cannon and Andrea Smith (Downers Grove, IL: IVP Academic, 2019), especially 177-82.

[127]On this process of victim-led reconciliation, see Myers and Enns, *Ambassadors of Reconciliation* 1:65-71.

center sit stories that need to be spoken and heard:

> The story of the injury itself is a gift, because if it is entered into by those who caused the pain, it allows the abuser to take responsibility for the abuse, and for both the abuser and the abused to move toward healing. In this way, story continues to be a way forward for Indigenous people to seek harmony in all relationships, even though those relationships contain painful stories.[128]

If the offender does not truly engage the process, then the community must treat the offender differently, as a "Gentile and a tax collector" (Mt 18:17). Again, modern punitive readings have equated this to an ejection or shunning by the community, but the context of Matthew's Gospel should quickly dissuade this type of thinking. Jesus has ministered to "Gentiles and tax collectors," even calling a tax collector as one of his disciples! The offender who does not meaningfully reconcile is not removed from the community's gaze or efforts, but in fact the efforts of the community change toward the offender in a different way—"the recalcitrant offender needs to be evangelized."[129]

The community discourse began with a positive example, the child, and closes with a parable indicating how not to be. The parable is predicated on the system of economic injustice, using the story of rulers and debts owed to teach about forgiveness. Scholars differ on how to understand this parable, centering especially on whether the king in the story is meant to be analogous to God.[130] The specific context of this community discourse, and especially the preceding verses and the lead-in question asked by Peter, should give the most interpretive weight. The parable does not equate the king with God but rather puts on display the corrupt nature of a "world captive to the logic of retribution."[131] None of the characters exemplify Christ's response to Peter to be people of forgiveness (seventy-seven times, Mt 18:22). Rather, the characters are all negative exemplars of limited forgiveness and therefore ultimately bound to retribution and a punitive ethic—the very thing Christ has instructed his disciples to avoid. If we do not smash the endless cycle of retribution with the hard work of reconciliation, then we ourselves become bound and captive to a punitive ethic, because "if two of you agree on earth about anything you ask, it will be done for you" (Mt 18:19), and "So my heavenly Father will also do to every one of you, if you do not forgive your brother or sister from your heart" (Mt 18:35; see Mt 6:14-15).

REINFORCING THE TEACHINGS (MATTHEW 19:1–20:34)

With the conclusion of the fourth discourse in Matthew 18, the following two chapters of narrative and teaching revisit and reinforce many themes and topics from the community discourse and other earlier sections of Matthew. There is a reason for the repetition and reinforcement of Jesus' teachings here. Matthew indicates that Jesus "left Galilee and went to the region of Judea beyond the Jordan" (Mt 19:1). Up until this point in the narrative, Jesus has been primarily in Galilee, with occasional forays into northern areas and areas on the other side of the Jordan River, places seen as more Gentile regions. The early sections of Matthew have established Jerusalem as

[128]Aldred, "Alternative Starting Place," 150.

[129]Myers and Enns, *Ambassadors of Reconciliation* 1:68.

[130]The variety of issues and interpretive options for this parable can be found in Klyne Snodgrass, *Stories with Intent: A Comprehensive Guide to the Parables of Jesus* (Grand Rapids, MI: Eerdmans, 2008), 61-77.

[131]Myers and Enns, *Ambassadors of Reconciliation* 1:79.

a place of corrupt leadership and danger for Christ (see Mt 2:1-23). With this section, Jesus now begins to move toward Jerusalem, traveling through Judea. Jesus and his followers are participating in the ceremonies and traditions of their nation, with a trek to Jerusalem and temple for Passover. This caravan of people would have been quite large, as Jerusalem's population would have greatly increased during this time.[132] Celebratory songs of ascent from the book of Psalms would have been sung as they ascended the mountain on which Jerusalem sat. At the same time, Jerusalem is a place of danger for Christ, and he has already foretold several times his impending death at the hands of the leaders (Mt 17:22). Despite this risk from his own people and ultimately from the Roman authorities, Jesus will not cease to be who he is—a medicine man for his people who challenges the imperial society that has entrapped the imaginations of even his disciples. Matthew indicates that even in this time of communal ceremony and celebration, people come for healing (Mt 19:2), including the healing of two blind men shortly before entering Jerusalem (Mt 20:29-34).[133]

Jesus reinforces and expands on his teachings on divorce, emphasizing in a greater way how male and female coupling must be grounded in the original vision of the Hebrew creation story (Mt 19:3-12; see Mt 5:31-32), while also acknowledging the sacred nature of eunuchs (and by extension others) who for different reasons do not or cannot participate in the marital covenant. Whereas the earlier teachings from the community discourse spoke of those "like" children (Mt 18:3), Jesus makes it clear in Matthew 19:13-15 that children were not solely used as an analogy. Children, as those who are most vulnerable and those lowest on the social hierarchy, are the citizens of Creator's kingdom: "Matthew's Jesus asks the audience questions along the lines of his injunctions in chapter 18: Are you ready to abandon what you have and follow Jesus in order to 'enter the kingdom of heaven' (19:23)? Can you welcome to your communities the 'others' who are like these little children and who have no evident parents or economic power?"[134]

This episode with the children reinforces the teachings of the community discourse, as does the parable of the workers in the vineyard (Mt 20:1-16). The parable, laden with meaning as parables always are, reinforces a point that has been weaved through much of the last few chapters concerning the desire for upward mobility and social power. It is no doubt spoken in hopes that his own disciples will abandon notions of envy or one-upmanship, as "human perceptions on ranking are without significance and will be stood on their heads in the kingdom."[135] Unfortunately, imperial logic and the hegemonic drift is still deeply ingrained, as is made clear in Christ's encounter with John's and James's mother as she asks for a special spot of honor for her sons (Mt 20:20-28). Their response indicates not only that the disciples continue to misunderstand the nature of this new community called the kingdom of the

---

[132]For geography and logistics of this annual pilgrimage, see A. D. Riddle, "The Passover Pilgrimage from Jericho to Jerusalem: Jesus' Triumphal Entry," in *Lexham Geographic Commentary on the Gospels*, ed. Barry J. Beitzel and Kristopher A. Lyle (Bellingham, WA: Lexham, 2017), 395-407.

[133]This healing further establishes Jesus as the one chosen to minister on Creator's behalf, as the blind men call out to him as the Son of David, the messianic healing shepherd for the people. See Zacharias, *Matthew's Presentation*, 79-103; Baxter, "Healing and the 'Son of David.'"

[134]Eunyung Lim, *Entering God's Kingdom (Not) like a Little Child: Images of the Child in Matthew, 1 Corinthians, and Thomas*, Beihefte zur Zeitschrift für die neutestamentliche Wissenschaft 243 (Berlin: de Gruyter, 2021), 67.

[135]Snodgrass, *Stories with Intent*, 371-72.

heavens, but also that there continues to be an expectation that Jesus will confront the Romans and establish a new Israelite kingship. The disciples' vision is too small, held captive by the imperial logic of the Roman Empire, such that they cannot yet imagine this new way of life that Jesus teaches.

The encounter with the rich young man in Matthew 19:16–30 serves as an example of the difficulty those higher up on the social ladder will have with Christ's teaching. Terry LeBlanc writes, "It is imperative that we understand that Jesus does not challenge the rich young man's attestation that he has fulfilled all the law. As improbable as it would seem to us, it appears that he has. Yet, as the young man hears Jesus' admonition, we have a very clear sense that he is so fixed on his wealth that he is left relationally isolated."[136] A wall of wealth separates him. Like Jesus and his contemporaries, Indigenous peoples of Turtle Island are well-acquainted with how wealth and greed breed destruction of communities, individuals, relationships, and the land.[137] The desire to find the passage to India by Columbus and other early colonizers was quickly supplanted by a frenzied and demonic desire for gold and wealth.[138] This rich young man sits in a place of privilege, but a religiously pious life has been coupled with great economic gain tied to the economic brutalities of the empire. The call to this young man is the same as that to the disciples in the community discourse to cut off those things that harm the community and those on the margins (Mt 18:6-9). It is only this action that can provide the means of entering a kingdom guided by a shalom vision.[139] This act will restore him to a community and to alternative treasures.

While the promise of "treasure in heaven" (Mt 19:21) is often understand futuristically and disconnected from present physical realities, Jesus has taught that this kingdom is already near (Mt 4:17; 10:7; 12:28). Furthermore, the kingdom in Matthew is "of the heavens," which encompasses the entirety of the community of creation, the seen and the unseen.[140] Jesus is not asking the rich young man to embrace poverty but to find very present riches within creation and community. These types of riches will not partake of oppressive economic systems, will not take advantage of those on the margins, and will not seek individualistic gain and upward social mobility.

JESUS IN JERUSALEM (MATTHEW 21:1–22:46)

Jesus enters Jerusalem in a triumphal procession. The narrative has made it clear that this is a place of danger for him, and Jesus has indicated many times that he will suffer and die at the hands of the leaders. But this reality has not held Jesus back; he is compelled by his purpose and vision despite increasing friction and hostility. One of his core teachings has been to redefine what this new community would look like. He has taught about this shalom-shaped kingdom in Galilee and in Judea, and now he must confront the corrupt Jewish and Roman leadership in Jerusalem. Jesus signals the different nature of this kingdom in his "triumphal entry" (Mt 21:6-11). Jesus himself has orchestrated the entry to be

---

[136]LeBlanc, "Toward an Indigenous Eschatology," 241.

[137]For example, Black Elk describes gold as "the yellow metal that makes the Wasichus [Western Europeans] crazy." Black Elk and John G. Neihardt, *Black Elk Speaks: The Complete Edition* (Lincoln: University of Nebraska Press, 2014), 68.

[138]The brutal details of Columbus and the colonizers can be read in David E. Stannard, *American Holocaust: The Conquest of the New World* (New York: Oxford University Press, 1993), particularly chaps. 3-4. For historical first-person account, see Bartolomé de Las Casas, *In Defense of the Indians*, trans. Stafford Poole (DeKalb: Northern Illinois University Press, 1992).

[139]Woodley, *Shalom*, 35.

[140]On this, see the discussion under Mt 4:1-25.

this way (Mt 21:1-5), following in the tradition of his ancestor King David (2 Sam 19–20) as well as the prophetic tradition in Zechariah 9.[141]

> In deliberately presenting himself before Jerusalem as its messianic king, Jesus has chosen an OT model which subverts any popular militaristic idea of kingship. The meek, peaceful donkey-rider of Zech. 9.9 is not a potential leader of an anti-Roman insurrection. In 20.25-28 Jesus has spoken of a type of leadership which is completely opposed to the world's notions of kingship and authority, and now he models it in the "meekness" of his royal procession to the city.[142]

Notable also is the nonhuman participation in this ceremony. Matthew indicates that it is a donkey and her colt who participate in this process, leading to the somewhat humorous portrait of Jesus riding both animals (Mt 21:7).[143] The point, though, is that an untrained colt is involved in this process and allows Jesus to ride. While Mark 11:2 explicitly states that the colt has never been ridden, in Matthew it is the presence of the colt's mother that indicates that the colt has not yet been trained.[144] As the community of creation is full of beings with agency, the mother and colt willingly participate with Jesus to provide him his ride.

Jesus moves immediately to a forceful show of his kingly role, the role of his work as medicine man and prophet, as he drives out sellers and flips tables (Mt 21:12-13). The verb "drove out" in Matthew 21:12 is used elsewhere to describe his work of exorcism (Mt 8:16; 9:33; 10:1, 8). This act is both symbolic and an act of purification—a responsibility that was supposed to belong to the religious leadership. To reinforce this message to the failed leadership and the nature of this new community, Jesus performs another symbolic act of cursing the fig tree (Mt 21:18-22) and speaking three parables (Mt 21:33–22:14), with the parable of the tenants adapting "the vineyard of Isa 5:1-7, and recast(ing) the story to serve as a juridical parable, a self-indicting mirror, for the religious leaders."[145] Jesus' work of healing also continues for those in need as the blind and the lame seek him in the temple for healing, and the children, the very ones to whom the kingdom belongs (Mt 19:13-15), offer him honor and praise in Matthew 21:14-17.

Direct confrontation between the religious leaders and Jesus occurs a number of times in this section as they plot to entrap him by what he says (Mt 22:15). Matthew provides a small but important detail, indicating that these Pharisees are working with "the Herodians" (Mt 22:16). While very little is known of this group, their designation indicates their strong alignment and support of the Roman leadership in the form of the Herodian dynasty, and their alignment with the Pharisees suggest they are Jewish. This underscores the critiques Jesus has made throughout the Gospel against the religious leadership of his day. The leaders have forsaken their role as the shepherds and healers of Israel. They have aligned with the colonial powers in order to cling to their own power and authority, and by so doing continue to propagate and partake of injustices against their people.

In some of the final encounters of this section, Jesus displays his wisdom and alignment with the greatest teachings of his own people as he

---

[141] For more on the rich Davidic traditions infused in this section, see Zacharias, *Matthew's Presentation*, 112-28.

[142] Richard F. France, *The Gospel of Matthew*, NICNT (Grand Rapids, MI: Eerdmans, 2007), 775.

[143] Mark's version of the entry in Mk 11:1-11 more explicitly focuses on the colt.

[144] See Craig S. Keener, "The Unridden Donkey Colt: Mark 11:2 in Light of Equine Development and Pedagogy," *BBR* 32 (2022): 23-29.

[145] Snodgrass, *Stories with Intent*, 295.

responds to the question of what the greatest commandment is (Mt 22:34-40). But he also must correct an especially errant group of religious leaders when the Sadducees seek to trap him with a hypothetical scenario (Mt 22:23-33). While there continue to be questions in scholarship about the Sadducees, it is certain from several sources that they did not believe in resurrection or an afterlife, and it is possible that they did not believe in spiritual beings either (Acts 23:8).[146] Christ's response to the Sadducees moves beyond their trap and gets to the heart of the issue—the Sadducees have an incomplete view of reality, and because of this they have a distorted view of Creator. Like Indigenous peoples throughout the world, Jesus lived with the reality of the spirit world present all around him. Martin Brokenleg writes, "We believe that the spirit world always belongs to us and we to them. They are always ready to welcome us, always ready to hold us and embrace us in every possible way."[147] This is a profound disconnection of the Sadducees from their people, from their place, and ultimately from their Creator: "Belonging means not just to people, but it also means to belong to a location on the earth. It means to belong to a particular place in the spirit world."[148] Jesus' words are the medicine that the Sadducees need; it is not simply that they are mistaken on a doctrinal point but that they are deeply disconnected from who they are meant to be. They are disconnected from the community of creation, from the community to which they are called to lead, from their ancestors, and ultimately from Creator. God is the God of the living, including their ancestors Abraham, Isaac, and Jacob (Mt 22:32).

THE JUDGMENT DISCOURSE (MATTHEW 23:1–25:46)

The final extended discourse in the Gospel of Matthew is as lengthy as the Sermon on the Mount, but this time it is filled with words of indictment, sorrow, and expected futures.[149] The discourse begins as an address to both the disciples and the crowds, and calls out the hypocrisy of the current religious leadership in Jerusalem, as "they do not practice what they teach" (Mt 23:3), something that is explicated in each "woe" against the leaders (Mt 23:13-36). Jesus sees in the current religious leadership of his day the opposite of what is expected for shepherds of Israel. They pursue instead the ideals of hierarchical power and prestige, following imperial logic. Rather than helping those heavily burdened by Roman colonization, they place further loads on people (Mt 23:4), and the things they do are for honor in this corrupt system (Mt 23:5-7).

Jesus has taught for many years, including many encounters with the religious leaders. But now, even with the Messiah in their midst, they cannot turn to the better way. Jesus moves to a series of denouncements of the current religious leadership for the harm they bring to the entire nation. Reading this from a modern individualistic ethic may cause readers today to see these as judgments only on individuals. However, a communitarian worldview like that of Jesus and Indigenous peoples today is the proper lens by which to read this discourse.

---

[146]On this, see F. Parker, "The Terms 'Angel' and 'Spirit' in Acts 23,8," *Biblica* 84 (2003): 344-65.

[147]Brokenleg, "Circles of Courage," 5.

[148]For an example study of the importance of connection with the spirit world and how traditional ceremonies support this belonging, see Damian Costello, "Black Elk's Vision of Waníkiya: The Ghost Dance, Catholic Sacraments, and Lakota Ontology," *Journal of NAIITS* 16 (2018): 40-56.

[149]Most commentators do not include Mt 23 in the final discourse. For arguments as to why this is a better understanding of Matthew's structure, see Jason B. Hood, "Matthew 23–25: The Extent of Jesus' Fifth Discourse," *JBL* 128 (2009): 527-43.

A judgment on the leadership of the Jewish nation of Jesus' day will affect the whole, as none of us stands alone; all are part of an interconnected web of relationships—a little yeast works through the whole dough (Gal 5:9). The religious leaders' hegemonic drift and collusion with the Roman Empire has had an effect on the whole of the nation. As bad shepherds, they have led their people astray and reject the means of healing and restoration in the person and work of Christ. Jesus desired to gather Jerusalem and its leadership into his new shalom kingdom as a hen gathers her chicks, but they were not willing (Mt 23:37).

Just as healing and wholeness in the ministry of Jesus had communal and social effects, so too do the sins of leaders affect the whole. Jesus moves to the Mount of Olives with only his disciples, where he foretells what will happen to the temple and Jerusalem. The current Jewish leadership will come to persuade the people to call for Jesus' death (Mt 27:22-25), and the Roman leadership, who holds ultimate control over Jerusalem, will not hesitate to flex their tyrannical muscle to crucify a Jewish prophet who is making good trouble. The peoples and their temple are intertwined and have interrelated futures, which is why the judgment against the religious leaders is quickly followed by Jesus foretelling the destruction of Jerusalem and its temple (see the disciples' question, Mt 24:1-3). The hypocrisy and injustices of the current religious leadership have brought about disharmony and unjust practices to the Jerusalem temple. The current religious leadership is no longer the shepherds of Israel chosen by God; that role now sits with the disciples of Jesus. And the place of forgiveness and healing is no longer the temple but now resides with Jesus himself. The book of Hebrews will contemplate and expand on what is here implicit in the narrative: Jesus is the great and final high priest and the final sacrifice, and as such now fulfills a unique space for encounter with God that the temple once was.

Modern, futuristic readings of Matthew 24 thrust the details of the chapter to the time of the second coming of Christ and the consummation of history. But the specific question asked by the disciples, the visionary and apocalyptic language drawn from Daniel 7 and other Hebrew Scriptures, and the historical details of the fall of Jerusalem in 70 CE should dissuade this futuristic reading.[150] In the tradition of Jewish prophets before Jesus, and following the tribal laws of his people, prophets were judged and vindicated based on whether what they said came to pass. This clearly was the case when Jerusalem fell and the temple was destroyed in 70 CE.

The final sections of the discourse consist of parables of watchfulness (Mt 24:44) oriented toward the future, with Matthew 25:1 being the only instance of Jesus stating what the kingdom of the heavens *will be* like. The discourse culminates with a futuristic scene of judgment, when people from every nation stand before the Son of Man and the righteous are separated from the unrighteous. The basis of this separation aligns with the ethos of the shalom kingdom that Jesus has taught and exemplified through his ministry—practicing solidarity with those on the margins, lifting them up and ministering to their basic needs. This alignment with the teachings of Jesus centers practice as the identifying marker of alignment with the Jesus way. In its history the church has so often centered the articulation of correct doctrine, and this reality coupled with dualism

[150]For more on this, particularly the usage of imagery from Dan 7 and the "one like a son of man" and its usage to refer to the events of Jesus' death and culminating in the destruction of the temple, see N. T. Wright, *The New Testament and the People of God*, Christian Origins and the Question of God 1 (Minneapolis: Fortress, 1992), chap. 10.

has fostered situations throughout church history in which Christians could confess "Jesus is Lord" while simultaneously trading slaves, stealing lands, and subjugating peoples. This climactic vision at the conclusion of the discourse warns us away from a hypocrisy (condemned by Jesus earlier in the discourse) that has no alignment between one's lifeways and cognitive beliefs.

MEAL, ARREST, AND TRIAL (MATTHEW 26:1-75)

In this final and climactic section of Matthew, the clash of kingdoms that began at the outset of the Gospel results in the death of the Christ. Jesus has been preparing his followers for his death (Mt 12:39-40; 16:4, 21-23; 17:22-23; 20:17-19; 26:2), and the majority of this section is devoted to Jesus' final night with the disciples. This establishes an inner-narrative vindication of Jesus following the Jewish teachings about prophets in Deuteronomy 18:22. He has predicted his own death at the hands of the religious leaders, his betrayal, his death, and his resurrection, all of which come to pass in the closing chapters.

After being anointed as a portent of his upcoming burial (Mt 26:6-13), Jesus celebrates the Passover meal with his disciples. This is the celebration that has brought Jesus along with thousands of other pilgrims to Jerusalem, and even in the midst of threats and betrayals, Jesus will celebrate with his people the story of their liberation from Egypt in the exodus. It is during this meal of remembrance that Jesus attaches new meaning and significance to the bread and wine passed among them. Despite Christ's knowledge that Judas will betray him (Mt 26:20-25) and all the disciples will fall away (Mt 26:31), the bread and wine are still passed around. Christ's final passion prediction is a tangible act of communion with the faint-hearted, indicating the significance of his upcoming death and its ability to bring people into Creator's family. As Communion is now a sacrament in the Christian church, it should not be missed that the initiation of this ceremony integrated with, adapted, and added to a currently existing ceremony of the Jewish tradition. This new ceremonial feast became a common component of the church gathering since the earliest of times, with the ceremony itself changing from a weekly practice of eating together the "love feast" (1 Cor 11; Jude 12) to modern expressions that vary in frequency, wording, form, and so on.

The instituting of the Lord's Supper provides for Indigenous followers of Jesus today an example of the contextual adaptation of a sacred tradition and ceremony. Certain components of the original Passover and its subsequent celebration were directly relevant to Jesus' life and teachings, but there was not a one-to-one alignment. Jesus added something new to a ceremony that his people had been observing for many generations. In so doing, the original meaning and intent of Passover was not dismissed but honored while also seen and understood in a new way. Indigenous followers of Jesus have likewise sought to honor their cultural traditions and bring them authentically into their lifeways and their communal ceremonies of thanksgiving.[151] Despite the church's practice of contextualization throughout history, the modern colonial project has made this an exceedingly difficult process for Indigenous peoples today.[152] Contextual and cultural adaptation and worldview integration has been

[151]On the issue of culture and contextualization, see also my and Chris Hoklotubbe's essay, "Turtle Island Biblical Interpretation," in the current volume.

[152]For examples of pagan practices brought in and syncretized into Christian practice, see Frank Viola and George Barna, *Pagan Christianity? Exploring the Roots of Our Church Practices* (Carol Stream, IL: Tyndale House, 2010).

and continues to be a part of localized Christian expressions throughout the global church. One effort to control this by hegemonic establishments is to use "syncretism" to label practices with which they do not approve, and "contextualization" for practices they do approve (or at least tolerate).

Indigenous theologians, such as the late Richard Twiss, resisted the policing of these movements of the Spirit and labeled such efforts as syncretism while also pointing out how this type of cultural contextualization happens in every culture where the gospel takes root.[153] Under colonization, the dominant culture and its participants are often blind to their own histories of cultural syncretism while being fiercely (and genocidally) opposed to these same movements in Indigenous and minority populations. Indigenous ceremonies were banned by governments and demonized by the church such that some of the greatest opponents to Indigenous expressions of Christian faith today are Indigenous peoples who have adopted the European brand of Christianity. Despite this persecution arising from colonization, some Indigenous Christians have sought to follow Jesus the way God made them and with the culture they were born into. This encompasses cultural ceremonies and practices as well as Indigenous worldviews and epistemologies, with the ultimate aim of articulating, valuing, and dignifying Indigenous contextual theologies and praxes.[154] The work of Indigenous believers today to integrate their cultural practices, as well as the worldviews and lifeways these ceremonies are tied to, finds resonance in the institution of the Lord's Supper.[155] Jesus celebrated and entered fully into the ceremony of his people, even while transforming it and imbuing it with a new meaning. Indigenous followers today follow Jesus' example in engaging their culture as the gospel imbues their practices with new meaning, whether this be smudging, sweat lodge, powwows, or pipe ceremonies.[156]

Steven Charleston considers Jesus' time in the garden of Gethsemane to be Jesus' third vision quest. In this sacred liminal space, surrounded by the community of creation—that is, an olive grove on a mountain—Jesus expresses his deep and profound human need in the face of what is to come. This scene has resonances with the role of the sun dancer in many First Nations. A sun dancer participated in the Sun Dance, a traditional ceremony held by several First Nations, primarily those located in the plains. Dancers prepared themselves with prayers and fasting. During the ceremony, a sun dancer danced their prayers and also sang songs, offered prayers, engaged in fasting, and sometimes took part in ceremonial piercing. All of this was done on behalf of the people. Charleston states: "No ordinary person could receive a vision to become a Sun Dancer to this level. The idea that one dance by one person could fulfill the deepest need of a crying humanity for all time is a sacrifice beyond precedent. . . . [Jesus] is the Sun Dancer for all people, for all of creation, for all

[153]See Richard Twiss, *Rescuing the Gospel from the Cowboys: A Native American Expression of the Jesus Way* (Downers Grove, IL: InterVarsity Press, 2015), chap. 1.

[154]See Casey Church, *Holy Smoke: The Contextual Use of Native American Ritual and Ceremony* (Cleveland, TN: Cherohala, 2017); Twiss, *One Church, Many Tribes*; Treat, *Native and Christian*; Charleston and Robinson, *Coming Full Circle*; Clara Sue Kidwell, Homer Noley, George E. Tinker, and Jace Weaver, *A Native American Theology* (Maryknoll, NY: Orbis Books, 2001). For lessons we can learn from the African context, see Vince L. Bantu, "Early Christian Foundations for Indigenous Theological Self-Determination," *Journal of NAIITS* 15 (2017): 45-50.

[155]This is true also of John's baptism, which had connection with the purification ceremonies of Judaism while also changing the practice into something new.

[156]For discussion on contextual practices, see Church, *Holy Smoke*. Non-Indigenous readers should not appropriate these traditions without Indigenous participation and leadership.

time. Through his Dance, all life will be blessed forever."[157]

After his arrest, Jesus is brought before a court before the religious leaders. Jesus remains silent before the false accusations, but once he does speak, his condemnation is assured. The high priest says, "Tell us if you are the Messiah, the Son of God" (Mt 26:63). In terms of the identity and roles of Jesus, this question and his response sits as the culmination of the Gospel. Jesus responds to the high priest, stating, "You have said so. But I tell you, From now on you will see the Son of Man seated at the right hand of Power and coming on the clouds of heaven" (Mt 26:64). In this exchange, the various titles of Jesus (which represent the various functions and roles of Jesus as the Messiah) converge: the (Davidic) Messiah, Son of God, and Son of Man. Jesus' response gives the religious leaders a clear charge with which to hand over Jesus to the Romans. But it also clues in readers to view the unfolding narrative in a different way—as a coronation of Jesus to a place of leadership and prominence in Creator's inbreaking kingdom.

DEATH AND BURIAL (MATTHEW 27:1-66)

At the close of the trial before the high priest, the response of Jesus in Matthew 26:64 opens a visionary window through which to view the events that unfold in the current section. With the response of Jesus that "from now on" they will see the coronation of the Son of Man, the components of the narrative now paint two portraits as readers are invited into a process of viewing what will unfold from the earthly standpoint and the spiritual standpoint. Jesus stands before Pilate, who is the wielder of absolute Roman power. Given the option to release Jesus, the crowd instead calls for the release of the criminal Barabbas. From the spiritual vantage point, this is a typological and satirical reenactment of the Jewish day of atonement, as Jesus will stand on behalf of all people.[158] This is followed by humiliation and torture at the hands of the Romans, including a mock robing, scepter holding, and a crown of thorns (Mt 27:27-31). Yet from the spiritual vantage point, this mocking is in fact reflective of his vindication and coronation to a place of leadership and prominence alongside Creator. Following this is Jesus' walk to the site of crucifixion, where he is lifted up and nailed to the cross, with a sign declaring that he is the king of the Jews (Mt 27:37), meant as an intentional warning to any who wished to challenge Rome's authority. But from the spiritual vantage point, Christ is not being lifted up in humiliation but to a place of honor beside God in the heavens, and the sign meant as intimidation and mocking is instead a spiritual declaration that this man indeed is the supreme servant (i.e., king) of his people.

From the cross, Jesus cries out words of lament from the Psalms and then dies, after which there is an earthquake and other symbolic events that cause the Roman soldiers to state, "Truly this man was God's Son" (Mt 27:54). This statement by the Roman soldiers, rather than a confession of faith, is an admission of guilt for the torture and execution that they have just presided over, as they recognize what others have come to believe (Mt 14:33) and now confirm as witnesses to Jesus' admission before the high priest (Mt 26:64). This declaration at the cross forms a bookend with the trial scene,

[157]Charleston, *Four Vision Quests*, 140. See also Clyde Holler, *Black Elk's Religion: The Sun Dance and Lakota Catholicism* (Syracuse, NY: Syracuse University Press, 1995); Ella Deloria, "The Sun Dance of the Oglala Sioux," *The Journal of American Folklore* 42 (1929): 354-413.

[158]See Hans M. Moscicke, "Jesus, Barabbas, and the Crowd as Figures in Matthew's Day of Atonement Typology (Matthew 27:15–26)," *JBL* 139 (2020): 125-53.

and from the spiritual vantage point the words are an admission of the Roman soldiers' defeat, as the "supernatural events demonstrate the enormous power at Jesus's disposal and they concede their defeat in the face of this superior force."[159] In recognizing the error of their ways, they acknowledge that Jesus is Lord and Caesar is not.

As I have said above, the community of creation is a community of living beings with agency and relationship with both Creator and humanity. With this in mind, the environmental events during the crucifixion should not be viewed as simply occurring for humanity but as an active response of creation to what is unfolding. The land to which Jesus belongs is covered in darkness during Christ's time of agony on the cross (Mt 27:45). At the time of day when the sun normally sits at the height of the sky and gives its light as per its creational duty (Gen 1:14-19), darkness reigns as the creation groans at Jesus' suffering. As Jesus breathes his last, the same land that was covered in darkness now breaks, just as Christ's body has broken to death. Yet, death is not new for the community of creation. In fact, death is built into the creational system of reciprocity, sustenance, and new life. The apostle Paul states, "What you sow does not come to life unless it dies" (1 Cor 15:36), and Jesus says in the Gospel of John, "Unless a grain of wheat falls into the earth and dies, it remains just a single grain; but if it dies, it bears much fruit" (Jn 12:24). The breaking of Jesus' body is present also in the breaking of the land in an earthquake, part of a continuous cycle that has occurred since creation began. Christ participates in this creational cycle.

The significance of Christ's death, however, is unique within the death-to-new-creation process, signaled immediately by Matthew with two symbolic and apocalyptic elements. First, the veil of the temple is torn, which signifies the conclusion of the temple's function in the life of Israel as it has culminated in the death of Israel's Messiah and so emphasizes that Jesus is uniquely "God with us."[160] Second, while Jesus participates in the death-to-new-creation process just as the community of creation always has, his death becomes the means of new life for those who have *preceded* him as well as those who *followed* him. This is something that sets apart this death from all other deaths. All of creation, including humanity, relies on the death of others for life. But only one death is able to impart new life to those who come before, symbolically displayed in the raising of past saints in Matthew 27:52-53, a process of new creation that the land itself participates in as the rocks split to open the tombs.

In this final vision quest of Jesus, Matthew notes, "Many women were also there, looking on from a distance; they had followed Jesus from Galilee and had provided for him" (Mt 27:55). At this time of Christ's greatest work to be good medicine for the whole world, his male disciples are not present; only women are present with him at the cross and in fact have been helping him prepare for this moment as the supporters of his vision quest. For Christ to fully represent humanity and all of creation in this most sacred act, the presence of the feminine is necessary:

> Women are not just accidental bit players in a male story. They are spiritually present because they have a weight of authority men do

[159]David C. Sim, "Rome in Matthew's Eschatology," in Riches and Sim, *Gospel of Matthew*, 104.

[160]For an in-depth analysis and discussion of the torn veil in Matthew, see Daniel M. Gurtner, *The Torn Veil: Matthew's Exposition of the Death of Jesus*, SNTSMS 139 (New York: Cambridge University Press, 2007).

> not have; without them, things would be out of balance. Women complete the circle of sacred vision. They infuse the vision with the holiness of their being, with the archetype of the female that is essential to the order and harmony of all creation. . . . They are there because they are part of a moment no male could fulfill.[161]

RESURRECTION AND GREAT COMMISSION (MATTHEW 28:1-20)

The sacred role of the women continues as they are present for the burial of Jesus by Joseph of Arimathea and are then there at the tomb when it is revealed to be empty (Mt 27:57-61; 28:1-10). An angel from the spiritual realm is present as the earth breaks once more, but this time it is the birth pangs of Jesus' resurrection as mother earth again plays her sacred feminine role as "the womb of the resurrection."[162] In the Olivet discourse, Jesus spoke about earthquakes in various places, describing them as birth pangs (Mt 24:7-8), and the apostle Paul speaks of the creation groaning in labor pains (Rom 8:22). Just like a seed in the soil must crack open and disrupt the soil around it to break forth, so too does the earth quake as the firstborn of the new creation breaks forth as God raises Christ from death (Rom 8:29; Col 1:15, 18). The women, like midwives who have completed their work to shepherd this new resurrection life, can now bring the male disciples back into the story as these women are the first proclaimers of the bodily resurrection of Jesus, whose feet they have touched (Mt 28:9).[163] Matthew indicates that the current religious leaders continue in their collusion with the Romans even to the time of Matthew's writing of his Gospel, in order to squash the voices of the women and by extension the rest of the disciples (Mt 27:62-66; 28:15).

The closing verses of the Gospel of Matthew bring to culmination several themes that have run through the book. Jesus was born into the kingly line of David and exhibited true kingship in his works of service as medicine man and teacher through the gospel, calling his disciples to a radical community ethic in this new shalom kingdom. His final hours saw him lifted in humiliation and death while simultaneously being lifted to a position of authority and leadership beside Creator. Jesus recognizes this in his final words, saying, "All authority in heaven and on earth has been given to me" (Mt 28:18). Because this new kingdom is not like other empires, Jesus does not establish his rulership or lay claim to new lands, nor does he place the disciples in hierarchical authority structures. As Jesus commissions his disciples to go and make disciples of all nations, the various threads of encounters with Gentiles now move into the expansion of this new community to be multiethnic. Just as Jesus himself encountered Gentiles and intentionally ventured into Gentile territory, so now the disciples will continue what Jesus started.[164] This new community will be a community of learners (disciples) who will identify with Jesus and this new community through the ceremony of baptism. The disciples are charged with passing on Christ's radical teachings of this shalom community. The Great Commission is the next phase in the disciples' work first

[161]Charleston, *Four Vision Quests*, 154-55.

[162]Stated by Chrysologus; see Thomas Aquinas. See John Henry Newman, ed., *Catena Aurea: Commentary on the Four Gospels, Collected Out of the Works of the Fathers: St. Matthew* (Oxford: John Henry Parker, 1841), 1:976.

[163]On the grasping of Jesus' feet, see Allison, *Studies in Matthew*, 107-16. For more detailed discussion on the resurrection narratives in the Gospels, see N. T. Wright, *The Resurrection of the Son of God*, Christian Origins and the Question of God 3 (London: SPCK, 2003).

[164]For more on this, see Michael F. Bird, *Jesus and the Origins of the Gentile Mission*, LNTS 331 (New York: T&T Clark, 2006).

begun in Matthew 10 but that had been restricted initially to Israel (Mt 10:5-6).

Modern readers, particularly Indigenous and those of other colonized nations, encounter this commission much differently from most Western readers, as missionary efforts for hundreds of years have been deeply enmeshed with colonization. The result of this has been a consistent understanding of mission as triumph. But this language and understanding is problematic:

> God's glory does not come through the triumph of one group over the other as one succumbs to the mission of the gospel, but rather through the open embrace and welcome that God through Christ demonstrates to each person. We should, therefore, replace the concept and language of "mission" with the concepts and language of "welcome and embrace." "Mission" must die in order that the invitation and welcome of gospel may live.[165]

As Gene Green discusses, the doctrine of discovery has malformed the Christian mind to see empty lands as needing to be filled by Christian peoples, and the peoples of those lands as empty and godless receptacles for the good news that colonists will provide. This understanding of mission is brought back to the reading of the Great Commission in Matthew and is present in modern missiology.[166] Yet, while the church must fully repent of and learn from the myriad of bad practices and theologies that arose from the Great Commission, this one small portion of text cannot be the sole passage that forms the impulse to evangelism, and indeed it holds very little instruction as compared to Matthew 10.[167] In Matthew it is the disciples (those first commissioned in Mt 10) who need to constantly hear and rehear the teachings of Jesus. Through the story, non-Israelites are the first worshipers of Jesus (Mt 2:1-12), display great faith (Mt 8:5-13), and can even confront Jesus with the complicated histories of his people and "sass" him (Mt 15:21-28). These are not paternalistic encounters exclusively focused on the salvation of one's soul but exchanges between people that encompass a holistic and integrated salvation that involves listening to one another (Mt 15:24-28; 18:15-16).

A close reading and deep encounter with Jesus in the Gospel of Matthew should in no way result in disciples who feel they have attained enlightenment (overrealized eschatology) such that they can lord it over peoples and lands. As they go to baptize and teach others what Jesus *first commanded them*, there is an expectation of constant reinforcement of Jesus' teachings within the life of the one who now witnesses. In the act of teaching, disciples are reminded that their desires for power will often be shaped by the empire (Mt 18:1-5; 20:20-28), that they will often be tempted to limit their forgiveness (Mt 18:21-35), that they will seek to silence the marginalized (Mt 19:13-15; 20:29-34), and that they will seek to separate themselves from those they deem godless (Mt 15:23). Jesus' teachings of the shalom kingdom of God are the cure to the colonial perspective and colonial mission practice. When followers of Jesus succumb to hegemonic drift, the result is a model of outreach based on imperialistic

[165]Gene L. Green, "The Death of Mission: Rethinking The Great Commission," *Journal of NAIITS* 12 (2014): 108.

[166]For reflections from several different disciplines on the legacy of the Great Commission, see the essays in Mitzi J. Smith and Jayachitra Lalitha, eds., *Teaching All Nations: Interrogating the Matthean Great Commission* (Minneapolis: Fortress, 2014).

[167]The Great Commission was specifically used by early discovery proclamations as grounds to subjugate peoples and lands. See Katerina Friesen, "The Great Commission: Watershed Conquest or Watershed Discipleship," in *Watershed Discipleship: Reinhabiting Bioregional Faith and Practice*, ed. Ched Myers (Eugene, OR: Cascade Books, 2016), 32-35.

values instead of Christ's life and teachings. These are the haunted stories we must face in the modern church.[168]

Carmen Rae Lansdowne suggests that the cure to the modern discussion and practice of mission is an intercultural theology that brings three direct challenges:

> First, indigenous/settler communities (or any dominant/oppressed society) cannot continue to operate on dependency models where the oppressed only have any freedoms under or by the grace of the oppressor(s). Second, that difference doesn't challenge access to resources, nor is it an ontological challenge in a way that switches who wins and who loses—it changes the game and there are enough resources, and enough truths, for all. Lastly, intercultural theology proposes that dialogue is itself the end, not a means to an end.[169]

This impulse to mission, or, as Green suggests, the impulse to "welcome and embrace," by Jesus and the disciples would have naturally been situated in people rooted in their own traditions. This fact has relevance for today: "If the missionary has no sense of belonging to any particular place, mission from *everywhere* becomes mission from *nowhere*. Rootlessness cannot sustain cross-cultural mission after Christendom."[170] This witness of welcome-and-embrace is exemplified in the book of Acts as Jewish followers of Jesus maintain their cultural and ethnic distinctives even as they begin to recognize that Jesus accepts the nations with their own cultural and ethnic distinctives. The Gentiles can stay rooted to their people and their land even as they choose to join this new multiethnic community of faith.

A final point here about the Great Commission relates to Christ's instructions to go out to the nations. "Nations" here is a complex entity: a communal grouping tied to a culture and landscape(s), a collective of individuals with their own agency, and a collective political entity. Jesus' words do encompass the idea of individual encounter with the gospel to bring about repentance, but it is a mistake to read his words as relating solely to individuals, as evangelism and mission are so often envisioned. The Great Commission is also about societal witness and communal transformation. Importantly, participating in God's work with the nations no longer involves gathering the nations to one place but is now a going out to the nations. In the Hebrew Bible, there are several visions of the nations coming before God for judgment (Dan 7:13-14), or the nations coming before God in Jerusalem as gifts of tribute (Is 66:19-20). These visions are revised and reimagined by Jesus. This is because the person of Christ has been given authority, because the Holy Spirit is uniquely present in creation (Mt 3:16), and because God is uniquely present in Christ. This is how God is with us (Mt 1:23). The temple's functioning has ceased (Mt 27:51) and will come to its end (Mt 24). The Jesus community is now decentralized from Jerusalem. Any hegemonic effort to gather to one location—and by extension to gather to one way of being, one worldview, one expression, or one creed crafted by a later church council—works against the reality that there is no central location for gathering in order to encounter Creator and follow Jesus as Lord. The Great Commission's exhortation to go out is not in order to gather back. Instead, it

[168]See Elaine Enns and Ched Myers, *Healing Haunted Histories: A Settler Discipleship of Decolonization* (Eugene, OR: Cascade Books, 2021).

[169]Carmen Rae Lansdowne, "Bearing Witness: Wearing a Broken Indigene Heart on the Sleeve of the Missio Dei" (PhD diss., Graduate Theological Union, 2016), 219-20, emphasis original.

[170]Friesen, "Great Commission," 32.

re-places the peoples of God into the communities and lands to which they belong, enabling them to encounter "God with us" in their own place and in the life, teachings, death, and resurrection of the Christ. The presence of Jesus will be wherever we are and as whoever we are (Mt 28:20).

SELECTED BIBLIOGRAPHY

Aldred, Ray. "An Alternative Starting Place for an Indigenous Theology." PhD diss., Toronto School of Theology, 2020.

———. "The Land, Treaty, and Spirituality: Communal Identity Inclusive of Land." *Journal of NAIITS* 18 (2019): 1-17.

Allison, Dale C. "Matthew's First Two Words." In *Studies in Matthew: Interpretation Past and Present*, 157-62. Grand Rapids, MI: Baker, 2006.

———. *Studies in Matthew: Interpretation Past and Present*. Grand Rapids, MI: Baker, 2006.

Anderson, G. P. "Parables." In *Dictionary of Jesus and the Gospels*, 2nd ed., 651-53. Downers Grove, IL: InterVarsity Press, 2013.

Apetagon, Byron. *Norway House Anthology: Stories of the Elders*. Vol. 1. Winnipeg: Frontier School Division, 1991.

Bantu, Vince L. "Early Christian Foundations for Indigenous Theological Self-Determination." *Journal of NAIITS* 15 (2017): 45-50.

Barclay, John M. G. *Paul and the Gift*. Grand Rapids, MI: Eerdmans, 2015.

Baxter, Wayne S. "Healing and the 'Son of David': Matthew's Warrant." *NovT* 48 (2006): 36-50.

Bernier, Jonathan. *Rethinking the Dates of the New Testament: The Evidence for Early Composition*. Grand Rapids, MI: Baker Academic, 2022.

Bird, Michael F. *Jesus and The Origins of The Gentile Mission*. LNTS 331. New York: T&T Clark, 2006.

Black Elk and John G. Neihardt. *Black Elk Speaks: The Complete Edition*. Lincoln: University of Nebraska Press, 2014.

Brokenleg, Martin. "Church—*Wocekiye Okolakiciye*: A Lakota Experience of the Church." In *Coming Full Circle: Constructing Native Christian Theology*, edited by Steven Charleston and Elaine A. Robinson, 133-49. Minneapolis: Fortress, 2015.

———. "Circles of Courage." *Journal of NAIITS* 18 (2020): 1-10.

Brueggemann, Walter. *The Land: Place as Gift, Promise, and Challenge in Biblical Faith*. 2nd ed. Overtures to Biblical Theology. Minneapolis: Fortress, 2002.

Bryan, Liz. *The Buffalo People: Prehistoric Archaeology on the Canadian Plains*. Edmonton, AB: University of Alberta Press, 1991.

Burkhart, Brian Yazzie. "What Coyote and Thales Can Teach Us: An Outline of American Indian Epistemology." In *American Indian Thought: Philosophical Essays*, edited by Anne Waters, 15-26. Malden, MA: Wiley-Blackwell, 2004.

Carter, Warren. "Matthean Christology in Roman Imperial Key: Matthew 1:1." In *The Gospel of Matthew in Its Roman Imperial Context*, edited by John K. Riches and David C. Sim, 143-65. JSNTSup 276. New York: T&T Clark, 2005.

———. *Matthew and Empire: Initial Explorations*. Harrisburg, PA: Trinity Press International, 2001.

———. "Matthew and the Gentiles: Individual Conversion and/or Systemic Transformation?" *JSNT* 26 (2004): 259-82.

———. *Matthew and the Margins: A Socio-political and Religious Reading*. JSNTSup 204. Sheffield: Sheffield Academic, 2003.

Charleston, Steven. *The Four Vision Quests of Jesus*. New York: Morehouse, 2015.

Charleston, Steven, and Elaine A. Robinson, eds. *Coming Full Circle: Constructing Native Christian Theology*. Minneapolis: Fortress, 2015.

Church, Casey. *Holy Smoke: The Contextual Use of Native American Ritual and Ceremony*. Cleveland, TN: Cherohala, 2017.

Clark-Soles, Jaime. *Women in the Bible*. Louisville, KY: Westminster John Knox, 2020.

Cooper, John W. *Panentheism, the Other God of the Philosophers: From Plato to the Present*. Grand Rapids, MI: Baker Academic, 2006.

Costello, Damian. *Black Elk: Colonialism and Lakota Catholicism*. Maryknoll, NY: Orbis Books, 2005.

———. "Black Elk's Vision of Waníkiya: The Ghost Dance, Catholic Sacraments, and Lakota Ontology." *Journal of NAIITS* 16 (2018): 40-56.

Crossley, James G. *The Date of Mark's Gospel: Insight from the Law in Earliest Christianity*. New York: T&T Clark, 2004.

Davies, W. D., and Dale C. Allison. *Matthew 1–7*. International Critical Commentary 1. New York: T&T Clark, 1988.

Davis, Kate Rae, and Richard Twiss. "Dancing Prayers: An Interview with Richard Twiss." *The Other Journal: An Intersection of Theology & Culture* 21 (2012): n.p. www.theotherjournal.com/2012/12/10/dancing-prayers-an-interview-with-richard-twiss/.

Deloria, Ella. "The Sun Dance of the Oglala Sioux." *The Journal of American Folklore* 42 (1929): 354-413.

Deloria, Vine, Jr. *The World We Used to Live In: Remembering the Powers of the Medicine Men*. Golden, CO: Fulcrum, 2006.

Enns, Elaine, and Ched Myers. *Healing Haunted Histories: A Settler Discipleship of Decolonization*. Eugene, OR: Cascade Books, 2021.

Esler, Philip F. "The Righteousness of Joseph: Interpreting Matt 1.18-25 in Light of Judean Legal Papyri." *NTS* 68 (2022): 326-43.

Evans, Craig A. *Matthew*. New Cambridge Bible Commentary. New York: Cambridge University Press, 2011.

Fejo, Wali. "The Voice of the Earth: An Indigenous Reading Of Genesis 9." In *Earth Story in Genesis*, edited by Norman C. Habel and Shirley Wurst, 140-46. The Earth Bible 2. New York: Sheffield Academic, 2000.

France, Richard F. *The Gospel of Matthew*. NICNT. Grand Rapids, MI: Eerdmans, 2007.

Fretheim, Terence E. *God and World in the Old Testament: A Relational Theology of Creation*. Nashville: Abingdon, 2010.

Friesen, Katerina. "The Great Commission: Watershed Conquest or Watershed Discipleship." In *Watershed Discipleship: Reinhabiting Bioregional Faith and Practice*, edited by Ched Myers, 26-41. Eugene, OR: Cascade Books, 2016.

Green, Gene L. "The Death of Mission: Rethinking the Great Commission." *Journal of NAIITS* 12 (2014): 81-110.

Gundry, Robert H. *Matthew: A Commentary on His Handbook for a Mixed Church Under Persecution*. 2nd ed. Grand Rapids, MI: Eerdmans, 1994.

Gurtner, Daniel M. *The Torn Veil: Matthew's Exposition of the Death of Jesus*. SNTSMS 139. New York: Cambridge University Press, 2007.

Hagner, Donald A. *Matthew*. 2 vols. Word Biblical Commentary 33A-B. Dallas: Word Books, 1993.

Hall-Smith, Beverley Moana. "Whakapapa (Genealogy), a Hermeneutical Framework for Reading Biblical texts: A Māori Woman Encounters Rape and Violence in Judges 19–21." PhD diss., Flinders University, 2017.

Hanson, Kenneth C. "The Galilean Fishing Economy and the Jesus Tradition." *Biblical Theology Bulletin* 27 (1997): 99-111.

Hascall, John S. "The Sacred Circle: Native American Liturgy." In *Native and Christian: Indigenous Voices on Religious Identity in the United States and Canada*, edited by James Treat, 179-83. New York: Routledge, 1996.

Heart, Bear. *The Wind Is My Mother: The Life and Teachings of a Native American Shaman*. New York: Berkley, 1998.

Hengel, Martin. *The Four Gospels and the One Gospel of Jesus Christ: An Investigation of the Collection and Origin of the Canonical Gospels*. Harrisburg, PA: Trinity Press International, 2000.

Holler, Clyde. *Black Elk's Religion: The Sun Dance and Lakota Catholicism*. Syracuse, NY: Syracuse University Press, 1995.

Hood, Jason B. "Matthew 23–25: The Extent of Jesus' Fifth Discourse." *JBL* 128 (2009), 527-43.

———. *The Messiah, His Brothers, and the Nations:(Matthew 1.1-17)*. LNTS 441. London: T&T Clark, 2011.

Irwin, Lee. *The Dream Seekers: Native American Visionary Traditions of the Great Plains*. Norman: University of Oklahoma Press, 1996.

Jeffers, James S. *The Greco-Roman World of the New Testament Era: Exploring the Background of Early Christianity*. Downers Grove, IL: InterVarsity Press, 1999.

Joerstad, Mari. *The Hebrew Bible and Environmental Ethics: Humans, Non-humans, and the Living Landscape*. Cambridge: Cambridge University Press, 2019.

Johnson, Elizabeth A. *Creation and the Cross: The Mercy of God for a Planet in Peril*. Maryknoll, NY: Orbis Books, 2018.

Kapolyo, Joe. "Matthew." Pages 1131-96 in *Africa Bible Commentary*, edited by Tokunboh Adeyemo. Grand Rapids, MI: Zondervan, 2006.

Keener, Craig S. "Adultery, Divorce." In *Dictionary of New Testament Background*, ed. Craig A. Evans and Stanley E. Porter, 6-16. Downers Grove, IL: InterVarsity Press, 2000.

———. *The Gospel of Matthew: A Socio-rhetorical Commentary*. Grand Rapids, MI: Eerdmans, 2009.

———. *Miracles: The Credibility of the New Testament Accounts*. Grand Rapids, MI: Baker, 2011.

———. "The Unridden Donkey Colt: Mark 11:2 in Light of Equine Development and Pedagogy." *BBR* 32 (2022): 17-40.

Keeney, Bradford. *Shamanic Christianity: The Direct Experience of Mystical Communion*. Rochester, VT: Destiny Books, 2006.

Kidwell, Clara Sue, Homer Noley, George E. Tinker, and Jace Weaver. *A Native American Theology*. Maryknoll, NY: Orbis Books, 2001.

Kimmerer, Robin Wall. *Braiding Sweetgrass: Indigenous Wisdom, Scientific Knowledge and the Teachings of Plants*. Minneapolis: Milkweed Editions, 2013.

Lansdowne, Carmen Rae. "Bearing Witness: Wearing a Broken Indigene Heart on the Sleeve of the Missio Dei." PhD diss., Graduate Theological Union, 2016.

Las Casas, Bartolomé de. *In Defense of the Indians*. Translated by Stafford Poole. DeKalb: Northern Illinois University Press, 1992.

LeBlanc, Terry. "Toward an Indigenous Eschatology: Caution, Circle Ahead." In *Indigenous People and the Christian Faith: A New Way Forward*, edited by William H. U. Anderson and Charles Muskego, 229-46. Wilmington, DE: Vernon, 2020.

LeBlanc, Terry, and Jeanine LeBlanc. "Liberation: Self and Community in Relationship." In *Evangelical Theologies of Liberation and Justice*, edited by Mae Elise Cannon and Andrea Smith, 170-91. Downers Grove, IL: IVP Academic, 2019.

Levine, Amy-Jill. "Matthew." In *Women's Bible Commentary*, edited by Carol A. Newsom, Sharon H. Ringe, and Jacqueline E. Lapsley, 465-77. Louisville, KY: Westminster John Knox, 2012.

Lim, Eunyung. *Entering God's Kingdom (Not) like a Little Child: Images of the Child in Matthew, 1 Corinthians, and Thomas*. Beihefte zur Zeitschrift für die neutestamentliche Wissenschaft 243. Berlin: de Gruyter, 2021.

Luz, Ulrich. *Matthew 1–7*. Translated by James E. Crouch. 3 vols. Hermeneia 61A. Minneapolis: Augsburg, 2007.

Mahuika, Nēpia. "A Brief History of Whakapapa: Māori Approaches to Genealogy." *Genealogy* 3 (2019): 1-13.

Meier, John P. *Mentor, Message, and Miracles*. Vol. 2 of *A Marginal Jew: Rethinking the Historical Jesus*. New York: Anchor Bible, 1994.

Mniyo, Samuel I., Robert Goodvoice, and Dan Beveridge. *The Red Road and Other Narratives of the Dakota Sioux*. Lincoln: University of Nebraska Press, 2020.

Montague, George T. *Companion God: A Cross-cultural Commentary on the Gospel of Matthew*. Rev. ed. New York: Paulist Press, 2010.

Moscicke, Hans M. "Jesus, Barabbas, and the Crowd as Figures in Matthew's Day of Atonement Typology (Matthew 27:15–26)." *JBL* 139 (2020): 125-53.

Muddiman, John. "Fasting." In *Anchor Bible Dictionary*, edited by David Noel Freedman, 2:773-66. New York: Doubleday, 1992.

Myers, Ched. *Binding the Strong Man: A Political Reading of Mark's Story of Jesus*. 20th anniversary ed. Maryknoll, NY: Orbis Books, 2008.

Myers, Ched, and Elaine Enns. *Ambassadors of Reconciliation*. Vol. 1, *New Testament Reflections on Restorative Justice and Peacemaking*. Maryknoll, NY: Orbis Books, 2009.

Obomsawin, Alanis. "Is the Crown at War with Us?" 2002. www.nfb.ca/film/is_the_crown_at_war_with_us/.

Parker, F. "The Terms 'Angel' and 'Spirit' in Acts 23,8." *Biblica* 84 (2003): 344-65.

Peeler, Amy. *Women and the Gender of God*. Grand Rapids, MI: Eerdmans, 2022.

Pennington, Jonathan T. *Heaven and Earth in the Gospel of Matthew*. NovTSup 126. Boston: Brill, 2007.

———. *The Sermon on the Mount and Human Flourishing: A Theological Commentary*. Grand Rapids, MI: Baker Academic, 2017.

Peterson, Wendy L. "A Gifting of Sweetgrass: The Reclamation of Culture Movement and *NAIITS: An Indigenous Learning Community*." PhD diss., Asbury Theological Seminary, 2018.

Piotrowski, Nicholas G. *Matthew's New David at the End of Exile: A Socio-rhetorical Study of Scriptural Quotations*. NovTSup 170. Boston: Brill, 2016.

Porton, Gary G. "Sadducees." In *Dictionary of New Testament Background*, edited by Craig A. Evans and Stanley E. Porter, 1050-52. Downers Grove, IL: InterVarsity Press, 2000.

Posthumus, David C. "Transmitting Sacred Knowledge: Aspects of Historical and Contemporary Oglala Lakota Belief and Ritual." PhD diss., Indiana University, 2015.

Rand, Silas Tertius. *Legends of the Micmacs*. Wellesley Philological Publications. Cambridge, MA: Longmans, Green, 1894.

Riches, John K., and David C. Sim, eds. *The Gospel of Matthew in Its Roman Imperial Context*. New York: T&T Clark, 2005.

Riddle, A. D. "The Passover Pilgrimage from Jericho to Jerusalem: Jesus' Triumphal Entry." In *Lexham Geographic Commentary on the Gospels*, edited by Barry J. Beitzel and Kristopher A. Lyle, 395-407. Bellingham, WA: Lexham, 2017.

Robinson, John A. T. *Redating the New Testament*. Philadelphia: Westminster, 1976.

Seow, C. L. "Face פנים." In *Dictionary of Deities and Demons in the Bible*, edited by Karel van der Toorn, Bob Becking, and Pieter W. van der Horst, 2nd rev. ed., 322-25. Grand Rapids, MI: Eerdmans, 1999.

Sim, David C. "Rome in Matthew's Eschatology." In *The Gospel of Matthew in Its Roman Imperial Context*, edited by John K. Riches and David C. Sim, 91-106. JSNTSup 276. New York: &T Clark, 2005.

Simpson, Leanne Betasamosake. *As We Have Always Done: Indigenous Freedom Through Radical Resistance*. Minneapolis: University of Minnesota Press, 2017.

Smith, Mitzi J. *Womanist Sass and Talk Back: Social (In)Justice, Intersectionality, and Biblical Interpretation*. Eugene, OR: Cascade Books, 2018.

Smith, Mitzi J., and Yung Suk Kim. *Toward Decentering the New Testament: A Reintroduction*. Eugene, OR: Cascade Books, 2018.

Smith, Mitzi J., and Jayachitra Lalitha, eds. *Teaching All Nations: Interrogating the Matthean Great Commission*. Minneapolis: Fortress, 2014.

Snodgrass, Klyne. *Stories with Intent: A Comprehensive Guide to the Parables of Jesus*. Grand Rapids, MI: Eerdmans, 2008.

Stannard, David E. *American Holocaust: The Conquest of the New World*. New York: Oxford University Press, 1993.

Stanton, Graham N. *A Gospel for a New People: Studies in Matthew*. London: T&T Clark, 1992.

Treat, James, ed. *Native and Christian: Indigenous Voices on Religious Identity in the United States and Canada*. New York: Routledge, 1996.

Turner, David L. *Matthew*. Baker Exegetical Commentary on the New Testament. Grand Rapids, MI: Baker, 2008.

Twiss, Richard. *One Church, Many Tribes: Following Jesus the Way God Made You*. Minneapolis: Chosen, 2000.

———. *Rescuing the Gospel from the Cowboys: A Native American Expression of the Jesus Way*. Downers Grove, IL: InterVarsity Press, 2015.

Twiss, Richard, Terry LeBlanc, and Adrian Jacobs. "Culture, Christian Faith and Error." *Journal of NAIITS* 1 (2003): 5-35.

Uytanlet, Samson L., and Kiem-Kiok Kwa. *Matthew: A Pastoral and Contextual Commentary*. Asia Bible Commentary Series. Carlisle, UK: Langham Global Library, 2017.

Viola, Frank, and George Barna. *Pagan Christianity? Exploring the Roots of Our Church Practices*. Carol Stream, IL: Tyndale House, 2010.

Wainwright, Elaine M. "A Transformative Struggle Towards the Divine Dream: An Ecofeminist Reading of Matthew 11." In *Readings from the Perspective of Earth*, edited by Norman C. Habel, 162-74. The Earth Bible 1. Sheffield: Sheffield Academic, 2000.

Wallace, Mark I. *Finding God in the Singing River: Christianity, Spirit, Nature*. Minneapolis: Fortress, 2005.

———. *When God Was a Bird: Christianity, Animism, and the Re-enchantment of the World*. Groundworks: Ecological Issues in Philosophy and Theology. New York: Fordham University Press, 2018.

Warrior, Robert Alan. "Canaanites, Cowboys, and Indians: Deliverance, Conquest, and Liberation Theology Today." In *Native and Christian: Indigenous Voices on Religious Identity in the United States and Canada*, edited by James Treat, 93-104. New York: Routledge, 1996.

Weaver, Dorothy Jean. "'Thus You Will Know Them by Their Fruits': The Roman Characters of the Gospel of Matthew." In *The Gospel of Matthew in Its Roman Imperial Context*, edited by John K. Riches and David C. Sim, 107-27. JSNTSup 276. New York: T&T Clark, 2005.

Westman, Tony, Shelah Reljic, and Peter Jones. "Salmon People." 2015. www.nfb.ca/film/salmon_people/.

Woodley, Randy S. "The Harmony Way: Integrating Indigenous Values Within Native North American Theology and Mission." PhD diss., Asbury Theological Seminary, 2010.

———. *Shalom and the Community of Creation: An Indigenous Vision*. Prophetic Christianity. Grand Rapids, MI: Eerdmans, 2012.

Wright, N. T. *The New Testament and the People of God*. Christian Origins and the Question of God 1. Minneapolis: Fortress, 1992.

———. *The Resurrection of the Son of God*. Christian Origins and the Question of God 3. London: SPCK, 2003.

Zacharias, H. Daniel. "The Land Takes Care of Us: Recovering Creator's Relational Design." In *The Land: Majority World and Minoritized Theologies of Land*, edited by K. K. Yeo and Gene L. Green, 69-97. Eugene, OR: Cascade, 2020.

———. *Matthew's Presentation of the Son of David: Davidic Tradition and Typology in the Gospel of Matthew*. London: T&T Clark, 2017.

Zinga, Dawn, and Sandra Styres. "Pedagogy of the Land: Tensions, Challenges, and Contradictions." *First Nations Perspectives* 4 (2011): 59-83.

Zolbrod, Paul. *Diné Bahane': The Navajo Creation Story*. Albuquerque: University of New Mexico Press, 1987.

GOSPEL OF MARK

Kay Higuera Smith

INTRODUCTION

Mark's Gospel is no history according to the norms of contemporary historiographers. But that was not Mark's goal. Mark tells us a story about Jesus and points to a way forward for the early followers of Jesus. Yet the order of events is sometimes difficult to square with the other Gospels. What, then, was Mark's goal? We might find a hint in the word *gospel*, which means, literally, "good news." In the historical context in which it was written, it appears as an ironic response to empire. The Caesars had used the phrase "good news" to describe their own economy. Mark, however, uses the language of empire with irony in order to disrupt empire. Jesus in Mark announces a different economy—one that the God of Israel is establishing as an alternate way of being to the powers and promises of Rome. This is truly the "good news," to which Caesar can offer only a grotesque mimicry.

Place of writing. Most argue that Mark was written from Rome. However, there is a counterargument that it was written from Galilee, a region north of Samaria and Judea, in the lands populated both by those who called themselves the people of Israel and by Syrian and eastern subjects of the empire.[1] Either setting is possible; however, given that the Gospel shows a preference for rural rather than urban life, I will assume here that it was set in Galilee and reflects the perspectives of some early Galilean rural followers of Jesus.

Mark's Gospel does not just reflect a regional dispute, nor can we reduce it to a political tug-of-war. In the ancient world, one could not separate "religion" and "politics." For the people of Israel who treasured the words of the Torah, Writings, and Prophets (known to Christians as the Old Testament and to contemporary Jews as the Tanakh), God's regency could not be separated from how humans structured and organized themselves on earth.[2]

The theme of how humans structure themselves in the two kingdoms is key for this Gospel writer. We must read this Gospel through the lens of first-century hearers to appreciate this perspective. Many non-Westerners, or non-Anglo-Europeans, today have an easier time comprehending this perspective because they may have been raised in a similar environment, in which the spheres of life—family—*familia*—and village or people are not separated in how people understand their own identities.

Time of writing. It is generally agreed that Mark's Gospel was written after 70 CE, around the same time as the destruction of Herod's

[1]See Adela Yarbro Collins and Harold W. Attridge, *Mark: A Commentary*, ed. Harold W. Attridge, Hermeneia (Minneapolis: Fortress, 2007), 8, where she argues that the internal evidence of the Gospel implies an eastern provenance where Aramaic was spoken, such as the region of the Galilee.

[2]Henceforth, I will refer to the collective writings of the Hebrew Bible, and/or its Greek translation, the Septuagint (abbreviated LXX), as the Tanakh in order to avoid the triumphalist implications of the phrase "Old Testament."

temple in Jerusalem. This dating is based on statements in Mark 13 that predict the destruction of the temple. An earlier date is certainly possible, given that Jewish historian Josephus mentions others prophesying the destruction of the temple (*J. W.* 4.3.2). A date at or near the beginning of the Jewish War, around 66–68 CE, is thus a more probable date. It reflects the persecutions that the early followers of Jesus would endure and the political upheavals caused by the Jewish War.[3]

MARK'S WORLD AND OUR WORLD

As more and more people from throughout the globe are gaining a voice in interpreting the Bible, we are beginning to experience a sea change in the assumptions being brought to the reading of Scripture. All of us come to Scripture with a set of assumptions that are borne out of our traditions, our life experiences, and our social and historical locations. For instance, many African Americans, because of their social memory of the tyranny of the slave system, read the story of the exodus from Egypt in light of that historical experience. Native American Bible readers, however, tend to read the exodus story very differently. My Native American Christian friends have shared with me the pain of hearing Anglo-European preachers compare them to the Canaanites, whose lands the Hebrews in Exodus were commissioned to conquer. For those White preachers, just as the Israelites were destined to conquer the Canaanites, so White Anglo-Europeans were destined by God to conquer Native Americans. An interpretation that is redemptive for one group is destructive for another. Assumptions based on historical and social memory, often unconsciously, shape the interpretations that make sense to us.

In this commentary on the Gospel of Mark, I am making my assumptions explicit as a Latina and Californiana, one whose identity has been shaped by *abuelos* and *abuelas*, *tíos* and *tías* telling stories at innumerable family gatherings that form my own social memory. My memories are shaped by notions of outsider status vis-à-vis the larger Anglo-European world of the rural California in which I grew up. As the elders told their stories, I heard of disenfranchisement, loss of land and properties, and inexorable efforts by Anglo-Europeans to reshape the geography, landscape, and history of my family's ancestral homeland. I also heard stories of our ancestors doing the same thing to the Native Americans in generations past. My *abuela* was philosophical. "We did it to the Native Americans; now the *gringos* are doing it to us," she would say. Boundaries were an issue. The elders maintained detailed genealogies of multiple generations in California. Yet they recognized that while our families had stayed in place, boundaries had shifted over us, offering us little voice in how those boundaries were framed. Thus, issues of justice, status, boundaries and borders, who has power and how power is wielded, land, food, and access to resources formed the urgent questions that dominated conversation among the adults as I grew into adulthood. These are the assumptions shaping the interpretations I bring to the text of Mark.

The people who first heard Mark read brought different sets of urgent questions based on their own social location and history. It is crucial that we attune ourselves to those urgent questions as well, as they will shape the meaning just as much, if not more so, than our own contemporary questions. Exegesis, or detailed analysis of the Bible, involves a careful and intuitive back and

[3]Collins and Attridge, *Mark*, 14, date the Gospel to sometime between 66 and 69 CE.

forth between these two sets of urgent questions—the ancient and contemporary.

History. In the first century, the regions about which Mark wrote were under provincial, colonial control by the Roman Empire. While the area is often referred to in contemporary literature as Palestine, that term did not develop until after the Second Jewish Revolt, in 135 CE. In Mark's time, these regions were called Judea, Samaria, Galilee, Idumea, and the Ten Cities of the Decapolis. The Northern Kingdom of ancient Israel had been conquered by Assyria in 722 BCE, while the Southern Kingdom, called Judah or Yehud, was utterly destroyed by the Babylonian Empire in 587/586 BCE, including its capital city, Jerusalem, and its temple, built by King David's son Solomon. Through these events, both the Northern and Southern Kingdoms, which were heirs to the biblical King David's united monarchy (ca. 1000 BCE), fell to the powers of multiple subsequent major empires.

Shortly after the Babylonians destroyed Jerusalem, the Persian Achaemenid Empire took control of the region, allowing the Yehudean elite, who had been taken captive to Babylon, to return to rebuild Jerusalem and the temple around 539/538 BCE. Thus began the building of what would be called the Second Temple, which lasted in some form until the time of the writing of Mark's Gospel. Achaemenid rule was harsh, as it levied heavy taxes to finance warfare against unending rebellions and insurrections.

In time, the region was conquered by Alexander of Macedonia in 330 BCE, and after his death, by the Ptolemaic and Greek/Seleucid successor empires. In 63 BCE it was conquered once more, this time by the Romans. This history of empire after empire ruling over the region is the historical context in which the Gospel of Mark was written. It was a period of rigid taxation and harsh policies, which led to multiple rebellions, none of which were successful. The most well-known rebellion by the Judean populace against Rome was the Jewish War, which lasted from 66–70 CE, at which time the Roman general Vespasian—by now emperor—and his son, Titus, brutally destroyed Jerusalem and the Second Temple, whose reconstruction had only just recently been completed.

This brief history highlights one of the most significant historical precursors to Mark's Gospel, which is the lengthy history of enslavement and oppression under one empire after another. First the Assyrian, then the Babylonian, followed by the Achaemenid, Ptolemaic, Greek-Seleucid, and Roman Empires imposed heavy taxes, diverted local resources, enslaved the populace, and at times forbade the practice of Israelite ancestral laws. In a period in which there was no concept of separation of religion and state, those who followed the Jerusalem temple cult experienced this oppression as an aberration that had to be corrected, by either violence or divine fiat.

Geography. In order to consider how to interpret Mark with regard to social identity, we must consider geography, economics, and other social institutions in addition to history. Geography shapes the social memory of various groups. The Galilee was where, according to Mark, Jesus' entire ministry was focused, with short forays into the regions of Syria to the north, the Decapolis to the southeast, and Galaunitis to the northeast. The Sea of Galilee, today called the Kinneret, was surrounded by a region which was several days' walk from Jerusalem. This distance contributed to an independence from Jerusalem that we see mirrored in Mark's Gospel. Moreover, Galilee's history was different from that of Jerusalem in the south. The Galilean region was conquered by the Assyrians in 733–732 BCE. It was part of the Northern Kingdom of Israel, whose primary city, Shomron (Samaria), was conquered in 722 BCE (see 2 Kings 15:29). According to tradition, the cities near Shomron were then repopulated with people from the nations around the empire, eroding the Israelite population (see 2 Kings 17:24). However, it appears that this did not occur in the Galilee, resulting in a consistent Israelite population there, albeit possibly a small one, at least until the time of the Israelite Hasmonean kings, who subsequently annexed Galilee as part of their Israelite/Jewish kingdom.[4]

Nevertheless, despite Galilee having a well-established Israelite/Jewish population, Herod Antipas, a client-ruler under Rome, established two major Hellenistic cities in Galilee during his reign, Sepphoris and Tiberias (4 BCE–39 CE). Strikingly, despite their proximity to the towns and villages to which Jesus traveled, we do not have a mention in any of our Gospels of either city. Given the imperial nature of these cities and their complicity in Herodian interests, our Gospels' distinct avoidance of them makes a political statement, distancing them from Herodian political interests. Geography, then, helps us understand that Mark's focus on Israelite Galilee alone and, as we will see, his association of Jerusalem with death would have communicated strong political as well as spatial interests.

Economics. Economically, Galilee in Mark's era was agricultural, marked by the presence of major landowners who lent the tillage of the land out to sharecroppers and poor tenant farmers. Under both Roman rule and the temple system, taxation was burdensome. For a small peasant farmer, it only took a drought or bad farming season to lose everything. This resulted in Galileans being more likely to disdain those associated with the empire and with the temple system as it was being operated. Here, those of us within Latinx cultural spaces can see that Mark's people also operated with concerns about how status was apportioned, who had the power to create boundaries and borders, and who controlled access to land, food, and resources, all within their concept of the justice of Israel's God.

All of these historical, geographic, and economic elements reinforce a social identity for Mark's people that shows them to have been independent, rural, somewhat detached from Jerusalem, and sharing a different social memory than the Judeans to the south while still having a strong Israelite/Jewish distinctiveness in their own right.

Roman state institutions, such as the military and a system of taxation and control of the land, dominated the region. In addition to these Roman state institutions, there were three ancient Israelite institutions that are central to understanding the Gospel of Mark and thus call for some sustained discussion. These are the institutions of temple, synagogue, and the system of biblical law. To be sure, these Israelite institutions, given the context of empire, necessarily also reflected Roman or Hellenistic values as well. Nevertheless, their unique roles in religion and society demand attention. Primary among these institutions was that of the temple system itself.

The temple: Site of the sacred. The Gospel of Mark represents a vigorous challenge to the

[4]On this, see 1 Macc 5:14-23; 11:63; 12:47; Josephus, *Ant.* 14.91. In 168 BCE, a family of priests, nicknamed the Maccabees and later more formally known as the Hasmoneans, formed a dynasty with significant self-rule under the Seleucid Empire. The Hasmoneans created a dynasty of priest-princes under the Seleucid dynasty.

temple of King Herod, a client-king under Rome, which was built during the time of Jesus. Too often, however, readers of the Gospel of Mark interpret Jesus' challenges to the Herodian temple in Mark as a challenge to Judaism or to Israelite religion in general. Nothing could be further from the truth. Rather, the challenge by Mark's Jesus was to Roman imperial power and social hierarchies precisely as they replaced the intrinsic symbolic power of the sanctuaries of Yahweh narrated in the Tanakh. For Mark, the challenge was to the Herodian temple's institutional power to define sacred space. It is crucial to understand this system to understand Mark's depiction of Jesus.

The temple was the central symbol of the Judaic systems of Mark's time. As such, it epitomized the category of sacred space. Mark's depiction of the temple makes sense only in the context of the temple's power and development over time as a symbol of the sacred.

THE TEMPLE SYSTEM AND MARK'S GOSPEL

The temple system that existed at the time of Jesus was the third structural system that had represented the sanctuary of Israel's God Yahweh. The first was the tabernacle described in Exodus 26, the second was Solomon's temple, and the final temple, called the Second Temple because it was a massive reconstruction of Solomon's temple rather than a new temple, was built by the Jewish/Idumean client-king of Rome, Herod. Each sanctuary contained symbols that represented an idealized conception of Israel's God and the social makeup of Israel's people. The symbols associated with Herod's temple represented a departure from those symbols associated with the tabernacle and the First Temple, and in these departures readers can see Mark's challenges to its authority to broker Yahweh's beneficence to the people of Israel and the nations.

The first sanctuary was the tabernacle, whose construction by Moses is detailed in Exodus 26, and had two important characteristics: inclusivity and mobility.[a] Male and female Israelites, those who had physical disabilities, and even certain people from the nations were invited into its courts.[b] The tabernacle, as a symbolic world, marked the extension of the sacred in an outward direction, from a divine center out to the people of Israel and beyond.[c] Its courts were open to women, willing participants from most nations, and those with blemishes or who were unable to walk or see.

The tabernacle was also portable. It was constructed so that it could be taken down and transported with the Israelites as they traveled through the wilderness. Thus, it represented a migratory model where all of Israel interacted with the sacred. Where the people went, the realm of the sacred accompanied them. Its symbolic space conveyed fluidity, motility, and ease of access to the sacred.

The second sanctuary was the tenth-century BCE temple built by Solomon, son and successor of King David, which is referred to as the First Temple. While taking on greater administrative responsibility than the tabernacle, Solomon's temple still offered open access to all of the people of Israel, although that access may have begun to exclude those unable to walk or see.[d] Its courts were still open to women and willing participants from the nations, however. Nevertheless, because it was a permanent building, it now shifted the value system from fluidity to the notion of a fixed sacred center.

Solomon's temple stood in various forms of repair and disrepair until its destruction by the Babylonians in 586 BCE (see 2 Chron 36:14-21). It was rebuilt under the Persian emperor Cyrus around 515 BCE. This rebuilt structure was called the Second Temple and is our third sanctuary, or structural system. It also endured various stages of decay and reconstruction until Herod undertook his massive reconstruction around 20 BCE.

With Herod's temple came architectural and symbolic developments that shifted away from those of the tabernacle and First Temple. The symbols inscribed in the architecture of Herod's rebuilt Second Temple mirrored Roman imperial power rather than the symbolic power of inclusion or mobility marked by the previous sanctuaries.[e] Moreover, Herod's temple inscribed a social hierarchy that marginalized not only the nations but now also the women of Israel and, much more likely, those with disabilities, who, according to Leviticus 21:16-24, had previously received access to the sacred courts.[f] As such, it apportioned out the sacred in concentric circles to smaller and smaller groups, excluding many who once had access. In his construction projects, Herod followed the architectural conventions of imperial Rome. It was the salient architecture and symbols of Rome rather than of the tabernacle or the First Temple that Herod inscribed in the Second Temple.

Mark responds harshly to precisely this social imaginary inscribed in Herod's temple. Given the history of tabernacle and temple in Israel, however, astute readers will recognize that it is not Jewish or Israelite symbols that Mark rejects; it is Roman imperial symbols inscribed in the very architecture of a sanctuary built for Israel's God.

---

[a]The tabernacle largely conformed to ancient Near Eastern altars and places of sacrifice. See Mark K. George, *Israel's Tabernacle as Social Space* (Atlanta: Society of Biblical Literature, 2009), 60.

[b]Only priests, however, could access its inner tent. On the inclusion of those with certain disabilities, see Lev 21:16-24. Those who fell into the categories of "the lame and the blind" were free to enter within the boundaries of the tabernacle courts and were considered pure. However, if a priest suffered any of the conditions, he was not allowed to make sacrifice for the people. He could, on the other hand, along with the other priests, partake of the sacrifices as food and thus was considered pure (Lev 21:22); see also George, *Israel's Tabernacle*, 118. The only Israelites excluded from the temple were those who had a skin disease, had mutilated genitalia, or were born of an illicit marital union (Lev 13:2-23; Deut 23:1-2). Jacob Milgrom notes that those males among the nations willing to undergo circumcision also could participate in the temple cult if they chose (Ex 12:48-49; Num 9:13-14; see also Lev 19:34). This leaves open the likelihood that females from among the nations also enjoyed full participation, as circumcision is listed as the only entrance rite. It is important to clarify, though, that while the circumcised *gerim*, or non-Israelites, were able to perform certain commandments, such as eating the paschal sacrifice, they were not bound by them, leaving them in a class by themselves. Nevertheless, Milgrom plainly references "the biblical *gēr*, who could enter the Tabernacle court to offer his sacrifices." See Milgrom, *Leviticus 17–22: A New Translation with Introduction and Commentary*, AB (New York: Doubleday, 2000), 1501. Milgrom also makes a distinction between performative and prohibitive commands, such as purification requirements (1496-99). The *gerim*, like the Israelites, were bound by those prohibitive purification requirements but not the performative ones (Lev 22:17-25; Num 15:14-16). Among the people of the nations, it appears that Ammonites, Moabites, and first- and second-generation Egyptians and Edomites also were not included in the assembly of the Lord (Deut 23:1-8). This is striking, as the list of nations limits itself only to a few tribal neighbors. There appears to be no other exclusion of people from the nations who willingly chose to bring offerings.

[c]George claims that while scholars disagree as to whether people from the nations were able to access the courts of the tabernacle, the specific prohibitions against the people of Ammon, Moab, Egypt, and Edom imply that those from other tribal groups indeed were able to gain access (*Israel's Tabernacle*, 126n127, following Jacob Milgrom, *Leviticus 1–16: A New Translation with Introduction and Commentary* [New York: Doubleday, 1991]). This assumes, however, that being included in the assembly of the Lord also implied access to the temple courts.

[d]Second Samuel 5:8 refers to David's hatred of the "lame and the blind," possibly because they had been used to taunt him (2 Sam 5:6). The narrator adds, "Therefore it is said, 'The blind and the lame shall not come into the house'" (2 Sam 5:8). The source of this saying is not known; however, it may refer to a tradition of excluding "the blind and the lame" from the sanctuary, which may have developed by the time of the writing of 2 Samuel. Anthony R. Ceresko identifies several scholars who interpret the text to imply a later development in temple history. See Ceresko, "The Identity of 'the Blind and the Lame' (*iwwer upiseah*) in 2 Samuel 5:8b," *CBQ* 63, no. 1 (January 2001): 27. Ultimately, he rejects this option in favor of the prohibition being interpreted as against entering David's own palace. However, Craig Evans shows that the targumic

tradition indeed interpreted the "house" of 2 Sam 5:8 to be the temple itself. See Evans, "A Note on Targum 2 Samuel 5.8 and Jesus' Ministry to the 'Maimed, Halt, and Blind,'" *Journal for the Study of the Pseudepigrapha* 15 (April 1997): 79. If this is the case, then the previous restriction excluding those with blemishes from offering sacrifices as priests by the time of the writing of 2 Samuel may have extended to a refusal of access to the temple courts for all who were lame or blind or had a blemish (Lev 21:16-24).

[e]David Jacobson, "Herod's Roman Temple," *Biblical Archaeology Review* 28, no. 2 (2002): 27. The Temple Mount was expanded far beyond the boundaries of the previous temple systems. Massive steps led progressively through each gate, opening into more and more exclusive courts. The porticoes aligned with the market scheme of Roman porticoes in general, a fortress was added, and storehouses for the economic wealth of Israel were expanded.

[f]See Evans, "Note on Targum 2 Samuel 5.8," where he recounts how regulations limiting participation for those with observable physical disabilities had become well developed by the time of the writing of the Qumran Dead Sea Scrolls as well as the Aramaic Targums, with the Targums going so far as translating "the blind and the lame" from 2 Sam 5:8 as "the sinners and the guilty" (79). This testifies to a tradition that assigned blame to those with disabilities (on this, see Jn 9:2). Evans comments: "Implicit is the assumption that the sick and impoverished are seen as the non-elect" (80). 1QSa 2:5b-6 seems to support such a development in its own community, stating, "No man with a physical handicap—crippled in both legs or hands, lame, blind, deaf, dumb, or possessed of a physical blemish in his flesh . . . may en[ter] to take place in the congregation of the m[e]n of reputation." See Michael Wise, Martin Abegg, and Edward Cook, eds. and trans., *The Dead Sea Scrolls: A New English Translation* (New York: HarperCollins, 2009); see also 1QM 7:4-5; 11Q19 45:12-13; 11Q20 12:6; 1QSa 2:5-8. Mishnah Hagigah 1 lists a taxonomy of those not required to fulfill the commandments of Israelites, including sacrificing in the temple, and it includes "a deaf-mute, an imbecile, and a minor; and a *tumtum* [intersex], and a hermaphrodite, and women, and slaves who are not emancipated; and the lame, and the blind, and the sick, and the old, and one who is unable to ascend to Jerusalem on his own legs." All of these developments point to practices by the time of Mark's writing that ranged from full exclusion of those with disabilities to limited expectations of participation of the full polity of Israel.

In response to the social imaginary reflected in the Herodian temple, Mark rejects the temple's claims to be a site of the sacred and locates the sacred in the person of Jesus instead. For Mark, the Herodian temple in Jerusalem has been irredeemably compromised. Its chief priests, deemed to possess the highest status as sculpted into the temple architecture, are corrupt and depraved. Sacred space is not being manifested in the temple. It is, however, manifested in the body of Jesus. Sacred space cannot be brokered by wealthy priests, installed and sustained by the Roman Empire. But it is brokered by Jesus as God's only Son. For this reason, Mark appears to look back to the symbolic model of the tabernacle of Exodus 26 and its geographic fluidity and social expansiveness for comprehending the sacred. He locates the sacred in unexpected places, such as in Galilee and in rural, inconsequential locations where Jesus is present. Jesus, not the scribes and lawyers from Jerusalem, is the authoritative broker of the sacred. Mark's critique, then, is not of Israelite tradition in general but of the way that the Herodian temple and its retainers do not reflect what Mark portrays as legitimate Israelite norms and values. Mark's Gospel does not reject the category of sacred space; it redirects it.

The synagogue. The second Israelite/Jewish institution we must understand is the ancient synagogue, a site that represented nonaligned territory for Mark. We cannot project what we know about contemporary rabbinic Jewish synagogues onto the ancient Mediterranean world, for they are distinct institutions. Instead, we can imagine what could almost be described as a secular role for the ancient synagogues. The word *synagogē* in Greek means simply "a gathering place." It is likely that ancient synagogues were used as much for the village elders to apprise their neighbors of information about crops, water conditions, or market days as for the purposes of reading and discussing the Torah, or Pentateuch, of Moses.

THE SYNAGOGUE

Synagogues were small, localized gathering places and not formally part of, or necessary for, the operation of the temple cult. Therefore, while Mark often challenged the claims by the temple system to constitute sacred space, readers do not see this challenge of synagogue spaces. They are neutral territory for Mark.

Mark presents Jesus as teaching or healing in the synagogue in Capernaum (Mk 1:21; 3:1) and elsewhere in the Galilee (Mk 1:39; 5:22). To be sure, when Jesus taught in the synagogue in his hometown of Nazareth, he was not well received (Mk 6). But that was not because the institution of the synagogue rejected him. Rather, it was because he was in his hometown (more on that later). Nevertheless, Jesus in Mark prophesied that the institution of the synagogue would turn against his followers in the future (Mk 13:9). But that may just reflect the more secular function of synagogues in general.

Mark's Gospel does not represent a rejection of Jewishness or Judaism or its institutions, such as the synagogue. Rather, the synagogue is often the site of an inner-Judaic dispute between Jesus and other authoritative groups as to what constitutes the people of God, who has the authority to define the people of God and act as broker of the system's beneficence, and what is the most appropriate social imaginary in light of Israel's biblical tradition to determine the nature of the people of God. Mark's Gospel will take up and answer these disputes by claiming that Jesus is the authoritative interpreter of the biblical tradition and broker of God's beneficence. The synagogue itself is neutral territory in which the disputes occur.

Biblical law. The third institution crucial to understanding Mark's Gospel is the system of biblical law that operated in Mark's and Jesus' day. Mark's Jesus often gets into challenge-and-response disputes with those who claim to be arbiters of biblical law. Biblical law, which draws from the Torah, has always required interpretation over time, as does any legal system. As such, the disputes in Mark's Gospel are not about its authority but about its interpretation. By Mark's day, a tradition of Israelite sages and legal experts had developed to carry out careful interpretation. We will discover that, when biblical law is discussed in Mark, the issue is never its validity; the issue is how to interpret it.

LAWYERS, SCRIBES, PRIESTS

In the Second Temple period, various groups arose whose training was in the interpretation of biblical law. Among these, three important groups are mentioned in Mark's Gospel. One of these groups was the lawyers, whose task was to interpret biblical law for the people of their time. Another group comprised scribes. Some ancient scribes, due to their literary skills and their intimate knowledge of the biblical books, which they had learned while painstakingly copying scrolls, also engaged in biblical interpretation and in communicating biblical regulations to the populace. Finally, priests often became adept at biblical interpretation because of the importance of precise application of the biblical injunctions regarding carrying out the temple cult. Because each of these groups makes an appearance in Mark's Gospel, it is important to understand how they functioned for Mark. It should be no surprise that differing collections of scribes, lawyers, and priests would coalesce around different interpretational streams of the biblical books. Mark's disputes with these groups, then, were not disputes of an outsider to the Judaic systems of the day. Rather the variety of disputes shows a lively and energetic set of inner-Judaic disagreements occurring in the first century, to which Mark's Jesus contributes.

QUMRAN COVENANTERS

Beside Mark's people, another group that entered into disputes with the scribes, lawyers, and priests was the Qumran covenanters, who wrote and transcribed the Dead Sea Scrolls and lived roughly contemporaneously with Jesus and Mark. Like Mark, they rejected the Herodian temple and the priestly families that controlled it, even though they themselves were priests. Like Mark, they still considered themselves Israelites and Jews. Their critique was not of the notion of the temple as such. Instead, for them, it was the current administrators of the temple whom they portrayed as defiling it. Because of this, the covenanters refused to enter Herod's temple. They are not present in the Gospels, but their writings have confirmed that it was indeed possible to condemn the Herodian temple aggressively while maintaining a covenant commitment to the people of Israel and to sacred space centered in a temple cult. In this sense, our knowledge of the Qumran covenanters comes to bear in understanding Mark. The Qumran Covenanters give a second example, along with the Jewish followers of Jesus, of an Israelite group faithful to the promises of Israel but also critical of the retainers of the temple system as it then operated. This will be the interpretive lens through which we interpret Mark as well.

PHARISEES AND SADDUCEES

Another interpretive circle, which is well represented in this Gospel, is the Pharisees. In most cases, Mark writes of them as adversaries to Jesus. However, readers must keep in mind that, in many ways, they shared more interpretive assumptions about the Bible with Mark's Jesus than did other interpreting communities of the era. In Mark, Jesus' disputes with the Pharisees represent inner-Judaic conflicts rather than a rejection of Judaic norms and practices.

One final interpretive circle that bears mention is the Sadducees. Mark only mentions them once, describing them as a group that denied the doctrine of the resurrection from the dead (Mk 12:18). While Mark does not often mention them, we know from other sources that they tended to be concentrated among the elite. However, we know little more about them than that they followed only the Torah of Moses and appear to have rejected the other books of the Tanakh. Jesus was closer to the Pharisees in this regard. The influence of the Sadducees gives us just one more example of the number of interpretive circles within the Second Temple Judaic systems and reflected in the Gospels or known from other histories. All of these groups were contending to be the authorized interpreters of biblical law. There was no single, uniform interpreting authority. Each circle vied for primacy in claiming to have found the determinative interpretation of the biblical tradition. Jesus entered this contentious world not as an outsider, rejecting all Judaic systems but as an insider, contending for a social imaginary based on his own understanding of the biblical tradition.

Given this short treatment of history, geography, economics, and awareness of ancient social and ideological systems, I will approach Mark with three major assumptions.

The first assumption is that the lens through which first-century Judean and Galilean Jews comprehended the world was a social memory that was attentive to temple, synagogue, biblical law, and a variety of interpreting circles vying for authority, all living under the iron fist of Roman colonization. Just as we, in the twenty-first-century United States, make sense of the world assuming an individualist perspective with individual rights and obligations, so ancient Israelites would have made sense of the world through the lens of a people committed to a narrative of being called by God to be "a light to the nations" (Is 42:6) in the context of this social history. Yet, ancient Israelites experienced cognitive dissonance between their understanding of their unique calling in the cosmos and their actual experience of having been oppressed by one empire after another from those very nations.

The second assumption is that this lens, or social memory, especially in light of the terrible burdens wrought by Roman colonization, would have caused ancient Israelites to identify with the disenfranchised and those marked as deviant by these mighty empires. As such, we might expect first-century Jewish writers to be suspicious of institutions that perpetuated oppression, marginalization, and disenfranchisement. These might be political institutions, but they just as easily could be social institutions. Kinship, for instance, along with all the expectations built into that social institution, is subject to severe critique in the Gospel of Mark. Other institutions such as the temple system, Jewish norms as promulgated by existing Jewish groups such as Pharisees and Sadducees, and government, including the experience of colonization under the oppressive rule of the Romans, are subject to scrutiny in Mark's Gospel.

In light of the second assumption, the third assumption is that this lens of cognitive dissonance vis-à-vis Israel's covenant with Yahweh, on the one hand, and the larger world, on the other, is likely to have resulted in a critique of marginalizing behavior in those institutions. By the same token, we as contemporary readers, in order to enter into Mark's world, need to be open to critiquing institutional readings that we have inherited that in themselves reinforce dominance of one group over others or the silencing of voices outside the social center. As readers who are committed to listening to and hearing the voices outside the social center, I invite you to join with me in affirming interpretations that challenge the single readings of the powerful, which have dominated Gospel interpretation throughout Western history.

BEGINNINGS (MARK 1:1-20)

The task of the gospel is set forth in the first verse, which claims to be presenting "the beginning of the good news of Jesus Christ, the Son of God" (Mk 1:1). "Good news," in the context of the occupation by Rome, is both ironic and subversive. The Roman emperor had proclaimed himself to be the bringer of good news. Mark's claim challenges the imperial claim and goes further yet, announcing the deliverance of not only a people but the cosmos itself. Mark refers to Jesus as "Christ," which in this context is a descriptor rather than a title. The Greek word *Christos* is a translation of the Hebrew word *mashiakh* and literally means "anointed one" or "one who is anointed with oil." In ancient Israel, the two offices whose ordination or coronation were marked by the ritual of anointing with oil were those of priest and king (Ex 28:41; 29:7; 1 Kings 1:34). By calling Jesus *Christos*—"anointed one"—Mark is making status claims for Jesus that all ancient Israelites would have recognized. "The good news of Jesus *Christ*" is that he fulfills the offices of both priest and king, both of which challenge Roman authority and Israelite collusion with Rome.

Mark's introduction also refers to Jesus as "the Son of God." In Psalm 2:6–7, the divine reference to "my son" could refer either to the hoped-for king who would restore Israel or to the collective people of Israel itself. Over time, within the Israelite tradition of interpretation that emerged under the boot of empire, the tradition gave preference to the former meaning. In this sense, Mark is making eschatological claims about Jesus as the royal redeemer sought for in Israel's traditions. But the latter meaning stayed alive as well. Mark's readers may just as easily have seen the reference to Jesus as "my son" being a claim that Jesus embodied the collective people of Israel in his own identity. Either meaning is a claim for Jesus to exercise authority among the people of Israel and in the cosmos.

From the outset, Mark's Gospel makes a cosmic claim about Jesus. Jesus is the one Israel's Scriptures describe: the hoped-for ruler who would be God's beloved son, anointed as priest/king, embodying the people, and instituting God's reign again over the cosmos. Mark's Gospel reflects an expectation that the cosmos is not in order and that history must correct it. It does so by anchoring its claims in Israel's prophetic scriptural traditions. At the outset, the Gospel has Jesus citing Malachi 3:1, where the prophet promises a messenger to prepare the way for Yahweh to refine the temple and witness against those who exploit with sorcery, adultery, and false witness, who commit fraud against workers, and who oppress the disenfranchised (Mk 1:2; Mal 3:5 LXX). Mark 1:2–3 also cites Isaiah 40:3–8, which promises that "the glory of the Lord shall appear, and all flesh shall see the salvation of God" (Is 40:5 LXX). Mark roots every significant event in the prophetic words of Israel's ancient seers, who looked forward to a day when injustice would cease and when justice for the exploited, the workers, and the disenfranchised would drive the economy of the people of Israel. Thus, the "good news" about which Mark writes, if read in this prophetic context, cannot be interpreted responsibly to refer to some notion of individual salvation as it is comprehended in the post-Enlightenment Western world. Such a notion would have made no sense to Mark's readers. To be sure, individual salvation was bound up with the hoped-for task of God manifesting rulership over Israel and the nations. But the two could not be separated. Good news for one had to be good news for all.

Mark goes on to introduce Jesus more fully only after first introducing John, the contemporary prophet, who immerses repentant Israelites in water as a response to their acknowledging their wrongdoing (Mk 1:4). The Gospel's narrative is shaped in ways that invoke Scripture at every turn. It is saturated with references and allusions that paint the stories through the medium of rich biblical imagery. This concept of good news was not original to Mark or to Caesar. Mark draws from Israel's scriptural traditions, where this language first emerges (Is 40:9; 41:27; 52:7; 60:6; 61:1; Nah 1:15; Ps 40:9; 96:2; 1 Chron 16:23). In introducing John, Mark tells us very little, describing him as a self-denying prophet in the wilderness, outside the halls of power, proclaiming a baptism—or ritual water immersion—"of repentance." The Judeans from Jerusalem were coming to him "confessing their sins" (Mk 1:5).

John's austerity is manifested in that he wears only camel's hair wrapped with a leather belt and eats only locusts and wild honey (Mk 1:6). This description, however, tells us a great deal. For John is not any prophet—he is the embodiment of one of Israel's greatest prophets, Elijah. In 2 Kings, Elijah is described as "a hairy man, with a leather belt around his waist" (2 Kings 1:8).

The parallels with Elijah do not stop at his appearance. He is a forerunner for the Messiah/Christ, or "anointed one." He is the promised messenger, "the voice of one crying out in the wilderness" who prepares the way (Mk 1:2-3; see Mal 3:1; Is 40:3). Malachi 4:5 proclaims, "See, I will send you the prophet Elijah before the great and terrible day of the Lord comes." This man John, who immerses Jesus in water, is himself the embodiment of that great prophet who was to come. To be sure, Mark is clear to acknowledge Jesus as the greater of the two (Mk 1:7), but there is no doubt that Mark is relaying events of cosmic significance for Israel's understanding of its redemption and restoration.

By creating an undeniable association between John and Elijah, Mark reveals the interpretive lens through which this Gospel story will unfold. For Mark, as for many other ancient writers who identified as Jews or Israelites, the Scriptures of Israel were alive and being enacted in history in their own time and place. The ancient Israelites, like many Indigenous peoples in the Americas, had a circular view of time, in which history was not perceived as linear but as operating in cycles.[5] In such a conceptualization, the idea is that the biblical characters and events are being reenacted in the here and now but have new meaning given the new context. Seen through this lens, then, John embodies all the hopes and dreams that Israelites placed in Elijah, the one who would announce the coming priest/king. Jesus, whom Mark identifies as that anticipated redeemer, also embodies ancient hopes and dreams being reenacted in Mark's story. The key, then, to interpreting Mark is to view every event by invoking circular time through the lens of Scripture as a first-century Israelite would have viewed it. In this conceptualization, John is both John the Baptizer *and* Elijah; Jesus is both a first-century Galilean Israelite *and* Christ/Messiah, Son of God, embodiment of Israel, anointed priest/king and proclaimer of the good news, refiner of the temple, and bringer of salvation.

Mark reintroduces Jesus in Mark 1:9, claiming that he came from Nazareth in Galilee. Here is one of the first challenges to sacred space as conceptualized in the Second Temple period. This is a striking detail. The Gospels of Matthew and Luke place Jesus' home in the revered city of Bethlehem, birthplace of the ancient King David, with a subsequent move to Nazareth (Mt 2:23; Lk 2:4-5, 39). Mark has no real interest in Bethlehem as a place of birth, never even mentioning the city. Mark's Jesus is a Galilean through and through. Sacred space for Mark is where Jesus is present. There is no need to ascribe honor to Jesus by placing his birth on sacred soil. Nazareth was not a town of distinction. Never mind. Jesus himself needed no such validation.

In a world in which nonelite people often have no voice in interpreting the Bible, it is worthwhile to stop and note a peculiarity of Mark's Gospel. The writer of this Gospel wrote in a common form of Greek. It is unsophisticated and sometimes tedious. This could indicate that the writer was not highly educated

[5]See, e.g., Donald L. Fixico, *The American Indian Mind in a Linear World: American Indian Studies and Traditional Knowledge* (New York: Routledge, 2003).

or sophisticated in the use of Greek. For instance, in Mark 1:10, Mark transitions from one event to another with the word *euthys* ("immediately"). This is a common occurrence in Mark, and sometimes the phrasing becomes tiresome: "and *euthys* . . . and *euthys* . . . and *euthys*." In fact, Mark's Greek is so unsophisticated that the writer of Luke, when drawing from Mark, was forced to correct the grammar and lack of elegance while retelling the stories. Nonprofessional readers can take comfort in knowing that one was not required to be an elite or highly educated individual to tell the story of the good news of Jesus Christ. Every *euthys* in Mark can remind us that the message is for all people.

Mark's presentation of Jesus as anointed king and prophet is reinforced in the story that follows Jesus' baptism. Readers are told, "The spirit immediately drove him [Jesus] out into the wilderness" (Mk 1:12). This act of the Spirit brings to mind the miraculous physical translations from one place to another that occur in the stories of Elijah and Elisha (2 Kings 2:1-12; 5:26). Ancient readers would have seen this as confirming Jesus as not only king/priest but also anointed prophet. The forty-day period Jesus spends in the wilderness also brings to mind Moses' forty days on the mountain with Yahweh, where he neither ate nor drank (Ex 24:18), but once again, it evokes Elijah, who went forty days without food on a mountain with God (1 Kings 19:8). Through this story, Mark confirms Jesus' status as Son of God, Messiah/Christ, and anointed ruler and prophet.

The focus now turns to Jesus' Galilean ministry. Mark 1:9 states that Jesus came from Nazareth in Galilee to be baptized by John. The setting for the baptism by John is the Judean wilderness, and thereafter Jesus is driven deeper into that wilderness by the Spirit to be tested. It is only after these events that Mark's attention turns, for the next several chapters, back to Galilee.

There Jesus begins "proclaiming the good news of God" (Mark 1:14). In introducing Jesus as preaching good news, Mark once again is telling us something crucial about Jesus' nature. Readers have already been introduced to the phrase "good news," from which comes our word *gospel*, but, like everything else to which Mark has introduced us, this phrase also is laden with prophetic and messianic significance. The phrase appears in Isaiah 61:1-3 LXX, where it is worth quoting in its entirety:

> The spirit of the Lord is upon me,
> because he has **anointed** [*echrisen*] me,
> he has sent me to bring **good news**
> [*euangelisasthai*] to the poor,
> to heal the brokenhearted,
> to proclaim release to the captives,
> and recovery of sight to the blind,
> to summon the acceptable year of the Lord,
> and the day of retribution,
> to comfort all who mourn,
> so that to those who mourn for Sion be
> given glory instead of ashes. (NETS)

By employing the phrase "bring good news"—*euangelisasthai*—from which we get the English word *evangelize*, and the word "anointed"—*echrisen*—from which we get the English word *Christ*, Mark is signaling to readers that Jesus is the promised proclaimer of the "good news" of the restoration of "Sion," or Mount Zion, on which the city of Jerusalem is built, referenced in Isaiah 61:1. What's more, this proclaimer in Isaiah 61:1-3 is a messiah—an anointed one—sent by Yahweh to address the needs of those experiencing poverty, those whose hearts are crushed, those who are imprisoned, blind, and in mourning. This good news is transformational for a people. It looks to the centuries-old longings of the people of Israel, which are not just spiritual in a disembodied sense but comprehend all social institutions. This is the good news Mark presents to the readers.

Jesus calls his Galilean hearers to believe in this good news with the words, "The time is fulfilled, and the kingdom of God has come near; repent, and believe in the good news" (Mk 1:15). Jesus consistently preaches this "kingdom," or *basileia*, in the context of healing, restoring, feeding, or providing for the people. These references are at times political and at times eschatological. In most cases such categories are indistinguishable.

Mark's presentation of Jesus links the preaching of the *basileia* with his work of healing and restoration, thus giving a sense of what this *basileia* looks like. It is another way of structuring ourselves as humans in the cosmos and of perceiving new norms and possibilities. In Mark's Gospel, Jesus challenges many of the conventional norms, systems, and social structures that people took for granted as to how they organized themselves in the cosmos and what level of human thriving they were willing to accept. In these references, there is no indication that Jesus imagined an exclusively geographic or nationalist entity but rather this *basileia* is a notion that comprehends the political while not being limited to it. Instead, Jesus' construction of a new system seems to describe a different religious, social, political reality, involving collectively entering into a space whose values, norms, and social expectations are defined by adherence to a certain set of standards and principles propounded from a specific interpretation of the Scriptures. The *basileia* is something one receives (Mk 10:15) or enters into (Mk 10:23-25), but it is also political (Mk 11:10). It is immanent—accessed by individuals in the present (Mk 12:34)—but also future (Mk 14:25; 15:43). It is both individualized and political, both immanent and future. As such, it is dynamic, multivalent, and grounded in paradox. This dynamic social, religious, and political vision drives the teaching, healing, and the ultimate suffering and death of Jesus in Mark.

This teaching of the *basileia* will require adherents. We often focus on the search for the historical Jesus, but we must also attend to the search for the historical people who supported, sustained, and furthered Jesus' word and work. Thus, Mark ends this section with Jesus choosing the brothers Simon and Andrew and the brothers James and John (Mk 1:16-20) as his first followers. Both sets of brothers are fishermen. Jesus does not choose highly educated scribes or lawyers as his first disciples. He chooses peasants who toil in physical labor and thus would be viewed as of generally low status in the Herodian temple system but whose voices, as Israelites, matter to Jesus and to Mark.

JESUS' WORK IN GALILEE (MARK 1:21–9:49)

One of the hallmarks of the Gospel of Mark is its geographical focus. Geography plays a major role in the structure of Mark's Gospel. Its formative stories and narratives are set in Galilee. Jesus is introduced as a man from a city in Galilee, Nazareth (Mk 1:9). Jesus quickly develops a reputation in the region as he performs exorcisms, heals, and preaches about an alternate kingdom or regency (Greek *basileia*) to challenge the vision of the Roman Empire. This regency is overseen by the God of Israel, who seeks the welfare of the people of Israel first and then through them the nations, who all suffer under the tyranny of human regents. Inevitably, this leads to an indomitable narrative drive away from Galilee and toward Jerusalem, from which there can be no turning back. Jerusalem will be the city of destiny and, ultimately, the city of death. But there is good news, as death will not hold Jesus. Instead, in his death, in an ironic twist, Jesus again demonstrates the power of the regency about which he preached, overcoming death through resurrection and sending an angel to urge his followers to return to the place where it all began—Galilee (Mk 16:7). This geographic focus on Galilee as a place of new beginnings and Jerusalem as a place of death dominates Mark's Gospel.

Jesus makes his home in Capernaum in Galilee (Mk 2:1), and it is in Capernaum that some of Jesus' most significant miracles occur. Galilee, a place not considered sacred in the canon of Israel's Scriptures, becomes a site of the sacred because Jesus is there. Jesus begins not only proclaiming the *basileia* there but also enacting miracles that reinforce the claim that Jesus' own presence created sacred space in this unexceptional region.

Mark's Gospel contrasts this notion of sacred space as embodied in Jesus with that promulgated by the temple institution. One way it does so is by presenting Jesus' healings and exorcisms as a challenge to the authority of the temple system to broker access to the divine.[6] Jesus' healings are primarily of those who may not have been permitted to enter into the sacred precincts of the temple. These included women; those who could not walk, see, or hear; and those with physical disabilities in their limbs or their skin. Mark's Jesus appears intent to heal and enfranchise into Israel's social center the very people who have been disenfranchised by the Herodian temple system.

As noted above, the architecture of Herod's temple reflected a particular social hierarchy that also set forth a particular value system based on a certain notion of holiness and shaped by Greco-Roman norms and social assumptions. At the top of the hierarchy were priests, then male Israelites, followed by female Israelites, all of whom were expected to manifest robust physical health and wholeness. Outside the temple courts proper and, correspondingly, on the periphery of the social system, were Israelites who were disabled, possessed, maimed, or unable to hear or see, as well as people from the nations. The message is that only the "purest" people—as defined by the Herodian temple priesthood—may approach God, while the "impure" are relegated to regions outside the body proper of Israel.

It is precisely this social hierarchy that Mark's Gospel consistently and systematically defies. Mark categorically rejects not only the sacred space of Herod's temple but also the social hierarchies it inscribes. Mark's Jesus turns these hierarchies upside-down. It is those who are disabled, afflicted, and unable to hear or see whom Jesus attends to, and thus such people are symbolically brought to the center of the social hierarchy as constructed in Mark's Gospel. These are the disenfranchised of Israel. They are joined by those who are poor and thus often not able to afford to bring the offerings and sacrifices that would allow them to participate in temple life; by people from the nations, and to a lesser extent, by women. To understand Mark's portrayal of Jesus, then, we must understand social hierarchies in ancient Judea and Galilee. These were not just "religious" hierarchies. Rather, they were social, political, religious, economic, and biological categories that were inscribed in the state monument and that manifested in physical bodies who had the status to occupy the social center and who was relegated to the margins. Mark's Jesus defies these social hierarchies and turns them virtually on their heads. The principle of rejecting hierarchies constructed during the Greco-Roman era that

[6]See William R. Herzog II, *Jesus, Justice, and the Reign of God* (Louisville, KY: Westminster John Knox, 2000).

marginalized and disenfranchised people is central to Mark's Gospel.

We also must understand the most urgent social values that enshrined these systems. In the case of the temple priestly elites, it was a certain cosmic interpretation of holiness. Ancient priestly systems operated in a way that convinced practitioners that they were maintaining order in the cosmos. That is, as long as they carried out the priestly cult according to the divine directions, the cosmos would continue to operate efficiently—the stars would stay in their trajectories, the rains and winds would come at the right times to fertilize the fields, and wars and social upheavals would not occur. Outside the realm of order was the realm of chaos. The task of the priests was to avert that realm and keep it at bay. In Leviticus, Yahweh, the God of Israel, explains to the people, "Be holy, for I am holy" (Lev 11:44-45). To remain holy would ensure the continued existence of the cosmos itself. Order represented holiness; disorder represented the profane.

For the Second Temple priestly tradition, this holiness had to be produced metaphorically in the bodies of the Israelite people proper. Such a system was sublime in one way but also carried within it a kind of social violence. Just as the lambs meant for sacrifice were to be without blemish, so were the priests who brought the sacrifice (Lev 21). By the time of the Herodian temple, this expectation of holiness extended to all male Israelites who came near the temple. In this system, the physical body mirrored the collective body. Yet there was an inherent social violence in this system that was not inscribed in earlier iterations of the temple and sanctuary. While the earlier tabernacle allowed entry to women, people with blemishes and disabilities, and willing people from the nations, the Herodian temple system excluded all these groups, as they did not represent in their body the "holy" (whole, hale) Israelite male. Women, along with those Israelites who could not display wholeness in their bodies, ended up being relegated to the margins of the polity of Israel through no fault of their own. Mark's Gospel addresses this social violence.

Jesus in Mark cares about holiness also. But in Mark, Jesus picks up on a different value system, also enshrined in Torah. That value system is the notion that holiness extends out from the divine to embrace and transform those who are not holy rather than precluding greater and greater numbers of people from the category of holiness. We might call this value system that of *wholeness*, representing not the wholeness of the physical body as ideal but the wholeness of the people of Israel. In this model, holiness works, but it does so to enfranchise all of Israel rather than to exclude.

Mark demonstrates this by presenting Jesus as operating with a notion of holiness whose force is centrifugal rather than centripetal. The force flows outward, from the holy to the unholy, rather than inward.[7] This is most observable in Jesus' healings. Mark depicts Jesus—not the inner sanctum in the temple—as being the center of holiness. Jesus is not defiled by the disabled, the leper, the woman, or the non-Israelite. Rather, his touch, or the power that goes out from him—often only with his words—makes the "unholy" holy. The holiness flows out from the center to the periphery and thus has a centrifugal force. This model reinforces a social imaginary of wholeness. The

[7]See Richard Bauckham, *Bible and Mission: Christian Witness in a Postmodern World* (Grand Rapids, MI: Baker, 2003), 65-81. He refers to concentric circles fanning out from Israel geographically in terms of mission. However, there is no mention of purity functioning in this way. Rather, Bauckham is referring to early Christian missionary practice.

holy center sanctifies the margins. This social imaginary recalls that of the tabernacle and represents a challenge to and rejection of the social imaginary enshrined in Herod's temple. This is a central feature of Mark's Gospel. It includes a rejection of the temple's priestly claims to enact and regulate sacred space and time. But this manifestly is not a challenge to Israelite religious social identity itself, as many Christian interpreters have imagined. Instead, as shown here, it is a challenge that looks back to earlier models of the sanctuary in order to enshrine a social imaginary that enfranchises all the "lost sheep" among Yahweh's people (Jer 50:6).

A new vision in Galilee (Mark 1:21-45). Jesus' ministry begins in earnest in the city of Capernaum, situated on the northern shore of the Sea of Galilee, an otherwise unremarkable village. Although Mark says that Jesus is from Nazareth in Galilee (Mk 1:9), Jesus carries out no ministry in Nazareth. We will see the reason in Mark 6, where there is a rejection scene in Nazareth. Luke, in contrast, places this rejection scene at the beginning of Jesus' work, explaining why he moved to Capernaum to launch his work. However, Mark will use the rejection scene later in the Gospel to reinforce challenges to kinship norms in the ancient Mediterranean.

Mark 1:21 introduces two institutions discussed above: the Sabbath, a category of sacred time enshrined in biblical law whose existing norms and regulations Jesus will contest, and the synagogue, a place of gathering for Torah reading but also for the communal needs of the village. The third institution discussed above—the temple itself—can be imagined to be at play too in its role as the broker of the beneficence of Yahweh to Yahweh's people.

Notice that Jesus' first action in entering the synagogue on the Sabbath is to teach (Mk 1:21-22). In describing the events thus, Mark is positioning Jesus as the authoritative voice in that social space. His teaching with authority seems to surprise the attendants: "He taught them as one having authority, and not as the scribes" (Mk 1:22). From this we are left to speculate how the scribes may have taught, but given that their role was to conserve the tradition, it is likely that their approach to interpreting Torah was to convey how traditional interpreters had approached the biblical text rather than to presume to offer fresh interpretations. Right away, then, Mark has Jesus making claims about his own authority to interpret Scripture.

Mark 1:23: "Just then [*euthys*] there was in their synagogue a man with an unclean spirit." The Mishnah, edited around 200 CE but containing earlier traditions, lists those who were not obliged to enter the temple, and includes in that list those with mental disabilities.[8] Nowhere in the Gospel is possession by an unclean spirit defined as a mental disability, but it is likely that the behavior of such a person would have precluded their being allowed to enter the temple in Jerusalem. Here in Galilee, however, such a man freely enters the synagogue because it does not connote sacred space as does the temple. Moreover, by naming the spirit that possessed the man as unclean or impure, Mark demarcates this fellow's status from those who would be able to access the temple unhindered. Mark then places in the mouth of this unclean spirit a pronouncement about who Jesus is: "the Holy One of God" (Mk 1:24). In doing so, he makes claims about the supernatural nature of the

[8]By that time, it appears that earlier injunctions against access to the sanctuary by priests with physical disabilities now applied to all Israelites and was expanded further to include those who were controlled by demons (*Mishnah Hagigah* 1.1; *Babylonian Talmud Rosh Hashanah* 28a, citing an earlier *baraita*). See David Bar-Cohn, "*Tzara'at* Purification: A Vestige of Demonic Exorcism," The Torah, 2023, https://thetorah.com/article/tzaraat-purification-a-vestige-of-demonic-exorcism.

spirit. It may be unclean, but it sees what humans cannot see.

Mark here appears to be developing a Christology, a set of criteria that explain Jesus' nature as divine. The LXX of Psalm 15:10 makes a distinction between Yahweh, whom the psalmist is addressing, and "your [Yahweh's] holy one."[9] We seem to have here, then, a rudimentary Christology, in which Mark is making claims about Jesus' nature as divine by employing the language of Scripture.

In any case, Jesus rebukes the unclean spirit, saying, "Be quiet and come out of him!" (Mk 1:25). It is too soon for Jesus' nature to be fully disclosed. The man convulses while the unclean spirit, "crying with a loud voice, came out of him" (Mk 1:26). This results in the synagogue attendees marveling at Jesus' authority to teach and to command unclean spirits.

Examining this little story through the lens of our social institutions, we can see that the entire narrative is about challenging those institutions. The narrative, that is, is political as well as spiritual. Jesus challenges the guild of scribes and their regulatory model of interpretation. He claims for himself the authority to interpret Torah. He challenges the structural hierarchies of the Jerusalem priesthood and the temple system itself, although from faraway Galilee, by claiming for himself the authority to set free the man with the unclean spirit, making it possible for him to be granted access to the inner precincts of the temple courts. Jesus also challenges particular understandings of sacred time in this narrative in that he initiates this exorcism of the unclean spirit on a Sabbath. In all these ways, then, these simple acts are all political. Mark's Jesus challenges the regulatory norms and ideals of those who claimed to represent the *polis*—the people of Israel—norms that included the authority to broker who could access sacred space, who could determine the use of sacred time, and how Scripture was interpreted to answer those questions. In the temple system in Jerusalem, the man from whom Jesus exorcised the unclean spirit would have been turned away. He would have in effect been disenfranchised from the blessings and beneficence that the temple could bestow on him, blessing his crops and ensuring a prosperous future. Jesus' act immediately enfranchises him. He has not undergone any form of purification. Jesus' own purity, his own holiness, extends and makes the impure pure.

This exorcism is the first of three events in which someone who is not whole—someone who in the social imaginary of Herod's temple was not invited to participate fully in Israel's political and religious life—is made whole. This first event is followed by Jesus healing Simon's mother-in-law of a fever (Mk 1:30-31). In itself, it is an unremarkable story, but if we examine it through the lens of social identity and who has access to the inner courts, the healing of a woman—Simon's mother-in-law—reinforces Jesus' challenge to the architectural divisions of Herod's temple. Women ought to have as much access to the beneficence to be bestowed on all the children of Israel as male Israelites do.

There is a transitional section from Mark 1:32-39, followed by a third significant healing story, relating a healing of a leper (Mk 1:40-44). Leprosy was another category that precluded the sufferer from access to the temple courts. In this case, unlike that of those with physical infirmities, those possessed by demons, and women, the decree follows

[9]Isaiah 49:7 also, in the Hebrew, makes a distinction between Yahweh, the Redeemer of Israel and [Yahweh's] Holy One. However, the LXX translates the phrase in a way that removes the distinction.

traditional biblical law (see Lev 13–14). The Hebrew word for leprosy, *tsara'at*, describes a condition that is not the same as Hansen's disease, the leprosy that we are aware of today. Its Greek equivalent, *lepra*, mirrors the Hebrew meaning rather than the modern one. In humans, it would have referred to a skin disease characterized by scaly, scabrous, patchy lesions on the flesh.[10] In the narrative in Mark 1:40-44, the testimony of this healing narrative is that Mark's model of the centrifugal force of holiness, centered in Jesus' own body, is a direct challenge to the authority of the priests to mediate the divine.

LEPROSY (*LEPRA*)

Leprosy was not a condition that was transmittable like a virus, and the reason it resulted in people's ostracism was that, by the time of the Herodian temple, it rendered a person unfit to enter the inner courts of the temple, as did blindness, deafness, and physical disabilities. The ancients did not know about viruses, so the issue was not about the transmissibility of a virus but rather of a form of cultic uncleanness. It conveyed uncleanness for the same reason as the other disabilities. The ideology surrounding the Herodian temple system demanded that the individual body of the Israelite must be whole in order to display God's ideal of holiness and wholeness.

Moreover, there was much anxiety in the temple cult about crossing boundaries. Scaly or scabrous skin marked a breaching of the boundary between inside and outside the body. In leprosy, blood and pus, which are meant to remain inside the body, found an irregular avenue to exit the body. Just as the priestly ideology imagined a body politic for Israel that was whole and hale, it imagined a physical body whose boundaries were secure and impermeable. By the same token, unlike those who were blind, deaf, or disabled, *lepra* did render a person unclean for accessing the earlier sanctuaries. Nevertheless, touching a leper did not mean one would contract leprosy as a disease. Just as mold or mildew can be removed from a house or a scaly skin disease disappear, so it was possible for the *lepra* to leave one's body. This meant that lepers could look forward to regaining access to the temple courts once they went through a purification baptism in water. This option was not available to those who were blind, deaf, or disabled, unless they were healed. In any case, all of these physical conditions rendered the person, whether temporarily or permanently, physically unable to model the ideal of the whole and hale body and thus disenfranchised that person from the beneficence of the temple system.

This first collection of healing narratives, all performed in the Galilee, far from the sacred space of the temple in the holy city of Jerusalem, is profoundly political. This is so in the sense that each healing reinforces claims about the nature of the people of Israel and who can claim to be enfranchised among the people and to receive the beneficence of its body politic, the operation of sacred space and time and the authority to mediate them, and the authority to teach and to interpret Torah and biblical law and to arbitrate its interpretation.

Challenge and response (Mark 2:1–3:6). In the ancient Mediterranean world, the

[10]It also was used to refer to defects or scaly erosions, possibly including mold and mildew, on fabrics and buildings. As such, lepers may simply have been suffering from a condition such as psoriasis or eczema, and leprous buildings may just have had mold or mildew.

challenge-and-response pattern was a rhetorical approach used to make status claims over against an opponent. One of the primary value systems of the Hellenistic world was the honor/shame system. The primary value for men was to enhance their honor. To be shamed, whether through military or rhetorical prowess, was to lose status and the ability to claim authority in any social group.[11] Jesus in Mark challenges the honor/shame system entirely, turning it on its head and claiming honor for those the dominant culture attempted to shame, and shame for those it attempted to honor. Sometimes, though, as in this case, Jesus exploits the system and claims honor for himself at the expense of those who assert their own authority in the society. In these honor/shame challenge-and-response motifs, Jesus claims the authority to broker forgiveness of sins (Mk 2:1-12), determine which groups are included within the people of Israel (Mk 2:13-17), fix sacred time for fasting and eating (Mk 2:18-22), and adjudicate what constitutes work on the Sabbath (Mk 2:23–3:5).

In each of the above cases, Jesus, through a challenge-and-response rhetorical move, wrests the authority from the Pharisees and their scribes, from the Herodians, and from the temple system itself. This is why the response is so heated (Mk 3:6). Whereas the response from the Galilean populace was so enthusiastic that Jesus had to stay in the wilderness to avoid the excessive crowds (Mk 1:45), the response from those who claim authority to define the norms and regulations of Israelite life is to destroy him (Mk 3:6). Mark lays out these two distinct responses in all their sharp contrast.

The context of these challenges throughout is the preaching of the kingdom or regency (*basileia*) of God (Mk 1:15). Within a few short chapters, Mark presents Jesus as more than a mere teacher or miracle worker. Each healing, exorcism, or rhetorical challenge takes aim at the central identifying social systems of the Herodian temple system: the challenge to fix sacred space and time, to interpret Torah and biblical law, and to adjudicate the social boundaries of the people of Israel.

Challenge to kinship and status norms (Mark 3:7–6:6). There are two further challenges that are contested, even within the Jesus tradition itself. First is the challenge to kinship norms. Mark appears to be intent not only on challenging the traditional norms of kinship in the ancient Mediterranean world but also on making that challenge explicit, even against those claiming to be Jesus' disciples. Mark especially singles out Jesus' mother and her family in an effort to deny to them any claims of status based on kinship. Mark lays out a status hierarchy based on fictive kinship rather than traditional kinship. For Mark, faithfulness to Jesus is the only mark that ascribes status; traditional kinship means little.

To make these challenges overt, Mark's Gospel constructs framing narratives, sometimes called inclusions or intercalations, or even Markan "sandwiches," in which material is framed around a narrative in order to shape the interpretation of the surrounded narratives. Jesus' mother and his siblings are mentioned in two separate narratives, both of which represent challenge and responses and which frame a literary "sandwich," the inner narrative of which in turn helps the reader interpret the frames. In this case, it is Jesus' own mother who makes the challenge, and Jesus' response is to reject her claims to special kinship status.

[11]To be sure, in a society influenced by Aristotelian gender norms, it was the opposite for women. Women gained honor by behaving as if they were shamed—covering themselves and remaining indoors.

The first kinship challenge comes in Mark 3:19–35, where Mark creates a literary frame-and-intercalation in order to constrain any status claims by Jesus' mother or brothers. The first frame sets up Jesus' family as wanting to restrain him because, they claim, "he has gone out of his mind" (Mk 3:21). The word translated "restrain" can just as easily be translated as "seize by force," and the term translated into English as "he has gone out of his mind" may very easily mean that they are charging Jesus with having gone astray. The closing frame specifies Jesus' mother and siblings as those sending and calling to him while "standing outside" (*exo*) the packed crowds (Mk 3:31-32). This mirrors Mark's language in Mark 4:11, where he claims that those who are "outside" (*exo*) cannot comprehend his teaching. The language reinforces the unflattering presentation of the mother and siblings. When told that his traditional kin are outside, Mark has Jesus denying that traditional kinship claims confer any kind of unique status in his vision of the *basileia* (Mk 3:33-35). Instead, a new kinship group—a fictive kinship group—is formed. Status in this group is gained simply by doing the will of God and is available both to men and women. In this way, Mark offers a view of kinship status that shifts from traditional kinship status claims to fictive kinship status claims. All followers of Jesus have equal status. Even kinship does not confer unique status.

To bolster Mark's challenge to traditional kinship status claims, the two kinship narratives in Mark 3 frame a literary sandwich around a narrative about scribes from Jerusalem accusing Jesus of practicing his deeds empowered by the prince of demons, Beelzebul (Mk 3:22-30). In creating this literary sandwich, Mark's Gospel further aligns Jesus' mother and his siblings with the scribes from Jerusalem.

We have already seen Mark's challenge to the sacred space claims made about the temple and Jerusalem; we have seen him ignore or be unaware of the sacred space claims of the tradition that places Jesus' birth in Bethlehem. Here we see Mark's challenge to the scribes as well. These scribes, who are from Jerusalem, accuse Jesus not only of being possessed by Beelzebul but of actually performing his deeds using the power and authority of Beelzebul (Mk 3:22). This is why the claim that Jesus "has gone out of his mind" is better translated as "has gone astray." Mark associates the family challenge with the Beelzebul challenge. In both cases, Jesus is not accused merely of being a victim of evil but of being the perpetrator of evil. Jesus' response to both challenges—that of the family and of the scribes from Jerusalem—is first to display the illogic of their claims: "How can Satan cast out Satan?" (Mk 3:23) and then to double down and reverse the challenge, accusing his challengers, both family and scribes, of blasphemy against the Holy Spirit (Mk 3:28-30). Just as the scribes from Jerusalem are blaspheming because they deny the divine source of Jesus' beneficence to the people, so his family is blaspheming because they interpret his acts as insanity at best or being led astray at worst. Their claims to status or to special treatment because of their traditional kinship relationship to Jesus are illegitimate and invalid, just as are the scribes' claims based on traditional interpretations of Levitical norms.

There is a second narrative that invokes Jesus' family in order to deny status based on traditional kinship. In Mark 6:1, Jesus returns to his *patrida*, which we assume to be his hometown of Nazareth. As is his wont, he attends synagogue on the Sabbath and teaches there. Many of those present are "astounded" at his wisdom (Mk 6:2). But then Jesus' hearers seem to turn on him based on traditional kinship assumptions. His kinship status does not earn him the requisite level of honor required for them to listen to him.

It is Mark's framing of Jesus' response, however, that reinforces Mark's own rejection of kinship status. First, Mark rejects the assumption that Jesus cannot claim to be an authoritative teacher because his kinship status identifies him as a poor peasant. Second, Mark appears to reject any claims to traditional kinship status that Mary, James, Joses, Judas, or Simon—those of Jesus' "own house"—may claim in Mark's own time and place. Mark's Jesus claims status based on his own authority to mediate the sacred to the people of Israel.[12]

Another traditional social norm Mark challenges is the status of those who claim authority as the twelve disciples of Jesus. This is a recurring theme in Mark's Gospel. We know that the apostle Paul acknowledged the authority of Jacob (a.k.a. James, Jesus' brother) and the Twelve, but he does not seem to have seen their status claims as worth anything more than his own status claim to apostolic authority (Gal 1:13–2:14; 1 Cor 9:5). Mark appears to have the same ambivalence, not only toward the kinship claims made by Jesus' family members, whose status claims would have been based on traditional kinship, but also toward Peter and the Twelve, whose status claims would have been based on having been with Jesus from the beginning (Acts 1:21-22). Neither Paul nor, in all likelihood, Mark, met this criterion. Given that, Mark appears to ascribe no special status to the Twelve throughout the Gospel, refusing their claims to honor based on their relationship to Jesus.

This ambivalence toward Jesus' inner circle spills out often. In Mark 4:1-13, Mark narrates Jesus getting into a boat because of the great crowds and teaching them a parable about a sower and seeds. Afterward, when "those around him and the twelve," ask him about the meaning of the parable, Jesus at first responds, "To you has been given the secret [or mystery] of the *basileia* of God," adding that for "those outside" (Greek *tois exo*), God has purposely hardened their hearts, paraphrasing Isaiah 6:9-10 to make the point (Mk 4:11-12). A cursory reading might lead one to assume that "those around him and the twelve" are not among "those outside." Yet Mark 4:13 goes on to clarify that they also do not understand the parable, implying that they are indeed among "those outside." Readers will see this pattern of the twelve, especially the inner circle, repeatedly failing to believe or understand. All of this undermines the status claims of the Twelve to a unique revelation over against those who came later, including, very likely, the writer of Mark.

Instances abound in the Gospel of Mark in which Jesus' inner circle of disciples do not understand. In Mark 4, at the height of the storm, they fearfully waken the soundly sleeping Jesus. His response to them is, "Have you still no faith?" (Mk 4:40). The implication to the reader is to answer in the affirmative. At the end of the story in Mark 6, Mark adds an explanatory note: "For they did not understand about the loaves, but their hearts were hardened" (Mk 6:52). Mark uses this same phrase about hardness of heart to describe the unbelieving witnesses to Jesus' healing in the synagogue (Mk 3:5) and some Pharisees who are trying to test him (Mk 10:5). The indictment of the disciples is harsh. Just as the doubters among the synagogue witnesses and Pharisees have hardened hearts, so do Jesus' closest disciples, despite the miracles they witness. Like the family who amazes Jesus because of their unbelief (Mk 6:6), the disciples too have no

[12]This is in marked contrast to the Gospels of Matthew and Luke, both of which include infancy narratives whose central defining feature is the claim of status based on traditional kinship.

faith. In this way, Mark repeats the theme of the faithlessness of Jesus' inner circle. For Mark, the only status to be claimed is earned based on one's faithfulness to Jesus.

When we examine these editorial configurations in this way, we begin to recognize that, in the first century, the disparate fellowships of Jesus-loving assemblies may have comprehended Jesus in manifold ways. Given their wide geographic distribution, this is not surprising. Geography and history shape the urgent questions we ask. What is important for our purposes is that such distinct communities were able to negotiate those differences without the backing of military power or imperial might, as began to happen in the fourth century CE when the church became the religion of empire. For now, the relationships between the various groups are marked by contention, but each group treasures a different gospel lens that enshrines the values that it understands to be primary in its pursuit of the *basileia* of God—a gospel lens shaped and honed in the context of each group's own geographic, historical, and social location.

The Gospel of Mark includes two crossing stories in which Jesus shows mastery over the stormy and primordial sea (Mk 4:35-41; 6:45-52). The sea itself is traditionally a site of cosmic warfare in Israel's Scriptures. The waters are a central part of Israel's creation account, and all the waters are collectively called "seas" (Gen 1:9-10). Ancient creation accounts in the region often included a cosmic battle between the divine and the sea, in which the divine represented cosmic order and the sea primordial chaos. The Sea of Galilee, while actually a large freshwater lake, would have been conceived as connected in the primordial depths to all other waters. Called in Hebrew the Kinneret (see Num 34:11; Josh 13:27), its size and location result in its being subject to large and tempestuous storms. These storms would have reminded ancient Galileans of the primordial battle between Tiamat, the goddess of the sea, and Marduk, the storm god, described in the *Enuma Elish*, an ancient Babylonian creation story, as well as ancient Hittite and Greek mythologies, which also contain stories of a cosmic battle between the deities in the sea and those of earth or sky. The crossings and the miracles that occur on the tempestuous sea reinforce once again Jesus' cosmic power and authority, even over the primordial depths.

These crossings also invoke the idea of crossing boundaries. The Sea of Galilee contained several trading ports, as goods and commodities were shipped across the sea to the region of the Galilee on the western shore, populated mostly by Israelites, and the regions on the eastern shore—the Decapolis to the south and the tetrarchy of Herod Philip to the north—populated largely by people from the nations. The Sea of Galilee was an important site for boundary crossing and all the social repercussions that carried. Crossing boundaries is a significant theme in Mark.

In one case in particular, crossing over the sea also represents a crossing of social boundaries while challenging both the power of empire and of the Herodian elites to define those boundaries (Mk 5:1-20). Right after Jesus demonstrates his power over the fearful, primordial depths by walking on the sea, he and his disciples land on the eastern shore, and, readers are told, arrive at the region of the Gerasenes, a region populated by people from the nations.[13] Upon disembarking, Jesus and his

[13]The location has been disputed because the region is far from the shore, and the narrative itself implies that the shore is close. Matthew has corrected Mark's location, calling it the region of the Gadarenes (Mt 8:28). Matthew may have done this also to limit the assumption that the characters involved in the narrative were non-Israelites and because Gadara is closer to the Sea of Galilee.

disciples encounter a non-Israelite man with an unclean spirit who has been living among the tombs. Contact with this man represents a threefold crossing of boundaries between insider/outsider categories of pure and impure with respect to the temple cult. Jesus crossed the sea and in doing so placed himself in a situation to cross even more boundaries. Mark is narrating a story in which, for the first time, Jesus extends the beneficence of the *basileia* to a non-Israelite. The supernatural power Jesus employs highlights the groundbreaking nature of the event.

This event is not only groundbreaking because a non-Israelite experiences the benefits of the *basileia*, however. It is also groundbreaking because Mark is subtly signaling Jesus' power not only in the spiritual but also the political realm. After an amplified description of the power of the unclean spirit, Mark has Jesus ask the man, "What is your name?" He replies: "My name is Legion, for we are many" (Mk 5:9). We do not know whether it is the man who replies or the spirits possessing him. However, the name Legion would have caused any ancient reader to recognize the reference. The legion was the unit of organization used by the occupying Roman army, consisting of approximately forty-eight hundred to fifty-five hundred infantrymen and employed particularly in areas where civil or political unrest made violent outbreak likely. As such, Roman legions represented the power of Rome to crush dissent or efforts at self-rule. It may be that the Israelites had been unable to throw off the chains of the Romans, represented by their legions, but such overriding power, when Jesus faces it, is dispatched with a word. The legion begs Jesus not to send them out of the region. He accedes to its wishes, just as he does not dispatch the Roman soldiers occupying the region. But he does send this Legion into a group of swine, an animal viewed as ritually unclean in Israelite tradition, and those swine rush headlong into the sea to be drowned. The legion still is in the region, but its power is now inert. By cloaking the language in that of demonic warfare, Mark, in addition to displaying Jesus' groundbreaking supernatural power, makes a strong political statement that, at the same time, is sufficiently ambiguous to deter outright accusations of insurrection.

Readers are beginning to see that Jesus' healings and miracles, in almost every case, have either a cosmic component, as in the stilling of the storm, or a social/political/religious component, such as in the casting out of the legion of demons. Readers are also noticing that to separate any of those components, when thinking about the ancient Mediterranean, is impossible. Each category is deeply entwined in the others.

In examining a primarily social component, with cosmic, political, and religious implications, I have noted that almost every time Jesus carries out a healing or exorcism in Mark, it results in someone who has become one of the outcasts of Israel becoming re-enfranchised into the people and able to reap the full benefits of the temple cult, and thus the blessings promised to the people of Israel. This is true of Jesus' other miracles as well. In Mark 6:33-44 he feeds five thousand men, along with women and children, and in Mark 8:1-10, he feeds four thousand people with food left over.[14] In the first case, Jesus' feeding of the people occurs in the context of teaching (Mk 6:34). The feeding itself is a mark of the *basileia* preached and imagined by Jesus. The *basileia* is a place of

[14]These two accounts may be two versions of the same story. While Matthew follows Mark in relating both stories, Luke relates only the first of the two. Both evoke the story of the prophet Elisha feeding the people in 2 Kings 4:2-44.

wholeness and satisfaction; it is a place where there is sufficient food and drink and where needs are fulfilled. The feeding is not a food fest. The amounts of food supplied are simple and basic. Yet these stories, enmeshed with the stories of the stilling of the storm and walking on the sea, help Mark's readers to perceive the nature of this *basileia* that Jesus preaches. It is not limited to any sphere, whether cosmic, social, political, religious, or economic. Yet it comprehends all of those spheres. It is life giving and peace inducing. This is the *basileia* that Jesus in Mark's Gospel imagines as an alternate way of being human in the world.

More challenge-and-response narratives follow, but one stands out because Jesus concedes the challenge. The challenge is by an outsider who solicits access to the benefits of Israel. First, in Mark 7:1-23, the scribes from Jerusalem reappear, along with the Pharisees, to challenge Jesus' authoritative claims to interpret biblical law based on the direction of the flow of unclean to clean or vice versa. Then, in Mark 7:18, Jesus again reprimands his own disciples for their lack of understanding. However, in a third challenge-and-response narrative, the challenger makes such a strong challenge that Jesus has to concede. In this case, it is a Syrophoenician woman—another non-Israelite—who so insightfully responds to Jesus' challenge that it results in her convincing him to heal her daughter. By now readers have been trained to recognize that if a person from the nations is involved, the narrative is a significant one. In this case, the event makes a larger statement about who may partake of the benefits of the *basileia* (Mk 7:24-30). In the case of the Syrophoenician woman, here is a person twice marginalized from the perspective of Israel's covenant identity. She is from the nations *and* she is a woman. These two elements of the story help us understand why this is the only challenge-and-response in which Jesus concedes to the respondent. By presenting a woman from the nations prevailing in this challenge-and-response, Mark is also making claims not only about access but also agency in the *basileia.* It will not be male Israelites only who will have access and agency. People from the nations, including women, will also be enfranchised and have access to honor and agency in this divine system.

For readers today, who do not operate with the gendered honor/shame system that informs this interaction, the story leaves us feeling ambiguous. To be sure, we have an example of a strong, intrepid woman, but in order to accomplish her task, she must put up with the shame of being called a "dog" and respond in a way that restores her honor. Contemporary women often flinch at such stories. How often have we had to overlook microaggressions and efforts to shame, discredit, or belittle us in order to make our own claims for legitimacy? The good news, of course, is that she responds to Jesus with grace and a strong answer. He affirms her answer and heals her daughter. She attains her objective through her wit, insight, and wisdom.

This narrative is followed by a miracle (Mk 8:1-10), a challenge-and-response by the Pharisees (Mk 8:11-13), and another indictment of Jesus' disciples for lacking understanding. They do not perceive. Their hearts are hardened (Mk 8:14-21). All of this language evokes Jesus' descriptions of those who are outside the *basileia* of God (see Mk 3:5; 4:12; Jer 5:21; Ezek 12:2). These challenge-response narratives are followed by the healing of another man who likely would not have been able to participate fully in the Herodian temple cult (Mk 8:22-26). All of these narratives reinforce themes of a new vision of the people of God, the *basileia* of God, and the boundaries that define them.

From there, Jesus and his disciples travel to Caesarea Philippi, which was in the region controlled by Philip II, son of King Herod and half brother of Herod Antipas, ruler of the Galilee. This geographic location, which was the site of the convergence of Philip's political power and the cult power of the ancient polytheistic deities, is a fitting place for a striking conversation Jesus has with his followers. Here, Peter proclaims Jesus as the Messiah, but the proclamation is quickly followed by Jesus rebuking Peter.

Once again, the inner circle of disciples—in this case Peter himself—is indicted, not only for unbelief but for collusion with Satan (Mk 8:27-33). Once again, readers see that, while Peter has the courage to claim Jesus as Messiah, he also fails to see the entire drama of Jesus acting in history. At first the story is hopeful. Jesus questions his inner circle as to who he is. After the others, Peter then responds with a powerful claim: "You are the Messiah" (Mk 8:29). Then, however, after Jesus begins to disclose to Peter and the others that the "Son of Man" must suffer (Mk 8:31), Peter rebukes Jesus, fearing that Jesus is predicting a violent fate for himself. Jesus responds, "Get behind me, Satan! For you are setting your mind not on divine things but on human things" (Mk 8:33). Once more, the disciples in the inner circle, especially Peter, are not only without understanding and hard of heart but represent Satan's work in the world. The indictment could not be more severe. Lest we be too hard on Peter, few could have imagined Jesus' ministry, calling, and ultimately suffering and death for his people. To be sure, Peter fails, but Mark may be telling us that if Peter failed, how much more would you and I have failed.

Jesus' rebuke of Peter is followed by an important speech in which he outlines the cost to be paid to enter into the *basileia*. Those who have power and authority are called on to lay it down. The phrase "Son of Man" (*huios tou anthropou* in Greek, *bar enosh* in Aramaic), used in Mark 8:31, refers to Jesus himself.[15]

Those who want to follow Jesus must be willing to suffer. They must take up the cross, which, in the context of Roman colonization, is a sober and terrifying risk (Mk 8:34-38). To seek after the *basileia* means to take one's own life in one's hand. Here again, we see a subtle critique of Roman brutality. Jesus chooses the particular instrument of Roman execution for insurrectionists as an image describing the potential fate of his followers. He understands the implications of his preaching, that it is a threat to Roman imperial power. The kind of power wielded by Rome, in which those with the greatest military and coercive physical force have the right to rule, is precisely the kind of power Jesus wholly rejects. Nevertheless, Peter's fear of facing death for the sake of the *basileia*, is a fear that Jesus attributes not just to ignorance but to Satan.

The final important event that I will consider before Jesus makes his fateful journey to Jerusalem, and the inevitable death that will await him there, is his transfiguration on the high mountain. Readers are not told on which mountain the event occurs, but the story is filled with supernatural phenomena. Jesus takes the three key disciples, Peter, James, and John, up onto the mountain. Thereupon, Jesus "*metemorphōthē* [lit. "was metamorphized"] before them, and his clothes became dazzling white" (Mk 9:2-3). In addition to this

[15]This phrase is often translated as a generic term for a human being (see Ezek 2:1; Dan 8:17). Moreover, whenever Jesus uses the phrase in Mark, it is in the third person (see Mk 2:10, 28; 8:31, 38; 9:9, etc.). We do not have an instance in which Jesus uses the phrase unambiguously to refer to himself. However, in Mk 8:31, the meaning makes most sense in the context if it is a third-person reference to Jesus himself.

metamorphosis, Moses and Elijah, the two prophets who have served as harbingers of the coming of a new era, appear alongside Jesus. We have come full circle in the Galilean ministry. Just as Mark associated Jesus with Elijah in Mark 1 while narrating a scene in which a voice from heaven claims, "You are my Son, the Beloved" (Mk 1:11), so Elijah is present in Mark 9 when a voice from heaven proclaims Jesus as "my Son, the beloved" (Mk 9:7).

As in Mark 8, Peter's response is wholly inappropriate (Mk 9:5-6). One last time, Mark shows Jesus trying to demonstrate to his disciples his true nature as a being from heaven, greater than or equal in status to Moses and Elijah. But, once again, they fail to understand (Mk 9:32). Jesus will travel to Jerusalem, to his dreadful fate, frightfully alone, with neither his traditional kin—his family—nor his fictive kin—his apostles—understanding what he has to do and why.

ON THE ROAD TO JERUSALEM (MARK 10:1–11:10)

After devoting several chapters to Jesus' crossing and recrossing the Sea of Galilee, preaching, teaching, healing, and exorcising, and after this major epiphany, readers are told abruptly, "He left that place and went to the region of Judea and beyond the Jordan" (Mk 10:1). Mark introduces a sense of purpose and direction in this section. In an important story about a conversation with a man who has many possessions, the man approaches Jesus "as he was setting out on a journey" (Mk 10:17). There is a sense here of directionality, and readers will soon discover that the direction is the city of Jerusalem. For Mark, it is the city of death. There is no hint of Jerusalem as sacred space. Rather, the holy city will be the place of the greatest display of the unholy. Yet Jesus is resolute in his journey toward it.

On that journey, however, Mark continues to relay important concepts about the *basileia* preached by Jesus, such as the hindrance that great wealth poses to entering (Mk 10:17-27). This is a narrative whose interpretation tends to identify the social location of the interpreters. Those living in affluent suburbs, areas in which food and housing insecurity are relatively unknown, tend to interpret this dialogue metaphorically. People in this social group tend to add, often unconsciously, an extra layer of interpretation, claiming that Jesus here is not telling rich folks to give up their goods but to put God first. This may indeed be a legitimate interpretation, but it does require a second level of meaning appended to it, a level not explicit in the text. However, those who live in poverty and with continual food and housing insecurity are much more likely to interpret it literally. The message for them is clear. Those who are rich will not be able to operate as effective disciples because their wealth will always be a lens through which they view what constitutes discipleship, forming obstacles to their entering into the *basileia*. Those who live in poverty, however, encounter many fewer obstacles and thus garner honor and dignity by Jesus' words. Often, those in affluent circumstances claim that they only read the plain sense of Scripture. They may be blind to the ways that they read through the lens of their affluence. It is not wrong to read through the lens of affluence. But it is wrong to announce such a reading to be the "plain sense" of Scripture and to deny the significance of alternate readings to those who do not share that affluence, especially when the alternate reading is a simpler and more intuitive reading. In a plain-sense reading, those with great wealth face the greatest obstacles to entering the *basileia*. The implication of the plain sense is that those who live in poverty are able to operate in the *basileia* more freely and intuitively, thus rendering them deserving of higher status. In either case, however, Mark calls all of us, whether rich or poor, to service to that same *basileia.*

Returning to the text, the disciples, now "greatly astounded," ask Jesus, "Then who can be saved?" (Mk 10:26). Peter, in another flood of emotion, points out that he and the other disciples have left all to follow Jesus. Jesus replies to this that there will be reward in heaven for those who have left all, including family, to follow him, but he then adds a striking phrase in this context: "But many who are first will be last, and the last will be first" (Mk 10:31). To the careful hearer of Mark, who has heard the repeated references to the disciples' hardness of heart and lack of understanding, there might be a veiled threat to Peter here. But ultimately, the claim is about reward. Mark wants to show that those of the lowest status who embrace the *basileia* of Jesus have unique insights that can lead them to reap a great reward.

Mark's Gospel offers a relentless critique of the hierarchical models that assign status based on traditional kinship, political or religious power, or wealth, arguing that the last will be first, including even among Jesus' closest disciples. Who else are the last in Mark's Gospel? Those among Israel who are afflicted to the point that they cannot access the benefits available to Israel through the temple system, those people from the nations fully outside the temple system, those whose kinship status does not afford them respect in society, those who have no possessions; and those who, because of gender, are forced into a lower-status group. These are the people whom Mark's Jesus elevates to the social center in his presentation of the *basileia* of God.

This new status structure is highlighted again in Mark 10. James and John, two of Jesus' earliest disciples (Mk 1:19), sensing the end, ask to sit at Jesus' right and left hand in his glory (Mk 10:37). Once more, members of the inner circle are shown to be obtuse in their thinking.

In Mark's version of the narrative, Jesus deflects the request by James and John, but it leads to one of the most important and urgent commandments of the Markan Jesus:

> You know that among the gentiles those whom they recognize as their rulers lord it over them, and their great ones are tyrants over them. But it is not so among you; but whoever wishes to become great among you must be your servant, and whoever wishes to be first among you must be slave of all. For the Son of Man came not to be served but to serve and to give his life a ransom for many. (Mk 10:42-45)

This command, a strong and direct command by Mark's Jesus, has largely been ignored in church history. Our social structures, rather than being constructed in contrast to the Gentiles, whose rulers "lord it over them," for the most part have been modeled precisely on those Gentile social hierarchies. Once Christianity became the religion of empire in the fourth century, then church leaders modeled church structures on imperial structures rather than on this vision of the *basileia*. Many Protestants tell themselves that they have rejected such hierarchies. To be sure, they may not ordain and appoint bishops and popes, but their church polities tend to be hierarchical, with the male senior pastor wielding almost imperial levels of authority. This has resulted in sexual abuse and harm to generations of church members.[16] Church

[16]See Kate Shellnutt, "Hundreds Accuse Independent Baptist Pastors of Abuse," *Christianity Today*, December 12, 2018, www.christianitytoday.com/news/2018/december/independent-fundamentalist-baptist-church-abuse-scandal.html; Peter Smith and Travis Loller. "Secret Recordings Show Southern Baptist Dispute on Sex Abuse," ABC News, June 10, 2021, www.news10.com/news/secret-recordings-show-southern-baptist-dispute-on-sex-abuse/; and Wietse de Boer, "The Catholic Church and Sexual Abuse, Then and Now," *Origins* 12, no. 6 (March 2019), https://origins.osu.edu/article/catholic-church-sexual-abuse-pope-confession-priests-nuns?language_content_entity=en.

leaders have the opportunity to take seriously Jesus' command and to model a kind of leadership that listens, enfranchises, and extends holiness to all. Here again we see opportunities to enfranchise those on the social margins who are passed over by church elites who read through the lens of assumed power, wealth, and privilege. The subversive nature of Mark's words is passed over and does not make it into the sermons of contemporary pulpit preachers without significant editorial refashioning.

Jesus finally arrives in Bethphage and Bethany, two villages on the outskirts of Jerusalem (Mk 11:1). He will make Bethany his headquarters in his early days in Jerusalem (Mk 11:11-12). It is in Bethany that a woman with a costly alabaster jar of ointment will break it and anoint him with its precious contents.

IN JERUSALEM (MARK 11:11–14:52)

In Mark 11, readers see Mark's most careful literary attempts to undermine the authority of the temple as sacred space and by extension the authority of the chief priests, scribes, and lawyers who derive their authority from it. Mark's literary structuring is clearly discernible. At times it is even awkward, providing clues that we are dealing with editorial structuring rather than a historic retelling of the story. Mark creates another literary sandwich, inserting a story about Jesus acting violently in the temple within two stories about a fig tree. In the first story, Jesus curses the tree (Mk 11:12-14). This is followed by the events in the temple (Mk 11:15-19). The following morning, as Jesus returns to the temple, he and the disciples find the leaves withered (Mk 11:20-25).

This editorial activity tells us that, for Mark, the temple is no longer the locus of gravity as a sacred site for Israel. This is not to say that Mark rejects an Israelite social identity or value system. Mark affirms the social category of sacred space but reassigns it to Jesus. Mark accomplishes this through his telling of the temple rejection scene.

Not surprisingly, the chief priests and scribes take umbrage at Jesus' attack on the temple. It is their interpretation of biblical law, which could not but occur through the lens of their own power base, that Jesus is attacking. Their power is threatened by his power. It is at this point, claims Mark, that they begin to plot Jesus' death (Mk 11:18).

Mark locates the narrative about the withering of the fig tree on Jesus' third entry into the temple in so many days. On this day, Mark records three challenge-and-response narratives (Mk 11:27-33; 12:13-17, 18-27), followed by a transitional narrative in which a scribe asks about the greatest commandment (Mk 12:28-34). After more teaching, Jesus leaves the temple for the last time (Mk 12:38–13:1).

Mark then takes us to the Mount of Olives, where Jesus gives an eschatological speech, but only to Peter, James, John, and Andrew. There are warnings about deception, false messiahs, wars, earthquakes, famine, persecution, and exhortations, but there also are promises (Mk 13:1-37). It is clear that Mark's Jesus is looking for a cataclysmic end to the world as they know it.

Mark then records an important narrative that in some form appears in all four Gospels. This is the narrative of the woman anointing Jesus with costly oil (Mk 14:3-9). Sadly, this story has been politicized in order to shame and silence women. Mark never identifies the woman (Mk 14:3), although Jesus honors her and immortalizes her act (Mk 14:8-9). Despite this, by the late sixth century, Christian tradition assumed the woman was Mary Magdalene and assigned her an identity as a prostitute, even though Mary Magdalene is never stated to be the woman in the anointing scene, nor is she named as a prostitute in any of the Gospels. The Western Roman tradition employed the motif of the Magdalene as prostitute despite little or no evidence.

Much was at stake in naming the Magdalene as a prostitute. In Roman culture, a public woman was by necessity a shamed woman. The Gospel of Luke presents Mary Magdalene and other women—both married and single—as traveling freely and openly with Jesus and his male disciples (Lk 8:1-3). In light of this, church theologians, influenced as they were by Roman culture, could not but associate her with sexual indecency. Mary as prostitute was born out of this patriarchal construction of reality. This is one reason it is a necessity to read the New Testament in color and with a careful eye to gender. Most of us who have spent any time in Christian circles have likely accepted this construction of Mary Magdalene as prostitute, never noticing that nowhere in Scripture is she named as such. Interestingly, the Eastern church, less influenced by Roman gender ideology, never conflated Mary Magdalene with the woman in Mark 14 or Luke 7, nor with Mary of Bethany in John 12:1-8. Because of this, the Eastern Orthodox churches honor Mary Magdalene as the faithful apostolic witness presented in the tradition.[17]

While there are many technical problems with the who and the where in this narrative, what is important here is that all four Gospels relate a story of a woman doing a task normally reserved for priests: anointing with oil. This is explicit in Mark and Matthew. When she anoints Jesus' head, the reader cannot but recall that the task of consecrating a king or priest was carried out by anointing the head with oil (2 Sam 2:4-7; Ex 29:7). In the Scriptures of Israel, it is often a prophet who anoints the king (2 Sam 12:7; 1 Kings 1:34; 1 Chron 29:22). In this way, while to be sure Jesus explains that she is anointing him for burial, the woman nevertheless evokes the role of a prophet. In Luke and John, where she anoints Jesus' feet, we can still infer a prophetic role (Lk 7:37-38; Jn 12:3). Just as the ways of this world exalt the head, so the ways of the *basileia* exalt the feet. In anointing Jesus' feet, then, the unnamed women in Luke and Mary of Bethany in John are demonstrating the antithetical nature of Jesus' hierarchies. Those who carry out the roles of women and slaves are those who are to be emulated. The woman functions as a prophet and models the new norms of the *basileia* for all disciples.

Jesus then celebrates the Passover with his disciples (Mk 14:17-25). Here, in ritual form, Jesus blesses the bread and wine, claiming, "This is my body" (Mk 14:22) and, "This is my blood of the covenant" (Mk 14:24). In this way, Jesus has ritually resignified the sacred nature of the bread and wine of the covenant to represent his own body. He then again foretells his fate, claiming, "I will never again drink of the fruit of the vine until that day when I drink it new in the kingdom of God" (Mk 14:25).

Next, Mark relates that "they went out to the Mount of Olives" (Mk 14:26). Mark does not say what happened to Judas Iscariot (see Jn 13:26-30). Nevertheless, in the next scene, Mark's Jesus is overt about his disciples' unfaithfulness, predicting that all of them will become deserters (Mk 14:27-28). Jesus' words quickly come to pass, as Peter and those in Jesus' closest circle fail to watch with him, and Jesus prophesies Peter's denial (Mk 14:27-42). Judas, "one of the twelve," who mysteriously disappeared, now reappears with "a crowd with swords and clubs, from the chief priests, the scribes, and the elders" (Mk 14:43). Mark's

[17]See Ann Graham Brock, *Mary Magdalene, the First Apostle: The Struggle for Authority*, Harvard Theological Studies 51 (Boston: Harvard Theological Studies, 2003), 168-69.

Gospel has already presented the chief priests, scribes, and elders as opposing Jesus (Mk 8:31; 11:27). Just as Jesus predicted, all of Jesus' disciples, presumably the other eleven, "deserted him and fled" (Mk 14:50). They do not understand Jesus; they are ignorant, unseeing, and hardhearted. They fail Jesus at his greatest moment of need. Yet the message is also to all of us who seek to follow Jesus. We too are ignorant, unseeing, and hardhearted. We too fail Jesus when he calls on us. For Mark, the Twelve represent those followers of Jesus who seek with their whole hearts to do right but might nevertheless fall short. The Twelve ultimately will be redeemed, giving hope to us all.

TRIAL AND DEATH (MARK 14:53–15:39)

Mark now leads readers to Jesus' death. Once again, the chief priests, scribes, and elders are arrayed against Jesus, this time before the high priest. The high priest during the Herodian temple period was an office appointed by Rome, which caused many to question his legitimacy. Mark never mentions the name of the high priest, but in Matthew, Luke, and John, he is identified as Caiaphas (Mt 26:3, 57; Lk 3:2; Jn 11:49; 18:13-14, 24, 28). Luke and John further elaborate that Caiaphas held the high priesthood in some relationship with his father-in-law, Annas.[18] It may be that, given Annas's influence, he continued to operate in an unofficial capacity during Caiaphas's exercise of the office. This dependence on Roman support is related in all four Gospels, with Jesus being subject to an early trial before the high priestly family and then being sent by them to Pilate (Mk 15:1; Mt 27:1-2; Lk 23:1; Jn 18:28).

Jesus before Pilate (Mark 15:1-15). The chief priests, elders, and scribes have Jesus bound and led to Pilate. All four Gospels reference this early meeting with the chief priests and their delivery of Jesus to Pilate. All four also present Pilate as attempting to exonerate Jesus against the wishes of the Jewish leadership. Readers are told that Pilate sought a way out of having to crucify Jesus.

This characterization, however, is puzzling in light of what we know about Pilate from historical sources. Pilate was a ruthless leader who often purposely provoked the Judeans and the Samaritans, showing that he had no concern about their opinions. Pontius Pilate was a Roman prefect who served as governor over Judea from 26–36 CE. As prefect, Pilate possessed the jurisdiction to execute criminals in the name of Rome. He was known for his disdain for the Israelite people and their practices (see Josephus, *Ant.* 18.3.1-2). Pilate's inhumanity was so well-known that, in 36 CE, the Roman emperor ordered him home to stand trial for executing people without proper trials and for inordinate cruelty. Church historian Eusebius says that after this, the Roman emperor ordered him to kill himself, which he did.

Yet in the Gospels, Pilate appears as both a just and a weak man, neither of which aligns with what we know about him from Josephus. In Mark, followed by Matthew and Luke, he offers the insurrectionist Barabbas to appease the crowds (Mk 15:6-15; see also Jn 18:39-40). In Matthew, he washes his hands of the killing (Mt 27:24). Three times in Luke, he claims that he finds no basis to accuse Jesus (Lk 23:4, 14, 22). John too presents him as finding no basis for accusation (Jn 18:38).

Recall that from the perspective of the Israelite establishment, the Evangelists represented a subaltern group of Israelite Jews and a growing contingent of people from the nations

[18]Josephus asserts that Caiaphas was appointed by the Roman governor after Annas, leading to some confusion about the periods in which the two exercised their offices. See Lk 3:2; Acts 4:6; Jn 18:13, 24; Josephus, *Ant.* 18.33-35.

who looked to the God of the Israelites as the true God. Thus the Evangelists portray the Jerusalem elite, and not Pontius Pilate, as the true accusers and as responsible for Jesus' death. For them, it was the Jerusalem elite who were betraying the plans and purposes of God and who thus were guilty.[19]

Second, the Evangelists had good reason to present Rome in a better light while openly challenging the Jerusalem Israelite elites. They were all likely writing in the late first century CE, after the Herodian temple had been destroyed. At this point, the high priest and the Jerusalem elite had lost their political power, although they retained social power. Nevertheless, they were no longer an immediate threat to the Evangelists and to their constituent readers and hearers. In contrast, Rome had become much more powerful and thus a greater force to contend with. This may have caused the Evangelists to shift the blame to the now-impotent Jewish authorities and away from Rome.

Finally, the early followers of Jesus were making inroads among Roman citizens, and they had the challenge of explaining to Roman citizens why they should follow a man who had been executed by their own empire. For all these reasons, if our Gospel writers presented the narrative in a way that exonerated Pilate, it would have made their message more effective throughout the empire.

Nevertheless, crucifixion was a Roman form of execution, not an Israelite/Jewish one. Therefore, as careful readers, we must look to Rome, not to the temple establishment, as the perpetrators of the execution. It is very unlikely that Pilate, who often purposely goaded the Israelite Judeans and the Samaritans, would have been worried about their opinion. Rather, it seems more plausible that the Evangelists minimize Pilate's role in order to place the blame squarely on the Jerusalem Israelite elites, who, by the time of writing, had no power to retaliate or to stand in the way of Roman citizens embracing the *basileia*.

Mark says that thousands had thronged the streets of Jerusalem for the Passover festival. Although there is no evidence outside the Gospels to corroborate this, Mark writes that it was a custom at this time for the Roman prefect to offer the people a choice as to whom Rome would crucify (Mk 15:6). The people cry out to Pilate to make good on the custom and to release to them Barabbas, "who had committed murder during the insurrection" (Mk 15:7). Readers have often been horrified that the people would have chosen an insurrectionist and murderer over the peaceful and loving Jesus. Recall, however, that most of the people in Jerusalem did not know of Jesus or of his ministry. They had come into the city from all over the empire for the festival. But many local Galilean and Judean Jews, suffering under Roman oppression, did know of and honored insurrectionists who had risen up against the oppressive Roman Empire. To be under the crushing boot of the Roman Empire was to be without rights, without justice, and without hope. For many Israelites, insurrection would have offered the only possibility of freedom from Rome's cruel yoke. It may be, then, that Barabbas was a local hero to the Israelites, which might explain their choice of him over the relatively unknown Jesus. Looking at the situation through the lens of

[19]Their portrayals, tragically, have resulted in centuries of violence by later Christians against Jews. Mark and the other Gospel writers may themselves have been marginalized Jews challenging the social center. But when imperial Christianity took up the same challenge later, it resulted in the victims becoming the victimizers. See Peter Tomson, *Presumed Guilty: How the Jews Were Blamed for the Death of Jesus* (Minneapolis: Fortress, 2005); Paula Fredriksen and Adele Reinhartz, eds., *Jesus, Judaism, and Christian Anti-Judaism: Reading the New Testament After the Holocaust* (Louisville, KY: Westminster John Knox, 2002).

how marginalized groups negotiate social and political power makes this suggestion plausible and understandable.

Crucifixion (Mark 15:16-39). Roman crucifixion was a brutal form of execution. Generally the victim was forced to carry the crossbar to the site of the crucifixion, where the upright beam would have been reused on one victim after another. The positioning of the prisoner led to a long, agonizing death, which occurred generally by blood loss or by asphyxiation as the muscles used for breathing became exhausted.

Crucifixions were commonplace under Rome, often occurring thousands at a time (Josephus, *Ant.* 17.10.10). Their purpose was as much to humiliate and deter as to punish. Crucifixions were common in cases of suspected or real sedition or insurrection. In Jesus' case, it is likely it would have been for sedition, given the evidence in the Gospels. From the type of execution to the way it was carried out, the evidence implies that it was because of Roman interests that Jesus was crucified as much as the interests of the temple elite. Here again, norms and conventions of behavior supported brutal violence and suppression of those who sought to put forth alternate visions of human society.

Resurrection (Mark 15:40–16:5). Mark mentions only Jesus' faithful female disciples as having the courage to observe the crucifixion directly. Among them, Mark names Mary Magdalene and Mary "the mother of James the younger and of Joses, and Salome" (Mk 15:40-41). These two women are also the first to the tomb after Jesus' burial (Mk 16:1). Jesus is buried by Joseph of Arimathea, whom Mark refers to as "a respected member of the council" (Mk 15:43). It is a surprise that Mark refers to Joseph as a member of the council, because in Mark 14:64, Mark reported that "all of them"—including the council (see Mk 14:55; 15:1)—"condemned him [Jesus] as deserving death." It may be that Mark was referencing the majority, as Luke 23:51 implies, but the Greek text also allows for the possibility that Joseph either had abstained from or not been invited to the council's interrogation of Jesus. The final possibility is that Joseph, as a pious Israelite, wanted to ensure that a fellow Israelite received a proper burial, whether or not he supported his cause. To be sure, Matthew and John refer to Joseph as a disciple of Jesus (Mt 27:57; Jn 19:38), but such a presupposition is not required by either Mark's or Luke's description of him (see Lk 23:50). In any case, the Joseph narrative explains how a poor itinerant such as Jesus could manage to be buried in a stone tomb, a burial reserved only for the wealthy in Jerusalem during this era.

The Sabbath day, following the day of crucifixion, would not have allowed for any ministrations to Jesus' body. The women's behavior, in avoiding the tomb on that day, demonstrates that for them sacred time and biblical law were to be revered. On the first day of the week those same women who witnessed the crucifixion come to the tomb and find it occupied not by Jesus' body but by "a young man, dressed in a white robe"—presumably an angel, based on the description of the clothing—who announces to the women that Jesus of Nazareth, whom he claims they are seeking, "has been raised" (Mk 16:5-6).

The angel then tells the women to tell the disciples and Peter that Jesus has arisen and that they will see him if they return to Galilee (Mk 16:7). Mark says that the women do no such thing, saying nothing to anyone out of fear (Mk 16:8). In the manuscript tradition, this is the most likely ending of Mark. Some ancient manuscripts add Mark 16:9, and others add Mark 16:9-20. However, it appears that both endings were added later to provide a more satisfying conclusion to the book.

Let us consider, however, two final important elements in Mark 16:7-8. First, once again, Mark privileges Galilee as a site of the sacred, over Jerusalem. Mark presents Jesus' post-resurrection appearance as occurring in Galilee, not Jerusalem. The second important narrative element to note in Mark 16:1-8 is the role of the women. Although Mark presents Mary Magdalene and Mary as the first to witness the empty tomb, Mark makes no effort to present them as the first evangelists, as do the other Gospels (Mt 28:1-8; Lk 23:55–24:10; Jn 20:1-18). For Mark, the women merely flee in fear (Mk 16:8). In either case, the women attest to the stone having been rolled away and to the angel testifying that Jesus has risen from the dead (Mk 16:4-7). Death has no dominion over Jesus. Life wins. Jesus has overcome the suffering, the persecution, the crucifixion at the hands of powerful Rome and its cronies in Jerusalem. For Mark, Jesus has overcome.

CONCLUSION

Mark's Gospel provides a key first-century witness not only to the story of Jesus but also to the manifold social identities of that era. Some groups, represented by Mark's perspective, valued the fictive kinship of the assemblies of Jesus-followers above all other markers of social identity. For Latinxs, traditional kinship, that is, *familia*, is a central identifying social value. While a simple reading of Mark might cause Latinxs to feel estranged from their social identity, Mark makes clear that the true *familia* is the *familia* centered on the resurrected Christ. A close *familia*, in this sense, makes perfect sense. As I read Mark in the context of my own hybrid cultural identity, being both Latina and White, I see a brother in Christ navigating the powerful hierarchies that seek to silence and exploit and instead finding another way, which enfranchises and enfolds those on the boundaries.

Mark challenges all the traditional social-identity markers of sacred space, time, and ritual. Jerusalem is not the sacred city for Mark; it is a site of death. The temple is not a sacred site; it has been profaned by the ungodly cronies of Rome who operate it. Rituals of food and Sabbath are challenged in Mark, although rarely rejected. Instead, Mark's Jesus generally tends to claim to be the authoritative interpreter when it comes to such rituals. In Latinx culture here in the western United States, rituals are much more accepted than they are in much of Anglo-European culture. For instance, Latinxs are much more likely to light a candle to memorialize the death of a person or to set aside time that is sacred for the family. Sacred space is often created by traditions that revere particular gathering places. Often this has to do with the strong tradition of Catholicism in Latinx culture in the United States. But there are also strong traditions within Indigenous culture and within Latinx Pentecostalism that value sacred time, space, and rituals as well. That these categories are contested opens up the possibility for contemporary Latinxs to see each type of social identity as contingent and as offering possibilities for change and engagement.

Mark has little respect for claims about any unique authority to be ascribed to the twelve disciples in Jesus' inner circle. Mark, as one very likely not from Jerusalem and as one not inclined to accept symbolic imagery as authoritative, presents the Twelve as uniquely stubborn and faithless. Here again, Latinxs can recognize that social identity is shifting and fluid. Some may find great comfort in traditional images and symbols; others, like Mark, may find them unhelpful. The Gospel tradition supports both.

It is incumbent on us, as Latinxs, to explore the deep and profound questions that arise from our unique social histories and geographies. If we simply accept unquestioningly the assumptions of Anglo-European Christianity, then we are in some sense accepting social-identity markers that do not take into account our own stories and narratives. When we read these Gospels as conversations rather than as dogmatic pronouncements, we can see that many of the social-identity signifiers in Latinx culture are present in one or all the Gospels in rich ways. To be sure, they are contested, but nevertheless they are enshrined in the Gospel tradition.

SELECTED BIBLIOGRAPHY

Bar-Cohn, D. "Tzaraʿat Purification: A Vestige of Demonic Exorcism." TheTorah.com, 2023. https://thetorah.com/article/tzaraat-purification-a-vestige-of-demonic-exorcism.

Boer, Wietse de. "The Catholic Church and Sexual Abuse, Then and Now." *Origins* 12, no. 6 (March 2019). https://origins.osu.edu/article/catholic-church-sexual-abuse-pope-confession-priests-nuns.

Brock, Ann Graham. *Mary Magdalene, the First Apostle: The Struggle for Authority*. Harvard Theological Studies 51. Boston: Harvard Theological Studies, 2003.

Ceresko, Anthony R. "The Identity of 'the Blind and the Lame' (*iwwer upiseah*) in 2 Samuel 5:8b." *CBQ* 63, no. 1 (January 2001): 23-30.

Eusebius. *The History of the Church*. Translated by G. A. Williamson. New York: Dorset, 1965.

Evans, Craig. "A Note on Targum 2 Samuel 5.8 and Jesus' Ministry to the 'Maimed, Halt, and Blind.'" *Journal for the Study of the Pseudepigrapha* 15 (April 1997): 79-82

Fredriksen, Paula, and Adele Reinhartz, eds. *Jesus, Judaism, and Christian Anti-Judaism: Reading the New Testament After the Holocaust*. Louisville, KY: Westminster John Knox, 2002.

García Martínez, Florentino, and Eibert J. C. Tigchelaar, eds. and trans. *The Dead Sea Scrolls Study Edition*. Vol. 1. Leiden: Brill, 1997.

George, Mark K. *Israel's Tabernacle as Social Space*. Atlanta: Society of Biblical Literature, 2009.

Herzog, William R., II. *Jesus, Justice, and the Reign of God*. Louisville, KY: Westminster John Knox, 2000.

Jacobson, David. "Herod's Roman Temple." *Biblical Archaeology Review* 28, no. 2 (2002): 19-25, 60-61.

Milgrom, Jacob. *Leviticus 17–22: A New Translation with Introduction and Commentary*. AB. New York: Doubleday, 2000.

Netzer, Ehud, and Rachel Laureys-Chachy. *The Architecture of Herod, the Great Builder*. Grand Rapids, MI: Baker Academic, 2008.

Shellnutt, Kate. "Hundreds Accuse Independent Baptist Pastors of Abuse." *Christianity Today*, December 12, 2018. www.christianitytoday.com/news/2018/december/independent-fundamentalist-baptist-church-abuse-scandal.html.

Smith, Peter, and Travis Loller. "Secret Recordings Show Southern Baptist Dispute on Sex Abuse." ABC News, June 10, 2021. www.news10.com/news/secret-recordings-show-southern-baptist-dispute-on-sex-abuse/.

Tomson, Peter. *Presumed Guilty: How the Jews Were Blamed for the Death of Jesus*. Minneapolis: Fortress, 2005.

Wise, Michael, Martin Abegg, and Edward Cook, eds. and trans. *The Dead Sea Scrolls: A New English Translation*. New York: HarperCollins, 2009.

GOSPEL OF LUKE

DIANE G. CHEN

INTRODUCTION

Among the four Gospels, the Gospel of Luke distinguishes itself as the only one with a sequel, the Acts of the Apostles. This lengthy double work begins with the birth of John the Baptist, takes the reader through the life of Jesus, and traces the spread of the gospel by the early church from Jerusalem to Rome.

The original autograph of the Gospel is no longer extant, but a copy, written in papyrus and dating back to around 200 CE, contains the postscript "Gospel according to Luke." Apparently, some scribe chose to identify Luke as the author of the manuscript. Other notable early church fathers, namely, Clement of Alexandria, Irenaeus, Tertullian, Eusebius, and Jerome, also attribute Lukan authorship to this narrative. This broad agreement among patristic writers from the second to the fifth century is sufficiently robust for us to accept that Luke wrote both the Gospel and the book of Acts.

Who, then, is Luke? The church fathers identify him as a physician from Syrian Antioch and a companion of Paul. These descriptors are consistent with what is said of him in Paul's letters (Col 4:14; 2 Tim 4:11; Philem 24). Moreover, some accounts in Acts are written in first-person plural. These "we-passages" suggest that the author was with Paul on certain occasions (Acts 16:10-17; 20:5-15; 21:1-18; 27:1–28:16), concurring with the claim elsewhere that he was Paul's coworker.

From the prologue, we learn that Luke was not an eyewitness but a second-generation Christian (Lk 1:2-3). His sophisticated style of writing points to a highly educated individual, fluent in the Septuagint (the Greek translation of the Hebrew Scriptures) and in Greco-Roman literary conventions. The general agreement among scholars is that Luke was a Gentile convert, but a Diaspora Jew could be just as learned and have as universal an outlook about God's salvation. Ethnicity aside, it is more important to acknowledge the skillful historian in Luke, who handled the information on Jesus with care, faithfulness, analytical clarity, and theological insight.

The Gospel of Luke must postdate the Gospel of Mark, since the author had Mark as a source.[1] If the dating of Mark is around 66–70 CE, and if the passages in Luke in which Jesus predicts the fall of Jerusalem reflect the manner in which Rome actually sacked Jerusalem in 70 CE (Lk 19:43-44; 21:20-24), then the Gospel of Luke may be reasonably situated somewhere between 70 and 90 CE.

The setting for the writing of this narrative is indeterminable, even though the addressee is identified as one "most excellent Theophilus" (Lk 1:3; Acts 1:1), a man of standing. Nothing

[1]Markan priority (the idea that Mark is the earliest of the four Gospels) and the Four Document Hypothesis (that Mark, Q, and L are the sources behind Luke; and Mark, Q, and M are the sources behind Matthew) are widely accepted for explaining the relationship between the Synoptic Gospels.

more is known about him, his faith community, their location, or the circumstances that prompted the penning of this narrative. Intended to appeal broadly, Luke–Acts would have enjoyed a good reception from Jewish and Gentile Christians alike, with its emphasis on the universality of God's salvation.

Luke's Gospel is neatly laid out in five segments: (1) The infancy narrative (Lk 1:1–2:52) records the parallel annunciations and birth stories of John and Jesus, connecting the Messiah's arrival with Israel's hope of deliverance in the Old Testament. (2) A time of preparation (Lk 3:1–4:13) depicts John's baptism of repentance for the people and introduces Jesus at his baptism qua commissioning and subsequent testing in the wilderness. (3) Jesus' Galilean ministry (Lk 4:14–9:50), beginning with his inaugural sermon at Nazareth, is filled with miracles, healings, and teachings. His identity remains a point of speculation until its revelation in Peter's confession and the transfiguration. (4) The travel narrative (Lk 9:51–19:27) recounts Jesus' final journey to Jerusalem, during which he teaches his disciples about prayer, commitment, use of money, perseverance, and the values of God's kingdom. (5) The passion narrative (Lk 19:28–24:53) begins with Jesus' entry into Jerusalem, traces the events through holy week, and culminates in his resurrection and ascension.

Significant thematic elements can be gleaned from the author's selection, arrangement, and narration of what Jesus did and taught. The Gospel of Luke emphasizes that Jesus is not only the Messiah of Israel but also the Savior of the world (Lk 2:30-32; 3:5-6). Gentile characters are depicted as having faith that surpasses even that of the Jews (see Lk 7:9; 8:39; 17:18; 23:47). The messianic identity of Jesus, however, is not immediately obvious to his contemporaries. In addition to a kingly portrayal (Lk 1:31-33; 19:38; 23:37-38), Luke also presents Jesus as God's eschatological prophet by comparing him with Elijah, Elisha, and Jonah (Lk 4:24-27; 7:1-17; 11:29-32). Ultimately, it is Luke's depiction of Jesus as God's divine beloved Son that rises above all other descriptions. Jesus enacts God's mercy and life-giving power on earth and models what it means for God's children to be perfectly faithful and obedient to their Father in heaven (Lk 2:49; 3:22; 9:35; 20:9-16; 22:42; 23:34, 46).

As the Son carries out his Father's mission, he embodies God's salvation in releasing people from bondage (Lk 4:18-19). In particular, Luke highlights Jesus' compassionate ministry to the nobodies, be they poor, widowed, laden with illnesses and diseases, demon-possessed, sinful, ostracized, or despised. Tax collectors and Samaritans are featured as the wrong people doing the right thing in Jesus' interactions and in his parables (Lk 5:27-29; 7:29, 34; 10:29-37; 17:11-19; 19:1-10). By contrast, religious leaders such as the scribes, the Pharisees, and the temple authorities who reject Jesus and his message will receive severe judgment (Lk 5:20-21; 7:30, 39; 13:14; 15:1-2; 20:1-47; 23:1-5). Indeed, the ethos of God's kingdom is completely countercultural, promising to lift up the lowly and bring down the elite, rewarding humble-hearted faith and punishing prideful self-righteousness. In the end, following Jesus on a path of suffering is daunting, but for those who persevere in faith, the reward and glory in the life to come will far outweigh the temporary hardship of this life.

As a Chinese immigrant growing up in Hong Kong, then still a British colony, and for the last four decades living as an immigrant in the United States, I have been pondering what it means to be both a Hong-Konger and a Chinese American, especially in light of the recent political upheaval in the city of my birth. At times it feels like I belong to both worlds, at other times to neither world. Either way, there is a nagging otherness, however faintly detected, that colors my reading of Luke. Like it or not, I will always be numbered among the minorities in this country, and because of that Jesus' compassion for outsiders draws me to this Gospel. It allows me to celebrate my otherness as a blessed place to encounter the living God. In God's kingdom, some tension with the social structures of this present world is a rather redemptive and contemplative place to be. I hope this short commentary resonates with those who also feel that they are neither here nor there. In God's family, the "other" has come home.

PROLOGUE (LUKE 1:1-4)

Following the convention of Greco-Roman writings of his time, Luke introduces his narrative with a prologue. Although the addressee is Theophilus ("one who loves God"), the intended audience would have included his community of faith. Without the tools of recording available to us today, eyewitness accounts were a valuable source of information for historians in the ancient world. Since Luke did not accompany Jesus in his earthly ministry, he traced the information available to him back to those eyewitnesses who faithfully passed on what Jesus taught and did. In addition to factual veracity, Luke's expressed goal is to use a well-organized narrative to help his readers understand the truth, in particular the significance of what they have already learned about Jesus—how all the events surrounding him represent the fulfillment of God's promise of salvation.

GOD REMEMBERS: JOHN'S BIRTH ANNOUNCED (LUKE 1:5-25)

Among the four Gospels, Luke is unique in relating the birth of John, the forerunner of the Messiah. Reaching back into the Old Testament, the story of John's birth is full of anticipation as God sets in motion his plan of salvation for Israel and the world.

Set in the Roman Empire during the time when the better part of Palestine was ruled by Herod the Great, a pro-Roman vassal king who was half Jew and half Syrian, the story begins with Zechariah the priest and his wife, Elizabeth. Both are descendants from pure priestly lines and have lived a righteous life before God. But a cloud of suspicion hangs over them because of Elizabeth's barrenness. In those days, childlessness would have been attributed to a divine curse. People might have looked at them with suspicion and wondered, "What terrible sin did they commit that God closed her womb?" Imagine the social stigma that hung over them, not to mention not having a son to carry the family name, care for them in their old age, and bury them when they died. These concerns would have resonated in a traditional, male-centered Chinese context, where childlessness was considered a terrible shame for the same reasons. In the old days, a barren couple with means might even have bought a son from peasants who could not afford to raise all their children. By contrast, Zechariah's and Elizabeth's acceptance of their lot from God is all the more exemplary, for they could easily have become resentful and blamed God for their adversity.

One day, Zechariah has an encounter with the archangel Gabriel that will change his and Elizabeth's life forever. Given the large number of priests on active duty, officiants for prayer services at the temple were chosen by lot. For the lot to fall on Zechariah was a once-in-a-lifetime opportunity. While offering incense just outside the holy of holies, he is terrified to see an angel appearing at the right side of the altar.[2] When the angel tells Zechariah that his

---

[2]The right is considered the superior side.

prayer has been answered, one might assume the prayer was for a son. But would the couple still have been praying for a child now that Elizabeth was far beyond child-bearing age? One would think they had given up hope a long time ago. Since this encounter occurs during a prayer service, could Gabriel be referring to Zechariah's prayer for Israel's restoration? After all, this child to be born will be filled with the Holy Spirit and his life dedicated to preparing God's people for repentance and reconciliation.[3] In God's sovereign efficiency, the long-awaited messianic hopes of Israel and the aching desire of this faithful priestly couple will soon be fulfilled in one fell swoop.

Incredulous, Zechariah asks, "How will I know that this is so?" (Lk 1:18). He asks for a sign as proof, but he will receive a sign of punishment. Because of his unbelief, Zechariah is rendered mute until Gabriel's words come to fruition. This sign, ironically, strips him of the pleasure of telling people the good news himself. Subsequently, Elizabeth becomes pregnant, and the stigma she and her husband endured for many decades will soon be removed.

GOD SURPRISES: JESUS' BIRTH ANNOUNCED (LUKE 1:26-56)

The scene shifts from the sacred environs of the Jerusalem temple to the home of a young girl named Mary in a backwater village of Nazareth in Galilee. The contrast between Zechariah's and Mary's statuses is notable in gender, age, and social standing, yet the same divine messenger is dispatched to both. Gabriel's appearance likewise shocks Mary, who could not have been more than twelve to fourteen years old. Already betrothed to Joseph, a Davidide, she receives an even more unfathomable message: she will bear a holy child who is the Davidic king promised by the prophets of old. Through Mary, a lowly virgin maiden, God will bring Israel's Messiah into the world. As if it were not counterintuitive enough that a king should be born of a peasant girl, her out-of-wedlock pregnancy would have been especially scandalous to the uninitiated (see Mt 1:18-19).

Mary, too, poses a question, "How can this be?" (Lk 1:34). Unlike Zechariah, her question stems not from unbelief. She simply cannot imagine how conception is possible without her having had relations with a man. When told that the Holy Spirit will bring this to pass, she responds in total submission. Without her asking for a sign, Gabriel provides one anyway: her aged relative Elizabeth's pregnancy bears witness to divine intervention, and Mary's is no different. Even though both women are beneficiaries of God's grace and honored to be chosen to carry John and Jesus in their wombs, the nine months of gestation must have been very awkward under the eyes of social scrutiny.

Nevertheless, joy and the presence of the Holy Spirit characterize the meeting of Mary and Elizabeth. Mary's hymn praises God for his mercy and celebrates Yahweh's saving action as a reversal of conditions, in which the lowly are lifted up and the proud are cast down. Because God helped the poor and the powerless in the past, he will surely help them again. The theme of reversal will be sounded again and again as the narrative progresses, separating those who receive God's salvation from those who refuse it.

THE FORERUNNER IS BORN (LUKE 1:57-80)

In due time, Elizabeth gives birth to a son, whom she names John ("God has been gracious"), as instructed by the angel. Relatives reject the idea at first and insist that the child

[3]The description of John's mission recalls the role of Elijah the eschatological prophet (Mal 4:5-6).

be named after his father, the norm in patrilineal cultures. But as soon as Zechariah concurs with his wife, his punishment is over, and he begins to prophesy.

The name Zechariah means "God remembered," a theme that pervades his prophecy concerning John and Israel. Convinced of God's faithfulness, Zechariah declares that God will rescue his people from the hands of their enemies. Israel has suffered much oppression from foreigners in its history, and at present it is the Romans. For Zechariah, God's covenant with Abraham remains valid. By God's mercy, Israel will emerge from darkness into light and from oppression into peace. The Messiah is coming, and John will prepare his way.

In describing the birth announcements of John and Jesus, Luke employs the literary technique of step parallelism. These are matching birth annunciations by the same angel, matching miraculous births, matching pronouncements of the child's future role, and matching hymns by Mary and Zechariah about God's salvation. Yet, at every turn, Jesus is presented as superior to John. For example, Jesus is Son of the Most High, while John is prophet of the Most High. Jesus is conceived by the Holy Spirit, an unprecedented event in human history, whereas John's conception, while miraculous in terms of God opening the womb of a barren woman, has antecedents in the Old Testament.[4] The parallelism reminds us that John and Jesus are about the same mission, but while John signifies continuity with Israel's past and its messianic hopes, Jesus embodies a new and definitive trajectory, where salvation is not only for Israel but also for the world.

THE ARRIVAL OF A MOST UNLIKELY KING (LUKE 2:1-40)

Luke's reference to Augustus Caesar's worldwide census is more than a timestamp marking Jesus' birth. Two important theological points are noted in relation to the Roman emperor. First, Jesus is Messiah of Israel as well as Savior of the world, whose regime stands in contrast to Caesar's.[5] Second, even though the census is a tool of subjugation, conducted to register subjects for taxation, Augustus is an unwitting instrument of God to bring Joseph and Mary from Nazareth to Bethlehem, the town from which the Messiah was expected to come (Mic 5:2; Mt 2:6).

In modern Christmas pageants, the scene where the innkeeper turns Joseph and Mary away is actually missing from the biblical text. The Greek word *katalyma* can refer to a guestroom or an inn. It is likely that the living quarters of Joseph's relative are already occupied, so the couple ends up staying where the animals are sheltered.[6] There Mary gives birth to Jesus, her firstborn, and she places him in a manger.

The king of Israel has arrived under the humblest of circumstances in a town belonging to one of the smallest clans of Judah. The shepherds in the field, who are the first to receive the news, also come from the most despised of professions. In ancient times, shepherds were hired hands, working out in the fields, moving from pasture to pasture, vulnerable to attacks by wild animals. People would not choose to be a shepherd if they had other options. Yet in an ironic twist of reversal, these lowly shepherds are honored by an angelic appearance announcing the birth of Jesus. Before their eyes, the armies of heaven

[4]E.g., Sarai, Rebekah, Rachel, Samson's mother, and Hannah.
[5]The Roman emperor also had the title *Sōtēr* ("Savior").
[6]Ancient homes often had separate spaces for animals and people under the same roof.

glorify God and promise peace to all the earth because of the Messiah's coming. And the sign they receive—a baby wrapped in cloth lying in a feeding trough—is unusual enough to be quite unmistakable.

Whether terrified or baffled by that glorious spectacle, the shepherds hurry off to Bethlehem in search of the Messiah. Because they believe what they have seen and heard, they are blessed with an intimate encounter with Jesus and his parents. Returning as eyewitnesses, they bear testimony to heaven's affirmation that this child in the manger is truly Israel's long-awaited Messiah.

On the eighth day, Jesus' parents bring him to the temple to be circumcised. They name him Jesus, the name given by the angel, meaning "Yahweh saves." That Mary and Joseph can afford only a pair of cheap birds and not a lamb for sacrifice is suggestive of their modest means. Though poor, they abide by the law and dedicate their firstborn to God, setting him apart for God's service.

Some Chinese parents dedicate their child to a temple god in exchange for a good life, more children, or prosperity for the family, with the hope that they will be well taken care of in their old age. This attitude differs from the Jewish dedication of the firstborn to God because everything belongs to Yahweh in the first place. In either culture, though, it is reasonable to hope for a blessed life when parents offer up their most precious firstborn child, especially a son. Jesus' parents, however, receive a painful prophetic word instead.

Two elderly and pious folks, Simeon and Anna, meet the holy infant and acknowledge his role in the restoration of Israel and the enlightenment of the nations. But this path of salvation will not be smooth, for Simeon prophesies that Jesus will cause some to rise and others to fall, implying a mixed response to his mission. As a result, Mary's soul will be pierced; she will suffer deep anguish in witnessing her son's death. Her role as the Messiah's earthly mother, while honorific, will be a bittersweet one.

FILIAL ALLEGIANCE REFOCUSED (LUKE 2:41-52)

Of the four Gospels, only Luke has an account of Jesus as a youth. From the time he was old enough to make the trip, Jesus has been going with his parents to Jerusalem to observe the Passover. As one of the three Jewish pilgrimage feasts of the year, Passover commemorates the night that God rescued the Israelites from Egypt, when the angel of death spared their firstborn by passing over their homes, whose doors were marked with the blood of the lamb. The feast also anticipates God's deliverance in the future, for the one who saved Israel will save again as promised.

This year, unbeknown to his parents, Jesus stays back when the family's traveling party leaves Jerusalem. By the time Mary and Joseph realize his absence, return to Jerusalem, search for him, and locate him at the temple, it has been three anxiety-filled days. Here is Jesus, sitting among the scribes, discussing the law. While his parents are probably relieved, they are equally upset with him. Mary chides him as a mother would: "Child, why have you treated us like this?" (Lk 2:48). Her reprimand is understandable because Jesus' action would strike any parent as oddly irresponsible and out of character. Jesus' reply, "Did you not know I must be about my Father's *business*?" (Lk 2:49, my translation), is telling. Most English translations read "my Father's *house*" (e.g., NRSV, NIV, NLT, CEV, ESV), because, after all, he is at the temple, but the Greek word for "house" is not in the text. The phrase *en tois tou patros mou* is more ambiguous: "in/among/

about the [something] of my father." The common translation fails to capture the theological truth in Jesus' answer. The Son of God will spend his life carrying out the mission assigned to him by his heavenly Father, and this event marks the beginning of that shift as the role and place of his earthly parents begin to recede.

JOHN'S PROGRAM AND JESUS' BAPTISM (LUKE 3:1-22)

The narrative time advances to the beginning of John's and Jesus' public ministry. Tiberias is now the sitting Roman emperor, and jurisdiction over Palestine is split between Pontius Pilate, the Roman governor in charge of Judea, and vassal kings Herod Antipas and Philip, who oversee Galilee and the surrounding regions. Also introduced are Caiaphas, the high priest, and his predecessor and father-in-law, Annas. These political and religious forces will play a significant role in the rejection of Jesus. Their mention strikes an ominous tone, hinting that conflict will arise even as deliverance comes to God's people.

John appears in the wilderness of Jordan and embarks on his mission as foretold by the angel (Lk 1:16-17). With a baptism of repentance for the forgiveness of sins, he prepares the people for Jesus' coming. Speaking of John as a "voice of one crying out in the wilderness" (Lk 3:4; see Is 40:3), Luke's citation from Isaiah underscores the universality of God's redemptive plan, that "all flesh shall see the salvation of God" (Lk 3:6; see Is 40:5).

True repentance manifests itself in human relationships, as indicative in John's ethical program. He warns the crowd not to assume that Abrahamic ancestry guarantees salvation. Rather, from peasants to tax collectors and soldiers, generosity and justice must characterize their treatment of one another. The haves must share with the have-nots, tax collectors must not overcharge, and soldiers must not extort money from the powerless. Such teachings were radical in a social structure where people did whatever they could to seize honor, influence, and wealth, even at another's expense. No wonder the crowds speculate about whether John is the Messiah, a misconception he is quick to correct. He anticipates the Coming One as infinitely loftier, with the power to judge and to send the Holy Spirit.

Here the author momentarily steps out of logical sequencing and mentions Herod's imprisonment of John *before* recounting Jesus' baptism, an event where John is obviously still present. In fact, Luke does not describe the actual baptism but the trinitarian scene that follows. As Jesus prays, the Holy Spirit descends on him, and a voice from heaven declares: "You are my Son, the Beloved, with you I am well pleased" (Lk 3:22; see Ps 2:7; Gen 22:2; Is 42:1).[7] With these words, the Father commissions his Son as Israel's servant-king.

FROM JESUS TO ADAM (LUKE 3:23-37)

Lest the reader glaze over the genealogy as simply a list of names that trace Jesus back to Adam, Luke's version makes several important theological points. First, since Jewish genealogies normally proceed from the ancestor downward, by going up the generations, Luke places Jesus at the position of prominence before all his forefathers. Second, this genealogy confirms Jesus' Davidic descent (Lk 3:31; see Lk 1:27; 2:4). Third, Jesus' lineage is traced back beyond Abraham to Adam, the first man, signifying that Jesus is not only the Messiah of Israel but also the Savior of the world. Last, the

[7]The sense that God the Father is speaking directly to Jesus the Son here is different from Mt 3:17, "This is my Son, the Beloved, with whom I am well pleased," which functions as an introduction of Jesus to the crowd.

parenthetical statement, that Jesus is "the son (as was thought) of Joseph" (Lk 3:23), indicates that although people normally think of Joseph as Jesus' father (Lk 4:22), in reality it is God, Jesus' Father in heaven, who determines the course of his life and to whom he owes total allegiance (Lk 2:49).

TEMPTATIONS AND TESTING (LUKE 4:1-13)

Jesus' encounters with Satan are often referred to as temptations. The Greek word *peirasmos* can mean "temptation," "trial," or "test." As Satan tries to lure Jesus into disobedience, the Son of God is at the same time tested and prepared for the challenges ahead.

As he is led by the Holy Spirit into the wilderness, Jesus' experience during these forty days evokes comparisons with Israel's forty years in the desert. The devil first entices Jesus to turn stone into bread, stating his entitlement for provision as God's Son. Jesus' situation recalls the time when the Israelites complained to Moses about their hunger and even pined for the food in Egypt (Ex 16:3). In refusing to take matters into his own hands, Jesus cites Deuteronomy 8:3, "One does not live by bread alone" (Lk 4:4), a phrase set in a larger context of God using hunger to train Israel to rely on divine sustenance. This unwavering trust in God to provide for his needs is a principle that Jesus lives by and teaches his disciples (Lk 9:3-4, 12-17; 10:4-7; 11:3; 12:22-31).

Next, the devil boasts of his dominion over all the world's kingdoms and purports to give them to Jesus in exchange for a bow of worship. The truthfulness of this claim is highly suspect, and Jesus retorts with Deuteronomy 6:13, "Worship the Lord your God, and serve only him" (Lk 4:8). This is another indictment of Israel's past failure in false worship, from the golden calf to the gods of the Canaanites. In Psalm 2:8, Israel's king is promised the nations as his heritage, so Satan's offer adds nothing to what Jesus already possesses by virtue of his divine and royal status.

Finally, the devil takes Jesus to the pinnacle of the temple and goads him to force God's hand of protection by invoking Psalm 91:11-12. Once more, Jesus' reply recalls Israel's failure in Deuteronomy 6:16. At Massah, the people tested God, but Jesus refuses to fall into the same trap and gives the rejoinder, "Do not to put the Lord your God to the test" (Lk 4:12).

These accounts present Jesus as more than just thumping his Bible at Satan. All three vignettes call to mind the failures of the exodus generation. God's people stumbled, but Jesus overcomes as the model Israelite. As Messiah, not only can he identify with the weaknesses of God's people, but he also leads them to faithful obedience and victory. Defeated, the devil leaves Jesus until his reappearance in Luke 22. In the meantime, satanic opposition continues in the form of unclean spirits and other obstacles to human flourishing (Lk 4:33-34; 8:27-28; 13:11, 16).

While these temptations are specifically designed to derail Jesus at the start of his mission, we may identify with Israel's lack of trust, whether in complaining about our problems, finding our own ways to solve them without waiting on God, or being drawn to earthly power and recognition. As a Chinese immigrant, I find that the combination of a strong work ethic and an aspiration for upward mobility in a new homeland—both good things in and of themselves—can tempt me to put my agenda before God's agenda. To many immigrants, chasing after the so-called American dream seems a responsible and dignifying thing to do, but will that ambition for security soon overshadow God's priority in our lives? After all, temptations often come disguised as something positive, or else we would not fall for them that easily. Even seemingly good things, as in the case of sustenance, honor, and protection for Jesus, can draw us into disobedience. Therefore, only with a laser focus on God, as Jesus models here, will we be able to detect Satan's manipulations, resist his temptations, and pass the tests of faith.

SALVATION AS RELEASE AND REVERSAL (LUKE 4:14-44)

Filled with the Holy Spirit, Jesus emerges from the wilderness and embarks on his public ministry. In the sermon preached at the synagogue in Nazareth, he lays out his messianic mission. Applying the reading from Isaiah 61:1-2; 58:6 to himself, Jesus claims to be the Servant of Yahweh who brings release from bondage and the reversal of conditions. Even though Jesus will not overthrow the Romans, he will bring true restoration to people in their relationship with God and with one another.

Initially, the villagers are pleased that Nazareth's hometown son has given a gracious word. Yet Jesus exposes their selfish and narrow-minded attitudes when he applies the proverb "Doctor, cure yourself" to them, pointing out that they expect him to benefit them only. To further explain the broad scope of his mission, Jesus cites Elijah's aid to the Sidonian widow at Zarephath (1 Kings 17:8-24), and Elisha's healing of Naaman, the Syrian general, from leprosy (2 Kings 5:1-14). Both were Gentiles, thus unclean to the Jews. Moreover, Naaman was doubly unclean as a leper, and the widow was poor and powerless. In other words, not only will Jesus not serve the people of Nazareth exclusively, but he tells them he is sent to bless those outsiders and nobodies whom they dislike. Filled with indignation, the villagers become incensed. If I were one of them, I might have felt slighted as well. In Chinese, there is a derogatory saying, "The thumb that turns outward and not inward," used to denounce an ingrate who sides with outsiders against their family members. Gone is the villagers' earlier approval of Jesus as they now want to hurl him over the cliff, fulfilling exactly Jesus' words that "no prophet is accepted in the prophet's hometown" (Lk 4:24).

A rapid succession of vignettes next situates Jesus in Capernaum, proclaiming the good news and doing the very things mentioned in his sermon at Nazareth. The power of Jesus is in his words. He teaches with authority, and he rebukes unclean spirits and Simon's mother-in-law's fever. His reputation spreads like wildfire, and many receive healing. The crowds try to keep Jesus among themselves, but to no avail, for the good news of God's kingdom must be spread everywhere, both near and far.

A SINNER TURNED DISCIPLE (LUKE 5:1-11)

How often does a carpenter tell a fisherman when and where to fish? Probably never. Peter could have shrugged off Jesus' command to drop his nets in deep water during the day as ignorant and insulting, especially when he and his crew just worked all night and caught nothing. Any seasoned fisherman would know that the fish could see the net in broad daylight and steer clear of the trap. Moreover, he would be shamed if they returned empty-handed again, not to mention owing additional wages to pay with money he did not have. Perhaps remembering Jesus' healing of his mother-in-law causes Peter to carry out the order, albeit reluctantly: "If you say so, I will let down the nets" (Lk 5:5).

What a revelation from a little bit of faith in concrete action! So many fish are caught that Peter's boat and that of his partners, James and John, are filled to the brink of sinking. Most people would have focused on the miraculous catch and the fortune it would bring, but Peter immediately recognizes his unworthiness in Jesus' numinous presence. His reaction is reminiscent of Isaiah's cry, "Woe to me!" when the prophet saw a vision of God's throne (Is 6:1-5). Falling on his knees, Peter entreats, "Go away from me, Lord, for I am a sinful man" (Lk 5:8). Jesus' response is not a rebuke but an invitation to discipleship. Immediately, leaving the security of their trade and family, Peter, James, and John follow Jesus to a new life of catching people.

We are so used to reading in the four Gospels that the disciples respond immediately when Jesus calls that we underestimate how radical that decision must have been. My father and my uncle ran a small business started by my grandfather, and there has always been an unspoken expectation, or at least hope, that the next generation would keep it going. In the Chinese context, what is best for the family takes precedence over individual aspirations, and maintaining the family business is an expression of filial piety and gratitude. I wonder, therefore, how the disciples' families reacted to their abrupt departure to follow this new rabbi. Did they resent them for abandoning their obligations? Were ties irreparably severed? Even though much of Jesus' itinerant ministry took place in Galilee, so the disciples could still visit their families on occasion, shifting one's primary loyalties from one's family of origin to Jesus could have created considerable relational tension. Even though Jesus promises his disciples divine recompense for having left home and family to follow him (Lk 18:28-30), each must count the cost—and the cost is very high—before making that irreversible commitment (Lk 9:23-24, 57-62).

JESUS' INTERPRETATION OF THE LAW (LUKE 5:12–6:11)

In this section, Luke presents a series of accounts to illustrate the mixed responses to Jesus. On the one hand, he heals the sick and reaches out to outcasts. On the other hand, he faces opposition from the respected teachers of the community. Jesus brings many people to wholeness—a leper, a paralytic, a man with a withered hand, and tax collectors and sinners. Even allowing the disciples to pluck grains on the Sabbath to eat is part of his holistic restorative mission. But the scribes and the Pharisees criticize Jesus for breaking purity and Sabbath laws. In these situations of conflict, the divide between the Messiah and the religious elite over the true meaning of the law is made apparent.

Lest one accuse all scribes and Pharisees of being nitpicky, legalistic hypocrites, it is worth considering the vantage point of those whose way of life was centered on pleasing God and obeying the law. What kind of a rabbi blatantly transgresses purity and Sabbath laws, and even declares a man's sins forgiven? According to the Old Testament, holiness involves ritual purity and moral uprightness (Lev 11–21). Some foods are unclean, as are Gentiles. People with diseases, demons, and handicaps are likewise viewed as unclean. Since physical blemishes were thought to be punishment from God, these sufferers' moral standings are also suspect. Tax collectors were despised for being especially unclean, for they served the Romans by cheating their fellow Jews. As for the Sabbath law, all work was prohibited on the day of rest (Ex 20:8-11; Lev 23:2-3; Num 15:32-36; Deut 5:13-14). While there may be exceptions in the oral traditions of the rabbis, where breaking the Sabbath law is permissible in a life-and-death situation, the incidents here do not fall into that category.[8] Finally, Jesus' pronouncement of forgiveness usurps God's prerogative, which is tantamount to

[8]Such discussions are found in the Mishnah (*Yoma* 8:6; *Baba Qamma* 5:6) and the Talmud (*Babylonian Talmud Megillah* 3b). These provisions may go back to the time of Jesus.

blasphemy. Therefore, from his opponents' perspective, Jesus' seeming disregard of the law and claim to divine authority are dangerous.

In these conflict stories, Jesus exercises both authority and compassion. First, every encounter is a teaching moment. Jesus calls everyone to repent—the unrighteous and the righteous, in particular those who *think* they are righteous. Second, in showing compassion Jesus puts his own status at risk. He contracts uncleanness by reaching out to those who are unclean. He touches a leper who probably has not felt a human touch for a long time, and he mingles and eats with Levi and his friends, most of whom are tax collectors. Third, Jesus heals with an authoritative command: "Be made clean" (Lk 5:13); "Stand up and take your stretcher and go to your home" (Lk 5:24); "Stretch out your hand" (Lk 6:10). The instant efficacy of Jesus' words stands in sharp contrast to ancient magicians who relied on incantations and objects to activate their spells. Fourth, Jesus' refutations are swift and authoritative. To answer the charge of blasphemy, Jesus fires back with a rhetorical question as to whether it is easier to say, "Your sins are forgiven you," or "Stand up and walk" (Lk 5:23). In reality, physical and spiritual healings are two sides of the same coin, and the effectiveness of his healing signifies God's approval. On another occasion, when the disciples are accused of breaking the Sabbath law by rubbing grains with their hands for food, Jesus compares himself to King David, who prioritized the well-being of his companions over the stipulations of the law by feeding them with the bread of the Presence, which only priests were allowed to eat (1 Sam 21:1-6). In every round of argument, Jesus reduces his opponents to silence.

Jesus embodies what the law teaches, but his enemies, who are highly knowledgeable about the law, are blinded by their obsession to impose the law and monitor people's adherence to it. Should not a healing on the Sabbath in the synagogue—where the law is read and explained—be the perfect context to bring an ostracized man with a withered hand physical, communal, and spiritual wholeness? Have these legal experts memorized the words of the law but failed to appropriate its true intention?

The two short parables on the old and new garments and wineskins identify the reason for the conflict. Jesus' new program is completely grounded in God's law, but the scribes and the Pharisees insist on their old interpretation and praxis. The two are incompatible, and Jesus' message is lost to the religious leaders. Furious at his strong rebuttals, they become increasingly bent on plotting his demise.

KINGDOM ETHOS AND VALUES (LUKE 6:12-49)

After a whole night in prayer, Jesus chooses twelve disciples. The list of names is almost identical across the Synoptic Gospels, except for two where Luke differs from Matthew 10:2-4 and Mark 3:16-19. It is difficult to determine whether Simon the Zealot is the same person as Simon the Cananaean, or whether Judas, the son of James, also goes by the name Thaddeus. More important is the number twelve, as in the twelve tribes of Israel. Here Jesus calls his disciples "apostles," for in addition to following him they will be sent to spread the good news and "catch people" for God (see Lk 5:10).[9]

There is some overlap between Jesus' teachings in the next section and the Sermon on the Mount in Matthew 5–7. These materials

[9]The Greek word for "apostle" is *apostolos*, meaning "messenger" or "one who is sent."

reflect the theme of reversal already introduced in Mary's song (Lk 1:46-55), as well as the ethics of mercy and integrity that are to characterize Jesus' followers.

Instead of the eight blessings in Matthew's Beatitudes (Mt 5:3-11), the Lukan Jesus proclaims four blessings and four matching woes. Poverty, weeping, hunger, and being hated are typical predicaments of those under oppression. By pronouncing them blessed, Jesus promises God's deliverance from their dire straits. On the contrary, to those who are enjoying wealth, laughter, abundance, and popularity, Jesus anticipates a rude awakening. Just as God redeems those who seek after him from the worst of situations, he condemns those who reject him by emptying them of their self-congratulatory fortunes.

The last set of blessings and woes concerning prophets whom people hated and false prophets whom people praised harks back to Jesus' identification with Elijah and Elisha (Lk 4:25-27).[10] Jesus' lament, "No prophet is accepted in his hometown" (Lk 4:24), is a reference to his prophetic predecessors as well as an anticipation of his own rejection as God's end-time prophet.

Blessedness is a highly coveted state of being for the Chinese, for it connotes prosperity, safety, happiness, and all that makes life smooth and worry-free. Especially around the Lunar New Year, families post auspicious red posters on their doors with the Chinese word for blessing (*fú*) for good luck. For Cantonese people, the poster is sometimes deliberately hung upside-down, because in the regional dialect, the word for "upside-down" sounds like the word for "arrival," which makes for a nice pun, that blessing will come to the home. Therefore, when Jesus names the poor, the weeping, the hungry, and the hated as blessed, these preconditions of blessedness grate against traditional Chinese sensitivities, making the paradigm shift to Jesus' way of thinking all the more challenging.

In the rest of Luke 6, Jesus describes human interactions that reflect the values of God's kingdom. "Be merciful, just as your Father is merciful" (Lk 6:36). In a world where balanced reciprocity is the cultural norm, repaying love with love or generosity with generosity is expected. But Jesus calls his followers to a much higher standard of *unbalanced* reciprocity. They are to love their enemies, bless those who curse them, lend without expecting a repayment, turn the other cheek, and go the extra mile. Another way to be over-the-top merciful is to resist the temptation of judgmentalism and extend forgiveness, lest God apply the same harsh measures that one uses on others back on oneself.

Jesus' disciples are also to be people of integrity and not hypocrites who pretend to be someone they are not.[11] To point out the speck in another's eye without recognizing the log in one's own eye is symptomatic of a hypercritical spirit that lacks self-awareness. Such inconsistency is unbecoming of Jesus' followers, whose behavior is compared to the fruit of a tree. A tree that is healthy and solid to the core can produce nothing but good fruit, but the same applies to a bad tree that bears bad fruit. There is only so much one can hide behind hypocrisy, for sooner or later, "each tree is known by its own fruit" (Lk 6:44), and what is concealed inside will be completely exposed.

At the end of his teaching, Jesus exhorts his disciples that lordship demands obedience. Putting his words into action is likened to building a house on rock that can withstand

[10]For a prophet people hated versus one people loved, see Jeremiah and Hananiah (Jer 27–28).

[11]The Greek noun *hypokritēs* refers to a person who is playacting.

strong floods. A disciple must be well-grounded against the ravages of life, be they temptations, persecutions, or sufferings. Otherwise, without a foundation built on a practiced obedience to Jesus' words, the house of faith will collapse under the slightest provocation.

JESUS THE PROPHET: IN THE STEPS OF ELISHA AND ELIJAH (LUKE 7:1-17)

Luke is fond of pairing stories that highlight a male and a female character, as in the healing of the centurion's slave in Capernaum and the raising of the dead son of the widow in Nain.[12] The contrast in status between the two is stark. The centurion is a ranked Roman officer who because of his generosity is held in high esteem even by the Jewish community—which is quite an unusual acknowledgment given the hatred the Jews had of their foreign overlords. The widow is doubly destitute, having lost both husband and son, with no one to provide for her. But death is no respecter of persons. The centurion's valued slave is critically ill, and the widow's son has just died.

These miracles contain theological truths beyond the life-giving power of Jesus. First, saving lives is more important than legal observance. Jesus shows no reticence in entering a Gentile's home to heal the centurion's slave, and he contracts corpse impurity by touching the bier carrying the widow's deceased son to halt the funeral procession. Second, God-honoring faith is not unique to Israel. Jesus praises the centurion for his exemplary trust in his willingness and power to heal. Third, divine compassion reaches down to the bottom of the social ladder. The widow's plight moves Jesus into action, for without the son, the mother is as good as dead herself.

These stories echo Jesus' identification with Elijah and Elisha in Luke 4:25-27. Just as Elisha healed Naaman the leper without ever laying eyes on him (2 Kings 5:1-14), Jesus heals the centurion's slave from a distance. Just as Elijah brought the son of the widow in Zarephath back to life, Jesus here also "gave [the young man] to his mother" (1 Kings 17:23).[13] Although the crowd rightly identifies Jesus as a great prophet, they have yet to grasp his true identity as God's Son and Israel's Messiah.

JOHN AND JESUS: TWO APPROACHES, ONE MISSION (LUKE 7:18-35)

Not long after Jesus' baptism, John was locked up in prison by Herod (Lk 3:19-20). He now sends messengers to inquire about Jesus' messianic identity. Jesus uses his actions to answer in the affirmative: the blind see, the lame walk, the leper is cleansed, and the dead are raised. His sermon in Luke 4 (with its quotation from Is 58:6; 61:1-2) and his answer here in Luke 7 form bookends around a plethora of salvific actions. Jesus' track record bears witness to God's endorsement and the Spirit's empowerment, leaving no doubt that he is indeed the Coming One for whom Israel has been waiting.

Even though John's and Jesus' ministries are very different in form, style, and location, each plays a unique role in God's plan of salvation. Both are misunderstood by their compatriots: John's ascetism is denounced as demonic and Jesus' table fellowship with sinners as profane revelry. Using child's play, Jesus illustrates the extent to which the Pharisees and the lawyers miss the point of his and John's mission. In this game, a cue is given to solicit an appropriate response. The opponents of John and Jesus,

[12]Other examples include Zechariah and Mary, Simeon and Anna, Jairus and the woman with a flow of blood, and the woman with a bent back and the man with dropsy.

[13]Luke quotes 1 Kings 17:23 (LXX) verbatim in Lk 7:15, clearly alluding to Elijah's story in recounting Jesus' miracle.

however, neither dance to their music nor echo their wailing with weeping. They remain trapped in self-righteousness, forfeiting God's purpose for themselves.

FAITH IN ACTION: FORGIVEN AND GRATEFUL (LUKE 7:36-50)

This is another story of contrast and reversal, in which the so-called wrong person does the right thing and the so-called right person does the wrong thing. Ultimately, Jesus' astute judgment determines who is right and who is wrong.

The provocative nature of the scene is jarring. A woman reputed to be a prostitute enters the house of Simon the Pharisee where Jesus is dining, and in front of everyone she anoints Jesus' feet with expensive perfume, weeps, and wipes her tears off his feet with her hair.[14] Imagine the immediate associations her actions would generate: sexual innuendo, uncleanness, extravagance, and disrespect. Neither does Jesus escape unscathed by her seemingly scandalous overtures. Imagine the side glances as the murmuring begins. "He should have known who that is and stopped her." "What kind of a rabbi tolerates such filth and shows such disregard for purity laws?" "Of all places, inside a Pharisee's house! What insolence!" The tension in the room is palpable. If this entire scene were played out at a Chinese dinner gathering, nobody would openly criticize the guest of honor so as to save face for the host, but the looks of condemnation would speak volumes.

With a simple parable, Jesus forces Simon to speak truth to the situation. Between two debtors, the one with the greater debt forgiven will love the creditor more than the one who is forgiven a lesser debt. In Jesus' assessment, the woman's unbridled outpouring of love is her expression of deep gratitude for having her many sins forgiven. The Greek preposition *hoti* in Luke 7:47 is better translated as "hence" (NRSV; see NLT, TNIV) than "for" (NIV, ESV, NAS, NKJV). Her love is not a precondition for her forgiveness but a result of it. By contrast, Simon loves little or not at all because he does not consider himself sinful in the first place. In fact, the woman has replaced Simon as host by showing Jesus true hospitality with her tears and her kisses. Her sins have already been forgiven, and she knows it. It is Simon and the other guests who need to hear Jesus' pronouncement of her forgiven status. Unmoved, they complain that Jesus has again usurped divine prerogative (see Lk 5:20-21). In the end, Jesus affirms the woman's faith and sends her away in peace, leaving Simon and his friends to their self-righteous indignation.

HEARING AND DOING (LUKE 8:1-21)

In ancient Judaism, rabbis had only male disciples. It is noteworthy, then, that Luke names Mary Magdalene, Joanna, Susanna, and other women who support Jesus and his disciples with their own resources. These women are not peripheral onlookers but faithful followers of Jesus like their male counterparts. Some will even reappear in the passion narrative (Lk 23:49, 55; 24:10).

The parable of the sower illustrates a mixed response to the gospel. Jesus is the sower, and the seed is the word of God. Liberally he sows anywhere and everywhere, over the footpath, into rocky soil, among thorns, and in good soil. Depending on where the seeds land, different outcomes emerge. Like birds snatching the

[14]Ancient dinner parties, if modeled after the Greco-Roman symposium, were not as private an affair as we would assume. People were allowed to listen in on the discourse around the table after dinner, especially when the guest of honor was someone of note.

seeds from the footpath, Satan quickly steals the word of God from the hearers' hearts, eliminating any hope of germination. Crop failure occurs among the rocks and the thorns, as the plant is unable to reach maturity due to shallow roots and a lack of nutrients. In life, difficult trials and earthly pleasures contribute to stunted spiritual growth, and God's word is ultimately abandoned. Against these odds, some seeds fall into good soil, mature, and result in fecundity. Even though many reject Jesus and his gospel, those who believe will bear fruit and yield a hundredfold harvest (see Lk 8:5-8).

"What type of soil are you?" "How do I become good soil?" These are questions a well-meaning Christian might ask. Among the Chinese immigrant community is the conviction that diligence will yield the desired result. "Work hard and you will eventually achieve the American dream." But can we, even industrious Chinese Christians, turn ourselves into good soil by mere human resolve and hard work? The answer is no, which is humbling. Soil is a *passive* image. Bad soil cannot simply become good soil by itself. The point, therefore, is not self-improvement but awareness of the reality of the mission field and the necessity of God's transformative power. Even with Jesus as the sower par excellence, there are obstacles against faithful receptivity to the good news, be they Satan, the hardness of the human heart, or competing loyalties in this world. Bearing true spiritual fruit entails not just hearing the word of God but doing it. The ability to abide by Jesus' word lies not in sheer will or good intentions but in the empowering of the Holy Spirit. Like a lamp that brightens a room, Jesus' disciples are to fulfill their intended function in God's salvific agenda. Because they hear Jesus' word and do it, they are counted as members of Jesus' spiritual family, a kinship that surpasses even the closest of ancestral earthly ties.

FAITH OVERCOMES FEAR (LUKE 8:22-56)

Fear, faith, and life weave through the four miracle stories in this section. In each story, a crisis erupts and Jesus intervenes, breathing life into a deadly situation. The four pericopes are recounted chronologically, tracing Jesus' movements across the Sea of Galilee to the Gentile territory of the Gerasenes and back, availing his saving mission to Jews and Gentiles alike.

The calming of the stormy sea demonstrates Jesus' authority over nature. Since ancient people viewed the sea as a symbol of chaos that only God could control (see Ps 107:28-29), the implicit answer to the disciples' question in Luke 8:25, "Who then is this?" is that Jesus their master possesses the same power God has over creation, which includes life and death. With Jesus on the boat, why do they fear for their lives? No wonder the disciples are rebuked for their lack of faith and, implicitly, their ignorance of Jesus' identity.

Across the lake, Jesus encounters a frightful madman who may as well be dead. Everything about him is unclean—a Gentile possessed by thousands of demons and living among the tombs.[15] The saddest thing of all is that he is entirely alone—nameless, naked, out of his mind, and rejected by his people because they cannot subdue him. Just as the people fear this uncontrollable maniac, the unclean spirits in him fear Jesus. While they recognize his authority and status as Son of the Most High God, their fear reeks of defiance. They challenge Jesus through their human host ("What have you to do with me?"), yet plead with him not to send them back to the abyss. Why does Jesus yield to the demons by sending them into the

[15]A Roman legion was five thousand to six thousand soldiers strong.

pigs? Shouldn't he consider the owners' economic loss and expel the demons without harming the pigs? But this is precisely the point. Jesus is not acquiescing to the unclean spirits, but this madman, written off by his people, is worth far more than two thousand pigs (see Mk 5:13). The resulting mania displayed by the pigs proves that the demons have left the man and latched onto new hosts. Ironically, the fear of the demoniac now shifts to Jesus, and the townspeople ask him to leave. The man, now restored to physical, mental, spiritual, and communal wholeness, has become a disciple. His days of screaming and self-torture are over; with the same voice he will return home to proclaim God's salvation among the Gentiles.

The last two stories are presented as a literary "sandwich," with the healing of the hemorrhaging woman inserted within the account of the raising of Jairus's daughter. The interpolation indicates that these two events are mutually interpretive. The woman has been sick for twelve years, and Jairus's daughter is twelve years old. The girl dies, and the woman is as good as dead, for all her attempts to seek healing from doctors have failed. The power differential between Jairus and the woman is striking. He is the respected head of the synagogue, whereas she is impoverished and perpetually unclean due to an unstoppable hemorrhage. Jairus, because of his status, has easy access to Jesus, for the crowd would readily have stepped aside for him. The woman, however, is not even supposed to be in public because she renders ritually unclean anyone she touches. Fear is in the air. Jairus is afraid for his daughter's life, and the woman is afraid to be discovered.

Much to the woman's dismay, Jesus does not allow her to slip away even though her bleeding has stopped immediately upon touching the fringe of his robe. Her testimony of her healing and his commendation of her faith serve as a pronouncement that she is no longer unclean, removing the stigma that has been beleaguering her for many years.

Meanwhile, because of the interruption, Jairus's greatest fear has materialized. By the time Jesus arrives at his house, his daughter has died. Once again, as with the raising of the dead son of the widow in Nain, Jesus performs the greatest of all healings with one powerful command: "Get up!" Indeed, the Messiah has the power to save both the living and the dead.

JESUS' IDENTITY REVEALED (LUKE 9:1-50)

Luke 9 is transitional as the disciples move from being observers to participants in Jesus' mission. It is also pivotal in revealing the identity of Jesus, whose ministry in Galilee is coming to an end.

Having witnessed the teachings and powers of Jesus, the disciples are now given the authority to do the same. Charged not to bring anything for the journey, they must rely on others' hospitality wherever they go (see Lk 8:1-3). To be effective, these apostles-in-training must be unencumbered by the necessities of life, trust in God's provision, and focus only on proclaiming God's kingdom. A mixed reception is to be expected, as has been the case for Jesus (see Lk 8:5-8). Some towns will embrace their message; others will reject it, in which case Jesus instructs them to shake the dust of that place off their feet. This is a symbolic gesture that Jews performed when leaving a Gentile territory to signify their riddance of ritual impurity. Ironically, the rejection of the gospel by Galilean towns is tantamount to spiritual uncleanness, which is much worse than ritual uncleanness.

In the story of the feeding of the five thousand, even though Jesus' disciples have witnessed his miraculous powers many times over, when asked to find food for the people, they resort to human means. Did they not learn to trust God for daily provisions when Jesus sent them into the villages? Yet they still fret over the impossibility of buying food for all. Nevertheless, Jesus enlists them to organize the crowd and distribute the loaves and fish he has multiplied. The frugal Chinese reader may approve of the disciples picking up the leftovers so as not to be wasteful, but the lesson runs deeper. These twelve baskets further remind the disciples of what Jesus can do with anything, no manner how insignificant, when it is offered for his use. If the Messiah can provide more physical food than one can eat, how much more abundantly will he give spiritual nourishment to those who commit themselves to him?

A miracle of this scale inevitably raises the question of Jesus' identity, whether it comes from the masses or from King Herod. To the casual observer, Jesus is a teacher, healer, exorcist, and miracle worker. The most natural category with which to identify him is that of a prophet, be he a redivivus John the Baptist, Elijah, or some other ancient prophet (see Lk 4:24-27; 7:1-17). But Jesus is more than a prophet; he is the Son of God and the Messiah of Israel, a truth known to the readers since the infancy narratives but only gradually disclosed to the characters in the narrative.

When Jesus asks, "Who do you say that I am?" Peter's reply is spot on: "The Messiah of God" (Lk 9:20). Without denying Peter's identification, Jesus forbids his disciples to publicize that fact, in light of the shocking prediction of his suffering that immediately follows. To the Jews, the notion of a suffering Messiah is a contradiction in terms. If Jesus' own disciples cannot accept that the salvific way of Jesus is one of suffering, how can they proclaim the gospel with integrity? Furthermore, Jesus' suffering and death have implications for them. He challenges his followers to take up their cross daily, which, in the days of the Roman Empire, implied a shameful and horrific death. Discipleship is not for the faint of heart, but life will emerge from suffering and death, with glory awaiting those who remain faithful to the end.

The event of the transfiguration gives Peter, James, and John a glimpse of Jesus' transcendent glory. The Messiah is more than a human king; he is the divine Son of God. In this account, the cloud, the mountain, the three attendants, and God's voice recall the giving of the law to Moses in Exodus 24. Appearing in resplendent glory, Jesus stands with Moses and Elijah to talk about his *exodos* (Lk 9:31). The Greek word *exodos*, translated "departure," carries layers of meaning. In secular usage, it is a euphemism for death. Yet *exodos* also harks back to God's deliverance of his people from bondage in Egypt. The three glorified figures discuss Jesus' impending death, the means by which God will accomplish the final exodus. There may be a veiled reference to Jesus' final departure from this earth in his glorious ascension as well (Lk 24:51). All these threads cohere with Jesus' prediction of his suffering and death in the wake of Peter's confession.

The disciples are understandably terrified, as reflected in Peter's nonsensical ramblings on building shelters for Jesus, Moses, and Elijah. God has the last word when a voice comes from the cloud: "This is my Son, my Chosen, listen to him" (Lk 9:35). At Jesus' baptism, God said, "You are my Son" (Lk 3:22). Here, God speaks directly to the disciples, commanding them to heed the word of the Son of God and servant of God par excellence (Is 42:1; Deut 18:18). Then the spectacle is over.

Jesus is left alone with his disciples, and he instructs them not to tell anyone what they have seen. This experience will become a source of encouragement and hope for Peter, James, and John. Although they will later witness Jesus' death, they are already assured of his life beyond the cross.

While these three disciples are mesmerized by Jesus' glory on the mountain, down below the others are struggling to exorcise a demon from an epileptic boy. Even though previously they had power over demons (Lk 9:1), their present faithlessness renders them ineffective. The disciples are too prideful; they jostle for positions of greatness and look down on others who are not one of the Twelve. Using a child of low status as an example, Jesus teaches them that true greatness seeks identification with the least. In a culture where honor is coveted, the lesson of humility is counterintuitive and undoubtedly difficult to embrace.

THE COST OF DISCIPLESHIP (LUKE 9:51-62)

Luke 9:51 is a turning point in Luke's narrative. Jesus resolutely sets his face toward Jerusalem, ready to embark on the definitive journey that will culminate in his death. Dubbed the "Travel Narrative" (Lk 9:51–19:27), this section is full of teaching materials. Given the passion predictions already sounded by Jesus (Lk 9:21-22, 44), it comes as no surprise that the first response the group encounters is rejection from a Samaritan village.[16] Regardless of the fact that Samaritans and Jews have a long history of enmity between them (see Jn 4:9; 8:48), John's and James's retaliatory and violent tactic, that Jesus authorizes them to call down fire to destroy the village, deserves strong rebuke. Have they forgotten Jesus' teaching on forgiving and loving one's enemies (Lk 6:27-28; 11:4)?

The radical commitment required of those who aspire to become Jesus' followers is at the heart of three conversations between Jesus and some would-be disciples. In each case, Jesus asserts his priority over home and family, which are precious to most people. First, an itinerant ministry means the absence of a stable homestead and constant reliance on others' hospitality. This would have been humbling and shameful in the ancient world, as such favors put the receiver indebted to the giver, not to mention an increased power differential between them. Second, commitment to Jesus supersedes the noblest of familial duties. A man wishes to complete his filial obligation and bury his father before returning to follow Jesus. While this is a noble request, a healthy father could mean a long time before the duty can be fulfilled. Given the primacy of Jesus' mission, family must take second place, hence Jesus' answer, "Let the dead bury their own dead" (Lk 9:60). Third, because God's kingdom work is urgent, Jesus' disciples must press forward. Unless the determination to follow Jesus is strong, lingering sentiments, even bidding one's family a fond farewell, can hinder one's progress. Although Jesus' demands may appear stringent, those who have left earthly families must believe that they will receive just recompense when Jesus welcomes them into his spiritual family (Lk 8:21; 18:28-30).

I have often struggled with Jesus' requirements, since filial piety is as highly valued in the Chinese context as in the Jewish world. Would Jesus really make his disciples choose between him and family, when the fifth commandment clearly states, "Honor your father and your mother" (Ex 20:12)? In traditional Chinese moral thought and praxis, obedience, caretaking, burial, and ancestral worship constitute the filial duties of children to their

[16]*Passion* in "passion narrative" refers not to a feeling, as in passionate, but to suffering, from the Latin word *passio*.

parents, to express gratitude for giving them life and nurturing them to adulthood. Yet Luke depicts Jesus as distancing himself from his earthly family to follow the bidding of his heavenly Father unencumbered (Lk 2:49; 8:19-21; esp. Mk 3:20-21, 31-35). It is not that Jesus delights in tearing people away from their families, but allegiance to the things of this world, even good things, be they loved ones or possessions, is a deal-breaker (see the rich ruler in Lk 18:18-31). Jesus asserts the priority of his lordship in the starkest of terms; he seeks absolute loyalty, not because he belittles human relationships but because the mission is urgent and the salvation of the world is at stake. If, in the life of discipleship, there comes a time when one must choose between Jesus and family, may we have the faith to entrust our loved ones to the one whose faithfulness is boundless.

SENDING THE SEVENTY (LUKE 10:1-24)

Lest Jesus' disciples think that they are the only ones authorized to participate in Jesus' mission (see Lk 9:49-50), Jesus sends seventy messengers as his heralds with the same power and instruction previously given to the Twelve in Luke 9:1-6. As before, this group is to bring nothing and rely on God's provision through people's hospitality. Because the mission is urgent, traveling light makes practical sense.

Despite the good news that the seventy proclaim, a mixed response is again anticipated. Peace will remain with those who extend hospitality and receive the message, but destruction will come on those who reject it. The symbolic action that Jesus tells them to perform—to wipe from their feet the dust of the ground of those inhospitable cities—denotes a strong statement of separation, analogous to how Jews would leave a Gentile territory. Sadly, the unrepentant towns of Chorazin, Bethsaida, and Capernaum are all Jewish. They will receive even harsher judgment than sinful Gentile cities such as Sodom, Tyre, and Sidon, for Israel has rejected its Messiah.

Brimming with joy, the Seventy return with reports of effective ministry. This is certainly a cause for celebration, though Jesus refocuses them on the cosmic battle between God and Satan that is played out on the world's stage. It is exciting to cast out demons, but the greater reason for lasting joy is being given citizenship in heaven. Spiritual insight is a gift that the Father chooses to dispense through his Son. Since God's ways defy human expectations, Jesus chooses to reveal divine mysteries to those who, like infants, are of low status. From those who profess to be wise and intelligent, such as the scribes and the Pharisees, God conceals profound spiritual truth. The pattern of reversal is once more in play. This gospel, embodied in the words and life of Jesus, can be perceived only with eyes of faith and embraced only with hearts of humble obedience.

A BOUNDARY-CROSSING SAMARITAN (LUKE 10:25-37)

Eternal life is not a uniquely Christian concept, as the Jews also believed it to be God's promise to the righteous (see Dan 12:1-3). Between the lawyer's first question and Jesus' answer, a legitimate conclusion may be drawn, that loving God and neighbor is the path to inheriting eternal life. It is the lawyer's second question that betrays his questionable motive. Implicit in "Who is my neighbor?" is the opposite question, "Who is *not* my neighbor?" Purity laws dictate that boundary setting is necessary to set Israel apart from all that is unclean. The lawyer is hiding behind the law to justify his unneighborly attitude.

The parable of the merciful Samaritan is one of the best-known of Jesus' parables. Typically, the lesson drawn from it is one of compassion, showing mercy to a person in need, even an enemy. More can be said, however, when the decisions made by the priest and the Levite are considered, for they are subject to stricter purity stipulations than regular Jews. When they spot the half-dead man from afar, it is difficult to tell whether he is dead or alive. If the man were dead or should he die in their care, they would contract corpse impurity. The priest and the Levite both pick the safer course of action. They would rather give the severely injured man a wide berth than risk coming into contact with a dead body. Motivated by self-preservation while using the law of purity as justification, their inaction speaks volumes about their religious and moral priorities.

Then comes a Samaritan. He, too, is subject to the law concerning corpse impurity, but moved by compassion, he chooses to stop and tend to the victim's wounds.[17] Putting aside the historical enmity between his people and the Jews, the Samaritan takes an even greater risk by bringing the Jewish man to an inn and paying for his care, for he could have been implicated as the aggressor. His actions indicate that true neighborliness knows no boundaries.

In the end, the reluctant lawyer admits that the wrong person—the Samaritan—has done the right thing, and the right people—the religious leaders such as himself—have been found wanting when it comes to embodying the precepts of God's law.

In Chinese, there is a saying, "Everyone must sweep the snow in front of their door, but don't bother with the frost on the neighbor's roof-tiles." In other words, "Mind your own business." Even when something evidently unjust or wrong cries out for action, there is often inertia and apathy. For sure, acts of justice and mercy are costly, and it is much easier to pretend not to notice—or, worse, to stand and stare but not say a word or lift a finger. From the human point of view, the Samaritan has everything to lose and nothing to gain by helping the injured man, yet he exemplifies the risk-taking mercy that characterizes both Jesus and God (see Lk 7:13; 15:20). Just as the lawyer cannot use the law to justify himself, neither can I invoke a Chinese idiom as an excuse for my self-protective indifference toward the needs and sufferings around me. When we pray for opportunities to be Jesus' hands and feet in this world, will we rise to the occasion when our prayers are answered?

MARY AND MARTHA (LUKE 10:38-42)

Martha receives a bad rap in this story, because she, the worker bee, is said to be "distracted by many things" (Lk 10:41), while Mary, the attentive learner, sits at the feet of Jesus and assumes the posture of a disciple. This distinction between Martha and Mary has caused some consternation among women in modern-day churches, as though being a Mary were more spiritual than being a Martha. But then, without the Martha-types, much would be left undone. If the sisters were to be evaluated through the lens of Chinese hospitality, Martha would have earned high marks. In that traditional patriarchal society, the place of women is in the home, especially the kitchen. The ability to whip up a delicious meal for a lot of guests in a short amount of time is highly prized. On the contrary, for Mary not to be cooking alongside her sister would be frowned upon, not only by a Chinese Martha but by the invited guests as well.

The difference between the sisters, in the context of Jesus' days, is Mary's willingness to let go of conventional expectations and extend hospitality to Jesus in a way that pleases her

[17]Samaritans accepted the Pentateuch, hence the Mosaic law, as authoritative and binding.

honored guest. She risks public disapproval to meet Jesus where his mission and heart are, and this profound eagerness earns her praise. Martha's act of hospitality is noteworthy and would normally have been appropriate. But Jesus' presence is unique, hence a unique form of hospitality is called for, and Mary has taken hold of that truth and acted on it.

THE FATHER WHO ANSWERS PRAYERS (LUKE 11:1-13)

Although Luke's version of the Lord's Prayer is shorter than Matthew 6:9-13, the key elements are the same. Reminiscent of ancient Jewish prayers such as the Amidah and the Kaddish, Jesus' prayer opens with a declaration of God's fatherhood and kingship, together with the expressed hope that the whole universe will acknowledge God's rulership and sovereignty. How can that be? The answer lies in the phrase "hallowed be your name" (Lk 11:2), whose implied subject is God. In spite of Israel's failure that has ruined God's reputation among the nations, God promises to forgive and give Israel a new heart and a new Spirit, so God's people will again sanctify Yahweh's holy name by their obedience (Is 29:23; Ezek 36:16-32).

The three petitions that follow point to God's role as Israel's Father, who provides for his children, forgives them when they do wrong, and protects them from harm. The middle petition in particular expects God's children to extend mercy to others because they themselves have received mercy (see Lk 6:36). These petitions reflect the disciples' total dependence on God, whose parental image is steeped in divine love and accountability.

Next Jesus turns to the posture and attitude of prayer. The parable of the friend at midnight assures the disciples how willing God is to provide what is needful. While the homeowner scrambles to find bread to feed an unexpected guest, the emphasis is not on his persistence but his willingness to be shamed for such an understandable but ill-timed request.[18] In order to do right for his guest, the homeowner bothers his sleeping friend and his family, hoping that their friendship will accommodate the late night intrusion. If this friend ultimately lends a hand despite his initial reluctance, how much more eagerly will God respond to the needs of his children? This view of God undergirds the triple encouragement in the next two verses to ask, seek, and knock, provided that the request is legitimate.

In case the disciples are still unsure of God's goodness, Jesus offers one final analogy from human experience. Any loving parent would not give a child something harmful, such as a snake or a scorpion, when the child asks for a fish or an egg. If imperfect earthly fathers know to do that, how much more will Israel's heavenly Father give the best gift—the Holy Spirit—to those who ask him (see Lk 24:49; Acts 1:4-5)?

FOR OR AGAINST JESUS (LUKE 11:14–12:12)

Out of an assortment of vignettes interspersed with miscellaneous teaching materials, two main themes emerge: Jesus' indictment of those who are against him and Jesus' exhortation to those who align themselves with him.

Jesus identifies three symptoms of unbelief among his opponents. First, they attribute the power behind his exorcisms to Beelzebul, the prince of demons. Jesus debunks their illogical reasoning by asking why Satan would create a coup aimed at his own downfall. Surely the devil would not endorse, let alone empower, Jesus to cast out demons. Rather,

[18]This parable makes a point different from the parable of the widow and the unjust judge in Lk 18:1-8, which is about persistence in prayer.

exorcism proves that the Satan has succumbed to the stronger power of the Holy Spirit through Jesus and those he has sent out to do the same (Lk 9:1; 10:17). This is not a civil war within Satan's domain but an invasion by a formidable foe.

Second, nonbelievers demand signs. Jesus' teachings and actions are the best signs that point to his identity and mission (Lk 7:20-23), yet without the eyes of faith, his opponents are blind to that reality. They see, yet they do not perceive, because they refuse to let go of their preconceived notion of the Messiah. Therefore, Jesus rightly condemns this unbelieving generation as evil and says that the only sign for them is the sign of Jonah. The point of contact has less to do with the three days Jonah spent in the belly of the fish and the three days Jesus will spend in the tomb than with the messages of both prophets. The Ninevites heeded Jonah's warning, repented, and were spared. Now Jesus is the second Jonah announcing the arrival of God's kingdom. Between salvation and judgment, will this generation choose wisely?

Third, hypocrisy is unbelief masked in self-righteous religiosity. Jesus minces no words in indicting the Pharisees and the scribes for the inconsistencies between their outward behaviors and inward motives. They meticulously adhere to purity laws to flaunt their flawless piety, such as performing ceremonial cleansing before they eat, while harboring moral filth in their greedy and wicked hearts. The Pharisees crave the limelight and love to be showered with respect and accolades. They tithe more than what is legally required yet ignore justice, the true mark of devotion and love of God. The legal experts likewise position themselves as the authoritative interpreters of the law. They impose strict obligations that become more of a burden for people than a faithful participation in their covenantal relationship with God. They follow the pattern of their predecessors who rejected and killed God's prophets, and they are doing the same to Jesus. By exposing their hypocrisy, Jesus further incites their hostility toward him. Once the good news is preached, it forces a decision: "Whoever is not with me is against me, and whoever does not gather with me scatters" (Lk 11:23). There is no room for compromise or doublemindedness.

So, what words of exhortation does Jesus have for those who choose to follow him?

The starting point is repentance. The parable in Luke 11:24-26 first appears as counsel to those freed from demon possession. Such persons are advised to fill the void left by the unclean spirit with a wholesome Spirit, lest the demons take advantage of the vulnerability and re-inhabit their prior host with even stronger diabolic forces. This principle applies similarly to anyone who has turned away from wickedness to follow Jesus. An injection of new, wholesome habits and thinking will prevent old ways from retaking their territory with a vengeance.

A regenerated life bears effective witness, as illustrated by the metaphor of a body filled with light. Notwithstanding the scientific inaccuracy of how ancient people perceived the eye as a source rather than a receptor of light, the contrast that Jesus makes between light and darkness is clear. Light signifies truth, life, and salvation, whereas darkness implies falsehood, death, and condemnation. If one is filled with light from within, that light also brings illumination to one's surroundings. Having received Jesus' light, a believer becomes a conduit of light to others.

Therefore, upon hearing the word of God, Jesus' disciples must put it into practice. Obedient action allows God's word to take root. If even Gentiles, be they the Ninevites at the time of Jonah or the queen of the South who sought after Solomon's wisdom, could turn toward the God of Israel, then God's elect have no excuse.

Given the hostility toward Jesus, his disciples will not escape persecution. They must remember that they are precious to God, who cares for them down to the minutest detail. Even the number of the hairs on their heads is counted. If God attends to common sparrows, which are a dime a dozen, how much more those who belong to him? Hence Jesus' disciples must stand firm in the face of opposition, rely on the guidance of the Holy Spirit in times of crisis, and not let the fear of human authorities cloud their fear of God. Otherwise, they will be in danger of committing the unforgivable sin. Blasphemy against the Holy Spirit is tantamount to apostasy, of which the consequence is eternal damnation. At the end of all things, faithful perseverance will yield its ultimate reward. In the meantime, opposition is inevitable, and Jesus' disciples must face it with unwavering trust.

TREASURES IN HEAVEN (LUKE 12:13-34)

The kingdom Jesus proclaims is not a physical one, in which power, wealth, and security reign supreme. Rather, those who enter God's kingdom adopt spiritual values that transcend this earthly life to the life eternal. The parable of the rich fool and Jesus' ensuing exhortation contrast the view of life in these opposing kingdoms. Jesus' message is relevant to the haves as well as the have-nots. The rich may obsess over their bountiful possessions, and the poor may worry about their basic means of survival. Either attitude, however, displaces God from the center of life by failing to show gratitude in times of plenty and trust in times of need.

Both the man who asks Jesus to settle a dispute between him and his brother and the fortunate landowner in Jesus' parable receive a windfall for which they have not labored. The man's inheritance is a gift from father to son and the bumper crop a gift of nature. Through the parable of the rich fool, Jesus exposes the man's greed, symptomatic of the underlying problems of godlessness and self-determination.

Peppered with first-person pronouns, the rich man's soliloquy is telling. He muses on building bigger barns to store his grains and enjoying life for many years to come. There is no word of thanks to God, nor any mention of family, community, and plans to help the poor. This man is a fool, not because he is unintelligent but because there is no space for God in his life. His plan may display practical foresight by earthly standards, but it carries no heavenly value. In Ecclesiastes 10:14, the Teacher wisely demurs, "Fools talk on and on. No one knows what is to happen, and who can tell anyone what the future holds?" Likewise, whatever grand plan the rich fool devises for years of security and enjoyment is ineffectual, for his life is on loan to him. If God takes it back that very night, where does that leave him? As the saying goes, "You can't take it with you." Earthly wealth, powerful as it seems, is useless for alleviating spiritual poverty.

For the poor, Jesus also has a word of exhortation. The obstacle barring them from being rich toward God is not what they have but anxiety over what they lack. Continuous fretting over the basic stuff of life—food, clothing, and shelter—is equally unproductive. Will God not feed them as he does even unclean birds? Will the one who counts the hairs on their heads not clothe their bodies as he does transient flowers and grasses? Jesus' rhetorical questions are hyperbolic to solicit a resounding vote of confidence: "Of course God will!" It is understandable, yet futile, for those who live at a subsistence level to worry. They are in fact better positioned than the rich to trust God daily (see Lk 21:1-4). With every step of faith, those who believe in Jesus' words of assurance accumulate treasures in heaven for the life to come.

My Chinese parents taught me to save for the rainy day, live within my means, enter a profession that offered financial security, and prepare for the future so as not to be a burden to society in my old age. While they have given good counsel that stands me in good stead in life, I wonder how much of a safety net is too much. I hope I am not the rich fool, but I do practice the discipline of saving. I also hope I am not compulsively anxious, but the planner in me is prone to worry. In light of the vast inequality in the world between rich and poor, powerful and powerless, what do appropriate stewardship and trusting in God's provision look like in concrete terms? If Jesus' followers are called to radical discipleship, the issue of money is a revealing litmus test (see Lk 18:18-31). Theologically, we affirm that everything belongs to God, but is that true in our consideration of what we have, what we want, and what we need? Do we even dare to have an honest conversation with Jesus about the inherent greed in the deeper recesses of our hearts?

Such is the paradox of the kingdom of God. Worldly kingdoms chase after riches and goods, yet all that effort amounts to nothing. On the contrary, because their Father in heaven is trustworthy, God's children are free to be generous toward others (see Lk 21:1-4). Whether they have a lot to give away or only a little to spare, they can count on God to provide for them, even to the extent of giving them the kingdom. The choice between the kingdom of this world and the kingdom of God is obvious, but discipleship is challenging, requiring self-examination and vigilance in the midst of a perverse generation.

ESCHATOLOGICAL VIGILANCE (LUKE 12:35-48)

Although the kingdom of God has impinged on the present in the person and ministry of Jesus, its final consummation lies in the future. In this realized eschatology, the certainty of God's final salvation must be embraced alongside the uncertainty of knowing God's timeline.

Constant readiness is an anticipatory posture, as shown in the following three examples. First, servants must be ready to attend to their master, who may return at any hour from a wedding banquet. Second, a homeowner must always be on guard against burglars, who come at the most unexpected hour. And third, a manager must remain faithful to his assigned responsibilities when the master is absent. In all three, a coming is bound to happen, and one must not be caught unawares, for the consequence of complacency is dire. In the spiritual and eschatological sense, when God ushers in the age to come and separates the righteous from the unrighteous, those who are not ready and have not stored up treasures in heaven will be found wanting. At that time, their rejection will be final.

The proclamation of God's kingdom must be met with a response, for with knowledge comes responsibility. There is no excuse for those who hear Jesus' warnings but fail to heed them. This is especially so for Jesus' disciples, who have been entrusted with the secrets of God's kingdom and empowered to proclaim the good news. Much is expected of them, but as costly as it is to follow Jesus, its eternal reward far outweighs their temporary sacrifice (Lk 18:28-30).

CALL TO REPENTANCE (LUKE 12:49–13:9)

A deep sense of foreboding and distress is expressed by Jesus toward his impending death and its aftermath. Fire represents severe divine judgment, and baptism connotes tremendous suffering. Whereas Jesus' death will seal God's covenant with the faithful for their salvation, it will pronounce condemnation on the unrepentant.

Jesus' message will cause division. At his birth the angels announced that the Messiah's coming would bring peace among those whom God favors (Lk 2:14). But Simeon predicted that Mary's child was "destined for the falling and the rising of many in Israel and to be a sign that will be opposed" (Lk 2:34). The division that Jesus brings is not divisiveness but separation, setting believers apart from nonbelievers, and the penitent from the impenitent. Allegiance toward Jesus will challenge even familial ties, the closest of human relationships.

Will the crowd recognize the wickedness of the times, come to terms with their sinfulness, and repent while there is still time? To those who bring up recent tragedies in which some Galileans were murdered by Pilate and others crushed by the tower of Siloam, insinuating that these victims were more deserving of God's wrath, Jesus issues a stern warning. Death is an equalizer, for all are culpable before God. Without repentance, everyone perishes.

Despite the ominous threat of judgment, Jesus concludes his teaching on a hopeful note. A barren fig tree is at the verge of being cut down by its owner, but the gardener asks for one last chance to nurture it back to fruitfulness. Likewise, Jesus petitions God for more time on behalf of Israel. Judgment will not be suspended forever, but a window of opportunity remains. If the people still refuse to listen, then their fate is sealed.

SABBATH HEALING AT ITS BEST (LUKE 13:10-17; 14:1-6)

Many points of contact exist between the healing stories in Luke 13 and Luke 14. Both take place on the Sabbath, on which Jesus performs a healing in plain sight of the religious elite, who interpret it as a violation of the Sabbath law. In both incidents, Jesus uses his opponents' own circumvention of the same law to expose their hypocrisy.

The first healing cures a woman who has been suffering from a bent back for eighteen years. Jesus speaks of her illness as a form of satanic oppression, from which she needs deliverance. Given the ancient belief that sickness and handicap were curses from God for some egregious sin, this woman would have been deemed unclean and ostracized by her community. Her restoration, therefore, is physical, spiritual, and relational. For Jesus to call her a "daughter of Abraham" is an acknowledgment of her rightful place among God's people. The leader of the synagogue, however, blames the woman for showing up on the Sabbath for healing when she does not have a life-threatening ailment. Imagine his logic: "What is one more day of stooping over if she has not stood up straight for eighteen years?" The leader is wrong on two counts: Jesus, not the woman, is the one who initiates the healing; and Sabbath is the best day of the week for this to happen. If Sabbath signifies God's gift of rest, then one more day of bondage is one day too many. Furthermore, Jesus charges his opponents with holding a double standard. If they untie their beasts of burden to lead them to water on the Sabbath to keep them alive, why not free a human being from a life-diminishing condition? Is a daughter of Abraham not more deserving of compassion than a farm animal?

Jesus makes the same argument in his healing of a man with dropsy, a disease of retaining water, causing the body to swell. The man cannot conceal his illness any more than the woman her crooked spine, so he, too, lives under a stigma of divine curse and its attendant social shunning. This time, Jesus asks the lawyers and Pharisees whether it is lawful to heal on the Sabbath. Their silence communicates an implicit disapproval, based on the same rationale that healing can wait until after the Sabbath so as not to transgress the law. But for Jesus dropsy, too, is life-diminishing and necessitates immediate rectification, so he heals the man. He then argues that if the Jews are allowed to transgress the Sabbath law in order to save a child or an ox from drowning in a well, it is entirely legitimate for him to give this man a new lease on life, for in his present condition he is a walking dead man.

Legally, the religious experts may have a point. Jesus' detractors prioritized the stringent adherence to the law of the Sabbath. To them, if life was not in danger, why make an exception? But Jesus, as Lord of the Sabbath (Lk 6:5), embodies God's compassion and affirms the value God places on human life and flourishing. Jesus is not choosing to give life to the neglect of the Sabbath law; rather, he is demonstrating the true meaning of the Sabbath, which represents God's gift of rest and restorative wholeness.

GOD'S COUNTERCULTURAL KINGDOM (LUKE 13:18-30; 14:7-24)

Sprinkled around the aforementioned stories of healing are various teachings on the kingdom of God. Seen together, they serve as a commentary on Jesus' opponents. As the journey toward Jerusalem progresses, the rift between the two sides continues to widen.

Appearances can be deceiving. Like a mustard seed or yeast, the kingdom of God may seem small, even invisible like yeast in a dough, yet its growth is unmistakable over time. To seek after such a countercultural kingdom, one must look where the world is not looking.

Entry into God's kingdom cannot be based on casual associations with Jesus, as if one could gain admission simply by mentioning Jesus' name. Rather, discipleship requires effort and commitment. Not many can get through the narrow door of the kingdom of God. The self-righteous religious leaders may consider themselves eligible, when in fact they will be rejected. On that day, inside Jesus' house, the seats alongside the patriarchs and the prophets at God's eschatological banquet will be occupied by true believers, including Gentiles. Indeed, as Jesus warns, "Some are last who will be first, and some are first who will be last" (Lk 13:30).

Watching the social dance of his fellow guests at the house of the leader of the Pharisees, Jesus speaks against a culture that craves honor. To begin with, he points out the folly of an overinflated sense of self-importance. Instead of making a beeline for the best seat at a wedding banquet, one should take the least honorable seat to avoid being shamed when told to vacate it for someone with greater honor. Exaltation belongs to God alone.

The second parable has to do with inclusion and exclusion in God's kingdom. In a cultural milieu in which status was determined by honor and shame, the composition around a dinner table mirrored the rules of social and economic compatibility. This way, a host avoided being shamed by a table companion of lesser status, and he could expect a return invitation based on the dynamics of balanced reciprocity. This accounting of debit and credit, returning favor for favor, kept the social hierarchy intact. The rich mingled with the rich, and the poor with the poor, with no incentive to cross any social barrier or level any playing field.

Against this cultural backdrop, Jesus challenges his dinner host to disrupt the status quo by extending invitations to people who are in no position to return the favor. Then, in the ensuing parable, Jesus turns the table on his haughty audience. God is the host, and the religious leaders the first round of invited guests. When the time comes to show up for the meal, because they produce all sorts of lame excuses—none of which is as urgent as it sounds—they forfeit their place at the banquet. Since this banquet signifies one's membership in God's kingdom, losing a place is tantamount to final condemnation (see Lk 13:27). God will instead fill their vacancies with those who never expect to be invited—the poor, the crippled, the blind, and the lame—the very class of lowly people with whom the Pharisees and scribes are loath to associate. Again, those who are first (or *think* they are first) will be last, and those who exalt themselves will be humbled.

EXPECTATION OF REJECTION (LUKE 13:31-35; 14:25-35)

Like a mother hen protecting its chicks under its wings, Jesus has repeatedly shown his Jewish compatriots the way back to God, but his opponents refuse to listen. By their hardness of heart, they have sealed their own condemnation. Their plot to kill God's final prophet continues to brew, from the mob in Nazareth (Lk 4:29), to now Herod Antipas (Lk 14:31), to the temple leadership in Jerusalem (Lk 19:47; 20:19; 22:2). Even though Jesus faces rejection wherever he goes, Jerusalem is singled out to epitomize Israel's rejection of God's eschatological prophet.

Amid mounting threat from his enemies and heightened danger ahead in Jerusalem, Jesus reminds his traveling companions to count the cost of discipleship. A builder should not commit to constructing a tower with inadequate resources, nor a king to fighting a battle with insufficient troops. Similarly, following Jesus for the long haul fetches a very high cost. Jesus takes priority over everything that is important on earth, whether possessions, family, even life itself. The demand of discipleship is encapsulated in the terrifying image of carrying one's cross, which in the Roman Empire meant a torturous and shameful death. If Jesus' way to glory must come by way of suffering and death, why would his followers expect otherwise?

LOST AND FOUND (LUKE 15:1-32)

As a triptych of parables, the lost sheep, the lost coin, and the lost son are meant to be interpreted together. In increasing severity, the lostness progresses from one out of a hundred, to one of ten, and finally one of two. One may even find in the third parable two lost sons in need of reconciliation with their father. Without Jesus, the loss is total—two out of two.

The first two verses of the chapter are key to a proper reading of these parables. Jesus is criticized by the scribes and the Pharisees for transgressing purity laws in his table fellowship with tax collectors and sinners. This complaint is not new (Lk 5:30; 7:34), and these verses remind the modern reader to first situate the parables within the context of Jesus' ministry among the Jews before jumping too quickly to read them through the lens of evangelism among the unchurched.

The parables of the lost sheep and the lost coin are similar in structure. Both the shepherd and the woman diligently look for what they have lost and find it. In the Old Testament, Israel's leaders are identified as shepherds. But they are so bad that God has to get rid of them and appoint his own shepherd to tend to his people instead (Jer 23:1-4; Ezek 34:1-31; Zech 11:4-17). In the first parable, Jesus identifies himself with the shepherd, whose concern for the lost sheep far exceeds that of the bad shepherds as represented by the scribes and the Pharisees. The second parable, of the woman who loses a coin, follows the same line of thought. Jesus' point is simple but powerful: God will stop at nothing to search for lost sinners until they are found, and their repentance is worthy of celebration in heaven. This runs counter to the grumbling of Jesus' opponents, for not only do they consider Jesus' companions as hopelessly unredeemable, but they also discount Jesus' ministry as fulfilling God's salvific purpose.

In the third parable, Jesus inserts the Pharisees and the scribes into the story, exposing their narrow-minded religiosity while teaching them the merciful wideness of God's fatherly love. The story begins with a man and his two sons, but the younger one is a scoundrel. By demanding his share of the inheritance while his father is still alive, he implicitly wishes him dead. No explanation is offered for the seemingly foolish acquiescence of the father to the young man's insolent demand. A Chinese father would have given his son a sharp rebuke, horrified and indignant that he dared to even think about asking for such a thing.

Armed with money to spend and no shortage of youthful indiscretions, the young man soon squanders everything in a foreign land. Left with nothing, he takes a job feeding pigs, and the owner treats him so poorly that he almost starves to death. As a Jew, this young man has rendered himself unclean in every conceivable way, from his immoral escapades to his tending unclean animals for a Gentile farmer. As a son, he has repudiated all ties with his family by his departure. In his shamelessness and shamefulness, he has practically disowned himself. All this is not lost to the prodigal, so that when he decides to go home, he expects to be no more than a hired hand, a position even below that of a household slave.

Meanwhile, having lost his son, the father waits day after day, yearning for his return. Dirty, sick, and emaciated, the son's fragile frame finally appears from afar. Filled with compassion, his father sprints toward him, robes flying and legs showing, disregarding all concerns for dignity, and embraces his beloved child. Even before the son can finish his apology, his father has already fired off a series of instructions to reinstate the prodigal's sonship and status. This is not naivete on the part of the father but pure grace and extravagant love.

The father's grace is risky, as the second half of the parable suggests. Hearing the music from the party that celebrates his brother's return, the older son's indignation is understandable. If the prodigal gets off so easily after the terrible things he has done, what guarantee is there that he will not do it again? To add insult to injury, the older brother's dutiful work has not earned him even a goat to enjoy with his friends, let alone the fatted calf that his father slaughtered for this undeserving rascal. Again, if this were a Chinese family, in which duty and obligation can sometimes be viewed as more important than love and affection, the older brother would have garnered much sympathy from the reader. It is also not uncommon for the oldest child to carry the weight of responsibility for both the family trade and the caretaking of aging parents, and for the youngest to be spoiled by overindulgent parents. The script of this parable, with the older son working in the field and the younger one gallivanting around in revelry, fits the Chinese stereotype quite well.

Once again, the father reaches out to his older son, who is lost in his own way. He reminds him that he does not have to earn the goat, or anything else, for that matter, because he is a son, not a slave, and all his father's possessions already belong to him. Sadly, the older son is so angry that he cannot even bring himself to call his father "Father," and he distances himself from his brother by calling him "this son of yours" (Lk 15:30). By contrast, at his lowest point, the prodigal still remembered he was his father's son (Lk 15:17-18, 21).

Ironically, as the story concludes, the son who severed his ties with his family is back in the house, whereas the one who never left is standing outside. Will the older son join his father to welcome his younger brother home? Will this act of reconciliation transform his own sense of sonship? These are questions that the scribes and the Pharisees need to ponder. If they claim to love and honor God, do they recognize that justice, mercy, and love lie at the heart of God's law?

FAITHFUL STEWARDSHIP (LUKE 16:1-31)

Jesus tells two parables to illustrate the wise and proper use of earthly resources in God's kingdom economy. The main character of the first parable is a steward. He is not a slave but an employee with substantial power to manage his master's affairs. Although no detail is furnished, this man is accused of financial misconduct and is about to be terminated. Since he offers neither denial nor defense, the charge is assumed to be true.

Like the prodigal son desperate to find a solution to his dire straits, this steward ponders his options to avoid the worst-case scenario. His soliloquy lays out his strengths and weaknesses. Too proud and too feeble, he quickly rules out begging and manual labor. His strength, however, lies in his creative scheming. He is decisive and proactive once he has charted out his course of action, wasting no time to seize the short window of opportunity. Since his firing is not yet public knowledge, he is still the steward as far as his master's debtors are concerned. So, when he approaches them to doctor the debt agreements, they are none the wiser. Moreover, he takes advantage of the social dynamics of patronage and balanced reciprocity to make the debtors his clients, obligating them for a return favor in the future. Everything proceeds as planned, and the debtors are more than willing to reduce the amount they owe by altering the loan agreement.

Despite the steward's egregious dishonesty, the master commends him for his shrewdness. In one fell swoop, the debtors are relieved of a sizable burden of debt, the steward has secured a future after his dismissal, and the master, in spite of additional financial loss, gains social status as a generous creditor. It is an ingenious win-win-win solution that works only because honor was even more valuable than material wealth in that culture.

No one would dispute that the steward is a dishonest swindler, but he is presented not as a model of integrity but of shrewdness. If such a negative character can outwit his master to extricate himself from a crisis, how much more should the disciples of Jesus be street-smart and use earthly resources to further God's kingdom. Even so, no matter how useful money can be, Jesus issues a stern warning against divided loyalties in trying to serve God and wealth.

Next, the parable of the rich man and Lazarus addresses the eternal consequence of misusing earthly wealth. The two characters could not be further apart in social status and fortune. The nameless rich man, dressed in finery and feasting daily, never lifts a finger to help Lazarus, a beggar at his gate, who is hungry, sickly, and covered with sores. Lazarus's name, which means "God has helped," hints at the divine vindication soon to come.

The grand reversal happens when both men die. Despite an elaborate burial, the rich man finds himself in Hades, parched and tormented, while Lazarus is nestled in the bosom of Abraham in a place of rest and bliss. From his place of suffering, the rich man appeals to Abraham, but his cry for mercy shows little remorse. That he knows Lazarus by name means that he was not unaware of the beggar's presence outside his gate, yet he did nothing. Even now, he treats Lazarus like a servant, asking Abraham to send Lazarus to cool his tongue with water and to warn his brothers of his sorry state. No, the rich man, self-centered as before, has not changed one bit.

Abraham rejects the rich man's request because the rich man's brothers have all they need to know from the Scriptures to avoid this dreadful fate. This parable is not about the afterlife; it is really about this life, for obedience to God now determines one's destiny in the life to come. The rich man receives his just deserts because he did not make use of his earthly time and resources to do good, give alms, and help the poor. Consequently, he gets a taste of his own medicine and receives no mercy when the tables are turned.

RESPONSIBILITY AND FAITH IN DISCIPLESHIP (LUKE 17:1-19)

The disciples must begin to take on the responsibility of shepherding others in the journey of faith. This requires a tenacious love that corrects the wrongdoer and forgives the penitent sinner as many times as needed. Because caring for the flock is crucial to the survival of the Christian community, Jesus will hold his disciples accountable should they cause anyone to stumble and lose their faith. As they are slaves to God, obedience is a duty. Therefore, faithfulness, not the expectation of a reward, must characterize their posture always. Rather than worrying about whether they have enough faith for the task, Jesus assures them that the power of God will work through whatever faith they have, even faith as small as a mustard seed, when they put their trust in him.

Following this discussion is a miracle that illustrates what the eyes of faith see that others do not. Ten lepers, brought together by a skin disease that renders them ritually unclean and unwelcomed in their communities, call out to Jesus for alms. Without giving them anything, Jesus tells them to show themselves to the priest. In view here is the requirement that a priest must verify a leper's recovery before the person may reenter life in the community.[19] Earlier on, Jesus gave the same instruction to another leper after healing him (Lk 5:14), but here he has not yet done anything to heal them. The lepers could have ignored Jesus, but they obey nonetheless and head off to the priest, and on the way all are made clean.

Ten are healed, but only one is truly saved. The Samaritan's realization of the numinous in Jesus recalls Peter and the miraculous catch of fish (Lk 5:8-9). The leper attributes his healing to God and thanks Jesus in worship. The text does not say whether the other nine are Jews, but Jesus is amazed at this foreigner's faith and finds it exemplary, like that of centurion whose slave he healed (Lk 7:9). In Jesus' ministry, outsiders have demonstrated faith that surpasses that of Israel, foreshadowing their receptivity when the gospel is later preached far and wide in the book of Acts.

PERSISTENCE UNTIL THE DAY OF THE SON OF MAN (LUKE 17:20–18:8)

The kingdom of God is no longer a future reality; it is here, embodied in Jesus' saving

[19]On leprosy, see Lev 13:1-59; Num 5:2-3.

words and deeds. Neither is it a physical political power with boundaries and armies, but rather it is the reign of God over all who profess faith in Jesus. In Luke 17:21, the Greek preposition *entos* should properly be rendered "among" (NRSV, NLT) or "in the midst of" (ESV, TNIV) and not "within" (NIV, NKJV). Contextually, it does not make sense for Jesus to tell the Pharisees who do not believe in him that the kingdom of God is *within* them as an inner spiritual reality. Rather, he encourages them to acknowledge that God's reign has already been made manifest through him, for the one who is to come is *already among* them (see Lk 11:20).

Because God's kingdom is both present and future, Jesus' disciples must live faithful and vigilant lives, for they will suffer rejection before the Son of Man returns. They must not be like the people at the time of Noah or the Sodomites at the time of Lot, completely oblivious of the imminent catastrophe when God wiped them out with flood and fire. The crisis of judgment evokes a sense of urgency, and there is no time to linger or look back like Lot's wife. In order to be saved, Jesus' followers must flee from those slated for destruction lest they too perish along with the sinners.

What enables the disciples to persevere? Like the widow in the parable in Luke 18:1-8, they do so with persistent prayer, in order not to be discouraged. The power differential between the judge and the widow is obvious. The former enjoys elite status, whereas the latter sits at the bottom of the social ladder. It is bad enough that the widow has no male advocate to plead her case, but the person who has the power to right the wrong turns out to be impious and arrogant. What chance does she have when the odds are stacked against her? Jesus' caricature of the unjust judge reminds me of old Chinese movies I saw as a child in which poor peasants had to bribe a magistrate to get a favorable verdict. I remember wondering how people could be placed in a position of authority to adjudicate between right from wrong when they themselves did not act justly. Apparently, unjust judges—as oxymoronic as it sounds—do exist, and this character, however exaggerated by Jesus' description, would have struck a realistic note with Jesus' audience.

Using the only weapon she possesses, that of persistence, the widow brings her petition repeatedly until the judge relents. A piece of humorous detail is lost in the English translation. The NRSV states that the judge is willing to grant her justice so that she does not wear him out (Lk 18:5). The Greek verb *hypōpiazō* literally means "to give someone a black eye." The image of a haughty judge being beat up by a feisty widow is rather comical. If the powerless widow can cause a self-serving and uncaring judge to do the right thing, how much more will God, who is totally unlike this judge, attend to his own when they cry out to him? Therefore, if Jesus' disciples endure to the end like the widow does, the Son of Man will find faith on earth when he returns to vindicate them.

SPIRITUAL INSIGHT (LUKE 18:9–19:27)

This section is bookended by two parables. The opening parable, featuring a Pharisee and a tax collector, illustrates the principle of reversal: "All who exalt themselves will be humbled, but all who humble themselves will be exalted" (Lk 18:14). The ending parable of the ten pounds stresses faithful action in matters pertaining to God's kingdom. Both themes are played out in the three incidents sandwiched between them.

The opening scene of the first parable appears incongruous. While the sight of a

Pharisee praying at the temple is expected, that of a tax collector would not be. One even wonders how the Pharisee would have spotted the tax collector, who, due to his uncleanness, was probably relegated to the Court of the Gentiles even though he was a Jew. Details aside, Jesus' audience would have endorsed the Pharisee's picture-perfect piety. He stands tall and prays with confidence, reciting his moral and ritualistic achievements to all within earshot. He tithes regularly and fasts beyond what is required. Without doubt, he sees himself as more righteous than *that* tax collector of ill-gotten gains. In stark contrast, the tax collector stands far away, too ashamed to lift his head, mourning over his own sins. His short but heartfelt confession differs strikingly from the Pharisee's self-aggrandizing verbosity. Much to the chagrin of his audience, Jesus renders the tax collector, not the Pharisee, justified before God. By his humility, the sinner is put back in a right relationship with God, while the pompous saint remains oblivious to his self-deception.

Humbleness of heart and lowliness of status like that of a child are requisite to entering God's kingdom. These values subvert the cultural ideal in which people crave honor and despise shame. As a result of Jesus' countercultural ethos, few will be saved even though many are invited. The sower sows the word of God liberally, but only the seeds that land in good soil yield a bountiful harvest (Lk 8:8, 15). The ruler in the next story is a perfect example of this principle.

A very rich ruler wants to know what he must do to inherit eternal life. When Jesus asks him about his adherence to the Mosaic law, he is ready with a respectable answer, for he has been practicing the commandments since childhood. It is not until Jesus challenges him to sell everything to give to the poor that his enthusiasm wanes. The affluent man's unwillingness to part with his treasure contrasts sharply with the disciples' renunciation of their livelihood to follow Jesus (Lk 5:11, 28; 18:28). It is not that rich people cannot be disciples, or that money is intrinsically evil, but because wealth often comes with status, comfort, and influence, these worldly perks are especially difficult to relinquish in exchange for a life of hardship, even if the road of suffering will eventually lead to eternal life.

The journey to Jerusalem is coming to an end, and Jesus makes the third prediction of his death and vindication.[20] Due to divine concealment, the disciples remain obtuse, as they have yet to see the whole picture from a post-resurrection perspective. Meanwhile, with increasing trepidation, they continue with Jesus to Jerusalem.

Outside Jericho, Jesus encounters a blind beggar, who is at the opposite end of the economic spectrum from the rich ruler. Having found out that it is Jesus of Nazareth passing by, the beggar cries out, refusing to be silenced, "Son of David, have mercy on me!" (Lk 18:38-39). When given a chance to state his request, he says, "Lord, let me see again" (Lk 18:41). Instead of a temporary fix, such as money, this beggar asks boldly for a new lease on life. If he regains his sight, he will be able to find work and participate in the life of his community. Most importantly, he trusts that Jesus can and will heal him. In spite of his blindness, he sees Jesus as Messiah and Lord, and because of that simple faith, he is made whole.

Continuing with the theme of spiritual insight, the next pericope introduces a notorious character in Jericho who is eager to see Jesus. Infamous for overcharging his fellow Jews and colluding with the Romans, Zacchaeus the

[20]For the first two passion predictions, see Lk 9:22, 44.

chief tax collector is hated and despised.[21] Yet he wants to see Jesus so badly that he risks being ridiculed and climbs a sycamore tree for a better vantage point. His small stature is the obvious reason, but maybe the crowd is also blocking his view on purpose.

To everyone's annoyance, Jesus sees the tax collector, summons him down from his high perch, and invites himself to his home. Jesus has just pushed all the wrong buttons of pious religiosity and social correctness. If accepting hospitality signifies consent and identification, how can a respected rabbi get himself mixed up with transgressors of purity and moral laws? When Jesus says to Zacchaeus, "I *must* stay at your house *today*" (Lk 19:5), he is invoking a divine necessity. The necessity is not for a place to stay but Zacchaeus's salvation. As with the woman at the house of Simon the Pharisee (Lk 7:48) and the hemorrhaging woman (Lk 8:48), these words are for the unforgiving spectators to hear. Even the word *today* communicates the immediacy of God's salvation in Lukan parlance (see Lk 4:21; 19:9; 23:43).

Zacchaeus's willingness to share his wealth with the poor and make retributions over and above the legal requirement is indicative of his repentance. Imagine the joy in his voice as he rattles off his promises to make amends. Unlike the rich ruler, Zacchaeus's wealth is no longer a barrier to his salvation, and he freely gives it away. This lost son of Abraham has been found, and there is much reason to celebrate (see Lk 15:1-32).

The journey toward Jerusalem ends with the parable of the ten pounds, which is about a nobleman, his citizen, and his ten slaves. Two story lines are interwoven here. The first pertains to a nobleman who receives authority to rule but is opposed by his citizens, which foreshadows the hostility that Jesus will face in Jerusalem. The stakes are much higher now, as the conflict culminates at the religious, economic, and political center of Jewish life. In the end, however, the nobleman's rule prevails, and the rebel citizens are destroyed (see Lk 20:9-19).

The second thread has to do with what the nobleman's ten slaves have done in the master's absence with the pound that each was given.[22] A pound was worth about three months' wages, enough to make something of it. A pattern soon emerges as each slave gives his report. Those who have generated a positive return on the money are rewarded according to their capabilities. But the slave who knows what is expected of him but does absolutely nothing is severely rebuked, and his portion given to the most productive slave. Like Zacchaeus, faithfulness is evidenced by concrete action. With the road ahead strewn with danger and suffering, Jesus' disciples must not be complacent but always be prepared for action.

ENTRY INTO JERUSALEM AND CLEARING THE TEMPLE (LUKE 19:28-48)

From the Mount of Olives, Jerusalem comes into full view two miles away. On its slope lie the small hamlets of Bethany and Bethphage. Jesus is in control even as death awaits him. The disciples sent to fetch the colt encounter exactly what Jesus told them. Normally, kings and generals rode stallions, but a borrowed colt fits the humility of this Messiah-King. As with horses ridden by kings, this colt, too, has never been ridden; its use hints at Jesus' royal status. Jesus' symbolic action daringly echoes the prophecy of Zechariah, in which *God* will return to Zion on the day of salvation as a triumphant and humble king riding on a donkey (Zech 9:9).

[21]Ironically, the name Zacchaeus means "innocent" or "pure."
[22]*Pound* could also be "mina" (Greek *mna*).

Whether the disciples and the crowd understand the full implication of the symbolism is doubtful, but they spread out their cloaks on the ground—the equivalent of the modern-day red carpet—to escort Jesus into Jerusalem, all the while praising God in exuberant joyfulness. They even replace "the one who comes" in the pilgrim song of Psalm 118:26 with "the *king* who comes" (Lk 19:38). During Passover, Jewish messianic fervor ran high. Were the people expecting Jesus to overthrow the Romans and dethrone Tiberius? A few days later, the crowd's chant and cheer will deteriorate into rant and jeer. For now, only the Pharisees remain unmoved, irritated by the surge of support for Jesus.

The exhilaration soon gives way to lament, as Jesus agonizes over Israel's inability to embrace the peace he brings. How ironic it is for Israel not to recognize its own Messiah! Yet the reason for Israel's blindness is divine concealment, not unlike how the disciples cannot grasp Jesus' passion predictions before the time is ripe (Lk 18:34). On the one hand, Jesus' salvific mission cannot be fully understood until after the resurrection. On the other hand, dullness is a means of God's judgment on human hardheartedness (Lk 8:10; see Is 6:9-13). Persistent rejection of Jesus will yield God's rejection, leading to the fall of Jerusalem. The city, together with its magnificent temple, will be demolished by its pagan enemies, and the underlying cause will be its failure to "recognize the time of [its] visitation from God" in the person and mission of Israel's Messiah (Lk 19:44).

Jesus' ensuing action at the temple is an indictment of its leadership. Seeing all the commercial activities at the temple, he chases the vendors away, charging them and the powerbrokers behind them with turning God's house of prayer into a robber's den (Lk 19:46; see Jer 7:11; Is 56:7). The temple authorities are particularly culpable, for they have much to gain financially from letting merchants do business in prime locations within the temple precincts. One might argue that moneychangers and sellers of sacrificial animals are essential for pilgrims who travel from afar, but if the din of buying and selling extends into the Court of the Gentiles, how can the temple effectively provide a place of prayer and reflection for foreigners when they come to Jerusalem to worship Israel's God?[23]

Like Jesus' ride into Jerusalem, his clearing of the temple is also a symbolic action to condemn the corruption of the temple authorities. As soon as he is gone, the commercial activities will likely resume, so it is not as though the temple were reformed by this singular act of protest. Nevertheless, the battle lines are clearly drawn. The crowds are mesmerized by Jesus' teachings, and the Jewish leaders must proceed with care if they want to find a way to kill him, lest they invite unwanted attention from the Romans, who had no tolerance for any hint of rebellion during pilgrimage feasts, especially the Passover.

CHALLENGES AND RIPOSTES (LUKE 20:1–21:4)

In a context where honor and shame governed the dynamics of social interactions, the challenges and ripostes in this chapter are not simply a display of one-upmanship to defend one's honor. The temple elites are actively looking for ways to trap Jesus and condemn him.

In the first challenge, on the source of his authority, Jesus' rejoinder is a counterquestion about his opponents' view of John's authority. Acknowledging John's prophetic status would mean admitting that Jesus, who aligns himself

[23]The reason for the moneychangers was that temple currency had to replace Roman coins to alleviate purity concerns.

with John, also receives his authority from heaven. Because the religious leaders have rejected John's baptism of repentance, but the crowds have embraced it (Lk 7:29-30), Jesus' rebuttal forces them into a corner. If they were to say what they really thought of John, the people would be furious at them. If they were to affirm John's prophetic status, they would be guilty of rejecting God's messenger. In the end, their refusal to given an answer amounts to an admission of defeat.

The next challenge pertains to the issue of sovereignty. The question on whether to pay taxes to Caesar pits Roman law against Mosaic law, as though one must choose one over the other. The Greek word *phoros* means "tax" or "tribute," an emblem of shame for the Jews. Paying tribute with a Roman coin acknowledged not only the lordship of Tiberius, whose head was on the coin, but also his title, "son of a god," which was blasphemous. If Jesus were to say no, he would be accused of rebelling against Caesar. If he were to say yes, the crowd would turn against him and the leaders could legitimately charge him with blasphemy. Steering clear of the binary trap, Jesus gives a nuanced response. Paying tribute to the emperor does not compromise God's sovereignty, for all earthly rulers are subject to divine sanction. If the Jews cannot give God what belongs to God, that is, their wholehearted loyalty, then any objection to showing allegiance to Caesar is but a sham.

The third attempt to trap Jesus comes from the Sadducees, who do not believe in the resurrection, yet they have devised a hypothetical situation to test Jesus' understanding of the Mosaic law that presupposes resurrection to be true. Two Mosaic laws are pitted one against the other—the provision of levirate marriage, in which a kinsman-redeemer marries a relative's widow to perpetuate the family name for the deceased (Deut 25:5-10), and the prohibition of polyandry, which prevents a woman from having more than one husband (Deut 17:17). This is a trick question because the two laws cannot be upheld simultaneously in the posited scenario, regardless of whether the woman ends up as the wife of all eight husbands or only the last one. Again, Jesus refuses to choose one of the two options laid out by the Sadducees. Instead, he exposes the basic flaws in the question itself. First, it is a mistake to assume that marriage for procreation is needed in eternity, when people no longer die. Second, the Sadducees' interpretation of Moses is faulty. At the burning bush, Moses called God the God of Abraham, Isaac, and Jacob, all of whom were long dead by then. But if Jesus and the Sadducees agree that God is the God of the living, then the patriarchs must have been alive as far as Moses was concerned, and the only way for that to happen is through the resurrection. As such, the Sadducees' premise that there is no resurrection is fundamentally mistaken.

During these tense interchanges, Jesus twice goes on the offensive. The parable of the wicked tenants foreshadows the killing of the Son of God by the leaders of the Jews. The allegorical correlation is obvious. The vineyard is a common metaphor for Israel (see Is 5:1-7; Jer 2:21; 12:10), and the first two servants represent prophets previously sent by God whom Israel rejected. When God, the owner of the vineyard, finally sends his beloved son, the tenants become all the more emboldened. Instead of respecting the heir, they murder him, which leads to their downfall. Citing Psalm 118:22, Jesus condemns the ignorance and audacity of the Jewish leaders. He is the cornerstone, the most important piece of stone in the building, against which all other stones are laid. Yet these unfaithful builders toss it aside, not knowing that this very piece of stone will eventually become their stumbling block when God punishes them for their unbelief and mistreatment of him.

The obtuseness of Jesus' opponents is also apparent in their inability to solve Jesus' riddle. According to Psalm 110:1, God places the Messiah, David's Lord, in an honorific position at God's right hand, so the challenge is to explain how the Messiah can be David's Lord and David's son, or how David can be both inferior and superior to the Messiah at the same time. Jewish messianic expectation conceived of an unending succession of human Davidic kings, not one who was seated next to God in heaven. Jesus is the only one who fits this role, because even though he is of Davidic descent by human ancestry (Lk 1:32), his messiahship is eternal and his enthronement is in heaven. Without the humility to accept Jesus as who he really is, these legal experts will never have the spiritual insight into his true identity.

As these debates draw to a close, Jesus warns his audience of the hypocrisy of the scribes, who enjoy public acclaim for their knowledge and praxis of the law, yet use their position to oppress the poor. Because they take advantage of those most vulnerable, such as powerless widows, their shameless display of piety will result in severe judgment.

Speaking of authentic piety, the quiet devotion of a widow who contributes two copper coins into the temple treasury is not lost to Jesus.[24] Giving God all that she has to live on, she puts herself entirely at God's mercy. The deeper her trust in God's provision, the greater her generosity, which far exceeds the large sums that the rich ostentatiously throw into the offering receptacles. The principle of reversal continues to ring true in God's kingdom, where the humble are exalted and the poor are blessed.

APOCALYPTIC DISCOURSE (LUKE 21:5-38)

Earlier, Jesus lamented over Jerusalem and predicted its destruction (Lk 19:41-44). Now, in response to his disciples' fascination with the beautiful stones and grandeur of Herod's temple, he reiterates the judgment on Jerusalem, which is but the beginning of an escalation of tribulation toward the end of time.

Since leaving Galilee, Jesus has been preparing his disciples for the challenges ahead. Here he reminds them of three important things. First, they must have discernment and not chase after false messiahs who claim to deliver them from their enemies. Second, they must show courage in the midst of calamities. Knowing that such trials are necessary acts of divine judgment within the larger scheme of God's plan of salvation will enable them to face these afflictions. Third, they must have perseverance when they are persecuted on all sides, from family and friends to synagogues and Gentile courts. When brought before the authorities, they will bear testimony with words that Jesus himself will give them. Should they suffer martyrdom, their final salvation will be their vindication.

It might have been hard for Jesus' disciples to imagine Jerusalem's demise, with the temple structures towering above them in apparent invincibility. By the time of the writing of the Gospel of Luke, though, Jerusalem had already fallen, in 70 CE. Luke's description of the fall of Jerusalem may reflect how Rome actually destroyed the city. According to Jesus' prediction, Jerusalem would find itself under siege, surrounded on all sides by its enemies. With no supplies coming in and no escape route going out, famine and weakness would set in, leaving the people defenseless and vulnerable to plunder, slaughter, and captivity.

[24]A *leptos* had the smallest valuation among the currency circulated at that time, equivalent to 1/132 of a denarius (the daily wage of a day laborer).

Jesus identifies these horrific times with the days of vengeance, of which the prophets of old repeatedly forewarned God's people.

The end of the age, however, will not follow immediately after the destruction of Jerusalem. The earth and its nations will continue to be ravaged by calamities, but there will still be time for repentance and faithful discipleship. Jewish apocalyptic language speaks of the sun and moon turning dark and the stars falling from the sky as portents of God's severe judgment (see Joel 2:10-11, 30-31; Rev 6:12-13; 8:12). While the wicked will be gripped with a sense of foreboding, Jesus' disciples will anticipate with joy the second coming of the Son of Man, riding on a cloud, to bring about their final redemption.

Until then, watchfulness is to characterize the life of discipleship. Jesus' followers must know how to interpret the times in which they live. Just as trees sprouting spring leaves signal the approach of summer, these tribulations point to the nearness of the end. Because the disciples do not know exactly when Jesus will return and when God will bring in the final judgment, they must remain vigilant, pray always, and not be distracted by the pleasures and worries of life. In doing so, they will emerge victorious beyond the time of trial.

Jesus' exhortation about the end times paints a big picture of God's judgment and salvation. The focus is not in identifying that one singular event that marks the end of time but in being aware of God's activities in the present. Even the fall of Jerusalem, traumatic as it was for the Jews, is one of many precursors before the final judgment. More important, then, is to heed Jesus' word by maintaining a posture of vigilant anticipation and faithful witness. That way, whether God ushers in the age to come during one's lifetime or not, the promise of salvation is assured.

JUDAS'S BETRAYAL AND THE LAST SUPPER (LUKE 22:1-30)

The challenges from the temple authorities in Luke 20 are but a preview of their full-fledged assault, set in motion by Judas's offer to hand Jesus over to them. In order to arrest Jesus by stealth, what better coconspirator than a traitor from within the inner circle, who has knowledge of Jesus' whereabouts away from the public eye? Behind the human machinations, though, is Satan's orchestration. At the conclusion of the temptations in the desert, Satan "departed from [Jesus] until an opportune time" (Lk 4:13). That time is now. The devil begins with entering Judas, but soon more people will succumb to his diabolical maneuvers.

At the time of Jesus, Passover and Unleavened Bread were celebrated as one feast.[25] Since the law stipulated that the Passover meal be eaten within the city limits, visitors had to rent a place, buy an unblemished lamb to be slaughtered and sacrificed at the temple, have the lamb roasted, and purchase supplies such as wine, bitter herbs, and unleavened bread. Knowing that he is a marked man, Jesus sends his most trusted disciples to run these errands. Peter and John are told to find a man with a water jar, follow him to a designated house, and greet the owner with a prearranged question.[26]

The Passover meal commemorates God's past deliverance and rekindles hope in God's future salvation. Each item of food and cup of wine has its symbolic meaning. Led by the head of the household, the exodus story is retold and the Hallel (Ps 113–118) is sung. As host, Jesus presides over the meal and injects meaning into the bread and cup to explain his

[25]Passover was on the fourteenth of Nisan and Unleavened Bread from the fifteenth to the twenty-first.

[26]Carrying a water jar was usually a woman's task, so this man would be easy to spot.

impending death. Breaking the loaf, he declares, "This is my body, which is given for you" (Lk 22:19). His death is not a defeat in the hands of his enemies but a voluntary, self-giving, and substitutionary act on behalf of his own. Similarly, in reference to the wine he says, "This cup that is poured out for you is the new covenant in my blood" (Lk 22:20). Jesus' death, violent though it will be, ratifies the agreement between God and Israel, recalling the occasion in which Moses dashed the blood of the sacrificial animal on the people to formalize their pact with God (Ex 24:6-8). Furthermore, Jesus' death seals the new covenant that God established through Jeremiah to forgive the people's sins and inscribe the law on their hearts (Jer 31:31-34). As such, the Messiah's death is the means by which God will accomplish the act of salvation. By taking one loaf and one cup to represent his body and blood for his disciples to eat and drink, Jesus inextricably binds himself to them—by his death they will live. In gratitude and in obedience to Jesus' command, "Do this in remembrance of me" (Lk 22:19), Christians ever since have been observing the sacrament of the Lord's Supper (1 Cor 11:23-26).

Despite the enormous implication of Jesus' death and their connection to it, the disciples still fail to grasp its deep significance. When Jesus discloses that one among them will betray him, they become preoccupied with identifying the traitor and pointing the finger away from their own fragile loyalties. The argument over who is the greatest among them could have been a distraction to defuse the tension, but the disciples have definitely missed the example that their Lord and teacher has just set for them. True greatness is exhibited in humility, lowliness, and servanthood, not self-promotion (see Lk 9:46-48). It seems that the disciples are still caught up in the euphoria of hailing Jesus as king and the delight in watching him reduce the temple elites to silence. The lesson Jesus is teaching them, in life and now in death, stands in striking contradistinction to the prevalent pursuit of honor and status so valued in that cultural milieu. To their credit, at least they have not peeled off at the first sign of trouble, and for that Jesus promises them roles of authority in God's kingdom. But immediately before them, a series of trials awaits.

ARREST AND PETER'S DENIAL (LUKE 22:31-62)

Even in the hour of darkness, Satan can wield his power only if given permission by God to do so. Knowing that the disciples will soon be targeted by the devil, Jesus assures Simon and the others that he has already prayed for them. Even if they stumble amid these trials, their faith will not fail, and they will recover.

The disciples are far from ready to overcome an enemy as formidable as Satan himself. Their weaknesses are in full display in this section. First, Peter is overconfident of his ability to stay loyal to Jesus, claiming that he will go with him to prison and to death. Little does he know that Jesus' prediction of his triple denial will soon come to pass. Second, the disciples tend to overreact and fight spiritual battles with earthly weapons. When Jesus suggests that they should have a sword among them, perhaps to defend themselves, they promptly produce two, at the ready to use when threatened. Soon after, at Jesus' arrest, one of the disciples wields his sword and lops off the ear of the high priest's slave, right in front of the religious leaders and their armed officers. Behind this act of compulsive aggression lies the inclination to fight violence with violence, a marked departure from Jesus' teaching on loving one's enemies (Lk 6:27-36). Third, despite Jesus' repeated exhortations about prayer, the disciples are ill-equipped to wage the real spiritual battle.

At the garden on the Mount of Olives, Jesus tells them to pray in order not to fall into temptation. But, overcome with sorrow, they fail to stay awake and keep watch. Without prayer, they are powerless against Satan's onslaught.

The account of Peter's denial of Jesus, described in extensive detail, is shot through with irony. Initially, Peter follows at a safe distance, up to the courtyard of the house of Caiaphas, where Jesus has been taken. His earlier bravado to follow Jesus to prison and to death soon crumbles. A servant girl identifies him as Jesus' companion, which he quickly refutes. Soon afterward, another man recognizes him as one among Jesus' group, and he denies it again. Even if Peter had been caught by surprise the first two times, the third challenge, coming an hour later, would have given him time to rethink his previous responses. Yet when a third person singles him out as a Galilean and links him to Jesus, Peter loses it. His fear turns into anger, and he snaps back a third denial. Even before he can finish speaking, the cock crows. It is hard to imagine the feeling when Jesus' and Peter's eyes met at that fateful moment, like a dagger piercing through the heart. One hopes that in his tears of regret Peter will remember that Jesus has prayed to protect his faith despite his colossal failure.

In sharp contrast to the disciples' cowardice, Jesus continues to stay the course. In deep anguish, he prays in the garden that his Father's will be done, even though he would rather the cup of suffering be removed. When Judas arrives with the authorities to arrest him, he shows no resistance and even heals the slave whose ear is cut off by his disciple. None of this is passive acquiescence to evil, but rather it is unwavering trust in God to provide the needed strength to deal the devil his ultimate defeat.

JEWISH AND ROMAN TRIALS (LUKE 22:63–23:25)

All four Gospels recount the trials of Jesus. There are overlapping details as well as elements distinctive to each. In Luke, within a span of a few hours, Jesus is interrogated before the Jewish ruling council, the Roman governor of Judea, and the ruler of Galilee. These proceedings are peppered with false accusations and insults, as each party finds what is expedient, not what is true, to move Jesus toward his death sentence. By the end of the morning, the guilty verdict is pronounced.

The mockery begins when Jesus is held at Caiaphas's house, and so does the irony. The guards taunt him by making him prophesy, ignorant that Jesus is indeed God's eschatological prophet. Likewise, the Sanhedrin asks Jesus about his kingship even though the members of the ruling council do not for a moment believe that he is a king. The titles "Messiah" and "Son of God" both carry royal connotations (see Ps 2:7; 2 Sam 7:14).[27] If Jesus admits to any form of kingship, they can use it to formulate a political charge of insurrection to take to the Romans. To the Jewish authorities, however, the primary justification for killing Jesus is religious. Jesus has often been criticized for breaking the Sabbath and purity laws, but the sin most worthy of death is blasphemy.[28] So when he says, "The Son of Man will be seated at the right hand of the power of God" (Lk 22:69), and does not deny that he is the Son of God, his enemies charge him with blasphemy. In their view, a man who elevates himself to the same level as God deserves to die.

[27]"Messiah" means "anointed one."

[28]This charge was already levied on Jesus back in Galilee when he pronounced forgiveness of sins to the paralytic (Lk 5:21) and the sinful woman (Lk 7:48-49).

Before Pilate, the Jewish leaders claim that Jesus calls himself a king, forbids the Jews to pay taxes to the emperor, and created a stir among the people from Galilee to Judea. To Roman ears, these accusations directly challenge Caesar's sovereignty. They also test Pilate's ability to avert a rebellion, if indeed an insurrectionist is active during the Jewish Passover when messianic sentiments run high. Neither Pilate nor Herod is particularly invested in the truth. They shuttle Jesus back and forth between them, each conducting a cursory questioning that yields either silence or a few inconclusive words from Jesus. Herod even joins his soldiers to dress Jesus up as a sick parody of a king before returning him to Pilate. The newfound friendship between the two that day underscores both Roman and Jewish complicity in Jesus' death.

At every turn, Jesus' accusers are relentless, accusing him and agitating the crowd into a frenzy to call for his crucifixion. The Jewish leaders turn a blind eye to justice by offering Jesus, an innocent man, to Pilate in exchange for Barabbas, a real insurrectionist and a murderer. Three times Pilate points to Jesus' innocence, and twice he offers to have Jesus flogged and released, but the Jews drown him out until he capitulates. Out of expediency, Pilate acquiesces to their demands, sets Barabbas free, and hands Jesus over to death. In the final analysis, perhaps this set of proceedings is but a farce and a nuisance to the Roman governor, for whom there is little incentive to render a judgment of rectitude.

CRUCIFIXION, DEATH, AND BURIAL (LUKE 23:26-56)

Criminals slated for crucifixion were normally required to carry the crossbeam of their cross to the place of execution. In Jesus' case, a hapless bystander, Simon of Cyrene, is forced into this service. The picture of Simon carrying the cross and walking behind Jesus is a vivid reminder of Jesus' words to those who desire to be his disciples, that they must take up their cross daily to follow him (Lk 9:23). A large crowd gathers on the way to the Skull, or Golgotha in Aramaic. In contrast to the exuberant crowd who welcomed Jesus as he rode into Jerusalem, Jesus now tells the mourning women not to weep for him but for the severe judgment that will befall this city and its rebellious people. When that time comes, one will not want to bring children into this world; one would rather be crushed by boulders or destroyed by fire than be alive when God's just fury is unleashed. That disaster will be much more horrific than Jesus' imminent execution.

Even so, the mocking and scoffing continue with Jesus hanging on the cross in between two criminals. The Jewish leaders, the soldiers, and the criminal on one side of him all deride and taunt him in like manner: "Save yourself! Isn't that what the Messiah or King of the Jews is supposed to do?" Jumping down from the cross would mean immediate self-vindication and defiance of Roman power, which used crucifixion as a deterrent because it was such a cruel and shameful punishment.[29] To ancient people, the shame of the cross was even worse than the physical torture, as the victims were crucified naked for all to see and their dead bodies left hanging for vultures to pick clean. Jesus, however, is still engaged in God's saving work to the end of his life. He asks his Father to forgive his enemies and acknowledges the penitence of the other criminal next to him. By believing that Jesus is truly a king whose power transcends that of the Romans, this

[29]Crucifixion was reserved for the worst of offenders, such as runaway slaves and political rebels. Roman citizens could not be subject to this form of execution.

man is promised entry into the place of eternal bliss.

The Messiah does not save himself. He is sent to embody God's salvation for others in life and in death. As Jesus hangs on the cross, bloodied and gasping for air, darkness envelopes the land for three hours. While darkness may be indicative of Satan's death-dealing assault, it also shields the shame of the crucified Messiah and bars Jesus' enemies from gloating over his dying frame. Right before he dies, the curtain of the temple that separates the holy of holies from the sanctuary is split into two, symbolizing that full access to God is now available through the death of the Messiah. With his final breath, the Son of God, whose entire life is about his Father's business (Lk 2:49), yields himself in obedience and in trust: "Father, into your hands I commend my spirit" (Lk 23:46).

The just verdict of Jesus' innocence is finally rendered, ironically, by a Roman centurion. Like the criminal who asked to be remembered by Jesus, this Gentile officer sees what the powers that be refused to acknowledge all along. Throughout the entire passion narrative, there is not a moment in which the author depicts Jesus as being at the mercy of his enemies. Despite the fact that Jesus' death is a fait accompli, it is not the death of a victim but that of a righteous sufferer.[30] As the final chapter of the narrative will prove, the alleged victory of Satan and his accomplices is short-lived.

With sundown fast approaching and the Sabbath beginning shortly, Joseph of Arimathea has little time to give Jesus a proper burial. As a member of the Sanhedrin, he would have had the social standing to ask, or bribe, Pilate for Jesus' body. Having wrapped Jesus in linen, he then places him in a new rock-hewn tomb, affordable only for the wealthy. Even though Jesus died a criminal condemned by the Romans, he now receives a burial fit for a king (see Jn 19:39-41). Spices and ointment will be prepared by the women who have followed Jesus from Galilee to Judea. From the cross to the tomb, they have remained faithful and courageous—a striking contrast to Jesus' male disciples, who are nowhere to be seen. As the day of preparation comes to an end, Joseph, the women, and Jesus all pause for their Sabbath rest.

AN EMPTY TOMB (LUKE 24:1-12)

After the Sabbath, a cadre of women disciples—Mary Magdalene, Joanna, Mary, and others—return at daybreak with freshly prepared spices to anoint the body of Jesus. This procedure, normally done by women, is different from the Egyptian custom of embalming. The aromatics are used to counter the stench of a decomposing corpse. Imagine the horror when they find the tomb open and empty, which in and of itself is not an iron-clad proof of Jesus' resurrection. Tomb robbery may have accounted for his disappearance, but what robber would steal the body and take the trouble to remove the linen cloth wrapped around it? An answer finally comes from two dazzling angels, who chide the women for seeking a living Jesus among the dead. They also remind them of Jesus' earlier predictions, which referred not only to his suffering but to his vindication (Lk 9:22; 18:32-33).

Too little credit is given to these women when they bring the incredible news back to the disciples. The cultural bias in the ancient world toward dismissing testimonies given by

[30]Jesus' last words in Lk 23:46 echo that of the righteous sufferer of Ps 31:5. Compare also the soldiers dividing his clothing by casting lots in Lk 23:34 with Ps 22:18, and their offering him sour wine in Lk 23:36 with Ps 69:21. Psalms 22; 31; 69 are psalms of lament.

women does not negate that Mary Magdalene and the others are telling the truth. Peter runs to the tomb, whether to verify the women's report or to see for himself, and returns just as baffled. The angels have spoken; Jesus has risen and is risen indeed.

ON THE ROAD TO EMMAUS (LUKE 24:13-35)

This resurrection appearance story is found only in the Gospel of Luke. Word about the women's angelic encounter at the tomb has spread among other followers of Jesus, causing much consternation. It is the topic of conversation between Cleopas and his unnamed companion as they travel to Emmaus, about seven miles from Jerusalem. Even though these are followers of Jesus, their knowledge of his identity remains incomplete. They understand him as "a prophet mighty in deed and word" (Lk 24:19) and even wonder whether he might be "the one to redeem Israel" (Lk 24:21). Jesus' death, however, seems to have shattered that hope. A crucified Messiah is a contradiction in terms, and they do not know what to make of the latest news that Jesus is alive again. The two have bits of information about Jesus, but they are struggling to piece together the puzzle.

The missing piece is what Scripture says about the Messiah suffering before entering into his glory. Joining Cleopas and his companion on their walk to Emmaus, Jesus admonishes the two for being foolish and unbelieving, longing for a Messiah to defeat the Romans and restore Jerusalem to its former splendor. To have a Messiah shamefully nailed to a Roman cross defies logic, but the suffering of the Messiah has been in God's plan all along according to the Scriptures. Although Luke does not indicate which specific texts in Moses and the Prophets Jesus cites in his explanation, the songs of the Suffering Servant in Isaiah, such as Isaiah 52:13–53:12, might shed some light.

Upon arrival at their destination, Cleopas and his companion urge Jesus to stay with them. This invitation is more than cordial hospitality, for they have already been experiencing an inner transformation, listening to Jesus open up the Scriptures to them. Their willingness to learn paves the way for more revelation. The moment of recognition comes when Jesus, reversing his role from guest to host, takes bread, blesses it, breaks it, and gives it to them. These actions recall the feeding of the five thousand (Lk 9:16) but especially the final Passover meal (Lk 22:19), when Jesus used the bread and cup to explain the significance of his sacrificial death. As soon as the penny drops, Jesus vanishes.

Without delay, the two retrace their steps to Jerusalem. When they find the Eleven, they learn that Jesus has already appeared to Simon Peter, the one who is especially in need of the assurance that Jesus, whom he denied three times, has truly been raised from the dead. Imagine the poignancy of the reunion between Peter and his Lord in light of that unforgettable backward glance Jesus gave him when the cock crowed (Lk 22:61-62).

COMMISSIONING AND ASCENSION (LUKE 24:36-53)

In the midst of all the excitement, Jesus suddenly appears. The disciples' joy immediately turns into fear, and they mistake him for a ghost. The confusion is understandable since, in his risen body, Jesus seems to be able to appear and disappear from one moment to the next, uninhibited by the constraints of time and space. It is unquestionable that Jesus has been raised bodily, for he bears the scars of his agony on his nail-pierced hands and feet, and he even eats a piece of fish in front of the disciples to dispel any last trace of doubt.

Like Cleopas and his companion, the disciples now have the post-resurrection perspective to understand how the Old Testament anticipates the suffering and vindication of the Messiah. Moreover, they can look back on the teachings of Jesus, his passion predictions, and his death on the cross as a continuous revelation of God's salvation for Israel and the world.

It is, however, not enough for the disciples to know of Jesus' resurrection. Now that they have the complete story, they must bear witness to what they have seen and heard. They are tasked with the message of the gospel—from a sinner's repentance to the forgiveness of sins through the death of the Messiah and his vindication by the power of God—to be spread from the Jews to the Gentiles and from Jerusalem to the nations. But they cannot do so by their own strength; they must wait to be empowered by the Holy Spirit, whom God has promised and Jesus will send.

The final scene of the narrative finds Jesus and his disciples in Bethany, back on the Mount of Olives, where Jesus began his ride into Jerusalem. While he is blessing them for the last time, he is taken into heaven. With great joy the disciples worship him, and they return to the temple praising and blessing God.

The Gospel of Luke has come full circle, beginning and ending at the temple. Luke brings his narrative of the life of Jesus to a close and situates Jerusalem as the launching pad for the mission of the early church. In Acts, the sequel to this work, the early church will carry the gospel from Jerusalem, Judea, and Samaria to the very ends of the earth (Acts 1:8).

SELECTED BIBLIOGRAPHY

Bailey, Kenneth E. *Poet and Peasant and Through Peasant Eyes: A Literary-Cultural Approach to the Parables in Luke*. Combined ed. Grand Rapids, MI: Eerdmans, 1983.

Borgman, Paul C. *The Way According to Luke: Hearing the Whole Story of Luke–Acts*. Grand Rapids, MI: Eerdmans, 2006.

Chen, Diane G. *God as Father in Luke–Acts*. SBL 92. New York: Peter Lang, 2006.

———. *Luke*. NCCS. Eugene, OR: Cascade, 2017.

González, Justo L. *The Story Luke Tells: Luke's Unique Witness to the Gospel*. Grand Rapids, MI: Eerdmans, 2015.

Green, Joel B. *The Gospel of Luke*. NICNT. Grand Rapids, MI: Eerdmans, 1997.

———. *The Theology of the Gospel of Luke*. New Testament Theology. New York: Cambridge University Press, 1995.

Hultgren, Arland J. *The Parables of Jesus: A Commentary*. Grand Rapids, MI: Eerdmans, 2000.

Johnson, Luke Timothy. *Prophetic Jesus, Prophetic Church: The Challenge of Luke–Acts to Contemporary Christians*. Grand Rapids, MI: Eerdmans, 2011.

Karris, Robert J. *Eating Your Way through Luke's Gospel*. Collegeville, MN: Liturgical Press, 2006.

Neyrey, Jerome H. ed. *The Social World of Luke–Acts: Models for Interpretation*. Peabody, MA: Hendrickson, 1991.

Peterson, Eugene H. *Tell It Slant: A Conversation on the Language of Jesus in His Stories and Prayers*. Grand Rapids, MI: Eerdmans, 2012.

Snodgrass, Klyne. *Stories of Intent: A Comprehensive Guide to the Parables of Jesus*. 2nd ed. Grand Rapids, MI: Eerdmans, 2018.

Wright, Catherine J. *Spiritual Practices of Jesus: Learning Simplicity, Humility, and Prayer with Luke's Earliest Readers*. Downers Grove, IL: IVP Academic, 2020.

GOSPEL OF JOHN

Miguel G. Echevarría

INTRODUCTION

Authorship. The Gospel of John is technically anonymous. Like the Synoptic Gospels, the author makes no attempt to identify himself. Even the title "According to John" is not definitive evidence of the author's identity—for it was added when the Gospel began circulating together with the Synoptics. The Gospel's anonymity, however, is not sufficient reason to discard its authenticity. F. F. Bruce remarks: "It is noteworthy that, while the four canonical Gospels could afford to be published anonymously, the apocryphal Gospels which began to appear from the mid-second century onwards claimed (falsely) to be written by apostles or other persons closely associated with the Lord."[1]

Aside from any explicit identification of the author, the Gospel of John claims to have been written by the "disciple whom Jesus loved" (Jn 13:23, 19:26, 20:2, 21:20). John 21:24 describes this disciple as "the one who has born witness about these things" and "wrote them down."[2] This verse, along with others such as John 1:14, testify that the beloved disciple was an eyewitness to the life, death, and resurrection of Jesus.

Some argue that the beloved disciple is an idealized figure, who was historicized by a later redactor.[3] Others contend that he is Lazarus, because Jesus is said to have loved him (Jn 11:3, 36) and accounts of the beloved disciple only occur after Lazarus's resurrection in John 11.[4] Still others contend that the beloved disciple is Thomas, for he asks to see Jesus' side, information only the beloved disciple would have known, and evidence points to a school of Thomas that shows interest in the Gospel of John.[5] Though these arguments have their merits, the traditional view is still the most plausible: that the beloved disciple is John the Son of Zebedee. He was, after all, one of the twelve (Jn 13:23) and one of the sons of Zebedee (Jn 21:1-14), making him an eyewitness to the events surrounding the historical Jesus. That's why he records events not found in the Synoptics, such as Jesus turning water into wine (Jn 2:1-11) and Jesus' conversation with a Samaritan woman, events to which a direct witness would have been privy (Jn 4:1-45).

D. A. Carson and Douglas Moo provide insight into distinguishing the beloved disciple from Peter and the other disciples: "That

---

[1]F. F. Bruce, *The Gospel of John: Introduction, Exposition and Notes* (Grand Rapids, MI: Eerdmans, 1983), 1.

[2]C. H. Dodd claims that Jn 21:24 only applies to verses Jn 21:20-23 (*Historical Tradition in the Fourth Gospel* [Cambridge: Cambridge University, 1963; repr., 1989], 12). George R. Beasley-Murray, who is no friend of the traditional view of authorship, argues that this contention is unlikely, for the "immediate historical sequence of 'who has written these things' in v 24 by the 'many other things' which Jesus did and which could hardly be written (v 25) leads the reader to relate the statement to chaps. 1–20 as well as to chap. 21" (*John*, Word Biblical Commentary, vol. 36 [Nashville: Thomas Nelson, 1999], lxxi). Translations in this chapter are the author's unless otherwise indicated.

[3]Rudolph Bultmann, *The Gospel of John: A Commentary*, ed. G. R. Beasley-Murray (Philadelphia: Westminster, 1971), 11-12.

[4]Gary M. Burge, *John*, The NIV Application Commentary (Grand Rapids, MI: Zondervan, 2000), 26.

[5]See James H. Charlesworth, *The Beloved Disciple: Whose Witness Validates the Gospel of John?* (Valley Forge, PA: Trinity Press International, 1995), 225-87.

he is one of the seven who go fishing in chapter 21 and, by implication, is not Peter, Thomas, or Nathanael, suggests he is one of the sons of Zebedee or one of the two unnamed disciples (21:2)."[6] And since James is the other "son of Zebedee" (Mt 10:2; Mk 1:19; Lk 5:10), who was martyred in Acts 12, John is the disciple and son of Zebedee who authored the Gospel of John.[7] Patristic evidence supports this conclusion. Irenaeus, for instance, attributes the Gospel to "John the disciple of the Lord, who leaned back on his breast, published the Gospel while he was a resident at Ephesus in Asia" (*Adv. Haer.* 3.1.2). Clement of Alexandria says that John wrote a "spiritual Gospel" (quoted by Eusebius, *Eccl. Hist.* 6.14.7). And the Muratorian Canon (ca. 180–200 CE) affirms that John the disciple wrote the Fourth Gospel.

While these arguments are well and good, that the church has decided to recognize John as the fourth canonical Gospel should be enough for Christians to accept its inspiration and authority. This is not a license to deny the traditional authorship of John's Gospel—it simply allows us to consider the canonical status of the Gospel as sufficient proof of its acceptance. For roughly twenty centuries, Christian communities from different tribes, tongues, and nations have read John's Gospel for encouragement and hope amid life's daily struggles—what many Latino/a people call *lo cotidiano*—knowing that Jesus has gone to "prepare a place" for them (Jn 14:3). The canonical status of John's Gospel was enough for them, as it should be for us.

Date. Since the nineteenth century, suggestions for dating the Gospel of John have ranged from 55 CE to the late second century. But with the discovery of Papyrus 52 (a short fragment containing John 18:31-32), which scholars usually ascribe to the early second century (ca. 117–138 CE), proposals for dating the Gospel from the mid to late second century have pretty well been ruled out. Thus, it is plausible to date John's Gospel anywhere from the late first century (80–100 CE) to the early second century (100–120 CE).[8]

John A. T. Robinson argues that John's Gospel was written before the first Jewish-Roman war (66–70 CE).[9] Few scholars are willing to date the Gospel that early. Unlike the Synoptics, John makes no reference to the temple. So, it's likely he wrote his Gospel after the temple's destruction in 70 CE, possibly ten to twenty years after this catastrophic event, which would have been long enough for his original audiences not to have required comment on what was once the central place of Jewish life.[10] We can argue, then, albeit tentatively, that John penned his Gospel somewhere between 80 and 90 CE.[11] Shortly thereafter, likely in the '90s, he published his three epistles.[12]

[6]D. A. Carson and Douglas J. Moo, *An Introduction to the New Testament* (Grand Rapids, MI: Zondervan, 2005), 237.

[7]G. K. Beale and Benjamin Gladd, *The Story Retold: A Biblical-Theological Introduction to the New Testament* (Downers Grove, IL: IVP Academic, 2020), 126.

[8]Colin Kruse, *John: An Introduction and Commentary*, Tyndale New Testament Commentaries, vol. 4 (Downers Grove, IL: InterVarsity Press, 2003), 30; Raymond E. Brown, *The Gospel According to John (i–xii)*, The Anchor Bible, vol. 29 (New York: Doubleday, 1966), lxxx-lxxxvi.

[9]John A. T. Robinson contends that all the NT books were completed before 70 CE. For his discussion of John and his epistles, see *Redating the New Testament* (Eugene, OR: Wipf & Stock, 2000), 254-311.

[10]See also Kruse, *John*, 31.

[11]For a more thorough discussion of the dating of John's Gospel, see D. A. Carson, *The Gospel According to John*, The Pillar New Testament Commentary (Grand Rapids, MI: Eerdmans, 1991), 81-86.

[12]See Marianne Meye Thompson, *1-3 John*, The IVP New Testament Commentary Series (Downers Grove, IL: InterVarsity Press, 1992), 20-21.

Setting. The traditional opinion is that John wrote his Gospel while a resident in Ephesus. Early evidence for this is found in the writings of Irenaeus (*Adv. Haer.* 3.1.2) and Eusebius (*Hist. Eccl.* 3.23.1–4). Ephesus is also the place where John wrote his epistles.

Some speculate that John's Gospel addresses the deficient beliefs of his followers in Asia Minor, such as matters related to the incarnation of Jesus, which he also addresses in his letters (Jn 1:1-18; 1 Jn 1:1-4; 4:2; 2 Jn 1:7).[13] While this is historically plausible, and may even be supported in the text (Jn 1:19-28, 35-42; 3:22-36; 10:40-42), we will not speculate about how John may (or may not) have been correcting deviant views among his earliest followers. We will focus on how John's Gospel reveals that Jesus is the Messiah.

Basic Outline. This commentary will follow a fourfold structure for the Gospel of John. The Prologue introduces the preexistence and incarnation of Jesus (Jn 1:1-18). The Book of Signs progressively reveals the identity of Jesus through seven messianic signs (Jn 1:19–12:50). The Book of Exaltation focuses on the crucifixion, resurrection, and ascension of the Messiah to the Father (Jn 13:1–20:31).[14] The seventh sign, the raising of Lazarus, bridges these two sections, anticipating Jesus' own resurrection (Jn 11:1-44; 12:1-11, 17-19).[15] The Epilogue concludes the Gospel, affirming John's eyewitness testimony to the events related to the historical Jesus (Jn 21:1-25). Below is an outline of the structure, which includes some further details.

I. Prologue (Jn 1:1-18)

II. The Book of Signs (Jn 1:19–12:50)

- The Appearance of Jesus and His Early Disciples: Transition to Signs 1–2 (Jn 1:19–1:50)
- The Cana Cycle: Signs 1–2 (Jn 2:1–4:50)
- The Jerusalem Cycle: Signs 3–7 (Jn 5:1–12:50)

III. The Book of Exaltation (Jn 13:1–20:31)

- The Farewell Discourse: Preparation for Exaltation (Jn 13:1–17:26)
- The Trials, Death, and Empty Tomb: The Exaltation of Jesus (Jn 18:1–20:31)

IV. Epilogue (Jn 21:1-25)

PROLOGUE (JOHN 1:1-18)

John begins his Gospel with the phrase "in the beginning." These familiar words evoke the creation account in Genesis 1, which begins the very same way (Jn 1:1; cf. Gen 1:1).[16] The interpretive context for John's prologue therefore includes the initial pages of Genesis. This expanded framework is essential for understanding important themes such as "Word," "light," and "life."[17]

---

[13]For instance, Thompson, *1-3 John*, 20.

[14]Andreas J. Köstenberger, *A Theology of John's Gospel and Letters: The Word, the Christ, the Son of God*, Biblical Theology of the New Testament (Grand Rapids, MI: Zondervan, 2009), 167. Often this section is labeled the Book of Glory. Already in the Book of Signs, Jesus' "glory" is spoken of in verses such as Jn 1:14; 2:11, 8:54, and 11:4. Moreover, the very "signs" in Jn 1:19–12:50 and Jesus' "exaltation" in Jn 13:1–20:31 are intended to reveal God's glory. All this leads us to conclude that the designation Book of Glory is not exact. I have chosen instead to designate Jn 13:1–20:31 as the Book of Exaltation, since this section emphasizes the "lifting up" of the Son of Man (e.g., Jn 17:1, 5, 24). See Köstenberger, *John's Gospel and Letters*, 167-68; George Mlakuzhyil, *The Christocentric Literary Structure of the Fourth Gospel*, Analecta Biblica: Investigationes Scientificae in Res Biblicas 117 (Rome: Editrice Pontificio Istituto Biblico, 1987), 161-62.

[15]Köstenberger, *John's Gospel and Letters*, 168.

[16]John cites *en archē* verbatim from Gen 1:1 LXX.

[17]James F. McGrath argues that in the prologue John uses imagery and traditions that would have been familiar both to him and his opponents in order to defend his communities' beliefs about Jesus ("Prologue as Legitimation: Christological Controversy and the Interpretation of John 1:1-18," *Irish Biblical Studies* 19.3 [1997]: 98-120). While I will not investigate potential historical strife between hypothetical Johannine communities and their opponents, I do agree that John uses Jewish tradition, particularly the Genesis account, to set forth a high Christology.

John affirms that the Word (*logos*)[18] was with God in the beginning of creation (Jn 1:1-2).[19] According to Genesis 1, God "speaks" his good creation into existence (Gen 1:3, 6, 9, 11, 14, 20, 24, 26).[20] Thus, God made all things through his "Word," the very agent in creation, the one about whom John says: "All things came into existence through him, and not one thing was made without him" (Jn 1:3). If that were not enough, John also declares that the Word is one and the same with Israel's God (Jn 1:1). He is the one who created Eden for humanity to enjoy—until his people fell into sin, ruining paradise (Gen 3).

John makes a further declaration about the Word—he is one and the same with Jesus, who "took on flesh and dwelt among us" (Jn 1:14). John has affirmed, then, that the Word is the creator God, Yahweh, who has taken on full humanity in the person of Jesus. Jesus was not created. He is, in fact, the creator of all things, who has always existed separately and independently from the world.

As he called light into darkness at the beginning of creation (Gen 1:3-5), Jesus has returned to illumine a world that has receded into darkness (Jn 1:4-5). In so doing, he will redeem what he has created, bringing life out of death (Jn 1:4-5, 9).[21] We can say that he is bringing forth a new creation, where we will no longer experience the effects of the curse, like suffering and death (cf. Gen 3).[22] And as the darkness could not prevent the presence of the light in the original creation, it has no power to thwart Jesus from shining his light into a world in need of renewal (Jn 1:5). There is nothing, as John says elsewhere, that will stop Jesus from "making all things new" (Rev 21:5).[23]

To make sure that humanity was ready for his coming, God sent John the Baptist into the wilderness. There, he testified about the "light," so that people would know that Jesus was about to renew all things (Jn 1:6-8). Later in the Gospel, Jesus speaks of him as "the lamp that burned and shined" (Jn 5:35). Through his witness as the lamp, John let the work of Jesus be seen in his ministry, so that "all might believe through him" (Jn 1:7).

But John is not supposed to be the exclusive witness to the "light." All believers are to witness to Jesus' redemptive work, showing the world that the savior has come to roll back the darkness of sin and death. One of the ways we do this is by working toward removing racial inequalities in society, such as making sure people receive equal justice in civil and criminal matters, advocating for equal opportunities for

[18]Jewish tradition notes that the *logos* is God's preexistent partner in creation (e.g., Prov 8:22-30; Eccl 1:1-9). She seeks to dwell among humans, but they do not accept her, so she returns to the heavens (Prov 1:20-32; Job 28). While I do not deny a connection to such contexts, I believe the primary allusion in John 1:1 is to the creation account in Genesis. I will note the exegetical implications of this connection in the remainder of the section.

[19]Margaret Davies, *Rhetoric and Reference in the Fourth Gospel*, Journal for the Study of the New Testament Supplement Series 69 (Sheffield: Sheffield Academic, 1992), 120.

[20]Andreas J. Köstenberger, "John," in *Commentary on the New Testament Use of the Old Testament*, ed. G. K. Beale and D. A. Carson (Grand Rapids, MI: Baker Academic, 2007), 421.

[21]While there are similarities with gnostic documents, such as the Testimony of Truth and the Gospel of Truth, John's prologue has clear allusions to the creation account in Gen 1. Unlike gnostic literature, John values the physical creation. He values it so much that he argues that Israel's God took on flesh to redeem that which he created—which includes both his human and nonhuman creation. That worldview is far from gnosticism, which values secret knowledge, so that humans might be delivered from the evil, physical world, rather than the acknowledgment of what God created as good and worthy of redemption.

[22]Beale and Gladd, *The Story Retold*, 131.

[23]Jesus as "light" is common throughout the Gospel of John (Jn 3:19-21; 8:12; 9:5; 11:9; 12:35-36, 46). In Jewish literature, "light" is linked to "joy, life, understanding, and ultimately God" (e.g., Job 5:14; Ps 18:28; Wis 7:26; *2 Bar.* 17:4; Thompson, *John*, 29). Darkness, on the other hand, is linked to "terror, gloom, and death" (e.g., Job 15:22-23; Ps 88:12; 91:6; 107:10).

employment and promotion, and eliminating housing practices like redlining, which group black and brown people into their own separate ghettos. Jesus cares about the physical world, which includes the disparities that exist among real flesh and blood people. That's why he came "in the flesh" to give humanity fullness of life on earth. Since Jesus' incarnation marks the beginning of his renewing work, racial equality—which is nothing other than making sure that people flourish from the moment they are conceived in the womb to the time Jesus takes them home—is something for which believers should strive. In so doing, we bear witness to the human flourishing people will experience when Jesus restores all things. This is the kind of witness that brightens a dark world, beckoning others to follow the God who is shining his renewing light into the darkness.

Before John concludes his prologue, he remarks that Jesus is the "unique" (*monogenēs*) Son of God full of "grace and truth" (Jn 1:14, 17).[24] These concepts recall the Mosaic Law's affirmation of God's "steadfast love and faithfulness" to his covenant people (Ex 34:6).[25] God is so loyal to the covenant that he sent his Son into the world to redeem his people from sin and death. The notion of sonship recalls 2 Samuel 7 and Psalm 2, which look forward to God's kingly Son, the Messiah, who will reign over the earth. The words God spoke to Moses are now fulfilled in Jesus—for God's "grace and truth" are now available to all who trust in Jesus, making us beneficiaries of the covenant promises of redemption (e.g., Gen 12, 15; Is 65–66).

The prologue ends with a final declaration of the importance of Jesus: Although "no one has seen God," the Son has made him known (Jn 1:18). At first glance, this affirmation seems inconsistent with the Old Testament, which is full of examples of people who have "seen God." Moses, for instance, is said to have spoken to God "face-to-face" (Ex 33:11; Deut 34:10). Israel's elders "saw the God of Israel" (Ex 24:9-11). And Isaiah, Ezekiel, and Daniel saw God in visionary experiences (Is 6; Ezek 1; Dan 7). Marianne Meye Thompson, noting examples from passages such as Exodus 33:20-23 and Deuteronomy 4:12-15, reconciles John's affirmation with the testimony of the Old Testament: "There are numerous interpretive moves [in the Old Testament] that seek to explain apparently direct visions of God as mediated or indirect encounters with God."[26] Unlike Old Testament figures, Jesus has "an unmitigated and direct vision of God," because he has been with him since the beginning of creation (Jn 1:1-3; cf. Gen 1).

With the content of the prologue in mind, the remainder of John's Gospel shows that Jesus is the one whom the Father has sent as his Son and Messiah (Jn 1:19–12:50), who was "exalted" for our transgressions (Jn 13:1–20:29), so that we might experience life in a new creation (Jn 20:30-31).

THE BOOK OF SIGNS (JOHN 1:19–12:50)

After revealing that Jesus is the creator and redeemer of the earth, John ties his identity to the promised Messiah. John makes this connection through seven messianic signs, beginning with Jesus turning water into wine (Jn 2:1-11) and concluding with Jesus raising Lazarus from the tomb (Jn 11:1-44). The Book of Signs, then, is a fitting designation for the first major unit in the Gospel. At strategic

[24]"Only begotten" is a common translation for *monogenēs* in John 1:14 and 1:18. In view of the glory revealed solely in the Son, it is best to render the term as "unique" or "one and only."

[25]Köstenberger, *John*, 422.

[26]Thompson, *John*, 36. I have included the words in brackets to clarify that Thompson's observations are based on the OT.

points, John inserts other scenes into the narrative, such as conversations with Nicodemus (Jn 3:1-21) and a Samaritan woman (Jn 4:1-45). The unit is rich in Old Testament allusions, recalling how Jesus fulfills the eschatological hopes of people like Moses, Ezekiel, and Isaiah.

The appearance of Jesus and his early disciples: Transition to signs 1–2 (John 1:19-1:50). John the Baptist and "the Jews" enter the narrative prior to the seven messianic signs. John's Gospel frequently paints a negative picture of "the Jews" of Jesus' time. We should recognize that John the author does not lump all Jewish people under the same term. Second Temple Judaism was far too complex—too variegated—for that kind of generalization. Groups like the Pharisees, Sadducees, and the Qumran community were all active in the first century. This makes it likely that John limits his use of "the Jews" to specific first century groups.

We should also note that intra-Jewish rhetoric is not uncommon in Second Temple literature. We see a parallel, for instance, in a thanksgiving hymn from Qumran, where the author speaks harshly of the community's enemies:

> And they, teachers of lies and seers of falsehood, have schemed against me a devilish scheme to exchange the Law engraved on my heart by thee for smooth things . . . . As for them, they dissemble, they plan devilish schemes. They seek thee with a double heart and are not confirmed in the truth. A root bearing poisoned and bitter fruit is in their designs (IQH 4:7).[27]

While the language is not as strong, John employs similar rhetoric against Jews who actively oppose Jesus (Jn 5:16-18; 7:1; 10:31, 39; 11:8), such as the Pharisees (Jn 7:32; 18:3) and chief priests (Jn 19:6, 15). Yet he does not depict all Jews, such as Nicodemus and Joseph of Arimathea, in the same light (Jn 3:11; 7:50; 19:38-42). He even describes Jews in a positive light, when he affirms that "salvation is from the Jews" (Jn 4:22) and affirms that Jesus himself is a Jew (Jn 4:9). We can therefore envision that John's pejorative use of "the Jews" is not a blanket term for all Jewish people, but a reference to members of the first-century religious establishment who oppose Jesus.

After clarifying these matters, we now turn our attention to the Jewish leaders' initial appearance in the Gospel, questioning John the Baptist about whether he is the Messiah (Jn 1:9). Although the people were genuinely anticipating an "anointed one" who would reign over the cosmos (2 Sam 7; Ps 2), the religious leaders are more interested in rooting out anyone who threatens their power, like any would-be Messiahs. That's why their question should not be taken at face value.

In response to their inquiry, John the Baptist confesses that he "is not the Messiah" (*christos*; Jn 1:20). So, the religious leaders move on to other anticipated figures, asking whether he is Elijah, the one to precede the arrival of the Messiah (Mal 4:5), or the Prophet, the one to lead Israel, just like Moses (Deut 18:15-19).[28] John denies each of these roles (Jn 1:21).

[27]Translation is from G. Vermes, *The Dead Sea Scrolls in English*, 3rd ed. (London: Penguin, 1987), 175. Gail R. O'Day cites this passage in her "The Gospel of John: Introduction, Commentary, and Reflections," in *The New Interpreters Bible Commentary*, ed. Leander E. Keck (Nashville: Abingdon, 2015), 8:545. See also her insightful discussion on the conflicts between various first century Jewish groups, including Jewish Christians, as the proper context for understanding John's negative portrayal of "the Jews" in pp. 540-53. For an overview of potential anti-Judaism scholarship on the Gospel of John, see Sonya Shetty Cronin, Raymond Brown, *"The Jews," and the Gospel of John: From Apologia to Apology*, Library of Biblical Studies 504 (London: T&T Clark, 2015).

[28]Burge points out that Deuteronomy 18:15-19 led to "enormous Jewish speculation concerning who this prophet would be and in some cases led to a conflation with the image of the Messiah. Other Jews distinguished the Messiah and the Prophet (see John 7:40; 1 Macc. 4:46; *T. Ben.* 9:2) and understood that he would simply be a forerunner. Qumran, for instance, looked for an eschatological 'prophet' who would accompany the Messiah (1 QS 9)" (*John*, 72).

Instead, he identifies himself as "the voice of one crying out in the wilderness: 'Make straight the way of the Lord,' as the prophet Isaiah said" (Jn 1:23). John recites an almost verbatim citation of the Septuagint (LXX) version of Isaiah 40:3.[29] In the larger context of Isaiah 40–66, this verse looks forward to a new act of salvation for God's people. As God delivered Israel from Egypt and led them to the land of Canaan, Isaiah looks forward to a new exodus from Babylon, culminating in a new heaven and earth (Isa 65–66).[30] By the first century, Babylon had come to personify any nation that oppressed God's people, including the Romans (Is 40:10-11; 51:9; 52; Rev 17–18). Isaiah's servant would bear the sins of the people, leading to a new act of salvation and restoration (Is 42:1-9; 49:1-9; 52:13–53:12). In view of this background, John's recitation of Isaiah 40:3 identifies his role as the herald of the Lord, the one who would accomplish the long-awaited new exodus.[31]

If he is not the Messiah, the Jewish leaders desire to know why John is baptizing (Jn 1:25). John specifies that his mission is to direct others to the coming Messiah (Jn 1:26-27). In view of exodus imagery, John's baptism evokes the memory of God leading Israel through the Red Sea, delivering them from slavery in Egypt and commencing their journey to the land of Canaan (Jn 1:24-28; cf. Ex 14–15), which then creates anticipation for one who would accomplish a much greater deliverance than what Israel experienced from Egypt (Jn 1:26-27).

The freedom the Israelites were expecting may be encapsulated in one powerful word, "liberation," which is a common hope for the people of God throughout history, who find solidarity with Israel's hope for deliverance. We see this, for instance, in Black and Latino/a theologies. After reflecting on the exodus from Egypt as a foreshadowing of the liberation of humanity in Jesus Christ, Gustavo Gutiérrez argues:

> The work of Christ is presented simultaneously as liberation from sin and all its consequences: despoliation, injustice, hatred. This liberation fulfills in an unexpected way the promises of the prophets and creates a new chosen people, which this time includes all humanity.[32]

The liberation of which Gutiérrez speaks, although grounded in the Scriptures, is often overlooked in favor of salvation as a departure into heaven. This is not what the Israelites expected—they anticipated a tangible deliverance from oppressive forces, which is a consequence of living under the power of sin. Nor is this what the world's marginalized populations anticipate when they read Israel's Scriptures, which includes people like them in the story of those who will be delivered from bondage to poverty, injustice, and racism. Gutiérrez's words are insightful for understanding how the promise of a new exodus is "good news" for all who trust that Jesus will deliver them from the power of sin and all its pervasive effects (Is 61; cf. Lk 4).

The echoes of a new exodus carry into the next scene, in which John sees Jesus and exclaims: "Look! The lamb of God who takes away the sins of the world [*kosmou*]" (Jn 1:29). The phrase "lamb of God" alludes to the Passover celebration in the exodus tradition, when the Israelites were to sacrifice a lamb and smear its blood on the lintels of their doors

[29]The only difference is that in Jn 1:23 the author exchanges *hetoimasate* for *euthynate* in Is 40:3.

[30]The expectation of a cosmic inheritance for God's people is also consistent with Second Temple literature. See, for instance, *4 Ezra* 6 and Sirach 44.

[31]See the helpful discussion in Beale and Ladd, *The Story Retold*, 134.

[32]Gustavo Gutiérrez, *A Theology of Liberation* (Maryknoll, NY: Orbis, 1988), 90.

(Ex 12). Those who followed these instructions were "passed over" by death and were later delivered from Egypt (Ex 12:23). There is a further allusion to Isaiah 53:7-12, which looks back on the original Passover, comparing the "servant" to a "lamb led to the slaughter."[33] When considering that Jesus takes away the sins of the "world," we can envision that he is the sacrifice of the new exodus, making it possible for all people to experience freedom from sin and all its repercussions (cf. 1 Jn 2:2).[34]

The presence of exodus imagery is heightened when John says that Jesus "baptizes with the Holy Spirit" (Jn 1:33). The cleansing of sin that Jesus, through the power of the Spirit, brings is connected to the promise of a new exodus. As God's Spirit delivered Israel through the Red Sea and gave them rest in Canaan (Ps 77; 104; Is 63:11-14; Neh 9), John's baptism symbolizes a new act of deliverance that Jesus would accomplish through his Spirit, leading his people to a new creation. His authority for the task is sourced in his identity as the promised Davidic king and servant, on whom the Lord has poured out his Spirit (Is 11:1-9; 42:1).[35]

John's vocation, then, is to announce that Jesus is the promised Messiah, who, through his suffering for sins, would deliver his people into a new creation. This new act of deliverance would be comparable to, albeit greater than, what God accomplished through Moses in Egypt. Though they hate anyone who contests their authority, the religious leaders will neither be able to hinder John from fulfilling his vocation nor stop Jesus from bringing redemption through his anguish.

Jesus' followers understood Passover imagery, calling Jesus the "lamb of God" (Jn 1:36), alluding to the sacrifice of a new exodus (Ex 14), and the Messiah and Son of God (Jn 1:41, 49), the promised Davidic king who would rule over the cosmos (2 Sam 7; Ps 2; 110). Phillip's statement to Nathanael ("We have found the one whom Moses in the Law and also the Prophets wrote. . . .") likely ties together "a host of expectations for a coming ruler that were rooted both in the Pentateuch and in the prophetic corpus of the Jewish Scriptures (e.g., Gen 49:9-12; Num 24:17-19; Mic 5:1; Isa 9; 11–12; Ezek 34)" (John 1:45).[36] Jesus' response to Phillip and Daniel ("you will see heaven opened, and the angels of God ascending and descending on the Son of Man") only strengthens his identity (John 1:51).

Although we will later expound on the allusion to the Son of Man figure in the book of Daniel, for now we affirm that Jesus' reply to his followers symbolizes the power and glory that will be revealed in his salvific ministry, things that are sourced in God's revelation to Jacob (Gen 28) and Daniel (Dan 7).[37] This final statement sets the stage for Jesus' signs, which progressively reveal his messianic identity. Along with the progression of the signs, we will also witness the religious leaders' increasing resistance to his authority.

Signs 1 and 2: The Cana cycle (John 2:1–4:54). John 2:1–4:54 records Jesus' first ministry cycle in Cana of Galilee, within which

---

[33]Beal and Gladd, *The Story Retold*, 134.

[34]John employs the term *kosmos* in keeping with its common use: "the sum total of everything here and now, the world, the (orderly) universe" (BDAG, 561). A reading that limits the death of Jesus to a particular group must account for the normative use of the word.

[35]Edward W. Klink III, *John*, Exegetical Commentary on the New Testament (Grand Rapids, MI: Zondervan, 2016), 136.

[36]Christopher M. Blumhofer, *The Gospel of John and the Future of Israel*, Society for New Testament Studies Monograph Series 177 (Cambridge: Cambridge University Press, 2020), 74.

[37]Klink, *John*, 154; J. Ramsey Michaels, *John*, The New International Commentary on the New Testament (Grand Rapids, MI: Eerdmans, 2010), 135-39.

Jesus performs his first two miraculous signs: turning water into wine (Jn 2:1-12) and healing an official's son (Jn 4:46-54). He also has discussions about eternal life with Nicodemus (Jn 3:1-21) and living water with the Samaritan woman (Jn 4:1-45). The sequence of events in Cana show that Jesus is the Messiah who is gathering a community of Jews and Gentiles—of whom many are social outsiders—into a new creation.

Sign 1: The wedding in Cana (John 2:1-12). The first messianic sign takes place "on the third day of the wedding in Cana of Galilee" (Jn 2:1). We should understand the reference to the "third day" from when John the Baptist witnessed about Jesus, which suggests that the wedding occurs on the seventh day of the week (Jn 1:19–2:1).[38] Raymond Brown contends that the Gospel frames the wedding on the seventh day so as to mark the beginning of a new creation in the same way in which Genesis 1–3 frames the original creation in seven days.[39] What is more, the reference to the "third day" also alludes to Jesus' coming resurrection on the "third day," when he would reveal himself as the first of many to rise from the grave, initiating a new creation (Gal 6:14-15; Col 1:18-20; Rev 1:13; 3:14).[40]

After noting the presence of Jesus' and his disciples, John sets the stage for the first sign, saying that the wine has run out (Jn 2:2-3). Wine was a staple at Jewish festivities. So, a lack of fermented goodness would have been perceived as a serious problem in a context where the host family was likely to lose honor.[41] The stakes are higher than individualist cultures may realize. Collectivist cultures, like those in the Middle East and Latin America, understand the shame associated with not meeting social expectations. So, when Mary wants Jesus to do something about the wine, what she really wants is for him to preserve the host family's honor before all the invited guests (Jn 2:3).

Jesus' response distances himself from the social responsibility of supplying wine for the wedding: "What does this have to do with me and you, woman? My hour has not yet come" (Jn 2:4; cf. 2 Sam 16:10).[42] As her son, Mary expects Jesus to oblige.[43] So, she instructs the servants: "Do whatever he tells you" (Jn 2:5). Her words sound remarkably like Pharaoh's instructions to starving Egyptians in Genesis 41:55. When people cry out for bread, Pharaoh directs them to Joseph: "Do whatever he tells you." As Joseph provided food for Egypt, Jesus would supply wine for the wedding. Since Mary's command in the Greek New Testament is remarkably similar to Pharaoh's in the Septuagint, it is unmistakable that John intends to draw our minds to the Joseph account.[44] Although it is not yet time (the "hour") for him to receive his

---

[38]Jey J. Kanagaraj, *John*, A New Covenant Commentary (Cambridge: Lutterworth Press, 2013), 20

[39]Brown, *John*, 105-6

[40]The fourth-century bishop Theodore of Heraclea notes that John's use of "the third day" is meant to allude to the fact that "he resurrected himself from the dead" (Joel C. Elowsky, ed., *John 1–10*, Ancient Christian Commentary on Scripture [Downers Grove, IL: IVP Academic, 2007], 89).

[41]See Bruce J. Malina and Richard L. Rohrbaugh, *Social-Science Commentary on the Gospel of John* (Minneapolis: Fortress, 1998), 70-71.

[42]The word-for-word translation of the sentence (*ti emoi kai soi gynai?*) is: "What to me and to you, woman?" The datives *emoi* and *soi* carry a sense of possession, conveying the responsibilities at the wedding that pertain to Jesus and Mary.

[43]Carson argues that, although Mary expected something from Jesus, it is unlikely that she anticipated a miracle at this point. It is more likely that Joseph has died, and Mary has become accustomed to relying on her firstborn son. It would have been natural, then, for Mary to turn to Jesus, as she would in other instances, for help in difficult circumstances (see *John*, 170-72).

[44]The respective verses read: *ho ti an legē hymin poiēsate* (Jn 2:5); *ho ean eipē hymin, poiēsate* (Gen 41:55 LXX). The minor differences are the use of *legē* in John 2:4 in place of *eipē* in Gen 41:55 LXX, although both are in the subjunctive mood, and the addition of *ti* in John 2:4. John could have purposely altered the passage or used another LXX version.

full glory, Jesus will perform his first miracle, providing a glimpse of the restoration he will accomplish.[45]

Jesus instructs the attendants to fill six large purification jars "to the brim" (Jn 2:5-7). He then tells them to "draw out" some of the contents and take a sample to the "head waiter" (Jn 2:7-8). The text does not tell us when the water becomes wine. All we know is that the head waiter tastes "water that had become wine" (Jn 2:9). It could have happened as soon as the water was poured in the jars, or while the attendants were carrying the contents to the head waiter. But too much discussion of such matters misses the point of the passage—that Jesus turns water into wine, giving us a glimpse of his identity.

Jesus' identity becomes clear when we read this sign in lieu of several Old Testament passages. Isaiah 25 associates wine with messianic expectations: that God would return to save his people from their oppressors, even death itself (Is 25:6). Jeremiah 31 connects wine with rejoicing and deliverance from exile (Jer 31:12). And Amos 9 links "sweet wine" with a time when Israel is restored to a prosperous land (Amos 9:13-14). What these passages have in common is the anticipation that the new age will bring deliverance from all oppression and into a permanent place of blessing, where God will "wipe away tears from all faces" (Is 25:8; cf. Rev 21:4). Thus, Jesus turning water into wine symbolizes that he is the anticipated Messiah who will lead his people out of exile in this sinful age and into a new creation. This new act of salvation, anticipated by prophets such as Isaiah, Jeremiah, and Amos, will liberate God's people from oppression in the present world. The kingdom that Jesus brings will transform the present earth into a place of justice, peace, and equity, exactly as God's people have anticipated for centuries. Though this is only the first of seven signs, it is enough for the disciples to "believe in him" (Jn 2:11).

Cleansing the Temple (John 2:13-25). After spending some time in Capernaum, Jesus heads to Jerusalem for the Passover (Jn 2:13). Upon entering the temple, he discovers people more concerned about economic profit than worshiping God through prayer and sacrifice (Jn 2:14). So, he uses a whip to drive people out of the temple, pours out the coins of the moneychangers, and turns over their tables (Jn 2:15). What seems like a fit of rage is actually a display of zeal for God's house, the kind the disciples recall from Psalm 69:9: "Zeal for your house will consume me" (Jn 2:17).

The context of the Psalm is a righteous sufferer upon whom "the reproaches of those who reproach you have fallen" (Ps 69:9). This figure is analogous to Isaiah's suffering servant who bears the iniquity of God's people (Is 53:6). When quoting Psalm 69:9, John recalls such Old Testament imagery, evoking the image of Jesus as the one who would suffer to restore his people to genuine worship of God. The locus of such worship would not be in a temple "made with human hands" (Mk 14:58). It would be Jesus' own body, the new temple, which he would resurrect three days after his death (Jn 2:18-22).

The original temple was intended to be a microcosm of the entire earth, where people would be at peace with God, just like Adam and Eve in Eden.[46] Thus, the resurrection of Jesus, the new temple, symbolizes the restoration of the

---

[45]The "hour" is common in John's Gospel, "referring to the time when Jesus will return to the Father through his death and resurrection" (e.g., Jn 4:23, 27; 13:1; 17:1; Kanagaraj, *John*, 21). In Jewish literature, "hour," as well as "time" and "day," is often used eschatologically, pointing to God's intervention in human history. See Dan 8, 10, 11, 12; *1 En.* 46–48; *3 En.* 30:2; *4 Ezra* 4:44-46.

[46]N. T. Wright, *History and Eschatology: Jesus and the Promise of Natural Theology*, The 2018 Gifford Lectures (Waco, TX: Baylor University Press, 2019) cites J. D. Levenson, *Creation and the Persistence of Evil: The Jewish Drama of Divine Omnipotence* (Princeton, NJ: Princeton University Press, 1994), 162-70. See Ps 78:69; Is 66:1-2; Jub. 1:26, 29; 50:5.

cosmos, when he will cleanse the present creation of sin and death, making it a suitable place of worship. Once again, John gives us a picture of what Jesus the Messiah has come to accomplish. And it is more than just salvation of souls, as some would lead us to believe. It encompasses souls, bodies, and all that God has made, redeeming everything from darkness and making all things worthy of being the dwelling place of God and humanity.

Jesus did many signs of this sort in Jerusalem, the kind that point to his identity, even though they are not all mentioned in the Gospel (Jn 2:23). John says these led many to "believe in him" (Jn 2:23). It is debatable whether they really understood what they were witnessing, or whether they were just impressed with Jesus' miraculous deeds. It could be that they were spiritually blind, as John 2:25 seems to insinuate, setting the stage for the conversation with Nicodemus.[47]

Conversation with Nicodemus (John 3:1-22). Jesus' conversation with Nicodemus is the first of three encounters with people in need of the Messiah. Each meeting shows that God does not discriminate based on whether someone is a member of the ruling elite, like Nicodemus, a foreigner, like the Samaritan woman (Jn 4:1-45), or the child of political royalty, like the official's son (John 4:46-54). All must experience the transforming power of Jesus.

Nicodemus comes to Jesus "at night," revealing his darkened spiritual state (Jn 3:1-2). He is need of the light, whom John has already identified as Jesus (Jn 1:1-5).[48] As the cosmos is in need of renewal, so too is Nicodemus. There is no escaping that everyone and everything, including privileged members of the ruling class, desperately need Jesus.

Jesus wastes little time with Nicodemus: "Unless one is born again, they are not able to see the kingdom of God" (Jn 3:3). As a member of the Sanhedrin, we can imagine what Nicodemus was thinking: "Who is this person to tell me, a member of the ruling class, that I need to be born again?" By now, readers of John's Gospel should know that Jesus is lord of creation, and Nicodemus is a mere creature. The power dynamics are therefore the opposite of what Nicodemus may perceive.[49]

Quite frankly, we are all like Nicodemus, in need of being "born again," whether we realize it or not (Jn 3:3). Jesus unpacks this metaphor as "being born of water and the Spirit," without which one "cannot enter the kingdom of God" (Jn 3:5). These words allude to Ezekiel 36:25-27, which anticipates the time when God would cleanse his people's hearts with clean water and transform them by the power of the Spirit.[50] These verses are surrounded by the larger context of Ezekiel 36–37, which shows that the spiritual renewal of God's people coincides with their resurrection to a restored Eden, where they will dwell under the rule of a Davidic king (Ezek 37:24-25). Nicodemus, nevertheless, could not envision this eschatological hope, even though he should have, for he taught Israel from the very Scriptures to which Jesus alludes (Jn 3:9-10).

With another scriptural allusion, Jesus tells Nicodemus that Daniel's Son of Man has

---

[47]Klink, *John*, 184.

[48]Note the negative associations with darkness in John 9:4; 11:10; 13:30; 21:31.

[49]Power dynamics are an important element in John's Gospel, especially in regard to how Jesus relates to authorities. Jesus shows that the lowly in the present age will soon receive the power and influence that groups like the chief priests and Pharisees try to preserve for themselves. Alicia D. Myers and Lindsey S. Jodrey also note the presence of power dynamics in John's Gospel ("Come and Read: Hermeneutics and Interpretive Perspectives in the Gospel of John," in *Come and Read: Interpretive Approaches to the Gospel of John*, ed. Alicia Myers and Lindsey S. Jodrey [Lanham, MD: Fortress Academic, 2020], 1-25).

[50]For a discussion of the options for interpreting "born of water and spirit," see Carson, *John*, 191-94.

descended from heaven, revealing that Jesus is the mysterious figure who brings the heavenly kingdom to the earth, transforming life as we know it (Jn 3:13; cf. Dan 7). To dwell in this kingdom, Nicodemus must believe that Jesus would be "lifted up" as "Moses lifted up the serpent in the wilderness" (Jn 3:14). The "serpent in the wilderness" recalls the time when rebellious Israel was plagued with poisonous snakes, but God saved his people when he instructed Moses to place a bronze serpent on a pole, so that "if a serpent bit anyone, they would look on the bronze serpent and live" (Num 21:8-9). According to Jesus, this event foreshadows the time when he would be "lifted up." In John's thought, the "lifting up" of Jesus encompasses his death, resurrection, and exaltation.[51]

John now strengthens God's concern for the cosmos: "For [*gar*] God loved the world in this way [*houtōs*]: he gave his unique Son, so that everyone who believes in him may not perish but have eternal life" (Jn 3:16).[52] Though translations such as the KJV, NIV, and ESV render the first clause in John 3:16 as "For God so loved the world," the adverb *houtōs* carries a forward-pointing sense rather than a superlative one, drawing the reader's attention to how God demonstrated his love for the cosmos—by giving his Son.[53] In view of the earlier allusion to Ezekiel 36–37, God intends to resurrect believers to a renewed earth, where Jesus will reign forever, just as Psalm 2 expects. After all, Jesus did not to come to destroy the cosmos, leaving us only with the hope of heaven—he came to save it (Jn 3:17-18).

To spend eternal life on the renewed earth, we must experience the renewing power of the Spirit, which comes through faith in the Messiah, just like Jesus told Nicodemus. This is the great equalizer of humanity. Regardless of ethnicity, class, nationality, or gender, all must trust in Jesus. If there was no exception for Nicodemus, then there is no exception for anyone—all need the total transformation that comes only through Jesus.[54] Whoever refuses to come to him shows that they prefer the darkness, rather than the transforming power of Jesus' light (Jn 3:19-21).

Conversation with a Samaritan Woman (John 4:1-40). On his way to Galilee, John says "it was necessary (*edei*)" for Jesus "to pass through Samaria" (Jn 4:3-4). John may be using *edei* to communicate that the route was shorter through Samaria.[55] In that sense, Jesus passed through Samaria out of convenience. More likely, though, the verb communicates the "eschatological necessity of God's plan, especially in regard to the saving work of Jesus (Jn 3:7, 14, 30; 9:4; 10:16; 12:34; 20:9)."[56] This sense fits with Jesus' mission to redeem the entire creation, including Samaritans. No one is outside of Jesus' redemptive plan.[57] That's why "it was necessary" for him to go through Samaria.

[51]Klink, *John*, 203.

[52]The postpositive conjunction *gar* is what conveys that the following context adds support to God's concern for the world. See the helpful discussion of this word in Steven E. Runge, *A Discourse Grammar of the Greek New Testament: A Practical Guide for Teaching and Exegesis*, Lexham Bible Reference Series (Bellingham, WA: Lexham, 2010), 52.

[53]Runge classifies *houtōs* as a "forward pointing adverb." For short, he calls it a "pro-adverb" (*Discourse Grammar*, 68-71).

[54]Allan Dwight Callahan recalls the moving story of Mary MacLeod Bethune upon hearing John 3:16 as a girl growing up in the Jim Crow South. When she heard her teacher read the verse, especially the word "whosoever," it meant to her that she had equal chance before God, leading to a life filled with confidence and determination ("The Gospel of John," in *True to Our Native Land*, ed. Brian K. Blount [Minneapolis: Fortress, 2007], 190).

[55]Bultmann, *John*, 176. See the similar use of *edei* in Josephus' *Life* 269 and *Ant.* 20:118.

[56]Klink, *John*, 235.

[57]Blumhofer claims that the need to pass through Samaria, as with every other use of *edei* in John's Gospel, is one of "theological necessity" (*Future of Israel*, 90).

To appreciate the wideness of Jesus' redemptive mission, we should consider that the Samaritans and Jews despised each other. The Samaritans were the descendants of the northern Israelites and colonists whom the Assyrians brought from Babylon and Media.[58] The Samaritans combined the worship of the God of Israel with the gods of Babylon and established Samaria as their place of worship.[59] By the time Jesus "passes through Samaria," there was longstanding enmity between the Jews, who considered themselves natives of the land and true worshipers of Yahweh, and the Samaritans, who were viewed as foreigners who had corrupted the worship of Israel's God.

Despite the animosity, the prophets anticipated the restoration of Samaria. Ezekiel, in the very context of renewal to which John has already appealed, takes two sticks in his hands so as to show how God would unite the northern and southern tribes when he comes to cleanse their sins and restore them to the land of their ancestors, where they will dwell under the rule of one king and one God (Ezek 37:1-28).[60] Jeremiah looks forward to the ten tribes, whom he calls Ephraim, being restored to faithfulness under a new covenant (Jer 31:1-37). Regardless of first century Jewish perceptions, the Samaritans have always been within the scope of God's redemptive plan.

All this enables us to grasp the significance of Jesus' conversation with a Samaritan woman at a village called "Sychar, near the piece of land which Jacob gave to Joseph, his son," where Jacob's well was located (Jn 4:5-6). This is the place where patriarchs Isaac, Jacob, and Moses came for water and met their prospective brides (Gen 24:1-27; 29:1-12; Ex 2:15-21).[61] Though they were viewed as outsiders, this geographical note reminds us that the Samaritans are closer to God's redemptive work than readers may imagine. No place or people are beyond God's salvation. As he worked at Jacob's well before, he does so again, offering water that renews relationships and heals old wounds.

When Jesus strikes up a conversation with the Samaritan woman, she has no clue about the identity of Jesus (Jn 4:7-8). All she knows is that hostility exists between Jews and Samaritans (Jn 4:9). Jesus does something unexpected, offering her "living water" that will become "a spring of water welling up to eternal life" (Jn 4:10, 14). The offer of "living water" recalls the "life giving water" in prophetic imagery that represents the cleansing and restoration of God's people (e.g., Zech 13:1; 14:8; Ezek 36:25-27; 47:1-12).[62] When God's people are restored, Ephraim and Judah will draw water with joy from the "fountains of salvation" (Is 12:3).[63] Later in John, Jesus associates "living water" with the Spirit (Jn 7:37-39). When glancing again at Ezekiel 36–37, we see that the Spirit is the one who will bring promised reconciliation and restoration to a new creation. This interpretive context brings to light that the offer of "living water" to the Samaritan woman symbolizes eschatological salvation. What the prophets anticipated for centuries is being fulfilled in the "gift" that Jesus offers a foreigner and enemy of the Jewish people (Jn 4:10).

The problem is that the woman does not comprehend Jesus' offer (Jn 4:15). So, he presses the matter further, revealing his

---

[58]Brown, *John*, 1:170.

[59]Klink, *John*, 235; Blumhofer, *The Future of Israel*, 91.

[60]Blumhofer, The Future of Israel, 92.

[61]Isaac met Rebekah through a servant.

[62]Blumhofer, *Restoration of Israel*, 96.

[63]Blumhofer, *Restoration of Israel*, 96.

knowledge of her relationships with men (Jn 4:16-18). In response, the woman acknowledges that Jesus is a prophet (Jn 4:19). Yet he is more than a prophet. That's why he goes on to explain that soon people will not worship in mount Gerizim in Samaria or the Temple in Jerusalem (Jn 4:22). God's cosmic salvation, which is sourced in a Jewish Messiah, is not for any particular people, neither Jew nor Samaritan, regardless of claims to salvific privilege (Jn 4:21).[64] The new age brings salvation for all "true worshipers" who "worship the Father in Spirit and in truth" (Jn 4:23).

When mentioning the Spirit, Jesus alludes again to prophets such as Ezekiel, who anticipate the time when the Spirit would usher in a new age in which God's people would experience restoration (Ezek 36:25-27; see also Joel 3). Worship in this era would not be centered in a particular place, but in the God who redeems creation through the work of his Spirit. This is true worship (Jn 4:24).[65]

The woman picks up on the messianic allusions in Jesus' words: "I know that the Messiah is coming, the one called Christ" (Jn 4:25). As we have noted, messianic expectations are associated with David's anointed son, who will rule peacefully over his people when he returns to restore all things (2 Sam 7; Ps 2; Ezek 36–37). Jesus' allusion to the redemptive work associated with the new age seems to be gaining traction with the woman. Though she has not yet understood his identity, the Samaritan woman seems to acknowledge the work of restoration, accomplished through the empowerment of the Spirit, associated with the Messiah. What Jesus then says makes it plain, using the words "I am" (*egō eimi*) to reveal himself as the promised one (Jn 4:26).

Unlike most English versions, the words *egō eimi* do not warrant the translation "I am he." Rather, this is one of several such statements in John's Gospel which should be rendered as "I am," bringing to mind God's self-revelation to Moses at the burning bush (Ex 3:14).[66] Jesus now speaks these same revelatory words to the Samaritan woman, revealing himself as the Messiah, God in the flesh, who has returned to redeem the cosmos, including those whom the Jews see as outsiders to the promises of redemption. The prophets, of course, such as Ezekiel and Jeremiah, knew better. They foresaw that, although salvation is "sourced in the Jews," it is not only for them—for it is through a Jew that the world would experience the blessing of salvation, including the Samaritans (Gen 12:3).

Subsequently, the Samaritan woman leaves the well and proclaims to fellow Samaritans: "Come! See a man who told me all I have done. Is this not the Messiah?" (Jn 4:29). Reflecting on this verse, Edward Klink argues: "The effect is not necessarily to challenge the possibility that he is the Messiah but to introduce a possibility not considered before. In a way, the Samaritan woman left the rhetorical challenge with Jesus and entered an entirely different rhetorical challenge, one involving the possibility of a Jewish Messiah for the Samaritans."[67] The woman, then, becomes a witness to the identity of Jesus. Through her testimony, many Samaritans believe that he is the "savior of the world" (Jn 4:39, 42; cf. Jn 1:29).

[64]In the clause *hē sōtēria ek tōn Ioudaiōn estin*, the prepositional phrase *ek tōn Ioudaiōn* carries a sense of source, suggesting that salvation originates in the promises to Jews like Abraham and David. This does not mean that it is exclusive to the Jews, for that would contradict John's view of cosmic redemption, which he reaffirms in John 4:42.

[65]In the prepositional phrase *en pneumati kai alētheia* in John 4:24, the conjunction *kai* conveys apposition, clarifying that worshiping "in the Spirit" is equivalent to worshiping "in the truth."

[66]See K.L. McKay, "'I am' in John's Gospel," *Expository Times* 107 (1996): 302-3.

[67]Klink, *John*, 247. See also Bultmann, *John*, 247.

The account of the Samaritan woman is a powerful testimony to Jesus' redemptive work—which is not exclusive to any particular people but available to all humanity, regardless of ethnicity or privilege. It also shows how God cares for foreigners and outsiders, those who are loathed or despised, perhaps because of their ethnicity or illegitimate residency. He loves such people so much that he offers them a place in his redemptive plan and uses them to witness to the grace that extends to all people. Jesus recognizes the full humanity of the "other," which makes the Samaritan woman worthy of proclaiming the arrival of the Messiah.[68]

If Jesus is our example, then we will also go to the outsider and offer them "living water." That means we will go to immigrants, regardless of whether they have proper documentation, to people living in illicit sexual relationships, to the communities to which our churches would not normally minister, and tell them about the Messiah who has come to deliver humanity from sin and death. After all, Jesus' work is not for any particular people, but for the entire world, including those with whom we have enmity or find unworthy of God's grace. As John has shown, those whom we shun have always been the focus of God's redemptive plan. In the new cosmos, we will enjoy sweet fellowship with those whom we once loathed. There, we will see redeemed Samaritans and Jews, former white supremacists and Hispanic immigrants, former pro-choice advocates and those who fought for the lives of the unborn, worshiping a brown skin Messiah. There is no limit to the extent of God's grace in Jesus Christ.

Sign 2: The healing of a royal official's son (John 4:43-54). The scene shifts back to Cana of Galilee, where Jesus performed his first sign. Jesus is welcomed to the area by people who had witnessed his miraculous deeds in Jerusalem (Jn 4:45-46). That does not mean they understand his identity. He is nothing more than a curiosity to them.

While visiting Cana, he is approached by a royal official whose son is at the point of death (Jn 4:46-47). The official asks if Jesus would come to Capernaum to heal his son (Jn 4:47, 49). Rather than leave the area, Jesus heals the boy from a distance, telling the official: "Your son lives" (Jn 5:50). The man "believes" Jesus and departs to his home (Jn 5:50). Upon his arrival, his servants inform him that his son has been healed, exactly as Jesus said (Jn 5:51-53). John confirms that this is Jesus' "second sign" (Jn 5:54).

It is important to note that the official believes before seeing evidence of his son's healing. This is far different from those who initially welcomed him into the region. Carson notes that their welcome "was fundamentally flawed, based as it was on too great a focus on miraculous signs (v. 45; cf. 2:23-25)."[69] Regardless of why they followed him, or when the official trusts in him, the restoration of the official's son is a picture of Jesus' mission—to bring life to a world in the throes of death. We would expect that someone well-versed in the Jewish scriptures, like Nicodemus, would have understood this. Instead, two unlikely people, a Samaritan woman and a Roman official, whom the Jews would have considered "outsiders to the covenants of promise," become beneficiaries of God's salvation.

The Jerusalem cycle: Signs 3–7 (John 5:1–12:50). John 5:1–12:50 records the remaining messianic signs. The seventh is the climactic

[68]Gerard S. Sloyan notes the pastoral implications of John 4: "An important avenue to reconciliation is acknowledging the full religious and human capacities of the 'other'" (*John*, Interpretation: A Bible Commentary for Teaching and Preaching [Atlanta: John Knox, 1988], 59).

[69]Carson, *John*, 238.

sign, foreshadowing the death and resurrection of Jesus. The section also features the Feast of Tabernacles and Jesus' interaction with Jewish leaders, providing insight into how the religious establishment saw Jesus as a threat to their authority. John 11–12 initiate a transition from the Book of Signs to the Book of Exaltation, which describes Jesus as being "lifted up" for the entire world (Jn 13:1–20:31).

Sign 3: Healing of a lame man (John 5:1-47). Jesus returns to Jerusalem during the "feast of the Jews" (Jn 5:1). John does not mention the name of the feast, wanting his readers to focus on Jesus' third messianic sign. Jesus tells a paralytic man: "Get up, take your bed and walk" (Jn 5:8). The man immediately "became well and took his bed and walked" (Jn 5:9). The man's healing should be understood within the larger matrix of prophetic expectations, especially Isaiah 35, which foreshadows the healing of the lame alongside the restoration of creation. When we set Isaiah 35 as the backdrop for reading John 5, we see that Jesus healing a lame man, though only described in two verses, is meant to evoke the grand picture of God restoring the earth, delivering it from sin and all its effects.

The Jewish leaders of that day disagreed. All they could think about was Jesus healing "on the Sabbath day" (Jn 5:9). Undoubtedly there are biblical passages that forbid work on the Sabbath (Ex 20:8-11; 31:15-16; Lev 23:3; 25:2; Deut 5:12-15). Among these is also the prohibition to "bear a burden" and bring it into Jerusalem, which likely covers the man carrying his bed (Jer 17:21-22).[70] The focus on the biblical injunctions against work on the Sabbath means the leaders missed the point of what Jesus was trying to evoke, especially when considering what the Sabbath represents in Jewish apocalyptic literature. For example, *4 Ezra* 7–8 and the *Life of Adam and Eve* 51 note that the Sabbath is intended to symbolize the rest from the curse that will take place in the new creation. When first-century Jews kept the Sabbath, relieving themselves from the pain and sweat of their brow they experienced the other six days of the week, they were to anticipate the day when people will experience eternal rest in a new Eden (cf. Ezek 36–37; Rev 22). The Jewish leaders of that day miss the typological significance of the third messianic sign. As a result, they decide to kill the man who has come to renew the earth (Jn 5:15-16).

They become even more upset when Jesus claims that his authority to "work" on the Sabbath is sourced in his status as God (Jn 5:17-18). Jesus' "work" means that he was in the process of renewing his creation, of bringing rest to the earth. Yet the leadership continues to miss the point of Jesus' words.

Jesus continues to press the issue, arguing that "as the Father raises the dead and gives life, so also the Son gives life to whom he desires" (Jn 5:21). Deuteronomy 32:39 and 1 Samuel 2:6 testify to God's prerogative to "give life" to real flesh and blood people. He heals wounds and diseases, making people whole (2 Kings 5:7; cf. Is 53). The one who believes in Jesus also believes in the Father, becoming a recipient of "eternal life" and "crossing over from death to life" (Jn 5:24).[71] Jesus, then, has the power to transfer a person's existence to a new creation, where they will experience true life. We experience a foretaste of the future through the power of the Spirit, who has begun the process of healing wounds and making people whole (e.g., Jn 1:4; 3:15-16; 4:36; 6:47; cf. Ezek 36–37; Joel 2).

---

[70]Thompson, *John*, 122.

[71]John's use of "eternal life" does not refer to heaven or spiritual bliss devoid of matter. Rather, it is in keeping with the way Second Temple texts such as *1 En.* 40:9 and CD 3:20 employ "eternal life" to refer to a future existence in the renewed cosmos.

The religious leaders, of course, do not agree with Jesus saying that he, like the Father, gives life (Jn 5:18). Before rushing to condemnation, we should not put too much hermeneutical distance between ourselves and the Jewish leadership, as if we were immune to the same error. We can also struggle to imagine how Jesus is in the process of healing and restoring lives, of delivering people from sin and all its effects, like social injustice, hunger, and poverty. Perhaps it would be helpful to listen to theologians such as Samuel Escobar, who argues that Christian mission, which is based on the ministry of the historical Jesus, leads us "into direct contact with pain, injustice, the dead end of economic poverty, the abyss of corruption."[72] Such insights enable us to envision that John's Gospel is "good news" to people suffering under repressive circumstances, for he really is "making all things new" (Rev 21:5). The marginalized and oppressed can begin to experience equity and justice in the present, through the renewing work of the Spirit, by trusting that Jesus is the God who grants new life (Jn 5:21-24). This is better than the promise of heaven, which suggests that God loves people's souls but sees fit to leave them in their present squalor and oppression. That's not the message of John's Gospel. Nor is it the witness of so many global Christians.

Jesus promises that his people will experience the fulfillment of the promised new age: "An hour is coming and is now here, when the dead will hear the voice of the Son of God, and those who hear will live" (Jn 5:25). Though we "already" experience the new age of restoration through the presence of the Spirit ("an hour . . . is now here"), we have "not yet" heard the Son of God call the dead out of the grave ("an hour is coming"). Soon, however, Jesus will raise the dead and complete his plan of restoration: "for an hour is coming when all who are in the tombs will hear [the Son of Man's] voice and those who have done good will proceed into eternal life, but those who have done evil to the resurrection of judgement" (Jn 5:28-29). This statement alludes to the promise of resurrection and judgment in Daniel 12:2-3: "Many of those who sleep in the dust of the earth will awake, some to eternal life and some to shame and eternal contempt. And those who are wise will shine like the brightness of heaven, and those who turn many to righteousness like the stars forever." Thus, in a single pericope Jesus identifies himself as the Son of God, alluding to Psalm 2, and the Son of Man, the figure in Daniel who will exercise dominion over the earth (Dan 7:14) and raise the dead (Dan 12:2-3). The ones who will be resurrected to life are those who believe Jesus is the Messiah. Those who oppose him will experience judgment.

The irony about the whole matter is that the first-century Jewish establishment was well-versed in the very words of Moses, which testify about Jesus (Jn 5:45-47). Though the entire Pentateuch looks forward to a new Moses, we can look to one specific text: "The Lord God will raise up for you a prophet like me from among you; it is to him that you will listen. . . . And whoever will not listen to my words that he shall speak in my name, I shall require it of him" (Deut 18:15, 19). Jesus is the prophet of whom Moses wrote. Since the religious leaders refuse to listen to him, as Moses required, they fail to understand his messianic identity. Consequently, they reject the one who has come to redeem them from the darkness of this sinful age, accomplishing an even greater redemption than Moses in the original exodus story.

[72]Samuel Escobar, *In Search of Christ in Latin America: From Colonial Image to Liberating Savior* (Downers Grove, IL: IVP Academic, 2019), 332.

Sign 4: Feeding the multitude (John 6:1-21). After his encounter with Jewish leaders, Jesus heads to "the other side of the Sea of Galilee" to perform his fourth messianic sign (Jn 6:1).[73] The sign takes place near the time of the Passover, which recalls Israel's deliverance from Egypt and God's provision in the wilderness (Jn 6:4). While looking back on these events, the Passover also anticipates a new deliverance and provision for God's people. This expectation forms the interpretive context of the fourth sign.

The fourth sign consists of Jesus turning five loaves and two fish into enough food to feed a large multitude (Jn 6:2-11). Jesus provides more than enough provision, instructing his disciples to collect the leftovers, which consist of "twelve baskets of fragments from the five barley loaves that remained" (Jn 6:13). When the crowd saw the sign, they remarked: "This is truly the prophet who has come into the world" (Jn 6:14). This response strongly suggests that the crowd believes Jesus to be the new Moses promised in Deuteronomy 18:15-18. Whether they understand the full implication of his identity is beside the point. The crowd utters enough truth for us to connect Jesus to the prophet who will accomplish salvation and supply eternal provision for his people (cf. Jn 6:22-59).

Later Midrashic texts, especially in the third and fourth centuries, associate the first deliver, Moses, with the second, the Messiah, "including the miraculous provision of bread from heaven at the time of the Messiah's self-revelation."[74] These thoughts were also swirling in the air of the first century. That's why, after seeing the sign, the crowd wants to make Jesus king (Jn 6:15). Knowing this, he withdraws from the crowd (Jn 6:15). While Jesus will certainly reign over the nations, as Psalm 2 says of God's Son, he would first be "lifted up" on the cross.

Commentators who chastise the crowd for their impulsiveness fail to consider that Jews had been oppressed for centuries, under countries like Assyria, Babylon, Greece, and Rome. They were longing to be delivered from their subjugation, longing for the Messiah. While they did not fully grasp how Jesus would establish his cosmic reign, they were right in seeing him as the king to deliver them from their enemies. Perhaps the world's oppressed have an easier time sympathizing with the crowd's desperation. Such people often live under the shadow of corrupt systems and governments, whose main concern is to maintain power and privilege, even if it means practicing exploitation and subjugation. So, they hope for a new leader to liberate them.

When reading about the eager crowd in John 6, we should realize that they, like so many oppressed peoples, wanted freedom from their oppressors—and they wanted it immediately! And who could blame them? They had been subjugated for centuries. At least they proclaimed the right leader as Messiah, regardless of whether they really understood what they were doing, or the full scope of Jesus' cosmic mission.

Sign 5: Walking on water (John 6:16-21). On the evening of the fourth sign, Jesus' disciples get into a boat and head to Capernaum (Jn 6:17). Along the way, they encounter a fierce storm (Jn 6:18). In the darkness of night, they see Jesus walking on the chaotic waters, evoking the image of Yahweh trampling on the waves of the sea in Job 9:8 (Jn 6:19). The scene

---

[73]The prepositional phrase *meta tauta* ("after these things") does not specify exactly when Jesus made his way to the Sea of Galilee. John uses these words to string together a narrative of selective stories that is sequential in nature, excluding accounts that are nonessential to John's theological argument. See Köstenberger, *John's Gospel and Letters*, 209.

[74]See the discussion in Blumhofer, *The Future of Israel*, 121.

is supposed to "open the eyes" of the disciples to Jesus' identity.[75] If that were not enough, Jesus tells the frightened disciples: "I am (*egō eimi*). Do not fear." The words *egō eimi* once more recall God's self-revelation to Moses at the burning bush, disclosing that Jesus is Yahweh in the flesh, who has come to establish his dominion over the creation. The account closes with the disciples gladly taking Jesus into the boat, shortly thereafter arriving at land (Jn 6:21).

When looking at the arrangement of John 6, we see that John sequentially arranges the fourth and fifth signs, Jesus feeding the multitude (Jn 6:1-15) and Jesus walking on the sea (Jn 6:16-21), so as to evoke the memory of Moses delivering his people from Egypt and through the chaotic waters of the Red Sea, identifying Jesus as the new Moses. As Yahweh, Jesus' act of deliverance will be far greater than anything Moses accomplished, leading his people out of the darkness of the present age and into a renewed earth.

Bread of life discourse (John 6:22-71). On the next day, the crowd that had eaten their "fill of the loaves" followed him to Capernaum (Jn 6:22-26). Recalling the example of Moses, the crowd challenges Jesus to perform a sign: "Our fathers ate manna in the wilderness, as it is written: 'He gave them bread from heaven to eat'" (Jn 6:31). Jesus corrects them, saying it was the Father who provided bread, not Moses (Jn 6:32). This bread was not meant to sustain the wilderness generation forever. Eventually, they died (Jn 6:49).

What Jesus provides is greater than anything Moses gave their ancestors. In the discourse, Jesus claims to be "the bread of life" (Jn 6:35), who has "come from heaven, so that anyone may eat of it and not die" but live forever (Jn 6:50-51). Jesus identifies the bread as his "flesh," which he gives for the world (Jn 6:51). As God gave his people manna in the wilderness, Jesus offers himself to a world in need of redemption. What was given during the time of Moses pointed to Jesus. Those who trust in Jesus will partake of a new exodus from this sinful age and into a place far better than Moses could have imagined.

With all that Jesus has said and done, there are still people who do not trust in him (Jn 6:64). Jesus is not surprised by this. He knew exactly who would not believe—even who would betray him, Judas Iscariot (Jn 6:64). This raises some poignant questions for us, the kind that affect our eternal destiny. Will we choose to believe that Jesus is the Messiah, like Peter (Jn 6:68-69)? Or will we reject him, like Judas Iscariot (Jn 6:66, 70-71)? John's Gospel will continue to give us reasons to believe that Jesus is the true Messiah.

The feast of tabernacles (John 7:1-52). Jesus continues his ministry in Galilee, appearing at the Feast of Tabernacles. The feast recalled the time when God provided for his people in the wilderness, following their deliverance from Egypt (Lev 23:42-43).[76] The feast lasted seven days, culminating with a celebration on the eighth day.[77] Each day there was a ceremonial pouring of water, which came to symbolize Israel's eschatological hopes (Num 28:7).[78] Following the exile, Zechariah 14:16-19 calls on all the families of the earth to head to Jerusalem to worship the Lord by keeping the Feast of

[75]The phrases *peripatounta epi tēs thalassēs* (Jn 6:19) and *peripatōn hōs ep' edaphous epi thalassēs* (Job 9:8 LXX) are similar, strengthening the likelihood that John associates Jesus with Yahweh. The differences are the case of the participles *peripatounta* (Jn 6:19) and *peripatōn* (Job 9:8) and John' omission of *hōs ep' edaphous*.

[76]Kanagaraj, *John*, 78; Callahan, "John," 195.

[77]Klink, *John*, 353; Köstenberger, "John," 452.

[78]Herman Ridderbos, *The Gospel of John: A Theological Commentary* (Grand Rapids: Eerdmans, 1997), 257.

Tabernacles. Those who failed to do so would receive no rain (Zech 14:17-19). Thus, the nations were to worship Yahweh to receive "life giving waters."[79]

Since the Jewish leaders "were seeking to kill him," Jesus makes his way to the feast "in secret" (Jn 7:1, 10). On the day marked by joyous celebration ("the great day"), Jesus proclaims: "If anyone thirsts, let him come to me and drink. The one who believes in me, as the Scripture says, 'Out of his heart will flow rivers of living water'" (Jn 7:38). John later tells us that the "living water" symbolizes the Holy Spirit (Jn 7:39).

It is impossible to link Jesus' promise to one specific text. More likely, Jesus evokes a matrix of passages that anticipate eschatological restoration. This includes texts such as Zechariah 14:16-19 and others such as Isaiah 44:3, which associate Yahweh "pouring out water on a thirsty land" with "pouring out the Spirit" on his people (see also Ezek 47:1-12; Joel 2:28).[80] What Jesus utters is loaded with symbolism, revealing that he fulfills the eschatological expectations associated with the Feast of Tabernacles.

In view of Zechariah 14, Jesus is the Lord whom all people should worship and receive "life giving water." John uses "water" as a metaphor for the promised Spirit who would be "poured out" on people, just as prophets like Isaiah and Joel envisioned. All who come to Jesus will receive the life-giving power of the Spirit. Although God sustained the original wilderness generation for a time, as the Feast of Tabernacles was meant to evoke, the Spirit will sustain us long after he has led us out of the wilderness of this dark world.

Subsequently, Jesus' words spark a division over his identity, some claiming that he is the Prophet, others that he is the Messiah (Jn 7:40-41). The people are unaware that Jesus fulfills both offices. Allen Dwight Callahan observes that the controversy "is a conflict of opinions about Jesus's natural origin and whether it disqualifies him from being a prophet."[81] They suppress Jesus' claim to heavenly origin—a fact they undoubtedly know (Jn 7:28-29)—and focus on his home country, claiming that no prophet comes from Galilee (Jn 7:52). This is an inaccurate claim, for Jonah was from this area (2 Kings 14:25). Regardless of what Jesus says or does, the religious establishment is bent on discrediting him, even if it means denying the truth.

The woman caught in adultery (John 7:53–8:11). The account of a woman caught in adultery is one of the most vivid examples of God's grace in the entire biblical tradition. In this story, Jesus freely forgives a woman caught in the act of sexual immorality, despite the expectations of the scribes and the Pharisees. It's exactly what we would expect of one who has come to redeem everything and everyone in the cosmos. John's Gospel has consistently shown that no one is beyond salvation, especially outsiders like an adulterous woman.

While the account fits John's theological emphasis, we must reckon with its exclusion from some of the earliest and most reliable manuscripts, such as $\mathfrak{P}^{66.75}$ (ca. 200 CE) and important fourth-century codices Sinaiticus (א) and Vaticanus (B). As far as we know, fifth-century Codex Bezae (D) is the earliest significant witness for its inclusion in John's Gospel. Add to this that the style and vocabulary of John 7:53–8:11 does not match that of the rest of John's Gospel, and that it seems to interrupt the focus on the Feast of Tabernacles in

[79]Callahan, "John," 195.
[80]Kanagaraj, *John*, 84; Blumhofer, *Future of Israel*, 139.
[81]Callahan, "John," 195.

John 7–8, and the case against its inclusion seems very strong.[82]

Despite the shaky evidence for its inclusion, we have sufficient warrant for believing the historicity of the encounter. Papias mentions that the *Gospel to the Hebrews* contains an account of a woman who was accused of many sins before Jesus (*Hist. eccl.* 3.39). The account is found in Western and Byzantine manuscripts, such as codices Bezae (D), Laudianus (E), and Boreelianus (F), giving it an established ecclesial heritage. Jerome was also familiar with the tradition, including it in the Latin Vulgate. Even though it may not have been original to John's Gospel, Bruce Metzger rightly claims that "the account [of a woman caught in adultery] has all the earmarks of historical veracity."[83]

Many Christian traditions have valued Jesus' encounter with the adulterous women, including those who still read the King James Version. Thus, we cannot simply ignore the story, as if it has no value, or never happened.[84] For centuries, the account has shown believers how Jesus pardons a woman whom religious leaders deem unworthy of forgiveness, having committed the "unpardonable" sin of adultery.

The story should cause us to reflect on how we may be too eager to condemn people for committing any number of unforgivable sins. Those whom we judge look a lot like the people whom Jesus embraces. There is certainly a cost for embracing such "sinners." We may be labeled heretics, or any number of slanderous terms meant to identify us with those outside of orthodoxy, not unlike how the first-century religious establishment attempted to label Jesus. Yet, the eternal price for not doing so outweighs any sufferings associated with the present age.

In short, the story of a woman caught in adultery should remind us of how no one is outside the scope of God's salvation. After all, we are all like the adulterous woman, having gone after other lovers (e.g., Jer 22:20; 30:14). Yet Jesus is merciful to forgive us, as he forgave the adulterous woman (Jn 8:10-11). Seen in that light, the story is in keeping with John's emphasis on the universality of salvation, which extends to those deemed the worst of sinners, even if it was not original to the narrative.

Back to the feast of tabernacles (John 8:12-59). The scene shifts back to the Feast of Tabernacles. Once more, Jesus clashes with the religious leaders, having the audacity to claim: "I am [*egō eimi*] the light of the world [*kosmos*]. Whoever follows me does not walk in darkness but will have the light of life" (Jn 8:12). Jesus again uses the words *egō eimi* to reveal that he is Yahweh, the God who delivered his people from slavery in Egypt. His self-identification as the "light" recalls John's prologue, which reveals that Jesus is the very embodiment of the God who shined his creative light in the primordial darkness

[82]Bruce Metzger, *A Textual Commentary on the Greek New Testament*, 2nd ed. (Stuttgart: Deutsche Bibelgesellschaft/German Bible Society Stuttgart, 1994), 188. See also Beasley-Murray, *John*, 143-44. Chris Keith notes that when the account does appear, it is found in ten different places in the manuscript traditions, such as after John 7:36, 44, 52, and 21:25 ("Recent and Previous Research on the Pericope Adultarae [John 7.53–8:11]," *Currents in Biblical Research* 6 [2008]: 377-404). Sloyan notes that the placement of the pericope in various places "testifies both to its existence as an independent narrative and to the sense of the copyists that it belonged with Jesus' teaching in the temple (cf. John 8:2) as part of his final eschatological warning" (*John*, 95).

[83]Metzger, *Textual Commentary*, 188.

[84]Köstenberger, for instance, acknowledges that commentators agree the account "was inserted at a later time" and moves on to discuss John 8:12-59 ("John," 456). Bultmann also omits commenting on the story, saying that it did not belong to the original form of John's Gospel nor the ecclesiastical story (*John*, 312n2). While acknowledging the lack of early reliable evidence, both Klink (*John*, 386-96) and Michaels (*John*, 493-50) see the value of discussing the account of a woman caught in adultery.

(Jn 1:1-5; cf. Gen 1). Only when we take the echoes of Genesis, Exodus, and the prologue of John's Gospel into consideration can we fully grasp the cosmic implications of Jesus' declaration—he has come to deliver the world out of the darkness of sin and death, an act of salvation greater than the one in Egypt, and shine the light of a new creation.[85]

Despite Jesus' claim, the Pharisees remain in darkness.[86] No matter how often Jesus tells them that he has come to accomplish the will of the Father, they still attempt to discredit him, accusing him of being a Samaritan and having a demon (Jn 8:48). Despite how they are depicted in John's Gospel, we should be aware that the Pharisees held that Yahweh would liberate Israel and raise the dead. They even anticipated the coming of the Messiah.[87] Such beliefs are in line with historic Judeo-Christian expectations. Their dissent, of course, is significant: they do not believe that Jesus fulfills Jewish hopes.

When they accuse Jesus of being a Samaritan, the Pharisees attempt to align Jesus with those who combine the worship of Yahweh and idols (Ps 106:34-37), and the accusation of having a demon attempts to align him with those who follow Satan (*Jub.* 19:28-29).[88] But Jesus turns the tables on them, aligning them with the originator of all unfaithfulness: "You are of your father the devil, and your will is to do what your father desires" (Jn 8:44). Abraham, then, is not their father, as they claim (Jn 8:53). If they were Abraham's offspring, they would have rejoiced to see Jesus' arrival (Jn 8:56). Instead, they pick up stones (Jn 8:58), confirming their true familial affiliation (Jn 8:44).

Sign 6: Healing a blind man (John 9:1-41). John shifts from the Feast of Tabernacles to Jesus' sixth messianic sign: healing "a man blind from birth" (Jn 9:1).[89] It is important to recognize that the Old Testament suggests that sickness may be the result of an individual's sin (cf. 2 Kings 14:6) or that of their parents (Ex 20:5; Deut 5:9). That's why the disciples ask: "Who sinned? This man? Or his parents?" (Jn 9:2). In this case, neither. It was God's will that the man be born blind, so that his powerful work might be displayed in him (Jn 9:3).

Before performing the sign, Jesus once again says: "I am [*egō eimi*] the light of the world [*kosmou*]" (Jn 9:5). This powerful statement reaffirms that Jesus is the creator God who has come to renew the cosmos, delivering all people and all things from slavery to sin (Gen 1; Jn 1; cf. Jn 8:12). As at other points in the Gospel, the statement prepares the reader for a glimpse of the cosmic restoration Jesus has come to accomplish.

We might expect that Jesus would heal the blind man immediately—but he doesn't. He does something laced with the kind symbolism we have come to expect of John's Gospel: He "spits on the ground and makes mud with the saliva" (Jn 9:6). He then takes the mud he just mixed[90] and "smeared" it on the man's eyes. Klink summarizes the symbolism well: "In

---

[85]See Beale and Gladd, *The Story Retold*, 142.

[86]Lynn Cohick ("Pharisees," *Dictionary of Jesus and the Gospels*, ed. Joel B. Green, 2nd ed. [Downers Grove, IL: IVP Academic, 2003], 675-76) observes that the Pharisees have the authority to convene a council with the chief priests to stop the spread of Jesus' influence, lest Rome take the temple and nation (Jn 11:48); they possibly hold power over synagogue membership (Jn 9:13-41); and they are likely among those who would have had authority over Jewish legal matters (Jn 1, 9).

[87]N. T. Wright provides a helpful discussion of the identity of the Pharisees (*Christian Origins and the Question of God*, vol. 1, *The New Testament and the People of God* [Minneapolis: Fortress, 1992], 184-203).

[88]See Klink, *John*, 421.

[89]See John Painter, "John 9 and the Interpretation of the Fourth Gospel," *Journal for the Study of the New Testament* 28 (1986): 31-61.

[90]The pronoun *autou* modifies *pēlon*, suggesting that this is the mud Jesus had just made.

light of the already established creation motif in the Gospel, the reader is encouraged to understand 'his mud' to be a reference to creation of humanity from the earth" (Gen 2:7).[91] The late fifth and early sixth century African presbyter Ammonius of Alexandria remarks that Jesus "wanted to show with the mud that he himself is the one who made Adam from the earth."[92] As he made humankind from mud once before, Jesus uses mud to symbolize his messianic work of new creation. While the man's life is transformed by the healing, the allusion to a new creation strongly suggests that this sign is intended to reflect what Jesus will do for the entire earth.

Jesus then tells the man: "Go. Wash in the Pool of Siloam (which is translated sent). So, he went, washed, and returned seeing" (Jn 9:7). The command to wash in the pool is reminiscent of Elijah sending Naaman to wash in the Jordan, so that his flesh might be restored (2 Kings 5:10-13).[93] As Naaman headed to the Jordan to be cleansed (albeit after some coaxing), the blind man goes to the pool and his sight is restored.

This miracle is in keeping with Isaiah's anticipation that the Lord would return and "open the eyes of the blind" (Is 53:5). This would occur as an essential event in the restoration of people and the land on which they would dwell, when they would at last see "the glory of the Lord" (Is 35:2). This connection only serves to strengthen the messianic significance of the sixth sign, through which we perceive that Jesus is the Lord who will soon bring restoration and healing. Like other events in John's Gospel, this sign is a microcosm of the future.

When the religious leaders press the man (now made well) for his opinion of Jesus, he utters astounding truth: "From eternity it has not been heard that a man opened the eyes of a man born blind. If this man were not from God, he could do nothing" (Jn 9:32-33). The power to restore sight is so unprecedented that it must be sourced in God himself. There is simply no other explanation. The man later reveals his trust in Jesus—which is the only proper response to Jesus' restorative work (Jn 9:38).

Despite the miracle, the religious leaders remain blind to the fact that Jesus is "the light of the world" (Jn 9:18, 41). They cannot fathom that Jesus is doing what prophets like Isaiah predicted. Roughly twenty centuries later, not much has changed. We still struggle with envisioning the wholeness that Jesus brings to people. We have difficulty fathoming that Jesus has initiated the course of salvation that will continue until the entire creation is restored, which includes bringing justice and equity to the earth. We may attribute this incredulity to a soteriology focused on delivering souls from the present creation (as if it were evil) and into a bodiless existence in heaven. Justo González argues that this problem is rooted in Gnosticism:

> Long before the time of Constantine, some Christians developed a theology that made it possible for them to claim faith without taking the risk faith implied for any oppressed group. This theology was gnosticism. The gnostics were well aware of the evil and injustice that abound in the world. Their solution, however, was not to oppose that evil but rather to surrender this world to the powers of evil, and to turn to a wholly different realm for their hope for meaning and vindication. . . . The physical world was not part of the divine plan for creation but is rather the result of a mistake. In this world,

[91]Klink, *John*, 439.

[92]Elowsky, ed., *John 1–10*, 324.

[93]Köstenberger, "John," 460; Brown, *John*, 1:32.

> and the material bodies that are part of it, our souls are entrapped, although in truth they belong to the spiritual world. Salvation thus consists of being able to flee this material world.[94]

Quite simply, we should avoid a view of salvation that has more in common with Gnosticism than historic Christianity. The former cannot envision how the Messiah's healing of a man born blind gives us a glimpse of the restoration of the full humanity of people who have been denied justice and equity in the present age, preferring a gospel of heavenly escapism. We should hold, instead, that the messianic signs in John's Gospel reveal that Jesus has come to bring wholeness, and thereby dignity, to people who have longed for it, just like the man born blind.

The good shepherd discourse and the feast of dedication (John 10:1-42). The good shepherd discourse is situated within the framework of John 9:1, when Jesus encounters a man born blind, and John 10:21, when members of the crowd ask: "Are these the words of someone possessed by a demon? Would a demon be able to open the eyes of the blind man?"[95] These verses function as an *inclusio*, setting the context for Jesus' self-disclosure as the promised shepherd.

In the discourse, Jesus declares openly: "I am [*egō eimi*] the good shepherd" (Jn 10:11). The familiar words *egō eimi* recall that Jesus is Yahweh, the same God who revealed himself to Moses at the burning bush. His self-designation as the "good shepherd" evokes the framework of Ezekiel 34, where God promises to send a shepherd who would care for his people, unlike all the bad shepherds throughout Israel's history, including the ones in their current context. Ezekiel identifies the "one shepherd" as God's "servant David" (Ezek 34:22-23). This suggests that when Jesus identifies himself as the "good shepherd," he links himself "to Israel's hope and expectations for a Davidic messianic ruler," evoking stories of David (e.g., 2 Sam 7; 1 Chron 17).[96] Within such stories, God promises that a new David would shield his people from affliction (2 Sam 7:10; 1 Chron 17:9). Ezekiel describes this as a time when the shepherd would "tend his people with justice" (Ezek 34:16).[97] Jesus' declaration thus brings to mind the hope of God's salvation through his Davidic Messiah, who would exercise loving oversight of his people.

He loves his flock so much that he willingly "lays down his life for his sheep" (Jn 10:11, 18). These words recall the servant of Isaiah 53, who hands over his life for God's wayward people. Those who hear the voice of the promised shepherd will follow him to "pasture" (Jn 10:4, 7), which is reminiscent of Yahweh leading the Psalmist to the place where his soul is renewed (Ps 23). In keeping with the theme of cosmic redemption, Jesus says that this promise is not only for Israelites, but also for gentiles: "I have other sheep who are not of this fold; it is also necessary for me to lead them" (Jn 10:16).

On a canonical level, Jesus' declaration recalls the hope of a new exodus into a renewed creation, that is, a better pasture. While people like the Psalmist would have rejoiced to hear Jesus' words, at the Feast of Dedication the Jewish leaders desire to stone Jesus, accusing him of blasphemy (Jn 10:22-39). They reject

[94]Justo González, *Mañana: Christian Theology from a Hispanic Perspective* (Nashville: Abingdon, 1990), 141.

[95]There is no marker of transition that indicates otherwise, as in John 6:1 and John 7:37.

[96]Richard B. Hays, *Echoes of Scripture in the Gospels* (Waco, TX: Baylor University Press, 2016), 294.

[97]See Daniel I. Block, *The Book of Ezekiel: Chapters 25–48*, The New International Commentary on the Old Testament (Grand Rapids, MI: Eerdmans, 1998), 292.

that Jesus is the "one from above" who has come to shepherd his people into a place where they will experience the abundant life they never experienced in the present age.

When he identifies himself as the good shepherd, Jesus shatters the first-century religious establishment's self-perception. He displays that his leadership is "from above" while theirs is of this world. He shows that they are like all other leaders throughout Israel's history, like those against whom Ezekiel railed, who are more interested in preserving their authority than caring for people. What Jesus did, in effect, is threaten the status quo, which kept certain people in authority and everyone else in their place. But the religious establishment was engaged in a futile struggle. As John argues, the power that belongs to the devil, his followers, and all the darkness is in the process of being transferred to Jesus and his flock.

What we see in this account provides hope to marginalized believers, whose leaders may pose as good and kind, when they may just be interested in preserving their power.[98] Granted, many leaders usually don't envision themselves that way, believing that they are doing what is best for the sheep. Most people are not fooled. They know that their leaders are trying to preserve authority that will be handed over to Jesus anyway, when he exercises a rule characterized by justice and equity. Until that day, believers can trust that Jesus is the real shepherd, who truly has our best interests in mind, so much that he gave his life to lead us into a better pasture.

Sign 7: The raising of Lazarus (John 11:1-57). The raising of Lazarus is the seventh sign in the Gospel of John. This miraculous event anticipates Jesus' death and resurrection, which itself is a foretaste of the restoration of the cosmos (Jn 11:43-45; 20:30-31). But the religious establishment has "no eyes to see," as Isaiah would say, what Jesus evokes by raising Lazarus out of the tomb (Is 6:10; 32:3). They can only envision how this sign threatens their status. As a result, "the chief priests and the Pharisees gathered the council and asked: 'What should we do? For this man is performing many signs. If we allow him to continue like this, everyone will believe in him, and the Romans will come and take away our place and our nation'" (Jn 11:47-48). The chief priests and the Pharisees are committed to doing whatever it takes to preserve their place and privilege in Israel, even if it means putting an innocent man to death (Jn 11:53).

The anointing of Jesus (John 12:1-11). Six days before the Passover, Jesus arrives at Bethany, the site where he raised Lazarus from the dead (Jn 12:1).[99] While there, Jesus was treated to a dinner, where Lazarus and his sisters, Mary and Martha, were also present (Jn 12:2). The

[98]See the relevant discussion in Fernando F. Segovia, "The Gospel of John," in *A Postcolonial Commentary on the New Testament Writings*, ed. Ferando F. Segovia and R. S. Sugirtharajah (London: T&T Clark, 2009), 156-93. Self-interested leadership extends its tentacles beyond the United States, into places such as Latin America, where North Americans have often exerted power over Christian seminaries and denominations. In the 1960s and 1970s, for instance, the Seminario Bíblico Latinoamericano fought to rid itself of American control. On behalf of the seminary, Orlando Costas argued, "Someone, certainly a missionary . . . has said that the [Seminario Bíblico Latinoamericano] is a child that has grown and now doesn't want to recognize her mommy. I would say [that we are] like a 48-year-old man whose mother, for reasons of cultural conditioning, has not been prepared to recognize her son's maturity with the promptness that it should, but that is gradually becoming conscience of his duties and responsibilities" (David C. Kirkpatrick, *A Gospel for the Poor: Global Social Christianity and the Evangelical Left* [Philadelphia: University of Pennsylvania, 2019] 69, quoting Orlando Costas, "En el camino hacia un seminario autóctono notas de viaje: 1970," SBL Archives, San José, Costa Rica, 4.).

[99]For a solution to issues of chronology, see Carson, *John*, 427. Michaels refuses to see symbolism in the "six days" (*John*, 663). Klink, however, reminds us that "'six days' was significant at the beginning of the Gospel, the first six days of Jesus's ministry . . . . While this chronology might simply be a time designation in regard to the events surrounding Passover, it also gives emphasis to the last week of Jesus's ministry, just as it did for his first week" (*John*, 524).

presence of these figures shows continuity with the events of John 11.

While Martha serves dinner to Jesus and her brother Lazarus, Mary took a pound of expensive perfume and "anointed the feet of Jesus and wiped his feet with her hair" (Jn 12:3; cf. Lk 7:36-38). It was common to anoint someone's feet to prepare them for burial.[100] It was uncommon to do so while a person was living. Thus, Mary does something unprecedented: She prepares Jesus for his coming death and burial.

John mentions that the odor of Mary's perfume fills the entire house (Jn 12:3), which contrasts the "stench of decay about which Martha warned Jesus at Lazarus's tomb" (Jn 12:3; cf. Jn 11:39).[101] The perfume's fragrance suggests that Jesus' coming death would not lead to the decay of his body, but to his resurrection.[102] Unfortunately, this symbolism was lost on Judas, who was more concerned about the money for which the perfume could have been sold (Jn 12:5). Though he pretended that his concern was for the poor, as treasurer he had grown accustomed to skimming from the money bag, which is what he would have done with the funds from the perfume (Jn 12:5-6).

Jesus would not allow Judas to distract from the significance of the event. So, he makes sure that his followers understand that Mary has prepared him for death (Jn 12:7). This does not mean that Jesus was unconcerned for the poor; it simply means that he wants his followers to focus on the significance of his anointing. When Jesus ascends to the Father, they will again devote their attention to the poor, in keeping with commands in passages such as Deuteronomy 15:11. For now, they are to focus on what will soon happen to their Messiah.

Later, a crowd comes to see Jesus and Lazarus in Bethany (Jn 12:9). The Jewish leaders were not pleased that Jesus, after having raised Lazarus, was attracting more followers (Jn 12:11). So, they decide to kill him. Through their evil and ruthlessness, we see the lengths to which some people will go to preserve their power. Unlike the religious establishment, believers are to take their cues from Jesus, who gave his life for his followers, rather than trying to preserve it (e.g., Jn 15:13).

The triumphal entry (John 12:12-19). Jesus now enters Jerusalem, fully aware of his destiny (Jn 12:12). The people "took branches of palm trees and went out to meet him, exclaiming: 'Hosanna! Blessed is the one who comes in the name of the Lord, the King of Israel!'"[103] While there is no Old Testament precedent for this event, in the first century palm branches were a symbol of liberation for the Jews.[104] The Israelites waved them two centuries prior to Jesus' entry, when they welcomed Simon Maccabeus into Jerusalem as a political hero, having defeated the Syrians and repelling them from the temple (1 Macc 13:51).[105] Hopes for liberation were even minted on coins, bearing the image of a palm tree with the inscription: "for the redemption of Zion."[106] Thus, to wave palms in the air at Jesus' arrival would have symbolized that Israel's political liberation had arrived.

---

[100]Brown, *John*, 1:454.

[101]Thompson, *John*, 259.

[102]Thompson, *John*, 259.

[103]The *kai* is missing from some manuscripts (e.g., A Γ Δ) but found in reliable witnesses such as [2.*]א[b] and B. If the word is original, it functions appositionally, specifying that the "one who comes in the name of the Lord" is the "King of Israel." Thus, it is acceptable to represent *kai* in translation with a comma, as I have done above, conveying the sense of apposition in the sentence.

[104]Callahan, "John," 201. See, for instance, 2 Macc 10:7.

[105]Klink, *John*, 535. On the importance of the purity of the temple, see 1 Macc 2:50-65 and 2 Macc 6:24-28.

[106]William R. Farmer, "The Palm Branches in John 12, 13," *The Journal of Theological Studies* 3 (1952): 64.

Waiving palm branches has a further significance. A decade or so later John would write Revelation, where he depicts a heavenly scene: "A great multitude . . . from every nation, from all tribes and peoples and languages, standing before the throne and before the Lamb, clothed in white robes, with palm branches in their hands, and crying out . . . 'Salvation belongs to our God who sits on the throne, and to the Lamb!'" (Rev 7:9-10). This canonical connection enables us to envision that "waiving palm branches" at Jesus' arrival means that he is more than Israel's deliverer—he is the liberator of all people enslaved to the present age, including those who have been demonized for their concern for justice, the very thing that God promises for his people in their eschatological redemption (Is 65–66; Rev 22).

The crowd in Jerusalem cried out "Hosanna," which means, "Save us!" (cf. Ps 118:25-26). Regardless of how well they understood his identity, Jesus is their promised liberator. He is better than all the Maccabean figures. And he is undoubtedly better than any political savior. While we may be tempted to place our hope in temporal rulers, like presidents or elected officials, only Jesus can save us from sin and all its consequences. We must avoid thinking that our favorite politician will bring our respective nation into a permanent age of prosperity. Christians should not be swept away in such fervor. Our faith in politicians should be tempered by the fact that humanity's hope for freedom and deliverance is only in King Jesus. Anyone else is sure to disappoint.

Unlike false saviors, Jesus had the right to ride into the capital city, symbolically announcing his enthronement. By riding into Jerusalem on a donkey, Jesus fulfills the messianic expectations of Zechariah 9:9: "Do not fear, daughter of Zion! Look! Your king is coming, sitting on the foal of a donkey!" (Jn 12:15). When his kingdom is established, Jesus will bring lasting peace to the cosmos.

After seven identity-revealing signs, and several scenes with people like Nicodemus and the Samaritan woman, there is sufficient reason to believe that Jesus is the promised Messiah. We would think this would have been evident to those who witnessed Jesus' miraculous deeds and heard his powerful words. Yet John tells us that some persist in unbelief, while others believe in secret, afraid of being put out of the synagogue by the Pharisees (Jn 12:37-43). The Pharisees, and the rest of the Jewish establishment, cannot thwart God's plan to "lift up" Jesus for the world. Jesus will soon reverse the order of things, laying low the powerful and raising up the meek.

THE BOOK OF EXALTATION (JOHN 13:1–20:31)

John 13:1 opens the Book of Exaltation. This second major unit in John's Gospel leaves no doubt about Jesus' identity. When he is "lifted up," all will see that he is the promised Messiah and Son of God who has come to rid the world of darkness and initiate the process of restoring the earth. The farewell discourse explains this event to the disciples, along with the promise of the Spirit (Jn 13:1–17:26), and the passion and resurrection of Jesus give us a picture of what Jesus has in store for the world (Jn 18:1–20:31).

Farewell Discourse: Preparation for exaltation (John 13:1–17:26). The farewell discourse ensues with a farewell meal (Jn 13:1-38). The scene reveals that Jesus has full awareness of the absolute power the Father has bestowed on him. We see this when John records that Jesus knows that "the Father has given all things into his hands" (Jn 13:3).[107] We could only imagine what Israel's religious establishment would do with such power.

[107]See Segovia, "John," 183.

During the course of the meal, Jesus rises and washes his disciples' feet, displaying that the most powerful man in the universe has come to offer his life for the sins of his people (Jn 13:4-5; cf. Phil 2:6-7; Ezek 36:25-27). That Jesus would "serve" in this way identifies him with Isaiah's servant, who would suffer for the transgressions of Israel (Is 53:6). We must not miss the irony in John 13: The one with "all power" reveals that he will do what is fitting for people with "no power." And he will do so in the humblest way possible, giving his life on a cross, a means of execution so dehumanizing that it is reserved for the worst of criminals (Jn 10:15).

Jesus expects that his people will follow his example, exhorting them to "wash one another's feet" (Jn 13:14). Believers, then, are to serve in ways that people normally associate with those of low status. We are to humble ourselves, identifying with the lowly, as Jesus identified with the humble in his death. In so doing, we come closer to fulfilling our true vocation—to be like Jesus, who was treated like a criminal, having been stripped of his rights and dignity. In our day, it may mean finding solidarity with people on death row or immigrants in detention centers, those whom society has rendered powerless, rather than people in the Whitehouse or on Wallstreet.

The call to "wash one another's feet" is one and the same with the "new command" to "love one another" (Jn 13:34). While loving others is grounded in the Ten Commands or Ten Words given to Moses, the ability to obey God is associated with the new age. That's why Jesus calls it a "new command." Throughout their history, Israel struggled to keep the intent of the law, loving God and others, so they were sent into exile (Exod 20; Deut 28). The prophets anticipated the days when the Spirit would enable God's people to obey his commands (Ezek 36:25-27; Jer 31:31-34). When Jesus sends the promised Spirit, his people would be empowered to live as never before, loving God and neighbor from the heart (Acts 2, 8, 10).

Not all at the meal would receive the Spirit. During the course of the evening, Jesus identifies Judas as the one who would betray him (Jn 13:21-30). John records that he leaves "at night" to hand Jesus over to the religious leadership of the day—those who would do anything to protect their power (Jn 13:30). Their attempt, of course, is futile. It's only a matter of time before all authority is handed over to the true lord of the world. This is a good reminder that attempts to preserve power are useless—its all going to be given to Jesus anyway.

The remainder of the farewell discourse explains the nature of the place Jesus is preparing for his followers (Jn 14:1-31), his identity as the "true vine" (Jn 15:1-17), the promise of the Spirit (Jn 15:18–16:33), and a final prayer of protection (Jn 17:1-26). All this moves the narrative closer to the exaltation of Jesus, initiating the healing of the world.

Preparing a place (John 14:1-31). In the next section of the discourse, Jesus assures his followers that his departure is for their own good, so that he might prepare an eternal home for them: "In my Father's house [*oikia*] there are many rooms. But if it were not so, would I say to you that I am going to prepare a place [*topon*] for you? And if I go and prepare a place for you, I will come again and take you to myself, so that you will also be where I am" (Jn 14:2-3). Interpreters have proposed various meanings for the place Jesus will prepare for his people.

Some argue that the word *oikia* insinuates that Jesus gives his followers hope of a heavenly temple.[108] Others contend that Jesus promises

[108]Steven M. Bryan, "The Eschatological Temple in John 14," *Bulletin for Biblical Research* 15 (2005): 187-98; Kanagaraj, *John*, 144-45.

his people a heavenly abode with God.[109] Each of these readings overlooks that in John's Gospel *oikia* is a special metaphor that refers to an actual place where a person dwells (e.g., Jn 11:31, 12:3).[110] And we have no reason to think *oikia* in John 14:2-3 is any different, especially since Jesus uses the word in connection to an actual "place" (*topos*).[111] Add to this the idea that Jesus' mission in the Gospel is to restore his creation and the sense of John 14:2-3 is clear: Jesus will leave to prepare a physical dwelling for his followers.[112] When he returns, Jesus will dwell with his people in the renewed cosmos he will have established for them (Rev 21:1, 3; cf. Is 65:17–66:24).

Knowing the ambiguity in his disciples' minds, Jesus clarifies the way to where he is going: "I am [*egō eimi*] the way, the truth, and the life. No one comes to the Father except through me" (John 14:6). Once more, Jesus identifies himself with the words *egō eimi*. As Israel's God and creator of the cosmos, it is fitting that only through him will his people find their "way" to the Father.[113] That means humanity must trust that Jesus is the very embodiment of "truth" and "life," leading to an existence in a far better world (Jn 14:8-10).[114]

When Jesus leaves to prepare an eternal dwelling place, he will not leave his people alone; he will send the Spirit in his place (Jn 14:16-17, 25-26). The Spirit will remain with us until Jesus returns to consummate the present age (Jn 14:16). Until then, we can trust that the Spirit's arrival fulfills the prophets' eschatological expectations, of when God would empower his people to follow him in obedience (Ezek 36:25-27; Jer 31:31-34).

It is no coincidence that the present section emphasizes the coming of the Spirit along with the call to "keep [Jesus'] commands" (Jn 14:15, 21, 23). The Spirit will remind Jesus' followers about all the Messiah has said and done, enabling his people to "keep the commands" with which the old covenant community had such difficulty (Jn 14:26). One of the most important expressions of the Spirit indwelling God's people is that he will enable us to love one another, as Jesus calls his disciples to do in John 13:34-35 and 15:10. This kind of obedience is evidence that we really do love Jesus and will dwell with him forever (Jn 14:15, 21).

Keeping Jesus' commands—embodied in the call to love our neighbor—varies from one context to another. Christian academics, for instance, can love their neighbor by intentionally bringing women and persons of color into course lectures, making sure that students read their names, see their faces, and hear their contributions. In so doing, we take marginalized voices and bring them to the center of conversation. Ministers can include quotes in their sermons from Latino authors like Robert Chao Romero and Black preachers like Tony Evans, showing congregants that their insights are just as valuable as those from the majority group. But loving others is not just reserved for academics and ministers. All Christians are called to love people at the margins and make them the center of our love and attention. If Jesus really has gone to prepare a better place for us, where all will receive equal love and attention, then Christians should start living now in light of the future, thereby giving unbelievers a glimpse of the acceptance all will

[109]Thompson, *John*, 307; Bultmann, *John*, 602.

[110]Klink, *John*, 614. See also BDAG, 695.

[111]See the similar use of *topos* as a "physical place" in 2 Sam 7:10 and Tob 3:6 LXX.

[112]See Klink, *John*, 615.

[113]Brown notes that most ancient and modern interpreters have read John 14:6 as the promise of eternal life in heaven or the ascent of the soul to a place removed from spatial realities (*John*, 2:621)

[114]See Thompson, *John*, 309.

experience in the world that Jesus is preparing for his followers.

The true vine (John 15:1-17). At the inception of this section, Jesus declares: "I am [*egō eimi*] the true vine" (Jn 15:1). We are already familiar with *egō eimi* statements identifying Jesus as the God of Israel. So, we will give more attention, as the thrust of the passage requires, to Jesus' self-identification as the "true vine." Jesus uses a metaphor that Isaiah applies to Israel, whom he accuses of producing bad fruit, i.e., living unfaithfully to God, as evidenced by their wicked deeds (Is 5:1-7).[115] Israel was therefore a vine fit to be burned, which is another way of saying they deserved the judgment of exile (Is 5:1-2; Ezek 15:2-6; 19:10-14).[116] In identifying himself as the "true vine," Jesus reveals that he is a new kind of Israelite—one who is faithful to the Father, even to the point of "laying down his life" for his brothers and sisters, taking the punishment they deserve (Jn 15:13). In so doing, he will reverse the destiny of his people, enabling them to produce "good fruit" (Jn 15:3-8, 16), which is equivalent to saying he will empower them to "keep the commands" (Jn 15:10-11). This is the kind of obedience Jeremiah expected when God delivered Israel from exile and brought them into a restored land (Jer 31:31-40). John expands the focus of new covenant obedience to include people throughout the entire world who trust in Messiah Jesus.

In "laying down his life," Jesus fulfills the command to "love one another" (Jn 15:13, 17). In so doing, we have the perfect example of obedience—loving people to the point of giving our lives to deliver them from the oppression of sin. We should not underestimate how costly it is to follow this example. If Jesus paid with his life, at the very least we should expect to be maligned by those who criticize our justice advocacy. Following Jesus, however, most certainly includes being aware of the injustices associated with the curse of sin and death and, by the power of the Spirit, doing something about it. Is this not what God did when he "heard the cries" of the Israelites and sent Moses to redeem them from bondage in Egypt (Ex 3:9-11)? Is this not what God did when he "heard the cries" of humanity and sent Jesus to redeem the world from slavery to sin (Gal 4:6-7)? Scripture resoundingly testifies that we serve a God who is aware of injustice—and does something about it, even giving his own life. We should assume that he expects nothing less from his followers.

Undoubtedly, then, we must count the cost of following Jesus. The parable of the rich young man is a good example. When told to give away his money to follow Jesus, the young man refused, for he was very wealthy (Mt 19:16-22). He was not willing to exchange his "capital" for the promise of eternal life. Like the rich young man, God calls us to risk what we have acquired, like relationships and distinguished positions, in order to follow Jesus in sharing and living a gospel that delivers people from sin and all of its tangible effects, like poverty and racism. And those who lose what they have acquired for living faithfully have the prospect of reigning with Jesus in the new world—which is far better than the wealth and prestige associated with this passing world (Mt 19:27-30).

The Spirit's coming (John 15:18–16:33). As the farewell discourse draws to a close, Jesus warns his followers that the world will hate them, just as it has hated him (Jn 15:18-25). Such enmity

---

[115]Beale and Gladd, *The Story Retold*, 146; Köstenberger, "John," 490-91; Klink, *John*, 650.

[116]Klink, *John*, 650. John F. O'Grady argues for the close relationship between the Good Shepherd discourse and the parable of the vine due to structural and theological similarities ("The Good Shepherd and the Vine and the Branches," *Biblical Theological Bulletin* 8 [1978]: 86-89).

will manifest itself in their persecution, which they will not face alone (Jn 15:20). Jesus will send his Spirit, who will embolden his people to bear witness to his restorative work (Jn 15:26-27). The Spirit will also convict the world of sin and the coming judgment (Jn 16:5-11), guide his followers into "all truth" (Jn 16:13), and declare "the things that are to come" (Jn 16:13). The latter is especially important in the face of persecution, for it reminds us of the future judgment of the world and the renewal of all things. When Jesus ascends to the Father, the Spirit will assure us that no matter how difficult the persecution, or how much the darkness seems to overshadow the light, Jesus will return to makes things right.

Despite living in a hostile world, Jesus' followers have good reason to be courageous. No matter what happens now, Jesus will return to make his creation whole, including those suffering under oppression, just like the Israelites living under Roman rule. As Jesus overcomes a dark world through his suffering and resurrection, we have the hope of overcoming our present difficulties through the power of the Spirit, who will raise us to enjoy a place transformed by Jesus the Messiah. There, we will experience the wholeness for which we have longed—the deliverance from oppression and the full restoration of our dignity—when we at last "overcome the world" (Jn 16:33). That day will be especially sweet for those who have suffered great affliction in the present age.

High priestly prayer (John 17:1-26). Jesus' intercessory prayer for his followers, commonly known as the high priestly prayer, concludes the farewell discourse. The prayer is composed of three petitions. In the first petition, Jesus prays for the glorification of the Father and Son (Jn 17:1-18; see Jn 17:1). Jesus' entire ministry has been directed toward his "exaltation"—through which the Godhead will receive glory by granting "eternal life" to all whom the Father has given to him (Jn 17:2). For the majority of the Gospel, John has asserted that Jesus has come to give his followers life in a new world. Now Jesus assures his followers that they can begin to enjoy this existence in the here and now, knowing that the Father is the "only true God, and Jesus Christ whom you [the Father] has sent" (Jn 17:3).

In the second petition, Jesus intercedes for his followers (Jn 17:9-20). As he sends his disciples into a dark world, Jesus prays for their unity and protection from the evil one (Jn 17:12, 18). Jesus knows that the world will hate them, as it has hated him, despite that he has come to shine his light into the darkness (Jn 1:6-18). For the sake of his followers, he will die, rise from the dead, and ascend to the Father (Jn 17:20).[117] After his ascension, he will send his Spirit to empower his people to extend his mission to the ends of the earth (Jn 15:26-27). The Spirit will see to it that the evil one does not thwart the message of new creation: that the effects of living in a dark world, where different forms of oppression are entrenched in our societies, will give way to an earth transformed by the light of Jesus the Messiah. There, Jesus will reign over his people with justice and equity, just like Isaiah, Jeremiah, Ezekiel, and other prophets anticipated. That's the "good news" that Jesus' followers are to announce to the broken and hurting—not a platonic or gnostic vision of heaven that gives people no hope that their fortunes will ever be reversed on the earth.

In the third and final petition, Jesus prays for all who will believe in him through the witness of his disciples (Jn 17:20-26; see Jn 17:20). This is where the focus of the prayer extends beyond his first-century followers to all who will believe in the message that first

[117]Klink, *John*, 722.

originated with Jesus and his disciples. Jesus prays that we may be one and that one day we may be in his presence on a new earth, where all the pain of the present age will be no more (Jn 17:24). That's why Jesus was "sent into the world"—to redeem his entire creation, both human and nonhuman, in an act of cosmic restoration (Jn 17:24). As we take this message to the world, we should keep in mind that the "exaltation" of Jesus makes possible the restoration of a world enslaved to darkness, which carries out its oppression in a variety of individual and systemic ways. That the cross brings about a cosmic reversal of fortunes is good news for humanity, for they will soon be "lifted up" to enjoy their full humanization, like peace and joy—what the darkness has tried to keep people from enjoying since Adam and Eve were first exiled from the garden.

The trials, death, and empty tomb: The exaltation of Jesus (John 18:1–20:31). After his High Priestly Prayer, Jesus departs "with his disciples across the Kidron brook" and enters a "garden" (Jn 18:1). The garden scene is a major transition point in the Gospel, setting in motion a series of events leading to the exaltation of Jesus. As we've noted, this event marks the turning point for the cosmos, when the darkness begins to fade, and the light of a new creation breaks forth. But the darkness will not depart quietly. It would do its worst to preserve its power over the world, even if it means arresting and crucifying the lord of the universe.

John uses the garden scene to recall Genesis 1–3, so that we might envision that Jesus is on a mission to create a new paradise for humanity.[118] That Jesus was crucified and resurrected in a garden solidifies his mission, of which he is the first fruits (Jn 19:41; 20:15).[119] Unbeknownst to Judas and the officers of the chief priests and Pharisees, the events following Jesus' arrest serve to fulfill the purpose for which he came to the earth.

Trials of Jesus (John 18:12–19:16). After his arrest, the Jewish leadership puts Jesus through a series of trials (Jn 18:12). They have no intention of giving him a fair hearing. The establishment sees Jesus as a threat to their authority, so they will do whatever it takes, even if it means releasing an insurrectionist, to convict him of a crime worthy of death (Jn 18:40). Perhaps they were ignoring texts prohibiting legal injustice, like Leviticus 19:15. What we can say for certain is that the religious establishment is blind to what is increasingly clear to readers of John's Gospel: that Jesus is the real king, whose reign is about to change the political and social order of the cosmos.

The Jewish leadership first brings Jesus before Annas, Israel's former high priest. Predictably, he finds him guilty and sends him to Caiaphas, the current high priest (Jn 18:19-24). John does not tell us what happened during Jesus' trial before Caiaphas. From Matthew's account, we assume he was found guilty of blasphemy, making him worthy of death (Mt 26:57-75). In John's Gospel, however, Caiaphas only serves to send Jesus on to Pilate (Jn 18:28). Since the Jews were under Roman rule, only Pilate had the authority to put Jesus to death (Jn 18:30-31). Even though they were under Roman authority, the Jewish establishment turns to their oppressors to crucify an innocent man who threatens their authority.

Before we rush to judgment, we should reflect on how we are also prone to collude with power for personal gain, even if it means

[118]My reading is influenced by Klink, *John*, 733. Establishing the theological significance of the garden is uncommon in Johannine scholarship. See, for instance, Brown (*John*, 2:806), who argues against the presence of the motif, and Kanagaraj (*John*, 172) and Thompson (*John*, 362-63), who do not mention the theological implications of the garden.

[119]Klink, *John*, 733.

compromising our ethical standards. We should avoid this approach, even if we are oppressed or marginalized. Israel' prophets call God's people to repentance, trusting that only Yahweh will fulfill the kingdom promises (Deut 28–30; Is 1; Jer 35; Amos 9). He is the only one who will give us true authority under his reign and autonomy from our enemies (2 Sam 7; 1 Chron 17). In our desire to be free—which is good and right—we should always keep our trust firmly in Jesus, the promised Messiah who has come to liberate us from sin and all its repercussions, including repressive authorities.

When we are aware of our own sinful inclinations, we understand why the Jewish leaders of Jesus' day, as sinful as their actions were, colluded with Rome to kill their promised king. We must learn from their mistakes, reminding ourselves that power is reserved for Jesus, from which we will benefit when he establishes his reign on the earth (Rev 20–22). Our hope for any lasting deliverance and authority must be in him.

When Jesus stands before Pilate, the Roman governor asks: "Are you the king of the Jews?" (Jn 18:33). Jesus knows that this question comes from the Jewish leaders' accusations, who don't fully understand his identity (Jn 18:34). His answer is appropriate: "My kingdom is not of this world" (Jn 18:36). This was a different response than what Pilate was accustomed. He was used to rulers who laid claim to particular lands or territories—not an otherworldly kingdom, one that would soon overtake the entire earth. Jesus is a far bigger threat than Pilate or the first-century Jewish authorities imagine. Jesus has not just come for Judea or Rome; he has come for the entire cosmos. Although the king of the universe is before him, Pilate does not recognize him. Nor does he understand the suffering Jesus must endure to establish his reign. What Pilate does recognize is that Jesus has committed no crime, so he will try to release him (Jn 18:39). The crowd, however, is insistent on crucifying the king, choosing to have Barabbas released in his stead (Jn 18:40).

Knowing that his release could spark an insurrection, threatening his own authority, Pilate complies with the Jews (Jn 19:6-8, 12-16). As readers of John's Gospel, we know what Pilate and the Jewish leaders do not under stand: Power is slipping out of their hands. The more they try to preserve it, the more they are losing it. It's only a matter of time before all authority is handed over to Jesus. Since the path to his reign is through a bloody cross, Pilate plays his part in this cosmic drama.

At first, he tries to appease the Jews by flogging Jesus (Jn 19:1). The soldiers adorn him with a crown of thorns and a purple robe (Jn 19:2). Then their mocking ensues: "Hail, King of the Jews!" (Jn 19:3). Their taunting only confirms what is partially true—in reality, he is the king of the cosmos, including Rome, just as the Psalmist affirms (Ps 2:8). As their sovereign, he has the power to crush all rebellion (Ps 2:9-12). If the soldiers had any sense, they would stop mocking the king whose anger will soon be kindled against all insurrectionists (Ps 2:12).

Despite Pilate's attempts at releasing Jesus, the Jewish leaders cry: "Crucify! Crucify! . . . We have a law, and according to that law he deserves death, for he has made himself out to be the Son of God!" (Jn 19:6-7). They attempt to force Pilate's hand by appealing to their religious and political law. To add to the pressure, they threaten his loyalty to Caesar (Jn 19:12). Sensing his own authority is being threatened, he compromises the standards of justice he is supposed to uphold, handing Jesus over to be crucified (Jn 19:16). Before he does, we should note the cries of the chief priests: "We have no king but Caesar!" (Jn 19:15). By giving their allegiance to Caesar, Jewish leaders reveal their affiliation with those who oppose God.[120] This is something we have sensed throughout the narrative, only now proclaimed from their own mouths. As God's Son, Jesus will soon execute judgment on all who refuse to honor him as king (Ps 2:9-12). Since the Jewish leaders would rather align themselves with Caesar, their fate will be tied to those who refuse the authority of Jesus, like Pilate.

At the risk of casting all the blame on the Jewish establishment, we should recognize that both the Jewish leaders and Pilate had a role in crucifying Jesus. While our focus has been on the former's actions, we must stress that Pilate was no less culpable. He knew Jesus was innocent. He could have resisted the pressure from the Jewish leadership. Instead, he approved of the execution of God's son. Seeing the culpability of both parties promotes a reading of John's Gospel that does not place all of the blame for Jesus' death on the Jews. Such readings have been used to promote antisemitism, something which John, who himself was a Jew, would never have condoned.[121]

Death and empty tomb (John 19:16-42). The soldiers lead Jesus out to a place called Golgotha, where he is crucified between two other men (Jn 19:17-18). Since the entire Gospel has been looking forward to this moment, we should expect him nowhere else than at the center of the crucifixion scene. The stage is set for the death and resurrection of the king.

Pilate contributes to this expectation, inscribing the words: "Jesus of Nazareth, King of the Jews" (Jn 19:20). Though he writes this to insult the Jewish leaders, his words serve as a notice to all who read John's Gospel: The king is about to offer his life.[122] When he does, the darkness will flee, and the light of a new creation will shine forth. The signs in John's Gospel are a foretaste of what he is about to accomplish.

Before the scene's climax, the soldiers cast lots to determine who would keep Jesus' tunic (Jn 19:2-24). John tells us that their actions fulfill Psalm 22:18 (21:19 LXX): "They divided my clothing among them, and for my tunic they cast lots."[123] By quoting the Psalm, John identifies Jesus with David, who suffers innocently at the hands of his adversaries.[124] In the throes of his own injustice, Jesus shows that he is the greater David-like ruler whose reign will not be thwarted, despite the efforts of the people. Though David reigned over the land of Israel, Jesus' suffering establishes his rule over the earth.

After enduring the agony of the cross, Jesus says, "It is finished!" These are the Gospel's climactic words, with which Jesus acknowledges that he has completed the work assigned to him by the Father. Through his suffering and death, Jesus initiates the liberation of the world from the powers of sin and death (Jn 1:1-18, 29; 3:16-17; 4:34; 5:36; 10:10; 17:4). Soon the creation will be renewed, and the darkness will have no foothold on the earth. We can imagine how Jesus' final words reverberated throughout

---

[120]Klink, *John*, 785.

[121]For a reading that is conscience of an antisemitic understanding of "the Jews" in John's Gospel, see Hays, *Echoes of Scripture in the Gospels*, 302-18.

[122]Origen argues, "Whether in pretense or in truth, Christ is proclaimed king, and every letter bears witness of his reign, whether of Greeks, or Romans, or Hebrews. And for a crown above his head was written, 'This is Jesus the King of the Jews'" (Joel C. Elowsky, ed., *John 11–21*, Ancient Christian Commentary on Scripture [Downers Grove: InterVarsity], 311).

[123]John cites the exact words of Ps 21:19 LXX: *diemerisanto ta himatia mou heautois kai epi ton himatismon mou ebalon klēron* The English translation reflects the chapter and verse order of the BHS.

[124]See Beal and Gladd, *The Story Retold*, 149-50; Blumhofer, *The Future of Israel*, 199.

the cosmos, announcing the arrival of freedom and restoration. Soon God's Spirit will overwhelm the darkness, empowering his people to practice a heartfelt love for God and neighbor, exactly as the Old Testament prophets anticipated. Among other things, this means that racism will be replaced by acceptance, xenophobia will be substituted by hospitality, and abuse will be supplanted by genuine care. No one will be called a stranger or outsider in the restored cosmos because all will be at home with their God. Jesus' final words certainly speak more than we can imagine—but no less than what we have mentioned.

John mentions that not one of Jesus' bones were broken, fulfilling Passover imagery from Exodus 12:46 (Jn 19:33, 36) and revealing he is truly the "lamb of God who takes away the sins of the world" (Jn 1:29; cf. Is 53:7-12). As mentioned earlier, Passover imagery also alludes to Isaiah 53:7-12, which compares the servant to a lamb led to the slaughter. All this enables us to envision how Jesus is the lamb of God who offers his life to liberate his entire creation from the darkness that has ensnared it since Adam and Eve were exiled from the Garden of Eden. Rightly does Jesus accomplish a new exodus, delivering the world from an oppression greater than anything Israel experienced under Pharaoh.

Arising out of the tomb, which just so happens to be in a garden, Jesus is the first fruits of a world that will blossom into the renewed Eden. The remainder of John's Gospel records how Jesus shows his disciples that he has been raised from the dead, proving he is the victorious king who restores all things.

Appearances of the resurrected Jesus (John 20:1-29). When Mary Magdalene reports that Jesus' body is no longer in the tomb, Peter and the beloved disciple run to the tomb to see for themselves (Jn 20:1-4). When they arrive, all they find are linen cloths (Jn 20:5-7). Though they saw the empty tomb, John records that they were slow to "understand the Scripture, that Jesus must rise from the dead" (Jn 20:9). Despite the obtuseness of the disciples, the empty tomb reveals that Jesus really is the first installment of the resurrection that Daniel anticipates (Dan 12:1-2); he is the first Israelite to whom the Spirit has given new life (Ezek 36–37); he is the suffering servant who has risen to experience eternal life with his offspring (Is 53:10). In him, the promises of resurrection find their fulfillment, displaying to the cosmos a foretaste of the renewal of all things.

Following this scene, Jesus appears, in resurrected form, to Mary Magdalene and the disciples (Jn 20:11-23). Jesus "breathes" on his disciples and says, "Receive the Holy Spirit" (Jn 20:22). This scene recalls Genesis 2:7, when God fills Adam with the "breath of life," and Ezekiel 37:9, when God "breaths" on Israel's dry bones. In keeping with this pattern, Jesus' "breath" on his disciples signifies that he is giving them new life, as he did to Adam in the original garden and he will do for his people in a new garden.[125] In addition, God empowers his followers to be ministers of his renewing work in the world (Jn 20:23). All who believe their message will also receive the life-giving breath of God, ensuring that they will be resurrected into a renewed garden.

The purpose of the book (John 20:30-31). John records many signs which the historical Jesus performed. There are more, of course (Jn 20:30). But what he has recorded is enough to fulfill his purpose: "that you may believe that Jesus is the Christ, the Son of God, and that by believing you may have life in his name" (Jn 20:31). By now we should understand that "life" is more than a spiritual reality. Through

[125]See the discussion in Michaels, *John*, 1010-12.

the series of signs, chief among them being the bodily resurrection of Jesus, John reveals that "life" refers to making people whole, delivering them from slavery to the darkness of sin and death in the present age and into one far better.

EPILOGUE (JOHN 21:1-25)

The epilogue of John's Gospel records Jesus' third post-resurrection appearance, which portrays him enjoying a meal of freshly caught fish and bread with his disciples (Jn 21:1-14). According to Jerome, Jesus ate with his disciples so that "he might confirm the doubting apostles who did not dare approach him because they thought they saw not a body but a spirit."[126] This scene reveals once more that Jesus has risen bodily from the grave. A spiritualized resurrection was never the position of John or his earliest readers.

After the meal, Jesus confirms Peter's commitment to shepherd the early followers of Jesus, knowing that he too will suffer and die (Jn 21:15-19). Peter will follow in the footsteps of the great shepherd, Jesus, even to death. It's a good reminder for those of us who desire to follow Jesus. As was the case with our Lord, suffering will soon give way to our glorious resurrection from the grave, when we will enjoy life in a better world.

John's Gospel ends with the assurance that everything the beloved disciple has recorded is true (Jn 21:24). Jesus really is the long-awaited Messiah, the one people like Moses, Isaiah, and Ezekiel wrote about. Through his miraculous signs, culminating in his exaltation on the cross, Jesus shows that he is in the process of recreating the earth, making it into a new Eden. Soon the creation will undergo a cosmic resurrection, undoing the darkness that has overwhelmed it for far too long (cf. Rom 8). On the renewed earth, all power and authority will be handed over to King Jesus. Soon he will reign with the kind of equity and justice the world has yet to see. Those who suffered under abusive authority will flourish under the rule of God's Son and David's royal descendant.

Since all John says is true, we can look forward to the day when all the effects of sin are reversed and Jesus is reigning over a resurrected people, on a renewed earth. But we should not wait until then. The Spirit Jesus promises in the farewell discourse has now come, initiating the process of healing and redemption, of making people and the entire creation whole (Acts 2). That means that the Spirit works through believers to gradually remove the effects of the curse on earth, such as individual and systemic racism, global poverty, government oppression, and exploitation of migrant workers, which will have no place on the earth God is preparing for his people. When we consider the whole of John's Gospel, we see that humanity is called to believe in the Messiah who was crucified and resurrected to renew his creation, delivering it from the power of darkness. In so doing, we have the privilege of participating in the work of restoration that the Spirit has begun on the earth, anticipating the day when Jesus returns and gives eternal wholeness and rest to his creation.

SELECTED BIBLIOGRAPHY

Beasley-Murray, George R. *John*. Word Biblical Commentary. Vol. 36. Nashville: Thomas Nelson, 1999.

Blumhofer, Christopher M. *The Gospel of John and the Future of Israel*. Society for New Testament Studies Monograph Series 177. Cambridge: Cambridge University Press, 2020.

Bruce, F. F. *The Gospel of John: Introduction, Exposition and Notes*. Grand Rapids, MI: Eerdmans, 1983.

[126]Elowsky, ed., *John 11–21*, 381.

Bultmann, Rudolph. *The Gospel of John: A Commentary.* Edited by G. R. Beasley-Murray. Philadelphia: Westminster, 1971.

Burge, Gary M. *John.* The NIV Application Commentary. Grand Rapids, MI: Zondervan, 2000.

Callahan, Allan Dwight. "The Gospel of John." In *True to Our Native Land*, edited by Brian K. Blount, 186-212. Minneapolis: Fortress, 2007.

Carson, D. A. *The Gospel According to John.* The Pillar New Testament Commentary. Grand Rapids, MI: Eerdmans, 1991.

Charlesworth, James H. *The Beloved Disciple: Whose Witness Validates the Gospel of John?* Valley Forge, PA: Trinity Press International, 1995.

Hays, Richard B. *Echoes of Scripture in the Gospels.* Waco, TX: Baylor University Press, 2016.

Kanagaraj, Jey J. *John.* A New Covenant Commentary. Cambridge: Lutterworth Press, 2013.

Klink III, Edward W. *John.* Exegetical Commentary on the New Testament. Grand Rapids, MI: Zondervan, 2016.

Köstenberger, Andreas J. *A Theology of John's Gospel and Letters: The Word, the Christ, the Son of God.* Biblical Theology of the New Testament. Grand Rapids, MI: Zondervan, 2009.

Malina, Bruce J. and Richard L. Rohrbaugh. *Social-Science Commentary on the Gospel of John* Minneapolis: Fortress, 1998.

Michaels, J. Ramsey. *John.* The New International Commentary on the New Testament. Grand Rapids, MI: Eerdmans, 2010.

O'Day, Gail R. "The Gospel of John: Introduction, Commentary, and Reflections." In *Luke, John*, edited by Leander E. Keck, 421-742. Vol. 8 of *The New Interpreters Bible Commentary.* Nashville: Abingdon, 2015.

Ridderbos, Herman. *The Gospel of John: A Theological Commentary.* Grand Rapids, MI: Eerdmans, 1997.

Segovia, Fernando F. "The Gospel of John." In *A Postcolonial Commentary on the New Testament Writings*, edited by Ferando F. Segovia and R. S. Sugirtharajah, 156-93. London: T&T Clark, 2009.

Sloyan, Gerard S. *John.* Interpretation: A Bible Commentary for Teaching and Preaching. Atlanta: John Knox, 1988.

Thompson, Marianne Meye. *1–3 John.* The IVP New Testament Commentary Series. Downers Grove, IL: IVP Academic, 1992.

GENDER IN THE NEW TESTAMENT

LISA M. BOWENS AND AMY PEELER

Occasionally, students will sheepishly voice a question they might have contemplated for a long time: "Does God value men more than women?" There are many men in the Bible, and they seem to play all the most prominent roles. Add to that the passages that advocate for women's silence and submissiveness. Such realities make it understandable that some have concluded that the Bible is not good for women.

We, however, wholeheartedly disagree.

As Christians and scholars committed to the flourishing of theology in the academy and the church, God has called us to investigate and live out Scripture's word, and we can say with conviction and joy that it is a good word for all, including women. Many examples in the Bible—chiefly that of Jesus—free men from the bondage of an oppressive masculinity. Strength is expressed not in domination but in confident humility and service. A fresh generation of scholars is providing in-depth analysis of masculinity in ancient cultures and what implications the Christian life has for men's lives today.[1]

In this article, however, we have chosen to focus on the New Testament's good word to women. The commentary in your hands has probably already convinced you of that, so here we lift up some especially pertinent examples from the life of Jesus, the communities of those who were following him, and African American women who lived out this good word in their lives. We provide explanation for passages that seem, on the surface, quite negative toward women and lift up other texts that have empowered women as full bearers of the image of God and recipients of God's Holy Spirit.

At the same time, we recognize that not only have the Scriptures been used to relegate women to second-class status, these sacred texts have also been part of the tensions between the need to advocate for POC and women. Chastened by these struggles and realizations we assert that the NT's advocacy for women is one powerful aspect of its valuing of the beauty of difference in the body of Christ. Equally powerful is the use of the NT by African American women to speak to their own "tridimensional oppression of gender, *race*, and class."[2]

Consequently, womanist readings of Scripture emerged in the twentieth century in order to speak to these dimensions of African American female existence because too often White feminist readings could not and did not address this trifold oppression of Black women. For womanists, one need not choose between advocating against racism and for women. The experiences of Black women demonstrate the intricate links between each of these spheres.

[1]For example, Brittany E. Wilson, *Unmanly Men: Refigurations of Masculinity in Luke-Acts* (Oxford: Oxford University Press, 2015); Zachary Wagner, *Non-toxic Masculinity: Recovering Healthy Male Sexuality* (Downers Grove, IL: InterVarsity Press, 2023).

[2]Raquel St. Clair, *Call and Consequences: A Womanist Reading of Mark* (Minneapolis: Fortress Press, 2008, 6, italics original).

While womanist readings of Scripture are more prominent now than ever, in the nineteenth century Black women biblical exegetes, such as Jarena Lee, Zilpha Elaw, and Julia Foote, were reading and interpreting Scripture in ways that took all of these elements into account, utilizing Scripture to protest racism, sexism, and classism. Often called proto-womanists, their own experiences as African American women in America shaped how they understood the biblical text and at the same time the biblical text shaped how they understood their experiences as Black women in America.[3] This dialectical relationship between the text and experience foregrounds their voices as interpreters who believe Scripture to advocate for women, including Black women, as preachers and teachers equal to their male counterparts in every way.[4] As will be demonstrated in what follows the New Testament's good word to women appears in the text itself and in the lives of later African American women interpreters who proclaim this good word to all they encounter.

GOSPELS

Many acknowledge that Jesus was supportive of women. So what do readers do with the encounter in which Jesus seems to call a woman a dog?

The conversation appears in both Matthew 15:21-28 and Mark 7:24-30, with several intriguing differences, but the story largely remains the same. A woman who is not a Jew begs Jesus to heal her daughter from an unclean spirit. Matthew indicates that Jesus simply ignores her initially, telling his disciples that he was sent for the lost sheep of Israel. Both evangelists record his words to her thus: "It is not good to take the bread of the children and cast it to the dogs." Why, we cry out in frustration, is Jesus being so callous? Some have suggested he is testing the woman, and others that he is making a point for the disciples. Whatever the intent, the exchange gives the woman an opportunity to demonstrate a reality of his kingdom, showing herself to be the wisest of disciples.[5] I'll embrace humility, she says, for even if all I receive is crumbs, at your table, that would be more than enough. In my tradition (Amy Peeler's), which uses the Book of Common prayer, her statement shines forth in the words of the Prayer of Humble Access, which congregants pray from the perspective of the woman: "We are not worthy so much as to eat the crumbs from your table." She understood and enacted the Christian principle of descent, the posture of humility. In the prayer, we then say, "But you are the same Lord whose property is always to have mercy." And in this encounter, Jesus did. By healing her daughter immediately, he not only gave her what she asked for, but he showed that she now stood in the position of a child of God. "Let the children be satisfied first," he had told her (Mk 7:27 NASB). When she put herself in the place of a disciple, showing that she trusted that even Jesus' crumbs were sufficient and that she was willing to humble herself to receive them (following Jesus' pattern of discipleship [Mt 16:21; Mk 8:34]), she was satisfied immediately, before even some of the disciples understood who Jesus really was and what he could do for them. So even this difficult story can

[3]For example, Mitzi J. Smith calls these women "proto-womanists interpreters" in "'This Little Light of Mine': The Womanist Biblical Scholar as Prophetess, Iconoclast, and Activist," in *I Found God in Me: A Womanist Biblical Hermeneutics Reader*, ed. Mitzi J. Smith (Eugene, OR: Cascade, 2015).

[4]For more on this dialectical relationship between Scripture and experience see Lisa M. Bowens, *African American Readings of Paul: Reception, Resistance, and Transformation* (Grand Rapids, MI: Eerdmans, 2020).

[5]C. Clifton Black, *Mark*, Abingdon New Testament Commentaries (Nashville: Abingdon Press, 2011),

teach powerful lessons. Jesus' conversation with her seems to be his way of asking if she'd be willing to humble herself, and when she was willing, he treated her, an outsider to the people of Israel, as a daughter of God. She becomes a lived example of the dynamic of reversal which runs throughout the gospels (Mt 23:12; Lk 1:51-53).

However, not only is this woman an example of humility, she is also an example of tenacity and perseverance. Her tenacity as well as her humility leads Jesus to see that, although a Gentile, she too is included in God's plan.[6] I (Lisa Bowens) agree with both Richard Bauckham and Lynn Japinga, who underscore the power of her unrelenting voice: "As has been often said, this is one of the most remarkable stories in the Gospels, the only one in which someone in conversation with Jesus leads him to change his mind."[7] This "someone" is a woman who "challenged him [Jesus] to be more inclusive. She reminded him that there was enough grace to go around. *She talked back*. Jesus listened to her, changed his mind, and healed her daughter as she asked."[8] Her dialogue with Jesus highlights the simultaneity of her humility and strength as well as her willingness to recognize herself and her child as worthy of God's care. Both Peeler and Bowens interpret the woman as outstanding among the followers of Jesus. For Peeler, the woman exemplifies faith and humility in her willingness to receive anything, even crumbs, from God's table trusting that God's mercy is enough. For Bowens, she is an exemplar of persistence and tenacity in her demand to receive mercy from God and be seen as a child of God. God's mercy is not only sufficient but abundant enough to share. Jesus is moved and challenged by the woman's plea and grants her request. In praising and agreeing with the woman and meeting her need, Jesus affirms that she is a daughter of God.

Much more often, Jesus' interactions with women demonstrate the way in which he cared for and honored them, including the many women he healed, for example, Peter's mother-in-law (Mt 8:14-15; Mk 1:30-31; Lk 4:38-39), the woman with the issue of blood (Mt 9:20-22; Mk 5:25-34; Lk 8:43-48), Jairus's daughter (Mt 9:18-26; Mk 5:21-43; Lk 8:40-56), and the crippled woman (Lk 13:10-17), as well as the women with whom he engaged in honest conversation (the Samaritan woman, Jn 4) and the issues he stood against that hurt women (such as lust and divorce, Mt 5:27-33).

One of the most well-known stories, Jesus' rescue of the woman caught in the act of adultery, may not have been original to the first writing of the Gospel, but certainly resonates with the character of Jesus. This story from John 7:53 to John 8:11 does not appear in the earliest and best manuscripts of the New Testament, but scholars conclude it may have been added later by a scribe who knew the story from the life of Jesus and believe it should

---

[6]Francis Moloney, *The Gospel of Mark: A Commentary* (Peabody, MA: Hendrickson, 2002), offers the following in regard to this passage. "The description of the Gentiles as 'dogs' (κυνάρια) is not surprising when some such setting for the saying is recognized. . . . He [Jesus] insists that 'the children,' Israel, be fed first, claiming that it is improper to take that bread and cast it to the Gentiles ('the dogs')," 146-47.

[7]Richard Bauckham, *Gospel Women: Studies of the Named Women in the Gospels* (Grand Rapids, MI: Eerdmans, 2002), 42-43.

[8]Lynn Japinga, *From Daughters to Disciples: Women's Stories from the New Testament* (Louisville, KY: Westminster John Knox, 2021), 41-42 (emphasis added). One could also argue that Jesus' encounter with his mother in the Gospel of John is another instance where Jesus, in conversation with another woman, changes his mind (Jn 2:1-11). When his mother tells him that the guests are out of wine at the wedding celebration in Cana, she expects him to do something about it. Yet Jesus responds to her that his hour has not yet come (Jn 2:4). Nevertheless, his mother tells the servants to do whatever he tells them, which demonstrates that in some sense she expected him to act despite his initial reservation (Jn 2:5). Mary's insistence leads him to perform what John calls the first sign in the Gospel (Jn 2:11).

be included. As the story goes, this shamed woman is used as a pawn in the leaders' persistent efforts to trap Jesus. His initial reaction appears careless. He ignores their question and her plight by taking a moment to draw. His silence, however, diffuses a tense situation. In the breathless pause to figure out what in the world Jesus is doing—when he has their attention—he calls attention to the sin of all those gathered. Anyone who is perfect could rightfully stone her. Readers of John's Gospel have no doubt by this time that Jesus who has come from the Father and continually does the will of the Father is perfect. Instead of stoning her for her offense or rendering to her the condemnation of which she is deserving, he sends her off charged to walk in newness of life. He has saved both her physical and her moral life. Because Jesus is so often in the business of meeting the holistic needs of those he encounters, this late addition fits the picture of Jesus readers have come to expect.

Other important events unfold in the relationship in which Jesus befriends two sisters during his earthly ministry, Mary and Martha of Bethany. Luke gives us the well-known account of their different responses to Jesus' visit. Martha shows him hospitality, by receiving him into her house and serving his needs. Mary, on the other hand, sits at his feet and listens to his teaching. Jesus does not disparage hospitality, but chides Martha for her worry about it. He also proclaims as necessary and good the path Mary chose. In so doing, Jesus' words stand against countless cultures who assert that a woman's place is in the kitchen. A woman's place, he says, is first and foremost as a disciple. John records Mary in the same position when she anoints Jesus' feet with costly perfume (Jn 11:2; 12:3). John also shares the story of the death of their brother Lazarus (Jn 11). Jesus weeps with them in their grief, teaches them about his status as the resurrection, and raises their brother. They give a glimpse of Jesus' close relationships and provide templates for faith and discipleship.

Everything from ancient Gnostic texts to contemporary films have hinted at a particularly intimate relationship between Jesus and Mary Magdalene, but the New Testament makes no more, and no less, of a claim for her other than that of being a faithful disciple, and this is no small claim at all. Jesus had restored her life when he cast out seven demons from her, and then she became one of the many disciples (male and female) who followed him faithfully (Lk 8:2). Luke specifies that the women gave of their resources to support his ministry. When the twelve—except for John—had abandoned him, Mary Magdalene and a handful of other women were there, at the cross (Mt 27:56; Mk 15:40; Jn 19:25), at the tomb (Mt 27:61; Mk 15:47), and at the resurrection (Mt 28:1; Mk 16:1; Lk 24:10; Jn 20:1, 18). Mary and the other women became the evangelists to the evangelists. If God was truly opposed to women telling the good news to men, Jesus would not have appeared to them first.

EPISTLES

The writings of Paul have a certain reputation for being the foil to Jesus. Whereas Jesus was inclusive, Paul says all the wrong things. A handful of verses get the bulk of the attention: chiefly 1 Timothy 2:8-15; 1 Corinthians 11:2-16; 14:34-35, but also the descriptions of the officers of the church that assume males and the household codes where women are encouraged to submit to their husbands (Eph 5; Col 3; also found in the writings of Peter [1 Pet 3:1-7]). Thankfully, we learned that any dismissive attribution of misogyny to Paul not only misreads these texts, but also willfully ignores others. This is not to ignore that Paul was a man of his own shockingly patriarchal time, but the Spirit who inspired him to write these texts is the same Spirit who participated in the creation of women in the image of God (Gen 1:26-27). The commentary provides specifics on each challenging passage, but we have learned not only to live with, but actually to celebrate the Epistles by keeping these points at the forefront:

Paul wanted women to be educated. As the addressees of the letters are of mixed gender, Paul and the other Epistle writers desire women to learn the deep theology and ethics sent in their correspondence. Even the passages that appear most limiting for women include an affirmation for women learning (1 Tim 2:11; 1 Cor 14:35). Education is a key step in full flourishing.

Paul did not hinder the outpouring of the Spirit and subsequent expression of gifts by women. Luke's history of the church leaves no room for disagreement. At Pentecost, just as Joel prophesied would happen, the Holy Spirit fell on both men and women (Acts 2:17-18). Later in that account the daughters of Philip prophesy (Acts 21:8-9). Paul knows that women are praying and prophesying in the Corinthian congregation and only gives them instructions for how to do so properly (1 Cor 11:5). When the Pauline literature enumerates the gifts of the Spirit in Romans 12, 1 Corinthians 12, and Ephesians 4:11-12, it enumerates *no gender* barriers to the expression of the gifts. Paul works alongside and praises the work of female disciples like Priscilla, Phoebe the deacon, and Junia, who was such a vocal witness for the gospel that she went to prison for it (and whom many interpreters believe to have been an apostle).

Paul argued that the coming of Jesus Christ radically impacted all things, including relationships between men and women. Just as Christ destroyed the barrier wall between Jews and Gentiles on both a future/spiritual and present/practical level and neutralized the power of masters over their Christian siblings, Christ also obliterated the oppressive hierarchy of men over women (Gal 3:28; 1 Cor 11:11).

Christians with many different views on gender roles can affirm these points of agreement. The affirmations create common ground on which all can stand and then respectfully dialogue about different applications of these principles.[9]

NINETEENTH-CENTURY AFRICAN AMERICAN FEMALE HERMENEUTS

Many early African American female biblical interpreters embraced Jesus' and Paul's interactions with women such as those discussed above. They also grasped the importance of women in the New Testament and in the early church, and by doing so seized the significance of these narratives for themselves. These women lived in a time when it was debated whether or not Black people had souls, much less could experience conversion. They also lived in a time when Black people were not considered human, or if human, of an inferior lot. In addition, during this period society deemed enslaved African American people as property. It is important to note the use of biblical texts to deny Blacks' humanity, with White preachers often preaching about the curse of Ham on the African race that supposedly destined them for enslavement, or the mark of Cain, which some White interpreters erroneously espoused as the curse of Black skin on

[9]For additional recent discussions on women and the New Testament, see Nijay Gupta, *Tell Her Story: How Women Led, Taught, and Ministered in the Early Church* (Downers Grove, IL: IVP Academic, 2023); Joy A. Schroeder and Marion Ann Taylor, *Voices Long Silenced: Women Biblical Interpreters Through the Centuries* (Louisville, KY: Westminster John Knox, 2022); Carla Works, *The Least of These: Paul and the Marginalized* (Grand Rapids, MI: Eerdmans, 2020), particularly 52-86.

African Americans. As a result of such views, many Whites believed that African Americans were inferior to them and were supposed to be poor, uneducated, and manual laborers. Thus, many Whites sought to keep Blacks illiterate and enslaved. Against such a racialized environment with its gender and class oppression, Black women like Jarena Lee, Zilpha Elaw, and Julia Foote, dared to speak out and to resist and protest this tridimensional oppression and they did so in many ways, but two of the ways in which they did so was to lift up women in the biblical text and to lift up texts that spoke to their own transformational encounters with the God of Scripture. By engaging Scripture in this manner, they indeed certified the inestimable value of all women, including African American women.

Jarena Lee. Jarena Lee, a nineteenth century preacher (1783–1850[?]), speaks out against church tradition that contradicts the Word of God regarding women preachers and instead lifts up Mary as the first minister: "Did not Mary *first* preach the risen Saviour, and is not the doctrine of the resurrection the very climax of Christianity—hangs not all our hope on this, as argued by St. Paul [1 Cor 15:12-22]? Then did not Mary, a woman, preach the gospel? for she preached the resurrection of the crucified Son of God."[10] Lee argues here that Mary Magdalene is the first preacher, since Paul in 1 Corinthians 15 contends that the resurrection is central to the Christian faith. If this is the case, then Mary becomes the first proclaimer of the gospel because she declares to the disciples that Jesus is risen. Indeed, Mary is an evangelist to the evangelists. In a fascinating exegetical move, Lee utilizes the apostle, often employed to silence women, to condone and sanction women preaching, for Mary proclaims what is in the apostle's eyes the very heart of the gospel. In her autobiography, Lee also makes a bold move by centering the death of Jesus as a death that legitimates a woman's right to preach:

> For as unseemly as it may appear now-a-days for a woman to preach, it should be remembered that nothing is impossible with God. And why should it be thought impossible, heterodox, or improper, for a woman to preach? seeing the Saviour died for the woman as well as the man. If a man may preach, because the Saviour died for him, why not the woman? seeing he died for her also. Is he not a whole Saviour, instead of a half one? as those who hold it wrong for a woman to preach, would seem to make it appear.[11]

Jesus' death for both women and men demonstrate that his death calls both to proclaim this mighty act of God. In fact, Lee's own ministry demonstrates that God calls women, for when she proclaims the gospel, sinners are awakened and converted. She reveals that many families have come to her and professed that through her they came to receive the gospel, and she confesses that God speaks through her, a "poor coloured female instrument."[12]

Zilpha Elaw. A number of these early Black women hermeneuts experienced powerful conversions and often had numerous divine encounters with God, what some today would call mystical experiences. For example, Zilpha

[10]*The Life and Religious Experience of Jarena Lee, a Coloured Lady, Giving an Account of Her Call to Preach the Gospel. Revised and Corrected from the Original Manuscript, Written by Herself* (Philadelphia: 1836), reprinted in William Andrews, *Sisters of the Spirit: Three Black Women's Autobiographies of the Nineteenth Century* (Bloomington: Indiana University Press, 1986), 36. For more detailed discussions regarding Jarena Lee, Zilpha Elaw, and Julia Foote, see Bowens, *African American Readings of Paul.*

[11]Andrews, Sisters of the Spirit, 36.

[12]Andrews, Sisters of the Spirit, 37.

Elaw (1790–?), another early female African American preacher, says of one of her supernatural experiences that she did not know whether she was in the body or outside of the body (echoing Paul's ascent in 2 Cor 12) and that while praying her spirit entered into a heavenly realm. In their autobiographies, women, like Elaw, describe these transformative encounters, how God calls them to preach the gospel, and how they wrestle with this calling due to feelings of inadequacy for the task, and because they knew the opposition they would face, not only because of their gender, but also because of their race. Elaw, although born free, courageously traveled to the slave states to preach the gospel, and she records Whites' astonishment at her presence. "Many of the slave holders . . . thought it surpassingly strange that a person (and a female) belonging to the same family stock with their poor debased, uneducated, coloured slaves, should come into their territories and teach the enlightened proprietors the *knowledge of God* [Rom 11:33; 1 Cor 15:34; 2 Cor 10:5; Col 1:10]. . . . *But God hath chosen the weak things of the world to confound the mighty* [1 Cor 1:27]."[13] Here, Elaw's statements bathed in scriptural language underscore the power of her presence to defy the racist and sexist assumptions of her day. The fact that God chooses what some believe are beyond God's choice, the weak things of the world to confound the mighty, demonstrates the destruction of racial and gender barriers, barriers that society deems permanent.

Julia Foote. Julia Foote (1823–1900) tells of a number of angelic visitations and her experience of accepting the call to preach. She also writes about how her acceptance of this call resulted in her excommunication from her church and severe opposition from women, men, Black, and White. Yet she refused to stop even though some tried to make her believe that her calling was not real. Indeed, Foote appeals to Pentecost in Acts:

> I could not believe that it was a short-lived impulse or spasmodic influence that impelled me to preach. I read that on the day of Pentecost was the Scripture fulfilled as found in Joel ii.28,29; and it certainly will not be denied that women as well as men were at that time filled with the Holy Ghost. . . . Women and men are classed together, and if the power to preach the Gospel is short-lived and spasmodic in the case of women, it must be equally so in that of men.[14]

For Foote, that women and men received the Spirit on Pentecost demonstrated that God intended women as well as men to proclaim the gospel. She goes on to describe Paul's language regarding women: "When Paul said, 'Help those women who labor with me in the Gospel,' he certainly meant that they did more than to pour out tea. . . . Paul gives directions, to men and women, how they should appear when they prophesy or pray in public assemblies; and he defines prophesying to be speaking to edification, exhortation and comfort."[15] The apostle's commands on how women are to appear in public assemblies

[13]*Zilpha Elaw, Memoirs of the Life, Religious Experience, Ministerial Travels and Labours of Mrs. Zilpha Elaw, an American Female of Colour: Together with Some Account of the Great Religious Revivals in America [Written by Herself]* (London: 1846), reprinted in Andrews, *Sisters of the Spirit*, 92. In this quote, Elaw reveals the slaveholders' characterizations of the enslaved (poor, debased, and uneducated) and the way the slaveholders characterize themselves as "enlightened proprietors." Her repetition of their characterizations heightens all the more Whites' astonishment regarding her presence in the South and why, as she relates in her autobiography, she was constantly followed.

[14]Julia Foote, *A Brand Plucked from the Fire: An Autobiographical Sketch by Mrs. Julia A. J. Foote* (Cleveland, OH: W. F. Schneider, 1879), reprinted in Andrews, *Sisters of the Spirit*, 208.

[15]Andrews, Sisters of the Spirit, 209.

when they speak in the congregation means that they are not silent participants or mere hostesses. They are an integral part of the worship service, proclaiming prophetically, "Thus saith the Lord." Foote buttresses her argument by proceeding to speak of women martyrs in the early church who died for the faith. This part of her argument leads her readers to ask, If women can die for the faith, can they not also preach the faith for which they suffer death?

CONCLUSION

Paul's coworkers, Jesus' care, the women as first witnesses of the resurrection, examples of Christian women's lives throughout history, all provide evidence that the New Testament affirms and continues that which stands at the fount of Israel's Scriptures: the image of God present in the creation of females just as it is in males (Gen 1:26-27). As redemption of God's good creation, Jesus Christ has come to save all, sanctify all, empower all, and will redeem all, spirit and body. Women do not lose their identity in Christ, they remain women, but in him by the power of the Spirit they are freed from any false narrative of second-class status any culture might impose on them. The very brief foray into the lives of some of the nineteenth-century Black women preachers illustrates that the biblical text shaped their identity, their call, and their relationship with God and society. They refused to allow society, including the church, to consign them to dehumanizing categories, such as inferior, because of their race or their gender. Does God value men more than women? Our brief examinations of women in the biblical text and African American women hermeneuts of the nineteenth century rings out a resounding no! Or, to use a biblical phrase, *mē genoito* (God forbid!)

Nothing, however, affirms the image of God in humanity with such radical power as that which stands at the heart of the Christian narrative, the incarnation itself. When God deigned to come dwell within creation, God did so by being born of a woman. God entered the world through *her*. Even more, the story told by both Matthew and Luke, vigorously upheld in the doctrinal tradition, affirms that God not only entered the world through her but took his body from her and her alone. The virginal conception is not just a quaint story to reenact at Christmas. It proclaims that God became human and did so by considering the body and life of a woman worthy of the presence of God. Any misreading of the New Testament that insinuates women are "less than" has to stand before the incarnate Lord himself, and will therefore, inevitably have to bow before the one who proclaims in body, word, and deed the inestimable value of women.

ACTS

Jordan J. Cruz Ryan

INTRODUCING ACTS

Acts of the Apostles tells the story of what the author calls "the Way," the movement of believers in Jesus, who they held to be the Jewish Messiah. It narrates the formation of their community in Jerusalem and the expansion of the movement to Jews and non-Jews alike across the Roman Empire. Acts is thus a story of the movement of people and God in the homeland and diaspora, living in conquered, assimilated, and colonized regions. Acts is the sequel to the Gospel of Luke and continues the story of Jesus through his followers. Its setting in the Roman Empire makes it a potential source of hope for people groups who have historically experienced the oppression of imperialism and colonialism.

A FILIPINO AMERICAN BIBLICAL HERMENEUTIC: OUR CONTEXT

I am Tisoy (half-Filipino), born and raised in Canada, and have been transplanted to the United States. The approach that I employ in this commentary requires biblical exegesis in tandem with the exegesis of culture, both ancient and modern. The history of oppression and colonization of the Filipino people looms large in the culture and experience not only of Filipinos in the Philippines, but also of Filipino Americans.[1] Therefore, faithful Filipino American hermeneutics need to be oriented toward decolonization. To any reader who might find the language of decolonizing uncomfortable, I would suggest that what should instead make us feel uncomfortable is the history and legacy of invasion, genocide, and colonization, not the efforts to undo their effects.

The people of what we now call the Philippines were invaded and oppressively colonized by Spain from 1571 until the outbreak of the Philippine Revolution in 1896, in which the Filipino people successfully revolted against Spain, resulting in the Philippine Declaration of Independence in 1898.[2] In the following year, the American imperial conquest of the Philippines, including the Philippine-American war (1899–1902) and the subsequent campaigns of "pacification" (until 1913) began. The American conquest was bloody and rife with atrocities committed against the Filipino people.[3] The number of Filipino lives lost to the American invasion and pacification was extremely high.[4] Some suggest that the mass amount of Filipinos who lost their lives as a result of the

[1]See the seminal work of E. J. R. David, *Brown Skin, White Minds: Filipino -/ American Postcolonial Psychology* (Charlotte, NC: Information Age, 2013), e.g., 37-49.

[2]Classic overviews of this period are found in Teodoro A. Agoncillo, *Introduction to Filipino History* (Quezon City: Garotech, 1974); Renato Constantino, *A History of the Philippines: From the Spanish Colonization to the Second World War* (New York and London: Monthly Review, 1975).

[3]See Luzviminda Francisco, "The First Vietnam War: The U.S.-Philippine War of 1899," *Bulletin of Concerned Asian Scholars* 5, no. 4 (1973): 2-16.

[4]E.g., Francisco, "The First Vietnam War," 14.

Philippine-American war and its aftereffects should be understood as a genocide.[5] During the war and the years that followed, Filipinos were inaccurately depicted in America as a people needing to be civilized, unworthy of self-government, as "ignorant," as "savages,"[6] needing to be educated and evangelized. These depictions and attitude toward Filipinos have contributed to the formation of the context in which Filipino Americans find themselves today. For Filipino Americans, it is long past time to move away from thinking of Spain as our "Roman empire." Spain is our Babylon, Japan is our Parthia, America is our Rome, and we are living in the midst of it.

The historical and ongoing racism and oppression faced by Filipinos in America is well documented.[7] Filipino Americans experience racism in America at an alarming rate, with 99% directly experiencing a racist event on a regular basis.[8] E. J. R. David's work has brought the harmful psychological effects of the "colonial mentality" in the Filipino American context to light.[9] Colonial mentality is internalized oppression that comes as a result of centuries of colonization and outward oppression.[10] Recently, Gabriel Catanus has shown that this same concept can be extended to Filipino American faith, terming it "colonial spirituality," defined as "manifestations of the colonial mentality in Filipino American spirituality and religious practices."[11] This underscores the pressing need for a decolonial reading and approach to biblical interpretation for the Filipino American community.

Filipino and Filipino American history is marked by incredible stories of resistance to oppression both at home and in the diaspora. To quote the historian Renato Constantino, "Filipino resistance to colonial oppression is the unifying thread of Philippine history."[12] Filipinos have something unique to offer to the global church as a result of those experiences.[13] It is particularly important to recall the nonviolent People Power Revolution of 1986 that toppled the US-backed, neocolonial Marcos regime. The revolution was theologically informed and heavily involved church leadership.[14] Filipino *American* history also bears witness to remarkable resistance to oppression. Filipino Americans were major leaders in twentieth century labor organization, protecting the rights of workers who experienced injustice and oppression.[15] From the canneries of Alaska and Seattle to the sugar plantations of Hawaii, to the asparagus fields and grape vineyards of

[5]E.g., Floro Quibuyen, "Rizal and Filipino Nationalism: Critical Issues," *Philippine Studies* 50, no. 2 (2002): 193-229 (220-23); Dylan Rodríguez, *Suspended Apocalypse: White Supremacy, Genocide, and the Filipino Condition* (Minneapolis and London: University of Minnesota Press, 2010), 120-39; or alternatively, as a race war, cf. Paul A. Kramer, "Race-Making and Colonial Violence in the U.S. Empire: The Philippine-American War as Race War," *Diplomatic History* 30, no. 2 (2006): 169-210.

[6]Yen Le Espiritu, *Filipino American Lives Across Cultures, Communities, and Countries* (Berkeley and Los Angeles: University of California Press, 2003), 52-53; Rodríguez, *Suspended Apocalypse*, 120-39.

[7]For a brief introduction, see David, *Brown Skin, White Minds*, 37-49. On historical oppression of Filipino Americans, see also Fred Cordova, *Filipinos, Forgotten Asian Americans: A Pictorial Essay, 1763-Circa 1963* (Dubuque, IA: Kendall/Hunt, 1983), 115-21.

[8]Alvin N. Alvarez and Linda P. Juang, "Filipino Americans and Racism: A Multiple Mediation Model of Coping," *Journal of Counseling Psychology* 57, no. 2 (2010): 167-78.

[9]David, *Brown Skin, White Minds*, 51-154

[10]David, *Brown Skin, White Minds*, 76.

[11]Gabriel J. Catanus, "Uncovering a FACE: Filipino American Christian Ethics," PhD diss., (Loyola University, 2021), 142.

[12]Renato Constantino, *A History of the Philippines: From the Spanish Colonization to the Second World War* (New York: Monthly Review, 2008), 9.

[13]I am indebted to Rei Lemuel Crizaldo for this idea.

[14]See (e.g.) Edicio de la Torre, *Touching Ground, Taking Root: Theological and Political Reflections on the Philippine Struggle* (Manila: Socio-Pastoral Institute, 1986).

[15]Cordova, *Filipinos, Forgotten Asian Americans*, 73.

California,[16] Filipino Americans have fought passionately for justice and resisted oppression through action and activism. We bring that ongoing history of resistance with us to our reading of Scripture, and carry the Bible's messages of redemption, freedom, and subversion with us in our struggle to thrive and survive in diaspora.[17] This Filipino struggle to resist, survive, and thrive is what has given birth to the "theology of struggle," a theological tradition distinct to the Philippines. The signature feature of this tradition is the idea that, like Jesus who suffered, but whose suffering had meaning and purpose, and whose suffering resisted the powers that be, those who suffer due to oppression, poverty, or coloniality can refuse to suffer passively and instead struggle in the midst of their suffering.[18]

As Joaquin Jay Gonzalez III has shown in his ethnographic study on the Filipino American church (both Catholic and Protestant), the Filipino American community expresses its faith in action through civic engagement and activism, taking action against various injustices.[19] Christian faith has historically played a major role in Filipino American activism.[20] Gonzalez describes the activities of the Filipino American church in terms of the concepts of *kasamahan* and *bayanihan*. *Kasamahan* is community organization referring to "the inward-focused kinship and ethnic ties and relationships that Filipino American churches help to establish and nurture," and *bayanihan* is community action, "the church-inspired, outward linkages and networks that Filipino American groups use to engage and contribute to U. S. and Philippine society."[21]

Filipino Americans are the third largest Asian American ethnic group in the United States, behind only Chinese Americans and Indian Americans. Recent census data shows that there are over 4 million Filipinos in the United States,[22] and that almost 1 in 5 Asian Americans are Filipino.[23] Despite this, Filipino Americans are extremely underrepresented and marginalized across the various facets of American public life and are regarded as "forgotten Asian Americans."[24] This underrepresentation extends to higher education.[25] There

---

[16]Cordova, *Filipinos, Forgotten Asian Americans*, 73-81.

[17]For an example of a hermeneutic of resistance in the Philippine context, see Lily Fetalsana-Apura, *A Filipino Resistance Reading of Joshua 1:1–9*, International Voices in Biblical Studies 9 (Atlanta: SBL Press, 2019).

[18]For an excellent overview of the theology of struggle, see Lisa Asedillo, "The Theology of Struggle: Critiques of Church and Society in the Philippines (1970s–1990s)," *Indonesian Journal of Theology* 9, no. 1 (2021): 62-92; cf. de la Torre, *Touching Ground*; Fernandez, *Toward a Theology of Struggle*.

[19]E.g., see the chapter conclusions in Gonzalez, *Filipino American Faith in Action*, 146-48, 1174-177.

[20]See, for example, the connection between Christianity and labor organization in Gonzalez, *Filipino American Faith in Action*, 54.

[21]Gonzalez, *Filipino American Faith in Action*, 9-10.

[22]United States Census Bureau, "Selected Population Profile in the United States: Filipino alone or in any combination," 2018.

[23]Supplementing the census data cited above, see also Gustavo López, Neil G. Ruiz, and Eileen Patten, "Key facts about Asian Americans, a diverse and growing population," *Pew Research Center*, 2017, www.pewresearch.org/fact-tank/2017/09/08/key-facts-about-asian-americans/; E. J. R. David, "Why Are Filipino Americans Still Forgotten and Invisible?" *Psychology Today*, 2016, www.psychologytoday.com/us/blog/unseen-and-unheard/201604/why-are-Filipino-Americans-still-forgotten-and-invisible.

[24]See, e.g., David, "Still Forgotten and Invisible"; Erwin S. de Leon and Gem P. Daus, "Filipino American Political Participation," *Politics, Groups, and Identities* 6, no. 3 (2018): 435-52; Allan Aquino, "Filipino Americans," in *Encyclopedia of Asian American Issues Today*, ed. Edith Wen-Chu and Grace J. Yoo (Santa Barbara, CA: Greenwood Press, 2010), 25-30; James A. Tyner, "Filipinos: The Invisible Ethnic Community," in *Contemporary Ethnic Geographies in America*, ed. Ines M Miyares and Christopher A. Airriess (Lanham, MD: Rowman & Littlefield, 2007), 251-70; Rick Bonus, *Locating Filipino Americans: Ethnicity and the Cultural Politics of Space* (Philadelphia: Temple University Press, 2000), 1-2. *Filipinos, Forgotten Asian Americans*, esp. Cordova's prologue on p. xiii.

[25]Jonathan Y. Okamura and Amefil R. Agbayani, "Pamantasan: Filipino American Higher Education," in *Filipino Americans: Transformation and Identity*, ed. Maria P. P. Root (Thousand Oaks, London, and New Delhi: Sage, 1997), 183-97.

are very few New Testament scholars of Filipino descent in permanent positions in colleges and universities, and even fewer who work in Christian confessional settings. Despite this, 89% of Filipinos in America are Christians, 65% being Catholic and 21% being Protestant.[26] While Filipino Americans are well represented in the Kingdom of God, we have not been given a voice or a seat at the table when it comes to the interpretation of Christian Scripture.

This shows that invisibility is a hallmark of the Filipino American experience. We carry this invisibility with us in our reading of the text, and the experiences of marginalization that come with it. This means that a Filipino American hermeneutic involves identification with the representation of marginality, marginalization, and marginalized people in Scripture. It also means that we should look and listen carefully to the text of Acts and its depiction of the marginality of the early church, the Jewish communities of the Mediterranean diaspora, and of various characters in the narrative in order to gain theological insight into how we might deal with the marginalization that we face as Filipino Americans in the church and in the academy today.

To summarize, a Filipino American hermeneutic for biblical interpretation will be 1) oriented toward an understanding of coloniality and imperialism in the biblical world and in ours; 2) committed to challenging and undoing the harmful effects of coloniality and imperialism; 3) grounded in contextual insights and issues drawn from Filipino and Filipino American history, making use of our counter-colonial and anti-oppressive historiographical traditions in our encounters with the Bible; 4) an instantiation of the Filipino theology of struggle, but transposed to the Filipino diaspora in the United States; 5) rooted in and attentive to the communal, collectivist nature of our culture; and 6) a recognition of and challenge to invisibility in our world and in the biblical world.

THE AUTHOR AND DATE

The author of Acts is the same person who wrote the Gospel of Luke. Acts begins by mentioning and summarizing the author's "first book" (Acts 1:1-2), and identifies "Theophilus," who is also the addressee of the Gospel of Luke, as the addressee of the work. The author wrote in Greek and was skilled with the language. Throughout the narratives of Luke and Acts, they also display considerable knowledge of Jewish Scripture and culture. In particular, the author displays very good knowledge of ancient synagogues,[27] and Luke contains the most material related to synagogues of any of the four Gospels.

A group of passages written in the first-person plural (the "we-passages") in the second half of Acts imply that the narrator was a companion of Paul for those parts of his travels. These passages suggest that the author traveled with Paul on these occasions. Patristic sources identify the author of Luke–Acts as "Luke," who was a companion of Paul.[28] According to the Anti-Marcionite Preface, he was an Antiochean Syrian, and according to the Muratorian Fragment, he was "zealous for the Law" (4-5). The name "Luke" is mentioned in the New Testament in Colossians 4:14, 2 Timothy 4:11, and Philemon 24. If Colossians 4:14 refers to the author of Luke–Acts, then it appears to exclude him from a group of

[26]Pew Research Center, "Asian Americans: A Mosaic of Faiths," 2012, www.pewforum.org/2012/07/19/asian-americans-a-mosaic-of-faiths-overview/.

[27]See Jordan J. Ryan, *The Role of the Synagogue in the Aims of Jesus* (Minneapolis: Fortress, 2017), 171-205, 219-32.

[28]E.g., Irenaeus, *Against Heresies*, 3.1.1.

Paul's coworkers who are "of the circumcision" (Col 4:11). Although other interpretations are possible, this is frequently taken as evidence that Luke was not circumcised. The author of Acts is thus often considered to be a "God-fearer," a non-Jew who was associated with the synagogue. However, the possibility that the author was Jewish cannot be ruled out.

Scholars tend to date Acts to one of three ranges: pre-70 CE; 70–90 CE; or 90–130 CE.[29] The strongest argument for the late dating depends on the hypothesis that Luke knew and used Josephus' *Antiquities* (ca. 93 CE), particularly in his discussions of Jewish revolutionary figures (i.e., Judas the Galilean, Theudas, the Egyptian).[30] While there are parallels between the discussion of these revolutionaries in Luke–Acts and *Antiquities*, direct dependence creates more problems than it solves. There is disagreement between the two in terms of the chronology of Judas and Theudas (Acts 5:36-37), and their accounts of the Egyptian are also substantially different (Acts 21:38).[31] The parallels could be explained in other ways, such as shared sources, commonly circulating knowledge of relatively recent events in the region, or even Josephus's dependence on Luke (though this is unlikely for the reasons above). I consider the late dating to be improbable, or at least based on tendentious foundations. The middle date is primarily based on the interpretation that Luke 19:43-44 refers to the destruction of Jerusalem, which took place in 70 CE and his likely use of Mark, which mentions the destruction of the Temple (Mk 13:32). The strongest argument for the early date is the ending of Acts, which concludes with Paul in prison, but does not mention his death. If the middle date is correct, then Luke–Act looks back on and reflects on the violent revolution and its horrific results, and if the early date is correct, then Acts is written during a time of rising political tension and revolutionary sentiment in the Jewish homeland.

GENRE

Acts follows common Greco-Roman conventions for history writing. However, Luke routinely cites the Jewish Scriptures, and was probably heavily influenced by the historical narratives of the Septuagint, the Greek translation of the Jewish Scriptures. Acts is thus most comparable to Greco-Roman works of history in the Jewish tradition, such as 1-2 Maccabees.[32]

SETTING: CITIES OF THE ROMAN EMPIRE

The story of Acts takes place across the cities of the Roman Empire. Luke's history of the early church is thus an *urban* story, set in places that are ethnically and socio-economically diverse and that experienced Roman imperial domination. Many of the cities featured in Acts are also literal Roman colonies, meaning that they were settled or resettled by a core of Roman military personnel and elites in order to establish political or military control of a region and to reward veterans with land.[33] Roman provincial cities were filled with the architecture of empire, blending the grandeur of Roman forms with local traditions.

[29]See Karl Armstrong, *Dating Acts in its Jewish and Greco-Roman Contexts* (London and New York: T&T Clark, 2021); Jonathan Bernier, *Rethinking the Dates of the New Testament* (Grand Rapids, MI: Baker Academic, 2022).

[30]Steve Mason, *Josephus and the New Testament*, 2nd ed. (Peabody, MA: Hendrickson, 2003), 234-35.

[31]See discussion in Bernier, *Rethinking*; and Armstrong, *Dating Acts*, 86-93.

[32]Cf. Osvaldo Padilla, *The Acts of the Apostles: Interpretation, History and Theology* (Downers Grove, IL: IVP Academic, 2016), 62-72.

[33]See Charles Gates, *Ancient Cities: The Archaeology of Urban Life in the Ancient Near East and Egypt, Greece, and Rome*, 2nd ed. (London and New York: Routledge, 2011), 335.

CRITICAL ISSUES

Luke–Acts and Roman Imperialism. Luke's stance toward Roman imperialism is disputed.[34] Some scholars interpret Luke–Acts as an apologetic work meant to demonstrate that the church was not a political danger to Roman interests, or even as a relatively pro-Roman text. Others read Luke–Acts as resisting or critiquing of Roman imperialism to various degrees.

In my opinion, Acts is literature of survival written for a multiethnic minority group made up primarily of dominated peoples living amid the empire that dominated them. Followers of the Way had to resist assimilation as well as pressure from local authorities and from members of the majority culture. Acts depicts followers of Jesus being arrested by various authorities no less than eleven times in total. The protagonists are frequently regarded by their accusers as disturbing the established societal order: they are "turning the world upside-down" (Acts 17:6). This makes good sense if we remember that Luke's Gospel presents us with a vision of the Reign of God as a great reversal, an upside-down Kingdom in which the lowly are elevated and rulers are cast down from their thrones (Lk 1:52), in which the first are last and the last are first (Lk 13:30), and in which the poor are blessed and the rich are woeful (Lk 6:20, 24).

When Paul is arrested in Jerusalem, Luke insists on Paul's innocence. However, his innocence illuminates the injustice of the Roman order and the corruption of Roman officials, as Paul is imprisoned for almost five years without being convicted of a crime. With the exception of Sergius Paulus (Acts 13:7, 12), Luke's portrayal of Roman authorities is generally negative. If Luke wrote Acts to demonstrate that the Way is compatible with Roman interests, then he did not do a very good job. It is much more likely that Acts was written for believers in Jesus who could expect to experience hardships like those faced by Peter, Stephen, Jason, Paul, Silas, and Barnabas than it was for Roman authorities.

Luke–Acts does not overtly advocate the violent overthrow of Rome. However, that does not mean it must be pro-imperial. Acts neither encourages revolt nor assimilation, but instead presents its readers with the challenge of living faithfully in the midst of empire, which requires resistance by necessity, but also *survival*. Here, the Filipino American experience is relevant. As Filipino Americans, our context requires us to resist oppressive systems as well as assimilation to the imperial theology of the "American dream," while nevertheless living and thriving in the colonizer's house. This necessitates a way of peaceful and faithful resistance rather than violent revolution. Our Exodus is toward our Egypt,[35] just as Paul's is toward Rome. Acts is not a Scriptural instantiation of colonial mentality, and the Way was no model minority.

Acts and Judaism (or Acts Within Judaism?). Acts sometimes depicts Jews persecuting or posing a danger to the protagonists and other followers of Jesus. As a result, Acts has lamentably been read through the lens of Christendom and supersessionism in order to support anti-Judaism and antisemitism. It should go without saying that nothing can or should ever justify anti-Judaism or antisemitism. The danger of anti-Judaism will be confronted throughout our reading of Acts.

There is growing recognition in scholarship that Acts presents the early church as being in

[34]For a good overview, see Drew J. Strait, "The Gospel of Luke," in *The State of New Testament Studies: A Survey of Recent Research*, ed. Scot McKnight and Nijay K. Gupta (Grand Rapids, MI: Baker Academic, 2019), 315-33 (322-29).

[35]Eleazar S. Fernandez, "Exodus-Toward-Egypt: Filipino-Americans' Struggle to Realize the Promised Land in America," in *A Dream Unfinished: Theological Reflections on America from the Margins* (Maryknoll, NY: Orbis, 2001), 167-81.

continuity with Judaism rather than breaking with it. The primary protagonists of Acts, Peter and Paul, are Jews who place themselves firmly within their Judaism (e.g., Acts 15:7-11; 24:14; 28:17). Indeed, Paul says that "according to the Way, which they call a sect, I worship the God of our ancestors, believing everything laid down according to the law or written in the prophets" (Acts 24:14). In the latter chapters, Luke directly presents the accusations leveled against Paul by his fellow Jews as an internal dispute (Acts 25:19). Internal division and critique are themselves a part of the Jewish Scriptural tradition as well as Second Temple literature. However, when a text like Acts is read in thoroughly non-Jewish Christian contexts in which Jews are "others," especially through the lens of Christendom, interpretation can too easily fall into anti-Judaism. We can combat this by recovering the historical context of the protagonists of the story, by reading the Peter and Paul of Acts as being within Judaism and Acts itself as being either within or at least in continuity with Judaism.[36]

ROOTS IN THE PROCLAMATION OF JESUS (ACTS 1:1-5)

Luke begins the second part of his two-volume work by referring the reader back to his first book, in which he "wrote about all that Jesus began to do and teach" (Acts 1:1). Beginning a new volume with a reference to previous ones was common in the ancient world (e.g., Polybius, *Histories* 2.1; 3.1).[37] By opening his second volume in this way and by directly drawing the reader's mind back to the end of his Gospel, Luke situates his story of the early church in direct continuity with Jesus' actions and teachings.

Just as Luke roots the life of the ancient church in the deeds, teaching, suffering, and resurrection of Jesus, so too should Christian readers today who identify with Luke's original audience see the life of the church today as rooted in those same things. The reference to the "suffering" of Jesus in Acts 21:3 is significant for the Filipino American context. The memory and depiction of Jesus as one who suffers has been an important image for Filipinos (and by extension, Filipino Americans), who identify in their suffering as a historically oppressed people with the suffering Jesus and who can also draw hope from the image of the risen Jesus, who presented himself to his disciples *after* his suffering.[38] The Jesus in whom Luke roots the story of the church is not only the victorious Jesus but a Jesus who suffered and overcame. Luke depicts Jesus as someone who "struggles," meaning that his suffering has purpose (Lk 9:22; 18:31-33; 24:25-27), and who overcomes and rises again (Lk 24:5).[39] The image of Jesus crucified, one whose suffering is purposeful and not passive, is a prevalent image for Filipino Christians and was a key symbol of inspiration during the People Power Revolution, a movement in the homeland that extended to the Filipino American community as well.[40] Christ crucified continues to be the most important image of Jesus among the Filipino people.

---

[36]Naturally, this will depend on how the reader views Luke's identity, whether it is a Jewish believer in Jesus, a Gentile convert, or a Gentile "Godfearer" with close proximity to Judaism.

[37]See Craig S. Keener, *Acts: An Exegetical Commentary*, 4 vols. (Grand Rapids, MI: Baker Academic, 2012), 1:651.

[38]See Fernandez, *Toward a Theology of Struggle*, 98-105.

[39]Fernandez, *Toward a Theology of Struggle*, 103.

[40]See Allan J. Delotavo, "A Reflection on the Images of Christ in Filipino Culture," *Asia Journal of Theology* 3, no. 2 (1989): 524-31; Delotavo, "Images of Christ in Filipino Culture and Atonement Experiences: A Case in the Contextualization of the Gospel Message," *Asia Journal of Theology* 15, no. 1 (2001): 140-50; James Zarsadiaz, "Raising Hell in the Heartland: Filipino Chicago and the Anti-martial Law Movement, 1972–1986," *American Studies* 56 (2017): 141-62.

The resurrected Jesus appears to the apostles and speaks specifically about the kingdom of God (Acts 1:3). This casts the reader's mind back to the mission and proclamation of the kingdom of God in Luke's Gospel. The "good news of the kingdom" (Lk 4:43) that Jesus proclaimed in the synagogues of Galilee entails good news for the poor, release to captives, recovery of sight for the blind, and freedom for the oppressed (Lk 4:18).[41] It is a kingdom that belongs to the poor (Lk 6:20) and is difficult for the rich to enter (Lk 18:24-25). It is important for Christians today, especially those from people groups who have experienced oppression, erasure, and invisibility, not to forget that the Christian community is rooted in the proclamation of *this* kingdom, a kingdom that belongs to the marginalized rather than to the powerful.

A CALL TO FAITHFULNESS IN THE MIDST OF EMPIRE (ACTS 1:6-11)

The apostles gather with the risen Jesus at a moment positively dripping with eschatological expectation. Their question, "Lord, is this the time when you will restore the kingdom to Israel?" reflects a yearning for liberation from colonial oppression (Acts 1:6; see Lk 24:21). There is a stark contrast between the hope for restoration expressed by the apostles as members of a colonized people and the imperial nationalism of a colonial nation. A decolonized Filipino American reading of the apostles' question about the restoration of the kingdom to Israel recognizes the yearning for freedom from oppression in the form of independence from a colonial power. Jesus' response (Acts 1:7) is not a rejection of the apostles' hope for restoration.[42] The problem is with the timing and not with the content of their hope.[43] Jesus redirects the apostles' attention and efforts toward *witness* (Acts 1:8). Being Jesus' witnesses will involve the realization of the radical, socially transformative teachings of Jesus as depicted in Luke in community as well as verbal proclamation. Because the hope for the restoration of the kingdom to Israel had not been realized, it is clear that Jesus' instruction to witness in occupied Jerusalem, Judea, Samaria, and the ends of the earth would necessarily require the apostles to live faithfully in the midst of empire.[44] Contemporary Filipino American followers of Jesus have to navigate the challenge of being a faithful witness in the midst of colonized spaces.

Jesus is taken up by a cloud, and the apostles are informed that he "will come in the same way as you saw him go into heaven" (Acts 1:11).[45] This scene evokes the Danielic vision of the Son of Man "coming with the clouds of heaven" to the Ancient of Days, to whom "dominion and glory and kingship" is given, "that all peoples, nations, and languages should serve him," an everlasting dominion (Dan 7:13-14). Luke's description of the "taking up" of Jesus is thus a reminder and symbol of his eternal kingship over all peoples, nations, and languages.

Acts 1:6-11 communicates that, whatever the political circumstances may be on earth, the apostles are commissioned to be faithful witnesses in the midst of them. Moreover, even in the midst of oppression and colonization,

[41]See Jordan J. Ryan, *The Role of the Synagogue in the Aims of Jesus* (Minneapolis: Fortress, 2017), 190-200.

[42]E.g., C. K. Barrett, *A Critical and Exegetical Commentary on Acts*, International Critical Commentary (Edinburgh: T&T Clark, 2004), 1:77; Mikael C. Parsons, *Acts*, Paideia (Grand Rapids, MI: Baker Academic, 2008), 28; Keener, *Acts*, 1:683.

[43]To paraphrase Keener, *Acts*, 1:683.

[44]See United Church of Canada, "Living Faithfully in the Midst of Empire," Report to the Thirty-Ninth General Council 2006, 32.

[45]Adrian P. Rosen, "The Ascension and Exaltation of Jesus in Lukan Theology," *Asian Journal of Pentecostal Studies* 19, no. 2 (2016): 202.

there is hope. The apostles are commissioned to the struggle of faithful witness in an unjust world. For some of them, it will bring death (e.g., Acts 12:2), imprisonment (e.g., Acts 5:17-42), and murderous threats (Acts 9:1). Like Elisha taking up Elijah's mantle, the apostles are now commissioned to carry on the prophetic ministry that Jesus began in the narrative of Luke's Gospel, a struggle that culminated in death on a Roman cross.[46]

THE RETURN TO JERUSALEM AND MATTHIAS REPLACES JUDAS (ACTS 1:12-26)

The apostles return to Jerusalem (Acts 1:12), just as they were instructed, to the "room upstairs" where they were staying (see Lk 22:12). This small community will form the beginning of the Jerusalemite church. Women were included among the earliest community, and Mary the mother of Jesus is specifically named as being among them (Acts 1:14). In fact, women are named as being among Jesus' followers since his Galilean ministry (Lk 8:2).

The presence of Mary, Jesus' mother, with the community is specifically noteworthy for the Filipino American context. Filipino, and by extension, Filipino American society and Filipino American Christianity are much more matriarchal than Western society.[47] Of Jesus' family members who are present (Acts 1:14), only Mary is named, and this recognizes her importance within the family and within the community. As Joseph Chieh writes, the portrait of Mary in Luke, as one who embodies the liberating message of the Magnificat that she proclaims, "offers hope to millions of Asian women who are struggling to liberate themselves from poverty, racism, classism, the caste system, militarism and all forms of oppression."[48]

The Eleven need to replace Judas, and Matthias is added to their number in his place (Acts 1:15-26). There must be twelve, since Jesus told them that they "will sit on thrones judging the twelve tribes of Israel" (Lk 22:30). An Israel judged by the Twelve is by necessity a liberated Israel, free from the machinations of empires.

THE DAY OF PENTECOST (ACTS 2:1-13)

Jesus' promise is realized at Pentecost (Acts 1:8). Pentecost was celebrated seven weeks after Passover (Lev 23:15-21). It was thus a kind of Sabbath of Sabbaths, a day especially fitting for liberation (see Lk 13:16) and for its proclamation (see Lk 4:16-21).[49]

The very first thing the Holy Spirit empowers the apostles to do is "to speak in other languages, as the Spirit gave them ability" (Acts 2:4). This highlights the importance of language and the cultural translation that comes along with it in Spirit-empowered witness. The crowd is able to hear the apostles speaking in their native languages (Acts 2:8). The people groups listed whose native languages were spoken are not restricted to the Roman Empire but include places beyond the reach of the Roman hegemony, such as Parthia (Acts 2:9-11). The ministry of the Spirit is thus not solely Western-facing but rather radiates out from Jerusalem in all directions.

---

[46]Rosen, "Ascension and Exaltation," 205-6.

[47]From a specifically Filipino American context, see, e.g., Cordova, *Forgotten Asian Americans*, 147-53 (esp. 147-48); Kevin L. Nadal, *Filipino American Psychology: A Handbook of Theory, Research and Clinical Practice* (Hoboken, NJ: Wiley, 2011), 164; David, *Brown Skin, White Minds*, 10-11; Gabriel J. Catanus, "Seeing Mary Jane," *Inheritance* 57 (2017), www.inheritancemag.com/stories/seeing-mary-jane.

[48]Joseph Chieh, "Asian Women's Mariology in Christological Context," *Marian Studies* 46 (1995): 87-88.

[49]Liberation is "the process of salvation and the process of development (humanization)," as stated by Edicio de la Torre, *Touching Ground, Taking Root: Theological and Political Reflections on the Philippine Struggle* (Manila: Socio-Pastoral Institute, 1986), 98.

This scene can be understood in light of the narrative of the tower of Babel in Genesis 11:1-9.[50] It is tempting to view the event of Pentecost as breaking the curse of Babel, as (for example) Gregory of Nazianzus did (*Oration* 41.15-17). However, we must instead recognize Pentecost as a repudiation of all that Babel stood for. It is no coincidence that the tower of Genesis 11:1-9 was called by the same name as the Babylonian empire ("Babel" in Hebrew), or that it was located where that empire eventually took root. The Lord's counteractions against the building of the tower (Gen 11:6-9) were not simply an explanation for the existence of multiple languages. They were a rejection of the monocultural hegemony of Babel and the empire that took root there.[51] In the Canadian church context, the monolingual hegemony of Babel is reminiscent of the horrors of church-run residential schools, where Indigenous children were forbidden to speak their ancestral languages in an attempt to force them to assimilate by erasing their traditional languages and cultures. Similarly, English was imposed on the Philippines by American colonization, such that it is now one of the official languages of the Philippines, while a number of Filipino indigenous languages are endangered. God's action at Babel should not be understood as a curse but instead as life-affirming and liberating.

The gift that is the diversity of languages remains, both in the world as we know it and in the narrative of Acts. According to Acts 2:6, the crowd is not made to understand the apostles' language (likely Aramaic or Hebrew), but instead the apostles speak in the various languages of the crowd. This ensured the multiculturalism and multilingualism of the church from its outset and, if anything, affirms and continues the divine counteractions of Genesis 11:6-9 against monocultural hegemony and the arrogance of the empire-building projects that come with it.

The Spirit-empowered multilingualism of the Pentecost proclamation is a reminder to the Asian American church of the value of its many languages and cultures. Our churches today are multilingual, just as the apostles' proclamation was on that day. Multiple services in different languages are commonplace, allowing the churches to serve broader segments of the Asian American population and to bridge generation gaps while also serving new immigrants. The multilingualism of the Asian American church reflects the situation of the first proclamation at Pentecost and of the first three thousand who made up the initial core of the Jerusalem church (Acts 2:41).

This story also reflects the experience of diaspora peoples in a way that second- and third-generation (and beyond) diaspora Asians can identify with. The loss of language is one of the challenges regularly faced by Filipino Americans and other Asian Americans. Many of us who were born in the diaspora do not speak the language of our parents' homeland fluently or as our first language. Acts 2:5 specifically identifies the crowd as being composed of "Jews from every people under heaven." Rather than hearing the apostles speaking in Aramaic or Hebrew, the diaspora Jews in the crowd "heard them speaking in the native language of each" (Acts 2:6).

---

[50]See, specifically in Asian/Asian American scholarship, Eleazar S. Fernandez, "From Babel to Pentecost: Finding a Home in the Belly of the Empire," *Semeia* 90/91 (2002): 29-50; Amos Yong, "The Future of Evangelical Theology: Asian and Asian American Interrogations," *Asia Journal of Theology* 21, no. 2 (2007): 371-97.

[51]See a similar argument made by Fernandez, "From Babel to Pentecost," 30-32, though Fernandez's argument relies more on historical-critical grounds.

PETER'S SPEECH (ACTS 2:14-40)

Through his citation from Joel (Acts 2:17-20), Peter affirms both that the crowd is witnessing prophecy and the fulfillment of biblical prophecy. Moreover, his citation of this particular passage indicates that the Pentecost event is *eschatological* (Acts 2:17), not because this pouring out of the Spirit will result in the end of the world but because it indicates the end of the present order and the dawning of a new one. This new order is one in which young men and women, and slaves, both men and women, will be filled with the Spirit and prophesy (Acts 2:17-18).[52] In this new eschatological reality, the Spirit is poured out on and empowers all.

Peter follows his citation of Joel with a proclamation of the victory, vindication, and exaltation of the crucified Messiah, who was raised from the dead (Acts 2:23-36). Peter implicates both the hearers of his speech, his fellow Israelites (Acts 2:22), and the Roman authorities, saying, "This man . . . you crucified and killed by the hands of those outside the law" (Acts 2:23). The mention of the direct role played by the Roman authorities is a reminder of the injustice of Jesus' death. People who have lived under the oppression of colonial regimes are all too familiar with the violence that comes to anyone who is perceived as a threat to the colonial order.[53]

Contemporary Christian readers of Acts must actively reject any use of the text to justify anti-Judaism or antisemitism, not simply on the basis of exegesis but also because there is an ethical responsibility to do so.[54] The Jewish crowd's implication in the death of Jesus needs to be understood within the context of the rhetoric of Peter's speech, which seeks to draw the hearers into the narrative. It also cannot be forgotten that Peter holds Gentiles responsible as well (Acts 2:23). Furthermore, Jesus was killed "according to the definite plan and foreknowledge of God." However we interpret this passage, a responsible reader and world citizen understands that none of this can or should ever justify Christian anti-Judaism.

Peter's third point is that Jesus was resurrected (Acts 2:24). He was raised, as the Greek text says, "set loose from the pains of death," because death was unable to keep Jesus under its power. The resurrection demonstrates the ultimate victory of Jesus in his struggle and is a triumph in the face of the injustice of his death. That resurrection and the new order it represents is a source of hope to those who struggle.

My father, who has worked for decades among the poor and homeless of Toronto's inner city, often reminds me that the believers among the homeless and urban poor often identify strongly with the image of Christ's suffering on the cross and that the resurrection is a source of hope for them. This is reflected in the Filipino and Filipino American context as well. As Eleazar Fernandez writes, "The experience of the resurrection is discernible in the lives of the Filipino people who have opted to struggle for a better tomorrow. This is their current situation as well as a hoped-for reality."[55] For Filipino Americans, death's inability to hold Jesus and his victory over injustice through the struggle of the crucifixion and the

[52]Willie James Jennings, *Acts*, Belief: A Theological Commentary on the Bible (Louisville, KY: Westminster John Knox, 2017), 34-35.

[53]See Fernandez, *Toward a Theology of Struggle*, 98-105.

[54]Readers who want to better understand these issues are encouraged to refer to the wealth of literature on Jewish-Christian relations and to listen to Jewish voices. E.g., see Paula Fredrickson and Adele Reinhartz, eds., *Jesus, Judaism and Christian Anti-Judaism: Reading the New Testament After the Holocaust* (Louisville, KY: Westminster John Knox, 2002).

[55]Fernandez, *Toward a Theology of Struggle*, 105.

vindication of the resurrection can serve as a source of hope. This is a hope for the resurrection and victory in the struggle against injustice, marginalization, and oppression that has been undertaken by the Filipino American community throughout our history.[56]

Peter concludes with the declaration that God has made Jesus, who was crucified, "both Lord and Messiah" (Acts 2:36). The paradox of the shame, vulnerability, and suffering represented by crucifixion juxtaposed with Jesus' status as both Lord and Messiah makes this a compelling point for people who have experienced injustice as well as oppression or marginalization. He is a Lord and Messiah who suffers with the people and who struggles in his suffering.[57] In this contrast between David and Jesus there is an instantiation of the upside-down kingdom that the Lukan Jesus proclaimed, a situation in which the first and last are inverted (Lk 13:30) and in which the lowly are exalted (Lk 1:52). In this "political poverty" we see the "powerless power" of the kerygma.[58]

Peter's declaration to "the entire house of Israel" that "this Jesus whom you crucified" (Acts 2:36) has been made Lord and Messiah appears to implicate Israel as a whole in Jesus' death. All of Israel, which includes Peter and the other apostles, did not literally crucify Jesus. Peter's aim is not to indict all of Israel for all time but to call his listeners to repentance.[59] This rhetoric needs to be understood as being *in continuity with* early Judaism, particularly Second Temple Judaism, rather than necessitating an antagonistic break with Judaism. Similar rhetoric about sin and repentance is common in Jewish literature of the Second Temple period (e.g., *Jub.* 1:18-24; *1 En.* 89–90; Bar 1:13–2:10; *Pss. Sol.* 1:1-8; Tob 13:9; 14:4-5) as well as in the prophetic literature of the Jewish Scriptures (e.g., Is 48; Hos 10–11; Zeph 1:2-13; Amos 2:4-16; Jer 3:6-25, to name just a few well-known examples). It should go without saying that none of these texts necessitates or invites an anti-Jewish or antisemitic response.

Finally, Peter connects repentance and baptism in the name of Jesus Christ to forgiveness and the gift of the Holy Spirit (Acts 2:38): "For the promise is for you, for your children, and for all who are far away, everyone whom the Lord our God calls to him" (Acts 2:39). The idea that the promise of salvation is for Jews and for Gentiles is in line with Hebrew Bible and Second Temple period Jewish eschatological expectations (e.g., Is 2:2-4; Tob 14:6).

THE ACTIVITIES OF THE JERUSALEM CHURCH: *KOINŌNIA* AND *BAYANIHAN* (ACTS 2:41-47)

The activities of the early Jerusalem church deeply resonate with the experience of many Filipino American and other Asian immigrant churches. The three thousand who are baptized after Peter's speech (Acts 2:41) habitually "devoted themselves to the apostles' teaching and fellowship, to the breaking of bread and the prayers" (Acts 2:42). The focus on the activities of teaching, fellowship, breaking bread, and prayer signals a group with a robust community life. This diverse group has emerged united. This is the effect of baptism, as Yanan

[56]See Gonzalez, *Filipino American Faith*, 146-48, 172-74, on more recent faith-based activism; see Cordova, *Forgotten Asian Americans*, 73-80, 115-20, on examples of historical organization and resistance; see the essays in Robyn M. Rodriguez, ed., *Filipino American Transnational Activism: Diasporic Politics Among the Second Generation*, Global Southeast Asian Diaspora 1 (Boston: Brill, 2019) on current activism among second-generation Filipino Americans.

[57]See Fernandez, *Toward a Theology of Struggle*, 102-3.

[58]Quoting de la Torre, *Touching Ground*, 94, 96.

[59]See Gene L. Green, *Vox Petri: A Theology of Peter* (Eugene, OR: Cascade, 2019), 268.

Melo writes, "We all rise from the waters as disciples—as followers of Jesus unified in diversity."[60]

The apostles teach the people. We can infer from Acts 2:44-45 that they likely passed on the teachings of Jesus, which would already have been known to the reader from Luke's Gospel. The act of selling goods and giving the proceeds to those in need reflects Jesus' exhortation to "sell all that you own and distribute the money to the poor," a teaching that appears twice in Luke's Gospel (Lk 18:22; see also Lk 12:33).

The communal breaking of bread is reflected in the practice of many contemporary Asian immigrant and Asian American or Asian Canadian churches. Postservice meals are a regular feature of community life in many Asian American and Asian Canadian churches. These communal meals, which often feature Asian food, are crucial for community and identity formation, helping to build the *koinōnia*. Joyce del Rosario's writing on the connections between Filipino potlucks and Filipino American theology underscores the centrality of communal meals to Filipino American culture.[61] It is over these meals that true community building and cultural formation can take place. Joaquin Jay Gonzalez writes, "Within Filipinized churches, food helps build *kasamahan*."[62] The *koinōnia* of the early Jerusalem church and the habitual practice of breaking bread together are connected.

Acts 2:45 reports that all who believed held all things in common and that they sold their possessions and distributed the proceeds "to all, as any had need." This is acting on Jesus' teachings and putting them into practice in community. It is Jesus' exhortation to "sell all that you own and distribute the money to the poor" (Lk 18:22; see Lk 12:33) in action. In this passage is a glimmer of the realized eschatology of the upside-down kingdom, presented here by Luke as an ideal for his readers to strive toward.

The communal spirit represented by the actions of the believers in Acts 2:44-45 finds a recontextual expression in the community orientation of immigrant communities in North America whose cultural values eschew individualism. This is particularly true for Filipino communities, since our culture is so thoroughly communally and family oriented. As Gabriel Catanus writes, Filipino American Christian ethics are in part a "spirituality of belonging."[63] In the *koinōnia* of the Jerusalem church, there is an overlap of the ancient context with our own in the concept of the *bayanihan* spirit, the spirit of community. The term *bayanihan* means "being a community" and is famously expressed in Filipino art and imagination by the image of a community relocating a neighbor's house by carrying it together on their backs using bamboo poles. I vividly remember my mother telling me a story about my grandparents' house being moved in this way, and it has remained with me as an image that expresses core Filipino values. We reflect the biblical practice of the *koinōnia* through our *bayanihan* spirit.

A number of other core Filipino values are related to community. *Kapwa* ("others," or *kapwa-tao*, "other beings") refers to unity with others and the recognition of shared identity,

[60]Yanan Melo, "Coming Home to the River: On Baptism, Displacement, and the Filipina/o Migrant Experience," *Inheritance*, May 27, 2021.

[61]Joyce del Rosario, "Did You Eat? What Filipino/a/x American Theology Brings to the Table," *Faith and Leadership*, January 26, 2021.

[62]Gonzalez, *Filipino American Faith*, 98. By *kasamahan*, Gonzalez specifically means "community organization," "inward-focused kinship and ethnic ties" (9), which is a somewhat particular usage of the term within his research.

[63]Gabriel J. Catanus, "Uncovering a FACE: Filipino American Christian Ethics" (PhD diss., Loyola University, 2021), 149.

and *pakikisama* ("going along with others") refers to prioritizing group goals or maintaining harmony, even if these things are not personally advantageous.[64] *Pakikipagkapwa-tao* is a compound word including elements of both *pakikisama* and *kapwa-tao*, expressing interpresonalism. According to Jove Jim Aguas, "In 'pakikipagkapwa-tao' the other is regarded as a subject or person and there is deep respect for his dignity and inherent worth as a fellow human being" that is "manifested in a basic sense of justice and fairness and in concern for others."[65]

In "Brown Girl Glossary of Terms," Filipino American poet Barbara Jane Reyes includes the term *Pakikipagkapwa-tao*, under which she writes (among other things) "one body together, shouldering a nation. One bamboo hut at a time. One set of lungs breathing. One heart."[66] Practiced within a Christian context, the concept of *bayanihan* and other Filipino values can be a gift to the broader church as expressions and examples of *koinōnia*.

In a 2004 publication, Reta Halteman Finger studied the impact of Western culture on the history of interpretation of the community of goods from Martin Luther through to the dawn of the twenty-first century. She found "significant negative reaction and even hostility toward the intense communal sharing described in these texts. Few commentators except those from Anabaptist traditions respond positively toward these texts as a lifestyle that ought to be emulated in some way by Christians."[67] Western cultural or contextual values including the union of church and state, the abstraction of spiritual qualities, classism, paternalism, commitment to capitalism, and antipathy toward communism all contributed to this surprising antipathy to the community of goods.

I have often seen majority-culture students wrestle mightily with this passage (and Acts 4:32-35) as they attempt to produce interpretations and applications that mitigate or reframe the meaning of the passage so that it means something entirely other than what is intended, or draws clear lines of distinction between the early Jerusalem church and "Marxism" or "socialism." The logic that undergirds this generally seems to be (1) that the passage describes a redistribution of goods according to need (which is correct); (2) that the redistribution of goods on the basis of need is necessarily "Marxist" or "socialist"; (3) American values are Christian values; (4) "Marxism" and "socialism" are contrary to American values; and thus (5) the passage is reinterpreted. This reinterpretation is such that the passage either cannot be describing the actual redistribution of goods, or is viewed not as an ideal but as a problematic practice that will soon be done away with, or is clearly and fundamentally differentiated from "Marxism" or "socialism," as though that distinction were the central preoccupation of the text, which can then be deployed as a critique of Marxism.[68] McCarthyism thereby becomes one of the prevailing hermeneutics of the American church.

---

[64]See V. G. Enriquez, *From Colonial to Liberation Psychology: The Philippine Experience* (Manila: De La Salle University Press, 1994), 45; David, *Brown Skin, White Minds*, 109-10. On *kapwa* theology and the *koinōnia*, see my comments on Acts 4:32-35. For more on *pakikisama*, see David, *Brown Skin, White Minds*, 108, 118.

[65]Jove Jim S. Aguas, "The Filipino Value of Pakikipagkapwa-Tao Vis-À-Vis Gabriel Marcel's Notion of Creative Fidelity and Disponibilitè," *Scientia* 5, no. 2 (2016): 25-26.

[66]Barbara Jane Reyes, "Brown Girl Glossary of Terms," in *Letters to a Young Brown Girl* (Rochester, NY: Boa, 2020), 25.

[67]Reta Halteman Finger, "Cultural Attitudes in Western Christianity Toward the Community of Goods in Acts 2 and 4," *Mennonite Quarterly Review* 78, no. 2 (2004): 235-70 (266).

[68]See the interpretation of H. C. Macgregor, "Acts," in *The Interpreter's Bible*, ed. George Arthur Buttrick (New York: Abingdon, 1951), 9:73. See a response to the problematic reading of this passage in Justo L. González, *Acts: The Gospel of the Spirit* (Maryknoll, NY: Orbis, 2001), 71-73.

This misguided McCarthyist exegetical endeavor is an instantiation of the syncretistic blending of Christianity with American civil religion, or what Jonathan P. Walton more provocatively terms "White American Folk Religion" (WAFR).[69] As Walton writes, "WAFR requires the exchange of the kingdom of God for the United States of America."[70] The desire to map New Testament practice and theology onto the orthodoxy of American civil religion will only result in distorting and stretching New Testament teaching in order to dress American civil religion in its skin.

A BEGGAR AT THE TEMPLE (ACTS 3:1-10)

This episode contrasts the grandeur of public monuments with the reality of poverty as Peter and John encounter a beggar at one of the gates of the temple complex. The disparity between the experience of the beggar and the splendor of the temple is better interpreted as a representation of the reality of urban poverty, wherein the city's destitute frequent and populate public space, than as an explicit critique of the Jewish temple itself, which soon becomes the site of the apostles' public preaching. Archaeological studies have laid bare some of the experience of ancient urban poverty, revealing an existence marked by low life expectancy, malnutrition, squalor, parasites, disease, appalling living conditions for those who had dwelling places, and poor food quality.[71]

The man is brought by others to a key public space in Jerusalem so that he can request alms from people passing by. Nothing in the text indicates that he was barred from the temple courts due to his disability. Aiding those in need was an important dimension of early Jewish thought and practice, both in Second Temple sources and in the teachings of the rabbis.[72] To take just one example from each, Tobit 4:6-7 states, "To all those who practice righteousness give alms from your possessions," and Yose bar Yohanan of Jerusalem teaches, "Seat the poor at your table" (Mishnah *Avot* 1:5).

Peter and John are intentional about making eye contact with the man. My father, who has worked with the homeless and urban communities in need for close to forty years, taught me from a young age to outwardly acknowledge the value and human dignity of street and street-involved people. There is little doubt that the destitute of the ancient world experienced being ignored and treated as less than human. The instruction to "look at us" calls the man to meet Peter and John's stare and make eye contact, drawing the attention of and acknowledging someone who is used to being ignored.[73]

By healing in the name of Jesus, Peter is continuing the ministry of healing that Jesus himself undertook in the Gospel of Luke. Jesus'

---

[69]Jonathan P. Walton, *Twelve Lies That Hold America Captive: And the Truth That Sets Us Free* (Downers Grove, IL: InterVarsity Press, 2019), 17. See, e.g., Peter Gardella, *American Civil Religion: What Americans Hold Sacred* (Oxford: Oxford University Press, 2014); Raymond Haberski Jr., *God and War: American Civil Religion Since 1945* (New Brunswick, NJ: Rutgers University Press, 2012).

[70]Walton, *Twelve Lies*, 17.

[71]See Jinyu Liu, "Urban Poverty in the Roman Empire: Material Conditions," in *Paul and Economics: A Handbook*, ed. Thomas R. Blanton IV and Raymond Pickett (Minneapolis: Fortress, 2017), 23-56. On life expectancy and osteoarchaeology, see David A. Fiensy, *Insights from Archaeology* (Minneapolis: Fortress, 2017), 99-128. On poverty specifically in Roman Palestine, see Gildas Hamel, *Poverty and Charity in Roman Palestine: The First Three Centuries C.E.*, 2nd ed. (Berkeley: University of California Press, 2019), esp. 41-45 (on the diet of beggars), 58-60 (on disease and death); Keener, *Acts*, 2:1056-59.

[72]E.g., B. Z. Rosenfeld and H. Perlmutter, "The Attitude to Poverty and the Poor in Early Rabbinic Sources (70–250 CE)," *Journal for the Study of Judaism* 47 (2016): 411-38. On poverty from a theological and Filipino perspective, see Melba Padilla Maggay, *Rise Up and Walk: Religion and Culture in Empowering the Poor* (Oxford: Regnum, 2015).

[73]See Joseph A. Fitzmyer, *Acts of the Apostles: A New Translation with Introduction and Commentary*, AYB 31 (New Haven and London: Yale University Press, 1998), 278.

mission of healing, the restoration of the body, is part of the realization of the kingdom of God.[74] It is an outpouring of the renewal and blessings that come with the reign of God. Where God reigns, there is healing. The healing is done freely, without expectation of compensation. Health care and healing, especially for those in need, are values central to Filipino American identity, values that are embodied in the tireless work of Filipino health-care workers in North America, including my own mother.[75] Within a Christian context, we can understand the selfless work of healing and care to be kingdom work done in imitation of Jesus, just as the apostles imitate Jesus by carrying on his work of healing.

PETER SPEAKS AT SOLOMON'S PORTICO (ACTS 3:11-26)

Peter denies that it is by their own power or piety that the man is able to walk (Acts 3:12). Instead, he speaks out against and names the injustice of Jesus' death (Acts 3:13-15). He specifically names the injustice of the release of Barabbas, a man with blood on his hands, over Jesus (see Lk 23:13-25). Peter's focus on this particular injustice does not absolve the Roman colonizers of their role but highlights the role played by the people. It is in the name of this Jesus, who suffered a deep injustice, that the man has been healed (Acts 3:16). Saying the name of *this* victim of injustice has power.

The incident Peter raises here is a miscarriage of justice. It is crucial to resolve that we can recognize this as an injustice *and also* not regard that injustice as justification for Christian acts of anti-Judaism or antisemitism. In the midst of naming this injustice, Peter refers to "the God of Abraham and Isaac and Jacob" as "the God of our ancestors" (Acts 3:13), which clearly situates him *within* ethnic Israel, not apart from it. Furthermore, Peter acknowledges that the people acted out of ignorance, as did their rulers (Acts 3:17), and that through this God was able to fulfill the prophecies of messianic suffering (Acts 3:18). Nevertheless, Peter still names and addresses the matter. Injustices that result from ignorance must also be confronted.

The apostles will continue to persist in naming this injustice throughout the story. This speaks deeply to Filipino Americans, whose long history of activism and speaking out in the homeland and diaspora against injustice has made us the rabble-rousers of Asian America.[76] Filipino Americans have recently been particularly visible and vocal in taking to the streets in protest against anti-Asian violence, reviving the activist slogan "Isang Bagsak!" and encouraging our fellow Asian brothers and sisters with the admonition "Mabuhay!" ("Live!").[77] When we march to speak truth to power, we follow in the footsteps not only of Carlos Bulosan, Larry Itliong, Liliosa Hilao, and José Rizal but also the apostles.

Peter's call to repentance (Acts 3:19) is accompanied by an invitation to participate in the coming eschatological renewal and restoration centered on the person of Jesus, the Messiah (Acts 3:20-21). The call to repentance is thus accompanied by a message of hope for

[74]Ryan, *Role of the Synagogue*, 209.

[75]On Filipino health-care workers in North America, see Catherine Ceniza Choy, *Empire of Care: Nursing and Migration in Filipino American History* (Durham, NC: Duke University Press, 2003). Filipinos make up a disproportionate number of health care workers in the US.

[76]See Zarsadiaz, "Raising Hell"; Jordan J. Ryan, "No Model Minority, Part II: Filipino Americans, the Bible, and Resisting Racism," *Reclaim*, January 12, 2021.

[77]"Isang Bagsak!" means literally "one down," a cry of solidarity followed by a clap in unison used by Filipino worker-activists in cooperation with Mexican colleagues during the Delano Grape Strike.

restoration, which has been so vividly illustrated for the crowd through the bodily restoration of the man who could not walk (Acts 3:9, 11). The promise of restoration would likely have resonated with Peter's Jewish audience, who were under the colonial authority of the Roman Empire and whose ancestors had endured the machinations and rule of various imperial powers and kingdoms for centuries.

Peter speaks of "universal restoration" (Acts 3:21), the same restoration announced by the prophets (e.g., Is 2:4; 49:6). This is not a new development but a realization of what had always been God's plan, which is for the good of all peoples.

PETER AND JOHN ARE ARRESTED (ACTS 4:1-4)

Peter and John are arrested in the midst of their public speech (Acts 4:1). The stated reason for this is that the temple authorities listed in Acts 4:1 are greatly disturbed "because they were teaching the people and proclaiming that in Jesus there is the resurrection of the dead" (Acts 4:2). Jesus was arrested by the priests and officers of the temple police (Lk 22:52), and subsequently condemned and executed by the Roman authorities (Lk 23:24, 33) under the accusation that he had been stirring up sedition, forbidding the people to pay taxes, and claiming to be "the Messiah, a king" (Lk 23:2). In the eyes of the authorities, Peter and John are persisting in the same sedition that Jesus was executed for. From their perspective, the arrest is warranted. From the perspective of Luke and his readers, Peter and John are speaking truth to power, bearing witness to and recounting (Acts 3:13-15) an injustice that these same authorities were involved in (albeit in ignorance; see Acts 3:17).

The temple captain (*stratēgos*; see Lk 22:52) was a high-ranking member of the priesthood who functioned, among other duties, as the local chief of police (see, e.g., Josephus, *Ant.* 1.652).[78] This scene thus depicts an encounter between the two apostles and the police that ends with Peter and John being arrested while they have gathered a large crowd of at least five thousand people (Acts 4:4) in a public space and are bearing witness to an injustice to that crowd.

This passage resonates with the experiences of Filipino and other activists in Asia who have spoken truth to power in their home countries and experienced detention or arrest.[79] It also resonates with the experience of people of color in Canada and the United States who have faced arrest from their own police or governmental powers while speaking out against injustice. It is crucial, however, to recognize that while there is an overlap in the experience of arrest by police, we must not transfer our experiences of authoritarian regimes to the Jewish authorities, who themselves experienced the imperialism and colonialism of Roman rule. This arrest is the first of many that the followers of Jesus will experience in Acts.

PETER AND JOHN BEFORE THE AUTHORITIES (ACTS 4:5-22)

Peter and John are brought before an assembly of the authorities, which includes the high priest and members of the high priestly family (Acts 4:5-6). They are placed "in the middle" of them (*mesos*, Acts 4:7), a detail that might reflect the semicircular shape of the Sanhedrin's meeting chamber (Mishnah *Sanhedrin* 4:3), a

[78]See Barrett, *Acts*, 219; Joachim Jeremias, *Jerusalem in the Time of Jesus* (Philadelphia: Fortress, 1981), 163.

[79]See Cristina Jayme Montiel, *Living and Dying: In Memory of Eleven Ateneo de Manila Martial Law Activists* (Manila: Ateneo de Manila University Press, 2007); de la Torre, *Touching Ground*, 163.

common shape for council meeting houses throughout the Roman Empire.[80] The question posed to Peter and John in Acts 4:4 is meant to determine the legitimacy of the authority with which they act.[81] It also allows both the judges and the accused to get to the heart of the matter: Peter and John's performing a healing in the name of Jesus of Nazareth, who was recently arrested and executed.

We are told that Peter is "filled with the Holy Spirit" as he responds (Acts 4:8). This reminds us that Jesus warned his disciples that they would be arrested and tried (Lk 21:12), that this would provide opportunity to testify, and that they would be given "words and a wisdom that none of your opponents will be able to withstand or contradict" (Lk 21:15). Peter maintains that the man was healed by Jesus Christ of Nazareth, the same Jesus who was arrested and executed by some of the same authorities whom Peter and John are now standing before, and God raised this Jesus from the dead (Acts 4:10). He is proclaiming that a man who was accused of sedition by the very council that he found himself before (Lk 22:66–23:2), and executed for that sedition by the Roman authorities, is the Messiah and that God raised him from the dead, thus vindicating him. Thus, "There is salvation in no one else" but Jesus (Acts 4:12).

The man's presence is a demonstration of the truth of Peter and John's words and of the restoration that the name of Jesus brings to the destitute. For the reader of both of Luke's volumes, his presence is also a manifestation of the good news that Jesus proclaimed to the poor (Lk 4:18; 6:20). However, the authorities are afraid that the apostles' message will spread and attempt to silence them by threatening them (Acts 4:16-18, 21). As Willie James Jennings writes, "The weapon of choice is fear, fear of imprisonment, torture, or worse."[82] This Jesus that Luke's readers know and the upside-down kingdom that he proclaims pose a threat to the order of power in the world. He brings good news to the poor but woes to the rich, proclaims a kingdom in which the first are last and the last are first, and casts down rulers from their thrones and uplifts the lowly.

We must not, however, turn these Jerusalemite authorities into cartoon villains. The context of Jerusalem in the first century was colonial. Rome is not specifically named in this story, but its presence is hardly hidden. Indeed, Roman forces were billeted at the Antonia Fortress, which adjoined the temple complex, where this episode is likely set. As with John's narrative of the plot against Jesus' life (Jn 11:45-53), the fear that the authorities feel is almost certainly a fear of the Roman authorities, and so their fear is ultimately born out of a concern for the well-being of the people and the nation. To neglect the colonial situation is to ignore the historical context of the text.

THE DISCIPLES PRAY (ACTS 4:23-31)

The disciples' prayer begins by acknowledging God's sovereignty (Acts 4:24).[83] This divine sovereignty is in stark contrast to the threat of other powers named in what follows. The prayer, citing Psalm 2:1-2 (LXX), expresses the threat posed by "the gentiles" and the "kings of the earth" (Acts 4:25-26). Within an early Roman-period context, "the gentiles" (*ethnē*) is sometimes used by Jewish and New Testament

[80]See John B. Polhill, *Acts*, NAC 26 (Nashville: Broadman, 1992), 142.

[81]See Gaventa, *Acts of the Apostles*, ANTC (Nashville: Abingdon, 2003), 92-93.

[82]Jennings, *Acts*, 48.

[83]See Keener, *Acts*, 2:1166. See, e.g., (as per Keener, *Acts*, 1166n1217), Wis 8:3; 13:3, 9; 2 Macc 5:17, 20; 6:14; 9:13; 3 Macc 5:12; Josephus, *Ant.* 1.20, 72; 5.93. See also Fitzmyer, *Acts*, 308.

authors as a synecdoche to refer to the Romans (e.g., *Pss. Sol.* 2:20, 24; Lk 18:32; 21:24; Mk 10:33). This citation of Psalm 2:1-2 identifies the threat that the powers that be, the "kings of the earth," and the Romans ("the gentiles") pose to the followers of the crucified Messiah. Followers of that same crucified Messiah today who are historically marginalized or who belong to people groups that have experienced the pains of colonization can identify with the challenges faced by Jesus' first disciples.

Acts 4:27 names Herod Antipas and Pontius Pilate, along with "the gentiles and the peoples of Israel," as the ones who have "gathered together" (as per Acts 4:26) against Jesus, God's anointed. These same powers continue to pose a threat to Jesus' followers (Acts 4:29). "The gentiles" and "the peoples of Israel" in Acts 4:27 are both synecdoches, meaning that they represent smaller parts of those groups. It is not Luke's nor the apostles' intention for the reader to think that all Jews conspired against Jesus or continue to pose a threat to the followers of Jesus (who are Jews themselves), nor that all Gentiles conspired against Jesus or pose a threat to his followers. The point is that there were both Romans and Jews among the authorities who "gathered together" with Herod and Pilate against Jesus in Luke's passion narrative, and those same authorities now threaten Peter and John.

It is not surprising to see local elites grouped together with the colonial authorities. Local elites are often placed in the difficult position of having to align themselves with colonial overlords in order to maintain the status quo and to prevent the outbreak of violence, thus also benefiting from the patronage of the colonizers.[84] As E. P. Sanders says of the Jerusalemite aristocracy, "The eminent had to answer to Rome. They were responsible for good order."[85] Being between the people and the Romans was a delicate balancing act, and the threats issued by the Jerusalemite elites are correctly perceived by the followers of Jesus as having a connection to the colonial overlords ("the kings of the earth") represented by Pilate and Herod Antipas. The power differential between local elites, such as Caiaphas (Acts 4:6), and imperial agents or authorities must be recognized.[86]

The pouring out of the Holy Spirit and speaking of the word of God with boldness also reflects Peter's earlier citation of Joel, with its description of the pouring out of God's Spirit, signs on the earth, and sons and daughters prophesying (Acts 2:17-21). Prophecy involves not just foretelling but forthtelling, speaking truth from the margins about the way that things are. Being Jesus' witnesses (see Acts 1:8) will require the followers of Jesus to speak truth about the injustice of his death and to confront the powers that be who are threatened by the idea of a Messiah who proclaims a kingdom in which the first are last and the last are first (see Lk 13:30). This is an example for contemporary followers of this same Messiah, who understand the need to pray for courage to persist in speaking Spirit-filled truth to power, especially when power attempts to silence truth.

THE BELIEVERS ELIMINATE POVERTY (ACTS 4:32-35)

This passage presents readers with an image of the ideal community of followers of Jesus. The

[84]On this passage and elites in our society, see the recontextualization of this passage within a Latin American context in Justo L. González, *Acts: The Gospel of the Spirit* (Maryknoll, NY: Orbis, 2001), 63-64.

[85]E. P. Sanders, *Judaism: Practice and Belief 63 BCE–66 CE* (London: SCM Press, 1992), 330.

[86]See Adele Reinhartz, *Caiaphas the High Priest* (Minneapolis: Fortress, 2013), 11-23 (esp. 20-22). See also Jeremias, *Jerusalem in the Time of Jesus*, 158-60; Josephus, *Ant.* 18.91-95.

believers eliminate poverty among themselves (Acts 4:34) through sharing and distribution to those who have need (Acts 4:32, 35). Luke repeats his statement from Acts 2:44 that the believers held all possessions in common and expands on it, informing readers that they eschewed private ownership (Acts 4:32). The repetition underscores this foundational characteristic of the earliest community of followers of Jesus. This sharing and distribution is done alongside the apostles' powerful witness to the resurrection of Jesus. For Luke, these two things go hand in hand as distinguishing features of the ideal community of followers of Jesus. The two are correlated, not separate movements within the community. The resurrection bears witness to the reality of the outbreak of the kingdom and the realization of the good news that Jesus proclaimed to the poor (Lk 4:18; 6:20).

It is striking that the believers in Jesus eliminate poverty within their community in such a relatively short period. It is done from the grassroots, the outworking of discipleship (see Lk 12:32-34; 14:33; 18:22) to the risen Lord. This resonates with the experience of Filipino Americans and others who hail from community-oriented cultures in which the community is crucial to survival and flourishing. The elimination of poverty comes not through the accumulation of private property but from unity in community, one heart with many hands hoisting a bamboo hut together. This is "*kapwa* theology."[87] *Kapwa* is a core Filipino value. It reflects something intangible that we all recognize in the way we relate to others, a spirit that is beautifully and inexplicably reflected in every Filipino gathering I have known. It is the recognition of shared identity, of unity with others in one's inner being (*loob*).[88] *Kapwa* theology is driven by that same sense of shared identity with others, leading us to seek the best for the community on the basis of self-sacrificial Christian love and our sense of unity with others, a concept that reflects the sense of unity in community seen in Acts 4:32.

This passage and its parallel in Acts 2:44-47 are among the passages that most resonate culturally with Filipinos living in the United States and Canada out of the entirety of Acts. In passages like these, we see our own foundational values, which are so alien and invisible within the individualistic-dominant culture of North America. It reminds us that our values are not foreign to the kingdom of God and that we have something that the rest of the church can stand to learn from. In his celebrated essay, "Freedom from Want," Carlos Bulosan, our own Filipino American poet, writes, "Our march to freedom is not complete unless want is annihilated."[89] Bulosan was writing about his experience as an impoverished and exploited immigrant worker in America. We also learn from our passage that establishing freedom from want was a priority of the earliest community of believers in Jesus alongside witness to the resurrection.

A decolonized reading must resist any attempts to undermine the message of this passage or to make it compatible with the values of American capitalism and imperialism. Cordova's history of Filipinos in America starkly reminds us that Filipino workers who fought for their rights as workers were accused of communism in the mid-twentieth century. In fact, Bulosan himself was blacklisted. We can take comfort in that the Jerusalem church has been likewise accused of

[87]See Joyce del Rosario, "Can There Be a Postcolonial Theology While Living in the Colonizer's House?," *ChristianityNext* 2 (2018): 41-58.

[88]See David, *Brown Skin, White Minds*, 109-10; del Rosario, "Can There Be a Postcolonial Theology," 52-53.

[89]Carlos Bulosan, "Freedom from Want," *Saturday Evening Post* (Indianapolis), March 6, 1943.

communism by some mid-twentieth-century Christian interpreters.[90] One such interpreter even calls the community sharing of the Jerusalem church "a 'communistic' experiment" that was responsible for their later poverty.[91] However, this interpretation flies in the face of the evidence, both biblical and extrabiblical (Acts 11:27-30; Josephus, *Ant.* 20.5; Tacitus, *Annals* 12.43; Suetonius, *Divus Claudius* 18), that the later need of the Jerusalem church stemmed from a major famine.[92] We should recognize that problematic readings of this sort are driven by a McCarthyist hermeneutic that insists on the notion that "communism" is a major cause of poverty that allegiance to capitalism can save us from. Decolonizing our interpretation necessitates collective resistance to the authority of such hermeneutics and recognizing ideologies that enable making the ephah small and the shekel great for what they are.

POSITIVE AND NEGATIVE EXAMPLES (ACTS 4:35–5:11)

Barnabas, who will later play a significant role in the narrative of Acts, is first introduced as a positive example of selfless discipleship within the Christian community. This establishes Barnabas as a just and reliable character for the reader, preparing for his return in a more significant role later on. The story of Ananias and Sapphira is a negative contrast to Barnabas's positive example. As Peter's response to Ananias indicates, the primary issue is not their personal greed, nor their attachment to personal property. As Peter states, the property was Ananias's and Sapphira's to begin with, and the proceeds were at their disposal (Acts 5:4). If greed was their motivation, then why did they give at all? The issue is the lie, their misrepresentation of a part as the whole.

Evergetism, performing works of giving and benefaction in a public or association setting, was highly valued as a way to gain honor. Mediterranean society in the Roman period was an honor/shame culture.[93] Honor can be broadly understood as social capital or standing within a society or community, and evergetism was a way to accrue honor.[94] For example, inscriptions in public spaces (called "evergetistic inscriptions"), which could variously include Greco-Roman public buildings, streets, and synagogues (as well as churches in later centuries), that gave the name of the person who provided the funds for the construction were commonplace. This practice exemplifies and vividly demonstrates the importance of public acts of giving within the honor/shame society of the Roman Empire.

Ananias and Sapphira wanted to present themselves as better and more generous givers than they really were in an attempt to match the standard of generosity that had been set in the community, exemplified by Barnabas. Ananias and Sapphira attempted to take advantage of a community practice undertaken for the good of all by believers who were filled with the Holy Spirit in order to misrepresent their evergetism as greater than it was. Their lie, meant to accrue honor for themselves, dishonors that Holy Spirit.

Our cultural context can shed light on this text. The Jerusalem believers exhibited *kapwa*

---

[90]González, *Acts*, 71.

[91]Macgregor, "Acts," 73.

[92]González, *Acts*, 71.

[93]Julian Pitt-Rivers, "Honour and Social Status," in *Honour and Shame: The Values of Mediterranean Society*, ed. J. G. Peristiany, The Nature of Human Society (Chicago: University of Chicago Press, 1966), 21-77.

[94]Bruce J. Malina and Richard L. Rohrbaugh, *Social-Science Commentary on the Synoptic Gospels*, 2nd ed. (Minneapolis: Fortress, 2003), 369-70.

in their community of sharing: they were "of one heart and soul" (Acts 4:32). Ananias and Sapphira are *walang kapwa* (without *kapwa*).[95] Being *walang kapwa* is to be "rock bottom," someone who will inevitably do wrong.[96] Filipino Americans and other Asian Americans with similar values will recognize that the lack of community spirit and unity with others exhibited by Ananias and Sapphira is an incredible offense and the root cause of their sin, the driving force behind the lie they tell. The point of the story is not that God is vengeful and violent but that there is a need for accountability and consequences for actions.

OCCUPY SOLOMON'S PORTICO (ACTS 5:12-16)

The followers of Jesus have become a movement. They gather in the premier public of the city, at Solomon's portico, and occupy it (Acts 5:12).[97] In that public space and in the streets, they cure the sick and exorcise unclean spirits, providing health care to those in need. This is not ancillary to the outbreak of the kingdom but is in fact the kingdom in action, "the outpouring of the renewal and blessings that come with God's reign," the physical restoration of the people of God.[98]

A MASS ARREST (ACTS 5:17-42)

As sometimes happens to leaders of movements that subvert the social order in the streets and public squares, the apostles experience a mass arrest (Acts 5:17-18). This is at the instigation of the high priest and "the sect of the Sadducees" (Acts 5:17). The Sadducees were closely associated with the priesthood and the aristocracy.[99] The point is that the mass arrest was initiated by certain members of the elite class, which follows from the previous arrest narrative in Acts 4. It is a grave mistake to see this as a conflict between "the Christians" and "the Jews" or as a Jewish persecution of Christians. Rather, this narrative depicts a conflict between a sect of Jews and some members of the aristocracy of Jerusalem who saw this movement as a threat to the precarious order they sought to protect.

The apostles are set free by an angel of the Lord (Acts 5:19-20). The image of an angel opening the doors of the prison is powerful. Luke's readers know that the proclamation of release to the captives is part of the messianic mission (Lk 4:18). As Jennings writes, "The power to free people from bondage is of the new order just as the power to imprison is of the old order."[100] God is a liberator of the imprisoned. In this age of mass incarceration and for-profit prisons, this image presents a powerful counternarrative. I vividly recall my father coming home from visiting members of the Regent Park and Church on the Street community in Toronto who were in prison and hearing his lament for the lack of justice in our justice system.

The apostles are swiftly rearrested and brought before the council. This is the third arrest in the story. The high priest's comments in Acts 5:28, as well as the apostles' response in Acts 5:29, remind us of something significant: the apostles are guilty of what they have been arrested for and charged with. They were forbidden from speaking or teaching in the name

[95]David, *Brown Skin, White Minds*, 112-13; Enriquez, *From Colonial to Liberation Psychology*, 63.
[96]Enriquez, *From Colonial to Liberation Psychology*, 63.
[97]See Jonathan Bernier, "Occupy Solomon's Portico," in *Reading the Bible in an Age of Crisis: Political Exegesis for a New Day*, ed. Bruce Worthington (Minneapolis: Fortress, 2015), 265-84.
[98]Ryan, *Role of the Synagogue*, 209.
[99]See, for example, the influential study of the Sadducees and the aristocrats in Sanders, *Judaism*, 317-40.
[100]Jennings, *Acts*, 62.

of Jesus (Acts 4:18), and they were caught in the act of doing exactly that (Acts 5:25-26). Although they are guilty of what they are arrested for, their arrest is unjust. Guilt and justice are not always correlated in human legal systems, modern or ancient.

Before the council, the apostles proclaim their obedience to God over any other authority, and they persist in bearing witness to the injustice of the execution of Jesus, which some of these same elites were involved in, and to his subsequent vindication in the form of his resurrection (Acts 5:29-32). Their witness is a counternarrative to the justice of the human courts, pointing to the greater justice of God that is evident in the story of Jesus' death and resurrection. Moreover, they proclaim that Jesus has been exalted "as Leader and Savior" (Acts 5:31), which points to his greater authority, over and above that of the council. This passage is a reminder that followers of Jesus ultimately owe their allegiance to God alone and not to national authorities.

Gamaliel intervenes when the council is enraged and desires to kill the apostles (Acts 5:33-34). He is a Pharisee (Acts 5:34) and thus a member of a minority party in this council meeting. Gamaliel is nevertheless respected by the populace, a man of the people. Gamaliel also appears in the Mishnah (Mishnah *Orlah* 2:12; Mishnah *Rosh Hashanah* 2:5; Mishnah *Yevamot* 16:7; Mishnah *Sotah* 9:15; Mishnah *Gittin* 4:3) and in other rabbinic literature. Jewish sources present Gamaliel as someone who was widely respected. Josephus describes Gamaliel's son, Simeon, as "of a very noble family" (*Life* 190), and an encomium in the Mishnah states, with intentional hyperbole, "When Rabban Gamaliel the Elder died, the glory of the Torah came to an end."[101]

Gamaliel's comparison of the followers of Jesus to the followers of Theudas and Judas the Galilean underscores that the apostles are perceived as leaders of a subversive political movement. Those movements were not of God, so they failed. If the apostles' movement is of God, then the council will be "found fighting against God" (Acts 5:39). As the narrative will reveal, the movement does not fail but spreads throughout the Mediterranean world.

Well-intentioned preachers and commentators have sometimes attempted to portray Gamaliel as a negative figure in this narrative, as a passive intellectual or someone who simply sits back and lets things play out rather than getting involved.[102] These interpretations certainly address real problems in our modern context. However, it stretches the narrative to view Gamaliel as a negative figure and even more to turn him into a negative example. At worst, he is portrayed as an ambiguous figure, at best he is relatively (though not wholly) sympathetic.[103] The most important points here are that he prevents the apostles' deaths and leaves the possibility open that their movement is of God. We must remember that this is not his movement. To treat him as a negative exemplar because he does not get involved ignores that Gamaliel the Elder was a part of another movement of Jews who were concerned with maintaining faithfulness to the God of Abraham. That movement was none too comfortable with the colonial powers either.[104] We

[101]Trans. Jacob Neusner, *The Mishnah: A New Translation* (New Haven, CT: Yale University Press, 1988), 465.

[102]Discussed in González, *Acts*, 85-86. E.g., Luke Timothy Johnson, *The Acts of the Apostles*, Sacra Pagina (Collegeville, MN: Liturgical Press, 1992), 102-3.

[103]See Gaventa, *Acts*, 110.

[104]In fact, Gamaliel's son, Simeon, supported the revolt against Rome (Josephus, *Life* 190-203). Later Jewish tradition holds that he was executed by the Romans (*Avot de Rabbi Nathan* 38:3).

must also thoroughly resist the impulse to turn every single Jewish authority figure who is not a follower of Jesus in the New Testament into a caricature of problematic authority figures in our own context. At any rate, Luke paints a generally positive picture of Gamaliel, who prevents the apostles from being killed by speaking up.

The apostles are not killed, but they receive corporal punishment before being released. This indicates that the apostles are now convicted criminals. Despite the pressure they face from the authorities, they persist in their teaching and proclamation in both public and private. Both the New Testament and the Mishnah set floggings by Jewish authorities in public places (Mt 10:17; 23:34; Mk 13:9; Acts 22:19; Mishnah *Makkot* 3:12). It was thus a great act of public shaming. That the apostles rejoice because they are deemed worthy to be dishonored "for the sake of the name" (Acts 5:41), that is, for the sake of Jesus' name (Acts 5:40), is a reminder of the complete reversal of societal values that being a disciple of Jesus entails. They do not suffer passively but struggle for the sake of Jesus' name. To struggle actively in suffering as the apostles do is to struggle alongside Christ.

THE COMMUNITY COMBATS DISCRIMINATION (ACTS 6:1-7)

This narrative depicts the community responding to an act of discrimination. It is important that we understand the historical context. This is not a matter of Jews discriminating against non-Jews. The two groups in Acts 6:1, the Hebrews and the Hellenists, are both groups of Jewish believers in Jesus. The "Hebrews" are Jews who are local to the Jewish homeland and whose primary culture and language are the dominant culture of Jerusalem. The "Hellenists" are Diaspora Jews who have relocated to Jerusalem, whose primary culture and language reflects the Greco-Roman culture of the broader Mediterranean world.

The neglect of the Hellenist widows resonates as a story of invisibility and powerlessness, an image of vulnerable members of a minority group being passed over by members of the dominant culture. This stands out as particularly egregious to those of us whose cultural contexts emphasize respect and care for women, such as the matriarchal, family-oriented culture of Filipinos in North America. This neglect shows that some in the community are *walang kapwa*, lacking recognition of the unity and interconnectedness of themselves with others. This passage also speaks to a situation all too common in Asian ethnic communities in North America, wherein those who grew up locally and speak English fluently and with an American or Canadian accent discriminate against or shame immigrant community members whose first language is the language of their homeland and who speak with what Westerners perceive to be accented English.[105] This discrimination comes out of the colonization of our minds and works against our core values as Christians and as Asian North Americans. For contemporary Asian North American followers of Jesus, aspiring to the *koinōnia*, to our community values, requires us to decolonize our minds and reject discrimination.

In order to combat this discrimination, the community appoints seven deacons, who are tasked with ensuring fair distribution (Acts 6:5). Notably, all the men who are selected have Greek names, which implies that

[105]See Leny Mendoza Strobel, "Coming Full Circle: Narratives of Decolonization Among Post-1965 Filipino Americans," in *Filipino Americans: Transformation and Identity*, ed. M. P. Root (Thousand Oaks, CA: Sage, 1997), 62-79.

they are all Hellenists. The solution is to empower the people experiencing discrimination and to place them in charge of ensuring equity and justice. No longer invisible, they are seen and heard. One of them, Nicolaus, is a proselyte from Antioch, which means that he was not an ethnic Jew but a Gentile convert to Judaism. That his status as a proselyte from Antioch is mentioned at all implies that Luke intends to highlight Nicolaus's minoritized status. Representation mattered to the earliest community of followers of Jesus, and so too should it matter to followers of Jesus today.

STEPHEN IS ARRESTED AMID POLARIZATION (ACTS 6:7-15)

Jerusalem is polarized by the movement. According to Acts 6:7, many join the movement, including some of the priests. However, we learn in Acts 6:9-11 that some members of a few different communities in Jerusalem are staunchly opposed to Stephen. Most of the groups listed in Acts 6:9 are trans-diasporic associations of Jews who live in Jerusalem but come from elsewhere in the Mediterranean world. Synagogues could be either public assemblies, similar to town halls, or voluntary associations that belonged to a specific group of Jews, similar to a club, who had something in common. The "synagogue of the Freedmen" (Acts 6:9) was most likely an association synagogue whose membership was made up of former slaves. Not all opposition comes from elites. As a result of false charges brought against him by his opponents, Stephen is arrested and brought before the council. This is the fourth arrest.

STEPHEN'S SPEECH (ACTS 7:1-53)

Stephen retells key events from Israel's Scriptural history. This retelling serves as his defense against the charge that he has been speaking "against this holy place [the temple] and the law" (Acts 6:13). One of the through lines of Stephen's speech is that the foundational figures of Israel's past exemplified faithfulness, even though they faced opposition. By reviewing Israel's history in this way, Stephen shows how both he and Jesus continue that story.

As other scholars observe, Stephen pairs positive figures in the history of Israel with negative exemplars of people who opposed or rejected them: Abraham was obedient to God but was opposed by the Egyptians, who enslaved and mistreated his descendants for four centuries (Acts 7:2-8); Joseph was sold into slavery by his brothers, though God was with him and rescued him (Acts 7:9-16); Moses was raised up by God as a liberator and prophet (Acts 7:17-43), but the people (whom Stephen calls "our ancestors") turned back to Egypt in their hearts and made the golden calf (Acts 7:39-42); the prophets were sent by God but were persecuted and killed by the audience's ancestors (Acts 7:52).[106] Finally, the Righteous One (Jesus) came, but Stephen's audience "have become his betrayers and murderers" (Acts 7:52). Stephen is thus able to turn the tables on his accusers and claim that it is *they* who have not kept the law (Acts 7:53). Stephen's knowledge and deployment of Jewish history allows him to show his accusers that they stand on the wrong side of their own history. Thus, as Mikeal Parsons writes, "Stephen is not pitting Christianity over against Judaism; rather, he is aligning himself and his group with what he considers to be the 'best' in Jewish history."[107]

In the popular 2019 Filipino film *Alone/Together*, Filipino American actress Liza

[106]Following here Parsons, *Acts*, 107-8.
[107]Parsons, *Acts*, 108.

Soberano delivers a monologue about Filipino painter Juan Luna's masterpiece, *Spoliarium*: "Luna's *Spoliarium* reveals to us the tragic character of our own history, of the colonized and the oppressed. The very substance of our collective memory. Our history is tragic, but no matter how tragic the past is, we must not forget. [Looking straight at the camera] We must never forget. To forget is to deny the present any significant meaning."[108] Selective versions of US history that are designed to glorify the state and maintain the status quo of injustice want us to forget, because history is powerful. The way we present and deploy our histories has an incredible capacity to speak truth to power and can enable decolonization. Historical narratives can also be liberative in the hands of the oppressed, providing a means to challenge the status quo, to lament past injustices, to understand why present injustice persists, to seek justice, and to effect change. This is why it is essential for Filipino Americans to remember our colonial history and to confront the pain of the American invasion of the First Philippine Republic. It is also why Filipino Americans must remember our history in the United States, our resistance against injustice, the manongs, and the history of anti-Filipino violence in the United States.[109]

Another theme of Stephen's speech is the idea that the Israelites were a people of perpetual foreigners without a home. This theme should resonate with Asian North Americans, who experience the pains of being treated like perpetual foreigners in the land we call home. Too many of us, including those who were born in North America or who have called North America home for many years, know the exclusion implied in the barbed question, "Where are you from?" As a half-Filipino living in the United States who is asked this question on a regular basis, I am reasonably certain that the answer that those who ask me that question are looking for is not "Toronto."

STEPHEN IS KILLED (ACTS 7:54-60)

The audience, which includes the council members as well as Stephen's accusers, reacts with anger to Stephen's speech. He has, after all, turned the tables and accused them of acting contrary to the law. Stephen's vision of the "Son of Man standing at the right hand of God" (Acts 7:56) parallels Jesus' words before the same council in Luke 22:69. Both call to mind the Son of Man of Daniel 7:13-14, who appears before the throne (see Dan 7:9) of the Ancient of Days. Within the story of Acts, the reader might also recall that Jesus was "taken up" by a cloud, just as the Son of Man comes with the clouds before the Ancient of Days in Daniel 7:13.

The Jerusalem council (Sanhedrin) did not have the authority to directly sentence someone to capital punishment without Roman permission.[110] The reader should recall that Jesus had to be handed over to Pilate (Lk 23:1), whose verdict was required in order for Jesus to be crucified (Lk 23:24). This means that Luke depicts Stephen's martyrdom as an extrajudicial act of mob violence: a lynching. Tragically, this proves Stephen's point at the cost of his own life. However, Stephen does not die alone. The Spirit fills him in Acts 7:55, ensuring that God is with him even in this terrible moment.

[108]This scene was widely used on social media in 2020 to remember the period of martial law under Marcos and to address present challenges in the Philippines. See also Leny Mendoza Strobel, *Coming Full Circle: The Process of Decolonization Among Post-1965 Filipino Americans*, 2nd ed. (Santa Rosa, CA: Center for Babaylan Studies, 2015), 61.

[109]See Cordova, *Forgotten Asian Americans*.

[110]See Keener, *Acts*, 2:1432-35.

Regardless of who did or did not participate in the lynch mob, it is imperative that we firmly resist any attempt to use this passage as a basis for anti-Jewish sentiment, nor should we equate ancient Jews with the White-supremacist lynch mobs of American history. Mob violence was common throughout the Roman world. It has also been common throughout the history of human civilization. Thus, as Craig Keener writes, this narrative "says nothing about specifically 'Jewish' hostility, Stephen himself being Jewish."[111] What we can do is note the overlap between this story and the experience of minority groups in the United States today in the experience and trauma of extrajudicial killings on a community. What we must not do is read our own experiences of violence at the hands of White supremacists back into the text and project our legitimate trauma onto ancient or contemporary Jews.

Our people have suffered too many extrajudicial killings.[112] As I write this, the Filipino American community has recently been shaken by the news of the death of Angelo Quinto, who died while in police custody a few days after an officer knelt on his neck. Death at the hands of mobs has also been a painful part of Filipino American history, including the violence in Watsonville and Yakima Valley. Ethnic minorities in America know all too well that justice for extrajudicial killings, whether they are the result of police brutality, mob violence, or anything else, is rare. As Stephen's speech implies, there is a clear parallel between Stephen's death and the unjust death of Jesus. For Filipinos reading about the death of the protomartyr, Stephen, it is hard not to be reminded of author Jose Rizal, who suffered an unjust death at the hands of the Spanish authorities of his own day as a result of his criticisms of colonial society. His death had a galvanizing effect on the Filipino people. Through the lens of the theology of struggle, Stephen, Rizal, and the Filipino people at home and in the United States can be seen as imitators of Christ in their own ways.

SAUL AND THE PERSECUTION OF THE JERUSALEMITE CHURCH (ACTS 8:1-3)

We are informed that Saul, who is first introduced at the scene of Stephen's death (Acts 7:58), approved of the killing. This is our first impression of the characterization of the eventual protagonist of the story: he approves of the extrajudicial killing of a man whose primary duty was to ensure the fair treatment of minoritized widows.

This passage describes what Luke labels a "persecution" of the followers of Jesus in Jerusalem. Rather than viewing this as a "Jewish" persecution of "Christians," we could view this as resistance by local colonized elites who were involved in the unjust killing of Jesus of Nazareth to a Jewish messianic movement centered around that same Jesus, a movement that has directly challenged their authority by publicly accusing them of injustice on multiple accounts. The method of the crackdown is mass arrest, carried out home to home by Saul (Acts 8:3). This mass arrest is the fifth arrest. This crackdown brings the followers of Jesus to Judea and Samaria, in fulfillment of Jesus' instructions to his followers (Acts 1:8). Even in this moment of scattering and mass arrest, Jesus' will is carried out.

Stephen is buried and mourned (Acts 8:2), acts that were important within the culture of early Judaism. For example, Tobit takes great personal risks in order to bury the bodies of

[111]Keener, *Acts*, 2:1433.

[112]On fatal police violence against Filipino Americans, see E. J. R. David and Kevin Nadal, "On Police Violence, Race-Based Trauma, Mental Health Among Fil-Ams," *Inquirer*, February 26, 2021. Historically, see the witness to anti-Filipino lynchings and violence throughout Carlos Bulosan, *America Is in the Heart: A Personal History* (Seattle: University of Washington Press, 2014).

his countrymen who were killed by the Ninevite authorities (Tob 1:16-20). In Tobit 1:17, providing the dead who had been unjustly killed with a proper burial is listed alongside feeding the hungry and clothing the naked as acts of justice that characterize Tobit as a righteous man. So too is mourning important in many Asian American cultures, and we should remember that both mourning and lament are biblical practices. The burial of Stephen was an act of courageous justice, one that came at great personal risk. It was also an act of resistance. Stephen was not buried quietly; he was buried with "loud lamentation." This mourning was a public act of honoring and remembering Stephen. By honoring and remembering those whose lives were taken unjustly, we continue to bear witness to the injustice of their deaths, just as we have seen the followers of Jesus do in the narrative of Acts. Our Asian American community in the United States has recently gathered in lament for the lives lost to anti-Asian hatred throughout the Covid-19 pandemic. We continue to remember and lament those whose blood cries out from the ground.

WITNESSES IN SAMARIA (ACTS 8:4-25)

Philip arrives in Samaria, thus fulfilling Jesus' earlier statement that the apostles would be his witnesses in Samaria (Acts 1:8). This happens as a result of the scattering caused by the persecution (Acts 8:1, 4). Persecution does not prevent the church from bearing witness; it only carries the witness further. The "city of Samaria," which had recently been renamed Sebaste in honor of Caesar Augustus, was the chief Samaritan city (Acts 8:5). There was history here. The city had been attacked and destroyed by Jewish ruler John Hyrcanus at the end of the second century BCE and had been recently rebuilt by Gabinius and Herod the Great, hence its renaming after the first Roman emperor.[113] There was long-standing ethic tension between Jews and Samaritans that sometimes spilled into violence (Josephus, *Ant.* 20.118).

Despite this history, the proclamation of Jesus the Messiah was also for the Samaritans (Acts 8:5-6). Philip performs the same deeds of healing and restoration (Acts 8:7) for the people of Samaria that Jesus commissioned his followers to do among the Jewish people (Lk 10:1-12, 17-20). The outpouring of the blessing that comes with the outbreak of the kingdom of God (see Acts 8:12) was for the Samaritans as well, and it was Philip, a Jew, who performed these deeds and bore witness to the Messiah to them. These acts brought joy to a people who had been dominated by their Jewish neighbors and by Herod and the Romans. The renaming of the city bore witness to that recent history. That Luke still calls it "the city of Samaria," rather than its imperial name, Sebaste, is deeply significant for colonized peoples. Recovery of names is a part of decolonization.

Filipino Americans may find parallels to their experience in the Samaritans, insofar as the Samaritans are a people who experienced colonization and who were much less visible in broader society in the Roman Empire than their Jewish neighbors. Even the emperor Augustus was familiar with Jewish customs and, according to Suetonius, claimed to practice a Sabbath fast (Suetonius, *Divus Augustus* 76). Ancient Samaritans also receive considerably less attention in contemporary scholarship than ancient Jews or Christians.[114]

---

[113]Daniel M. Master, "Samaria/Sebaste," in *The Oxford Encyclopedia of the Bible and Archaeology* (Oxford: Oxford University Press, 2013).

[114]For an excellent overview of scholarship on Samaritans, see Ingrid Hjelm, "What Do Samaritans and Jews Have in Common?," *CurBR* 3, no. 1 (2004): 9-59. According to Hjelm, "For more than 1,500 years, Samaritan history and traditions could be relegated to a minor, or even a neglected, status in biblical studies" (46).

They were and are in a sense invisible Israelites, much as Filipinos are invisible Asian Americans. Nevertheless, the Samaritans are seen by God, receive the Holy Spirit, and experience the blessings of the outbreak of the kingdom.

The incident with Simon Magus highlights the problem of power. Simon wanted to be "someone great" (Acts 8:9) and used words and magic to accrue renown from even the greatest of society in Samaria (Acts 8:10). In an honor/shame culture, that "greatness" translated into social capital and thus power. Simon Magus's problem is not that he is a magician. The problem is that he believes that the ability to lay hands on others so that they might receive the Holy Spirit is *power* that he can buy. The power that comes from the Spirit requires repentance, not money. This is the way of the upside-down kingdom.

A NUBIAN EUNUCH (ACTS 8:26-40)

Interpreting this passage requires an intersectional approach to the central figure of the narrative.[115] Luke identifies the man that Philip encounters as "an Ethiopian eunuch" (Acts 8:27). However, the reference to the Kandake, a dynastic title rather than a proper name, suggests that the man in question was not from the Nubian kingdom of Meroë.[116] The term *Ethiopian* refers to the darkness of the man's skin, and thus he is literally identified by his blackness.[117] The identification of the man by his skin color would have indicated foreignness to Luke's ancient readers. This is recognizable to Filipino Americans, since the brownness of our skin is problematically regarded as a signifier of perpetual foreignness in our context.

The man was apparently of high socioeconomic status as a court official, a fact further indicated by his possession of a scroll and a chariot.[118] However, he was also a eunuch. As someone who had been castrated, he would have been perceived as a person of ambiguous gender and sexual identity. Lucian of Samosata writes that eunuchs were "neither man nor woman but something composite, hybrid and monstrous, alien to human nature" (*Eunuchus* 11). This ambiguity would have resulted in stigma and demonization of the sort expressed by Lucian.[119] As a eunuch, he was also most likely a slave.[120] Thus, the story of the Nubian eunuch is "an instance of a slave choosing to convert of his own accord," a slave who has agency of his own.[121]

This passage is the first instance of a Gentile being baptized and becoming a follower of Jesus. That Gentile is a castrated, dark-skinned, Nubian slave. However, that a person of such a complex multifaceted identity was the first Gentile believer in Jesus has been mostly overlooked in the reception history of this passage in the church.[122] It is in stark contrast to the

[115]See, e.g., Marianne B. Kartzow and Halvor Moxnes, "Complex Identities: Ethnicity, Gender and Religion in the Story of the Ethiopian Eunuch (Acts 8:26-40)," *Religion and Theology* 17, no. 3-4 (2010): 184-204; Brittany E. Wilson, "'Neither Male nor Female': The Ethiopian Eunuch in Acts 8.26-40," *NTS* 60, no. 3 (2014): 403-22.

[116]See, e.g., discussion in Keener, *Acts*, 2:1550-52.

[117]See D. K. Williams, "Acts," in *True to Our Native Land: An African American New Testament Commentary*, ed. Brian K. Blount (Minneapolis: Fortress, 2007), 225-28.

[118]See Gaventa, *Acts*, 142-43.

[119]Parsons, *Acts*, 120; Jesse J. Lee, "On Distracting and Disappearing Joy: An Exegetical Comparison of the Ethiopian Eunuch and the Slave-Girl Rhoda in Acts," *Horizons in Biblical Theology* 40 (2018): 67.

[120]Kartzow and Moxnes, "Complex Identities," 197-98.

[121]Christy Cobb, *Slavery Gender, Truth, and Power in Luke–Acts and Other Ancient Narratives* (Cham, Switzerland: Palgrave Macmillan, 2019), 31.

[122]Heidi J. Hornik and Mikeal C. Parsons, *The Acts of the Apostles Through the Centuries*, Wiley Blackwell Bible Commentaries (Chichester, UK: Wiley-Blackwell, 2017), 107.

story of Cornelius in Acts 10, a man of unambiguous high status, whose high-profile conversion sparks discussion in the church. However, although the Nubian eunuch's story was apparently invisible and unknown to the leadership of the Jerusalemite church according to Luke's narrative, Luke brings his audience into this story of the forgotten *true* first Gentile believer.

SAUL ENCOUNTERS THE PERSECUTED ONE (ACTS 9:1-19)

Saul attempts to carry his violence against the followers of Jesus beyond the Jewish homeland. There was a large Jewish Diaspora community in Syria, and the synagogues of Damascus would have functioned as ethnic associations serving that community.

Western readings of this passage tend to center Saul and his repentance as a reflection of the guilty sinner who is saved. Rather than focusing on guilt, Filipino American readers might tend to center the figure of Jesus. In saying, "I am Jesus, whom you are persecuting" (Acts 9:5), Jesus identifies himself as a co-sufferer with his people in their struggle. This is an expression of the theology of struggle, the identity of those who struggle in their suffering with the crucified Lord. That powerful image of Christ as participant in the struggle of the oppressed is the beating heart of the will to resist for the Filipino American church. When we cry, "Isang bagsak!" the cross is the divine unity clap.[123]

Jesus is literally invisible, but his voice is nevertheless heard (Acts 9:7). He is not passive in his struggle, but even as Saul persecutes him, Jesus brings the oppressor to his knees. He calls him not only to repentance but to service (Acts 9:15), to repair what has been broken (Acts 9:18-22), and to suffering, not in vain but for a cause (Acts 9:16). In short, Jesus calls Saul to the struggle. He who once was an oppressor is now called "brother" (Acts 9:17).

This former-oppressor-turned-brother now joins with the disciples in Damascus (Acts 9:19) and proclaims Jesus as the Son of God (Acts 9:20) and Messiah (Acts 9:22) in the synagogues. As local Jewish ethnic associations, the Damascus synagogues provided community for local Jews and were a natural place for Saul and the Damascus-based disciples to carry their message. However, that proclamation is not without controversy. News of Saul's mission preceded him, which meant that the Jewish community in Damascus was probably already aware of the challenge that the movement of Jesus-followers posed to the Jerusalemite authorities. By proclaiming that a man who had been condemned by both the imperial authorities and the colonized elites in Jerusalem was the Son of God and the Messiah, Saul was presenting a message that subverted the authority of their homeland authorities. It was thus a potential threat to the stability and security of the community. Luke does not explain why Saul's fellow Jews in Damascus hatch a plot to kill him. However, in light of what I have just said, rather than seeing this as the result of "Jewish" malice against "Christians," it might be better understood as a necessary survival strategy for an ethnoreligious minority diaspora community. Beyond the pragmatics, this is also the result of a theological divide over the Messiahship of Jesus. Saul continues to learn what it means to suffer with a purpose in Jerusalem. There he finds acceptance with the apostles, with Barnabas's help

[123]"Isang bagsak!" is a protest slogan used by Filipinos during the labor organization movements in the US and by the People Power revolution in the Philippines. Literally meaning "one down," it has the sense of "rise and fall together" and is followed by a "unity clap," a single clap by all those present signifying unity.

(Acts 9:26-27), but also finds himself in danger from some of his fellow Hellenistic Jews when he speaks boldly in Jesus' name (Acts 9:28-29). In a twist of irony, Saul now experiences for himself what it is like to be in danger as a result of speaking in the name of the persecuted one whom he met on the road to Damascus.

IMAGES OF RESTORATION (ACTS 9:31-43)

This passages presents us with three images of restoration and the kingdom of God in action: the peace experienced by the church in Judea, Galilee, and Samaria; the healing of Aeneas; and the raising of Tabitha. The healing of Aeneas, who was paralyzed, and the raising of Tabitha both mirror miracles performed by Jesus (Lk 7:11-17). The messianic work of liberation from sickness and death that Jesus' ministry brought is being carried on through the apostles.

Luke gives both Tabitha's Aramaic name and her Greek name, Dorcas (Acts 9:36), both of which mean "gazelle." The practice of having two names, one in the mother tongue and the other in the lingua franca, is also a well-known phenomenon in the Asian American context and functions as a survival and assimilation strategy in America. Tabitha is characterized by her devotion to good works and acts of charity. This highlights the crucial role that women have always played in the church's work of justice, a work that continues to be driven by many Asian American women in the church today.[124] Her craftwork, making tunics and other clothing, was valued by her community and becomes a part of how she is remembered (Acts 9:39). Her resurrection demonstrates fully what the reader already knows to be true: the chains of death are already broken. The struggle is not over, but the final liberation is already assured.

CAN THE OPPRESSOR BE SAVED? PETER AND CORNELIUS (ACTS 10:1–11:18)

This narrative and the story of Saul's Damascus road experience in Acts 9 both ask a crucial question: Can the oppressor be saved? The story of Cornelius is not the story of the first Gentile to become a follower of Jesus. That honor belongs to the Nubian eunuch. Cornelius is the first *colonizer* to be redeemed. This illustrates the transformative power of God at work in the world through the followers of Jesus and the Spirit. It presents the reader with a radical vision for the transformation and redemption of the whole world.

Acts 10:1 introduces Cornelius by identifying him as (1) an officer in the Roman army (2) who is a member of the Italian cohort and (3) is located in Caesarea. The "Italian cohort" probably refers to a Roman auxiliary unit that was originally raised in Italy, the Roman homeland, though it would have drawn replacements from local regions.[125] Cornelius is a Roman name, indicating his status as a Roman citizen.[126] He is a centurion, not a rank-and-file soldier, a man both with and under authority (see Lk 7:8), a representative of Rome's military power and presence. As Alexander Kyrychenko writes, "For the indigenous population, the Roman centurion was Rome."[127] Moreover, Cornelius was located in Caesarea, a colonial Roman city on the Levantine coast, built in Roman fashion, the base of the

---

[124]See, e.g., Lisa Asedillo Pratt and Grace Y. Kao, "On Becoming Asian American Christian Ethicists," in *Asian and Asian American Women in Theology and Religion: Embodying Knowledge*, ed. Pui-lan Kwok (Boston: Brill, 2020), 223-39.

[125]Alexander Kyrychenko, *The Roman Army and the Expansion of the Gospel: The Role of the Centurion in Luke-Acts* (Berlin: de Gruyter, 2014), 165; Keener, *Acts*, 2:1737.

[126]Kyrychenko, *Roman Army*, 165.

[127]Kyrychenko, *Roman Army*, 182.

imperial presence in the region, and site of an imperial temple dedicated to Augustus and Roma, the personification of Rome itself. All of these clues that Luke uses to characterize Cornelius point the reader toward Rome. Cornelius was not just any Gentile. Cornelius was a colonizer.

The difference in setting between Cornelius and Peter highlights the imbalance in their statuses and identities. Cornelius was a homeowner (Acts 10:22) and a slave owner (Acts 10:7), living in Caesarea, a newly founded Roman imperial colony built by Herod the Great. Peter was residing in a house that he did not own, the house of a tanner, a trade considered to be particularly low class.[128] That house was in Joppa, a city that had been under Jewish control since the mid-second century BCE (e.g., 1 Macc 10:76; Josephus, *Ant.* 13.91-92).

Cornelius is no underdog: he is a representative of Rome and has all of the power in this narrative.[129] Yet, in a staggering reversal, Cornelius will soon fall at Peter's feet (Acts 10:25), an image of a world turned upside-down. Once more, God brings the oppressor to his knees, this time by his words, as he instructs Cornelius to send for Peter (Acts 10:3-6).

Peter's dream and the divine declaration that "What God has made clean, you must not call profane" (Acts 10:15) is a powerful statement that speaks to the fact that no one, regardless of their ethnicity, should be considered untouchable or someone to be avoided. This is meaningful to Asian Americans, who have long battled the harmful stereotypes that we are literally dirty, that our food is strange and dangerous, and because of these things we are bearers of disease. It is these stereotypes that fueled the spike in anti-Asian violence and hatred during the Covid-19 pandemic in 2020–2021. This is an old strategy for othering ethnic groups. According to the Roman general Pompeius Trogus, for example, the Jews had their origins in diseased people who were expelled from Egypt to prevent the spread of their diseases (Justin, *Epitome of Pompeius Trogus* 36.2).

Cornelius sends a soldier and his slaves to find where Peter is staying (Acts 10:7), an image that Luke's readers would likely have recognized as typically being terrifying, much like how Black and brown Americans, including brown Asians, know the rush of fear when the police knock on the door or pull us over. This reminds us again that, by colonial standards, Cornelius has all of the power, and yet it is still he who falls before Peter. When Peter asks why Cornelius sent for him (Acts 10:29), Cornelius responds by saying that he and his household are there "to listen to all that the Lord has commanded you to say" (Acts 10:33). White American Christians have much to learn from Cornelius's example. Although he has all the worldly power, Cornelius the centurion, an officer of an occupying army, humbles himself before Peter, a colonized Jew, and above all *he listens.*

We Christians of color have much to learn from Peter's example, who proclaims good news to the oppressor, confronting, resisting, and liberating by bearing witness to truth. This example is a challenge for we who have experienced colonization to proclaim a faithful decolonized gospel, even to those that slaughtered and colonized our ancestors, so that we might be redeemed and liberated together from sin and systems of oppression. Colonizers need redemption and liberation as well. As Leny Strobel writes, "How can the colonizer

[128]Keener, *Acts*, 2:1725.

[129]See Revelation Enriques Velunta, "Cornelius the Centurion Meets the Ethiopian Eunuch in a Jeepney," in *Scripture and Resistance*, ed. Jione Havea (Minneapolis: Fortress, 2019), 62.

give that which he doesn't have? He is not free. He is not whole. For if he was, then he would not have needed to destroy others who were not like him."[130]

Filipino American followers of Jesus have no choice but to proclaim that good news from within the colonizer's house, just as Peter did.[131] Like Peter's message to Cornelius, the message we are challenged to proclaim includes the good news of the life of Jesus, the resurrection, and forgiveness of sins (Acts 10:40-43), *as well as* the message of ethnic egalitarianism in the eyes of a God who shows no partiality (Acts 10:34-35). This message cuts both ways for Peter as a Jew and for Cornelius as a Roman, the proclamation of peace as opposed to violence (Acts 10:36), and a confrontation of the injustice caused by colonizer's instrument of death, the cross (Acts 10:39).

Cornelius, as a Roman officer, would have known the cross for what it was: an instrument and symbol of colonial violence. He would have known that it was the very army he served that put the Messiah, the Lord of all (Acts 10:36), to death on it. In this moment we see the realization of the vision of Isaiah 2:2-4, of Gentiles streaming to be taught the ways of the God of Jacob and of swords beaten into plowshares. This passage from Isaiah is a reminder that Peter's message of ethnic egalitarianism is not an overturning of some perceived Jewish prejudice or supremacy. Rather, it is a realization of a powerful truth in the Jewish tradition that has always been there: God's redemptive work is ultimately for all peoples.

The Roman military and the imperial cult were closely intertwined. This was especially true for centurions.[132] Although soldiers could worship whatever deities they saw fit in their private lives, participation in the Roman imperial cult was expected of members of the Roman army.[133] Thus, Tertullian writes, "The entire religious life of a soldier is to worship the military standards, to swear by the standards, and to place the standards before all gods" (*Apology* 16.8). For Cornelius, Peter's declaration that Jesus is "Lord of all" (Acts 10:36) would conflict with his religiopolitical allegiance to Rome and its emperor.

It is as Cornelius listens and as Peter bears witness that the Holy Spirit falls on the colonizers. Thus, they are disarmed. As the Jerusalemite believers say in response to Peter's report of the incident at Caesarea, "God has given even to the Gentiles the repentance that leads to life" (Acts 11:18). Salvation is available to Gentiles such as Cornelius, but an act of *repentance* is required. Change is required, a turning away from systems that oppress. Salvation and liberation are available for colonized and colonizer alike, but the colonizer has further to fall in order to participate in the reality of a world turned upside-down.

FORCED MIGRATION AND FAMINE IN THE DIASPORA (ACTS 11:19-30)

Forced migration of Judean followers of Jesus carries the good news as far as Phoenicia, Cyprus, and Antioch (Acts 11:19), though it is initially spread only internally to other Jews. This shows that some of the first international "missionary" efforts were carried out by people who had left their homes by necessity in order to escape an oppressive situation. This should resonate with the experiences of many immigrants, including my own Filipino Canadian

[130]Strobel, *Coming Full Circle*, 21.

[131]See the language of del Rosario, "Can There Be a Postcolonial Theology."

[132]Justin R. Howell, "The Imperial Authority and Benefaction of Centurions and Acts 10.34-43: A Response to C. Kavin Rowe," *JSNT* 31, no. 1 (2008): 33-36.

[133]See, e.g., Brian Campbell, *The Roman Army, 31 BC–AD 337: A Sourcebook* (New York: Routledge, 1994), 127.

family, who left the Philippines during the period of martial law under the Marcos regime and came to Canada to seek a better life. Indeed, it resonates with many of our stories, as colonial and neocolonial situations continue to lead us or our forebears to migrate. This passage also reminds us of the importance of diaspora communities as a place where the good news spreads, which is the case in many Asian American communities. It is believers from Cyprus and Cyrene, Hellenized regions outside the Jewish homeland, who take it on themselves speak to and to proclaim the Lord Jesus to Hellenists as well (Acts 11:20). It is *they*, who are native to Hellenized areas, who are able to bridge the cultural divide and successfully proclaim the Lord Jesus to the Hellenists (Acts 11:21).

The severe famine predicted by the prophecy of Agabus (Acts 11:28) confronts the Antiochene community with a coming crisis. Other historical evidence also indicates serious and widespread food shortages during the reign of Claudius.[134] The response of the Antioch church is to send relief, each according to their ability to the Judean believers (Acts 11:29). Relief has been a part of the work of the church from the beginning. This act should also be understood in light of the background of a broader concern among Diaspora communities to send money to the Jewish homeland (e.g., Cicero, *Pro Flacco* 67-68; Josephus, *Ant.* 16.167-173). The actions of the Antiochene believers find a parallel and can be recontextualized in the self-sacrificial efforts of diaspora Filipinos worldwide, and particularly overseas Filipino workers who give generously and send much of what they earn to family and those in need in the homeland. This is a survival strategy for our neocolonial context. It is no wonder, then, that at the time of writing, the highest-grossing Filipino film of all time is *Hello, Love, Goodbye*, a story about an overseas Filipino worker in Hong Kong who experiences exploitation and abuse as she sacrifices deeply to send her earnings to her family in the Philippines.

PETER IS LIBERATED FROM PRISON (ACTS 12:1-19)

The church in Judea suffers violence at the hands of the colonial authorities. The "King Herod" of Acts 12:1 is Agrippa I, the Roman-educated and -appointed client-king, who was a close friend and agent of the emperors Caligula and Claudius (Josephus, *Ant.* 18.143, 237; 19.274-275). Regardless of his apparent popularity, Agrippa I was undeniably part of the Roman imperial regime. He has James, brother of John and the son of Zebedee, executed in an act of state violence. James is killed "by the sword" (Acts 12:2), referring to decapitation, which was a preferred Roman method of execution.[135] We are not directly told why Agrippa had James executed, but within the narrative of Luke–Acts, the church is made up of followers of a man who was executed by the Roman authorities, and Gamaliel's speech in Acts 5:35-39 groups the followers of Jesus together with revolutionaries who "rose up" (Acts 5:35, 37), strongly implying that the early followers of Jesus were a threat to the order that authorities sought to preserve. For Luke, a direct statement of the reason for James's execution was thus apparently unnecessary. Peter is also arrested in order to curry favor with Agrippa's Judean subjects (Acts 12:3), which implies that popular sentiment had turned against the followers of

[134]E.g., specifically referring to a famine in Judea, Josephus, *Ant.* 20.51, 100-101. On these shortages more generally across the Roman world, see Bruce W. Winter, "Acts and Food Shortages," in *The Book of Acts in Its Graeco-Roman Setting*, ed. David W. J. Gill and Conrad Gempf (Grand Rapids, MI: Eerdmans, 1994), 59-78.

[135]See Keener, *Acts*, 2:1872-73.

Jesus. The arrest of James and Peter are the sixth and seventh arrests in the narrative. Agrippa's intent to publicly execute Peter at Passover is implied in Acts 12:4, which creates a strong parallel to the arrest and execution of Jesus. The church prayed "fervently" for Peter through his imprisonment (Acts 12:5), demonstrating their care and compassion for him and their belief and trust that God can and will set the imprisoned free. There is a lesson here for the church today about the need to pray and care for those in prison and those who are victims of state and police violence rather than assuming that their imprisonment is just.

Peter is imprisoned and chained between two soldiers, awaiting execution, when he is liberated by an angel of the Lord, and the chains literally fall off. It is fitting that this happens during Passover: just as God liberated Israel from slavery, so too is Peter liberated from chains. In this moment, we are reminded that this kind of liberation is also part of the mission of Christ, who proclaimed that the Spirit of the Lord "has sent me to proclaim release to the captives" (Lk 4:18). This passage and others that depict God literally freeing prisoners are frequently spiritualized in the worship music and teaching of the White evangelical church. This spiritualization ignores that the intended sense of the text is to depict Peter's *actual* liberation from prison. The text reminds us that God is present even in the midst of oppressive state violence and that he desires the liberation of the unjustly imprisoned. Perhaps we have much to learn, theologically and biblically, from those imprisoned unjustly, as Peter was. Edicio de la Torre, a Filipino Catholic priest, theologian, and activist, was imprisoned for nine years during the period of martial law under the Marcos regime. Reflecting on his imprisonment, he writes, "Prison is like a novitiate. You learn a spirituality, a spirituality for struggle. It's a time to gather yourself together as a human being. . . . In prison, I made my decision to be with the poor forever."[136]

Before Peter leaves, he brings the good news of his liberation to some of his fellow Christ-believing Jews in Jerusalem. The house of Mary, mother of John Mark, is the place of gathering and prayer (Acts 12:12). That the house used for gatherings is specifically identified as belonging to a woman is significant and is part of a broader trend in earliest Christianity: Nympha (Col 4:15) and Lydia (Acts 16:15) are also women who open their homes to the church. Rhoda's joy at seeing Peter free and alive, and the skepticism that she is met with when she announces that Peter is at the gate (Acts 12:15-16), creates another strong parallel to Luke's passion-and-resurrection narrative. Again, a woman carries good news to the church, but is not believed until they see with their own eyes. Peter's instruction to tell James and the brothers and sisters that the Lord brought him out of prison (Acts 12:17) will allow the others to know that he is safe, but it is also a proclamation that can bring encouragement to a church living in the midst of violence: the Lord has literally liberated Peter and broken his chains!

THE DEATH OF AGRIPPA I (ACTS 12:20-25)

Agrippa's death is presented as divine justice enacted against an oppressor, and the placement of this story directly after the narrative of James's death and Peter's arrest underscores this. Within the context of Luke's story, Agrippa is an oppressor and a tyrant directly responsible for the death of one of the Twelve. His plan to execute Peter shows that he is willing to bloody his hands in order to increase his public standing,

[136]De la Torre, *Touching Ground*, 163.

his execution of his own soldiers in Acts 12:19 further demonstrates his brutality, and his dispute with the Tyrians and Sidonians reveals him to be competent but ruthless in his political dealings. We must recognize, however, that Agrippa certainly had supporters. Josephus, for example, calls him "a person most worthy of admiration" (*Ant.* 18.129) and depicts him as having a good reputation (*Ant.* 19.328-331). Luke may also hint at Agrippa's popularity in Acts 12:22. Powerful political figures, even ones who commit acts of oppression like Agrippa, are rarely universally loved or universally despised. Filipinos who remember the Marcos regime know this well, as do many ethnic minorities in the United States who recently endured a national leader who consistently perpetuated harmful racist tropes, policies, and stereotypes between 2016 and 2020, yet was loved by many of our evangelical siblings.

Josephus provides a parallel account of the death of Agrippa that helps to supplement Luke's narrative. Josephus sets the death of Agrippa during an imperial festival at Caesarea honoring the emperor (*Ant.* 19.343). Both Josephus and Luke could be correct: such a festival, celebrating Caesar, would make for a good "appointed day" (Acts 12:21) on which to deliver a public address proclaiming peace. Josephus relates that the "royal robes" (mentioned by Luke in Acts 12:21) were of a brilliant reflective silver, which helps to explain why Luke mentions the robes and why the people flatter Agrippa by acclaiming him as a god (Acts 12:22), a detail also mentioned by Josephus (*Ant.* 19.345). The imperial festival setting in Caesarea and Agrippa's close connections to the emperor illuminate the severity of what he has done. Like the emperor, he too fancied himself deserving of acclamation as a god. Thus, he is struck down by an angel of the Lord (Acts 12:23). Agrippa is eaten by worms, which calls to mind the death of Antiochus Epiphanes, another king and violent oppressor who claimed divinity and was consumed by worms (2 Macc 9:9). The contrast between the death of Agrippa and the increase of power of the word of God punctuates this scene.

The God we know from Luke–Acts casts down rulers from their thrones and uplifts the lowly (Lk 1:52). The deification of rulers and of the state itself is an affront to God and must be resisted by his people. Hence, we must recognize the blasphemies and other dangers of Christian nationalism, which has recently gripped the church in the United States, as well White American folk religion.[137] For those of us with a colonized past, Christian nationalism can appear to be attractive to our colonized minds. However, let us not forget that the American invasion of the Philippines and subsequent slaughter of our people was framed as a missionary effort. We must remember our history, both the history of the early church and our own history of colonization by those who claimed to be bearers of the good news, both Spanish and American, but were instead bearers of the sword of oppression. The blood of our ancestors cries from the ground as a witness against the intertwining of the sword and the cross.

SAUL AND BARNABAS ARE SENT OUT (ACTS 13:1-12)

The diverse origins of the prophets and teachers of the church at Antioch (Acts 13:1) leap off the page. The scene is reminiscent of the fellowship of Christians of different Asian diaspora origins in the Asian American church. Although it is the teachers and prophets who lay their

[137]See Andrew L. Whitehead and Samuel L. Perry, *Taking America Back for God: Christian Nationalism in the United States* (New York: Oxford University Press, 2020); Walton, *Twelve Lies*.

hands on them and send them out, Saul and Barnabas are not selected by them but are set apart and called by the Holy Spirit (Acts 13:2-3).

That the Spirit called these two in particular makes very good sense and provides an exemplar of Luke's ideal "missionaries." They are both ethnically Jewish, meaning that they come not from the dominant, colonial ethnic group but from a colonized ethnic minority. However, while both have close ties to their homeland and to their Jewish identities, they have also been immersed in the broader culture of the Greco-Roman world, and thus of the people that they will minister to, both Jews and Gentiles. I am often dismayed by the way that the people of my mother's homeland are presented as the objects of White American missions that too often seem to be aimed primarily at making them American rather than followers of the crucified Christ, often prioritizing "proclamation" over development or justice initiatives in one of the most Christian nations in the world.[138] In the words of Barbara Jane Reyes, "They want to bring you Jesus, even though they see your people nailing themselves to crosses on Good Friday. Moreover, they think they brought you light bulbs, feminine hygiene products, and feminism."[139]

Cyprus is the first place Barnabas and Saul are sent to (Acts 13:4). Notably, Cyprus is Barnabas's home (Acts 4:36). Cyprus was culturally and ethnically predominantly Hellenistic, as its material culture shows. It also had a sizable Jewish population (mentioned by Josephus, *Ant.* 13.283; Philo, *On the Embassy to Gaius* 282). In Salamis, Barnabas and Saul's activities are focused on the local Jewish synagogues. Barnabas is a Cypriot Jew: these are his people. Synagogues in the diaspora were typically a kind of religio-ethnic association, similar to a club, based on shared Jewish ethnic and religious identity, though they could also be based on other shared aspects of identity as well, such as sectarianism, or a common profession. Synagogues also often provided accommodations for Jewish visitors.[140] Using the synagogues as a starting point will become a part of Paul's missionary method going forward.

The mention of the Jewish magician or pseudoprophet, Bar-Jesus (Acts 13:6), in Paphos implies that Barnabas and Saul's efforts there were also focused on the Jewish community. Nea Paphos was a Hellenistic city that was conquered by the Romans in the first century BCE and had since become the local Roman administrative center, as implied in Acts by the presence of the proconsul, Sergius Paulus (Acts 13:7), at Nea Paphos. Sergius Paulus was the local colonial administrator, and this scene (Acts 13:6-12) again depicts the early church bearing witness and proclaiming good news to a colonizer, who is surprisingly open to their message (Acts 13:7, 12). They are opposed by Bar-Jesus (Elymas), the court pseudoprophet and magician. Paul denounces him as an "enemy of justice [*dikaiosynē*]" who "makes the straight paths of the Lord crooked" (Acts 13:10, my translation). His supernatural blinding reveals his lack of spiritual sight. Court pseudoprophets continue to exist in the halls of power in every time and place who could rightly be called "opponents of justice" who "make the straight paths crooked."

It is during this encounter (Acts 13:9) that Luke begins to consistently refer to Saul as Paul. He has headed into the Greco-Roman world and has to put on his Diaspora Romano-Jewish identity. His two names speak to the two worlds

[138]See, e.g., Al Tizon, *Whole and Reconciled* (Grand Rapids, MI: Baker Academic, 2018), 37-56. See also Strobel, *Coming Full Circle*, 4-5.

[139]Reyes, "Brown Girl Glossary," 24.

[140]Lee I. Levine, *The Ancient Synagogue: The First Thousand Years*, 2nd ed. (New Haven, CT: Yale University Press, 2005), 406.

that he inhabits as a Diaspora Jew. This dual identity is something Asian Americans understand well, as we exist *both* as Asians and as North Americans simultaneously, immersed to different degrees in our diasporic cultures as well as the majority culture. Those of us who are mixed race (such as myself) carry those two identities in our bodies as well as in our minds.

TEACHING IN PISIDIAN ANTIOCH (ACTS 13:13-52)

Pisidian Antioch was a literal Roman colony. This meant that a significant number of Roman colonists had been given land and power within the city and that the colony was tasked with the military goal of maintaining and defending Roman occupation.[141] Administration, and thus political power, was in the hands of the colonists.[142]

The Jewish Diaspora community is the center of Paul and Barnabas's activity in Pisidian Antioch. It is a reminder of the importance of diaspora communities for newly arrived people to connect with others. By going to the synagogues, Paul and Barnabas are carrying on a pattern established by Jesus during his Galilean ministry (Lk 4:15, 43-44). This section provides the fullest account of Paul's synagogue teaching in Acts. The description of the Sabbath synagogue service in Acts 13:14-15 presents the reader with a slice of Diaspora community life. The readings from the Jewish Scriptures, specifically the Law and the Prophets, served not only to form the community spiritually but also to form community identity and maintain ties to the homeland and the broader Jewish community, conveying Jewish history, culture, narrative, and values. Teaching and discussion typically followed Scripture readings in synagogues, a practice that stemmed at least as far back as the first public readings of Scripture outside the temple (Neh 8:7-8).

Paul's message for the ethnically mixed audience of Jews and Gentiles "who fear God" (Acts 13:16) draws on Israel's rich history and relates it to their present context. This selective overview of the biblical past reminds the hearers of their foundational history as a people, highlighting God's faithfulness to Israel. Beginning with Acts 13:23, Paul then relates that scriptural narrative of faithfulness to their own times, presenting Jesus as a continuation of God's faithfulness to his people, a savior (Acts 13:23) through whom forgiveness of sins is proclaimed (Acts 13:38-39).

Paul's retelling of biblical history begins with the exodus, the story of liberation from Egypt. It is likely that this foundational story resonated strongly with his Diaspora synagogue audience, who were perpetual foreigners in Pisidian Antioch. Exodus is also an important narrative for the Filipino American church. In *America Is in the Heart*, Bulosan relates that, when he was a child, his brother read him "the story of a man named Moses who delivered his persecuted people to safety in another land" when he was young, and how José Rizal was like a Moses for Filipinos but was killed by the Spanish colonizers. In one of the last chapters of *America Is in the Heart*, Bulosan writes of a class he taught to Filipino and Mexican immigrant laborers in California on the state of the United States, including US history. He describes how he used Old Testament biblical narratives as "historical analogies" for the workers, particularly the stories of Moses, Ruth, and Job, and how it was only among these laborers that he "understood the full significance of Moses's flight." He recognized that these were stories of persecuted

[141]Barbara Levick, *Roman Colonies in Southern Asia Minor* (Oxford: Oxford University Press, 1967), 5-6.
[142]Levick, *Roman Colonies*, 189.

immigrants and told the laborers, "All these persecutions happened a long time ago in an ancient land. . . . But they are significant to us because we are undergoing similar persecutions. We who came to the United States as immigrants are Americans too."[143]

Paul's speech finds its apex in the proclamation of Jesus (Acts 13:23-39), who is the culmination of salvation history, the Savior brought by God to Israel in fulfillment of his promise (Acts 13:23). Paul teaches that this Savior was rejected by his own people (Acts 13:27) and unjustly killed at the hands of the Roman authorities (Acts 13:28). He specifically names the fact that Jesus was killed even though there was no cause for a sentence of death. That injustice and suffering is also a part of the story of salvation history, but it is not the end of the story because God raised Jesus from the dead (Acts 13:30). This shows that Jesus is ultimately victorious, that he was vindicated by God, and that he has prevailed over death and over the injustice done to him. The resurrection of Jesus is the ultimate fulfillment of salvation history, because it is the fulfillment of God's promise to Paul and the synagogue members' shared Israelite ancestors (Acts 13:33-37, citing Ps 2:7 and Ps 16:10), and so Paul rightly calls it "good news" (Acts 13:33). It is through Jesus that Paul proclaims full salvation and liberation to his audience, because it is by Jesus that there is liberation from sin for all who believe (Acts 13:38-39). This is good news indeed: Jesus has overcome through struggle, has been vindicated in the face of the injustice of his violent death, and has triumphed over sin and death!

Paul's message of hope is well received, so he and Barnabas are asked to speak again on the next Sabbath (Acts 13:42-43). However, the large crowd of Gentiles that shows up to the synagogue on the next Sabbath upsets Paul and Barnabas's Jewish hosts. Luke is not clear about why this creates "jealousy" (Acts 13:45), but we might guess that the invasion of minority space by outsiders from the majority culture, and a sudden visibility due to the appearance of visitors carrying a message that was apparently controversial within the Jewish community, could be factors. Paul and Barnabas's declaration that they are now "turning to the gentiles" (Acts 13:46) indicates a new focus on those who were previously outsiders to salvation history. It does not indicate that Paul, Barnabas, or God has turned away from Jews. The text they cite about being a light to the Gentiles comes from Isaiah 49:6, which is spoken to God's servant, Israel (Is 49:3), and follows a statement about God gathering Israel to himself. By citing this, Paul and Barnabas are taking on the task of being *representatives* of Israel as a light to the Gentiles. Hence, we find them yet again in a synagogue in the very next city that they visit.

ICONIUM, LYSTRA, AND DERBE (ACTS 14:1-20)

The ministry in Iconium is again based in the local synagogue and results in an ethnically mixed group of new believers composed of Jews and Gentiles together (Acts 14:1). We are not told why the movement is divisive in Iconium, but we do get some clues: it is divisive for both Jews and Gentiles (Acts 14:4-5), and thus opposed by some of both groups, and local rulers are involved in the attempt to mistreat and stone Paul and Barnabas. It is also worth noting that during the reign of Claudius, the same time that this narrative is set, Iconium was renamed Claudiconium in recognition of

[143]Bulosan, *America Is in the Heart*, 45-46, 312.

its adoption of Roman ideals. It was also a "double community" in this time, with a Roman colonial population as well as a local population, which makes it likely that the Gentile "rulers" would have included local Roman colonial authorities.[144]

Lystra was also a Roman colony.[145] The healing of the man who had never walked strongly parallels Peter and John's earlier healing of another man who was unable to walk from birth in Jerusalem (Acts 3:1-10). Like Peter and John, Paul also looks intently at the man, making eye contact with someone who was probably frequently overlooked (see comments on Acts 3:1-10 above). Once again, Paul and Barnabas's message is accompanied by restorative acts of care.

By mistaking Barnabas for Zeus and Paul for Hermes (Acts 14:11-13), the crowds mistake the messengers for the message.[146] In Greco-Roman religion, the gods frequently appeared in human guise, which partly explains their misunderstanding. In the Asian American church, there is a temptation to accord more authority than we should to charismatic teachers, which can unfortunately play on our positive cultural values of respect and honor. Those of us who are in positions of honor and authority can learn from the example of Paul and Barnabas, who are grieved at being mistaken for being divine (Acts 14:14). Rather than using Jewish Scripture, which would have been culturally irrelevant to most of their Gentile audience, Paul and Barnabas instead draw on examples from creation and providence from creation to direct their hearers to the living God.

The mob's attempt to lynch Paul by stoning him (Acts 14:19) is yet another instance of the recurring theme of violence that followers of Jesus face throughout the narrative of Acts. Faithful discipleship persists in struggle, as violence is not suffered in vain. Paul is not abandoned but is surrounded by the Lystran disciples after being left for dead and rises in their midst (Acts 14:20).

THE END OF THE FIRST JOURNEY (ACTS 14:21-28)

Derbe, like Pisidian Antioch, Iconium, and Lystra, was also a Roman colony.[147] This underscores that Paul's very first missionary journey brought him to proclaim good news to people who had literally experienced colonization, Jews and Gentiles alike. Paul and Barnabas encourage and strengthen the disciples in Lystra, Iconium, and Pisidian Antioch by teaching them, "It is through many persecutions that we must enter the kingdom of God" (Acts 14:22). These were cities where Paul and Barnabas had just experienced persecution. Discipleship entails suffering, but that suffering is not without purpose. Rather, it is a struggle, for we enter the kingdom of God through it.[148] For people who have endured the pains of oppression and colonization, this passage is a reminder that the kingdom is for us and that the history of the suffering church is our history too. Decolonizing our hermeneutics, remembering our history, and understanding our own experiences will help us to see how our Christian history and our history as colonized people overlap. This is our story too.

[144]Stephen Mitchell, "Iconium and Ninica: Two Double Communities in Roman Asia Minor," *Historia* 28, no. 4 (1979): 409-38.
[145]Levick, *Roman Colonies*, 195-97.
[146]See González, *Acts*, 167.
[147]Bob Wagner and Mark Wilson, "Why Derbe?: An Unlikely Lycaonian City for Paul's Ministry," *TynBul* 70, no. 1 (2019): 57.
[148]Though not in the sense of "by it."

THE JERUSALEM COUNCIL (ACTS 15:1-21)

The question of whether one must be circumcised in order to be saved is a crucial one. It is important to understand it in context. Circumcision had always been required to be a part of God's covenant people. It is biblical. Circumcision was an ethnic boundary marker, something that set Jews apart from Gentiles. The ethnic boundary marker laws, such as circumcision, keeping kosher, keeping the Sabbath, and ritual purity, had served the Jewish people well as part of their survival strategy as people living faithfully in the midst of empire, in diaspora, and through colonization. These were good and part of God's plan of providence and grace. Nevertheless, now that God's people included Gentiles as well, the markers of a people of God made up of Jews and Gentiles together would need to be envisioned.

To require Gentiles to be circumcised and to keep the Torah would have required them to set aside their own ethnic identity and adopt Jewish ethnic boundary markers. The issue is not merely that this would create division in the church; it is that this requirement would create a church that would be uniform rather than diverse, a church that would not include Jews and Gentiles *together*. For Paul and Barnabas, circumcision was a matter of inclusion. It was about unity in diversity.

Some believers maintain that "it is necessary for them to be circumcised and ordered to keep the law of Moses" (Acts 15:5). These believers have tradition on their side. This is the way it has always been. They have Scripture. Yet, whether intentional or not, these early conservative believers are demanding assimilation, to make "them" more like "us." To require Gentiles to be circumcised and to keep the Torah would require them to set aside their own ethnic identity and adopt Jewish ethnic boundary markers. This requirement would create a church that is uniform rather than diverse, a church that does not include Jews and Gentiles together. For Paul and Barnabas, circumcision was a matter of inclusion. As Peter argues, God has cleansed the hearts of Gentiles by faith (Acts 15:9), "he has made no distinction" between "them" (Gentiles) and "us" (Jews). Thus, faith plays an important role in maintaining a church that is truly united in its diversity. Moreover, Peter argues that ordering Gentiles to be circumcised and to keep the Law of Moses places a "a yoke that neither our ancestors nor we have been able to bear" on the necks of Gentile disciples (Acts 15:10).

Asian and Asian American Christians are often pressured to assimilate to the culture, biblical interpretation, and theology of the White, Western church. This has been particularly true for Filipinos and thus also Filipino Americans, due to our colonial history. The insistence on traditional US norms such as patriotism, patriarchal gender roles, individualism, and capitalism, things that are foreign to our way of being and to our discipleship to Christ, as Christian values compromises the gospel. This is what Gabriel Catanus calls "colonial spirituality."[149] That said, we must reject the problematic notion that this incident depicts "Jews" discriminating against Gentiles or maintaining an ethnic superiority. This controversy is specific to followers of Jesus and only exists within the framework of Christ-belief. The controversy depicted in Acts 15:1-5 is not identical to our situation, but the overlap in meaning and experience of this controversy within the ancient church speaks clearly to our context as Asian Americans in the church today.

[149]Catanus, "Uncovering a FACE," 142.

Western culture is too often sold to us as Christianity. As Leny Strobel writes in a dialogue with God,

> I have been angry with the white missionaries and white people who robbed me of the opportunity to know You on my own terms. I have felt this fakery I have lived by, this cultural Christianity; and part of that cultural Christianity includes the oppression of people, their being judged as inferior people. All my life I've lived feeling inferior to white people, beholden to them for their intelligence, affluence, productivity, and cultural creations. After I became a Christian, I wanted even more to become like them, for to be like them is to be like You. I do not believe that any longer.[150]

Acts envisions a diverse community in which there are different ways of being a follower of Jesus, both Jewish and Gentile together. Although many of us from all ethnic and cultural backgrounds might implicitly understand this in concept, in practice, Asian American Christians are often made to feel as though our values and culture are "foreign" not just to the United States, but to the church, even when those values are actually just contrary to Western culture and not to orthodox Christian faith. As this controversy in Acts 15 reminds us, there are different ways of being that are faithful within the church.

Peter's response to the controversy calls back to his earlier experience in Acts 10–11, where he saw the Spirit poured out on Gentiles (Acts 15:7-8). He underscores that God has "made no distinction between them and us" (Acts 15:9). This is a lesson that Peter had to learn, with divine help (Acts 10:15, 34). That there is no distinction means that Jewish believers can be Jews, and Gentile believers can be Gentiles. James reminds the assembly and the reader that God's taking a people for his name from among the Gentiles has always been part of the divine plan, as witnessed in Jewish Scripture (citing Amos 9:11-12).

TIMOTHY, A MULTIETHNIC BELIEVER, JOINS THE MISSION (ACTS 15:36–16:5)

The separation of Paul and Barnabas over John Mark contrasts sharply with the message of ethnic unity declared at the Jerusalem council. Barnabas and John Mark leave on their own journey (Acts 15:39). Paul takes Silas with him, and they are joined by Timothy in Lystra (Acts 16:1-3). Timothy is immediately characterized by his biethnicity: his mother was Jewish and his father was Greek. Multiethnicity in antiquity was complex, just as it is today. Timothy was forced to navigate his layered, overlapping identities. Multiethnic people carry diversity in their bodies, and Timothy represented both the unity and the fault lines between Jewish and Greek believers in his flesh. Despite having just argued that Gentile believers do not need to be circumcised, Paul circumcises Timothy (Acts 16:3), allowing him to be accepted as a Jew by his Jewish brethren who know of his paternal Greek heritage. Although Luke does not say so directly, we should recognize that by being circumcised, Timothy would complicate his Greek identity, likely compromising his ability to be accepted as a Greek by his father's people.

This incident speaks to the way that mixed people can experience feeling or being regarded as other than or less than the parts of their lineage. In a North American context, it is extremely difficult for me as a person with brown skin to identify as White or to claim my father's Newfoundland Irish ethnic heritage. I will inevitably be racialized as

[150]Strobel, *Coming Full Circle*, 4.

something-other-than-White. My Filipino *kababayans* are typically much more accepting of my Filipino identity. Yet, we are aware that my experience, context, and thus identity are distinct. It is another way of being. According to Lisa Asedillo Pratt and Grace Kao, "Being mixed should neither be perceived as alien to being Asian . . . , nor seen as 'less than' or 'more than' (e.g., persons of Asian heritage who are racially mixed with white are often viewed as 'more beautiful' than if they were 'just' Asian), but simply as one of the many ways of being Asian American."[151]

Timothy's example shows us that mixed, multiethnic people are not invisible. We are represented in the scriptural narrative of the church's beginnings. In fact, Timothy's multiethnicity proves advantageous for him as he accompanies Paul and Silas through Macedonia and Achaia, homelands of Hellenistic peoples and cultures, and interacts with Diaspora Jewish communities in those regions. So too can our layered and overlapping ethnic identities be received by us as a gift, albeit one that comes with deep complexities.

TO MACEDONIA (ACTS 16:6-15)

This new journey is directed explicitly by the Spirit, culminating in a visionary call to Macedonia. Macedonia had risen to power in the fourth century BCE under the leadership of Philip II and Alexander the Great and had played a role in the Hellenization of the Mediterranean world. However, Macedonia was invaded and occupied by Rome, coming under full Roman control in the second century BCE. The journey into Macedonia is the first passage to be narrated in the first-person plural, implying the author's participation in that journey. The good news is carried into Europe from the east, rather than vice versa.

Philippi was a Roman colony during this time, having been settled twice by Roman colonists. The heavy Romanization of the city is reflected in its archaeological remains, including its inscriptions, which are predominantly in Latin despite being located in a region populated primarily by people of Greek ethnicity and language.[152] The term "place of prayer" (*proseuchē* in Greek) that Luke refers to is frequently used to refer to Jewish synagogues in the Diaspora. This "place of prayer" may or may not have been a building; it could have been an open-air meeting. Its location outside the walls is not unusual or unique, since access to a body of water for purposes of ritual purity, among other things, was convenient for Jewish communities.[153] Paul and his companions knew the trans-Diaspora culture of their people well enough to be able to find and connect with them quickly. Lydia is the first known and named baptized follower of Jesus in Europe. By the end of the chapter, her home will become the place of gathering for local believers (Acts 16:40). It is a woman who paves the way for others to follow and who also opens her home to Paul and his companions.

SHAKING THE FOUNDATIONS IN PHILIPPI (ACTS 16:16-40)

There is no mention of conflict in Philippi until Paul casts a spirit of divination out of a slave girl. This narrative depicts the economic exploitation of a slave girl, who is further oppressed by the spirit that enables the divination that her masters exploit for monetary gain.

[151]Pratt and Kao, "On Becoming Asian American Christian Ethicists," 231.

[152]Eduard Verhoef, *Philippi: How Christianity Began in Europe—The Epistle to the Philippians and the Excavations at Philippi* (London: Bloomsbury, 2013), 7-10, 16-19.

[153]Anders Runesson, Donald D. Binder, and Birger Olsson, *The Ancient Synagogue from its Origins to 200 C.E.: A Source Book* (Leiden and Boston: Brill, 2008), 239.

Although Paul does so out of irritation, his exorcism of the spirit would have freed the slave girl from its oppression and from that particular form of exploited work. The exploitation of bodies for monetary gain is an all-too-familiar reality for overseas Filipino workers in the United States, who are too often treated as expendable flesh for the neocolonial gain of their US employers.

The girl's masters drag Paul and Silas to the marketplace. The marketplace, or agora, of a Greco-Roman city was typically where public buildings, and thus the local authorities, could be found. Due to Philippi's status as a Roman colony, the authorities were Romans, but local chief magistrates (called *duoviri*) rather than imperial officials.[154] The charge that Paul and Silas's accusers bring against them is noteworthy. Paul and Silas are accused of "disturbing the city." Their Jewish ethnicity is specifically brought up, which has the effect of turning them into "others," outsiders who cannot be considered *true* Romans or Philippians. That othering is followed by the accusation that they are "advocating customs that are not lawful for us, being Romans, to adopt or observe" (Acts 16:21). This pits the accusers' colonial Roman identity against Paul and Silas's foreign, Jewish identity. They are, as Eric Barretto writes, "accused of disrupting the fundamental ethnic ordering of this colony."[155] Ironically, the accusation that what Paul and Silas are proclaiming is not lawful for Romans is not completely untrue. Following Jesus Christ would necessarily require turning away from the imperial cult and subverting the *pax deorum* (peace of the [Roman] gods).

Paul and Silas are severely flogged with rods (Acts 16:22-23), a Roman form of corporal punishment. This happens without a trial (Acts 16:37). Here is illegitimate violence wielded by the authorities without trial. It is imperial violence administered by local colonial magistrates against the bodies of colonized ethnic others. Paul himself writes that he was beaten three times in this way in 2 Corinthians 11:25, a sure sign that he continued to run afoul of the Roman authorities. Paul and Silas are then arrested and placed in maximum security in the innermost cell (Acts 16:24). This is the eighth arrest.

Prisons are often means of oppression and suppression used by tyrants, (neo)colonial authorities, and empires. I think of Jose Rizal, Edicio de la Torre, and the Filipino American activists and organizers in Bulosan's *America Is in the Heart*, who all spent extended time in prison for their resistance against different colonial powers. In the United States, prison continues to oppress, with its system of for-profit, privatized prisons, and crackdowns against undocumented immigrants, an issue that concerns Filipinos in particular among Asian American groups.[156] God shakes the prison to its foundations, throws open its doors, and unfastens the prisoners' chains. This is the second time that God has liberated one of the protagonists of Acts from prison, showing God's consistent concern for the freedom of the imprisoned. This is the second time that God has shaken the earth in Acts (see Acts 4:31). In both cases, the earth quivers in the face of the oppression of God's people, showing God's presence with the powerless who are faithful in the midst of their suffering. The captives are released, just as Jesus himself proclaimed (Lk 4:18). It is not only Paul and Silas who are liberated but the whole prison.

[154]Verhoef, *Philippi*, 7; W. M. Ramsay, "The Philippians and Their Magistrates," *JTS* 1, no. 1 (1899): 114-16.
[155]Eric Barretto, *Ethnic Negotiations: The Function of Race and Ethnicity in Acts 16* (Tübingen: Mohr Siebeck, 2010), 178.
[156]See Catanus, "Uncovering a FACE," 191-96.

A colonial spirituality insists that Christian freedom is spiritual freedom from sin and nothing more, but Luke–Acts presents us with a much wider and more inclusive vision of what freedom is: as we have seen, God shakes the foundations not only of this prison in Philippi but of arrest, imprisonment, and injustice themselves.

Paul's shout to the jailer, "Do not harm yourself" (Acts 16:28), shows compassion and regard for the human life and dignity of a literal oppressor. The oppressor is not free and so seeks salvation, allowing Paul to proclaim salvation to him if he places faith on the Lord Jesus (Acts 16:30). Jailer and prisoner are liberated and saved together, each in different ways. Paul and Silas are even shown hospitality in the jailer's house, and they share food together, an act of fellowship in ancient Mediterranean culture and in ours. It is unlikely that the jailer was Jewish, so this scene also depicts Paul and Silas accepting Gentile food and sharing it with Gentiles. We know from Paul's letter to the Galatians that this practice was unacceptable to some Jewish followers of Jesus (Gal 2:12), so this scene would have been an all the more striking act of unlikely fellowship. The juxtaposition of the jailer washing Paul and Silas's wounds with Paul and Silas baptizing the jailer and his family is a powerful image of the upside-down kingdom in action. Both prisoners and jailer are washed and cleansed of their wounds.

Paul's response to the police (Acts 16:37) exemplifies a willingness to speak out against injustice and insist on recognition of that injustice even when it does not benefit him, since he is free to go (Acts 16:35-36). The police's response reminds us of the privilege and benefits of citizenship in the Roman world, which overlaps considerably with the US Filipino context, where many of us lack the power that citizenship provides and the ability to be heard as "true" Americans.

TURNING THE WORLD UPSIDE-DOWN (ACTS 17:1-9)

The Thessalonian narrative gives us some insight into Paul's activity in synagogues. He attends the gatherings on the Sabbath, when the Jewish Scriptures were read aloud, and argues on the basis of Jewish Scripture (1) that it was necessary for the Messiah to suffer and die, and (2) that Jesus was that Messiah (Acts 17:1-3). This reflects the norms of ancient synagogues in this period, in which interpretation and discussion of Scripture was a regular feature of gatherings.[157] Paul draws on the shared culture of his people's Diaspora communities to proclaim Jesus' death, resurrection, and messiahship, standing within that culture rather than apart from it. The strategy bears some fruit. Acts 17:4 hints at the diverse demographic composition of the early Thessalonian church. It was a multiethnic church with a mixture of people of different social statuses. It is significant that the Thessalonian church included some of the city's leading women, who would likely have been key and influential members of the community. The continuing prominence of influential women in the ancient church before Constantine is attested archaeologically in a donor inscription discovered in the early Christian meeting place discovered at Legio (Meggido) in the Jezreel Valley, which names four women: Primilla, Cyriaca, Dorothea, and Chreste.[158]

[157]See Ryan, *Role of the Synagogue*, 42-45.

[158]Yotam Tepper and Leah di Segni, *A Christian Prayer Hall of the Third Century CE at Kefar 'Othnay (Legio)* (Jerusalem: IAA, 2006), 41.

Controversy ensues, which erupts into mob violence (Acts 17:5). The accusation leveled against Jason and the other believers whom the mob seized is important. Jason is accused of harboring Paul and Silas, "who have been turning the world upside down" (Acts 17:6), and the believers are accused of "acting contrary to the decrees of the emperor, saying that there is another king named Jesus" (Acts 17:7). Although Jewish anti-Roman sentiment ran high at this time, we should recognize the effect of colonial mentality, the psychological effects of colonization, on conquered or colonized people living in the midst of empire.[159] Colonial mentality can foster support for the powerful colonizers and of the status quo, the present order, as well as the impulse to show one's loyalty to it. These accusations characterize the early followers of Jesus in the mind of the reader and show how the movement was perceived. They are significant not because the mob is wrong but because they have perceived correctly. The Way that Paul and Silas proclaim is a threat to the *ordo*, the hierarchical ordering of Roman imperial society, with the emperor at the top. The implied reader will remember that Luke's first volume proclaimed the kingdom of God as a world turned upside-down (Lk 1:52; 4:18-19; 6:20-26; 13:30), and we see that same upside-down kingdom reflected in Paul's own writings, in which the weak shame the strong (1 Cor 1:27-28) and the humble are exalted (Phil 2:8-9). The way of Jesus casts down the hierarchy and turns the world upside down. Proclaiming Jesus' kingship is incompatible with the supremacy of the emperor. Jason and the others pay bail (Acts 17:9), indicating that this should be counted as the ninth arrest.

ADAPTABILITY IN ATHENS (ACTS 17:16-34)

Athens was the traditional heart of Greek thought and culture, and functioned as a symbol of those things during the Roman period, although it had waned in power and influence. In Athens, Paul goes not only to the synagogue but also to the agora, the marketplace and public square that lay at the heart of public, economic, and civic life in Greco-Roman cities. This brings Paul into the broader public eye and into debate with Epicurean and Stoic philosophers.

The philosophers think that Paul is either babbling or "a proclaimer of foreign divinities," understanding Jesus to be a deity and "resurrection" (*anastasia* in Greek) to be his consort.[160] It might seem that the philosophers are sophisticated for wanting to hear from Paul, but Paul and his proclamation are identified by their foreignness. According to the Roman geographer Strabo, the Athenians were known for their "hospitality" to foreign things and gods (*Geogr.* 10.3.18) and were lampooned by comics for it. That said, Athens was not a welcoming place for foreign people, who were treated as second class.[161] This fascination with foreign culture or religion but not necessarily foreign people overlaps all too well with what the Asian American community experiences of exoticism. The Areopagus narrative has the flavor of exotic spectacle: the Jewish Paul and his foreign message are displayed in public by learned people for intellectual consumption and consideration.

Paul's speech exemplifies his cultural and contextual adaptability, representing the sorts of approaches that he might have typically taken when witnessing to Gentiles. It stands in contrast to the method of the synagogue

[159]Revolts against Rome in Judea occurred in 66–70 CE and 132–135 CE. The Diaspora revolt in Cyrenaica, Cyprus, and Egypt took place in 115–117 CE.

[160]See Parsons, *Acts*, 243; John Chrysostom, *Homily on Acts* 38.1.

[161]See Craig A. Keener, *Acts*, New Cambridge Biblical Commentary (Cambridge: Cambridge University Press, 2020), 434.

ministries in Thessalonica and Berea and to the synagogue teaching in Pisidian Antioch (Acts 13:16-41). Paul's typical references to the Jewish Scriptures are absent. Instead, Paul focuses on God as transcendent Creator of the *kosmos* (universe), who does not live in things made by human hands. The speech highlights the universal parenthood of God for all humanity, who are his offspring. Since God is the Creator and progenitor of all, he is for all and can be found by all, since he is not far from each of us (Acts 17:27). In order to present this message, Paul draws on things from the Athenians' own context, including the monuments of their city (Acts 17:23) and their own thinkers (Acts 17:28). Paul is thus able to adapt his message for different cultural contexts and even draw on those contexts without compromising the substance of his proclamation.

Although it has fixed elements, the gospel can be proclaimed and expressed without compromising its substance in many different cultural contexts and forms. No culture has a monopoly on it. Ultimately, it is the "foreign" elements of Paul's proclamation that turn off his intellectual elite audience. They scoff at the resurrection of the body, an idea common in Judaism but foreign to the high Hellenistic thought of Achaia. Even the educated intellectual elite who appear open to new ideas will scoff at foreign ideas that they find trite, uneducated, or strange. Tokenism and exoticism only carry them so far.

CORINTH (ACTS 18:1-17)

Corinth was once a leader of the Achaian League, a league of Greek states. The league defied and was broken by the Roman Republic in 146 BCE, and Corinth was crushed. In 44 BCE, Rome founded a new colony on the site. The result was a hybrid culture, a thoroughly Roman city that nevertheless laid claim as a legitimate heir to its Greek heritage.[162] Its Romanization is reflected in its material culture, particularly its public architecture and layout, which were characteristically Roman.[163] However, as Ekaputra Tupamahu has shown, Corinth's culture included remarkably diverse languages and ethnic groups, which hints at diaspora communities thriving in the midst of empire.[164]

In Corinth, Paul encounters Priscilla and Aquila, Jews who had been expelled from Rome by the emperor Claudius and with whom he finds kinship and community (Acts 18:2-3). In the same way, Filipinos often find *bayanihan* and *kasamahan* with our *kababayans* (fellow Filipinos) in North America, as well as fellowship and support with other Asian Americans. Work and working together with *kabayans*, as Paul does with Priscilla and Aquila, is also the experience of overseas Filipino workers in the United States and elsewhere. The expulsion of Jews from Rome may have been linked to internal division in the Jewish community over Christ-belief (see Suetonius, *Divus Claudius* 25.4). This imperial expulsion highlights the vulnerability, perceived foreignness, and thus "danger" to public order of the Jewish Diaspora community in places such as Rome. Filipinos and other minority groups face similar challenges in the United States today.

Paul again focuses his activities on the synagogue but is met with opposition (Acts 18:5-6).

---

[162]See Benjamin W. Millis, "The Social and Ethnic Origins of the Colonists in Early Roman Corinth," in *Corinth in Context: Comparative Studies on Religion and Society*, ed. Steven J. Friesen, Daniel N. Schowalter, and James C. Walters (Boston: Brill, 2010), 13-35.

[163]For an introduction, see John McRay, *Archaeology and the New Testament* (Grand Rapids, MI: Baker Academic, 2005), 311-38.

[164]Ekaputra Tupamahu, *Contesting Languages: Heteroglossia and the Politics of Language in the Early Church* (New York: Oxford University Press, 2023), 49-84.

Shaking off the dust and going next door to the house of Titius Justus, apparently a Gentile worshiper of the God of Israel with a Roman name, symbolizes Paul turning toward Gentiles in his Corinthian ministry.[165] However, Paul's efforts in the synagogue community are far from fruitless. Crispus, a synagogue official called an *archisynagōgos*, becomes a Christ-believer, along with all of his household (Acts 18:8, 17; see 1 Cor 1:14). An *archisynagōgos* was an influential member of a synagogue community. The title was a prestige granted to benefactors who oversaw the reading and interpretation of Scripture.[166] Despite the internal division within the Corinthian synagogue community, God tells Paul that he is with him and that no harm will come to him, so Paul can speak without fear (Acts 18:9-10). Paul is enabled to teach the word of God for an extended period in Corinth because of God's presence with him. God comforts Paul by reminding him of the many in Corinth who belong to his people (Acts 18:10). The community of the people of God should be a refuge in the midst of hardship.

As the proconsul of Achaia, Gallio was a high-ranking imperial official operating by the authority of the Roman senate. Gallio is well-known from Roman sources. He was the brother of Seneca the Younger and had close connections to the emperor at the time, Claudius, and was later a friend of Nero. He is mentioned in an inscription discovered at Delphi as a "friend" of Claudius.[167] The incident at Gallio's tribunal presents some interpretive difficulties. Is Paul accused of persuading people to worship God in a manner contrary to Jewish law (i.e., Torah) or Roman law? It is more likely that it is Roman law, and that the accusation is that the association that met at Titius Justus's house should be considered a permitted religion (*religio licita*) under Roman law. Judaism was an established *religio licita* due to its antiquity, but Paul's association's ties to the Jewish community and thus to Judaism were being called into question. Gallio's response, that the issue is "a matter of questions about words and names and your own [Jewish] law" (Acts 18:15), implies that this is the heart of the accusation. He declines to judge the matter and drives them away from the tribunal (Acts 18:16). Gallio is hardly an ally or hero. His actions betray an ambivalence and lack of care for his minority Jewish constituents and their community concerns.

The seizure and beating of Sosthenes, an *archisynagōgos*, by a mob in front of the tribunal is a horrific scene of majority-group mob violence against a prominent member of a minority community and the callous complicity of the colonial, imperial authorities that allow it to happen without consequence. Since the Jews were expelled from the tribunal (Acts 18:16), this violence must have been carried out by the non-Jewish Corinthian crowd. That the beating of a prominent Jewish community member could be carried out right in front of the tribunal, and moreover in front of the proconsul, demonstrates the crowd's confidence that they could engage in this act of violence without retribution. The Jewish minority community suffers violence simply for taking up too much space in the halls of power. This passage speaks *deeply* to the experiences of Filipino Americans whose ongoing invisibility in the church and society is reinforced by anger and derision from the majority culture whenever we try to take up

[165]The language of Titius Justus's house being next door implies that the "synagogue" of Corinth had a building.

[166]See Ryan, *Role of the Synagogue*, 50-52.

[167]Inscriptiones Graecae 7.1676.

space. For example, the spike in racially motivated violence against Asian Americans of 2020–2021 was not just about the Covid-19 pandemic. That the violence has been directed not only at Chinese Americans alone, who were despicably scapegoated for a pandemic that they could not possibly have caused, but at Asians in general points to broader issues. It is a repudiation of us for taking too much space in US society, for the faulty perception that we have succeeded at the "American dream" despite being perpetual foreigners. It has showed us what American society truly thinks of its so-called model minorities.

PRISCILLA AND AQUILA IN EPHESUS (ACTS 18:18-28)

Paul leaves Achaia with Priscilla and Aquila to return to Syria by way of Ephesus and Judea. The stop at the synagogue in Ephesus anticipates future ministry in that city and also depicts a warmer welcome than in Corinth by the Jewish community members, who want Paul to stay longer.

Apollos is characterized as passionate, eloquent, and well-versed in the Scriptures. However, his knowledge is incomplete, which is evident to Priscilla and Aquila when they hear him speak in the Ephesian synagogue (Acts 18:26). We should note that Apollos is willing to be taken aside, to learn, and to be corrected by both Priscilla and Aquila. Priscilla is named first in the Greek text. The instruction and correction she provides to Apollos alongside Aquila results in Apollos becoming a more effective proclaimer of Jesus' messiahship (Acts 18:27-28). That Priscilla is a woman is important, since it highlights the role that women played in instruction and in passing on the oral teachings of the Way. Would that the charismatic, educated male leaders in the church today might take note of Apollos's example and be willing to learn from the Aquilas *as well as* the Priscillas of our own time.

PAUL RETURNS TO EPHESUS (ACTS 19:1-10)

Acts 19 contains a collection of several narrative traditions about Paul's extended ministry in Ephesus, which took place over two years (Acts 19:10). Ephesus was the third largest city of the Roman Empire, with a population size estimated at 250,000 (based on its size and particularly the size of its theater), making it a veritable metropolis by first-century standards, with a diverse population and a considerable economy driven by Ephesus's sizable harbor and famed temple of Artemis.[168] The stamp of Roman imperial culture and propaganda is visible in the material culture of the city at the time of Paul discovered through archaeological excavations, including a statue of Julius Caesar, a colossal statue of Mark Antony, an imperial temple dedicated to Roma and Augustus, and a coin commemorating Nero issued by Ephesus.[169] Not long after the time of Paul, the city boasted two more imperial temples, one dedicated to Domitian and one to Hadrian.

The first narrative at Ephesus involves disciples who were baptized in John's baptism but have not heard that there is a Holy Spirit and who do not understand that John's teaching points to the one who came after him, Jesus (Acts 19:2-7). For Luke, belief in and baptism in the name of Jesus is inseparable from life in the Spirit.

Paul's teaching and discussion in the synagogue at Ephesus involve the kingdom of God,

[168]For a good introduction to the city in relation to the NT for nonspecialists, see Edwin M. Yamauchi, *New Testament Cities in Western Asia Minor* (Eugene, OR: Wipf & Stock, 2003), 79-114. More recently, see the scholarly historical novel by David A. deSilva, *A Week in the Life of Ephesus* (Downers Grove, IL: IVP Academic, 2020).

[169]Yamauchi, *New Testament Cities*, 83-84.

the central theme of Jesus' teaching in Luke (Acts 19:8). Some traces of the distinctive material culture of the Jewish community over the centuries in Ephesus have survived in the archaeological record, including mention of the Jewish community in a funerary inscription, a menorah carved into the steps leading to the Library of Celsus, lamps featuring menorahs, and a glass depicting the menorah, shofar, and *lulab* (a frond of a date palm tree).[170] Culture and identity are frequently expressed through the things we use and own.

Paul moves his teaching to the "lecture hall [*scholē*] of Tyrannus" when some in the synagogue community speak ill of the Way. This yet again underscores Paul's cultural adaptability and his ability to function both in Jewish and in Hellenistic scholastic and cultural spaces. Naturally, Paul's methods and message likely would have differed based on which venue he was in and thus which audience. This reminds us of the distinct modes of teaching in Paul's teaching in the synagogue at Pisidian Antioch and at the Areopagus in Athens. Luke is thus able to claim that all, both Jews and Greeks, "heard the word of the Lord" (Acts 19:10). Similarly, Asian Americans often have to function in two worlds and to move fluidly between them.

THE SONS OF SCEVA (ACTS 19:11-20)

Exorcism is also described in a number of Second Temple Jewish sources other than the New Testament (e.g., Josephus, *Ant.* 8.46-48; Tob 8:2-4; *Jub.* 10:3-13; 4Q560 1:3-5; 11Q11 5:6), indicating that belief in the demonic and the need to counter the sort of oppression that demons represented were widespread. Indeed, Luke and the other Evangelists present exorcism as a crucial part of Jesus' itinerant ministry. Demonic reign was understood to be another kind of oppressive rule (e.g., *Jub.* 1:20; 1QS 1:17-18; 4Q390 2) that ancient Jews and followers of Jesus confronted. The sons of Sceva were supposedly the sons of a high priest, but Luke's readers would have recognized Sceva as a Latin name and thus perhaps an intentionally humorous false name for a Jewish high priest.[171] In short, these would-be exorcists were fakes. Their attempt to use the names of Jesus and Paul in their exorcism is more fakery. Names did have power in ancient Jewish and Christian exorcism, and these exorcists recognize the power that Jesus' name has. However, their intent is to exploit it (along with Paul's name) for their benefit without discipleship to the one whose name they want to use for power. As a result, they are dominated and overpowered by the demon. For Luke, liberation from demonic dominion comes from God and requires discipleship to Jesus, the sort that Paul represents (Acts 19:11-12), rather than lip service. The story of the sons of Sceva reminds us that the name of Jesus (as well as that of Paul) continues to be used by those who seek power without discipleship. It is crucial for us to recognize the ways that the name of Jesus was used to justify colonial power and oppression over Filipinos and countless other people groups elsewhere in ways that demonstrate a lack of discipleship to the Christ behind the name.

A SILVERSMITH SPARKS A RIOT (ACTS 19:21-41)

The Ephesian temple of Artemis was the jewel of Roman Ephesus. Second-century geographer Pausanias remarks that "all cities worship Artemis of Ephesus" and that her temple's size surpasses all other buildings,

[170]Yamauchi, *New Testament Cities*, 110.
[171]See Gaventa, *Acts*, 267.

contributing to her renown (*Description of Greece* 4.31.8). The Artemision's fame brought visitors and their money from around the Mediterranean world. A proconsular edict from 44 CE preserved in several inscriptions at Ephesus calls the Artemision the ornament of the whole province (of Asia) because of the size of its construction, its antiquity, and the "abundance of its revenues."[172] It also functioned as the treasury of bank of Ephesus, the monetary heart of the city.[173]

Demetrius correctly perceives that Paul's teaching that "gods made with hands are not gods" (Acts 19:26) is a threat both to the economic interests of the silversmiths and to the majesty of the Artemision itself (Acts 19:27). The Artemision featured a famous image of Artemis (Ephesian Artemis) that was copied and sold in the form of smaller statues. Demetrius is concerned with preserving the temple economy that he benefits from monetarily as well as the majesty of the temple that was the crowning glory of his city.

It is also true in our own context that rejecting idolatry threatens mammon-worship (see Lk 16:13) intrinsic to exploitative economies. Demetrius's fear is primarily about preserving the economy of Ephesus along with being about the "majesty," what we might think of as the greatness of the polity he belongs to. Similar idolatry exists in our own society in the form of wholehearted allegiance to the national economy and greatness, and willingness to sacrifice for it and thus *to* it. Our own US-based overseas Filipino workers are exploited for cheap labor and thus sacrificed to the idol of the US economy.

The riot that ensues takes place at the theater. This was one of the grandest theaters of the ancient world and a common location for large public gatherings. Luke describes the events that unfold as marked by confusion (Acts 19:29, 32). The mob continually shouts, "Great is Artemis of the Ephesians" (Acts 19:28, 34), an assertion of civic identity that by nature excludes Jews and Christ-believers. In tandem with this, outsiders of different sorts are the mob's targets: Gaius and Aristarchus (Acts 19:29), who are Macedonians, and Alexander, who is a Jew (Acts 19:33). The response of "Great is Artemis of the Ephesians" to the Jewish community when they put Alexander forward is telling: this is about who counts as a *true* Ephesian, and Jews, who would not acknowledge Artemis or her temple, do not. Thus, Alexander, the spokesperson for the Jewish community, is silenced. It is instead the city scribe who speaks and dismisses the assembly, telling them to pursue formal charges rather than be charged with rioting (Acts 19:35-41).

Filipinos and other Asian American Christians are regarded as perpetual foreigners and so frequently face tests or queries of whether we belong or count as "true Americans." We face pressure in our churches and other Christian institutional spaces to assimilate, to proclaim the greatness of the United States of America, to hold the same cultural values, and to defend the economic status quo that we as "foreigners" are perceived to threaten. Sadly, many Filipino Americans and other Asian Americans adopt colonial mentalities, seeing their own culture as inferior to Western culture or White American culture, neglecting their own heritage so that they can fit in, succeed, or escape racial trauma. This is magnified in church contexts, in which Euro-American

[172]Inscriften von Ephesos Ia.18; G. H. R. Horsley, "The Inscriptions of Ephesos and the New Testament," *NovT* 34, no. 2 (1992): 147-48.

[173]Yamauchi, *New Testament Cities*, 103.

theology or ways of reading Scripture are presented as normative and orthodox.

FURTHER TRAVELS (ACTS 20:1-16)

Paul revisits the regions of Macedonia and Greece, and sails from Philippi to Troas. The first-person plural "we-passages" resume at Troas (Acts 20:5), implying that the narrator has rejoined Paul. Luke continues his practice of identifying the geographic and ethnic origins of Christ-followers, highlighting the diversity of Paul's companions (Acts 20:4). There are some notable references to the Jewish festivals of Unleavened Bread (Acts 20:6) and Pentecost, since Paul hopes to be in Jerusalem on Pentecost. The festivals are an important element of Jewish faith and culture, which both Luke and Paul recognize. In Troas, Paul's lack of attention to the need of a young person in his audience results in Eutychus falling. This story reminds us of the value of the life of young people to communities. Receiving the boy alive brings them comfort.

THE FAREWELL AT MILETUS (ACTS 20:17-38)

Paul's farewell to the Ephesian elders at Miletus is comparable to the farewell testaments attested in other Jewish and Christian literature, a genre that includes predictions and exhortations for the disciples or family of the figure bidding farewell. Paul's farewell reveals the character of his ministry: it was "service" (lit. "being a slave") with humility (Acts 20:19), it was both public and house to house (Acts 20:20), it was to both Jews and Gentiles (Acts 20:21), and he proclaimed the kingdom (Acts 20:25) and taught about repentance toward God and faith toward "our Lord Jesus" (Acts 20:21). Luke's depiction of Paul exemplifies Christian ministry in the struggle, through tears, trials, and danger (Acts 20:19). Paul apparently expects further danger in Jerusalem, danger that may endanger his life (Acts 20:24), and thus thinks that that the Ephesian elders will not see his face again.

The instructions Paul gives to the elders anticipate danger for them (Acts 20:18-35). It is now up to the elders to shepherd the flock. Some of the danger will come from within the fold, from those who distort the truth. It is worth noting that other New Testament texts speak to distortions of truth among the churches in Asia Minor in general and in Ephesus in particular (Rev 2:1-7; 1 Tim 1:3-7; possibly 1 Jn 2:18-19). In our own context, the danger of those who distort the truth can still come from both without and within as well.

Acts 20:32 reminds the hearers that God and the message of his grace are edifying and can give "the inheritance" to those who are sanctified. Grace and its inheritance are connected here to sanctification, the transformative work of the Spirit, and are not separate from it. Finally, Paul reminds his hearers that he did not aim for economic gain from those he ministered to but worked to support himself (Acts 20:33-34). The practical upshot of this is that it provides an example to Paul's hearers and thus also to Luke's readers "that by such work we must support the weak" (Acts 20:35), which here means those who are in economic need. This calls back to the collection for the Jerusalem church and to the *koinōnia*, which distributed goods as they were needed. The work of supporting those in need is part of the essential instruction that Paul leaves his hearers and Luke's readers. Paul cites a saying of Jesus that "it is more blessed to give than to receive" in support (Acts 20:35). Although this teaching is not attested in the canonical Gospels, it nevertheless reflects Jesus' concern for those in need, which the reader is familiar with from Luke's first volume. We do not work to accumulate wealth. Work helps us to support those who are in need. This once again reminds us of overseas Filipino workers and other Filipino Americans and Canadians (such as my own Lola) who work hard with their own hands not only for their own benefit but to send money and goods to those in need in the homeland.

A STOPOVER IN CAESAREA (ACTS 21:1-16)

Paul and his companions arrive at Caesarea Maritima. Here we again encounter Philip, one of the seven deacons appointed to ensure fair treatment of Hellenistic Jewish widows (Acts 6:5). This picks up where Philip's story left off in Caesarea (Acts 8:40). Philip's four daughters who can prophesy casts the reader's mind all the way back to Peter's citation of Joel's prophecy that God's Spirit would be poured out on all flesh, and sons and daughters would prophesy (Acts 2:17). The colonial church today insists on control over women's spirituality and voices, but the Spirit was poured out on *all* flesh, so these women prophesy and stand in the long tradition of Jewish and Hebrew women prophets: Anna (Lk 2:36), Huldah (2 Kings 22:14), Noadiah (Neh 6:14), Miriam (Ex 15:20), and Deborah (Judg 4:4). Agabus, another figure associated with the Judean believers, who previously foretold the famine (Acts 11:27-28), reappears here in Caesarea as well. His warning to Paul (Acts 21:11) takes the form of a prophetic symbolic action reminiscent of the ones performed by the prophets of Israel's Scriptures. Paul and those around him now know beyond a shadow of a doubt that he will be handed over to the Romans by his own people. His story at this point parallels Luke's story of Jesus, who was aware that he would suffer and die in Jerusalem (Lk 9:22) but set his face toward it all the same (Lk 9:51).

IN JERUSALEM (ACTS 21:17-36)

When Paul and his companions arrive in Jerusalem, we encounter another familiar figure connected to the Judean believers: James the Just (Acts 21:18). The meeting with James is narrated in the first-person plural. Thus, the author of Luke–Acts implies that they made direct contact with a person who knew Jesus during his lifetime. While James and the elders praise God for the news of what God has done among the Gentiles, James also informs Paul that many of the (presumably Jerusalemite) Jewish believers have falsely been told that Paul has been teaching Diaspora Jews to abandon Torah, not to circumcise their children, and not to "observe the customs" (Acts 21:21). Although this is false, it reflects the legitimate fear of assimilation in the diaspora and the loss of culture that comes with it. For Jews, the loss of their ethnic boundary markers would also have been a rejection of the covenant and the ongoing story of divine grace that it represented. Paul's inclusive teachings, which allow Gentile believers to retain their ethnic identities, are garbled and wrongly portrayed as a threat to traditional Jewish values and identity. James thus encourages him to outwardly demonstrate his adherence to his Jewish identity, religion, and culture.

Ironically, it is while Paul is at the temple doing what James encouraged him to do that he is accused of teaching "everyone everywhere against our people, our law, and this place" (Acts 21:28) and of bringing Greeks into the temple. It is Paul's known association with Trophimus, a person of Gentile ethnicity, that leads to the latter accusation (Acts 21:29). While Greeks could enter the Court of the Gentiles, the inner courts were marked off by a barrier called the *soreg*, which included warnings that foreigners should not go beyond the barrier on penalty of death.[174] These garbled accusations come from Jews from Asia who recognize Paul (Acts 21:27) and are presumably in Jerusalem for the festival of Shavuot (Pentecost). The Roman soldiers' quick response is likely because the garrison at Jerusalem was billed at the Antonia, a looming fortress on the Temple Mount that adjoined the temple complex, which was constructed by Herod the Great and named for Mark Antony. The location of the fortress and its Roman garrison was intentional, an ever-present warning to Herod and Rome's Jewish subjects who gathered at the temple meant to deter trouble. The soldiers save Paul from further violence, but they also arrest him, binding him with chains as Agabus predicted (Acts 21:33), and take him to the barracks, presumably at the Antonia.

This is the tenth arrest. The arrest may have saved Paul from the violence of the mob, but it is unjust. He has not done what the mob accuses him of. The arrest is also a case of mistaken identity in part, since the tribune believes that Paul is "the Egyptian," a violent revolutionary Jewish prophet of Egyptian origin. According to Josephus (*J. W.* 2.261-263), this revolutionary brought thousands of men (four thousand according to Luke but thirty thousand according to Josephus) from the wilderness to the Mount of Olives and intended to attack Jerusalem and conquer the Roman garrison. His forces were defeated by the Romans, but he escaped, leading to the possibility that Paul could be mistaken for him. This case of mistaken identity calls to mind Luke's narrative of Jesus' descent from the Mount of Olives to Jerusalem.

PAUL'S DEFENSE (ACTS 22:1-29)

By clearing up his identity, showing his knowledge of Greek, and stating that he is from Tarsus, Paul is given the opportunity to speak to the crowds. The defense is essentially his testimony, a retelling of his origin story, particularly his encounter with Jesus and how he went from persecuting members of the Way to being one himself. In Paul's retelling of his own story, he portrays himself as a persecutor, and thus, it is a story of the transformative power of Jesus Christ who can call an oppressor to the struggle. Paul's defense teaches us that there is hope for redemption for even an oppressor like him. The crowd listens to his story until he speaks of being sent to the Gentiles (Acts 22:21-22). The survival of Israel had depended on its people's ability to separate themselves from the Gentiles who had sought to absorb and dominate them. It is thus understandable why some might see Paul's teaching as an attack on the Jewish people and on the law (see Acts 21:28).

Naturally, the Romans do not grasp the matter at hand, because this is an internal issue, but the tribune nevertheless "ordered him to be examined by flogging, to find out the reason for this outcry against him" (Acts 22:24). This representative of empire does not understand what Paul has done wrong but assumes that he must be guilty and will use violence to extract a confession from him. Torture is substituted for a fair trial. This is the "justice" of colonial empires. Paul points out that what they intend to do is illegal, because he has not been tried and condemned. It is the privilege that Paul's Roman citizenship from birth affords that saves him from being tortured to extract a confession. There is some overlap here with our context, in which those in our community who lack citizenship are not afforded the same opportunities and privileges and can be subject to a privation of freedom. Many immigrants in the Asian community are all too familiar with

[174]Two of these warning signs, inscribed on stone in Greek, are attested archaeologically.

the "golden cage" and pain of family separation caused by the deficiencies of US work visas.

PAUL TESTIFIES BEFORE THE JERUSALEMITE COUNCIL (ACTS 22:30–23:11)

This section is the first of several episodes that bring Paul before the various powers that be of Judea in his day. The first of these is the high priest, Ananias, and the local Jerusalemite council. When Paul proclaims the clarity of his conscience, Ananias orders him to be struck in the mouth, but Paul vehemently protests the injustice of this abusive violence (Acts 23:1-3). Josephus portrays Ananias as a hoarder of wealth who cultivated a friendship with the Roman procurator Albinus and who had agents who took the priestly tithe by violence (*Ant.* 20.205). He eventually met his fate at the hands of his own people, as during the revolt against Rome the people burned his house down and he was eventually killed by the rebels (*J.W.* 2.246, 441). Paul's sharp response to Ananias is probably his harshest to anyone in Acts. Even while being tried, he is not afraid to speak truth to power and to confront the abuse he experiences (Acts 23:3). Paul's statement that he did not know that Ananias was the high priest (Acts 23:5) may be genuine but may also be a critique, in that Paul did not recognize him as high priest because he was not acting like one, since it is unlikely that someone who previously had close ties to the Jerusalem authorities would not recognize the high priest.[175]

Paul finds allies in the Pharisees on the council by revealing his own Pharisaic allegiance and belief in the resurrection of the dead. It is worth noting that Paul *continues* to identify as a Pharisee (see also Phil 3:5) while also being a follower of Jesus and that the two should not be seen as mutually exclusive (see Acts 15:5). As a result, the council is deeply divided over Paul along sectarian fault lines. Paul is a divisive figure in the streets and in the halls of power. As a result of the violence that threatens to engulf the council over this disagreement, the tribune orders the soldiers to take Paul by force (Acts 23:10) and bring him back to the barracks (presumably the Antonia fortress). Since Paul had previously been released (Acts 22:30), this is the eleventh arrest. The Lord's words to Paul while he is once again imprisoned inform him that he is to be sent to testify in Rome (Acts 23:11). Paul will need to keep up his courage, as he is being sent into the heart of imperial power to testify just as he has in Jerusalem.

PAUL IS SENT TO CAESAREA (ACTS 23:12-35)

A conspiracy to assassinate Paul is foiled by his nephew. Assassination of dissidents, especially of someone like Paul who lacked political power, is a violent political strategy that values suppression and silence over human life. In our own context, Bulosan bears witness to an attempt to lynch key Filipino American activists and organizers in San Jose by five White men.[176] Filipino Americans today also live in the more recent memory of the assassinations in the homeland of church-based activists and Benigno Aquino Jr. during the martial law period.

The assassination attempt leads the tribune to transfer Paul to Caesarea to be tried before Felix, the governor. The events that unfold are an almost farcical parody of justice. Paul is escorted by a total of four hundred infantry and seventy horsemen. Although this show of military might to safely transfer Paul to Caesarea may have saved his life, the tribune is hardly an

[175]See Parsons, *Acts*, 315.
[176]Bulosan, *America Is in the Heart*, 206-9.

ally, nor is this an act of justice. In his letter to Felix, the tribune (now named as Claudius Lysias) states that Paul "was charged with nothing deserving death or imprisonment" (Acts 23:29) and that he is sending Paul to Felix so that the accusers can state what they have against him (Acts 23:30). In other words, the charge against Paul remains unclear at best and suspect at worst, yet Paul has been imprisoned and is being sent under guard by a small army to the highest imperial authority in the land.

Upon arrival in Caesarea, Paul is imprisoned in "Herod's praetorium," which refers to the promontory palace constructed by Herod the Great. Paul is already in the belly of the imperial beast. Caesarea was a Roman city in Jewish territory, featuring a Roman layout as well as an imperial temple and Greco-Roman entertainment structures. It was the seat of Roman administration in the region, a port city that faced west toward the heart of the empire, and the praetorium was its nerve center.

THE HEARING BEFORE FELIX (ACTS 24:1-27)

Felix was a former slave who had amazingly worked his way into a high-ranking imperial post (Tacitus, *Histories* 5.9; Suetonius, *Divus Claudius* 28). The period of his administration was marked by increasing anti-Roman sentiment, to which Felix responded with violence (Josephus, *Ant.* 20.160-161). He had also had a previous high priest, Jonathan, assassinated (Josephus, *Ant.* 20.162-164).

The accusations against Paul brought by Tertullus are that (1) he is an "agitator among all the Jews" and (2) a ringleader of "the sect of the Nazarenes," who (3) tried to profane the temple, which is why he was seized (Acts 24:5). This final accusation is a specifically intra-Jewish issue and seems to be the primary thrust of the case against Paul, repeating the false accusation raised by the Jews from Asia (Acts 21:28-29). The former two accusations are vague but attempt to paint Paul as a threat to the order of society and thus to Roman interests.

Paul's defense addresses all of Tertullus's accusations. He does admit to being a member of what they consider to be a sect, which Paul refers to as "the Way" rather than "the Nazarenes." Nevertheless, he stresses that this Way is in continuity with Jewish faith and practice, including worship of the God of his ancestors and belief in the Law and the Prophets, adding his belief in the hope for the resurrection, a belief that not all Jews held but that was certainly common and not deviant (Acts 24:14-15). He is not on trial for doing or believing something that is contrary to Jewish faith or law (Acts 24:15, 21). Ultimately, Paul's defense rests on what the reader knows to be true: there is no clear crime that Paul has committed.

Felix nevertheless keeps Paul in custody for two years, despite not finding him guilty. The motivation for this appears to be that Felix wants to receive a bribe from Paul. We must recognize this as a miscarriage of justice: an innocent man is held indefinitely despite having been tried and not having been found guilty of any particular crime. The colonizer cannot be relied on for justice. They are not there to bring justice to the colonized. The colonizer is there for their own benefit. We can expect no justice in a system where there is colonizer and colonized. Felix, a slave-turned-colonial-master, steals the liberty of another person for profit, a stunning exemplar of colonial mentality.

When Felix and his Jewish wife, Drusilla, hear Paul speak "concerning faith in Christ Jesus," what they hear includes talk of "justice, self-control, and the coming judgment" (Acts 24:24-25). This implies that Paul's account of "faith in Christ Jesus" necessarily entails those things and that they are not separate from that faith. The talk of those things frightens Felix, because indeed justice and divine judgment are a natural threat to an unjust representative of imperial authority.

NEW HEARINGS IN A NEW POLITICAL LANDSCAPE (ACTS 25–26)

Porcius Festus has replaced Felix. The political landscape continues to shift. The days of Pilate, Antipas, and Caiaphas, the high authorities of the region at the beginning of the story, are now long gone. Paul, however, remains imprisoned although he has not been found guilty of a crime. Festus's administration saw the further rise of revolutionary violence and political tension in Judea, particularly connected to the Sicarii, a group of Jewish revolutionaries. Josephus informs us that during his rule, Festus was engaged in military action against revolutionaries, particularly against an unnamed "impostor" who had promised deliverance and freedom (*Ant.* 20.185-188). These were the tumultuous years directly leading up to the First Jewish Revolt against Rome.

Pressure from members of the Jerusalemite elite to have Paul transferred to Jerusalem leads to Festus arranging another hearing in Caesarea. Again, the accusations against Paul cannot be proven (Acts 25:7-8), further underscoring the ongoing absurdity of Paul's lengthy imprisonment by the imperial authorities. Luke indicates that Festus's suggestion that Paul go up to Jerusalem to be tried before him is motivated not by justice but by the desire to curry favor with the Judean elites who want Paul to be transferred there (Acts 25:9; note the repetition of *charis* ["favor"] from Acts 25:3). Like Felix before him, for Festus Paul's case is an opportunity to exploit for his own benefit. It is abundantly clear that imperial authority cannot be relied on for justice. Yet, Paul appeals to the emperor's tribunal, to be tried by the highest authority in the Roman Empire (Acts 25:10-11). This would probably have come as a shock to Luke's original readers, who have just seen the failings of the imperial authorities in matters of justice on full display. Yet, it is also a way to survive if only a little longer, as this appeal will carry Paul away from Jerusalem, a city that he has to be escorted away from under the watch of almost five hundred soldiers. The slow process of the imperial justice system will ironically extend Paul's life and witness.

The conversation between Festus and Agrippa II (Acts 25:13-22) illuminates Festus's confusion about the accusations against Paul, since he informs Agrippa that Paul was not charged with the crimes he had expected (Acts 25:18). It is not immediately clear what crimes Festus might have expected, but we are later informed that they were things that would have deserved the death penalty (Acts 25:25). Festus's concern is not with the Jewish religion or Jesus, whom he does not seem to be familiar with (Acts 25:19). We should remember that by Festus's time as governor, Jesus' crucifixion must have seemed to be a relatively insignificant incident in the past to the local Roman authorities.

Paul's hearing before Agrippa II and Bernice is a scene of pageantry and colonial power, including both Roman military tribunes and local Caesarean city leaders (Acts 25:23). The purpose of the hearing is ostensibly so that Festus can indicate the charges against Paul in his letter to the emperor (Acts 25:26-27). The charges are still unclear. This fully illuminates the absurdity of the scene and the perversion of justice it represents. Paul's defense mostly reiterates his story. Notably, he opens by highlighting his own Jewish faith (Acts 26:4-8) and presents his hope for the resurrection, a hope shared by many Jews, as the reason why he is imprisoned

(Acts 26:6-8). Toward the end of the speech, he also states that he was seized in the temple because of his proclamation of repentance to the Gentiles (Acts 26:20-21). The retelling of Paul's story exemplifies the subversive nature of salvation history and the reign of God. Paul owns his deeds as a persecutor. Jesus, who identifies with the persecuted, first brings Paul to his knees, then stands him on his feet (Acts 26:16). The oppressor is disarmed and then transformed. This is a testimony to the disruptive power of Jesus Christ at work in the world, bearing witness to the hope of Jewish and Gentile followers of Jesus alike.

Paul's message appears to be insanity to Festus (Acts 26:24). Nevertheless, it is Paul's sincere hope that his audience will become like him, "except for these chains" (Acts 26:29). Even in chains, Paul still hopes for the salvation of those that keep him bound, including the imperial and colonial elites who hold his people captive at a time when anti-imperial sentiment is about to spill into revolution. The opinion of the highest authorities in the region is ultimately that Paul "is doing nothing to deserve death or imprisonment" (Acts 26:31) and that Paul could have been set free had he not appealed to the emperor (Acts 26:32). Paul did not pose the severe violent threat to Roman and Herodian order or authority that both Agrippa II and Festus dealt with while in power.

Some might take this speech and Agrippa's conclusion as an indication that Luke intends to show that the Way is not a threat to authority or that it is compatible with Roman imperialism. However, what this narrative shows is only that the charges laid against Paul by members of the Jerusalem elite, namely, the issues of resurrection and his proclamation of repentance to the Gentiles, are viewed as obscure intra-Jewish matters and of little concern to Roman law. In fact, the Caesarea trial narratives reveal the injustice of the Roman officials and of the Roman legal system, as Paul is kept in chains for years without just cause. The Way is not a violent revolutionary movement like the ones that Festus and Agrippa put down. Yet, the narrative has consistently depicted followers of the Way being arrested, at the center of public disturbances, and running afoul of authorities. The Way does not entail the violent overthrow of Rome, but it does require a radical faithfulness lived out in the midst of empire that is contrary to the imperial order and its values.

THE SEA JOURNEY (ACTS 27)

Paul begins his journey west to Rome, the heart of the empire, as a prisoner. Luke describes a difficult, multileg voyage. The journey from Fair Havens (Crete) is particularly fraught with danger. Paul's warnings are not heeded by Julius the centurion, and the ship is endangered by a violent storm. Nevertheless, Paul has been informed by an angel that he must stand before the emperor, so he has confidence in the ship's safety. Paul also provides encouragement for his jailers, companions, and fellow prisoners by urging them to eat before they throw the wheat overboard, and gives thanks to God for the food in the midst of the crisis (Acts 27:33-38). These are acts of hope in the midst of turmoil. The soldiers' plan to kill the prisoners so that they do not escape (Acts 27:42-43), which is prevented by Julius, shows a callous lack of regard for the humanity of prisoners and a deeper commitment to their punishment than to their lives and dignity, a problem that also plagues our own society today. The reader will remember that Paul has not yet been convicted of any crime. The impulse to secure and punish imprisoned bodies heedless of innocence or guilt is no excuse for violence.

MALTA (ACTS 28:1-10)

Luke refers to the people of Malta as *barbaroi* (Acts 28:2), a Greek term for foreign, particularly non-Greek-speaking, people. Inscriptions from Malta show that Punic (a Semitic language related to Phoenician) was likely the common language.[177] Nevertheless, these people, who are identified by their otherness, show the shipwrecked survivors an uncommon *philanthrōpia* ("kindness" in the NRSV, literally "love to humankind"), providing them with the human necessity of heat by building a fire. This hospitality shown by *barbaroi* can be read as an intentional subversion of Luke's ancient readers' stereotypical expectations.[178] The incident with the snake (Acts 28:3-6), initially taken by the group's Maltese hosts as divine justice and a sign of Paul's guilt, is actually a divine sign showing Paul's innocence and that he is under God's care (see Acts 27:24). However, the sign is misunderstood as evidence of Paul's divinity. The notion that Paul must have been a murderer implies that it was clear that he and others were prisoners. Nevertheless, the group's Maltese hosts provide care for them all the same, in contrast to the soldiers who wanted to kill the prisoners. This did not escape John Chrysostom, who wrote in the fourth century, "Let those who say: 'Don't do good to those in prisons' be ashamed! Let us be shamed by the barbarians [*barbaroi*], because they did not know who these people were, but out of circumstance alone, they perceived that they were human, and consequently regarded them worthy of kindness."[179] For his part, Paul heals Publius's father and cures the people of the island who come to him with diseases (Acts 28:8-9).

It is curious that Luke does not tell us that Paul engaged in the sort of teaching and proclamation activity at Malta that we are accustomed to from him. Was Paul's good news not also for these people that Luke calls *barbaroi*? Patristic commentators widely regarded Paul's time on Malta as having a missionary character.[180] Both Eusebius and John Chrysostom, for instance, regard Paul's healing work as evangelistic (Eusebius, *Commentary on Isaiah*, on Is 11:10-16; Chrysostom, *Homilies on Acts* 54). Acts of care for the body such as healing are not separate from missionary activity. Jesus' healing ministry was part of the outbreak of the kingdom (Lk 4:18; 7:22), and healing in Acts is usually done in the name of Jesus (Acts 3:6, 16; 4:10, 30; 9:34; 16:18; 19:13). Healing and health care are crucial to Filipino American culture, due to the extremely high proportion of health-care workers in the Filipino American community. Within a Christian context, their efforts can be understood as missional, kingdom work in service to the well-being of others.

PAUL IN ROME (ACTS 28:11-31)

Luke has made it clear that Paul's arrival in Rome was inevitable. Paul's story thus further imitates Luke's story of Jesus, whose arrival, imprisonment, and passion in Jerusalem were similarly inevitable. When Paul does arrive in Rome, it is as a prisoner with limited freedom and under the guard of a Roman soldier (Acts 28:16). Luke tells us that he lived there in this way for two years and at his own expense (Acts 28:30). This now amounts to almost five years of imprisonment in various forms without a conviction. Paul's arrival in Rome, as

---

[177]See, e.g., Colin J. Hemer, *The Book of Acts in the Setting of Hellenistic History* (Winona Lake, IN: Eisenbrauns, 1990), 152.
[178]Joshua W. Jipp, "Hospitable Barbarians: Luke's Ethnic Reasoning in Acts 28:1-10," *JTS* 68, no. 1 (2017): 23-45.
[179]John Chrysostom, *Homilies on Acts* 54; see Ronald H. van der Bergh, "The Missionary Character of Paul's Stay on Malta (Acts 28:1-10) According to the Early Church," *Journal of Early Christian History* 3, no. 1 (2013): 90.
[180]See van der Bergh, "Missionary Character."

a colonized person called to the heartland of the empire, and then having limited freedom when he arrives, resonates with the story of many Filipino American immigrants and US-based migrant overseas Filipino workers (who may intend to return to the Philippines), past and present. Like Paul, Filipino immigrants to the United States are colonized people who are called to the heartland of the empire that colonized them and then experience the limitation of freedoms that the immigration process entails. The so-called golden cage of US work visas that do not provide work authorization for spouses and children, leaving them "caged" at home, is too often the cause of family separation, or the breakdown of the family, which is central to Filipino and Filipino American life and culture. Freedom remains elusive for immigrants in the "land of liberty."

Paul is greeted by believers in Rome, though he has never been there, who bring him courage. So too are we often encouraged when we meet *kababayans* in the diaspora or when we have fellowship with other Asian Americans. The existence of believers in Rome implies that Paul is not the first to bring the good news there, nor that he is there to found a new community in an unevangelized city as he did on his missionary journeys. Why Rome, then? To "stand before the emperor" (Acts 27:24).

The gathering of the Jewish community provides Paul with another opportunity to connect with his fellow Jews (his own ethnic *kababayan*), to proclaim his innocence and allegiance to his people and ancestral customs (Acts 28:17), and to later testify to Jesus and the kingdom of God (Acts 28:23). Perhaps because he is under arrest, his teaching takes place at his own lodgings rather than the synagogue. The mixed results (Acts 28:24-25) cause Paul to cite Isaiah 6:9-10 and conclude, "This salvation of God has been sent to the gentiles; they will listen" (Acts 28:28). Here, Paul and Luke are wrestling with the fact that not all of Israel has accepted the proclamation of Jesus the Jewish Messiah. Paul's solution to this dilemma is that the Gentiles will listen. This does not preclude Jews from "this salvation of God" (Acts 28:28), however, since Paul continues to welcome all who come to him (Acts 28:30), presumably including Jews, and some Jews *are* persuaded by Paul (Acts 28:24). More importantly, Paul's citation of Isaiah 6:9-10 to support the conclusion of Acts 28:28 places his own circumstances in line with rather than in opposition to Jewish tradition (see Acts 28:17). Indeed, "it is for the sake of the hope of Israel" that he is in chains (Acts 28:20).

Acts ends with Paul imprisoned in Rome for two years (Acts 28:30-31). While imprisoned, Paul continues to welcome visitors. Luke summarizes his proclamation as centered on the kingdom of God and the Lord Jesus Christ. The mention of the kingdom of God ties the ending back to the resurrected Jesus' teaching at the beginning of the story, and moreover to Jesus' ministry according to Luke's Gospel. That kingdom, the reader will recall from Luke, is an upside-down, eschatological reversal of the present order, and Paul is in continuity with Jesus in proclaiming it. Luke does not tell us what happened after those two years. However, 2 Timothy 4:6-7 hints at Paul's imminent death, and other early Christian writings outside the New Testament bear witness to a widespread tradition that Paul was martyred by Nero (e.g., *1 Clement* 5:5-7; Tertullian, *Scorpiace* 15; *Acts of Paul* 11:5; Eusebius, *Hist. eccl.* 2.22; 2.25.5). Roman historian Tacitus writes that Nero scapegoated Christians for the great fire of Rome in 64 CE in order to deflect blame from himself (*Annals* 15.44.26-27), and if Paul was imprisoned, he would have been an easy target for Nero. If this is how Paul met his fate, then he died as a member of a minority group that was scapegoated and blamed by the emperor himself for a disaster that they did not cause. Let the Asian American reader understand, as our communities were scapegoated for the Covid-19 pandemic in the United States and suffered violence as a result.

Luke's omission of Paul's death is only a problem if Acts was written after Paul died. Otherwise, it may simply present the reader with the situation when Acts was written. Whatever the case may be, the foundational history of the Way concludes with the kingdom of God and the lordship of Jesus, the Jewish Messiah, being proclaimed "with all boldness" in the heart of empire. For Filipino American followers of Jesus, who live in the heart of our own colonizer, this ending invites us to do the same.

SELECTED BIBLIOGRAPHY

Selected Works by Filipino and Filipino American Authors in Biblical Studies and Theology

Asedillo, Lisa. "The Theology of Struggle: Critiques of Church and Society in the Philippines (1970s–1990s)." *Indonesian Journal of Theology* 9, no. 1 (2021): 62-92.

Asedillo Pratt, Lisa and Grace Y. Kao, "On Becoming Asian American Christian Ethicists." In *Asian and Asian American Women in Theology and Religion: Embodying Knowledge*, edited by Pui-lan Kwok, 223-39. Boston: Brill, 2020.

Asis, Michael Demetrius H. *The Filipino Christ and the Historical Jesus.* Manila: Ateno de Manila University Press, 2021.

Catanus, Gabriel J. "Uncovering a FACE: Filipino American Christian Ethics." PhD diss., Loyola University, 2021.

Delotavo, Alan. "Images of Christ in Filipino Culture and Atonement Experiences: A Case in the Contextualization of the Gospel Message." *Asia Journal of Theology* 15, no. 1 (2001): 140-50.

Fernandez, Eleazar S. "Exodus-Toward-Egypt: Filipino-Americans' Struggle to Realize the Promised Land in America." In *A Dream Unfinished: Theological Reflections on America from the Margins.* Edited by Eleazar S. Fernandez and Fernando F. Segovia, 167-81. Maryknoll, NY: Orbis, 2001.

———. "From Babel to Pentecost: Finding a Home in the Belly of the Empire." *Semeia* 90/91 (2002): 29-50

Fetalsana-Apura, Lily. *A Filipino Resistance Reading of Joshua 1:1–9.* International Voices in Biblical Studies 9. Atlanta: SBL, 2019.

Maggay, Melba Padilla. *Rise Up and Walk: Religion and Culture in Empowering the Poor.* Oxford: Regnum, 2015.

del Rosario, Joyce. "Can There Be a Postcolonial Theology While Living in the Colonizer's House?" *ChristianityNext* 2 (2018): 41-58.

Tizon, Al. *Whole and Reconciled.* Grand Rapids, MI: Baker, 2018.

de la Torre, Edicio. *Touching Ground, Taking Root: Theological and Political Reflections on the Philippine Struggle.* Manila: Socio-Pastoral Institute, 1986.

Velunta, Revelation Enriques. "Cornelius the Centurion Meets the Ethiopian Eunuch in a Jeepney." In *Scripture and Resistance*, edited by Jione Havea, 59-72. Minneapolis: Fortress, 2019.

Selected Resources on Acts from Underrepresented Perspectives

Barretto, Eric. *Ethnic Negotiations: The Function of Race and Ethnicity in Acts 16.* Tübingen: Mohr Siebeck, 2010.

Cobb, Christy. *Slavery Gender, Truth, and Power in Luke–Acts and Other Ancient Narratives.* Cham, Switzerland: Palgrave Macmillan, 2019.

González, Justo L. *Acts: The Gospel of the Spirit.* Maryknoll, NY: Orbis, 2001.

Jennings, Willie James. *Acts. Belief: A Theological Commentary on the Bible.* Louisville, KY: Westminster John Knox, 2017.

LETTER TO THE ROMANS

Jarvis J. Williams

INTRODUCTION

My ethnic, social, and theological location. In my exposition of Romans that follows, I present a contextualized commentary of Romans grounded in grammatical-historical exegesis but honest about my specific mixed African American and multiethnic social location. The goal of my exegesis is to explain Paul's letter to the Romans in its first-century social setting (1) to communicate his intent and (2) to apply his message to the Romans to my own theological context and specific diverse multiethnic social location. I hope that the wider church in different social locations and theological contexts from my own will have ears to hear so that they can benefit from both my exegesis and my application with an eye toward applying my exegesis to their own social contexts.

I am an African American Southern Baptist professor of New Testament with a multiethnic heritage writing within a particular stream of soteriological Calvinism. My family has African, African American, European, Spanish, and additional multiethnic ancestry. Additionally, my wife is a Latina from Costa Rica; her mother is a Latina from Nicaragua, and my wife's father is a native of Costa Rica. Our son has the multiethnic heritages of both my wife and me, as he has African, African American, Hispanic, European, and additional ethnic ancestry as part of his beautiful diversity. Our middle-class Black and Brown multiethnic family lives in a middle-class Black, Brown, Asian, and White multiethnic community in an ethnically diverse city, but our community is also a socially diverse neighborhood.

I serve as a nonstaff elder/pastor of preaching at a predominantly White multiethnic church in an urban context in Louisville, Kentucky in a historically predominantly poor Black and working-class community, but now a multiethnic and gentrified community that continues to change rapidly. Our church's pastoral staff and nonstaff pastors are ethnically diverse. Our lead pastor is an African American, we have staff who are African American, Hatian, Asian, and White, and our other pastors (staff and nonstaff) are White, with two additional African American elders, and Hispanic. Our church also has diverse Asian, Black, Brown, and White nonpastoral staff and a diverse group of White, Black, Asian, Brown, and additional ethnically diverse nonstaff leaders.

Our church is also socially diverse, as we have a few wealthy, several middle-class, and multiple poor members from a diversity of ethnicities. It is politically diverse, with members on many different political spectrums. By God's grace, our congregation is a place where image-bearers with names like Chanekwa, Sue, Malcolm, Paco, Ray-Ray, Jada, Jevonte, Mookie, Pookie, Frank, Huhn, Dominic, Miguel, Ann, Jaquan, Becky, Raphael, Tom, Frank, Sarah, and people with last names like Lee, Kim, Ok, Rodriguez, So, Torrez, Martinez, Smith, Washington, and Chong can find a home. As a result,

I write this commentary with an eye toward illuminating the text of Romans for saints reading this commentary within a similar context as mine and with an eye toward giving insights from the text to, and encouraging the broader Christian community from, different ethnic, ecclesiological, and theological contexts from my own.

Authorship. Scholars disagree on the authorship of several books in the New Testament.[1] However, virtually every New Testament scholar agrees Paul wrote Romans. In Romans 1:1, Paul states he wrote the letter. Additionally, the Greek style, theological themes, and key Greek terms in the letter give scholars reasons to believe Paul wrote the letter. He used an amanuensis named Tertius (16:22) to write the letter.

Date. Dating ancient texts is difficult. There are scholars who suggest Paul wrote Romans possibly in the AD 50s (maybe AD 55–58).

Setting. Jewish converts to Christianity or Gentile proselytes who converted to Christianity on the day of Pentecost possibly took the gospel to Rome and helped establish house churches there (Acts 2:10-11). New Testament scholars disagree about the social setting of Romans. Traditionally, scholars have suggested Paul wrote Romans to a mixed Jewish and Gentile audience. Scholars have also estimated the population of Rome at the time Paul wrote Romans was approximately one "million people."[2] These residents included a diverse group of Jews and Gentiles from different parts of the Roman empire. Scholars further estimate "40,000-50,000" of those residents were Jews.[3] However, in recent scholarly conversations, interpreters question a traditional understanding of the social setting of Romans, arguing instead that Paul's audience in Rome was exclusively a Gentile Christian audience.[4]

Related to this discussion is Emperor Claudius's expulsion of the Jews from Rome (Acts 18:1-2). This expulsion occurred in the late 40s, before Paul wrote the letter. Around the mid-50s (AD 54), the emperor permitted the Jews to return to Rome. Many scholars believe the Christians in Rome were a Jewish majority prior to the emperor's expulsion of Jews from Rome. The view goes as follows. After Jews returned to Rome, however, non-Christian Jews and Jewish Christians established the house churches in Rome to be constituted by a Gentile Christian majority. This diversity could perhaps explain the divisions Paul addresses in Romans 14–15 (e.g., Rom 15:7-12). Scholars suggest that one of the tensions in Romans 14–15 is that many members of the house churches in Rome were Gentiles with different convictions regarding kosher foods (Rom 1:5-6, 13; 11:13), while at least some of the leaders of those house churches were Jewish (e.g., Rom 16).[5] In this commentary, I assume the position that Paul wrote the letter to a mixed Jewish and Gentile audience of Christians in house churches in Rome based on his direct comments to Jews and Gentiles throughout the letter (e.g., Rom 1–3; 9–11; 14–15).[6]

Purpose and message. Paul wrote Romans to introduce his gospel to Christians living in Rome, for he wanted their help to take the gospel from Rome to Spain (Rom 15:23-24). Paul had not visited the Christians in Rome prior to writing this letter (Rom 1:8-14;

[1]For example, scholars have labeled the following letters as so-called deutero-Pauline letters: Ephesians, Colossians, 2 Thessalonians, 1–2 Timothy, and Titus. My view is Paul wrote all thirteen letters in the NT that bear his name.
[2]Craig Keener, "Romans," in *NIV Cultural Backgrounds Study Bible* (Grand Rapids, MI: Zondervan, 2016), 1945.
[3]Keener, "Romans," 1945.
[4]For a detailed discussion, see A. Andrew Das, *Solving the Romans Debate* (Minneapolis: Fortress, 2007).
[5]Keener, "Romans," 1945.
[6]Scholars debate the merits of the above premise.

15:23-24). When he arrived at Rome, he did so in chains as a prisoner of the gospel (see Acts 28:11-31). Paul may also have written the letter to resolve social tensions between Jews and Gentiles in the small house churches throughout Rome (Rom 14–15). These tensions relate to disputes over foods between two groups that Paul identifies as the weak and the strong.

Outline.[7]

1. Paul's introduction to the Romans (Rom 1:1-17)
   A. Salutation about the gospel of God (Rom 1:1-7)
   B. Thanksgiving and eager desire to preach the gospel in Rome to Gentiles (Rom 1:8-17)

   Theological theme: the saving power of Paul's multiethnic gospel and his multiethnic vision for a multiethnic world
2. Universal condemnation of Jews and Gentiles apart from faith in Jesus, the Jewish Messiah (Rom 1:18–3:20)

   Theological theme: the impartial multiethnic display of God's wrath
3. Jews and Gentiles can be justified the same way: by faith in Jesus Christ (Rom 3:21–4:25)

   Theological theme: the justification of Jews and Gentiles by faith in Christ
4. The certainty of hope in present suffering because of the certainty of future salvation (Rom 5:1–8:39)

   Theological theme: cosmological redemption in the face of ethnocentrism and racism
5. God has not forsaken his promises to Israel (Rom 9:1–11:36)

   Theological theme: God's faithfulness to his multiethnic people
6. Obey the gospel! Paul's gospel horizontally applied to multiethnic relationships (Rom 12:1–15:33)

   Theological theme: love one another!
7. Commendations, a warning, and a benediction (Rom 16:1-27)

   Theological theme: honor our sisters in our churches

PAUL'S INTRODUCTION TO THE ROMANS (ROMANS 1:1-17)

Salutation about the gospel of God (Romans 1:1-7). Paul begins this letter in common Greco-Roman fashion. He identifies himself as the author (Rom 1:1), states to whom he writes the letter (Rom 1:7), and offers a prayer of goodwill to the recipients (Rom 1:7).[8] One of the major differences between Paul's salutation here in comparison with the salutations both in his other letters and in other ancient letters is his long biblical and theological parenthesis in Romans 1:2-6.

In Romans 1:2-6, Paul first emphasizes his authority by calling himself an "apostle" (Rom 1:1). The term *apostle* basically means a "messenger" or "sent one."[9] Paul is a messenger of the gospel of Jesus Christ, although he became an apostle in an abnormal way, unlike those who were part of the eyewitness community who had walked with and seen the resurrected Christ (1 Cor 15:1-8). Paul's apostleship came by means of an "abnormal birth"

[7]There are many outlines of Romans. My outline shares similarities with and differs from the many scholarly outlines of the letter. See critical commentaries of Romans for various outlines of Romans.

[8]For a discussion of first-century letters, see E. Randolph Richards, *Paul and First-Century Letter Writing: Secretaries, Composition, and Collection* (Downers Grove, IL: InterVarsity Press, 2004).

[9]Unless otherwise indicated, all translations of biblical texts in this commentary are my own. For a few examples of the noun for "apostle," see Mt 10:2; Mk 3:14; 6:30; Lk 6:13; 9:10; 11:49; 17:5; 22:14; 24:10. For a few examples of the verb "to send," see Rom 10:15; 1 Cor 1:17; 2 Cor 12:17.

(see 1 Cor 15:8). As an apostle, he is uniquely set forth and commissioned by the Lord to "preach immediately Jesus in the synagogues" (Acts 9:20). Paul, then, uses an explosive phrase to identify himself as a loyal devotee to Jesus Christ: "slave of Jesus Christ" (Rom 1:1).

The history of slavery in both the Greco-Roman world and in the United States is complex. Slavery in the two contexts has a few points of continuity and many points of discontinuity. One fundamental difference is that slavery in the Greco-Roman world was not based on biological racism, racial hierarchy, or White supremacy.[10] Instead, while slavery in antiquity was a form of oppression, the enslaved in Paul's world became slaves voluntarily as indentured servants, by force due to being captured in war, or for other reasons.[11] The phrase "slave of Christ" would have evoked power, ownership, obligation, and loyalty in the minds of Paul's original audience. Readers in the modern world should not understand the phrase "slave of Jesus Christ" as either a justification of or as support for the perpetuation of race-based slavery.[12] Paul here uses an ancient concept (slavery) to communicate his devotion to Jesus Christ without intending to validate the practice of slavery, either ancient or modern slavery.[13]

After Paul identifies himself as a "slave of Christ Jesus" and as a "called apostle" (or as a "called sent one"), "who has been set apart for the gospel of God" (Rom 1:1), he parenthetically explains the content of the "gospel of God"

[10]For a bibliography, see Colin Kidd, *The Forging of the Races* (Cambridge: Cambridge University Press, 2006). I use the phrase "White supremacy" here to mean an ideology of White superiority that has historically manifested itself by means of power dynamics and acts of discrimination (and at times violent acts of discrimination) against non-White people. White supremacy also manifests itself when the social construct of White and those who are socially categorized as White are presented as the standards of truth, beauty, and righteousness, and when the value of those who are categorized into non-White groups is judged by the standard of the social construction of White. In this definition, it is imperative for readers to understand that the categories of race, White, whiteness, blackness, and so on are all social constructs, not biological realities. Regardless of the color of one's skin, all human beings are created in the image of God, and they all have dignity, beauty, and value. However, the constructs of race, White, and Black historically had nothing to do with biological realities but were social fictions created for the purpose of establishing a racial hierarchy within society. As numerous scholars have recognized and thoroughly documented, race is a biological fiction but a social reality. God created one human race filled with many diverse ethnicities (groups of diverse people from different cultures, with different values, dialects, geographies, with different shades of skin, etc.). Human beings, after sin entered creation, created and constructed the idea of different superior and inferior races of people within the one human race for the purpose of a racial hierarchy. For my brief discussion of these complex issues and for a bibliography, see Jarvis J. Williams, *Redemptive Kingdom Diversity: A Biblical Theology of the People of God* (Grand Rapids, MI: Baker Academic, 2021), 3-7, 9-18, 152-73.

[11]For primary texts on the complexity of slavery in Greco-Roman antiquity, see Thomas Wiedemann, *Greek and Roman Slavery* (New York: Routledge, 1980); Sandra R. Joshel, *Slavery in the Roman World* (Cambridge: Cambridge University Press, 2010).

[12]Racialized (i.e., the act of ascribing racial characteristics to humans within humanity for the purpose of dehumanization and for the purpose of a racial hierarchy) theological efforts are well documented in the scholarly literature. For a few examples, see the arguments and bibliography in Rebecca Anne Goetz, *The Baptism of Early Virginia: How Christianity Created Race* (Baltimore: Johns Hopkins University Press, 2012); Carolyn Renée Dupont, *Mississippi Praying: Southern White Evangelicals and the Civil Rights Movement, 1945–1975* (New York: New York University Press, 2013); Richard A. Bailey, *Race and Redemption in Puritan New England* (Oxford: Oxford University Press, 2011); Donald G. Mathews, *At the Altar of Lynching: Burning Sam Hose in the American South* (Cambridge: Cambridge University Press, 2017); Mary Beth Swetnam Mathews, *Doctrine and Race: African American Evangelicals and Fundamentalism Between the Wars* (Tuscaloosa: University of Alabama Press, 2017). For responses of the enslaved to racist theological constructs, see Emerson B. Powery and Rodney S. Sadler Jr., *The Genesis of Liberation: Biblical Interpretation in the Antebellum Narratives of the Enslaved* (Louisville, KY: Westminster John Knox, 2016), Kidd, *Forging of the Races*.

[13]For work that shows African American reception of Pauline texts on slavery and African American scriptural resistance of race-based slavery, see Powery and Sadler, *Genesis of Liberation*; Lisa Bowens, *African American Readings of Paul: Reception, Resistance and Transformation* (Grand Rapids, MI: Eerdmans, 2020). For examples of African American reception of Scripture as an exercise in hope, see Esau McCaulley, *Reading While Black: African American Biblical Interpretation as an Exercise in Hope* (Downers Grove, IL: InterVarsity Press, 2020).

in Romans 1:2-6. The phrase "gospel of God" occurs in other New Testament texts (Mk 1:14; Acts 20:24; Rom 15:16; 2 Cor 11:7; 1 Thess 2:2, 8-9; 1 Tim 1:11). The noun "gospel" (*euangelion*) and its cognate verb "to announce the good news" (*euangelizō*) refer to an announcement. Paul's gospel is an announcement that God has fulfilled all his saving promises for Jews and Gentiles and for the world through the death and resurrection of his Son, Jesus, the Jewish Messiah.[14] Paul's parenthetical remarks in Romans 1:2-6, in which he explains "the gospel of God," support this reading.

First, Paul says God promised the gospel of God "beforehand through his prophets in the holy scriptures" (Rom 1:2). The prophets refer to the Old Testament prophets, for Paul quotes Isaiah and other prophets throughout the letter (e.g., Rom 9:27–10:21). The phrase "holy scriptures" refers to the Hebrew Scriptures, which Christians today identify as the Old Testament.

Second, Paul asserts the "gospel of God" pertains "to his Son, who came to be from the seed of David in accordance with the flesh." Paul's remarks mean God's preexistent and eternal Son entered this world as a Jewish man and descendant of David. Thus, the "gospel of God" is about God's preexistent Son who became a Jewish man and a descendant from the messianic seed of David in accordance with the promise of 2 Samuel 7:12-14 (see Ps 2; 110).

Third, Paul states that "the gospel of God" is about God's Son, who is Jesus Christ, our Lord, and who was appointed to be God's Son with power in accordance with the Spirit "at the resurrection of the dead" (Rom 1:4).[15] Some scholars understand Paul's remarks here to mean God adopted Jesus as God's Son at his resurrection. However, Paul's high Christology both in his salutation and throughout Romans speaks against this adoptionistic Christology. Paul identifies Jesus as the content of the "gospel of God" when he says it is the gospel about his Son (Rom 1:3). Paul also calls Jesus "Christ" (Rom 1:1) and "Lord" (Rom 1:4). Both Christ and Lord are divine titles when applied to Jesus (e.g., Rom 9:5–10:13). Paul says grace and peace come from "God, the Father, and the Lord Jesus Christ" (Rom 1:7). The term *Lord* refers to Yahweh, Israel's one and only God, in the Old Testament (e.g., Joel 2:28-32). Although the Greek term for "Lord" (*kyrios*) can simply refer to a human "sir/lord" or "master" (e.g., Mt 18:25), here in Romans, "Lord" (*kyrios*) always refers to a divine title concerning Jesus sharing in Yahweh's "divine identity" (Rom 4:8; 9:28-29; 10:12; 12:19; 14:4, 11).[16] Paul identifies Jesus as Lord by applying Old Testament texts to him that clearly refer to Yahweh in their Old Testament contexts (e.g., Rom 10:8-9, 13).

Paul likely identifies Jesus as "God" with the Greek term *theos* in Romans 9:5, but he refers to the Father alone as *theos* in every other

[14]Of course, there are many features of this "good news" (e.g., Jesus' death and resurrection, repentance, justification, etc.), but the term *gospel* basically refers to an announcement of what God has done to fulfill his saving promises through his Son, Jesus Christ. For the idea of gospel as announcement with the noun *euangelion*, see Rom 1:1, 9, 16; 2:16; 10:16; 14. For verses that use the verb *euangelizō* ("to announce as good news"), see Gal 1:8-9, 11, 16, 23; 4:13; Eph 2:17; 3:8; 1 Thess 3:6; Heb 4:2, 6; 1 Pet 1:12, 25; 4:6; Rev 10:7; 14:6. For examples where *euangelion* ("good news") occurs in the Greek translation of the Old Testament (also called the LXX), see 2 Sam 4:10. For the verb *euangelizō* ("to announce as good news"), see 1 Sam 31:9; 2 Sam 1:20; 4:10; 18:19-20, 26, 31.

[15]Some take the Greek verb *horisthentos*, which I translate as "to appoint," to mean "to declare." However, none of the other occurrences in the New Testament means "declare," but to "appoint" or to "determine." E.g., Lk 22:22; Acts 2:23; 10:42; 11:29; 17:26, 31; Heb 4:7.

[16]See 1 Cor 3:5, 20; 4:4-5, 19; 6:13; 7:10, 12, 17; 2 Cor 3:17; 6:17-18; 10:8, 18; 13:10; Gal 4:1; Phil 2:11. I borrow the phrase "divine identity" from Richard Bauckham, *Jesus and the God of Israel* (Grand Rapids, MI: Eerdmans, 2008).

occurrence in his uncontested letters.[17] Finally, in Romans 1:9, Paul refers to the gospel of God's Son. The "gospel of God" (Rom 1:1) and the gospel of God's Son (Rom 1:9) are the same gospel. Thus, God's (the Father's) installment of Jesus (his eternal Son and the Lord) to be the exalted Jewish Messiah with power at the resurrection is a high christological statement referring to the moment in history when God finally installed the Messianic king over Zion in all of his messianic (divine) glory at his resurrection (Ps 2; 16:9-11; 110).

Fourth, the "gospel of God" concerns God's appointing of Jesus to be God's Son by means of God's resurrecting power when he raised Jesus from the dead (Rom 1:4). Paul means the resurrection of Jesus was the moment in history when God installed Jesus (his eternal Son) as David's messianic descendant and as the king over Zion (Ps 2:6). Jesus' resurrection/exaltation and ascension were the moment in history where God told his preexistent Son, who became a Jewish man incarnate within history, to sit by his right hand after his resurrection and exaltation until he appoints his enemies as a footstool under his feet (Ps 110:1). Jesus' resurrection and exaltation was the moment in history when he began to reign over the throne of David as the Jewish God-man and Messiah. Jesus, the preexistent Son of God, took on Jewish flesh within history as a descendant of David to be exalted as the promised seed of David to rule as King over Zion forever.

Fifth, Paul says "we received grace and apostleship" through Jesus "on behalf of his name" (Rom 1:5). Recent scholarship on grace in Paul shows that grace is "unconditional" but not "unconditioned." That is, grace in Paul's world was understood as a gift that creates reciprocity between the giver and the recipient. Paul believed God gave grace "*unconditionally* to *unworthy* recipients," but this grace transformed them so that they would meet God's expectations of responding with a life of faithful obedience to Jesus Christ.[18] Paul's remark that God gave him and others "grace and apostleship for the obedience of faith amongst the Gentiles" supports this interpretation of grace (Rom 1:6). The grace God gave to Paul to preach the "gospel of God" was for the purpose of giving the Gentiles this grace so that they would be transformed by it and live in obedience to the gospel along with Jewish followers of Christ. Their obedience to the gospel would flow from their faith in the gospel of God's announcement about Jesus, his Son (see Rom 6:1-23). The Christ-followers in Rome are those whom God effectually called to believe the gospel of God about Jesus Christ, his Son (Rom 1:6). As a result, Paul prays that all "beloved ones of God in Rome" would experience God's saving grace and peace, which come from both "God, the Father, and the Lord Jesus Christ" (Rom 1:7).

Thanksgiving and eager desire to preach the gospel in Rome to the Gentiles (Romans 1:8-17). Paul now thanks God for the faith of the Roman Christians, and he expresses his eager desire to visit them. He is thankful their faith in Christ was announced in the known world (Rom 1:8). He calls God as his witness to the fact that he fervently prays for an opportunity to visit them so that they could mutually encourage one another with their spiritual gifts (Rom 1:9-12). He laments that his previous efforts to visit the Romans were unsuccessful (Rom 1:13). He insists he deeply desired to bear

---

[17]Rom 1:9, 19, 24, 26, 28; 2:16; 3:4-6, 25, 29-30. For an argument in favor of taking *theos* as a reference to Jesus in Rom 9:5, see George Carraway, *Christ Is God over All: Romans 9:5 in the Context of Romans 9–11* (New York: Bloomsbury T&T Clark, 2013).

[18]The language of "unconditional" and "unconditioned" grace comes from John Barclay, *Paul and the Gift* (Grand Rapids, MI: Eerdmans, 2015).

gospel fruit among them as he did among other Gentiles (Rom 1:13). He felt obligated to preach the gospel to all Gentiles (to both Greeks and barbarians, sophisticated and unsophisticated Gentiles; Rom 1:14-15), for the gospel reveals God's saving power, resulting in salvation for all people who believe it, with no ethnic restriction (Rom 1:16-17).

Many scholars agree Romans 1:16-17 provides the thesis of the book: the gospel is both the power of God unto salvation and the revelation of God's righteousness for those who believe.[19] These verses support Paul's previous comments in Romans 1:15 about his strong desire to preach the gospel to those in Rome. Paul declares he is not "ashamed of the gospel" (Rom 1:16). Such remarks should be understood in light of ancient Mediterranean values of honor/shame. Honor and shame were determined by group members within a particular community.[20] Paul is not put to shame by group members of a particular community opposed to the gospel because the gospel is God's saving power (Rom 1:16). God manifests the power of the gospel in the salvation of all who believe. Salvation here refers to deliverance from God's future wrath (see Rom 2:7-10; 5:9). In Paul's letters, salvation often refers to a future hope (Rom 5:9-10; 9:27; 10:9, 13; 11:14, 26) that has invaded the present evil age (Rom 8:24).

Recent scholarship argues that *pistis* ("faith") in Paul's writings connects to propositional beliefs, trust, trustworthiness, loyalty, and faithful obedience to God through faithfulness to Jesus Christ, and that *pistis* in Paul's letters is also participatory.[21] Scholars continue to debate the meaning of *pistis* in Paul.[22] Here Paul's point is that humans experience the saving power of the gospel by faith. The saving power of the gospel for all who have faith in Jesus saves both Jews and Gentiles who believe, since Paul defines "everyone who believes" as "Jew and Greek" (Rom 1:16).

Romans 1:17 is parallel to Paul's remarks in Romans 1:16. The former verse further defines how the gospel manifests God's power through the salvation of sinners: "namely, God's righteousness is revealed in it from faith to faith. As it is written: 'the righteous one by faith shall live'" (Rom 1:17). Paul's words here introduce readers to an explosive Pauline phrase ("the righteousness of God"). Many commentators on Romans have written much about this verse.[23] *Righteousness* is one of those important Pauline words with a *dik-* prefix (*dikaiosynē*, "righteousness"; *dikaioō*, "to justify"; *dikaiōsis*, "justification"; *dikaios*, "righteous"; *dikaiōma*, "righteous requirement").

The attached phrase "of God" connects "righteousness" to God. In context, the phrase seems to refer to God's forensic righteousness being revealed as a gift by faith through the gospel to all who believe, since Paul connects Romans 1:16 ("the gospel is the power of God

---

[19]For one example of many, see the exposition and bibliography in Thomas R. Schreiner, *Romans*, rev. ed., Baker Exegetical Commentary on the New Testament (Grand Rapids, MI: Baker Academic, 2019).

[20]On honor and shame, see David A. deSilva, *Honor, Patronage, Kinship, and Purity: Unlocking the New Testament Culture* (Downers Grove, IL: InterVarsity Press, 2000).

[21]See Teresa Morgan, *Roman Faith and Christian Faith: Pistis and Fideis in the Early Roman Empire and Early Churches* (Oxford: Oxford University Press, 2015); Jeanette Hagen Pifer, *Faith as Participation: An Exegetical Study of Some Key Pauline Texts*, WUNT 486 (Tübingen: Mohr Siebeck, 2019).

[22]See recently Kevin W. McFadden, *Faith in the Son of God: The Place of Christ-Oriented Faith Within Pauline Theology* (Wheaton, IL: Crossway, 2021).

[23]For a history of interpretation, see N. T. Wright, *Paul and His Recent Interpreters* (Minneapolis: Fortress, 2015). For recent scholarship on the righteousness of God and an argument for a traditional reading of God's righteousness against the covenant-faithfulness reading, see Charles Lee Irons, *The Righteousness of God: A Lexical Examination of the Covenant-Faithfulness Interpretation*, WUNT 386 (Tübingen: Mohr Siebeck, 2015).

resulting in salvation to everyone who believes") with Romans 1:17 ("God's righteousness is revealed in it") with the word "for" (*gar*) in Romans 1:17. Additionally, the "righteousness of God" in Romans 1:17 is another way of talking about "being justified" (Rom 3:24).[24] This is a reasonable interpretation since Paul easily moves from talking about the "righteousness of God" (Rom 1:17) and to "being justified" with a verb form (*dikaioō*, Rom 2:13) similar to the noun (*dikaiosynē*, Rom 1:17). Paul likewise easily moves from saying the law will justify no one (*dikaioō*), affirming the present manifestation of the righteousness of God "by faith in Jesus Christ to all who believe" in Romans 3:21-22, to the necessity of all "being justified" (*dikaioumenoi*) freely as God's redemptive gift in Jesus Christ (Rom 3:24) because both Jews and Gentiles are guilty of sin (Rom 3:23).

This line of argument, together with Paul's remark in Romans 1:18 (that the gospel reveals God's wrath), suggests the "righteousness of God" in Romans 1:17 refers both to God's forensic act of justifying all Jews and Gentiles who believe/have faith in Jesus Christ from his future wrath, and to the act of rendering the not-guilty verdict in their favor in God's law court on the day of judgment because he counts the guilty righteous in Christ (see Rom 2–4).[25] He counts the guilty righteous in Christ because he does not reckon/count their sins against them but instead covers their sins by the blood of Jesus Christ, who was handed over for their sins and raised for their justification (Rom 4:1-25). Christ's righteousness is in fact imputed to those who are united to Christ by faith so that in Christ they are no longer condemned by their sin (Rom 4:1-25; 8:1).

Paul cites Habakkuk 2:4 in Romans 1:17. Habakkuk 2:4 has a complex history of interpretation, with different renderings of *beʾĕmûnātô* in the Hebrew Bible ("his faithfulness"), the Greek translation of the Old Testament (LXX, "my faith"), and in Paul ("by faith"). These different translations express different points and raise questions as to whether Paul's remarks refer to one's personal faith or to God's faithfulness. Habakkuk cries out to the Lord with complaints about the pervasive injustice in his context (Hab 1:2-4, 12-17). Yahweh promises Habakkuk that the enemies of his people will receive their just deserts because of their arrogance and unjust ways (i.e., because of their unfaithfulness; Hab 2:1-3, 5-20), but the "righteous person will live by his faithfulness" (Hab 2:4 NIV). Habakkuk agrees Yahweh has been and will continue to be faithful to his people (Hab 3:1-19).

The "righteous one" in Paul's citation of Habakkuk 2:4, when he says that "the righteous one by faith shall live," refers to the one who has faith/trust in God. This faith/trust results in salvation for all who believe, and God's saving righteousness is revealed through the gospel in the lives of those who have faith/trust in the announcement of God's gospel about his Son, Jesus Christ (Rom 1:1-6), a faith/trust that is the basis of receiving God's forensic declaration and saving righteousness as a gift because of Christ's death for their sins (Rom 3:21-26). Paul reads Habakkuk 2:4 as referring to eternal life given by faith to those who believe/trust the announcement of the gospel and to whom God renders his saving, forensic, and justifying verdict of not guilty on their behalf in his presence because of God's saving action for them in Christ and their participation in this salvation by their faith in Christ.

[24]So also, Irons, *Righteousness of God*.

[25]For a recent monograph that argues interpreters should read Paul's remarks about salvation in Romans from the perspective of the last judgment, see Brendan Byrne, *Paul and the Economy of Salvation: Reading from the Perspective of the Last Judgment* (Grand Rapids, MI: Baker Academic, 2021).

THEOLOGICAL THEME: THE SAVING POWER OF PAUL'S MULTIETHNIC GOSPEL AND HIS MULTIETHNIC VISION FOR A MULTIETHNIC WORLD (ROMANS 1:1-17)

In the introduction, Paul communicates his gospel-mission was to the Jew first but primarily to the Gentiles. He also communicates the saving power of his gospel extended to all Jews and Gentiles who believe (Rom 1:5, 13-16). Thus, he demonstrates that his gospel is a multiethnic gospel. One cannot separate Paul's gospel message and mission from the ethnic question: Are Jews and Gentiles the people of God by faith in Christ? His gospel proclaims that a Jewish Messiah, who died for our sins and was resurrected for our justification, brings salvation to ethnic Jews and ethnic Gentiles who hear and trust in the gospel by faith.

One can define a Gentile as any ethnicity that is not Jewish ethnicity. At a basic level, this is what I mean when I say ethnic reconciliation touches the very heart of Paul's gospel: namely, the Jewish Messiah died for the sins of ethnically diverse Jews and Gentiles, and God resurrected him from the dead to save them from their sin, to justify them by faith, to reconcile them to God and to one another, and to make them part of the people of God (see Rom 5:6-10; Eph 2:1-21).

Of course, Paul's gospel centers on the cross and the resurrection of Jesus Christ as matters of "first importance," as Jesus died for our sins and God raised him from the dead (1 Cor 15:1-4). Yet, Jesus' death for sinners and resurrection from the dead are inseparable from his Jewish identity and his death for the sins of Jewish and Gentile people. God in and through Jesus (the Jewish Messiah) has acted once and for all to reconcile to one another Jews and Gentiles (Rom 3:21–4:25; 5:6-10; 14:1–15:33). Because of God's saving action in Christ for Jews and Gentiles, they are now empowered by the Spirit to live in pursuit of reconciliation in the real world, where problems of racism, racial discrimination, and ethnic divisions persist in both church and society (Rom 8:1-11; 14–15). Paul's introductory remarks about his gospel-mission should make it apparent to everyone with ears to hear that the gospel as the power of God unto salvation for everyone who believes is a multiethnic gospel that in fact has the power to save many people from diverse ethnicities when they place their faith in Jesus. Ethnocentrism, racism, and any other form of racial or ethnic discrimination or prejudice thus stand antithetical to the gospel and have no place among the people of God or in their churches.

Paul's multiethnic gospel-mission has the power to save diverse sinners from God's wrath and to transform them and to make them the people of God as members of the same spiritual family and of the same local church (when possible) by the power of the Spirit. And, when context and social locations allow, Paul's multiethnic gospel about a Jewish Messiah who saves Jews and Gentiles has the power to create multiethnic, gospel-believing churches that beautifully reflect the power of the gospel to save ethnically diverse image-bearers from God's wrath, and to transform them into a diverse people who live in community with each other in specific local and global church communities. Paul's multiethnic vision must not be limited to the Black-White divide in the United States. For obvious reasons because of the history of slavery, Jim Crow, and its aftermath, the racial and ethnic conciliation conversation in the United States, or the conversation about racial and ethnic relations in certain Christian contexts in the United States, continues to focus almost exclusively on the Black-White divide or on the racism among Whites and Blacks. However, many Black and White Christians in the United States fail to apply Paul's multiethnic gospel and multiethnic vision to a global people, to issues of anti-Asian racism, or to the various forms of racism experienced by additional ethnicities besides Whites and Blacks. Blacks and Whites have often made Paul's multiethnic gospel exclusively about them to the neglect of the many tongues, tribes, peoples, and nations for whom Christ died.

Moreover, although many African Americans and others within so-called minority ethnic groups are quick to point out the racism and the racist ideas of certain Whites, many so-called ethnic minorities often fail to address our own racism and ethnocentrism against White people and against other ethnic minorities in our own lives and congregations, or the intraracial racism that exists among members of the same communities (e.g., colorism in Black communities). Sadly, in 2020, there were numerous reports of anti-Asian racism. Many were reports of crimes committed against Asians by Black and Brown people. The media basically ignores this reality since it does not fit within the popular "blame every racist act on White supremacy" trope. While certain Whites were also complicit in anti-Asian racism, numerous reports stated that many anti-Asian racist incidents were committed by Black and Brown people.

I am aware that historically the terms *race* and *racism* are connected to power and specifically to the power of White supremacy and that race and racism are indeed social constructs. I am also aware that historically those who were racialized as White used this racialized category to exploit and control the social and economic destinies of enslaved Africans and (eventually) African Americans during a certain period in this country. However, because of the Bible's teaching of original sin and because of sin's power to rule and reign over all people and systems regardless of ethnic identity, Christians of any ethnicity can also be complicit in racism. I have worked this out in detail elsewhere.[26] For my purposes here, I simply say that sin is original (Rom 5:12), an individual transgression, and a structural power (Rom 3:23; 6); and racism is both an individual transgression and a structural power. A clear example of this is the aftermath of Jim Crow today in the effects of the systematic dehumanization of Blacks through the act of redlining. Jim Crow is gone, but the systemic impact of this racist policy on Black communities and on other communities of color is still apparent in numerous underserviced Black and Brown communities in the United States.[27]

However, Christians who are ethnic minorities must be neither naive nor arrogant. We must realize that we are capable of being racist against other ethnicities. It is startling and sad to see how many ethnic minorities hate members within their own group because of racist ideas. It is also startling and sad to see how ethnic minorities, many of whom know what it is like to suffer because of racism, will likewise appropriate racist attitudes and behaviors toward White people in the name of antiracism or justice. The destructive power of sin and its impact on individuals and systems operate to create a diverse and multifaceted version of either racism or ethnic or racial discrimination and prejudice within diverse

[26]Jarvis J. Williams, *Redemptive Kingdom Diversity: A Biblical Theology of the People of God* (Grand Rapids, MI: Baker Academic, 2021).

[27]For examples of the devastating effects of redlining in the modern era from primary texts and from the data, see Richard Rothstein, *The Color of Law: A Forgotten History of How Our Government Segregated America* (New York: Liveright, 2017).

communities. In my view, White racism, Black racism, Brown racism, Asian racism, and other forms of racism do not directly correlate one-to-one to one another. White racism, for example, is connected to the social construct and ideas of White supremacy and whiteness, and it has been perhaps the most pervasive racist power in the colonies and in the United States since 1619 and since the nation's founding in 1776. However, my point here is that though racism appears in many forms, racism is a deadly cancer that appears in numerous ethnic communities. Just look, for example, at the racism between Black and Asian communities in Los Angeles in the wake of the Rodney King riots and the racism that exists between ethnic minorities in many communities in the United States today.

Paul's gospel is a multiethnic gospel with a multiethnic vision and reveals God's saving power for a multiethnic world. Christians should proclaim this power to all people without ethnic restriction, seek to obey this gospel in the power of the Spirit, and apply this gospel in ways that will enable them to be agents through whom an ethnically diverse group of Jews and Gentiles will believe, be saved from God's wrath, and be transformed by the power of the Spirit as they live in community with one another and with Spirit-empowered love for one another.

GOD'S UNIVERSAL CONDEMNATION OF ALL JEWS AND GENTILES WITHOUT FAITH IN JESUS, THE JEWISH MESSIAH (ROMANS 1:18–3:20)

Paul's gospel is the power of God resulting in salvation for all believing Jews and Gentiles without ethnic restriction (Rom 1:16). The saving power of the gospel for all people without ethnic restriction is crucial because God's wrath is currently revealed now against every unrighteous human deed that suppresses the truth by the unrighteous pattern of life of the unrighteous (Rom 1:18-32). God's wrath will be revealed in the day of judgment against all people, without ethnic restriction, who reject the truth of the gospel (Rom 2:1–3:20). With the word "for" (*gar*) and with the same verb "to reveal" (*apokalyptetai*) in Romans 1:18 as in Romans 1:17, Paul links his remarks in Romans 1:18-32 about God's current and abiding wrath in the present time with his comments about the gospel in Romans 1:16-17. God's saving righteousness "is revealed" through the gospel (Rom 1:17), and God's wrath "is revealed" against those who disobey the gospel (Rom 1:18-32).

God's wrath is complex in Paul's letters. Often, God's wrath refers to a retributive future day of wrath on the day of judgment at the end of history, reserved for all Jews and Gentiles who reject the gospel of Jesus Christ (e.g., Rom 2:8; 3:5; 4:15; 5:9; 9:22; see also Eph 2:3; 5:6; Col 3:6; 1 Thess 1:10; 2:16; 5:9).[28] However, in Romans 1:18 Paul refers to the current manifestation of God's wrath in the here and now through sinful behavior. God reveals God's wrath in Romans 1:18-32 by handing the unrighteous over to do the desires of their hearts, so that they live in rebellion against God and against his gospel about Jesus since they reject God's revelation of the truth.

On three occasions, Paul asserts that "God gave" the unrighteous over to carry out the sinful proclivities of their hearts because they refuse to yield their lives to the truth of the gospel (Rom 1:24, 26, 28). God reveals just wrath against those who suppress the truth in unrighteousness, because God reveals his

[28]For an argument against God's retributive wrath in the New Testament, see Stephen H. Travis, *Christ and the Judgment of God*, 2nd ed. (Grand Rapids Academic, MI: Baker, 2009).

divine nature to them through creation and through their human consciences (Rom 1:18-20). Still, this revelation does not move them to worship the Creator instead of the creation. Instead, they reject this revelation and glory in exchange for a lie (Rom 1:25), resulting in God's handing them over to a perverted mind/will to do the very rebellious things they desired (Rom 1:21-32).

In Romans 1:24-27, Paul states that God handed over the unrighteous to rebel against the original design of creation for humanity and to practice various forms of sexual immorality. God's wrath results in all who suppress the truth doing "the things that are not fitting" (Rom 1:28). In Romans 1:29-31, Paul lists numerous different Greek terms to describe the different ways in which God manifests just wrath on those who suppress the truth by giving them over to a depraved mind and a rebellious pattern of life against God.

In Romans 1:29, Paul states that "God gave" them over to practice "all unrighteousness," "evil," "covetousness," "full of envy, murder, selfishness, deceit, meanness," and to be "gossipers". In Romans 1:30, he also states that "God gave" them over to be "slanderers, haters of God, insulters, arrogant, prideful, schemers of evil, and disobedient to parents." In Romans 1:31, Paul states that God gave them over to be "foolish, disloyal, lacking any kind of human affection, and merciless." Those whom God hands over to practice these things know better, but they both practice these vices and are pleased with those who practice them, even though they know God will condemn those who practice such things (Rom 1:32).

Scholars debate whether the content of Romans 2:1-29 is Paul's view, the view of a Jewish interlocutor, or the view of a Gentile interlocutor sympathetic to Judaism.[29] The important point for my purposes here is Paul's remarks represent his own views.[30] Whereas Paul primarily criticizes Gentiles and Gentile vices in Romans 1:18-32, Romans 2:1-29 highlights Jewish vices. Paul's remarks in Romans 2:1 point in this direction when he says his interlocutor's judgment of those who practice the vices in the previous verses is "without excuse," because the interlocutor condemns himself since he practices the same vices. The Old Testament Apocrypha criticizes the types of vices Paul mentions in the previous verses as Gentile vices (see Wis 11–14). By mentioning these vices at this point in his argument, Paul takes his first step in the argument of Romans 1–3 of setting Jews and Gentiles on the same footing of condemnation before God and showing that both groups fail to obey God.

Paul quickly points to a future day of wrath when Jews who live in disobedience to the truth of the gospel will suffer God's just condemnation (Rom 2:1-8). He states that this judgment will come for both Jews and Greeks (Rom 2:9), while God's eternal "glory" and "honor" will come to both Jews and Gentiles who obey the truth of the gospel since God remains impartial to one's ethnic distinction when he judges (Rom 2:11). God desires both Jews and Gentiles to obey him; he will judge both groups with his unrelenting wrath in the day of wrath at the end of history (Rom 2:12-16). Paul, then, criticizes his Jewish interlocutor for self-righteous hypocrisy (Rom 2:17-24). He also enlightens his interlocutor that a true Jew is one whose heart is circumcised by the Spirit, whether Jewish or Gentile, not one whose flesh only is circumcised (Rom 2:25-29).

---

[29]For discussions of these views, see arguments and bibliography in Rafael Rodríguez, *If You Call Yourself a Jew: Reappraising Paul's Letter to the Romans* (Eugene, OR: Cascade, 2014). For additional discussion of issues related to the speaker in Rom 1:18–3:20, see also Douglas Campbell, *The Deliverance of God* (Grand Rapids, MI: Eerdmans, 2009).

[30]Contra Campbell, *Deliverance of God.*

Because of Paul's assertions that God will judge both Jews and Gentiles without ethnic restriction, Paul then asks whether Jews have an advantage over Gentiles (Rom 3:1-20). In Romans 3:1-2, Paul answers in the affirmative, that Jews have an advantage over the Gentiles in that God gave Jews the oracles of God. That is, the Jews, not the Gentiles, received the Torah from Yahweh at Sinai (Ex 20). However, the Jews do not have an advantage over the Gentiles in God's eschatological judgment as a result of receiving the oracles of God at Sinai, because both Jews and Gentiles are "under sin" and because God requires both groups to obey him and his law (Rom 3:9-20). The Jewish law will justify neither Jews nor Gentiles, "for through the law comes the knowledge of sin" (Rom 3:20). Paul will argue later the law brings death and condemnation (Rom 7), but God's saving action in Christ brings freedom from condemnation and grants the life-giving power of the Spirit to those in Christ (Rom 8).

THEOLOGICAL THEME: THE IMPARTIAL MULTIETHNIC DISPLAY OF GOD'S WRATH (ROMANS 1:18–3:20)

Many in the modern world shun talking about the wrath of God, despite its prominence in the Scriptures. One of the primary arguments Paul makes in Romans 1–3 is the righteous God and Father of our Lord Jesus Christ is a God of fierce and unrelenting wrath. He will display this wrath both within history and at the end of history against all (Jews and Gentiles) who refuse to repent and follow Jesus by faith. Paul speaks of God's wrath both being displayed in the present evil age against all ethnic groups in the everyday rhythms of life as he hands the rebellious over to practice their rebellion against him (Rom 1:18-29), and in a future day of wrath to be poured out against all ethnic groups who reject Christ at the end of history (Rom 2:1-29).

As I argue above, Paul's remarks about the current revelation of God's wrath in the here and now speak to God's act of giving disobedient and hardened sinners over to their disobedience to commit the sinful desires of their hearts. Paul mentions a litany of vices to which God hands them over in Romans 1:18-32. These vices pertain to idolatry, sexual immorality, and other relational/social sins.

God's judgment will fall on all sinners who reject Christ regardless of ethnic distinction, because sin is original (Rom 5:12), a power (Rom 6:1-23), and an individual transgression (Rom 3:23). Sin is also a cosmic power that rules and reigns over people, creation, and systems as an evil tyrant (Rom 6:12-13; 8:18-22). God demands and expects Jews and Gentiles to obey him (Rom 1–3). Instead, all (Jews and Gentiles) have sinned and fallen short of God's glory (Rom 3:23). When sinners are full of envy and unrighteousness, lie, slander, gossip, are merciless, are without affection, plot evil deeds against their neighbors, insult others, and the like, they personify God's wrath by their ungodly behavior as they live in complete rebellion against God's revelation in Torah and in Christ. They manifest that God's wrath abides on them as he allows them to be intoxicated by their own self-deceptions of their own ungodly reality.

As a result, the ungodly ones, who live in disobedience to the gospel of God both inside and outside the church, store up wrath for themselves in the day of wrath. Furthermore, those who refuse to live in light of the transformative power of the gospel likewise store up wrath for their ungodly acts in the day of wrath when God will judge every soul of a person who does evil, the Jews first and also the Greeks. God will deliver over to a rebellious life now those who refuse to be obedient to the truth of the gospel because of their hardened unbelief, and God will destroy the ungodly with indestructible wrath at the end of history if they refuse to repent. God's judgment is multiethnic. God will pour out eschatological destruction on diverse sinners from different ethnic communities throughout the world on that great and terrible day of wrath at the end of history when Jesus returns, because the wrath of God is ethnically impartial. A diverse and multiethnic people will be saved from God's wrath if they repent, believe, and follow Jesus as the Jewish Messiah, but a diverse and multiethnic people will likewise experience God's wrath on the day of judgment unless they repent and believe in Jesus.

JEWS AND GENTILES CAN BE JUSTIFIED THE SAME WAY: BY FAITH IN JESUS CHRIST (ROMANS 3:21–4:25)

In Romans 3:21–4:25, Paul's argument takes a positive shift. Romans 1:18–3:20 teaches Jews and Gentiles (all people without ethnic restriction) will suffer the wrath of God now in the current age and at the end of history because of their unbelief. Now, Paul says in Romans 3:21–4:25, Jews and Gentiles (without ethnic restriction) can be justified by faith in Jesus Christ apart from the works of the law. I understand the latter section to further unpack Paul's remarks in Romans 1:16-17 about the gospel's power to save all who believe and about the revelation of God's righteousness in the gospel.

Paul makes a redemptive-historical shift in his argument with the words "but now" in Romans 3:21. God's wrath is revealed through unrighteousness when God hands over the rebellious to practice rebellion because of their disobedience to God (Rom 1:18-32) and at the end of history against those who refused to submit to the truth revealed in Jesus Christ (Rom 2:1–3:20). "But now," in this current age of redemptive history, "apart from the law the righteousness of God is manifested, being testified to by the law and the prophets, that is, the righteousness of God by faith in Jesus Christ to all who believe" (Rom 3:21-22). These two verses, and in fact the entire section of Romans 3:21-26, constitute the basis of many exegetical debates.[31]

I understand these verses to mean God justifies (reveals the "righteousness of God" to) Jews and Gentiles by faith in Christ apart from Jews or Gentiles keeping/living by the Mosaic covenant in accordance with "works of the law" (Rom 3:22). "Works of the law" refer to the Mosaic covenant (Ex 20-Deut). The idea here is that living a Jewish way of life in compliance with the law of Moses is not how one is justified. Instead, Jews and Gentiles are justified by faith in Christ as Jews and as Gentiles apart from the works of the law. This is supported in part by the fact that Paul says God in Christ is the God of both Jews (those who received the law) and Gentiles (those who did not receive the law), for God justifies both Jews (those with the law) and Gentiles (those without the law) by faith in Christ (Rom 3:28-30). Consequently, God establishes the intent of the law through faith by justifying Jews and Gentiles by faith in Christ (Rom 3:31; Gal 3:24). Yes, the Law and the Prophets testify and point to the moment in history when God would reveal his righteousness to Jews and Gentiles with faith in Jesus

[31]For a discussion of the complex exegetical issues in this section, see commentaries on Romans. For a few accessible commentaries that discuss the exegetical issues of these verses and of the entire letter, see Schreiner, *Romans*; Douglas J. Moo, *Romans*, NICNT (Grand Rapids, MI: Eerdmans, 1996); Ben Witherington III and Darlene Hyatt, *Romans* (Grand Rapids, MI: Eerdmans, 2004); Craig S. Keener, *Romans*, NCC (Eugene, OR: Cascade, 2009); and the bibliographies in these commentaries.

Christ (e.g., Is 40–66).[32] However, the law does not justify anyone, because it only reveals a knowledge of sin (Rom 3:20) and brings further condemnation on those who disobey it (Rom 7).

Just as God promises to judge a multiethnic group of Jews and Gentiles for the same reason (namely, because of their disobedience to the truth of the gospel; Rom 1:18–3:20), God likewise chooses to save a multiethnic group of Jews and Gentiles by faith in Christ for the same reason: namely, "for there is no distinction between Jews and Gentiles" (Rom 3:22). That is, "all" (both Jews and Gentiles) have sinned against God and have failed to honor him to the degree that he demands (Rom 3:23). Consequently, "all" (both Jews and Gentiles) need to be "justified freely by God's grace through the redemption that is in Christ Jesus" (Rom 3:24). In Romans 3:20, Paul says that no one "will be justified" by obedience to the law, because the law gives knowledge of sin. In Romans 3:24, he now says everyone must be "freely justified" by God's grace through Christ's redemptive work.

As I argued earlier about the "righteousness of God" in Romans 1:17 and in Romans 3:21-22, the Greek verb *dikaioumenoi*, which Paul uses here and which I translate as "justified," is a forensic term.[33] The verb means here "to declare to be in the right" or "to declare not guilty." The opposite verdict would be condemnation. A form of this Greek verb occurs in a legal context in the Greek translation of the Old Testament (Septuagint or LXX) where the judge exonerates the righteous and condemns the ungodly when there is a dispute between them (Deut 25:1). When Paul says, "there is no condemnation for those who are in Christ Jesus" (Rom 8:1), he conceptually means those in Christ Jesus now stand justified, not condemned, by God (see Rom 8:31-30). Judgment awaits all ethnic groups who reject Christ, disobey God within history, and continue in their disobedience until the end of history on the day of wrath. However, God's wrath will not fall on those who trust in Jesus by faith and who obey him now until the end of history (see Rom 1–3). This "not guilty" or justification pronouncement connects to faith in Christ and to redemption by the blood of Christ, according to Romans 3:24; 4:1-25.

Scholars debate issues of translation and theology in Romans 3:25. One of the major debates pertains to the proper way to translate the Greek term *hilastērion*.[34] Paul states that God offers Jesus to be a *hilastērion*. This term occurs in the Greek Old Testament to refer to the mercy seat (LXX Ex 25:17, 20-21; 31:7; 35:12; 38:5, 8; Lev 16:13-15). Some translate Paul's use here to refer to Jesus' death for sins as an act of "expiation" (RSV), a "propitiation" (ESV, NASB), or as a "sacrifice of atonement" (NIV).[35]

---

[32]"The Law and the Prophets" is a stock phrase for the Jewish Scriptures (Mt 7:12; 11:13; 22:40; Lk 16:16; 24:44; Jn 1:45; Acts 13:15; 24:14; 28:23; Rom 3:21; see also LXX = Greek translation of the Hebrew Scriptures and Apocrypha; Sirach 1:1; 2 Macc 15:9; 4 Maccabees 18:10).

[33]Scholars fiercely debate Paul's understanding of justification. For a summary of the debate, see comments and bibliography in Stephen Westerholm, *Perspectives Old and New on Paul: The "Lutheran" Paul and His Critics* (Grand Rapids, MI: Eerdmans, 2004). For a recent book on justification, see Thomas R. Schreiner, *Faith Alone: The Doctrine of Justification* (Grand Rapids, MI: Zondervan, 2015). For a few examples of the verb in the LXX, see Gen 38:26; 44:16; Ex 23:7; Deut 25:1; 2 Sam 15:4; Tob 12:4; Ps 18:10; 50:6. For a few examples of uses in the New Testament, see Rom 2:13; 3:4, 20, 24, 26, 28, 30; 4:2, 5; 5:1, 9; 8:30, 33; Gal 2:16-17; 3:8, 11, 24; 5:4.

[34]For recent work on *hilastērion*, see Stephen J. Hultgren, "Hilasterion (Rom. 3:25) and the Union of Divine Justice and Mercy Part 1: The Convergence of Temple and Martyrdom Theologies," *JTS* 70, no. 1 (2019): 69-109; Hultgren, "Hilasterion (Rom. 3:25) and the Union of Divine Justice and Mercy Part 2: Atonement in the Old Testament and in Romans 1–5," *JTS* 70, no. 2 (2019): 69-109. See also his bibliography and interaction with a history of scholarship.

[35]*Expiation* refers to God's act of cleansing sin. *Propitiation* refers to God's act of satisfying or assuaging divine wrath. "Sacrifice of atonement" allows for both expiatory and propitiatory ideas to be present, but it emphasizes God's act of providing a means of atonement through the death of Jesus to deal with the problem of sin through a sacrificial death for the transgressors.

Scholarship on the meaning of this term is plentiful. Here I simply note that Paul's basic point is to reiterate that God presented Christ to die in order to provide a solution to the human plight of sins, which God passed over in the previous age under the law, in order to demonstrate himself to be a just God who deals with sin and a God who justifies sinners who have faith in Jesus (Rom 3:25-26). The presence of blood in Romans 3:25 supports this use of *hilastērion* in relation to Jesus' death. That is, Paul asserts that God presented Jesus to be a *hilastērion* "by his blood" (Rom 3:25). Blood here evokes the image of the Old Testament sacrificial system (see Lev 16). Paul also connects Jesus' blood with redemption (Rom 3:24) and with justification, salvation, and reconciliation (Rom 5:9-10).

God's verdict of justification (or not guilty) on behalf of those who have faith in Jesus connects in Romans 4 to the forgiveness of sins (Rom 4:8) and to the Lord not reckoning to human beings their sins (Rom 4:9). Paul says God "reckons" or "credits" faith to one's account as righteousness (see Rom 4:5), just as David says in Psalm 32 and just as Abraham demonstrates by his faith in Genesis 15:6 (Rom 4:1-25). In Romans 4:25, Paul says Jesus died for our transgressions and was raised for our justification. In Romans 3–4, Paul associates the verdict of not guilty with Jesus' death and resurrection. God reckons sinners as not guilty because God does not credit their transgressions against them (see Rom 4:1-25). Rather, God justifies them and imputes to their credit Christ's righteousness by faith (Rom 3:21–4:25).[36]

God's work of justifying Jews and Gentiles by faith in Jesus Christ causes Paul to raise this question: "Where is boasting" in oneself before God (Rom 3:27)?[37] He says boasting is excluded because one is justified by faith apart from "works of the law" (Rom 3:28).[38] The latter phrase is also debated.[39] But it should be understood as works done in obedience to Torah, that is, works in obedience to the stipulations of the Mosaic covenant (see Ex 20:1–Deut 29:29). Paul comments in Romans 1–3 that the law cannot justify (Rom 3:20). He further explains that the law does not give Jews an advantage over Gentiles in the day of judgment (Rom 3:1-2, 9-18).

As a result of Paul's argument for the universal condemnation of all Jews and Gentiles apart from faith in Christ and the justification of all Jews and Gentiles by faith in Christ, Paul asks an important ethnic and soteriological question: "Is God the God of the Jews only? Is he not also the God of Gentiles?" (Rom 3:29). This question, and his previous argument in Romans 1–3 about the gospel and judgment, is one of many reasons why Paul's gospel cannot be separated from the Jew-Gentile question, because the question is, Who are and who can become the people of God? Must Jews be justified by faith in Christ to be part of the people of God even though they had the law, and must Gentiles embrace a Jewish way of life in accordance with the law in addition to being justified by faith in Christ before they can become

[36]For a discussion of the imputation of Christ's righteousness, see Brian J. Vickers, *Jesus' Blood and Righteousness: Paul's Theology of Imputation* (Wheaton, IL: Crossway, 2006).

[37]For a detailed discussion on early Jewish soteriology in comparison with Rom 1–5, see Simon J. Gathercole, *Where Is Boasting? Early Jewish Soteriology and Paul's Response in Romans 1–5* (Grand Rapids, MI: Eerdmans, 2002).

[38]The debate relates to the question of the reference of these works. For recent discussion, see Matthew J. Thompson, *Paul's "Works of the Law" in the Perspective of Second-Century Reception* (Downers Grove, IL: InterVarsity Press, 2020).

[39]For the various discussions related to justification and "works of the law," see Westerholm, *Perspectives Old and New*; Stephen J. Chester, *Reading Paul with the Reformers: Reconciling Old and New Perspectives* (Grand Rapids, MI: Eerdmans, 2017). For recent discussion of the reception history of Paul's "works of the law" language, see Thomas, *Paul's "Works of the Law."*

part of the people of God? Are Jews the people of God because of their Jewish identity apart from faith in Christ, and can Gentiles become part of the people of God as Gentiles by faith in Jesus Christ?

These remain massively important soteriological questions. Paul's answer emphatically states that God, because of justification by faith in Christ, is the God of both Jews and Gentiles (Rom 3:20). This one God "will justify the circumcision by faith and the uncircumcision by faith" (Rom 3:30). This one God does not create separate ways of salvation or different sets of requirements in Christ for Jews and Gentiles.[40] Instead, this one God makes individuals within both ethnic groups part of the people of God by justifying them by faith in Jesus Christ, the Jewish Messiah, without eradicating their ethnic identities. They are justified by faith in Christ (Rom 3:21–4:25), and by the Spirit living in them they become transformed Jews and transformed Gentiles in Christ (Rom 12:1–15:33). Thus, according to Paul, the one God has definitively acted in history in Christ, the Jewish Messiah, to justify a multiethnic group of Jews and Gentiles by faith to make them one multiethnic people of God with many diverse ethnic groups. This truth is in fact a significant component to Paul's gospel of God that he preached to Jews and Gentiles (see Rom 1:1-7, 16-17).

THEOLOGICAL THEME: JUSTIFICATION OF BOTH JEWS AND GENTILES BY FAITH IN JESUS CHRIST (ROMANS 3:21–4:25)

Since the beginnings of Christianity, Christians have struggled with ethnic division. Of course, the ethnic division of the early church was Jewish and Gentile. This division was complex, with its own theological/ethnic/political/geographic/ethic particularities. In certain expressions of Christianity these days, however, the ethnic problem has primarily been Gentile versus Gentile division.

Paul's argument in Romans 3:21–4:25 should remind all Christians from every ethnic group throughout the world that God acts to justify diverse Jews and diverse Gentiles by faith in Jesus Christ, whose blood bleeds red for every ethnic group. Jesus was crucified for a multiethnic people and for a multiethnic bride (namely, the church). God raised him from the dead to justify them by faith. There are massive implications of this for the people of God. Justification by faith is first rooted in Jesus' death for the sins of diverse tongues, tribes, peoples, and nations and in his resurrection from the dead. His death and resurrection are a great theological equalizer in the presence of God for those from different ethnic groups scattered throughout the world.

The same God who created one human race also created all the ethnic groups throughout the world. Paul's remarks about justification by faith in this section remind us that this same God, the one and true God, likewise justifies a diverse people and makes them right before him and with him by faith in Christ so that every ethnic group is placed on an equal footing before God in the judgment and so that a multiethnic people of God will participate in the soteriological blessings now and at the end of the age. A powerful implication of this truth is Jews are justified by faith in Christ *as Jews*, and Gentiles are justified by faith in Christ *as Gentiles*. Neither Jews nor Gentiles stop being ethnic Jews or ethnic Gentiles. Rather, they are transformed Jews and transformed Gentiles in Christ. This means they must put on the new person in Christ and strip off the old Adam, while imposing neither their Jewish nor Gentile identities on others. They must consider one

[40]Contra Gabriele Boccaccini, *Paul's Three Paths to Salvation* (Grand Rapids, MI: Eerdmans, 2020).

another to be more valuable than themselves as they love the brothers and sisters for whom Christ died in the gospel (see Rom 12–15; 1 Cor 10; Eph 4–5; Phil 2:1-10). As Paul says, God is the God of Jews and Gentiles (Rom 3:29). God justifies them both by faith in Christ without eradicating their Jewish and Gentile identities. Jewish and Gentile distinctions are still present in Christ, but they no longer are marks of separation, for God justifies them both by faith in Jesus Christ alone, and he transforms them by the Spirit (Rom 8:1-17).

As we will see in Romans 12–15, Paul argues that God transforms Jews and Gentiles by the renewing of their minds. One evidence of this transformation is Jewish and Gentile unity in the gospel and love for one another flowing from what God has done for them in Christ to make them together the people of God. Paul's "therefore" in Romans 12:1 links Romans 12–15 with Romans 1–11, chapters that focus on God's work of justifying Jews and Gentiles by redeeming them in Christ in accordance with Paul's gospel. God's work of justifying a multiethnic people of Jews and Gentiles should provide the motivation for diverse Christians to live in multiethnic Christian community when social location provides spaces to do so. Paul's remarks should also provide the motivation for this diverse, justified people to work toward the flourishing of ethnically diverse image-bearers inside and outside the church by pushing against all forms of racial injustice and ethnic division in both churches and communities. God's work to justify a multiethnic group of Jews and Gentiles by faith in Christ is a significant biblical, theological, and spiritual truth that should guide us in our efforts against any form of racism or hostility against multiethnic Christian communities. Because of justification by faith, Jews and Gentiles stand on equal footing in Christ in the presence of God.

THE CERTAINTY OF HOPE IN PRESENT SUFFERING BECAUSE OF THE CERTAINTY OF FUTURE SALVATION THROUGH CHRIST (ROMANS 5:1–8:39)

Romans 5:1–8:39 begins a new section in the letter. Paul infers from his previous argument in Romans 1–4, seen with the term "therefore" in Romans 5:1. His primary theme in Romans 5:1–8:39 is the certainty of hope in present suffering because of the certainty of future salvation through Christ. Paul specifically mentions hope in Romans 5:4-5, and he concludes the section with hope in Romans 8:1-39. Throughout Romans 5–8, the certainty of hope through Christ in suffering is real because Jesus died for our sins to justify us by faith, to deliver us from God's wrath, and to reconcile us to God (Rom 5:1-10). God through Christ reversed Adam's curse (Rom 5:12-21).[41] Jesus liberated us from the tyrannical power of sin (Rom 6:1-23). The law condemns Jews and Gentiles, but Jesus liberates Jews and Gentiles from the enslaving power of the law through his death and resurrection and through the indwelling power of the Spirit, who enables us to walk in the Spirit and not in accordance with the flesh (Rom 7:1–8:11; see Gal 5:16-26). By the Spirit, we are no longer slaves to the flesh. We are led by the Spirit of adoption, by whom we can cry out to God as our Father since God makes us his heirs (Rom 8:12-17). We have the certainty of hope in suffering because our current afflictions cannot compare to our future redemption (Rom 8:18-25). Our confidence is grounded in Jesus' prayers for us, the Spirit's prayers for us, and God's ability to

[41]For Paul's belief that Jesus reverses the Deuteronomic curse, see Marvin Pate, *Reverse of the Curse: Paul, Wisdom, and the Law*, WUNT 114 (Tübingen: Mohr Siebeck, 2000).

work out all things in accordance with our soteriological good (Rom 8:18-30). We know absolutely nothing will or can separate us from God's love in Christ (Rom 8:31-39).

In Romans 5:1, Paul states believers have current peace with God "because we have been justified by faith." Just as God justifies Jews and Gentiles by faith in Jesus Christ (Rom 3:22, 24, 30), so also God gives us peace "through our Lord Jesus Christ" (Rom 5:1). Those who are justified by faith in Christ experience this peace. That is, we stand before God reconciled as his friends, no longer his enemies (Rom 5:8-10), because God has justified us by faith in Christ (Rom 5:1). This interpretation seems plausible given Paul's remarks about reconciliation in Romans 5:9-10. Paul says our future deliverance from God's wrath is certain "because we have been justified by Jesus' blood" (Rom 5:9). In Romans 5:10, he asserts we will certainly be delivered by Jesus' life (i.e., his resurrection), "because we were reconciled to God through the death of his son while we were enemies" with God.

Paul connects the certainty of our future hope to suffering. He says, "We boast in the hope of the glory of God" (Rom 5:2). I understand this to mean the justified ones exalt in the certainty that God will glorify/honor them with eternal life in the day of judgment, even as they suffer now, if they endure suffering with him now (see Rom 8:17). Paul connects boasting and the endurance of suffering ("afflictions") with this hope (Rom 5:3). He also states, "We boast in afflictions," since "we know that affliction produces endurance, endurance character, and character hope" (Rom 5:3-4).[42] Paul brings this chain of events flowing from hope in Christ to a climax in Romans 5:5 when he says, "And hope does not disappoint." That is, hope is certain, because "God's love is poured out in our hearts through the Holy Spirit who was given to us" (Rom 5:5). The Spirit living in those who are justified by faith guarantees the certainty of future hope and brings the proleptic nature of this hope into the present for those who suffer afflictions in this present evil age (Rom 5:1-6; see Rom 8:1-17).

Furthermore, in Romans 2:1-6, Paul emphasized God's eschatological wrath would be poured out on the last day on all who rejected the truth of his gospel, whereas in Romans 2:7, he suggested God would give "eternal life" to those who pursued "glory" and "honor" and "immortality," corresponding to the "endurance" (the same term for endurance as in Rom 5:3-4) of "good work." Once more, Romans 8:28-30 points in this direction when Paul asserts God works all things together for those who love God for the good of the saving purposes of the people of God because God foreknows them (i.e., sets his covenantal love on them; Rom 8:29), predestines them to be conformed to the image of Jesus, effectually calls them to saving faith in Christ, justifies them, and glorifies them (Rom 8:30).

The justified have current certainty in future hope even as they suffer afflictions now because this certainty is grounded in God's love for them, which he displayed through Jesus' death for their sins and his physical resurrection from the dead (Rom 5:6-11). While the justified ones were weak sinners (Rom 5:6, 8), God displayed his love to them in that "Christ died for our sins" (Rom 5:8). His death was not a noble death for a noble cause (Rom 5:7). Rather, he, the righteous one, died for ignoble and unrighteous people (Rom 5:6, 8).

[42]In Paul's world, ancients generally boasted in strength, not in weakness. For a discussion of primary texts, see Neil Elliott and Mark Reasoner, eds., *Documents and Images for the Study of Paul* (Minneapolis: Fortress, 2011), 32; Duane F. Watson, "Paul and Boasting," in *Paul and the Greco-Roman World*, 2nd ed. (New York: Bloomsbury T&T Clark, 2016), 90-112.

"Therefore," the justified ones can be confident that God will save them from his wrath through Christ since he has justified them by "the blood of his Son" (Rom 5:9). Since the justified were reconciled to God by Jesus' death while they were God's enemies (i.e., they hated God, and God hated them [Ps 5:5]), they know with absolute certainty they will be saved from God's judgment through Jesus' resurrection life (Rom 5:10).

This hope is certain because Jesus is the last and perfect Adam (Rom 5:12-21). Jesus' act of faithful righteousness reverses the effects of Adam's unrighteousness (Rom 5:12-21). Because of Adam, sin entered the world, with the result that all who enter the world participate in sin, but Jesus' act of obedience triumphed over Adam's act of disobedience (Rom 5:12-21). God liberates sinners from sin through Christ, the second Adam, as they die with him in baptism and as they are raised to walk with him in the newness of a transformed life of resurrection. As a result, the justified make every effort in the power of the Spirit not to let sin reign as an evil tyrant over their lives because they know sin produces death, but God's gift is eternal life (Rom 6:1-23). The law kills and enslaves the Jew in Adam, under the law, and all people in Adam under the law (Rom 7:1-23). But Christ liberates the Jew in Adam from the condemnation of the law, and all people in Christ from the condemnation of the law through Jesus' death and through the indwelling power and presence of the Spirit (Rom 8:1-17).

Consequently, all things will work out for the soteriological good of God's people when they do not know what to pray in afflictions, because Jesus and the Spirit pray for them (Rom 8:18-30). God set his covenantal love on them (Rom 8:29) when he predestined (determined in advance) them to be conformed to the image of Jesus, with the result that they would be part of the family of God among many brothers and sisters (Rom 8:30). God also effectually called them to saving faith in Jesus Christ (Rom 8:30). He likewise justifies them whom he effectually calls (Rom 8:30). As a result of this chain of salvation, God glorifies them with eternal life—that is, those whom he set his covenantal love on, those whom he predestined, those whom he called, and those whom he justifies (Rom 8:29-30). God's redemptive acts to save his people and to guarantee their soteriological destinies in and through suffering reminds the justified that since God is for his people in Christ, neither anyone nor anything can separate them from his love in Christ (Rom 8:31-39).

THEOLOGICAL THEME: COSMOLOGICAL REDEMPTION IN THE FACE OF ETHNOCENTRISM, RACISM, AND MULTIETHNIC DIVISION (ROMANS 5:1–8:39)

As I stated in the introduction to the commentary, I am an African American with a multiethnic heritage. My wife has multiethnic Hispanic ancestry, with parents from Nicaragua and Costa Rica. My son has the beautiful multiethnic heritages of my wife and me. As an African American with a mixed ethnic heritage from the southeastern part of Kentucky, I grew up in a context where I and my family experienced overt racism and covert racism from certain Whites because we were African American, and overt racism and racist attitudes from certain African Americans because they did not think we were Black enough (whatever that means!). This is quite ironic, because my oldest aunts and uncles attended segregated schools because they were Black. They are Jim Crow survivors! They had threatening experiences whenever they attempted to cross the racist color line because they were Black, and they suffered the same racist attacks as the so-called nonmixed African Americans because they too were racialized as Black. The difference was they were lighter skinned and/or mixed.

Growing up, I was often called "nigger" and a host of other racist terms by racist Whites, and at times I feared for my safety because I am Black. My family and I were also at times shunned, mocked, and looked down on by certain African Americans who dehumanized us with names such as nigger-white, half-breed, high-yellow, Uncle Tom, sellouts, and so on because of our (as they called it) high yellow and light black skin. Fellow African Americans who thought they were self-proclaimed authorities on blackness often called each other "nigger," and they called us light-skin Blacks "niggers" too. The lighter-skinned African Americans would make fun of the darker-skinned African Americans in my neighborhood because of their dark skin, while the darker-skinned African Americans would in turn make fun of both the lighter-skinned African Americans because of their light skin and the darker-skinned African Americans because of their dark skin, while they also mocked African Americans who were lighter than they because they were not too light or too dark. If this all seems silly, that's because it is!

These complex interracial, intraracial, and interethnic interactions remind us that the creation is in absolute chaos because of original sin, individual transgressions, and the cosmic power of sin. Creation is enslaved to sin and its power. Instead of honoring God's beautiful creativity of a multiethnic diversity of humans who have a diversity of beautiful skin colors and ethnic heritages, fellow image-bearers would rather despise, shame, and dehumanize the beautiful multiethnic diversity of humans that God created to display his creative glory and power.

Paul's comments about hope in suffering remind the people of God that no one nicely and neatly fits into one specific social context. Although creation is in agony right now as those within it await the redemption of their bodies, the people of God have tasted that redemption now in Christ. As a result, the multiethnic love and unity that will be perfectly realized on the last day can be experienced in part now by faith in Jesus and the transformational power of the Spirit as the ethnically diverse people of God love one another. Thus, ethnically diverse Christians all over the world should make every effort in the power of the Spirit to live considering that unity right now. This is not easy. Living this way is hard! In fact, it is easier not to do this. Yet, the people of God must pursue this kind of multiethnic unity whenever and wherever possible, in the church and in society, as we seek to proclaim Christ to the world, obey Christ in the world, and love our neighbors as we love ourselves. God's multiethnic people should pursue a multiethnic, global gospel vision in ways consistent with their contexts and their social realities in the face of racism and ethnocentrism, and to the shame of racists and ethnocentrists in the name of Jesus Christ.

GOD HAS NOT FORSAKEN HIS PROMISES TO ETHNIC ISRAEL (ROMANS 9:1–11:36)

Romans 9–11 is one of the most contested sections in the letter. In my commentary below, I simply state what I understand to be the basic message of the chapters and support this interpretation with a discussion of selected texts. This section is integral to the argument Paul has made in Romans 1–8. Romans 1–8 seems to present a problem for Paul's Jewish interlocutor, who rejects Jesus but is the ideal Torah-observant Jew. The problem is some might think God has forsaken his promises to ethnic Israel since Paul has argued there is no advantage for Jews over Gentiles in the judgment and since many Jews in his day rejected Jesus as the Jewish Messiah. Thus, in Romans 9–11, Paul's primary message seems to be the following: God has not forsaken his promises to Israel. The apostle summarizes this message in Romans 9:6 with the words, "It is not as though the word of God has fallen." In Romans 11:1-2, Paul returns to the premise in Romans 9:6 by saying one reason his Jewish interlocutor should know God has not forsaken his promises to Israel is Paul himself is a Jew, he too is an Israelite, he too is from the seed of Abraham, and he too is from the tribe of Benjamin.

Paul makes these remarks about God's faithfulness in Romans 9:6 after agonizing over the fact that many Jews reject Christ (Rom 9:1-3) and after emphasizing the many benefits Jews have received related to the fathers and the Messiah (Rom 9:4-5). Paul defends the basic premise that God has not forsaken his promises to Israel by arguing God never promised to save all Jews or all people without exception (Rom 9:6-29). Rather, God has chosen by divine election to save only some Jews and Gentiles without ethnic restriction.

After Paul states that God's word to the Jews has not become void (Rom 9:6), he begins to explain this: not all "those from Israel are from Israel." Here Paul presents his Jewish interlocutor with two competing Israels, one ethnic and one spiritual, one that consists only of ethnic Jews and one that consists of ethnic Jewish Christ-followers and ethnic Gentile Christ-followers (see Rom 2). Paul's remarks in Romans 9:7 seem to support this reading when he says all children of Abraham are not the "seed of Abraham" since God only had one promised child, namely, Isaac (see Gen 21:12). God reckons only the children of the promise (i.e., those who have faith in Christ), not the children of the flesh (i.e., ethnic descendants of Abraham), as his seed (Rom 9:8). That is, ethnic Jews descending from Abraham without faith in Christ are not children of the promise, but they are children according to the flesh (Rom 9:9). However, God promised Sarah a child in accordance with his promise (Rom 9:9; see Gen 18:10, 14). Paul continues this same line of argumentation about the certainty of God's promise to bless a remnant by referring to his promise to Isaac and Rebecca to give them a promised offspring (Rom 9:10-13). Paul asserts that before the twins (Jacob and Esau) were born and before they made a choice to do anything good or evil, God had already determined to make the older (Esau) serve the younger (Jacob) so that this "promise in accordance with election might stand, not of works but of him who calls" (Rom 9:11-12). God's promise also stands in accordance with the Lord's words in Malachi: "Jacob I have loved, but Esau I have hated" (Rom 9:13; Mal 1:2).

Interpreters generally argue here for either individual election or universal/corporate election based on Paul's citation of Malachi 1:2. Those who argue for individual election point out the obvious: Jacob and Esau were real individuals. Those who argue for corporate election likewise point out the obvious: Jacob represents Israel (Gen 32:28), and Esau represents the Edomites (Gen 36:29). I, on the other hand, agreeing with many commentators, suggest Paul refers to both corporate and individual election. Space prevents me from defending this interpretation in detail. However, one basic argument is Paul begins Romans 9 lamenting Israel's lack of salvation, crying out that he would even wish himself to be accursed from Christ for them if it were possible (Rom 9:1-5). He develops his premise about God's faithfulness by appealing to corporate promises to Israel that involved individuals: not all Israel is Israel, not all children of Abraham are the promised children (Rom 9:6-13).

Paul continues in Romans 9:14-25 to defend why Jewish unbelief does not prove God has forsaken his promises to Israel and that he therefore is not unrighteous. His argument is God can show his mercy to whomever he wishes to show his mercy (just as he did to Moses in Ex 33:19; see Ex 33–34), and he can display his wrath against whomever he wants to display his wrath. Paul's chief example of a vessel of wrath is Pharaoh (Rom 9:14-18; see Ex 9:16; also Ex 15), whom God raised up to destroy so that he would show his glory throughout the ends of the earth (Rom 9:17).

Paul, then, infers from Romans 9:19-29 that God can do whatever he wants. This section has its own set of exegetical and theological challenges (single versus double predestination, one versus two decrees of God, etc.). But Paul argues that God as the Creator has the right to create/predestine some people to be the objects of his saving mercy and others to be the objects of his eternal wrath in order to display and highlight his glory over the vessels of mercy, which he created for the honor of salvation through the destruction of the vessels of wrath, that he prepared for eternal destruction (Rom 9:19-29). This interpretation seems on target because of Paul's earlier comments about election and salvation (Rom 9:1-5, 13) and about God's divine prerogative to give his saving mercy and divine wrath to whomever he chooses (Rom 9:18). That is, Paul starts Romans 9:1-5 lamenting Israel's salvation and continues in Romans 9:6-13 by explaining that God has always promised only to save those whom he desires to save by divine election as he uses Jacob and Esau as historical examples. In Romans 9:14-29, Paul says God's divine prerogative to predestine some to salvation and others to destruction while holding both groups responsible for the decisions they make for or against the gospel in no way makes God unjust.

Furthermore, Paul refers to God's act of creating from one lump, the same lump, two distinct groups of people (Jews and Gentiles) to participate in two different eternal destinies (eternal salvation or eternal damnation; Rom 9:21-23). In Romans 9:24, Paul says God calls "some" from the Jews and from the Gentiles. In Romans 9:25-29, Paul refers to a litany of Old Testament texts that speak to God's desire to save only a remnant/elect of Jews (see Hos 2:21, 25 [Eng. 19, 23] in Rom 9:25-26; Is 10:22 in Rom 9:27; Is 28:22 in Rom 9:28; Is 1:9 in Rom 9:29). Thus, in Romans 9:19-29, Paul describes the eternal destinies of both individuals and nations. He seems to argue specifically for a double predestination of individuals: God's predestination of some unto salvation and his predestination of others unto condemnation, while likewise suggesting God holds both groups responsible for the decisions they make.

In Romans 9:30–10:13, Paul reintroduces the righteousness language from Romans 1–3 to reinforce the point that Jews who reject Christ fall short of receiving his righteousness because they pursued it by means of law, whereas Gentiles who receive and participate in God's righteousness do so because they pursued it by faith apart from works of the law. The Jews who reject Christ stumble over Christ in their efforts to keep Torah, just as Isaiah promised (Rom 9:32-33; see Is 8:14; 14:13; 28:16). However, the Gentiles receive the promise of God's righteousness because they confess with their mouth that Jesus is Lord and believe in their hearts that God raised him from the dead so that they could be saved (Rom 10:1-12). They experience the promise prophesied in Joel that "anyone who calls on the name of the Lord will be saved" (Rom 10:13). Only those who hear the gospel about Jesus and believe will be saved and receive God's righteousness as a free gift (Rom 10:14-21).

In Romans 11, Paul turns his attention primarily to the issue of Jewish salvation to restate the premise in Romans 9:6: namely, God's word of promise regarding the salvation of ethnic Israel has not failed (Rom 11:1-2). To the contrary, just as in the days of Elijah the prophet, God has a remnant of Jews to whom he has chosen to give his saving mercy "in accordance with the election of grace" (Rom 11:5), not by works of law (Rom 11:2-6; see 1 Kings 19:10, 14, 18). Consequently, what Israel pursues by law (namely, righteousness; Rom 11:7; see Rom 9:31-32), she has failed to obtain (Rom 11:7). However, those whom God has chosen within Israel and among the Gentiles to obtain God's righteousness have obtained it by faith in Christ (Rom 9:30-31; 11:7), while the rest (i.e., nonelect Jews within Israel) "are hardened" in accordance with God's promise in the Scriptures (Rom 11:7-10; see Deut 29:3; Is 6:9; 29:10; Ps 35:8; 68:23).

Yet, Paul insists God's hardening of some within Israel does not mean that God has permanently hardened all of Israel (Rom 11:11). Instead, the hardening of some within Israel results in the saving blessing of some among the Gentiles (Rom 11:12-13). The salvation of some among the Gentiles will result in the salvation of some among the Jews as God provokes them to jealousy through the salvation of the Gentiles (Rom 11:14). Paul reminds the Gentiles of God's deep longing to "save some" of the Jews through Paul's gospel ministry (Rom 11:13-14) so that they will receive "life from the dead" (Rom 11:15), just as many Jews' rejection of the gospel resulted in the "reconciliation of the world" (i.e., Gentile salvation; Rom 11:15). Additionally, Paul warns the Gentiles to avoid arrogance because of their salvation and because of God's hardening of some Jews, lest God cut off Gentiles from the olive tree of salvation as he hardened some of the members of the natural (ethnic) olive tree of Israel (to whom and through whom the promises of salvation were originally given; Rom 11:16-24).

Paul concludes this section of the letter in Romans 11:25-36 with a final word of hope regarding Jewish salvation and a word of praise regarding the mysterious way in which God saves both Jews and Gentiles through Christ. He links Romans 11:25-36 with the previous section with "for" in Romans 11:25. Here Paul restates the premise he articulated earlier in Romans 9 regarding God's commitment to fulfill the promises to save the Jewish people by the Jewish Messiah (see Rom 9–11). Paul informs the Christians in Rome that he does not want them to be ignorant about "this mystery" (Rom 11:25). In Paul, the term *mystery* often refers to something previously hidden but now revealed in Christ through Paul's ministry (see 1 Cor 2:1; 15:51; Eph 1:9; 3:3; 5:32; 6:19; Col 1:6; 4:3).

The mystery relates to the way by which God will in fact fulfill his saving promises to elect Jews and save elect Gentiles. Paul says this hardening of some Jews within Israel is not eternal but temporal. It will last "until the fullness of the Gentiles should enter" (Rom 11:25). "The fullness of the Gentiles" refers to the time in history when God's designated number of Gentiles come to faith in Christ and participate in God's promises of salvation. These promises were originally given to Israel and promised to extend to the ends of the earth through Israel (see Is 40–66). This interpretation is likely because Romans 9–11 is about the salvation of Jews and Gentiles, and because

Paul has just recently referred to the "salvation of the Gentiles" (Rom 11:11) in the context of God's election of grace to choose a remnant of some Gentiles (Rom 9:23-26) within Israel to believe in Christ and be saved (Rom 11:5). Paul hopes the salvation of ethnic Jews will happen through his ministry to the Gentiles as their salvation provokes Israel to jealousy (Rom 11:13-14).

In Romans 11:26, Paul says, "and so," or "in this manner," or "like this," "all Israel will be saved." This verse has multiple exegetical and theological difficulties. At least five important questions emerge from this verse: (1) How will all Israel be saved? (2) Who are the "all"? (3) Who is Israel? (4) When will "all Israel" be saved? (5) Does Paul refer to a "temporary hardening" of all within Israel or to a "partial hardening" to some within Israel? Scholars have spent much time seeking to explain this verse. Given the need for brevity, I simply attempt to answer each of the following questions with a sentence about Paul's basic point: God has not forsaken his promises of salvation to Israel because a large number of Jews (i.e., "all Israel") will be saved as a result of being provoked to jealousy, both through Paul's ministry to the Gentiles and through the salvation of the Gentiles.

This salvation occurs within history through Paul's apostolic ministry, and it will culminate at the end of history. When God pours out wrath in the future day against Jewish and Gentile unbelief, a large number of ethnic Jews (i.e., "all Israel") will be saved because they are being saved throughout history.[43] "All Israel" here does not refer to elect Jews and Gentiles who make up the church as the people of God, since Romans 9–11 as a whole has primarily focused on one question: Has God forsaken his promises to ethnic Israel? Instead, Paul seems to refer only to elect Jews who come to faith in Christ, who are being saved within history, and who will therefore be saved from God's wrath, along with believing Gentiles, at the end of history.[44] This interpretation seems accurate since Romans 11:26 occurs in the context of Israel's salvation in Romans 9–11, where Paul has gone to great pains to explain the reason many Jews reject Christ and the reason some Gentiles confess and believe that Jesus is Lord (see Rom 9:30–10:13). Furthermore, that Paul refers to the salvation of some elect Jews within Israel is supported by Paul's remarks about an elect group of faithful Jews and a remnant of faithful Jews who have obtained salvation earlier in Romans 9–11 (see Rom 9:11; 11:5, 7).

In Romans 11:26, Paul grounds his remarks about the certainty of the salvation of some Jews in the Scriptures. In the Hebrew text, Isaiah promises a redeemer will come "to Zion" (Is 59:20). The Greek version of Isaiah says a deliverer will come "on account of/for the sake of Zion." However, Paul says "a deliverer will come from Zion" (Rom 11:26). There is perhaps more than one reason why Paul's citation differs from the Hebrew and Greek versions of Isaiah 59:20. Yet, in context, Paul may simply emphasize the deliverer is a "Jewish" deliverer—hence Paul's words that the deliverer will come "from Zion." Paul reminds believers in Rome that God's saving promises to Israel remain fixed and certain because they connect to the Jewish messianic deliverer who comes from Zion. This argument supports his previous assertions that God will also save some within Zion (see Rom 11:5, 7). When the Jewish messianic deliverer comes, he will fulfill God's

[43]For a similar view and a discussion of additional interpretive options, see Benjamin L. Merkel, "Romans 11 and the Future of Ethnic Israel," *Journal of the Evangelical Theological Society* 43, no. 4 (2000): 709-21.

[44]See also Merkel, "Romans 11 and the Future."

covenant by saving some within Zion when he turns "ungodliness from Jacob/Israel" and when he forgives "their sins" (Rom 11:26-27). This reading is reasonable since Paul again discusses the election of some Jews (Rom 11:28).

The Greek in Romans 11:28 poses significant challenges in understanding. It roughly translates into English as "on the one hand, enemies because of you in accordance with my gospel; on the other hand, beloved ones in accordance with election because of the fathers." These two statements lack a Greek verb, which makes interpretation difficult. However, in context, Paul appears to communicate the following: in accordance with his gospel, which is the power of God unto salvation for both believing Jews and Gentiles (Rom 1:16), by which God will judge "the secret things of humans through Christ" (Rom 2:16), Jews who reject Christ are God's enemies and headed toward judgment. However, because God made promises to the fathers to save a remnant according to the election of grace (i.e., a reference at least to the promises to Abraham, Isaac, and Jacob: see Rom 9:6-13; 11:5, 7; and to David regarding the Messiah: Rom 1:2-3; 9:5; see also 2 Sam 7:12-14), elect Jews are now considered "beloved ones" through Christ (i.e., recipients of God's saving promises).

Evidence for this reading occurs further when Paul asserts that God's gifts and calling of his people are "irrevocable" (Rom 11:29). Just as the Gentiles were once disobedient to God and God showed them mercy because of Israel's unbelief (Rom 11:30), in a similar way many Jews are disobedient to the gospel and God will show them mercy because of the Gentiles' obedience (Rom 11:31-32). Paul concludes this specific argument by stating, "God shut up all people for disobedience so that he would show mercy to all" (Rom 11:32). Given the overt Jewish and Gentile context of the letter and the discussion of Jewish and Gentile salvation in Romans 9–11, Paul likely asserts here that God has chosen to shut up under sin's condemnation all ethnic groups without ethnic restriction (see Rom 3:9, 20; see also the argument of Rom 1–3), so that he can display his saving mercy to all ethnic groups without restriction by faith in Jesus Christ (see Rom 1:16; 3:21–4:25; 9:1–10:21). Contextual restrictions require the reader to interpret Paul's use of the term *all* in a selective ethnic sense in Romans 11:32 since he has already established that only the elect/remnant of Jews and Gentiles will be saved as vessels of mercy (Rom 9:19-29; 11:5, 7). Paul has also already made it explicitly clear that only those with faith in Christ are justified before God and therefore saved (Rom 3:21–4:25; 5:6-10). Paul concludes this section by praising God for his saving purposes as he expresses that God's ways are incomprehensible and that to him alone belong glory and honor (Rom 11:33-36).

THEOLOGICAL THEME: GOD'S FAITHFULNESS TO HIS JEWISH AND GENTILE MULTIETHNIC PEOPLE (ROMANS 9:1–11:36)

The people of God have a long history of suffering. From the very beginnings of Israel's ethnic identity as a people in the Old Testament, God's people suffered, and their God either delivered them from or walked with them in their suffering (see Ex 1–15). In fact, in both the Old Testament and the New Testament, suffering is one of the many marks of the people of God. Often throughout history, the suffering of God's people has been connected to their ethnic identity. In the modern world, for example, there are Christians who suffer because they are Christians, and there are Christians who suffer because they are Christians identified within a particular ethnic, racial, geographic, or tribal group. In certain contexts, Christians suffer for their faith in Christ regardless of their ethnic identity. In other contexts, Christians suffer because of their faith and their ethnic identity since their Christian faith is viewed as inseparable from their ethnic identity.

Those of us living out our faith in a diverse multiethnic community can certainly expect suffering to come to us because of our faith in Jesus Christ and because of a commitment to a gospel-centered and Spirit-empowered multiethnic vision. However, we will also experience much pain because of the intentional and unintentional wounds that we cause one another in a multiethnic context. Those from one ethnic group in the same body of Christ might not be able to relate to, understand, empathize with, or sympathize with the unique experiences of others. Also, mixed people of color with multiethnic families in multiethnic contexts in which they are the minority culture often simply feel like they do not belong because they do not fit nicely and neatly into one specific ethnic or cultural context.

While those in those contexts try so hard in the power of the Spirit to pursue a God-centered, Christ-exalting, and Spirit-empowered multiethnic vision in our communities, we and our ethnically diverse brothers and sisters continue to fall short of living in light of the vision for unity to the degree that Jesus prayed and for which he died. Consequently, those of us in multiethnic communities who experience much multiethnic joy and multiethnic pain in our fellowships might be tempted to think that God has forsaken his promises to save and unify a multiethnic people of Jews and Gentiles by faith in Christ because of the difficulty of pursuing a multiethnic vision of the gospel, even in churches where there is a clear vision.

Romans 9–11 reminds us that God has not and will not forsake his soteriological promises to his multiethnic people. These promises include saving a multiethnic Jewish and Gentile people for a multiethnic purpose, even as this people suffers as the multiethnic people of God in a world hostile to God's gospel and hostile to a multiethnic gospel vision. God's promises to save a multiethnic people match and overcome sin's power by the power of the Spirit because the gospel of Jesus Christ is truly the power of God, resulting in salvation to Jews and Gentiles who believe. This power will be manifested throughout a multiethnic world as the gospel continues to go forward, regardless of whether individual churches remain resistant to this vision or cannot see this vision worked out in their church contexts due to monoethnicity.

OBEY THE GOSPEL! PAUL'S GOSPEL HORIZONTALLY APPLIED TO MULTIETHNIC RELATIONSHIPS (ROMANS 12:1–15:33)

Romans 12–15 infers from Paul's argument in Romans 1–11, evident from the word *therefore* in Romans 12:1. Paul's basic message to the Romans in these chapters is to obey the gospel and live in multiethnic love for one another as the people of God. Interpreters might be tempted to read Romans 1–11 as doctrine/theology and Romans 12–15 as ethics. I reject such an artificial division. Paul's ethical exhortations in Romans 12–15 are very much theological exhortations and should be connected to his argument in Romans 1–11, since Paul grounds his ethical exhortations in God's saving action for Jews and Gentiles in Christ and since he instructs Jewish and Gentile Christians how to live as the people of God, whom God has redeemed in Christ.[45]

[45]For my recent work on the relationship between Paul's soteriology and ethics in Galatians, see Jarvis J. Williams, *The Spirit, Ethics, and Eternal Life: Paul's Vision for the Christian Life in Galatians* (Downers Grove, IL: InterVarsity Press, 2023).

Paul begins this section with an exhortation to these Christians in Rome to present themselves to God as "living sacrifices" (Rom 12:1). He says obedience is the right thing for them to do since they have participated in God's saving mercies in Christ. Paul restates the command from Romans 12:1 in Romans 12:2 by exhorting them not to be "conformed to the world" but to be "transformed" by their mind's renewal. If they heed Paul's command, the result will be that they will "test so as to prove" God's "good and perfect will" (Rom 12:2). He continues in Romans 12:3–15:13 to explain specific ways in which they should present themselves as living sacrifices to God.

Some from Western Christian traditions might be tempted to read Paul's remarks in only individual terms. However, it is important to realize Paul does not envision the Christian life to be lived in isolation from Christian communities in the house churches in Rome. Certainly, everything Paul states in these verses applies to individuals, because there cannot be any Christian communities apart from *individuals* who make up Christian communities. My point, however, is Paul expects these commands to be obeyed among the people of God in the various Christian communities/churches and in the various social contexts in which these house churches exist in Rome.

Paul exhorts the Christians in Rome not to be arrogant or to consider themselves to be more important than others (Rom 12:3). Rather, he exhorts them to use their gifts to serve one another in ways that are consistent with the gifts God has given to each person to build up the body of Christ with diverse gifts (Rom 12:3-8). Paul commands the Christians in Rome to love one another (Rom 12:9-13), to bless those who persecute them (Rom 12:14), to rejoice with those who rejoice (Rom 12:15), and to weep with those who suffer (Rom 12:15). He repeats his command to be humble toward one another from Romans 12:3 in Romans 12:16. He repeats the command to bless those who persecute them from Romans 12:14 in Romans 12:17 when he exhorts them not to repay evil for evil but rather to make every effort to do "good things in the presence of all people." He exhorts them to keep peace with everybody, if it is possible (Rom 12:18). That is, he wants them to love their neighbors as themselves as occasion might allow.

Paul urges the Christians in Rome not to seek their own vengeance against their enemies by their own means in evil ways but to give the place of wrath against their enemies to God, since the Scripture says vengeance is his and that he will repay all of the enemies of the people of God (both inside and outside the church) with divine retribution (Rom 12:19). Instead of going tit-for-tat with their enemies and scheming ways to execute their own justice in unjust ways, Paul says Christians should feed their enemies if they are hungry and give them something to drink if they are thirsty. This will in fact bring an expression of judgment on their heads, as it demonstrates the people of God are entrusting them to God's perfect justice on the day of wrath even as they suffer at the hands of their enemies in this present age (Rom 12:20; see Prov 25:21).

The Christians in Rome should not be conquered by evil but must conquer all forms of evil with good (Rom 12:21). Insofar as it is possible, the Christians in Rome must live righteously under the authority of an unjust government since God generally provides the government to keep civil order (Rom 13:1-7), while there are many corrupt governments that rebel against God's intent for government. The Christians in Rome must love one another because their love fulfills the entire law. Their salvation in Christ requires them to put away every work of darkness and to put on every weapon of the light by walking in obedience to the gospel as the people of God in the Christian communities of faith and in society (Rom 13:8-14). Otherwise, they will be swallowed up in the day of salvation with God's wrath (see Rom 2–3).

In Romans 14:1–15:12, Paul exhorts the weak Christians in Rome to receive and love the strong Christians. He also exhorts the strong Christians in Rome to receive and love the weak Christians. The "weak" and "strong" groups are weak and strong with respect to how they interact with certain foods and certain days (Rom 14:5-6). The nature of the weakness and strength of these two groups in Rome is not clear from the text. The weakness may refer to one's social location, spiritual status, or one group's decision to be unmoved by the other. However, Paul begins Romans 14:1-12 with a reference to one being "weak in the faith," saying that the Christians in Rome should not quarrel over differing opinions related to food or special days. Given Paul's remarks earlier about "works of law" in Romans 3 and the Jewish and Gentile complexities of salvation and election in Romans 9–11, these foods and special days perhaps are references to Torah. Still, it is not entirely impossible that Paul speaks here about certain Roman festal days and Roman cultic days. Paul wants the Christians in Rome to love one another and to receive one another, instead of forcing one another to violate one's own conscience regarding these meals and days, because both the weak and the strong will stand before the judgment seat of Christ (Rom 14:10). He reminds the Christians in Rome that Jesus became a servant for the Jew for the truth of the gospel "so that he would confirm the promises of the fathers and so that the Gentiles would glorify God on behalf of mercy," in accordance with the promises of Scripture (Rom 15:8-9; see Deut 32:43; 2 Sam 22:50; Ps 117:1; Is 11:10).

Paul concludes this section in Romans 15:14-29 by reminding the Gentile Christians in Rome that he has served them in a priestly manner as an apostle to the Gentiles and that he presents the Gentiles as acceptable sacrifices to God in Christ. Having explained to them his gospel in the previous chapters, Paul expresses interest to visit them so that they will financially help him take the gospel to Spain (Rom 15:22-24, 28). Finally, Paul asks the Christians in Rome to pray that God will deliver him from those who disobey the gospel in Judea and to pray that his ministry will be accepted by the saints there when he visits the poor in Judea (Rom 15:30-32; see also Rom 15:25-27).

THEOLOGICAL THEME: LOVE ONE ANOTHER! (ROMANS 12:1–15:33)

Throughout Romans 12:1–15:12, Paul uses beautiful familial language when he discusses how the people of God should conduct themselves in the house churches in Rome and in the larger society as the people of God. The Jewish and Gentile Christians in Rome had in common the gospel of Jesus Christ, which focused on Jesus' death and resurrection, the power of God unto salvation for Jews and Gentiles who believe. Paul suggests that one piece of evidence that the Christians in Rome are in fact Christians is their love for one another in their multiethnic and social diversity.

For the apostle Paul, love is no optional attribute or virtue. God's love in offering Jesus to die for Jewish and Gentile sinners and Jesus' love by voluntarily giving up his life in death for sinners is the model for how Jewish and Gentile Christians in Rome should love one another (Rom 5:6-10). Without love, the Christians in Rome and all Christians will live isolated, selfish, and fragmented lives in opposition to the pursuit of the multiethnic redemptive vision for which Jesus died and to which Paul's gospel calls us. As an African American Christian New Testament scholar with a multiethnic heritage, a multiethnic family, in a multiethnic church, I am constantly in contexts where I am an ethnic minority within majority-cultural Christian and non-Christian contexts, as I seek to live in pursuit of a multiethnic vision of the gospel. My reality can be (and is!) exhausting! I am reminded on a regular basis that actualizing a redemptive multiethnic vision of the gospel comes with great costs and is utterly impossible without a sacrificial love for others rooted in Jesus' death and resurrection and the life-giving power of the Spirit.

Spirit-empowered love moves ethnically diverse Christians to live sacrificially for one another, to consider each other to be more valuable than ourselves, and to consider the best motives of one another unless we give reason to question otherwise, but this kind of love is neither easy nor automatic. Rather, it is hard and exhausting work! Spirit-empowered love is the kind of love that will enable churches and the people of God to move from a naive pursuit of colorblindness, from cultural-warrior efforts to shut down conversations of goodwill about race and ethnic division, from vague and superficial chatter about unity, from generic talk about racial reconciliation, from accepting destructive ideological propaganda in the disguise of so-called antiracism, and from simply being content with diversity (whatever that means!).

Of course, Christians should not judge people "based on the color of their skin but on the content of their character." Who in their right Christian mind would deny this? However, what people often mean today by *colorblind* is not that we should refrain from making racist judgments of people because of the color of their skin. Rather, they mean that we do not or should not see skin color when we see people, that we should ignore ethnic difference, or that ethnic difference or racialization does not play a role in how we perceive others, or that the color of one's skin plays no role in how one experiences the world or how the world experiences that person. Sadly, there are numerous examples that demonstrate that real or imagined ethnic differences and differences based on skin color in fact do affect how humans experience the world and how the world experiences them.[46] I love Hallmark movies, but life is not one.

Those who quote Dr. Martin Luther King Jr.'s statement to support the idea of colorblindness outlined above seem to forget that when he spoke his words about judging people by their character instead of the color of their skin, he immediately pointed out that he dreamed for the day when his Black kids would hold hands with White kids. In other words, he immediately pointed out color and ethnic difference after he spoke against race-based and racist evaluations of people because of the color of their skin. Whatever Dr. King meant by the statement that we should judge people based on their character instead of their skin color, he could not have meant that we should

[46]For examples from ancient primary texts, see Denise Kimber Buell, *Why This New Race: Ethnic Reasoning in Early Christianity* (New York: Columbia University Press, 2004); Gay L. Byron, *Symbolic Blackness and Ethnic Difference in Early Christian Literature* (New York: Routledge, 2002); Benjamin Isaac, *The Invention of Racism in Classical Antiquity* (Princeton, NJ: Princeton University Press, 2004); Rebecca F. Kennedy, C. Snydor Roy, and Max L. Goldman, eds., *Race and Ethnicity in the Classical World: An Anthology of Primary Sources in Translation* (Indianapolis: Hackett, 2013). For an argument against color prejudice against Blacks in antiquity from primary texts, see Frank M. Snowden Jr., *Blacks in Antiquity: Ethiopians in the Greco-Romans Experience* (Cambridge, MA: Belknap, 1971); Snowden, *Before Color Prejudice: The Ancient View of Blacks* (Cambridge, MA: Harvard University Press, 1991). For examples of this in the US, see Colin Kidd, *The Forging of Races: Race*

not see the color of one's skin or that we should deny or ignore ethnic difference. He pushed against an entire White-supremacist system of racism that made value judgments about people because of the color of their skin. Dr. King pleaded with our country to stop perpetuating White supremacy and racism. He was not pleading with our country to pretend that we do not see skin color or to stop seeing skin color. He instead pleaded with this country to stop seeing dark skin with contempt and to stop privileging White skin.

Furthermore, Paul specifically talks about Jews and Gentiles and often points out ethnic difference for the purpose of emphasizing unity in Christ in the midst of ethnic difference (Rom 1–15; see Gal 2:11-14; Eph 2–3). Revelation talks about Christ redeeming some from every tongue, tribe, people, and nation (Rev 5:9). Paul's gospel neither ignores nor is blind to ethnic distinctions, but he emphasizes that Jesus (a Jewish Messiah) is the God of both Jews and Gentiles so that they should live in reconciled and transformed community with one another in their ethnic differences.

Spirit-empowered love modeled after Jesus' sacrificial love for his people will move Christians to pursue relentlessly a God-centered and Spirit-empowered vision of multiethnic community whenever and wherever it is possible. This kind of love is a reflection of the saving power of the gospel. Perhaps the reason so few of us see this kind of robust multiethnic love in our churches is that pursuing this vision is hard and that maybe why so few of our churches and denominations believe or obey the very gospel we claim to preach and defend.

COMMENDATIONS, A WARNING, AND A BENEDICTION (ROMANS 16:1-27)

In Romans 16, Paul commends many partners in ministry. Many of them are female servants of the Lord. Paul commends Phoebe as a faithful "servant" of the church in Cenchreae (Rom 16:1). He urges the saints in Rome to welcome her in a manner "worthy of the saints" and to help her in "whatever she needs" (Rom 16:2). Paul identifies Phoebe as a "helper of many" and of Paul (Rom 16:2). Paul identifies both Aquila (husband) and Priscilla (wife) as his "fellow workers in Christ Jesus" (Rom 16:3), who "risked their lives for his life and whom all the churches of the Gentiles" thank (Rom 16:4). Paul commands the saints in Rome to greet many women: Mary, who worked hard for them (Rom 16:6); Junia (Rom 16:7), who, with Andronicus, was a "fellow prisoner and worker" with Paul; Tryphaena and Tryphosa, who "labored in the Lord" (Rom 16:12); Persis, the beloved (Rom 16:12), who "worked hard for the Lord"; Rufus's mother and Paul's (Rom 16:13); and the sister of Nereus (Rom 16:15).

In Romans 16:17-19, Paul urges the Romans to take note of those in the midst of their Christian communities who cause divisions contrary to the teaching they received and to avoid them. He declares these troublemakers are not serving the Lord Jesus but their own selfish appetites (Rom 16:18). Because the Romans' faithful obedience has reached all (Rom 16:19; see Rom 1:8-15), Paul urges the Christians in Rome to be "wise with respect to the good and innocent with respect to evil" (Rom 16:19). In Romans 16:20, Paul reminds the Christians in Rome that the "God of peace will crush Satan" under their feet "quickly" (Rom 16:20). He concludes Romans 16:21-23 sending greetings from Timothy, his fellow

---

and Scripture in the Protestant Atlantic World, 1600–2000 (Cambridge: Cambridge University Press, 2009); Goetz, *Baptism of Early Virginia*; Mathews, *At the Altar of Lynching*; Rothstein, *Color of Law*.

worker in the gospel; from Lucius, Jason, and Sosipater, his compatriots in the gospel; from Tertius, his amanuensis (secretary) to whom he dictated the letter; from Gaius, Paul's host and the host of the entire church; from Erastus, the steward of the city; and from Quartus the brother. Romans 16:25-27 is bracketed in the Greek New Testament to mark the absence of some of these verses in some ancient manuscripts. These verses are a prayer in which Paul offers a final farewell by wishing God's blessings on the Romans and a praise to God.

THEOLOGICAL THEME: HONOR OUR SISTERS IN OUR CHURCHES (ROMANS 16:1-27)

In some theological traditions women have no public voice in the church, although they essentially do much of the work. In other theological traditions, women have more opportunities to use their gifts than in others. Celebrating and honoring faithful sisters in Christ in the church is essential to having a healthy church that flourishes. Especially in multiethnic contexts where diverse brothers and sisters are seeking to live in the light of God's redemptive work in Christ to reconcile diverse sinners to God and to one another, churches must pursue ways in which they can empower an ethnic diversity of faithful sisters in Christ to use their gifts to build up the body.

SELECTED BIBLIOGRAPHY

Bailey, Richard A. *Race and Redemption in Puritan New England*. Oxford: Oxford University Press, 2011.

Barclay, John. *Paul and the Gift*. Grand Rapids, MI: Eerdmans, 2015.

Bauckham, Richard. *Jesus and the God of Israel* (Grand Rapids, MI: Eerdmans, 2008).

Bowens, Lisa. *African American Readings of Paul: Reception, Resistance and Transformation*. Grand Rapids, MI: Eerdmans, 2020.

Buell, Denise Kimber. *Why This New Race: Ethnic Reasoning in Early Christianity*. New York: Columbia University Press, 2004.

Byrne, Brendan. *Paul and the Economy of Salvation: Reading from the Perspective of the Last Judgment* (Grand Rapids, MI: Baker Academic, 2021).

Byron, Gay L. *Symbolic Blackness and Ethnic Difference in Early Christian Literature*. New York: Routledge, 2002.

Campbell, Douglas. *The Deliverance of God*. Grand Rapids, MI: Eerdmans, 2009.

Carraway, George. *Christ Is God over All: Romans 9:5 in the Context of Romans 9–11*. New York: Bloomsbury T&T Clark, 2013.

Chester, Stephen J. *Reading Paul with the Reformers: Reconciling Old and New Perspectives*. Grand Rapids, MI: Eerdmans, 2017.

Das, Andrew A. *Solving the Romans Debate*. Minneapolis: Fortress, 2007.

deSilva, David A. *Honor, Patronage, Kinship, and Purity: Unlocking the New Testament Culture*. Downers Grove, IL: InterVarsity Press, 2000.

Dupont, Carolyn Renée. *Mississippi Praying: Southern White Evangelicals and the Civil Rights Movement, 1945–1975*. New York: New York University Press, 2013.

Elliott, Neil, and Mark Reasoner, eds. *Documents and Images for the Study of Paul*. Minneapolis: Fortress, 2011.

Gathercole, Simon J. *Where Is Boasting? Early Jewish Soteriology and Paul's Response in Romans 1–5*. Grand Rapids, MI: Eerdmans, 2002.

Goetz, Rebecca Anne. *The Baptism of Early Virginia: How Christianity Created Race*. Baltimore: Johns Hopkins University Press, 2012.

Hagen Pifer, Jeanette. *Faith as Participation: An Exegetical Study of Some Key Pauline Texts*. WUNT 486. Tübingen: Mohr Siebeck, 2019.

Irons, Charles Lee. *The Righteousness of God: A Lexical Examination of the Covenant-Faithfulness. Interpretation*, WUNT 386. Tübingen: Mohr Siebeck, 2015.

Isaac, Benjamin. *The Invention of Racism in Classical Antiquity*. Princeton, NJ: Princeton University Press, 2004.

Joshel, Sandra R. *Slavery in the Roman World*. Cambridge: Cambridge University Press, 2010.

Keener, Craig S. *Romans*. NCC. Eugene, OR: Cascade, 2009.

———. "Romans." In *NIV Cultural Backgrounds Study Bible*, 1945-79. Grand Rapids, MI: Zondervan, 2016.

Kennedy, Rebecca F., C. Snydor Roy, and Max L. Goldman, eds., *Race and Ethnicity in the Classical World: An Anthology of Primary Sources in Translation*. Indianapolis: Hackett, 2013.

Kidd, Colin. *The Forging of the Races*. Cambridge: Cambridge University Press, 2006.

Mathews, Donald G. *At the Altar of Lynching: Burning Sam Hose in the American South*. Cambridge: Cambridge University Press, 2017.

Mathews, Mary Beth Swetnam. *Doctrine and Race: African American Evangelicals and Fundamentalism Between the Wars*. Tuscaloosa: University of Alabama Press, 2017.

McCaulley, Esau. *Reading While Black: African American Biblical Interpretation as an Exercise in Hope*. Downers Grove, IL: InterVarsity Press, 2020.

McFadden, Kevin M. *Faith in the Son of God: The Place of Christ-Oriented Faith Within Pauline Theology* (Wheaton, IL: Crossway, 2021).

Merkel, Benjamin L. "Romans 11 and the Future of Ethnic Israel." *Journal of the Evangelical Theological Society* 43, no. 4 (2000): 709-21.

Moo, Douglas. *Romans*. NICNT. Grand Rapids, MI: Eerdmans, 1996.

Morgan, Teresa. *Roman Faith and Christian Faith: Pistis and* Fideis *in the Early Roman Empire and Early Churches*. Oxford: Oxford University Press, 2015.

Pate, Marvin. *Reverse of the Curse: Paul, Wisdom, and the Law*. WUNT 114. Tübingen: Mohr Siebeck, 2000.

Richards, E. Randolph. *Paul and First-Century Letter Writing: Secretaries, Composition, and Collection*. Downers Grove, IL: InterVarsity Press, 2004.

Rodríguez, Rafael. *If You Call Yourself a Jew: Reappraising Paul's Letter to the Romans*. Eugene, OR: Cascade, 2014.

Powery, Emerson B., and Rodney S. Sadler Jr. *The Genesis of Liberation: Biblical Interpretation in the Antebellum Narratives of the Enslaved*. Louisville, KY: Westminster John Knox, 2016.

Schreiner, Thomas R. *Faith Alone: The Doctrine of Justification*. Grand Rapids, MI: Zondervan, 2015.

———. *Romans*. 2nd ed. Baker Exegetical Commentary on the New Testament. Grand Rapids, MI: Baker Academic, 2019.

Snowden Jr., Frank M. *Blacks in Antiquity: Ethiopians in the Greco-Romans Experience*. Cambridge, MA: Belknap, 1971.

———. *Before Color Prejudice: The Ancient View of Blacks*. Cambridge, MA: Harvard University Press, 1991.

Travis, Stephen H. *Christ and the Judgment of God*. 2nd ed. Grand Rapids, MI: Baker, 2009.

Watson, Duane F. "Paul and Boasting." In *Paul and the Greco-Roman World*, 90-112. 2nd ed. New York: Bloomsbury T&T Clark, 2016.

Westerholm, Stephen. *Perspectives Old and New on Paul: The "Lutheran" Paul and His Critics*. Grand Rapids, MI: Eerdmans, 2004.

Wiedemann, Thomas. *Greek & Roman Slavery*. New York: Routledge, 1980.

Williams, Jarvis J. *Redemptive Kingdom Diversity: A Biblical Theology of the People of God*. Grand Rapids, MI: Baker Academic, 2021.

———. *The Spirit, Ethics, and Eternal Life: Paul's Vision for Christian Life in Galatians*. Downers Grove, IL: Intervarsity Press, 2023.

Witherington, Ben, III, and Darlene Hyatt. *Romans*. Grand Rapids, MI: Eerdmans, 2004.

Wright, N. T. *Paul and His Recent Interpreters*. Minneapolis: Fortress, 2015.

FIRST LETTER TO THE CORINTHIANS

Gene L. Green

INTRODUCTION

The Corinthian church was a community divided. The apostle Paul founded the church during his so-called second missionary journey, around 51 CE (Acts 18:1-18). Some short years later, in 54 CE, he wrote the letter-essay known as 1 Corinthians to the congregation. Despite the eighteen months he spent in Corinth (Acts 18:11) and the years between the founding of the church and the writing of this letter, Paul declares that the Corinthian Christians are still "mere infants in Christ" (1 Cor 3:1).[1] The cultural norms of the city, not the gospel, orient their conduct and theology. The congregation has rival factions because of their adherence to one leader over another, they elevate rhetoric over the wisdom and power of the cross of Christ, they haul each other into court, they embrace sexual immorality, and they exercise their liberty to the hurt of fellow believers. Economic and social stratification mark their celebration of the Lord's Supper, and some regard themselves as superior in their use of the spiritual gifts. In accordance with current views about death, members of the church deny the future resurrection of believers. This congregation is divided against itself since its members conform "to the pattern of this world" (Rom 12:2) instead of being transformed by the gospel.

The world of the first Christians in Corinth was radically different from ours today. Yet as we read this letter along the grain of their cultural matrix, watching carefully how the apostle Paul brings the gospel to bear on their troubling situation, we begin to understand how to recontextualize his message today as we closely examine the norms that govern our church's life together and in the world. The task is not simply to find parallels between them and us or to seek applications of the message but to hear what the Spirit of God said to them and says to us today through the apostle's words.[2]

THE LAND

The story of any people begins with the land. Geography, history, and culture are inextricably bound together. The city of Corinth was extremely rich since it was situated on the isthmus that joined the mainland of Greece to the north with the peninsula known as Peloponnese to the south. Its situation gave the city strategic control over the movement of people and trade between the north and the south. But it also controlled one of the main east–west trade routes of the Mediterranean Sea. Ships

[1]Unless otherwise indicated, biblical quotations in this commentary follow the NIV.

[2]"No se trata de forzar un 'paralelismo' entre una situación antigua y otra actual, ni de hacer una simple 'aplicación' del texto, sino de descubrir qué fue lo que el Espíritu decía a aquella iglesia en medio de su compleja situación humana, que abarca no solo sus ideas religiosas sino todos los aspectos de su vida: socio-económicos, políticos, culturales. Si acompañamos el trabajo de indagación histórica con una investigación igualmente seria del contexto actual de la iglesia, tendremos los elementos que nos ayudarán a interpretar el mensaje de esta carta para hoy." Irene Foulkes, *Problemas Pastorales en Corinto. Comentario Exegético-Pastoral a 1 Corintios* (San José, Costa Rica: Editorial SEBILA, 2011), 28.

navigating from Italy to Asia Minor encountered contrary winds and high seas when they attempted to sail around the southern tip of the Peloponnese. Strabo, the ancient geographer, quotes the ominous ancient proverb that says, "But when you double Maleae forget your home" (*Geogr.* 8.6.20-23).[3] The city had two harbors, Cenchreae to the east, on the Saronic Gulf, and Lechaion, situated to the north on the Gulf of Corinth. Strabo explains, "The one leads straight to Asia, and the other to Italy; and it makes easy the exchange of merchandise from both countries that are so far distant from each other." Goods and even ships could be hauled across the isthmus on the dry canal known as the *diolkos*, a purpose-built road dating from 600 BCE. Given its location, Strabo remarks, "Corinth is called 'wealthy' because of its commerce."

THE HISTORY OF CORINTH

The classical period. The city of Corinth had two histories. Before the coming of the Romans, Corinth was a member of the twelve-city Achaian League (Polybius, *Histories* 2.41-43). The Achaian cities were devoted to democracy and rejected rule by the Macedonians and their king Antigonus II Gonatas, who had captured the city in 244 BCE. Polybius comments, "The Achaeans always followed one single policy, ever attracting others by the offer of their own equality and liberty and ever making war on and crushing those who either themselves or through the kings attempted to enslave their native cities." The devotion to liberty ran deep in Corinth, so the Roman "liberation" of Achaia from Macedonian rule was celebrated with tremendous enthusiasm. Rome was expanding to the east during this period and styled itself as the great liberator of the Greeks. In 196 BCE the Roman general Titus Quintius Flamininus announced freedom for the Greeks at the games held in Isthmia just outside Corinth. The herald announced that the Roman Senate and Flamininus had "restored . . . freedom, without garrisons and without imposts, and to the enjoyment of their ancient laws, [to] the Corinthians" and other cities of Achaia. Plutarch describes the scene: "At first, then, the proclamation was by no means generally or distinctly heard . . . but when silence had been restored, and the herald in tones that were louder than before and reached the ears of all, had recited the proclamation, a shout of joy arose, so incredibly loud that it reached the sea" (*Titus Flamininus* 10.4-5). But the Roman liberation of Achaia from the Macedonians meant that now the Achaian cities would pay taxes to Rome. "Freedom" came with a price tag.

The Romans continued their eastern campaign by conquering and subsequently plundering Macedonia in 168 BCE. After Lucius Mummius quelled a Macedonian resistance movement against Rome in 149 BCE, the Roman Senate sent him south to wage the Achaian War (146–145 BCE) due to unrest in the Peloponnese. The Romans unleashed such force against the Achaians that Pausanias said, "It was at this time that Greece was struck with universal and utter prostration" (*Description of Greece* 7.17.1). Mummius brought in thirty-five hundred calvary and twenty-three thousand foot soldiers to Achaia. He wasted the city of Corinth and set it on fire, killed men by the sword, took women and children captive, and plundered the city's riches to assure that it would not rise again (7.16). Antipater of

[3]This and all following citations from Greek and Latin literature are from the *Loeb Classical Library* (Cambridge, MA: Harvard University Press), unless otherwise indicated. Maleae was located on the southern tip of the Peloponnese. To "double Malaea" (*kampsas*) means to "sail around Malaea." The lexeme was commonly used to refer to sailing past a certain point of land (as in Herodotus, *Histories* 4.42.4, "They rounded the pillars of Hercules and came to Egypt").

Thessalonica captures the agony and pathos of the Corinthian tragedy in an epigram:

> I, Rhodope, and my mother Boisca neither died of sickness, nor fell by the sword of the foes, but ourselves, when dreadful Ares burnt the city of Corinth our country, chose a brave death. My mother slew me with the slaughtering knife, nor did she, unhappy woman, spare her own life, but tied the noose round her neck; for it was better than slavery to die in freedom.[4]

Achaian independence was over. Corinth lay empty for one hundred years, with only a few Greeks remaining among the ruins.

Roman Corinth: The land and the people. Not long before his death in 44 BCE, Julius Caesar decided to reestablish the city of Corinth, now as a Roman colony.[5] Rome founded colonies throughout the empire in order to secure its hold on the conquered territories that were brought under its control. These colonies were "mini-Romes," with Latin being the dominant language, government according to the Roman order, and often freedom from taxation thrown in for good measure. Luke identifies some Jews from the city—Aquila, Priscilla (Prisca), and Sosthenes—using their Latin names (Acts 18:2, 8, 17), and it was not uncommon for Greek families in the city to adopt Latin names as well. Corinthian coins from the period bear Latin letters, and most of the inscriptions found in the city are in Latin, save for those related to the panhellenic Isthmian games. The architecture during the Roman period was Italian style, and the emperor's images were decked out in Roman dress. Members of the Corinthian church also included Latins such as Titius Justus, Gaius, Erastus, and Quartus, Fortunatus, and Achaicus (Acts 18:7; 19:22; Rom 16:23; 1 Cor 16:17).[6] If Erastus is indeed the same person identified in the famous inscription bearing his name, he was a civic benefactor and member of the city's ruling class.[7]

Corinth was a Roman colony on Greek soil, an occupied land, and the Latins held the greatest riches and power.[8] However, through the years more Greeks came to Corinth, likely in search of the economic benefits the city offered. But Latin influence, wealth, and power dominated. The Jewish population was on the rise as well (Acts 18:1-4, 12-17); Philo is the first to reference the presence of Diaspora Jews in the city (*On the Embassy to Gaius* 281).[9] Given the advantages of its location, the city rapidly grew to approximately eighty thousand people, with another twenty thousand in the surrounding countryside.[10] Corinth was a diverse city where one group held power.

Julius Caesar sent the poorest of Roman society to colonize Corinth, the *liberti* (former slaves) and the lower-class *plebs*, along with

---

[4]W. R. Patton, trans., *The Greek Anthology*, LCL (New York: Putnam's Sons, 1919), 2:269.

[5]Strabo, *Geogr.* 8.23: "Now after Corinth had remained deserted for a long time, it was restored again, because of its favourable position, by the deified Caesar, who colonised it with people that belonged for the most part to the freedmen class."

[6]Romans was likely written from Cenchreae, one of the ports of Corinth (Rom 16:1-2), or Corinth itself.

[7]David W. J. Gill, "Erastus the Aedile," *TynBul* 40 (1989): 293-301; Andrew D. Clarke, "Another Corinthian Erastus Inscription," *TynBul* 42 (1991): 146-51. The inscription reads: "[praenome nomen] Erastus for his aedileship laid (the pavement) at his own expense ([praenome nomen] Erastus pro aedilit[at]e s(ua) p(ecunia) stravit)." Gill notes that aediles "were responsible for the maintenance of public streets and buildings, which included the marketplaces, they managed the revenues derived from such places, and they served as judges" (294). See Gill regarding the discussions on the relationship between this title and the *oikonomos* in Rom 16:23.

[8]David W. J. Gill, "In Search of the Social Élite in the Corinthian Church," *TynBul* 44 (1993): 323-37.

[9]Archaeologists have located an inscription naming the city's synagogue, although it dates from the fourth to fifth centuries CE.

[10]Donald Engels, *Roman Corinth. An Alternative Model for the Classical City* (Chicago: University of Chicago Press, 1990), 84.

veterans from the Roman army. These colonists from Rome were given a land grant, and some, such as Gnaeus Babbius Philinus, took advantage of the city's strategic location and became rich in the process.[11] The six-mile-long dry canal, the *diolkos*, was still in operation and allowed goods and even small ships to portage between the Gulf of Corinth and the Saronic Gulf. The city adopted a service economy, and its wealth helped revive the Achaian economy that had been severely depressed.

However, the majority of those in the city remained poor, so much so that Crinagoras writes, "What inhabitants, O luckless city, have you received, and in place of whom? Alas for the great calamity to Greece! Could, Corinth, that you be lower than the ground and more desert than the Libyan sands, rather than wholly abandoned to such a crowd of scoundrelly slaves, you should vex the bones of the ancient Bacchiadae."[12] The noble free city of old had a new and entirely different social cut. The church in Corinth reflected the social matrix of the city. Paul comments, "Not many of you were wise by human standards; not many were influential; not many were of noble birth" (1 Cor 1:26). When the church celebrated the Lord's Supper, "one person remains hungry" while others ate their own private supper and got drunk, "humiliating those who have nothing" (1 Cor 11:21-22). In the second century, the orator Alciphron remarked on the economic disparity of the city, saying, "I learned in a short time the sordidness of the rich there and the misery of the poor" (*Epistle* 3.24), with young men and women being among the poor who could not sustain themselves well.[13] The city was also home to countless slaves who had no means to chronicle their own stories. They appear as members of the Corinthian church (1 Cor 7:21) since the gospel provides a place for all. The city, though rich, experienced famine, possibly around the time of the church's founding.[14]

Corinth became the administrative center of the Roman province of Achaia and the home of the Roman proconsul. City government was according to Roman style, with two *duoviri* who had jurisdiction over civil cases, while the proconsul held both administrative and judicial powers over criminal cases. The city had a senate, the *decuria*, and an administrator of the games held in Isthmia, the *agōnothetēs*. Acts tells the story of one of the proconsuls, L. Iunius Gallio, before whom Paul was accused at the *bēma* in the city's forum (Acts 18:12-17). His brother, the philosopher Seneca, remarked that Gallio did not finish his one-year term because he "began to develop a

[11]Jerome Murphy-O'Connor, *St. Paul's Corinth: Texts and Archaeology* (Collegeville, MN: Liturgical Press, 2002) 27. His name suggests he was previously a slave. He was elevated to the highest ranks in the city. The inscription on the Babbius monument reads: "Ganaeus Babbius Philinus, aedile and pontifex, had this monument erected at his own expense, and he approved it in his official capacity as duovir."

[12]Patton, *Greek Anthology* 9.284. Murphy-O'Connor writes, "The rigorously exclusive Bacchiadae ruled Corinth from ca. 750 to ca. 657 BC" (*St. Paul's Corinth*, 49).

[13]He said Corinth was "a town charming indeed to look upon and abounding in luxuries, but inhabited by people ungracious and unblessed by Aphrodite." Alciphron paints a picture of the poor in the city: "For example, at midday, after most people had bathed, I saw some pleasant-spoken, clever young fellows moving about, not near the dwellings but near the Craneium and particularly where the women who peddle bread and retail fruit are accustomed to do their business. There the young fellows would stoop to the ground, and one would pick up lupine pods, another would examine the nutshells to make sure that none of the edible part was left anywhere and had escaped notice, another would scrape with his fingernails the pomegranate rinds . . . to see whether he could glean any of the seeds anywhere, while others would actually gather and greedily devour the pieces that fell from the loaves of bread—pieces that had by that time been trodden under many feet."

[14]Commenting on Claudius's reign, Tacitus, *Annals* 12.43, says, "Scanty crops too, and consequent famine were regarded as a token of calamity." So, too, Suetonius, *Divus Claudius* 18.2, remarks on the "scarcity of grain because of long-continued droughts."

fever in Achaia and took ship at once, insisting that the disease was not of the body but of the place" (*Epistulae morales* 104.2). One of the city's aediles, Erastus, is named in a now-famous inscription. This may well be the same person identified by Paul in Romans 16:23 as the "city's director of public works."

The religious landscape of Corinth was as diverse as its cultural matrix, as Paul's comment in 1 Corinthians 8:5 suggests when he speaks of the "so-called gods, whether in heaven or on earth (as indeed there are many 'gods' and many 'lords')."[15] Among the deities worshiped in the city were Apollo, Demeter and Kore, Hera, Poseidon, Helios, Dionysius, Asclepius, and Aphrodite, who was the city's protector. The imperial cult was also a prominent feature of the city's religious landscape.[16] The celebration of the imperial cult "as an annual event . . . was one important way for a province to demonstrate to the emperor and the Roman Empire its loyalty and support of *Romanitas*. It was an event of enormous significance for the province and its capital, and it brought with it great prestige." It was "enthusiastically embraced in the Roman colony of Corinth."[17] The city celebrated the deified Julius Caesar, the founder of the Roman colony, and the temple of Augustus's sister Octavia was adjacent to the forum. It was elevated on a platform, giving it a prominence over all the other temples within the city. The Corinthians venerated Claudius and other members of the imperial family as well.[18]

Religious observance bound Corinth to the imperial power of Rome. One could not simply avoid the worship of the gods in Corinth since meat that had been sacrificed to them was available in the market (*macellum*; 1 Cor 10:25), invitations to dine in the precincts of temples such as that of Asclepius were not uncommon (1 Cor 8:10), and the worship of the gods, including the imperial cult, was considered a civic duty. The gods gave the community identity and were the city's protectors and benefactors. Maintaining the *pax deorum* ("peace of the gods") was a social obligation. Abandoning the worship of the gods was an antisocial act.

The gospel and the Corinthians. Luke tells the story of the evangelization of Corinth in Acts 18:1-18. Paul had preached in Athens previously, where the reception of the gospel was less than robust (Acts 17:32-33), and he was quite distressed when confronted with the prospect of preaching Christ in Corinth (Acts 18:9-10; 1 Cor 2:3). This was a low point in his ministry, following the abuse he endured in Macedonia as well (Acts 16:1–17:15). Paul carried on, first supporting himself through making tents but then dedicating himself wholly to preaching after receiving support from the Macedonian churches (Acts 18:2-3; 2 Cor 11:7-9). After his eighteen-month stint in Corinth (Acts 18:11), the Alexandrian Jewish Christian Apollos came to the city, where he was well-received (Acts 18:27–19:1). Apollos was trained in the art of rhetoric, which may be the reason he was so popular among the Corinthians (Acts 18:24-25; 1 Cor 1:12; 3:4). In this respect Paul was hardly his match (2 Cor 10:10).

[15]See Daniel N. Showalter and Steven J. Friesen, *Urban Religion in Roman Corinth: Interdisciplinary Approaches* (Cambridge, MA: Harvard University Press, 2005); Nancy Bookidis, "The Sanctuaries of Corinth," *Corinth* 20 (2003): 247-59. Pausanias mentions "a sanctuary to all the gods" (*Description of Greece* 2.2.8), thus leaving no deity without proper civic honor.

[16]See, for example, Bruce W. Winter, *After Paul Left Corinth. The Influence of Secular Ethics and Social Change* (Grand Rapids, MI: Eerdmans, 2001) 269-86; S. R. F. Price, *Rituals and Power: The Imperial Cult and Asia Minor* (Cambridge: Cambridge University Press, 1984); Ittai Gradel, *Emperor Worship and Roman Religion* (Oxford: Clarendon, 2002).

[17]Winter, *After Paul Left Corinth*, 269-70.

[18]Winter, *After Paul Left Corinth*, 272-74.

Sometime after departing from Corinth, Paul sent them a letter now lost to us (1 Cor 5:9-11). While the apostle was in Ephesus during his so-called third missionary journey, news about the church's problems arrived via some from Chloe's household (1 Cor 1:11-12; 16:8, 19; Acts 19). A more official delegation also crossed the Aegean Sea to see Paul, and likely they delivered the letter Paul references that possibly contained numerous queries (1 Cor 7:1; 16:15-18). Paul wrote 1 Corinthians in response. Paul also dispatched Timothy to the city but expected the letter to arrive before Paul's young associate (1 Cor 4:17; 16:10-11).

The city of Corinth presented unique cultural challenges that mitigated against the deep rooting of the gospel in the lives of the new followers of Christ. The city was marked by economic disparity, social divisions, various approaches to practices associated with the temples in the city, and cultural differences between the Latin, Greek, and Jewish communities. It was known as a litigious city (1 Cor 6:1-11) where prostitution was fully accepted (1 Cor 6:12-17). Popular philosophies found their home in the city, and those with developed rhetorical skills were celebrated. From old the city celebrated freedom as the highest value, while power and pride-filled honor were high cultural norms. Paul struggled to orient the lives and theology of the Corinthians around the gospel through his own teaching, letters, and associates sent to them. He persisted with them as a father with his beloved children (1 Cor 4:14-17).

Today's "Corinth." My reading of 1 Corinthians and its history is from the standpoint of an older White male born in the United States. The Corinthian landscape is both radically dissimilar and strikingly, and painfully, similar to my own. My nation and people celebrate freedom, yet we have a deep history of slavery and repression of those who are "others" due to our constructions of race. Mine is the richest nation in the world, yet poverty is the lot of many fellow citizens. We who trace our ancestry back to Europe are colonists in the land of the First Peoples of North America, whom we killed and removed as the Romans did to the inhabitants of the Greek city of Corinth, and we have mapped and reconstructed the land according to our own culture and language. A libertine approach to sexuality is woven into the warp and woof of our contemporary life, as it was in Corinth. Our congregations are marked by divisions that circle around theological or political differences, economic disparity, and ethnic divisions, making it difficult to find a common table, the Lord's table, where we share one bread and one cup. The church's theology is not well informed by the apostolic writings; who today pays any mind to the apostle's insistence on the resurrection of the believers (1 Cor 15) with its glory-filled affirmation of human bodily existence? We are lovers of litigation and power and believe that the best leaders are those who put on the best show. Indeed, church services appear more like stage productions, complete with lights, cameras, and special effects, instead of places where community members share their spiritual gifts (1 Cor 12:7).

The question 1 Corinthians puts to me is how my White privilege, economic independence, and position as "doctor" or professor become subject fully to the gospel of the cross of Christ, where God's true power and wisdom are found (1 Cor 1:20-25). This is a challenging book for any "Latin" like me who enjoys economic, political, and cultural power. First Corinthians thunders, but do I, do we, hear God's voice in its booming cadences?

Paul to the Corinthians. Some scholars understand 1 Corinthians as a series of responses to an eclectic mixture of problems the apostle Paul needed to address. For example, Ben Witherington says there are five issues Paul dealt with: partisanism centered on Christian leaders, continued adherence to cultural norms and values, pride centered on spiritual gifts, sexuality, and varied views on eschatology.[19] Others attempt to find a common thread that runs through the whole. Walter Schmithals sees the Corinthian problem as adherence to Gnostic viewpoints, while Craig Blomberg says that the church suffered from dualistic thought related to a triumphalist overrealized eschatology.[20]

The letter presents as Paul's response to reports he had received about the church (1 Cor 1:11) and answers to the letter that the Corinthians had put to the apostle (1 Cor 7:1). The reports included information about the divided nature of the Corinthian church because of their allegiance to this or that leader (1 Cor 1:10–4:21), immorality in the community such as incest (1 Cor 5:1-13), lawsuits (1 Cor 6:1-11), and prostitution. The letter sent to Paul included queries about marriage (1 Cor 7:1-40), eating meat that had been offered to idols (1 Cor 8:1–11:1), and worship (1 Cor 11:2–14:40), which included notes about gender roles (1 Cor 11:2-16), the Lord's Supper (1 Cor 11:17-34), and spiritual gifts (1 Cor 12:1–14:40).[21] Paul returns to a problem he heard about, that being the denial of the resurrection of the dead (1 Cor 15:1-58), and rounds out the letter with notes about the collection for the Judean church, his travel plans, and Apollos's visit (1 Cor 16:1-12). The letter has to do with social divisions and conflict in the community, and adherence to common societal norms and practices instead of the gospel.[22] The Corinthian situation is most clearly seen through the lens of intersectionality given the interrelationship of its varied problems. In the end, the Corinthians were not living according to the gospel of the cross of Christ.

Paul to the American church. In 2021, an insurrection was attempted in Washington, DC, at the US Capitol as part of the protest against the 2020 Presidential election results. Among the banners waved by those who breached security and went on the attack at the Capitol Building were some that said "Jesus Saves" and "God, Guns & Guts Made America. Let's Keep All Three." The gospel of Christ had been reinterpreted in the support of Christian nationalism and political factionalism that revolved around adherence to a persuasive political leader. A particular vision of America's history and culture

---

[19]Ben Witherington III, *Conflict and Community in Corinth: A Socio-rhetorical Commentary on 1 and 2 Corinthians* (Grand Rapids, MI: Eerdmans, 1995).

[20]Walter Schmithals, *Gnosticism in Corinth. An Investigation of the Letters to the Corinthians* (Nashville: Abingdon, 1971); Craig Blomberg, *1 Corinthians*, NIV Application Commentaries (Grand Rapids, MI: Zondervan, 1995). For a concise review of positions, see Thomas R. Schreiner, *1 Corinthians*, Tyndale New Testament Commentaries (Downers Grove, IL: IVP Academic, 2018), 8-16.

[21]Scholars often note that Paul divides each new topic with the expression *peri de*, "now concerning," indicating perhaps that each topic of the Corinthians' letter to Paul is treated in order (1 Cor 7:1, 25; 8:1; 12:1; 16:1, 12). Mitchell, however, notes that the expression was simply a common way to introduce a new topic known to both the author and reader. See Margaret Mitchell, "Concerning *peri de* in 1 Corinthians," *NovT* 31 (1989): 229-56. While Mitchell is correct about the broader use of *peri de*, we must ask how Paul might have known about the common topics were it not through some communication from or about the Corinthian church. Paul acknowledges that the letter contained various points—"the matters"—to which he responds.

[22]Schreiner, *1 Corinthians*, 14-15; Bruce W. Winter, "The 'Underlays' of Conflict and Compromise in 1 Corinthians," in *Paul and the Corinthians. Studies on a Community in Conflict; Essays in Honour of Margaret Thrall*, ed. T. J. Burke and K. Elliott, NovTSup (Leiden: Brill, 2003), 139-55.

merged with Christian language; the banner of Christ flew among the same crowd where the Confederate flag was unfurled, the symbol of states that fought to preserve slavery. Almost all of the insurrectionists were White; people of color were conspicuously absent. The troubles boiling over in Washington showed the depth to which those who attend Christian churches can be seduced by cultural values that have no roots in the gospel. At present I watch a church deeply divided along political and racial lines. Never has the message of the cross jumped from the pages of 1 Corinthians with such urgency as it does on this confused and agonizing day. It is unclear where the church in the United States is headed, but my hope and prayer is that the bride of Christ will find her way through the teaching of the prophets, Jesus, and the apostles, and follow the one who called her.

OUTLINE OF 1 CORINTHIANS

- I. Letter greeting and thanksgiving (1 Cor 1:1-9)
- II. Responding to the reports about the Corinthians (1 Cor 1:10–6:20)
  - A. Divisions over leaders (1 Cor 1:10–4:21)
  - B. Immoral cultural norms in the community (1 Cor 5:1–6:20)
    1. Incest (1 Cor 5:1-13)
    2. Lawsuits (1 Cor 6:1-11)
    3. Prostitution (1 Cor 6:12-20)
- III. Paul's responses to the Corinthians' concerns and issues (1 Cor 7:1–16:12)
  - A. About marriage (1 Cor 7:1-40)
  - B. About meats sacrificed to idols (1 Cor 8:1-11:1)
  - C. About worship (1 Cor 11:2–14:40)
    1. Gender roles (1 Cor 11:2-16)
    2. The Lord's Supper (1 Cor 11:17-34)
    3. Spiritual gifts (1 Cor 12:1–14:40)
  - D. The resurrection of the dead (1 Cor 15:1-58)
  - E. About the collection, travel plans, and Apollos's return (1 Cor 16:1-18)
- IV. Letter closing (1 Cor 16:19-24)

LETTER GREETING AND THANKSGIVING (1 CORINTHIANS 1:1-9)

The opening of Paul's letter to the Corinthians follows the standard practice of the day of beginning with the name of the author, the name of the recipient, and an initial prayer or thanksgiving. As a person of his day, he adopted and adapted common letter-writing conventions.[23] We should not imagine that Paul simply took pen in hand when he composed the letter but rather that he employed the services of an amanuensis, to whom he dictated the epistle. Paul added a final greeting in his own hand at the end (1 Cor 16:21; see 2 Thess 3:17; Rom 16:22). An amanuensis could have an editorial role, although the final contents of the communication were approved by the author.[24] Paul does not name his amanuensis here. Although the composition is Paul's, he writes along with Sosthenes (1 Cor 1:1). The majority of the first-person verbs are in the singular (over 70 percent), so clearly Paul was the principle person responsible for the contents.

We do not know who carried the letter to the Corinthians, but it may have been borne in the hands of those who had brought news of the church to Paul when he was in Ephesus (1 Cor 16:17; 1:11). The role of the messenger would commonly include offering explanatory

[23]A helpful, brief introduction to ancient letter-writing norms and practices is Abraham J. Malherbe, *Ancient Literary Theorists* (Atlanta: Scholars Press, 1988).

[24]See E. Randolph Richards, *The Secretary in the Letters of Paul* (Tübingen: Mohr Siebeck, 1991); Richards *Paul and First-Century Letter Writing: Secretaries, Composition, and Collection* (Downers Grove, IL: InterVarsity Press, 2004).

comments.[25] Reading aloud was the practice in the day, so when the letter arrived, someone would have read it to the gathered community (see Acts 8:27-30; 1 Tim 4:13). Paul is not a lone figure, despite his apostolic credentials, but writes together with others to a community that itself is embedded in the larger community of Christians throughout the Mediterranean world: "together with all those everywhere who call on the name of our Lord Jesus Christ" (1 Cor 1:2). The "rugged individualism" that Herbert Hoover celebrated at the time of the Great Depression and that continues to characterize the American social landscape is absent in this letter, as Paul demonstrates here and throughout a communitarian perspective rather than individualism and a mythical self-reliance.[26]

Paul addresses "the church of God in Corinth, to those sanctified in Christ Jesus and called his holy people" (1 Cor 1:2). Paul continues to emphasize the Corinthians' unity by calling them the "church" or assembly of the people of God (Paul never uses the term to refer to a building). But their corporate identity traces back to the way God separated them and called them to be holy. Paul stresses God's initiative in setting them apart ("sanctified" marks them as converted to Christ, as in 1 Cor 1:30; 6:11), and now they share a common identity, as did Israel as God's holy people (see 1 Pet 2:9; Lev 19:2). This socially disparate community finds its existence as one people because of God's initiative. Their identity as a "holy people" also has a moral dimension. The letter opening anticipates the struggles Paul will have to bring this reality into their daily existence. In the opening words of the letter, Paul shows the way forward beyond the factionalism that characterized the church and the immoral practices that marked life in the city of Corinth (1 Cor 6:9-11).

Instead of voicing the standard greeting found in ancient letters (*chairein*, meaning "Rejoice!") Paul offers a blessing: "Grace [*charis*] and peace to you from God our Father and the Lord Jesus Christ" (1 Cor 1:3). *Grace* summarizes the saving work of God through Jesus Christ (Rom 3:24; 5:15; Eph 2:8; 2 Thess 2:16), while *peace* is not an emotional disposition but describes the relationship of the people with God; it is the fruit of God's reconciliation with us (Rom 5:1). Paul's blessing is more than a formality but embraces the totality of the divine benefits he desires for these believers.

The opening thanksgiving (1 Cor 1:4-9) is surprising given the problematics of the Corinthian church. Paul sees God's grace in them despite the deep moral and community failures that mark the church. Not only does he thank God for the saving grace God has given them, but he celebrates the knowledge and wisdom they have from God and the spiritual gifts that mark their community (see 1 Cor 12-14). He affirms their eschatological anticipation (1 Cor 1:7), knowing that God can keep them and transform them (1 Cor 1:8). And he celebrates their fellowship and communion together (*koinōnia*) with Christ, even in the face of the grave divisions that mark the community's life (1 Cor 1:10-17). His celebration rests in God's activity in every verse ("because of his grace," "in him you have been enriched," "you do not lack any spiritual gift," "He will also

---

[25]Richards, *Paul and First-Century Letter Writing*, 201-2; Hans-Josef Klauck, *Ancient Letters and the New Testament: A Guide to Context and Exegesis* (Waco, TX: Baylor University Press, 2006), 65. Klauck cites a papyrus text that reads: "The rest (i.e., anything else that remains) learn from the one who carries the letter to you. For he is no stranger to us." W. L. Westermann and E. S. Hasenoehrl, eds., *Zenon Papyri: Business Papers of the Third Century B.C. Dealing with Palestine and Egypt* (New York: Columbia University Press, 1934), 3:6.14-16.

[26]Herbert Hoover, campaign speech, 1928, www.digitalhistory.uh.edu/disp_textbook.cfm?smtID=3&psid=1334.

keep you firm," "God is faithful" and is the one "who has called you").

The confidence Paul expresses is breathtaking given the depth of the Corinthians' divisions, moral lapses, and disordered theology. While the social forces have molded them, Paul places greater confidence in God's transforming power (Rom 12:1-2). Paul possesses an unwavering eschatological focus ("wait for the Lord Jesus Christ to be revealed," "blameless on the day of our Lord Jesus Christ" [1 Cor 1:7-8]). What God starts, God finishes. The eschatological hope expressed here is at the same time a call to actualize God's calling in their lives. Eschatology and ethics are bound together in Paul's understanding of the Christian life. In our age focused on the now and the immediate, Paul's long-view theological perspective comes as a strong corrective and a source of hope.

RESPONDING TO THE REPORTS ABOUT THE CORINTHIANS (1 CORINTHIANS 1:10–6:20)

Divisions over leaders (1 Corinthians 1:10–4:21). Paul begins the body of this letter by naming the first of many problems to follow. This is a church that is divided because of their adherence to one leader over another (1 Cor 1:10-17). The thread of Paul's argument is hard to follow at first glance. Paul starts by addressing the problem of rivalry in the church based on the way they honor one leader over others. The argument turns, abruptly it seems, in 1 Corinthians 1:18–2:16, where Paul extensively discusses wisdom (1 Cor 1:17, 19-27, 30; 2:4-7, 13), foolishness (1 Cor 1:18, 20-21, 23, 25), and the cross of Christ (1 Cor 1:17-18, 23; 2:2, 8). The other themes that run through the section are weakness (1 Cor 1:25, 27; 2:3) and power (1 Cor 1:17-18, 24, 26; 2:4-5). Then, in 1 Corinthians 3:1–4:21, Paul makes a sharp turn back to the Corinthians' celebration of one leader over another, focusing primarily on Apollos and himself. The transitions are marked by the hinge in the final clause of 1 Corinthians 1:17 ("not with wisdom and eloquence, lest the cross of Christ be emptied of its power") and the resumption of the leadership discussion in 1 Corinthians 3:1-4, beginning with the vocative in 1 Corinthians 3:1: "Brothers and sisters, I could not address you as people who live by the Spirit but as people who are still worldly—mere infants in Christ." It may seem that Paul is rambling as he dictates since the discussion about wisdom and foolishness, power and weakness, and the cross appear disconnected from the problem of rivalry. What is Paul doing as he calls for concord among them (1 Cor 1:10)?

Apparently, the Corinthians viewed Paul, Apollos, and Cephas (Peter) as if they were some of many itinerant philosophers who traveled through the ancient world to present their particular brand of "wisdom." They styled the apostles as sophists, "those rhetoricians whose ability in oratory was such that they could both secure a public following and attract students to their school."[27] People such as Dio Chrysostom were like the rock stars or celebrities of the ancient world. He describes the type of scene he would encounter when visiting

> the greatest cities, escorted with much enthusiasm and éclat, the recipients of my visits being grateful for my presence and begging me to address them and advise them and flocking about my doors from early dawn, all without my having incurred any expense or

[27]See Bruce W. Winter, *Philo and Paul Among the Sophists: Alexandrian and Corinthian Responses to a Julio-Claudian Movement* (Grand Rapids, MI: Eerdmans, 2002), 3-4; Duane Litfin, *Paul's Theology of Preaching: The Apostle's Challenge to the Art of Persuasion in Ancient Corinth* (Downers Grove, IL: IVP Academic, 2015).

> having made any contribution, with the result that all would admire me and perhaps some would exclaim, Ye gods! how dear and honoured is this man To whatsoever town and folk he comes. (*Discourses* 47.22)

The orators had their faithful followers, who viewed others as rivals. Some centuries before, Diogenes of Corinth describes the tensions: "That was a time, too, when one could hear crowds of wretched Sophists around Poseidon's temple shouting and reviling one another, their disciples, as they were called, fighting with one another" (8.9). The tension between the orators and their disciples could become so intense that it issued in violence (Philostratus, *Vitae sophistarum* 587-588). While the tensions between the "disciples" of Paul, Apollos, and Peter did not rise to this level, Paul describes their divisions as "rivalries among you" (1 Cor 1:11, my translation). The NIV translation, "quarrels," does not capture the thought; the term Paul uses brings into sharp relief the rivalry, discord, strife, and tension that marks the church.[28] The community is marked by jealousy (1 Cor 3:3) and division (1 Cor 1:10). The Corinthian believers have bought into the "cult of rivalry" that marked Greek society.[29]

Paul was not an eloquent orator (2 Cor 10:10), and he did not gain adherents to the gospel through his rhetorical power (1 Cor 1:17). Apollos, on the other hand, was known for his rhetorical training (Acts 18:24). Both he and Paul had been with the church (Acts 18:1-18, 24-28). We may suppose that Cephas (the Aramaic form of the given name Peter) also traveled and came through Corinth (1 Cor 9:5) and was honored in the church, possibly among the Jewish believers. While the Corinthians divided up as disciples behind these three leaders, Paul states simply that he is aligned with Christ (1 Cor 1:12; see 1 Cor 3:23).

But the problem goes beyond misconceptions about the nature of leadership within the church. Paul drives to the heart of the matter and exposes a fundamental misunderstanding of the nature of the gospel. The message of the cross is not simply another philosophy or form of wisdom among the many such currents of the day. The proclamation about Christ and his crucifixion is "the power of God and the wisdom of God" (1 Cor 1:24). Paul counters Jewish misconceptions about the Messiah; for them the message "Christ crucified" runs contrary to their triumphalistic notions embodied in the "signs" and "power." God's salvation comes through the death and resurrection of Christ. Paul eschews the power of rhetoric (1 Cor 2:1-5) and points to the cross of Christ as that place where the power and wisdom of God are found (1 Cor 1:18-23). God's true wisdom is located in Christ Jesus, "who has become for us wisdom from God—that is, our righteousness, holiness and redemption" (1 Cor 1:30).

Both the form and content of Paul's preaching were contrary to standard practices of the day (1 Cor 1:21).[30] Paul's focus on the cross runs counter to the way discussion about crucifixion was not socially acceptable. As Roman senator and orator Cicero says,

> How grievous a thing it is to be disgraced by a public court; how grievous to suffer a fine, how grievous to suffer banishment; and yet in the midst of any such disaster we retain some degree of liberty. Even if we are threatened with death, we may die free men.

[28]BDAG, 392.

[29]Ceslas Spicq, *Theological Lexicon of the New Testament*, trans. and ed. James D. Ernest (Peabody, MA: Hendrickson, 1994), 3:71.

[30]*Tou kērygmatos* (NIV, "what was preached") focuses on not only the content but the form of Paul's proclamation (Litfin, *Paul's Theology of Preaching*, 198-99).

> But the executioner, the veiling of the head and the very word "cross" should be far removed not only from the person of a Roman citizen but his thoughts, his eyes and his ears. For it is not only the actual occurrence of these things but the very mention of them, that is unworthy of a Roman citizen and a free man. (*Pro Rabirio Perduellionis Reo* 16)

What Cicero and others would not talk about, Paul proclaimed publicly as the center of the gospel.

Those who became followers of Christ were not the elite and rich of the city. The social composition of the church was not mainly patricians, people of higher social status and privilege (1 Cor 1:26-31), although some in the church did enjoy high social status. Not many in the church were trained in philosophy and rhetoric ("wise"), not many who had either social or economic power ("influential"), and few were born higher class ("noble"). The bulk of the church did not come from the educated urban elite of Corinth but were those of low status. God chose these people so that no one could boast, except in God (1 Cor 1:27-29, 31). Paul turns the importance of being one of the elite on its head. Compare Paul's perspective with that of Pliny the Elder, who chronicled the ten greatest and highest objects of humanity's pursuit: "To be a first-class warrior, a supreme orator and a very rave commander, to have the direction of operations of the highest importance, to enjoy the greatest honor, to be supremely wise, to be deemed the most eminent member of the senate, to obtain great wealth in an honorable way, to have many children, and to achieve supreme distinction in the state" (*Natural History* 7.43.139-140). God chose those below and on the margins.

First Corinthians 2:6-16 marks a dramatic move as Paul affirms wisdom, but not on philosophical terms. Rather, the perspective is that of the divine wisdom, as in 1 Corinthians 1:24, 30. Paul and other preachers do speak wisdom, divine wisdom (1 Cor 2:6-7), but this is none other than the wisdom contained in the gospel, which the world rejects as foolishness, as 1 Corinthians 2:8 clarifies (1 Cor 1:23-24). It has to do with the cross. Paul does not speak of some esoteric wisdom that only an elite group of Christians understand but that which this world does not understand (1 Cor 2:6). Paul strikes the contrast between those who receive this wisdom with those who do not. The wisdom of God found in the cross is perceived and received only by those who have the Spirit of God (1 Cor 2:10-16).

Paul identifies another problem. Although the Corinthians have the Spirit of God, he cannot speak to them as those "who live by the Spirit" since they act as "people of the flesh, as infants in Christ" (Gal 5:25; 1 Cor 3:1 NRSV). The evidence of their state is that there is jealousy and competitive rivalry among them (1 Cor 3:3). They have divided into sectarian groups over against each other as they exalt one Christian teacher over another (1 Cor 3:4; 1:11-13). Their conduct is that of humans who do not have the Spirit of God.

In 1 Corinthians 3:5-9 Paul clarifies the true role of Christian ministers. They are not leaders of philosophical schools, great rhetors to be praised and defended, but rather servants (1 Cor 3:5) and those who are "co-workers in God's service" (1 Cor 3:9). In God's work they play a subordinate role. One plants, another waters, but God causes the growth (1 Cor 3:6-7). In the end, the church does not belong to any minister but rather to God (1 Cor 3:9). For that reason the Corinthians should not exalt one minister over anther (1 Cor 3:5; 4:6). Paul received the sharpest criticisms in the church (1 Cor 4:3), but the apostle is not out to defend himself but to turn the Corinthians back to the gospel.

Paul sees the church as a whole as God's temple, the divine dwelling (1 Cor 3:10-17). The section serves as a warning to the leadership in the church who would attempt to steer the Corinthians into rivalry and division.[31] The imagery of laying the foundation and building on highlights the way large-scale construction was an ongoing process in the ancient world. Temples were not built in a day but were under construction for years (Jn 2:20) just as the construction of a cathedral in Europe could span generations. Those who promoted rivalries in the church were engaged in a destructive act that bore dire consequences (1 Cor 3:16-17). People recognized that there were severe consequences for those who profaned a sacred temple. Charles Talbert remarks,

> In antiquity, in order to protect temples that were repositories of great wealth from plunderers of various sorts, two stratagems were used. On the one hand, temple police functioned as a small mercenary army to protect the temple precincts. On the other hand, a curse of the deity was leveled against anyone who violated the sanctuary. . . . It was not uncommon to hear stories of tragic end of those upon whom such a curse came.[32]

Paul wraps up the argument by stating that since the wisdom of this world is foolishness, the Corinthians should not exalt Christian leaders as if they were leaders of philosophical schools (1 Cor 3:19-21). The disciples of the many rhetors would invoke the name of the founder of the philosophy or the name of the principal teacher to support their arguments and affirm their position. Paul states that the situation in the church should be different. *All* the ministers belong to them and not just the one that each faction honors (1 Cor 3:21-22). And all the groups in the church, not just one of them, belong to Christ (1 Cor 3:23; 1:12).

In the first paragraph of 1 Corinthians 4:1-21, Paul returns to the question of the place of Christian leaders in the plan of God (1 Cor 4:1-5). They are simple servants and stewards (1 Cor 4:1). The first term originally referred to the slaves who rowed on a galley but came to mean simply one who carried out the commands or decisions of another. A steward was a person in charge of the goods, property, or slaves of another (Lk 12:41-45; 16:1-10), or a class of public servants (Rom 16:23). What they administer are "the mysteries God has revealed" (see 1 Cor 2:7), the open secret of the gospel. Paul underscores the subordinate position of the ministers from the start.

Following on, Paul rebukes the Corinthians for their pride (1 Cor 4:6-8, 10) and in contrast speaks of his own weakness (1 Cor 4:9, 11-13). In their pride, the Corinthians criticized Paul, but Paul responds to their exalted self-image (1 Cor 4:8) with biting sarcasm, which deals a blow to their idea that they have arrived (1 Cor 4:9). The Corinthians think of themselves as wise, strong, and those with honor, whereas Paul and the apostles are considered to be, according to the sufferings they endured, those who are foolish, weak, and without honor (1 Cor 4:10). Paul ends the section with a list of sufferings he and other apostles endured due to their labors. Paul was clearly the opposite of all that they expected of the great rhetors (see 1 Cor 2:1-4). The Corinthians possibly held an over-realized eschatology,

---

[31]It is unlikely that Paul is critiquing the work of Apollos here since he affirms that Apollos watered the seed of the gospel that Paul planted (1 Cor 3:6).

[32]Charles H. Talbert, *Reading Corinthians: A Literary and Theological Commentary* (Macon, GA: Smyth & Helwys, 2003), 20.

which meant that they thought they were already experiencing the full benefits of the new age, as Talbert says, "beyond suffering, beyond tragedy, beyond poverty, beyond hard times" (1 Cor 4:8).[33] Theirs was a triumphalism that was not joined with a theology of suffering. Paul states that the apostles endure all the sufferings and humiliation of this age. In a culture where honor and shame were chief concerns, the argument is striking.[34]

In the close-out of the section, Paul seeks to reel the Corinthians back in. He appeals to them as their spiritual father (1 Cor 4:14-17). According to the rabbis, if a person teaches another man's son the Torah, "it is as if he had begotten him (b. Sanhedrin 19b)."[35] As a father, Paul can then exhort them to be imitators of his way of life, which was so despised among them (see 1 Cor 11:1; Phil 3:17; 1 Pet 5:3). For this reason, Paul sends Timothy to the church to "remind you of my way of life in Christ Jesus" (1 Cor 4:17). The apostle tells them that what they have received from him is just what he has taught other congregations. He does not change the message according to the audience (1 Cor 4:17; see 1 Cor 1:2; 11:16; 14:33). Paul contemplates coming to Corinth to have a showdown with those who are proud (1 Cor 4:18-19). Though Paul may be lacking according to the standards of the culture, he will confront them in the power of God (1 Cor 4:20-21).

The city of Corinth was a diverse community consisting of Latins, Greeks, Jews, and barbarians, according to Favorinus.[36] Given that the city was a hub for trade in the Mediterranean, undoubtedly those from the provinces of Macedonia, Asia, and Egypt made their way to the town, as had the Jewish Diaspora (Acts 18:4). This was a Latin colony on Greek soil, so some traditional Greeks adopted Latin names, offering them new status in the city. The Latins were the representatives of the colonial imperial power and wealth. On the other hand, Favorinus and others note that the city was becoming Hellenized. The new residents of the city looked back to the glory of Greek culture and wedded themselves to it by acts such as support of the traditional Isthmian games.

This cultural move was a means of establishing their legitimacy on the land, much in the same way that Tammany Societies emerged through early European colonization of North America. Adopting Native American dress was common in a bid to link the European colonists' history with that of the First Peoples of the land.[37] Mixed in were the barbarians, those who were neither Greek nor Latin, although Jews were sometimes tagged as such (see Juvenal, *Satires* 6.158). The gospel came into this cultural matrix with the story of a crucified Jew and the astounding move of bringing all these communities into the Jewish story. When Paul reminds the church of Israel's history, he draws

---

[33]Talbert, *Reading Corinthians*, 21.

[34]David A. deSilva, *Honor, Patronage, Kinship, and Purity: Unlocking New Testament Culture* (Downers Grove, IL: InterVarsity Press, 2000), 23-93.

[35]Talbert, *Reading Corinthians*, 21-22.

[36]"But if someone who is not a Lucanian, but a Roman, not one of the masses but of the equestrian order, who has emulated not only the language but also the sensibility and the manner and the dress of the Greeks . . . in order to achieve this one thing above all else, namely both appear and to be Greek, then should this man not deserve to have a bronze statue set up by you? Yes, he even deserves one in every city—by you, on the one hand, because he, though the Roman, has been thoroughly Hellenised, just as your very own patrimonial city has been . . . , and, on the other hand, by all the Greek cities, because he pursues philosophy and has both aroused many of the Greeks to join him in the pursuit of philosophy and has caused not a few of the barbarians. Why, it seems he has been equipped by the gods for just such a purpose" *Korinthiakos* 25, cited in Marcin N. Pawlak, "Corinth After 44 BC: Ethical and Cultural Changes," *Electrum* 20 (2013): 147.

[37]The Boston Tea Party is a vivid example of the practice. See Philip J. Deloria, *Playing Indian* (New Haven, CT: Yale University Press, 1999).

the circle around them all: "Our ancestors were all under the cloud and . . . they all passed through the sea" (1 Cor 10:1). Jewish history was instructive for everyone (1 Cor 10:6).

The cultural soup of Corinth boils over from the beginning of the letter. Paul, Apollos, and Cephas were all Jews who passed through the city with the same gospel. Yet Apollos held appeal given his Greek name and rhetorical finesse. Both Greeks and Latins, whether adoptive or natural born, would have found his presentation appealing. The Jewish wing of the Corinthian community would have been attracted to Peter, the Rock who had walked with Jesus in Galilee and Jerusalem. Paul was the founder and, though he was no rhetorical match, did have his followers among the body. The cultural divisions in the church also become vivid when Paul discusses the matter of eating meats offered to idols (1 Cor 8–10), a practice the Jewish community would have abhorred. Others ate freely, most likely those Gentiles of higher social strata. Some waffled, not knowing what to do. Add to the mix the social disparities that were rooted in education or lack thereof, social and economic status, and family birthright with accompanying social honor (1 Cor 1:26-27). Some were slaves (1 Cor 7:17-24), some were *liberti*, while others were freeborn.

The ethnic and social matrix of the city makes thinking about a common table almost impossible, yet Paul affirms, "Because there is one loaf, we, who are many, are one body, for we all share the one loaf" (1 Cor 10:17). Paul's message speaks loudly into the North American situation as well as the social realities in many countries where the gospel has been received. How do followers of Christ who are Black, Latinx, central and east Asian, White Europeans, and people who hail from the Caribbean—Jamaicans, Bahamians, and Haitians—find common cause and unity in the gospel? Despite the cultural streams of Corinthian life and the way cultures and names were adopted, Paul eschews asking Latin and Greek men to be circumcised although he brought a Jewish story. Jews were not pushed into violation of their ancestral traditions by insisting that they eat meat that had been offered to the gods. Yet the contemporary church in North America remains divided and holds a history of European cultural norms being imposed on converts such as Native Americans when they turn to Christ.[38]

God's plan, over and again, is to honor those who are the least in society (1 Cor 1:26-31). The gospel story begins on the margins in Galilee with the Messiah, who was from a poor family and whose opening recorded sermon highlighted God's good news for the poor, the sick, and the imprisoned (Lk 4:18-19). That same care emerges in the Corinthian story as it does throughout this land and over the world. The gospel's story of redemption resonates deeply in the Black and Latinx communities and has found its way powerfully outside the North Atlantic corridors of power. The center of the faith currently is in the Majority World, where most Christians live and the powerful vitality of the gospel is strong within minority communities, despite the way members of my community, the White European community, have traditionally dominated leadership and theological discussion. The Black community sees within the cross of Christ a sign of God's solidarity with their community, which knows too well the lynching

[38]Michael O. Emerson and Christian Smith, *Divided by Faith: Evangelical Religion and the Problem of Race in America* (Oxford: Oxford University Press, 2000); David Wallace Adams, *Education for Extinction: American Indians and the Boarding School Experience, 1875–1928* (Lawrence: University Press of Kansas, 1995); Richard Twiss, *Rescuing the Gospel from the Cowboys: A Native American Expression of the Jesus Way* (Downers Grove, IL: InterVarsity Press, 2015).

tree. As James Cone says, "God's loving solidarity can transform ugliness—whether Jesus on the cross or a lynched black victim—into beauty, into God's liberating presence."[39] Members of the Latinx community regard the exodus story as paradigmatic of their liberation from political oppression in home countries and from economic ruin. Women around the globe are reading texts such as Luke–Acts and the whole biblical narrative and discovering the strength of female witness and leadership that resonate with Paul's socially disruptive claim in Galatians 3:28.

The gospel holds good news for the poor and oppressed, for those who have been "outside" in society, such as the foreigner and women.[40] The message of the cross did not fully take hold in Corinth despite Paul's reaching, so he reaches back to it over and again to address the myriad social and economic problems of the church. Jesus' crucifixion and resurrection together are the heart of the story Paul tells and lives (even though at times he uses "the cross" as shorthand for the whole story, as in 1 Cor 1:23; see 1 Cor 15:1-8). Paul's boldness on this count is striking given the social stigma associated with the cross. Christianity is not about cultural dominance, political power, nationalism veneered with Christian rhetoric, gender dominance, or economic prosperity, as in the so-called prosperity gospel. It is about the cross, all the way down.

Immoral cultural norms in the community (1 Corinthians 5:1–6:20). The divisions in the church were not the only Corinthian problems that found their root in the maladaptation of the gospel to culture. The contextualization of the gospel into the languages and cultures of the world is one of the marvels of Christianity. The church hears the good news in Greek, Hebrew, English, French, Spanish, Creole, and Swahili. Worship is led with guitars and drums, organs and choirs, or no instruments at all. The gospel dialogues with culture as each people group helps us to see dimensions of God's plan that our own group has missed. Christians in collectivist cultures help us see the corporate dimensions of faith, and those from honor/shame cultures give us insight into this critical value range in the New Testament world. But the gospel also comes as a critique and corrective to existing habits of mind, values, and practices. No New Testament author abides idolatry (as in 1 Jn 5:21), and the apostles arrest abusive treatment of women (as in 1 Pet 3:7). God affirms culture; Jesus is the Son of God incarnate as a Jewish male which is culture-affirming. But God opposes those practices that are antithetical to the good news. In this section, Paul address three areas where the Corinthians have not allowed the gospel to critique their culture: incest (1 Cor 5:1-8), lawsuits (1 Cor 6:1-11), and prostitution (1 Cor 6:12-20). Paul also addresses the Corinthians' misunderstanding of his previous correspondence to them (1 Cor 5:9-13), which deals with the church's handling of immorality.

Incest (1 Corinthians 5:1-13). In 1 Corinthians 5:1, Paul responds to another topic reported to him by those from Chloe's household (1 Cor 1:11): "It is actually reported that there is sexual immorality among you, and of a kind that even pagans do not tolerate: A man is

[39]James H. Cone, *The Cross and the Lynching Tree* (Maryknoll, NY: Orbis, 2011), 162.

[40]"Yet God choses those who are foolish and weak in the eyes of the dominant culture to bring about God's will. It is not the wise and strong who are entrusted by God, but the disenfranchised, the frail, the outcast. It is the stone rejected by those whom society admires that God uses as a foundation for God's work. In fact, salvation comes even to the powerful and privileged via the marginalized." Demetrius K. Williams, "The First Letter of Paul to the Corinthians," in *The Peoples' Bible*, ed. Curtiss Paul DeYoung et al. (Minneapolis: Fortress, 2009), 1598.

sleeping with his father's wife."[41] The identification of the man's partner as "his father's wife" indicates that she is his stepmother. Her act is not addressed, so we may assume she was outside the Christian community in Corinth.

In general, people in Paul's day were tolerant of a variety of sexual encounters beyond the bonds of marriage. Cicero, for example, endorses free rein for the young, at least for a season, as long as no harm came to others:

> Let some allowance be made to age; let youth be allowed greater freedom; let not pleasures always be forbidden; let not that upright and unbending reason always prevail; let desire and pleasure sometimes triumph over reason, provided that in such matters the following rule and limitation is observed: let a young man be mindful of his own repute and not a despoiler of another's; let him not squander his patrimony; nor be crippled by usury; nor attack the home and reputation of another; nor bring shame upon the chaste, taint upon the virtuous, disgrace upon the upright; let him frighten none by violence, quit conspiracy, keep clear of crime. Lastly, when he has listened to the voice of pleasure and given some time to love-affairs and these empty desires of youth, let him at length turn to the interests of home life, to activity at the bar and in public affairs. (*Pro Caelio* 18.42)

Plutarch advised a wife to be patient if her husband goes out to gratify his sexual desire outside the marriage bed: "If therefore a man in private life, who is incontinent and dissolute in regard to his pleasures, commit some peccadillo with a paramour or a maidservant, his wedded wife ought not to be indignant or angry, but she should reason that it is respect for her which leads him to share his debauchery, licentiousness, and wantonness with another woman" (*Moralia* 140B). The boundaries within the church were much tighter, and the tension between Christian views of sexuality and those of the surrounding culture generated various problems within the church (e.g., see 1 Thess 4:1-8).

But the situation in the Corinthian church was unique since a man had relations with his stepmother, an act "that even pagans do not tolerate," Paul says (1 Cor 5:1). Jewish law prohibited such unions (Lev 18:8), and the Romans disapproved as well. Craig Keener notes, "Relations between sons and stepmothers were often notoriously uncomfortable in antiquity. They also could prove sexually tempting: given the typical practice of Romans (and especially Greeks) marrying younger wives, second marriages often yielded stepmothers in the age range of elder sons."[42] Such behavior was widely censured. In this case, it may be that the mother had passed on, but even in such a case, the practice was condemned. Cicero says, "The pontiffs shall inflict capital punishment on those guilty of incest" (*De legibus* 2.9.22). Elsewhere he expresses horror at such a union: "And so mother-in-law marries son-in-law, with none to bless, none to sanction the union, and amid naught but general foreboding. Oh! to think of the woman's sin, unbelievable, unheard of in all experience save for this single instance!" (*Pro Cluentio* 5.14–6.15).

John Chow suggests that the issue at hand was the possible loss of inheritance if the man

[41]The Greek is more concise: "Someone has his father's wife." Every translation is an interpretation; the NIV captures the idea, as does the NRSV's rendering "for a man is living with his father's wife" and the CEB's "a man is having sex with his father's wife." Paul regards the union as *porneia*, "sexual immorality," a wide-ranging term associated with many types of illicit sexual unions. See Aline Rousselle, *Porneia: On Desire and the Body in Antiquity* (Cambridge, MA: Blackwell, 1988). On ancient views regarding incest, see Craig S. Keener, "Adultery, Divorce," in *Dictionary of New Testament Background*, ed. Craig A. Evans and Stanley E. Porter (Downers Grove, IL: InterVarsity Press, 2000), 12-14.

[42]Craig S. Keener, *1–2 Corinthians*, New Cambridge Biblical Commentary (Cambridge: Cambridge University Press, 2005), 48.

did not marry his stepmother.[43] We cannot be sure whether the core issue was economic, since the motivation could be desire and no more. Regardless of the driving cause, Paul censures the act and is outraged that the Corinthian church approves and is proud of the union (1 Cor 5:2). The Corinthians are given to arrogance and boasting (1 Cor 4:6, 18-19; 8:1; 13:4) so in some sense their response is not out of character. But some suggest that the man was a person of status, a patron perhaps, and the community would have been loath to dishonor such a person.[44] Social power trumped gospel values. Paul, on the other hand, prescribes a different course of action—grief and the expulsion of the person from the community (1 Cor 5:2; the language echoes Deut 17:7; 19:19; 22:21, 24; 24:7). Exclusion from social fellowship, even from the common meal, would mean full disenfranchisement. In a collectivist society, the impact would have been devastating. Such folk are to be removed from the community to keep the community pure, but the hope is that the person will be turned from their errant ways.[45]

The action Paul prescribes (1 Cor 5:3-5) appears to be informed by the disciplinary procedure Jesus laid out (Mt 18:15-20). The goal of excommunication looks with hope to the person's restoration (1 Cor 5:5). Paul recognizes that if the church does not act to address open sin in its midst, the consequence will be the corruption or spread of sin through the rest of the community (1 Cor 5:6). Paul uses the imagery of yeast and the Passover. Jewish law prescribed cleaning the house of yeast before the Passover sacrifice (Ex 12:15-21). Paul says that the time to clean out the old leaven of sin is already passed since Christ, our Passover, has been sacrificed. The sin should not be condoned but should have been dealt with already.

In 1 Corinthians 5:9-12 Paul addresses a misunderstanding that arose in Corinth about Christian association with those who engaged in immoral practices. We do not have a copy of this prior letter but only this reference to it. Paul called them not to mix in close social association with those in the church who were actively engaged in sin. They heard him saying that they should not have social intercourse with anyone in the surrounding society who lived in this way. To interpret the letter that way would have meant that they would need to lead a completely separated or monastic life (1 Cor 5:9-10). Paul's view is that Christians are called to live in society but not according to those norms that are antithetical to Christian virtue. He clarifies that they should not associate with anyone who claims to be part of the community yet engages in the vices listed in 1 Corinthians 5:11. The reason Paul brings up the letter is clear; he is now exhorting them to "expel the wicked person from among you" (1 Cor 5:13; a reference to Deut 17:7; 19:19; 22:21, 24; 24:7). In a collectivist culture, the group has a responsibility for the conduct of the individual.[46]

As I write this, the story broke of the immoral behavior of an extremely prominent Christian leader. He did his best to cover up his sexual sin, and some around him aided in the process, refusing to believe the victims. Public and private comments have come in from

[43]John K. Chow, *Patronage and Power: A Study of Social Networks in Corinth*, LNTS (Sheffield: Sheffield Academic Press, 1992), 114-40.

[44]Keener, *1–2 Corinthians*, 49.

[45]Bruce J. Malina and Jerome H. Neyrey, *Portraits of Paul: An Archaeology of Ancient Personality* (Louisville, KY: Westminster John Knox, 1996), 186-87.

[46]Malina and Neyrey, *Portraits of Paul*, 154-57.

Christians disillusioned and bewildered since the man was looked up to as a model of Christian conduct and faith, a champion of the evangelical movement. Years ago my wife and I attended a church that was beset by moral failures, including three people convicted of murder. We discovered later that the pastor was involved in three adulterous relationships. He and others covered the sin, including two who later committed murder. Christian institutions and churches may not celebrate the sins as did the Corinthians, but most reading this will know situations where immorality in the community was left unchecked or where victims' credibility is constantly questioned. The result is that people's faith is damaged, and the silence in the face of the vices signals to others that such behavior is tolerated; "a little yeast leavens the whole batch of dough" (1 Cor 5:6). The sins may be sexual in nature, but they can also be greed and theft, overblown pride, perpetual lies that are not addressed with the truth, violence against women, and racism in subtle and overt forms. Paul's address in 1 Corinthians 5 is a thunderous call to assure that the leaven is swept out. Jesus laid out the need to address sin in the community, and Paul took the teaching to heart. Although such social control may not have the same effect today as it would among those of a dyadic culture where the group had greater influence on the behavior of the individual, the church must bring socially destructive sin to light and not tolerate its growth in the community. Christ our Passover has already been sacrificed, so our community keeps the festival "with the unleavened bread of sincerity and truth" (1 Cor 5:8).

Lawsuits (1 Corinthians 6:1-11). Corinth was known for litigation. Dio Chrysostom describes its "lawyers innumerable perverting judgment" (*Virtue* 9). He was aggrieved when a statue of him was stolen and no judicial action was taken:

> Nay, that statue of mine neither ran away nor tried to do so nor had any such intention at all; therefore we are left to conclude that the Corinthians themselves banished it, not only without holding any trial, but also without having any charge at all to bring against it. And would any one have believed this to the discredit of the Corinthians, whose forefathers were pre-eminent among the Greeks for cultivating justice? (*Corinthian Discourse* 16)

Bruce Winter outlines the injustice inherent in the courts of the day. Those of lower rank in society could not take those of a higher rank to court, there were cliques among jurors that could sway a verdict and oppress the innocent, bribes were not uncommon, the rich and the powerful received "justice" but the poor could not, and our contemporary rules of evidence were not in place then.[47] When a dispute arose in the church, Paul is aghast that they would take the case before the "unrighteous" (1 Cor 6:1 NRSV; not "ungodly," as the NIV), an apt description of the Corinthian courts. Moreover, the courts were venues where personal enmity and revenge were commonplace. Judicial proceedings were public and often designed to dishonor a person (see Acts 18:12-17).[48] Injustice in the judicial system is not a new thing.

Paul offers an alternative model to resolving disputes that would otherwise go to the courts, where justice was hard to find. After reminding them of their future role as judges of the world and angels (1 Cor 6:2-3), he shames them, asking whether there were nobody wise enough in the church to handle such matters (1 Cor 6:4-5; see their claims to be "wise" in 1 Cor 3:18; 4:10). Paul even echoes the teaching

[47]Bruce W. Winter, "Civil Litigation in Secular Corinth and the Church," *NTS* 37 (1991): 561-67.
[48]David F. Epstein, *Personal Enmity in Roman Politics 218–43 BC* (New York: Croom Helm, 1987), 1-2, 19-20.

of Jesus that it is better to be wronged than do wrong to a fellow believer (Mt 5:38-42; see Rom 12:17, 19; 1 Pet 2:23; 3:9). Retaliation has no place in the church, as sweet as revenge may seem at first. Paul likely has in mind the way that the courts were used to dishonor and damage the social standing of another. Best to turn the other cheek than enter the downward spiral of enmity. Paul's prescription is arbitration in the church (1 Cor 6:5; the term "to judge" was used of arbitration). Winter notes, "Provision existed in Greek, Roman and Jewish legal systems for the use of arbitrators who acted in a legal capacity with the agreement of the defendant and the plaintiff."[49]

Paul amplifies the statement in 1 Corinthians 6:1 about the "unrighteous" in 1 Corinthians 6:9-10, including a vice list that focuses on those who are sexually immoral, idolators, greedy, drunkards, slanderers, and grifters, reminding them of their own conversion to Christ out of such practices.[50] They are righteous in Christ (2 Cor 5:21) and morally transformed by the Spirit of God (Rom 8:1-17).

Some who read this will remember the O. J. Simpson trial. The celebrity football player was charged with the murder of his wife and her friend, yet he walked free. Though he was guilty, his star power and the media coverage helped tilt the verdict in his favor, although later he was convicted as the responsible party in a civil trial. Others will remember the injustice surrounding the death of Trayvon Martin, an African American youth who was shot and killed in cold blood, yet his white assailant was acquitted. Michelle Alexander has chronicled the racial injustice in American courts.[51] Today questions remain about the ability to obtain justice in the courts if someone is poor or a person of color. Do the courts remain the domain of the "unrighteous"? Justice is difficult, if not impossible, to obtain for many. Yet contemporary courts are governed in ways that seek to minimize injustice, including the rejection of bribes and the seating of impartial juries, though justice is hardly even in the balance. Recourse can exist in civil and criminal cases. The conditions that prevailed in the Corinthian court are not entirely a one-for-one equivalent to the contemporary courtroom. Paul wants justice to be done, but not any justice motivated by revenge. He longs for wise assessment by those competent to judge. The question today is not simply whether Christians may take each other to court but whether the church will support wise and fair justice in our systems and speak up against distorted justice or revenge. The venue will vary according to the place where justice is needed.

Prostitution (1 Corinthians 6:12-20). That Paul needed to address the Corinthians about prostitution is a surprise, at least until we consider that prostitution was condoned in Corinth and cities throughout the Roman Empire. Archaeologists have discovered a brothel in Pompeii on a principle street, and there was another in Thessalonica's agora. Philo notes that men from other nations visit harlots from the age of fourteen, but the Jews

[49]Winter, "Civil Litigation in Secular Corinth," 569.

[50]In recent years considerable debate surrounds Paul's use of *malakoi* and *arsenokoitai* in 1 Cor 6:9. As Thiselton notes, the debate is about whether the terms refer "to homosexual relations in general, or more narrowly to male prostitution, sacred male prostitution, pederastic practices, or concepts of maleness and effeminacy in the Greek and Jewish world of the day." See Anthony C. Thiselton, *The First Epistle to the Corinthians*, New International Greek Testament Commentary (Grand Rapids, MI: Eerdmans, 2000), 439-44; see also Keener, "Adultery, Divorce," 14-15; Keener, *1–2 Corinthians*, 54-55. The contemporary literature on sexual orientation and gender identity is legion; dealing with all the issues involved is beyond the scope of this study.

[51]Michelle Alexander, *The New Jim Crow: Mass Incarceration in the Age of Colorblindness* (New York: New Press, 2012).

do not visit them at all (*On Joseph* 42-43). Greek and Roman perspectives were quite different. According to Talbert, in Roman cities such as Corinth, prostitutes registered with the *aedile* (Tacitus, *Annals* 2.85), and moralists condoned the practice as a safeguard against adultery.[52] The worst thing that one could do would be to enter a sexual liaison with another man's wife. Philip of Thessalonica wrote an epigram to commemorate the construction of a boat:

> I, a boat constructed from the Cyprian's trade, have come to the sea which gave the goddess her birth. On adept in beauty formed me and called me "Courtesan" because I am the friend of every man. Board me joyfully, I do not demand a high price. I receive all who come. I take foreigners as well as citizens. As you did on land, so now row me over the depths of the sea.[53]

The Corinthians justified the practice of visiting prostitutes by an appeal to Christian liberty, "I have the right to do anything" (1 Cor 6:12; see 1 Cor 10:23). Paul echoes their position. They also appeal to nature: "Food for the stomach and the stomach for food" (1 Cor 6:13), that is, the body is designed for food, and food is for the body, so the body is designed for sex. It is as natural a function as eating. Paul counters that the body is rather for the Lord and has an eternal destiny (1 Cor 6:14; Rom 6:12-13; 1 Cor 15). One cannot separate the body from Christ himself so to engage in prostitution, which means that Christ is involved in the act (1 Cor 6:15-17). Indeed, the body is the temple of God's Spirit (1 Cor 6:19) and has been redeemed by Christ. In a practice known as sacred manumission, a purchase price for freedom of a slave was paid to the slave owner within a temple and an inscription was placed on the site that read, "For freedom So and So was set free." The freed slave now had an obligation to the deity. So, Paul says, they have been freed but are obligated to Christ: "You are not your own" (1 Cor 6:19).[54] Christian freedom is not license. The resounding conclusion is, "Therefore honor God with your bodies" (1 Cor 6:20).

Paul's words could not be more relevant for our era, which celebrates all forms of sexual expression outside marriage. Paul reminds us that our bodies are for the Lord and that one cannot separate what one does with the body from one's relationship with Christ. Christian liberty cannot devolve into sexual license (Jude 4). Current cultural norms regarding free sexual expression have found their way into the church at an astounding pace, with prominent Christian leaders not being exempt from sexual immorality. While the root problem is not the availability and sanction of prostitution but the way some regard sexual liaisons as expressions of freedom and the natural desires created by God. Paul has a higher view of the body—it is for the Lord while, at the same time, affirming marriage (1 Cor 7:1-16). Paul holds a high theology of the body.[55]

Paul does not address the wider issue of why women become involved in the sex trade—his problem is with the "johns." Financial necessity, childhood sexual abuse, seduction of young women by pimps, addiction to drugs, male dominance, and ethnicity (Indigenous women are especially

[52]Talbert, *Reading Corinthians*, 48.

[53]A. S. F. Gow and D. L. Page, *The Greek Anthology: The Garland of Philip and Some Contemporary Epigrams* (Cambridge: Cambridge University Press, 1968), 1.140. The Cyprian was Aphrodite, the patron deity of prostitutes.

[54]Adolf Deissmann, *Light from the Ancient East* (Grand Rapids, MI: Baker, 1978), 322-23.

[55]See Beth Felker Jones, *Faithful: A Theology of Sex*, Ordinary Theology Series (Grand Rapids, MI: Zondervan, 2015); Jones, *Marks of His Wounds: Gender Politics and Bodily Resurrection* (New York: Oxford University Press, 2007).

targeted for sexual exploitation) are all factors that snare women into the profession. Paul does not address the wider social issues surrounding prostitution, but he cuts off the road to the brothel for the Corinthian men. The church's ongoing task is to call not only for sexual purity but sexual safety and justice in society, asking the broader questions about why people are caught in prostitution and how to address the causes and not only the outcomes.[56]

PAUL'S RESPONSES TO THE CORINTHIANS' CONCERNS AND ISSUES (1 CORINTHIANS 7:1–16:12)

Paul begins the second part of the body of this letter with responses to the letter the Corinthians sent to him: "Now for the matters you wrote about" (1 Cor 7:1). As noted previously, Paul begins with the Greek words *peri de*, which are repeated at various points in this section of the epistle (1 Cor 7:1, 25; 8:1; 12:1; 16:1, 12), perhaps—if not likely—marking out his various responses. The section also mentions issues he heard about, such as the divisions that are evident when they celebrate the Lord's Supper (1 Cor 11:17-34; see 1 Cor 11:18) and the denial of the resurrection of believers (1 Cor 15:1-58; see 1 Cor 15:15).

Marriage (1 Corinthians 7:1-40). Paul's begins his response to the Corinthians' queries with an extensive discussion about marriage (1 Cor 7:1-16), changing one's social situation (1 Cor 7:17-24), and "the virgins" (1 Cor 7:25-40). In this chapter Paul argues that the single life is preferable over marriage, a surprising position given that Jewish perspectives on marriage were quite positive, rooted as they were in Genesis 2:18-25 (see Tob 8:4-9). The Essenes did not prescribe marriage, but they were the exception to the rule. Jesus affirmed marriage and spoke against divorce and remarriage (Mk 10:2-12). Matthew's rendition of the teaching includes the famous exception clause regarding infidelity (Mt 5:31-32; 19:3-12). But he also taught that marriage was an institution delimited by this age and would not carry over into the time of the resurrection (Mt 22:23-33), a long way from Mormon teaching on "celestial marriage" that lasts beyond the grave and is an essential element of becoming divine.

Over against Jewish views and Jesus' teaching, some in the early church found warrant for denying marriage as well as forbidding eating meat (1 Tim 4:3). Such asceticism may have had its roots buried in the soil of an incipient Gnosticism, could have been the product of an overrealized eschatology, or in Ephesus may have sprung from Gentile perspectives on Artemis, "a 'virgin unmarried goddess. Her priests were most likely celibate or castrated men."[57] Religious celibacy was even known in Corinth (Apuleius, *Metamorphoses* 11.6). Another possible framing of the problem is the Stoic and Cynic debate about marriage. Both philosophical schools understood the obligations inherent in marriage and, according to Will Deming, asked, "Should the intelligent, informed, morally upright person take on such responsibility?"[58] The Stoics, on the one hand, responded positively. The universe was governed by divine principle, and one had to live in harmony with it. The Cynic answer to the question was not so positive. The

[56]On the church's social commitment, see the fifth paragraph of the Lausanne Covenant, on "Christian Social Responsibility," 1974, www.lausanne.org/content/covenant/lausanne-covenant#cov, along with the commentary by John Stott, www.lausanne.org/content/lop/lop-3#5.

[57]Aída Besançon Spencer, *1 Timothy*, NCC (Eugene, OR: Cascade, 2013), 106.

[58]Will Deming, *Paul on Marriage and Celibacy: The Hellenistic Background of 1 Corinthians 7* (Grand Rapids, MI: Eerdmans, 2004), 54.

Cynic ideal was freedom for the pursuit of philosophy and from the encumbrances of this life, including all concerns for "food, clothing, house, home marriage, children, etc.; freedom from all ties which morality, law, state, and community life in general may put upon the individual."[59] Whatever the root cause, some Corinthians opted for an asceticism with regard to sex within marriage; 1 Corinthians 7:1 appears to be a quote from their letter to Paul: "It is good for a man not to have sexual relations with a woman."

Paul responds by falling out on the Stoic side of things but with a distinctly Christian rationale: "But since sexual immorality is occurring," or perhaps better, "because of the temptation to sexual immorality" (1 Cor 7:2). The point is that because of such temptations (1 Cor 7:5), conjugal relationships should be maintained within the marriage bond. Paul understands the mutuality inherent in marriage (1 Cor 7:2-4), a position refreshingly devoid of male dominance. But he also offers that abstinence may be acceptable for a season of prayer (1 Cor 7:5). Paul's position is somewhat similar to that in Mishnah *Ketubbot* 5:6, which goes so far as to prescribe the number of days one may abstain given a person's profession. Paul, however, says such abstinence may occur if there is "mutual consent." In the end, Paul recognizes that some have the gift of marriage, while others do not (1 Cor 7:7; Mt 19:11-12). The single life is an option open to Christians, as is marriage. Some, like the late Dr. John R. W. Stott, remain single throughout their life, while others, including me, have enjoyed decades of marriage. We each have our gift, Paul affirms. Paul counsels sexual mutuality within marriage yet does not leave room for coercion or force in sexual relationships. Sexual domination or manipulation is antithetical to the love and honor that should characterize the marriage bond (Eph 5:25; 1 Pet 3:7).

Paul demonstrates his preference for the single life (1 Cor 7:8-9) yet does not prescribe divorce, even if one is married to someone outside the faith (1 Cor 7:10-14). He recognizes that the unbelieving spouse may wish to break the bond of marriage (1 Cor 7:15-16), but his hope is that the nonbeliever will be saved through the life and testimony of their spouse (see 1 Pet 3:1-2). Among the Romans, husbands and wives had the same rights regarding divorce. Divorce as well as remarriage was common. Seneca highlights how common this was as he asks:

> Is any woman ashamed of being divorced, now that some noble ladies reckon the years of their lives, not by the number of the consuls, but by that of their husbands, now that they leave their homes in order to marry others, and marry only in order to be divorced? Divorce was only dreaded as long as it was unusual; now that no gazette appears without it, women learn to do what they hear so much about. Can any one feel ashamed of adultery, now that things have come to such a pass that no woman keeps a husband at all unless it be to pique her lover? (*De beneficiis* 3.16)

Paul's teaching about marital fidelity and commitment contrasts sharply with societal norms.

The complex issues that may arise to strain the marriage bond are not fully addressed in Paul's words. He does not touch on physical or emotional spousal abuse, nor does he deal with varied forms of marital infidelity. Paul addresses a particular set of questions and in doing so reflects on the fundamentals of God's plan for humanity in Genesis and Jesus' teaching (1 Cor 7:10; Mt 5:32; 19:9), the same

[59]Deming, *Paul on Marriage and Celibacy*, 60-61.

touchpoints that should be applied today. At the same time, when touching those matters not addressed by Jesus, Paul offers theological counsel (1 Cor 7:12)—the work of theology is never done. Not every issue is addressed in Scripture; therefore wise, theologically rooted reflection is incumbent on the church.

Paul allows the question of marriage to open a wider discussion about changing one's social status because of one's faith (1 Cor 7:17-24). Paul does not regard the gospel as a vehicle for changing ethnicity (1 Cor 7:17-20). Gentiles do not have to become Jewish to follow Christ, nor does the Jew need to adopt Gentile identity. Conversion to Christ does not entail cultural conversion, as was prescribed when Indigenous peoples turned to Christ.[60] Paul steps aside, however, to discuss the issue of slavery and lets slaves know that they may take advantage of freedom while recognizing that one may serve Christ in whatever state one is in (1 Cor 7:21-24). This text and others where Paul and Peter tell slaves how to live as Christians within their bondage (Eph 6:5-8; Col 3:22-25; 1 Pet 2:18-25) are not wholesale endorsements of slavery meant to preserve the institution, as was believed in the antebellum South and is believed even among some Christians today. Not long ago I met a PhD student from an evangelical seminary who fully endorsed slavery given Paul's teaching about slaves submitting to their masters. Unsurprisingly, *The Negro Bible—The Slave Bible*, an edition of Scripture published for slaves in the "British West-India Islands," completely cut out this and surrounding chapters in 1 Corinthians as well as Galatians 3.[61] God's plan for humanity, however, is equality and freedom (Gal 3:28; Gen 1–2), themes that led eventually to the abolition of slavery.[62]

Paul spends considerable time discussing questions regarding "virgins" (1 Cor 7:25-39), a topic raised by the Corinthians themselves ("Now about virgins" in 1 Cor 7:25; see 1 Cor 7:1). Who are the virgins? It is not likely that they are "virgin daughters," since Paul never mentions their "father," the word *daughter* is absent from the discussion, and *virgin* was not a common way to speak of a person's daughter. "Virgins" may be "spiritual wives," those in a "spiritual marriage" without sexual relations. Although such unions existed in the early centuries of the church, there is no evidence for them at present. Alternately, they may be those who are promised in marriage, an interpretation that holds more merit. As previously, Paul opts for singleness (1 Cor 7:25-40), although he concedes that marriage is no sin. He refers to "the present crisis" (1 Cor 7:26) a possible reference to a current famine, which makes singleness a preferable option.[63] The counsel is situational.

As both Deming and Winter illustrate, the questions regarding marriage, singleness, and social status that Paul addresses in this chapter were part of the common discussions of the day.[64] Paul finds a way forward through the teaching of Jesus (as in 1 Cor 7:10),

[60]On the grim story of forced assimilation of Indigenous peoples in the United States, see Adams, *Education for Extinction*.

[61]*The Negro Bible—The Slave Bible: Select Parts of the Holy Bible, Selected for the Use of the Negro Slaves, in the British West India Islands* (Blountsville, AL: Fifth Estate, 2019).

[62]The defense of slavery was rooted in various biblical texts (Gen 9:25-27; 17:12, Deut 20:10-11; Rom 13:1, 7; Col 3:22; 4:1; 1 Tim 6:1-2), while abolitionists returned to the whole arc of biblical teaching regarding equality and justice, affirming that all people were of one blood (Acts 17:26). Hermeneutics and theology were at the heart of the debate. See Mark A. Noll, *The Civil War as a Theological Crisis* (Chapel Hill: University of North Carolina Press, 2006), 33-50.

[63]See the discussion of the passage in Winter, *After Paul Left Corinth*, 215-68.

[64]Deming, *Paul on Marriage and Celibacy*; Winter, *After Paul Left Corinth*; Bruce W. Winter, *Seek the Welfare of the City: Christians as Benefactors and Citizens* (Grand Rapids, MI: Eerdmans, 1994), 145-64.

theology (as in 1 Cor 7:22, 29), a keen understanding of his context and current realities (as in the philosophical discussions of the day and current conditions in 1 Cor 7:26), and his own informed judgment (1 Cor 7:12). Paul's epistle does not provide an answer to every one of today's questions regarding status, marriage, singleness, and social conditions but does show the contemporary Christian an approach to theological wisdom for dealing with the complexities of human existence in the world. Prooftexting is not the same as sound theological reflection that is rooted in Scripture, informed by the theological tradition, responsive to context, and developed through sound reflection. Paul faced issues that we do not face, and we face realities he did not contemplate. Yet reading the whole arc of Scripture; attending to the teaching of the Old Testament, Jesus, and the apostles; and sound theological judgment provide the necessary moral guidance to face our own present crises.

About meats sacrificed to idols (1 Corinthians 8:1–11:1). The relevance of 1 Corinthians 8–10, which deal with the question of whether one should eat meat that had been previously offered to idols, is not immediately evident to most Western Christians. Having mentioned this in a class on 1 Corinthians, a student at the back of the class raised her hand. Rose was from Nigeria and posed the question: "If a friend invites me to dinner and then tells me that the goat meat we are eating had been offered to their gods, should I eat it?" The application of the passage became apparent to everyone as her concerns and perspectives became part of the discussion. Reading together with those of different cultures often brings fresh and vibrant insights into the faith. In the ensuing discussion, we looked at ancient and contemporary questions, including those from Asia regarding ancestor veneration.[65] The contextual considerations brought us back to discussions about how white Christian America often places freedom as the highest good, regardless of the consequences for others (see 1 Cor 9). Intercultural study of Scripture and theology, as represented in this volume, is the way all theology should be done. We read together as one holy, catholic, apostolic church that has a place at the table for all members of the Christian community, both contemporary and ancient.

In this whole section Paul addresses two issues that arose in the Corinthian church, both of which had to do with food. The first is whether or not a Christian can eat meat that was sacrificed in pagan temples and subsequently went on sale in the *macellum* or marketplace where people bought provisions. The second question is whether a Christian may dine in the *triclinia* located in the idol temples such as that of Asclepius. Both concerns appear in 1 Corinthians 8; 10. How, then, does 1 Corinthians 9 fit into the argument? Paul addresses the issue of Christian freedom here (1 Cor 9:1) but also the attendant social responsibility placed on Christians for the good of others (1 Cor 9:19-23; 8:9-13). Paul makes it clear that certain social circumstances limit the use of Christian freedom, and he uses himself as an example of this in 1 Corinthians 9 (1 Cor 9:3-6, 12, 15, 19). While the specific issue is the eating of meat offered to idols, the principle Paul works over is responsible use of Christian freedom.

---

[65]Finny Philip, "1 Corinthians," in *South Asia Bible Commentary*, ed. Brian Wintle (Udaipur, India: Open Door Publications; Grand Rapids, MI: Zondervan, 2015), 1569; Dachollom Datiri, "1 Corinthians," in *Africa Bible Commentary: A One-Volume Commentary Written by Seventy African Scholars*, ed. Tokunboh Adeyemo (Grand Rapids, MI: Zondervan, 2006), 1387.

Understanding food and dining customs in ancient Corinth is necessary in order to interpret 1 Corinthians 8; 10. There were two types of sacrifices in the temples that dominated the landscape. One could offer a sacrifice, burn a portion on the altar, offer part of the animal to the priests, and then use the rest in a private banquet in a dining room or *triclinium* of the temple. Invitations would be sent to people's peers and clients, such as this one from Oxyrhynchus Papyrus 110: "Chaermon [the host] invites you to dine at the banquet of the Lord Serapis in the Serapeum tomorrow, that is, the 15th, from the ninth hour."[66] If invited to such a feast, should a Christian attend? Paul contemplates this issue in 1 Corinthians 8:9-13; 10:1-22.

Paul's response to this situation is negative. If a Christian eats in the temple of a god, likely affirming their freedom since "An idol is nothing at all in the world" and "There is no god but one" (1 Cor 8:4), such an act may embolden a weak believer who cannot separate in their mind eating the food with the cult of idolatry. In other words, that person is drawn back into idolatry due to their fellow's exercise of freedom and "is destroyed by your knowledge" (1 Cor 8:11). For Paul, the well-being of the other takes precedence over one's knowledge and freedom.

But Paul takes the issue a step further in discussing that, in the end, one cannot eat such meat in the confines of a temple without truly participating in the cult. Place matters, and so eating in the temple of an idol will of necessity mean participating in the worship of the god (1 Cor 10:14-22). Paul carefully notes that he is not backtracking on his previous teaching—an idol is nothing (1 Cor 10:19-20). But the active power behind idolatry is demonic, and Paul cannot contemplate the participation of believers with demons (1 Cor 10:18-22). He reminds the church of Israel's participation in idolatry and the divine judgment that ensued (1 Cor 10:1-13).

The other type of sacrifice was public rather than private. After the sacrifice, the animal was divided; a small part was burned on the altar, a portion given to the priests, and the rest was given to the civic magistrates. Any remaining meat went for sale in the public market, the *macellum* in Corinth, and could be purchased by the populace (1 Cor 10:25). The Jewish community refused to each this meat since it was idol meat (1 Cor 8:1, 4, 7, 10; 10:19) and had not been killed according to the dictates of Jewish law. Whether Christians could eat such meat was a topic raised at the Jerusalem Council (Acts 15:29; 21:25). In contrast, Paul states that one may eat this meat (1 Cor 10:25), but he lays out clear qualifications that look to the effect of a person's actions on other members of the Christian community. If eating this meat is going to embolden a fellow believer to eat in violation of their conscience, best not eat the meat (1 Cor 8:7-13). The weak believer cannot disassociate the meat from the cult and is thereby drawn back into idolatry. Community welfare trumps knowledge and the exercise of freedom.

A final table custom is the invitation to eat at someone's house. Should a Christian go and eat in a nonbeliever's house even if the meat served was sacrificed to idols? Paul raises this possibility in 1 Corinthians 10:27-30. Dining in a private home was commonplace, as those of higher status and great wealth would invite their friends and clients to a banquet. Social obligations within patron/client relationships would place a demand on one of lower honor

[66]Greg H. R. Horsley and Stephen Llewelyn, eds., *New Documents Illustrating Early Christianity* (North Ryde, NSW: The Ancient History Documentary Research Centre, Macquarie University, 1981–), 1.5.

to respond positively to the invite. In his fifth satire, "How Clients Are Entertained," Juvenal paints the scene: "So if after a couple of months it is his pleasure to invite his forgotten client, lest the third place on the lowest couch should be unoccupied, and he says to you, 'Come and dine with me,' you are in seventh heaven! what more can you desire?" In a community filled with those of lower status (1 Cor 1:26), this situation must have been common.

Paul's approach is consistent: one may go and eat at the banquet in a home and should not ask questions about the provenance of the meat (1 Cor 10:27). If, however, someone remarks that the meat is idol meat, it is best not to eat it for the sake of the other's conscience. The person is likely one who is weak in the faith (1 Cor 10:28-30; see 1 Cor 8:7-8). Love for the other guides the way forward (1 Cor 8:1). Christians should be those who do not "seek their own good, but the good of others" (1 Cor 10:24; 12:7).

In 1 Corinthians 9, Paul takes up the issue of freedom, in the first instance with reference to his apostleship (1 Cor 9:1). But the application is much wider, both for the Corinthians and the contemporary reader. Some Corinthians believed that to have freedom meant that one should make full use of it in all circumstances. Paul had already warned them about the deleterious effects of using one's freedom if it meant harm to others: "Be careful, however, that the exercise of your rights does not become a stumbling block to the weak" (1 Cor 8:9), that is, something that will lead them into sin (Rom 14:13, 15, 21; Gal 5:13). The Corinthian problem with freedom also manifests in the way its exercise leads them to exceed all moral bounds and brings them into activities that are out of bounds even for the free person in Christ (1 Cor 6:12-20; 10:23-24).

Paul puts himself forward as a free person who voluntary limits his freedom for a higher good. As Margaret Mitchell remarks, "In chap. 9, in the form of a mock defense speech, Paul presents himself as the example of the proper non-divisive, conciliatory behavior to which he calls the Corinthians."[67] For example, he claims that he has the right to live from the gospel (1 Cor 9:3-11, 13-14), but instead of affirming this right and demanding support, he has not made use of this (1 Cor 9:12, 18, 23). Not using one's rights does not mean losing one's rights. There is a small step from this to the concerns that Paul expresses about the way the Corinthians are handling the issue of idol meats. We should read the argument of 1 Corinthians 9 in the glare of the concluding affirmation of 1 Corinthians 8: "Therefore, if what I eat causes my brother or sister to fall into sin, I will never eat meat again, so that I will not cause them to fall."

The Corinthian church was marked by division and diverse practices, and they handled the strife similar to the way people managed political strife. To be conciliatory in conflict and to yield to the position of one's opponents means losing some of one's own freedom.[68] Compromise implies loss of one's rights. Some ancient voices rose against such approaches to conflict. Aelius Aristides appeals in one of his speeches: "You are proud of the fact that you are free. . . . Therefore if for no other reason, then for the sake of being free and doing what you wish, abandon this present conduct so that you may not suffer anxieties which will be as great as your present audacity." In order to maintain harmony, he

[67]Margaret M. Mitchell, *Paul and the Rhetoric of Reconciliation. An Exegetical Investigation of the Language and Composition of 1 Corinthians* (Louisville, KY: Westminster/John Knox, 1991), 130.
[68]Mitchell, *Paul and the Rhetoric of Reconciliation*, 130-38.

argues, one must at times forgo the use of freedoms. He continues: "Imitate the form and fashion of a household. What is this? There are rulers in a household, the fathers of the sons and the masters of the slaves. How do these administer their households well? Whenever the rulers do not think that they can do anything, but voluntarily give up some of their authority."[69]

Paul adopts a similar approach. Overall community concerns, especially the concern for others, take precedence over individual or factional claims. Mitchell concludes,

> Political realism dictates that everyone cannot have their way in everything. What is required for concord is a redefinition of freedom from an individualistic to a corporate perspective. Factionalism can be stopped only by compromise, where each side ceases to think only of what it is their right to do, and instead makes concessions to the other side for the sake of the greater good.[70]

So in 1 Corinthians 9:1-14 he speaks of his rights, in 1 Corinthians 9:15-18 he affirms that he does not use them, in 1 Corinthians 9:19-23 he states that his purpose is to serve others, and in 1 Corinthians 9:24-27 he shows how he exercises self-discipline, a section that is the prelude to 1 Corinthians 10.

While I once taught that 1 Corinthians 8–10 did not hold immediate relevance for contemporary Christians, Rose brought a different perspective from Nigeria. Our contemporary strife in society and the church also move me to regard these chapters as some of the most relevant for the American church. Cultural differences certainly played a part in Paul's discussion in this community of Jews who would not eat idol meat ever and Gentiles who were accustomed to the practice. Economics and social rank played a role as well, since those with greater wealth bought meat and held banquets that others were obliged to attend. In facing the Corinthians' factionalism and strife, Paul places love and the well-being of others as the highest virtue while never once letting loose of his commitment to freedom. Paul prescribes empathy that sees and hears the effects one's theology and actions have on others rather than an approach to community that is full steam ahead, hang the consequences. In the midst of strife, Paul is a community builder across the social divides of the day and also across the theological divides. He never derides the weak but opts for building up others rather than holding an unwavering commitment to prideful use of knowledge (1 Cor 8:1). Indeed, true knowledge is not simply found in the confession but in the exercise of love (1 Cor 8:2). Self-referential righteous arrogance and theological sword-wielding do not promote love and demonstrate that one does not truly know.

About worship (1 Corinthians 11:2–14:40). In these chapters Paul addresses issues arising within corporate worship, touching first on proper male and female conduct in the gathering of the saints (1 Cor 11:2-16), moving on to problems surrounding the Lord's Supper (1 Cor 11:17-34), and finally discussing the gifts of the Spirit in relationship to the body of Christ and the virtue of love (1 Cor 12:1–14:40). Gordon Fee suggests that there may be another overarching theme that ties together these chapters with the discussion on the resurrection in 1 Corinthians 15.[71] In 1 Corinthians 11:2 Paul refers to the "traditions" he

[69]Aelius Aristides, *Oration* 24.22, 32-33, cited in Mitchell, *Paul and the Rhetoric of Reconciliation*, 130-31.

[70]Mitchell, *Paul and the Rhetoric of Reconciliation*, 131.

[71]Gordon D. Fee, *The First Epistle to the Corinthians*, New International Commentary on the New Testament (Grand Rapids, MI: Eerdmans, 1987), 491-92.

handed down to them. The same language about the transmission of sacred traditions appears in 1 Corinthians 11:23 regarding the Lord's Supper and 1 Corinthians 15:1-3 in the discussion of the apostolic preaching and the resurrection. The traditions were the central truths of the faith, passed on orally from the apostles to the churches before the composition of the Gospels and Epistles. The reference is not to "human tradition" (Col 2:8) but rather to those that come from the Lord (1 Cor 11:23) or have been handed down by his authoritative messengers, the apostles (2 Thess 2:15; 3:6; Rom 6:17). The Corinthians affirmed that they faithfully kept the traditions the apostle had handed down to them (1 Cor 11:2), but Paul questions their judgment when it comes to the Lord's Supper and the teaching on the resurrection (1 Cor 11:16-17, 22; 15:3). Throughout this section, Paul questions whether they have truly held the sacred traditions they received. His judgment is at variance with their assessment of themselves.

Gender roles (1 Corinthians 11:2-16). Paul includes an extensive reflection on head coverings in the context of worship (1 Cor 11:4-5). The discussion intersects his understanding of gender roles, with a particular focus on the marriage relationship (1 Cor 11:3). The section is best read in light of Paul's understanding of human origins, which is rooted in the Old Testament (Gen 1:27; 3:16; 5:1; 9:6; Wis 2:23; 1 Cor 11:3, 7-12), his observation from nature about birth (1 Cor 11:12), and head-covering customs in the symbolic world of Paul's day.

Ancient reliefs carved in stone often depict Roman men and women with their heads covered, using part of their garment brought up over the head. In marriage scenes women appear with the *stola* covering their heads, and in reliefs depicting sacrifices those serving as priests have part of their toga draped over their heads.[72] Plutarch, the priest of Apollo at Delphi (located about 125 miles from Corinth), discusses head coverings extensively in his book *Roman Questions* (266C-267C), wherein he explains Roman customs to the Greeks. Plutarch's discussion centers on worship and honor. He asks, "Why is it that when they worship the gods, they cover their heads, but when they meet any of their fellow-men worthy of honour, if they happen to have the toga over the head, they uncover?" (266C-D). He comments, however, that they sacrificed to the god called "Honor" with the head uncovered (266F). On the other hand, women commonly had their head covered while in mourning (though there were exceptions, Plutarch notes in 267A-B). He notes, "It is more usual for women to go forth in public with their heads covered and men with their heads uncovered" (267A-B). Head covering for women was associated with marriage (267B-C).

Paul walks into this ancient discussion, commenting on the Corinthian Christian women's practice of uncovering their heads while in worship and men's habit of covering their heads (1 Cor 11:4-6). Paul regards such actions as dishonoring their respective heads (1 Cor 11:3). Women may have uncovered because they viewed the faith as liberation from marital obligations, and men may have covered since they regarded their role as priests within the community. While we cannot be sure of the exact cause, Paul rejects both practices. Men should uncover in worship—contrary to Roman custom—and women should remain covered—in harmony with Roman custom. In

[72]An easily accessible source for illustrations is Everett Ferguson, *Backgrounds of Early Christianity* (Grand Rapids, MI: Eerdmans, 2003), 73, 189, 191. There is no evidence for the contemporary Jewish custom of head covering for men in worship until the second century CE.

one go, Paul distances the Corinthians from common Gentile practices in worship and affirms the symbolic world of the marriage relationship. In our contemporary symbolic world of marriage, the wedding ring may serve as a rough conceptual equivalent. We should not, however, draw the line between Paul's injunction to men as equal to taking off a fedora or baseball cap in church. More was at stake.

Contemporary discussions have laser-focused on 1 Corinthians 11:3: "But I want you to realize that the head of every man is Christ, and the head of the woman is the man, and the head of Christ is God." The second clause may be understood as the NIV footnote: the head "of the wife is her husband" (so the NRSV: "the husband is the head of the wife").[73] Does "head" map to the concept of "having authority over," or is the mapping to the concept of "source" or "origin"? The former sense is rare in Greek literature, although LXX translates *rosh*, the ruler of a community (Judg 11:11; 2 Sam 22:44; Ps 18:43; Is 7:8-9; Lam 1:5), with the Greek term for "head" (*kephalē*). On the other hand, "head" could mean the "source" of a river (Herodotus, *Histories* 4.91) or have the theological meaning of "source," as in the Orphic fragment (21a), "Zeus is the head, Zeus the middle, and from Zeus all things are completed."[74] Paul's use is closer to the latter, since the core of his discussion is about origins in 1 Corinthians 11:8-12, where he references the story of human creation and the natural process of birth (woman came from man, man comes from woman). His reflection on headship elsewhere points to the idea of source rather than rulership (Eph 4:15-16; Col 1:18-20; 2:19). Paul's teaching stresses honor and mutuality (see Gal 3:28) and not dominance and control, the latter being the common approach to the passage among many contemporary Christians who support patriarchal views.

Peter and Paul do not allow the faith to become weaponized against the institution of marriage, nor do they use the faith to support male dominance (1 Pet 3:7; Eph 5:25-33). Both show how married women may live as Christians within the extant structures of society (1 Pet 3:1-6; Eph 5:22-24), curtail male dominance and control (1 Pet 3:7; Eph 5:25-33), and leave open the door for a redefinition of the nature of the institution. Although Peter and Paul call slaves to be subordinate to masters (1 Pet 2:18-25; Eph 6:5-8), the church has been instrumental in changing the orders of Roman society and so eventually sought to abolish slavery.[75] Christians today should not conclude that the apostles wished to endorse Roman conceptions of marriage as permanent for all time. The character of the marriage bond has changed in light of love, the fundamental equality of men and women as people made in the image of God, and the revision of extant social structures in relation to Christ (Gal 3:28).

Paul and Peter are on the move in their radical teaching that men should love and honor their wives. They do not endorse

[73]The passage is not about male authority over all women. Paul does not extend counsel regarding marriage to gender norms for all society. Both women and men are created in the image of God (Gen 1:26-27), sharing equally in moral and mental capacities and in social responsibilities.

[74]Henry George Liddell, Robert Scott, and Henry Stuart Jones, *A Greek-English Lexicon*, 9th ed. with revised supplement (Oxford: Clarendon, 1996), 945.

[75]"To subordinate" (*hypotassō*) emerges from the Roman concept of "the orders," where some were superordinate (such as the emperor or masters) and some were subordinate (such as ordinary citizens and slaves). The apostles teach how to live out the faith amid existing orders but leave open the question of changing the orders in light of God's creation and redemption. Few Christians today would endorse government under the rule of a king or emperor, and fewer still regard slavery as a permanent institution. The marriage relationship, though permanent, should not be fixed within Roman conceptions of the institution. See John H. Elliott, *1 Peter*, AB (New York: Doubleday, 2000), 486-89.

systems, ecclesial or familial, that are patriarchal to the exclusion of women's principal roles in either. Women, like men, may pray or prophesy in the church (1 Cor 11:4-5). They are in full possession of gifts that serve the whole congregation (1 Cor 12:7). Women such as Phoebe (Rom 16:1-2), Priscilla (Acts 18:24-26), Nympha (Col 4:15), and others had leadership and teaching roles in the churches.[76] The theology and pattern of female leadership in the church was laid down in the New Testament and continues to be developed today.

The Lord's Supper (1 Corinthians 11:17-34). The Lord's Supper began as a common meal that Jesus celebrated with his disciples at the time of the Jewish Passover (Mt 26:17-30). The practice of celebrating the memorial of Jesus' death, resurrection, covenant, and coming continued in the early church and remains a central celebration of the church until this day.[77] As the gospel went forth from the Jewish confines in Judea out into the Gentile world, it entered a conceptual world where banqueting was a common practice. Voluntary associations were common, and as Valeriy Alikin notes, "Almost all of these societies were local, consisting of people living in the same city; in general, they were small, with an average membership of less than fifty. . . . The common feature of all the clubs and associations was that on certain occasions their members dined together. Communal feasts were held at regular intervals," as occurred in the church with its weekly gatherings. "The meetings had a bipartite structure: they consisted of a supper . . . and a symposium . . . afterwards."[78] Banqueting also occurred in the confines of temples, where the meal was celebrated in the presence of the deity (see comments on 1 Cor 8:9-13; 10:1-22), but also within private homes (1 Cor 10:27-30).

Social stratification marked such meals (Lk 14:7-11), with better food and wine offered to those who ranked higher up the social scale. In his fifth satire, Juvenal describes the scene at one such occasion: "And what a dinner after all! You are given wine that fresh-clipped wool would refuse to suck up, and which soon converts your revellers into Corybants. . . . The great man himself drinks wine bottled in the days when Counsels wore long hair. . . . Tomorrow he will drink a vintage from the hills of Alba or Setia" that has been well aged. As for the food, "See now that huge lobster being served to my lord, all garnished with asparagus. . . . Before you is placed on a tiny plate a shrimp hemmed in by half an egg—a fit banquet for the dead" (*Satires* 5.25-36, 80-91). Such social stratification marks the Corinthians' celebration of the Lord's Supper in this community, where most rank lower on the social scale, including slaves (1 Cor 1:26; 7:21-22). The disparity between the classes is so marked that "one person remains hungry and another gets drunk" (1 Cor 11:21). Instead of eating the common Lord's Supper, "some of you go ahead with your own private suppers" (1 Cor 11:21). In banquets held by voluntary associations, people usually had access to better-quality food than they normally could eat, but this was far from the case in the Corinthian Christians' celebration, which mimicked more socially stratified gatherings.[79] Paul does

---

[76]See, for example, Dorothy A. Lee, *The Ministry of Women in the New Testament: Reclaiming the Biblical Vision for Church Leadership* (Grand Rapids, MI: Baker Academic, 2021); Cynthia Long Westfall, *Paul and Gender: Reclaiming the Apostle's Vision for Men and Women in Christ* (Grand Rapids, MI: Baker Academic, 2016); Bonnie Thurston, *Women in the New Testament: Questions and Commentary* (Eugene, OR: Wipf & Stock, 1998).

[77]Valeriy A. Alikin, *The Earliest History of the Christian Gathering: Origin, Development and Content of the Christian Gathering in the First to Third Centuries* (Leiden: Brill, 2010).

[78]Alikin, *Earliest History of the Christian Gathering*, 18.

[79]Alikin, *Earliest History of the Christian Gathering*, 19.

not commend them for allowing social disparities to mark their common celebration. They should eat together or eat at home (1 Cor 11:33-34). The Christian gathering is to be a place where hierarchies based on class or gender are dissolved as guests celebrate with one another in the presence of the Lord.

The core of the Christian banquet is the Lord's Supper, where the bread and the wine celebrate their union with Christ, their participation in the new covenant, and the community he formed (1 Cor 11:23-26). Paul harks back to the words and actions of the Lord Jesus (Mt 26:26-29; Mk 14:22-25; Lk 22:14-20) as he reminds the rich that the meal is not for abundant feasting or becoming inebriated but rather to commemorate the death of the Lord and to proclaim that death until he returns. "Received" and "passed on" are words pointing to the transmission of sacred tradition (see 1 Cor 15:3). Paul reminds them of what they already know. The bread represents his body, and the words "which is for you" allude to his propitiatory death (Is 53:12; see 1 Cor 15:3; Gal 3:13; 2 Cor 5:21; Rom 5:6, 8). "In remembrance of me" should be read in light of the Jewish perspective that held that remembrance was more than a mental process but included a participation in what one remembered (Ex 13:3, 9; Deut 16:3). When Jesus took the cup of wine (1 Cor 11:25), he referenced the new covenant of Jeremiah 31:31-34 (see Ex 24). As in the first covenant, the new is ratified with the blood of the Lamb (Ex 24:8), but the new includes the forgiveness of sins. In the act, there is a visible proclamation of the gospel and an affirmation of the eschatological expectation of the Lord's return (1 Cor 11:26; Mt 26:29). Past, present, and future all coalesce in the Supper.

Paul refers to the way that the Lord's Supper has become yet another venue where the Corinthians' social divisions are manifest (1 Cor 11:18, 27-32) and offers the most solemn warning to those who continue to celebrate the Supper in the context of division. If the gathering is practiced in a sinful way, it will bring dire consequences. Paul's hope, however, is for redemption, as always (1 Cor 11:32).

The Lord's Supper stands as a witness against the contemporary church, which divides itself along socioeconomic, gender, and ethnic lines. The vision of the church Paul promotes is rooted in the Supper that Jesus inaugurated, where all had an equal place at the table, regardless of language or age, skin color or sex, riches or poverty. The table, the cup, and the bread do not belong to any one group that invites others to participate but rather belongs to all as members of the same family.

Spiritual gifts (1 Corinthians 12:1–14:40). First Corinthians 12–14 is part of a larger section that addresses questions about public worship (1 Cor 11:2–14:40). At the beginning of the long discourse on spiritual gifts, Paul includes the expression *peri de*, which may indicate that he is responding to yet another question the Corinthians put to him (see 1 Cor 7:1 and comments). Here Paul focuses on the gifts of the Spirit in the worship of the church. The heart of the teaching is 1 Corinthians 13, where Paul clarifies that the most important virtue for community life is love, the primary fruit of the Spirit (Gal 5:22). Paul does not suggest that love is a substitute for spiritual gifts but instead affirms that the gifts are to be used out of love for the other (see 1 Cor 12:7).

Paul earlier accused the church of being fleshly (1 Cor 3:1-3) and immature in the faith. Despite their moral infancy, Paul recognized that they did not lack spiritual gifts (1 Cor 1:7). In other words, the presence of the gifts in the church is not a sure sign of spiritual maturity. Indeed, the gifts of the Spirit have become sources of pride and division. Some are arrogant because of the gifts they exercise (1 Cor 12:21), while others consider themselves to be inferior and not essential members of the church (1 Cor 12:15-17). Others try to bring abuses of the gifts under control and attempt to prohibit the use of at least one spiritual gift (1 Cor 14:39; see 1 Thess 5:19-20).

Paul's argument in 1 Corinthians 12–14 divides into five sections; the first is about the gifts (1 Cor 12:1-11), the second about the body of Christ (1 Cor 12:12-27), the third returns to the gifts (1 Cor 12:28-31), the fourth is a discourse on love (1 Cor 13:1-13), and the fifth turns back to the spiritual gifts. In the same way, Paul begins Romans 12 with a reflection on the body of Christ (Rom 12:4-5), then moves to discuss the gifts (Rom 12:6-8), and finally concludes with a brief section on love (Rom 12:8-9). The apostle's teaching concerning the body of Christ is not an ontological description of the nature of the church but rather a functional analysis of life together as the church. It is a piece of practical theology. In Paul's view, the church functions as the body of Christ when each member uses their gift for the benefit of others (1 Cor 12:7) and for the church's building up (1 Cor 14:3-5, 12, 26; see 1 Pet 4:10-11). Herein lies Paul's antidote to the factionalism that has beset the Corinthian congregation—spiritual service to one another for the good of the whole.

Paul first differentiates Christian worship and confession inspired by the Spirit of God from what occurred in the various religions of the day. Being carried away by some god or demon (1 Cor 10:20-21) is not the same as the inspiration of the Spirit of God (1 Cor 12:1-3). Lucian talks about such alien power: "A sort of god carries us away wherever he wills, and it is impossible to resist him" (*Dialogues of the Dead* 19.1). Lucan discusses the oracle at Delphi, not far from Corinth, saying, "For, if the god enters the bosom of any, untimely death is her penalty, or her reward, for having received him; because the human frame is broken up by the sting and surge of that frenzy, and the stroke from heaven shatters the brittle life" (5.115-119). Paul views the Spirit's work as something other than uncontrolled, demonic inspired frenzy, since "the spirits of prophets are subject to the control of prophets" (1 Cor 14:32).

Paul points the Corinthians to unity amid diversity in 1 Corinthians 12:4-6. The basis of unity is that all the gifts have a divine trinitarian source: the Spirit (1 Cor 12:4), the Lord (1 Cor 12:5), and God the Father (1 Cor 12:6). He retraces the theme of unity in diversity over and over again in the following verses (1 Cor 12:12, 14, 19-20, 27; see Rom 12:4-5); unity does not imply uniformity. Paul calls all these gifts *charismata*, that is, manifestations of the grace of God (*charis*) inspired by the Spirit of God. Peter states the perspective plainly: "Each of you should use whatever gift you have received to serve others, as faithful stewards of God's grace in its various forms" (1 Pet 4:10). Like Peter, Paul reminds the Corinthians that no person among them is devoid of a spiritual gift and that the gifts are given to benefit others: "Now to each one the manifestation of the Spirit is given for the common good" (1 Cor 12:7). Paul names the gifts in 1 Corinthians 12:8-10, but the list is hardly comprehensive (see 1 Cor 12:27-31). Peter's taxonomy of the gifts is simpler; there are gifts of speaking and gifts of service (1 Pet 4:11). Such gifts did not vanish at the end of the first century CE.[80]

The discussion about the variety of gifts and the body would have sounded familiar to the

[80]See Talbert, *Reading Corinthians*, 105-6, for reference to the way the gifts were active in the first centuries.

Corinthians (1 Cor 12:12-31). The metaphor of the body appears repeatedly in ancient literature; Paul is not speaking about a mystical union that melds all believers into a body. Rather, this same imagery often appears where an author speaks out against discord in community, especially political discord. Mitchell assembles many examples of this use of the metaphor.[81] For example, in Livy we hear Menenius Agrippa speak about the revolt of many members of the body against the belly (2.32.9–2.33.1). "This fable," Mitchell notes, "is told in a deliberative speech urging the plebs to cease from *seditio* and work for *concordia*."[82] The plebs belonged to the lower classes of society. The body metaphor frequently speaks about the political organization of society, stresses the interdependence of the various members of the body, and contends against discord in community. Aelius Aristedes talks about the divided people of Rhodes, saying, "Rather you destroy it [your city] by your actions, while you honor it with your speech, and you await the victory of Cleomentes the Laconian, who chopped up his [own] body, beginning with his feet." He goes on to ask, "And how shall you differ from the women who tore Pentheus apart when you yourselves have torn apart with your own hands the body of the city which you all share?" Plutarch, like Paul, highlights the necessary members of the body: "And yet the illustration of such common use by brothers Nature has placed at no great distance from us; on the contrary, in the body itself she has contrived to make most of the necessary parts double and brothers and twins: hands, feet, ears, nostrils" (*Moralia* 478D; see 1 Cor 12:22). Those who are most necessary are of the upper classes. Contrary to the common discourse on the body politic, which focused on the hierarchies of society and the need to maintain them, Paul's discourse focuses in on mutuality and the honor ascribed to even the lowliest member of the body. All members are necessary and should therefore receive honor (1 Cor 12:21-26). Down to the end, Paul opts for unity in diversity, helping them recognize that all the Corinthians are members of the body, but not all possess the same gifts (1 Cor 12:27-31).

Paul's discussion about love (1 Cor 12:31–13:13) is the best-known passage from 1 Corinthians and likely the most recognizable discourse from all his writings. Surprisingly for us, Paul's discussion is not about the marriage bond but rather life together in community. While the gifts are important in the life of the church, the virtue of love must prevail. Paul does not place love over against the gifts but lets the church know that they should be other-directed in their use of the gifts, which are in the end for the welfare of others (1 Cor 12:7). The gifts and all personal sacrifice have no value unless they are demonstrations of love (1 Cor 13:1-3). In 1 Corinthians 13:4-7 Paul describes the character of this love, and then in 1 Corinthians 13:8-13 he lays out its permanence and superiority.

The love Paul describes is not an attitude or emotion but a commitment to the well-being of the other. As such, it bears up under injustices ("patient"); does good to all, even to those who do it evil ("kind"); does not desire what belongs to another ("not envy," although the thought may be a counterpoint to rivalry as in 1 Cor 3:3); does not pridefully parade its own virtues ("not boast"); is not arrogant ("not proud"); does not treat others shamefully ("does not dishonor others"); seeks the best for others and not itself ("not self-seeking"); is not quick tempered ("not easily angered"); does

[81]Mitchell, *Paul and the Rhetoric*, 157-64.

[82]Mitchell, *Paul and the Rhetoric*, 158.

not seek to retaliate ("keeps no record of wrongs"); does not delight in the wrong others do ("not delight in evil") but identifies with the good and honest ("rejoices with the truth"). Love always protects, believes, hopes, and perseveres in all circumstances (1 Cor 13:4-8). Indeed, love will endure even when the gifts are no longer needed due to Christ's revelation (1 Cor 13:8-13). Love is permanent. Paul's perspective is eschatological, looking forward to the time of the revelation of Christ (1 Cor 13:12). The present time is an era of partial revelation that the apostle compares to looking into a polished mirror of metal, but the time of full revelation, face to face, is coming (see 1 Pet 1:7).

In 1 Corinthians 14, Paul speaks about the way that the gifts should function in the context of the assembly of the Corinthian believers, with special attention given to the gifts of tongues and prophecy. The love that members of the church show one another is not a substitute for the gifts (1 Cor 14:1). Rather, the gifts are for the edification or building up of the church (*oikodomeō* in 1 Cor 14:4, 17; *oikodomē* in 1 Cor 14:3, 5, 12, 26). In ancient literature, the terms referred to the construction of buildings such as temples or houses or could have a metaphorical sense, as here. In the Old Testament, God can build Israel and establish her as a nation (Jer 1:10; 24:6). Jesus utilizes the imagery to talk of establishing the church (Mt 16:18), and Acts speaks of the founding the Christian communities the same way (Acts 9:31). Paul describes his ministry as one of building, not destroying (2 Cor 10:8), save for tearing down false teaching (2 Cor 10:4-5). Previously Paul warned church leaders to take care with how they build (1 Cor 3:10-17). Now Paul tasks Corinthian believers with building the community through their ministry to one another via the gifts of the Spirit (see 1 Thess 5:11). Building is opposite of the destructive and divisive way the Corinthian church is functioning. Love is the motivation, which emanates in the mutual activity of building up the church instead of tearing it down (1 Cor 8:1; Eph 4:16). Building up means more than "a pale ideal of inward-looking personal development" but rather points to "constructive as opposed to destructive relations."[83]

The second major issue running through this chapter is the maintenance of proper order in the use of the gifts, especially tongues, interpretation of tongues, and prophecy. In 1 Corinthians 14:1-25 the overarching concern is that tongues should be interpreted in the assembly so that the church may be edified or well-constructed (1 Cor 14:5, 13). If tongues are not interpreted, prophecy has more value than tongues, since prophecy builds up the church. Prophecy is the greater gift due to its impact on the church (1 Cor 14:5, 19, 23-24). Paul carefully argues that tongues should not be suppressed, although proper order should be maintained in community gatherings (1 Cor 14:39-40; see 1 Thess 5:19-22).

Paul's statement about women in the church merits careful attention (1 Cor 14:34-35). Some, like Fee, have argued that these verses are a textual interpolation by a scribe since the Greek manuscripts do not uniformly have these verses in this position, and their teaching appears to be at variance to what Paul said previously about women's active participation during community worship (1 Cor 11:5, 13).[84]

---

[83]Edwin Judge, "Cultural Conformity and Innovation in Paul: Some Clues from Contemporary Documents," *TynBul* 35 (1984): 23-24.

[84]Fee, *1 Corinthians*, 699-710; Hans Conzelmann, *1 Corinthians. A Commentary on the First Epistle to the Corinthians*, Hermeneia (Philadelphia: Fortress, 1975), 246; Richard A. Horsley, *1 Corinthians* Abingdon New Testament Commentaries (Nashville: Abingdon, 1998), 188-89; and see the NRSV.

This text also "stands in tension with much of Paul's teaching in this period (esp. Rom 16:1-7), but could be explained along the lines of 11:2-16," where the apostle discusses head coverings.[85] Paul is concerned about the disruption of proper order in this chapter as well.[86] Either this passage is a non-Pauline addition to the text or, if genuine, should be viewed within the context of the disruptions within the Corinthian community, similar to the way some women were throwing off head coverings in 1 Corinthians 11. The apostle's affirmations elsewhere about women's roles in this and other communities provide clarifications of Paul's overall teaching on women in the church. The apostle affirms their active part but, as with men as well, does not endorse disruptive activity in the church.

First Corinthians 12–14 is a symphony of inclusion. Every person in the community has a place at the table, not because some of higher social status granted it but because the Lord has given each a gift. Every person is essential and worthy of honor since what they bring contributes to the whole. The church will not be fully built up unless each person recognizes and is enabled to make their contribution. Early Christian worship was dynamic, inspired by the Spirit, a place where everyone could participate (1 Cor 14:26). First Corinthians 12; 14 are central texts in contemporary discussions about charismatic gifts in the church, as indeed they should be. But the theological implications of the chapters are broader. If indeed all members of the church have a role to play, what then of the voices and theological perspectives of those members of the church who live outside the West and the traditional corridors of theological reflection in the North Atlantic region? We are currently witnessing a global rise in biblical and theological reflection coming from Africa, Asia, Latin America, and Oceania. And within North America, African American, Asian American, Latinx, and Indigenous Christian communities are offering fresh visions of the faith and deepening our understanding of the gospel of Jesus Christ. As Justo González said in 1990, there is a "macroreformation" occurring as churches around the globe are "self-theologizing" in dialogue with Scripture, inherited theological traditions, and their contexts.

> From Asia, Africa, and Latin America, as well as from ethnic minorities in North America and in other places, and from women all over the world, have come stunning visions of the meaning of the gospel, and a number of theologians in the traditional centers of theological learning have seen the value of these insights. The dialogue that has resulted means that theology will never be the same again.[87]

This volume represents part of that macroreformation that González celebrates.[88]

Yet most seminary and Christian college and university curricula offer few, if any, courses on these global developments, and syllabi are largely devoid of bibliography from the Majority World, leaving students and Christian leaders wondering whether anything good can come out of "Nazareth" (Jn 1:46). Majority World and minority

---

[85]Keener, *1–2 Corinthians*, 117-18.

[86]Thiselton, *First Epistle to the Corinthians*, 1150-61.

[87]Justo L. González, *Mañana. Christian Theology from a Hispanic Perspective* (Nashville: Abingdon, 1990), 49.

[88]The bibliography emanating from the Majority World and minority communities in North America and beyond is legion. Various accessible introductions are available, such as Jeffrey P. Greenman and Gene L. Green, eds., *Global Theology in Evangelical Perspective: Exploring the Contextual Nature of Theology and Mission* (Downers Grove, IL: IVP Academic, 2012); Gene L. Green, Stephen T. Pardue, and K. K. Yeo, eds., *Majority World Theology. Christian Doctrine in Global Context* (Downers Grove, IL: IVP Academic, 2020).

authors and teachers hear a contemporary version of 1 Corinthians 12:21: "The eye cannot say to the hand, 'I don't need you!' And the head cannot say to the feet, 'I don't need you!'" Women have been relegated to the role of observers rather than participants in theological discussion within many theological faculties and churches, as if their perspectives were suspect and carry no value. The theological academy of the West, especially those that represent more conservative theological positions, have neglected to hear Paul's explanation of God's plan: "But God has put the body together, giving greater honor to the parts that lacked it, so that there should be no division in the body, but that its parts should have equal concern for each other" (1 Cor 12:24-25). Christians through history, around the globe, within minoritized communities, and women from all quarters have a place at the table since this is their table, set by the Lord and inspired by the Spirit of God. Racial prejudice, patriarchy, and misogyny have no place at this table. As the final document of the Latin American Theological Fellowship meeting, CLADE III, declares: "La persona del Espíritu Santo actúa con poder en el mundo. Lo hace primordialmente por medio de la Iglesia ortogándole vida, poder y dones para su desarrollo, madurez y misión."[89] All members of the body are necessary, regardless of their location in the world, society, or history.

The resurrection of the dead (1 Corinthians 15:1-58). The most extensive discussion of the resurrection of the dead in the New Testament appears here in 1 Corinthians 15. Paul consistently affirms the resurrection of the body (Rom 8:11, 23). In one of his earliest writings, 1 Thessalonians, Paul addresses the topic as well but not the to the extent that he does here (1 Thess 4:13-18). The Thessalonians were ignorant about the destiny of deceased believers (1 Thess 4:13), but the situation in Corinth is different. Some Corinthian believers have denied the resurrection of believers (1 Cor 15:12), most likely rejecting the teaching they received from the apostle. Their denial most likely stemmed from the common belief that death was final and that the gods could not raise dead bodies. This idea was absent from Greek and Roman thought. In his play *Eumenides*, Aeschylus has the god Apollo say, "But when once a man has died, and the dust has sucked up his blood, there is no rising again" (647-648; no *anastasis*, "resurrection," as in 1 Cor 15:12-13, 21, 42). There was hopelessness in the face of death since, as the character Corydon says in Theocritus's *Idlyll*, "While there's life there's hope; it's the dead who have none" (4.42). The most common funerary inscription from the period, found in both Latin and Greek, says, "I was not, I was, I am not, I care not."[90] There were notions of an afterlife, as reflected in an epigram from Antipater of Thessalonica: "All men have the same way down to Hades; if mine is quicker than others', I shall be face to face with Minos the sooner."[91] Food offerings were sometimes placed in the tomb or sarcophagus of the dead, but the idea of a resurrection of the body was not found outside Judaism. Although some in the Jewish community denied the possibility of the resurrection of the dead, it was more commonly affirmed. Luke points out the difference between the Sadducees and the Pharisees

[89]"The person of the Holy Spirit works powerfully in the world. He does this primarily through the Church, giving it life, power and gifts for its development, maturity and mission." *CLADE III: Tercer Congreso Latinoamericano de Evangelización, Quito, 1992* (Buenos Aires: FTL, 1993), 856.

[90]Ferguson, *Backgrounds of Early Christianity*, 248-49.

[91]Gow and Page, *Greek Anthology*, 1:35.

on the matter in Acts 23:8 (see Dan 12:2; 2 Macc 7:9, 14, 23; *Pss. Sol.* 3:12).

The beliefs of that day are not far removed from contemporary Christian beliefs about death. Most often, homilies for the dead and discussions about the deceased focus on the person's continued life with the Lord but disembodied existence. "She has gone to be with the Lord," or "He's in a better place now." Mention is hardly ever made of the resurrection of the body, perhaps due to the Western Christian heritage that finds deep roots within Greek thought. Indeed, early on Christians began to slip away from the teaching about the resurrection of the dead in favor of the more Greek notion of the immortality of the soul without a bodily resurrection. For example, one funerary inscription from 145 CE says, "Most excellent earth covers the body of Banao, but my soul is in paradise and rejoices in the company of the young, victorious martyrs."[92] Yet the resurrection of the dead is embedded in both the Nicene-Constantinopolitan Creed (381 CE) and the Apostles' Creed (390 CE): "We look for the resurrection of the dead"; "I believe in . . . the resurrection of the body."

But as God created humans as bodily creatures (Gen 2:7), so God's plan through Christ is to restore humanity through the resurrection of the body. Paul can conceive of an intermediate state between death and resurrection (2 Cor 5:6-8; Phil 1:20-24); his belief is that as Christ was raised from the dead, so too will God raise those who have died. The resurrection of the dead, along with the divine creation of humans, entails the value of human life in the body in the present era. The apostolic faith does not comport with views such as Gnosticism or Docetism that minimize the value of the humanity of women or any ethnic group considered "other" by a society. Paul recognizes that undoing the theology of the resurrection has ethical implications for the present (1 Cor 15:29-34).[93]

So central is the union between the resurrection of the believer and the resurrection of Christ that Paul affirms that to deny the believers' resurrection is in fact to deny Christ's resurrection (1 Cor 15:13, 16; see Phil 3:21). Christ is "the firstfruits of those who have fallen asleep," that is, died (1 Cor 15:20), the first portion of the eternal harvest and the guarantee of the harvest to come. For Paul, the Christian hope is not life eternal in heaven but rather the resurrection. The resurrection of Christ is the core of the gospel. If Christ has not been raised, our faith is in vain and we have no salvation (1 Cor 15:14-19). Christianity is not simply a moral code to follow but the promise of immortality and the triumph over death and hell (1 Cor 15:54-57).

Paul returns to the sacred tradition he handed down to the Corinthians (1 Cor 15:1-2; see 1 Cor 11:2 and comments), which in this text centers on the death and resurrection of Christ (1 Cor 15:3-8). As in 1 Thessalonians 4:14, Paul roots his theology of the resurrection in the early Christian creed regarding Jesus' sufferings and glorification (see Acts 17:3). In 1 Corinthians 15:3 the apostle affirms Christ's atoning death for our sins (2 Cor 5:21; Rom 3:24-26) and that this was God's plan predicted in the Scriptures (Is 53:12). He actually died, was buried, and was raised physically on the third day—not simply as a spirit (1 Cor 15:4; Rom 4:25; Lk 24:36-43). Christianity knows nothing of an Easter faith without the bodily resurrection of Jesus in history. This, too, was

[92]Cited in Richard Lattimore, *Themes in Greek and Latin Epitaphs* (Urbana: University of Illinois Press, 1962), 305. On ancient views regarding the body, see Dale B. Martin, *The Corinthian Body* (New Haven, CT: Yale University Press, 1995), 6-37.
[93]See Jones, *Marks of His Wounds*.

God's plan predicted in biblical texts that offer the earliest testimony to Christ's death and resurrection (Is 53:10-11; Ps 16:10). Paul adds the testimony of the eyewitnesses to Christ's resurrection to confirm the ancient divine testimony (1 Cor 15:5-9).[94] The resurrection of Christ was the center of the apostle's preaching and early Christian faith (1 Cor 15:9-11). Christianity is not simply a moral code but the proclamation of the death of death. In the face of untold suffering, the church has found a way to carry on—whether in the Roman Colosseum, through racial and sexual violence, and through religious persecution against believers.

Paul ties the resurrection of the believers with the resurrection of Christ. To deny the former is to deny the latter (1 Cor 15:12-19). If the dead are not raised, then the conclusion is that Christ has not been raised. And if Christ was not raised, all preaching and faith are useless, the church offers false testimony, we are still in our sins, there is no hope for the dead, and therefore "we are of all people most to be pitied" (1 Cor 15:19). Denial of the resurrection of believers is the beginning of the denial of Christ and the unraveling of the Christian faith. The gospel stands or falls on the reality and theology of the resurrection.

Paul turns to affirm the resurrection of Christ and the believers in 1 Corinthians 15:20-28, affirming that the destinies of Adam and Christ entail the destiny of humanity. Through Adam death entered the world, but through Christ the hope of the resurrection to life comes to those who believe (1 Cor 15:22-23; Rom 5:12-21). The death of death comes through the resurrection of Christ (1 Cor 15:26). If the dead are not raised, Paul asks, why would he subject himself to dangers as he does (1 Cor 15:30-34)? And if the dead are not raised, why do the Corinthians baptize for the dead (1 Cor 15:29)? This verse is one of the most enigmatic of the New Testament and can only be understood as a reflection on a particular Corinthian practice that likely had its roots within ancient funerary practices, possibly post-burial commemorations of the dead.[95] This is no warrant for the Mormon practice of baptizing for the dead. Paul is using the Corinthian custom simply to show that their practice is an implicit affirmation of the resurrection.

In 1 Corinthians 15:35-58 the apostle launches a discussion about the nature of the resurrected body in response to the Corinthians' query (1 Cor 15:35). Doubts prevail since the Corinthians have framed the resurrected body within what they know of common human existence. While Paul affirms the resurrection of the dead, the resurrected body is a different kind of body (1 Cor 15:38), whose characteristics are imperishability so it will not die (1 Cor 15:42), glory and power in the place of dishonor and weakness (1 Cor 15:43). This body is dominated by the power of the Spirit and is not merely natural (1 Cor 15:44; see 1 Pet 3:18). He returns to discuss the nature of Adam and the resurrected Christ (1 Cor 15:44-48), driving to the point that the nature of the resurrected body will be like that of the resurrected Christ (1 Cor 15:49). Paul returns to the latter point in his letter to the Philippians, where he says that Christ "will transform our lowly bodies so that they will be like his glorious body" (Phil 3:21).

As in 1 Thessalonians 4:13-18, Paul says the resurrection of the dead is an eschatological event (1 Cor 15:52). Although he does not

[94]On the importance of testimony in epistemology, see Gene L. Green, *Vox Petri: A Theology of Peter* (Eugene, OR: Cascade, 2019), 19-31.

[95]Richard E. DeMaris, "Corinthian Religion and Baptism for the Dead (1 Corinthians 15:29): Insights from Archaeology and Anthropology," *JBL* 114 (1995): 661-82. For a survey of views, see Thiselton, *First Epistle to the Corinthians*, 1240-49.

mention the parousia or coming of Christ in 1 Corinthians 15, the final consummation will occur when Christ comes (1 Thess 4:15-17). As in 1 Thessalonians, Paul includes some explanation of the transformation that will happen to the living believers (1 Cor 15:51-52; 1 Thess 4:15-17). Paul's thought about the transformation of the living and dead believers is more developed in his epistle to the Corinthians. The expectation of the final redemption of their bodies is calculated to encourage the believers to "stand firm" through all adversity (1 Cor 15:58). There is hope even in the face of death (1 Cor 15:55-57).

The power of Paul's argument surpasses the doubts that some Corinthians expressed about the resurrection of the believers. Paul lets loose with the most astounding vision of life that eclipses death and the despair it levels against the human community (1 Thess 4:13). This teaching, while inspiring hope, is not designed to lead the church to turn from the injustices and violence in cities and rural areas and only offer an eschatological Band-Aid to the problems and pain. These are words directed to those who are sounded by the worst of the human condition—death—in order to offer hope and resolve. Christians have endured through the worst through the centuries. But they have also taken the gospel of life and sought to address the violence of poverty, sickness without health care, racial exploitation, and violence against women and the weakest—the born and the unborn. The hope of the resurrection is not a replacement for the work of justice in the world, as Jesus himself taught (Lk 4:18-19), but it does provide the resolve to carry on in the face of the strongest scorching winds.

About the collection, travel plans, and commendations (1 Corinthians 16:1-18). Before the final greetings to close the letter (1 Cor 16:19-24), Paul takes up two more topics, likely addressing questions he received from the Corinthians (see 1 Cor 7:1 and comments). The first is the collection for the believers in Jerusalem (1 Cor 16:1-4), a concern mentioned over and again in the New Testament (Acts 11:29; Rom 15:26-27; 2 Cor 8–9) and a gracious response to the appeal from James, who was the leader of the Jerusalem church (Gal 2:10). Paul also recounts for them his own travel plans, which include a return to the church (1 Cor 16:5-9), and inserts an embedded letter of commendation for Timothy, whom Paul sent to the church (1 Cor 16:10-11; 4:7; see Phil 2:19-24). Paul responds to the Corinthians' query about the plans Apollos has to return to Corinth (1 Cor 16:12) before giving a final exhortation about watchfulness, having courage, being strong, and doing all out of love (1 Cor 16:13). The section rounds out with a letter of commendation regarding Stephanas, Fortunatus, and Achaicus, who most likely brought the letter from the Corinthians to Paul (1 Cor 16:15-18; 7:1). They also brought support for Paul (1 Cor 16:17; see Phil 4:14-19).

LETTER CLOSING (1 CORINTHIANS 16:19-24)

Paul closes the letter to the Corinthians with final greetings from the churches in the province of Asia as well as Aquila and Priscilla; he was in Ephesus when he wrote the letter (1 Cor 16:19-20; see Acts 18:2, 18, 26; Rom 16:3-5). In addition to bringing greetings, Paul encourages the Corinthians to greet one another with a holy kiss (1 Cor 16:20; Rom 16:16; 2 Cor 13:12; 1 Pet 5:14). Paul is connected and seeks to bring all the churches into network and assure that the churches themselves function as whole units rather than an amalgamation of individuals. Christian community, both across the empire and within the cities where the churches were located, was one of the apostle's highest values. He connected the congregations through his own travels, through sending messengers and letters, and by making sure that the letters were circulated among the churches (Col 4:16). This was the ancient "holy internet" that utilized the roads, sea lanes, and communication technology of the day—letters—penned through amanuenses and carried by messengers. In order to assure that the communications received were indeed from the apostle, he fought against fraud by including a final greeting in his own hand (Gal 6:11; Col 4:18; 2 Thess 3:17). Letter writing in the name of another was known (2 Thess 2:2).

Paul closes the letter with a curse formula (1 Cor 16:22; see 1 Cor 12:3), a prayer for the Lord's coming (1 Cor 16:22)—surprisingly transliterated from Aramaic, a blessing in the form of a wish-prayer (1 Cor 16:23), and an affirmation of his love for the church (1 Cor 16:24).

In the end, Paul loves the Corinthian church. Despite the depth of their internal problems, he approaches them out of deep parental love (1 Cor 4:14-15; Gal 4:19-20; 1 Thess 2:7-12). Above all, he calls the Christian community to the bond of love as the Lord commanded. In an age of fragmentation in the church, ethnic and socioeconomic tensions, gender marginalization, immoral practices, and teaching not aligned with the gospel, 1 Corinthians provides a road map for the way forward. Paul brings the church back to the core of the gospel as he addresses every single issue, turning them to Christ and to one another. The relevance of 1 Corinthians for our day means that it should be taught and studied deeply in our churches, so wanting in understanding of the core of the gospel.

SELECTED BIBLIOGRAPHY

Books

Adams, David Wallace. *Education for Extinction. American Indians and the Boarding School Experience, 1875-1928*. Lawrence: University Press of Kansas, 1995.

Alikin, Valeriy A. *The Earliest History of the Christian Gathering: Origin, Development and Content of the Christian Gathering in the First to Third Centuries*. Leiden: Brill, 2010.

Barrett, C. K. *A Commentary on the First Epistle to the Corinthians*. BNTC. London: Adam and Charles Black, 1971.

Blomberg, Craig. *1 Corinthians*. NIVAC. Grand Rapids, MI: Zondervan Academic, 1995.

Bruce, F. F. *1 and 2 Corinthians*. NCB. London: Oliphants, 1971.

Chow, John N. *Patronage and Power. A Study of Social Networks in Corinth*. LNTS. Sheffield: Sheffield Academic Press, 1992.

CLADE III. Tercer Congreso Latinoamericano de Evangelización, Quito, 1992. Buenos Aires: FTL, 1993.

Conzelmann, Hans. *1 Corinthians: A Commentary on the First Epistle to the Corinthians*. Hermeneia. Philadelphia: Fortress, 1975.

Deissmann, Adolf. *Light from the Ancient East*. Grand Rapids, MI: Baker Academic, 1978.

Deloria, Philip J. *Playing Indian*. New Haven, CT: Yale University Press, 1999.

Deming, Will. *Paul on Marriage and Celibacy: The Hellenistic Background of 1 Corinthians 7*. Grand Rapids, MI: Eerdmans, 2004.

deSilva, David A. *Honor, Patronage, Kinship, and Purity: Unlocking New Testament Culture*. Downers Grove, IL: IVP Academic, 2000.

Elliott, John H. *1 Peter*. AB. New York: Doubleday, 2000.

Engels, Donald. *Roman Corinth: An Alternative Model for the Classical City*. Chicago: University of Chicago Press, 1990.

Epstein, David F. *Personal Enmity in Roman Politics 218-43 BC*. London, New York, and Sydney: Croom Helm, 1987.

Fee, Gordon D. *The First Epistle to the Corinthians*. NICNT. Grand Rapids, MI: Eerdmans, 1987.

Ferguson, Everett. *Backgrounds of Early Christianity*. Grand Rapids, MI: Eerdmans, 2003.

Foulkes, Irene. *Problemas Pastorales en Corinto.* Comentario Exegético-Pastoral a 1 Corintios. San José, Costa Rica: Editorial SEBILA, 2011.

Garland, David E. *1 Corinthians.* BECNT. Grand Rapids, MI: Baker Academic, 2003.

Gow A. S. F., and D. L. Page. *The Greek Anthology: The Garland of Philip and Some Contemporary Epigrams.* 2 vols. Cambridge: Cambridge University Press, 1968.

Gradel, Ittai. *Emperor Worship and Roman Religion.* Oxford: Clarendon Press, 2002.

Green, Gene L. *Vox Petri: A Theology of Peter.* Eugene, OR: Cascade, 2019.

Gundry, Robert H. *The Church and the Tribulation: A Biblical Examination of Posttribulationism.* Grand Rapids, MI: Zondervan, 1973.

Horsley, Richard A. *1 Corinthians.* ANTC. Nashville: Abingdon, 1998.

Johnson, Alan F. *1 Corinthians.* IVPNTC. Downers Grove, IL: IVP Academic, 2004.

Jones, Beth Felker. *Faithful: A Theology of Sex.* Ordinary Theology Series. Grand Rapids, MI: Zondervan, 2015.

Jones, Beth Felker. *Marks of His Wounds: Gender Politics and Bodily Resurrection.* New York: Oxford University Press, 2007.

Keener, Craig S. *1–2 Corinthians.* NCBC. Cambridge: Cambridge University Press, 2005.

Klauck, Hans-Josef. *Ancient Letters and the New Testament: A Guide to Context and Exegesis.* Waco, TX: Baylor University Press, 2006.

Lattimore, Richard. *Themes in Greek and Latin Epitaphs.* Urbana: University of Illinois Press, 1962.

Lee, Dorothy A. *The Ministry of Women in the New Testament. Reclaiming the Biblical Vision for Church Leadership.* Grand Rapids, MI: Baker Academic, 2021.

Martin, Dale B. *The Corinthian Body.* New Haven, CT: Yale University Press, 1995.

Malherbe, Abraham J. *Ancient Literary Theorists.* Atlanta: Scholars, 1988.

Malina, Bruce J. and Jerome H. Neyrey. *Portraits of Paul: An Archaeology of Ancient Personality.* Louisville, KY: Westminster John Knox, 1996.

McCaulley, Esau. *Reading While Black: African American Biblical Interpretation as an Exercise in Hope.* Downers Grove, IL: IVP Academic, 2020.

Mitchell, Margaret M. *Paul and the Rhetoric of Reconciliation: An Exegetical Investigation of the Language and Composition of 1 Corinthians.* Louisville, KY: Westminster/John Knox, 1991.

Murphy-O'Connor, Jerome. *St. Paul's Corinth: Texts and Archaeology.* Collegeville, MN: Liturgical, 2002.

The Negro Bible-The Slave Bible. Select Parts of the Holy Bible, Selected for the use of the Negro Slaves, in the British West India Islands. Intro. by Joseph Lumpkin. Blountsville, AL: Fifth Estate Publishers, 2019.

Noll, Mark A. *The Civil War as a Theological Crisis.* Chapel Hill: University of North Carolina Press, 2006.

Price, S. R. F. *Rituals and Power: The Imperial Cult and Asia Minor.* Cambridge: Cambridge University Press, 1984.

Perkins, Pheme. *First Corinthians.* Paideia. Grand Rapids, MI: Baker Academic, 2012.

Shogren, Gary S. *Primera de Corintios: Un Comentario Exegético-Pastoral.* Viladecavalls (Barcelona), España: Clie, 2021.

Showalter Daniel N. and Steven J. Friesen. *Urban Religion in Roman Corinth.* Interdisciplinary Approaches. Cambridge, MA: Harvard University Press, 2005.

Schreiner, Thomas R. *1 Corinthians: An Introduction and Commentary.* TNTC. Downers Grove, IL: IVP Academic, 2018.

Schmithals, Walter. *Gnosticism in Corinth: An Investigation of the Letters to the Corinthians.* Nashville: Abingdon, 1971.

Spencer, Aída Besançon. *1 Timothy.* NCCS. Eugene, OR: Cascade, 2013.

Stott, John. *Basic Christian Leadership: Biblical Models of Church, Gospel and Ministry.* Downers Grove, IL: IVP Books, 2002.

Talbert, Charles H. *Reading Corinthians: A Literary and Theological Commentary.* Macon, GA: Smyth & Helwys, 2003.

Thiselton, Anthony C. *The First Epistle to the Corinthians*. NIGTC. Grand Rapids, MI: Eerdmans; Carlisle, UK: Paternoster, 2000.

Thurston, Bonnie. *Women in the New Testament: Questions and Commentary*. Eugene, OR: Wipf and Stock, 1998.

Treggiari, Susan. *Roman Marriage: Iusti Coniuges From the Time of Cicero to the Time of Ulpian*. Oxford: Clarendon, 1991.

Trenchard, Ernesto. *La Primera Epístola del Apóstol Pablo a los Corintios: Un Comentario*. Madrid: Literatura Bíblica, 1980.

Twiss, Richard. *Rescuing the Gospel from the Cowboys: A Native American Expression of the Jesus Way*. Downers Grove, IL: InterVarsity Press, 2015.

Westfall, Cynthia Long. *Paul and Gender: Reclaiming the Apostle's Vision for Men and Women in Christ*. Grand Rapids, MI: Baker Academic, 2016.

Winter, Bruce W. *After Paul Left Corinth: The Influence of Secular Ethics and Social Change*. Grand Rapids, MI: Eerdmans, 2001.

Winter, Bruce W. *Philo and Paul Among the Sophists: Alexandrian and Corinthian Responses to a Julio-Claudian Movement*. Grand Rapids, MI: Eerdmans, 2002.

Winter, Bruce W. *Seek the Welfare of the City. Christians as Benefactors and Citizens*. Grand Rapids, MI: Eerdmans; Carlisle, UK: Paternoster, 1994.

Witherington, Ben. *Conflict and Community in Corinth: A Socio-Rhetorical Commentary on 1 and 2 Corinthians*. Grand Rapids, MI: Eerdmans; Carlisle, UK: Paternoster, 1995.

Woodley, Randy. *Living in Color: God's Passion for Ethnic Diversity*. Downers Grove, IL: InterVarsity Press, 2004.

Articles and Book Chapters

Bookidis, Nancy. "The Sanctuaries of Corinth." *Corinth* 20 (2003): 247-59.

Clarke, Andrew D. "Another Corinthian Erastus Inscription." *TynB* 42 (1991): 146-51.

Datiri, Dachollom. "1 Corinthians." In *Africa Bible Commentary. A One-Volume Commentary Written by 70 African Scholars*, edited by Tokunboh Adeyemo, 1377-98. Nairobi: WordAlive; Grand Rapids: Zondervan, 2006.

DeMaris, Richard E. "Corinthian Religion and Baptism for the Dead (1 Corinthians 15:29): Insights from Archaeology and Anthropology." *JBL* 114 (1995): 661-82.

Gill, David W. J. "Achaia." In *The Book of Acts in Its Graeco-Roman Setting*, edited by David W. J. Gill and Conrad Gempf, 433-53. Vol. 2 of *The Book of Acts in its First Century Setting*. Grand Rapids, MI: Eerdmans; Carlisle, UK: Paternoster, 1994.

———. "Erastus the Aedile." *TynB* 40 (1989): 293-301

———. "In Search of the Social Élite in the Corinthian Church." *TynB* 44 (1993): 323-337.

Judge, Edwin A. "Cultural Conformity and Innovation in Paul: Some Clues from Contemporary Documents." *TynB* 35 (1984): 3-24.

Keener, Craig S. "Adultery, Divorce." In *Dictionary of New Testament Backgrounds*, edited by Craig A. Evans and Stanley E. Porter, 6-16. Downers Grove, IL: InterVarsity Press, 2000.

Mitchell, Margaret M. "Concerning *peri de* in 1 Corinthians." *NovT* 31 (1989): 229-56.

Pathrapankal, Joseph. "1 Corinthians." In *Global Bible Commentary*, edited by Daniel Patte, 444-54. Nashville: Abingdon, 2004.

Pawlak, Marcin N. "Corinth after 44 BC: Ethical and Cultural Changes." *Electrum* 20 (2013): 143-62.

Philip, Finny. "1 Corinthians." In *South Asia Bible Commentary*, edited by Brian Wintle, 1555-84. Udaipur, India: Open Door Publications; Grand Rapids, MI: Zondervan, 2015.

Treggiari, Susan. "Divorce Roman Style: How Easy and How Frequent Was It?" In *Marriage, Divorce and Children in Ancient Rome*, edited by Beryl Rawson, 31-46. Oxford: Clarendon, 1991.

Williams, Demetrius K. "The First Letter of Paul to the Corinthians." In *The Peoples' Bible*, edited by Curtiss Paul DeYoung et al., 1594-1609. Minneapolis: Fortress, 2009.

Winter, Bruce W. "Civil Litigation in Secular Corinth and the Church." *NTS* 37 (1991): 559-572.

———. "The 'Underlays' of Conflict and Compromise in 1 Corinthians." In *Paul and the Corinthians: Studies on a Community in Conflict. Essays in Honour of Margaret Thrall*, edited by T. J. Burke and K. Elliott, 139-55. NovTSupp. Leiden: Brill, 2003.

SECOND LETTER TO THE CORINTHIANS

Julie Newberry

INTRODUCTION

Addressed to a community with whom Paul has a close but fraught relationship, 2 Corinthians treats a range of sensitive subjects. Paul defensively explains his travel plans and changes to them (2 Cor 1:15–2:4; 2:12-13; 7:2-16; 9:1-5; 12:14; 13:1, 10), and he nuances his counsel about church discipline (2 Cor 2:5-11). He discusses the giving and receiving (or not) of financial support (2 Cor 2:17; 8:1–9:15; 11:7-12), and he rebuts those who interpret his weaknesses and sufferings as a mark against him—specifically, against his authority as an apostle (e.g., 2 Cor 10:1–13:4).

Indeed, these issues all relate to an underlying question about the validity and shape of Paul's apostolic vocation, which has apparently been called into question by more conventionally impressive rivals.[1] As an apostle of the crucified and risen Lord Jesus, Paul cannot with integrity resort to self-exalting domination or self-promotion of the sort practiced by his "superapostle" competitors. Nevertheless, Paul does have authority and needs to use it to redress various problems in Corinth. How can he defend and exercise his apostolic vocation—against the objections of those who interpret Paul's behavior, abilities, and experiences as disqualifying—without tacitly accepting terms of debate that run counter to the cruciform lordship of Christ? Further, how might Paul's example help Christians navigate questions of vocation, weakness, authority, and community today, in our varied social locations?

I broach these questions from a social location marked by historically deep privilege, an exegetical liability in this context. How can someone like me—a heterosexual, cisgender, thirty-something, typically abled, White American Christian from a middle-class family, who has had access to excellent education and is happily employed—even begin to interpret a letter such as 2 Corinthians, so focused on cruciform apostleship and the Christocentric (re)interpretation of suffering?[2] Three approaches suggest themselves.

First, where I inhabit positions of privilege, I can speak of and to my contexts. I can confess how parts of this letter's history of interpretation have perpetuated abusive power dynamics, contrary to Paul's teaching and example. I can also highlight how Paul's approach to ecclesial conflict provides guidance for White Christians when our theologically motivated concern for racial justice creates

[1]Though he assumes that the letter is composite, Victor Paul Furnish recognizes that "apostleship—specifically Paul's authority as the apostle to and for the Corinthians—is the pervasive underlying theme of canonical 2 Cor." See Furnish, *II Corinthians: A New Translation with Introduction and Commentary*, AB 32A (Garden City, NY: Doubleday, 1984), 34; see also, e.g., 37. See also Judith A. Diehl, *2 Corinthians*, Story of God Bible Commentary (Grand Rapids, MI: Zondervan Academic, 2020), 19-20.

[2]On the cruciformity—i.e., cross-shaped-ness—of Paul's life and thought, see the work of Michael J. Gorman, including "2 Corinthians: Paul's Defense of Cruciform Ministry," in *Apostle of the Crucified Lord: A Theological Introduction to Paul and His Letters* (Grand Rapids, MI: Eerdmans, 2017), 287-337.

tension in majority-White church spaces. Second, I can underscore how 2 Corinthians encourages those who—like Paul—experience invalidation in Christian ministry, including due to racial/ethnic prejudice and the classism that is often intertwined with it. Paul's christologically grounded inversion of cultural assumptions about qualifications for ministry calls into question (especially White) Christians' tendency to evaluate preachers/teachers of color based on White cultural standards. Third, because we exist at the intersection of multiple social categories, I can draw on insights that arise for me as a person whose privilege is tempered by real, if less life-altering, experiences of marginality—for example, as a single, child-free woman working in a male-dominated field and in a (Protestant, evangelical) subculture that strongly favors marriage and parenting.[3]

The commentary below weaves these three angles of approach into a close reading of Paul's letter as a whole. This procedure entails working assumptions about two contested issues: the literary integrity of 2 Corinthians and, relatedly, its place in Paul's complicated relationship with the Corinthian believers.

Though the Pauline authorship of 2 Corinthians is rarely questioned, the literary unity of this letter is hotly debated. Seeming digressions, jarring shifts in topic, and internal tensions lead some to propose that the canonical 2 Corinthians is composed of fragments of two or more letters.[4] However, given the lack of manuscript evidence supporting partition theories, attempts to identify discrete letters within 2 Corinthians are necessarily somewhat speculative, and no proposal has achieved the status of scholarly consensus. In my judgment, a compelling case can be made for the letter's literary integrity. Moreover, whether or not the initial addressees of 2 Corinthians received it as a single letter, the vast majority of subsequent readers have encountered it as such. I will accordingly assume the letter's literary unity in the reflections that follow.

How does this singular letter fit into Paul's rocky relationship with the Corinthian believers?[5] Canonical evidence suggests that Paul made at least three trips to Corinth and wrote at least four letters to this community. First, Paul and coworkers founded the Christian community in Corinth (Acts 18:1-18; 1 Cor 4:15; 2 Cor 10:13-14). After leaving, Paul wrote them a first (no longer extant) letter, about which we know because he refers to it in 1 Corinthians 5:9-10. Our 1 Corinthians is thus at least the second letter Paul wrote to this community, penned in response to both questions they sent by letter (1 Cor 7:1) and an oral report delivered by "Chloe's people" (1 Cor 1:11).

Paul closes 1 Corinthians with travel plans: rather than a brief stop on his way from Ephesus to Macedonia, he will visit Corinth after his trip to Macedonia, perhaps staying a few months (1 Cor 16:5-9). For some reason, Paul instead made a (surprise?) second visit to the Corinthians on his way to Macedonia

[3]The above accurately reflected my social location when I wrote this chapter, in mid-2020. By the time I received the proofs (October 2023), several aspects of my social location had changed significantly. I retain the original description, however, because it indicates the perspective from which I wrote this analysis of 2 Corinthians.

[4]Furnish, who adopts a "two-letter hypothesis," reviews arguments for and against seeing 2 Corinthians as a composite text and discusses several partition theories (*II Corinthians*, 30-41). Shelly Matthews, who treats the letter as a literary unity, also summarizes the debate. See Matthews, "2 Corinthians," in *A Feminist Commentary*, vol. 2 of *Searching the Scriptures*, ed. Elisabeth Schüssler Fiorenza (New York: Crossroad, 1994), 2:196-217, esp. 198-201.

[5]In this and subsequent paragraphs, I roughly follow the reconstruction proposed by Mark Allan Powell, *Introducing the New Testament: A Historical, Literary, and Theological Survey*, 2nd ed. (Grand Rapids, MI: Baker Academic, 2018), 310-14.

(2 Cor 1:15-16). A major conflict arose, prompting Paul to defer his next visit and instead send a third, difficult letter (2 Cor 1:23–2:4). Now lost, this letter apparently included a call to discipline whoever had been at the center of the conflict (2 Cor 2:3-5, 10).

Paul writes 2 Corinthians (his fourth known letter to the community) partly in joyful response to Titus's report of the Corinthians' penitent reception of this third letter (2 Cor 7:2-16). Real points of tension remain unresolved, however. Rival teachers have apparently introduced a model of Christian ministry that more easily conforms to wider societal norms, offering displays of spiritual and rhetorical prowess that Paul seems to lack.[6] Paul counters this challenge not by proving that he actually fulfills these cultural ideals better than his rivals but rather by calling those ideals into question in light of the revelation of God in Christ crucified and resurrected. From what we can tell, this approach bore fruit. As others have noted, Paul's letter to the Romans appears to be written from Corinth (Rom 16:23; see also 1 Cor 1:14). Far from alluding to ongoing tensions, Romans relates that the region of Achaia (where Corinth was located) has contributed to the collection of which Paul writes at length in 2 Corinthians 8–9 (Rom 15:25-27).

INITIAL GREETING (2 CORINTHIANS 1:1-2)

Already in his formulaic greeting, Paul implicitly begins to defend his apostleship. Though not unique to 2 Corinthians, his self-description as an "apostle of Christ Jesus by the will of God" (2 Cor 1:1) carries particular weight in light of rivals' claims that Paul fails to conform to cultural expectations for teachers (e.g., 2 Cor 11:5-15). In anticipation of later chapters' Christocentric apologia for his ministry, Paul portrays himself as an "apostle of Christ Jesus" (2 Cor 1:1), paving the way for the contrast he will draw between himself and his coworkers (who proclaim Christ—not themselves) and rivals who (in Paul's view) do otherwise. Whatever others may say, Paul is and remains an apostle, appointed by none other than God (2 Cor 1:1).

Paul's tacitly self-defensive opening can shape our responses when church communities question the vocation of Christian ministers who do not conform to current cultural norms for pastors and other leaders, whether because of race/ethnicity, personality, marital status, education, ability, or other factors. For any who receive invalidation from other believers because they do not "look" or "sound" like a "proper leader"—which, in American evangelicalism, is often envisioned as an assertive White male who is married with children—Paul's self-introduction offers a critical reminder. The validity of our calling depends on God, and our faithfulness is measured by our conformity to the Lord Jesus, whom we proclaim, not by our (non)conformity to whatever other norms the church invents or takes over from the wider culture.[7]

---

[6]As Guy Nave observes, the Corinthian Christians—a socially diverse community in which many seem to have been of lower socioeconomic status (1 Cor 1:26)—would have pragmatic reasons to favor such an approach. See Nave, "2 Corinthians," in *True to Our Native Land: An African American New Testament Commentary*, ed. Brian K. Blount, Cain Hope Felder, Clarice J. Martin, and Emerson B. Powery (Minneapolis: Fortress, 2007), 325.

[7]Though she is not primarily engaging with 2 Corinthians, Mandy Smith reasons in a way reminiscent of Paul's letter when reflecting on her struggle to accept that she could live into her pastoral vocation in ways consistent with her cultural and personal tendencies as an artistic, introverted Australian woman. See Smith, "Who Am I That I Should Lead?," *Christianity Today*, April 1, 2020, www.christianitytoday.com/pastors/2020/spring/hildegard-bingen-who-am-i-that-i-should-lead.html. Nave offers the historical example of Richard Allen, "a freed slave and the founder of the African Methodist Episcopal Church," whose confidence in his vocation helped him persevere despite objections raised by both White and Black people ("2 Corinthians," 309).

Canonical evidence suggests that this would have been a heartening word also for Paul's cosender, Timothy, who was apparently more timid than the average first-century leader (1 Cor 16:10; 2 Tim 1:6-10). Paul's mention of Timothy in 2 Corinthians 1:1, and later of Titus and other envoys (2 Cor 8:16-24), also reminds us that—despite the tendency today to elevate individual intellectual productions (perhaps especially in White/Western contexts)—Paul's letters leave no doubt about the cooperative, communal nature of his work. After identifying the recipients of the letter, Paul offers a typical greeting (2 Cor 1:1-2) and then shifts to the next conventional letter component: a thanksgiving or blessing.

OPENING BLESSING AND ILLUSTRATION (2 CORINTHIANS 1:3-11)

Rather than thanking God for the Corinthians (see 1 Cor 1:4), Paul blesses God as the one who "consoles us in all our affliction" (2 Cor 1:3-4).[8] This "us" is Paul and his coworkers, in distinction from the Corinthian believers ("you," 2 Cor 1:6), but Paul insists on the deep interconnection of the two groups, in affliction and in consolation (2 Cor 1:6-7). Anticipating his handling of his perceived weaknesses later in the letter, Paul begins to develop a Christocentric, theologically grounded, and ecclesially oriented (counter)interpretation of his potentially shameful sufferings. Far from disqualifying him as an apostle, Paul's afflictions unite him to Christ in a special way: "The sufferings of Christ are abundant for us" (2 Cor 1:5). Furthermore, it is precisely in these afflictions that Paul and his coworkers experience God's consolation "through Christ" (2 Cor 1:5)—all for the sake of the church in Corinth (2 Cor 1:6).

Paul illustrates the point through an anecdote about a recent experience of suffering and consolation in the province of Asia (2 Cor 1:8-11). He and his coworkers faced the prospect of the ultimate human affliction: death. Paul will later claim to be "hard-pressed" but not so as to be "straitened" or "narrowed" (2 Cor 4:8).[9] In this case, however, he and his companions felt otherwise. They "were so surpassingly weighed down [*bareō*] beyond [their] power that [they] despaired even of life" (2 Cor 1:8, my translation). Just here, though—in this crushing affliction—God met them with consolation (see 2 Cor 1:4). Having in themselves "the sentence of death" served to make Paul and his colaborers "rely not on [themselves] but on God who raises the dead" (2 Cor 1:9). Since God's resurrection power has been demonstrated most fully in Christ (2 Cor 4:14), it is indeed "through Christ" that the consolation Paul receives can abound (see 2 Cor 1:5).

Paul's opening blessing and anecdote thus already begin to reframe his experience of shameful afflictions as part of—rather than a deviation from—his enactment of Christocentric apostleship toward the Corinthians. Clearly, Paul's is no "prosperity gospel" model of apostleship. However, neither does he exult in suffering for its own sake. He blesses God not for the afflictions themselves but for the comfort that God provides during suffering, equipping Paul to minister to others who suffer in various ways (2 Cor 1:4, 6)—including the Corinthians, whose own endurance in affliction bolsters Paul's hope for them (2 Cor 1:7).

For Christians who understand the affirmation of Christ's lordship to entail our pursuit of a multiethnic ecclesial community and our

[8]The word translated "consoles" is *parakaleō*; this word group occurs multiple times in the letter and, depending on context, may be translated with English terms such as "comfort," "console," "encourage," or "exhort."

[9]My translation: *thlibomenoi all' ou stenochōroumenoi*.

opposition to White supremacy and racial/ethnic injustice, the work can be exhausting and the progress demoralizingly slow. White Christians are often positioned such that we can "opt out" of this work if we find it too controversial or unrewarding. By framing his ministry in terms of suffering that is real but not without significance—a significance rooted not in his immediate temporal success but in his participation in suffering and consolation through the crucified and risen Lord Jesus—Paul provides theological guidance for White Christians as we seek to grow in the hope and love necessary to persist in racial justice work that flows from the gospel.

CONFLICT WITH THE CORINTHIANS, PART ONE: CHANGED ITINERARY AND COMMUNITY DISCIPLINE (2 CORINTHIANS 1:12–2:13)

Paul's case study of recent affliction-and-consolation culminates in an implicit request for the Corinthians to join others in praying for him and his team (2 Cor 1:10-11). Even as Paul reaffirms his close relationship with the Corinthians, though, hints of conflict emerge in his firm (defensive?) insistence on his forthrightness (2 Cor 1:12) and the intelligibility of his letters (2 Cor 1:13; see 1 Cor 5:9-13; 2 Pet 3:15-16). In the following verses, one reason for this insistence comes into focus: the divergence of Paul's travel from the plans outlined in 1 Corinthians has raised doubts about his trustworthiness (2 Cor 1:15–2:13).

Lest his perceived unreliability seem to call into question the reliability of the Lord he proclaims, Paul insists that God can be trusted, as demonstrated by the giving of the Holy Spirit as a guarantee (2 Cor 1:17-22). Paul further explains that, in keeping with the faithfulness of the God he serves, he altered his itinerary not out of fickleness but rather because of his deep commitment to and abiding relationship with the Corinthians. Following his tumultuous second trip to Corinth, he sent a letter prior to coming again precisely because he hoped to smooth things out before his next visit to this beloved community (2 Cor 1:23–2:4).

Paul will return in 2 Corinthians 2:12-13 to the anxiety he experienced while awaiting news of their reaction to this letter, but he digresses in 2 Corinthians 2:5-11 to address the penitent response of which he has since learned. He emphasizes the need to restore to fellowship the person who received communal discipline in connection with the conflict. Foreshadowing his later comments about which sorts of grief are or are not conducive to Christian flourishing (2 Cor 7:8-10), Paul cautions that the individual who grieved the community should not be pushed into overwhelming grief himself but rather should receive consolation (2 Cor 2:5-8), lest the believers "be outwitted by Satan" (2 Cor 2:11).

Satan, after all, would presumably be only too glad for what started out as "godly grief," grief that "produces a repentance that leads to salvation" (2 Cor 7:10), to morph into the sort of ostracization that leads offenders to despair and/or permanently divides Christians from each other. The nuanced model that Paul offers—one in which wrongs are redressed in a way that avoids letting Satan co-opt this process for nefarious purposes—remains instructive today, not least for White Christians who find ourselves having conversations with other White Christians about the gospel's implications for racial justice and multiethnic community. Paul's emphasis on the need for appropriate discipline invites White Christians to the work of confronting White-supremacist and/or racist tendencies in ourselves and our circles of influence, despite the conflicts this may create. Paul's model also reminds us, though, to do this work in a spirit of love, with the aim of fostering repentance and reconciliation rather than ostracization, despair, and division.[10]

Paul's call to modulate communal discipline reflects his perspective after learning that the Corinthians received his letter penitently. In 2 Corinthians 2:12, he recalls the period before he knew their response. Whereas he had previously changed his itinerary in ways that troubled the Corinthians, Paul now upends his travel plans to go to Macedonia, seeking an update on them from Titus (2 Cor 2:12-13)—who, as the Corinthians would already know, had been sent to them (2 Cor 7:6-7). The jubilant thanksgiving in 2 Corinthians 2:14 anticipates the happy resolution of the tension Paul felt, but this thanksgiving also leads him into a tangent from which he will not return until 2 Corinthians 7:5-6.

PAUL'S MINISTRY, PART ONE: A DEFENSIVE DESCRIPTION AND EXHORTATIONS (2 CORINTHIANS 2:14–7:4)

References to Macedonia and Titus (2 Cor 2:14; 7:5-6) bracket a long segment of the letter that explicates and implicitly defends Paul's ministry (2 Cor 2:14–7:5). Along the way, Paul draws several contrasts between himself (and his coworkers) and certain unnamed rivals, whom he will discuss more openly in 2 Corinthians 10:1–12:21. Unlike Paul and his team, these competitors conform to cultural norms for the behavior of respectable teachers, including by accepting monetary compensation for teaching (2 Cor 2:17) and by using commendatory letters to establish their credibility (2 Cor 3:1). Paul's repeated discussion of the mixed responses to his preaching may further suggest that he and his rivals differ as to their "success" rates in ministry (2 Cor 2:15-16; 4:3), perhaps in part due to Paul's perceived rhetorical and other weaknesses.

Paul does not contest these "facts" so much as their interpretation. Faced with concerns about the validity of his apostleship vis-à-vis others' more conventionally impressive ministries, Paul needs to assert his apostolic authority without compromising his Christocentric (and hence cruciform) understanding of the nature of his apostleship. To this end, Paul characterizes his vocation in terms of two paradoxically juxtaposed realities: the greatness of his apostolic ministry in Christ, on the one hand, and the reality of Paul's own weaknesses (up to and including his very mortality), on the other. As he often does, Paul makes his case by drawing Israel's Scriptures into conversation both with the story of Jesus and with God's ongoing work by the power of the Holy Spirit through Paul and others in the church.[11]

Divinely bestowed competency, divinely written commendation: Who is sufficient? (2 Corinthians 2:14–3:6). When Paul bursts into thanksgiving in 2 Corinthians 2:14, one expects the catalyst to be Titus's good report (see 2 Cor 7:5-7). However, as sometimes happens when Paul waxes doxological, the thanksgiving leads him into another train of thought. Having thanked God, "who in Christ always leads us in triumphal procession and through us spreads in every place the fragrance that comes from knowing him" (2 Cor 2:14), Paul uses this olfactory imagery as a springboard for an extended reflection on the character of his ministry in light of mixed responses

[10] I frame this paragraph as an intra-White-community conversation because the burden of educating White Christians about racial/ethnic injustice should not be placed on Christians of color.

[11] For a still-illuminating study of the role of Israel's Scriptures in Paul's letters, see Richard B. Hays, *Echoes of Scripture in the Letters of Paul* (New Haven, CT: Yale University Press, 1989).

to it.[12] He freely acknowledges that the reception of his message varies; what some experience as the scent of life, others find to be the smell of death (2 Cor 2:14-16; see also 2 Cor 4:3-4). Whereas his rivals may have spun this mixed reception as a sign of failure on his part, Paul portrays it as a mark of his integrity. Anticipating the letter's later defense of his seemingly unprofessional refusal to accept financial support from the Corinthians (2 Cor 11:7-12; 12:14-15), Paul contrasts himself and his team with others who are "peddlers of God's word" (2 Cor 2:17).[13] He is not out to make a financial profit and hence is not concerned primarily with the number of converts. However others may respond, Paul's mission is simply to proclaim the gospel of Jesus Christ, accountable to God rather than to the pollsters (2 Cor 2:17).[14]

For majority-White churches, Paul's example provides guidance as we count the cost of acting on the conviction that racial/ethnic injustice and de facto segregation are affronts to the gospel of Jesus Christ—in whom, according to Paul, differences that once divided us are no longer barriers to unity (Gal 3:27-28). What might it look like in our contexts to prioritize faithfulness to Christ—including opposition to racism, White supremacy, and any other powers that try to usurp Christ's lordship—over concern for membership numbers and the financial viability of a congregation? How might such an approach shape whether and how our Sunday services address instances of police violence against Black, brown, and Indigenous people, for example?[15] Committing to bear bolder witness in this area may come at a price. However, in light of Paul's dismissive characterization of those who boost their success rate by being mere "peddlers of God's word" (2 Cor 2:17), we do well to ask ourselves: What is the cost when we tacitly tolerate racist, xenophobic, and other patterns of thinking and acting that undermine the integrity of our confession that Jesus Christ is Lord of all?[16]

Following Paul's instructive assertion of his integrity in 2 Corinthians 2:17, he anticipates a potential objection, asking rhetorically, "Are we beginning to commend ourselves again?" (2 Cor 3:1). Given that Paul goes on to discuss the issue of receiving commendation from other human beings, the contrast seems to be between Paul and his team's alleged

[12]As often noted, the reference to fragrance evokes "the odor of incense used in religious sacrifices" (Nave, "2 Corinthians," 313). On the historical background for the image of a "triumphal procession," as well as the implications of Paul's imagery for Christians' ongoing efforts to resist colonialism and other forms of oppression, see Nave, "2 Corinthians," 312-13.

[13]On why Paul's refusal to accept their funds may have seemed unprofessional and/or offensive, see, e.g., Margaret Thrall, *I and II Corinthians*, Cambridge Bible Commentary on the New English Bible (Cambridge: Cambridge University Press, 1965), 172.

[14]The end of 2 Cor 2:17, with its emphasis on Paul's sincerity and God-given vocation, implies that those who are "peddlers" of the gospel are not merely accepting financial support (see 1 Cor 9; Phil 4:10-20). More problematically, they are (according to Paul) ministering out of insincerity and without a divinely authorized, Christocentric vocation.

[15]See Esau McCaulley, "Preaching Against Racism Is Not a Distraction from the Gospel," *Christianity Today*, August 9, 2019, www.christianitytoday.com/pastors/2019/august-web-exclusives/racism-preaching-against-not-distraction-from-gospel.html.

[16]As Matthews argues, "Paul's voluntary acceptance of status loss and subsequent suffering" as a Jesus-follower and apostle is instructive for those reading 2 Corinthians from a position of privilege, but it is important to underscore that such sacrifice "must be motivated by radical love for and accountability to the oppressed rather than by compulsion to sacrifice self" in a self-abnegating way ("2 Corinthians," 215). Additional pastoral complexities arise in the case of marginalized groups, for whom "the message that glory is located in humiliation and suffering" has sometimes been used as a tool of oppression (215). Such abuses should be ruled out if we attend to the theological basis for and christological shape of Paul's example and exhortation. See also Nave's analysis of the distinction between how the hope of (eschatological) glory rightly functioned to empower and encourage enslaved people to move toward justice—and, conversely, how slave masters sought to pervert such hope into an argument for acquiescing to unjust suffering (315-16; see also 326).

self-commendation (i.e., they had offered no conventional endorsement from other human beings to authenticate themselves) and the divergent approach of their rivals, whose credibility receives formal certification through letters of recommendation (2 Cor 3:1).

In the ancient world, a person traveling to a new place might bring a letter of commendation from an acquaintance who had social connections to the destination.[17] We still rely on analogous letters in some contexts, such as for graduate-school applications. Now as then, this system makes a certain amount of sense. Unfortunately, it also tends to reinforce the privilege of those who have access to impressive connections, to the detriment of others—thereby perpetuating long-standing (and in our contexts, frequently racialized) inequities. How does Paul navigate the issue of letters of recommendation in his context?

Taking the Pauline corpus as a whole, we see that Paul adopts but radically transforms the practice of recommendation writing. He does sometimes commend those whom he is sending (back) to a given community (e.g., Phil 2:19-30), including in 2 Corinthians (2 Cor 8:16-24). Without erasing the social particularity of those he commends, however, Paul consistently grounds his recommendation in their relationship to the church in Christ—not in a person's social status in the eyes of the world. Thus, though Romans 16 implies that Phoebe is a woman of some means, Paul introduces her as a "sister" in the Lord and a "deacon" of a local church (Rom 16:1).[18] Her wealth comes up only indirectly, in connection with her benefaction toward Paul and other believers (Rom 16:2). To take another example, Onesimus may be legally enslaved, but when sending him back to his owner, Philemon, Paul introduces Onesimus not as a slave but as his own child in the faith (Philem 10), to be welcomed as Paul himself would be welcomed (Philem 17).[19] Paul's manner of commending people reminds us not to allow culturally determined (in our contexts, often implicitly White, male, upper- and middle-class) norms to determine whom we commend and how/why we commend them.[20] Instead of being governed by the value his culture places on a person, Paul commends individuals in ways that foreground their divinely given status in and service of the church.

Though 2 Corinthians 3 deals with the question of Paul's (non)reception of commendation rather than his giving of commendation, his reasoning follows a similar pattern here. He models an ecclesiological and theological (christological, pneumatological) reconfiguration of the practice of bolstering one's credibility with letters of formal endorsement. Paul reasons that the Corinthian

[17]See, e.g., Hays, *Echoes of Scripture*, 126, citing William R. Baird (126n13).

[18]The Greek *diakonos* could also be translated as "servant" or "minister."

[19]Paul mentions Onesimus's slavery once, when calling for this status to be relativized (if not eliminated) in light of his primary identity as brother in Christ (Philem 16). On the interpretive cruxes and interpretation history, see Demetrius K. Williams, "No Longer a Slave: Reading the Interpretation History of Paul's Letter to Philemon," in *Onesimus Our Brother: Reading Religion, Race, and Culture in Philemon*, ed. Matthew V. Johnson, James A. Noel, and Demetrius K. Williams, Paul in Critical Contexts (Minneapolis: Fortress, 2012), 11-45.

[20]By extension, we should also be aware that conventional means of commendation in our society are often fraught with historic and ongoing systemic injustices. For example, when graduate programs are evaluating applications, how much weight is placed on recommendation letters written from institutions that—for reasons of historically deep, structurally entrenched racial injustice—remain less accessible to people of color than to their White peers? What other kinds of evidence might be incorporated to mitigate the influence of White privilege on the application process? Similar questions could be asked in relation hiring a pastor, choosing which popular theologian to read in a small group, and more. On the ways in which marginalized communities might be emboldened by Paul's insistence on the commendation provided by the work of the Spirit (rather than by human letters), see also Matthews, "2 Corinthians," 214.

believers already have his letter of recommendation: more than that, they *are* themselves the ecclesiologically embodied "letter" that commends his ministry (2 Cor 3:2).[21] This letter is "of Christ" (2 Cor 3:3), the ultimate sender who authorizes its commendation of Paul's ministry (see also 2 Cor 10:18). Though the letter has been "ministered" by Paul and his coworkers—couriers, in the analogy—it is written not with these ministers' human resources (e.g., ink) but rather "with the Spirit of the living God" (2 Cor 3:2-3).[22]

A play on writing imagery sets up the next movement of Paul's argument, with its complex intertextual reasoning about his ministry and its varied results.[23] Paul juxtaposes the image of his ecclesially embodied recommendation "letter" (*epistolē*)—which is "inscribed" (*engraphō*) on the heart (2 Cor 3:2; or "tablets of fleshy hearts," 2 Cor 3:3, my translation)—with a mixed metaphor that combines references to two other writings: his rivals' conventional letters of recommendation, inscribed with ink (*engegrammenē . . . melani*), and the Mosaic law, inscribed on "tablets of stone" (2 Cor 3:3; see Ex 31:18; 32:16; 34:1-4, 27). Expanding on the latter image, Paul goes on to contrast the covenant "of letter" (*grammatos*) and that "of spirit" (*pneumatos*, 2 Cor 3:6).[24] This comparison leads into discussion of how Paul's ministry relates to that of Moses, including with respect to Moses' veiling of his face (2 Cor 3:7–4:6; Ex 34:29-35).

Moses, Paul, and (un)veiled glory (2 Corinthians 3:7–4:6). We come now to one of the more puzzling passages in 2 Corinthians. By way of preface, it may be helpful to review the portion of the exodus narrative that is Paul's primary intertext here. The Lord has delivered Israel from Egypt (Ex 1–15); the people have heard and agreed to keep the Ten Commandments, including the commandment against idols (Ex 20:1-21). God then calls Moses to go up Mount Sinai to receive divinely crafted stone tablets, on which the Lord writes the covenant (Ex 24:12–31:18). Moses' absence on this errand is extended, and the people despair of his return. Under the leadership of Aaron, they make a golden calf to worship, which Aaron identifies with the god(s) who brought them out of Egypt, prompting the people to offer sacrifices before the idol (Ex 32:1-6). This does not go over well with the Lord. When God proposes eliminating the people and starting over with Moses, Moses—as representative of the people before God—intercedes on their behalf (Ex 32:7-14). However, Moses himself is so enraged when he sees the people's idolatrous behavior that he breaks the stone tablets of the covenant (Ex 32:19). Later, in Exodus 34, the Lord tells Moses to hew two new tablets and go back up Mount Sinai to receive the covenant again (Ex 34:1-4).

A curious wrinkle in the ensuing narrative merits mention. The Lord initially asserts that the new (Moses-made) tablets will again be divinely written on (Ex 34:1), but later God tells Moses to write on the tablets (Ex 34:27). Moses' role in the writing of the (renewed) covenant arguably provides a precedent for Paul and his colleagues' part in "ministering" the commendatory letter of Christ that the Corinthians themselves are—albeit written, in

---

[21]This recalls Paul's reasoning in 1 Cor 9:2 (Thrall, *I and II Corinthians*, 131).

[22]The analogy of couriers comes from Hays, whose translation of *diakonētheisa* as "ministered" I follow; Hays argues that this unexpected diction prepares for the subsequent discussion of Paul's and Moses' ministries (*Echoes of Scripture*, 127).

[23]On Paul's wordplay here and the translation difficulties involved, see Hays, *Echoes of Scripture*, 130-31.

[24]2 Corinthians 3:6 also recalls Paul's emphasis on the Spirit's role in writing the "hearty" letter of recommendation that the Corinthians themselves are (2 Cor 3:3).

the Corinthians' case, on hearts rather than on stone tablets (2 Cor 3:3).[25]

Before taking up Paul's comments about Moses' face and veiling later in Exodus 34, we should note that the apostle's contrast between tablets of stone and of hearts evokes several other Old Testament passages.[26] Though the end of 2 Corinthians 3:3 is sometimes rendered as "human hearts" (e.g., NRSV), the Greek might more literally be translated as "fleshy [*sarkinos*] hearts."[27] This rendering makes it easier to notice Paul's echo of Ezekiel 11:19; 36:26. Both passages describe the restoration of God's people in terms of the replacement of stony hearts with "fleshy [*sarkinos*] hearts," enabling obedience to God's statutes (Ezek 11:19; 36:27). Given 2 Corinthians 3's repeated references to the Spirit (esp. 2 Cor 3:3-6, 17-18), it is worth noting that these passages also describe this transformation in terms of God giving the people a (new/divine) s/Spirit (Ezek 11:19; 36:27).

This imagery of "fleshy hearts" being written on recalls additional Old Testament passages in which hearts are the loci of the writing of God's law. Particularly important is Jeremiah 38:33 LXX (31:33 MT), in which the writing of the law on the hearts of God's people is a mark of the new covenant (see also Ezek 37:27). Paul reinforces the link to Jeremiah in 2 Corinthians by describing himself and his coworkers explicitly as "ministers of a new covenant" (2 Cor 3:6).

For readers who catch these echoes of Israel's Scriptures, Paul's development of the letter/tablet/heart imagery not only underscores the parallel between his ministry and Moses' but also suggests that the work now underway is even greater than the covenant renewal wrought through Moses following the golden calf incident.[28] As a minister of Christ's letter that is written on "tablets of fleshy hearts" (2 Cor 3:3), Paul participates in the promised restoration of God's people to a relationship with the Lord that is even more intimate and transformative than the one mediated by Moses at Sinai.

This is, to be sure, a remarkably bold claim for Paul to make about his ministry. Accordingly, in keeping with his theocentric reframing of the letter image (2 Cor 3:1-3), he immediately reiterates that whatever sufficiency he and his team have for this vocation comes from God (2 Cor 3:4-6). Like Moses—who in the Greek translation of Exodus 4:10 objects to God's calling by claiming, "I am not sufficient" (*ouch hikanos eimi*, my translation)—Paul hastens to underscore his inherent insufficiency for the task entrusted to him.[29] Nevertheless, as Moses' personal inadequacy was beside the point because all depends on God's equipping (Ex 4:11-12), so also Paul can name his own insufficiency in the course of affirming that he does have sufficiency—that is, from God (2 Cor 3:5-6; see also 2 Cor 2:16). In this way, Paul emphasizes

[25]On "ministering," see again Hays's translation (*Echoes of Scripture*, 127). Given Paul's reference to the Holy Spirit's role in "writing" the letter that the Corinthians are (2 Cor 3:2-3), it is interesting to note that the stone tablets were written on by "the finger of God" (Ex 31:18; Deut 9:10), a phrase taken elsewhere in the canon as periphrasis for the Holy Spirit (Lk 11:20; compare Mt 12:28; also noted by Hays, *Echoes of Scripture*, 128n21).

[26]See also Hays's discussion of these and the Exodus echoes in *Echoes of Scripture*, esp. 127-31.

[27]My translation, here and subsequently with this phrase; so also, e.g., Hays, *Echoes of Scripture*, 128.

[28]For reflection on verbal and thematic links between the OT passages evoked in 2 Cor 3, see Carol K. Stockhausen, "2 Corinthians 3 and the Principles of Pauline Exegesis," in *Paul and the Scriptures of Israel*, ed. Craig A. Evans and James A. Sanders, LNTS (Sheffield: Sheffield Academic Press, 1993), 143-64, esp. 155-58.

[29]Moses expresses concern specifically about his speaking abilities (Ex 4:10); compare Paul's alleged lack of rhetorical excellence (2 Cor 10:10). Stockhausen points out that Ex 4:10 contains the only "parallel use of ἱκανός . . . in the Septuagint" and argues that it "determines Paul's use of the word in 2 Corinthians 3" ("2 Corinthians 3," 146; see also 147).

the weightiness of his ministry without adopting the self-exalting practices of his more conventionally impressive rivals. He also paves the way for his engagement with Moses' story in the remainder of 2 Corinthians 3.

Although 2 Corinthians 3:6 is grammatically and logically bound up with the surrounding verses, its reception history is such that it will be helpful to pause over the end of this verse before taking up Paul's subsequent discussion of Moses' veil. Paul writes that God made him and his coworkers "ministers of a new covenant, not of letter but of spirit [or Spirit], for the letter kills, but the Spirit [or spirit] gives life" (2 Cor 3:6). From the patristic era on, this verse has sometimes been taken as authorizing "spiritual" or "figural" interpretations of the (especially OT) Scriptures.[30] However, though some sorts of figural reading are indeed scripturally warranted and theologically appropriate, it is anachronistic to interpret 2 Corinthians 3:6 as establishing such a hermeneutical principle.[31] Moreover, such an interpretation of the verse has too often led from the appropriate affirmation of figural reading to a problematic privileging of "spiritual" interpretation over against literal interpretations of the Old Testament, sometimes due to theologically problematic and pastorally disastrous antibody and/or anti-Jewish tendencies.[32]

The danger of anti-Jewish interpretations is particularly acute in treatments of 2 Corinthians 3, since Paul does portray his ministry as in some sense greater than Moses'.[33] This passage has been and sometimes still is interpreted as denigrating Moses/the Old Testament and/or as providing grounds for Christians to deride Jews who do not believe that Jesus is the Messiah. Even when not intended to foment anti-Judaism, such interpretations can nevertheless have that result. In a post-Holocaust world in which anti-Judaism continues to be a deadly force, Christians must take very seriously this passage's history of effects.

In doing so, we are forced to ask whether the difficulty arises only from (mis)interpretations or whether Paul's argument itself may be supersessionist and/or anti-Jewish. A full answer to that question would require more space than is available here, not least because much depends on the (contested) definition of key terms such as *supersessionist*. For now, I offer three framing observations to guide further reflection.

First, it is important to read this passage in the context of all of Paul's letters (not least

[30]For example, Augustine of Hippo evokes this verse when describing how Ambrose's figural interpretations of the OT helped Augustine overcome his negative perception of many OT passages. In this context, Augustine does deprecate the literal sense of the passages in a way that may allow for anti-Judaism, unfortunately. See Augustine of Hippo, *Confessions*, trans. Henry Chadwick, Oxford World Classics (Oxford: Oxford University Press, 1992), 6.4.6.

[31]Hays, though he has written much on the figural interpretation of the NT, emphatically rejects the view that "Paul is distinguishing between literal and spiritual modes of exegesis" in 2 Cor 3:6 (*Echoes of Scripture*, 130). Of course, this is not to deny that Paul sometimes engages in figural interpretations of Israel's Scriptures (e.g., Rom 15:4; 1 Cor 10:1-6). Moreover, reading the OT in this way is central to the Christian confession not only of the canon's coherence but also of the integrity of God's identity. For one discussion of the theological stakes of figural reading, see Ephraim Radner, "The Discrepancies of Two Ages: Thoughts on Keble's 'Mysticism of the Fathers,'" *The Anglican* 29, no. 2 (2000), http://anglicanhistory.org/essays/radner/keble.pdf.

[32]Hays traces such readings back as far as Origen and notes the danger of "Gnosticism and arbitrariness" when the literal sense is "discarded . . . in favor of esoteric allegorical readings" (*Echoes of Scripture*, 124; see also 130-31, 150-51). See also Jane Heath, "Moses' End and the Succession: Deuteronomy 31 and 2 Corinthians 3," *NTS* 60, no. 1 (2014): 37-60, esp. 37-38.

[33]Jewish NT scholar Daniel Boyarin offers an incisive review of three books that portray different postures toward Judaism in relation to these issues. See Boyarin, "The Subversion of the Jews: Moses's Veil and the Hermeneutics of Supersession," *Diacritics* 23, no. 2 (1993): 16-35.

Rom 9–11, which takes up the question of "unbelieving Israel" more explicitly) and in relation to the entire Christian canon (including Israel's scriptural traditions, which are evoked by the NT at practically every turn). Hatred toward non-Christian Jews and the denigration of the Tanakh/Old Testament are ruled out by the wider context of Paul's letters and the shape of Christian Scripture as a whole.

Second, as others have observed, the logic of Paul's argument in 2 Corinthians 3 has more nuanced implications than may appear at first glance. He does craft an argument from the lesser to the greater, in which his and his coworkers' ministry outshines Moses'. However, the force of an argument from the lesser to the greater depends on the starting assumption of the high valuation (not the devaluation) of the "lesser" member in the comparison. By setting up a comparison between his ministry and Moses', Paul already evinces a high view of Moses' ministry.[34] Whether this rhetorical device still allows for supersessionism depends in large part on how one defines that term.

It depends also on what one makes of a third observation: as shown above, Paul understands his "greater" ministry to be itself a fulfillment of Israel's scriptural traditions, including specifically the prophecies of Ezekiel and Jeremiah.[35] These Scriptures thus remain able to speak an authoritative word about Paul's apostleship. Indeed, throughout this segment of 2 Corinthians, what we would call the Jewish Tanakh or the Christian Old Testament provides the interpretive matrix within which Paul articulates a defense of the forthrightness of his ministry and the varied responses it has evoked.

Admittedly, none of the foregoing observations changes the fact that Paul's interpretation of Israel's scriptural traditions in 2 Corinthians 3 is not one that could be accepted by Jews who do not believe that Jesus is the Messiah. Such readers may indeed experience Paul's handling of Scripture as invalidating.[36] This sort of hermeneutical disagreement does not ipso facto entail anti-Judaism on Paul's part, particularly in his historical context.[37] Nevertheless, the history of the church makes lamentably clear how easily Christians can slide from disagreement to deprecation and worse. Moreover, even if the form of Paul's argument implies a high valuation of Moses/Torah, there is no denying that Paul differentiates his ministry from Moses' in rather stark terms, contrasting his own ministry "of the Spirit" and "of justification" with Moses' ministry "of death" and "of condemnation" (2 Cor 3:7-9).[38]

---

[34]See, e.g., discussion in Susan Grove Eastman, "Unveiling Death in Second Corinthians," in *The Ways That Often Parted: Essays in Honor of Joel Marcus*, ed. Lori Baron, Jill Hicks-Keeton, and Matthew Thiessen (Atlanta: SBL Press, 2018), 79-102, esp. 88-89. See also Hays, *Echoes of Scripture*, 132-33.

[35]As Margaryta Teslina observes of the new covenant language that Paul echoes from Jeremiah, "Though the occasion for this new covenant is the people's failure to remain faithful, the making of a new covenant does not signify their rejection, but an attempt to bring them back to their Lord once and for all (cf. Jer. 32:40)." See Teslina, "In the Image of Moses, in the Image of Christ: Pauline Hermeneutics in 2 Corinthians 3" (paper presented in the New Testament: Epistles and Apocalypse section of Society of Biblical Literature Pacific Coast Regional Meeting, Fullerton, CA, 2017), 12.

[36]See Boyarin, "Subversion of the Jews," as well as discussion of his view (esp. vis-à-vis Hays's) in Eastman, "Unveiling Death," esp. 90-91, 94, 100.

[37]In the first-century context, such interpretive disputes existed within ongoing (intra-Jewish) debates about the continuation of the Jewish tradition. See Boyarin, "Subversion of the Jews," 27-28; Matthews, "2 Corinthians," 205, 214. Teslina draws attention to another possibility for reading this passage as something other than straightforwardly anti-Jewish: "The entire letter is aimed to contrast Paul's ministry with that of the super-apostles," whom Teslina plausibly takes to be Jewish believers in Jesus (see 2 Cor 11:22-23); thus, 2 Cor 3 "must be understood as an argument not against Judaism *in toto*, but against the ministry of these particular Jewish Christians" ("In the Image," 2; see also, e.g., Hays, *Echoes of Scripture*, 126).

[38]See also Eastman, "Unveiling Death," esp. 88-89.

The import of Paul's strong language hinges to some extent on one's interpretation of contested terms and shifting metaphors within 2 Corinthians 3, particularly in relation to the image of (veiled) glory. This imagery evokes Exodus's claim that, after Moses re-receives the covenant on new stone tablets (Ex 34:1, 10, 27; see 2 Cor 3:3, 6), his face shines as a result of his encounter with the glory of the Lord on Mount Sinai (Ex 34:5-8, 29).[39] Though Moses' glorious visage terrifies the Israelites, they are allowed to gaze on it while he delivers the reestablished covenant (Ex 34:30-33). Moses then veils his face—but only until he returns to the Lord's presence (Ex 34:33-34; see also 2 Cor 3:16). Though subsequent encounters occur in the tent of meeting, Moses follows the same procedure. After meeting with the Lord, Moses allows the people to see his authenticating radiant visage while he relates God's message; then he covers up again till his next trip to the Lord's presence (Ex 34:34-35).[40]

In 2 Corinthians 3, Paul describes the glory of Moses' countenance using the verb *katargeō*, which is often translated in ways that suggest either a gradual dimming (e.g., "fade," REB) or a definitive displacement (e.g., "set aside," NRSV). The former translation implies that the shining of Moses' face gradually decreases between his meetings with the Lord; the veil prevents observation of this fading.[41] This would cohere with 2 Corinthians 3:13, provided one takes the noun *telos* there to mean "end" in the sense of "termination, ceasing to be."[42] However, such an interpretation requires that Paul use *katargeō* in an uncharacteristic way, as well as engage in uncharacteristically sloppy scriptural interpretation.[43] After all, in Exodus, Moses covers his face precisely because it is still shining with terrifying brightness—not because it is ceasing to shine. Translations of *katargeō* that suggest definitive displacement ("set aside" [NRSV], or perhaps better, "render inoperative") avoid this problem. Moses' face keeps its glory in Paul's account, as in Exodus, but that glory is (in effect) no longer glorious because of the greater glory that has come in Christ (2 Cor 3:10).

If this second interpretation of *katargeō* is preferred, it remains to determine the sense of *telos* in 2 Corinthians 3:13. Some, such as Richard Hays, have argued that *telos* here means "end" in the sense of "goal."[44] Moses veils his shining face to prevent the Israelites from seeing the glorious goal of the law—that is, ultimately, the glory of God in Christ.[45] However, in addition to raising questions about why Moses would obfuscate the aim of the revelation he delivered, this line of interpretation again stands in tension with the Exodus account.[46] As noted above, Moses unveils precisely while telling the people the words of God—words that, according to Paul, ultimately point to Jesus as the Christ.

[39]Scott J. Hafemann, "The Glory and Veil of Moses in 2 Cor 3:7-14: An Example of Paul's Contextual Exegesis of the OT—a Proposal," *Horizons in Biblical Theology* 14, no. 1 (1992): 31-49, esp. 33-34.

[40]Eastman, for example, also emphasizes that Moses unveils while receiving and delivering God's words for the people ("Unveiling Death," 81). On the cultural overtones of male veiling, see Eastman, "Unveiling Death," esp. 82-86.

[41]This view is held, for example, by Thrall, who works with a translation that uses "fade" (NEB); see *I and II Corinthians*, 133-36.

[42]Hays, who rejects this interpretation, notes that many modern commentators have adopted it (see *Echoes of Scripture*, 136).

[43]See discussion in Hays, *Echoes of Scripture*, 133-36, 146. On the translation of *katargeō*, see also, e.g., Hafemann, "Glory and Veil," 37-40.

[44]Hays, *Echoes of Scripture*, 136-140.

[45]According to Hays, "Patristic interpreters unanimously understood the phrase *to telos tou katargoumenou* as a reference to Christ as the true significance or fulfillment of the old covenant" (*Echoes of Scripture*, 137).

[46]Hays acknowledges but seems to dismiss this difficulty about why Moses would obfuscate the aim of the revelation he delivered as among the "silly objections" to Hays's preferred interpretation (*Echoes of Scripture*, 136, 139-40).

Presumably, though, the actual moment of mediating revelation would be the most important one for a veil, if the point of veiling were to prevent perception of the law's end/goal in Christ.[47]

While this sense of *telos* ("goal") may be in play at some points in 2 Corinthians 3–4, another understanding of *telos* in 2 Corinthians 3:13 allows for greater coherence between Paul's argument and Exodus.[48] To see how this is so, we will need to zoom out a bit. As Scott Hafemann observes, Moses was in God's presence before, but it is only after his "unique experience of God's glory in [Exodus] 34:1-9" that Moses' face shines, such that he "himself bears the glory of God with him back to the camp." If Hafemann is correct to infer that Moses' radiance "is the means by which YHWH will place his presence in the midst of his people" (see Ex 33:1-3, 12-17; 34:8), then "Moses becomes . . . the mediator" not only "of the covenant Law, but of the covenantal presence of God."[49] Moses thus fulfills in a deeper way the mediatorial role that the people requested for him earlier, after briefly experiencing the awe-inducing holiness of God for themselves (Ex 20:18-23; see also Ex 24:16-17).[50] Hafemann's interpretation has important implications for the question of why Moses veils his still-shining face after he has performed this mediating role by relaying God's words—as well as for how we might interpret *telos* in 2 Corinthians 3:13.

In short, the veil serves to protect the people, who, as Hafemann notes, are described as fearing Moses' glowing face (Ex 34:30).[51] The "end" (*telos*) of the glory at which they are not able (2 Cor 3:7) or permitted (2 Cor 3:13) to gaze is a specific (terrifying) consequence or outcome.[52] It is the destruction-by-divine-holiness that would otherwise befall the "stiff-necked" (Ex 33:5 NETS)—or, in Paul's terms, hard-minded (2 Cor 3:14)—people. They could not survive continuous exposure to God's glory, and yet, through Moses, they are granted the ongoing (albeit veiled) presence of God's glory (see Ex 33:1-5; 34:30; cf. Ex 33:15-17; 34:9).[53] Moses' reason for covering his face is therefore not to prevent the people from discerning the law's ultimate aim (i.e., Christ) but rather to keep the people from being consumed by a glory that would be too much for them. The veiling is thus, as Hafemann puts it, "an act of grace."[54]

How does this relate to Paul's "unveiled" ministry, with its greater glory? Recurring comments about contrasting responses to Paul's ministry suggest that his reasoning about Moses relates to the charge that Paul is a rather unimpressive speaker, whose preaching has had embarrassingly mixed results (2 Cor 2:15-16; 4:2-4). Again, Paul does not deny but rather reinterprets the evidence. His greater forthrightness—no "veiling" and, concretely, no fancy rhetoric (2 Cor 2:17; 4:2; 10:10; see also 1 Cor 2:1-2)—is

[47]Hays again recognizes this difficulty but dismisses it, maintaining that Paul "apparently disregards" Exodus's portrayal of Moses as unveiled while delivering God's word to Israel (*Echoes of Scripture*, 140).

[48]On the ambiguity of *telos* here and possible connections to Deut 31, see Heath, "Moses' End," 51-52.

[49]Hafemann, "Glory and Veil," 34.

[50]Importantly, as Hafemann observes, the people's fear is not portrayed negatively in this earlier theophany, when their fear serves to bolster their resolve against sin (esp. idolatry) and expresses appropriate reverence for God ("Glory and Veil," 34, in conversation with Moshe Greenberg).

[51]Hafemann, "Glory and Veil," 34.

[52]See Hafemann, "Glory and Veil," esp. 40-42.

[53]As Hafemann suggests, Ex 33:3, 5 suggests that "the effect of [God's] presence" on the people has changed following the golden calf incident: "Rather than sanctification [as in Ex 20], God's presence in the midst of his people now means judgment for" them ("Glory and Veil," 34; see also 35-36, 43).

[54]Hafemann, "Glory and Veil," 35, citing also Ex 34:6-7. Hafemann ultimately sees both mercy and judgment in the veiling ("Glory and Veil," 35-36).

warranted by the definitive good news he proclaims, a more glorious hope than was accessible through Moses (2 Cor 3:10-12). However, the effect of Paul's forthrightness is indeed that some experience exposure to the glory of God in Christ as a revelation that brings death (2 Cor 2:15-16), the very thing that would have happened to the Israelites if Moses had not worn a protective veil.[55]

In accounting for the fact that some reject his message to their own harm, Paul extends and relocates the metaphor of the veil. For those who experience Paul's unveiled ministry as death-dealing, the veil that once covered Moses' face still obscures their reading of the old covenant/"Moses"—that is, the Scriptures associated with Moses (2 Cor 3:14-15).[56] Viewed from another angle, the veil now covers their "hearts" (2 Cor 3:15, my translation)—perhaps suggesting that in their cases hearts of stone, or "hardened" minds (2 Cor 3:14), have not yet been replaced with the "fleshy hearts" on which the Spirit writes (see above on 2 Cor 3:3). Shifting the metaphor yet again, in 2 Corinthians 4:3 Paul describes the gospel he preaches as itself being that which is "veiled to those who are perishing." For such people, there is an important sense in which Paul's gospel, as gospel ("good news"), remains concealed (2 Cor 4:3).[57]

These permutations of the veiling metaphor have a common thread. Whereas the veil served a protective function in Moses' day, now it becomes a hindrance to receiving life in Christ through the transformative work of the Spirit, who facilitates life-giving receptivity to God's revelation. Though there may be some sense in which the present veil is the same veil that Moses used (2 Cor 3:14), Paul attributes the ongoing and now-destructive concealment not to Moses but rather to the "god of this world" (2 Cor 4:4). Conversely, the possibility of life-giving receptivity to Paul's message depends on the revelatory action of the true God, revealed in Jesus Christ (2 Cor 4:4-6). As promised in the prophets (see above on 2 Cor 3:3, 6; see also 2 Cor 6:16–7:1), now not only Moses but all God's people can receive even fuller revelation as transformative rather than as fatal. This is so precisely because of the gift of the Spirit, who writes on their fleshy hearts (see 2 Cor 3:3, 6, 17-18).[58] Like Moses—who removed his veil while meeting with the Lord (*kyrios*, Ex 34:34 LXX)—anyone "in Christ" (2 Cor 3:14) has the "veil" removed upon "turn[ing] to the Lord" (*kyrios*, 2 Cor 3:16), that is, "the Spirit" (2 Cor 3:17-18).[59]

Speaking always in the presence of the Lord, before whom "the veil is removed" (2 Cor 3:16; see also 2 Cor 2:17; 4:2; 12:19), Paul cannot veil himself or his gospel (2 Cor 3:18), not even if such a "veil" might make his message more appealing and less hazardous to those who have not yet "turn[ed] to the Lord" (2 Cor 3:16) to be transformed by the Spirit (2 Cor 3:17-18). To the extent that Paul and his coworkers "commend [them]selves," they do so precisely through their

[55]Hafemann does not fully address the "negative" side of responses to Paul's "unveiled" preaching; see "Glory and Veil," 43-44.

[56]The immediate focus seems to be on Jews who do not believe Jesus is the Messiah, though Paul might make similar claims of Gentiles who read Israel's Scriptures without registering their witness to Jesus. On the shift from Moses-as-individual to Moses-as-Scripture, see Hays, *Echoes of Scripture*, 145.

[57]In this context, the "end of the glory" would indeed seem to be its goal/aim in Christ. Thus, the reading I advance here fits well with Heath's suggestion that *to telos tou katargoumenou* may be ambiguous and for a reason: "The nature of the Israelites' end (and that of the Mosaic icon at which they gaze) is open to a twofold consummation, according to whether or not they turn to 'the Lord' (2 Cor 3.16-18)"—an interpretation Heath sees as consonant with Moses' words in Deut 31 ("Moses' End," 51-52).

[58]See similarly, e.g., Hafemann, "Glory and Veil," 43-44.

[59]See discussion, e.g., in Hays, *Echoes of Scripture*, 143-44, and (on Paul's alteration of Ex 34:34 LXX), 146-47. On Paul's use of "Lord" here in relation to subsequent trinitarian distinctions, see also Thrall, *I and II Corinthians*, 136-38.

forthright teaching (2 Cor 4:2; see 2 Cor 3:1). Such frank preaching is off-putting or worse to those who experience Paul's message as bringing judgment and death—the result (*telos*) avoided in Moses' case through protective veiling (see also 2 Cor 2:15-16; 4:2-6; Ex 34:30).[60] However, this outcome has to do not with a failing on Paul's part but with the imperceptivity of those who experience the gospel as "veiled" because their own "minds" have been "blinded" by "the god of this world" (2 Cor 4:3-4). In contrast, the true God is the one who provides the illumination needed rightly to perceive the transformative "light of the gospel of the glory of Christ, who is the image of God" (2 Cor 4:4; see also 2 Cor 4:6).

Treasure in jars of clay: Mortal weakness and divine empowerment (2 Corinthians 4:7–5:10). The divine source and hence sure hope of Paul's ministry fosters resilient but humble confidence. Paul and his teammates do not "lose heart" (2 Cor 4:1, 16)—or, stated positively, they are "confident" (see 2 Cor 5:6, 8)—despite the fact that their undeniable vulnerability to suffering might seem to invite discouragement (2 Cor 4:7–5:10; see also 2 Cor 1:8-11). To convey this paradoxical reality, Paul develops a new metaphor, stating that he and his coworkers have the surpassingly glorious "treasure" of their ministry "in clay jars" (2 Cor 4:7).

The Greek term translated as "clay jars" (*ostrakinos*) comes up numerous times in the Old Testament, where such jars could be used to preserve other (sometimes important) items but were also susceptible to being contaminated and/or shattered (e.g., Lev 11:33; Is 30:14; Jer 32:14 [39:14 LXX]; Lam 4:2). As implied by the use of the same term in 2 Timothy 2:20, clay jars themselves were seen as less valuable than containers made of materials such as gold or silver. In 2 Corinthians 4, Paul's use of the image allows him to name at once the preciousness of the gospel he preaches and the humble vulnerability of the mortal life in which he carries this treasure: a life less impressive, humanly speaking, than some—notwithstanding the surpassing greatness of the treasure it bears.

Paul's words in 2 Corinthians 4 offer encouragement to any who find themselves living out a vocation that feels beyond their means. More specifically, given that Paul addresses a situation in which his authority has been called into question because of his failure to conform to certain (e.g., rhetorical) norms of the wider culture, his reflection speaks to and for those who—due to race/ethnicity, gender, education, personality, abilities, or other factors—may not fit the culturally typical profile for the vocation to which God calls them.

Paul exemplifies the experience of divinely given qualification within apparent disqualification. Anticipating his later litany of trials (2 Cor 11:23-33), he builds on the image of a treasure-filled but breakable jar by describing the contradictions that attend his ministry. He and his coworkers are "pressed-hard," yet this pressure does not narrow their ability to minister (see also 2 Cor 6:12); they are "at a loss" (*aporoumenoi*), "but not totally at a loss" (*exaporoumenoi*, 2 Cor 4:8, my translation). The list culminates in the ultimate paradox, the meeting of death and life in the bodies of Paul and his coworkers as they risk their lives to bear embodied witness to Jesus' death and resurrection (2 Cor 4:10-11; see also 2 Cor 3:18; 13:4). Christological precedent thus undergirds Paul's countercultural understanding of his weaknesses as opportunities for the demonstration of God's power (see 2 Cor 4:7; 3:4-6; 12:8-10). If he and his team dare to speak a message that endangers their very survival, they do so for the sake of Christ's people—not least the believers in

[60]Hafemann maintains that Jewish interpretive traditions tend to view Moses' veiling as protective ("Glory and Veil," 31).

Corinth—and in the sure hope of being raised by the God who raised Jesus from the dead (2 Cor 4:11-15; see also 2 Cor 1:3-7).

The reason Paul and his coworkers do not despair, despite the physical toll of their ministry, is their hope of still-greater glory to come and the sobering prospect of Christ's final judgment (2 Cor 4:16–5:10). Though Paul refers to a glory beyond the present life, he makes clear that his hope is not for disembodied existence but for life in a no-longer-mortal body (2 Cor 5:1-4; see also 1 Cor 15). This hope is firm because it is rooted in God, who not only raised Jesus from the dead (2 Cor 4:14) but has also given to believers a "guarantee" in the sending of the Spirit (2 Cor 5:5)—that is, the Spirit through whom Christians experience a transformative encounter with God even now (2 Cor 3:17-18). Paul's theologically grounded hope enables him to live out his ministry with a view not to mere human commendation (2 Cor 3:1) but rather to the coming judgment that the risen Lord will pass on every person's actions in the body (2 Cor 5:10), that "clay jar" of mortal life in which Paul carries around the great "treasure" of the gospel (2 Cor 4:7).

In sum, Paul (re)interprets his potentially shameful, even life-threatening experiences in terms of the larger narrative of God's work in the world, particularly the death and resurrection of Christ, the sending of the Spirit, and the prospect of eschatological judgment. Analogous (re)interpretation of our lives and callings, including sufferings and setbacks in our attempts to live into the lordship of Christ, can orient and empower those of us seeking (from whatever social location) to foster unity and justice within and beyond the church walls. For White Christians who are committed to pursuing multiethnic community and racial justice but who may be fond of the delusion that we can seek Christ's kingdom without having to suffer for it, Paul's christologically grounded description of his ministry reminds us that bearing witness to the crucified Lord may well increase our inability to evade suffering—at least, in the short term of this life. Even so, Paul also reminds us that the eschatological goal of kingdom work is well worth whatever trials we may voluntarily confront for the sake of bearing faithful witness to Christ, the risen Lord and ultimate judge of all.

Paul's positive appeal: Be reconciled with God in Christ (2 Corinthians 5:11–6:13; 7:2-4). The mention of Jesus' role as judge allows Paul to pivot again to the question of his and his teammates' qualifications and their commendation or lack thereof (2 Cor 5:11-13). Though he has been defensively describing his ministry, Paul insists that his point is not to commend himself. Rather, he is providing an opportunity for the Corinthians to commend him (2 Cor 5:12-13; see also 2 Cor 3:1-3; 12:11). Paul does not go long before shifting the focus back to Jesus, the love of whom motivates Paul and his coworkers in their bold, perilous ministry (2 Cor 5:14-21). Paul again highlights Christ's death and resurrection and believers' participation in this reality as the ground for uncompromisingly frank proclamation of the gospel. Christ "died for all," and therefore there is an important sense in which "all have died" and now ought to "live . . . for him who died and was raised for them" (2 Cor 5:14-15). This participation in the life of the risen Christ is a participation in "new creation" (2 Cor 5:17), something only God could bring about (2 Cor 5:18).[61] Paul accordingly emphasizes that his appeal to the

[61]Note also the echo of Gen 1:3 in 2 Cor 4:6 (e.g., Thrall, *I and II Corinthians*, 139). As others have argued, the NRSV's translation of 2 Cor 5:17 ("there is a new creation") is preferable to the more individual-focused rendering found, e.g., in the RSV ("he is a new creation"). Though both are defensible translations, the former appropriately registers the cosmic dimension of redemption according to Paul (e.g., Rom 8:19-25).

Corinthians is not on his own behalf, nor is it for the sake of his own glory or commendation. Much as Paul depicted himself and his colaborers as couriers in the metaphor of the commendatory letter (2 Cor 3:1-3), he now describes his team as "ambassadors for Christ," emissaries through whom God invites the Corinthians to reconciliation in Christ (2 Cor 5:20-21).

It is from this vantage point, as coworkers of God in inviting the Corinthians to reconciliation, that Paul exhorts them "not to accept the grace of God in vain" (2 Cor 6:1). He underscores the urgency of the matter with a quotation from Isaiah 49:8 LXX (2 Cor 6:2), here taken to convey God's favorable disposition toward the believers in their present moment. Interestingly, subsequent verses call the Corinthians to be reconciled with Paul and his team (2 Cor 6:3-4, 11-12). The implication of the juxtaposed invitations—to reconciliation with God and to renewed receptivity toward Paul—seems to be that Paul views reconciliation with himself and his coworkers (i.e., God's colaborers) as bound up with the Corinthians' genuine acceptance of reconciliation with God in Christ.

This is again a very bold claim, but it coheres with the wider letter. Paul has already argued that the ministry entrusted to him surpasses even that of Moses, the paramount Old Testament mediator between God and God's people. Further, as becomes clear in 2 Corinthians 11:2-4, the tension between Paul and the Corinthians is due in part to the influence of interlopers who, in Paul's view, are leading the Corinthians away from the true gospel. In this context, one can see why Paul would frame receptivity to himself (one of God's authorized "ambassadors," unlike his theologically erring opponents) as an urgent element of rightly receiving God's grace.[62]

In 2 Corinthians 6:3-10, Paul elaborates on the ways in which he and his coworkers demonstrate their authenticity as ministers of the gospel. He again asserts his forthrightness in ministry (2 Cor 6:3; see also, e.g., 2 Cor 4:2) before highlighting other ways through which he and his coworkers "have commended [them]selves" (2 Cor 6:4-10). The list includes items one might expect the Corinthians readily to appreciate, such as knowledge (2 Cor 6:6; see also 1 Cor 1:5, 18-25). However, Paul also deems commendable certain seemingly shameful experiences, such as being beaten and imprisoned (2 Cor 6:5), and he describes his team's purportedly commendable service with paradoxical statements that underscore the countercultural character of service to the crucified and risen Lord. Though Paul and his coworkers are viewed "as impostors," in fact they are "true" (2 Cor 6:8). Though they are seen "as unknown" (perhaps specifically without formal/human commendation?), they are "well known" (2 Cor 6:9)—having been made "manifest," as Paul earlier stated, to God, and hopefully also to the believers in Corinth (2 Cor 5:11, my translation). To the Corinthians, so easily swayed by others' fancy letters and impressive rhetoric, Paul and his companions may appear "as having nothing." In a more important sense, however, these true servants of God "posses[s] everything" (2 Cor 6:10).

Paul's positive invitation to the Corinthians is that they re-realize this truth, warmly reciprocating the love of Paul and his team rather than pulling back in search of something more impressive by the standards of their culture

[62]See also Nave, "2 Corinthians," 318. Whereas Nave expresses reservations about Paul's close association of reconciliation with himself and with God, I would argue that the wider epistolary context makes Paul's move theologically acceptable, albeit not one to be imitated too hastily.

(2 Cor 6:11-12). It is a request Paul reiterates in 2 Corinthians 7:2-4, where he also reaffirms his commitment to and concern for the Corinthian believers.

Paul's cautionary command: "Do not be unequally yoked" (2 Corinthians 6:14–7:1). Between these two appeals, in 2 Corinthians 6:14–7:1, Paul includes a catena of Old Testament intertexts (2 Cor 6:16-18), bracketed by instructions to avoid "be[ing] unequally yoked with unbelievers" (2 Cor 6:14) and instead to maintain holiness in all of life (2 Cor 7:1).[63] A string of rhetorical questions gives a sharp edge to the pericope (2 Cor 6:14-16), but it is not immediately clear what Paul's concrete concern is or why he brings it up now.[64]

In some (not least evangelical) contexts, the warning against being "unequally yoked" is often taken to mean that Christians ought not to marry (or date) non-Christians.[65] Whatever one thinks of this counsel, the use of 2 Corinthians 6:14–7:1 as a prooftext is puzzling, since the passage does not directly address marriage.[66] Closer examination of the scriptural intertexts that Paul cites, as well as the literary setting of the catena within the letter, will shed light on what 2 Corinthians 6:14–7:1 may be about in the first instance, providing a firmer foundation for analogous reasoning about issues not explicitly treated here.

Paul bases the call to holiness in these verses on scriptural promises (2 Cor 7:1) that the holy God will be present among God's people. Extending his earlier engagement with the motif of the (new) covenant (see especially 2 Cor 3), Paul initially draws on passages that frame this promised presence in covenantal terms. Leviticus 26:11, quoted in 2 Corinthians 6:16, includes God's presence among the blessings that will come if the people adhere to the covenant established through Moses (Lev 26:1-13); the wider context also warns of the consequences of failing to do so (Lev 26:14-39). Ezekiel 37:27, evoked later in 2 Corinthians 6:16, promises God's presence in the context of looking forward to the divine establishment of an everlasting covenant of peace with God's people (Ezek 37:26), which will prompt the nations' recognition of the Lord's sanctifying work (Ezek 37:28).

Consistent with themes in the wider context of both Leviticus 26 and Ezekiel 37 (esp. Ezek 37:24, 28), the next passages from which Paul quotes highlight the obligation placed on God's people by divine presence. Thus, 2 Corinthians 6:17 echoes Isaiah 52:11, with its call to holiness as part of a promised restoration of God's people, whom God will accompany as they return from exile (Is 52:12; see also Ex 33:1-5, 12-17; 34:8). Paul also incorporates language from God's promise in Ezekiel 20:34

---

[63]"Unequally yoked" is my translation; NRSV has "mismatched."

[64]Due to the perceived thematic shift and prevalence of terms not typical of Paul, some view 2 Cor 6:14–7:1 as a non-Pauline passage (added by Paul or a later interpolation); others have attempted to identify it with the (otherwise lost) letter to which Paul refers in 1 Cor 5:9. See discussion, e.g., in Furnish, *II Corinthians*, 27; Matthews, "2 Corinthians," 207-8. The latter proposal seems implausible, since 2 Cor 6:14–7:1 speaks of separation from people understood to be nonbelievers, which seems to closer to the Corinthians' *mis*understanding of Paul's earlier letter than to Paul's clarification of its import in 1 Cor 5. See Furnish, *II Corinthians*, 27.

[65]Some English translations encourage this interpretation. E.g., according to the NEB, the Corinthians should "not unite [themselves] with unbelievers," since the latter "are not fit mates for" the Corinthians (2 Cor 6:14). Thrall, in a commentary on the NEB, infers from 2 Cor 6:14 that "it is foolhardy [for believers] to risk moral corruption by contracting [marriage with unbelievers] where it does not already exist" (*I and II Corinthians*, 157).

[66]The unusual term *heterozygeō* ("unequally yoked") may evoke Lev 19:19 (see also Deut 22:10)—which, on a literal level, is about animals. Paul can reason from OT animal regulations to instructions for the church (e.g., 1 Cor 9:8-10), but he does not explicitly do so here. For Paul's fullest extant counsel about marriages between believers and unbelievers, see 1 Cor 7, esp. 1 Cor 7:12-16, 39.

to "receive" the people (LXX; 2 Cor 6:17, my translation)—a promise pointedly qualified in the following verses by the Lord's insistence that only the faithful will be allowed to enter into the promised land (Ezek 20:33-38). Similarly, after the lines evoked in 2 Corinthians 6:18, 2 Samuel 7:14 goes on to state that God's promise to David's descendant—described elsewhere in Scripture as a covenant (e.g., 2 Sam 23:5; 2 Chron 7:18; 21:7; Jer 33:21)—includes the promise of discipline, should David's offspring stray (2 Sam 7:14).[67]

As noted, Paul brackets this covenant-focused catena with calls to holiness in the sense of being set apart from polluting influences (2 Cor 6:14-16; 7:1). Whose contaminating fellowship are the Corinthians supposed to avoid, though? The initial characterization of the issue—in terms of the danger of being "unequally yoked" with "unbelievers"—would seem to suggest that Paul is urging the Corinthians against some kind of close connection/partnership with people who are totally outside the church. This impression finds support from the subsequent contrasts drawn between Christ and Beliar (Satan) and between God's temple and idols (2 Cor 6:15-16). However, if we treat 2 Corinthians as a coherent whole, it is telling that this seeming digression is framed by appeals to the Corinthians to renew their love for Paul and his team (2 Cor 6:11-13; 7:2-4). Perhaps the strong characterization of the threatened contamination in 2 Corinthians 6:14-16 and 2 Corinthians 7:1 anticipates Paul's later depiction of his rivals in Corinth as proclaimers of a different gospel, a different Christ, and a different Spirit from that which Paul and his coworkers proclaim (2 Cor 11:3-4). If so, Paul's implied assertion is that these rivals—despite their insistence otherwise (e.g., 2 Cor 11:23)—are not truly believers at all, not truly proclaimers of or participants in the new covenant (see also 2 Cor 11:13-15; Gal 1:6-9).[68] As counterfeit Christians, they should be avoided for the sake of the holiness of the community at Corinth.

It is worth emphasizing that Paul takes a much more conciliatory approach in 1 Corinthians when addressing factions that have formed around himself and others whom he considers legitimate ministers of the gospel (1 Cor 1:10-17; 3:1–4:6).[69] In the church's current, polarized moment, we must learn from Paul to distinguish between those conflicts that arise over perversions of the gospel and those conflicts that stem from mere preferences for this or that teacher or style. We can glean further pointers on this score from Paul's more direct discussion of his rivals beginning in 2 Corinthians 9. First, though, Paul ties up a loose thread related to Titus's report in Macedonia and then transitions into an exhortation concerning the Jerusalem collection, in service of which Titus and others are to return to Corinth prior to Paul's third visit.

[67]The LXX speaks of David's "offspring" (*sperma*, 2 Sam 7:12 NETS), most immediately Solomon. Christian tradition interprets the promise ultimately in relation to Jesus; in 2 Corinthians, Paul extends this reading to God's people in Christ, giving the verse a breadth of reference that may account for deviations from Septuagintal wording. Paul (or his source) not only makes the reference to children plural but also, as Matthews notes, explicitly adds mention of "daughters" ("2 Corinthians," 208—though Matthews does not otherwise find evidence in this letter of Paul "acknowled[ing] the presence of real women in Corinth"; see 202).

[68]Nave similarly argues that, if we take 2 Cor 6:11–7:3 as originally included in this epistolary context, it seems to serve as an exhortation to "the Corinthians to separate themselves from [Paul's] opponents in Corinth" ("2 Corinthians," 317).

[69]Note that Peter, with whom Paul had sharp conflict (Gal 2:11-14), is among those toward whom he takes a conciliatory approach in 1 Cor 1:10-15. In view of this past practice, I would nuance Nave's judgment that Paul in 2 Corinthians displays a problematical my-way-or-the-highway attitude. See Nave, "2 Corinthians," esp. 328. The harshness of Paul's response to his rivals in 2 Corinthians reflects his perception of the spiritual threat these rivals pose to his beloved Corinthians (2 Cor 11:4; see also Gal 1:6-9; 5:7-12).

CONFLICT WITH THE CORINTHIANS, PART TWO: RESOLUTION AND CLARIFICATION (2 CORINTHIANS 7:5-16)

Paul's reaffirmation of his approval of and care for the Corinthian believers in 2 Corinthians 7:3-4 leads him finally back to the question of Titus's update about their response to Paul's letter of rebuke. Having gone to Macedonia in search of news about the Corinthians, Paul found consolation when Titus arrived with a good report (2 Cor 7:5-7, 13; see also 2 Cor 1:3-7; 2:13-14). Paul delicately avoids rehearsing the offense that prompted his reproachful letter; the Corinthians no doubt knew the details all too well. Instead, he focuses on the Corinthians' penitent response, marked by grief over sin as well as eagerness to rectify the situation and demonstrate their integrity (2 Cor 7:9-12)—presumably through the communal discipline that Paul both commends and tempers in 2 Corinthians 2:5-11. Though Paul admits that he once regretted grieving them with his letter, he now insists on the salutary character of the grief they experienced (2 Cor 7:9-10).

Christians grappling with racial and ethnic injustice would do well to lean on the distinction Paul draws here between, on the one hand, godly sorrow that leads to repentance and salvation and, on the other hand, worldly sorrow that leads to death. For White Christians in particular, the dawning realization of our ongoing benefit from and complicity in others' oppression can provoke a range of feelings, including grief. Not all feelings of grief in relation to whiteness and racial injustice are equally conducive to the sort of personal and societal reformation to which faithfulness would call us, however. Paul's discussion of godly grief can help us to identify and move toward properly Christian grief, expressed in (ultimately life-giving) repentance. Such grief differs from deadening "worldly grief" (2 Cor 7:10), which takes at least three forms in relation to White people's reaction to seeing whiteness, White privilege, and racial injustice.[70]

First, there is the worldly grief of regretting consequences more than the unjust biases, behaviors, and systems that led to them. This sort of "grief" finds expression, for example, when White people lament the disruption caused by protesters seeking racial justice but are not (or are less acutely) grieved by the reality of racial injustice. Such grief tacitly values property and (White) convenience/comfort over the lives of Black, brown, Asian, Indigenous, and other minoritized people—all human beings created in the image of God. Such grief also walls us off from true repentance, which requires criticism of ourselves rather than of other people's responses to us and to our shared world.

Second, there is the worldly grief of White despair. Despair tells us that, yes, things are bad with respect to racial/ethnic injustice, but it is a hopeless case—or at any rate, we are a hopeless case. This grief seems to take the problem seriously, which may make those who experience it think that we have done our due diligence simply by feeling bad. In fact, though, this grief lets us off the hook. How can I be expected to repent if I am a hopeless case? Despair invites a sort of self-loathing that masquerades as repentance but accomplishes nothing. If the pseudo-repentance of self-loathing is intolerable, we even may shift from despair to the more comfortable feeling of denial. Either way, we effectively reject the invitation to repentance that leads to life.

[70]I write in summer 2020, in the wake of protests over the murder of George Floyd, Breonna Taylor, Ahmaud Arbery, and others—and over the systemic injustices these murders highlight. All three sorts of worldly grief described below have been on display in some White responses to protests.

Third, there is what we might call the worldly grief of White self-victimization. This variety of grief occurs when white Christians try to reframe ourselves as the ones who are suffering. To be sure, all human beings suffer, and there is and should be a space for naming and lamenting every suffering. However, when White people foreground our personal trials (or our sufferings as members of some other group) *in contexts where the conversation is about race*, we are appropriating space that is not ours to take, recentering the conversation on ourselves in a way that reinscribes our privilege. Consciously or otherwise, we attempt to shield ourselves from the painful realization that—whatever our real grievances against the world may be—we have been complicit in, have benefited from, and have been malformed by racism and its systemic effects. The outcome of this third sort of worldly grief, again, is that we miss the opportunity to do the hard work of repentance that leads to life.

Godly grief in the face of racial/ethnic prejudice and injustice, White supremacy, and associated evils is more honestly self-reflective than grief-over-consequences, more tolerable and fruitful than despair, and more just and loving than White self-victimization. In the context of racialized injustices, godly grief for a White person will involve listening to people of color long enough to find out about the root issues that they protest, rather than fixating on the tangible consequences of protest that inconvenience "us." It will involve admitting that we have failed where we did not have to fail (contra despair) and that (contra self-victimization) we have failed in ways that we can and should repent of, regardless of how others may also have failed us in various contexts. Such godly grief leads to repentance because we know that God in Christ has provided for our forgiveness and freed us from the power of Sin so that we no longer have to be subject to its dominion—a freedom into which Paul elsewhere exhorts believers to live actively (e.g., Rom 6).

The Corinthians' openness to such true repentance brings joy to both Titus and Paul (2 Cor 7:13-16). Pastorally, Paul's strong affirmation reinforces their faithful response to correction. Rhetorically, this praise also encourages openness to the request he will now make concerning Titus's return to arrange for their participation in an important fundraising project (see 2 Cor 8:6, 16-24; 9:3).

JERUSALEM COLLECTION (2 CORINTHIANS 8:1–9:15)

Paul had already mentioned this endeavor—sometimes called the Jerusalem collection—in 1 Corinthians 16:1-4. There, as in 2 Corinthians 8–9, Paul assumes the Corinthians' knowledge of and openness to contributing to the project, which involved collecting financial support from primarily Gentile churches and delivering this aid to impoverished believers in Jerusalem. Repeated references to the collection in Paul's letters demonstrate the high value he placed on the project. In Romans, Paul's request for prayer in connection with the delivery of the collection suggests he had apprehensions about its (and his) reception in Jerusalem, by both Jews who did believe in Jesus and Jews who did not (Rom 15:25-32). Nevertheless, he was intent on completing the project. Why?

Beyond providing material relief to Jerusalem believers, the collection seems to have had symbolic overtones for Paul. As others have suggested, it may be his attempt to live out the commitment recorded in Galatians 2:1-10, where the Jerusalem leaders approve of Paul's Gentile-inclusive mission and ask only that he remember the poor, which he expresses eagerness to do. Paul may also have seen taking the (Gentile) collection to Jerusalem as a fulfillment of Old Testament passages such as Isaiah 60:3-7.[71]

Whatever his own reasons for valuing the collection may have been, in 2 Corinthians 8–9 Paul makes a rhetorically powerful case for the Corinthians' participation. He broaches the matter with yet another reference to Macedonia, praising the believers there for their sacrificial contribution (2 Cor 8:1-5). Paul thus sets up a competition of sorts (2 Cor 8:8), establishing a high bar for the Corinthians' giving. He increases the pressure by praising the Corinthians and calling on them to excel yet again, this time in giving (2 Cor 8:7). Further, he reminds the Corinthians of their own past commitment to contribute (2 Cor 8:10-11), which Paul had used to motivate the Macedonians' participation (2 Cor 9:2). In short, both Paul and the Corinthians will be shamed if the Macedonians find out that the Corinthians do not willingly give to the collection (2 Cor 9:1-5).

Perhaps there can be healthy competition within Christian community (e.g., Rom 12:10). Given the Corinthians' tendency to divisive rivalry (e.g., 1 Cor 1:10–3:23; 12:12–13:13), however, Paul's compelling case for contributing to the collection does come with pastoral risks.[72] Although the Jerusalem collection was a historically particular project without exact parallel today, the practice of giving/receiving between differently located Christians remains fraught. How can we encourage generous giving by those who have financial means, without creating a toxic sort of competition among them? In our own contexts, we might add: How can we foster generosity while discouraging patronizing attitudes toward its recipients, whether less privileged communities in our own city or brothers and sisters elsewhere in the world? Today, these questions take specific, often racialized shapes due to factors such as the legacy of modern colonialism, the transatlantic slave trade, and Jim Crow; the ongoing process of globalization; and the effects of mass and social media. As we seek to think through giving/receiving with theological-pastoral nuance and humility, four aspects of Paul's reasoning about the Jerusalem collection in 2 Corinthians prove instructive.

First, although Paul does give a competitive edge to his discussion by invoking the example set by the hard-pressed but generous Macedonians (2 Cor 8:1-8), he ultimately frames contributions to the collection in terms not of competition but of mutuality and sufficiency within the church (2 Cor 8:12-15). What matters finally is not how much the Corinthians give, whether more or less than the Macedonians. Instead, the aim of the collection is to foster mutuality within the translocal church, such that everyone has enough (2 Cor 8:11-14).[73] Likewise today, the point of sharing resources is not to compare the

---

[71]For discussions of what is at stake for Paul in the Jerusalem collection, see, e.g., Matthews, "2 Corinthians," 208-9.

[72]Nave alludes to some of these complexities in "2 Corinthians," 320.

[73]As Awet Iassu Andemicael rightly observes, "Paul is not writing about financial equality between the Corinthians and the Jerusalemites, but about matching up the abundance or surplus of the former and the need of the latter. Paul is seeking universal sufficiency, not necessarily quantitative equality. In absolute terms, some may have more ('the one who had much') and some, less ('the one who had little'). Nevertheless, everyone in the system has enough—no one has too much or too little." See Andemicael, "Grace, Equity, Participation: The Economy of God in 2 Corinthians 8:8-15," *Anglican Theological Review* 98, no. 4 (2016): 628. On the theological grounding of and christological basis for this aspect of Paul's exhortation, see 628-31. For a discussion of 2 Cor 3 that emphasizes the motif of mutuality throughout the letter, see Teslina, "In the Image."

amount given by particular congregations or congregants, nor is the point to create unhealthy sorts of dependence or manipulative power relations between individuals or congregations. Rather, in giving/receiving, individuals and communities live into the unity of the church in Christ so that each member of this larger body has enough. We give and receive for *ecclesiological* reasons.

Second, Paul provides crucial *christological* scaffolding for this call to self-sacrificing mutuality. While the generosity of other believers may provide a bit of healthy peer pressure, the definitive precedent for generous giving is not the Macedonians but Jesus (2 Cor 8:9). By highlighting Christ's own gracious gift of himself for the salvation of God's people, Paul reminds those with more financial resources of their own dependence on Christ's grace (2 Cor 8:9).[74] This remains an important word—not least for majority-White congregations, who may lose sight of our dependent status because of our (in many cases) greater financial resources.[75]

Third, Paul opens and closes his discussion of the collection by emphasizing God as the source of all Christian giving, a theological insight that leads Paul to praise God. Generous giving reinforces church unity to the glory of God, as believers thank God for providing through other members of the household of faith (2 Cor 9:11-14; see also 2 Cor 8:19). Indeed, the divine gift of the Corinthians' willingness to give is itself something for which thanks is due to God (2 Cor 9:13-15; see also 2 Cor 8:1). By couching his appeal in these *theological-doxological* terms, Paul reconfigures the problematic power dynamics that might otherwise be created by a relationship of financial giving and receiving. As Stephen Fowl argues in relation to Philippians, such theological (re) framing of economic support disrupts the patronage system that normally would have governed such exchanges in the ancient world, where the generosity of "patrons" enhanced their social status, securing them the loyalty and praise of their beneficiaries ("clients").[76] Even for contemporary societies that do not operate with an acknowledged system of patron-client relations, analogous sub-Christian power dynamics can arise in the context of giving/receiving. This reality is indicated, for example, by the fact that we would (correctly, and disapprovingly) term "patronizing" a majority-White church that gave financial aid with the expectation of accolades

---

[74]The semantic range of the Greek word *charis* allows for wordplay not easily conveyed in English. This term names both Christ's grace/gift of himself (2 Cor 8:9) and the grace/gift the Corinthians should enact by contributing to the collection (2 Cor 8:6-7, 19). Participating in the collection is itself a gift/grace (2 Cor 8:1, 4; 9:14), made possible by God's grace/gift (2 Cor 9:8), prompting the further "grace" of thanksgiving (2 Cor 8:16; 9:15). On the "hermeneutical puzzle" created by this wordplay in the context of Paul's larger argument, see Andemicael, "Grace, Equity, Participation," esp. 622-27. Building on Kathryn Tanner's understanding of *kenōsis* and John Barclay's analysis of 2 Cor 8–9, Andemicael concludes, "If the soteriological act of Christ does not diminish Christ in any way, then the human act of giving, in imitation of Christ, need not diminish the Corinthian givers—certainly not to the point of beggaring them financially" ("Grace, Equity, Participation," 624).

[75]One might also note the relevance of what Willie James Jennings calls "Gentile forgetfulness"—the phenomenon in which White/European Gentiles arrogantly forgot the grace of our own inclusion in the (Jewish) people of God and, in so forgetting our place in God's story, have tended also to jettison the humility and openness to others that once made our own inclusion possible. For a condensed version of his argument, see Jennings, "Overcoming Racial Faith," *Divinity Magazine* (2015): 4-9, esp. 6-7, https://divinity.duke.edu/sites/divinity.duke.edu/files/divinity-magazine/DukeDivinityMag_Spring15.WEB_.compressed.pdf.

[76]See Stephen E. Fowl, "Know Your Context: Giving and Receiving Money in Philippians," *Interpretation* 56, no. 1 (2002): 45-58. Compare Matthews's judgment that the Corinthians would have perceived Paul's refusal to receive their financial support as "signaling his unwillingness to enter into a relationship of *mutuality*" ("2 Corinthians," 211, emphasis added).

from and/or control over a non-White recipient congregation.[77] Paul's theological-doxological emphasis offers us a more faithful framework for understanding and enacting giving/receiving—including across differences of race, ethnicity, and culture that may be bound up with financial inequalities—as a graced participation in the generosity of God, to the glory of God.[78]

Fourth and finally, Paul also draws on several Old Testament passages, thereby highlighting the scriptural grounds for christologically informed, theologically grounded giving/receiving within the translocal church.[79] Specifically, Paul again evokes Exodus before echoing a psalm and Isaiah. Paul's allusive discussion of his ministry in relation to Moses' earlier in the letter (2 Cor 3:1–4:6) primed the Corinthians to think about their experiences in connection with the narrative of Exodus.[80] Now, Paul invites them to draw further inferences from another scene in Exodus, when the Lord first provides manna for Israel following their escape from Egypt (Ex 16:1-36). Paul focuses on the issue of distribution. According to Exodus 16:18 (quoted in 2 Cor 8:15), every Israelite ended up with the right amount of manna for each household's daily need.[81] Likewise, the Jerusalem collection aims to make sure that every believer has enough—which, at the moment, means that the Corinthians need to share financial resources with those in Jerusalem (2 Cor 8:13-14).

Then as now, affluent Christians have a range of reasons for resisting the economic vision Paul sketches, but one factor can be the fear that giving will threaten one's own sufficiency of supply. In 2 Corinthians 9, Paul helpfully addresses and reframes this concern, in part through further engagement with the Old Testament. He affirms that God will meet the Corinthians' own needs as they participate in providing for others (2 Cor 9:8). At the same time, Paul also refocuses the Corinthians' attention on the spiritual fruitfulness that God will bring about through their generous giving. Paul echoes two additional scriptural passages in articulating these points.

The most obvious intertext is Psalm 112:9 (Ps 111:9 LXX), from which Paul offers a marked quotation:

---

[77]For a reflection on the dynamics of giving/receiving across lines of political/ethical/hermeneutical disagreement, in this case in a global context, see A. Katherine Grieb, "Philippians and the Politics of God," *Interpretation* 61, no. 3 (2007): 256-69. Drawing on the teachings of Philippians, Paul's approach to the Jerusalem collection, and the contemporary example of an Anglican bishop from the Pacific Islands, Grieb emphasizes the need "to set up structures that will facilitate the giving and receiving of financial gifts, so necessary to the spiritual health of the whole body, in a way that does not compromise either giver or receiver, while the doctrinal argument" in question (in her case study, the Anglican Communion's stance on LGBTQ+ issues) "runs its course" (267).

[78]The *charis* wordplay (see note above) reinforces the idea that the Corinthians' generosity is in fact a "practical result of participating in the very life of Christ, of living fully in the theological realm into which Christ has drawn believers" (Andemicael, "Grace, Equity, Participation," 627).

[79]The four points listed here are not unrelated; see Hays's discussion of the "ecclesiocentric" hermeneutics reflected in Paul's engagement with Ex 16 in 2 Corinthians (*Echoes of Scripture*, 88-104).

[80]See also 1 Cor 10:1-11; as Hays suggests, that earlier letter lays the hermeneutical groundwork for the less explicitly developed allusions we find here (*Echoes of Scripture*, 91).

[81]Following Plummer, Hays rightly observes that Exodus does not specify how everyone ends up with the appropriate amount; moreover, if we infer that God miraculously (re)distributes as needed, this might seem to undermine Paul's call to generosity among believers (*Echoes of Scripture*, 88). Andemicael offers a helpful way forward when she emphasizes the christological inflection that distinguishes the situation in 2 Corinthians: "What makes the redistribution of the manna seem miraculous, almost magical, is the narrative invisibility of the mechanism of redistribution"; however, "in 2 Corinthians 8, we see the mechanism of God's action turned inside out, making visible God's non-reductive assumption of human agency into God's divine agency" ("Grace, Equity, Participation," 632). On the influence of Deut 8 on Paul's engagement with Ex 16, see Hays, *Echoes of Scripture*, 89-90.

Table 14.1. 2 Corinthians 9:9 and Psalm 112:9

2 Corinthians 9:9 (my translation)	Psalm 112:9 (111:9 LXX, my translation)
As it is written, "He scattered, he gave to the needy; his righteousness remains forever."	He scattered; he gave to the needy; his righteousness remains forever and ever; his horn will be exalted in glory.

The context of Psalm 112 suggests that the agent of "scattering"—an activity here set in near-synonymous parallelism with "giving to the needy"—is the person who fears the Lord (Ps 112:1), whose blessedness this psalm recounts. Such a person, guided by God's commandments (Ps 112:1), generously provides for those in need (Ps 112:9). Paul's quotation thus invites the Corinthians to enter into the role of being the blessed person who "gave to the needy"—in this case, by giving to the poor in Jerusalem.

Paul offers an agricultural image for the promise of enduring righteousness with which Psalm 112:9 concludes: Those who give generously will augment their "harvest of . . . righteousness" (2 Cor 9:10). Thus, though Psalm 112 does emphasize the material prosperity of the blessed person whom it describes (Ps 112:3), Paul instead fixates on the psalm's portrayal of that person's righteousness when describing the fruits of generosity. To the extent that he gestures toward material blessings that may arise from generous sharing, Paul makes clear that the aim of a fruitful material yield is additional giving. After evoking Isaiah 55:10, he affirms that God will "multiply [the Corinthians'] seed *for sowing*" (2 Cor 9:10, emphasis mine)—which in this context suggests that God will give to generous givers still more resources, not for hoarding but rather for continued generosity (see also 2 Cor 9:8).

Stepping back from 2 Corinthians 8–9, we can ask: What might it look like to inhabit such a notion of the church and its giving/receiving today? Awet Iassu Andemicael describes the task well:

> Paul challenges us, as Christians and as the church, to an entirely different level of engagement in the world—not as philanthropists who use our economic power to rescue those less fortunate, or victims who depend on the goodwill of others for our survival, but together as beloved citizens of the kingdom of God, members of God's household, and fellow participants in God's economy.[82]

Concretely, one might consider the case of predominantly White congregations that have ongoing relationships with predominantly non-White church communities. For complex reasons of historical and ongoing racial/ethnic injustice, non-White congregations often have fewer financial resources than their majority-White counterparts. As a result, one of the tricky issues that can arise in such partnerships is financial assistance. If a Latinx church is struggling to buy a van to transport elderly members to and from services, for instance, is it appropriate for an affluent White church—for whom a single van might be a very doable expenditure—to pitch in? If so, how should such financial partnership be approached? How should the project be "spun" to White church members? How should the offer be made to the Latinx congregation? It would be inappropriate for me to offer specifics since each situation would have its own contextual complexities, but Paul's reasoning with the Corinthians provides an ecclesiological, Christocentric, theological-doxological, and

[82]Andemicael, "Grace, Equity, Participation," 637.

scriptural framework on which we can build as we prayerfully discern the way forward in conversation with each other.

PAUL'S MINISTRY, PART TWO: A "FOOLISH" DEFENSE (2 CORINTHIANS 10:1–12:21)

Following the doxological climax of his reasoning about the collection (2 Cor 9:15), Paul abruptly shifts to another lengthy discussion of his apostleship (2 Cor 10:1–12:21). Earlier asides contrasting Paul and his coworkers with unnamed others (e.g., 2 Cor 2:17–3:1) give way to a more direct apologia for Paul's ministry, delivered in a tone of exasperation. The believers in Corinth, themselves the fruit of Paul's apostolic labors (2 Cor 10:7-8, 14), should surely recognize the validity of his apostleship. Instead, they are being swayed by rival teachers who have cast a shadow on the ministry of Paul and his team. As mentioned above, many of the charges leveled at Paul reflect fundamental disagreements between him and his opponents regarding the shape and proper use of apostolic authority. How can he respond to these criticisms without ceding too much ground to a problematic conception of apostleship?

Paul begins by emphasizing that, as a matter of principle, he does not play the game his would-be rivals are setting up.[83] Although, like all mortal human beings, Paul in one sense lives "in the flesh" (2 Cor 10:3), he does not subscribe to the modes of conflict and standards of greatness associated with this life ("according to the flesh"; see 2 Cor 10:1-5).[84] While others frantically compare themselves with each other, vying for top status, Paul focuses on fidelity to his own God-given vocation. He accordingly insists—as he had already in 1 Corinthians 1:31—that whoever boasts should "boast in the Lord" (2 Cor 10:17).[85] In the context of 2 Corinthians 10, such boasting is based on the commendation of the Lord, whose judgment is the one that counts (2 Cor 10:18; see also 2 Cor 12:19) and who assigns each person's "sphere of action"—in Paul's case, a sphere that includes the believers at Corinth (2 Cor 10:12-16).

Having made clear that he rejects the vision of greatness set forth by his rivals, Paul nevertheless moves in 2 Corinthians 11:1–12:13 into a self-defense that largely plays out according to the rules of their game—with one critical difference. As might be expected given 1 Corinthians 1:18-31, Paul inverts the value system used to measure greatness. He frames this rhetorically risky move as a "foolish" defense (2 Cor 11:1; 12:11) and articulates it with sharp irony and a degree of ambiguity.

Counterinterpretations (rather than outright denials) of seemingly dubious aspects of Paul's ministry bookend this self-defense (2 Cor 11:2-12; 12:12-21). Compared to his ostensibly more professional rivals, Paul is admittedly not an eloquent speaker (2 Cor 11:6). Nonetheless, he has performed "the signs of a true apostle" in Corinth (2 Cor 12:12), and he will demonstrate his apostolic authority in person by taking disciplinary measures, if need be, the next time he visits (2 Cor 12:20-21; see also 2 Cor 13:1-4). It is also true that, unlike the "superapostles" and many teachers of that day, Paul has not accepted the Corinthians' financial support for his ministry among them. However,

[83]Nave helpfully suggests a comparison with Martin Luther King Jr. and other civil rights advocates who "lived out their faith in a violent racist society without allowing that violence to force them to adopt the human standards of violence" ("2 Corinthians," 322).

[84]My translation/NRSV alternate translation.

[85]In 1 Cor 1:31, the phrase underscores the need to "boast" in the counterintuitive wisdom and power of God in Christ, rather than in one's own status. See also Jer 9:22-23; LXX 1 Sam 2:10.

this practice is an expression of—not a mark against—his parental commitment to these children in the faith (2 Cor 11:7-12; 12:13-18).

Before we consider Paul's argument between these bracketing statements, it is worth pausing over the still-complex issue of financial support for ministers of the gospel. The Pauline corpus makes clear that Paul was not in principle opposed to accepting any financial support from churches, but his refusal to receive funds from the Corinthians reminds us that there can be pastoral advantages to bivocational ministry and other arrangements that reduce a pastor's financial dependence on a congregation (see 1 Cor 9:3-18; Philem 4:10-18; 1 Thess 2:9; 2 Thess 3:7-9). Such models of ministry have long been common among less affluent churches in the United States, including many churches in which the majority of congregants are BIPOC, and similar arrangements may become necessary for a wider range of churches in the wake of the economic disruptions caused by Covid-19. Paul highlights the theological-pastoral benefits of such a practice, even as his struggles with the Corinthians also alert us to the need in such cases to avoid even the perception of profiteering on the sly.[86]

Within Paul's framing (re)interpretations of his financial practices and other supposed weaknesses (2 Cor 11:2-12; 12:12–13:4), his "foolish" boast begins with spiritual credentials. As a Jew, he can match anyone's status claims (2 Cor 11:22). As a minister of Christ, he even claims superiority to his opponents (2 Cor 11:23), provided greatness be (re)defined in terms of suffering for the gospel of Christ.[87] According to this way of thinking, what attests to Paul's apostolic authority is precisely his endurance of a wide range of shameful experiences for the sake of Christ—from undergoing imprisonment and flogging to facing opponents from multiple sides, from enduring physical need to living with exhausting concern for other believers (2 Cor 11:23-33). This inversion of standards, as the Corinthians ought to know from Paul's earlier canonical letter, is not merely rhetorically convenient but christologically grounded (1 Cor 1:18-31).

At the beginning of 2 Corinthians 12, Paul edges toward more straightforward boasting when discussing mystical experiences (2 Cor 12:1-5). Even here, though, he guards against the glory-seeking self-commendation into which his rivals would draw him. Paul introduces these spiritual experiences as the experiences of someone he knows (2 Cor 12:2). When it becomes clear that this anonymous person is Paul (2 Cor 12:2, 6-7), he repositions himself yet again to avoid falling into the trap of accepting his opponents' vision of Christian leadership. He shifts attention away from his impressive mystical experiences to the "thorn . . . in the flesh" that keeps him grounded and self-consciously dependent on Christ, spiritual highs notwithstanding (2 Cor 12:6-10).

In the "foolish defense" of 2 Corinthians 10–12, Paul walks a fine line indeed. He defends his God-given apostleship and authority against naysaying rivals while also refusing to adopt his opponents' terms of debate in any except a subversive way that recenters attention on the glory of God in the crucified and risen Jesus Christ (e.g., 2 Cor 13:3-4). Paul's reconfiguration of the grounds on which a ministry is evaluated and validated poses an important challenge to us today, not least in relation to attempts at multiethnic worship. As

[86]Some may have perceived the Jerusalem collection as a covert way for Paul to collect money for himself (2 Cor 12:16-18); see, e.g., Matthews, "2 Corinthians," 209, 211; Nave, "2 Corinthians," 328.

[87]As Matthews observes, "The passage is an ironic contrast to lists of impressive achievements . . . commonly compiled on behalf of notable public figures" ("2 Corinthians," 212).

a White person, I think in particular of the oft-given advice that White people would benefit from putting ourselves under the pastoral leadership of a person of color. One reason why many White people find this difficult to do is our strong preference for a particular sort of worship service and preaching that we may think of as "normal," "educated," or "orderly"—but that is in fact distinctively "White" (often also middle class, associated with particular denominations, etc.). Much as the Corinthians were inclined to prefer the preaching of the "superapostles" who better met their cultural expectations for teachers, those of us in the dominant culture today may find it difficult to appreciate styles of preaching and worship that reflect the rhetorical preferences and pastoral concerns of another culture. Blind to the particularity of our own ways of knowing, being, speaking, organizing, singing, and listening, we assume that anything different from our conventions must be simply a falling short of the (unacknowledgedly White) norm. Paul reminds us that what matters is not how well a preacher measures up to any culturally determined standard—whether of eloquence, formal education, or financial "success"—but rather the power of God in Christ working in and through that person by the Spirit in the preaching of the gospel.[88]

Paul's reasoning about his "thorn in the flesh" can also be a source of encouragement for those who feel they are afflicted by weaknesses that actually do undermine their capacity for ministry, such as chronic physical- or mental-health challenges. Enacting his insight from 2 Corinthians 1:3-4, Paul offers us the consolation he himself received. In 2 Corinthians 12:7-10, we find a precedent for praying that painful weaknesses be removed, as well as a model for thinking well about—even coming to a place of acceptance in relation to—cases where those petitions are not granted. Paul thus reminds us that what others (and perhaps we ourselves) perceive as our weaknesses may be precisely the point where Christ's power most gloriously shows up in our ministry.

This encouragement carries particular weight for (White and other) Christians who inhabit more privileged social locations and nevertheless find themselves afflicted by some "thorn in the flesh" that no amount of prayer, medication, and effort will remove. For those struggling to find their footing in the midst of sudden, extreme, and/or prolonged suffering, communities of privilege can be difficult spaces indeed. The person who suffers is an unwanted reminder of the human vulnerability that even White privilege cannot finally erase, however much it may lessen the blow in particular cases.[89] Paul does not deny our basic vulnerability; indeed, mortality has been a recurring theme in this letter (e.g., 2 Cor 1:8-11; 4:16–5:10). Instead, Paul invites us to the recognition that God's power can shine through our precarious lives—not only by the removal of difficulties but also precisely in the midst of unresolved suffering.

CLOSING WORD (2 CORINTHIANS 13:1-13)

The final chapter of 2 Corinthians includes a brief description of Paul's travel plans

[88]Paul would no doubt insist that all Christians practice Spirit-led discernment when finding a church home, avoiding any leader who distorts the gospel or exercises pastoral authority in abusive ways. However, there is a difference between fundamental theological conflict and mere differences in style or emphasis. To borrow from a famous North African theologian: if an interpretation of Scripture does not contradict the rule of faith or the law of love, then it is theologically permissible. See Augustine of Hippo, *On Christian Teaching*, trans. R. P. H. Green, Oxford World Classics (Oxford: Oxford University Press, 2008).

[89]This difficulty is especially acute in churches influenced by the so-called prosperity gospel. On the challenge Paul's letter presents to this movement, see Nave, "2 Corinthians," 310.

(2 Cor 13:1-4), a farewell (2 Cor 13:11-12), and a benediction (2 Cor 13:13). As he often does, Paul shapes this conventional component to meet the pastoral-theological needs of the present case. Consistent with the letter's emphasis on his cruciform apostolic authority, Paul affirms that whatever discipline he may impose when he visits the Corinthians will arise from and cohere with his witness to Jesus Christ—the Lord who "was crucified in weakness" but now "lives by the power of God" (2 Cor 13:4). Paul's final words to the troublesome but beloved Corinthians thus reinforce the Christocentric, theologically grounded, and ecclesially oriented manner in which he has been reasoning throughout the letter.

As I have suggested at several points above, these undergirding commitments can guide Christians today as we seek prayerfully to discern how 2 Corinthians speaks into our contexts, not least in relation to our understandings of Christian ministry and leadership. Paul's christological reconfiguration of apostolic authority offers a salutary challenge—a *paraklēsis* in the fullest sense, at once an encouragement and an exhortation—to Christians formed in ecclesial contexts where White culture is the unmarked norm. For White Christians who feel ill-equipped to do our small part in encouraging the church toward greater multiethnic unity and christologically grounded antiracism, Paul reminds us that our weaknesses are not disqualifying but rather create space for God's power to show through us more clearly. For Christians of color who find themselves leading in majority-White church spaces, Paul models the truth that conformity to the dominant (White) culture's assumptions about leadership is not the standard of faithfulness for Christ's ministers. Further, by calling into question the cultural assumptions that governed the Corinthians' judgments about what makes for an authoritative teacher, Paul also provides a crucial corrective for White Christians whose interest in attending a church led by a person of color may be dampened by our (often unreflectively White) cultural assumptions about what counts as competent preaching and pastoral leadership.

The glory of God revealed in Christ, "crucified in weakness" but now alive "by the power of God" (2 Cor 13:4), invites us all to ongoing transformation by the power of the Spirit (2 Cor 3:17-18). Such transformation equips us to live ever more fully into the reality of new creation (2 Cor 5:17), in which worldly (including White) standards of greatness and expressions of authority no longer govern our evaluation of Christian leaders.[90]

SELECTED BIBLIOGRAPHY

Andemicael, Awet Iassu. "Grace, Equity, Participation: The Economy of God in 2 Corinthians 8:8-15." *Anglican Theological Review* 98, no. 4 (2016): 612-38.

Augustine of Hippo. *Confessions*. Translated by Henry Chadwick. Oxford World Classics. Oxford: Oxford University Press, 1992.

———. *On Christian Teaching*. Translated by R. P. H. Green. Oxford World Classics. Oxford: Oxford University Press, 2008.

Boyarin, Daniel. "The Subversion of the Jews: Moses's Veil and the Hermeneutics of Supersession." *Diacritics* 23, no. 2 (1993): 16-35.

Diehl, Judith A. *2 Corinthians*. The Story of God Bible Commentary. Grand Rapids, MI: Zondervan Academic, 2020.

Eastman, Susan Grove. "Unveiling Death in Second Corinthians." In *The Ways That Often Parted: Essays in Honor of Joel Marcus*, edited by Lori Baron, Jill Hicks-Keeton, and Matthew Thiessen, 79-102. Atlanta: SBL Press, 2018.

[90]Thanks to Mary Lynn Myers for expert help with copyediting; remaining errors are my own.

Fowl, Stephen E. "Know Your Context: Giving and Receiving Money in Philippians." *Interpretation* 56, no. 1 (2002): 45-58.

Furnish, Victor Paul. *II Corinthians: A New Translation with Introduction and Commentary.* AB 32A. New Haven, CT: Yale University Press, 1984.

Gorman, Michael J. "2 Corinthians: Paul's Defense of Cruciform Ministry." In *Apostle of the Crucified Lord: A Theological Introduction to Paul and His Letters*, 287-337. Grand Rapids, MI: Eerdmans, 2017.

Grieb, A. Katherine. "Philippians and the Politics of God." *Interpretation* 61, no. 3 (2007): 256-69.

Hafemann, Scott J. "The Glory and Veil of Moses in 2 Cor 3:7-14: An Example of Paul's Contextual Exegesis of the OT—a Proposal." *Horizons in Biblical Theology* 14, no. 1 (1992): 31-49.

Hays, Richard B. *Echoes of Scripture in the Letters of Paul.* New Haven, CT: Yale University Press, 1989.

Heath, Jane. "Moses' End and the Succession: Deuteronomy 31 and 2 Corinthians 3." *NTS* 60, no. 1 (2014): 37-60.

Jennings, Willie James. "Overcoming Racial Faith." *Divinity Magazine*, 2015, 4-9. https://divinity.duke.edu/sites/divinity.duke.edu/files/DukeDivinityMag_Spring15.WEB_.compressed.pdf.

Matthews, Shelly. "2 Corinthians." In *A Feminist Commentary*, vol. 2 of *Searching the Scriptures*, edited by Elisabeth Schüssler Fiorenza, 196-217. New York: Crossroad, 1994.

McCaulley, Esau. "Preaching Against Racism Is Not a Distraction from the Gospel." *Christianity Today*, August 9, 2019. www.christianitytoday.com/pastors/2019/august-web-exclusives/racism-preaching-against-not-distraction-from-gospel.html.

Nave, Guy. "2 Corinthians." In *True to Our Native Land: An African American New Testament Commentary*, edited by Brian K. Blount, Cain Hope Felder, Clarice J. Martin, and Emerson B. Powery, 307-32. Minneapolis: Fortress, 2007.

Powell, Mark Allan. *Introducing the New Testament: A Historical, Literary, and Theological Survey.* 2nd ed. Grand Rapids, MI: Baker Academic, 2018.

Radner, Ephraim. "The Discrepancies of Two Ages: Thoughts on Keble's 'Mysticism of the Fathers.'" *The Anglican* 29, no. 2 (2000). http://anglicanhistory.org/essays/radner/keble.pdf.

Smith, Mandy. "Who Am I That I Should Lead?" *Christianity Today*, April 1, 2020. www.christianitytoday.com/pastors/2020/spring/hildegard-bingen-who-am-i-that-i-should-lead.html.

Stockhausen, Carol K. "2 Corinthians 3 and the Principles of Pauline Exegesis." In *Paul and the Scriptures of Israel*, edited by Craig A. Evans and James A. Sanders, 143-64. LNTS. Sheffield: Sheffield Academic Press, 1993.

Teslina, Margaryta. "In the Image of Moses, in the Image of Christ: Pauline Hermeneutics in 2 Corinthians 3." Paper presented at Pacific Coast Regional Society of Biblical Literature meeting. Fullerton, CA, 2017.

Thrall, Margaret E. *I and II Corinthians.* The Cambridge Bible Commentary on the New English Bible. Cambridge: Cambridge University Press, 1965.

Williams, Demetrius K. "No Longer a Slave: Reading the Interpretation History of Paul's Letter to Philemon." In *Onesimus Our Brother: Reading Religion, Race, and Culture in Philemon*, edited by Matthew V. Johnson, James A. Noel, and Demetrius K. Williams, 11-45. Paul in Critical Contexts. Minneapolis: Fortress, 2012.

LETTER TO THE GALATIANS

Eric C. Redmond

INTRODUCTION

A book that proclaims liberty rather than legalism resonates well with African Americans' historical emphasis on freedom.[1] In the long American conflict in which the descendants of slaves have fought to overcome the oppressive whiteness of the culture, Brad Braxton's words are an appropriate description of the experience of many: "So many African Americans were (and are) shackled by conscious and subconscious capitulation to white ways of thinking and being." For such thinking, Galatians provides "An 'ideological Emancipation Proclamation . . . that might shine a beacon of liberation upon contemporary African American experience."[2]

Galatians proclaims a message in the face of a competing ideology. Both thoughts are vying for the label of "truth" to don their message. Both proclaim a means of becoming right with God, but only one does so through a trail of freedom. Yet only the message of *liberation from attempts to be righteous before God by keeping the law* offers an emancipation that gives life and hope amid the oppressions fostered by injustice.

Author. The author addresses himself as "Paul" and "apostle" (Gal 1:1, 2; 5:2).[3] He introduces his apostleship by describing it as being something not given by the commission of humanity, but directly from the resurrected Christ and the Father. The writer develops these ideas in a testimony of his calling and sending by the Lord (Gal 1:11–2:21). The testimony offers details that accord themselves with what is recorded about the apostle Paul in Acts, including his (1) former advancement in Judaism, (2) persecution of the church, (3) visit to the apostles in Jerusalem, (4) calling to the Gentiles, and (5) charge to remember the poor.[4]

The writer appeared among the audience with physical ailments in his body, maybe even a disease of the eyes (Gal 4:12-16). Yet the audience received him graciously. In the writer's mind, he has a fatherly affection for the Galatians (Gal 4:19).

The author adds the final greetings in his own handwriting, which is the characteristic of an authentic Pauline work.[5] The writer had taken bodily abuse for the sake of the Lord (cf. Acts 16:22-23). Internally, the evidence points to the apostle Paul as the writer of this letter.[6]

---

[1]The present writer gives great thanks to his undergraduate faculty assistant, Ms. Leah Marie McDonald (Moody Bible Institute, class of 2023), for making tremendous suggestions and edits to this work to bring it to successful completion.

[2]Brad R. Braxton, *No Longer Slaves: Galatians in the African American Christian Experience* (Collegeville, MN: Liturgical Press, 2002), x.

[3]See also Acts 9:1-12; Rom 1:1; 2 Cor 1:1.

[4]Compare Gal 1:14 and Acts 22:3; Gal 1:13 and Acts 9:1-5; 22:4-5, 19-20; 26:9-12, 14; Gal 1:18 and Acts 9:26-29; Gal 2:7 and Acts 9:15-16; 22:4; 26:17-20; Gal 2:10 and Acts 24:17.

[5]Gal 6:11, 17; cf. 1 Cor 16:21; Col 4:18; 2 Thess 3:17; Philem 19.

[6]Such a view of Pauline authorship has attestation prior to that of modern evangelical scholarship. "That Galatians is a genuine, authentic Epistle is indisputable" writes W. G. Kummel in his *Introduction to the New Testament* (Nashville: Abingdon Press,

Audience. "The churches of Galatia" (Gal 1:2) raises a question about which region of churches is the recipient, whether North Galatia (a people group in what is now Northern Turkey) or South Galatia (a Roman province in Southern Turkey). The debate surrounding the recipients is known as the North Galatia Theory (ethnic Galatia) versus South Galatia Theory (mixed Galatia). The theories on the identity of the Galatians have significance for the ethnic identity of the Galatians. If "Galatians" refers to people of "North Galatia," the letter was written to those identifying ethnically as Galatians.[7] If it refers to the people of "South Galatia," the letter was written to people Paul visited with Barnabas when they were commissioned and sent from Antioch in Acts 13–14.

The argument in favor of the South Galatia theory posits the following:

- Paul's common practice was to write to churches he had visited. He has traveled to the southern region (Acts 13–14). The NT is silent on any travels of Paul to North Galatia.
- In the discussion about those who participated in the collection for the saints in Jerusalem, Paul mentions "the churches of Galatia" (1 Cor 16:1). An entourage that carried the relief gift included believers from South Galatia (cf. Acts 20:4).
- Paul visited the region of Phrygia and Galatia after departing from Lystra and Iconium (Acts 14:6-21; 18:23). Those in this region would have met Barnabas on Paul's journey to Galatia such that addressing Barnabas in this epistle was important (Gal 2:1, 9, 13).
- Paul writes to a people with knowledge of the Old Testament. It is doubtful that Jews lived in North Galatia.[8]
- Paul does not reference the conclusions reached at the Jerusalem Council in Acts 15, even though their deliberations have significance to much of what Paul writes to the Galatians. If the letter does not include a reference to the Jerusalem Council because the council convened after Paul had visited the churches, the churches would be those of South Galatia, which were visited prior to the Council.

In contrast, the following arguments favor the North Galatian Theory :

- *Galatian* was a term used for the Gaulic region in the North in Paul's day.
- In Galatians, Paul does not mention the personal attacks he experienced in South Galatia (cf. Acts 14:5, 19). Yet this would be an argument from silence and might favor a North Galatians view instead.
- It is common for the Lukan writer of Acts to use a phrase like "Phrygia and Galatia" to indicate geographical locations (e.g., Northern Galatia), such as "Pisidian" Antioch (Acts 13:14) and "Lyconia" for Lystra and Derbe (Acts 14:6).

1975), cited in D. A. Carson, Douglas Moo, and Leon Morris, *Introduction to the New Testament* (Grand Rapids, MI: Zondervan, 1992), 290. Similarly, Henry Alford wrote, "Of all the Epistles which bear the characteristic marks of St. Paul's style, this one stands foremost" (Henry Alford, *The Greek New Testament: With a Critical Revised Text: A Digest of Various Readings, Marginal References to Verbal and Idiomatic Usage, Prolegomena, and Critical and Exegetical Commentary* [London: Longmans, Green, 1872], 1). For the sake of this work, "Paul" will be used for the writer since the letter bears the name of Paul. Space limitations do not permit longer discussions on debate about the authorship of this letter.

[7]Philip Freeman, *The Galatian Language: A Comprehensive Survey of the Language of the Ancient Celts in Greco-Roman Asia Minor* (Lewiston, NY: Edwin Mellen Press, 2001), 3.

[8]Joseph A. Pipa Jr., *Galatians: God's Proclamation of Liberty* (Fearn, Scotland: Christian Focus, 2010), 10.

As Paul usually wrote to churches he established on his missionary journeys, it is more likely that he wrote to the churches of South Galatia (cf. Acts 13:1–14:28). As Carson and Moo write, "From all this it appears that there is no final proof for either the North Galatian or the South Galatian theory. But it sure seems that, while the South Galatian theory comes short of a complete demonstration, the arguments in its favor are considerably more compelling than those for North Galatia."[9]

Occasion. Seemingly Paul is writing to believers who have been seduced by a different gospel message than the one he had preached to them (Gal 1:6; 3:1). The good news presented to the Galatians involved them working to make themselves righteous before God rather than finding that Christ has worked for them alone to provide them righteousness. Rather than being an *euangelion* of freedom, it is a proclamation that enslaves and makes having Christ no advantage toward their salvation (Gal 5:1-2). The attack on the Galatians by the false teachers occurs prior to the Jerusalem Council and its conclusion about the sanctification of Gentile believers and their fellowship with Jewish believers.[10] Paul distinguishes the false teachers from the Galatians (Gal 1:7; 4:17), maybe even recognizing a strong leader among them (Gal 1:9; 5:10).[11] He implies that the opponents were not believers at all (Gal 1:6-7).[12]

The false teachers taught a gospel of legalism, with an emphasis on the necessity of circumcision for salvation (Gal 6:12, cf. Gal 5:2-6). They promoted the necessity of keeping Jewish feast days (Gal 4:10). As a result of entertaining the need for keeping circumcision and the Jewish feast days, the Galatians began to reconsider the gospel that they had learned; they embraced the thought that justification required circumcision, and having been justified they also sought to be sanctified by keeping the law (Gal 5:4; cf. Gal 4:21).[13]

These false teachers also led the Galatian believers into *license* (Gal 5:13-26). In their attempt to accomplish their purposes of gathering followers from among the Galatian believers and avoiding being persecuted for Christ,[14] the false teachers made direct attacks on Paul, for discrediting him would be necessary in order to discredit the gospel the Galatians had embraced through his preaching. Thus, Paul found it important to write to Galatia to defend the motives of his ministry

[9]D. A. Carson and Douglas J. Moo, *An Introduction to the New Testament* (Grand Rapids, MI: Zondervan, 2009), 461. However, it might be wisest to conclude with James Dunn, "The only obvious conclusion to draw from all this is that the evidence briefly reviewed is actually decisive on neither side. In particular, the difficulties of correlating Galatians with Luke's account in Acts make it doubtful whether, or at least to what extent, we can use the details of Acts to fill out the picture in Galatians" (James D. G. Dunn, *The Epistle to the Galatians* [London: Continuum, 1993], 7). My position here respects the work of scholars like Martinus C. de Boer and J. Louis Martyn who hold to a North Galatia view (see Martinus C. de Boer, *Galatians* [Louisville, KY: Westminster John Knox Press, 2011]; J. Louis Martyn, *Galatians* [New Haven, CT: Yale University Press, 2004]).

[10]Initially, it seems that the Jerusalem Council debate will concern the need for the Gentile to be circumcised in order to gain salvation (Acts 15:1). However, en route to the council, as Paul and Barnabas share testimony of the Gentiles receiving Christ according to faith as they served among them, the church receives the report of the working of God (Acts 15:2-4). Therefore, they discuss a different but remaining question of whether or not the Gentiles must *keep* the law of Moses and circumcision for sanctification (Acts 15:5). The council will "not trouble those Gentiles who are turning to God," but trust that those who have turned will refrain from practices that would offend fellow Jewish believers (Acts 15:19-21). It is to "brothers" in the faith (Acts 15:23, 32, 33) that they are removing "further burden[s]" (Acts 15:28).

[11]Carson, Moo, and Morris, *An Introduction to the New Testament*, 295.

[12]Carson, Moo, and Morris, *An Introduction to the New Testament*, 295.

[13]Paul does not indicate who introduced the earliest Galatian believers to the gospel, but only recognizes the fact of their belief having been taught to them in Gal 1:6, 3:2.

[14]Paul presents these two motives among the opponents in Galatia in Gal 4:17, 6:12.

among them and the content of his gospel proclamation (Gal 1:10; 5:11).

Structure. Galatians has two macrosections that make up its contents. First, Paul *reasons* with the believers in Galatia by arguing with them from his apostolic experience and scriptural revelati*on* (Gal 1–4). In the second macrosection, Paul appeals to the believers to exhort them toward responses to *grace* (Gal 5–6).

In Galatians 1–4, after giving a nonstandard introduction to the letter (Gal 1:1-4),[15] Paul very forcefully condemns the proclamation of a gospel than the one he preached (Gal 1:5-9). He appeals to his personal experience in receiving the gospel as a revelation and only being affirmed by the church leaders in Jerusalem (Gal 1:10-2:10). Paul relates an experience in which he rebukes Peter for a departure from the gospel (Gal 2:11-21).

Galatians 3–4 provides a long argument on justification by faith rather than by "works of the law." Paul begins by questioning the Galatians' experience with the gospel that he had preached (Gal 3:1-7). Paul builds the remainder of the argument from the OT scriptures (Gal 3:10–4:21).[16] In Galatians 3:10-29 he brings the narrative of Abraham's life to the center to show that faith alone always has been the instrument to accomplish justification (Gal 3:10-29). Following the discussion of Abraham, the writer will dismantle the opponent's arguments for the necessity of circumcision for salvation, showing that circumcision is a powerless advantage to one maturing in Christ (Gal 4:1-20). Finally, the first macrosection concludes with an allegory that utilizes Sarah and Hagar to explain the end of slavery to the law for the believer and the believers' position as free in Christ based on justification by faith (Gal 4:21-31).

In the second macrosection, Paul appeals to the believers to exhort them toward responses to grace (Gal 5–6). He made a case for depending on grace for salvation rather than on works in Galatians 1–4. Now he will explain the significance of a grace-based salvation for continuing into Christian maturity.

To do so, Paul will explain the significance that freedom has to both license (Gal 5:1-15) and living the Christian life in obedience to the Spirit (Gal 5:16-26). The final chapter will focus on the doing of good works to the full body, including those who stumble (Gal 6:1-5), teaching of the word (Gal 6:6), and all persons (Gal 6:7-10). His final warning lays to rest the seeking of circumcision (Gal 6:11-18).

The unifying idea across the book is *the truth of the gospel* (cf. Gal 1:6-7; 2:5, 14; 4:16; 5:7). Paul writes to the Galatians to confront a "different gospel" (Gal 1:6)—a distortion of the gospel (Gal 1:7), to preserve the true gospel message (Gal 2:5), and to foster continued sanctification in and by means of that gospel (e.g., "step," "running," Gal 2:14; 5:7). There are not two messages of good news that provide salvation; certainly, there cannot be competing ones. Salvation by grace and salvation by works are mutually exclusive for Paul. There is one gospel only and to this gospel Paul persuades his readers as the message of truth.

This is the gospel that was revealed in Paul by grace (Gal 1:11, 12), that was at stake in his controversy with Peter—that Peter would live by law before Jews but in the freedom of grace before Gentiles (Gal 2:14). Paul writes to say that the truth of the gospel *demands a response*

[15]Paul does not give his customary greeting or offer a prayer for the church as he does in all of his other letters to churches. See Rom 1:7-15; 1 Cor 1:2-9; 2 Cor 1:1-7; Eph 1:1, 15-17; Phil 1:1-11; Col 1:2-14; 1 Thess 1:1-10; 2 Thess 1:1-4.

[16]For references to OT scriptures and the use of the term "Scriptures" in this section, see Gal 3:6-8, 10-13, 16, 18, 22; 4:21-23, 27, 30).

of faith to receive all that God has provided. God has provided two things to the believers: A righteous *standing* before God in Christ (Gal 3–4), and a righteous *walk* as the believer lives in the power of the Spirit (Gal 5–6; cf. Gal 3:1-3; and especially Gal 5:16-26).[17]

The following is a more detailed outline of Galatians:

I. Paul's reception of the Gospel by revelation established the truth of his message, corresponding to the scriptural call for faith (Gal 1:1–4:31).

A. Opening: Paul addresses the churches in Galatia who are blessed by God in the work of Christ (Gal 1:1-5).

B. The Galatians' response to the gospel exposes them to a distortion of the good news found in Christ (Gal 1:6-10).

C. Paul's reception of Christ by revelation, transformation from a persecutor, and recognition of his gospel (Gal 1:11–2:10).

D. The truth of the gospel was challenged by Peter's duplicity and clarified in Paul's correction and confession (Gal 2:11-21).

E. The Galatians' consideration of their own personal merit before God and the emptying of the truth of Christ crucified (Gal 3:1-5).

F. The model of Abraham's faith for all and the anticipation of God's original promise (Gal 3:6-9).

G. Contrast of the law's operation with the declaration of righteousness by faith, based on Christ's work against the curse (Gal 3:10-14).

H. The promises spoken to Abraham and his seed and the identification of Christ as the seed who inherits the promises (Gal 3:15-20).

I. The combination of the law's imprisonment and promise in Christ in the provision of righteousness (Gal 3:21-25).

J. The Galatians as Abraham's seed and the reception of the Spirit of God's (the Father's) Son (Gal 3:26–4:7).

K. The application of a biblical revelation to the Galatians and the formation of Christ in them (Gal 4:8-20).

L. The illustration of Abraham's two sons and the influence of the law on inheritance (Gal 4:21-31).

II. The purpose of freedom through Christ from slavery to keeping the law for sanctification (Gal 5–6).

A. The believer's standing in new freedom and dependency on the Spirit to satisfy the demands of the law (Gal 5:1-26).

B. The believer's doing of good to the stumbling and the teacher of the truth (Gal 6:1-10).

C. The closing example of Paul's lived gospel verses the Judaizers' gospel of hypocrisy, with benediction (Gal 6:11-18).

OPENING: PAUL ADDRESSES THE CHURCHES IN GALATIA WHO ARE BLESSED BY GOD IN THE WORK OF CHRIST (GALATIANS 1:1-5).

The language of divine calling for ministers is familiar to the experiences of the traditional African American church. Paul establishes his apostleship as a divine appointment, and the terseness of the language raises the significance of the issues he will address. The gospel is central to the concerns at hand, as Paul identifies Jesus as the one whom the Father raised from the dead.

[17]The phrase, "and a righteous walk as the believer lives in the power of the Spirit," does not intend to imply synergistic sanctification in which the Spirit is helped by the believer or in which the believer and the Spirit have equal roles in the believer's sanctification. Christ accomplishes sanctification in the believer through the works of the believer mysteriously, by grace (cf. 1 Cor 15:10; Eph 1:4; Phil 1:6; 2:12-13; Col 1:29; 1 Tim 4:10).

Paul adds "our" as an indication of an inclusive faith that does not turn away people struggling with theological understanding or maturity in Christ. The gospel concerns the present age and is not open to Marx's "opiate of the people" label.[18] It delivers from the present evil age upon the return of Christ. For Paul there is no separation of the doctrinal truth of the resurrection and the practical, effective truth of the deliverance. Consistently in his writings, Paul seeks for God to be made known beautifully and as praiseworthy as we speak his gospel truthfully and have lives that conform to the implications of the resurrection.

THE GALATIANS' RESPONSE TO THE GOSPEL EXPOSES THEM TO A DIFFERENT GOSPEL (GALATIANS 1:6-10)

Paul expresses astonishment at the Galatians' embracing of a false gospel and warns them to examine those who distort the message they previously received. His warning is significant to American communities of color facing false gospels like prosperity theology—a theology that takes advantage of peoples' hope to escape poverty and experience full enfranchisement of the American dream.[19]

Paul skips the prayer of thanksgiving often found at the beginning of his discourses.[20] Instead he launches into his astonishment over the Galatians' departure from grace. The introduction of the gospel as a message of grace stands in contrast to effort from anyone other than Christ.

Paul's condemnation of the opponents to hell ("accursed") might be troubling to members of honor-shame communities.[21] It is easy to read into this verse horror stories of discipline done harshly or biasedly by a church or cult. However, preserving the truth of the gospel requires removal of those who falsely teach against it, lest the church be characterized by a false gospel. One can anathematize a false gospel and false teachers and do so with grace toward the family, friends, congregation, and those deceived.

Paul's previous correspondence with the churches of Galatia called them to anathematize those teaching a false gospel. The double emphasis in the correspondence along with the reference to the past exhortation reveals the seriousness of what is at stake.

Identifying himself as a *slave* (or *servant*) could provoke the most gruesome images of mistreatment to people on the basis of skin color.[22] However, Paul's servanthood is "of Christ" (cf. 1 Cor 7:21-23). Paul speaks of his ministry, and not of a Roman industry; he would have anathemized a gospel that supported chattel slavery.

---

[18]Karl Marx, "Introduction," in *A Contribution to the Critique of Hegel's Philosophy of Right*, trans. A. Jolin and J. O'Malley, ed. J. O'Malley (New York: Cambridge University Press, [1843] 1970), www.marxists.org/archive/marx/works/1843/critique-hpr/intro.htm; Andrew M. McKinnon, "Reading 'Opium of the People': Expression, Protest and the Dialectics of Religion," *Critical Sociology* 31 (2005): 15–38. Karl Marx drew an analogy between religious practice and opium because he viewed each as having numbing effects toward the painfulness of life in this present world. The hallucinatory nature of each was to present an alternative world as reality—for the opium addict, the world in which the drug abuser was to inebriated to see reality; for the religious adherent, the promise of a better world to come.

[19]Eddie Glaude speaks of prosperity theology in the Black church as "a theology that suits a vision of capitalism that is devastating our communities and country" (Eddie S. Glaude Jr., "Too Many Black Churches Preach the Gospel of Greed," *New York Times*, Mar 19, 2015, www.nytimes.com/roomfordebate/2014/06/25/has-capitalism-become-incompatible-with-christianity/too-many-black-churches-preach-the-gospel-of-greed, accessed August 6, 2020). See also Kareem Abdul-Jabbar, "Prosperity Gospel Is War on the Poor," *Time Magazine*, Jun. 8, 2015, https://time.com/3912366/kareem-abdul-jabbar-prosperity-gospel/, accessed August 6, 2020.

[20]For Paul's opening prayers of thanksgiving see Rom 1:8-12; 1 Cor 1:49; Eph 1:15-23; Phil 1:3-6; Col 1:3-8.

[21]The Greek term *anathema* has the sense of "condemn to hell."

[22]Among many examples in her work, Lisa Bowens records that in his 1843 work, *In Slavery as It Relates to the Negro or African Race*, Josiah Priest, a proslavery advocate, "aligns Ham's character with that of his descendants" so that "just as Ham's character was always evil and morally corrupt, so too is the character of all his prosperity." Bowens continues by noting,

Or someone could accuse Paul of seeking to please people by proclaiming a gospel of grace (which he addresses in Gal 5:16-23). But preaching grace enslaves him to Christ, who gives the message of grace. The purity of motive rests in gaining God's approval alone.

PAUL'S RECEPTION OF CHRIST BY REVELATION, TRANSFORMATION FROM A PERSECUTOR, AND RECOGNITION OF HIS GOSPEL (GALATIANS 1:11–2:10)

The apostle responds to two concerns raised by his opponents. If one could show the origin of Paul's gospel to be human rather than divine, his message would have no basis for legitimacy in the lives of the Galatians; the gospel only is a product of sociology of knowledge and human choice. However, if his message has an origin in the mouth of God, it carries the weight of the words of OT prophets who spoke words directly from the Lord.

Paul is not a simple peddler of another's philosophy. He declares his gospel message came from Christ via revelation. Historically, this accords with Paul's life (Acts 9:3-8; 22:6-11; 26:12-18; 1 Cor 9:1; 15:8). Paul received the same direct revelation the other apostles experienced in the course of Jesus' three-year ministry.

Those familiar with Paul's former life would remember that he once vehemently opposed the gospel he now knows by revelation from Christ. "In Judaism" pits him directly against the Jewish Christian opposition—the Judaizers. Paul offers details about his former life in Judaism to support the claim that he did not receive his gospel from humans or subscribe to a message taught to him (Gal 1:1, 11-12). Only by divine revelation (Gal 1:15) could such an opponent to the church of God become a servant of Christ.

First, Paul was not simply a receiver of a message from other humans, as evidenced by his previous persecution of the church. In Acts, the writer shows Paul giving consent to the death of Stephen and obtaining authority to imprison and kill believers (Acts 8:1-3; 9:1-2). Paul's reputation as a former persecutor was known to the Galatians. An image of persons responsible for burning African American churches in the south in the 1990s might come to mind for the reader.[23] However, a more apt picture of one who persecutes for their faith would be the photos of members of ISIS beheading Egyptian believers for their faith.[24]

Second, Paul did not receive his gospel message as human teaching because he was a student of Judaism with both zeal for his studies and advancement beyond his peers. He was sold to his Jewish studies and traditions.

Third, in his support of the divine origin of his gospel message are his encounter with Jesus and postconversion experience. Testifying like one at a prayer service in the Afro-Baptist traditions, Paul speaks of his conversion as an act of divine calling and grace. The preconversion summons points to the direct providence of God in Paul's experience with the gospel message he preaches. Paul understands his own conversion to be a work extending from eternity past to the present (e.g., *election*, cf. Eph 1:3-5).

As Jeremiah was called to preach God's word to the nations (Jer 1:5), so Paul comes in the vein

"Corresponding to this view, many Southern preachers proclaimed that the curse of Canaan was a curse of black skin as well as perpetual slavery. Augustine Calmet related, in his popular dictionary, that Ham's skin became black upon Noah's pronouncement of a curse on Canaan and Ham" (Lisa M. Bowens, *African American Readings of Paul: Reception, Resistance, and Transformation* [Grand Rapids, MI: Eerdmans, 2020], 17).

[23]Moira Lavelle, "The Fire Last Time: The 1990s Wave of 145 Church Burnings—Map July 2, 2015," The World—PRX blog, https://theworld.org/stories/2015-07-02/fire-last-time-1990s-wave-145-church-burnings-map, accessed Aug. 5, 2020.

[24]Jared Malsin, "Christians Mourn Their Relatives Beheaded by ISIS," *Time Magazine*, Feb. 23, 2015, https://time.com/3718470/isis-copts-egypt/, accessed Aug. 5, 2020.

of Jeremiah preaching God's gospel to persons of all nations. For Paul, the calling of God is grace and not based on effort on the part of Paul.

Paul describes in his divine encounter that God was pleased "was pleased to reveal his Son *in* me" (Gal 1:15-16 NIV).[25] Paul was acted on and did not seek out even the salvation himself.[26] Salvation is a work in which the Lord, setting Paul apart for salvation from eternity past, and summoning Paul by grace, reveals the Son in Paul by the Lord's pleasure. It would be hypocritical for Paul to speak of salvation (i.e., justification) in terms of works of the law, for that would be vastly incongruent with his experience of salvation by grace.

God's plan of salvation purposed Paul to preach Christ to people in Gentile lands, not exclusively, but primarily. Acts does not hint at Paul consulting with "flesh and blood" (humans) for the message he preached to the Gentiles. It is not that Paul's internal calling is sufficient for him to do ministry. Instead Paul is free from the need to have the apostles teach him the message of the gospel; he had received conversation at Jesus' hands directly. His trip to Arabia is unrecorded in Acts.[27]

Important for Paul's argument is that he had three years to work out his understanding of the gospel apart from any talk with the twelve.[28] After three years, he finally made his way to Jerusalem for a visit with the apostle Peter. In those fifteen days together there would have been opportunity to compare notes. But Paul already would have been firm in his understanding of justification according to grace, given the extensiveness of his time without interacting with the Jerusalem church.

The emphasis on his lack of contact with all other apostles except James removes Paul from the accusation of being persuaded into his belief by agreement with a majority in authority. Identifying "James the Lord's brother" would seem to pose a historical problem, for the writer of the epistle bearing the name James was not one of the twelve. Paul seems to use "apostle" in a broader sense to refer to James's leadership in the Jerusalem church. Many African American and Pan-African traditions do the same, identifying their leaders by the title *apostle*.[29]

The solemn oath gives Paul's audience a tone of truthfulness that invites the listener to accept Paul's words as an accurate portrayal of the history of his acquisition of the gospel message. Paul keeps the law of not bearing a false witness, which helps the reader later to interpret the "law of Christ" statements. That is, Paul keeps the ethical code of the Mosaic law not in order to gain righteousness or maintain the civil or ceremonial codes but as a product of his faith in Christ.[30]

---

[25]Translated as "to" in the ESV, *en* in the Greek may indicate "in" in certain constructions.

[26]The aorist of the verb *eudokēsen* indicates a "pleasing" completed perfectively in the past.

[27]Timothy George notes, "It is important to recognize that both Luke and Paul wrote their distinctive accounts with a clearly defined purpose in mind. Neither Acts nor Galatians was intended to be a day-by-day journal of Paul's activities; each is a selective account of what Paul said and did, designed to show, in the case of Acts, his strategic role in the worldwide mission of the church and, in the case of Galatians, the divine derivation and independence of his apostolic mission" (Timothy George, *Galatians* [Nashville: B&H Publishers, 1994], 123).

[28]Consistent with the previous footnote, the "three years" are not specified in Acts but seem to begin at Acts 9:26.

[29]As an honor and shame culture, African Americans routinely have given honorific titles to their leaders in churches and denominations, including *apostle*. In some churches within the Wesleyan traditions, *apostle* is a title in their organizational structure akin to *organizer*, *founder*, *church planter*, or *senior pastor*. For more, see C. Eric Lincoln and Lawrence H. Mamiya, *The Black Church in the African American Experience* (Durham, NC: Duke University Press, 1990), 275; Robert Joseph Taylor, Linda M. Chatters, and Jeff Levin, *Religion in the Lives of African Americans: Social, Psychological, and Health Perspectives* (Newbury Park, CA: SAGE Publications, Inc., 2004), 142.

[30]Even where Paul keeps ceremonies in Acts, such as participation in Pentecost or in the Nazarite vow, he does so as a cultural custom, not as a means of achieving righteousness (cf. Acts 18:18; 20:16; 21:23). This is evident in James's affirmation of Paul's

Acts 11 seems to be the reference point for Paul's trip to Syria and Cilicia, Gentile regions. Among Jewish people, he was infamous, and could not have received or been taught the gospel by churches of Judea professing Christ. In Paul's absence of visiting Judea, word spread in Judea of Paul's conversion from persecutor of the church to preacher of the gospel.

That the people in Judea gave glory to God for Paul's conversion shows their agreement with God on "the faith [Paul] once tried to destroy" (Gal 1:23). Renown and fame go to God for converting Paul from one who sought to destroy the faith that proclaimed grace in Christ to one who preached the gospel of justification by faith.

Paul's defense of the origin of his gospel as something not of human origin turns to his first major meeting with "those who seemed to be influential" (Gal 2:1, 6 [2x] ESV). The event transpired fourteen years after the visit to Cephas (cf. Gal 1:18). Paul travels with Barnabas and Titus, each of whom become important to the later narrative of Paul's consistent proclamation of a gospel of divine origin (Gal 2:3, 9, 13).

The meeting in Jerusalem was private and small; Paul was not being political, hoping to win enough votes for his viewpoints and thus gain approval of his ministry. Reading of Paul's submission to examination by church leaders may sound foreign to modern sensibilities about autonomy and soul competency, but such submission is for the sake of the propagation of the gospel.[31] Those in Jerusalem approved of his message that did not require "those among the Gentiles" to keep the law or to maintain salvation.

Paul's team refuses circumcision for the Gentile Titus. If Paul had agreed to Titus's circumcision—the most significant physical mark of Judaism and identification with the Abrahamic covenant—then one would have understood keeping the law of circumcision as necessary for Gentile conversion.

An unknown group of Jewish believers had been brought in by a faction within the churches of Jerusalem holding to the need for the Gentiles to keep the law. The motivation of the faction is evident in making moves "secretly." They wanted to move Paul and his companions from freedom to slavery. The "slavery" versus "freedom" paradigm clarifies that the content of Paul's gospel message is not bringing people into the slavery of keeping Jewish law. Instead, it is about offering the freedom to be led by the Spirit (Gal 5:16-23).

Paul's stance against the circumcision of the Gentile companion preserved the truth of the gospel for the Galatians.[32] Paul spoke truth to those who attempted to power over him with an ecclesial form of slavery.

Those leading the church in Jerusalem did not make any additions to Paul's gospel message. The second reference to "those who seemed to be influential" brings the yet known group back to the fore without associating them with the false brethren. Seemingly, Paul is watching a dynamic in play in which church members submit to a certain group of people who apparently wield considerable authority.

Paul perceives a need to respect "those who seemed influential" the way Africans and Pan-Africans tend to respect their elders and

preaching of salvation by faith to the Jews in Gentile regions coming with his offer to Paul to participate in the vow to waylay Jewish believers' concerns about Paul preaching against Jewish customs (Acts 21:20-24).

[31]In some Baptist practices, "soul competency" refers to the power of the individual to be competent to live the Christian life faithfully without any accountability. But such a belief can lead to unchecked heresy or moral breaches. See Russell Moore, "Creeping Creedalism! The Moderates Were Right," Russell Moore site, June 2, 2004, www.russellmoore.com/2004/07/02/creeping-creedalism-the-moderates-were-right/; also, *Mars Hill Audio Journal* 74, Mars Hill Audio. Submission to authority allows others to discern whether Paul and Barnabas are true to the gospel message as they preach far and wide.

[32]See Gal 2:14; 4:16; 5:7; cf. Eph 1:13; Col 1:5.

ancestors. Paul does not make his evaluation of the influential on a basis as one of equal educational, class, or financial status. Instead, Paul's evaluation of those with influence rests in his understanding of God and intention to please him. The OT and NT reveal God as one who shows no partiality.[33] God stands against all forms of unwarranted favoritism, including those based in *bias* against gender, race, ethnicity, nationality, age, sexual orientation, marital status, familial upbringing, physical abilities or appearance, and religious beliefs. If God is impartial, the election of Israel and the church are excluded from discussions of partiality, but must remain matters of mercy and divine mystery.[34]

Paul is welcomed into fellowship with the apostles as one in agreement on the message of the gospel. His stewardship holds the same responsibility as Peter's ministry to the Jewish people. Both commitments are trusts given as works of God rather than social assignments by churches. They make Paul and Peter instruments through whom the Lord will serve.

James, Peter, and John seemed to be the influencers on whom rested the greatest weight of evaluation of Paul's ministry. Designating some as "pillars" in local congregations has its origin in this passage, even though modern parlance is giving honorific labels to people based on their longevity and faithfulness within the life of an assembly.

The evaluation of the three evaluators is that a work of the grace of God is taking place through Paul's ministry. They therefore offer to Paul a gesture of formal welcoming of agreement on the message set before them (Gal 2:1-2); they all share in the same message and work in what the one is doing in Jerusalem and the other is doing among Gentiles. Modern churches do something very similar when they use such language to take the baptized into membership.

Very significant is that their fellowship includes service to the poor as part of the work of the message Paul preaches and set before them. We see this in Acts and the letters area of Paul—an idea that flows from the gospel.[35]

THE TRUTH OF THE GOSPEL RECEIVED CHALLENGED BY PETER'S DUPLICITY AND CLARIFIED IN PAUL'S CORRECTION AND CONFESSION (GALATIANS 2:11-21)

Paul stood against Peter when the apostle to the Jews attempted to portray "works of the law" (Gal 2:16) as the truth of the gospel (Gal 2:14). It is important to see that Paul describes Peter's actions in Galatians 2:12-15 as "works of the law." This is not a simple social concern or fellowship concern.

Peter's practice prior to the visitation from those in the Jerusalem church was to eat with Gentiles. When the Jewish contingent came, Peter became concerned that the circumcision faction of the church would criticize Peter for fellowshipping with those without circumcision because they were not justified. This put the truth of the gospel in jeopardy (Gal 2:5, 21).

What Peter, the rest of the Jewish believers, and Barnabas believe is that they can have fellowship with the uncircumcised because the Gentiles do not need a requirement of the

[33]Deut 10:17; 2 Chron 9:7; Job 34:19; Acts 10:34. Moore, "Creeping Creedalism!"

[34]Following Scripture, Christian faith understands God to be a faithful judge who administers his rule impartially (1 Sam 16:7; Ps 7:9; Prov 16:11; 17:15; Jer 17:10; Acts 10:34-35). When he speaks of his election of Israel, the basis is God's freedom to love as a pleases, not on the basis of Israel being greater toward him than other nations (Deut 7). Similarly, God's foreknowing of believers, relationally, so that they become his own and are vouchsafed for salvation from eternity past, has his love as the basis, not the believer's merit (Rom 8:28-39; Eph 1:3-7).

[35]See Acts 11:29-30; 24:17; 2 Cor 9:6-15.

Mosaic Code to be justified.[36] The hypocrisy is that Peter lives like the Gentile believers, not in moral vice, but apart from keeping the Mosaic code. Paul and Peter, both of fully Jewish lineage and now Christian, no longer keep the law for justification. So certainly those born apart from the law do not need to keep it.

Faith in Christ does not seem to have in mind the faithfulness of Christ (Gal 2:16, 17). Nowhere up to this point in Galatians could such a rhetorical conclusion about Christ's faithfulness be drawn. "Justification in Christ" is equivalent to "justification by faith in Christ." Faith is the instrumental means and Christ is the sphere. However, in the shortened form grammatically the phrase "in Christ" shows the means and sphere are the same. One is justified in a mysterious union with Christ who died and rose again.

Paul moves from a construction analogy to the spiritual and theological conclusion (Gal 2:18). If Paul claims justification by works while not following the law as a means for justification, he transgresses by stepping across the boundary he has said is wrong. He is like one who tears down an edifice, saying it is wrong to remain standing, then rebuilding the same edifice.

Elsewhere Paul will speak of dying to sin (Rom 6:2) and dying to the law (Rom 7:4). In the former he has ended sin's ability to reign over him because he has died with Christ and is united to him. In the latter, Paul is free from keeping the Mosaic code because he died to his marriage to that code when he died with Christ. Like one becoming free from keeping the law of marriage that binds a husband and wife together mysteriously until the death of the spouse, so Paul finds himself unbound from the legal code to which he has died in his crucifixion. The inability to keep the law brings him to the place of needing faith in Christ to obtain righteousness.

The image Paul uses to express his mysterious union to Christ in his death on the cross reveals that Paul's death to the law takes a law trusting Paul away: Paul himself has been put to death by means of crucifixion! A new Paul "lives," having the power of Christ's resurrected life in him. Paul lives in his human body as one hidden behind the cross and risen from the empty tomb. The threefold description of Christ as "the Son of God," "who loved me," and "gave himself for me" links Paul's justification to three things. First, he links it to the power and promises of God in Christ to save his people (Gal 2:20). Second, he ties it to the elect and eternal love of God for sinners, which Paul applies personally to himself as an individual ("me," Gal 2:20). This is a truth each believer can claim: "God loves me," and "God loves you." The believer can proclaim that Christ saves on the basis of love.

Third, Paul bases his justified living through faith on the work of Christ's substitutionary atonement.[37] Again, it is personal for Paul and not generalized to the church. Each believer—Jew or Gentile—needs not keep the law for each

---

[36]The concern of Jewish fellowship with Gentiles was the potential for the nation of Israel to adopt the unrighteous ways of the nations. The nations were unrighteous because they did not practice the moral righteousness of the Mosaic law. But righteousness according to the law no longer is an issue, for the believing Gentiles are found to be righteous by faith.

[37]The phrase *paradontos eauton hyper emou* indicates a handing of oneself over on behalf another. This phrase would carry this sense even without the redundancy of *paradontos*. As Ernst Riesenfeld writes, "In christological sayings *hyper* is used to show the thrust of the work of salvation . . . [the] death and passion of Christ are for men and accrue to their favour," and "A typical group is formed by expressions of the same content in which ὑπὲρ ἡμῶν is combined with the verb (παρα)δίδωμι" (Ernst Harald Riesenfeld, "ὑπέρ," in *Theological Dictionary of the New Testament*, ed. Gerhard Kittel and Gerhard Friedrich [Grand Rapids, MI: Eerdmans, 1972], 8:508-9, 510). Riesenfield cites Gal 2:20 as an example. See also M. J. Harris, "*hyper*," *New International Dictionary of New Testament Theology*, ed. Colin Brown (Grand Rapids, MI: Zondervan, 1978), 3:1196; Bruce K. Waltke, "The Theological Significations of *Anti* and *Huper* in the New Testament" (ThD diss., Dallas Theological Seminary, 1958), 2:295-301.

is crucified with Christ like Paul. Christ works to provide the righteousness of God in love.

"The grace of God" describes the work of Christ on behalf of Paul: "then Christ died" (Gal 2:21). It summarizes "justified in Christ" (Gal 2:17), "crucified with Christ" (Gal 2:19) and "Christ lives in me," "loved me," and "gave himself for me" (Gal 2:20), and "Christ died" (Gal 2:21). Paul's "works of the law"—personal effort to obtain righteousness—would nullify the mysterious union, death of Christ, resurrection of Christ, election, and Christ's substitutionary atonement. But he will place faith in Christ alone—in his person as the divine Son and the work he has done for righteousness because that is the purpose for which Christ died in the history of redemption. His language derives from the Jewish legal context of will, contracts, and testaments: "Nullify" (Gal 2:21).[38] Those who would cause believers to add keeping works of the law to salvation would annul the work of Christ on behalf of sinner.

THE GALATIANS' CONSIDERATION OF THEIR OWN PERSONAL MERIT BEFORE GOD AND THE EMPTYING OF THE TRUTH OF CHRIST CRUCIFIED (GALATIANS 3:1-5)

Paul turns to two new lines of argument for justification by faith being the truth of the gospel. The first appeals to the Galatians' experience (Gal 3:1-6). The second reviews the message of justification through redemptive history (Gal 3:7-29), largely focusing on Abraham (Gal 3:6, 7 [2x], 14, 16, 18, and 29).

The Galatians' Christian experience with the Spirit in the gospel questions their bewitching as foolishly out of sync with Abraham's experience. The Galatians had not judged rightly the message of the gospel, which Paul lets them know forcefully. Strong was the voodoo-like power of those preaching the false gospel, as it had the ability to make the Galatians deny their own collective visual experiences.[39] Paul's preaching rests the message of justification on the work of the Messiah.

The Galatians should see for themselves that their experiences with the Spirit negate justification by works of the law (Gal 3:2-4). Language for reception of the Holy Spirit has great association with Pentecostalism and charismatic Christian expressions. The Galatians' justification by the hearing of faith followed the reception of the Spirit and did not occur as a result of circumcision, maintaining the Sabbath, or maintaining strict food regulations. The question of their beginnings ties together work of the Spirit in the perfecting of the Christian walk (e.g., sanctification) to the believer's justification.

THE MODEL OF ABRAHAM'S FAITH FOR ALL AND THE ANTICIPATION OF GOD'S ORIGINAL PROMISE (GALATIANS 3:6-9)

God, who sent the Spirit and works miracles, did not respond to circumcision or other works of the law. Miracles could not and cannot be conjured on queue by human efforts. The writer ties the working of the Spirit according to the hearing of faith to the narrative of the life of Abraham. The reference to Genesis 15:6 introduces Abraham as one who believed what God had promised: an offspring through whom all nations would be blessed. Only later will Abraham circumcise his son (Gen 17). Paul makes the case from the Scriptures of the Jewish people that righteousness only comes by faith throughout all of redemptive history. Galatians 3:6 begins

---

[38]Ben Witherington III, *Grace in Galatia: A Commentary on St. Paul's Letter to the Galatians* (Grand Rapids, MI: Eerdmans, 1998), 192.

[39]Gerhard Delling, "βασκαίνω," in *Theological Dictionary of the New Testament*, ed. Gerhard Kittel (Grand Rapids, MI: Eerdmans, 1964), 1:595.

the first of a cache of OT references to support his argument.[40]

To speak of "Scripture" "foreseeing" affirms the truthfulness of the written prophetic words of Scripture. The ancient writer saw ahead God's counting of the Gentiles as righteous on the basis of faith, so preaches the good news in cryptic form. The blessing of all nations exceeds the scope of Abraham's lifetime to accomplish. The promise pointed to one to come from Abraham's loins who had the ability to bless all nations. Because Abraham's promise of blessing to the nations did not invite the nations to work, only those who exercise faith receive the blessings of the "man of faith" (Gal 3:9).

CONTRAST OF THE LAW'S OPERATION WITH THE DECLARATION OF RIGHTEOUS BY FAITH, ON THE BASIS OF CHRIST'S WORK AGAINST THE CURSE (GALATIANS 3:10-14)

To rely on the works of the law to proclaim one righteous before God actually does the opposite, placing one under a curse. As the blessing of Abraham is his justification, the cursing should be thought of as damnation. Every person fails to keep the law, ensuring damnation status for himself or herself.

Habakkuk's message stands against a declaration of righteousness according to the law.[41] The ambiguity in translations is inconsequential since Paul is speaking of the appropriation of eternal life. At issue is the apostle's use of the LXX to obtain "faith" rather than the Hebrews Bible's "faithfulness" (*emunah*).[42] Over 1400 years prior to the Protestant Reformation Paul demonstrates that "works of the law" is a matter of keeping the law to obtain righteousness. One does not need to propose that scholars sharing this view of Paul's theology are imposing Luther on Paul.[43]

In place of his own, Christ receives the cursing on himself. Paul reasons from Deuteronomy 21:23 combined with knowledge of the wood of Roman crucifixes coming from trees. Christ did not hang on a living tree, but on the product of a tree.[44] The Watchtower Society's false emphasis on "the tree" (Acts 5:30; 13:29; 1 Pet 2:4) as the only accurate description of Jesus' place of crucifixion fails to understand Roman crucifixion and the apostolic reading of the significance of Deuteronomy 21:23.[45] Christ, being cursed for us, provided this blessing of Abraham in himself so that in Abraham justification (Gen 15:6) might be experienced by Gentiles (cf. Gen 12:7). If the

[40]See Gen 12:3; Deut 27:26; Hab 2:4; Lev 18:5; Deut 21:23; and Gen 12:7.

[41]Habakkuk's language of "upright" and "righteous" are established in the law (Ex 23:7; Num 23:10; Deut 4:8; 16:18, 19; 32:4; also in Moses' writings, but chronologically before the giving of the tablets of the law, see Gen 6:9; 18:23).

[42]Daniel I. Block, "Christotelic Preaching: A Plea for Hermeneutical Integrity and Missional Passion," *SBJT* 22 (2018): 26. Elliott Johnson makes a good case for "live by faith" on the basis of the parallel of *emunah* and *uppelah* ("puffed up") (Elliott E. Johnson, "Literal Interpretation," Dean Bible Ministries, https://deanbibleministries.org/dbmfiles/notes/2014-ChaferConf-009-Johnson-Paper.pdf, accessed Aug 15, 2020).

[43]For more on views related to the imposition of Luther's theology on Paul, see Stephen Westerholm, *Perspectives Old and New: The "Lutheran" Paul and His Critics* (Grand Rapids, MI: Eerdmans, 2004), 88-97.

[44]Compare to Gen 40:19; Deut 21:22; Josh 8:29; 10:26.

[45]Jehovah's Witnesses deny Jesus' death on a cross, instead teaching he died on a "tree" (*xylon*) or what they describe as a single pole. At the Jehovah's Witnesses website, JW.org, the organization states, "Many view the cross as the most common symbol of Christianity. However, the Bible does not describe the instrument of Jesus' death, so no one can know its shape with absolute certainty. Still, the Bible provides evidence that Jesus died, not on a cross, but on an upright stake," and "The Bible also uses the Greek word *xylon* as a synonym for *stauros*. (Acts 5:30; 1 Peter 2:24) This word means 'wood,' 'timber,' 'stake,' or 'tree.' *The Companion Bible* thus concludes, 'There is nothing in the Greek of the NT even to imply two pieces of timber.'" The teaching intends to deny that Jesus was crucified. See also, Trevor R. Allin, "Did Christ Die on a Cross or a Stake?," Bethinking, www.bethinking.org/jehovahs-witnesses/did-christ-die-on-a-cross-or-a-stake, accessed March 8, 2022.

works of the law provide cursing, the reception of the Spirit comes only by faith.[46]

THE PROMISES SPOKEN TO ABRAHAM AND HIS SEED AND THE IDENTIFICATION OF CHRIST AS THE SEED WHO INHERITS THE PROMISES (GALATIANS 3:15-20)

Paul moves to an example about human-made covenants. If two human parties institute a covenant, the terms of agreement are cemented by the act of ratification. If this holds true in earthly affairs, even more it holds true for God-made covenants, which is the nature of the Abrahamic covenant. For the Lord's words and actions in Genesis 15 ratified the covenant between he and Abraham's posterity.

As a collective noun, "offspring" remains ambiguous in the initial promise as to whether the recipient is singular or plural (cf. Gen 13:15). It would appear to be collective in order for all nations to be the recipient of the blessings of the promise. However, Isaac is the promised son from Abraham's loins, which would seem to make the object of the blessing singular. But Isaac does not fulfill the scope of the blessing. The terms of the blessing are then passed from Isaac to Jacob, and from Jacob to his sons.

As the promises are reiterated, clarified, and ratified, God includes the offspring of Abraham (Gen 13:15) and says they will be innumerable (Gen 13:16). The unidentified offspring will be a physical descendant (Gen 15:1-5) and God grants a covenant to seal what he promises to the seed. The promise included the grant of specific land to Abraham's seed (Gen 12:7, 17), which is included in the covenant (Gen 15:18-20). As the children of Israel never obtained the land in fulness as promised, the land promise of the covenant pointed to one offspring who would receive the land. God's promise to Abraham had been fulfilled in a generation living under Joshua's leadership in terms of giving them the land, rest from enemies, and making them prosper in the land (Josh 21:43-45). But even that generation did not secure all that was granted to them (Josh 23:4-10; Judg 1:27-36).

So like Isaac, Joshua and his generation were Abraham's seed but not his seed who entered and received the land.[47] Jesus is the only descendant of Abraham with the responsibility of obedience necessary to receive all that God had promised. Paul identified him by the promise, "I will give the land to the seed."[48] Paul reads the OT story of Israel in order to recognize the sense of "offspring" in the land promise. The promises of America and her "dream" for many African Americans has failed as housing and employment discrimination often keeps home ownership and economic prosperity out of reach.[49] Unlike America and her unsuccessful promises, the Lord is faithful to his promises—to see that nothing he promised to Abraham failed.

The giving of the law 430 years after the covenant was ratified cannot change the terms of the divine covenant any more than one could change the terms of a covenant between two humans. Paul's argument is that the covenant promise comes only by faith because Abraham

[46]The Hebrew Bible promises the coming of the Spirit (Is 32:15; 44:3; Ezek 11:19; 36:14, 26-27; 39:29; Joel 2:28).

[47]See Judg 1:1–2:5 for land remaining to be conquered. While the conquest was complete, the occupation left much land yet to be received. While they had been given the land, they had only possessed the gates of their enemies (Gen 22:17).

[48]Elliott E. Johnson, "What I Mean by Historical-Grammatical Interpretation and How That Differs from Spiritual Interpretation," *GTJ* 11 (1990): 167.

[49]For more on the failure of the American dream for African Americans, see Reniqua Allen, "The American Dream Isn't for Black Millennials," *New York Times*, Jan. 5, 2019, www.nytimes.com/2019/01/05/opinion/sunday/american-dream-black-millennials-homeownership.html; Joslyn Armstrong et al., "'A Dream Deferred': How Discrimination Impacts the American Dream Achievement for African Americans," *Journal of Black Studies* 50 (April 2019): 227–50; Nigel Chiwaya and Janell Ross, "The American Dream While Black: 'Locked in a Vicious Cycle,'" NBC News, Aug. 3, 2020, www.nbcnews.com/specials/american-dream-while-black-homeownership/.

was a receiver of the covenant rather than a solidifier. Abraham was asleep when God alone bound himself to keep the promises to "give" to Abraham and his descendants what he promised (Gen 15:12, 18). Abraham simply believed God (Gen 15:6). The offer of the land as a gift nullifies the need for works and is nullified doubly by the word of promise.

The law acts to reveal transgressions, making evident the need for one to come worthy of receiving the promises as one who did not transgress the law. Even that law was too holy for Moses to receive directly, so angels mediated, as the Lord gave mediation. Reading the OT, Paul recognizes that the law couldn't offer life as did the Abrahamic covenant.

THE COMBINATION OF THE LAW'S IMPRISONMENT AND PROMISE IN CHRIST IN THE PROVISION OF RIGHTEOUSNESS (GALATIANS 3:21-25)

Human legal systems allow for bias in interpretation, application, and sentencing, leading to inequities in profiling, arrests, sentencing, and even distribution of capital punishment. They often protect real criminals behind racial and economic injustices in a "white collar paradox" that favors the wealthy.[50] The law of God puts all equally in need of something that will offer life rather than imprisonments and subsequent judgment. As that promise of life is tied to the seed who will receive the land, only trusting the promise in the seed—Jesus, Messiah, provides the blessing of atonement for the imprisoned.

The coming of "faith" seems to be a reference to Christ based on the like phrase "until Christ came."[51] A "guardian" (ESV), "disciplinarian" (NRSV), or "schoolmaster" (KJV) was a slave to whom a son was committed from the time he left his nurse's care,[52] who controlled and disciplined the child,[53] offering round-the-clock supervision and protection to those under their care.[54] The law disciplined us in the way of righteousness through the revelation of sinfulness until the dawning of the messianic age of grace. It is then that Christ performs the works of the law needed to achieve righteousness so that we might be righteous by belief in him.

THE GALATIANS AS ABRAHAM'S SEED AND THE RECEPTION OF THE SPIRIT OF GOD'S (THE FATHER'S) SON (GALATIANS 3:26–4:7)

Paul will introduce "baptized into Christ" for the first time in his writings (Gal 3:27).[55] The putting on of Christ frees one from need of guardianship as one arrives at the intended destination of having met the required righteousness for salvation in him. This is a common metaphor in Paul demonstrating the new identity one has such that one should put to death the sinful ways of the pre-Christian life.[56]

---

[50]Adam Cohen, "How the Supreme Court Favors the Rich and Powerful," *Time*, March 3, 2020, https://time.com/5793956/supreme-court-loves-rich/. See also Sarah Lustbader, "Wealthy and Connected Defendants Like Roger Stone Get Off Easy All the Time," *Washington Post*, Feb. 14, 2020, www.washingtonpost.com/outlook/2020/02/14/wealthy-connected-defendants-like-roger-stone-get-off-easy-all-time/.

[51]To make the case for justification by faith, Paul seems to contrast the age of the law with the age of faith—the very thing he will do beginning in Gal 4:1 to explain what he has stated in Gal 3:23-29: "I mean that. . . ." The coming of faith contrasts with being under the time the law functioned as a schoolmaster. It is that time that is done away when Christ comes to complete redemption—a coming described temporally: "Now before faith came . . . until Christ came . . . now that faith has come."

[52]F. F. Bruce, *The Epistle to the Galatians: A Commentary on the Greek Text* (Grand Rapids, MI: Eerdmans, 1982), 182.

[53]G. Walter Hansen, *Galatians* (Downers Grove, IL: InterVarsity Press, 1994), 107.

[54]Timothy George, *Galatians* (Nashville: B&H Publishers, 1994), 265.

[55]See also Rom 6:3; Eph 4:5; Col 2:12.

[56]Rom 6:11-14; Eph 4:17-24; Col 3:5-12.

The appropriation of Galatians 3:28 to the role of women and men in the church and home seems to be a matter of attempting to appropriate some of the terms to a contemporary concern, for this is not a verse within a Haustafel unit. Contextually, there is no mention of church structure, pastor qualifications, the relationship of husband and wives to one another. Instead, the mentioning of Jew and Greek relates to sonship (Gal 3:28). Both Jews and Greeks are sons of Christ. Both bondservants and free are sons of Christ Jesus, each one's sonship is equal, and their sonship is equal across ethnic lines. Sonship does not do away with slavery status, for Paul distinguishes "slaves" and "free." But the verse would have made Christian Jews treat Christian Greeks as their spiritual equals—not demanding Greeks to become Jews to have Christ, while yet recognizing ethnic differences of "Jew" and "Greek." The oneness offered in Christ does not flatten out every distinction; it only flattens them out in sonship in Christ. "Male" and "female" are not made indistinguishable in Christ.

The equality has to do with the Galatians' inheritance as believers (Gal 3:9, 14, 16, 18, 22). The inheritance rests on their position in Christ: "until Christ came" (Gal 3:24), "in Christ Jesus" (Gal 3:26), "into Christ" (Gal 3:27), and "in Christ Jesus" (Gal 3:28). This stands in contrast to their position under the law: "imprisoned" (Gal 3:23), "our disciplinarian" (Gal 3:24), and "subject to a disciplinarian" (Gal 3:25). Under the law (and thus, outside of Christ), there are Jews (circumcised) and Greeks (uncircumcised), there are slaves (indentured) and free (owners), men (inheritors), and women (who are inheritors based on their husband's positions). In Christ, all inherit the blessings of Abraham based on spiritual sonship.[57] Rather than making an egalitarian society, Paul recognizes egalitarian sonship with respect to inheritance; there is enfranchisement for all in Christ's kingdom.[58]

The believer's possession by Christ provides all promised to Abraham and his offspring. The offspring is spiritual, not simply ethnic, for believers become sons by Christ's adoption. They do not become Jews. Yet the sonship is spiritual and national for Jewish believers—those who share both ethnic and spiritual identity with Abraham. The promise to Abraham was life and land blessing. Abraham understood this based on the choice to be buried with Sarah in the cave of Machpelah. His full expectation was that the God who promised him land would provide him life to see that land. As offspring of Abraham, because we share his faith, we inherit what our father Abraham passed to us.

The explanation of inheritance of sonship provided in the redemption in Christ from slavery finds an analogy in the slave and son relationship under guardianship. The slave and the child have the same position in a household, with the exception of the child's status as a future owner of the father's inheritance.

"The elementary principles" is the master to whom the unbeliever subscribes his worldview, ambitions, what passes for wisdom, and even "common sense."[59] Many of these basic principles often guide believers with justifications like, "But this is just American," "this is the way our family has done things for generations," or "our people always do this."

[57]Thanks goes to Dr. Elliott E. Johnson, Dallas Theological Seminary, for discussions helpful to clarifying the sense of these first century cultural terms within the context of Gal 3:26–4:7.

[58]This conclusion on egalitarianism and enfranchisement only intends to discuss Paul's argument here. It does not intend to speak to an entire Pauline or NT theology on how the enfranchisement of all in Christ's kingdom effects the transformation of political and relational realities with respect to how people engage one another in the present age.

[59]*Stoicheia* ("elementary principles") are the "rudimentary religious teachings, possessed by the whole human race"; David R. Bundrick, "TA STOICHEIA TOU KOSMOU (GAL 4:3)" *JETS* 34 (1991), 345-64.

Prior to the protoevangelium,[60] the eternal decree established the death of Christ and the salvation of the elect. The plan was put into effect in history with the first gospel pronouncement of a deliverer (cf. Gen 3:15).

"Born of a woman" points to Paul having Genesis 3:15 in mind. Here, maleness is important because the introduction of sin into the world came by Adam and not Eve, as evident in the sequence of Genesis 3 (she saw, ate, he ate, then . . .) and NT teaching (Rom 5:12-21; 1 Tim 2:13-15). The male human disobeyed and brought sin to humankind and into the created order. Another male human is needed to restore the breach of God's law by the first, lest it appears that the woman human was responsible for the evil in the world. The woman human, instead, receives word that she would give birth to the deliverer seed, which Mary did (cf. Mt 1:18; Luke 1:31, 35; 2:7).

The Son was born under the law (Lk 2:22-24). Jesus also kept the law completely in his lifetime, fulling the standards of the law intended for Israel to keep (Mt 5:17); he never broke the law (2 Cor 5:21; Heb 4:15; 7:26; 1 Pet 2:22). By being under same law as all members of Israel and bearing the law's requirements without failure, Jesus paid the purchase price of righteousness on behalf of those who failed at keeping the law with their works (cf. Rom 8:3).

Sharing the righteous status of the Son, the believer is brought into a relationship with the Father as an adopted child. Through redemption—a work of the Son alone—the believer enters a status of which one might be qualified to receive an inheritance from the Father.

The indwelling of the Spirit brings the believer into mysterious and familial union with the Father and Christ. The Spirit cries out from the hearts of believers tenderly and dependently. It is the Spirit who maintains the Sonship purchased by Christ. As the Spirit of God's Son, by dwelling within believers, cries out to God as his Father, we too are the ones crying to God our Father; we are sons for as long as the indwelling Spirit lives within to cry out to the Father.

The Spirit of God acts as cosmic abolitionist so that the Spirit's presence in *sons* guarantees that believers have been separated from slavery. Sonship is a legal concept; it would not be right to say "daughters and sons" for that term, as "daughters" did not have Roman rights to "sonship" even though daughters in Israel had sonship rights in the absence of sons to inherit (Num 27:1-11; 36:1-13; Josh 17:3-6). As sons of the Heavenly Father, believers will be recipients of the inheritance he gives. There is no discussion here of the contents of the inheritance, but only its certainty.

THE APPLICATION OF A BIBLICAL REVELATION TO THE GALATIANS AND THE FORMATION OF CHRIST IN THEM (GALATIANS 4:8-20)

Except for the experience of house slaves—who were treated with more kindness than the slaves who worked the cotton and tobacco fields—the hope of slaves in America was total freedom. No romanticized pictures of US slavery, such as those in *Gone with the Wind* and depicted on food product labels, should be accepted as truth.[61] Paul revisits the distinction between the

[60]"Protoevangelium" refers to the first pronouncement of the gospel in Gen 3:15. The verse speaks of the deliverance of Adam and Eve from the judgment of sin through the work of a male offspring who does conflict with evil and evil's offspring, suffers a minor wound, and is yet triumphant over evil.

[61]In the wake of the death of George Floyd, American companies began to acknowledge the problem of romanticized images of US slavery in film and marketing of consumer goods. See Alina Selyukh, "Aunt Jemima Will Change Name, Image as Brands Confront Racial Stereotypes," NPR, June 17, 2020, www.npr.org/sections/live-updates-protests-for-racial-justice /2020/06/17/879104818/acknowledging-racial-stereotype-aunt-jemima-will-change-brand-name-and-image, accessed August 21, 2020.

believer's former status as slave and the new status as those simply free from slavery. The description of the believers' lifestyle reveals an ethos of idolatry. The acceptance of a false gospel leads to worship of a false god and false Christ.

The proclivity to see works as a means of righteousness reveals the *self* as king. We hope to present ourselves as sufficient to God rather than rely on the working of another on our behalf. Religious pilgrims who are seeking a god via human works show the idolatries in the world. The Judaizers, though monotheistic and well-meaning, shared this philosophy as those clinging to works of the law for righteousness. The deception is that human-effort gods are not actually deified.

"We have come to know" him is a natural way for someone to speak of a relationship with God in Christ. This is an adequate understanding of being introduced as an adopted child to one's new Forever Parent. Yet, as Charles Booth wrote, "We see the purpose of God dating far back before the foundation of this world, before there had yet risen on it the sun and the moon by whose aid our days and months and years are measured. They tell us of God's purpose, choice, election, and predestination long before the creation of any one of those who were thus to be brought to the kingdom prepared for them from the foundation of the world."[62] The weakness and worthlessness of the elementary principles stand in contrast to the strength and worth of being known by God in the justification of sinners forever.

The elementary principles are powerless and empty in comparison to the eternal gospel of grace. Paul invites the Galatians to consider why they would wish to return to such emptiness. The specific elements of the principles to which he is referring are the Mosaic covenant practices of observation of holy days.

The Jewish calendar had weekly, yearly, and periodic year practices. Labeling these observations under "weak and worthless" negates them as having value for righteousness, and aligns them with other elementary principles unnamed included within the broader mentioning of the term. Just as the seven principles of Kwanzaa appear to offer strength and honor for a Pan-African people disenfranchised by a majority culture, so the observation of Jewish practices seemed to offer value to God for people of the old covenant.

If the Galatians turned from Paul's gospel to works for sanctification, there was no need for Paul to have preached to them. Yet Paul had labored among them without attempting to gain righteousness by the observation of days, even if he maintained observation of days for cultural identification (cf. Acts 18:18; 20:16; 21:23).

Paul's hope is that the preaching yields formation of Christ in the lives of the Galatian believers (Gal 4:19). With the sort of familial address common to modern churches of historic African American origins, Paul entreats the brothers and sisters rather than commanding them. Paul is wise not to pit his commands against the demands for circumcision, observation of days, and the call for believers to keep the law. The entreaty is personal and vulnerable: "I. . you . . . I am . . . you are. . . . You did me. . . . You know."

Paul preached to the Galatians with sickness in his eyes, even indicating a detour in his agenda that made the preaching come to them first. They gave reception to Paul as if he was an angel or even Jesus. They demonstrated such love toward Paul that they would have sacrificed their own sight to improve his. Paul now has anguishing desire for the Galatians to hope for their own formation in Christ even if it means bodily suffering for rejecting the false gospel of justification by works of the law (Gal 4:19).

[62]Charles Octavius Booth, *Plain Theology for Plain People* (Bellingham, WA: Lexham Press, 2017), 61.

Paul, in weakness, could not work for their favor, but needed the work of their free and honorable reception and the potential sacrifices of their own sight. Their reception of Paul demonstrates them as those not working to earn Paul's preaching of the gospel; he came of his own accord, and they simply received.

The contrast in their present embracing of a different gospel effectively makes Paul their enemy with his gospel message. The questioning of this change in disposition leaves self examination of their incongruence in the hands of the Galatians.

The self-centered motives of the Judaizers are affirmed by acts of shutting believers out of fellowship so that believers will come crawling back to them with a willingness to say that justification by works of the law is the gospel (Gal 4:17). The Galatians' opponents use exclusion to make the believers long to regain fellowship with those who have flattered them.

Paul does not deny the goodness of being celebrated, as long as the intention is good. "My little children" (Gal 4:19) is endearing, most likely also in contrast to empty and inconsistent flattery by the circumcision party. Rather than shutting out some, Paul is embracing the Galatians as if he gave birth to them—which he did in one sense.[63] Yet the real child endearment Paul seeks is for his labors to produce Christlikeness in them.

THE ILLUSTRATION OF ABRAHAM'S TWO SONS AND THE INFLUENCE OF THE LAW ON INHERITANCE (GALATIANS 4:21-31)

Paul addresses those who wish to live with the law as rule over them (Gal 4:21). The "law" in this first usage seems to refer to the Mosaic law's 613 commandments and prohibitions. The second usage uses the verbal link of "law" when referring to the first five books of the Hebrew Bible, Genesis through Deuteronomy.

Paul illustrates the influence of the law on inheritance in the contrast between the inheritance of Isaac—the heir according to promise, and Ishmael—the heir according to human effort. In history, the heirs of Abraham are born not according to a natural process from the slave girl, but according to a supernatural process from the freed woman. Paul will tell the story in history (Gal 4:21-23), provide an extended analogy (Gal 4:24-27), and then appropriate the story and analogy to the Galatian's identity (Gal 4:28-31).

Abraham had two sons.[64] God had promised Abraham that he would have numerous offspring, and that through him, the whole world would be blessed. Ishmael was born to Abraham naturally, through human effort without faith in what God had promised. The free woman had a child because God did something supernaturally when she was ninety years old. The child born by trust in the

[63]Paul's relationship to them via the gospel was analogous to the relationship of a father to his own child. This is a recurring theme in the Pauline corpus, both in the sense of having introduced some to the gospel (e.g., "birthed") and in becoming an intimately close companion as a result of the gospel (1 Cor 4:15; Phil. 2:22; 1 Thess 2:11-12; 1 Tim 1:2; Tit 1:4; Philem 10).

[64]Abraham is considered to be the father of the faith in the three great monotheistic religions—Judaism, Christianity, and Islam. His two sons, Ishmael and Isaac, are the source of conflicts between Muslims and Jews, and Muslims and Christians. For Islam believes that Ishmael was the son of promised blessing, and that they are the offspring of Ishmael, and thus, the people of God. But the Genesis narrative, which the Qur'an itself reveres, points out something different. For more, see Charles Halton, "Jon D. Levenson Talks to Charles Halton About Abrahamic Religions," *Los Angeles Review of Books*, March 12, 2013, https://themarginaliareview.com/jon-d-levenson-talks-to-charles-halton-about-abrahamic-religions/; Timothy George, "Is the God of Muhammad the Father of Jesus?," *CT*, February 4, 2002, www.christianitytoday.com/ct/2002/february4/is-god-of-muhammad-father-of-jesus.html; Jon D. Levenson, "The Idea of Abrahamic Religions: A Qualified Dissent," *Jewish Review of Books*, Spring 2010, https://jewishreviewofbooks.com/articles/244/the-idea-of-abrahamic-religions-a-qualified-dissent/; Wendy Murray Zoba, "Islamic Fundamentals," *CT*, March1, 2000, www.christianitytoday.com/ct/2000/marchweb-only/21.0c.html.

promises of God to do what cannot be done by natural human effort is the child of the free woman. This is what the law speaks to those who want to keep the law to please God.

Paul turns to write in a method similar to the way in which Jordan Peel's modern work, *Us*, allegorizes an African American family who has embraced the White American dream in their lifestyle choices and parenting and marriage.[65] The two women, one slave and one free, represent two covenants. The woman who gives birth by natural process corresponds to the covenant from Mount Sinai—the covenant to which the circumcision party appeals for righteousness. This is the slave girl, Hagar, who corresponds to the present city of Jerusalem. The absence of a description of Hagar as "Egyptian" is important for seeing that her African heritage is not the basis of Paul's comparison or argument.[66] A noninheriting offspring comes from Hagar, indicating that the analogous offspring—the Judaizers, as those enslaved to the law of Mount Sinai—will not inherit the blessing of Abraham.

The woman who gives birth by the supernatural process corresponds to a heavenly Jerusalem (Gal 4:26). Sarah, once was barren, miraculously receives an heir *through the promise to Abraham*. Analogous to her offspring are those who believe in Paul's gospel message of justification by faith. Isaiah 54:1-8 reveals that a redeemed bride (Israel), married to the Lord himself, will bear children more numerous than in her former days of captivity.

Paul understands believers are united to the ascended Christ as the redeemed bride is married to Christ (Gal 4:27). He concludes that the Jerusalem—the Jewish descendants of his day were returning to the barren days of captivity.

THE BELIEVER'S STANDING IN NEW FREEDOM AND DEPENDENCY ON THE SPIRIT TO SATISFY THE DEMANDS OF THE LAW (GALATIANS 5:1-26)

Christ's work transfers the one exercising faith from slavery under the law to freedom in Christ—freedom in grace. The standing firm against returning to slavery make a double wall against the works of the law providing sanctification for those freed by Christ's redeeming work. Paul throws the weight of his experiences with the gospel (Gal 1:10-2:21) and the Galatians (Gal 4:12-20) against the circumcision party's promotion of circumcision for believers.

Acceptance of *circumcision* is the concern (Gal 5:3, 4 ["severed"], 6, 11, 12 ["emasculate"]). The Judaizers claim that circumcision advantages Jews and Gentiles before God as it did Abraham. But it renders idle the advantage of Christ's righteousness that was accomplished in the cross.

Circumcision brings with it the demand to keep the full law in order to obtain righteousness. In a creative and jarring use of circumcision imagery Paul indicates that the cutting of the foreskin for the sake of keeping the law severs a person from Christ and his blessings (Gal 5:4). Justification unto righteousness is zero sum with respect to grace: it is all grace or falling away.

Because of the Spirit and the completed work of Christ, righteousness is already and not-yet for the believer. The inaugurated eschatology is evident in the present experience of faith pointing forward to the righteousness to come.

The equity of Jews and Gentiles on the basis of the work of Christ (Gal 3:28) means both gained the justification and sanctification of Christ apart from works of the law. Paul specifically uses "circumcision" and "in circumcision" here for Jews

[65]Jordan Peele, *Us* (Los Angeles: Monkeypaw Productions, 2019).

[66]Nyasha Junior recognizes, "Although [Paul] describes her as the slave woman, he does mention that she is Egyptian. . . . He is not interested in the women as multi-faceted characters but as symbols of opposing covenants" (Nyasha Junior, *Reimagining Hagar: Blackness and the Bible* [Oxford: Oxford University Press, 2019], 27).

and Gentiles in order to focus on the problem of the act rather than the ethnic identity.

The Judaizers want Jewish works for Gentiles, but not full ethnic proselytizing of Gentiles into Judaism (Gal 5:3, 6). Once thought a better health option for boys, circumcision has no significance to health or righteousness. What matters is faith working through love (Gal 5:6).

Paul draws in the concept of running from ancient games to show progress being made and then interrupted.[67] Those promoting circumcision have interrupted the Galatian believers from following the truth of the gospel. The apostle leaves no room for compromise or syncretistic practice.

The summons to faith in Christ is a consistent Pauline idea (Gal 5:8).[68] A summons negates works as the means by which one becomes justified.

Like the working of yeast, leaven from one batch of baking could be held a few days and then inserted into a new batch, helping the new batch to expand. A small persuasion away from the truth could influence a complete corruption of the truth and a full turning away from its message. "To tolerate a trifling error inevitably leads to crass heresy."[69]

Nevertheless, Paul affirms his faith in the Galatians to believe the truth rather than any other view of the gospel. It is the Spirit of the Lord who will work in the affections of the Galatians to solidify them in the truth (cf. Gal 5:16).

Paul also promises the judgment of the circumcision party. Each person who promoted circumcision will face judgment, regardless of their power or influence in their society. They should not be thought of as friends of the Galatians, even if they present themselves as friendly (cf. Gal 4:17). They should not be thought of as friends of God, for they stand in his judgment (cf. Gal 1:8, 9).

The troublemakers claimed that Paul preached the necessity of circumcision. Paul therefore juxtaposes his earlier experiences with the gospel (Gal 1:9–2:21) and his gospel experiences with the Galatians (Gal 4:12-20) against the allegation. If Paul's message were the same as the circumcision party's, they would have no need to attack him (Gal 5:11).

The familiar nature of the brotherly address gives a tone of warmth to an otherwise grating discourse (cf. Gal 4:20).[70] It softened the invitation to weigh their experience with Paul against the position of the circumcision party.

Some of the opponents also might have wrongly inferred a denigration of the law by Paul preaching of the grace of Christ.[71] Experiencing offense for proclaiming justification by faith is congruent with the need for courage, boldness, and zeal on the part of believers.[72]

Well-known in the Roman Empire was the practice of self-emasculation among the Galli—priests of the goddess Cybele. An annual ritual witnessed the castration of many.[73] Paul

[67]In 1 Cor 9:24-27, Paul seems to be drawing upon races in the Isthmian Games. John Fotopoulos, *The New Testament and Early Christian Literature in Greco-Roman Context: Studies in Honor of David E. Aune* (Leiden: Brill, 2006), 97.

[68]Rom 1:6, 7; 9:24; 1 Cor 1:9; Eph 4:1, 4; 1 Thess 2:12; 5:24; 2 Tim 1:9.

[69]Martin Luther, "Commentary on Galatians 5:9" in *Martin Luther's Commentary on Galatians* (Grand Rapids, MI: Zondervan, 1939), www.studylight.org/commentaries/mlg/galatians-5.html, accessed August 20, 2020.

[70]Paul uses *adelphoi* ("brothers") to address the Galatians nine other times: Gal 1:11; 3:15; 4:12, 28, 31; 5:11, 13; 6:1, 18.

[71]The question of Paul and the possible denigration of the Mosaic code arises in Acts, in part, as a matter of Paul telling Gentiles there was not a need for circumcision and the report coming to believing Jews in Jerusalem that Paul was speaking against the law (Acts 21:20-24, 28). Some may have inferred the same in Galatia with respect to Paul preaching against a need for circumcision.

[72]On boldness, zeal, and courage in proclaiming the gospel in the NT, see Acts 4:13, 29, 31; 9:27, 28; 13:46; 14:3; 19:8; 26:26; 28:31; 2 Cor 3:2; Eph 6:19, 20; Phil 1:14, 20; 1 Thess 2:2.

[73]Classicist Sarah Bond notes, "The priests of Cybele called galli, likely due to the Gallus River that ran beside the original temple for Cybele, were supposed to be eunuchs. They castrated themselves yearly on a festival held on March 24, reportedly using primitive instruments. But we also have surviving castration clamps that are decorated with deities and likely used in

pronounces his personal desire for self-judgment on the circumcizers with gritty imagery. While they are in the act of cutting on the male genital organ of everyone, they should turn the knife on themselves and completely remove their own genitals. Paul wishes to prevent false teachers from having the strength to continue their severing messages.

The dangerous temptation of moral license always exists (cf. Rom 6:15-23; Eph 5:3-13; Col 3:5-10; 1 Thess 4:1-8). Living under a system that espouses freedom allows the possibility that some will use freedom for unrighteous activity rather than righteous activity. Such a person seems to think absence of a guardian law code also means absence of obedience, holiness, or morality. However, the summons to freedom from the works of the law does not give the believer permission or rationale for using one's "rebellious human nature" without restraint.[74]

Paul marks love as the path to moral righteousness. Freedom is not the ability to be autonomous in the exercise of one's choices and desires, neither is it escape from authority organization or authority. Instead, within the familial relations of redeemed people adopted into the same family, those justified by grace maintain ethical treatment toward one another by a means that keeping the law does not provide. When family members act in love toward one another, they do not need rules to provide consideration and right treatment toward the other members of the family. One only needs law where there is an absence of the application of love. Were the Judaizers to accuse those holding to justification by faith of embracing a theology of living lawlessly, their case would be cancelled by Paul's understanding of the relationship of love to the law (cf. Lev 19:18).

Paul says fulfillment of the whole law lies in obedience to love one's neighbor not apart from the command to love God.[75] The one loving God with his entire heart, mind, soul, and strength displays this in the world by means of loving one's neighbor. It is not possible to conjure such love without the power the Spirit of grace. The seams of the false gospel show through the absence of love. The Galatians are biting and devouring one another, like wild beasts attacking and savagely eating their prey.

"Walk" is a term for how the believer lives (as reflected in the NRSV).[76] The righteousness the Galatians desire is not achievable apart

---

a religious context" (Sarah Bond, "What 'Game of Thrones' Gets Right and Wrong About Eunuchs and Masculinity," *Forbes Magazine*, August 20, 2017, www.forbes.com/sites/drsarahbond/2017/08/20/what-game-of-thrones-gets-right-and-wrong-about-eunuchs-and-masculinity/#6a0e33c2c55f.

[74]Hawthorne recognizes six uses of *sarx* ("flesh") in the Pauline literature: (1) physical matter (2 Cor 12:7), (2) human body (2 Cor 7:1), (3) human person or race (1 Cor 1:29; Rom 3:20), (4) a morally neutral sphere (Rom 4:1; 1 Cor 10:18), (5) a morally negative sphere (1 Cor 1:26; Phil 3:3-4), and (6) rebellious human nature (Rom 7:5; 1 Cor 5:5). Hawthorne cites the uses of *sarx* in Gal 5:13 and those to follow in Gal 5:16-24 in the last category (General F. Hawthorne, Ralph P. Martin, and Daniel G. Reid, eds., *Dictionary of Paul and His Letters: A Compendium of Contemporary Biblical Scholarship*, [Downers Grove, IVP, 1993], 77-81). Similarly, Douglas Moo suggests the usage in Gal 5:16-17 represents the fallen human condition (Douglas J. Moo, "Sin in Paul," in *Fallen: A Theology of Sin*, ed. Christopher W. Morgan and Robert A. Peterson [Wheaton: Crossway, 2013], 107-30).

[75]See also Rom 13:9; Jas 2:8.

[76]Rom 6:4; 8:4; 13:13; 2 Cor 5:7; 10:3; Gal 5:16; 6:16; Eph 2:10; 4:1, 17; 5:2, 8, 15; Phil 3:17 (see also Phil 3:18); Col 1:10; 2:6; 4:5; 1 Thess 2:12; 4:1, 12; 2 Thess 3:11. Friedrich Hauck and Seigfried Schulz note, "Sparta and the Doric branch maintained sexual discipline more strongly than Athens, Corinth and the Ionic sphere. It was here, however, that homosexuality developed and this then spread over the whole of Greece and was practised rather than censured even by notable figures. Lesbianism was much less common. In a fateful way both opened the door to unnatural perversion" (Friedrich Hauck and Seigfried Schulz, "πόρνη, πόρνος, πορνεία, πορνεύω, ἐκπορνεύω," in *Theological Dictionary of the New Testament*, ed. Gerhard Kittel and Gerhard Friedrich (Grand Rapids, MI: Eerdmans, 1968), 6:583. On pederasty and pedophilia in the Roman world and the distinction between the two, see also Stuart Frost, "The Warren Cup: Highlighting Hidden Histories," *JADE* 26 (2007): 63-72; John Pollini, "The Warren Cup: Homoerotic Love and Symposial Rhetoric in Silver," *Art Bulletin* 81 (1999): 21-52;

from the power of the Spirit. The Spirit should guide the believer and the believer should yield to such guidance.[77]

The works following the desires of the flesh will result in forfeiture of inheritance in the kingdom. Paul lists fifteen works.[78] This list is representative of the acts and attitudes that show no love toward God or neighbor.

Sexual immorality would have covered all sexual activity outside of the confines of a heterosexual, monogamous, legal marriage, including the ancient practices of pedophilia and pederasty.[79] In today's world, this would include all print and digital (or virtual) forms of pornography (the etymology of which should make its sinfulness self-explanatory).

Although one might attempt to change Paul's concept of *sensual* to reflect something less rebellious and more enlightening, it will fail, even if stated in the language of James Baldwin: "To be sensual, I think, is to respect and rejoice in the force life, of life itself, and to be *present* in all that one does, from the effort of loving to the breaking of bread."[80]

Theophus Smith proposes that the *pharmakeus* ("witchcraft") in Black cultures of North America are known by vernacular terms of "conjuror," "conjure doctor," or "hoodoo doctor."[81] The semantic range of the term would seem to cover all dark magical acts of witchcraft, practices of occultism, voodoo and healing arts of witch doctors, and earthly theurgy.

The Scriptures consistently condemn the abuse of alcohol.[82] The modern license many believers exercise with alcohol use should meet with Paul's teaching here. Paul repeats a warning call for discernment: Anyone practicing anything in the range of Paul's opposed-to-the-Spirit acts will not inherit the kingdom of God.

To *inherit* is to receive something of considerable value which has not been earned.[83] Disobedience does not lose what it has never earned, nor prove that one is not a son. It does limit participation in God's reign in the kingdom of Christ.[84]

The believer should seek to be led by the Spirit at all times, countering conceit. Conceit manifests in two forms in the relationships within the body. The first is provoking—which could lead to the fleshly works of dissections, divisions, anger, rivalries, and so on. The second is envying, which is condemned in the list of vices.

Out of step with the Spirit's leading, conceit would carry an I-am-better-than-you-attitude

---

Craig Arthur Williams, *Roman Homosexuality: Ideologies of Masculinity in Classical Antiquity* (Oxford: Oxford University Press, 1999).

[77]It is beyond this work to discuss the mysterious nature of the working of the Spirit or whether the Wesleyan understanding is to be preferred to other understandings.

[78]The count for some is sixteen, based on the variant in Gal 5:21 that inserts murder between envy and drunkenness.

[79]For the nature of marriage as public (or "legal"), see Christopher Ash, *Marriage: Sex in the Service of God* (Leicester, UK: InterVarsity Press, 2003).

[80]James Baldwin, *The Fire Next Time* (New York: Vintage International, 1993), 43.

[81]Theophus H. Smith, *Conjuring Culture: Biblical Formations of Black America* (Oxford: Oxford University Press, 1994), 208.

[82]Prov 20:1; 23:29-32; 31:4-5; 1 Cor 5:11; Eph 5:18; 1 Tim 3:3; Tit 1:7.

[83]Definition of "inheritance" assumes the freedom of owner to give without reference to the behavior of the recipient, i.e., "The portion of possessions that transfers to an heir upon the owner's death." (Chad Chambers, "Inheritance," *The Lexham Bible Dictionary* [Bellingham, WA: Lexham Press, 2016], np., and "to receive (money, property, etc.) from someone when that person dies" ("Inherit," *The Britannica Dictionary*, www.britannica.com/dictionary/inherit). Hence, when speaking of God, R. E. Nixon states, "But that inheritance is not of right, it is by the free disposition of God, who is able in his sovereign pleasure to dispossess those who seem to have most title to it and give it to others of his choice" (R. E. Nixon, "Inheritance," *New Bible Dictionary* [Downers Grove, IL: InterVarsity Press, 1996], 506).

[84]My position sees the kingdom as a future, earthly reality, but does not require such an eschatological position. Whether earthly kingdom or new creation, sonship is unearned and given freely. An inheritance is given by the right of the owner, but, as in the case of the kingdom, might require obedience on the part of those with sonship to realize promises for being given a stewardship of responsibility or the like (cf. Luke 19:16-19).

or a why-aren't-you-showing-fruit-like-me-attitude. Either attitude could cause envy of the working of the Spirit in the life of another. Being out of step with the Spirit, both provoking and envying would lead to the devouring of which Paul warned.

THE BELIEVER'S DOING OF GOOD TO THE STUMBLING AND THE TEACHER OF THE TRUTH (GALATIANS 6:1-10)

Galatians 6 looks at the continuance of good works as a Christian to those who have fallen and to other various members of the local assembly. While a conceited reply to the working of the Spirit would be counter to the freedom Christ offers, stumbling into sin would not be. Gentleness utilizes resources of the Spirit to address the believer's stumbling. Harsh responses and apathy do not demonstrate the same reliance. Looking to oneself takes seriously the susceptibility of the believer to the power of the flesh.

Overcoming (or recovering from) the sin into which one has stumbled is too much for the believer to handle on their own. A member of the body walks with the one who has stumbled. Such actions flow from the Spirit as love, for Paul already indicated love filled the law. "Of Christ" reflects the understanding of the law of Moses in the life of the believer in light of the death and resurrection of Christ and the believer's union with him.

The believer's response to those stumbling into sin takes self-inventory in humility in order to prevent personal sin. Thinking one is above sin or morally superior to another who has fallen is an attitude rooted in sufficiency of works of law. If one works to achieve righteousness, failure (or lack thereof) depends on a perceived relationship to the law. This attitude lends itself to false thinking about one's sufficiency to overcome temptation and sin.

Testing one's own work removes comparison to others. The boasting is not glorifying of one's success. Because it is a "boasting" of self-inventory in humility, it is an acknowledgment of one's own culpability to stumble into sin. Such perspective keeps one from boasting (or gloating) in the sin of a neighbor. Each believer must steward his walk to take responsibility to fight yielding to sin.

Paul provides instruction on doing good toward the assembly's teachers. Teaching the truth of the Scriptures is labor worthy of pay (or "love offering" in some traditions).[85] It also shows the importance of every believer sitting under teachers of the word in community, as no one individual believer has exhaustive knowledge of the word. The sharing reflects a response of grace toward the teacher of truth and the teaching. There is no expectation in the assembly of Galatia that a teacher of truth should have to justify, request, beg for, or demand a salary (Gal 6:6). Persons receiving the spiritual benefits of teaching that helps one walk without stumbling should return the benefits of material goods toward the teacher.

The doing of good to the teacher of the word should consider the unmocking reaping process of God and encourage good toward all, with priority on the church. There are those who might think they can give to teachers sparingly rather than liberally—rather than sharing all good things. To such persons Paul inserts God into the process as one who is repaying the one who gives. The doing of good is not a means to impoverish the giver or make wealthy the teacher. The bountiful sharing reflects the fruit of goodness flowing from the Spirit rather than a fleshly act of selfishness or greed reflected in giving sparingly.

The measures of bountiful and sparing giving probably reflect one's giving in comparison to one's personal wealth rather than a specific

[85]See also 1 Tim 5:17-18, cf. 1 Cor 9:1-18.

amount of money in comparison to the amount of another's giving. He will see what actually is sparing or bountiful giving and produce proportionate bounty or spare in one's gain of monetary and material good. The sowing into another's ministry is not a gimmick guaranteeing a certain bounty. God is pleased with those who sow bountifully as an act of good in response to the good of the teaching of the word in truth by a teacher in the assembly (Gal 6:7).

The believer should do good toward all. The giving of monetary gifts should reflect the work of Christ to include all generally (Gal 3:28) and some especially. The doing of good is not exclusive to the body, just as the message of Christ is someone one stewards to the world.

The two spheres of sowing represent sparing and bountiful. One is accomplished by the rebellious nature toward oneself. The other is accomplished by the work of the Spirit to others in great sacrifice. The reaping of the Spirit cannot be works, for the entire book argues against such. But being reflective of the Spirit, the one who sews bountifully shows the working of eternal life within and reaps what is inherent.

THE CLOSING EXAMPLE OF PAUL'S LIVED GOSPEL VERSUS THE JUDAIZER'S GOSPEL OF HYPOCRISY, WITH BENEDICTION (GALATIANS 6:11-18)

The contrast between Paul's example of suffering for Christ and those who wish to boast in the flesh of the Galatians shows the grace of Christ resting on those who walk with Christ and find no benefit in circumcision or uncircumcision. What looks like a simple ending and benediction is another very structured message.

Paul preciously writes of issues with his eyes. Much like the highly recognizable and famous signature of President Barak Obama, Paul's personal signature is recognizable and common to his letters.[86] Here the largeness is part of his pattern of suffering (Gal 6:12, 14, 17).

Paul also returns the motives of the Judaizers: circumcision is for optics and self-preservation. To forgo circumcision is to be willing to be identified with Christ and to accept reproach for him. So not following the law is following Christ; it is to accept persecution for being identified with him and his atoning death for us on the cross.

Paul says explicitly that the issue of the opponents in Galatia is keeping the law in opposition to the cross of Christ. It is not simply a matter of socializing; it is a matter of the correct message of salvation. The cross is the place God establishes righteousness for the believer forever. Opponent wishing to add to the final and finished working of God stand in opposition to the working of the God of grace.

The circumcision party are hypocritical in the endeavors. They do not keep the law in all areas themselves, but calls for the Galatians to do so. They brag to themselves and others that the Galatians see works of the law as the means to pleasing Christ.

In great contrast, Paul will not stand on personal accomplishment, even though his motives toward the Galatian believers are pure. Just as the large letters of his signature point to suffering he received for the gospel, so his exaltation is to elevate the salvation work of Christ who was crucified.

Paul's distancing of himself from boasting excludes boasting in the death of Christ. Christ's redemption unites Paul to the world in its work. The double use of "crucified" shows that the work of the cross binds Paul and the world to one another. Earlier he is crucified "with" Christ in mysterious union. But the world is not mysteriously united by Christ's

[86] 1 Cor 16:21; Col 4:18; 2 Thess 3:17; Philem 19.

death; the world caused his crucifixion. Therefore, if speaking of suffering, the relationship is one of united calling: *Paul suffers for the world as a servant who preaches of the cross of Christ and the world persecutes him so that he is persecuted as if enduring the cross of Christ.*

Paul recognizes that Christ's atonement makes a new person, looking forward to the final glorification of the believer and redemption of the present creation. Paul wishes those who agree to experience peace and mercy while being persecuted for Christ (Gal 6:16). This includes his believing ethnic brothers and sisters who have trusted the work of God in Christ rather than their own human efforts to keep the works of the law.

To look on Paul's body was akin to US Union soldiers looking on the whipped back of the escaped slave "Gordon" (a.k.a. "Whipped Peter").[87] Greater than the sign of circumcision, Paul has physical signs of the beatings and weariness he had received from unbelievers as one faithful to the message of the gospel of grace. Asking for the believers to receive his message was not too much for Paul to expect. As in all of his writings, Paul exalts the grace of Christ and wishes it on those he serves.

SELECTED BIBLIOGRAPHY

Abdul-Jabbar, Kareem. "Prosperity Gospel Is War on the Poor." *Time*. June 8, 2015. https://time.com/3912366/kareem-abdul-jabbar-prosperity-gospel/.

Alford, Henry. *The Greek Testament*. London: Longmans, 1872.

Ash, Christopher. *Marriage: Sex in the Service of God*. Downers Grove, IL: InterVarsity Press, 2003.

John Fotopoulos. *The New Testament and Early Christian Literature in Greco-Roman Context: Studies in Honor of David E. Aune*. Leiden: Brill, 2006.

Baldwin, James. *The Fire next Time*. New York: Vintage International, 1993 (1963).

Blakemore, Erin. "The Shocking Photo of 'Whipped Peter' That Made Slavery's Brutality Impossible to Deny." History. February 8, 2019. www.history.com/news/whipped-peter-slavery-photo-scourged-back-real-story-civil-war.

Block, Daniel. "Christotelic Preaching: A Plea for Hermeneutical Integrity and Missional Passion." *SBJT* 22 (2018): 7–34.

Bond, Sarah. "What 'Game of Thrones' Gets Right and Wrong About Eunuchs and Masculinity." *Forbes Magazine*. August 20, 2017. www.forbes.com/sites/drsarahbond/2017/08/20/what-game-of-thrones-gets-right-and-wrong-about-eunuchs-and-masculinity/#6a0e33c2c55f.

Boothe, Charles. *Plain Theology for Plain People*. Bellingham, WA: Lexham Press, 2017.

Brad, Braxton. *No Longer Slaves*. Collegeville, MN: Liturgical Press, 2015.

Bruce, F. F. *The Epistle to the Galatians: A Commentary on the Greek Text*. Grand Rapids, MI: Eerdmans, 1982.

Bundrick, David. "TA STOICHEIA TOU KOSMOU (GAL 4:3)." *JETS* 34 (1991): 345-64.

Carson, D. A., Douglas J. Moo, and Leon Morris. *Introduction to the New Testament*. Grand Rapids, MI: Zondervan, 1992.

Carson, Donald A., and Douglas J. Moo. *An Introduction to the New Testament*. Grand Rapids, MI: Zondervan, 2008.

Delling, Gerhard. "βασκαίνω." Vol. 1 of *Theological Dictionary of the New Testament*, edited by Gerhard Kittel, 594-95. Grand Rapids, MI: Eerdmans, 1964.

George, Timothy. *Galatians*. Nashville: B&H, 1994.

———. "Is the God of Muhammad the Father of Jesus?" ChristianityToday.com. February

[87]See Erin Blakemore, "The Shocking Photo of 'Whipped Peter' That Made Slavery's Brutality Impossible to Deny," History.com, Feb 7 2019, www.history.com/news/whipped-peter-slavery-photo-scourged-back-real-story-civil-war, accessed Aug 21, 2020, for the very famous photo, which is part of the Library of Congress collection.

4, 2002. www.christianitytoday.com/ct/2002/february4/is-god-of-muhammad-father-of-jesus.html.

Glaude, Eddie S., Jr. "Too Many Black Churches Preach the Gospel of Greed." *New York Times*. March 19, 2015. www.nytimes.com/roomfordebate/2014/06/25/has-capitalism-become-incompatible-with-christianity/too-many-black-churches-preach-the-gospel-of-greed.

Halton, Charles. "Jon D. Levenson Talks to Charles Halton About Abrahamic Religions." The Marginalia Review of Books. March 12, 2013. https://themarginaliareview.com/jon-d-levenson-talks-to-charles-halton-about-abrahamic-religions/.

Hansen, G. Walter. *Galatians*. Downers Grove, IL: InterVarsity Press, 1994.

Hawthorne, Gerald F., Ralph P. Martin, and Daniel G. Reid. *Dictionary of Paul and His Letters: A Compendium of Contemporary Biblical Scholarship*. Downers Grove, IL: InterVarsity Press, 1993.

Johnson, Elliott. "Literal Interpretation." Dean Bible Ministries. Accessed August 15, 2020. https://deanbibleministries.org/dbmfiles/notes/2014-ChaferConf-009-Johnson-Paper.pdf.

Johnson, Elliott E. "What I Mean by Historical-Grammatical Interpretation and How That Differs from Spiritual Interpretation." *GTJ* 11 (1990): 157-69.

Junior, Nyasha. *Reimagining Hagar: Blackness and Bible*. Oxford: Oxford University Press, 2019.

Junne, George H. *The Black Eunuchs of the Ottoman Empire*. New York: Bloomsbury Publishing, 2016.

Kummel, W. G. *Introduction to the New Testament*. Nashville: Abingdon, 1975.

Lavelle, Moria. "The Fire Last Time: The 1990s Wave of 145 Church Burnings—Map." The World—PRX blog. July 2015. https://theworld.org/stories/2015-07-02/fire-last-time-1990s-wave-145-church-burnings-map.

Levenson, Jon D. "The Idea of Abrahamic Religions: A Qualified Dissent—Jewish Review of Books." Jewish Review of Books. December 6, 2018. https://jewishreviewofbooks.com/articles/244/the-idea-of-abrahamic-religions-a-qualified-dissent/.

Luther, Martin. "'Commentary on Galatians 5:9' in Galatians 5: Luther's Commentary on Galatians—Bible Commentaries." StudyLight.org. 1939. www.studylight.org/commentaries/mlg/galatians-5.html.

Malsin, Jared. "Christians Mourn Their Relatives Beheaded by ISIS." *Time*. February 23, 2015. https://time.com/3718470/isis-copts-egypt/.

Moo, Douglas J. "Sin in Paul." In *Fallen: A Theology of Sin*, edited by Christopher W. Morgan and Robert A. Peterson, 107-30. Wheaton, IL: Crossway, 2013.

Peele, Jordan, dir. *Us*. Los Angeles: Monkeypaw Productions, 2019.

Pipa, Joseph A. *Galatians: God's Proclamation of Liberty*. Fearn, Scotland: Christian Focus, 2010.

Selyukh, Alina. 2020. "Aunt Jemima Will Change Name, Image as Brands Confront Racial Stereotypes." America Reckons With Racial Injustice. *NPR*. June 17, 2020. https://www.npr.org/sections/live-updates-protests-for-racial-justice/2020/06/17/879104818/acknowledging-racial-stereotype-aunt-jemima-will-change-brand-name-and-image.

Smith, Theophus H. *Conjuring Culture*. Oxford University Press, 1995.

Sommerville, Diane Miller. "Rape, Race, and Castration in Slave Law in the Colonial and Early South." In *The Devil's Lane: Sex and Race in the Early South*, edited by Catherine Clinton and Michele Gillespie, 74-89. Oxford: Oxford University Press, 1997.

Zoba, Wendy Murray. "Islamic Fundamentals." ChristianityToday.com. March 1, 2000. www.christianitytoday.com/ct/2000/marchweb-only/21.0c.html.

LETTER TO THE EPHESIANS

Esau D. McCaulley

AUTHORSHIP, DATE, AND CIRCUMSTANCE

Since the time of F. C. Baur, Pauline authorship of Ephesians has been questioned.[1] These arguments were in part based on an evolutionary understanding of early Christianity in which Ephesians represents the triumph of the Petrine tradition (early catholic Christianity).[2] This particular way of articulating things no longer rules the day, but the basic skepticism about Pauline authorship of Ephesians remains in place.[3]

More recently, Cohick has highlighted the four main areas of concern, which are "(1) theology; (2) grammar, vocabulary, and syntax; (3) historical circumstances; and (4) relationship to Colossians."[4] These issues cannot be comprehensively litigated in this brief introduction. I can only note that the theological distinctives between the so-called undisputed letters of Paul and Ephesians can be explained by differing circumstances rather than different authors. Second, suggesting that the differences again in grammar, syntax, and vocabulary can only be explained by positing a Pauline imitator either excessively limits Paul's ability to be creative in his mode of expression, or downplays the role of scribes in the production of letters. Stated differently, we are dealing with literature, prose, and art, not mathematics. Writers (and Paul was a writer if nothing else) can enter into startlingly different registers depending on mood and situation.[5] Solutions to the historical issues and the relationship to Colossians have been answered elsewhere.[6]

If Paul indeed wrote Ephesians, he probably wrote it from Prison in Rome sometime around AD 62–63.[7] Ephesus, like many major Greek cities of its day, was a cultural melting pot. It was known for the Artemis cult on the one hand and the cult of the emperor on the other.[8] There was also an existing Jewish community (Acts 19:1-10).

The congregation seems to consist of mostly Gentiles who have left their pagan past

---

[1]Markus Barth, *Ephesians*, The Anchor Bible 34 (Garden City, NY: Doubleday, 1974), 1:32-50 remains to my mind the best reflection on the authorship questions. We must not commit the error of chronological snobbery in which only the most recent works are worthy of note. The most judicious recent study is that of Stephen E. Fowl, *Ephesians: A Commentary*, The New Testament Library (Louisville, KY: Westminster John Knox Press, 2012), 27, who concludes that he is not sure one way or the other. It is the confident and strident denial of Pauline authorship that outruns the evidence.

[2]Fowl, *Ephesians*, 22.

[3]I think that N. T. Wright's reflections on respectability and doubting of Pauline authorship are vital. See N. T. Wright, *Paul and the Faithfulness of God*, vol. 4, *Christian Origins and the Question of God* (London: SPCK, 2013), 58-60.

[4]Lynn H. Cohick, *The Letter to the Ephesians*, New International Commentary on the New Testament (Grand Rapids, MI: Eerdmans, 2020), 4.

[5]See the discussion of the problem of "false grouping" in Luke Timothy Johnson, *Constructing Paul*, vol 1. of *The Canonical Paul* (Grand Rapids, MI: Eerdmans, 2020), 38-41.

[6]On the relationship to Colossians and the historical reconstruction see Thielman, *Ephesians*, 9-18.

[7]Barth, *Ephesians*, 1:51-52.

[8]Frank Thielman, *Ephesians*, Baker Exegetical Commentary on the New Testament (Grand Rapids, MI: Baker Academic, 2010), 19-22.

to follow Jesus. Nonetheless, some aspects of that past continue to stalk the congregation. Therefore, Paul encourages them to live lives that reflect the high calling they have as Christians. The emphasis on the supremacy of Christ over authority and power is also relevant in a culture that has many claim-making deities and earthly rulers. Given some of Paul's personal comments (Eph 3:13; 6:19), some members may have struggled to reconcile their beliefs about the universal lordship of Jesus with the fact that their founding apostle was imprisoned. Paul responds by saying that the imprisonment shows that they are worth suffering for and that the gospel is itself a glory.

OVERVIEW

After a standard greeting that marks many of Paul's letters, the apostle recounts God's plan of salvation, redemption, transformation, and adoption of believers before turning to God's triumph over evil powers.[9] Paul underscores how the inclusion of the Gentiles was not some innovation in God's purposes; it was his plan before the foundation of the world. Chapter two highlights the inclusion of the Gentiles and the creation of one humanity out of two divided groups through the cross. Chapter three encourages a life together as Christians reflect God's wisdom to the watching world, where Paul invites the Ephesians to a love that defies comprehension. Chapter four depicts Christian life together as a community of mutual submission, forbearance, and sharing of gifts with the goal of fully maturing in Christ. Chapter five and the first half of chapter six considers how Christ and his kingdom transfigures social relationships in the household (wives/husbands; slaves/masters; parents/children). That chapter continues by reminding Christians that the armor of God is sufficient protection against spiritual powers, before concluding with a few personal matters and a benediction.

GREETINGS (EPHESIANS 1:1-2)

Paul opens his letter, as he often does, by giving his name and title. He is an "apostle" of Jesus the Messiah by the will of God. Hidden in this brief description is the tale of Paul's own life, God's wider purpose in redemptive history, and his sovereignty over human affairs. Paul is an apostle commissioned by Jesus, Israel's long-expected messianic king, to bring the good news of this strange kingship and Christ's reconciling death for sins to the varied ethnic groups of the world. I use to the term *ethnic group* because the Scriptures of the Old and New Testaments do not think in terms of races (Black, White, Latina, Asian), but people groups that are a mix of biological descent, culture, and belief system. Although Paul speaks often of Jews and Gentiles, he also clearly knows about the different ethnicities that cluster under the category of Gentile.

Paul's ministry to the Gentiles, then, is not some innovation, taken up as plan B after God's initial plan went awry. The inclusion of the Gentiles is a part of God's sovereign plan, which precedes creation itself.[10] Paul refers to the bringing of all things together under the lordship of Christ as God's eternal will and purpose finally made known on the other side of Christ's passion (Eph 1:9-10)

Paul addresses this letter to those in Ephesus calling them "saints" and faithful in the

---

[9]Cohick, *Letter to the Ephesians*, 1.

[10]See Victorinus's comments in M. J. Edwards, ed., *Galatians, Ephesians, Philippians*, Ancient Christian Commentary on Scripture (Downers Grove, IL: InterVarsity Press, 1999), 106.

Messiah Jesus. By calling the largely Gentile community "saints," he narrates them into the people of God. Just like the people of Israel in the old covenant were "set apart" or holy to the Lord, now the Gentiles are as well. Calling them saints speaks to the reality of who they are in Christ and to their vocation to be holy people of God.[11] Alongside this identity as saints, they are called the "faithful," those whose life is marked by trust in the Messiah.

Last, these Ephesian saints are "in Christ." This is a physical and existential reality. Through faith and baptism, the believer is united with Christ and lives out his or her existence with and in him.[12] The Christian life is encompassed on all sides by Jesus, the one who conquered death and rules all things. Our identity derives from him, our present and future are linked to his.

Paul concludes his introduction, as he often does, by speaking of the grace and peace that comes from God our Father and the Lord Jesus Christ.

Listening to his section "in color" involves recognizing the identity that Paul gives to all believers. There are no graduated callings to holiness based on ethnicity, gender, or class. All those in Christ are both holy and called to be holy. This is a gift, not a burden because the life with God is our great joy. Paul's words lift up those who live in a society where there are all kinds of limits placed on achievement and worth. He believes that holiness is available to us. Paul's words here remind the church in Ephesus and Christians throughout time that what matters most is not the name that society gives, but the identity given by our creator. He has called us and made us his own.

IN PRAISE OF GOD'S PURPOSES (EPHESIANS 1:3-14)

Following on from his greeting, Paul gives an extended blessing of praise to God. In its original language, this passage is one long sentence extending down to at least Ephesians 1:14. Paul praises God our Father and the Lord Jesus the Messiah for all the spiritual blessings that the Ephesians have due to their union with Christ. When Paul speaks of spiritual blessings, he does not have in mind merely "nonmaterial" blessings. Instead, he speaks of spiritual blessings as those things that have their origin in God himself and that are mediated to the Christian by the Spirit.[13] These blessings include God's election of all believers in and through Christ before the foundation of the world. This election was for a purpose. God chose the Ephesians and us "to be holy and blameless before him." God's rescue wasn't just from judgment, but toward holiness. This election or choosing is rooted in God's love (Eph 1:4). God's lovingly chose the Ephesians and us for adoption.

Normally in the Greco-Roman world adoption was of adults whose talents and gifts brought something to the family. It was rooted in an assessment of proved worth or potential. Being adopted signaled a break with one authority and the transferal into a new family with a new head.

Paul wanted the Ephesians to know that God chose them because he loved them and because it was a part of his wider plan to unite all things in Christ. God was not concerned with what the Ephesians brought to the family. Instead of choosing those qualified, he made those whom he chose worthy. He bestowed dignity and gave them gifts instead of using

[11]Pheme Perkins, "The Letter to the Ephesians," in *New Interpreter's Bible*, ed. Leander E. Keck (Nashville: Abingdon Press, 2000), 11:370.

[12]Andrew T. Lincoln, *Ephesians*, Word Biblical Commentary 42 (Dallas: Word 1990), 21.

[13]Francis Foulkes, *Ephesians: An Introduction and Commentary*, Tyndale New Testament Commentaries 10 (Downers Grove, IL: InterVarsity Press, 1989), 54.

their preexisting gifts and talents (as in the Greco-Roman world) to bring his family esteem.

The response to this election is the praise of God for the grace that he showed them in Christ. It is in and through Christ that Christians received redemption through his blood and the forgiveness of their wrongdoing.[14] God, according to Paul, did not barely muster enough grace to bring about forgiveness and redemption. God had more than enough to spare, being wealthy or rich in his grace. This grace abounded to the Ephesians as a manifestation of God's wisdom and understanding. This gracious act of saving, transforming, and adopting them into his family is the eschatological revelation of God's plan and purposes. These purposes are made clear in Christ. When the Ephesians recognize this plan for the wonder that it is, according to Paul, the only response is praise. The Ephesians turned to this gracious God when they heard the word of the truth, the gospel of their salvation, and received the Holy Spirit as the first fruits or down payment toward the larger inheritance that belongs to God's family.[15]

Seeing this passage as a text for the whole church involves recognizing that God's plan was always to bring different ethnic groups into God's family through Jesus' atoning and reconciling death. Paul's words would help Gentiles in Ephesus understand that their inclusion into God's people was not some hastily conceived alternative to a failed plan. According to Paul, this was God's plan from before the world was created: to gather a people from every tribe, tongue, and nation into one body. Christ, according to Paul, is God's wisdom on display, his plan made plain.

The Black Christian, the Latina Christian, the Asian Christian do not have to wonder about their standing among the people of God, based on the teaching of the New Testament. God always wanted to gather the varied people of the world into his family. What then is the problem? Too often the majority culture church in America has treated itself as the center of God's purposes. Ethnic minorities (Black, Asian, Latino, Indigenous Peoples) are then put in the place of Gentiles who are added to "the church" in the fullness of time. That is not what Paul says. All non-Jewish believers are the same. We are all added to Abraham's family. All of us ought to be humbled to find ourselves caught up in this grand story.

PRAYERS FOR THE CHURCH (EPHESIANS 1:15-23)

Paul turns from a blessing to a prayer for the church in Ephesus. His prayers for the church are anchored in two things about the Ephesians: (1) they trusted in Jesus the Messiah, and (2) they loved their follow believers. He prayed that God would give them a "Spirit of revelation and insight," perhaps an allusion to the Spirit that was to mark the coming son of David's ministry in Isaiah 11:2. The Spirit that empowers the Ephesians to understand all that God has done for them in Christ is the same Spirit that empowered Jesus' earthly ministry. Paul's prayer is that the Ephesians fully understand (1) the hope of their calling, (2) God's glorious inheritance of them—the saints are God's prized possession, and (3) the power that he works toward those who believe—the same power that God exercised when he raised Christ from the dead.[16]

---

[14]Mitzi J. Smith, "Ephesians," in *True to Our Native Land: An African American New Testament Commentary*, ed. Brian K. Blount, Cain Hope Felder, Clarice Jannette Martin, and Emerson B. Powery (Minneapolis: Fortress Press, 2007), 348-62.

[15]N. T. Wright, *Paul for Everyone: The Prison Letters* (London: SPCK, 2004), 9-10.

[16]Perkins, "Letter to the Ephesians," 382.

Christ has not merely defeated death, but has ascended (Eph 1:20) to God's right hand in power beyond all other authorities.[17] God has, according to Paul, made Christ the supreme head over all things for the good of the church (which is his body), which receives "the fullness," namely all of Christ who fills all things. Coming to grips with this world-transforming gospel is not the result of human effort. It is a gift of God mediated through his Spirit. Paul believes that if the Christian comes to understand all that they have in Christ, then their life would be changed. We would have the confidence that God's power working in the community is sufficient to overcome any obstacle.

What would it mean for the Christian of color to be marked by the "hope of their calling" and not the news cycle that tempts us to despair? We can look at the problems facing us: systemic racism, sexism, the indifference of other Christians, the long track record of trauma inflicted on us, and wonder if there is any way our future can be different from our past. But Paul reminds us that Christ has ascended beyond all powers and authorities. He also tells us that the same power that raised Christ from the dead is at work among us who believe. If we believe in a God who is supreme over spiritual powers (which themselves impact earthly rules) working on our behalf, then no problem is too big. Systemic racism and anti-Blackness are not more powerful than death.

Therefore, racism must bend the knee like all other powers. This might not be realized fully and visibly in our time, but all evil powers that oppose us have been defeated by Christ. Yes, Paul has much to say about the forgiveness of our individual sins. That forgiveness is part of his apostolic preaching. But in this Ephesians passage he emphasizes the message that powers have been defeated. And when we start talking about spiritual powers in North America, we cannot help but talk about the demonic grip of racism that has stalked us far too long.

FROM DEAD TO ASCENDED AND REIGNING WITH CHRIST (EPHESIANS 2:1-10)

In chapter two, Paul recounts the lives of the Ephesians before they came to know God. He uses an interesting image: referring to them as dead (Eph 2:1) in their sins and trespasses. Despite the fact that they were dead, Paul says that they walked around in those sins following the ways of the ruler of this age (Eph 2:2).[18] Paul depicts the world in opposition to Christ as dominated by spiritual powers that lead humanity away from their God-intended ends. This includes the materialism, greed, lust, violence, and racism that stalks the varied people of the world. All of us in different ways participate in this broken world until God, who does not lack mercy, calls us to life in Christ as a display of his love (Eph 2:4-5).

In Romans 6, Paul talks about dying to sin with Christ in baptism and being raised to new life by his resurrection from the dead. In Ephesians 2:6-10, Paul also speaks of being raised with Christ. In Ephesians, however, Paul has in mind Christ's ascension. The Christian is not merely raised from the dead with Christ, but rather they are somehow sharing even now in his divine perspective and rule.[19] This unthinkable gift is an act of pure grace so that Christians might engage in the good works he has given us to do (Eph 2:7-10).

What does it mean for the Christian to believe that we share a real union with the ascended Christ? It means that we are no longer limited to

---

[17]Smith, "Ephesians," 352.

[18]Karl Barth, *Epistle to the Ephesians*, trans. Ross M. Wight (Grand Rapids, MI: Baker Academic, 2017), 139.

[19]Cohick, *Letter to the Ephesians*, 152.

earthly options. We do not view reality from the perspective of the ups and downs of human vice and virtue. Instead, we see the world from the perspective of the Messiah who rules over all things. Therefore, we are not without hope. Our witness is never in vain. We can fight sexism, racism, and economic exploitation because we know that Christ is risen and, in the fullness of time, he will establish a kingdom rooted in righteousness and truth. Our vocation, then, is not to win our struggle by any means necessary. Our vocation is to trust that the sovereign God can do with our witness what he will with the assurance that in the end all will be well. Union with the ascended Christ does not remove the Christian from the world, but places our work in the world in the proper context. This is why Paul's discussion of the "good works prepared for us" is important (Eph 2:10). Paul probably had in mind more interior or personal good works in his day. In other words, he probably envisioned matters of personal holiness and assisting other members in the Christian community. The church lacked the political or economic power to do much more than that. For Christians with more resources and political influence, the call to good works is not decreased. We are still called to love our fellow Christians and pursue personal righteousness, but there is more available to us now. We can as a part of those good works assist those outside of the Christian community, something Paul himself supports in other contexts (Gal 2:10; 6:10).

CHRIST, OUR RECONCILIATION (EPHESIANS 2:11-21)

Paul continues his reconstruction of the Ephesians' past by calling on them to remember that those born Gentiles were called "the uncircumcision" by those who were the circumcision. Paul points out that even those who called the Gentiles "the uncircumcision" focus on a circumcision made with human hands instead of interior renewal.

Here Paul draws on an important point found in the Torah that God is concerned with the transformation of the human heart (Deut 30:6; Jer 4:4; Ezek 44:7, 9). Nonetheless, it is true that the Gentiles were excluded from citizenship in Israel, foreigners to the covenants of promise, and separated from the Messiah. Paul also says that they were without hope (Eph 2:11–12). He does not mean that Gentiles lacked any positive plans for the future. He has in mind the knowledge of the future rooted in God's own promises.

The gospel in a conjunction. The point is not to condemn their past, but to contrast their past with their present and future. Those who were far off have been brought near. Through Christ, God has brought Gentiles into a relationship with himself through the blood of his Son. Paul describes the Messiah as our "peace" the one who has destroyed or nullified the dividing wall of hostility.

Paul's language here deserves parsing out. In places like Romans 3:30-31, Paul explicitly says that faith does not nullify the law, but upholds it. In Romans 7:7-25, he goes a long way to assert that the law is holy, just, and good. Does Paul contradict himself in Ephesians? Scholars have put forward the following options to explain this contrast: (1) highlight the nullification language—the law itself is not destroyed; it simply no longer determines the people of God; (2) argue that Paul's point is the ceremonial law; (3) maintain that Paul claims that sin hijacked the law and used what was good for evil. It divided people.[20] Christ's death nullified the law in the sense that it can longer play that role. Instead it can do the work for which it was intended, namely articulate a vision for what it means to be human.

[20]Fowl, *Ephesians: A Commentary*, 90-96.

It seems that since Paul's focus is on reconciliation, the third option is the best.[21] Christ has put the enmity caused by the law, due to human sin, to death. The purpose of Christ's death, then, is to create out of the divided people of the world one new humanity defined and united at every point by Christ and his cross. This cross, according to Paul, is not only for the Gentiles (Eph 2:17). Both Jews and Gentiles have access to the Father through the Spirit because of Christ's death for them (Eph 2:18). This is a profoundly trinitarian account of the work of redemption. God the Son's actions mediated through the Spirit brings us into relationship with the Father.

The result of this work is that believing Gentiles are fellow citizens alongside believing Jews in God's commonwealth.[22] They are brothers and sisters in one family, its foundation being apostolic testimony (Eph 2:19-20). This testimony is their preaching about Jesus. We cannot shrink the extent of what this means. Paul doesn't merely mean the plan of salvation when he refers to the apostolic teaching. If the rest of the New Testament is faithful to the ministry and ethos of Jesus, then the foundation of the church is the person of Christ as it emerges over the whole of the canon. That means what Jesus says about the disinherited and justice remains central to the church. It also means that the Christology of the New Testament, who Jesus is—the God-man—is central to the health and well-being of the church. It means that God's gracious gift of salvation is crucial to the coherence of our ministry. Proclaiming the joyous fact that the church of believing Jews and Gentiles fulfills God's promises to Abraham, Isaac, and Jacob remains vital to followers of Christ.

The language of foundation adds a third layer. Alongside being a part of a kingdom and a family, the Ephesians are part of a new temple, developed crucially from the apostolic testimony.[23] But the cornerstone, the thing that keeps the family, kingdom, and temple together is not the apostles' testimony. It is Christ himself. The church is not held together by the preaching of Christ, but by Christ in their midst. It is the church's union with Christ that makes it into a temple. What unites the church? It is not that we share a common language, skin color, ethnicity, or culture. What unites the church is Christ and it is through him that we become a place where God's own Spirit dwells.

The vision for the church that Paul lays out in these verses is staggering. Although the Gentiles were described as the uncircumcision, there is a deeper reality at work. The Gentiles specifically as Gentiles were objects of God's concern. The Abrahamic promises themselves included a vision for their blessing (Gen 12:1-3). Therefore, the covenants depicted them as both alienated from God and loved by God. This is how the Ephesians were called to remember their past. They can see how they were never outside of God's purposes. This means that the gospel in principle is for everyone, including Black, White, Asian, Latino/a, First Nation, and the varied ethnicities of the world.[24]

We are a kingdom and a family. This kingdom and family has different values than those that marked the lives of believers beforehand we met Christ.[25] This family unites Jews and Gentiles. We must be careful here

[21]Fowl, *Ephesians*, 94.

[22]José-David Padilla, "Aliens, Sojourners, and Heavenly Citizens: The Inclusive Household of God," *The Bible Today* 56 (2018): 29-34.

[23]On the temple imagery see William S. Campbell, "Unity and Diversity in the Church: Transformed Identities and the Peace of Christ in Ephesians," *Transformation* 25 (2008): 161.

[24]Smith, "Ephesians," 354.

[25]Campbell, "Unity and Diversity," 19, calls the church an "alternative Society."

when applying Jew/Gentile reconciliation to what we experience in our day. In the North American context, it is not only the relationship between Jewish and Gentile believers that we must consider. It is the relationship between different ethnic groups within a largely Gentile church in North America (although we should remain grateful for the presence of Jewish Christians in our midst by attending more closely to their steadfast witness and the difficulties they experience). Do Paul's words to the church in Ephesus have anything to say to us? I think they do. Although Paul's emphasis is on Jew/Gentile unity, he speaks about what the blood of Christ is able to do. It can bring peace and unity.[26] But this peace and unity did not come without cost. It came through the cross. The cross reveals that God understands the depth of human sin, otherwise the incarnation of his Son would be unnecessary.

Within the North American church, there exist streams and communities that not only ignore racism and sexism, but suggest that those individuals who promote justice in these arenas are being needlessly divisive. But we who believe that racism and sexism are sins that are doing real damage to the church are not causing division. We are taking the fall seriously. If Christ's resurrection is real, then those sins do not have the last word. The resurrection gives us hope that no sin is more powerful than God. Therefore, we must battle these sins as a testimony to what we believe that God is able to do. As early twentieth-century African Methodist Episcopal (AME) cleric Reverdy Ransom wrote, "There is nothing to fear by forever demolishing every wall, religious, political, industrial, social, that separates man from his brotherman."[27] We can fight to overcome these sins and thereby bring unity across ethnic difference to the church because that unity is a visible manifestation of the universal saving power of the gospel.

Paul's statements about unity, then, address any divided church. He does not call them to come together. He says by virtue of Christ's own work they *are together*. The work of the church in every age is to make this unity manifest to the watching world. It is important to note that this unity is not rooted in a vague desire that we be together. It will not do to say, "Let's put aside our differences and come together." The apostolic testimony (including the bits about justice and righteousness) are nonnegotiables. Christ at the center of this community is not up for debate. What Paul articulates here is a Christocentric, Spirit-filled community of faith whose life together is an enacted parable of the gospel. Who is worthy of such a thing?

THE PLOT TWIST (EPHESIANS 3:1-7)

In this section, Paul explores his own ministry. After articulating God's glorious plan to unite all things in the Messiah, Paul reminds the Ephesians that this ministry is the reason that he is in prison (Eph 3:1). He was a prisoner for the sake of the Gentiles. Paul goes on to tell the church of the stewardship of God's grace given to him for the Gentiles' good. Paul did not discover this gospel. It was made known to him as a revelation or an apocalypse (Eph 3:3).

This is one of two places where Paul speaks of a revelation related to his vocation and calling. In Galatians 1:15-17, Paul speaks about the revelation of Jesus to him as Son, which allowed Paul to begin the ministry God had set him apart for before he was born. By the time

---

[26]See Lisa M. Bowens, *African American Readings of Paul: Reception, Resistance, and Transformation* (Grand Rapids, MI: Eerdmans, 2020), 195, for its relevance for Black/white relationships.

[27]Anthony Pinn, ed., *Making the Gospel Plain: The Writings of Reverdy C. Ransom* (Harrisburg, PA: Trinity Press International, 1999), 77, quoted in Bowens, *African American Readings of Paul*, 199.

he writes Ephesians, this vocation has led him to prison. Nonetheless, this gospel remains a grace that he stewards.

He describes the revelation he received as a mystery of Christ (Eph 3:5). God has now made this mystery known, not just to Paul, but to all the apostles and prophets. Paul has already referred to apostles and prophets as the foundation of the church (Eph 2:20). They are not foundational because of an inherent attribute or talent, but because the Holy Spirit revealed the mystery to them.[28]

What is this mystery? The fact that Gentiles are coheirs with Jews and sharers together in the promise in the Messiah Jesus (Eph 3:6).[29]

Why was Paul in prison? Why was he suffering? He is in prison as a direct result of the ministry that God gave him, namely to proclaim the creation of one new people in the Messiah Jesus.[30]

Paul's willingness to suffer is a challenge to the American church. We cannot have community, at least not Christian community, if we do not bear one another's burdens. One burden that too many Black and brown brothers and sisters have had to bear is living in a country where their status as bearers of the image of God is functionally denied. This tendency to deny the full humanity of ethnic minorities can be seen in Jim Crow laws in the South and the discriminatory restrictions on Asian and Hispanic immigration in the 1800s and 1900s. This dehumanization is in full view when racist tropes persist in media and popular culture.

But the moment that we begin to speak about anti-Black and -brown racism, we are called divisive or accused of losing focus on the gospel. This leads many majority culture pastors and leaders to avoid issues of controversy in the hopes of keeping peace. But issues of "divisiveness" in one community are matters of life and death in the other. Therefore, just as Paul was willing to risk going to prison, White pastors and churches must face the inevitable slander and misunderstanding that can arise when one partners with believers whose lives are impacted daily by injustice.

It is also instructive to attend to what captures Paul's imagination. What is the mystery revealed to him, the rest of the apostles, and the prophets by the Holy Spirit? We might expect Paul to speak of justification by faith. In many depictions of Pauline theology justification is the sine qua non of his theology. That Paul believes that we are justified by faith is not to be denied. What is important here and elsewhere is how justification functions in Paul's argument. He says that he is a steward or caretaker of the fact that the Gentiles are coheirs and members of the same body *through the gospel*. Paul is awed by what the saving message of the gospel does. It makes the Gentiles members of God's people alongside believing Jews. This is the plot twist that no one saw coming. If the epic of Israel begins with the promise to bless the varied ethnic groups of the world (Gen 12:3), then the question remained as to how that might happen. Of all the pictures of Gentile blessing that filled the imaginations of Jews in the Second Temple period, none imagined a Messiah like Jesus of Nazareth, whose life exemplified Torah faithfulness and whose death for sins and subsequent resurrection reconciled Israel and the world to God. None imagined that faith would be sufficient to bring Jews and Gentiles into

[28]Harold W. Hoehner, *Ephesians: An Exegetical Commentary* (Grand Rapids, MI: Baker Academic, 2002), 444.

[29]Sigurd Grindheim, "What the OT Prophets Did Not Know: The Mystery of the Church in Eph 3,2-13," *Biblica* 84 (2003): 531-53, rightly notes that the mystery involves the incorporation into the Gentiles into the people of God apart from the law.

[30]Aaron Sherwood, "Paul's Imprisonment as the Glory of the Ethnē: A Discourse Analysis of Ephesians 3:1-13," *Bulletin for Biblical Research* 22 (2012): 97-111.

the new kingdom and family created by his death and resurrection.

Paul considers himself a servant of this gospel and the community that it creates (Eph 3:7). If this reading of Ephesians 3:1-7 is accurate, we must wonder if the fruit of the gospel (the union of people across ethnic and racial difference) still captures our imagination. There are times and contexts where churches may not always be multiethnic. There are, for example, historic reasons for the existence of Black churches. Churches where minorities have a chance to lead and exercise their gifts are vital in a society that often devalues the gifts of Black and brown women and men. Nonetheless, we must also recognize the importance of multiethnic churches as a visible manifestation of what the gospel does. Even in contexts where individual churches cannot embody this reality, it is important that churches of diverse backgrounds work together in projects of common concern.

PAUL'S VOCATION (EPHESIANS 3:8-13)

Paul, when reflecting on his calling, recognizes that he is the "least of all the saints." He probably has in mind his persecution of the church (Gal 1:23-24). Despite his sinful past, God graciously gave him the task to preach the untraceable riches of the Messiah Jesus. The language that Paul uses here (*anexichniastos*) is important. It describes the riches of Christ as something that is beyond us.[31] It defies our ability to comprehend.

Paul's work as apostle to the Gentiles is to bring this mystery to light that have been previously hidden from all eternity with God (Eph 3:9). This statement again articulates the place of Gentiles in God's purposes. It stretches back into eternity because it was hidden in the God who created all things. God's status as Creator is important because it was linked to his ability to bring about his will in the future (Is 41:9-10; 43:14-15). According to the reasoning of the prophets, the one who created all things is the one being capable of bringing about his purposes in the end. He created with a purpose and that purpose will win out in the end over any agenda or person that tries to hinder it.

The inclusion of the Gentiles reveals to the rulers and authorities the manifold wisdom of God through the church. Who are these rulers and powers? These are the same powers that led humanity into sin (Eph 2:1-2; 6:12).[32] The church, brought into being by Christ's life, death, resurrection, and ascension, reveals God's manifold wisdom (Eph 3:10). The image that Paul uses to describe God's wisdom also occurs in descriptions of complex embroidered patterns.[33] God's wisdom revealed in and through the church is beautiful in its complexity. When the powers looked on the church, they saw how their schemes were like scribbles in the dirt in comparison with the master painter.

This display of wisdom was in accord with the eternal purpose God carried out in the Messiah Jesus (Eph 3:11). The Messiah is the reason that Paul and the Ephesians have confidence and boldness to approach God through faith (Eph 3:12). If what he has said about what the gospel is and what the gospel does is true, then the Ephesians should not let their hearts be troubled by his suffering for them. Instead, if the good news is truly good, then it is worth suffering to spread it.

Paul views his ministry of preaching the riches of Christ to the Gentiles as a privilege, not a burden. In his day, the Gentiles might be

[31]Fowl, *Ephesians*, 111.

[32]Thielman, *Ephesians*, 216-17.

[33]M. Barth, *Ephesians*, 1:345.

tempted to view themselves as a divine afterthought. In the same way, misuses of the Christian faith to oppress Black and brown people have led some to doubt their place in God's kingdom. Much like Paul, it is a privilege to make the place of all people in God's family clear. However, the witness is not just to the Gentiles. Paul believed that the witness was to the powers in the heavenly places. The church's unity across ethnic difference is a testimony to God's wisdom, authority, and power. The powers tried to create a society based on dishonesty, greed, oppression, and mutual hostility. God created a society (the church) rooted in sacrificial love, mutual forbearance, graciousness, and respect. When we see what God has created through his Son, the only conclusion we can offer is that God was wise to create through the passion of his son.

If the church together under the rule of the one true king is a manifestation of God's wisdom, then it is incumbent on us to do our best to foster that unity in our local churches and communities.

THAT THE CHURCH MIGHT KNOW THE UNKNOWABLE (EPHESIANS 3:14-21)

After explaining the nature of his apostolic ministry, Paul intercedes for the Ephesians. He speaks of bowing his knee to the Father (Eph 3:14). Kneeling is not, in the first place, a position of prayer. It is a statement about God's sovereignty. He is the one to whom every knee will bow (Is 45:22-24). In Isaiah, YHWH is the source of salvation for all. This sentiment fits well with Ephesians, which celebrates the inclusion of the Gentiles. Thus, it is no surprise that Paul describes God as the one from whom all the families of the earth derive their name. Naming suggests that the families of the earth receive their identity from the sovereign God who called them into being.

We can tell Paul's impending request is no small matter. He begins by acknowledging that the basis of his intercession is not the worth of the recipient, but rather the "riches of his glory" (Eph 3:16). Furthermore, to receive what Paul requests requires more than their own strength. Therefore, he asks for God's Spirit to strengthen the inner being of the Ephesians (Eph 3:16), that Christ might dwell within their hearts through faith. In other words, they need the power of God to do the inner work necessary to receive what he has for them.

But what does Paul want for them? He wants the Ephesians to have what all the saints have, an understanding of the height, width, and breadth of the love of Christ. Despite the fact that Paul prays that the Ephesians would have the strength to comprehend this love, he ultimately admits that this love surpasses knowledge (Eph 3:19). The result of comprehending the incomprehensible is that they would be filled with all the fullness of God. What does Paul mean by the fullness of God? Andrew Lincoln captures it well when he says, "The fullness of God, which is best explained as his presence and power, his life and rule, immanent in his creation, has been mediated to believers through Christ, in whom the fullness was present bodily."[34]

Paul closes this section of his letter with a praise. He addresses it to the one who can do more than we can ask or imagine. This is important because Paul has just asked God to do the seemingly impossible. He asked that God would grant the Ephesians the power to understand the incomprehensible. By stating here that God can do more than they could ask or imagine, he is noting that even their requests do not exhaust the limits of what God can do for and through the church. It is to the God that

[34]Lincoln, *Ephesians*, 214.

does more that we can imagine that Paul ascribes a glory that will last forever (Eph 3:21). This glory does not simply arise from what God has done in Christ's earthly incarnation. This glory also comes from the ongoing work of the church. For Paul, Christ and the church united to him are sources of God's eternal renown.

It is hard to escape the hint of mysticism and awe that permeates this section. It begins with Paul bowing his knee to the king of the universe. For the Christian of color who often has no governmental or societal support, it is the universal kingship of God that gives us hope. With God on our side, the future bursts with possibility.

The ancient world believed that people groups owe their origins to a single individual or father who forms a family that grows into a larger clan or nation. This clan or nation develops habits or customs that form a culture. Therefore Paul's claim that the families of the earth derive their identities from God is an affirmation of the potential good of culture (Eph 3:14-15). The cultures we create through our lives together have their origins in God. If they have their origins in God, then they find their final meaning and purpose in bringing honor to their Creator. We worship God in the cultural forms he himself has made. This insight opens the space for each people group to offer their gifts to God, not as separate closed-off entities, but as mutually enriching and intersecting displays of God glory.

When Paul asks God to grant us strength to understand the incomprehensible love of God, he speaks to a human tendency to deny that we are loveable. For people denied dignity and worth in a corrupt and broken society, God's unfathomable love is light in a dark place. The call for the disinherited is to believe that these words are true. People of color are those (alongside all our other brothers and sisters in Christ) deeply loved by God.

Christians are invited to comprehend that which is incomprehensible. Paul invites us to a life marked by communion with God that can only be experienced, never exactly understood. This is a life that does not exist alone. It is shared with all the saints. By saying that all the saints share in the love of God, he speaks to the union of the church across ethnicity, class, and culture. All of us are wrapped up in God's love (Eph 3:18). If we do indeed share in that love, it naturally follows that we love one another. God's own love for us compels us out into the world in love for our brothers and sisters.

God's gracious love for us also influences how we treat those outside the family of God. If we didn't have to do anything to earn God's love, our compassion toward the poor, the immigrant, and the outcast ought not to be based on a utilitarian analysis of what they can do for us. Our gracious and compassionate love toward others can function as an enacted parable of the gospel. This is not dissimilar to what God said to the Jewish people after the exodus. He told them to remember that they were in slavery. Because of God's compassionate love, he freed them. Therefore, they were to be compassionate toward the widow and the foreigner (Deut 24:17-22). In other words, the public policy of Israel toward the outsider was influenced by their experience of God's love. In a similar way, God's love toward us ought to impact how we live and move in the world.

Paul reminds us that the God we serve has better plans for his people than we have for ourselves. We do not have a better vision for the church or justice or society than God. He holds the future. The church does its best to listen to what he says about that future in his word and through listening to him in prayer. The church does not glorify itself through its holiness of life or service to those in need. It brings rightful acclaim to God.

THE CALL TO UNITY (EPHESIANS 4:1-7)

After concluding his doxology, Paul addresses the Ephesians directly, reminding them of his status as a prisoner of the Lord (Eph 4:1). This is a paradox. He has been entrusted with a gospel of the unimaginable goodness of God. He serves a God who can do more than the Ephesians can ask or imagine, but he remains imprisoned. Paul's ministry, then, mimics the cruciform ministry of Christ through his suffering for the church. What should be a shameful fact becomes a source of glory.

Paul calls on them to walk worthy of the calling to which God has called them. The calling is what has occupied Paul throughout this letter. In Ephesians 1:3-14, he argues that God planned to bring the Ephesians into his family before creation itself. In Ephesians 2:1-11, he tells them that God prepared good works for them to walk in. In Ephesians 3:7-13, he contends that the church united across difference is a manifestation of the wisdom of God.

Because such a lofty description might puff the Ephesians up, he calls them to humility, gentleness, and patience (Eph 4:2). No community could live up to all they are called to be in Christ. What does Paul counsel them? He encourages a gentle and patient attitude toward one another that will keep them from a legalism or harshness that destroys community. This is only possible if they are do everything with love. This is the same longing that he prayed would function as the ground of their life in God previously. Alongside an attitude energized by love, Paul encourages them to be to swift to guard the unity of the Spirt in the bond of peace. Stated differently, God's Spirit (the guarantee of our inheritance) unites us, making us one body. But that unity is a gift and a calling. Therefore, Paul encourages them to attend to that unity by maintaining peace. According to Paul, it is peace or harmony that functions to keep the church together.[35]

This unity is not only an aspiration, something achieved by the Ephesians. It is a reality given as a gift. Paul reminds them that they are one body (Eph 4:4). God has made believing Jews and Gentiles one through the cross. As a part of this one body, they also share in the one Spirit. This oneness of Spirit and body arise from the fact that their hope comes from a singular calling. Christians, according to Paul, do not hope for a variety of futures. There is a singular and assured life with God that functions as the guiding light for all believers. There is one Lord who rules over the church and the world. There is one faith. Referring to the "faith" includes the person in whom the Ephesians believe and the act of believing.[36]

What would it mean for the church in North America to walk in a manner worthy of the gospel, with all gentleness, humility, and patience? In every generation, that is a complex vocation. This much can be said: we must take seriously the new creation and new community brought about by the life, death, resurrection, and ascension of Christ. We must recognize that we have been gifted the Spirit, which allows us to live transformed lives. We must preach and teach the entirety of Christian tradition, not a truncated version of it. We need a vision of life together as all encompassing as the one God has for us.

Therefore, the Christian is well within her rights to point out patterns of life in the Christian community that fall short of that. No false peace should be permitted. Nonetheless, we also have to recognize that the journey is long and arduous. We must not lose heart. We strive and strain toward the likeness of Christ, but will not arrive

[35]M. Barth, *Ephesians*, 2:428-29.

[36]Mark D. Roberts, *Ephesians*, The Story of God Bible Commentary (Grand Rapids, MI: Zondervan, 2016), 121.

there until the Messiah's second advent. The church is always failing in some way. We do not love each other as we should; we do not display the fruit of the Spirit. Our witness is tainted by our greed and complicity with the values of the culture. But the good news is God is always calling the church back to its purpose and vocation. He does not give up on us, so we cannot give up on each other.

We are one body whether we like it or not. I am not allowed to give up on my brothers and sisters, even when they have failed me deeply, because God didn't give up on me when I failed him. I cannot quit my Christian family because we are all children of the one true God by adoption. This is not indiscriminate unity; it is unity rooted in our common faith. The Christian life together consists in reasoning from the common belief in Jesus and his vision for the kingdom to the life we live here and now.

SERVICE IN THE CHURCH AND SPIRITUAL MATURITY (EPHESIANS 4:7-16)

The common life referred to above is possible because of the gifts of the Spirit described in this portion of Paul's argument. Paul informs the Ephesians that each gift is the result of the gracious benevolence of the Messiah (Eph 4:7). To prove his point, Paul cites Psalm 68:18, which in his rendering refers to God giving spiritual gifts to the Ephesians.[37] Paul's use of Psalm 68:18 has been a source of confusion because in context the psalmist speaks of God ascending to Mount Zion with a host of captives and receiving gifts from people.[38] The best explanation of Paul's use of this psalm is that he read it christologically. Christ is the one who, like YHWH in the psalm, has defeated his enemies (Satan and other spiritual powers). In the wider context of the psalm, God's victory over his enemies leads to blessings coming to Israel. According to Paul, Jesus' defeat over his enemies leads to blessings coming to the church in the form of spiritual gifts.[39] Paul goes on to say that the one who ascended also descended to the lower parts of the earth. Again, we find ourselves in choppy exegetical waters. What does Paul mean by the "lower parts of the earth"? Scholars contend for two viable options: it refers to (1) Christ's descent into Hades, or (2) Christ's descent to the earth at the incarnation.[40] The second reading fits best with the context of Ephesians, which focuses on Christ's incarnation and ascension (Eph 1:20-23).[41] The purpose of this giving of gifts is that through the expansion of the church to cover the world, Christ's own presence among them would "fill all things." The world, then, would be bursting with the presence of God.

Paul then describes the people that he gives to the church as gifts: apostles, prophets, evangelists, shepherds, and teachers.[42] They are given to the church as gifts so that the church itself can be equipped to the work of ministry. That ministry is the building up of the body of Christ. This building lasts until the church attains the unity of the faith and the knowledge of the Son of God. Linked to this knowledge of God's Son is Paul's vision of the church's maturity. He hopes they will no longer be like children who are easily swayed. Instead, he wants the Ephesians to be adults with an unflappable security due to the hope they have in

[37]Thielman *Ephesians*, 264.

[38]Marvin E. Tate, *Psalms 51–100*, Word Biblical Commentary 20 (Grand Rapids, MI: Zondervan, 1990), 181.

[39]Fowl, *Ephesians*, 137; Theilman, *Ephesians*, 268.

[40]Fowl, *Ephesians*, 138-39.

[41]For a good defense of this reading see M. Barth, *Ephesians*, 2:434-35, and more recently Charles H. Talbert, *Ephesians and Colossians*, Paideia: Commentaries on the New Testament (Grand Rapids, MI: Baker Academic, 2007), 109-11. For a defense of a reference to Hades, see Theilman, *Ephesians*, 268-72.

[42]Lynn Cohick, *Ephesians*, New Covenant Commentary Series (Eugene, OR: Cascade Books, 2010), 109-10.

Christ that remains steady even as life changes around them. This shared goal of maturity would allow the Ephesians to speak the truth to one another in love (Eph 4:15) as they grow into the head, Christ. Here, Paul's "head" language is different from Ephesians 1:22. In that passage, Christ is the head of all things for the good of the church. Here he is the head of the church, in the sense of the goal to which we aspire and the source of our common life.

Jarena Lee, one of the early Black women preachers in the AME, claimed that the ability to preach effectively and in accord with the Scriptures is a work of the Holy Spirit.[43] This gift of the Spirit leading her to ministry was a manifestation of the reality depicted in Ephesians 4:7-8, God giving his gifts to his people as he wills. This idea that God would give these gifts to the enslaved and those who escaped cut against prominent ideas at the time about Black worth and intellectual abilities. But enslaved and liberated Black folk had a secure confidence in God's estimation of their worth. God calls people from a host of ethnicities to participate in apostolic, evangelical, catechetical, and shepherding work (Acts 13:1-3). The multiethnic participation in the ministry of the church embodies the reality that all have something to offer. The purpose of diversity is not a photo op. It is that the body might achieve the unity of the faith and the knowledge of God's Son. The goal is spiritual maturity. Unless we are going to claim that only one ethnicity or culture has been called to lead, then we must acknowledge that we are impoverished when the whole body of Christ across culture isn't given the freedom and space to do the ministry to which it is called.

Paul's vision for the church is a maturity and stability that allows it to know that Christ is the source and goal of its existence. If Christ is the goal of the church's existence, then it follows from that truth that we must attend to the example he set for us on earth. Jesus cared for the disinherited. The church that is growing in the way of Jesus is growing in the way of love, especially love of the neglected.

Paul wants the parts of the body working together. This leads us to ask what in our day might hinder the shared work of the body of Christ. Many things might contribute, but one of them is surely different understandings of the history and ongoing impact of racial discrimination and injustice. We can't have genuine unity and cooperation if I am forced to lie about what happened in the past and its implications for the presence. Stated differently, the inability to deal with racism and injustice impacts the unity, development, and growth of the body of Christ. A desire for unity, thus, can't be separated from a desire for truth. The church telling the truth frees the body to flourish in its ministry.

REACHING FULL MATURITY (EPHESIANS 4:17-24)

If the Ephesians are called to grow to full maturity and union with Christ rooted in love (Eph 4:16), a few things follow from that. Paul calls on the Ephesians to no longer live as Gentiles (who don't know God) in the futility of their minds. There is a focus on understanding and thinking in Ephesians 4:17-18. Paul maintains that life apart from God means that there is a different way of viewing the words that results in a set of practices (impurity, greed). Further, this existence detached from the life of God gives way to a callousness (*aselgeia*) toward the good, the just, and the true, with unbelievers indulging their desires (Eph 4:19).

The conjunction here reveals Paul's vision for a different experience for believers: "That is

[43]Bowens, *African American Readings of Paul*, 81-82.

not the way you learned Christ" (Eph 4:20). The Ephesians learned about the truth, what it means to be human and live in Jesus (Eph 4:21). As a result, they are to put off their own person with their desires that lie to them (Eph 4:22). Life in Christ for Paul gives birth to a new way of thinking in accord with the new person that the Ephesians have become (Eph 4:23). This new person lives a life of righteousness and holiness (Eph 4:24).

There are two important points to be made from this section of Ephesians. First, Paul thinks that coming to know Jesus should make a difference in how we think and how we live. This way of life stands in sharp contrast with the way that those apart from God live. The true and beautiful life is open to all who follow Jesus. Second, Paul speaks of a callousness that dulls one's moral code and leads to more degradation. He warns the Christians that this should not be true of them because they learned a different Christ. But this danger is real. Christians have the possibility of becoming so walled off from the pain and suffering of others that it opens the way for them to participate in their exploitation, or, at the very least, to be apathetic to others' desire for freedom. Paul's focus is on how callousness in nonbelievers leads to sensual indulgence. That does not mean that sensual indulgence is the only possible negative consequence. The Christian then must remain open to God's continual direction to avoid such an outcome.

THE CALL TO HOLINESS (EPHESIANS 4:25-32)

If the Ephesians are to reflect God in the world, then they must put away all falsehood and speak the truth to one another (Eph 4:25). This truth is necessary because the Ephesians are members of one another. Paul acknowledges that anger is a part of the human experience, but it need not give way to sin (Eph 4:26). Instead, the community of believers should deal with problems immediately rather than letting them linger so that the evil one gains no foothold (Eph 4:26-27). Those whose pre-Christian lives involved theft must become different people, not simply because stealing is wrong, but so that they might be able help others (Eph 4:28). The transformation extends all the way to our speech. Just like the thief used to exploit and harm the wider community, the unredeemed tongue also did damage. Therefore, just as the former thief's labor now adds to the community, Paul calls on the Ephesians to speak in such a way that gives life to the hearer (Eph 4:29). This mode of life in step with the Spirit keeps them from grieving God's Spirit (Eph 4:30) by falling back "into old pagan ways."[44] Instead of grieving the Spirit by harmful language, bitterness, wrath, and anger, Paul calls on the Ephesians to be a community marked by forgiveness and tenderness of heart. This forgiveness arises from the God who forgave them through Christ (Eph 4:32)

Doctrine is of course important, but equally important to Paul is how we live together as a community of faith. This involves truth telling because we are part of one another. For Paul, the union of believers in Christ is an ontological reality from which certain ideas flow. Lying to a fellow believer involves lying to oneself. What does this mean for the church of today? To be quiet about the racialized experience that I have as a Black man in America would be lying. It means that women must be encouraged and have the freedom to speak about misogyny and sexism. The goal is not simply venting but the transformation of the community to a more Christlike space. It is

[44]Cohick, *Letter to the Ephesians*, 301.

about not giving space for the devil to allow our divisions to wreak havoc on the church.

This call for transformation includes our speech and work. The healthy Christian community is one in which we use our gifts and our speech to build up the church. This may be a particular challenge in our day when social media rewards cruelty and slander more than encouragement. Paul's words will become flesh in our day when all our communication in person and virtual is life giving rather than discouraging. He also paints a picture of a community of compassion and forgiveness that arises out of God's forgiveness of us. This is an important claim. Despite the failures of the church to deal properly with racism, sexism, and injustice, there is always a possibility of reconciliation and forgiveness. This does not arise from some reservoir within the person themselves. It is a gift flowing from the cross. This forgiveness doesn't eliminate the truth-telling called for earlier, or the transformation of life ("Thieves must give up stealing"), but it does articulate the Christian hope for community on the other side of the truth-telling and transformation. We can be a family.

A NEW LIFE FOLLOWING CHRIST (EPHESIANS 5:1-20)

Continuing on from his command to forgive as Christ forgave, Paul calls on the Ephesians to further follow in the footsteps of their Creator. As children of God, they are to imitate him by walking in love. The paradigmatic example of this walking in love is the Christ who loved them and gave himself as a sacrifice and offering to God (Eph 5:1-2). The Ephesians and the wider body of Christ can be like God by offering their lives to him, like the Son did on the cross. Here, Paul comes close to Jesus' own statement that discipleship involves taking up one's cross and following him.

The sacrifice that Paul has in mind includes a holiness of life that includes fleeing greed, vulgar or foolish talk, and lust (Eph 5:3-5). These are things that should not even be named among believers. Of particular concern for Paul was greed, which he calls idolatry (Eph 5:5). Greed and idolatry can be linked because the pursuit of financial gain can, according to Paul, so capture one's life that it becomes a deity. Paul warns the Ephesians that those whose lives are marked by these things lack an inheritance in the kingdom of God and the Messiah (Eph 5:5). This warning allows the Ephesians to take the walk with God as a matter of utmost concern, but must be read in conjunction with Paul's previous statements about their election in Christ before the foundations of the earth (Eph 1:3-14). According to Paul, the Ephesians live within the following tension: (1) they were chosen in Christ before the foundation of the world; and (2) the way they live matters as it relates to inheriting the kingdom of God.

If Ephesians 5:1-5 looks at the life the believer lives in the presence of God, Ephesians 5:6-9 looks at dangerous associations. He warns them about outsiders who might deceive them with empty words (Eph 5:6). Interestingly, Paul uses familial language to describe this people, calling them sons (and daughters presumably) of disobedience (Eph 5:6). In the same way that God has created a family united by faith in his Son and invited them into his kingdom, there is a family and kingdom that lives in opposition to God. That family will in the end receive God's wrath (Eph 5:6).

When Paul tells the Ephesians not to be associated with them, he does not have in mind being cut off from the world. Instead, he means not participating in their dark deeds (Eph 5:7) because the church is a part of the light (Eph 5:8). Therefore their lives should reflect their change in circumstance. Life in the light produces the good, the righteous, and the true (Eph 5:9). This good, right, and true life calls for discernment. They must "find out what is pleasing to the Lord" (Eph 5:10).

They are to reject the works of darkness (Eph 5:11) and expose them for the death-dealing activities that they are (Eph 5:12). If the Ephesians do not expose them, God will in due course. Therefore, Paul advises the congregation to wake up and allow the light of Christ to shine on them, exposing and removing their sin (Eph 5:14)

All this calls for wisdom. They must attend to how they live (Eph 5:16). Since the days are evil, they must discover the best ways to make good use of life that God has given them. The shortness of life should not lead to a drunken hedonism that tries to exploit and indulge every deceptive desire (Eph 5:18). Instead, wise living involves being filled with God's Spirit, singing songs of thanksgiving for the gift of life itself (Eph 5:18-20).

It is important here to note who exactly functions as a model for human behavior here for Paul. It is God and his Son whose sacrifice for us that points the way. This pushes back on any normalization of a particular culture as the sole reservoir of godliness. African Americans and others are called to be like God, not Americans of European descent. The inescapably moral implication of meeting Jesus are also highlighted in this section because of the focus on God-honoring actions. Fornication and impurity and greed are ruled out of the Christian life. These instead mark the lives of the "children of disobedience."

God is not merely upset because the children of disobedience are not on his team, so to speak. The concern here is what opposition to God produces in their lives. Immorality such as greed and fornication often comes at the expense of the vulnerable. For example, pornography available online includes images of children being harmed or people who have been trafficked. There are victims. Even when there is no "legal victim," there remains the harm done to the souls of all involved in the production and the devaluation of persons that flow from it. In other words, fornication, power, and exploitation are not so easily disentangled. God is not merely a prude who steps on the desires of humans. He is a steward of persons, and directs our desires toward their proper ends. God is not simply concerned with the damage our sins do to others; he also cares about the damage done to our own souls. The lives we live reveal what we believe about reality. A life devoted to self-indulgence tells a lie about the purpose of our creation.

The mention of greed as idolatry is crucial. If greed becomes one's god, then similar to fornication, we cease to be sensitive to how our desires harm others. If greed is our god, then we do not care about how we get the more that we desire. Our only concern is that we get it. Paul thinks that better things are in store for a Christian. The Christian life is one of wisdom where in light of God's future we do two things: (1) we discern what pleases him; (2) we allow the Spirit to lead us to thanksgiving and praise of God for the gift of life itself. This a beautiful picture of Christian community that gives room for a pursuit of holiness, justice, and sacrifice in the name of God our Savior.

LIFE TOGETHER (EPHESIANS 5:21-33)

From the beginning, this section presents the interpreter with a series of difficulties, the first being how we understand Paul's call to submit to one another out of reverence to Christ. Does it conclude the previous section on the church's life together or does it inform Paul's statements about marriage that follow? On the side of the idea of submission concluding the previous section, we note that it is the last in a series of participles describing the church's activities including singing and giving thanks (Eph 5:20). On the side of mutual submission being a part of the next section, we note that most English translations begin Ephesians 5:22 with a call for wives to "submit" to their husbands.

The word for submission in Ephesians 5:22 is absent in the original Greek text. It must be inferred from the call to mutual submission outlined in Ephesians 5:21. What Paul says about the church submitting to another in Ephesians 5:21 can't be detached from married life as if the posture to which fellow believers are called outside of marriage differs from those inside of marriage. For example, Paul's calls to display the fruits of the Spirit (Gal 5:16-22) surely informs how believers interact with one another in marriage. So theologically, I am inclined to see the implications of Ephesians 5:21 spilling over into what Paul says about marriage. Grammatically, I am inclined to think that the link between mutual submission in Ephesians 5:21 and the call to submit in Ephesians 5:22 means that they should be read together.

A few more things to set the table before we talk about 5:21-33. What scholars called "household codes" occur here in Ephesians, in Colossians 3:18–4:1, and 1 Peter 3:1-7. They address relationships common to Greco-Roman households: husband/wives; enslaved/enslavers; parents/children.[45] In Cohick's helpful review, she points out that Greco-Roman writers to varying degrees based their advice on some assumed ontological difference between men versus women and slave versus free. In almost every case, men have some assumed ontological superiority over women and women's needs and desires are not considered of equal value.[46] Paul, by contrast, does not assume an ontological distinction between the different pairs. Furthermore, his focus is on how Christian faith redefines or transforms the status quo. In each pair, Paul limits the power of those whom society normally places at the top by telling them to use their power to serve others. Paul's most extensive comments, therefore, are not about justifying the power imbalances, but thinking through how Christ calls on those with power to set it aside for the flourishing of all.

Paul addresses wives, calling on them to submit to their husbands as to the Lord. This call for the wife to submit to her husband does not eliminate the call to mutual submission (Eph 5:21). In other words, the wife is not called to do something that is unknown to the wider body of Christ.

It does, however, reflect the reality that "it would be almost impossible from a cultural standpoint for Paul's audience to make sense of a direct statement for husbands to submit to their wives, for the social expectations would not have envisioned it. Moreover, the legal codes treated adult women as 'minors' which would have made nonsense of Paul's request."[47]

In other words Paul does seem to operate within the model of the Greco-Roman household, choosing to give a series of christological "motivations and justifications" for wives' submission that might be assumed.[48] These motivations do not serve to prop up a patriarchal institution that was wobbly and in need of Pauline support. Instead, he was trying to articulate the ways in which the gospel reorders all relational interactions, often with extended concern for those most at risk.

[45]Cohick, *Ephesians*, 342.
[46]Cohick, *Ephesians*, 342-47.
[47]Cohick, *Ephesians*, 352.
[48]Fowl, *Ephesians*, 187.

Paul does a few things here that are important. First, he says that they are to view their submission as "to the Lord." This does not mean that men play the role of God in the marriage. It is a way of saying that their submission has as a telos, service to God, and not the glorification of the husband.

Paul grounds his call for submission on the fact that the husband is the head of the wife.

There is an extensive debate on the meaning behind Paul's use of the head and body analogy that cannot be considered here.[49] Instead, I will focus on Paul's head language in Ephesians.

It might be best to begin with the church's submission to Christ as head and reason back from there to what Paul says about marriage.[50] Paul uses head language to refer to Christ twice in Ephesians. In Ephesians 1:21 he is made head over all things for the church's benefit. There the emphasis is his rule, not over the church, but the world. When he talks about Christ as head of the church in Ephesians 4:15-16, Christ is the source of growth and development toward its God-appointed end. The emphasis there is not on issuing commands, but facilitating development:

> Speaking the truth in love, we must grow up in every way into him who is the head, into Christ, from whom the whole body, joined and knit together by every ligament with which it is equipped, as each part is working properly, promotes the body's growth in building itself up in love. (Eph 4:15-16)

What does the submission to Christ then mean for the church? Fowl gets it correct when he says that "the church's submission to Christ results in the church's coming to love and desire for itself that which Christ desires and loves for the church."[51] The wife's submission to her husband, in a society where he held most of the legal and cultural power, involves a trust that has her full flourishing at the heart of all his activities.

Placing the flourishing and life of the wife as a priority clarifies Paul's instructions to the husband in Ephesians 5:25-30. He calls on the husband to love his wife as Christ loved the church by giving himself up for her (Eph 5:25). As we can see, the central connecting point of the analogy between Christ and the husband is not Christ's exercise of power, but his sacrifice. The work of washing and cleansing that Paul describes was often work reserved for women.[52] It now becomes the work that Christ does for his body, the church, and by extension husbands for their wives.

The point of Christ's sacrifice was the church's growth in holiness (Eph 5:27). This links with the earlier discussion on the flourishing of the church and the head as the source of growth. Christ died so that the church might become something that it could not become without him, holy and reflecting God in the world. The husband does not save the wife in the same way that Christ saves or sanctifies the church. He does, according to Paul, encourage her to become what God in Christ created her to be.

This is why Paul says that men should care for their wives in the same way that they care for their bodies (Eph 5:29). If one wants to function in a healthy manner, they feed and care for their body. This involves listening to what your body needs and in turn meeting those needs for your body. In the same way, love for one's wife involves listening to her

[49]See in various places Cynthia Long Westfall, *Paul and Gender: Reclaiming the Apostle's Vision for Men and Women in Christ* (Grand Rapids, MI: Baker Academic, 2016).

[50]Fowl, *Ephesians*, 187.

[51]Fowl, *Ephesians*, 188

[52]Westfall, *Paul and Gender*, 23.

needs and then providing for it so that she flourishes.

Paul alludes to Genesis 2:24 to speak about Christ and the church. It seems that one function of marriage is to picture or an anticipate the eschatological union between Christ and the church. Through the union, mutual sacrifice, and care, the husband and wife enact a parable of the gospel. This is why he concludes with a final call for the husband to love his wife and the wife to respect her husband (Eph 5:33).

Paul's words on marriage has been interpreted wrongly to justify behavior that has done damage to persons and the name of Christ. The point of Paul's argument is to help the Ephesians think through the ways in which what they believe about Christ changes the way that marriages function. Rather than relying on power given to husbands based in part on the assumed ontological inferiority of the wife, Paul calls on the husband to sacrifice. He calls on him to put the flourishing of the wife at the center of his concerns. This involves listening to the wife and thinking through how he, who had the cultural and legal power, could use that for her benefit. The telos of all this work would be for the husband and wife in their marriage itself to show the world something about Christ and his church.

PARENTS AND CHILDREN (EPHESIANS 6:1-4)

Paul moves on from discussing the relationships of husbands and wives to discussing children and parents. As with his discussion of marriage, Paul begins with those who have less social power. He calls on children to obey their parents (Eph 6:1). This would have been common advice in Greco-Roman and Jewish literature of the time.[53] As with the discussion of marriage, Paul again adds a christological reorientation of motivation. The children are to obey their parents "in the Lord." Parents are not respected simply because they have legal and social power. Instead, obedience can be seen as a manifestation of Christian discipleship.[54] Paul adds two reasons for this obedience. First, it is the just thing to do. Paul probably means that it is universally recognized as a good thing to do.[55] Second, the law itself speaks of the importance of honoring one's parents and the blessings that flow from giving such honor (Eph 6:2-3).

After discussing the parents as a couple, Paul has a particular word for fathers. He warns them not to anger children by mistreating them.[56] Instead they raise them to become virtuous Christians obedient to the Lord (Eph 6:4).

Too often, Paul's teaching about parenting is isolated from the rest of his thoughts on the Christian life. There is more to being a Christian parent than his brief notes here. The graciousness and patience that marks the Christian life more broadly also bears on the interactions between parents and children.

It is interesting to note that Paul's instructions on marriage and family appear in the appeal by African enslaved Christians to the House of Representatives in 1774.[57] They claimed that slavery interfered with Pauline prescriptions on marital and familial relationships precisely because children could be sold and removed from the authority of their parents, and wives and husbands could be

---

[53]Thielman, *Ephesians*, 396.

[54]Lincoln, *Ephesians*, 402.

[55]Theilman, *Ephesians*, 398.

[56]Talbert, *Ephesians and Colossians*, 142.

[57]*A Documentary History of the Negro People in the United States*, ed. Herbert Aptheker, vol. 1, *From Colonial Times Through the Civil War* (New York: Citadel Press, 1951), 8-9.

separated.[58] This is important because it shows how different aspects of the Christian tradition can be rightly used to push back on injustice. There are political and theological implications for Christian teaching on family that tend toward freedom. God's vision for the rightly ordered family carries with it the creation of societies (as pictures of God's future) that allow such families to flourish.

Finally, we see that those with power in society (husbands) are asked to consider carefully how to steward that power well to point their children toward God and away from anger. This does not eliminate the role of the wife, who also receives obedience from her children.

SLAVES AND MASTERS (EPHESIANS 6:5-9)

Last, Paul addresses the enslaved and their earthly masters. He calls on slaves to obey their masters with fear and trembling. Too often this fear has been assumed to be linked to the right of slave owners to turn to violence for disobedience. This is a poor reading of Paul.[59] Threats of violence as a means of persuasion would have been antithetical to beliefs about Christian love and mutual submission outlined throughout the letter. Nonetheless, he does envision slaves recognizing the social position society gives their owners. When Paul speaks of the labor the slaves offered to their master, his goal is not simply to promote obedience. He was giving the slaves a way to think theologically about the obedience they were already obligated to give. Rather than their obedience reflecting an ontological hierarchy where they played their role in society by staying in their place, they worked "as to the Lord."

This does not put the slave master in the place of God. It removes them as the person being served. The slave has a place to offer his service. It is to God, not merely their masters. This is because whether they are slave or free, God will reward people according to their actions (Eph 6:8). Here, in contrast to much writing of the time, Paul posits no intellectual, physical, emotional, or ontological difference between slave and free.

Paul's words to the masters are brief, but full of meaning. He calls on the masters to "do the same thing to them [i.e., the slaves]." If Paul seems to simply be giving a theological justification for the status quo in Ephesians 6:5-8, then Ephesians 6:9 upends that notion.

The same service that Paul calls on the slave to provide for the master, the master is called on to perform for the slave.[60] If the slave is to serve with fear and trembling, so is the master. This is a radical redefinition of the dynamics between slave and freedom this side of full manumission. They are to leave off threatening and remember that they have a master in heaven. Like with husbands and wives, Paul does not create a new social structure. Instead, he undercuts that structure by laying a new christological foundation that limits the damages that society put in place.

A full discussion of Paul and slavery and his misuse in the history of the church's witness is beyond the scope of this commentary.[61] Justification for slavery in North America did not arise from an unbiased reading of Paul; it was rooted

---

[58]Esau McCaulley, *Reading While Black: African American Biblical Interpretation as an Exercise in Hope* (Downers Grove, IL: IVP Academic, 2020), 156-57.

[59]See Cohick, *Ephesians*, 401-42; Fowl, *Ephesians*, 197.

[60]Cohick, *Ephesians*, 404-5. See however Pheme Perkins, "The Letter to the Ephesians," in *2 Corinthians–Philemon*, vol. 11 of *New Interpreter's Bible*, ed. Leander E. Keck, Accordance electronic ed. (Nashville: Abingdon Press, 2000), 453-54, who thinks that Paul's statements are much less radical. I believe Paul's words in Eph 6:9 are indeed as paradigm shifting as they appear.

[61]See a fuller discussion in McCaulley, *Reading While Black*, 137-63.

in a heretical theology of persons that claimed people of African descent were not fully human.[62]

A full analysis would involve taking seriously all that Paul has to say about the Christian life more broadly, and then reflecting on the implications of those teachings for the institution of slavery. The letter written by the enslaved to the Massachusetts House of Representatives cited above is a good model of this type of reading. It would also necessitate a contextually rich interpretation of the varied Pauline passages in conversation with ancient slavery and its points of connection and disconnection with the transatlantic slave trade and its aftermath. Suffice to say, the church's witness during that era is a matter of great shame and disgrace. Ecclesial support for slavery had more to do with greed, lust, and a desire for power than fidelity to Christ.

But we close our reflections of Paul and slavery with more than condemnation. We must ask ourselves what God was using Paul to do in the fullness of time. We would love an unrelenting call for abolition in Paul's letters, but that is not what we received. What did we receive? In Paul's letters and the wider biblical witness, we observe the call for a certain type of community, rooted in a particular vision of persons and the world. That vision and theological imagination, to my mind, and that of those early Black Christians, creates a way of thinking that could, if read properly, dismantle slavery.[63]

CONCLUDING COMMENTS (EPHESIANS 6:10-18)

Paul opened his letter by reminding the Ephesians of their eternal election in Christ before the foundation of the world (Eph 1:3-14). He informed them that the power at work in the church was the same power that God used to raise Christ from the dead (Eph 1:18-19). This resurrection and ascension places Christ above all things (Eph 1:20). He returns to this theme at the close of this letter by telling the Ephesians to be strong in the Lord (Eph 6:10). They are to do so by putting on God's armor to protect them from spiritual powers (Eph 6:12) so that they can be able to stand. Many of the weapons of warfare have their origins in passages like Isaiah 11:4-5, 52:7, and 59:17.[64] This means that, as important as the individual pieces of armor are, what is most important for Paul is that the Christian is equipped with the armor of God and the Messiah. They are the Christian's defense. This defense includes the belt of truth and plate of righteousness (Eph 6:14). God's armor also includes shoes shod with the gospel of peace, which refers to how like a good pair of shoes, the gospel of Christ's peace keeps you stable in a world prone to promoting imbalance.[65] Faith is the shield against the attacks of the enemy (Eph 6:16). Paul concludes by telling the congregation to take up the helmet of salvation, meaning the ready knowledge of all that God has given them in Christ and their inheritance that is theirs as God's own children and the sword of the Spirit, which is the Word of God empowered by the Spirit. That word is the message about Jesus, Israel's Messiah, as the crucified and risen king who invites all into his family who trust in him alone for salvation. The "word of God" here does not refer to the Scriptures. Nonetheless, it cannot be separated

[62]See Esau McCaulley, "Toward A Black Anthropology and Social Ethic: Why the Humanity and Jewishness of Jesus Matters," in *Who Do You Say I Am: On the Humanity of Jesus*, ed. George Kalantzis, David B. Capes and Ty Kieser (Eugene, OR: Cascade Books, 2020), 143-57.

[63]See McCaulley, *Reading While Black*, 137-63.

[64]Perkins, "Letter to the Ephesians," 460.

[65]Wright, *Paul for Everyone*, 74.

fully from them because Paul's own letters reveal that he uses the Scriptures to preach Christ.

Although Paul has moved on from a discussion of military equipment, his call to prayer cannot be separated from what came before (Eph 6:18). A good soldier maintains a close connection to his commanding officer and is ready to assist his fellow soldiers at any moment. Prayer accomplishes both those tasks. It keeps us connected to the one who fights for us. Paul himself calls prayer on his own behalf a matter of partnering with him in the struggle of his ministry (Rom 15:30). That is why he asks for the assistance of the Ephesians so that he might engage in his ministry with boldness as an ambassador in chains (Eph 6:20). Ironically, Paul's own suffering and imprisonment, as shameful as it may seem to the world, is the precise means by which he represents the upside-down nature of the Christian message.

The struggles of the Christian are not simply human. We battle spiritual forces. The hope that we have isn't our ability to overcome them, but that Christ our champion protects us and fights for us. This spiritual warfare involves more than a series of interpersonal temptations. We resist a whole world that exists in opposition to God. This includes the racism, sexism, and generally the devaluation of life and injustice. These injustices are not only a series of individual sins done by humans. There is also a spiritual element to the problems we face. The world needs Jesus. This does not mean that the Christian ignores laws and policies in favor of spiritual warfare. It is noting that laws and policies themselves can be manifestations of evil. The struggle against them involves facing darkness. In other words, Paul's statement about dark powers that themselves influence humans open up the possibility of talking about how evil can infect structures of society in such a way that the poor and needy are mistreated.

FINAL GREETINGS (EPHESIANS 6:21-24)

Paul ends his letter with a few practical notes. He is sending Tychicus to give an update on his status and to encourage their hearts (Eph 6:21-22). He concludes with a wish for peace and the love that comes from faith. This love has its origins in God the Father and the Lord Jesus (Eph 6:23). His final words serve as a fitting wish for readers of this commentary: Grace be with all who have an undying love for our Lord Jesus Christ.

SELECTED BIBLIOGRAPHY

Aptheker, Herbert, ed. *From Colonial Times Through the Civil War.* Vol. 1 of *A Documentary History of the Negro People in the United States.* New York: Citadel Press, 1951.

Barth, Karl. *Epistle to the Ephesians.* Translated by Ross M. Wight. Grand Rapids, MI: Baker Academic, 2017.

Barth, Markus. *Ephesians.* Anchor Bible 34. 2 vols. Garden City, NY: Doubleday, 1974.

Bowens, Lisa M. *African American Readings of Paul: Reception, Resistance, and Transformation.* Grand Rapids, MI: Eerdmans, 2020.

Cohick, Lynn H. *The Letter to the Ephesians.* New International Commentary on the New Testament. Grand Rapids, MI: Eerdmans, 2020.

Edwards, M. J. ed., *Galatians, Ephesians, Philippians.* Ancient Christian Commentary on Scripture. Downers Grove, IL: IVP Academic, 1999.

Foulkes, Francis. *Ephesians: An Introduction and Commentary.* Tyndale New Testament Commentaries 10. Downers Grove, IL: IVP Academic, 1989.

Fowl, Stephen E. *Ephesians: A Commentary.* The New Testament Library. Louisville, KY: Westminster John Knox Press, 2012.

Hoehner, Harold W. *Ephesians: An Exegetical Commentary*. Grand Rapids, MI: Baker Academic, 2002.

Johnson, Luke Timothy. *Constructing Paul*. Vol. 1 of *The Canonical Paul*. Grand Rapids, MI: Eerdmans, 2020.

Lincoln, Andrew T. *Ephesians*. Word Biblical Commentary 42. Dallas: Word 1990.

McCaulley, Esau. *Reading While Black: African American Biblical Interpretation as an Exercise in Hope*. Downers Grove, IL: IVP Academic, 2020.

Padilla, José-David. "Aliens, Sojourners, and Heavenly Citizens: The Inclusive Household of God." *The Bible Today* 56 (2018): 29-34.

Perkins, Pheme. "The Letter to the Ephesians." In *New Interpreter's Bible*, ed. Leander E. Keck. Vol. 11. Nashville: Abingdon Press, 1994–2004.

Roberts, Mark D. *Ephesians*. The Story of God Bible Commentary. Grand Rapids, MI: Zondervan, 2016.

Smith, Mitzi J. "Ephesians." In *True to Our Native Land: An African American New Testament Commentary*. Edited by Brian K. Blount, Cain Hope Felder, Clarice Jannette Martin, and Emerson B. Powery. Minneapolis: Fortress Press, 2007.

Talbert, Charles H. *Ephesians and Colossians*. Paideia: Commentaries on the New Testament. Grand Rapids, MI: Baker Academic, 2007.

Thielman, Frank. *Ephesians*. Baker Exegetical Commentary on the New Testament. Grand Rapids, MI: Baker Academic, 2010.

Westfall, Cynthia Long. *Paul and Gender: Reclaiming the Apostle's Vision for Men and Women in Christ*. Grand Rapids, MI: Baker Academic, 2016.

Wright, Tom. *Paul for Everyone: The Prison Letters: Ephesians, Philippians, Colossians, and Philemon*. London: SPCK, 2003.

LETTER TO THE PHILIPPIANS

M. Sydney Park

INTRODUCTION

Our current politico-social context. Considering the devastating effects of 2020 for the United States in terms of Covid-19 and racial enmity, it is painfully clear that our country has deep systemic issues that put our very lives at risk. To be sure, disease is not particular to United States, but endemic to all human life. Biological diseases are perennial, affecting all without discrimination against race, gender, or age. Yet, the high casualty in the United States (to date, worldwide 6.87 million, and the United States 1.13 million) was not due to the virus itself, but systemic corruption and incompetence in government.[1] Racism is also ubiquitous to all human society.[2] Yet, 2020 was also the year of shocking revelations about racism in America. Three prominent deaths of Ahmaud Arbery (Feb 23), Breonna Taylor (Mar 13), and George Floyd (May 25) brought the horrific realities of racism in America to every household in the country through mainstream news and video streams. George Floyd's death sparked unprecedented protests across the United States (over 2000 cities/towns) and the world (over 60 countries); in the United States alone, it is estimated that 15–26 million participated in the protests.[3] These protests were singularly different from all previous demonstrations against Black oppression in the United States in their racial composition—citizens of many races, including Whites, stood with Blacks to protest racism in America. We stand at a precipice of history: even as some in the United States approve and perpetuate racism, people of all colors, including White, hunger for and demand racial equity.

Our current ecclesiological-theological context. As the country moves forward toward equality for all, the validity of evangelical faith is on trial. My focus at this point is not with secularism, which rejects and critiques Christian faith, but with evangelicals of every color. The year 2020 revealed to the global audience that much of American evangelicalism is made up of nominal religious/cultural identity rather than authentic faith anchored in Scripture.[4] The facile, indeed eager embrace of nationalism and White supremacy among some White evangelicals is undeniable proof of the wide divergence of evangelical "faith" from the gospel as defined in the New Testament. Consequently, many White evangelicals of biblical faith are also now beginning to

---

[1]It is also likely that the necessary restrictive measures to limit the escalation of the virus (e.g., government and business shutdowns, social limitations, masks) perceived as curtailment of individual freedom and rights, contributed to the high death toll.

[2]E.g., the Bosnian War (1992–1995), Rwandan genocide (1994), and Nazi Germany (1941–1945).

[3]Tim Craig, "'The United States Is In Crisis': Report Tracks Thousands of Summer Protests, Most Nonviolent," *Washington Post*, Sept 3, 2020; www.washingtonpost.com/national/the-united-states-is-in-crisis-report-tracks-thousands-of-summer-protests-most-nonviolent/2020/09/03/b43c359a-edec-11ea-99a1-71343d03bc29_story.html.

[4]For a good descriptive study of Christian nominalism, see D. Inserra, *The Unsaved Christian: Reaching Cultural Christianity with the Gospel* (Chicago: Moody Publishers, 2019).

understand that racial reconciliation cannot be sidelined as secondary to the more "spiritual" doctrines of faith and simply labeled as "liberal social gospel."

The non-White evangelicals' riposte to the easy alliance of faith and nationalism also stands at a critical juncture. Given the prevailing politico-social tide toward racial equity, it is all too tempting and convenient to transpose secular ethos and logic to the church. The assumption that secular ideology and solutions equate to or enhance the biblical vision of racial reconciliation is alluring. Such imprudence will also result in deviation from Scripture, which is, in effect, another form of nominalism. The urgent question at hand is simply this: Although the promise of racial reconciliation in the New Testament has not yet been fully realized, does it offer genuine reconciliation that is *qualitatively different from* that of secular political/social égalité? Thus, the current historical moment presents a challenge to evangelicals of all color to reexamine the validity of the promise of reconciliation to both God and humans in Scripture. For reconciliation on both dimensions is accomplished on the single event of the cross of Jesus Christ (Eph 2:11-19). One cannot be separated from the other; the redemptive work on the cross is the only means by which all nations may participate in salvation with honor as God's creation, by faith as one body of Christ.

Toward an effective reconciliation: A way forward. The call to stand on Scripture as the foundation for racial reconciliation is not novel. There have been pivotal historical gestures toward biblical reconciliation such Billy Graham's famous removal of the red rope of segregation at his crusade in Jackson Mississippi in 1952 and the landmark SBC Resolution on Racial Reconciliation in 1995. Both instances were motivated by scriptural understanding of the unity of all people by salvation (Gal 3:28; cf. also Rom 10:12; 1 Cor 12:12-13; Gal 5:6; Eph 2:11-16; Col 3:11). Despite being biblically centered, both events *became* simply titular with eventually no will toward implementation of comprehensive racial reconciliation, which necessarily requires long-suffering faith. The comprehensive scale of racial reconciliation based on reconciliation with God is yet to be realized. And the solution cannot be "Go harder and longer!" as the issues of racial enmity are ultimately spiritual issues, which require authentic repentance and not just a sense of guilt, as well as a new ethos of cruciformity, regardless of ethnicity. The new path forward presented here does not displace but reaffirm the foundation of Scripture and amend a few critical points of deficiency in interpretation and application of biblical racial reconciliation.

Those who affirm faith in the eternal trustworthiness of God's word (Ps 119:89; Prov 30:5; Is 40:6-8; 55:10-11; 1 Pet 1:24-25; cf. also Mt 24:35; and Mk 13:31) must scrutinize Scripture carefully to rediscover, reclaim, and implement the reconciliation effected through the cross. To begin, the following broad questions on the uniqueness of gospel reconciliation may be posed. What are the theological and social contours (before and after) of biblical racial reconciliation? What are the mindset and ethics of a cross-reconciled community of all nations? The careful investigation of Scripture also requires honest self-evaluation. How and why did we deviate from the completed reconciliation of all races effected by the cross, one that is perfected in New Jerusalem (Rev 7:9-10)?[5] An authentic commitment of faith in Scripture

[5]A comprehensive analysis and answers to these questions extend well beyond the parameters of my comments on Philippians. As an initial prompter for discussion, I limit my focus below on the convergence of historical reality and theological truth in terms of ethnicity.

and Jesus Christ our Savior will necessarily insist on repentance from our personal and corporate sins of unfaithfulness (cf. 2 Chron 7:14), as well as commitment to reform toward the obligatory principles and character of cruciformed reconciliation.

The primary passage that accounts for both the vertical and horizontal dimensions of reconciliation is Ephesians 2:11-22 as it is the rationale for "neither Jew nor Greek" elsewhere in Paul's letters.[6] For Paul, spiritual and social reconciliations are not accomplished in two separate acts, nor in a two-stage process, but in the single event of the cross (Eph 2:13-16). Racial reconciliation is not a convenient slogan for Paul's missionary activity; rather, he proclaims the good news of Jesus Christ to the Gentiles *because* racial unity is central to the claim of reconciliation with God. Given this theological tenet, some oft-utilized rationale at odds with the comprehensive effect of biblical reconciliation can be concisely addressed.

Time and again, two forms of resistance against racial peace of the gospel message surface. First, although there is a concession to the fact that racism is sin, various arguments nevertheless minimize racial enmity as merely a universal or particular sin. Racism (including atrocities of slavery)—it is often said—is ancient and transcends time and ethnicity. Every race or ethnic group is guilty of enmity and or oppression of another throughout history. In this argument, the ubiquity of racism curbs both personal and corporate accountability and repentance. The rationale is similar to the deflection of responsibility in the claim "everybody lies" and is equally baseless in the court of humans and God. On the flipside, some argue so as to blunt the urgency of resistance against racism with the rationale that it is but one form of sin. The logic of "everyone is guilty" or "racism is only one sin among many" fails to acknowledge that both ubiquity and particularity of racial enmity is addressed in Ephesians 2:13-16. *All* sins have been put to death; negligence in one or few and cherry-picking sins to address are meritless and ultimately judged (Jas 2:8-13).

Of all the sins that humanity commits against one another, racial enmity is specifically tethered to the cross. And the universality of racism is effectively vanquished only by the cross with the result of racial unity. The history of slavery and racial oppression in the United States and the world is not obscured, but equally terminated. To claim reconciliation with God (i.e., salvation) and simultaneously persist in racial enmity and segregation is to redefine and champion "another gospel"—a gospel idolatrously shaped in our own image and to our own convenience—as much as some Jewish Christians attempted to reshape the gospel as *Jewish* gospel for the Galatians. For Paul, such a gospel is heterodoxy (*heteron euangelion* Gal 1:6), perversion (*metastrephō* Gal 1:7), and anathema (*anathema* Gal 1:9). Theological orthodoxy mandates coherent social behavior: Paul's harsh critique of Peter is not based on theological dissonance, but social deviance from theology. Specifically, Paul rejects and rebukes social behavior inconsistent to orthodoxy: "But after they [the Torah-observant Jewish Christians] came, he [Peter] drew back and kept himself separate for fear of the circumcision faction" (Gal 2:12, but see Gal 2:11-14). Peter's theological conviction is well attested in Acts 10:1-48 (esp. Acts 10:27-29, 34-35, 46-48) and Acts 11:1-18. Peter does not hesitate to "stay" with Gentiles, which would include table fellowship in Acts 10:48—a decision based on direct revelation from Christ, which he defends against

[6]See references on previous page.

criticism of associating and eating with Gentiles (Acts 11:3-18). In Galatia, Peter deviates from the racial unity of the gospel of Jesus Christ out of fear for the opinions of Jewish Christians who maintain dietary regulations (cf. Lev 11 and Deut 14:1-21). And consequently, he withdraws from table fellowship with Gentiles.[7] What Paul critiques is not just a form of hypocrisy, but as evident throughout Galatians, one that perverts the authentic racial reconciliation accomplished on the cross.

Second, the refusal to desegregate in order to pursue the racial unity of the cross is based on the rationale of history. For minorities, especially Black Americans, the call for racial integration in the church is met with justified skepticism. The horrors of slavery and ongoing persecution of Black Americans validate trepidation and misgivings. Despite reasonable fears, this argument likewise curtails the full effect of the cross and ultimately reshapes the gospel message by the idol of history and functions to reinforce racial enmity and past identity as slaves. If, indeed, human history of sin, in all its wretchedness, cannot be redeemed by the cross, there is no redemption with respect to either humans or God. Reception of forgiveness from God necessarily means granting forgiveness to others (Mt 6:12-15; 18:21-35; Mk 11:25; Lk 6:37). To be sure, Jesus requires that his disciples not only forgive, but love their enemies (see esp. Mt 5:44-48).

The refusal to forgive threatens our own forgiveness from God. The lack of courage to believe that true racial unity is possible through the cross is but a cynical disbelief in our own redemption, the sovereignty of God, *and* authentic solidarity of all races God has already effected. The result of this perspective is slavery to the history of sin and oppression with no hope of reform. The pathway to "a more perfect union" is accomplished by the cross of Jesus Christ, our Redeemer and Creator, not the US Constitution. As the law, whether secular or biblical, has no power to perfect anything (Heb 7:19). While secular law may provide some immediate relief in terms of racial equity, as long as sin persists, progress is always transient; the only place where sin has been decisively nullified is on the cross of Jesus Christ at Golgotha.

Given the lack of will on both sides as described above, the frequently quoted words of Martin Luther King Jr. in 1963, "It is appalling that the most segregated hour of Christian America is 11 o'clock on Sunday morning" lose their intended reformative power and wither to a guilt trip or worse, a slogan. If the current intent and effect of these words is to wait for White evangelicals to initiate racial reconciliation, based on the logic "they sinned, they need to ask us for forgiveness and initiate reconciliation," it is again, contrary to logic in Jesus' teaching: "forgive because you have been forgiven." But more significantly, it lacks agency in the power already available to all. Why wait, as though the perfect and enduring racial unity of the cross accomplished by God required the majority's or anyone's consent? Why deflect responsibility, and therefore cede agency, to White evangelicals, lest there is no will among evangelicals of color to pursue cruciformed reconciliation? My commentary on *Philippians* below is intended to embolden evangelical minorities, especially leaders, to proclaim the gospel in both vertical and horizontal dimensions in imitation of another minority, Paul.

The final obstacle to address is the weightier issue of our approach to Scripture. Conservative evangelicalism has traditionally prioritized with validity of the spiritual dimension of

[7]For a concise analysis of Jewish dietary restrictions and table fellowship with Gentiles, cf. David A. deSilva, *The Letter to the Galatians*, NICNT (Grand Rapids, MI: Eerdmans, 2018) 198-203.

the gospel—redemption from sin—over the social implications of salvation (e.g., economical, social, and political oppression). Regardless of social context, all need to hear the good news and be saved, which may not immediately affect the broader social context as neither Jesus, Paul, nor the rest of the New Testament authors directly aimed to reform the secular politico-economic-social structure of their day. For example, Jesus' mission was not to lead a political revolution against the Romans who occupied Judea in the first century, but to die on the cross to save not just the Jews, but all people throughout time. Paul's repeated exhortations to submit to the governing body (Rom 13:1; Titus 3:1; cf. also 1 Pet 2:13) as well as his directives to slaves to comply to the existing structure of slavery (Eph 6:5; Col 3:22) indicate not an endorsement of oppression and injustice of his day, but a prioritized goal of spiritual salvation for all social contexts. To be sure, while the visions of both Jesus and Paul did not seek to remedy their immediate social-political-economic concerns, the permanent salvation for all throughout the ages ultimately aims toward indelible reform in all social dimensions—corporate sins of social-political-economic dimension are sins deemed for certain judgment in the court of God (cf. Rev 7:15-17; 18:1–19:5).

On the other hand, the Social Gospel movement (1870–1920) sought to administer the ethics of the gospel (e.g., Mt 5–7 and Lk 6) to effect secular social reform, yet with scant attention to the theological core of repentance and salvation in the gospel message. Apart from the vertical crux, the horizontal consequence of good will loses the vital theological characteristic, thus its power; it becomes indistinguishable from secular social benevolence (e.g., the Peace Corps). While these efforts may be substantially beneficial, such an anemic presentation of the gospel is no gospel and must be rejected *tout de suite*.

The solution to the dilemma is to switch from a dualistic hermeneutic that prioritizes the spiritual over the social to the Old Testament mindset that maintains both spiritual and social axes as cohesive for human existence. Such a holistic hermeneutic is the bloodline that pulsates throughout Paul's letters, Jesus' teachings, and the Old Testament. For example, one charge leveled against Israel's ignorance of God and her idolatry (Is 1:2-4) is lack of social justice in Israel (Is 1:15-17, 21-23); where injustice reigns, Israel's worship is repugnant and rejected (Is 1:11-15) and her election is void (Is 1:10). That the social dimension affects the spiritual in Isaiah is not a reinvention, but reiteration of covenant requirements in the Ten Commandments/Decalogue (Ex 20:1-17; Deut 5:6-21) that encompass both vertical and horizontal relationships. Jesus affirms the validity of both axes of the covenant in Matthew 22:34-40 (cf. Mk 12:28-33) when he summarizes the Ten Commandments with two points: (1) "You shall love the Lord your God with all your heart and with all your soul and with all your might" (Deut 6:5); and (2) ". . . but you shall love your neighbor as yourself: I am the Lord" (Lev 19:18) and concludes, "On these two commandments hang all the Law and the Prophets." Echoing Isaiah's critique, the Markan parallel frames the nexus of both axes in terms of worship in the scribe's response: "'He [God] is one, and besides him there is no other'; and 'to love him with all the heart and with all the understanding and with all the strength' and 'to love one's neighbor as oneself'—*this is much more important than all whole burnt offerings and sacrifices*" (Mk 12:32-33, italics mine). In coherence, Jesus warns that "spiritual" work without implementation of his ethical teaching in Matthew 5–7 not only renders the spiritual work null and void, but results in exclusion of the workers from the kingdom of God *because* such division between faith and action is contrary to his teaching and salvation (Mt 7:21-23; cf. Lk 6:46-49; Jas 2:17-26). Hence, an authentic theological interpretation of the New Testament must account for the social axes of salvation and affect human relations to reflect said salvation.

While it is typical for advocates of a social gospel to cast their attention to social justice in the secular realm, the focus of New Testament social ethics is directed to the redeemed community. As much as Old Testament law mandated compassion for the marginalized in Israel's community (e.g., Ex 22:22; Deut 14:29; 16:11; 24:19; 27:19; Is 1:17; Jer 7:6; Ezek 22:7), the New Testament also exhorts and exercises compassion for the deprived in their community (Acts 6:1-3; 24:17; Rom 12:13; 1 Cor 16:1-3; 2 Cor 8-9; Jas 1:27). To be sure, this self-sacrificing compassion extends to outsiders as a testimony of redemption, with no explicit concern to change the broader secular system.

Further, redeemed relations are defined not by a sense of justice, but the cross. The logic in both Beatitudes of Matthew (5–7) and Luke (6:20-49) is not simply reversal of fortune, but Christocentric. Jesus' disciples are exhorted to embrace what is despised by the world: poverty (in spirit); mourning; meekness; hunger and thirst for righteousness; mercy; purity in heart; peacemaking; persecution; and revilement. Every human seeks to avoid these conditions, but Jesus Christ calls them "blessed" (Mt 5:3-10; Lk 6:20-21) when embraced for the sake of his name (Mt 5:11-12; Lk 6:22-23). "Love your enemies and pray for those who persecute you" in Matthew 5:44 is not justice, but cruciformed ethics applicable to all, rich and poor, in Christ, as it is framed with the purpose "so that you may be children of your Father in heaven" (Mt 5:45). The call to give a tunic to the one who has already taken the cloak is not justice (Mt 5:40; Lk 6:29), but extreme self-sacrifice that mirrors the cross as the only garment left is the loincloth (i.e., underwear)! Such self-sacrifice is the definition of discipleship to Jesus Christ (cf. Mt 16:24-26; Mk 8:34-38; Lk 14:25-27), hence, an emblem of faith to the world; secular social reform begins in the Church through the cross.

Similarly, racial reconciliation proclaimed in Ephesians 2:13-16 and throughout Paul's letters enjoins *the church*, and not the secular world to live as *one body* in the cruciformed ethics as outlined by Jesus. Biblical reconciliation is not mere tolerance of other races nor does it operate on the logic of equal rights. Rather, it is a self-sacrificing love and humble embrace for the "once foreign, now family" and "once foe, now friend" in the holy presence of God, who has redeemed us all through the humiliating and self-sacrificing death of his own Son. This uniquely precious reconciliation between all races has already been perfected on the cross, as it is impossible apart from the consummate solution to both individual and corporate sin. The commission of God's people to proclaim the good news (Mt 28:19) *is* commission to proclaim and embody racial reconciliation *in the church*. Historically, it is a commission the church has failed to implement based on the faith that *all sins* have been conclusively resolved by the "once for all" atonement of the cross. If the cross does not result in true racial reconciliation, that is, the death of the sin of racial enmity, there is no other solution: "For if we *willfully* persist in sin after having received the knowledge of the truth, there no longer remains a sacrifice for sins but a fearful prospect of judgment and a fury of fire that will consume the adversaries" (Heb 10:26-27, italics mine). The "adversaries" are not unbelievers, but Christians who profess faith *yet* continue to sin.

The final amendment required for a biblical interpretation of racial unity is the reading of Scripture, specifically, the New Testament and Paul's letters in its historical context of ethnicity.[8] Too often in modern proclamation for racial reconciliation, the classic Pauline phrase "Jew and Gentile" is misconstrued as a call for inclusion of minorities, typically directed to White evangelicals with the presumption that "Gentiles" refers to minorities while "Jews" signifies Caucasians. "Jew and Gentile" refers to the perception of the world from Israel's perspective as God's elect. Thus, it is *one* nation, Israel the elect, vis-à-vis the world. Israel's theological identity as the divinely elect must be seen also from her social/historical reality as the *minority* nation amid multiple nations: "It was not because you were more numerous than any other people that the Lord set his heart on you and chose you, for you were the fewest of all peoples" (Deut 7:7). The equation of one elect nation that is the minority does not apply to all minority nations/cultures either in ancient or modern times; it is the exclusive historical claim of Israel (e.g., Deut 4:37; 7:6-8). As election or redemption moves beyond ethnic boundaries in the New Testament, minority ranking of the elect (i.e., believers) in relation to the world is, nevertheless retained, as election before God necessarily results in sociological and cultural dissonance from the rest of the world (cf. Heb 11; 1 Pet 1:1). Namely, to be a Christian is to be a minority vis-à-vis the world.

In view of Israel's historical election, regardless of ethnic origin, all are "Gentiles." The modern issue of racial reconciliation as "White versus non-Whites" in the church is essentially an internal hostility among the Gentiles over privilege and power—Gentiles, who have all been "grafted in" (Rom 11:11-24). There is no justification for theological or ethnic priority apart from the common grace available to all, namely to both "Jew and Gentile": " . . . the righteousness of God through faith in Jesus Christ for all who believe. For there is no distinction, since all have sinned and fall short of the glory of God; they are now justified by his grace as a gift, through the redemption that is in Christ Jesus" (Rom 3:22-23; cf. also vv. 9-18). Thus, racial enmity based on skin color is theologically and historically incoherent to Scripture and must be set aside as secularism whenever it seeps into the church.

But Israel's election and thus minority status vis-à-vis the nations requires further elaboration in order to fully appreciate the truly groundbreaking nature of the nascent church in its proclamation of salvation by grace to all nations. As Israel's election is exclusive to her, one nation chosen by God for covenant relations, her purpose was to give testimony that Yahweh is the only true God to all nations through her faithful obedience to God's will and laws (Deut 4:5-8; cf. also Is 42:6; 49:6). Her privilege and responsibility as *the* elect over and against all other nations must be set in the context of ethnic oppression. Israel's covenant with Yahweh as a nation begins in the context of slavery, and deliverance from slavery is construed as the faithful outworking of Yahweh's promises to the patriarchs—election (Ex 2:24; 3:6, 14-17; 6:2-8; 32:13; Deut 4:36; 7:8; 10:15). Israel's oppression under Egyptian rule is cruel,

[8]Below, I address the ethnic misrepresentation of the apostle Paul in relation to racial reconciliation. However, misrepresentation of Jesus' ethnicity as well as the wider depiction of Jesus has a long history in scholarship. In the effort to modernize the historical Jesus for more accessibility, scholars' depiction of Jesus revealed their own image and culture more than Jesus of Scripture. Cf. Albert Schweitzer, *The Quest of the Historical Jesus: A Critical Study of Its Progress from Reimarus to Wrede* (London: A&C Black, 1911) 554-61. Such desire to reimagine Jesus in our own image was not limited to scholarship, but influenced the arts, especially European Renaissance art. The same impulse drives the current American political discourse on the Second Amendment (Jesus as pro-gun advocate) and race (Jesus as White).

including genocide, extending even to infanticide (Ex 1:8-22).[9]

Even as Israel enters the Promised Land, her conquest must be framed by the two factors of election and her minority status. Her victory in Canaan is entirely dependent on the contingencies of election—she must have faith in and be faithful to Yahweh alone (cf. Josh 1:1-9, 16-18). Lack of faith and faithfulness to Yahweh are detrimental to Israel (cf. Ex 32:1-35; Num 14:1-38; Josh 7:10-26) as her testimony to the nations of Yahweh and her election depends on both faith and faithfulness. Her war against all other nations is necessarily war against the idolatry of the nations and not simply ethnicity (e.g., Deut 7:1-5, 25-26), as Gentiles with faith in Yahweh were embraced into her midst.[10] Moreover, just as Yahweh demanded destruction of all idolatry of her neighbors, he showed no partiality in face of Israel's own idolatry in the wilderness and failure in Canaan. The primary thrust of Israel's election is not ethnocentricity, but singularity of her worship of the living God.[11] Ultimately, Israel's exile to captivity (Assyrian 733 BCE; Babylonian 586 BCE) is not perceived by her own prophets as a natural sociopolitical inevitability of one small nation in the midst of greater empires, but the consequence of Israel's failure of covenantal faith and faithfulness (e.g., Isaiah, Jeremiah, Ezekiel). Throughout her history, regardless of the glory in David's reign over a united kingdom, Israel was the minority vis-à-vis the nations.

Upon their return to Jerusalem from captivity, the Israelites complete the construction of the Second Temple (516 BCE), but never fully regain their national sovereignty, apart from the brief respite of the Hasmonean Dynasty (165–63 BCE) and Salome Alexandra's rule (76–67 BCE). By the first century, they are a client state under the Roman Empire with the presence of Roman prefects (e.g., Pontius Pilate) and soldiers. It is under these sociopolitical conditions that Jesus dies on the cross despite having the popularity to lead an ethnic/national revolution to "redeem" Israel from the Roman oppressors. In similar countercultural and counterintuitive fashion, Paul, a Jew from a country currently under Roman subjugation, proclaims the gospel message of Jesus Christ to all non-Jews, specifically, in Philippi, to Roman citizens. Paul's missionary activity in Acts and his letters to Gentiles must be read in light of these historical realities of Israel. Paul is a minority with an ethnic history of slavery and continued oppression under Rome who boldly persists in calling Gentiles, including those aligned with Rome, to form "one humanity" in Christ (Eph 2:15) as promised by the redemption of the cross. Paul's story is a model for all, but especially for minority Christians to pursue redemptive racial reconciliation without regard to their history of oppression nor to current racial prejudice. Paul in *Philippians* is a model of *how* a minority can transcend beyond the ethno-historical realities to form "one humanity" in Christ and the *content* of that new kinship in terms of mindset and ethics.

The reading of Philippians through the lens of racial reconciliation is not simply another "special interest" hermeneutics, but an interpretation of the New Testament's theological message seen through the sociopolitical history of Israel vis-à-vis Gentiles. Such a cohesive reading of both social and theological axes does not distract from but magnifies God's act of salvation in Jesus Christ to its fullest significance, which decisively altered

[9]Despite all the challenges twentieth century scholarship leveled against the Old Testament, the fact of Israel's slavery is never in dispute. Cf. John Bright, *A History of Israel*, 4th ed. (Louisville, KY: Westminster John Knox, 2000), 121.

[10]E.g. Caleb (Num 13:6, 30; 14:6, 24, 30, 38; 26:65; 32:12; 34:19; Deut 1:36; Josh 14–15; 21:12), Rahab (Josh 2:1-3; 6:17-25) and Ruth.

[11]This is the singular point effectively proclaimed by John the Baptist in preparation for Jesus' ministry, cf. Mt 3:7-10; Lk 3:7-9.

social reality of the first century in conformity to God's redemption. And it is the same expansive understanding of God's salvation that will redress and transform modern-day racial enmity.

INTRODUCTION TO PAUL'S LETTER TO THE PHILIPPIANS

Background of Philippi. Philippi (modern-day Fillipoi), which lies in northeastern Greece, was an ancient city with renowned history and status in Paul's day. It was named after Philip II of Macedon (father of Alexander the Great) in 356 BCE, who appropriated the territory under Macedonian rule to access nearby gold and silver mines.[12] It later became famous as the site of a Roman internecine battle, where Mark Antony and Octavian defeated Brutus and Cassius in 42 BCE. Upon victory, as veteran soldiers were settled in the city, it was established as a Roman colony by *ius Italicum*.[13] Thus, Philippian citizens enjoyed the rights and privileges of Roman citizens such as ownership of land (purchase and transference included) as well as the right to civil lawsuits. Roman rather than Greek culture was dominant in Philippi as evident from its architecture, coinage, clothing, language, and religion.[14] Since the city was strategically placed along the *Via Egnatia*, it was commercially and militarily significant.[15] In Paul's day, Philippi is recognized as "a leading city of the district of Macedonia and a Roman colony" (Acts 16:12). Philippi's elite status of Roman citizenship is recognized and utilized by Paul as he exhorts the Philippian believers to "live as citizens" (Phil 1:27; in NRSV "live your life"), which translates πολιτεύμαι and reminds them of their heavenly "citizenship" (Phil 3:20).

The gospel message comes to the Philippians as Paul, on his second missionary journey, answers the urgent call from a Macedonian man in his vision: "Come over to Macedonia and help us" (Acts 16:9). Paul immediately obeys as he perceives the vision as a divine directive (Acts 16:10) and the gospel of Jesus Christ is first introduced to Macedonia in Philippi. After a few days in Philippi, on Sabbath, Paul, Silas, and Timothy (cf. Acts 15:40; 16:1-5) seek a place of prayer "outside the gate by the river" (Acts 16:13) and evangelize to women gathered there. Lydia of Thyatira, a merchant of purple cloth along with her household, are the first converts in Philippi (Acts 16:14-15).

According to Acts, in various cities Paul and his companions visit, they seek out a synagogue in the city for worship and proclamation: Damascus, Acts 9:19-20; Salamis, Acts 13:5, Antioch Pisidia, Acts 13:14-48; Iconium, Acts 14:1; Thessalonica, Acts 17:1, Berea, Acts 17:10, Athens, Acts 17:16-17; Corinth, Acts 18:1-4; Ephesus, Acts 19:1, 8. In each of these cities, there is a sufficient Jewish population to necessitate a synagogue. The lack of a synagogue in Philippi indicates a scant Jewish presence. Instead, Philippi as a Roman colony was polytheistic and worshiped the multiple gods of Rome as well as the emperor.[16] Yet, given the constant assimilation of other cultures into the Roman Empire, it is most likely that other religions ("folk" religion; Silvanus; Thracian Rider) coexisted as subcultures

[12]P. Pilhofer, *Philippi: Die erste christliche Gemeinde Europas*, WUNT 87 (Tübingen: Mohr Siebeck, 1995), 1:78-81.
[13]Roman law granting cities outside Italy rights and privileges of Roman citizenship.
[14]See M. Bockmuehl, *A Commentary on the Epistle to the Philippians* (London: A&C Black, 1997), 4.
[15]Via Egnatia was a major east-west road stretching from Dyrrachium to Byzantium (from the modern-day western end of Albania to the eastern end of Istanbul) established in 2 BCE by the Romans. As it linked the Roman colonies in its path, it provided smooth transfer of Roman military and commercial goods. It is most likely the road Paul used to travel from Philippi to Thessalonica (Acts 16–17).
[16]Emperor worship began with the death of Julius Caesar (44 BCE) as he was declared *divus* (divine).

to the formal and dominant Roman religion.[17] While Jews enjoyed the protection of Roman law to practice their religion, Judea in the first century was occupied under Roman rule and they were prey to state-sanctioned persecution (e.g., banishment from Rome in 19 CE under Claudius). Luke's account of Paul's conflict and imprisonment in Philippi sets the Philippians' rejection of Judaism in sharp relief against other syncretistic and polytheistic cities in the first century.

Acts 16:16-24 is confirmation of antisemitism in Philippi. In the aftermath of casting out a demon of divination in the servant girl, who harassed Paul and Silas for days, her owners, angry at the loss of their profit, point to ethnicity as the offense to the magistrates: "These men, these Jews, are disturbing our city and are advocating customs that are not lawful for us, being Romans, to adopt or observe" (Acts 16:20-21).[18] In the Greek New Testament, the ethnic component in both clauses stands at the end to highlight the contrast: "being Jews" (*Ioudaioi hyparchontes*) and "being Romans" (*Rōmaiois ousin*).[19] The charge of being Jews and false allegation of promoting Jewish ways are sufficient to rile up both the crowd and magistrates to physical abuse ("stripped of their clothing" and "beaten," Acts 16:22) and imprisonment (Acts 16:23-24). Emphatically, this is the only recorded instance of Paul's, indeed, of all the missionary activities in Acts, where ethnicity is explicitly the reason for persecution.

Of course, their imprisonment becomes the context for God's miraculous sovereignty. In response to unfair persecution, Paul and Silas pray and worship God; and God answers by causing a tremendous earthquake that releases the prisoners' bonds and opens the jail doors. Paul and Silas give testimony to the gospel by demonstrating integrity and concern for the jailer's welfare. As Acts 16:27 indicates, the jailer's own life would be liable for the prisoners' escape. It is the combination of supernatural event and testimony of the apostles' character of worship and integrity that leads to the jailer's and his household's salvation (Acts 16:30-34).

Philippi is also the first of only two instances where Paul's Roman citizenship is mentioned (Acts 16:37; 22:25-29). As evident here, in Acts 22:25-29 and 25:16, Roman citizenship signifies elite status in the Roman Empire. It affords tremendous legal protection of rights against persecution and imprisonment without legal due process; breach of these rights had severe consequences.[20] Roman citizenship can be bought at significant cost, but Paul's privilege is even more elite—it is by birth (Acts 22:28). The elite status of Roman citizenship affords Paul and Silas the opportunity to not only clear their name, but more significantly, to vindicate the integrity of the gospel, as the magistrates apologize for wrongful imprisonment (Acts 16:35-39). The concern here is not personal injury, but the integrity of the gospel message.

After two years of work in Ephesus, Paul visits Macedonia and probably Philippi (although this is not explicit in Acts 20:1) to encourage the saints and heads toward Greece (most likely Corinth, Acts 20:2). After three months, he returns to Philippi and heads toward Troas (Acts 20:3-6). Both Timothy and Erastus also visit Macedonia/Philippi, perhaps

---

[17]Cf. Bockmuehl, *Philippians*, 5-8, for a salient assessment and especially on the evidence of a coin bearing the image of Thracian Rider on one side and Emperor Augustus on the other.

[18]"Jews," *Ioudaios*, can mean "Jewish Christian." The bulk of the instances of *Ioudaios* simply means "Jewish" in Acts (e.g., cf. Acts 2:5, 14; 9:22-23; 10:22, 28, 39; 11:19).

[19]The verbs *hyparchō* and *eimi* are semantically equivalent, meaning "to be."

[20]Cf. Craig S. Keener, *Acts*, NCBC (Cambridge: Cambridge University Press, 2020) 407n1754: the unlawfully beaten and imprisoned Roman citizen had both moral and legal ground against the perpetrators.

as an extension of Paul's desire and presence (Acts 19:21-22). That Paul points to the "churches of Macedonia" as models of financial generosity despite their own hardship (2 Cor 8–9; esp. 8:1-5) correlates well with the fact that Paul entered into a rare financial relationship with the Philippians (Phil 4:10-20).[21] The repeated visits as well as the rare financial support suggest that the relationship between Paul and the Philippians is of profound love that sprouts from spiritual maturity of the gospel, as evident in the letter.[22]

While the account from Acts provides the origin of the Philippian church, for unknown reasons neither Lydia nor the unnamed jailer are mentioned in the letter. Yet a tentative proposal for the composition of the church can be made. Many would have the privileged Roman citizenship and naturally their allegiance is to the Roman Empire (at least, prior to conversion). The congregation may be composed of both merchants and former or current servants to the Roman Empire. Finally, by the first century, the Roman Empire had approximately 10 million slaves (20 percent of the population), whether by war, debt, or punishment of criminals; human trafficking was fueled by consumer demand.[23] Naturally, some slaves would also be part of the congregation. Paul's use of *doulos* "slave" in Philippians 1:1; 2:7 and *douleuō* "to be subject, a slave to someone" in Philippians 2:22 has rhetorical and theological impact on both the free and enslaved.

Authorship and date. Pauline authorship of *Philippians* is virtually unquestioned. Provenance and date are determined by the fact that Paul writes from prison (Phil 1:13-14, 17). Paul was frequently imprisoned (2 Cor 6:5; 11:23) as the three additional "prison epistles" (Ephesians, Colossians, and Philemon) testify. Three locations along with corresponding dates surface as possibilities for *Philippians*: Rome (60–62 CE), Ephesus (54–55 CE) and Caesarea (57–59 CE). Determination of locale is based on two factors: distance from Philippi and internal evidence. Paul's use of *praitōrion* or "imperial guard" in Philippians 1:13, which signifies the presence of the praetorian regiment stationed in Rome, as well as the reference to "Caesar's household" (*ek tēs Kaisaros oikia*) in Philippians 4:22, give weight to Roman imprisonment. However, the distance between Philippi and Rome (approximately 1200 miles) makes multiple journeys for communication difficult.[24]

Paul was imprisoned in Caesarea for two years (Acts 24:27) and "imperial guard" may refer to Herod's rather than Nero's (Acts 23:35). Yet the distance from Caesarea to Philippi is comparable to Rome. Ephesus is the closest to Philippi, but untenable given that there is no textual evidence in the New Testament for Paul's imprisonment in the city.[25] To date, based on the internal evidence in *Philippians*, Rome remains as the best option; while the distance between the two cities requires a lengthy journey, travel was not uncommon in

[21]Paul studiously rejects financial support from the fledgling communities he establishes in Thessalonica and Corinth; cf. 1 Thess 2:9; 2 Thess 3:7–8; 1 Cor 9:6, 11–12, 18; 2 Cor 11:7; cf. also Acts 18:2–3. In both instances, Paul works to support himself in order to avoid allegations of financial impropriety.

[22]Hence, the popularized notion that Philippians is a "friendship" letter.

[23]Grant R. Osborne, *Revelation*, BECNT (Grand Rapids, MI: Baker Academic, 2002), 649. See also Richard Bauckham, *The Climax of Prophecy: Studies on the Book of Revelation* (London: T&T Clark, 1998), 338-83.

[24]Cf. D. A. Carson and Douglas J. Moo, *An Introduction to the New Testament*, rev. ed. (Grand Rapids, MI: Zondervan, 2005), 504. It appears there are four journeys in view in Philippians: (1) news of Paul's imprisonment; (2) Epaphroditus (Phil 2:25); (3) news of Epaphroditus's sickness to the Philippians; (4) the Philippians' concern for Epaphroditus (Phil 2:26). Carson and Moo project three further journeys: sending and return of Timothy (Phil 2:19) and Epaphroditus (Phil 2:25).

[25]Bockmuehl, *Philippians*, 27.

the first century (e.g., commerce/trade and military deployment). That Paul anticipates imminent death (Phil 1:20) gives further weight to Rome as an option, as an appeal to Caesar is final.

Purpose. On the practical level, Paul writes to thank the Philippians for the (financial) gift and service they sent through Epaphroditus (Phil 1:7; 2:25; 4:10-18, esp. Phil 4:18). The letter also alleviates the Philippians' concern for Epaphroditus, who has fallen sick since his arrival (Phil 2:25-29). Further, Paul relates that he will send both Timothy and Epaphroditus (Phil 2:19; 28) and exhorts the Philippians to receive them with honor.

Second, Paul writes to relate his own circumstance and welfare to the Philippians and ease their concern for him (Phil 1:12-26; 4:10-19).

Third, Paul writes to exhort the Philippians to press forward toward perfection in their love (Phil 1:9) and internal unity against external threats (Phil 1:27-30). Both these components are further developed in tight intrinsic coherence of soteriology and cruciformed ethics as well as persevering testimony and eschatology. For support of this theology, Paul provides models to follow (Christ, Phil 2:5-11; Timothy, Phil 2:19-24; Epaphroditus, Phil 2:30; himself, Phil 3:4-17; 4:8-9) and to avoid (Phil 3:2; 18-19). It is only after the dense theological elaboration of what "in Christ" means that Paul addresses the internal conflict of Euodia and Syntyche (Phil 4:2-3). Correct theology leads to correct ethics.

Finally, as I have argued above, while Philippians, as well as the rest of Paul's letters, may be read insightfully apart from the lens of ethnicity, the more historically accurate reading necessitates the social-political-ethnic component of the first century and the particularity of Philippi, especially in the context of Paul's mission in the city. As such, Philippians provides hope of biblical racial reconciliation as it is de facto between Paul and the Philippians. Hence, it also offers a blueprint for all, but especially minority leaders, to follow with confidence and eagerness to attain to the reality of the cross—both Jew and Gentile have been made one by Jesus, our peace (Eph 2:14-16).

GREETING (PHILIPPIANS 1:1-2)

As typical in Greco-Roman and New Testament tradition, the letter begins with the identification of the senders and recipients, followed by greetings. In Paul's letters, these components are modified as necessary for each occasion. Here, Paul designates himself and Timothy as "slaves" (*douloi*), typically translated by most English versions as "servants" of Christ Jesus. This is the only instance among his letters where *doulos* alone identifies Paul's role among his converts. In both Romans 1:1 and Titus 1:1, *doulos* is coupled with "apostle" (*apostolos*). In the bulk of his letters, only *apostolos* appears (1 Cor 1:1; 2 Cor 1:1; Gal 1:1; Eph 1:1; Col 1:1; 1 Tim 1:1; and 2 Tim 1:1). The names of the senders stand alone in the Thessalonian correspondences; and "prisoner" (*desmios*) is used in Philemon 1:1. As the last instance signifies, Paul's self-description varies to suit the occasion of the letter. In Philemon, he writes to argue for mercy on behalf of Philemon's slave, Onesimus. Paul's identity as "prisoner" lays rhetorical weight to Paul's appeal to Philemon—whatever loss (social and personal indignity) Philemon may incur from receiving Onesimus as an equal (Philem 1:15-17) and possibly releasing Onesimus for service to Paul (Philem 1:12-14), Paul risks a greater loss of his entire life for the gospel. Likewise, in *Philippians*, "slaves" is used with intent and import.

First and foremost, his self-identification as a "slave" of Christ Jesus underwrites the humble subordination of his apostleship, while "apostle" of Jesus Christ may highlight the authority of the apostle as "one sent by" Jesus Christ. The distinction between the two, despite the pragmatic epistolary function as described above, must be nuanced by the fact that there is no authority of an apostle without total submission as a slave to the sender, Jesus Christ, as Philippians 2:6-11 clearly demonstrates (cf. also Jn 14:9-10). To be a slave is to wholly subject one's will and subjectivity to another. Only such submission results in authority exercised by New Testament apostles.

Second, Paul's self-understanding as "slave" corresponds to the identity of Christ, who emptied himself by taking on the "form of a slave" (Phil 2:7). Jesus' profound humility is the model for all Christians, including leaders. Third, Paul's concern for the Philippians' progress in faith is specified as adoption of Christ's mindset, which includes that of a slave (Phil 2:5, 7). Fourth, an identity of the self in terms of humility and service would quickly resolve the issue of contention between Euodia and Syntyche (Phil 4:2). Thus, Paul's identification as a "slave" functions as a model for both his broader and specific exhortations to the Philippians.

Given the genuine affection between the apostle and the congregation, his humility and service expressed in the term *slave* is not titular rhetoric. In terms of ethnicity, Paul exhibits no residual anger or insecurity with respect to historical and current racism against Jews evident in the Roman Empire and Philippi. Rather, he as well as the Philippians are united under the spiritual identity as Christians (Phil 3:20; also 1 Cor 12:13) where all enmity is put to death on the cross.

This is the only instance among his letters where Paul greets the leaders of the church "with the overseers [*episkopois*] and deacons [*diakonois*]" to the more general audience of "all the saints in Christ Jesus who are in Philippi." The term *overseers* may refer to the office of elders (cf. 1 Tim 3:2; Titus 1:7; Acts); hence, *diakonois* carries the specific sense of ecclesial office rather than the general meaning of "servant." The use of both suggests that as one of the earliest churches Paul established, it has sufficiently progressed in faith to install leaders.

As in all the greetings in the New Testament letters, "grace" and "peace" have theological significance. "Grace" conveys God's mercy in deliverance of sinners. "Peace" is the result of God's grace with respect to relationship with God and his people.[26]

THANKSGIVING AND PRAYER (PHILIPPIANS 1:3-8)

Thanksgiving for his readers at the beginning of the letter is routine for Paul (apart from Gal and 2 Cor). In each instance, his gratitude is always tied to his prayers for the respective communities; it is a prayer report. Hence, thanksgiving is not simply "good thoughts" concerning the various communities he established, but specifically gratitude relayed to God in prayer. As evident in the bulk of his letters and *Philippians*, Paul is a man of constant prayer (Phil 1:3-4). The prayer report of Paul's thanksgiving typically lays out the various themes Paul will address in the letter. There are five intertwined themes densely packed in these verses that will be further developed in the letter: joy, partnership, mindset (to think), love, and God's sovereignty.

First, when Paul thanks God for the various churches, regardless of their spiritual maturity, he conveys his love for the redeemed. But here, he does so with joy. Indeed, he prays or wishes for the joy of the respective readers (Rom 15:13; 2 Cor 1:24; Gal 5:22; Col 1:11) and Paul himself takes joy in them (2 Cor 7:4; 1 Thess 2:19, 20;

[26]Cf. I. Howard Marshall, *The Epistle to the Philippians*, EC (London: Epworth Press, 1991), 4-5.

3:9; 2 Tim 1:4; Philem 1:7). Joy is a natural emotion for Paul in view of the salvation of his converts and disciples. Coherently, Paul elaborates that his constant prayer in gratitude for the Philippians is joyful.

In Philippians, however, the concept of joy is also a principal theme. The word "joy" (*charas*) occurs five times in the letter (Phil 1:4, 25; 2:2, 29; 4:1) and the verb "I rejoice" (*chairō*) appears nine times (Phil 1:18 [2x]; 2:17, 18, 28; 3:1; 4:4 [2x], 10). Paul takes joy, not simply on the virtue of their salvation, but *because* of their constant partnership in the gospel. This particular joy is based on sufficient spiritual maturity of the Philippians expressed through their wholehearted commitment of love and finances (Phil 2:25; 4:10-15). Paul qualifies the extent of their commitment as unswerving constancy: "from the first day until now" (Phil 1:5). Where there is love, there is joy, even when unrequited (e.g., the Corinthians); but, when there is reciprocity of love and devotion, joy is abundant.

Second, this mutuality of love is expressed through the key theme of "partnership" in this section and throughout the letter. The word translated "partnership" is *koinōnia* (Phil 1:5), which usually signifies "fellowship." Contrary to the diminished sense of "fellowship" as mere "social gathering" in our culture, *koinōnia* in the New Testament indicates active sharing and participation and carries this sense in all three instances in Philippians (Phil 1:5; 2:1; 3:10).[27] This sense of active participation is strengthened in the letter with two compound words of the *koinōn* root that reinforce the sense of cooperation with the preposition "with" (*syn*): "co-participant" (*ho synkoinōnos*)[28] in Philippians 1:7 and "I participate with someone" (*synkoinōneō*[29]) in Philippians 4:14. Apart from these, the sense of active participation is intensified throughout Philippians with fourteen other *syn*-compound words (Phil 1:27; 2:2, 17, 18, 25 [2x]; 3:10, 17, 21; 4:3 [4x], 14).

In this section, the Philippians' active partnership *in the gospel* is the reason for Paul's joyful thanksgiving in prayer (Phil 1:5) and confident hope that God will bring to completion the good work already operative among Philippians until the day of Christ (Phil 1:6-7). It is not simply temporal constancy of faith, but one that leads to active solidarity in Paul's imprisonment *and* in his defense and confirmation of the gospel (Phil 1:7). Such wholehearted unity with Paul requires authentic faith in the gospel and love for the one who brought the news of salvation to them. The faithful character of the Philippians described in this section is coherent with Paul's description of the Macedonians' generosity for the Jerusalem believers suffering famine (2 Cor 8:1-5), where two key words, *charas* and *koinōnia*, also appear (2 Cor 8:2, 4). They not only gave money when they themselves were experiencing "extreme poverty" (2 Cor 8:2); they "begged" for the privilege of participating in the financial support of fellow believers because they saw giving as "grace," "fellowship," and "service."[30] This true participation in the gospel and the fellowship of saints occurred as the Philippians first entrusted themselves to the Lord and by God's will (2 Cor 8:5).

Thus, both partners of the relationship (Paul and the Philippians) demonstrate remarkable character, which is only possible and normative for all redeemed through the cross. Paul feels no need to stress his authority as father and apostle

[27]*Koinōnia* is not a common word in the New Testament; it occurs only 19x and predominantly in Paul (13x).

[28]*Ho synkoinōnos* appears 4x in the New Testament (Rom 11:17; 1 Cor 9:23; Phil 1:7; Rev 1:9).

[29]*Synkoinōneō* appears 3x in the New Testament (Eph 5:11; Phil 4:14; Rev 18:4).

[30]"With much pleading, beseeching us for the grace [τὴν χάριν] and the participation [τὴν κοινωνίαν] of the service [τῆς διακονίας] for the saints" (2 Cor 8:4), author's translation.

of the Philippians, *because* they already conduct themselves on the assumption of his authority. The Philippians are wholly devoted to him in affection and financial support, not out of allegiance to individual personality, but because of faith in God and the message of salvation. Racial difference, elitism of Roman citizenship, and history of oppression matter not for either party; only love remains.

Third, while Paul's identity as a slave of Jesus Christ reflects Jesus Christ's humility and self-sacrifice, it does not signify absence of apostolic authority nor of responsibility to both God and the Philippians. Indeed, genuine love of a leader does not simper with sweet praises, but always exhorts those under their charge toward perfection that will be approved on judgment day ("day of Christ," Phil 1:6). The love of a true apostle necessarily mandates such a mindset. In Philippians 1:7 Paul states that it is only "right" (*dikaios*) for him "to think" (*phroneō*) of their progression in faith as specified in Philippians 1:6. *Dikaios*, used once more in Philippians 4:8, is a cognate of the more familiar Pauline term "righteousness" (*dikaiosynē*); the sense here is not simply "appropriateness" of human decorum, but "what is just before God." Clearly, Paul's love for the Philippians is more than simply emotions, but one that is always accountable to God (Phil 1:8). *Phroneō* introduced in Philippians 1:7 is highly significant in the letter, as it occurs ten times in Philippians (Phil 1:7; 2:2 [2x], 5; 3:15 [2x], 19; 4:2; 4:10 [2x]). The sense of *phroneō* is more than simple ability to form thoughts; rather, it conveys a certain "mindset," "disposition" that comprehensively affects every aspect of one's life.[31]

Fourth, Paul's mindset in Philippians 1:6-7 is specifically motivated by his love for the Philippians: "because I have you in (my) heart" (Phil 1:7). It is love that can be verified by God (Phil 1:8). The word "affection" (*splanchnon*) in Philippians 1:8 means "entrails" or "belly" as referent for emotions (i.e., love, compassion, heart) in the ancient world.[32] It is used eleven times in the New Testament with respect to believers' love for one another.[33] However, the verb "I have compassion" (*splanchnizomai*) is used twelve times in the New Testament, specifically in reference to Jesus Christ or God.[34] Paul's love for the Philippians is not only accountable to God, but has the shape of God's love for humanity.

Furthermore, the fact that the Philippians are participants in grace also justifies Paul's mindset. While the word "grace" (*charis* Phil 1:7) may specifically signify "financial giving," given that Paul also specifies "defense and confirmation of the gospel," *charis* conveys a broader meaning already relayed in Philippians 1:5. The Philippians are wholly invested in their salvation through active support in evangelism of the gospel. In view of the Philippians' fully orbed participation in the spread of the gospel, and his love for them, "it is only right" that Paul should desire further perfection among them.

Finally, in the midst of this mutual self-sacrificing love between Paul and the Philippians, God's sovereignty stands front and center. Without God's sovereignty such love would be impossible. Paul attributes both the beginning and the continuance of their faith ("good work" *ergon agathon*, Phil 1:6) as that contingent on God's sovereign work and will.

[31]The cognate *phronēsis* "mindset" was one of the chief virtues in Greek philosophy and conveys more than pure intellectual knowledge. It is "the right state of the intellect from which all moral qualities derive," see G. Bertram, "Φρήν," *TDNT* 9:220-35, 222; for its significance in Hellenistic Judaism, 227-30.

[32]BDAG, 1 & 2.

[33]Lk 1:78; Acts 1:18; 2 Cor 6:12; 7:15; Phil 1:8; 2:1; Col 3:12; Philem 1:7, 12, 20; and 1 Jn 3:17.

[34]Mt 9:36; 14:14; 15:32; 18:27 (parable of the unforgiving servant); Mt 20:34; Mk 1:41; 6:34; 8:2; 9:22 (plea from the epileptic's father); Lk 7:13; 10:33; and 15:20 (parable of the prodigal son). In the two parables, the reference is God the Father.

Neither he nor the Philippians can ultimately claim to be the cause of their salvation, their progress of faith, nor their precious love—hence, Paul's prayer in Philippians 1:9-11.

INTERCESSORY PRAYER (PHILIPPIANS 1:9-11)

Prayer reports are common in Paul's letters, but a record of his actual prayer only occurs here. The prayer fleshes out what Paul means by the "good work" God began and will complete in them (Phil 1:6). There are five elements to consider: love, knowledge and wisdom, moral and spiritual rectitude, righteousness of Christ, and exaltation of God, the Father. First, clearly, the Philippians already love, as evident in their relationship with Paul.[35] However, Paul prays for exponential growth in love: "that your love may *overflow more and more*" (Phil 1:9, emphasis mine).

Second, love, coupled with knowledge and wisdom, has a twofold purpose. This perfect love leads to the ability to approve by discernment "the things that matter" (translated "what is best").[36] This love does not accept uncritically, but through examination or testing of things discriminates between what is and is not christologically centered.

Third, love that exercises wisdom and knowledge should prevail in all dimensions of life in order to stand "pure and blameless" before God. Both words "pure" and "blameless" only occur here in Philippians and denote flawless character, measured not by human standards, but by God's. "Day of Christ" has already appeared in Philippians 1:6 and occurs again in Philippians 2:16 in the same sense—it refers to Jesus' parousia, hence, judgment day.

Fourth, but to stand blameless before God on judgment day cannot be confined to the arena of morality, separate from faith. It is, rather, ethics derived from the righteousness attained only by faith in Jesus Christ. The prominent Pauline word "righteousness" (*dikaiosynē*), with the theological significance of his other letters, appears here and three times more (Phil 3:6, and twice in Phil 3:9).[37] It refers to the right standing with God that results in ethics coherent with salvation. And finally, it is this mature, discriminating love that ensues from the righteousness of Jesus Christ that leads to glory and praise of God.[38]

In conclusion, this entire prayer and specifically the phrase "righteousness that comes through Jesus Christ" lays the foundation for the dense, theological core in Philippians 2 and 3. The broad concepts of love and wisdom introduced here gain specific soteriological shape in the paradigm of Christ in Philippians 2:6-11 and coherent illustrations of that model in Timothy (Phil 2:19-24), Epaphroditus (Phil 2:25-30), and Paul himself (Phil 3:4-10). In such coherence, the prayer, theologically reasoned and expanded in Philippians 2 and 3, ultimately aims toward the only internal issue specifically mentioned in the letter—the contention between Euodia and Syntyche (Phil 4:2-3).

THE ADVANCE OF THE GOSPEL (PHILIPPIANS 1:12-26)

As Paul relates his own situation of imprisonment and how it affects his mission in response to the Philippians' gift and message through Epaphroditus, he reveals his own mindset as one wholly dependent on Christ's

[35]While "love" (*agapē*) only occurs four times in *Philippians* 1:9, 16; 2:1, 2, as already discussed above, "love" is conveyed by different expressions.

[36]Cf. BDAG, 4.

[37]*Dikaiosynē* appears ninety-two times in the New Testament and fifty-eight times in Pauline epistles.

[38]"Glory" (*doxa*) occurs six times in the letter: Phil 1:11; 2:11; 3:19, 21; 4:19, 20. "Praise" (*epainos*) occurs only twice: Phil 1:11 and 4:8.

own mindset in Philippians 2:6-8. Two themes dominate this section: (1) the advance of the gospel; and (2) the priority of Christ and others.

Philippians 1:12-18 focuses on Paul's imprisonment and its effect. First, Paul states that his imprisonment, contrary to expectation, "has actually resulted in the progress of [*prokopē*] the Gospel" (Phil 1:12). *Prokopē* is used once more in Philippians 1:25. Even in jail, Paul's life serves as gain for the gospel and others; it is an entirely decentered understanding of the self. Second, this effect of advancement is construed as an explicit result of his imprisonment as "for Christ" (Phil 1:13). The cause of his imprisonment is relayed by the phrase *en Christō*, which is usually translated "in Christ." Here, it signifies cause rather than the typical sense of participation, although the latter cannot be ruled out in view of Philippians 2:6-8 and the call to adopt Christ's mindset in Philippians 2:5. The word for "imprisonment" or "chains" (*desmos*), already used in Philippians 1:7, occurs three times in this section (Phil 1:13, 14, 17). Imprisonment equates to shame in any culture, past or modern, as it implies moral culpability. Yet, what is culturally shameful becomes the occasion for honor and advancement (cf. Phil 2:6-11). That Paul is imprisoned, not because of any legal or moral infraction, but for the sake of Christ, becomes a well-known fact among the imperial guards and everyone else. Hence, the gospel is proclaimed as a *result* of Paul's imprisonment.

The second effect is also counterintuitive and coherent with the first. Logically, imprisonment would thwart further evangelism for fear of similar persecution. Instead, Paul states that his captivity has fueled "many" brothers with confidence in the Lord so that they boldly speak the word without fear (Phil 1:14). Risking dishonor or suffering for the sake of the gospel of Jesus Christ does not result in restraint, but in reverse, in escalation of evangelism. Significantly, it should be mentioned that the initial reason for Paul's arrest in Jerusalem, which ultimately ends in Rome, is that the gospel Paul proclaims is "*against* our people [of Israel], our law, and this place [temple]" along with the charge of bringing Gentiles into the temple (Acts 21:28, emphasis mine). Namely, Paul is charged with acts against his own people in his proclamation and inclusion of Gentiles. His incarceration is ethnically motivated for his own people *because* the gospel message proclaims salvation for all without distinction in terms of ethnicity, gender, or status apart from the law (Gal 3:28). As it will become clear below, the gospel nullifies old ethnic allegiances in order to reestablish a more enduring fealty of all ethnicities to Christ (cf. Phil 3:2-11).

In view of escalated proclamation by those emboldened by Paul's imprisonment, Paul observes not all do so out of good will (Phil 1:15-18). One group preaches Christ from "goodwill" (*eudokia*), "love" (*agapē*) and in "truth" (*alētheia*, Phil 1:15-18). Another group preaches Christ from "envy" (*phronos*), "rivalry" (*eris*), and "selfish ambition" (*eritheia*), "disingenuously" (*ouch hagnōs*) in order to stoke (further) affliction (*oiomenoi thlipsin egeirein*) for Paul in his imprisonment (Phil 1:15-17). These preach Christ in "false motives" (*propharis* Phil 1:18). These verses form a chiasm (ABB'A') to underscore the difference between the two groups. The first group is allied with Paul in his mission and suffering; they preach Christ, motivated by love and truth, to support his cause and plausibly risk sharing Paul's suffering (i.e., incarceration). Conversely, the second group preaches Christ in opposition to Paul. The characteristics of this group (vice list) provide a clear, contrasting portrait from the former; yet their precise identity and why Paul condones such tainted proclamation are unclear.

To their identity, some propose that they are Jewish Christians who insist on adherence to the law. However, such groups are thoroughly excoriated by Paul in Phil 3:2 and elsewhere (e.g., Gal 1:6-9; 2:11-14).[39] Or they may be Christians who proclaim Christ much like Paul (salvation by faith rather than law), but in competition to Paul as they are jealous of his success and prominence in the early church. The list of words that characterize this group are often found in Pauline vice lists (cf. Gal 5:19-21; 1 Tim 6:4-5). As such they represent behavior Paul definitively rejects (cf. Rom 1:29; 13:13; 2 Cor 12:20; Titus 3:9) as they reflect the mindset of the flesh (1 Cor 3:3) and not of Christ. Of the words describing this group, one word "selfish ambition" (*eritheia*), a cognate of "rivalry" (*eris*), appears once again in Philippians 2:3, as one of the characteristics Paul proscribes.[40]

Then how can Paul be so generous to this group, who evidently exhibit un-Christlike character? In contrasting this group with the other, clearly Paul does not blindly excuse motives of jealousy and malice. Nor does he state that the outcome of such tainted proclamation renders glory to God, especially, in view of Philippians 2:1-11 (and possibly Phil 3:18-19; also cf. 1 Cor 3:10-15). Rather, the purpose of this section is to convey to the Philippians *his own response* to such rivalry—he refuses to be goaded into participation in their petty, personal feud. Rather, he chooses to "rejoice" in the fact that Christ is proclaimed (Phil 1:18). In such a way, his generosity, composure, and joy function as an illustration of Paul's own conformity to Christ's mindset exhorted in Philippians 2:1-8, even in extreme situations. In turn, Paul's ungrudging will has a rhetorical force for whatever contention may exist between Euodia and Syntyche in Philippians 4:2-3.

Typically, for most, joy is a circumstantial emotion tied to external events and passively received ("something that happens to us"). For Paul, it is an act of will, regardless of life's situation. Paul launches the next section, beginning in the second part of v. 18 to v. 26, with the repetition of joy: "I will continue to rejoice" (*charēsomai* 1:18) and concludes with joy in Philippians 1:25. He provides three reasons for his joy.

First, even in the midst of captivity that may lead to death, he is not alone. He has the support and prayers of fellow believers, who actively love him by sending an agent to convey their hearts (Phil 1:19; Epaphroditus, Phil 2:25; 4:18). Second, God has not abandoned him; the Spirit of Jesus Christ actively assists him in his humiliating situation. Third, the succor of both the Philippians and Spirit of Christ provide Paul hope, not so much for release, but for honor and glory to Christ, whether by life or death (Phil 1:19-20). Given his willingness to accept either outcome of life or death in Philippians 1:20-21, "deliverance" (*sōtēria*) in Philippians 1:19 cannot mean "release" from prison. With the help of the Philippians' prayers and support, with the help of the Holy Spirit, Paul determines "deliverance," that is, further testimony to Christ will certainly be the result. What matters to Paul is not bodily existence, but whether by life or by death, the singular faith in and faithfulness to Christ. To wit, Paul's only concern is the proclamation of salvation without ethnic distinction for all, with perfect fellowship of all persons without ethnic distinction, and with God. This sublime singularity of faith edifies and exhorts the Philippians as well as modern-day believers to reorient their lives to boldly magnify

[39]Cf. Bockmuehl, *Philippians*, 77-78, for further discussion.

[40]*Eris* also appears in 1 Cor 1:11, where Paul addresses the issue of factionalism. The root issue of rivalry may be the same in the Philippian church (Phil 1:15-18 and 2:3), however, given Paul's irenic tone in Philippians the issue may be minor in comparison to the one in the Corinthian church.

(*megalynō* Phil 1:20) Christ exclusively, knowing that such faith does not lead to shame. Certain in God's faithfulness and sovereignty in this purpose, Paul rejoices.

In Philippians 1:22-26, Paul shifts the focus from his own concerns to that of the Philippians. Given the choice of life and death, Paul prefers death as it means he will be with Christ. As such, death is the far superior choice (Phil 1:22), thus gain (Phil 1:21). But bodily existence (life) means continuation of faithful testimony to Christ with further conversions and growth among the converts ("fruitful labor" Phil 1:22); hence, Christ is magnified ("to live is Christ" Phil 1:21). For the sake of the Philippians, Paul's continued existence signifies continued ministry with them, which leads to further progress (*protokē*), joy in their faith (Phil 1:25) and glory in Christ (Phil 1:26). Paul's choice between life and death is not self-centered, but wholly motivated by others' needs. Whether in context of imprisonment or ministry to the Philippians, Paul's motivation is not self-benefit, but that of both God and the Philippians. Thus, Paul's living presence with the Philippians ("in me" *en emoi*) will ensure their "boast" (*to kauchēma*) in Christ Jesus will abound (Phil 1:26; cf. 2:16). In such wholehearted selflessness, Paul anticipates both progress and joy of faith among the Philippians.

EXHORTATION FOR WORTHY CONDUCT OF THE GOSPEL (PHILIPPIANS 1:27-30)

These verses naturally form two discrete sections of exhortation: Philippians 1:27-30 and 2:1-5. Of twenty-five commands (imperatives) in Philippians, the first occurs in Philippians 1:27. There is a small interpretive difficulty in this section; namely, that with Philippians 1:27-30. Paul turns from his own affair to address the particular context of persecution and suffering of the Philippians from without. Along this line, "opponents" (*tōn antikeimenōn*) in Philippians 1:28 may have a specific referent. Undoubtedly, the Philippians are familiar with suffering, as Paul states that "during a severe ordeal of affliction" (*en pollē dokimē thlipseōs*), both their "abundant joy" (*hē perisseia tēs charas autōn*) and their "extreme poverty" (*hē kata bathous ptōcheia autōn*) lead to generosity for others (2 Cor 8:2). Moreover, suffering was neither rare nor sporadic, but pervasive for Christians in the New Testament (Mt 10:22; 24:9; Mk 13:13; Lk 21:17; Heb 10:32-34; 1 Pet 2:13-3:6; alienation from homeland, 1 Pet 1:1; 2:11; cf. also Acts).

Yet, apart from addressing the issue of the Philippians' struggle against the unbelieving world, there is no further detail to suggest that Paul addresses a specific situation. Moreover, the adverbial "only" (*monos* Phil 1:27) standing at the head of the verse most certainly gives weight to what follows, but cannot be seen as a new section from the preceding without the usual markers of either "now" (*de*) or "therefore" (inferential *oun*). Rather, it stands in parallel to Paul's pedagogical desire for the Philippians already conveyed in Philippians 1:6, 9-10, and 25. Indeed, Paul's role as champion for the Philippians' progress and joy in faith as long as he lives (Phil 1:25) begins (in terms of the letter) in Philippians 1:27 while absent from them. This structural coherence to the immediately preceding verses is validated by the fact that the exhortation in Philippians 1:27-29 is thematically parallel to Paul's own disposition in his incarceration described in Philippians 1:12-26, as Philippians 1:29-30 clarifies: "For he has graciously granted you the privilege not only of believing in Christ but of suffering for him as well, since you are having the same struggle that you saw I had and now hear that I still have."

Paul's first imperative for the Philippians is to be a united force against their opponents, contending for the faith of the gospel without fear—this is their singular (*monon*) objective. This mandate is fleshed out further with the following components. First, unity without fear spells out what "live your life in a manner worthy of the gospel of Christ" means. A life disposition that cohesively testifies to faith in Christ and the salvation he offers is not a lackadaisical attitude of "do what you can," but one that actively seeks to shine light, through our acts and mindset, to the inestimable worth of the gospel. This sense is highlighted by the use of *politeuomai*, which means "to live as citizens" (Phil 1:27) and not simply "to live one's life" as often rendered in English. Further, the concept of citizenship (*politeuma*) is reiterated in Philippians 3:20. "To live as a citizen" is to be read with specific reference to Roman citizenship, which affords legal privilege and elite social status to the citizen; it comes with prerogatives *and* necessary duty that reflects and brings honor and glory of the city. *Politeuomai* would readily be understood by those Philippians who held the honor of Roman citizenship. If Roman citizenship required a lifestyle of honor and glory for Rome, then how much more is necessary for a heavenly citizenship to the Lord, Jesus Christ? The conduct of heavenly citizenship is a constant lifestyle regardless of Paul's presence (Phil 1:27). There is no space for a duplicitous lifestyle with respect to believers' citizenry to impress prominent leaders. Rather, as Paul has demonstrated in Philippians 1:12-26 (cf. also Phil 1:2-11), the Philippians' primary goal as believers is to live a life worthy of the gospel so that, like Paul, whether free or jailed, whether in life or in death, the gospel of Jesus Christ is proclaimed with honor.

Second, one of the duties of citizenship is the defense of that empire (or country). Again, this is a concept familiar in Philippi, which was originally established with retired soldiers. In the secular world, regardless of various internal conflicts, in war, the citizens of respective countries must be a united front—otherwise, they court inevitable defeat. Likewise, if the Philippians are to contend successfully with enemies of faith, they must do so with "one spirit" and "one mind" (*en heni pneumati, mia psychē*); they do not fight individually, but in cooperation: "striving side by side" (*synathlountes*, *syn-* compound verb signifying cooperation). Internal unity, rather than armament, is the Philippians' weapon. Again, in the matter of unity, Paul has already provided a model in himself in Philippians 1:12-26. He is united with the Philippians and holds their benefit above his own. Still, he seeks ways to be united even with those who pit themselves against him.

Finally, despite the unceasing, merciless, and overwhelming intimidation of opponents, the Philippians are to resist without fear (Phil 1:28). God is the one who is at work in the Philippians' salvation life (Phil 1:6) and the reason for Paul's unwavering confidence of "deliverance" that will result in the exaltation of Christ either through life or death (Phil 1:19-20). Similarly, the Philippians are to rely on God's sovereignty in their lives as they face persecution from the world. "This" (*touto*) in Philippians 1:28 refers to all the components mentioned above (lives worthy of heavenly citizenship, internal unity, contending for the faith, and fearlessness). All these aspects of faith actively demonstrated will be a sign from God of the unbelievers' destruction, which in turn is salvation for the Philippians. At this point, Paul is not specifically forecasting an apocalypse for unbelievers in the sense of Revelation. Rather, he is pointing to the fact that if the Philippians adopt the mindset outlined in Philippians 1:27-28, they epitomize and therefore testify to salvation in Jesus Christ. Any opposition to this is already judged for destruction, especially, in light of Philippians 2:6-11; 3:18-19. Despite the constant oppression and what may appear to be defeat, victory has already been secured in the cross. As citizens of heaven, they must live in the certainty of this victory—fearlessly.

This section concludes with the rationale that drives the imperatives in Philippians 1:27-28. The critical word in Philippians 1:29 "it has been graced" (*echaristhē*),[41] is a cognate of the more familiar term "grace" (*charis*) and used once more in Philippians 2:9. "Grace" carries the theological sense of God's redemption of sinners apart from any works (e.g., Rom 3:24; Eph 2:5). *Echaristhē* frames suffering on behalf of Christ as not a burdensome onus, but as part and parcel of grace, namely, redemption from God. Such an understanding of "grace" subverts the all too common tendency to erode faith in Christ into cheap grace without full participation in Christ. Jesus himself defines discipleship in his name as one conformed to his own sufferings (Mk 8:34; cf. also Mt 10:38; Lk 9:23; 14:27). Receiving grace from God through faith in Jesus Christ comes with the mandate "to suffer" (*paschō*) "on behalf of him/ Christ" (*hyper autou*). *Paschō* is predominantly used for Christ's sufferings on the cross in the Gospels and intimates full rather than limited participation in Christ. The phrase "on behalf of Christ" (*hyper Christou*) has a definite article (*to*) and stands at the head of the verse, which turns the phrase into the subject of *echaristhē*: "The on behalf of Christ has been graced to you." The phrase "on behalf of him" (*hyper autou*) is repeated at the end for emphasis with clarification that ties "to suffer" (*to . . . paschein*) to the phrase. The preposition "on behalf" (*hyper*) in reference to Christ's death signifies substitutionary death—that is, Christ dies in place of all sinful humanity (Jn 11:50; Gal 3:13; 2 Cor 5:14); and in this substitution, of course, Christ represents sinful people.[42] In Philippians 1:29, however, the phrase does not signify substitution, but representation. Participation in Christ's suffering is how believers contend for their faith, that is, giving testimony of their salvation in Christ to the unbelieving world. In such exhaustive participation in their salvation ("in Christ"), believers are wholly aligned with their Lord, Jesus Christ, and with Paul (Phil 1:30). Apart from this complete engagement in salvation, there is no partnership. Just as Paul is an advocate for the gospel and the Philippians in every way, Paul calls the Philippians to join him in a fully committed partnership that shares in the sufferings of Christ.

EXHORTATION FOR INTERNAL UNITY AND HUMILITY (PHILIPPIANS 2:1-5)

The new section is marked by the first use of the inferential conjunction "therefore" (*oun*) in the letter and signifies that the imperative that follows in Philippians 2:1-5 is built on what Paul has already conveyed in Philippians 1:27-30. These verses provide specificity to "one spirit" and "one mind" in Philippians 1:27. Philippians 2:1 is a fourfold repetition of "if" (*ei*), a conditional particle in a first-class conditional clause; it signifies the assumption of truth, in this instance, reality. The only variance in the four clauses are the corresponding predicates: "encouragement" (*paraklēsis*) in Christ; "consolation" (*paramythion*) of love; "sharing" (*koinōnia*) of the Spirit; "compassion and sympathy" (*splanchna kai oiktirmoi*). The last clause is distinct from the previous three in that it provides two predicates without further modification.[43] This fourfold repetition of similar construction has the rhetorical effect of

[41]NRSV translation "he has graciously granted" does not account for the passive voice.

[42]Cf. Daniel B. Wallace, *Greek Grammar Beyond the Basics* (Grand Rapids, MI: Zondervan, 1997), 383.

[43]Cf. Moisés Silva, *Philippians*, BECNT, 2nd ed. (Grand Rapids, MI: Baker Academic, 2005), 90-91, who reads the phrase "compassion and sympathy" as a hendiadys "compassionate mercy."

forceful emphasis that ultimately hammers in the question: Are you saved?

The second half of an "if . . . then" construction appears in Philippians 2:2 with an imperative.[44] If indeed, the Philippians have experiential knowledge of salvation goodness, then Paul commands them to complete his joy. The "so that" (*hina*) clause explains what Paul means by "make my joy complete:" it is "of one mind" (*to auto phronēte*). The remaining clauses in Philippians 2:2-4 provide further details on this necessary singular mindset, which is coherent with salvation. First, this prototypical disposition is firmly tied to love. As the rest of the points in this section will demonstrate, the mindset in view is not an individual's integrity, apart from, but juxtaposed to interpersonal relations. Indeed, Paul commands not only to be "of one mind," but also "[to have] the same love." In other words, they are to be "in full accord and of one mind" (*sympsychoi, to hen phronountes*, Phil 2:2). There is clear emphasis on the need for a single mindset through the repetition of "same" (identical function of *autos*) and the use of "one" (*to hen*). Divergence from this particular mindset (cf. Phil 2:6-8) is counterproductive and deleterious to the unity of believers. The importance of this mindset or disposition is also emphatic in the repetition of the verb "to think" in the verse: "be of the same mind" (*to auto phronēte*) and "of one mind" (*to hen phronountes*). Full participation in this one mindset is expressed by *sympsychoi*, a *sun*-compound word translated as "united in spirit, harmonious, in full accord."

Philippians 2:3-4 reveals how love factors into Paul's command for a united, singular mindset. Unity in mindset and love excludes the following characteristic and behavior: "selfish ambition, rivalry" (*eritheian*, cf. Phil 1:15), and "vainglory, conceit" (*kenodoxian*). The mindset of selfishness, rivalry, and self-glory are not neutral facets of individuals, but antithetical and noxious behavior that divides rather than solidifies believers. The mindset coherent to salvation, the call to unity in the same mindset and love is humility—a mindset that considers others as more significant than the self. The word "humility" is a compound word "lowly mindset" (*tapeinophrosynē*) and introduces the concept of humility that is applied to Christ in Philippians 2:8 (*tapeinoō*) and the sense of humiliation in Philippians 4:12 and 3:21 (*tapeinoō* and *tapeinōsis*). The word translated "those more significant" is derived from *hyperechō*, which means "to have power or authority" and can be used to denote "excellence, greatness"; it is used two more times in the letter to signify the superiority of something over and against the other (Phil 3:8; 4:7). The translation "more significant" diminishes the sense of superior worth based on the power or authority held. The thrust of the word and the phrase is to consider others in the esteem and trepidation that we naturally have for those in positions of power and authority. The common disposition of a faithful community is the renunciation of hubris and egotism, and the embrace of authentic humility that leads to an honorable estimation and treatment of others. Humility does not signify absence of self-concern, but inclusion of other's interests, as Philippians 2:4 clearly states.

However, the natural inclination to diminish conformity to authentic humility, the absence of hubris, and find solace in Philippians 2:4, must ultimately reckon with Christ's utter relinquishment of his own rights and interest, as Philippians 2:5 firmly anchors the exhortation to the paradigm of Christ's mindset. The critical word "to think" (*phroneō*) appears again in Philippians 2:5 to connect and

[44]Notably, out of twenty-five imperatives, only three are aorist (Phil 2:2; 4:4, 21), while the rest are present.

reinforce the exhortation in Philippians 2:2: "Let the same mind be in you that was in Christ Jesus" (*ho kai en Christō Iēsou*). As the final phrase is verbless, there are two interpretive options. First, if "to be" is implied, then the verse highlights *imitatio Christi*. Just as Christ demonstrates profound humility and self-sacrifice, the Philippians should conform to Christ's model disposition; many English translations adopt this view. The second option highlights the soteriology of Philippians 2:6-8 as the capacity to renounce the sin of egotism (Phil 2:3), which is only possible through the salvation achieved by Christ. Such sense is evident in the ESV translation: "Have this mind among yourselves, which is yours in Christ Jesus." This requires an insertion of "yours" (*hymōn*) or "you have" (*echete*), which is more cumbersome than the simple "to be," but not implausible. As will become clear in the next section, the two options are not mutually exclusive, but held in tandem.

The call to unity in Philippians 2:1-4 is the prevailing exhortation in the letter. In the Greco-Roman world, "humility" (*tapeinos* word group) is predominantly negative ("lowly," "weak," or "servile") and the verb "to humble" is "to weaken," "to humiliate," "to oppress," and "to exploit."[45] W. Grundmann states, "The Greek concept of free man leads to contempt for lack of freedom and subjection."[46] In this cultural context, Paul's call to adopt humility as a life disposition in Christ challenges the Philippians to choose between the secular and Christian norm. To adopt Christ's mindset guarantees that the Philippians will invite further revulsion and mockery from fellow citizens of Philippi. Hence, the humility of Christ is hardly the clever evangelistic strategy that seeks shared values with the secular culture as common in modern times, as humility is not a shared value between the redeemed and unredeemed in the first century. The testimony to the unbelieving world that Paul routinely practices and advocates the Philippians to enact is radically cross-centered and gives testimony exclusively to the revelation of God in the cross (Phil 3:2-9; also cf. 1 Cor 1:17–2:5). Christ in victory and the glory of the resurrection has no meaning apart from Christ in humiliation and the weakness of the cross. The testimony of believers must be centered on the cross and all its horrific implications.

The cultural rejection of humility is still prevalent in the modern day, albeit on a slightly different rationale. Our culture, addicted to self-promotion, self-health, and promotion of individual rights as remedy for insecurities, loss of identity, personal and corporate victimization (due to race, gender, social status, etc.), rejects the call to humility, self-sacrifice, and submission to others as an oppressive exacerbation of a diminished and suffering selfhood. Accordingly, the call to take up the cross and adopt the mindset of Christ stands antithetical to human flourishing. The solution proffered in this perspective derives from secular culture and co-opts the gospel message, which now distorted, offers no benefits of salvation (Phil 2:1) nor resurrection power in Christ-formed unity (Phil 2:2-4). As it will become clear in Philippians 2:6-11 and 3:2-21, the confidence for those who follow the way of the cross exceeds any humanly conceived solution, as confidence ultimately flows from God's revelation and good pleasure. Current preoccupation with the self also suffers from astounding myopia as it dismisses the rich history of the various forms of suffering endured by the faithful in the Old Testament (cf. Heb 11), Jesus Christ (Mt 26:1–27:54;

[45]Cf. W. Grundmann, "ταπεινός," *TDNT* 8:1-26, esp. 1-5.

[46]Grundmann, "ταπεινός," 11. Cf. also E.-M. Becker, *Paul on Humility*, trans. W. Coppins (Waco, TX: Baylor University Press, 2020), 24-26.

Mk 14:1–15:39; Lk 22:1–23:47; Jn 18:1–19:37), the apostles (Acts), as well as early believers (e.g., 2 Cor 8:2; 1 Thess 1:6; 2:14; 2 Thess 1:4; Heb 10:32-34; 1 Pet 1:6; 4:12; 5:10). The solution to the diminished self must be anchored to salvation in both the benefits and obligations. Finally, unity as described in Philippians 2:1-4 exceeds the accord that may be found apart from faith or that formed by preservation of individual rights. It describes self-sacrificing love as demonstrated by Christ (Phil 2:6-8) offered to all regardless of all worldly social constructions of race, gender, and social status. It offers salvific healing and reflects the unity of the triune God. These issues briefly addressed here will gain further amplification in the next section.

THE MODEL OF CHRIST AND GOD'S RESPONSE (PHILIPPIANS 2:6-11)

Two historical-critical issues with a long history need a brief address prior to examining the passage and its theological implications: (1) Philippians 2:6-11 as a New Testament "Christ Hymn"; and (2) the soteriological-ethical divide.[47] First, Philippians 2:6-11 (along with Col 1:15-20 and 1 Tim 3:16) has long been deemed as a "hymn" by scholars and laity—that is, it is one example of a hymn employed in ecclesial worship in the first century. Several literary features are isolated as markers of a hymn: it is a self-standing unit, it begins with *hos* ("who"), and it contains anomalous or unusual grammar/vocabulary. Yet, none of these features are uniquely *hymnic*, but typical features of the New Testament. This issue moves beyond proper nomenclature to arguments for "preexistence" of the passage prior to Philippians. Again, such theories are mere speculation without hard evidence and by the fact that the passage is thoroughly coherent to the surrounding passages without any hint of displacement.

Second, while the ethics of a believing community is clearly the focus in Philippians 2:1-4, the description of Christ in Philippians 2:6-11 is indisputably relayed in the framework of salvation events—it moves through Christ's preexistence, incarnation, crucifixion, and exaltation. Thus, Philippians 2:6-11 relates salvation events and the hinge verse of Philippians 2:5 should be rendered, "Let the same mind be in you that was in Christ Jesus." The ethics commended in Philippians 2:1-2, 4 stand in contrast to sin in Philippians 2:3, which has been effectively put to death by Christ on the cross. Further, it is argued that Christ's mindset and actions in salvation events, as well as God's response to Christ, can hardly be seen as features that can be imitated by humans. Indeed, preexistence, incarnation, expansive atonement for all humanity, and total supremacy in all dimensions of life (heaven, earth, and underneath the earth) are particular to divinity rather than humanity. Yet these features are decidedly not in view in Philippians 2:5—the call to conformity is tethered to one aspect, that is, Christ's mindset. The apprehension against interpreting Christ as mere "moral teacher" apart from salvation is unfounded, as the basis of the exhortation in Philippians 2:1 and 2:12 clearly anchors the ethical exhortation in Philippians 2:2-5 to salvation. Salvation and corresponding ethics are not mutually exclusive, but the latter is the necessary consequence of the former. The fact that the profound humility and selflessness of Philippians 2:2-4 can only be a reality for the redeemed may be the reason why Paul describes

[47]For further details on these arguments, cf. M. Sydney Park, *Submission Within the Godhead and the Church in the Epistle to the Philippians: An Exegetical and Theological Examination of the Concept of Submission in Philippians 2 and 3* (London: T&T Clark, 2007), 10-37.

Christ and his redeeming work in terms of the same mindset.

Philippians 2:6-8 are unique in the New Testament in its elaboration of the impetus in salvation events. Often, the rationale for God's salvation in Scripture is his love for his people, whether Israel or all of humanity (e.g., Deut 4:37; 7:8; Jer 31:3; Jn 3:16; Rom 5:8; Eph 2:4; Titus 3:4; 1 Jn 4:9-10), which is decidedly absent in Philippians 2:6-8. Specifically, the mindset at work in the salvation of humanity begins with the Son's relationship with God the Father. Coherently, Philippians 2:6 describes Christ's preexistence, in keeping with John 1:1-4. Yet, in relaying Christ's mindset in terms of his relationship with the Father, operative in preexistence, Paul relates entirely unique information in Scripture. *Although* Christ was in the form (*morphē*) of God, he did not consider (*ēgeomai*) equality with God as something to take advantage of (*harpagmos*). First, "form" does not indicate that Christ's divinity vis-à-vis the Father was inferior in essence. As the end of the clause indicates, Christ had equality with God (*to einai isa theō*). The word "form" is used to highlight the extreme contrast in the "form of a slave" in Philippians 2:7. The most difficult word is *harpagmos*, which is only used here in the New Testament, but the verb (*harpazō*) conveys the sense of "taking hold of something violently" (e.g., Mt 11:12; Jn 6:15; Acts 23:10). Historically, there are two options: (1) either Christ did not think "to reach out and grasp" at equality with God, which he did not have; or (2) Christ did not think "to strenuously retain" his equality with God already in possession. The usage of *harpagmos* in conjunction with *ēgeomai* ("to consider") in Greek literature demonstrates another possibility proposed by R. W. Hoover. First, it indicates the sense of "taking advantage of something" rather than "grasping something violently." Second, it indicates that what is taken advantage of is something already at one's disposal.[48] Consequently, the thrust of Philippians 2:6 in conjunction with Philippians 2:7 states that while Christ is equal in divine identity and status with God the Father, he did not consider his equality as the occasion to promote his equality but emptied himself.

The term "he emptied" (*ekenōsen*) in Philippians 2:7 does not convey loss of divine identity, as it is modified by the phrase "by taking the form of a slave." It speaks to the uttermost contrast between "form of God" and "form of slave." As the parallelism of the remaining two phrases in the verse indicate, "form of a slave" is not a literal but metaphorical reference to Christ's incarnation: "being born in the likeness of man; and being found in human form." In the parallel, two notions are emphasized. The synonyms "likeness" (*homoiōmati*) and "shape" (*schēmati*) further elaborate "form" (*morphēn*). Likewise, "human" or "mankind" (*anthrōpos*) is repeated to emphasize Christ's human existence—he is fully human.

The primary force of the contrast in Philippians 2:7 vis-à-vis Philippians 2:6 is that becoming human is an act of not only humility but humiliation. It is not an indication of Platonic division between what is spiritual versus material; rather, it speaks to the extreme contrast of status. Divinity and humanity represent extreme ends of status and identity. God not only has complete agency over himself, but absolute sovereignty over all of his creation; by contrast a slave has no agency, even over his own body, but wholly submits to the will of another. God is in full glory, honor, and power, while the slave is powerless, humiliated, and treated with contempt. Christ in equality with God, in full honor, glory, and power, does not consider his divine identity and status in relation to the Father as

[48]R. W. Hoover, "The HARPAGMOS Enigma: A Philological Solution," *HTR* 64 (1961): 95-119.

the reason to promote his own rights and privilege. *But* he empties himself by becoming human. Christ's humility continues a downward spiral in Philippians 2:8. The mindset of self-emptying is so complete that he obeys to the utter extremity of death, even a death characterized wholly by humiliation—death on a cross. To be God is to be eternal whereas death only applies to creation after the fall (Gen 2:17). But the contrast of Philippians 2:8 is not simply between divinity and humanity, but between God and slave. "Form of a slave" in Philippians 2:7 is echoed in the crucifixion as it is a death allocated only to slaves and criminals.

The reversal to the descent from divinity to the lowest form of humanity comes in Philippians 2:9-11. The reversal is obviously not by human agency, nor by any human remorse of disciples, nor the authorities (Jewish and Roman) who executed the death sentence—there is no true remedy humans can effect for the certain finitude of death. The definitive panacea to death can only come from God the Father; yet note that there is no mention of the resurrection in Philippians 2:9-11. Just as Philippians 2:6-8 was framed in terms of Christ's mindset and actions, Philippians 2:9-11 is constructed as God's analogous response. Here in Philippians 2:9, God's exaltation of Christ is solely based on Christ's self-emptying mindset and actions in Philippians 2:6-8: "therefore" (*dio*) is inferential—it draws up conclusions to what has preceded in Philippians 2:6-8. God *approves* Christ's interpretation of his equality with God as the correct understanding of what it means to be God. In his self-emptying, humility, obedience to humiliating death, Christ *reveals* God's character.[49]

In response, God exalts him to the highest point by giving ("gracing," *echarisato*; cf. Phil 1:29) him "the name that is above every name." Such a name can only be YHWH, God's own name, what God avows to never give to another (Is 42:8; 48:11). In the Old Testament, a name conveys not only the identity of the person but the totality of the person. With respect to God, his name conveys all his glory and honor (Is 48:11). And Philippians 2:10 confirms that this name is "Jesus." In giving his own name to Christ, God confirms that Christ's mindset and actions in Philippians 2:6-8 divulge God's character to the world—God who loves at the risk of humility, humiliation, and death—and simultaneously confirms Jesus as Son of God. God's honor and glory bestowed to Christ is all-extensive in its sovereignty as every being in all three dimensions of the world, whether living or dead, whether human or angelic, submits and confesses that Jesus Christ is Lord (Phil 2:10-11). The confession that Jesus Christ is Lord is given even by human and spiritual enemies as demons in the Gospels fully recognize that Jesus Christ is the Son of God despite their rebellion (e.g., Mt 8:29; Mk 1:24; 3:11; 5:7; Lk 4:41; 8:28; and the temptation accounts in Mt 4:3, 5; Lk 4:3, 9).

God the Father responds in kind to Christ's self-emptying mindset and actions. And gracing the Son with his own glory, honor, and sovereignty, does not divest the Father of his glory, but fully redounds to his glory. The perfect inner unity within the Godhead, as expressed by both the Son and the Father, is indeed love, one that is not simply emotions, but comprises the same selfless mindset and actions toward the other. This divine love shared by the Father and the Son is what is revealed for humanity in the salvation events from incarnation to exaltation.

Three conclusions can be drawn from Philippians 2:6-11 in addition to the remarks already made in Philippians 2:1-5. First, Paul has intentionally described Christ's extreme

[49]Cf. N. T. Wright, *The Climax of the Covenant: Christ and the Law in Pauline Theology* (Edinburgh: T&T Clark, 1991), 97.

humility in terms of salvation events as evident in the fact that resurrection has been eclipsed by exaltation. Exaltation, which must include resurrection, serves Paul's purpose of underscoring God's approval in parallel extremity to Christ in Philippians 2:6-8. Christ's mindset and actions of profound selflessness, which embrace loss of status to endmost humiliation of the cross, are the very mindset that leads to salvation for all, including the Philippians and Paul. Christ's disposition to "consider" the other as superior with honor and to give mind to "the things of others" is *salvific*. Namely, it is how the Philippians are saved. If indeed, the Philippians are saved (Phil 2:1) by Christ's self-renouncement, then they must adopt the same mindset as living proof of their salvation within the body of Christ. If indeed, the Philippians are saved, then they must live according to the mindset, which God has resoundingly approved (Phil 2:9-11)—for what is the point of salvation, if not to stand in God's good pleasure? *This* is their testimony of salvation to the unbelieving world. The mindset exhorted in Philippians 2:2-5 is not merely coherent with salvation; it is the daily perpetuation of salvation within the body of Christ for the salvation of others.

Second, as Christ's actions are matched by God's own supreme response to his Son, it is revealed that the mindset of Christ is precisely the definition of what it means to be equal with God. This divine internal relationship is utterly singular, as evident throughout history and today, equal rights for sinful humanity inevitably means exploitation and abuse of the other. One's own rights always prevail over others' and the preservation of self is a matter of existential crisis. Christ maintains his concern for the other even in the face of humiliation and death. Indeed, this mindset is the modus operandi of both the Father and the Son. Hence, only perfect unity exists within the Godhead based on the mutual volition "to consider the things of others" as more supreme. The exhortation in Philippians 2:2-5 is a call for the church to participate in this divine inner relationship as all barriers between the Holy God and sinful humanity are conclusively eradicated (cf. Eph 2:18; 3:12; Heb 10:19-22).

Within this framework of trinitarian relations, the key word "slave," first self-appropriated by Paul (Phil 1:1) and applied to Christ (Phil 2:7) can be further explored. As already elaborated above, the Philippian congregation would comprise some slaves, who represent the lowest, most despised status among humans. That "slave" is appropriated to both Paul and Christ (the only two times *doulos* appears in the letter) should not offend but elevate and give comfort to the slaves. Both Paul, their human shepherd, and Christ, the Great Shepherd, perceive their respective roles as slaves rather than self-aggrandizing authoritarian masters. And for both, neither their agency nor power is eradicated in their adoption of a slave mindset. The status of slave, so despised in culture, is inverted and redefined by not only the examples of Paul and Christ, but by God's overwhelming approval. Further, as the exhortation in Philippians 2:2-5 applies to all, slaves are not exempt in being treated with the honor and dignity of one in authority by the free.

The mindset and actions of Christ as slave upheld as the paragon for the free within the congregation has a forceful conviction for reform. Simultaneously, as Christ the Son of God volitionally adopted the identity of a slave on their behalf, the slaves must necessarily treat the free, as well as other slaves, with the same humility, no longer by law, but by the grace of salvation and their own agency. As both the free and slave adopt Christ's mindset of selflessness and sacrifice, the vision of the reconciliation of the cross truly takes effect and finally operates on the fact that old barriers of social division have been crucified.

Finally, the ethnic dimension requires a brief word based on the previous two points. Further elaboration on ethnicity will be made in Philippians 3:2-11. The fact that Paul is a *Jewish* apostle (as most New Testament apostles) cannot be underscored enough, in view of the content of exhortation to a congregation of mostly Gentiles. In view of his ethnic heritage of slavery and oppression and recent history of ethnic prejudice in Philippi, Paul shows no inhibition to embrace the humble, humiliating role of a slave with respect to God and the Philippians. Namely, there are no trigger points for offense *because* the heritage of wretched suffering and enmity has been crucified; they no longer define Paul as he is exclusively defined by Christ (Phil 3:2-11).

And by being wholly defined by Christ ("in Christ"), Paul participates in Christ's mindset and actions of a slave as he daily lives in self-sacrifice to God and the Philippians (Phil 1:12-26). His authority before the Philippians, as well as the rest of his converts, is entirely dependent on his consistent and exhaustive conformity to Christ. As it will become clear in the remainder of the letter, Paul is bold in his leadership; the "friendship" between them does not frustrate but emboldens his authority.

All the implications of Philippians 2:1-11 outlined above are chilling in the censure they level against modern-day churches, as the promises and exhortations of salvation apply with equal force and relevance for us as they did for the Philippians. Imagine what Sunday morning worship would be if all believers embraced Christ's humility, which risks humiliation and even death for the sake of the other. Imagine the unity of all races within the church, when such divine inner relations are operative. This is the promise and shape of racial reconciliation of the cross.

CONCLUDING EXHORTATION, TESTIMONY, AND FAITHFULNESS (PHILIPPIANS 2:12-18)

This section draws up concluding exhortations based on the preceding section with "therefore" (*ōste*). Given all the radical and difficult implications of the preceding exhortation, Paul begins his additional commands by calling them "beloved" (*agapētoi*) as reminder of the love between them, and significantly, of his love for them. The exhortation, no matter how devastating, is delivered because of love. Simultaneously, Paul does not hesitate to exercise his authority—he explicitly calls them to "obey" (*hypēkousate* only in Phil 2:12 in the letter). The mention of his presence and absence in Philippians 2:12 recalls the first exhortation in Philippians 1:27 to live as a citizen worthy of the gospel of Jesus Christ *by being of one spirit with one mind*. The repetition of his presence and absence in both verses functions as a bookend for the verses within. The content of worthy citizenry is specifically explained in Philippians 2:1-11. Further the phrase "live your life in a manner worthy of the gospel of Christ" in Philippians 1:27 stands in synonymous parallel to "work on your own salvation with fear and trembling" in Philippians 2:12. The command "to work on" (*katergazesthe*) does not convey that salvation is meritorious despite the fact that the verb is a cognate of "works" (*erga*), often used by Paul to renounce salvation by merit (cf. Rom and Gal). Undoubtedly, conformity to Christ's model in Philippians 2:6-8 will require sustained effort, but not as a means to earn salvation, but in view of its gracious bestowal from God. While the Philippians are to stand against opponents without fear, they are to embrace and embody their salvation with "fear and trembling" (*meta phobou kai tromou*). If God has truly begun the "good work" in Philippians in that they are saved (Phil 1:6), they will recognize that God is the one behind Paul's exhortation in Philippians 2:1-5 as God is actively effecting conviction and transformation toward the paradigm of Christ in Philippians 2:6-8—the paradigm that brought God great pleasure and glory (Phil 2:9-11). If there is any equivocation among the Philippians to give up their privilege and rights, they do so at the risk of God's displeasure and against his will and work already operative in them (Phil 2:13). The consequence of such resistance should cause "fear and trembling."

In coherence of the concept of trepidation in view of God's judgment, in Philippians 2:14 Paul uses another word used in the context of Israel's rebellion against God in the desert: "grumbling" (*gongysmōn*; cf. Ex 16 where the word is used five times; Num 17:20, 25). The second word "disputing" (*dialogismōn*) confirms the sense of rebellion. In Numbers 14:1-38 the Israelites who complained against God due to unbelief died by God's plague in the desert. To be sure, all those who lacked faith and consequently complained would not enter God's rest but die in the desert, apart from Joshua and Caleb (Num 14:38).[50] The type of complaint in view is not one that seeks understanding and clarification but one that sprouts from unbelief in God's faithful character and promises (cf. Heb 3:12-4:3; Jude 1:5).

In the call to avoid culpability in unbelief, Paul introduces the concept of testimony in Philippians 2:15. The exhorted blamelessness of the Philippians is set in contrast to the unbelieving and wicked culture of the secular world and is to function as testimony, "shining lights," against the dark backdrop of wickedness. While "crooked" (*skolias*) is used only once in Peter's sermon to describe the secular world (Acts 2:40), the word "crookedness" (*diestrammenēs*) also appears in the Gospels to describe wickedness that results from unbelief (Mt 17:17; Lk 9:41). The theme of testimony connects again back to Philippians 1:27 as they were called to stand in unity against their opponents, engaged in the same conflict that ensues from testifying to the gospel (Phil 1:28). The urgent call to avoid God's condemnation and to give testimony to the unbelieving world is firmly anchored to the conformity to Christ's mindset.

Much as a parent delights in the success of his children, the Philippians' obedience to Paul's strong commands in this section as well as the preceding has the purpose of producing joy and boast. The word for "boast" (*kauchēma*) was also used in Philippians 1:26: "so that I may share abundantly in your boasting [*to kauchēma hymōn*] in Christ Jesus." Likewise, the Philippians' obedience, approval from God, and their continued testimony to the world provide Paul with grounds for confidence before God—that he did not run/labor in vain. In the parallel between Philippians 2:16 and 1:26, there is mutuality of genuine investment between Paul and the Philippians. And in keeping with the self-sacrifice and responsibility of Paul already noted in Philippians 1, Paul explicitly describes his apostolic responsibility before God as one that is "poured out like a libation over the sacrifice and the offering of your faith." The words "sacrifice and offering" (*thysia kai leitourgia*) are used frequently in LXX to describe the Levitical sacrificial system (e.g., Num 15:8-10; 28–29). Here they are to be seen as a hendiadys and translated as "sacrificial service." The complex sentence conveys mutuality of sacrifice for both Paul and the Philippians. Paul's own life is sacrificed before God ("poured out") in order to offer up the Philippians' faith as a pleasing

[50]Cf. also Num 16:49, where 14,700 died in addition to 250 from Korah's rebellion; and Num 25:9, where 24,000 died.

sacrifice to God. Despite the adversity of such responsibility to God and his converts, Paul again chooses to rejoice. In keeping with the parallel to Philippians 1:12-30, the final verses (Phil 2:17-18) overflow with the will to rejoice as the verb "I rejoice" (*chairō*) is strengthened with the cognate "I rejoice with" (*synchairō*) at the end of Philippians 2:17 and then repeated in command form "you should rejoice" (*chairete*) and again emphasized with "you should rejoice with" (*synchairete*) in Philippians 2:18. Mutuality and coparticipation in joy as well as the formidable exhortation to adopt Christ's mindset is but a reflection of the mutual indwelling in the triune God.

CHRISTLIKE EXAMPLE OF TIMOTHY AND EPAPHRODITUS (PHILIPPIANS 2:19-30)

The remaining verses in Philippians 2 are naturally divided into two sections on Timothy (Phil 2:19-24) and Epaphroditus (Phil 2:25-30). The sections appear to be in essence a return to the discussion of Paul's affairs in relation to the Philippians. Yet, as it is evident in Philippians 1:12-26, the practical matters are shaped in coherence to the theological sections of the letter. And here, in relaying the message that he will send both Timothy and Epaphroditus to the Philippians, his description of both men ultimately serve to reinforce his exhortation in Philippians 2:1-5—they are models of Christ's mindset. Thus, the Philippians should receive them with honor.

Paul states that he will send Timothy soon for the purpose of hearing news of the Philippians, which will encourage him (Phil 2:19). His hope is that his own circumstances will allow him to send Timothy and that he will also visit them (Phil 2:24). In between these two sentences that relate logistics, Paul provides a brief yet targeted description of Timothy. Timothy plays a unique role in the apostle's life, as he is authentically concerned for the welfare of the Philippians (Phil 2:20). Timothy stands in contrast to "the many" who only seek self-interest rather than that of Jesus Christ (Phil 2:21). Clearly, Timothy already demonstrates the exhortation Paul directed in Philippians 2:3-4, as he will genuinely seek (*merimnēsei*) the interest of the Philippians. And concern for other believers is equated to prioritizing Christ's concerns. In Philippians 2:22, Paul states that the Philippians are already aware of Timothy's character as evident in his relationship with Paul. Timothy treats Paul as a son to a father—that is, with love, honor, and respect. Timothy does not deem himself as Paul's equal given that he fully participates in Paul's mission, much like Christ with respect to the Father. Further, Timothy "slaves" (*edouleusen*) with Paul for the purpose of the gospel. The word translated as "served" is not *diakoneō*, which is typically used to convey the act of service. Rather, it is *douleuō*, a cognate of *doulos*, meaning "I am subjected" or "I am a slave." This verb usually takes a dative for a direct object, "I am a slave *to someone*," but the direct object is missing in the verse. Instead, the Greek construction is "he slaves with me." The use of *douleuō* is an intentional link to the "form of slave" adopted by Christ in Philippians 2:7. Hence, in sending Timothy, Paul sends a model of conformity to Christ's humility, which in turn reinforces his exhortation in Philippians 2:1-14. As strenuous as conformity to Christ's mindset may be, Timothy is a living example, along with Paul (he slaves *with* Paul), that can be realized.

In Philippians 2:25-30, Paul turns to Epaphroditus. Clearly, there is much concern that Paul expresses concerning Epaphroditus as well as the Philippians because Epaphroditus almost died in representing the Philippians' love and service for Paul (Phil 2:27). Paul was anxious over Epaphroditus's illness, as believers should prioritize the concern of others (Phil 2:28).

Paul's marked relief in his healing (God's mercy), as well as the sorrow Paul would have felt in his death, is genuine love at work among believers. But Epaphroditus himself demonstrates selfless love as he also is distressed about the Philippians' concern over his health. There is a free-flowing devotion to the other between all three (Paul, Epaphroditus, and the Philippians) where concern for the other outweighs self-interest. In this passage, the love and concern of the Philippians for Paul first mentioned in Philippians 1:3-7 is reaffirmed; they sent Epaphroditus to serve Paul during his imprisonment.

Paul's description of Epaphroditus in Philippians 2:25, 29-30, again, reiterates the theological themes already outlined in the letter. Epaphroditus is described by five appositional nouns; the first three are in relation to Paul and the remaining two in relation to the Philippians. Paul states that he is "my brother [*adelphon*] and co-worker [*synergon*] and fellow solder [*systratiōtēn mou*]."[51] He begins with a familial term "brother" and adds two *syn*-compound words, "co-worker" and "fellow soldier," to emphasize the kind of participation that exists within the family. Epaphroditus is only mentioned in Philippians and there is no explicit description of his ministry, apart from his illness and his role as emissary to Paul. Whatever his activities may have been, as Paul gives full recognition of Epaphroditus as a coparticipant in the gospel, the theme of participation already evident in the previous chapters gains further emphasis. Paul's attitude is not that of elitism, but genuine consideration of others as his partners.

The two terms that describe Epaphroditus in relation to the Philippians are "your messenger [*hymōn . . . apostolon*] and minister" [*leitourgon*]. Again, Paul uses an unusual word for "messenger." In the New Testament, with respect to both spiritual and human messengers, "angel" (*angelos*) is used (Lk 7:24; 9:52; 2 Cor 12:7; Jas 2:25). "Apostle" (*apostolos*) in the New Testament predominantly carries the sense of authoritative agents of Jesus Christ with the commission of evangelism and pedagogy for the churches (cf. Mt 28:16-20; Eph 2:20; 4:11).[52] While *apostolos* appears most frequently in Paul, it is used in the sense of God's authorized agents rather than mere "messengers," apart from two instances: 2 Corinthians 8:23 and Philippians 2:25. In light of the fact that Paul replaced his usual identity as "apostle" with "slave," the fact that the only instance of "apostle" in Philippians is applied to Epaphroditus shows intent. Clearly, the term does not mean "apostle," but "messenger." However, that the typical term used to convey Paul's authoritative identity and status as God's agent is now applied to Epaphroditus could not be lost on the Philippians. As much as God the Father exalts the Son with his own status, name, and glory, Paul freely elevates Epaphroditus. The word "servant" (*leitourgon*) is a cognate of "service" (*leitourgia*), already used in reference to Paul's sacrifice and the Philippians' faith, which will be used again in Philippians 2:30 in reference to the Philippians' "service" to Paul. Epaphroditus's service on behalf of the Philippians to Paul would already require sacrifice of time, income, and energy, given the distance between Philippi and Rome. But due to illness, this "service" becomes "sacrifice" as he nearly died for the work of Christ. In his willingness to risk his life on behalf of both the Philippians and Paul, he mirrors Christ's extreme humility that extended to death on a cross. Hence, the Philippians are to

[51]The possessive pronoun "my' (*mou*) applies to all three nouns.

[52]*Apostolos* appears eighty times in the New Testament (twice in 1 Cor 15:9); once in Matthew; twice in Mark; six times in Luke; once in John; twenty-eight times in Acts; thirty-four times in Paul; five times in the General Epistles; and three times in Revelation.

receive him with all joy and honor, just as God the Father honored the Son.

The two models of Christ's mindset and actions not only reiterate the necessity of obeying Paul's exhortations in Philippians 2:1-14, but function as living examples testifying to the Philippians of the actual practice of Christ's humility and self-sacrifice, in hope that they might strive toward the actualization of Philippians 2:2-11 with full confidence.

RIGHTEOUSNESS BY FAITH IN CHRIST: POSITIVE EXAMPLE OF PAUL (PHILIPPIANS 3:1-11)

The entirety of Philippians 3 presents some difficulty for theological and structural coherence with what has preceded in the first two chapters. First, the beginning word "finally" (*to loipon*) is typically used in Paul's letters to signify a conclusion of a topic or the letter itself (2 Cor 13:11; Eph 6:10; 1 Thess 4:1; 2 Thess 3:1). "Finally" in Philippians 4:8 functions in this way as it concludes the letter and Paul discusses his own affair with final greetings. Here, however, Paul has not finished his theological discussion, given Philippians 3:2-21. Second, the subject of discussion in that passage prima facie appears to be an entirely separate discussion from the concerns addressed in the preceding chapters. Many seek to explain the sudden shift in topic as either a present threat among the Philippians from Jewish Christians advocating law observance, much like the churches of Galatia, or their threat is a trigger point for Paul, as he has vigorously refuted these opponents and/or their message in the past. Thus, he returns to his signature proclamation of "righteousness by faith" (Phil 3:9; cf. Galatians and Romans). For both these options the threefold imperatives in Philippians 3:2, "beware" (*blepete*), is translated as a warning, "look out" or "beware of." The presence of a threat also explains the tonal shift from a relatively harmonious and friendly style that reiterates the need for joy to what is a decisively impassioned and intolerant mode. The sharp denigration of enemies of the gospel in Philippians 3:2, 18-19 stands in obvious contrast to Paul's indulgence of preachers who still operate from a sinful mindset (Phil 1:15-17).

Yet, there are sufficient textual clues that point to another solution to these problems of incoherence. First, despite the anomalous usage of "finally," it may signify the conclusion of one aspect of the broader topic. In Philippians 2:1-11, as well as other supporting verses as I have outlined above, Paul presents the moral facet of salvation in Christ in order to fasten the mindset of humility and self-sacrifice to Christ, God, and specifically, to salvation events—the mindset advocated is not simply a "moral" virtue, but inextricably tied to salvation accomplished by the Triune God. In Philippians 3:2-11, Paul crystallizes the soteriological foundation for the moral presentation of salvation in Philippians 2:1-11, which he has already established in various ways. The rationale in Philippians 3:2-11 is not *imitatio Christi*, but righteousness by faith, which ultimately reinforces the exhortation of Philippians 2:1-5. This is evidence of an integrated perspective: a theology of "salvation by faith" is inextricably tied to praxis. As such, the statement, "To write the same things to you is not troublesome to me, and for you it is a source of steadfastness," in Philippians 3:1 indicates that what follows is a reinforcement of Philippians 1–2; "same things" (*ta auta*) does not refer to previously conveyed information, but what he has already written in the preceding. Philippians 3:1 essentially functions as a hinge between Philippians 1–2 and 3 with emphasis on Philippians 3 as the final point in his discussion. Second, the three imperatives at the head of Philippians 3:2 cannot be interpreted as warnings since the verbs stand without the required negation (*mē*) for such a translation. Thus, the imperatives function as pointers to something: "Look at!" rather than "Beware of."

In keeping with the two positive models of Christ's mindset in Timothy and Epaphroditus in the immediately preceding section (Phil 2:19-30), Paul provides a negative example in the Jewish Christians, who preach law observance alongside faith in Philippians 3:2-3. The introduction of these negative models serves as a platform for Paul's own model of faith for the Philippians in Philippians 3:4-11. While it may be claimed that the phrase "righteousness by faith" places this section in similarity to Galatians 2:16 and Romans 1:17; 10:4, there is a notable difference in Philippians 3:2-11 from these texts, which points to another purpose than the usual argument of faith versus law. Mainly, there is quite an emphasis on ethnicity in Philippians 3:4-6 vis-à-vis Philippians 3:2-3. Nowhere else in his letters does Paul relate in such detailed terms his *Jewish* privilege. Absence of ethnic privilege is the shape of Paul's signature proclamation of "righteousness by faith." My argument for an ethnic dimension in Philippians thus far has been largely dependent on Acts 16, but there has been no explicit reference to ethnicity in the letter itself—it has been an argument from silence, albeit conspicuous. But in Philippians 3:2-11, ethnicity is front and center, with one significant difference from my argument: Paul's Jewishness is presented not as a detraction in view of the historical and first century denigration of Jews, but as a virtue. The logic is of course, first, coherent to the boast of Jewish Christians who advocate law observance (Phil 3:2-3). Second, the position of privilege as the beginning point mirrors Christ's supreme identity and status in Philippians 2:6. Finally, while the positive interpretation of Jewish heritage may be laughable to the wider secular audience in Philippi, for believers saved by Jews (cf. Acts 16), who are now aware of the authority and power of Jewish apostles in the early church, the privilege of Israelites vis-à-vis Gentiles may well be recognized and honored. After all, "salvation is from the Jews" (Jn 4:22).

The negative model of those who privilege their Jewish ethnicity are thoroughly denigrated in Philippians 3:2. Paul labels them as "dogs" (*tous kynas*), "evil workers" (*tous kakous ergatas*), and "those who mutilate the flesh" (*tēn katatomēn*). The first slur is ethnic, as Gentiles were called "dogs" (cf. Mt 7:6; 15:26-27 and Mk 7:27-28), especially in the Mishnah (*m. Ned.* 4:3; *m. Bek.* 5:6) because dogs eat things considered unclean (e.g., garbage, feces, carrion). In view of Jewish dietary laws for clean food under the covenant (Lev 11), Gentiles ("dogs") signify exclusion from the covenant with YHWH. Paul reverses the slur to indicate the opponents' exclusion from the covenant by faith in Christ. Second, they are evildoers rather than the workers of righteousness they claim to be in their insistence that stricter adherence to the law, that is, the need for circumcision, proves their superior righteousness before God. "Evildoers" refers to people who live in rebellion against God's commands. Thus, the opponents are enemies, rather than righteous representatives or champions of God. And finally, "those who mutilate the flesh" (*tēn katatomēn*) is a play on the word for circumcision (*peritomē*). So, the opponents are "the mutilation" rather than "the circumcision," the outward sign of covenant relations with YHWH (e.g., Gen. 17:10-14, 23-27; Ex 4:25; 12:44, 48; Lev 12:3), which should reflect internal, moral, and spiritual righteousness before God (Deut 10:16; Jer 4:4; Ezek 44:7). In a nutshell, what Paul thoroughly rejects in these opponents is their ethnic promotion:

unless the Gentiles *become Jewish*, they are not truly saved. Paul does not renounce Jewish ethnicity itself, as he himself is Jewish, along with the Twelve *and Jesus*! Rather, he repudiates the promotion of Jewish ethnicity in salvation *because* their ethnic promotion is, ultimately, reliance on human nature, that is, the flesh (Phil 3:3). In direct opposition, those who live by faith are the circumcision, true worshipers by the agency of the Spirit of God and those who boast in Christ rather than the flesh (Phil 3:3). Each one of these components are further fleshed out in Paul's testimony in Philippians 3:4-11.

The list of Paul's personal privilege as a Jew listed in Philippians 3:4-6 is not mere "mano a mano" aggression against his opponents. The prerogatives set the stage for the downward movement of self-emptying (Phil 3:7-8) in conformity to Christ's self-emptying (Phil 2:6-8), which in turn serves to further animate the Philippians to also conform to Christ's mindset. Paul denounces boasting in the flesh not because he has no grounds for boasting; indeed, he has more than the opponents (Phil 3:4). In the six categories listed, the first two, "circumcised on the eighth day" and "of the people of Israel," are general descriptions for all Jews (Phil 3:5), as all Jewish males were circumcised on the eighth day according to law (Gen 17:12; Lev 12:3; both John the Baptist and Jesus undergo circumcision, Lk 1:59; 2:21). The next four components successively narrow the privilege further. The third component anchors the privilege to one tribe—that of Benjamin (Phil 3:5). The Benjamin tribe is one of the two faithful tribes in the Old Testament, remaining faithful to the Davidic monarchy (1 Kings 12:21). Jerusalem and the temple lay within its borders (Judg 1:21) and Israel's first king, Saul, hails from the tribe of Benjamin (1 Sam 9:1-2). The fourth component, "Hebrew born of Hebrews," indicates pure bloodline and perhaps upbringing of traditional Jewish culture along with its language rather than Judaism syncretized with Greek culture (i.e., Hellenists).[53] With respect to the law, Paul is a Pharisee, scrupulous in law observance. He was so zealous for Jewish election before God that he persecuted the church; and in terms of righteousness by law, Paul claims he was "blameless." Paul's pedigree and personal achievements are indeed worthy of boast if the goal was to promote Jewish ethnicity.

In Philippians 3:7-9 the downward descent is described in repetition of "loss" (*zēmian*) in Philippians 2:7-8 and the cognate verb "I have suffered loss" (*ezēmiōthēn*) in Philippians 3:8. In his acceptance of salvation in Jesus Christ, his former ethnic privilege becomes loss rather than "gain" (*kerdē*, Phil 3:7); and the cognate verb "I might gain" (*kerdēsō*) functions to emphatically contrast the "loss" (Phil 3:8). At this juncture, a critical distinction between Paul's own testimony in Philippians 3:4-11 and Christ's mindset and actions in Philippians 2:6-8 requires address. Without doubt, both passages begin with elevated status, mutatis mutandis. Christ's adoption of the form of a slave, obedience, humiliation of the cross, in contrast to equality with God requires willful self-emptying of genuine superiority. The same is not true of Paul's own self-emptying. The virtues listed are indeed superior qualities, but only from a *human perspective*. What Paul describes in Philippians 3:4-9 is a shift in his perspective—what he thought was gain, in view of the cross, is loss. By contrast, never at any point does Christ think his equality with God was somehow a detraction—equality with God remains the supreme virtue. Paul counts his virtues as loss in the realization that "there is no one who is righteous, not even one" (Rom 3:10; Ps 14:1-3) and

[53]Cf. Marshall, *Philippians*, 84.

"We have all become like one who is unclean, and all our righteous deeds are like a filthy cloth" (Is 64:6).[54] All human virtue, privilege, and advantage are, in reality, "dung" (*skybala*, Phil 3:8).

Whatever privilege we may claim over and against others, we have none before God. Human excellence, in all its noble accomplishments in spirit, mind, and body, cannot result in once-for-all atonement for all of humanity for all generations. The exchange between Paul's previously considered "gains" for the gain of Christ requires facing the truth concerning the human condition vis-à-vis God the Creator and Redeemer. Humans are at once lowly not only in the difference of essence (human vs. divine), but that of unholiness due to sin. If there is any temptation among the Philippians to adopt Christ's mindset from the logic of "although I am superior, I will follow Christ and be humble," in Philippians 3:2-9, Paul eviscerates such logic.

The exchange is made on the virtue of gaining something of far superior worth than his own privileges—the knowledge of Christ Jesus as Lord (Phil 3:9). But knowledge of Jesus Christ requires more than mere renouncement of his advantage as the exchange is comprehensive. All self-righteousness is put aside in order to be found in righteousness of God, by faith in Christ. Moreover, the exchange requires participation ("fellowship" *tēn koinōnian*) in his sufferings and becoming like him (*symmorphizō*) in his death (Phil 3:10). The logic here is not simply *imitatio Christi*, but salvation. Only in such full-throttled participation can the redeemed also share in the power of the resurrection and participate in resurrection from the dead (Phil 3:11).

Some concluding thoughts on the issue of ethnicity are necessary. Just as Paul laid aside the historical and current oppression of Jews, in his role as apostle to the Philippians, his ethnic privilege has had no significance in his teaching and his relations with the Philippians. He operates exclusively from the mindset of the cross. It is in this thoroughgoing participation with Christ that he claims authority to exhort, teach, and love the Philippians. This has groundbreaking implications for race relations in the modern-day church. It should be obvious that any claim to racial superiority in the name of Jesus Christ is not only meritless, but evidence of an unredeemed state. White superiority often linked with Christian nationalism is simply heresy. Christian leadership is not determined by ethnicity, but conformity to the cross. No minority called to lead needs to justify their call and their authority as long as the crucified mindset of Christ is evident. Just as a Jewish apostle leads with bold confidence to exhort Gentiles in the truly agonizing matters of faith, there should be no hesitation from minority leaders to pastor and disciple White believers. As long as genuine love of Christ as exemplified in Philippians 2:6-8 exists for the sake of the congregants, regardless of color, the promise of authentic reconciliation of races is only a promise waiting to be activated.

EXHORTATION TO RUN TOWARD THE END GOAL (PHILIPPIANS 3:12-21)

The pursuit of knowing Christ in his sufferings, death, and resurrection, in view of the salvation Christ accomplished, is an ongoing process that requires daily and persistent diligence. To claim that he has already achieved perfection would counter all that has been said in Philippians 3:4-9. What surfaces in Philippians 3:12-14 is Paul's unflagging single-minded pursuit of Christ. He is neither distracted by past failures or success, but constantly moves forward toward the goal as one in a race (Phil 3:13-14). The goal is qualified as the "heavenly

[54]The word translated as "filthy cloth" is *ʿiddâ* meaning "menstrual." Menstrual discharge signifies uncleanness in Lev 15:19-24.

call of God in Christ Jesus" and not one humanly appointed; it is one that comes with a prize, which is best seen as the resurrection mentioned in (Phil 3:11). In Philippians 3:15 Paul returns to a more generous tone. Despite the fact that he perceives his singular pursuit of knowledge of Christ as the mature mindset, he gives space for those who may disagree, with the caveat that God will reveal either the merit or deficiency of their disagreement. He concludes that regardless of minor differences of opinion, all should agree to what has already been attained (Phil 3:16). The emphasis falls on not reverting to unbelief, regardless of whatever level each believer has reached.

In Philippians 3:17 Paul boldly exhorts the audience to imitate him as well as to be watchful for those who walk in accordance with the example he and like-minded others provide. Paul is the only one in the New Testament who calls others to imitate him (1 Cor 4:16; 11:1; 2 Thess 3:7, 9), which some have interpreted as evidence of extreme hubris.[55] In all fairness, he also points to others as models of imitation, as he does here (1 Thess 1:7-8), and calls Timothy to be a model for imitation to others (1 Tim 4:12) in keeping with the presentation of both Timothy and Epaphroditus as models of a Christlike mindset in Philippians 2:19-30. To be sure, the call for others to imitate oneself requires bold confidence. But the charge of hubris against Paul seems to dismiss the content for imitation, which is, in this instance, the renunciation of all his privileges in order to adopt the mindset of Christ (Phil 2:2-8), participate fully in Christ's sufferings and death (Phil 3:10), and constantly pursue these goals without the assumption of perfection (Phil 3:12). Paul has effectively presented his own mindset as one that has been crucified in Christ. Imitation of such a model would only result in our benefit and encourage humility rather than pride. Perhaps one of the reasons why the modern church is incapable of demonstrating genuine faith with concomitant humility and self-sacrifice is that there are not enough models of such faith. Where these models exist, all should do well to follow their example.

Philippians 3:18-19 delivers a sharp critique against people Paul deems as "enemies of the cross of Christ." The main problem in these verses is the lack of precise identity of these "enemies." Are these the same that preach out of rivalry in Philippians 1:15-17? Or are they unbelievers who oppose and persecute believers (cf. Phil 1:28)? Another option may be that they are the Jewish Christians who advocate circumcision mentioned in Philippians 3:2. Or perhaps they are those who seek self-interest, whom Paul has mentioned in cursory form in Philippians 2:21. Despite the lack of clarity on the identity of these enemies, it is clear that Paul and the Philippians know their identity, as he has already spoken of these enemies often (Phil 3:18). Further, it is possible to gain a clearer picture of these enemies based on Paul's description.

First, despite the fact that these people embody the contrast to the gospel message as outlined in the letter, Paul nevertheless grieves for them (Phil 3:18). This factor does not rule out any of the options mentioned above; it simply speaks to his compassion for all who resist the gospel. Second, they are called enemies of the "cross of Christ" and not simply enemies of Christ. This may rule out the option of unbelievers, as what they oppose is "the cross." Third, if indeed they are believers who refuse the cross as a way of life, then the

[55]E.g., Elizabeth A. Castelli, *Imitating Paul: A Discourse of Power*, Literary Currents in Biblical Interpretation (Louisville, KY: Westminster John Knox, 1991).

description applied to them in Philippians 3:19 effectively likens them to unbelievers.

If indeed these enemies are those who claim salvation, but reject the cross as a way of life, such premature or nominal faith results in identity and destiny unqualified from unbelievers. The cross is the emblem of salvation in Christ, participation within the inner relations of the Godhead, participation in Christ, knowledge of Christ, and guaranteed resurrection. Lest all privileges and status are crucified on the cross, that is, exchanged for participation in Christ's sufferings and death, the flesh becomes their god, whom they serve. Such a mindset stands entirely antithetical to that of Christ in Philippians 2:6-8. Just as the Jewish Christians who rely on the law for righteousness in Philippians 3:2-3 do not represent authentic faith and worship, Paul presents the identity and destiny of true worshipers in Philippians 3:21. Those who are citizens of heaven await a Savior, who is sovereign over all things; and in his sovereignty he will transform our lowly body to be like his glorious body. Those who live out the cross on earth, in contrast to the enemies of the cross, have a destiny not only as citizens of heaven, but a Savior who will recognize and approve a self-emptying mindset, as much as God the Father approved the Son in Philippians 2:9-11. Our lowly, humiliated, and suffering human existence will be transformed in similarity to Christ's exaltation, to glory.

This section in Philippians 3:18-19 is in sum a qualification to the difference of opinion Paul allows in Philippians 3:15. Indeed, it may be said that what he hopes God will reveal to the objectors is relayed in Philippians 3:18-19. For Paul, there can be no alternative view on the centrality of the cross for the redeemed in faith and praxis. Those who reject the cross-centered lifestyle modeled by Christ, Timothy, Epaphroditus, and Paul do so at the peril of destruction.

FINAL EXHORTATION (PHILIPPIANS 4:1-9)

Paul concludes his exhortations in Philippians 4:1 by evoking the familial relationship between him and the Philippians. They are siblings, regardless of ethnicity or status. Within this family earnest love exists; hence, Paul states that he loves them and longs to see them; love is also reiterated at the end of the verse with "my beloved." He takes joy and pride in them, again, much as a parent takes pride and delight in their children. The final word of encouragement is to stand strong "in this way" in the Lord. The word *outōs* refers to all that he has argued, explained and exhorted in the letter, but most immediately in Philippians 3:17-21.

In Philippians 4:2-3, Paul raises the issue of contention between Euodia and Syntyche. That he raises the matter at the end of the letter may suggest that the issue must be minor, especially as Paul only devotes two verses to them. Yet it may be that he exercises extreme wisdom in addressing the issue of these two women, as they "have struggled beside me" (*gnēsie syzyge*) and colabored with Paul (*synēthlēsan*) in his ministry. His description echoes those of Timothy and Epaphroditus. Apart from their description, he does not mention any details besides the fact that they need to "to be of the same mind in the Lord." The words for "to be of the same mind" (*to auto phronein*) pick up on the exhortations for holding the same mindset in Philippians 2:2-5 as well as the mindset of Christ in Philippians 2:6-8. Hence it may be argued that the pivotal exhortations in Philippians 1:27–2:18 as well as the models of Christ's mindset in Timothy, Epaphroditus, and Paul himself, and the denigration of those who refuse the crucified life, may have the rhetorical weight of a Mack truck for these women. Whatever their disagreement may be, they need to "be of the same mind," which must be first anchored in Christ's mindset of Philippians 2:6-8. The fact that he mentions Clement suggests that he has some significance among the Philippians, but there is no other reference to him in the New Testament, and Paul provides no further detail.

In Philippians 4:4-7, Paul offers final exhortations centered on joy and peace. He exhorts them to joy, as he has done repeatedly throughout the letter. And in keeping with Philippians 2:17-18, it is repeated: "Rejoice! . . . again I will say, rejoice!" The first is qualified with "in the Lord always." The repeated emphasis on joy may possibly be due to the fact that the commands he has enjoined to the Philippians are tremendously difficult. For those who walk apart from the cross, obviously, the call to renounce all self-privilege and self-promotion is daunting and painful to embrace. For those who do walk in the mindset of the cross, there is a toll on the soul in the constant disposition of humility, humiliation, and self-sacrifice. For both, joy is a salve to all obstacles to cruciformed life. It is imperative to rejoice often in the knowledge of God's sovereignty and promises of deliverance. The second imperative calls the Philippians to show their "gentleness" (*to epiekes*) to all (Phil 4:5). Rather than aggression and hubris of self-glory, the Philippians are to demonstrate a testimony within and without the church, the gentleness that comes from humility and self-sacrifice, but even more as "the Lord is near." The nearness of the Lord conveys both his judgment and succor for faithfulness to his will as revealed in Jesus Christ in Philippians 2:6-8. Paul commands them further against anxiety. Whatever stressful and alarming situations may arise, the response should be prayer, supplication, and thanksgiving to God, for God will hear all our concerns. It is through this critical communication and worship before God that the Philippians will find relief. For God will hear and provide his own peace, which goes beyond human understanding and guards the hearts and minds to remain in Christ (Phil 4:7), just as God grants Paul peace in his imprisonment (Phil 1:14, 19-21).

Paul concludes his exhortation in 4:8-9 with a highly structured list of virtues, which are well-known in Stoic moral philosophy.[56] As noted by M. Bockmuehl, "Paul now offers cross-cultural Christian exhortation *in the language of Philippi*" for the purpose of evangelism and apologetics.[57] Six virtues are listed in Philippians 4:8: true, honorable, just, pure, pleasing, and commendable. Each is in a set pattern of "whatever is . . ." (*hosa estin*).[58] Paul follows this list with two parallel first-class conditional clauses: "if there is any excellence . . . if there is anything worthy of praise." This last feature is reminiscent of the same structure in Philippians 2:1 as well as the command "to think" on these things.

PAUL'S THANKSGIVING FOR PROVISION (PHILIPPIANS 4:10-20)

Some of the material in Philippians 4:10-20 has already been discussed above, so I will focus on some new information. As Paul has integrated the exhortations with his personal account in Philippians 1:3-26; 2:19-30 and of course, Philippians 3:2-16, he continues to merge the concepts he has previously discussed into his personal narration. Paul begins by reiterating the concept of joy he has commended in Philippians 4:4. Specifically, his joy lies in the Philippians' renewal of their concern for him (Phil 4:10). It

[56]See J. N. Sevenster, *Paul and Seneca* (Leiden: Brill, 1961), 157-58.

[57]Bockmuehl, *Philippians*, 250.

[58]In Greek, the verb "to be" is only given in the first and elided in the rest of the phrases; this is a common feature in Koine Greek.

appears that while the Philippians' love and concern for him remained constant, they had no opportunity to demonstrate that concern. The specifics of the situation are unclear. It may be that they had no one who could serve as a messenger to Paul. The honor given to Epaphroditus in Philippians 2:25-30 may indicate that he was a rare individual who sacrificed much to carry out the compassionate mission to Paul. Alternatively, it may mean that the Philippians, who were already struggling financially, had difficulty in collecting funds for Paul. That Paul addresses his perspective on finances may give weight to the latter option.

Despite the fact that Paul rejoices in their support, he makes it clear that he is not soliciting further funding. This statement is repeated in Philippians 4:17 and does not convey his pride, as again, it would subvert Paul's entire exhortation in the letter. Rather, in keeping with the authentic love between Paul and the Philippians, he wants to lay no further burden on people who have already suffered financially. In Philippians 4:11-13, Paul reveals his peace regardless of whatever situation may arise. The New Testament *hapax legomenon*, *autarkēs*, means "contentment" or "self-sufficiency," an ideal state in Stoic and Cynic philosophy.[59] At variance for Paul, the word conveys God-sufficiency rather than self-sufficiency.[60] Hence, he models the peace he enjoined in Philippians 4:6-7. He is content in both prosperity and poverty. And in Philippians 4:12, he calls this contentment a "secret." This secret is most likely explained in Philippians 4:13: "I can do all things through him who strengthens me." This verse has been wildly taken out of context in modern times to imply all kinds of ludicrous ability. The verse is firmly tied to the context of finding peace in various economic situations. His ultimate reliance in coping with either prosperity or need is the firm belief that God strengthens him to endure and prevail in every circumstance.

In Philippians 4:14, Paul again thanks the Philippians for participating in his trouble. In Philippians 4:15-16 Paul reveals the fact that the Philippians were the only church that entered this financial relationship when he departed Macedonia and once again in Thessalonica, where he took no support from the Thessalonians (1 Thess 2:9; 2 Thess 3:7-9). The love and affection conveyed throughout the letter between the apostle and the Philippians is based on a long history of love that extends even to rare financial sharing. Paul would not have accepted financial help from converts who did not demonstrate authentic faith. 1 Corinthians 9:1-27 indicates that Paul did not take support from the Corinthians, who continued to demonstrate a fleshly mindset (cf. 1 Cor 2:6-3:4).

In Philippians 4:17, Paul reiterates that he is not seeking the gift, but rather, the gift that will be counted as virtue with God. Indeed, Paul reassures the Philippians that what he has received is more than generous and that he is well supplied (Phil 4:18). He calls the gifts sent with Epaphroditus "a fragrant offering" and "a sacrifice acceptable and pleasing to God." Ultimately, the Philippians' gift to Paul is, as with all acts that originate from faith, a sacrifice to God. In full recognition of this, Paul uses sacrificial language for the Philippians' generosity (cf. Phil 2:17). In Philippians 4:19, Paul blesses the Philippians in the certainty that God will supply all their needs, not according to human standards, but God's standard of "riches in glory in Christ Jesus." The best reference for this is Philippians 2:9-11: as God bestowed unlimited, all-extensive glory to Christ, God will also respond

[59]Sevenster, *Paul and Seneca*, 113.

[60]F. F. Bruce, *Philippians*, NIBC, 2nd ed. (Peabody, MA: Hendrickson, 1989), 125.

similarly to the Philippians' need in view of their sacrifice. And Philippians 4:20 concludes with a doxology as in all his letters. All glory is directed to God, who is also our Father for all ages.

FINAL GREETINGS (PHILIPPIANS 4:21-23)

The final list of greetings is also typical in Paul's letters. But here, the greetings are general and Paul offers no specific greeting to individuals (cf. 2 Tim 4:19; Col 4:15; and 1 Cor 16:19-20). Rather, greetings are sent to "every saint in Christ Jesus" and "all saints" also send their greetings; perhaps "each" rather than "all" in the first greeting indicates intentional effort to ensure each are greeted specifically. He conveys greetings from brothers who are with him as well as greetings from those in Caesar's household. And the letter closes with a benediction that prays for the grace of Jesus Christ to be with their spirit. The benediction is a replica of the same in Philemon 1:25 (cf. also Gal 6:18). The letter closes with grace as it began with grace (Phil 1:2).

SELECTED BIBLIOGRAPHY

Bauckham, Richard. *The Climax of Prophecy: Studies on the Book of Revelation*. London: T&T Clark, 1998.

Becker, E.-M. *Paul on Humility*. Translated by W. Coppins. Waco, TX: Baylor University Press, 2020.

Bertram, G. "Φρήν." *TDNT* 9:220-35.

Bockmuehl, M. *A Commentary on the Epistle to the Philippians*. London: A&C Black, 1997.

Bright, John. *A History of Israel*. Louisville, KY: Westminster John Knox, 2000.

Bruce, F. F. *Philippians*. NIBC. Peabody, MA: Hendrickson, 1989.

Carson, D. A., and Douglas J. Moo. *An Introduction to the New Testament*. Rev. ed. Grand Rapids, MI: Zondervan, 2005.

Castelli, Elizabeth A. *Imitating Paul: A Discourse of Power*. Literary Currents in Biblical Interpretation. Louisville, KY: Westminster John Knox, 1991.

Craig, Tim. "'The United States Is in Crisis': Report Tracks Thousands of Summer Protests, Most Nonviolent." *Washington Post*. Sept 3, 2020; www.washingtonpost.com/national/the-united-states-is-in-crisis-report-tracks-thousands-of-summer-protests-most-nonviolent/2020/09/03/b43c359a-edec-11ea-99a1-71343d03bc29_story.html.

deSilva, David A. *The Letter to the Galatians*. NICNT. Grand Rapids, MI: Eerdmans, 2018.

Grundmann, W. "ταπεινός." *TDNT* 8:1-26.

Hoover, R. W. "The HARPAGMOS Enigma: A Philological Solution." *HTR* 64 (1961): 95-119.

Inserra, D. *The Unsaved Christian: Reaching Cultural Christianity with the Gospel*. Chicago: Moody Publishers, 2019.

Keener, Craig S. *Acts*. NCBC. Cambridge: Cambridge University Press, 2020.

Marshall, I. Howard. *The Epistle to the Philippians*. EC. London: Epworth Press, 1991.

Osborne, Grant R. *Revelation*. BECNT. Grand Rapids, MI: Baker Academic, 2002.

Park, M. Sydney. *Submission Within the Godhead and the Church in the Epistle to the Philippians: An Exegetical and Theological Examination of the Concept of Submission in Philippians 2 and 3*. London: T&T Clark, 2007.

Pilhofer, P. *Philippi: Die erste christliche Gemeinde Europas*. Vol. 1. WUNT 87. Tübingen: Mohr Siebeck, 1995.

Schweitzer, Albert. *The Quest of the Historical Jesus: A Critical Study of Its Progress from Reimarus to Wrede*. London: A&C Black, 1911.

Sevenster, J. N. *Paul and Seneca*. Leiden: Brill, 1961.

Silva, Moisés. *Philippians*. BECNT. Grand Rapids, MI: Baker Academic, 2005.

Wallace, Daniel B. *Greek Grammar Beyond the Basics*. Grand Rapids, MI: Zondervan, 1997.

Wright, N. T. *The Climax of the Covenant: Christ and the Law in Pauline Theology*. Edinburgh: T&T Clark, 1991.

LETTER TO THE COLOSSIANS

Dennis R. Edwards

From the outset it is important to understand that African Americans have not always viewed Paul as a friend. The reception of his writings among African American Christians has been mixed, ranging from what Abraham Smith calls "reverential appropriation" to outright rejection.[1] The instructions to slaves in Colossians 3:22 (along with Eph 6:5 and 1 Pet 2:18) were favorites of American slaveholders, so it is not surprising that African American "slaves and ex-slaves refused to respect texts that justified their exploitation."[2] Many people have recounted theologian, poet, and mystic Howard Thurman's story about how his grandmother, Nancy Ambrose—a formerly enslaved woman—welcomed his reading the Bible to her, but never from any of Paul's writings. She recalled how when the master's White minister preached, he'd typically turn to Paul's aforementioned instructions to slaves.[3] Yet, despite this oppressive use of Paul, a significant number of African American Christians find what Brian K. Blount calls "theology enabling liberating ethics."[4] For Blount, Pauline theology offers words of liberation—at least sometimes. Blount describes problems with Paul—and with the interpreters of Paul—yet acknowledges Paul's boundary-breaking teaching. "Paul's theology has as one of its primary goals the breaking down of religious, social, and political boundaries between Jews and Gentiles in the first-century believing communities."[5]

Lisa Bowens also sees Paul's boundary-breaking teaching and suggests that Paul's words can help African Americans in the quest for justice and equality.[6] Bowens gives several examples of early African American New Testament exegesis where Paul's words were used to combat the injustice of slavery and at times even to support the call of women to preach. Bowens asserts,

[1]Abraham Smith, "Paul and African American Biblical Interpretation," in *True to Our Native Land: An African American New Testament Commentary*, ed. Brian K. Blount, Cain Hope Felder, Clarice J. Martin, and Emerson B. Powery (Minneapolis: Fortress Press, 2007), 35-36. See also John Byron, *Recent Research on Paul and Slavery*, Recent Research in Biblical Studies 3 (Sheffield, UK: Sheffield Phoenix Press, 2008), 36-66. Some scholars assess the troublesome passages as deutero-Pauline, thereby acquitting Paul of endorsing sexism and slavery. Consequently, issues arising within second-century (or so) Christian contexts become the source of the problem rather than Paul.

[2]Brian K. Blount, *Then the Whisper Put On Flesh: New Testament Ethics in an African American Context* (Nashville: Abingdon Press, 2001), 120. The quotation is from his chapter titled "Paul: Theology Enabling Liberating Ethics—Sometimes." See also Clarice J. Martin, "The *Haustafeln* (Household Codes) in African American Interpretation: 'Free Slaves' and 'Subordinate Women,'" in *Stony the Road We Trod: African American Biblical Interpretation*, ed. Cain Hope Felder (Minneapolis: Fortress, 1991), 213-18.

[3]Howard Thurman, *Jesus and the Disinherited* (Boston: Beacon Press, 1976), 20.

[4]Blount, *Then the Whisper*, 119-57.

[5]Blount, *Then the Whisper*, 121.

[6]Lisa Bowens, "Liberating Paul: African Americans' Use of Paul in Resistance and Protest," in *Practicing with Paul: Reflections on Paul and the Practices of Ministry in Honor of Susan G. Eastman*, ed. Presian Burroughs (Eugene, OR: Cascade, 2018), 57. Also see Bowens's more recent work, *African American Readings of Paul: Reception, Resistance, and Transformation* (Grand Rapids, MI: Eerdmans, 2020).

> These early interpreters knew the power of Paul's words to shape reality and to give voice to the voiceless. Although Paul was constantly being used to silence, dehumanize, and subjugate them, these explicators reappropriated Paul as a figure of protest and resistance in opposition to the powers of oppression, evil, and slavery. Paul, these writers insisted, did not belong to the white slaveholder or to the white minister but to the slaves and even to women preachers. He was their companion, and likewise can become our companion in the fight for freedom and the struggle for justice.[7]

Although baggage accompanies African American readings of Paul, Colossians might still nourish the liberationist sensitivities of African American Christians. For example, in his commentary on Colossians, Scot McKnight recognizes the God who, paradoxically through the crucifixion of Jesus, conquers the evil powers that oppress humanity and foster division, thereby bringing freedom for life "in a new kind of community."[8] Brian J. Walsh and Sylvia C. Keesmaat interpret Colossians as a liberating text that subverts imperial power.[9] Additionally, Annie Tinsley analyzes Colossians as a liberating text, noting how Africans who would come to face the tyranny of European slavery are similar to the first readers of Colossians.[10] Even though the letter does not contain the characteristics of an overt anti-imperial manifesto, Colossians makes allusions and references to its Roman context, such as the image of victorious Roman generals parading conquered foes in Colossians 2:15, and the people groups named in Colossians 3:11.[11] To the extent that Colossians challenges the status quo of life under an empire, the letter resonates with marginalized people who know that faith in God runs counter to "tribalism, nationalism, and imperialism."[12]

This brief letter, with similarities to Ephesians, connections to Philemon, and some linkage to the Laodicean Christians of Revelation 3:14-22, celebrates reconciliation with God through Jesus Christ, while urging conciliation across ethnic and economic boundaries. The portrayal of Jesus Christ as the one who sustains the universe (Col 1:17), who embodies the fullness of God (Col 1:19; 2:9), who reigns over all cosmic forces (Col 1:16; 2:10), who defeats our spiritual opposition (Col 2:14-15) freeing us from condemnation (Col 2:16-23), bringing new life (Col 3:1-3), and removing the stigma of ethnic or societal marginalization (Col 3:11), serves as a beacon of hope that shines brightly for African Americans and other marginalized people. Oppressed people appreciate a champion who is stronger than the forces working against them. Harry O. Maier declares, "Indeed, in its affirmation of Jesus as the one in whom, through whom and for whom all things are made (1.16) and continue to hold together (1.17), by logical implication even Caesar, together with the cosmic powers he serves, is ultimately subject (Col 2.10). We have here the making of a Quiet

---

[7]Bowens, "Liberating Paul," 72.

[8]Scot McKnight, *The Letter to the Colossians*, NICNT (Grand Rapids, MI: Eerdmans, 2018), 1-4.

[9]Brian J. Walsh and Sylvia C. Keesmaat, *Colossians Remixed: Subverting the Empire* (Downers Grove, IL: InterVarsity Press, 2004).

[10]Annie Tinsley, *A Postcolonial African American Re-reading of Colossians: Identity, Reception, and Interpretation Under the Gaze of Empire* (New York: Palgrave Macmillan, 2013), 7.

[11]See Allan R. Bevere, "Colossians and the Rhetoric of Empire: A New Battle Zone," in *Jesus Is Lord, Caesar Is Not: Evaluating Empire in New Testament Studies*, ed. Scot McKnight and Joseph B. Modica (Downers Grove, IL: IVP Academic, 2013), 183-96 and McKnight, *Colossians*, 63-65.

[12]These three terms occur together a few times in McKnight, *Colossians*, 3-4.

Revolution."[13] The quiet revolution that Maier observes reverberates, despite how the household regulations of Colossians 3:18–4:1 might be a stumbling block for some readers, because at its heart Colossians is a message of hope, transformation, and triumph.

AUTHORSHIP AND DATE

Scholars dispute the authorship of Colossians, with some placing it among the so-called deutero-Pauline letters (along with Ephesians, 2 Thessalonians, 1 Timothy, 2 Timothy, and Titus). Detailed discussion of Pauline authorship is beyond the scope of this brief commentary, but views of authorship inform our thoughts surrounding the development of Pauline theology, ethics, and ecclesiology. For instance, one might ask, "To what extent does the Christology of Colossians 1:15-20 reflect the views of the earliest Christians?" And "do the household codes serve to reinforce societal hierarchies as part of ecclesial attempts to counter a somewhat more radical way of life flowing from Pauline egalitarianism (as in Gal 3:28)?" Pauline letters may have Paul as the primary author, but there are frequently fellow senders of the letter, typically Timothy.[14] This essay refers to Paul as the main author of the letter as, prima facie, the letter purports to be from Paul and Timothy (Col 1:1) with an imprisoned Paul penning the final greeting himself (Col 4:18).[15] If Paul indeed wrote Colossians, he did so around 53–55 CE, probably from a prison in Ephesus.[16] Scholars who uphold Pauline authorship view Colossians as one of the Pauline Prison Epistles (Ephesians, Philippians, Colossians, Philemon).[17] Scholars who conclude that Paul did not write the letter suggest a date late in the first century, or early in the second.[18]

SETTING

The city of Colossae was in the Lycus Valley of Asia Minor (modern-day Turkey). Although Colossae appeared to have a sizable Jewish population, the church was predominately Gentile, likely the fruit of Epaphras's evangelistic efforts (Col 1:7; 4:12) and not Paul's (Col 2:1). Paul writes to reaffirm what Jesus Christ accomplished on behalf of believers through his death and resurrection. The apostle also urges his audience to resist spiritual opposition (Col 2:4-23), called "the philosophy" at one point (Col 2:8). Additionally, Paul exhorts the believers who are bound together in a loving community to display upright ethical behavior in front of unbelievers through participation in the life of Christ (Col 3–4). As an African American male, born

[13]Harry O. Maier, "A Sly Civility: Colossians and Empire," *JSNT* 27, no. 3 (2005): 340.

[14]In 2 Cor 1:1; Phil 1:1; 1 Thess 1:1; 2 Thess 1:1; Philem 1:1, Timothy is listed as a coauthor. Other fellow letter senders include Sosthenes (1 Cor 1:1) and Silvanus (1 Thess 1:1; 2 Thess 1:1). There are also others who served as couriers or performers of the letters who were likely involved in the development of the letter (e.g., Phoebe in Rom 16:1-2; and Tertius in Rom 16:22; Tychicus in Eph 6:21 and Col 4:7).

[15]For detailed discussions of authorship, see David A. deSilva, *An Introduction to the New Testament: Contexts, Methods & Ministry Formation* (Downers Grove, IL: IVP Academic, 2018), 616-22; McKnight, *Colossians*, 5-18 and Paul Foster, *Colossians*, BNTC (London and New York: Bloomsbury T&T Clark, 2016), 61-81. McKnight accepts Pauline authorship while Foster does not. Both acknowledge the challenges and implications of decisions concerning authorship, and Foster admonishes, "Ultimately it needs to be remembered that the question of authorship, or the position one takes on it, is not the decisive issue. Rather, the significant challenge for commentators is to bring out the rich and finely crafted message of the letter" (p. 81).

[16]McKnight, *Colossians*, 34-39. Scholars debate the city where Paul was imprisoned, with Ephesus, Rome, and Caesarea as the most likely candidates (see following discussion of Philemon).

[17]Second Timothy purports to be a Pauline letter written from prison but is classified as a Pastoral Epistle (along with 1 Timothy and Titus).

[18]Foster, *Colossians*, 80, gives a range of 65–80 CE. He also tabulates the views of various scholars, listing their take on Pauline authorship, possible dates for the letter, and the likely location of Paul's imprisonment (73-78).

near the end of our nation's post–WWII baby boom, I approach Colossians with a cautious eye on the previously mentioned household codes, but also eager to embrace the letter's liberative, egalitarian, and hopeful elements.

THEMATIC OUTLINE

- Letter opening: Pastoral appreciation and intercessory prayer (Col 1:1-14)
  - Opening greetings from Paul and Timothy (Col 1:1-2)
  - Paul's gratitude for the Colossians' faith, hope, and love (Col 1:3-8)
  - Prayer for the Colossian's spiritual maturity and faithful endurance (Col 1:9-14)
- Main body of the letter: Christ's supremacy and Christian maturity (Col 1:15–4:1)
  - The reconciling work of the preeminent Son of God and its impact on the Colossians and Paul (Col 1:15–2:5)
    - Song of the Son's supremacy (Col 1:15-20)
    - The gospel of reconciliation through Christ (Col 1:21-23)
    - Paul's ministry of God's mystery (Col 1:24–2:5)
  - Calling the Colossians to live fully and freely because of Christ (Col 2:6-23)
    - Growing spiritually stronger (Col 2:6-7)
    - Experiencing Christ's liberating victory over evil forces (Col 2:8-15)
    - Rejecting religious restrictions (Col 2:16-23)
  - Urging heavenly life within harmonious households (Col 3:1–4:1)
    - Dying with Christ and being raised with him (Col 3:1-4)
    - Taking off the old humanity and putting on the new (Col 3:5-17)
    - Christian households within hostile territory (Col 3:18–4:1)
- Letter closing: Facing outward and moving onward (Col 4:2-18)
  - Proclaiming the mystery of Christ in words and actions (Col 4:2-6)
  - Connecting with fellow ministers of the gospel (Col 4:7-15)
  - Sharing, remembering, and blessing (Col 4:16-18)

INTRODUCTION

Paul writes primarily as a pastor addressing local groups of Christians, and not as a public theologian offering religious ideas while detached from a particular setting.[19] Pastoral teaching and admonition have always been central to African American Christians.[20] Generally speaking, African American Christianity demonstrates the utmost respect for pastors. This feature of our faith dates back to the times when enslaved preachers, who were sometimes illiterate yet knowledgeable of Scripture, used and interpreted the Bible for other enslaved people. Preachers became the most likely African Americans to learn to read, and for decades pastors were among the most educated members of the African American community. Consequently, because of their education and faith in Jesus, pastors influenced the daily decisions of entire neighborhoods. One might approach Paul's letters—and Colossians is no exception—as pastoral admonition to encourage and motivate all followers of Jesus.

---

[19]See Scot McKnight, *Pastor Paul: Nurturing a Culture of Christoformity in the Church*, Theological Explorations for the Church Catholic (Grand Rapids, MI: Brazos Press, 2019).

[20]See Esau McCaulley, *Reading While Black: African American Biblical Interpretation as an Exercise in Hope* (Downers Grove, IL: IVP Academic, 2020); Lloyd A. Lewis, "Colossians," in Blount et al., *True to Our Native Land*, 384.

LETTER OPENING: PASTORAL APPRECIATION AND INTERCESSORY PRAYER (COLOSSIANS 1:1-14)

Opening greetings from Paul and Timothy (Colossians 1:1-2). Paul affirms his apostolic calling and his understanding that Jesus of Nazareth is Israel's Messiah (Christ) as he greets the Colossians alongside his most frequent letter-writing partner, Timothy. At this point, Timothy figures as a brother but toward the end of Paul's life, Timothy will become a child (1 Tim 1:2; 2 Tim 1:2). There remains a long-standing practice in many African American churches of preachers identifying themselves as sons and daughters of the pastor under whom they received their calling, in much the way academics refer to their *Doktorvater* ("doctor father") or *Doktormutter* ("doctor mother")—the one who guided their research. Paul greets the holy and faithful sisters and brothers, describing them with one of his favorite phrases, "in Christ."

Scholars have written much to explain the *in* (or *with*) phrases of Paul ("in Christ," "in him," "in the Lord," "with Christ," and the like).[21] The phrase here in the greeting anticipates the all-encompassing work of Jesus celebrated a few verses later in Colossians 1:16 ("in him all things . . . were created"). For Paul, the *in* language can describe the relationship that humans have with Jesus, often expressed with weighty theological terms, such as *justification*, *salvation*, *redemption*, and *sanctification*, all of which are summed up by Michael Gorman through the term *participation*.[22] Those who live in Colossae also participate in the life of Christ. The believers are geographically, socially, and politically located in the gentile world of Colossae, but must demonstrate what life in Jesus Christ entails. Christians have always had to contextualize their faith. Jesus-followers living under repressive governments might express their faith differently than those in democratic nations. Urban Christians might practice hospitality differently from rural Christians. As scientific and technological advancements increase, Christians continually need to navigate societal changes. Marginalized people, such as African Americans, are among the most inspirational and faithful witnesses of what it means to be in Christ while living in uncaring—or even hostile—territory. Black churches, for example, were the center of community life, not just a source of spiritual inspiration. For African Americans who fled the segregated south to find new opportunities during the Great Migration, many churches in large cities in the north, such as Chicago and New York, served as critical connection points.

Paul offers his customary wish for grace and peace. Grace recalls God's kindness to those of low or no status (e.g., Israel in the Old Testament, Gentiles in the Jesus movement, the enslaved and women in all times and places). For Paul's Jewish hearers, peace suggests God's wholeness, *shalom*, found throughout the Hebrew Bible. Gentile hearers might also discern a subtle rebuke of pagan and secular notions of peace. To the Greeks *eirēnē* (the etymological origin of the name Irene) was a goddess. Under the Roman Empire, the *Pax Romana* or "Peace of Rome" was the political machinery that enabled the crucifixion of Jesus. God's peace stands in stark contrast to pagan and secular understandings of peace.

Paul's gratitude for the Colossians' faith, hope, and love (Colossians 1:3-8). In Paul's prayer of thanksgiving, he celebrates the faith,

[21]See the following and the references in their footnotes: Petr Pokorný, *Colossians: A Commentary* (Peabody, MA: Hendrickson, 1991), 127; McKnight, *Colossians*, 85

[22]Michael J. Gorman, *Becoming the Gospel: Paul, Participation, and Mission*, The Gospel and Our Culture Series (Grand Rapids, MI: Eerdmans, 2015).

hope, and love of the Colossian Christians.[23] There is a call and response aspect of this pastoral expression of gratitude. The call and response in African American Christianity describes the back-and-forth communication between leader (typically the preacher, or musical soloist) and the congregation (or choir), as each respond to what they've heard from the other. The communication need not be an invitation; it may be merely an affirmation. Nevertheless, sensory interaction is expected, and such interaction is prominent in this section. Hearing (Col 1:4, 5, 6), along with learning (Col 1:7) and making known (Col 1:8) reflect the pattern of communication between the leaders Epaphras and Paul with the Colossians. Epaphras taught the gospel (Col 1:7) so that the Colossians heard the word of truth (Col 1:5-6). The gospel bore fruit in the lives of the Colossians (Col 1:6), so in turn, Paul heard of their faith (Col 1:4), their hope (Col 1:5), and their love (Col 1:4, 8). Faith in Jesus and the community's faithfulness were communicated back and forth between the leaders and the congregation.

Paul lauds Epaphras as beloved fellow slave (*syndoulos*) and faithful minister (*diakonos*) of Christ (Col 1:7). While many English translations render *doulos* as "servant," it commonly refers to an enslaved person (e.g., Mt 8:9; Gal 3:28; 1 Tim 6:1).[24] It is virtually impossible for African Americans to read the word *slave* and not think of aspects of our history. Paul uses *doulos* to describe his own ministry (e.g., Rom 1:1; Gal 1:10; Phil 1:1). On the one hand, African Americans might view Paul's appropriation of *slave* to describe his own ministry as insensitive, or even offensive. After all, slavery was ubiquitous in his world, and Paul, a privileged Roman citizen, did not directly condemn the system (see discussion of Philemon below).[25] On the other hand, Paul might be honoring enslaved people by pointing to them as models of devotion. Early Christians knew what submission to earthly masters looked like (and for some what it felt like) and found that image to fit their relationship to Jesus Christ.[26] As I noted at the introduction, enslaved African Americans found, even within Paul's writings, language that condemned the institution of slavery. Perhaps rather than pity our forebears, we can see them instead as heroes; they persevered through hellish opposition.

Hope stands out among the trio of virtues and reflects the eschatological yearnings of marginalized people who await a new day that brings liberation from oppression. Paul tells the Colossians that "hope is laid up for you in heaven" (Col 1:5). Lloyd Lewis sees hope in Colossians 1:5 as both a future promise as well as a present reality and points out that "African American believers have preserved in hymns and sermons and in their poetry this same eschatological concern and tension. In hope they anticipate the future. At the same time they see in the Good News proclaimed and enacted signs of hope as God's new arrangement confronts injustice and evil."[27] Marginalized people in our time can take hope in the knowledge that the Colossian Christians—a small community within the vast Roman Empire—witnessed the gospel bearing fruit in their lives, as they participated in a growing, worldwide movement (Col 1:6).

Prayer for the Colossian's spiritual maturity and faithful endurance (Colossians 1:9-14). Paul's intercessory prayer in Colossians 1:9-14 amplifies the eschatological hope of alienated

[23]This trio of virtues also appears together in 1 Cor 13:13; 1 Thess 1:3; 5:8.
[24]*Oiketēs*, "household servant," also occurs in the New Testament (Lk 16:13; Acts 10:7; Rom 14:4; 1 Pet 2:18).
[25]See Mitzi J. Smith, "Slavery in the Early Church," in Blount et al., *True to Our Native Land*, 11-22; McKnight, *Colossians*, 103.
[26]See Byron, *Paul and Slavery*, 67-91.
[27]Lewis, "Colossians," 382.

people. The present time requires knowledge of God's will, spiritual wisdom, and understanding (Col 1:9), and strength to endure trials patiently (Col 1:11). Yet, there is the promise that all God's people, those who are upright and have been liberated, will enjoy a future inheritance (Col 1:12). The future is sure because God has already rescued and redeemed God's people (Col 1:13-14). The concepts of rescue and redemption resonate with African American Christians who see our story in the exodus account of God's deliverance of Israel out of slavery. In Exodus 6:6, God commands Moses, "Say therefore to the Israelites, 'I am the Lord, and I will free you from the burdens of the Egyptians and deliver you from slavery to them. I will redeem you with an outstretched arm and with mighty acts of judgment." The LXX uses the verb *rhyomai* ("I rescue") which occurs in Colossians 1:13, *and lytroō* ("I redeem"), a form of the word redemption found in Colossians 1:14. God's deliverance of Israel from slavery in Egypt has always served as a paradigm for African Americans who came to view God as a deliverer, not oppressor, contrary to the way slave owners depicted God. Rescue describes deliverance from captivity. Furthermore, for the Colossians, embedded in a world where slavery was ubiquitous, redemption signaled manumission—the release of enslaved people. God is a liberator. God liberates people from the bondage of sin.[28] Paul equates redemption to the forgiveness of sins. Since he views sin as an oppressive power (e.g., Rom 6:12-23), for Paul, forgiveness, like redemption, means deliverance, or liberation.

Freedom from the power, or dominion, of darkness means becoming subjects of the "kingdom of his beloved Son" (Col 1:13). Powerless people subjected to the whims of frail and fickle human leaders—an apt description of some of Rome's Caesars—surely appreciate the affirmation that Jesus is the true king. African Americans can discern from our sojourn in the United States the same dominion of darkness and power of sin that the Colossians recognized in aspects of the Roman Empire because the government sanctioned our oppression. Slavery, Jim Crow legislation, segregated schooling, and mass incarceration are a sampling of a host of legal forms of discrimination. Life in physical darkness mirrored the spiritual darkness under which enslaved people suffered. "Dark was the existence of the enslaved African for they were made to work long hours during the day and they did not own the night because it encompassed them as they lay exhausted in their dimly lit and meager dwellings."[29] The reign of Jesus brings light to his people (Col 1:12), a reign foreshadowed in the Old Testament. The KJV of Isaiah 9:6 says, "For unto us a child is born, unto us a son is given: and the government shall be upon his shoulder." The prophecy, which is often applied to Jesus, goes on to assert that for the promised Prince of Peace, "of the increase of *his* government and peace *there shall be* no end" (Is 9:7). Hence, the government of Jesus is superior to any human government.

MAIN BODY OF THE LETTER: CHRIST'S SUPREMACY AND CHRISTIAN MATURITY (COLOSSIANS 1:15–4:1)

The reconciling work of the preeminent Son of God and its impact on the Colossians and Paul (Colossians 1:15–2:5)

Song of the Son's supremacy (Colossians 1:15-20). Most scholars recognize a hymnic quality to Colossians 1:15-20, seeing it as a song that Paul either created or repeated. The song reflects the heart of the entire letter, tying

---

[28]McKnight, *Colossians*, 130-32.

[29]Tinsley, *Postcolonial Re-reading of Colossians*, 132.

together the earlier thanksgiving and prayer with the subsequent admonitions to the Colossians. Petr Pokorný points out the irony of the hymn's use of majestic language celebrating "an impoverished Jew . . . who was executed as one of the less significant mischief-makers."[30] This ironic portrayal of Jesus mirrors the lives of African Americans. We have been insignificant in the eyes of society yet believe that we are prominent in God's eyes. We adore a Savior who participated in our situation.[31] Jesus of Nazareth lived as an unimpressive figure from an insignificant town, yet through his resurrection from the dead he is revealed to be the unique Son of God. Jesus, the unique Son of God, is the image of God, demonstrating what God is like. How we see Jesus, therefore, is an indicator of how we imagine God. The popular *Head of Christ* painting by Warner Sallman, with the Roman-nosed, long-haired Lord in three-quarter profile, still persists as the prominent picture of Jesus in many churches. If Jesus, being the Son of God, looks European, it creates unnecessary distance between God and non-Europeans, specifically people with dark skin. Furthermore, a European Jesus denies the historical context of the New Testament. African Americans helped to lead the way in rejecting blond, blue-eyed Jesus, opting for a more historically accurate picture of the Lord. That Jesus took on the flesh of marginalized people in occupied territory and communicates that God appears as one who understands the plight of alienated people.

Pokorný observes, "Behind this hymn is the view of Christian worship as proclamation of the Lordship of Christ in the face of all powers that influence humanity and seek to determine its destiny."[32] The visible and invisible entities of Colossians 1:16 (thrones, dominions, rulers, and powers) can constitute a threat to humanity and they need to be disarmed (Col 2:15). The thrones, dominions, rulers, and powers refer to spiritual beings who are represented by or find some parallel in humans and their institutions.[33] In hearing such terms, the Colossians could not help but picture the Roman Empire, with the emperor at the head of the body politic, attempting to hold together all aspects of life within the empire. "The Christ who is head of the body, the church, parallels the emperor who is head of the body of his Empire, with the difference that Christ's is not a rule centered in military dominion over pacified enemies."[34] African Americans know how human institutions, such as corporations and governments, can exert discriminatory and oppressive force, quenching human flourishing or even threatening human existence. These institutions appear sovereign over human lives, but this Colossians hymn rebukes those institutions by asserting the sovereignty of Christ. Jesus Christ is what God looks like and embodies whatever God is (Col 1:19; cf. Phil 2:6). As firstborn Son (Col 1:15), Christ is supreme over all the world (Col 1:18) and creates peace (Col 1:20). The reconciliation Christ creates through his reign "is marked not by domination, but by self-giving."[35]

The gospel of reconciliation through Christ (Colossians 1:21-23). Through Christ's selfless service and giving himself through sacrificial death (Col 1:20)—humans become friends with God (Col 1:21). While under captivity to the cosmic powers (cf. Col 1:16; 2:8, 15), humans think and act in ways that make us enemies with God (Col 1:21). Reconciliation with God means

[30]Pokorný, *Colossians*, 69.
[31]See Thurman, *Jesus and the Disinherited*, 1-25.
[32]Pokorný, *Colossians*, 74.
[33]G. K. Beale, *Colossians and Philemon*, Baker Exegetical Commentary on the New Testament (Grand Rapids, MI: Baker Academic, 2019), 93; McKnight, *Colossians*, 152
[34]Maier, "Sly Civility," 340.
[35]Maier, "Sly Civility," 340.

liberation from the enslaving spiritual forces. Reconciliation also means that humans who were once alienated from God can become holy, blameless, and irreproachable—perfect offerings to God (cf. Eph 5:27; Heb 1:9). When the larger society views you and your people as unclean, blameworthy, and reproachable, as has been the case with African Americans, Paul's words to the Colossians provide spiritual balm to soothe damaged psyches. God makes friends with us even if the world opposes us. "If God is for us, who can be against us?" (Rom 8:31 NIV). Paul expects the Colossians to persevere in their faith (Col 1:23). As a building relies on the security of a firm foundation, the Colossians depend on the gospel as their source of hope.[36] Paul sees the gospel as advancing throughout the world (Col 1:6), and as what defines his work as servant.

*Paul's ministry of God's mystery (Colossians 1:24–2:5).*As a servant of the gospel, Paul completes his quota of physical suffering, which he does on behalf of Christ's body, the church (Col 1:24). Service for Christ means suffering, as we follow in the Lord's own steps. Christ is the Suffering Servant whose passion provides our redemption (cf. 1 Pet 2:24). Through suffering, God's word advances (Col 1:25), enabling the revelation of a previously hidden mystery (Col 1:26). Mystery (*mystērion*) is a frequent term in Pauline literature but does not function as it did in pagan religions to indicate esoteric knowledge that only the enlightened might know.[37] For Paul, mystery was something previously hidden, or not understood, about God's plans for the world that become evident to believers through Jesus Christ. Here, in Colossians 1:27, the mystery is that God intended for Gentiles—those who seemed far away from the God of Israel—to have hope for a glorious future with God, because Christ is alive within them. The reconciliation and peacemaking noted above (Col 1:21) constitutes part of the mystery. God has taken those who seemed to be the furthest away—at least in Jewish reckoning—to share in the inheritance (Col 1:12). There was a time in US history when White Christians did not know what to make of the souls of Black folk. Some thought we were beyond redemption. Others thought we could be saved, but were inherently inferior to White people.[38] Paul's words here are poignant for African American Christians. The unveiling of God's mystery means that Christ is in us just like he might be in any other believer providing for us the same glorious hope. There are no second-class subjects in the kingdom of God's beloved Son.

The apostle's suffering for Christ is a struggle from a distance (Col 2:5) on behalf of the Colossians and the neighboring Laodiceans (Col 1:29–2:1). In addition to encouragement and unity through love (Col 2:2), Paul desires his readers to experience the riches of understanding, knowledge, and wisdom (Col 2:2-3). There are spiritual insights that Paul has that he wants the Colossians (and Laodiceans) to know. Here lies a tension for marginalized people. African Americans and other alienated people were, in many cases, introduced to Jesus by their oppressors. Tinsley speculates that this invitation to acquire knowledge, "when applied to the conditions of the African before slavery, meant they would have the power that the missionaries had as they came over to their land; the power to cross oceans

---

[36]Beale, *Colossians and Philemon*, 117-18, explains how the vocabulary of Col 1:23 is drawn from the world of architecture.

[37]See Beale, *Colossians and Philemon*, 145-51; McKnight, *Colossians*, 196.

[38]Michael O. Emerson and Christian Smith, *Divided by Faith: Evangelical Religion and the Problem of Race in America* (New York: Oxford University Press, 2000), 25-30; Jemar Tisby, *The Color of Compromise: The Truth About the American Church's Complicity in Racism* (Grand Rapids, MI: Zondervan, 2019), 43-51.

and bring elaborate gifts and ultimately the same power that robbed them of their resources."[39] Furthermore, Tinsley avers that

> some would say that the enslaved desired knowledge into the ways of the enslaver so that they might live like them or gain revenge. To some extent this was true, but upon release from slavery they did not seek retribution but only the ability to care for themselves and live peacefully in society. . . . The knowledge they sought was not only to survive this present situation but also to live long enough to be free of it.[40]

For people who were forbidden to read, long denied formal education, begrudgingly educated in segregated schools, then—after danger and turmoil—permitted to attend desegregated schools, the appeal to spiritual knowledge means acquiring something different from the oppressors' faith. Paul's warnings against deception (e.g., Col 2:4, 8, 16) not only apply to strange religious ideas from outside of Christianity that were infiltrating the church, but to distortions within Christianity that marginalize fellow human beings.

MAIN BODY OF THE LETTER: CHRIST'S SUPREMACY AND CHRISTIAN MATURITY (COLOSSIANS 1:15–4:1)

Calling the Colossians to live fully and freely because of Christ (Colossians 2:6-23)

Growing spiritually stronger (Colossians 2:6-7). In Colossians 2:6-7 Paul returns to the building imagery of Colossians 1:10-12, with essentially the same vocabulary, and also employing his favorite word describing upright ethical living: *walk*. Part of faithful walking is to overflow, or abound, with thanksgiving. One might easily overlook the admonition to be thankful when that person has abundant material resources. There is a human tendency to take blessings for granted. But for those on the margins of society, thankfulness to God is especially poignant. Thankfulness when suffering is countercultural, so we recognize it as genuine when we see it. While African American Christianity is not monolithic, a common characteristic of our public worship experience is joy, and has been so from our earliest days when our existence was even more tenuous and life-threatening than it is now.[41] That joy is evidence of "overflowing with thankfulness" (Col 2:7 NIV).

Experiencing Christ's liberating victory over evil forces (Colossians 2:8-15). Paul captures our attention with a rare word in Colossians 2:8, drawn from the practice of slavery.[42] The Greek verb *sylagōgeō* ("I take captive") occurs only here in the New Testament and warns against the impact of following erroneous beliefs. The false teaching (*philosophia*) is hollow, deceptive, and relies on human traditions as well as *ta stoicheia tou kosmou* ("elemental principles of the world" NRSV), a term that occurs again at Colossians 2:20.[43] Paul lists some of the practices of the false teachers in Colossians 2:16-18, and also addresses religious restrictions in Colossians 2:21-22. Scholars debate the source and content of the philosophia, and some of the restrictions mentioned resonate

[39]Tinsley, *Postcolonial Re-reading of Colossians*, 145. This is not to say that Christianity was first introduced to Africa by European missionaries. It was not. However, in the case of many African Americans, the gospel came by way of slaveholding whites in the US.

[40]Tinsley, *Postcolonial Re-reading of Colossians*, 144.

[41]Pedrito U. Maynard-Reid, *Diverse Worship: African-American, Caribbean and Hispanic Perspectives* (Downers Grove, IL: InterVarsity Press, 2000), 67-68.

[42]See McKnight, *Colossians*, 224.

[43]*Stoicheia* occurs a few times in the New Testament (Gal. 4:9; Heb 5:12; 2 Pet 3:10, 12) and scholars debate its meaning. See Pokorný, *Colossians*, 113-21.

with aspects of Judaism.[44] We do not know the details of what the Colossians were up against, but Paul denounces whatever is "not according to Christ" (Col 2:8).

The irony for African Americans is that in Colossians 2:8 Paul warns against the power of religious beliefs to enslave, yet that is what happened to our forebears with Christianity, as it was part of the system that literally took us captive. If the Colossians were indeed mostly Gentiles, then these converts to Christianity had to wade through all sorts of competing beliefs in their attempts to understand how to best orient their lives in obedience to Christ. There is a parallel to the first Africans in America who arrived with religious beliefs and also observed the Christianity practiced by slaveholders.[45] The struggle continues. Many African Americans see the Christianity practiced by large segments of White society as holding us captive. Some Christians support White-supremacist ideas while simultaneously minimizing the voices and experiences of African Americans. Distorted religious views threaten our spiritual freedom in other ways. For example, African Americans continue to abandon Christianity because of the way it has been practiced, with some of us looking to find a spiritual home within traditional African religions.[46] The ideologies of American consumerism also seek to take us captive. Sometimes consumerist ideologies, as in the case of the so-called prosperity gospel, "come dressed up in the clothes of Christian faith."[47] In the third stanza of the Black National Anthem, "Lift Every Voice and Sing," James Weldon Johnson urges us to pray that we not be taken captive to worldliness, which might be found in American consumerist ideologies:

> God of our weary years,
> God of our silent tears,
> Thou who has brought us thus far on the way;
> Thou who has by Thy might Led us into the light,
> Keep us forever in the path, we pray.
> Lest our feet stray from the places, our God, where we met Thee,
> Lest, our hearts drunk with the wine of the world, we forget Thee,
> Shadowed beneath Thy hand,
> May we forever stand.
> True to our God,
> True to our native land.

Colossians 2:9-15 provide three reasons for the believers' confidence in their spiritual liberation. First, Jesus is fully God (Col 2:9; cf. 1:19) and reigns as head over all other spiritual entities (Col 2:10; cf. 1:16). Second, since Jesus possesses the fullness of deity, his followers are complete, having been brought to fullness in him (Col 2:10). The initiatory rite of baptism (seen here as spiritual circumcision) affirms this fullness (Col 2:11-12). There is no need for these Gentile converts to submit to the Jewish ritual of circumcision since Christ has spiritually circumcised them through baptism. Baptism here, as in Rom 6:3-6, symbolizes death and resurrection, mirroring the literal death and resurrection of Jesus. Fullness in Christ means new life, which includes the forgiveness of sins (Col 2:13). Forgiveness is an act of divine favor, or grace, and is pictured as the cancelation of written charges of indebtedness. When Jesus was

---

[44]McKnight, *Colossians*, 25-34.

[45]Vincent L. Wimbush, *The Bible and African Americans: A Brief History*, Facets (Minneapolis: Fortress, 2003); Allen Dwight Callahan, *The Talking Book: African Americans and the Bible* (New Haven, CT: Yale University Press, 2008).

[46]Sigal Samuel, "The Witches of Baltimore," *Atlantic*, Nov. 5, 2018, www.theatlantic.com/international/archive/2018/11/black-millennials-african-witchcraft-christianity/574393/.

[47]Walsh and Keesmaat, *Colossians Remixed*, 138.

nailed to the cross, he carried on him the charges against us (Col 2:14). Perhaps the nailing of written charges is an allusion to the *titlos* (notification) above Jesus on his cross, condemning him as King of the Jews (Jn 19:19). But with the crucifixion of Christ, the condemnatory charges disappear.

The third reason the believers can be sure of their spiritual freedom is that Christ's death on the cross disarmed and embarrassed the powers and authorities (Col 2:15). The reversal here is stark. "It is not the crucified Christ who is 'made a public example' on the cross but the hostile power, and the cross thus becomes the scene of triumph."[48] Making a public spectacle of the powers and authorities recalls the Roman army's victory procession, with the conquered being marched to their doom. God boldly disgraces the evil forces aligned against oppressed people. While such humbling does not always happen in our lifetimes, sometimes the downfall of despots occurs before an audience, as with the humbling of Pharoah when God delivered Israel from enslavement. The book of Revelation depicts God shaming evil powers while passages such as Romans 16:20; 1 Corinthians 15:25; Ephesians 1:22; and 1 Peter 3:22 depict Jesus visibly victorious over evil forces. Such divine reversal speaks to those who have had evil forces marshaled against them. African Americans and other marginalized people might find hope in a God who paradoxically turns the tragedy of the cross into victory. James Cone reflects on "the terrible beauty of the cross" as he compares the crucifixion of Jesus and the lynching of African Americans:

> As Jesus was an innocent victim of mob hysteria and Roman imperial violence, many African Americans were innocent victims of white mobs, thirsting for blood in the name of God and in defense of segregation, white supremacy, and the purity of the Anglo-Saxon race. Both the cross and the lynching tree were symbols of terror, instruments of torture and execution, reserved primarily for slaves, criminals, and insurrectionists—the lowest of the low in society. Both Jesus and blacks were publicly humiliated, subjected to the utmost indignity and cruelty.[49]

The physical cruelty many African Americans suffered mirrors the physical agony that Jesus of Nazareth endured. Allen Dwight Callahan affirms how "African Americans have seen in the Crucifixion the treachery they themselves have suffered individually and collectively."[50] Yet, the shame of the cross is replaced by its power, as the cross represents freedom from sin and triumph over spiritual enemies. The lynching tree is still a symbol of shame for America, but for some of us African Americans, the lynching tree also symbolizes our remarkable strength and resilience. Our faith and fortitude boldly communicate triumph over the genocidal forces aligned against us seen in the lynching tree.[51]

Rejecting religious restrictions (Colossians 2:16-23). Scholars debate the background of the competing religious claims in Colossae, yet it seems that for Paul, the rules and restrictions of Colossians 2:16-23 do not have their origins in Christ. Having grown up immersed in a form of American Christianity that might be described as "legalistic," I am well-acquainted

[48]Hooker, "Colossians," 1408.

[49]James H. Cone, *The Cross and the Lynching Tree* (Maryknoll, NY: Orbis Books, 2011), 31.

[50]Callahan, *The Talking Book*, 219-20.

[51]The Equal Justice Initiative's National Memorial for Justice and Peace in Montgomery, AL is a memorial to the legacy of African Americans who suffered domestic terrorism. The memorial condemns the evil of lynching while simultaneously urging the nation to both be and do better. The cross similarly recalls humanity's evil, but also invites humanity, through faith, to live into the *fullness* (Col 2:10) of being in Christ.

with a religious faith reduced primarily to rules and regulations. In my three decades of pastoral ministry, I've heard from countless African Americans whose experiences were similar to mine, even though we were in different denominations. Although anecdotal, my observations illustrate the human tendency to depend on particular actions (or lack of other actions) as the pathway to maturity or genuine spiritual enlightenment, i.e., wisdom (Col 2:23). Paul instructs the Colossians to "not let anyone condemn you" (Col 2:16) and "Do not let anyone disqualify you" (Col 2:18) in matters of certain religious rituals. It seems that it is possible for rituals to mask rather than highlight the reality of Christ.

Urging heavenly life within harmonious households (Colossians 3:1–4:1)

Dying with Christ and being raised with him (Colossians 3:1-4). African Americans and other marginalized people tend to be wary of any pie-in-the-sky-when-you-die religion that promises justice and freedom only in the afterlife, but urges passivity in the here and now. One tension within our community has been the appeal to personal piety on the one hand, and the call for social action on the other. The civil rights movement highlighted such tension as some Black churches were reluctant to behave in any way that might upset the White establishment, choosing instead to focus primarily on the upright behavior of its members. However, Black churches fueled the civil rights movement, providing leadership, meeting and rallying spaces, and all manner of support systems. While the admonition of Colossians 3:1-4 could be interpreted as a pie-in-the-sky perspective, the subsequent verses demonstrate the way heavenly perspectives impact earthly realities.

Based on the teaching of Colossians 1–2, particularly the notion of dying with Christ (Col 2:20), Paul makes a transition ("since then") to focus on practical ethical instruction, using the language of resurrection. The Colossians not only submit to Christ as king (Col 1:13), they participate in his life, even though Christ is not physically present on earth. The believers are raised with Christ (Col 3:1), have lives that are hidden with Christ (Col 3:2), and will be revealed with him in glory (Col 3:4). Without minimizing the reality of injustice in the present, participation in the life of Christ means spiritual safety and security no matter the circumstances. This is to say that God gives promises to Jesus-followers that societal forces cannot take away spiritual blessings (e.g., Rom 8:38-39). Paul's exhortation is a reminder that people might gain the world yet forfeit their souls (Mk 8:36). From his place of authority—the right hand of God (Col 3:1)—the Lord Jesus Christ rules and intercedes for his people.[52] Christ's rule and intercession not only compels his followers to live blameless lives, but also calls them to foster healthy community that dismantles ethnic and status boundaries (Col 3:11).

Personal piety and social activism need not be seen as oppositional binaries. The accomplishments of the civil rights movement are due, in part, to the moral integrity of the participants. Nonviolent protesters, propelled by faith in Jesus, demonstrated the righteousness of their cause while confronting rabid segregationists. Most thoughtful Americans are astonished to see the footage of abusive law enforcement officials whose water hoses, nightsticks, and dogs assailed honorable church-going protesters, while angry Whites cheered the onslaught. We also do well to remember that social activism is incomplete without spiritual transformation. We need Jesus for that, and the Lord's work of transformation, or redemption, reaches its climax at his return.

---

[52]McKnight, *Colossians*, 292.

Christ is currently not visibly present, but he will return to earth (Col 3:4). The promise of the parousia (second coming) means that whatever social progress we make before that time will always be incomplete.

Taking off the old humanity and putting on the new (Colossians 3:5-17). While waiting for the parousia, Christians must put to death behaviors consistent with a preconversion way of life (Col 3:7), and instead demonstrate their participation in Christ. The worldly behaviors listed in Colossians 3:5, 8-9 characterize those who are disobedient to God and therefore will experience God's wrath (Col 3:6). The first set of vices focuses primarily on inordinate sexual desires and material greed, which is idolatry (Col 3:5). The second vice list (Col 3:8-9) addresses sins that thwart unity.

Unity is a goal for the Christian community. The believers are to shed, like old clothes, the sinful behaviors that characterize the Roman way (Col 3:9), and take on a new self (Col 3:10) with new behaviors (Col 3:12-17). The new self, with its new knowledge, recognizes the unity of humanity (Col 3:11). Participation in Christ, who is all and in all, means that social barriers and ethnic distinctions cannot be allowed to separate the followers of Jesus from each other. The Jew-Gentile (Greek) contrast is attested elsewhere and reinforced with the circumcised-uncircumcised terminology.[53] The Greeks called anyone who could not speak their language, and so presumed to be uncultured, barbarian (*barbaros*). The noun *barbaros* was an onomatopoetic slur, as Greeks called non-Greek speakers babblers ("bar-bar-bar"). Scythians were from the region of the Black Sea, north of the Lycus Valley, and Greeks mocked them as savages. These ethnic and nationalistic contrasts are joined by an economic one: slave-free.[54] For Paul, when it came to ethnic, gender, and social differences, the church was to function more equitably than the broader Roman society.[55]

Harry Maier finds evidence that Colossae and nearby Hierapolis were ethnically diverse, but Colossae, especially, experienced societal attempts to assimilate the diverse cultures. Maier argues that the letter to the Colossians "presents a model of civic integration" that is different from "imperial acculturation."[56] Maier well captures the imagination with his assessment of Colossians 3:11.

> The utopian declaration of Col 3.11, that includes barbarians and Scythians, is a powerful geopolitical representation of the universal reach of Christ's rule and its power in turning enemies into friends. . . . The Roman imperial iconographic treatment of barbarians was to represent them in postures of submission or defeat. Colossians places an alternative cosmopolitan vision before its listeners' eyes. It portrays a unity of humankind brought about through the crucifixion of

[53]Depending on the one making the assessment, humanity could be divided into two groups: Jew and Gentile (or "Greek"), indicating different ethnic (which includes religious) differences. Paul makes this distinction in several places (e.g., Rom 1:16; 1 Cor 12:13; Eph 2:11-12). From a Greco-Roman perspective, Jews have such unique practices that first-century writers like Philo of Alexandria and Josephus explain and defend Jewish life. See Rebecca Futo Kennedy, *Race and Ethnicity in the Classical World: An Anthology of Primary Sources in Translation* (Indianapolis: Hackett Publishing Company, 2013), 243. Notice also how in Acts 16:20, the enslavers of a girl with supernatural power accuse Paul and Silas of not only depriving them of income, but of being Jewish, exploiting anti-Jewish sentiment.

[54]Col 3:11 is reminiscent of Gal 3:28 but lacks the male-female contrast. For possible reasons, see Pokorný, *Colossians*, 170; Harry O. Maier, *Picturing Paul in Empire: Imperial Image, Text and Persuasion in Colossians, Ephesians and the Pastoral Epistles* (New York: Bloomsbury, 2013), 94.

[55]See Scot McKnight, *A Fellowship of Differents: Showing the World God's Design for Life Together* (Grand Rapids, MI: Zondervan, 2015).

[56]Maier, *Picturing Paul in Empire*, 92-93.

> Jesus, a victorious death that triumphs over those 'estranged and once hostile in mind,' no longer enslaved to the now subjugated principalities and powers, and now joined them together in love and perfect harmony, and governed with peace (1.21; 3.13-15).[57]

Maier's analysis resonates with the perspective that many African American Christians have regarding unity with diversity. African American Christians have a lengthy history of being among those who have argued and advocated for the dignity and equality of all people. Furthermore, we have joined with other Christians who believe that being in Christ is key to dismantling the isms that divide humanity. Yet, in dismantling those divisions, we do not erase or ignore our ethnic distinctions. We do not advance the myth of colorblindness that minimizes our identity. The government should make it easier for people of diverse backgrounds to function in proximity to each other, having equal access to opportunities within that society. We do not, however, want the government to require the erasure of our cultural heritage. It is the church, those who are in Christ, that can present to the world a new community where ethnic distinctions are cause for celebration and not fear.

In Colossians 3:12, Paul addresses the entire community with terms that described Israel in the OT: *elect*, *holy*, and *beloved*. In so doing, he connects the Gentile followers of Jesus to the Jewish followers of Jesus, indicating their common spiritual heritage. The diverse Christian community, which shares in the life of Christ, nurtures its unity through virtues that stand in stark contrast to the vices listed in 3:8-9.[58] The ultimate virtue on the list is forgiveness. The admonition to forgive is prickly for African Americans, as well as other oppressed groups. There is no question that forgiveness is Christlike. The problem is that oftentimes African Americans are expected to not only forgive the injustices of a bygone era, such as slavery, but also be quick to forgive current injustices, such as the war against drugs that unfairly targeted us, racial profiling and brutality by police, or other acts of violence and discrimination. High-profile incidents, such as a White-supremacist shooting and killing nine people in a historic African American church in South Carolina in 2015, or a police officer shooting and killing a man in his own home (with the officer claiming she thought she was encountering an intruder in her own home), found African Americans offering forgiveness to the killers. Some have declared that the work of justice gets truncated with such public acts of forgiveness.[59]

Miroslav Volf offers help with his nuanced discussion of forgiveness.[60] He argues that forgiveness is, of course, the Christian response to injustice. However, Volf also addresses the interplay between honesty, forgiveness, and injustice, describing the journey that reconciliation takes.

> As to the journey, it follows the path that starts with remembering truthfully, condemning wrong deeds, healing inner wounds, releasing wrongdoers from punishment and guilt, repentance by and transformation of wrongdoers, and reconciliation between the wronged and their wrongdoers; and it ends with the letting go

[57] Maier, *Picturing Paul in Empire*, 90.

[58] For detailed discussion of each of the virtues, see McKnight, *Colossians*, 320-26; Beale, *Colossians*, 294-302, Pokorný, *Colossians*, 171-75.

[59] See Dennis R. Edwards, *Might from the Margins: The Gospel's Power to Turn the Tables on Injustice* (Harrisonburg, VA: Herald Press, 2020), 177-79.

[60] Miroslav Volf, *The End of Memory: Remembering Rightly in a Violent World* (Grand Rapids, MI: Eerdmans, 2006).

> of the memory of wrongdoing. We take this journey partially and provisionally here and now when we forgive and reconcile—and on rare occasions release the memory of wrong suffered. We undertake it once again, definitively and finally, at the threshold of the world to come.[61]

For Volf, releasing or letting go of the memory of wrongdoing is not amnesia. Rather, it is a "divine gift" that "grows out of a healed relationship between the wrongdoer and the wronged in a transformed social environment."[62] That social environment is the type of Christian community that Colossians envisions.

Christian households within hostile territory (Colossians 3:18–4:1). Right after we read about and reflect on diverse countercultural Christian community characterized by love (Col 3:14), peace (Col 3:15), thankfulness (Col 3:15), and gratitude (Col 3:16), we run into the household codes (Col 3:18–4:1) which appear to reinforce society's social divisions. As I noted in the introduction, the household codes (*haustafeln*) are a stumbling block to women, African Americans, and to anyone in solidarity with those marginalized groups.[63] On the one hand, the commands directed to women, children, and enslaved people, concur with the status quo.[64] The household codes appear to demonstrate agreement with Roman's hierarchical and oppressive society.[65] According to law and custom, the paterfamilias ruled the household, exercising complete authority over his wife, children, and slaves. It is not clear why Paul did not directly denounce patriarchy, child abuse, and slavery. It is true that the early Christians were initially a small movement with little societal clout; consequently, railing against the establishment may have only served to threaten Roman leadership who could destroy the nascent church.[66] Nevertheless, we are disappointed that while Paul saw the need to point out certain evils (as in Col 3:5-9), he apparently overlooked others. We cannot help but wonder if Paul's social position as a male Roman citizen obscured his perspectives on vulnerable members of society.

On the other hand, however, aspects of Paul's household instructions display "a notable deviation from societal norms."[67] The deviation is demonstrated in at least the following three ways:

1. The motivation given to those in the subordinate position is based on the lordship of Christ more so than on societal requirements (and such is the case for slave masters).
2. Paul commands those in dominant positions—husbands, fathers, and masters—not solely those in the subordinate roles.
3. Those in the subordinate position are addressed alongside those in the dominate position, suggesting that both groups are fellow members of the Christian community. Both

[61]Volf, *End of Memory*, 151.

[62]Volf, *End of Memory*, 146.

[63]Martin, "*Haustafeln*," 206-31.

[64]E.g., Marianne Meye Thompson, *Colossians and Philemon*, The Two Horizons New Testament Commentary (Grand Rapids, MI: Eerdmans, 2005) observes, "The household codes are worrisome because they appear to perpetuate societal patterns that lend themselves too easily to domination and abuse" (96).

[65]K. R. Bradley, *Slaves and Masters in the Roman Empire: A Study in Social Control* (New York: Oxford University Press, 1987) notes that Christianity spread among the "lower orders of society," and with regard to slavery, asserts, "The stress contained in these injunctions on servile obedience is remarkable for a religion which taught the spiritual equality of all mankind, and what this reflects is an unqualified acceptance of the existing social structure in which they found themselves by early Christians" (38).

[66]See Pokorný, *Colossians*, 178.

[67]Thompson, *Colossians and Philemon*, 93.

groups are present together and hearing the letter being read aloud.

Regarding the lordship of Christ as motivation, wives are to submit to their husbands, not so much because their husbands demand or require it, but because humility demonstrates Christlikeness, which is how one might understand "fitting in the Lord" (Col 3:18). Likewise, children are to obey their parents because it is acceptable, or pleasing to the Lord (Col 3:20). Enslaved people are to obey earthly masters out of fear of the Lord Jesus Christ (Col 3:22).[68] Additionally, those enslaved are to perform their tasks as an offering to the Lord Jesus, rather than to their earthly masters (Col 3:23), with the promise that God rewards with an inheritance (Col 3:24). We might imagine that for enslaved African American such a distinction in motivation, while not dismissing the injustice of the institution, allowed for some mental and emotional separation from the human master as well as the economic engine that drove slavery. Some enslaved people might come to believe that they were not working for the master of the plantation or for American capitalism. Instead, they adopted a heavenly perspective, laboring in humiliating earthly conditions while simultaneously existing in a superior spiritual condition because they were serving God while their masters were not.

While Paul reminds enslaved Colossians that wrongdoing will not go unpunished, he also points out that there is no favoritism or partiality when it comes to God's reckoning (Col 3:25; cf. Eph 6:8). Perhaps enslaved Christians in Colossae found some satisfaction knowing that God considers the actions of masters as well as that of slaves. The Greek word *prosōpolēmpsia*, translated as "favoritism" (NIV) or "partiality" (NRSV) describes judgment based on appearance.[69] The New Testament employs this vocabulary to teach that humans are prone to make judgments based on appearances (Jas 2:1, 9), but God does not (Acts 10:34; Rom 2:11; Eph 6:9). For the multitude of marginalized people—including African Americans—who have been continually judged and devalued based on physical appearance, the teaching that God does not show partiality is especially reassuring. It is also another way that we can see how much of the Christianity presented to the enslaved of the New World was hypocritical. American Christianity presented a God who showed partiality, apparently favoring White skin over dark skin. Even Scripture—specifically the so-called curse of Ham in Genesis 9:20-27—was used to justify God's apparent favoritism of Europeans.[70] According to racist interpretations of the so-called curse of Ham, God allegedly destined Africans to be enslaved to Europeans. Alongside enslavement came the demonization of Black skin.[71] One of the pillars that bolsters the system of racism is prejudice based on appearance. God does not make judgments based on physical appearance (1 Sam 16:7) and according to Colossians 3:25, God makes equitable judgments.

Regarding the direction of Paul's commands, we are not surprised that wives are instructed to submit, while children and slaves are instructed to obey. What does come as a surprise are the commands for husbands to love their wives, fathers not to provoke or

---

[68]*Kyrios* is used for both the human *master* as well as the *Lord Jesus*. The upper case in the English translations makes the distinctions clear.

[69]BDAG, 887.

[70]For more on the curse of Ham, a good place to start is Edwin M. Yamauchi, *Africa and the Bible* (Grand Rapids, MI: Baker Academic, 2004), 19-33.

[71]Gay L. Byron, *Symbolic Blackness and Ethnic Difference in Early Christian Literature* (London: Routledge, 2002).

embitter their children, and masters to treat their slaves justly and fairly. Rather than Paul telling husbands to demand that their wives submit, or give husbands license to coerce, he tells them to love their wives. Love must remain supreme (Col 3:14; cf. Eph 5:25-33). Even though society granted husbands dominion over their wives, Paul commands husbands to love. Furthermore, the admonitions of Colossians 3:12-13 may be behind Paul's additional instructions that husbands not treat their wives harshly (literally, "become embittered toward them"). Compassion, kindness, humility, meekness, patience, and forgiveness flow from love. Christian husbands, with respect to their relationships with their wives, are called to be noticeably different from their non-Christian counterparts, who treated their wives as possessions. Christian fathers, according to Paul, must take into account the way that their parenting impacts their children's psyche. Parents should not demoralize their children.[72] This command to fathers picks up on the vices in Colossians 3:8. For eons, anger and abusive language from parents—sometimes accompanied by physical abuse—have created dispirited children, who are likely to grow up and become abusive parents themselves.

The longest part of the household codes relates to the master-slave relationship.[73] As noted above, slaves are to obey their earthly masters while offering their labor to the Lord. At the same time, earthly masters are required to treat enslaved people justly and fairly. The term *dikaios* ("right" or "just"), an ever-present concept in Paul's writings, relates to behavior that reflects the character of God.[74] In context, just treatment of enslaved people forbids their exploitation even if falling short of manumission. However, the letter to Philemon, which likely accompanied this letter via the slave Onesimus (Col 4:9), suggests that Paul may have had more in mind. Paul's admonition that Philemon take back Onesimus "no longer as a slave but more than a slave, a beloved brother" (Philem 16), relates to *isotēs* ("fairness" or "equality") in Colossians 4:1. Some scholars see Colossians 4:1 as advocating that all slaves be treated the same, with none getting preferential treatment, while other scholars see Paul as requiring full social equality.[75] Paul tells earthly masters that they have a heavenly Master who sees if slaves are treated justly and equitably. For those on the margins of society, there is some consolation in knowing that God sees the ones who perpetrate injustice even if God does not visibly intervene in ways that we'd prefer. Colossians 4:1 is a sober warning for Christians who participate in or benefit from unjust systems; it is a message to all who possess relative power and privilege. God is the ultimate master to whom all must give an account.

African Americans have long viewed Christians who participated in the sale or ownership of enslaved people as offensive and hypocritical. Callahan recounts a 1774 petition from a group of enslaved people to the Massachusetts House of Representatives, where they "enlisted the words of Paul to argue against their status of perpetual servitude. It was slavery's conflict with Pauline commandments of family and communal life, they contended, that

[72]The verb *athymeō* occurs only here in the entire New Testament.

[73]Thompson, *Colossians and Philemon*, 94, speculates that since the letters to the Colossians and to Philemon were written at the same time and traveling to the same place, the Onesimus-Philemon relationship may have prompted this longer discussion of the slave-master relationship.

[74]See Beale, *Colossians and Philemon*, 328; McKnight, *Colossians*, 366; Thompson, *Colossians and Philemon*, 96.

[75]See discussion in Beale, *Colossians and Philemon*, 327-31 of both perspectives. Beale takes the view that Paul does not argue for freedom for slaves, but for impartiality in their treatment.

showed the institution to be inherently incompatible with Christianity."[76] Likewise, in current times we find Christians who benefited from injustice without acknowledging it to be offensive and hypocritical. It's not uncommon to hear White people—including Christians—who lament discussions of slavery or reluctantly endure antiracism trainings, say something like, "My family never owned slaves," or "I don't hate Black people."[77] While it is commendable that one's family did not own slaves, or to be free of hatred, it is disingenuous to deny how slavery caused America to prosper economically, with that prosperity overwhelmingly benefiting White people—even the non-slave-owners. If virtues such as compassion, kindness, and humility (Col 3:12) could be allowed to accompany the sobering perspective of Colossians 4:1—that the heavenly Master sees injustice and unfairness—then perhaps those in positions of relative power and privilege would do all they could to rectify situations rather than excuse their culpability. By Paul addressing those in dominant positions, and not just the subordinate position in society, he sowed seeds for societal transformation with Christians at the forefront as they developed equitable communities. Maier points out that since the household code here in Colossians addresses "those inhabiting traditional positions of power," it "unsettles the traditional absolute rule and exploitation of Graeco-Roman paterfamilias over their subordinates. A domestic peace in the house church marked by love, justice and equity insists that the Colossian church realize a civic identity that runs counter to the exploitative rule by domination of its imperial overlords."[78] While revolution might start from the bottom, positive change increases exponentially when those in power join in.[79]

Interestingly, Jonathan Edwards, son of the famous slaveholder, preacher, and intellectual of the same name, delivered sermons against the slave trade. One of his sermons included the following observation: "And as the apostle Paul requires masters to give their servants that which is just and equal, (Col 4:1) so if any were enslaved unjustly, of course he in this text requires of the masters of such, to give them their freedom."[80] In the earlier part of the sermon, Edwards takes Colossians 4:1 to apply to "the general duty of servants who are righteously in the state of servitude, as many are or may be, by hire, by indenture, and by judgment of a civil court. But they do not say, whether the servants in general of that day were justly holden in slavery or not."[81] For Edwards, Paul writes about the fair treatment of workers, and goes as far as to suggest that if actual slavery is in view, then the just and fair thing would be manumission. It is true that *doulos* is sometimes translated servant and may apply in the Greco-Roman world to those who were employed and were not actual slaves. However, interpretations that remove slavery from the context of Paul's words do a further disservice to those who were actually enslaved. Turning Paul's commands into words for how bosses should treat workers is a luxury our enslaved forbears did not have. All

[76]Allen Dwight Callahan, "Brother Saul," in *Onesimus, Our Brother: Reading Religion, Race, and Culture in Philemon*, Paul in Critical Contexts, ed. Matthew V. Johnson, James A. Noel, and Demetrius K. Williams (Minneapolis: Fortress Press, 2012), 144.

[77]See Robin J. DiAngelo, *White Fragility: Why It's So Hard for White People to Talk About Racism* (Boston: Beacon Press, 2018).

[78]Maier, "Sly Civility," 347.

[79]See Edwards, *Might from the Margins*, 80-84.

[80]Tryon Edwards, *The Works of Jonathan Edwards, D.D., Late President of Union College with a Memoir of His Life and Character* (Boston: John P. Jewitt & Co, 1854), 85 (emphasis original).

[81]Edwards, *The Works of Jonathan Edwards*, 85.

Bible readers do well to remember, and subsequently address, the reality of slavery rather than ignore or minimize it. Furthermore, even though chattel slavery is illegal, there are modern-day sexual, economic, and penal forms of exploitation that enslave vulnerable people.[82] Christians are still called to undermine and dismantle those systems.

The early believers heard the household codes of Colossians 3:18–4:1 while all the groups mentioned—husbands, wives, children, slaves, and masters—worshiped Jesus together. They listened to this letter (and the one to Philemon) while looking each other in the face. That is certainly not the way Christianity was practiced in the USA for much of our existence. Blacks worshiped separately from Whites. And when they were allowed to worship in the same buildings, seating was segregated. The Colossian Christians were called to dismantle the function of the ancient household even if not the form. This is to say that Paul pictured Christians living within their societal roles, but functioning as siblings in Christ. Consequently, the Christians must not exploit, dehumanize, or otherwise minimize their sisters and brothers. As Scot McKnight points out, "As with Philemon, so here: Paul opens the door for a new way of life in the household."[83] Lloyd Lewis observes,

> Though Paul's church was grounded in its own time and situation he insists on the power of God's new arrangement. In God's new arrangement masters are exhorted not only to show justice to their slaves but to demonstrate their recognition of equality (*isotes*) (4:1) with them. Through the church of which Christ is head, the situation exists in which social stratification begins to crumble along its hardened edges.[84]

While Paul did not rail against Roman injustices, he may have mitigated abuses, with Christians demonstrating a loving and increasingly equitable way of life. As noted earlier, Paul does not denounce the system that allows for patriarchy, child abuse, and slavery. However, he has already pointed out Christ's superiority over and defeat of spiritual forces (Col 1:16-17; 2:8). Evil spiritual forces are what undergird and empower society's unjust systems and structures. Christians are called to participate in Christ's work by confronting evil's power undergirding dehumanizing systems (Col 2:8, 20).

LETTER CLOSING: FACING OUTWARD AND MOVING ONWARD (COLOSSIANS 4:2-18)

Proclaiming the mystery of Christ in words and actions (Colossians 4:2-6). As the letter draws to a close, Paul's final admonitions address not only his evangelistic ministry, but also that of the Colossians. According to Colossians 4:2, evangelism starts with prayer. For Christians, according to Paul, conversation with God is prelude to conversations and other interactions with those outside the community of faith (Col 4:2, 5-6). The Jesus-followers must make prayer a central focus of their communal life. Not only are the Colossians to devote themselves, they must watch, or guard their prayers with attitudes of gratitude.[85] Thanksgiving is an important theme in Colossians (Col 1:3, 12; 2:7; 3:17; 4:2), as it is throughout Paul's writings (e.g., 2 Cor 4:15; 9:11, 12; Eph 5:4; Phil 4:6; 1 Thess 3:9; 1 Tim 2:1).

---

[82]Walsh and Keesmaat, *Colossians Remixed*, 212-14; Michelle Alexander, *The New Jim Crow: Mass Incarceration in the Age of Colorblindness* (New York: New Press, 2012).

[83]McKnight, *Colossians*, 367.

[84]Lewis, "Colossians," 387.

[85]See Rom 12:2 for similar language of *devotion* in prayer and Mt 26:41 for the combination of *watching* and *praying*.

Being thankful in prayer is not easy, especially when experiencing trials. Paul offers himself as an example. He reminds his readers that he is in prison (Col 4:3). Yet he does not bewail his imprisonment. Even though he is imprisoned because of his evangelistic efforts, Paul asks the Colossians to pray that a door be opened for more preaching opportunities. Paul describes his evangelistic proclamations as speaking the mystery of Christ. Mystery has already appeared in this letter, referring to Christ's presence within his followers (Col 1:26, 27) and to Christ himself (Col 2:7), and Paul feels obligated to communicate that mystery (Col 4:4). Paul's eagerness to communicate his message despite having been jailed for doing that very thing, prompts a comparison to Dr. Martin Luther King Jr. In his famous "Letter from a Birmingham Jail," Dr. King takes the opportunity to reaffirm his mission to combat segregation through civil disobedience and other forms of protest, and also to call others to share in the work. Dr. King even uses the word *thankful* on two occasions in the letter to describe his feelings about others ("some of our White brothers in the South" and "some noble souls from the ranks of organized religion") joining in the efforts for Blacks to gain civil rights.[86]

In more recent times, *salty* is used to describe the vulgar speech of old sailors (those experienced in traversing saltwater), but Paul has just the opposite in mind in Colossians 4:6. Beale compares Colossians 4:6 to Ephesians 4:29 and comments that Paul may "have in mind the metaphorical notion of salt being a preservative against corruption of food: words seasoned with salt will not corrupt or rot but will build up and benefit others."[87] Helpful speech accompanies a wise lifestyle (Col 4:5). Language surely matters, especially in a society characterized by racism and xenophobia. For example, people ought to avoid using derogatory terms to refer to those outside their own ethnic group and give careful thought to using language that invites communal connection. Every marginalized group is painfully familiar with the crude aspersions designed to demoralize them. African Americans have endured the "n-word" for generations and notice that even some Christians are not immune to the sickness of bullying others through insults, stereotyping, and vulgarities. While the proclamation of the gospel in the first century is different from the civil rights struggle in twentieth-century America, this section of Colossians evokes images of the movement led by Dr. King and other iconic figures. Many who engaged in nonviolent demonstration during the civil rights movement were Christians whose faith compelled them to work for justice. They committed themselves to prayer before their demonstrations while emotionally preparing to be arrested. Edward Gilbreath, in his trenchant analysis of Dr. King, remarks how "too many Christians in the public square today have allowed their politics to shape and define their faith. For Dr. King it was always the other way around."[88] Many African Americans who lived through or participated in the movement were upstanding citizens of impeccable behavior, who behaved wisely in public (cf. Col 4:5). Their speech was gracious (Col 4:6) so as not to invite the ire of White people who opposed the civil rights of African Americans.

---

[86]Martin Luther King Jr., "Letter from a Birmingham Jail," April 16, 1963, African Studies Center, University of Pennsylvania, www.africa.upenn.edu/Articles_Gen/Letter_Birmingham.html.

[87]Beale, *Colossians and Philemon*, 346.

[88]Edward Gilbreath, *Birmingham Revolution: Martin Luther King Jr.'s Epic Challenge to the Church* (Downers Grove, IL: InterVarsity Press, 2013), 167-68.

The marginalized have often gone the extra mile to demonstrate upright behavior so as not to summon suspicion from law enforcement or other segments of society. We often feel that if our presence is perceived as threatening, then the onus is on us to quash the qualms of others. Yet that ought not be the case. While we continue to be Christlike in our speech and actions, we recognize that Christians in privileged positions must also take up their responsibility to follow Paul's teachings. In the way that the household code of Colossians 3:18–4:1 addressed the powerful as well as the relatively powerless, so do these final admonitions. Those possessing relative power and privilege in society must conduct themselves wisely and graciously. Furthermore, all Christians—especially in the West—could take a cue from the Colossians regarding evangelism. The church's posture toward outsiders can be combative. Our evangelistic efforts have been tinged with an air of bravado rather than humility. While we must be ready to use words to share what we believe about Jesus (Col 4:6; cf. 1 Pet 3:15), our actions will typically speak more loudly.

Connecting with fellow ministers of the gospel (Colossians 4:7-15). The Great Migration describes the relocation of 6 million African Americans from southern states to primarily large cities in northern states during 1916–1970.[89] Southern churches bid farewell to members who embraced new Christian sisters and brothers in Northern congregations.[90] To affirm their good standing as church members, the Christian newcomers to the North often carried letters of commendation from the pastors of their home churches to present to their new congregations. Pastors could then readily identify new leaders and willing workers for their churches. In much the same way that Southern pastors commended their existing members to new congregations, Paul acknowledges fellow workers, starting with the two couriers of the letter, Tychicus (Col 4:7) and Onesimus (Col 4:8). In addition to carrying the letter to Colossae, Tychicus is to give his own update of Paul's circumstances. He may also be the one to read aloud and explain the letter to the Colossians, and perhaps to the Laodicean Christians meeting in Nympha's house (Col 4:16). Although we know little of Tychicus, Paul clearly trusted him (see Acts 20:4; Eph 6:21; 2 Tim 4:12; Titus 3:12). There's a tendency to skip or skim the endings of New Testament letters, except perhaps to grab a salient command or poignant benediction.[91] The letter endings, however, give us insights into Paul's circumstances as well as a brief glimpse into the life of early Christian communities. Ignoring the closing greetings might lead us to assume that Paul was a type of lone worker, traveling and ministering solo, without a team of partners. It is clear, however, that Paul had several others with whom he ministered. Paul's closing greetings, or "shout-outs," as my students have called them, typically depict fellow workers in favorable terms.

After mentioning the letter carriers, Paul next sends greetings from three coworkers who share his ethnic background: Aristarchus, Mark, and Jesus, called Justus (Col 4:10-11). Paul refers to the men literally as fellow workers who are "of the circumcision." They are the

[89]See Isabel Wilkerson, *The Warmth of Other Suns: The Epic Story of America's Great Migration* (New York: Random House, 2010); Thomas C. Holt, *Children of Fire: A History of African Americans* (New York: Hill and Wang, 2010), 237-83.

[90]L. H. Whelchel, *The History and Heritage of African-American Churches: A Way out of No Way* (St. Paul, MN: Paragon House, 2011), 161-71.

[91]The oversight occurs in academic circles as well as local church contexts. See Jeffrey A. D. Weima, *Neglected Endings: The Significance of the Pauline Letter Closings*, JSNT 101 (Sheffield, UK: JSOT Press, 1994), 12.

only Jews—at least at the time of Paul's present circumstances—who work alongside him. Paul approves of their work for the kingdom of God, a concept with especially Jewish undertones. Also, he notes how the presence of these men has been especially comforting.[92] Paul's comfort may come not only from shared experiences as evangelists, but also from the reality that these men understand his world, that of a Jewish believer in Jesus the Messiah.[93] Not only does Paul mention the ethnic background of these workers in a time when Jew-Gentile relationships could be strained and even hostile, he highlights the comfort these Jewish men give him. In our time, those who observe ethnic differences within groups are often accused of fostering division. The accusations tend to come from people who accept the myth of colorblindness (discussed earlier). The thinking appears to be that if we do not acknowledge ethnic differences, they will not become an issue. In reality, ethnic differences are already issues and ignoring those differences exacerbates, not ameliorates, tensions among people—including Christians. Furthermore, when ethnic minorities meet together apart from White people, or celebrate and share aspects of their cultural heritage, some White people become suspicious and even fearful. Many African American Christians who have worked in White-dominated ministries, have come to lament our situation. Our voices get minimized, our culture dismissed or appropriated, and our concerns ignored.[94] Because there are often so few of us working at one time in a particular setting, there are small numbers of others who share common circumstances, perhaps providing unique comfort in our situation. The fact that Paul finds comfort among those who best understand his world and journey of faith, encourages ethnic minorities to seek support from those who might best understand our situation. At the same time, we ethnic minorities continue to work alongside those of other ethnic groups. The point is that we don't have to reject, downplay, or otherwise minimize our ethnic identity to serve the Lord alongside White people.

Paul calls Aristarchus a "fellow prisoner" (cf. Acts 19:29; 20:4; 27:2; Philem 24).[95] Yet one of Paul's earliest coworkers, Barnabas (see Acts 11:30; 12:24; 13:2), is mentioned without a descriptor, suggesting that the Colossians already know him (Col 4:10). But Paul also wants the Colossians to know Mark, Barnabas's cousin (cf. Philem 24).[96] With the rift between Paul and Barnabas concerning Mark in view (Acts 15:36-40), we find that Colossians 4:10 suggests there had been a reconciliation between the two apostles.

Three more ministry partners extend their greetings to the Colossians (Col 4:12-14), Epaphras, Luke, and Demas (cf. Philem 23-24). Here we learn Luke's vocation as physician. The last word on Demas is that he abandoned Paul (2 Tim 4:10). Epaphras, likely the founder of the church, is a Colossian and agonizes in prayer on behalf of his people. The emotional connection between Epaphras and the Colossians is heightened knowing that he is one of them. Again, background and cultural identity

---

[92]*Parēgoria*, "a source of encouragement, comfort" (BDAG), occurs only here in the New Testament, but suggests "comfort in the profoundest sense of the term" (Pokorný, *Colossians*, 193).

[93]McKnight, *Colossians*, 391.

[94]E.g., Edward Gilbreath, *Reconciliation Blues: A Black Evangelical's Inside View of White Christianity* (Downers Grove, IL: InterVarsity Press, 2006).

[95]Aristarchus may not have currently been imprisoned with Paul, who may be speaking figuratively (see McKnight, *Colossians*, 388).

[96]The KJV refers to Mark as the nephew ("sister's son") of Barnabas, but *anepsios* means "cousin."

matter in human relationships, as Paul's remarks assume.

Paul goes on to give his own greetings, not only to the Colossians, but also to the Christians in nearby Laodicea, with special attention to the believers who meet in Nympha's house (Col 4:15). It's likely that the Laodicean Christians met in Nympha's home and the Colossians met in Philemon's (and Apphia's) home (Philem 1-2). We know little about Nympha, but it is safe to assume she practiced well the hospitality that was expected and necessary in her day (cf. 1 Pet 4:9). She may have been the patron of the church, having the financial means for about forty or so people to meet in her home.[97] We can only speculate as to how prominent women, such as Nympha, responded to the instructions to be submissive to their husbands (Col 3:18).[98] As with the commands to enslaved people (Col 3:22-25), the words to wives have been used for centuries to reinforce patriarchy, limiting the place of all women—not just wives—in the church and even in the broader society. Nympha prompts us to remember with respect all the women who served God's people—especially church leaders—tirelessly, and often with little recognition. In many denominations, women have been held back from pastoral leadership but nevertheless made innumerable and immeasurable contributions to the work of ministry. Women not only opened their homes, but also their wallets, to support God's work. In addition, they passed along the faith like Lois and Eunice (2 Tim 1:5) and taught the Scriptures like Priscilla (Acts 18:26). In some African American contexts, the wise words and faithfulness of "church mothers" exert powerful influence on entire congregations. Paul's greeting to Nympha prompts us to remember all women who serve the Lord, and especially those who were prevented from public speaking and leading. Lewis notes that "Paul's choice [of people to mention] shows us the breadth of the family of believers, for they were Jew (Jesus, called Justus) or Greek (Tychichus)(*sic*); slave (Onesimus) or free (Archippus); male (Luke) and female (Nympha)."[99] Paul's closing greetings give a glimpse into the way he viewed the Christian community: "There is no longer Greek and Jew, circumcised and uncircumcised, barbarian, Scythian, slave and free, but Christ is all and in all!" (Col 3:11).

Sharing and remembering (Colossians 4:16-18). Paul's request that the Colossians trade letters with the Laodiceans (Col 4:16) prompts speculation as to whether that latter letter is one that is already in the canon (unlikely), or is simply lost to us (likely).[100] We likewise wonder what unique message Paul may have had for the Laodiceans. Also, Paul's instructions for swapping letters reminds us that churches can stimulate connection rather than foster competition. This is to say that Paul's invitation for two different communities to share what they have heard and learned could be a model for current times as mutual sharing can strengthen relationships. Connection through sharing and remembering is how the letter to the Colossians ends. The last few verses reinforce my initial observation that Paul writes as a pastor. Part of pastoral ministry is helping to encourage connections

[97]Consider another woman, Lydia, who first hosted the Philippian Christians (Acts 16:14, 40). See Nijay K. Gupta, *Colossians*, Smyth & Helwys Bible Commentary (Macon, GA: Smyth & Helwys, 2013), 192-93.

[98]See the imaginative take on Nympha from Brian J. Walsh and Sylvia C. Keesmaat, *Colossians Remixed*, 49-57; 220-25.

[99]Lewis, "Colossians," 387.

[100]See N. T. Wright, *Colossians and Philemon*, TNTC (Grand Rapids, MI: Eerdmans, 1986), 159-62, who argues that Ephesians is the letter to the Laodiceans.

among the flock, while also helping them to remember. The object of remembrance is not only the work God has done through Jesus, which Paul has made clear throughout the letter (e.g., Col 1:3-8), but also the work that the community must do. Paul uses his pastoral authority to remind Archippus—with the entire church as witnesses—to complete whatever task he had been given (Col 4:17). We don't know what Archippus was supposed to do, but we can appreciate pastoral admonition. Some scholars suggest that Paul is giving Archippus a warning.[101] If we assume, as may be the case in some contemporary church circles, that calling a person to remember their duty is cause for shame or embarrassment, then it is easier to see Paul's words as a warning to Archippus. However, traditional African American churches have generally affirmed the pastor's role as spiritual leader and guide. Consequently, people are honored when the pastor calls them out by name, since the aim is often to affirm their responsibility in front of everyone. Marianne Meye Thompson's point about Paul's words to Archippus is apropos of how many African American churches have operated: "While Archippus thus has a specific, personal commission, it is not a private matter but the responsibility of the church together to encourage and exhort him to complete it."[102] Such will be the case with Paul's letter to Philemon. Finally, as Paul takes the writing utensil from his secretary to sign his own name, he requests the Colossians to remember his imprisonment (Col 4:18). Paul serves as a living witness of how faith in Jesus can be costly. His imprisonment is also a reminder that human systems are paradoxical. On the one hand, the Pax Romana—the Roman Empire's strategy for making Rome great—paved the way for some to advance in a variety of disciplines. On the other hand, the Roman Empire could be oppressive, thwarting human flourishing for others. The brilliant Paul, an apostle of the crucified yet risen Jesus, promoting faith, hope, and love, wishes his readers grace, even while languishing in prison. Paul was the casualty of an imperfect system. African American Christians know that until broken systems get fixed—if they ever will—there will always be the need for God's grace.

BIBLIOGRAPHY

Alexander, Michelle. *The New Jim Crow: Mass Incarceration in the Age of Colorblindness*. New York: New Press, 2012.

Bevere, Allan R. "Colossians and the Rhetoric of Empire: A New Battle Zone." In *Jesus Is Lord, Caesar Is Not: Evaluating Empire in New Testament Studies*, edited by Scot McKnight and Joseph B. Modica, 183-96. Downers Grove: IVP Academic, 2013.

Blount, Brian K. *Then the Whisper Put On Flesh: New Testament Ethics in an African American Context*. Nashville: Abingdon Press, 2001.

Bowens, Lisa M. *African American Readings of Paul: Reception, Resistance, and Transformation*. Grand Rapids, MI: Eerdmans, 2020.

———. "Liberating Paul: African Americans' Use of Paul in Resistance and Protest." In *Practicing with Paul: Reflections on Paul and the Practices of Ministry in Honor of Susan G. Eastman*, edited by Presian Burroughs, 57-73. Eugene, OR: Cascade, 2018.

Bradley, K. R. *Slaves and Masters in the Roman Empire: A Study in Social Control*. New York: Oxford University Press, 1987.

Brogdon, Lewis. *A Companion to Philemon*. Cascade Companions. Eugene, OR: Cascade Books, 2018.

[101]Pokorný, *Colossians*, 195

[102]Thompson, *Colossians and Philemon*, 108.

Byron, Gay L. *Symbolic Blackness and Ethnic Difference in Early Christian Literature*. London: Routledge, 2002.

Byron, John. *Recent Research on Paul and Slavery*. Recent Research in Biblical Studies 3. Sheffield, UK: Sheffield Phoenix Press, 2008.

Callahan, Allen Dwight. *Embassy of Onesimus: The Letter of Paul to Philemon*. New Testament in Context. Valley Forge, PA: Trinity Press International, 1997.

———. "Paul's Epistle to Philemon: Toward an Alternative Argumentum," *HTR* 86, no. 4 (1993): 357-76.

———. *The Talking Book: African Americans and the Bible*. New Haven, CT: Yale University Press, 2008.

deSilva, David A. *An Introduction to the New Testament: Contexts, Methods and Ministry Formation*. Downers Grove: IVP Academic, 2018.

De Vos, Craig Steven. "Once a Slave, Always a Slave? Slavery, Manumission and Relational Patterns in Paul's Letter to Philemon." *JSNT* 23, no. 82 (2001): 89-105.

DiAngelo, Robin J. *White Fragility: Why It's So Hard for White People to Talk About Racism*. Boston: Beacon Press, 2018.

Edwards, Dennis R. "Hermeneutics and Exegesis." In *The State of New Testament Studies: A Survey of Recent Research*, edited by Scot McKnight and Nijay Gupta, 63-82. Grand Rapids, MI: Baker Academic, 2019.

Emerson, Michael O., and Christian Smith. *Divided by Faith: Evangelical Religion and the Problem of Race in America*. New York: Oxford University Press, 2000.

Felder, Cain Hope. "The Letter to Philemon: Introduction, Commentary, and Reflections." In *2 Corinthians–Philemon*, vol. 11, *New Interpreter's Bible*, edited by Leander E. Keck, 881-905. Nashville: Abingdon, 2000.

Fitzmyer, Joseph A. *The Letter to Philemon: A New Translation with Introduction and Commentary*. AB 34C. New York: Doubleday, 2000.

Foster, Paul. *Colossians*. BNTC. New York: Bloomsbury T&T Clark, 2016.

Gilbreath, Edward. *Birmingham Revolution: Martin Luther King Jr.'s Epic Challenge to the Church*. Downers Grove, IL: InterVarsity Press, 2013.

Gilliard, Dominique DuBois. *Rethinking Incarceration: Advocating for Justice That Restores*. Downers Grove, IL: InterVarsity Press, 2018.

Gupta, Nijay K. *Colossians*. Smyth & Helwys Bible Commentary. Macon, GA: Smyth & Helwys, 2013.

Holt, Thomas C. *Children of Fire: A History of African Americans*. New York: Hill and Wang, 2010.

Hooker, Morna D. "Colossians." In *Eerdmans Dictionary of the Bible*, edited by David Noel Freedman, Allen C. Myers, and Astrid B. Beck, 1404-12. Grand Rapids, MI: Eerdmans, 2000.

Johnson, Matthew V., James A. Noel, and Demetrius K. Williams, eds. *Onesimus, Our Brother: Reading Religion, Race, and Culture in Philemon*. Paul in Critical Contexts. Minneapolis: Fortress Press, 2012.

Lewis, Lloyd A. "Colossians." In *True to Our Native Land: An African American New Testament Commentary*, edited by Brian K. Blount, Cain Hope Felder, Clarice J. Martin, and Emerson B. Powery, 380-88. Minneapolis: Fortress Press, 2007.

———. "Philemon." In *True to Our Native Land: An African American New Testament Commentary*, edited by Brian K. Blount, Cain Hope Felder, Clarice J. Martin, and Emerson B. Powery, 437-43. Minneapolis: Fortress Press, 2007.

Maier, Harry O. *Picturing Paul in Empire: Imperial Image, Text and Persuasion in Colossians, Ephesians and the Pastoral Epistles*. New York: Bloomsbury, 2013.

———. "A Sly Civility: Colossians and Empire." *JSNT* 27, no. 3 (2005): 323-49.

Martin, Clarice J. "The Haustafeln (Household Codes) in African American Interpretation: 'Free Slaves' and 'Subordinate Women.'" In *Stony the Road We Trod: African American Biblical Interpretation*, edited by Cain Hope Felder, 206-31. Minneapolis: Fortress, 1991.

Maynard-Reid, Pedrito U. *Diverse Worship: African-American, Caribbean and Hispanic Perspectives*. Downers Grove, IL: InterVarsity Press, 2000.

McKnight, Scot. *A Fellowship of Differents: Showing the World God's Design for Life Together*. Grand Rapids, MI: Zondervan, 2015.

———. *The Letter to Philemon*. NICNT. Grand Rapids, MI: Eerdmans, 2017.

———. *The Letter to the Colossians*. NICNT. Grand Rapids, MI: Eerdmans, 2018.

Pokorný, Petr. *Colossians: A Commentary*. Peabody, MA: Hendrickson, 1991.

Raboteau, Albert J. *Slave Religion: The "Invisible Institution" in the Antebellum South*. New York: Oxford University Press, 1978.

Smith, Abraham. "Paul and African American Biblical Interpretation." In *True to Our Native Land: An African American New Testament Commentary*, edited by Brian K. Blount, Cain Hope Felder, Clarice J. Martin, and Emerson B. Powery, 31-42. Minneapolis: Fortress Press, 2007.

Smith, Mitzi J. "Slavery in the Early Church." In *True to Our Native Land: An African American New Testament Commentary*, edited by Brian K. Blount, Cain Hope Felder, Clarice J. Martin, and Emerson B. Powery, 11-22. Minneapolis: Fortress Press, 2007.

Stevenson, Bryan. *Just Mercy: A Story of Justice and Redemption*. New York: Spiegel & Grau, 2014.

Thompson, Marianne Meye. *Colossians and Philemon*. The Two Horizons New Testament Commentary. Grand Rapids, MI: Eerdmans, 2005.

Thurman, Howard. *Jesus and the Disinherited*. Boston: Beacon Press, 1976.

Tinsley, Annie. *A Postcolonial African American Re-reading of Colossians: Identity, Reception, and Interpretation Under the Gaze of Empire*. New York: Palgrave Macmillan, 2013.

Tisby, Jemar. *The Color of Compromise: The Truth About the American Church's Complicity in Racism*. Grand Rapids, MI: Zondervan, 2019.

Van Dyke, Robert H. "Paul's Letter to Philemon: An Appeal Above and Beyond the Law." *Sewanee Theological Review* 41, no. 4 (1998): 384-98.

Volf, Miroslav. *The End of Memory: Remembering Rightly in a Violent World*. Grand Rapids, MI: Eerdmans, 2006.

Walsh, Brian J., and Sylvia C. Keesmaat. *Colossians Remixed: Subverting the Empire*. Downers Grove, IL: InterVarsity Press, 2004.

Weima, Jeffrey A. D. *Neglected Endings: The Significance of the Pauline Letter Closings*. JSNT 101. Sheffield, UK: JSOT Press, 1994.

Whelchel, L. H. *The History and Heritage of African-American Churches: A Way out of No Way*. St. Paul, MN: Paragon House, 2011.

Wilkerson, Isabel. *The Warmth of Other Suns: The Epic Story of America's Great Migration*. New York: Random House, 2010.

Wimbush, Vincent L. *The Bible and African Americans: A Brief History*. Facets. Minneapolis: Fortress, 2003.

Yamauchi, Edwin M. *Africa and the Bible*. Grand Rapids, MI: Baker Academic, 2004.

Young, Stephen E. *Our Brother Beloved: Purpose and Community in Paul's Letter to Philemon*. Waco, TX: Baylor University Press, 2021.

LETTERS TO THE THESSALONIANS

Marcus Jerkins

INTRODUCTION

Stephen King's *The Stand* is one of his most famous postapocalyptic pieces. The story surrounds two groups of people who represent the forces of good and evil before the end of the world and the beginning of another. The title *The Stand* is appropriate because that is exactly what those who are on the side of good are supposed to do: uphold decency, goodness, righteousness, and truth.

In a similar fashion, Paul exhorts the Christians at the city of Thessalonica to stand. It is worth noting that he uses the language of "waiting" (1 Thess 1:10; 1 Cor 1:7).[1] They are waiting with anticipation for their Lord. Paul reaches out to the Thessalonians—praising their past faithfulness to the gospel and their present allegiance to Messiah Jesus—in an effort to make sure that they do not lose either. In the process, Paul comforts and warns about the dangers of being thrown off because of faulty beliefs regarding the Lord's coming. In particular, since many of the Thessalonians are concerned that those who had already "fallen asleep" would miss the parousia (or return of Christ), Paul needs to clarify this for them. Death would not in any way diminish the great glory that believers—alive or asleep at the parousia—would experience when the Lord comes (1 Thess). Also, the Lord has not come yet, despite the concerns of a few Thessalonian believers, and several things would have to happen before he came (2 Thess). Waiting is the name of the game. The people of God are to continue in the things of God looking forward in faith and practice to the day they see Jesus.

As a boy, I remember being raised on the theology of my ancestors that looked sweetly at the coming of the Lord.[2] As Paul intended, the Lord's coming came as both a comfort and a warning. It blessed me to hear about the fact that death was not final, that life with Jesus was inexorable. During funerals in the Black church we sing "I shall wear a crown." This hope impels us to go on as we have in the face of injustice.

But there is also an admonition. We would often say, thinking of that great king who comes as a "thief in the night," that we should never let him "catch you with your work undone." The promise of the coming of Jesus offers to the oppressed both the comfort of justice being done and the attainment of paradise with the Savior and the warning that wickedness will not go unpunished by the Lord of glory.

Consequently, every aspect of these letters, and not merely their reflections on eschatology,

[1]In 1 Thess, Paul uses *anamenō*, while in 1 Cor, he uses *apodechomai*. Both have the same function in both passages. Paul speaks of the current status of the people of God, a people waiting with anticipation to see their Savior.

[2]See Cain H. Felder, "1 Thessalonians," in *True to Our Native Land: An African American New Testament Commentary*, ed. Brian K. Blount (Minneapolis: Fortress Press, 2007), 389-400; Cain H. Felder, "2 Thessalonians," in Blount, *True to Our Native Land*, 401-8, for other perspectives on African American engagement with some of the themes and ideas of these letters. See also Lisa M. Bowens, *African American Readings of Paul: Reception, Resistance, and Transformation* (Grand Rapids, MI: Eerdmans, 2020), for a more general analysis of African American interpretations of Paul the apostle.

offer the reader a peek into the early church. We get a chance to better understand how these small, beleaguered congregations survived to produce the sprawling churches of the modern era. These letters gave them hope and joy that allowed them to carefully manage the many crises they faced being part of this new sectarian, marginal group. It does us great benefit now to read these letters anew to see what the Spirit of God continues to say to us through them.

Before further analysis of these letters, I now turn to briefly discuss preliminary matters regarding them. This kind of investigation will allow us to explore the letters more deeply.

HISTORICAL BACKGROUND: THESSALONICA[3]

Founded in 316 BC, Thessalonica was founded by Cassander, a Macedonian military leader, after the disunification of the Hellenistic empire under Alexander the Great. Cassander named the city after the daughter of Philip II, the half sister of Alexander the Great. The city became prominent in part due to its location as a port city below the Hortiates mountains. By 187 BC, Thessalonica was given the ability to print its own coinage by King Philip V. That it was allowed to do so helped it gain high economic status among the cities throughout Macedonia.

In 168 BC, Rome brought Macedonia under its suzerainty and it became one of its territories, as part of its march to lay siege to the former empire of Alexander the Great. When they divided Macedonia, Thessalonica became the capital of the second district. Thessalonica's support for Rome granted it the privilege of being called the capital of the province of Macedonia. Also, the Romans built the Via Egnatia, a road that connected Thessalonica to Dyrrachium on the Adriatic Sea in the west.

Thessalonica chose wisely in support of Octavian and Mark Antony after the death of Julius Caesar in 44 BC. Their reward was to be declared a free city, which meant that they could receive a certain amount of autonomy and some support from Rome. When Paul came to Thessalonica, it was a financially prosperous city.

Its population was diverse. The evidence suggests that it contained Jews, Greeks, Thracians, and Italians. The diverse population meant a diversity of religions. Paul mentions how the Thessalonian Christians had "turned . . . from idols" and to worship the "living and true God" (1 Thess 1:9). The residents of Thessalonica likely worshiped Zeus, Asclepius, and Demeter. But they also worshiped Egyptian deities like Isis and Serapis. They also participated in the worship of the goddess Roma and in giving worship to Caesar. Acts also suggests that there was a synagogue in Thessalonica, indicating the presence of the practice of Judaism (Acts 17:1).

THE CHURCH OF THE THESSALONIANS

Paul wrote these letters to the churches of the Thessalonians, a predominantly Gentile church. Acts 17 reveals that Paul established this church during his journey in Macedonia. In both of

[3]For more information on the historical background of Thessalonica, see Eugene Boring, *I and II Thessalonians: A Commentary*, NTL (Louisville, KY: Westminster John Knox Press, 2015), 14-19; Abraham J. Malherbe, *The Letters to the Thessalonians: A New Translation with Introduction and Commentary*, AB 32B (New York: Doubleday, 2000), 14-15; Nijay Gupta, *1–2 Thessalonians*, NCCS (Eugene, OR: Cascade Books, 2016), 3-7. See also Beverly Gaventa, *First and Second Thessalonians*, Interpretation (Louisville, KY: John Knox Press, 1998), for a more theological and homiletical reading of the letters. Wayne Meeks, *The First Urban Christians: The Social World of the Apostle Paul*, 2nd ed. (New Haven, CT: Yale University Press, 1983), explores Paul's work in urban settings, and Peter Oakes, "Contours of the Urban Environment," in *After the First Urban Christians: The Social-Scientific Study of Pauline Christianity Twenty-Five Years Later*, ed. Todd Still and David Horrell (London: T&T Clark, 2009), 21-35, engages this topic also with reference to Thessalonica.

these letters, Paul speaks of the church as a persecuted body of believers. Acts 17 explores the persecution with origin from Jews who were jealous of the preaching of the gospel to the Gentiles. Paul himself focuses on the persecution the church received from their fellow Gentiles. But these two states of affairs are not contrary to one another. It is certainly possible that Paul received persecution that started with Jews who then motivated Gentiles to raise objections to the newfound faith of these Gentile believers.

Conventional scholarship suggests that Paul wrote the first letter around AD 49. Acts 18 locates the establishment of the church at Corinth around 51 as it mentions the ruler Gallio who held office during this time, circa 51. Since Paul established the church at Thessalonica before this point, it makes sense, it is argued, to see the congregation being constituted then. For other theological reasons, which cannot be fully explored here, many have concluded that this letter is Paul's earliest.[4] Paul would have written the second letter sometime after the first, maybe in the mid to late 50s.

But there is good reason to believe that Galatians may have been Paul's earliest letter.[5] If so, it may be that 1 Thessalonians was one of Paul's earliest but maybe not the earliest. Paul mentions that he was in Athens when he sent Timothy to check on the Thessalonians. It could be that he was still in Athens when Timothy returned but this is unlikely. He may have been in Corinth when we wrote 1 Thessalonians. He may have been in Corinth again when he wrote the second letter.[6]

AUTHORSHIP

Space does not permit a thorough engagement with scholarship on the question of Paul's authorship as it relates to 2 Thessalonians.[7] While 1 Thessalonians is undisputed among modern scholars, 2 Thessalonians is not. Many argue that it is pseudepigraphic, in that it sounds so much like 1 Thessalonians that it cannot have been written by Paul. Also, many charge that 2 Thessalonians presents a different eschatology.

The first argument is poor. Many of the same scholars who disqualify the Pastorals do so because they sound too different from the other letters. The second argument is better but still fails to grapple with the possibility that Paul saw 2 Thessalonians as an opportunity to clarify his theology of the Lord's coming. Paul does not argue the coming of Jesus will look like a burglary to Jesus' followers, they will be ready for it (1 Thess 5:4). There is no drastic shift in argument between the letters. But 2 Thessalonians argues that the parousia (the coming of Jesus) had not happened yet, because some people thought it had. Thus, Paul had to make sure no further misinformation would damage the church's faith. This explains a great deal of the nature of the letter in my view.

PURPOSE AND THEOLOGY

Paul wrote these letters for similar reasons. The first letter was meant to give comfort in the Thessalonian Christians' time of crisis. Paul wrote the first time to give an extra layer of assurance to them after Timothy left them. Paul wanted to affirm and strengthen the congregation even after Timothy's joyful report. Paul

[4]See Malherbe, *Letters*, 75.

[5]N. T. Wright, *Paul: A Biography* (New York: HarperOne, 2018).

[6]For the life of Paul, see Wright, *Paul*.

[7]N. T. Wright and Michael F. Bird, *The New Testament in Its World* (Grand Rapids, MI: Zondervan Academic, 2019), discuss the arguments for and against authorship. The arguments against Pauline authorship, in my view, are quite weak. Also on this view, see Malherbe, *Letters*, 350-69. The late Malherbe, former professor at Harvard and perhaps the most distinguished modern commentator on the letters, dismantles many of the conventional arguments for doubting the letter's authenticity.

encouraged the people with good news to sustain them. He wrote that they are remembered before God, that God is with them, and that they should wait patiently and steadfastly for the coming of Jesus.

Second Thessalonians continues in this same spirit except that Paul had heard that there was confusion regarding the nature of the coming of Jesus. Paul went into greater detail about Jesus' coming, arguing that Jesus, most assuredly, had not come yet. Things had to happen within the church and within the world that would signal the real parousia. In the end, given Paul's paranetic emphasis in both letters, his aim was the same: to offer clarity about the Lord's coming and help the people remain steadfast in their devotion to the Lord until they saw him face-to-face.

The Thessalonian correspondence offers us a theology wholly centered on the eventual appearance of the coming of the Lord. Paul offered consolation to those who endured a beleaguered present, giving them the expectation that a glorious future would break in on them. The Lord whom they sought would come to where they were to deliver them from the wickedness with which they had to contend. But Paul was clear: act like what you are expecting. Live by the power of the living Lord now because you will live by that power later.

But this message is not for individuals. The language and emphasis of these letters is that the community will be rescued together. As such, they rely on Jesus together and hold each other accountable to make sure that the Lord is pleased with how we interact with him and one another. The horizontal posture, how we live in community with one another, cannot be separated from the vertical posture, how we live with God. This way of being is essential to apocalyptic expectation. Those who wait on the Lord's appearance take seriously the necessity to live in a way that demonstrates hope in his coming.

OUTLINE OF THE THESSALONIAN CORRESPONDENCE

1 Thessalonians

1 Thessalonians 1:1 Opening Greeting

1 Thessalonians 1:2-10 Remembering Faith and Waiting for the Son

1 Thessalonians 2:1-16 Remembering the Preaching of Paul, His Coworkers, and the Bond of Persecution

1 Thessalonians 2:17-19 Paul's Prayer to Come to the Thessalonians

1 Thessalonians 3:1-10 Timothy's Report of Thessalonian faith

1 Thessalonians 3:11-13 Paul's Prayer for Preparedness for the Lord's Coming

1 Thessalonians 4:1-12 Instructions for Preparation for the Coming of the Lord

1 Thessalonians 4:13–5:11 Consolation, Commandments, and the Community in the Coming of the Lord

1 Thessalonians 5:12-24 Instructions for Living as a Waiting Church

1 Thessalonians 5:25-28 Closing Greeting

2 Thessalonians

2 Thessalonians 1:1-2 Opening Greeting

2 Thessalonians 1:3-12 The Current Tribulation and the Coming Judgment

2 Thessalonians 2:1-12 Clarity on the Coming of the Lord

2 Thessalonians 2:13-17 Instructions with a Prayer for God's Strength

2 Thessalonians 3:1-5 Paul's Request for the Church and Prayer for the Thessalonians

2 Thessalonians 3:6-15 Instructions for Living in Community

1 THESSALONIANS

Opening greeting (1 Thessalonians 1:1). The opening of 1 Thessalonians is not unusual for someone writing within the Greco-Roman world. Greco-Roman letters included "the name of the author, addressees, and a salutation."[8] The writer mentions his own name, Paul, and those assisting with the writing of the letter, Silvanus and Timothy (see Acts 15–16). They also mention the addressee. This letter is written "to the church of the Thessalonians." Where Paul might highlight the city, "to the church in Corinth" (1 Cor 1:2),[9] here he says, "the church of the Thessalonians."

But the greeting sets the theological tone of the letter. These people are not mere addressees. They are those who find their identity, "in God the Father and the Lord Jesus Christ." This, in the very least, demonstrates a binitarian framework for knowing the true God. It is indisputable that Paul thinks Jesus is God. And Jesus and God the Father are the very residence of the believer. The Godhead is established as both the Father and Jesus. Paul will certainly not exclude the Spirit, but, for now, he lists the Father and the Son as the place where the Thessalonians can be found (see Gal 4:4-6; 1 Cor 12:4-6). This mystical language suggests two realities. They as people are now identified with God the Father and his Son, Jesus Christ. Also, that they as a people live in God like a house. God's presence surrounded them as the pillar cloud did by day and the fire pillar by night (Ex 13:21-22). It may be that Paul wants less emphasis on the city in which this church is located but does want them to focus on their location in the realm of God. They are certainly living on earth but at the same time they are "seated in heavenly places with Christ Jesus" (Eph 2:6, author translation). As will become clear in the letter, the persecuted status of this church did not determine their condition, rather, it is their place in God that did.

Since they have found their identity in the Father and the Son, their location will play the most important role in who they truly are. They are found in the Father and the Son and are waiting on the Son to bring to full manifestation their communion with the Father. Though Paul never refers to the Thessalonians as God's children, it is quite obvious that the connection they have with God as God's family is assumed. These are no mere servants but members of the household of God.

It can be pointed out that Paul, unlike most of his other letters, never refers to his vocation in the beginning of this letter. It is clear that Paul speaks of his authority (1 Thess 2:7) and praises the Thessalonians' proper reception of what Paul and his associates preached to them as the very "word of God" (1 Thess 2:13). But, instead of discussing the usual sources of "grace and peace," namely, God and Jesus, Paul expresses this himself. Whether coming from God and Christ or from Paul, the effect is meant to be the same. But, here, it can show in a different way the priestly role of the apostle to confer the grace and peace of God on those over whom he has oversight (see Num 6:21-27).

Many Christian traditions take seriously the priestly blessings given by the minister. The Black church, however, though mostly found with low liturgy practices, the priestly blessing, the benediction, is absolutely essential. Many members of the Black church wait for the pastor to raise his or her right hand to offer a word of grace and peace over their lives for the week. In this incarnational moment, the pastor is considered a vessel of the Word of God,

[8]See Malherbe, *Letters*, 97-100; Gupta, *Thessalonians*, 38-39; Boring, *Thessalonians*, 45-54.
[9]See Malherbe, *Letters*, 98.

speaking protection and blessing that will walk out of the church doors with the believer.

The kind of liturgy is inconsequential. The polity is not the controlling issue. It is the fact that the Black preacher is a person who has to be empowered with the very real presence of God for a people who need the very real presence of God to make it for another week. To face the very present hells of this age, the Black member hopes to receive a word of grace and peace to overcome.

Remembering faith and waiting for the Son (1 Thessalonians 1:2-10).[10]

1 Thessalonians 1:2-3. Part of the pastoral role is to keep people in prayer. It is a fundamental part of Paul's communication with each church he served (Rom 1:9; Eph 1:16; Phil 1:4; Col 1:3). His letters frequently contain a mention of how much—unceasingly—Paul prayed for those over whom God had given him oversight. Prayer was and certainly still is an indispensable tool for building others up in their faith. It is also a necessary weapon used as a mechanism against the powers of darkness (Eph 6:18).

1 Thessalonians 1:4-5. Paul was aware that those who had received the message of the gospel had received it by grace. That is, they had been "chosen," by God, it was not by happenstance that they came to believe. God through his own power transformed them to become believers in the gospel. Salvation is not a mere choice based on human reason but the consequence of God's gracious persuasion to trust in him.

As such, what was preached was ordained by God. First Thessalonians 1:5 is one of the many instances in Paul (Rom 15:19; 2 Cor 11:12) where he speaks of signs and wonders following the declaration of the gospel. The skeptic who rejects the miracles of Jesus or the authenticity of Christian testimony about the beginnings of the early church due to a lack of eyewitness testimony should seriously reconsider his objections to Jesus, the Gospels, and Acts. Here, in this passage, we have the firsthand account of Paul that he himself was not only a witness to but a practitioner of the miraculous. Scholarship must give more attention to Paul as a miracle worker.

Paul and his coworkers confirmed the truth of the gospel through their miracles, just as the Gospel writers testified of Jesus. Paul called this back to the Thessalonians' attention so that they might be reminded of the authenticity of their chosen status and their place in God. God had orchestrated their salvation and stamped his approval on them. Also, the fact that Paul and the coworkers were capable of miracles proved their own ministerial authenticity.

1 Thessalonians 1:6-10. With the Jewish Scripture as their primary source of information about the faith, Paul and his coworkers were essential sources for knowledge of Christianity. And, in persecution, those who led them to the faith were the necessary examples to maintain the faith. Their initial reception was insufficient for its maintenance, even when it was received with Spirit-led joy. They needed human examples to confirm the validity of their trust in the living God.

Those in Macedonia and Achaia took notice. They saw the Thessalonians as authentic followers of the faith despite deterrents that arose to coax them to forsake it. Their witness spoke for itself. In the process of the conversion, the Thessalonians mimicked Paul and his associates. Their eagerness to listen to the gospel was apparent. Paul and his associates were well received and the gospel they preached found a welcome place in the lives of the Thessalonians.

[10]See Gupta, *Thessalonians*, 39-41; Malherbe, *Letters*, 105-122; Boring, *Thessalonians*, 55-76; Gaventa, *Thessalonians*, 13-22.

They forsook their former devotion to their idols and turned to the "living and true God." As we have noted, devotion to idols representing many different deities was the common religious affiliation of many in the congregation.

It may be that many in the congregation were God-fearers. These were Gentile believers who came to accept Jewish belief in the one God and attempted to be faithful to Jewish Scripture but stopped short of circumcision. Cornelius the Centurion was considered a God-fearer (Acts 10–11). And evidence from Acts suggests that future members of the church were in the synagogue when Paul initially preached at the beginning work of the church there (see Acts 13). So, it may be that members of the congregation kept their idols while participating in Jewish practice or there were some who continued to worship idols while others did not. But, because of their previous conversion to the living God, Paul knew that the Thessalonians were waiting for the Lord. Faith in Jesus' return shaped the way they conducted themselves in the world. The living Lord gave them hope that they would be rewarded in the day of judgment and be accepted by God. The Lord's appearance and salvation gave them much needed confidence to hold on to their hope.

Remembering the preaching and conduct of Paul, his coworkers, and the bond of persecution (1 Thessalonians 2:1-16).

1 Thessalonians 2:1-2. Paul reminds the Thessalonians of his initial encounters in this section. The first two verses reflect on the time when Paul was persecuted and mistreated in Philippi prior to his coming to Thessalonica. It is a reflection of joy, however, because, despite Paul's suffering, the people of Thessalonica received the gospel.

1 Thessalonians 2:3-8. And suffer he did. Paul speaks not only of his suffering but also of his "mistreatment" (*hybrizō*). But he was undeterred. As it is described in Acts 16–17, Paul continued his onward march to preach the message of the cross in Thessalonica with "courage in our God" (1 Thess 2:2) in the face of fierce resistance. Acts 16:22-23 portrays egregious acts of abuse. Paul was flogged and jailed without a trial in Philippi. Such would have been allowable in the ancient world, where there was little oversight of policing. Both as noncitizens, and possibly because they were Jews, they were more easily mistreated (see Acts 16:20). And since Paul and his companions were considered *peregrini*, the mere accusation of wrongdoing on the part of Paul and Silvanus prompted acts of violence against them in the name of justice. But Paul continued to preach the gospel with unflappability.

When the gospel was preached in Thessalonica (Paul refers to this as "our appeal"), it was done after a moment of state violence (so, naturally, questions would arise about the character of those who were punished). People today still assume that when people are punished for wrongdoing or when unarmed Black men are killed by police, that they did something to merit it. But we know that punishment can often be utilized by unjust people for unjust reasons. Probably, Gentiles abused Paul and Silvanus, not only for religious but also for ethnic reasons, because they were Jews. Similar ethnocentric identity politics still persist today. Paul explains, however, for him and his coworkers, that their intentions, aims, and speech were pure when they declared God's message. They did not do it to please people but God, who is the ultimate judge.

And, for good measure, Paul mentions that he could have asked for something in return for the great gift they had given the Thessalonians (see also 1 Cor 9:6-12). Other philosophers and traveling orators relied on the benevolence of their audience for sharing their wisdom. Paul was clear that he could have expected pay, some sort of honorarium, for preaching the wisdom of the ages to them (1 Cor 9:9-11). But he did not. So, in essence, Paul clarifies that there is every reason to trust them from the time they began their ministry in Thessalonica until the present moment.

Instead, Paul uses language mostly associated with women to speak of their conduct. They were "gentle" among the people (*nepios*), like a wet nurse (*trophos*) "caring" for her own children (1 Thess 2:7). Paul saw their role as those who give more than they took. He gave the milk of the gospel to those needing the sustenance of the kingdom of God. Such motherly language was not rare for Paul (Gal 4:19). It shows that Paul valued femininity in ways many men, in the name of masculinity, would hold in disrepute.

1 Thessalonians 2:8-12. Paul explains that he and his coworkers not only preached the gospel to them but gave their own "lives" for them. This language should be heard with all of its Christlike fervor. In other words, Paul and the others did for them what Christ did for all the world. The work of the minister was to continue to enact the mode of the cross for all whom she came into contact, resembling Christ over and over again. Paul and the others gave and self-funded their work in the beginning. Acts informs us that Paul was a tentmaker and used this skill to acquire funds to support himself in the work of the ministry (Acts 18:3). But it also appears that Paul received some support from the Philippians when spending time in Thessalonica (Phil 4:15-16).

Paul was a father and a mother to them; they were like his children. His conduct could not be in any way besides careful and scrupulous. The intimacy of the bond between him and them, and, indeed, all of them and God, demanded virtuousness and genuineness. The cause was beyond comparison; the very lives of those to whom Paul preached were on the line. To live the life that God had called them to lead, in his "kingdom and glory" (1 Thess 2:12), they had to heed the words of Paul and his associates. Believing the words preached by Paul and his associates would provide them with eternal life in this world and in the coming age. This age had seen the coming of God's Son to die and be raised. The coming age would be unambiguously characterized by the coming of the Son of God. The ambiguating corruption that obfuscates the thin veil between heaven and earth would be torn from the top to the bottom, exposing the dominance of God over the powers of Sin and Death for all eternity.

1 Thessalonians 2:13-16. Since the declaration of the gospel leads to this inexorable future, Paul constantly thanks God for his initial meeting with the Thessalonians and their ongoing relationship.[11] For the ministers did not merely give them the results of the deepest and most profound of human cogitations; they gave the Thessalonians something greater, "God's word" (1 Thess 2:13). And the Thessalonians received the message of God not as it came from human beings but as it came from the very God who made the world.

This reflection of Paul should spark a major examination of the role of the minister and all members of the body of Christ as it pertains to the high responsibility associated with the gospel. Oftentimes, the preaching of the word is desacralized. Paul and the other ministers shared with them the word that contained the potency that created the very cosmos (see Gen 1). When Paul says they were given the "word of God," Paul has in mind the message

[11]Boring, *Thessalonians*, 95-95; Malherbe, *Letters*, 166-67.

that enables life itself to continue. The Christian, then, should be careful about how we consider the rightful preaching of the word of God and Scripture on which it is based. The declaration of the gospel is a creative act where Christ is revealed and the age of new creation becomes ever more apparent, driving out darkness and bringing life from the dead. As such, the word of God creates space for God to "energize" the community (cf. Phil 2:13) to walk in their salvation (1 Thess 2:13).

The fact that Christ is the new center of their existence comes with negative consequences as well (1 Thess 2:14).[12] Paul compares the suffering that Christians endured from other Jews with the suffering of the Thessalonians. Paul reflects on the historical record, arguing that Jews killed Jesus and the prophets. Indeed, the refrain of Jesus himself, was that Jerusalem, the Pharisees and scribes, and other Jewish groups were responsible for the blood of the prophets (Mt 23:37; Lk 11:46-54; 13:34). In Luke–Acts, the emphasis falls on the elite of Jerusalem as the most responsible. Interestingly, Jesus held them accountable for crimes they did not directly commit. But their recalcitrance to the gospel made them indirectly responsible in the eyes of God, and therefore placed themselves under God's judgment.

Paul situates himself within the prophetic tradition of Israel, and therefore discusses the resistance of those who opposed his message in the manner of the prophets. Echoing Jesus, whom he considered part of that prophetic tradition, he describes the effort of Jewish persecution as "filling up the measure of their sins" (1 Thess 2:16). God is not without a response. Paul suggests that God will bring his wrath on them for their abuse of the prophets of God.

Such wrath would be expected against those who have resisted God's very words. Consequently, judgment, wrath, punishment, these are expected when injustice is done, when people have committed heinous acts of violence against others even out of fidelity to their understanding of God. It is not problematic at all, then, to be people of mercy who long for God's just judgment, as we also see in the book of Revelation: "Sovereign Lord . . . how long?" (Rev 6:10).

African Americans, on the whole, have been people of mercy but await the day of judgment. The hope of Black people is that God will not allow those who have committed terrible crimes against their brothers and sisters of a darker hue to escape guiltlessly. African Americans have longed for repentance on the part of racist depraved social groups who have repressed and subjugated them. But where there is no repentance, Black people request God's righteous judgment to come.

Paul's prayer to come to the Thessalonians (1 Thessalonians 2:17-19). Paul and his associates longed to come back to Thessalonica and continue to share the love and care of the gospel with the Thessalonians. Despite the intense opposition Paul faced while ministering to them, he wanted to make sure they would return to see the Thessalonians. We will discover that Timothy has already done this (1 Thess 3:2). Here, however, Paul explains that they all wanted to come to see the Thessalonians face-to-face.

In fact, Paul explains that "we wanted to come to you—certainly I, Paul, wanted to again and again—but Satan blocked our way" (1 Thess 2:18). This mention of Satan is the only time he is mentioned by name, although it is no doubt that Satan lurks behind the scenes in much of the discourse of persecution. We are not aware of the nature of the hindrance. It could be that Satan worked through Jews or

[12]Boring, *Thessalonians*, 97-109; Malherbe, *Letters*, 166-71.

non-Jews, perhaps some form of human opposition who were motivated by Satan (Mt 16:23; Lk 22:3). This may be what Paul has in mind.

The diligent search for a path to see the congregation again is to assure that their faith has been maintained. For Paul's chief aim is to make sure that they will be able to stand worthily before the Lord when he comes. They are the "joy" and "crown of boasting" of Paul and the other ministers. They are evidence that their labor, their sacrifice, was not for nothing, that God has won their hearts for his glory.

Timothy's report of Thessalonian faith (1 Thessalonians 3:1-10). Paul, remembering the past, recounts the reasons for sending Timothy to Thessalonica. Paul, not able to come himself, remained in Athens with other associates while they sent Timothy to check on the Thessalonians. Paul and the ministers were a bit uneasy about the status of the Thessalonian church members since this group of believers, young in the faith, had seen Paul's own suffering and suffered, too. Timothy's mission was to "strengthen" them and bring "comfort" to them. They wanted to make sure that they understood that persecution was normal for the real believer.

So, Timothy came and made certain that they were remaining faithful to the Lord who called them. And when Timothy returned, he gave a very favorable report of their faith. The Thessalonians wanted to see Paul and the others as much as Paul wanted to see the Thessalonians (1 Thess 3:6).

Such news brought Paul and the coworkers joy and encouraged them in their suffering. It may be that they continued their work in Athens. We see from the report of Acts 17 that Paul was brought before the Areopagus, which was not a mere philosophical debate.[13] It may be that Paul and the other ministers were in very real danger and were able to get out of it with little trouble. But, apparently, something else had occurred that threatened their lives. Perhaps, this was the attack of Satan that prevented them from returning to Thessalonica. Whatever the particular problem, Paul was concerned about the strength of the faith of the Thessalonians and hearing that they were still maintaining their devotion to Christ was quite encouraging.

The psychological dimension is just one aspect of why Paul and the others seek to know their good. Paul's ministry aimed toward strengthening the people of Thessalonica so that he and the others might "thank God . . . for all the joy that we feel before our God" (1 Thess 3:9). This statement probably refers both to Paul's current prayer to God for them and to Paul's eschatological expectation. Paul intends to present this community of believers before the Lord Jesus on the day of judgment. The current supplications he makes to God on their behalf anticipate the day when Paul will be able to give his account of stewardship and how he did his utmost to secure these believers in the faith (1 Thess 3:10-11). For this reason, Paul and the others are deeply concerned with returning to continue their work among the Thessalonians so that they may continue in their growth.

Paul's prayer for preparedness for the Lord's coming (1 Thessalonians 3:11-13). Paul, then, grants us insight into his life of prayer, what he is seeking God for in his ministry. He asks that God, the Father, will "direct our way to you" (1 Thess 3:11). The ministers are eager to support these new followers of Jesus so that they may increase in their love toward one another and so they might be found without blemish (1 Thess 3:12). Again, this is

[13]Craig Keener, *Acts: An Exegetical Commentary* (Grand Rapids, MI: Baker Academic, 2012), 3:2600-2607.

eschatological speech (cf. Eph 5:27). Paul's assignment is to build and nurture this community of believers to the end that they are prepared for the Lord's coming.

But why such a focus on the coming of Jesus? We will discuss this in more detail below and especially in our discussion on 2 Thessalonians. But it becomes essential to note the dynamic between the recounting of persecution and the expectation of the coming of Jesus. The day of the Lord is the day when all accounts are settled, the righteous are rewarded and the wicked are punished. This is why oppressed communities long for this day of all days. Paul wants to emphasize to them that they need not go back on their faith, but stay faithful to their calling in the Lord Jesus. Through their endurance, their maintenance of their faithfulness to God, in spite of massive resistance, their salvation will be revealed. And one day, the Lord whom they seek will complete the work of their salvation. Giving up on Jesus is not an option because one day Jesus will return for them. Paul's charge is to make sure that they were completely aware of this.

Instructions for preparation for the coming of the Lord (1 Thessalonians 4:1-12).

1 Thessalonians 4:1-2. While waiting for the Lord's coming, however, as Paul's prayer for them indicates, holiness and blamelessness were fundamental. Paul will now give instructions, a type of Christian *halakhah.* Among Jews, discussing the way one walks was metaphorical for proper conduct. The Wisdom Psalm, Psalm 1, provides a perfect example of this mode of tradition: "Blessed is the person who does not walk . . ." (Ps 1:1, my translation). Paul, then, turns to giving ethical instructions. But these instructions are not disconnected from the larger argument concerning the Lord's coming and their tribulation. Preparation for the Lord is part of the larger concern. Paul sent the letter, sent Timothy, and will seek to come to them again for their preparedness. To be ready for the Lord is to walk as if the one is waiting for the Lord to return.

Paul recounts that he gave them "commandments" when he was present with them. He will now discuss some of those "commandments" again in the letter. What he gave to them, we must be reminded, were not mere ethically based suggestions. Moreover, they were not prescriptions for good behavior that any philosopher might give. These were the charges that were given "through the Lord" (1 Thess 4:2). Paul echoes what he said in 1 Thessalonians 2:13, where he explained that he preached the very words of God to the people. The apostle relayed to the people the dictates of the kingdom of God because the people were being tried and proven for the kingdom of God. All of Paul's effort would go into making sure that they had what it took to be ready for their eschatological evaluation when they stood before the Lord.

1 Thessalonians 4:3-8. When Paul was dictating this part of his letter, I believe he probably shouted at this moment, "sanctification!"[14] The major, controlling point of this section of Paul's letter is that God has called the people to be holy. It was certainly essential in Jewish thought (Ex 19:6; Lev 20:7). As such, the people who fulfilled the law must also exemplify holiness. They must separate themselves from the impurities of the world. To be people of the gospel, they must be holy!

It is absolutely appropriate that Paul would name one of the most prominent sins at this juncture, sexual immorality. There are many vice lists in the New Testament and this sin seems to find its way into almost all of them. Paul's world is different from our own in many

[14]Malherbe, *Letters*, 224-42.

ways but in many ways it is the same. Back in the early 1990s the hip-hop duo Salt-N-Peppa had a hit song called "Let's Talk About Sex." This song came out at the height of the AIDS epidemic in America. In their song, they were appealing to us to open up discussions around something that is so beautiful, when understood properly, but can also be abused and misused when implemented in a flawed fashion. Paul was saying to the Thessalonians, reflect and converse on what I taught you about sex. Do not abuse it; use it the way God intended it.

In our time, sex has been severed from negative spiritual consequences. Sex is essentially understood to only have positive spiritual outcomes as a mode of self-expression. The more one expresses oneself through sex, when one is being pleasured, it is portrayed as good. Paul would have rejected this view of sex. For him and the early church, while sex was viewed as a gift of God, it could also be a site of rebellion against the living God. Paul never gets into details here of what he understands the misuse of sex to be, but he will make that clear in another letter (see 1 Cor 5–7). The "freedom" many discover in exhibiting their sexuality Paul would argue was a form of bondage and uncleanness in the sight of God.

In 1 Thessalonians 4:4, Paul speaks of the body as a "vessel," something he will say other times (Rom 9:21-23; 2 Cor 4:7; 2 Tim 2:21). In a literal sense, a "vessel" is a container. It is appropriate that Paul would speak of the body in this way because Paul will express what our bodies are meant to contain, the Holy Spirit, later in this section. For now, he engages his hearers with the thought that they must consider the necessity of avoiding impurity from this age.

This age is plagued by ignorance of God. The nations who worshiped idols and were separated from the God of Israel were unholy. They embraced and promoted desires that proved that they did not know God (1 Thess 4:5). The cutthroat tendencies of communities around the world where people harmed and tried to get over one another were condemned by God (1 Thess 4:6). Paul had shared this with them while he was with them; and he reiterates these points now because God "called" them to "holiness" not "uncleanness" (1 Thess 4:6-7).

And if God was the one who made such a call, and these standards come from God, when one disobeys, one disobeys God (1 Thess 4:8). Paul praised the Thessalonians for accepting what he shared with them as God's word (1 Thess 2:13). Now, he reminds them that they need to continue in the way that God had situated them because any rebellion is to be seen as a rejection of God himself.

Moreover, and this only heightens the danger and volatility of playing with uncleanness, the God one may reject had given the saints his Spirit. Paul sets in contrast the nature of unholiness which rejects the nature of God and God's giving nature. While God gives benevolently, humanity's rebellious nature is to reject God's benevolence. Those who choose to live in covetousness, fornication, and arrogance set themselves up in opposition to God and his way; they reject the very gift of God.

Again, Paul does not get into the minuscule details about what holiness is supposed to look like on the ground nor does he tell us what the Holy Spirit does. Paul's paraenesis in this letter is meant to remind the people of what they have already heard and what the Spirit will do in and through their lives. He makes plain that holiness is not just a consequent reality that comes with being filled by the Spirit. Rather, the commands of Paul suggest that the believer is supposed to work to maintain holiness. Yes, the Spirit is part of this process. But Paul suggests that the believer must make serious attempts at keeping herself pure before God, that is, rejecting bad behaviors that would threaten to take them back to the lives they left behind.

1 Thessalonians 4:9-12. Paul begins this next section with a phrase he will use in 1 Corinthians 7:1, 25; 8:1; 16:1, most likely addressing concerns that the Corinthians themselves raised. "Now concerning love of the brothers and sisters," in this case, may not mean that the Thessalonians had sent to Paul to ask whether or not they should love one another.[15] Rather, Paul and his team take this moment to encourage a stronger bond within the community. Such is expected when speaking to a beleaguered community. We must remember that Paul was trying to keep these saints together and settled in their faith. Paul's instructions are meant to do just that.

Paul reangles the subject of holiness to address *philadelphia,* the "love of brothers and sisters." Often this language speaks of love for blood-related family members (cf. BDAG, 1055). Such love in the church functions differently. Jesus commanded his followers to embrace nonrelatives as brothers and sisters because their bond is the gospel. In the reality of the kingdom of God, that is the strongest connection (Mt 8:21-22). Paul draws on this kind of thinking, arguing that familial love belongs to those who embrace Jesus as their Messiah. The members of the family around Macedonia knew the love of the Thessalonian church. They were aware of their faith. It stands to reason that they would be aware of their love for one another. In part, this would have been demonstrated through how they stuck together and remained faithful during their persecutions. But such should increase because the expectation of any Christian is growth, always. Paul challenged the believers to continue to become better in how they expressed their love with one another. They should be quiet, that is, stop saying things that cause division. He encouraged them to take care of their own things and to work with their own hands.[16] And all of this means that people should not steal. You will not take things from people whom you love! Moreover, if you love God and the people within the church, you will walk in a way that demonstrates love to those who are outside of the church. Proper conduct is essential for the growth and development of a healthy church. It blesses the church internally and increases the effectiveness of evangelism.

Consolation, commandments, and the community in the coming of the Lord (1 Thessalonians 4:13–5:11).

1 Thessalonians 4:13-18. Paul has spoken quite frequently about the coming of Jesus prior to this section. The imperatives he has issued have been in service of preparation for the Lord's coming.[17] The apostle and his coworkers' tasks centered on the necessity of ensuring the church is prepared for the Lord at this world-transforming meeting. Everything, therefore, that has preceded the explication we encounter in this section is necessary. The coming of Jesus is the culmination of not only the salvific project of God. The first age in that moment will give its last gasp and finally yield to the power of the age to come. It was incumbent, then, that Paul would send Timothy, send this letter, and do all he could to make sure that the Thessalonians were prepared. They had to be ready for this day, for on this day, they would finally meet their Lord.

[15]Malherbe, *Letters*, 246-47; Gupta, *Thessalonians*, 84-87; Boring, *Thessalonians*, 150-51.
[16]Malherbe, *Letters*, 246-47; Gupta, *Thessalonians*, 88-98.
[17]See Malherbe, *Letters*, 262-79; Boring, *Thessalonians*, 154-74; Gupta, *Thessalonians*, 91-100; Gaventa, *Thessalonians*, 61-79.

However, before we can engage in closer examination of this day, it is also essential to say what this day is not. As will become clear in this commentary, this day did not mark the time of the rapture. When Paul spoke of the coming of the Lord prior to this section, and as he goes into greater detail here, we must be clear about this: he had no inkling of what we call the rapture today. This view has become quite common in evangelical Christian doctrine in the past three hundred years.[18] In my reading of Scripture, it does not have a strong biblical basis. We will explore this briefly.

Many have argued based on this text that the Scripture predicted that there would be a day when Jesus would snatch away all of the people of God and there would be mass pandemonium in the streets because the rest of humanity would be left behind. This event would be the beginning of the Great Tribulation, the time when earth would be tossed into agony in preparation for the second coming of Jesus. The catching away, the "rapture," is the harvesting of God's people whom God promised to protect from wrath.[19] And since God promised to protect his people from wrath, so goes the logic, then God will not allow Christians to suffer with the rest of the world. Therefore, before this Great Tribulation, he would come to rapture the church. At the end of the seven years of tribulation, God will send Jesus back with the previously raptured church for a second coming. Then, there will be judgment, followed by a thousand years of peace and the wedding supper of the Lamb. At this moment, all of the world's troubles will be over as the people of God will reign with Jesus.

One of the major problems with this interpretation of the Scripture is that it lacks biblical evidence. The New Testament never says anywhere that the people of God will be snatched to heaven prior to the great tribulation. Jesus' discussions about the elect being caught up in the four winds are not references to the rapture but most likely the return from exile (Mt 24:29-31). Nowhere does Revelation speak of the church beings snatched away to escape the tribulation.

Furthermore, none of this has anything to do with particular Old Testament expectations for the earth or the body (see Gen 1–2; Is 66; Dan 12). For now, we are only able to discuss what Paul has said in 1–2 Thessalonians. One of the few things that the vision of the "rapture" gets right is the word *rapture* itself. The word used for "caught up" can be translated as "rapture." But the careful reader will note that there is a difference between being "raptured" and being "raptured away." Those who believe in the Rapture insert in the text something that is not there. After discussing being "caught up," Paul describes the "meeting" of the Lord in the air. Never does Paul say anything about being "caught up" to go back to heaven.

Rather, Paul describes the Lord's coming as his descent from heaven to meet the people of God so that they may forever be together in body and spirit. That is, the chief concern of Paul is not the going up of the saints but the coming down of Christ. Again, this focus is not alien to the repeated argument of the book, namely, the Lord is coming. And nowhere does Paul say that Jesus is coming to go somewhere else. Within the New Testament, and

[18]Some of the most popular and recent versions of this doctrine come from Tim LaHaye and Jerry Jenkins in their *Left Behind* series of novels. This series became so popular that it was made into a major Hollywood production. There are countless other books and other media portrayals that assume the rapture doctrine is the standard belief of Christianity. It, however, is not. Nor has it ever been. It is particular to a certain, though large, segment of Christianity.

[19]Being saved from the "wrath" of God or from "evil" does not necessarily mean being raptured away within Scripture (1 Thess 1:10; 5:9; cf. Rom 1:18; Gal 1:4).

within the Second Temple Jewish worldview, the idea was that God would transform the heavens and the earth. And the vision of it all that Paul focuses on is that the Lord intends to come to earth to raise the dead. The resurrection of the saints is a central idea in Pauline theology, something that should be central in our own. More can be said, but now it is important to turn to the text.

Paul introduces this discussion as a way to bring comfort to those who mourn. Unlike we, who live in a society shaped by Christianity, Paul is writing to a congregation of former worshipers of various deities. Their traditions about the hereafter would have been as varied as the gods they worshiped. They would not have shared Paul's understanding about the expectation of the resurrection. In fact, it was well-established in Greek theological perspectives that there was no resurrection. Paul's arguments about what God intended with the coming age would have sounded completely ridiculous to many of the Thessalonian hearers. Yet they had accepted the message of the cross and awaked to the reality of the coming resurrector.

So, if they were expecting the resurrection, what would happen to their loved ones who had already died? Paul would have preached to them about the coming judgment and the resurrection. But, as any preacher knows, people do not always receive the full message the first, second, or third time. Paul had to assure these believers that with this new worldview those who had died were not lost. Since their expectation was to meet the Lord in their bodies, it is likely questions arose concerning those who had already died.

Such thoughts would cause sorrow, of course. Grief is expected if one thinks her family members are somehow lost or will not experience the resurrection. Paul says no, the brothers and sisters who have died have not been lost. And, therefore, the proper way to handle their deaths is to not grieve as non-Christians do.

Some scholars have concluded that Paul is against grieving altogether. They argue that Paul has excluded grief since God will raise these people from the dead. But my reading of the text suggests that Paul has not proscribed grief. This would contradict everything he has said about grieving in other letters. This is certainly possible, but highly unlikely. The better reading is that Paul argues against the kind of grieving one might do when one is completely hopeless. Christian grief is unlike non-Christian grief. Our grief is with "hope." While we have lost loved ones for a time, we know that we will see them again.

Paul follows these words of comfort with the description of the Lord's world-transformative arrival. Space does not permit a thorough exegesis of each component of this depiction of the coming of Jesus. For now, we will provide a brief explanation with each phase of the description in the letter. First, Paul begins with the resurrection of Jesus Christ as the foundation of the promise. If they believe in Jesus' death and resurrection, then it is only logical to believe in their own participation in the resurrection. Therefore, those who have died have not been lost, they are like Jesus when he died; they will be raised from the dead with him. They will come "with" Jesus when he comes.

Second, those who are alive do not proceed those who have died. Those who are alive during the coming of Jesus will be transformed after the dead have been transformed. First, the dead are raised, then the living undergo some sort of bodily transformation, which Paul does not explain here.

Paul, then, explores the Lord's coming using language reminiscent of Moses' covenant meeting with God and the people of Israel. In Exodus 19:18-20, the Lord's presence descends on the mountain. The entrance of YHWH into earth's atmosphere is meant to generate reverberations throughout nature. In Exodus, the Lord's descent on Sinai caused the mountain to smoke. God lit the great mountain on fire. And more, the mountain began to shake as the trumpet blew louder and louder. The psalmist is able to speak of God's voice in a similar way (e.g., Ps 29). Or better yet, the response of nature to the presence of the all-powerful deity suggests nature knows exactly who God is, even when human beings seem to not get the notice.

In this description of the Lord's return, again, the echo suggests Paul considers Jesus to be YHWH. The blowing of the trumpet is never identified in Exodus. But it is clear in 1 Thessalonians 4 that the archangel blows the trumpet in preparation for the arrival of YHWH, the Lord.

But unlike God's encounter with the people of God at Sinai, all the people who are living are invited to come closer to God. Moses was warned to tell Israel not to approach the mountain of God (Ex 19:21). But the descent of Jesus is meant to entail the coming together of all of the people of God. Those who were dead are raised back. And those who are alive are going to be caught up in the air to "meet the Lord" (1 Thess 4:17). This is, indeed, beyond any mountain meeting. The people of God meet Jesus "in the clouds," and Paul further accents this, "in the air." The language may not be literal. When Paul speaks of the coming of Jesus in 1 Corinthians 15, he makes no reference to the air meeting. In this case, it may bespeak the intentionality of God to transcend all that humanity had ever known to this point. Or, it may also refer to how enraptured the church will be to see the arrival of their Lord.

Paul assures the believer, still maintaining his pastoral tone, that this is her eternal status. From this point on, all believers will always "be with the Lord" (1 Thess 4:17). There will no longer be any separation between the creature and the Creator. God will be all and in all (1 Cor 15:28). This is the end of life as humanity once knew it and the beginning of a new era where the church now experiences God without boundaries.

Such a promise is supposed to be comforting for an embattled people who have lost their place in the world because of their choice of Jesus. Paul requests that the people would "comfort one another" with the message of the Lord's coming (1 Thess 4:18). Though the world's current fake ruler and his ways rejected the people of God, it was comforting to know that the true ruler would embrace them. In 1 Corinthians 15:26 Paul speaks of the "enemy" as Death. Death is not given its status as an entity here. But the implications are no less. Death will no longer bind the people of God at the Lord's coming.

The modern church can learn a great deal from the tone of Paul's words of comfort. First, the fact that death should not be feared. Paul assures the believer that death is not final. In a world shaped by existentialist thinking, the afterlife can be quite scary. Well, to be fair, Paul's words suggest that many believers found death to be quite scary as well. But Paul urged the believer to recognize that God would ultimately have power over death. Those who belonged to Jesus would be rewarded with the same status. They, too, would be raised from the dead. More and more, the church should embrace biblical faith in the resurrection of the believer over against the more Platonic hope in a disembodied existence after death. God cares about our whole being, this means that God will raise our bodies from the dead.

Second, we should welcome the coming of Jesus. The "end times" as they are known today are also seen as a scary prospect for most people. But the coming of the Lord Jesus, the apocalypse, the revelation of Jesus Christ, is a time of wonderful fellowship. The coming of Jesus will not be disastrous for those who believe in Jesus. It will be a grand reunion in which all of the church's hopes and dreams come true. Life, then, will truly be complete. In the words of the Revelation writer, "Come, Lord Jesus" (Rev 22:20).

The day of Lord and the children of the light (1 Thessalonians 5:1-11). Paul continues the theme of the coming of Jesus by further expressing it as the "day of the Lord" (1 Thess 5:2).[20] The "times and the seasons" (1 Thess 5:1) are something that Paul once explained to them. He explained that the day of the Lord was something that would come like a "thief in the night" (1 Thess 5:2).[21] That is, the Lord's coming would come without warning. One day everything would be normal and the next, Jesus would appear, the dead would be raised, and new creation would be set forth in the world.

There is another side to the day of the Lord. Paul's pastoral concerns earlier caused him to focus on God's benevolent future for his people. The day of the Lord would mean "destruction" for others, however (1 Thess 5:3). Paul's argument is quite consistent with other accounts of the glorious appearing of Jesus resulting in two fates for God's human creatures. The "two ways" conception in Jewish thought comes to its culmination with the two promised futures. One can live in a future with God or a future without God. Those who proclaim "peace and safety," common speech among those who trusted in the protection Caesar provided, would suffer a fate they could not predict. "Sudden destruction" will come on those who trusted in the course of this age and its ruling powers (1 Thess 5:3).

The believer, on the contrary, would not be caught off guard. First, because they had been told about the coming of the Lord. They received the oracles of God that spoke of their future in the presence of God. Second, they were looking at the times and the changing seasons, recognizing that the Lord would be on his way. They were, therefore, not in "darkness" to be caught off guard. The day would not be like a "thief in the night" to them (1 Thess 5:2).

The church of the Lord Jesus Christ, "the children of light," will not be asleep when the Lord comes, however. First Thessalonians 5:5 introduces the notion that the people of God are also the "children of light." They are those who can be characterized by the "light," which is also symbolic of God (e.g., Jn 1:4-12; 1 Jn 1:5). God is of the light—indeed, it can be said that God *is* light—and drives out the darkness, as God did in creation (Gen 1:3-5). Those who belong to God are called by Paul the "the children of light" and he can also easily say, they are the "children of God" (Rom 8:16). Though Paul has not explicitly stated their identity in this fashion in this letter, he has implied it by speaking of the position of the church in God the Father.

It is this strong connection to the light of God that prevents the people of God from sleeping through the Lord's coming. Rip Van Winkle's story comes to mind. He is someone who was supposed to have slept through the American Revolution.[22] But the people of God do not live in the "darkness." So the

[20]See Gupta, *Thessalonians*, 101-10; Boring, *Thessalonians*, 174-89; Malherbe, *Letters*, 286-301.
[21]The "day of the Lord" is a phrase used quite often in the OT to signify a day on which God will demonstrate God's strength. See Is 2:12; 13:6, 9; Jer 46:10; Ezek 13:5; 30:3; Joel 1:15; 2:1, 11, 31; 3:14; Amos 5:18, 20. Obad 1:15; Zeph 1:7, 14; Zech 14:1; Mal 4:5.
[22]Irving Washington, *Rip Van Winkle, and The Legend of Sleepy Hollow* (New York: Macmillan, 1963).

characteristics of a night dweller do not apply to them. They "keep awake" and are "sober" (1 Thess 5:6). But those who are night people "sleep" and are "drunk." Then, as it is now, drunkenness is something associated with nighttime activities (1 Thess 5:7). Bad behavior is associated with the darkness. Therefore, Paul says that the people of God, those who are sanctified and characterized by good behavior, are people of the "day" (1 Thess 5:8). They even wear the armor of God while they act soberly (cf. Is 59:17; Eph 6:14).

The people of God, then, were not to live with their heads in the sand. But since they expected the entrance and full revelation of the power of God, they lived their lives with eyes wide open, looking to see the appearance of the Lord Jesus Christ. Paul and those to whom he wrote expected, it seems, that they might be able to see the Lord in their own lifetimes. But this was not a guarantee, of course. Paul would later explore the possibility of his own death with the Philippians before the coming of the Lord (Phil 1:21-26). Regardless, the theological implication meant for the church was to take on the demeanor of people characterized by a clear-eyed expectation that Jesus was to return. But this clarity of vision suggested full engagement with the world in which they lived. It did not involve otherworldly escapism. The ethical mandates prescribed by Paul suggested that the church should make this world better until the day in which this world meets its Lord.

On that day, the believer was to recognize that only good things awaited them. There will be no "wrath" but grace and peace (1 Thess 5:9-11). On that day, the church will only see "salvation" and "life." On that day the people of God would behold their coming Savior as a bearer of the long-awaited justice and mercy.

Instructions for living as a waiting church (1 Thessalonians 5:12-24). "But," Paul says, as he enters this next section of his letter with commandments for believers. In light of the coming of Jesus, Paul provides some final commandments that allow them to live as a church waiting for the "coming of the Lord" (1 Thess 4:15). They are to comfort and edify. They are to recognize and respect those who are assigned to lead them. These may be some of the elders whom Paul would have left in charge in his and his associates' absence. And this obligation to honor comes with the notion of "love," which also means to pay them (1 Thess 5:13). Reverencing and respecting leadership has everything to do with creating a peaceful environment in the church. This command is connected to the desire to keep a healthy atmosphere in the church where everyone is cared for (1 Thess 5:14).[23]

Among other ethical commands, still thinking of the overall care for the church, Paul urges people not to give evil back to people who do evil to them. People should rejoice, pray constantly, be thankful, allow the Spirit to flow freely, and, therefore, support prophecy, look for and reject evil, not go anywhere near evil (1 Thess 5:16-22).

Paul changes his view from the believer to what God will do for the believer in 1 Thessalonians 5:23-24. He offers what seems to be a prayer. God will sanctify the whole church, both collectively and individually. It appears that Paul has in mind that humans are tripartite beings, spirit, soul, and body. There is some precedent in Greek views of anthropology that human beings are dichotomous.[24] But Malherbe notes that Paul is anomalous in his description of the human as spirit, soul, and body. Paul can speak in other places of the

[23]See Malherbe, *Letters*, 316-17; Gupta, *Thessalonians*, 111-12.

[24]Malherbe, *Letters*, 337-38.

body and spirit or even the flesh and spirit. Paul nowhere else speaks of people with the spirit, soul, and body. We are left without real discussion of how the reader is supposed to distinguish the soul from the spirit. What is clear is that Paul somehow saw differences between these various parts of human beings.

Closing greeting (1 Thessalonians 5:25-28). At the conclusion of the letter, Paul requests prayer, proper treatment of others, and the reading of the letter. And, as is typical, a blessing closes out the letter. This is a fitting conclusion since Paul opens the letter with a blessing for the people of God.

CONCLUSION

1 Thessalonians is a pastoral letter meant to address various concerns the church of Thessalonica encountered or might encounter along their journey. Paul's intent was to urge the people of God to stand firm, to continue waiting for Jesus, expecting that Jesus would come to meet them. They were to adopt a posture commensurate with one who has heard good news and waits for its fulfillment. Despite obstacles and trials faced while waiting for that fulfillment, they were to continue waiting, knowing that the good news fulfillment would come as he promised. But, as is the case with most churches, those who waited heard other news that rebutted the word of fulfillment. So, Paul would have to write again to further assure the hearts of the believers of Thessalonica.

2 THESSALONIANS

Opening greeting (2 Thessalonians 1:1-2). Paul, Silas, and Timothy greet the church in the same way they did in the first letter. There is virtually no difference between the words Paul used before and this time.[25] The situation, as we will discover, had not significantly changed. The church was still being persecuted and they were still waiting on the Lord's coming. As such, Paul still wished the people of God to recognize their place in the Lord their God. This God was their Father and their Lord was Jesus Christ. Just as a few months prior to the writing of this present letter, they were still in need of the grace and peace of God to settle them during this turbulent period of their lives. The God who was able to keep them all of this time was still very much able to continue keeping them in his power.

The current tribulation and the coming judgment (2 Thessalonians 1:3-12).

2 Thessalonians 1:3-4. The announcement of grace in the greeting is followed by a repetition of pastoral thanksgiving seen in the first letter (1 Thess 1:1). Paul says, "We must always give thanks to God for you." In the first letter, Paul mentions they all have gratitude to God "constantly" for the saints in Thessalonica. Again, the reason is because they have believed and they continue to grow in their "faith" and "love" toward each other. Paul had heard of their growth that they had grown as he requested in the last letter (1 Thess 3:12). Their ability to endure in the face of hardship has provided Paul with the necessary evidence to rejoice over this congregation. Despite their trials, Paul and the others are excited about this congregation because they have been able to demonstrate their faithfulness to God in the face of immense opposition.

2 Thessalonians 1:5-12. Syntactically, the sentence from 2 Thessalonians 1:3 continues on into 2 Thessalonians 1:5. But for the sake of clarity, I am dividing up the verses. The thanksgiving that Paul begins in 2 Thessalonians 1:3 ends and Paul begins to speak of the expected judgment of God in 2 Thessalonians 1:5 and

[25]Malherbe, *Letters*, 379-80.

onward. The suffering of the saints is an exhibition of the "righteous judgment of God." We are not told exactly how the suffering and tribulation of the people of God demonstrates God's judgment. But Paul can say elsewhere that suffering is certainly a badge of honor (e.g., 2 Cor 11). Suffering most certainly connects the believer with Christ. Luke recounts that Paul encouraged believers to hold on to their faith because "through suffering" they would "enter the kingdom of God" (Acts 14:22). Suffering well, with hope and faith, can be a means by which God proves the believer (cf. 1 Pet 4:17).

Therefore, it is no wonder that Paul will go on to say that in their tribulations the Thessalonians are "to make you worthy of the kingdom of God." Suffering is part of God's sovereign will for the waiting church to count them worthy of God; but also a mechanism that exposes the wickedness of the world. God's righteous judgment will distinguish the wicked from the righteous. Those who are opposed to the will of God will always be on the side of those who have persecuted the children of God. They will be seen for who they truly are in the day of God's wrath. Their actions in the present, Paul is saying, foreshadow their place in the day of judgment.

Paul reminds them that God has their situations in hand, so they should rest with Paul and his associates. God will not allow the wicked to escape.[26] All of those who are deserving of judgment for their abuses of the people of God, will suffer the consequences. The only proper response is "rest." That is, giving God the space to do what God will do and not to act before God has chosen to act (Rom 12:19).

Why? Jesus is coming back. This was the central consolatory argument of the previous letter. Paul detailed the coming of Jesus in the previous letter to describe his intent to save. In this letter, he places heavy emphasis on Jesus' intent to destroy. Jesus' coming will involve bringing "angels of power" in his "revelation." Moreover, Jesus will come with "flaming fire" (2 Thessalonians 1:8). Indeed, God is a "consuming fire" (Deut 4:4; 9:3; Heb 12:29). Nonbelievers, those who oppose the gospel, will reward themselves with eternal wrath from the "presence of the Lord and from the glory of his might." Jesus comes to wreak havoc on those who fight him while he is honored and glorified by those who believe and trust in him. For those who believe and trust in him have believed and trusted in the word of the apostles about what God promised for "that day."

Paul concludes his remarks in this section by going back to the tone in which he started in 2 Thessalonians 1:11-12. He thanked God for the waiting church in the beginning; and now he ends with the notice that he constantly prayed for the church, that God would make them worthy, and God would fill the church with his blessed goodness. And with all of this, the name of the Lord Jesus would be glorified in the church and the people of God would be glorified in Jesus. Again, though the emphasis has shifted, Paul and his coworkers are still very much concerned with the celebration of the Lord's coming as a salve for this present pain. The Lord's coming would involve a reversal of fortune. Those who laugh now would wail later. Those who clap now would hang their heads later. Certain devastation awaited those who lived in comfort while thriving on the discomfort of others. God was not blind; God would reward the wicked for their wickedness.

Condemnation, then, is used as comforting news for the believer. Knowing how terrifying

---

[26]See Malherbe, *Letters*, 394-405.

God's wrath is contrasts with the benevolence of God's graciousness to those who accept it. The waiting church is meant to look forward to the day of judgment as a time when God will settle all scores, mete out reward and punishment, give everyone what she or he is due. It was supposed to be a welcome day, despite how bad the present was, because the present suffering would have to give way to God's delightful blessings. Today, believers are supposed to consider the coming wrath of God in a similar fashion. Racism, sexism, classism, and all other "isms" will have their place in the flames of Jesus. Everything that has opposed the plan and power of God will suffer on the divine ash heap of righteousness. All things will be destroyed that do not glorify God. This, indeed, is good news. Paul would probably argue today that the fact that all wickedness will be destroyed one day is good news.

Clarity on the coming of the Lord (2 Thessalonians 2:1-12). After declaring God's eschatological edict, namely, that everything will be judged when the Lord comes with wrath for the unjust and peace for the just (2 Thess 1:5-9), Paul switches gears to discuss portents for the Lord's coming.[27] Here, Paul expands on what to look for in order to discern the Lord's coming. Apparently, some in the congregation had heard that the Lord had already come. It may be that some interpreted the Lord's manner of coming as a thief to indicate that it had happened and they had not been aware of it. To be sure, Paul was very clear with them that the Lord's coming would not catch *them* by surprise as it would others (1 Thess 5:4). They were "children of the day." The night was not something for them to be scared of because they were in relationship with the true and living God. They would not be caught unaware.

But, as any preacher knows messages do not always make it through as intended. So Paul addresses them again by describing the expectation, the hope of their salvation. The hope, "the coming of our Lord Jesus Christ and our being gathered together to him," remains steadfast, certain, and still sure to come (2 Thess 2:1). But Paul cautions that the church should never be deceived if a "spirit," a "word," or a "letter" should come to them telling them that Jesus' day had come. Paul and his associates warn: if you did get some message saying this, it did not come from us. They would not have changed their former arguments concerning the day of the Lord. Indeed, Paul cautioned the Galatians to not even believe him if he came back and preached another gospel (Gal 1:8). What Paul first preached and taught to the Thessalonians still stood. They were expecting the resurrection as a grand meeting with the Lord Jesus Christ. Paul assured them that they should not be concerned about any message supposedly coming from them by a word of prophecy ("spirit"), some form of preaching or teaching (a "word") or a letter. The coming of the Lord's day would have obvious signals the church should have expected. There would be a great apostasy (2 Thess 2:3), first. It appears that Paul meant that many in the church would leave the faith; and a great decline among the people of God would herald the coming of the ever-living Messiah.

However, this decline would come alongside the "lawless one" being "revealed" (2 Thess 2:3).[28] Paul had spent a great deal of time discussing the problems with sinful behavior and how the Thessalonians should behave in light of their reception of the Spirit (1 Thess 4:8). It only makes sense that the one who would fight against the things of God

[27]See Malherbe, *Letters*, 416-17; Boring, *Thessalonians*, 262-71.
[28]Malherbe, *Letters*, 417-27.

would be known as the "man of lawlessness." He is the "son of destruction," which could be understood as a way of saying he is the epitome of what God will destroy in Jesus' revelation from heaven.

This person will fight against everything that is called God or seen as a god from the perspective of nonbelievers. This language may speak to his desire to be considered among the gods or to be set atop of the pantheon. And, in particular, it suggests that he will fight against the Jewish beliefs on the authority of the true and living God (1 Thess 1:9).

His "lawlessness" will be so reprehensible that he will be worse than the many other rulers who came before and desecrated God's temple (e.g., Dan 9:27).[29] He will sit in the very temple to be worshiped as God. The prospect of such a thing would have been unthinkable to both Jews and Romans as this would have certainly sparked a violent dispute.

Apparently, Paul had shared this information with them already (2 Thess 2:5). But the next verse provides one of the most mysterious verses in the New Testament. "And you know what is now restraining him, so that he may be revealed when his time comes" (2 Thess 2:6).[30] To what/who was Paul referring? Was it the church? Was it the Holy Spirit? Is what is preventing him something good or evil? Scholarship provides no definite answers. Whatever the proper answer was, if the readers knew it, it has been lost to history. We can only make guesses about what prevents the revelation of the "lawless one."[31]

Interestingly, Paul switches the gender of the term used for the preventing force in 2 Thessalonians 2:7. "What is now restraining him" is used in 2 Thessalonians 2:6. In 2 Thessalonians 2:7, it is, "one who now restrains." Again, we have no clue as to who this is. But the thing/person will be removed and the chief resistor of God will be revealed.

When he is revealed, however, as is the case in Daniel's prophecy, the Lord will overcome him. Daniel foresaw a moment when ungodly powers would attempt to desecrate the temple and defeat the people of God. In that moment, the Lord would defeat the ungodly forces and cleanse his temple (see Dan 7, 9, 11). But as the lawless one is revealed, so will the Lord of heaven. He will annihilate him with the "breath of his mouth, annihilating him by the manifestation of his coming" (2 Thess 2:8).

Paul, then, after describing the wicked one's destruction, continues the description of the lawless one. He links the revelation of the evil person with those who support his cause. He has already said that the "mystery of lawlessness" is revealing itself at present. Paul explains that this power is at work in this wicked person. He works through the power of "Satan" and will be able to perform, like many false prophets before him (see Deut 13:1-5), many signs and wonders of lies (2 Thess 2:9-19). In other words, this person will have power but it will be to deceive people to believe his lies. And those who will fall for his deception will be those who hated the truth of God that could save them. Those who believed the lies of the wicked one will be sent "a powerful delusion" so that those who did not accept the truth of Jesus will believe what the wicked one has said to them (2 Thess 2:11). God does this on purpose, so that they might be judged for their folly of rejecting the gospel (2 Thess 2:12).

---

[29]There is a long history of this occurring. Nebuchadnezzar (2 Chron 36:15-23) and Antiochus Epiphanes (1 Macc 1:57; 2 Macc 6:2) are known for desecrating the temple of God.

[30]See Gupta, *Thessalonians*, 132-40; Gaventa, *Thessalonians*, 107-20.

[31]However, see the thorough work of Colin Nichol, *From Hope to Despair in Thessalonica: Situating 1 and 2 Thessalonians* (Cambridge: Cambridge University Press, 2008), who argues cogently that the restrainer is a reference to the archangel Michael.

Instructions with a prayer for God's strength (2 Thessalonians 2:13-17). Paul repeats what he said in 2 Thessalonians 1:3. Paul says he and his associates should be thankful at all times for the church. They, a family beloved by the Lord, are the "first fruits" with respect to "salvation" and the "Holy Spirit." Paul's praise of the congregation is meant to commend and comfort them despite their present perilous circumstances. They were, indeed, the Lord's chosen, even though their lives did not seem to reflect this reality. They were "called . . . through our gospel" toward obtaining "the glory of our Lord Jesus Christ." Indeed, their unjust treatment would never prevent their inheritance of a glorious future.

But the present circumstances demanded strict fidelity to what they were taught. Paul repeats the language he mentioned earlier about the media of communication that had thrown them off (2 Thess 2:1-2). In this case, he did not mention the "spirit" but he admonishes the people to "maintain" and "hold on to" the traditions they were "taught" through "our word" or "letter." The apostolic stamp of approval was necessary as a sign of authentic doctrine. Paul was clear: neither he nor the others sent messages to them altering what they were taught in the beginning.

God has nothing but comfort for them, not confusion. Paul prays that the Lord Jesus and God the Father would give them comfort in the work they were doing. And he repeats the prayer for comfort. This suggests that Paul was trying as he had in 1 Thessalonians 4:18 to get the church to reckon with their troubled circumstances with the knowledge of God's presence with them. They will make it to the end, but they must be willing to hold on.

Paul's request for the church and prayer for the Thessalonians (2 Thessalonians 3:1-5). After this engaged discussion of the Lord's coming and how the church should understand its role in light of it, Paul indicates the letter's closing and that he will address concluding matters. Paul asks for prayer, as he had prayed for them. Paul's prayer request reminds the readers that he and his associates are struggling with the same problems as the congregation they are comforting. Paul asks that they might be "rescued" from wicked people (2 Thess 3:2). We must be transparent in our discussions about principalities and powers within biblical treatment. Indeed, the enemies are invisible, ultimately, but they work through people. And Paul asked that he and the others would be set free from any and all who would try to disrupt their lives as ministers of the word of God. Naturally, then, Paul would also speak to God's ability to protect them through their prayers but also to God's faithfulness and ability to keep them from the evil one, the devil (2 Thess 3:3-5). Paul and his associates believe that the Thessalonians will do what they have been commanded. And they believe that the Lord will cause the Thessalonians to be settled in the love of God.

Instructions for living in community (2 Thessalonians 3:6-15). An old adage says, "An idle mind is the devil's workshop." Paul may not have had something like this axiom in mind when he wrote this particular portion of his second letter to the Thessalonians.[32] The proper mode of being in this moment of the church's life is "waiting" in expectation of the Lord's coming. They were charged to keep their eyes open, to live in the day and eschew the night life. But some, it appears, were living in anticipation of the Lord's coming—but in the wrong way! So, they stopped working to feed themselves, chose to start problems among the church, and foolishness began to occur. Paul and his associates

[32]See Gupta, *Thessalonians*, 147-51; Malherbe, *Letters*, 448-54; Meeks, *Christians*, 64-65.

wanted to put a stop to this behavior. This was not *just* because an idle, troublemaker causes problems in the community. It is also because, and this is of the utmost importance, this kind of behavior bespeaks that one is not living in light of the eschatological realities Paul discussed with them when he was with them, in his letter, and has now reiterated.

To fight against this tendency for troublemaking, Paul uses himself and his associates as an example. Paul and the associates "command" the Thessalonians "in the name of our Lord Jesus Christ" (2 Thess 3:6). We should not ignore this invocation of the name of Jesus to strengthen both the authority and urgency of the command. Paul means business. Not that he did not in other commandments (2 Thess 2:13). But he wants the readers to understand the seriousness of this imperative. They cannot be nonchalant about what Paul is about to say. And we see why. They must stay away from people who are idle and not obeying the apostolic decrees (2 Thess 3:6). Paul is clear elsewhere that mingling with people who are disobedient can cause problems in the church and other leaders are as well (see 1 Cor 5). Bad influences affect the life of the church, so it is necessary for people to separate from brothers and sisters who cause confusion. To stop this idleness, Paul reminds them of his own example. Believers should work just like Paul and his associates worked. While they preached, they also held on to side jobs to subsidize their income (1 Thess 2:9; cf. 1 Cor 4:12). If they could work, while ministering to the congregation, surely these Thessalonians could as well. And, to make it clear, Paul wanted them to recognize that he did not have to work (2 Thess 3:9). Moreover, anyone who chose not to work should not receive food from the community. Paul had already told them this when he was with them in person (2 Thess 3:10). People who refuse to work but choose to stir up mischief in the congregation should be marked, identified, and separated from the congregation.

It needs to be said that the average preacher today serves the church under similar circumstances to Paul and his associates. Contrary to the popular depiction of preachers as money-grubbing, celebrity-aspiring crooks, modern preachers work very hard for the congregations. Especially for Black and brown ministers, who typically have a lower economic status within the United States, preachers often have to be at the very least bivocational. That is, they *have* to work more than one job to make ends meet while they attend to all of the needs of their congregation. Black and brown ministers are not strangers to labor in the Lord's vineyard and, oftentimes, the vineyards of others. They work not only to eat but also to feed the flock of God. While some pastors are privileged to make a living wage by serving their congregations, most Black and brown preachers do not. Yet, they still serve the Lord and their people faithfully to the glory of God.

Instead, people should be like Paul and not try to "burden" the community but try to build it up. People should work "quietly" and "earn their own living" (2 Thess 3:12). And when the church identifies the troublemakers they should not treat them as "enemies" but still as members of the family (2 Thess 3:14). As in Galatians, the church cannot get tired of doing what is right (Gal 6:9). The obligation of the believer is to do what is necessary both to "warn" those who are out of sync with the Lord Jesus, who is soon to return, and to do what we can to restore those who have gone astray (2 Thess 3:15-16).

Closing greeting (2 Thessalonians 3:16-18). As in the first letter, Paul turns from ethical commandments to offering a closing benediction. He prays that "the Lord of peace" will provide them with "peace" and be with them (2 Thess 3:16). This is a priestly benediction (Num 6:22-26). It was common in Jewish prayers to ask the Lord for his peace. But this is the only time we see the phrase in Paul and in the New Testament: "the Lord of peace." Typically, Paul will speak of the "God of peace" (Rom 15:33; 16:20; Phil 4:9; 1 Thess 5:23). It may be that Paul wants to emphasize that the Lord Jesus is watching them. They are "in God" and Jesus is in their midst watching to see if they will keep his commandments.

Paul splits his benediction, however. Paul mentions that he authenticates his letters the same way to identify himself. He does it in "every letter" (2 Thess 3:17). But this is the only time he will say he authenticates all of his epistles. It is clear why he would do this. Someone seems to have attempted to plagiarize his work or at least sound like him and the other apostles. Paul wanted to make sure the Thessalonians recognized it was him.

Last, Paul offers the exact same concluding benediction from the first letter (1 Thess 5:28). The prayer for peace is followed by a prayer for grace, which was combined in 2 Thessalonians 1:2. These are things that only God can give in this tumultuous environment. And Paul wanted the church to remember that despite their present chaos, the Lord remained with them.

Conclusion. Second Thessalonians offers more clarity on what Paul preached to the Thessalonian church but also leaves us in the dark in other ways. But the letter served as a powerful sequel to continue to remind the church of its place in Christ. God cared about them, Jesus was coming to see them, and God, in the meantime, would make his grace and peace abound among them.

They only needed to remember not to listen to ideas and doctrines not authorized by the apostles. If it did not comport with what they were already taught, and did not come with evidence of Paul's approval, throw it away. Furthermore, anyone who chose not to obey what they were commanded was to be shamed for their disobedience. This was serious business. The fate of the world had already been decided, Jesus was on his way back. The church has the obligation to live like they were expecting Jesus to return. The church was to certify that its behavior aligned with what they were expecting. The meeting with Jesus was, and certainly is, the height of all existence. Nothing greater is coming. So, Paul said to them, prepare yourselves for this wonderful time that the Lord has for you.

CONCLUSION OF THE COMMENTARIES

In both these letters, we the church are challenged to hear what the Spirit may be saying to us. Have we lost the sense of our sacred worth to God? Are we allowing the temporal things of this age to guide our approach to God or are we engaging this age with the lens of the eternal? Does our eschatology guide our present action?

Paul wanted to comfort the church with the promise of the Lord's coming. This embattled group of believers were in need of assurance that they had not given up their idols for nothing. The living God was on their side, despite all evidence to the contrary. In the first letter, Paul explored the concept of the Lord's coming to comfort those who had lost loved ones but to also warn that the Lord's coming could be any moment. Live justly. Never be complacent.

In the second letter, Paul reiterates this point, this time pointing out some clarifying points. The Lord had not come yet. So, still, live justly! Justice will be done against those who persecute the church. The church is therefore challenged to be on the right side of eternity even at the expense of being on the wrong side of history. That is, the circumstances may appear to be against us. But Paul's point is that eternity is for us. Salvation is near. Keep the faith. The Lord will return to the children of God. And the people of God will live with him forever.

BIBLIOGRAPHY

Boring, Eugene. *I & II Thessalonians: A Commentary*. New Testament Library. Louisville, KY: Westminster John Knox Press, 2015.

Bowens, Lisa M. *African American Readings of Paul: Reception, Resistance, and Transformation*. Grand Rapids, MI: Eerdmans, 2020.

Felder, Cain H. "1 Thessalonians." In *True to Our Native Land: An African American New Testament Commentary*. Edited by Brian K. Blount. Minneapolis: Fortress Press, 2007.

———. "2 Thessalonians." In *True to Our Native Land: An African American New Testament Commentary*. Edited by Brian K. Blount. Minneapolis: Fortress Press, 2007.

Gaventa, Beverly. *First and Second Thessalonians*. Interpretation. Louisville, KY: John Knox Press, 1998.

Gupta, Nijay. *1–2 Thessalonians*. New Covenant Commentary Series. Eugene, OR: Cascade Books, 2016.

Irving, Washington. *Rip Van Winkle, and The Legend of Sleepy Hollow*. New York: Macmillan, 1963.

Keener, Craig. *Acts: An Exegetical Commentary*. Vol. 3. Grand Rapids, MI: Baker Academic, 2012.

Malherbe, Abraham J. *The Letters to the Thessalonians: A New Translation with Introduction and Commentary*. Anchor Bible. New York: Doubleday, 2000.

Meeks, Wayne. *The First Urban Christians: The Social World of the Apostle Paul*. 2nd ed. New Haven, CT: Yale University Press, 1983.

Nichol, Colin. *From Hope to Despair in Thessalonica: Situating 1 and 2 Thessalonians*. Cambridge: Cambridge University Press, 2008.

Oakes, Peter. "Contours of the Urban Environment." In *After The First Urban Christians: The Social-Scientific Study of Pauline Christianity Twenty-Five Years Later*, edited by Todd Still and David Horrell, 21-35. London: T&T Clark, 2009.

PASTORAL LETTERS

Osvaldo Padilla

INTRODUCTION TO THE PASTORAL EPISTLES

Authorship.[1] All three letters begin with the name "Paul" as their author. For this reason Christians around the world believe that these letters were written by the apostle. Under the belief that the Bible is the Word of God and therefore trustworthy, the letters are viewed as part of those written by Paul just because they say Paul at the beginning. This was in fact the belief of the confessing church (with a few exceptions like Marcion) up until the eighteenth century. In 1792 the English clergyman Edward Evanson rejected the letters as Pauline (he also rejected Romans!). He viewed the letters as pseudonymous, the primary reason being the supposed harsh theology of the letters. In Germany, Friedrich Schleiermacher questioned the authenticity of First Timothy on a linguistic basis, although he admitted that his conclusions were more impressionistic than methodical. As the nineteenth century continued, more meticulous arguments were proffered by scholars like J. G. Eichorn, F. C. Baur, H. J. Holtzmann, and, later in the twentieth century and in English, P. N Harrison. By this time, it was not only First Timothy that was viewed as pseudonymous but all three Pastoral Epistles. It is no exaggeration to say that in most mainline Protestant institutions and in some evangelical institutions, the belief that Paul wrote these letters is no longer held (and for some Catholics, e.g., Lorenz Oberlinner). On the other hand, the vast majority of Christians in Africa, Asia, and Latin America believe that Paul did write the Pastoral Epistles. The main reason? Because that is what the Bible says.

This is not the place to provide detailed arguments for and against the genuine author of these epistles.[2] Generally speaking, the letters are rejected as Pauline for *linguistic* reasons (e.g., the vocabulary does not match the other "genuine" letters of Paul); for *historical* reasons (when did Paul write these letters? It is, so the argument goes, difficult to find from the Acts of the Apostles when Paul wrote them). Last, according to Johnson, there are "extra-evidential" reasons why the Pastoral Epistles are rejected. In his opinion, social pressure in the academy plays a significant factor in scholars not assessing the arguments carefully and therefore accepting what leading and powerful voices in the academy say.[3]

This commentary accepts the traditional view of the Pastorals' authorship, while recognizing that there are some difficult problems (esp. regarding when Paul wrote these letters). I accept the letters as genuine for the following

---

[1]What follows builds on Osvaldo Padilla, *The Pastoral Epistles,* TNTC (Downers Grove, IL: InterVarsity Press, 2022), 1-16.

[2]For that, readers are directed to the work of Jermo van Nes, *Pauline Language and the Pastoral Epistles: A Study of Linguistic Variation in the* Corpus Paulinum, LBS (Leiden: Brill, 2018), as well as the introduction of Luke Timothy Johnson's commentary, *The First and Second Letters to Timothy*, AB (Garden City, NY: Doubleday, 2001).

[3]Luke Timothy Johnson, *The First and Second Letters of Timothy*, AB (New Haven: Yale University Press, 2001), 55-99.

reasons. First, each letter does begin with "Paul, apostle. . . ." My belief in the trustworthiness of the Bible is a strong factor here. Of course I am aware that there were multiple pseudonymous gospels, acts, and letters in the first four to five centuries of the church that claim to have been written by Peter, Paul, Thomas, and so on. And of course I am aware that the Bible works within the conventions of the period in which it was written. However, my own research (and that of many others) leads me to the conclusion that the early, orthodox church viewed pseudonymity as unacceptable.[4] These are my two main reasons for accepting the traditional view.[5]

The supposed linguistic problem of the Pastorals remains unconvincing to me, especially in light of the small size of the Pauline corpus and the possibility (perhaps probability) that Paul may have used a secretary, who had some freedom in the act of composing these letters.[6] Two more reasons may be given. First, at least with respect to the Gospels, Simon Gathercole has made a convincing case that there were strong theological *Tendenzen* in pseudonymous gospels, especially toward Gnosticism.[7] Even if an advanced system of Gnosticism did not exist during the New Testament period, the Pastoral Epistles do not in any way show favor toward Gnosticism. On the contrary, there are texts that clearly reject any form of Gnostic teaching (e.g., 1 Tim 4:1-5; 6:20). The last reason for accepting the genuine authorship of the Pastorals is methodological and theological. In his challenging book, Benjamin L. White has asked the very uncomfortable question of why, that is, on what basis, scholars use the rhetoric of the "real" Paul or of "genuine letters from Paul" in contrast to "disputed Paulines" (this is the method of operation in the Society of Biblical Literature).[8] If you do not accept the biblical and early manuscript testimony that a group of letters are from Paul, where do you begin to distinguish what is real and what is not? This can cause a significant crisis. According to White, this crisis was already going on in the second century! This was revived in the eighteenth and nineteenth centuries. Here the key figure was F. C. Baur of the so-called Tübingen School in Germany. For Baur, there were only four genuine letters of Paul (the *Hauptbriefe*). These letters were Romans, 1–2 Corinthians, and Galatians. Why are these letters included and not, say, Colossians? White's argument is that ultimately it was Baur's particular Protestantism, and more specifically, Lutheranism, that led to his view that there were only four genuine letters of Paul.[9] Thus, the supposed Rankean objectivity of scholars like Baur and others was not real. It was their *theological*, specifically Lutheran ethos, that led to what White calls "the captivity of Paul." Eventually, three more letters were added to Baur's *Hauptbriefe*: 1 Thessalonians, Philippians, and Philemon. These seven letters have become those that show us the "real" Paul, while the others do not. This conclusion is apparently scientific; but I believe White (who does not accept the

[4]Some important works in this area include Stanley E. Porter and Gregory P. Fewster, eds., *Paul and Pseudepigraphy*, Pauline Studies (Leiden: Brill, 2013); Armin Baum, *Pseudepigraphie und literarische Fälschung im frühen Christentum: mit ausgewählten Quellentexten samt deutscher Übersetzung*, WUNT 2/138 (Tübingen: Mohr Siebeck, 2001).

[5]On the state of the Pastoral Epistles in the manuscript tradition and in the early church (e.g., Apostolic Fathers and Muratorian Fragment), see Padilla, *Pastoral Epistles*, 1-6. The evidence here is strongly supportive of Pauline authorship.

[6]Somewhat outdated but still fundamental is E. Randolph Richards, *The Secretary in the Letters of Paul*, WUNT 2.42 (Tübingen: Mohr Siebeck, 2001).

[7]See Simon Gathercole, *The Gospel and the Gospels* (Grand Rapids, MI: Eerdmans, 2022).

[8]Benjamin L. White, *Remembering Paul: Ancient and Modern Contests over the Image of the Apostle* (Oxford: Oxford University Press, 2014).

[9]White, *Remembering Paul*, 20-27.

Pastorals as Pauline) has raised some crucial questions as to how we know who the "real" Paul is.

To conclude, we will work in this commentary with the traditional view that Paul wrote the Pastorals. There are many scholars who, while not accepting Pauline authorship of the Pastorals, still view them as canonical holy Scripture, which are authoritative for the church today (e.g., the late I. Howard Marshall). While disagreeing with them on the question of authorship, this commentary will not sideline such scholars in the course of exegesis. In fact, any work on the Pastorals that is genuinely scholarly will constitute a conversation partner.

Date. One's decision on the authorship of the Pastorals has repercussions on the date of their respective compositions. Therefore, one would have to date 2 Timothy sometime between 64-67 CE, that is, during the final days of Paul as these are described in 2 Timothy. The dates for 1 Timothy and Titus are more challenging. I follow J. N. D. Kelly's observation that given the similarity of language and themes of 1 Timothy and Titus, these letters were written around the same period. However, suggestions as to what period are simply guesses.[10]

Occasion. Each of these letters has its own particular nuance. However, they all have in common a mandate to their recipients to attempt to preserve the genuine apostolic doctrine as the basis of belief for the respective churches. This is done by proclamation and teaching; but it is also crucial that godly leaders be present who can protect the flock.

But protect the flock from whom? There is no consensus as to who the false teachers were who troubled these churches in Ephesus and Crete. I have argued elsewhere that the false teachers were likely Jewish Christians who presented themselves as philosophers (see, for example, the Jewish philosopher Trypho in Justin Martyr's *Dialogue with Trypho*, who likely followed Platonic philosophy). But there was a tendency toward Gnosticism in their teaching. As Martin Hengel has suggested, there were Jews, especially among the Essenes, who combined teachings of Judaism with Gnostic tendencies (e.g., Colossians).[11] Furthermore, Paul compares the false teachers with Jannes and Jambres (2 Tim 3:8), who were viewed as powerful Jewish magicians. Perhaps, then, the false teachers were itinerant Jews who claimed to be Christians but who rejected the sound apostolic doctrine for Jewish Haggadah (1 Tim 1:3-7), Gnostic teaching, philosophy, and perhaps dabbled in magic. They targeted women in particular (see 1 Tim 2:9-15; 5:3-16), perhaps especially wealthy widows, and attempted to seduce them not only spiritually but also monetarily and physically.

Why the Pastoral Epistles? It is not necessary to read these letters as one corpus. However, there appears to be precedent in the early church to read them as such (e.g., Muratorian Fragment). What unites them is the fact that they are letters written to individual coworkers of Paul who were called to shepherd churches in Ephesus and Crete. The advantage of reading them as one corpus is that one may shed bright light on the other. On the other hand, some scholars read these as individual letters; and this is causing some to rethink the status of the letters as genuine. Thus, some scholars are not prepared to accept First Timothy as Pauline but will read Second

[10] J. N. D. Kelly, *The Pastoral Epistles*, BNTC (London: A&C Black, 1963), 34-36.

[11] Martin Hengel, *Judaism and Hellenism: Studies in their Encounter in Palestine During the Early Hellenistic Period*, trans. J. Bowden, 2 vols. (Philadelphia: Fortress Press, 1974), 1:43.

Timothy as a genuine letter of Paul.[12] This may lead to gains at the ecumenical level and so it is worth considering.

1 TIMOTHY: PART ONE

Salutation (1 Timothy 1:1-2). Paul introduces himself as the author of this letter. It is important to note that he describes himself not only by his name, Paul, but also by his vocation: *an apostle of Christ Jesus*. In the Pastoral Epistles he emphasizes that he has been appointed by the Lord to proclaim the gospel, particularly to the Gentiles (1 Tim 1:11; 2:7). This means that Paul's written words in these letters are authoritative for the beliefs and conduct of the church. This would entail that Christians should read these letters as the revelation of God.

This letter is addressed to Timothy, although the rest of the church was also to read it. Timothy is designated as "my true child in the faith" (1 Tim 1:2). Timothy was not Paul's biological son. His mother was a Jewish Christian and his father was Gentile (who at one point had embraced Judaism? Acts 16:1). Timothy came to faith through his mother and grandmother (2 Tim 1:5; cf. 3:15). Paul, while not the first to disciple Timothy, did become his mentor and spiritual father for most of the latter's life. This explains why Paul calls him his *child*.

Application. Throughout the Pastoral Epistles the importance of a mentoring relationship is both highlighted and implied, primarily in the lives of Timothy, Titus, and Paul. The concept of a devoted mentor-mentee relationship is lacking severely in many churches in North America. One often finds more vibrant relationships of this kind in other countries. For example, a close friend from the Romanian church used to tell me about his "confessor." I asked him what this meant: surely as a Protestant he did not have a priest who listened to confession of his sins and prayed for his forgiveness! He told me that he was referring to the older Christian man who had led him to faith in Christ. The two had a beautiful friendship of mentor-mentee, where my friend would speak, pray with, and even asked his mentor for help with sin patterns. His mentor provided him with advice and wisdom from his many years of living the Christian faith. My friend took this relationship very seriously, at times following his "confessor's" directions even when the advice did not seem to make sense to him.

In North America we often prefer *books* to teach us the "how to's" of Christian existence. Perhaps it is easier—less time consuming, less vulnerable, less embarrassing—to substitute a person with a book. We who live in North America should consider the mentor-mentee relationship of Paul and his coworkers and how it is practiced in churches around the world.

Christian teaching and love of God and neighbor (1 Timothy 1:3-11). This section constitutes the beginning or introduction to Paul's First Letter to Timothy. As such, it contains the principal themes of the letter.[13] We find in this section crucial words and phrases such as "different doctrine," "myths and endless genealogies," "love," "faith," "sound teaching," and "gospel." If we could summarize in a few words the main thrust of this section, the following may be said: only an existence based on sound doctrine can lead to the essential obligation of humans, namely, to love God and to love neighbor.

---

[12]See, for example, Jens Herzer, *Die Pastoralbriefe und das Vermächtnis des Paulus*, WUNT 476 (Tübingen: Mohr Siebeck, 2022).

[13]Greek and Roman speech and letter writers called the beginning of their pieces the *prooimion* or *exordium*. In this section they included the main themes of the rest of the speech or letter.

False doctrine. Paul begins the section in a negative fashion by encouraging Timothy to order certain people "not to teach different teachings" (1 Tim 1:3). The phrase *different teachings* is just one compound word in Greek: *heterodidaskalein*. This is false doctrine or false teaching. What did it look like? At least two things may be said in this respect. First, the false teaching consisted in "myths and endless genealogies" (1 Tim 1:4). This likely refers to the type of haggadic (i.e., narratives invented on the basis of Old Testament Scripture) material that we find in some Jewish works from the Hellenistic period (e.g., Jubilees, Ps. Philo, 1 Enoch). These stories filled in gaps of Old Testament genealogical trees, told of fallen angels who taught humans how to use herbs and roots for magical purposes, and so on. One can only imagine how seductive these stories were, especially for young Christians. The problem with the doctrines was not just their falsity; they could also lead Christians away from the center: Jesus Christ. The second type of false teaching is related to the law of Moses or Torah. In 1 Timothy 1:7 we hear that the false teachers are "desiring to be teachers of the law." Since the Torah is ontologically good (1 Tim 1:8; cf. also Rom 7:7, 16), Paul clarifies that their error is in teaching the Torah "without understanding either what they are saying or the things about which they make assertions." What *were* the false teachers saying about the Torah? Were they insisting, as the Judaizers in Galatia had, that in order to be truly part of the people of God it was necessary first to commit to keeping the Torah (which in the case of males, included circumcision)? We do hear in 1 Timothy 4:1-5 that the false teachers were urging the believers to abstain from certain material things that God had made and Christ had cleansed (e.g., foods). While we do not know with precision what the Jewish false teachers were insisting on, we can say that in their obsession with "myths and endless genealogies" as well as with their lack of understanding of the place of the law (1 Tim 1:8-11), *they were decentring Jesus Christ* from his place in salvation history. It had been revealed to Paul that in light of the advent of Jesus Christ the Torah could not have the central place it had occupied in the history of Judaism (see Gal 2:15-4:1). In fact, the Torah was just a *paidagogos* (a tutor, Gal 3:24), which meant that it was a servant for someone greater. This had been so from the beginning, although only in the coming of Christ had it been decisively revealed. In fact, in light of Jesus Christ, it becomes clear that the Torah "is laid down not for the righteous but for the lawless and disobedient" (1 Tim 1:9). *The problem with the false teachers vis-à-vis the law was that their teaching did not conform to the glorious gospel of Jesus Christ* (1 Tim 1:10-11). The Torah was likely being presented as the center of God's revelation. Paul is asking Timothy to insist that Jesus Christ is the center of God's revelation. Anytime something or someone is placed above him either in our interpretation of Scripture or in our relationship with God, it becomes destructive. Or, as Paul says, any such teachings "promote speculations" (1 Tim 1:4) and lead to "meaningless talk" (1 Tim 1:6).

Sound doctrine. In contrast to the destructive "different teachings" (1 Tim 1:3) stands the sound apostolic doctrine. Paul speaks of this doctrine in three ways: (1) *divine training* (1 Tim 1:4); (2) *sound teaching* (1 Tim 1:10), and *the glorious gospel* (1 Tim 1:11). The *gospel* or good news was preached by Jesus Christ himself (Mk 1:14-15). He entrusted this gospel to the Twelve and their closest disciples (Acts 1:15-26; 1 Cor 15:1-4), who were witnesses of his resurrection. Paul, "as . . . someone untimely born" (1 Cor 15:8), also was called an apostle by the risen Christ. The apostles and their companions passed down the teaching of Jesus (including the meaning of the crucifixion and resurrection) and further developed it by the guidance of the Holy Spirit (Jn 14–16). The New Testament is essentially the written testimony of the prophets and apostles (Eph 2:20). Although it is unlikely that the New Testament was complete when Paul wrote to Timothy, there certainly existed a summary of the apostolic teaching, submission to which was the hallmark of genuine churches.[14]

Often in the Pastoral Epistles (1 Tim 6:3; 2 Tim 1:13; 4:3; Tit. 2:1) this summary of apostolic doctrine is called "sound teaching." It was common for Greco-Roman moral philosophers (e.g., Seneca, Dio Chrysostom) to speak of their rational philosophical teaching as *sound* or *healthy*, providing intellectual medicine that would help the minds of people return from unsoundness. Paul is likely implying that the gospel of Jesus Christ is the true and only teaching that can bring healing and soundness to humans.[15] Sound teaching makes us whole because it comes from God himself.

Only sound doctrine can enable us to love God and neighbor. God's revelation of himself in Holy Scripture is given so that we might be reconciled to him and enjoy him in fellowship. But this relationship with God has also, as it were, both a vertical and horizontal obligation. From the beginnings of Israel's existence God told the nation that the Lord alone was their God and that they were to love their Lord with all their being (Deut 6:4-5). Irreducibly related to this command is love for other human beings, our neighbors: "You shall love your neighbor as yourself" (Lev 19:18). The Lord Jesus Christ, when asked what the greatest commandment was, answered, "'You shall love the Lord your God with all your heart and with all your soul and with all your mind.' This is the greatest and first commandment. And a second is like it: 'You shall love your neighbor as yourself.' On these two commandments hang all the Law and the Prophets" (Mt 22:37-40).

It is no coincidence, therefore, that Paul tells Timothy that the aim or goal of apostolic instruction, such as is found in 1 Timothy, "is love that comes from a pure heart, a good conscience, and sincere faith" (1 Tim 1:5). Only by relying on the gospel can we fulfill God's goal of love for our lives. For relying on the gospel is not relying on a formula but on the crucified and raised One, who himself is the gospel. We are reminded of Augustine's famous words in his treatise *On Christian Doctrine* (1.36): "Whoever, then, thinks that he understands the Holy Scriptures, or any part of them, but puts such an interpretation upon them as does not tend to build up this twofold love of God and our neighbor, does not yet understand them as he ought."

Application. How can reading 1 Timothy 1:3-11 from a Hispanic angle help us? As a whole, Christianity (including Roman Catholicism) among Hispanics tends to be focused on the incarnate Jesus Christ. There is less metaphysical interest and speculation on "God in himself" or on epistemology, namely, how we can know about God, as we find in medieval Christianity or post-Reformation dogmatics. Christian religion among Hispanics is more "concrete" or "tangible." Therefore, there are many spaces in homes or towns where images of Christ are present. During Holy Week, I recall as a child in the Dominican Republic

[14]We can see fragments of this apostolic teaching in the speeches in Acts (e.g., Peter, Stephen, Paul) as well as in some of the liturgical pieces of the New Testament (e.g., Phil 2:5-11; Col 1:15-20; 1 Tim 3:16). On the former see Graham Stanton, *Jesus of Nazareth in New Testament Preaching*, SNTSMS (Cambridge: Cambridge University Press, 1975). See also Irenaeus's "Rule of Truth," in *A. H.* 1.22.1.

[15]See Padilla, *Pastoral Epistles*, 62-63.

seeing men walking on their knees on the hot pavement with a cross on their shoulders; some would have a crown of thorns on their heads and whip themselves. Although I doubt that these spiritual exercises have biblical warrant or are healthy, the effect they tend to have is to remind us that the center of our faith is the incarnate Christ. This is in contrast to many expressions of Christianity in the West—especially in modern liberal Protestantism—which are more focused on an abstract God (not to say god) or self-improvement.

On the other hand, a Hispanic angle, while pointing (however imperfectly) to the incarnate Christ, is often focused on Jesus *as our example*. To be sure, this is part of the biblical picture of Jesus (see 1 Pet 2:19-23 and the presentation of Jesus in the passion narrative of the Synoptic Gospels as the righteous sufferer whom we are to imitate). But the biblical Christ is also the one who died for our sins and was raised from the dead for our justification. In this respect, the Hispanic tendency to view Jesus as primarily a righteous man who left us an example is something we can learn from in a negative way. This is a shortcoming of Hispanic Christianity that stands to learn from other traditions, where it is understood that the suffering of Jesus is not given us as a mimetic image to gain our salvation. The gospel is good news in that Christ atoned for our sins out of pure love; and we follow him out of gratitude.

The testimony of Paul the persecutor (1 Timothy 1:12-17). It is clear from the Pastoral Epistles that Paul's aim is ultimately to rehabilitate the false teachers, to rebuke them so that they would repent (see 2 Tim 2:24-25).[16] Yet, in light of the strong language used throughout these letters it is clear that this would be a very difficult task. Timothy may well feel overwhelmed with this task. To encourage Timothy in his assignment Paul narrates briefly how God was able to save him despite the fact that he had been "a blasphemer, a persecutor, and a man of violence" (1 Tim 1:13). The logic of this paragraph is the following: if God can save someone as lost as Paul used to be, he can also save the false teachers who are opposing the sound doctrine.

The language Paul uses to describe himself prior to his conversion paints the picture of someone who was full of insolence toward God. Scholars often ask how Paul can speak of himself in Philippians 3:6 as "blameless," while here speaking of himself as a blasphemer! The likely answer is that in the former passage he was describing himself apart from the reality of Jesus Christ. In fact, because he viewed Jesus and his followers as deceivers who were polluting Israel, persecuting the church was actually an act of justice and zeal, cleansing Israel as Phinehas and Elijah had done in the past. But when Paul was met by the risen Jesus on the road to Damascus, the Lord revealed to him that he was actually persecuting the Messiah himself (Acts 9:1-5). Paul's acts were now revealed for what they truly were: acts of blasphemy and hubris. Although Paul "had acted ignorantly in unbelief" (1 Tim 1:13), he deserved to be punished by God. But something different happened: "The grace of our Lord overflowed for me with the faith and love that are in Christ Jesus" (1 Tim 1:14). God's grace overflowed over Paul! This is *grace*: God's gift that is incongruous with what we deserve.[17] Paul's salvation/calling demonstrates that "Christ Jesus came into the world to save

[16]See Lyn M. Kidson, *Persuading Shipwrecked Men: The Rhetorical Strategies of 1 Timothy 1*, WUNT (Tübingen: Mohr Siebeck, 2020).

[17]See John M. G. Barclay, *Paul and the Gift* (Grand Rapids, MI: Eerdmans, 2015), 565-66.

sinners—of whom I am the foremost" (1 Tim 1:15). Paul's salvation would serve as "an example to those who would come to believe" (1 Tim 1:16). Timothy should thus be encouraged in his ministry, for God's arm was not too short to save both those who were struggling with the doctrine of the false teachers and the false teachers themselves. Remembrance of God's grace for him leads Paul to close this section with a doxology (1 Tim 1:17).

Application. ¡Un testimonio, por favor! It is the custom in many Hispanic churches in North America to ask members of the congregation to share *un testimonio*, a testimony of what God has done in their lives during the previous week. Because often there is no wide gap between the clergy and the congregants, people from the pew are at liberty, when the right moment comes, to share a testimony. It does not matter how well-spoken or not you are; how old or young; male or female. What matters is that God has been present in your life and sharing that experience will strengthen others who may be disheartened. And often the operative term in these testimonies is *grace*: God has been gracious to me! Paul also is giving a testimony in this text: God has been gracious to me! Timothy may thus be encouraged in his ministry: God could also show grace to the opponents.

Hymenaeus and Alexander (1 Timothy 1:18-20). In this section Paul mentions two concrete examples of men who "have suffered shipwreck in the faith" (1 Tim 1:19). The language of *shipwreck* used metaphorically was common in the Greco-Roman world, where the many shipwrecks in the Mediterranean Sea were often the subject of conversation. Paul speaks of the shipwreck of their *faith*. The word *faith* is used many times in the Pastoral Epistles, having three main references: (1) *faith* as that which one believes in, namely the apostolic doctrine centered in the gospel of Jesus Christ. This is the objective faith. Theologians often speak of this type of faith as *fides quae*. (2) *Faith* can also refer to the *act of believing*, placing faith in God/Christ. Theologians often speak of this type of faith as *fides qua*. (3) *Faith* can also refer to "religious practice," where the emphasis falls on the Christian's existence of devotion to God. All three senses of faith are intertwined. For example, *fides quae* ineluctably leads to devotion to God, otherwise it is not real faith. *Fides qua* is not "faith in faith," but faith in the Lord Jesus Christ, the center of apostolic doctrine. Hymenaeus and Alexander have suffered "shipwreck in the faith," with *faith* likely including all three senses above.[18]

Paul's response to Hymenaeus and Alexander has been to turn them over "to Satan." Although this phrase would seem to indicate the end of these two men, careful observation of the language suggests that Paul's goal is actually to *rehabilitate* them to the faith.[19] The situation is similar to what we find in 1 Corinthians 5:5.

Application. For different historical reasons, Hispanic culture, especially in the Caribbean and Brazil, is one where language of *Satan* or *the Devil* is very common. This is particularly evident in practices of Voodoo and Santeria. In most Hispanic cultures there tends to be strong awareness of the supernatural, often accompanied by fear of being cursed or hurt by Satan.

[18]On faith in Paul and the Pastoral Epistles, see Teresa Morgan, *Roman Faith and Christian Faith*: Pistis *and* Fides *in the Early Roman Empire and Early Churches* (Oxford: Oxford University Press, 2015). For those who can read German, the work of Mutschler is foundational: *Glaube in den Pastoralbriefen:* Pistis *als Mitte Christlicher Existenz*, WUNT 256 (Tübingen: Mohr Siebeck, 2010).

[19]The verb translated as *they may be taught* in 1 Tim 1:20 comes from the Greek *paideuō*, which gives the basic sense of *correcting*, not final punishment.

Yet, as a Hispanic reading, this passage of Scripture makes it clear that while Satan can inflict harm, he is ultimately under God's control. He can even be God's instrument to accomplish God's purposes (see, e.g., Job). Ultimately, therefore, Christians must not fear Satan the way one is afraid of an enemy who is impossible to beat. For Satan has already been defeated on the cross of Jesus Christ (Col 2:15).

Prayer in the household of God (1 Timothy 2:1-7). Prayer is crucial in the church, and so Paul instructs Timothy (and with him all church leaders) on different aspects of prayer. In this section we find the different *types* of prayers that the church should offer; the *objects* of prayer; and the *reason* or *basis* of prayer.

"I urge that supplications, prayers, intercessions, and thanksgivings be made . . ." (1 Tim 2:1). The first two terms, which can often be found together in Greek literature, refer to prayer in general, asking God to meet a need (BDAG, 213, 878). The last two types of prayers, *intercessions* and *thanksgivings*, can also appear together (BDAG, 340). By piling up these different terms for prayer Paul is emphasizing that the task of the church is to pray in all circumstances (cf. 1 Thess 5:17-18).

Who should we pray for? The word "everyone" or "all" in reference to all humanity (Greek, *anthrōpos*) appears three times in this section (1 Tim 2:1, 4, 6 [implied]). We should pray for all human beings. In 1 Timothy 2:2 Paul focuses on prayer for those in authority, perhaps because—humanly speaking—the fate of much of humanity is dependent on those who govern. When Paul wrote the Pastoral Epistles the Roman empire was in power over most of the then-known world. To be sure, some city-states were allowed to govern their own affairs. The Romans would not intervene much in these cases as long as disorder was kept to a minimum and the proper taxes were paid. Early Christianity, because it was often viewed as a movement within Judaism (cf. Acts 18:12-17) was allowed to meet as a group.[20] This was in contrast to many voluntary associations and cults, whose meetings were viewed as suspicious and often forbidden. In the late second century the philosopher Celsus accused the Christians of being a secret society that was spreading a false philosophy.[21]

Paul follows Jewish tradition in praying "for kings and all who are in high positions" (1 Tim 2:2) but not praying *to* the kings, as in emperor worship.[22] Jesus authorized this tradition for believers when he ordered them: "Give . . . to Caesar the things that are Caesar's and to God the things that are God's" (Mt 22:21).

Prayer for those in authority has the goal that society would "lead a quiet and peaceable life in all godliness and dignity" (1 Tim 2:2). The emphasis here falls on the authorities procuring *peace* for those they govern. Peace is better than chaos; peace is better than anarchy; peace is better than war. God desires peace for his creation. Interestingly, Paul links a situation of peace with an existence that is characterized by *all godliness and dignity*. In light of the statements in 1 Timothy 2:3-7, this likely

[20]The first century AD Jewish historian Josephus preserves a number of letters and decrees from the Roman Senate, Roman emperors, and city resolutions that would seem to indicate that the Jews had received special status to practice their way of life wherever they went. These rights included the freedom to assemble, freedom from military service, freedom to practice the Sabbath, and freedom to collect funds to send to Jerusalem for the temple. See Josephus, *Jewish Antiquities* books 14, 16, and 19. The important essay from Tessa Rajak should be read in conjunction with Josephus: "Was There a Roman Charter for the Jews?," in *The Jewish Dialogue with Greece and Rome: Studies in Cultural and Social Interaction* (Leiden: Brill, 2001), 301-33.

[21]See Origen, *Contra Celsum* 1.1 and passim.

[22]See Ezra 6:8-10; Josephus, *J.W.* 2.197, 409; Philo, *Flacc.* 49.

means that a calm, nonviolent society is one where the gospel can flourish. Of course, the gospel can also grow in times of war and disarray; but the ideal is a peaceful state where the preaching of the gospel would not be hindered. To summarize what Paul exhorts us to pray for, we can say that he calls on us to pray for humanity to live in a state of peace, not only because peace is better than chaos, but also so that the *Missio Dei* would prosper. This becomes clear in the following verses.

The reason to pray for humanity to live in peace is because "this is right and acceptable in the sight of God our Savior, who desires everyone to be saved and to come to a knowledge of the truth" (1 Tim 2:3-4). Paul could simply have said that prayer is acceptable to God. But we should note that he includes language of God as *Savior* and the verbal cognate *to be saved*. This is the clue that the reason for prayer has to do with the salvation of humanity: "God . . . desires everyone to be saved [*that is*] to come to the knowledge of the truth." What follows is likely a liturgical statement of the early church: "For there is one God; there is also one mediator between God and humankind, Christ Jesus, himself human, who gave himself a ransom for all" (1 Tim 2:5-6). The statement about there being *one God* is an echo of Deuteronomy 6:4, part of the precious *Shema*: "Hear, O Israel: The Lord our God, the Lord is one" (NIV). Just as there is only one God, there is also one mediator, *Christ Jesus, himself human*. This is a powerful statement, for it is likely operating within the framework of Jesus' preexistence, which would mean that Jesus shared in God's divine identity (see Phil 2:6-11). Therefore, the addition *himself human* is a statement about the incarnation, through which he became one with humanity (as the second Adam) and obtained our salvation through his very life and suffering. This is why the section ends with the statement that the incarnate Messiah Jesus *gave himself a ransom for all*. This is an echo of Jesus' statement in Mark 10:45, which itself goes back to the Servant of Isaiah 53:4-8. Rather than humans taking the punishment that we deserved as sinners, Jesus Messiah stood in our place and delivered us to be servants of God.

Application. In many of our traditions' prayer books, there is a section that guides us in praying for those in authority. As an Episcopalian, I pray the section in the Book of Common Prayer that asks for wisdom and guidance for those in authority, for God to keep the nation under his care, and for peace. These are good, biblical prayers. But it strikes me that these prayers could give the impression that our ultimate hope is in our particular nation being kept. There is nothing wrong with patriotism. But do we pray these prayers believing that our hope is in the United States being kept prosperous and protected (I mention the United States because most, if not all, the contributors reside in the United States)? I come from Latin America, and my country of origin was so corrupt that I honestly did not believe that my hope was in my country getting better—because I did not believe that the country *would* get better! Perhaps I lacked faith. But what if the United States, or other countries where we feel safe and prosperous, begin to crumble? My experience as a Hispanic helps me to pray, not only for the country where I now live and cherish, but ultimately for the kingdom of God. Our ultimate prayer from the Lord is *thy kingdom come!* Those of us who have lived in nations where there is no hope may have the clarity to tell our brothers and sisters in the United States to ultimately put their hope, not in the stability and prosperity of a country, but on the kingdom of God. Our hope is in his returning to this world, where his will shall be done as it is in heaven.

The conduct of men and women in prayer (1 Timothy 2:8-15). Paul continues the subject of prayer in these verses. He adjusts his lens to focus on prayer vis-à-vis our conduct as men and women in the household of God. There are likely three reasons why he proceeds in this way. First, although the Old Testament already spoke of the importance of our spiritual condition when coming before the Lord (see Ps 24:3-6, for example), the Lord Jesus made this central in his teachings on prayer. In particular, Jesus drove home the importance of harmonious relationships with our neighbors if we expect God to answer our prayers (Mt 5:21-26; 6:5-15). Paul is following this logic here, calling attention to our behavior toward one another when we pray. Second, Paul instructs in particular adult males and females in this section. Instead of addressing the congregations as a whole, he speaks of how "the men" should pray (1 Tim 2:8) and how "the women" should behave when they pray (1 Tim 2:9). Why does Paul proceed this way? The answer is that Paul is likely using the Greco-Roman philosophical construct of *oikonomia*, that is, giving instructions concerning the different members of an ancient household (e.g., fathers/husbands, mothers/wives, sons, daughters, and slaves). This becomes more explicit in 1 Timothy 5:1–6:2 and Titus 2:1-10, where Paul addresses the different ages and stations of a household. In the current section he limits his paraenesis to men and women. Third, Paul proceeds as he does in 1 Timothy 2:8-15 because it is probable that there were particular problems with this group of people in the church. We note that while the men receive only one verse in the exhortations, the women receive several verses. The reason for this is that the false teachers were targeting mostly wealthy women. It is not the case, however, that Paul is "targeting" women in the Pastoral Epistles! Recall that most of the rebukes in the letters are toward the false teachers, who were males.

The conduct of men (1 Timothy 2:8). The heart of the command that Paul gives the men has to do with "anger." As they lift up their prayers to God, their attitude and treatment toward one another must be "without anger or argument." As indicated above, this command looks like an application of Jesus' teaching as found in Matthew 5:21-26. There must be forgiveness and peace between the men when they pray.

The conduct of women (1 Timothy 2:9-15). These are some of the most contested verses in the church today. They are often used in a negative fashion to demarcate what women cannot do in church ministry. For those who argue that it is not biblical for women to be ministers or priests in the church, 1 Timothy 2:9-15 apparently represents the clearest articulation of the prohibition. In fact, however, these verses may actually obscure our understanding of women's ministry in the church. Why? Because when we look at Scripture as a whole there are many places where women are shown to be leading the entire congregation of Israel (Deborah, Huldah), speaking before the congregation what the Spirit reveals to them (1 Cor 11), and instructing men (Priscilla with Aquila in Acts 18). Furthermore, Paul calls some of the women who ministered alongside him his "coworkers," even speaking of Junia as an "apostle" (i.e., sent by the Lord for a task) in Romans 16:7. If 1 Timothy 2:9-15 were not part of Scripture; or if we were unaware of its contents, it would be very difficult to make an argument from Scripture against women instructing the entire church: the passages cited above would function as positive evidence that women *should* be part of the leadership of the church, no exceptions. It is therefore jarring when we read in

1 Timothy 2:11-14, "Let a woman learn in silence with full submission. I do not permit a woman to teach or to have authority over a man; she is to keep silent. For Adam was formed first, then Eve, and Adam was not deceived, but the woman was deceived and became a transgressor." Many of my readers may respond that these verses are not "jarring" to them at all; they seem like the most natural thing. I would argue that these verses may not appear "jarring" or strange because many of us have been in churches for years where these verses are concrete realities: only the men are the leaders, and therefore 1 Timothy 2:11-14 is expected, and is even declared "the clear teaching of Scripture." My point, however, is that actually 1 Timothy 2:11-14 is the exception, not the rule, of the biblical scope regarding the ministries of women. I am going to suggest below that this text is primarily about the character of women, not some universal teaching on the place of women in the ministries of the church.

As we will see in more detail in 2 Timothy 3, it appears that one of the significant problems addressed in the Pastoral Epistles was the conduct of some of the women in the churches. It would seem that these women—in part moved by the culture and in part moved by the false teachers—were behaving in immodest, libertine, and disrespectful ways, particularly in relationship to the male leaders of the church. Not only was this conduct contrary to the expected behavior of women who followed the faith, but the conduct could also cause the gospel to come into disrepute and thereby jeopardize the missional duty of the church. To stop this behavior Paul calls attention to two areas in which there needed to be changes. We can summarize these areas with the words *modesty* and *respect.*

Regarding *modesty*, in 1 Timothy 2:9-10 Paul concentrates on the deportment of the women. The language used here was common in the discourse of moral philosophers of the period: "modestly . . . decently . . . not with their hair braided, or with gold, pearls, or expensive clothes" (1 Tim 2:9 NRSV 1989).[23] The modesty that needed to be displayed was primarily social. That is, when meeting in the different households to worship, the women should not dress luxuriously, with expensive hairdos, clothing or jewelry. Paul is not prohibiting elegance or beauty; he is against lavish deportment that called more attention to the body or wealth of the women. If women wanted to dress "richly," they should do so in the department of *good works* (1 Tim 2:10).

Second, there is the matter of *respect*, particularly in the domain of public speech. 1 Timothy 2:11-12 suggests that instead of learning calmly and respectfully, some of the women were continually "interrupting the lesson."[24] One of the key terms used in 1 Timothy 2:12 is the uncommon Greek verb *authenteō*. The NRSV renders this with the phrase "to have authority." A better, more precise translation would be "to display authority arrogantly," or "to display authority with a heavy hand." We know from 1 Corinthians 11:2-16, 14:31-32 that women prophesied in public, that is, spoke messages from the Lord to the entire church. Paul directed the Christian women at Corinth to do this public speaking in a manner that was respectful to men (which in that period was demonstrated by wearing a veil). It appears that the situation in 1 Timothy, which is likely very similar to that in Corinth, had gone in the wrong direction: some of the women were not only speaking in public but were doing so in a

[23]For the primary sources, see Padilla, *The Pastoral Epistles*, 83-86.

[24]I. Howard Marshall, *The Pastoral Epistles;* ICC (London: T&T Clark, 1999), 453.

manner that was "arrogant" or "heavy handed." In short, this group of women were not showing *respect* to their male teachers or the males present in the household communities. In the Greco-Roman culture of Paul's time this would have been scandalous—ultimately endangering the relationship between the church and her neighbors. And so Paul prohibits these women from teaching (1 Tim 2:11-12).

Paul the apostle always sought to establish his injunctions on the basis of Scripture. And so he concludes this section by employing Genesis 2–3. The women should show respect to men because Adam was created first (1 Tim 2:13). In addition, Paul is going to provide an illustration from the same Genesis text: Eve had been deceived by the serpent, not Adam (1 Tim 2:14). This Scripture forms the basis for Paul's command that women be modest and respectful. It *illustrates* what can happen when women behave in an overly independent manner from their brothers.

We conclude this section by reflecting on how difficult it is to know how 1 Timothy 2:9-15 applies to the present-day church. A "minimalist" application would simply be the following: women should dress modestly when meeting for worship; women should honor men (in the same way that men should honor women!): that is, they should not speak to them disrespectfully, especially in a public setting. I myself am content with this "minimalist" application. But many scholars desire to go beyond this simple application by drawing "principles" from this text for use in the present. What principles should we draw from this text?

Application. An important leitmotif of *The New Testament in Color* is the thesis that our present reality has a profound effect on how we interpret Scripture. Our spiritual state, gender, ethnicity, socioeconomic location, and so on tend to be the lens through which we interpret the Bible. There is no such thing as "the view from nowhere." Yet this does not mean that we are hopelessly "captured" or "prisoners" of our current situations, such that a correct or plausible interpretation of the Bible is impossible. This book argues the opposite: our locations (women, men, Asian, Anglo, African American, Hispanic, rich, poor, etc.) may actually be aids in interpretation, for the Bible itself is cultural in that it was written, not in some cultural vacuum, but in ancient cultures that at times are strikingly similar to our present cultures. This is precisely why we need biblical interpretations from Christians of different ethnic backgrounds: the interpretation of my brother or sister from an Indian background, for example, may open vistas to the biblical text that have been obscured in my own ethnic background.

And so, instead of going beyond the "minimalist" application of 1 Timothy 2:9-15 offered above, I encourage the reader to consult commentaries written from different ethnicities (for example, the *Biblia Africana*). This should provide an exercise in hermeneutics that may in the long run be more helpful to the student than my own particular view of what principles can and cannot be drawn from this text.[25]

Leaders in the church: the offices of overseers and deacons (1 Timothy 3:1-13). Both explicitly and implicitly the Pastoral Epistles underline the importance of godly leadership in the church. The principle is the following: for the people of God to flourish, there must be present godly and capacious leaders. This is a principle that is found throughout the entire biblical canon.

---

[25]For those who want to know with more nuance my view of 1 Timothy 2:9-15, they may consult my commentary on the Pastoral Epistles.

In this section of 1 Timothy Paul speaks of two church offices:[26] overseer and deacon.[27] In what follows I put forth three points that help explain these verses, with a fourth point addressing contemporary application.[28] First, it is important to observe that the virtues expected of overseers and deacons are almost entirely the same virtues that *all* Christians should display. *All* Christians should be "self-controlled, respectable, hospitable" (1 Tim 3:2) and so on. When looking at the qualifications for deacons (1 Tim 3:8-13), the same applies. The ability to teach sound doctrine (see 1 Tim 3:2) may be said to be specific to overseers (and, I would argue, deacons as well; see below). But then we also have to remember that all Christians, to the extent that all should share their faith, need to be able to lay out clearly the meaning of the gospel. In a sense, then, even this specific qualification, that is, for the overseer to be able to teach, is not unique to the office. This does not mean that we should relativize the capacity to teach in such a way that there no longer exist lines of demarcation between overseers and lay Christians. The point is that "clericalism" can isolate those who serve in church offices from those who serve as laity. The Pastoral Epistles question the myth that church leaders are "super Christians," that they possess a spirituality that is a step above other Christians. But this is not true. Not recognizing this has often led to church leaders having to put on "airs" of superspirituality, which usually leads to hypocrisy, burnout, and a host of other maladies that are destructive of both congregation and pastors.

The second observation has to do with the titles themselves. It must be clear that the Greek words variously translated into English as "overseers," "deacons," and "elders" neither originated in the Bible nor were exclusive to the vocabulary of the church. It is the other way around. Theologically speaking, the reason for this state of affairs is that while the church is not *of* the world it interacts daily and profoundly *with* the culture in which it exists. Thus, when God reveals himself to his people he uses the common culture (which includes *language*. For example, Greek was the dominant language in the world of the New Testament: therefore, the New Testament was written in Greek). Without this divine *accommodation*,[29] humans could not comprehend God's revelation. Thus, revelation always goes down to the very roots of the culture God is addressing. Stated yet another way, there is no such thing as God revealing himself in a manner that is *a*cultural. The search for such a thing is not from the Bible but from Enlightenment philosophy. Practically speaking, in our case this leads to asking how and where the terms that Paul took-over to speak of church leadership were used. The short answer is that terms like *episkopos* ("overseer") were abundant, especially in the context of the city-state and voluntary associations.[30] And so we ask, "What did an *episkopos*

[26]An office refers to a position that exists irrespective of the individual who holds the office. For example, the office of president of the United States does not belong to any one particular individual (like a throne would belong to particular family, for example); the office exists to be occupied by whoever is voted in, irrespective of who that person is.

[27]On elders and their relationship to a church office, see under 1 Tim 4:14; 5:17-25 and Titus 1:5-9.

[28]For those who wish a detailed explanation of all the qualifications and virtues expressed in these verses, the commentary by Marshall, *The Pastoral Epistles*, 471-97, is strongly recommended.

[29]The language is Calvin's, who speaks of God accommodating himself to speak to us: "This, therefore, is a special gift, where God, to instruct the church not merely uses mute teachers but also opens his most hallowed lips. . . . He has from the beginning maintained this plan for his church, so that . . . he also put forth his Word, which is a more direct and more certain mark whereby he is to be recognized" (*Institutes* 1.6.1).

[30]Voluntary associations were unofficial syndicates made up of men and women who practiced the same profession. For example, there were voluntary associations of purple dyers, fishermen, physicians, and so on. As one scholar puts it, "These

do?" "Where did an *episkopos* work?" This leads to our third set of observations.

"Overseer" (which, again, I will argue is not synonymous with "elders"), in both its substantival and verbal form, was used in many different contexts in antiquity.[31] It is only a slight exaggeration to say that the essential activity of the *episkopos* was that of "looking after," with connotations of management and supervision attached to this "looking after." Thus, a good *episkopos* was one who constantly "looked after" a state (i.e., a large property) so that its conditions would not deteriorate. It is said of the gods that they "watched over" humans to protect them. There are multiple examples where the verb *episkopeō* basically means to visit a sick person. In the LXX the verb also expresses the act of "watching over" or "caring for" someone, although the term can also go into the semantic domain of "judging" or "judgment." Paul's audience, then, when hearing a form of the word *episkopos* would have quickly understood that the churches' overseer's task was to "take care" or "watch over" the believers in the different churches. The main task of the overseer would not have been preaching or teaching (we will return to this below). As leaders who had been appointed by God, the job of the overseers was essentially to care for the sheep (1 Pet 5:2!). This would have included primarily the type of work which today we call "pastoral" work: visiting those in need, looking after the sick, caring for the ill, managing the churches so that they would function well, and so on. Part of this "looking after" would of course have included instructing the believers in the Holy Scriptures (see 1 Tim 3:2; 4:6, 11; 2 Tim 4:1-5).

The CEB translates the next office with "servants." The Greek term *diakonos* stands for both the masculine and feminine, and this is likely why the CEB has rendered it "servants" instead of simply "deacons." It should not at all be surprising to understand *diakonos* in 1 Timothy 3:11 as referring to female deacons or "deaconesses," especially in light of the fact that in the ancient Greco-Roman world the women were the ones who often cleared the tables and did a lot of the "kitchen" related work. In so doing, they were "serving" (*diakoneō*). Lexically speaking, therefore, from very early on the noun *diakonos* and/or the verb *diakoneō* was used with women as the subjects (see *TDNT* 2:82). Thus, it would have been easy to use the label *diakonos* also as referring to women deaconesses. This is more than likely the case here.

There are very few differences between the concrete work of the overseer and the deacon as presented in 1 Timothy 3:1-13. The latter would have included more manual or practical work than the former, to be sure. However, we should be careful not to make facile differentiations such as the following: overseers (or elders) taught the Bible; deacons did the material work. One of the reasons why I think that deacons (male and female) also were teachers is the statement in 1 Timothy 3:9: "They must keep hold of the deep truths of the faith with a clear conscience." It is fascinating to note that in Titus 1:9, in speaking of the *overseer*, Paul says the following: "He must hold firmly to the trustworthy message as it has been taught, so that he can encourage others by sound doctrine and refute those who oppose it" (NIV).

---

associations provided members with a sense of belonging, along with some practical benefits such as opportunities for networking, regular banquets, and a decent burial" (Richard Ascough, *Associations in the Greco-Roman World* [Waco, TX: Baylor University Press, 2012], 1). The language of leadership in the voluntary associations were imitative of the language of the city-state.

[31]See the literature in *TDNT* 2:600-622; Kloppenborg, *Christ's Associations*, 280, 368n76. My examples above are drawn from here.

As we will comment in more depth under Titus 1:9, all we can say at the moment is that the statement in Titus 1:9 is strikingly similar in both language and concept to the expectations of deacons of 1 Timothy 3:9—*but in Titus 1:9 the reference is to the overseers.* To put it briefly now, I believe that deacons also were responsible for teaching, even if to a lesser amount than overseers. If this is true, it would also mean that female deacons or deaconesses could also instruct in the Holy Scriptures.

The fourth and last statement to be made on this passage is of a practical nature. Let us assume for the moment that the activities of the overseers can be applied to what today most of our churches call "the pastor." When we then carefully observe the duties of overseers and deacons/deaconesses as expressed in 1 Timothy 3:1-13 it is clear that the modern evangelical church has departed from what it means to be a pastor. The reader should not misunderstand. I am not saying that to be faithful to the biblical concept of pastor one must follow every biblical passage *au pied de la lettre* (i.e., with inflexible literalness). That is a misunderstanding of how to read the Bible, a misunderstanding that stems from fundamentalism. Application or extension of the Bible to the present is a complex activity that requires nuanced understanding of the Bible itself, the "large narrative" of the Bible with its christological center and telos, genre, contemporary culture, and so on. It is in this complex sense that I am saying that the modern evangelical church has changed the biblical concept of the pastor to one that has more in common with the modern CEO or white-collar conception of what it means to be a leader. The concept of pastor in the church today, as it has been seduced by modern culture, demands that a pastor must be someone who woes with charisma and is an outstanding speaker, capacious enough to hold the attention of the audience for thirty minutes (or usually longer!). This is his main job; and the staff and congregation must "free" him from other duties lest his weekly sermon suffer in content or delivery. As we said above, he must also brim with charisma; lead from the top-down; and so on. Especially in larger churches, it is often expected that associate pastors or nonclergy would do the so-called pastoral work of the church while the "senior" pastor studies and prepares throughout the week for preaching. Sadly, this model of pastoring has very little to do with the work of the pastor as seen above. In fact, we must admit that we have allowed the cultural concept of leadership to control the church. To be sure, preaching and teaching are important, even essential, activities of leaders in the churches. But so is the type of "watching over" or "looking after" that I have tried to explain above. Naturally, this type of "watching over" *is* carried out in preaching and teaching; but pastoral work that does not shepherd the congregants in the type of work mentioned above (e.g., visiting the sick, helping the poor in the community) ultimately has more to do with contemporary leadership culture than with the biblical concept of the pastor.

The great mystery (1 Timothy 3:14-16). With these verses we reach the end of the first section of 1 Timothy. At the same time, a number of topics that were mentioned in 1 Timothy 1–3 continue in the following section (1 Tim 4–6), although different motifs are accented. We can thus think of 1 Timothy 3:14-16 as the "hinge" of the book. For some scholars this section constitutes the center of all the Pastoral Epistles (e.g., Spicq, 103), and as such is crucial.[32] We have in 1 Timothy 3:14-15 a clear statement of purpose for Paul's writing of

[32]See, for example, Ceslas Spicq, *Les Épîtres Pastorales*, EBib (Paris: Gabalda, 1969).

the letter: "I hope to come to you soon, but I am writing you these instructions so that, if I am delayed, you would know how one ought to behave in the household of God." Interestingly, Paul does not immediately follow this statement with orders and commands. Instead, he *defines* for Timothy what *God's household* is, and then adds a statement about what the gospel is. The lesson here is that Christians cannot behave as Christians if they have not first come to a knowledge of the mystery from which true godliness springs (1 Tim 3:16), an enlarged way to refer to the gospel. Conduct (the imperative) is not possible with gospel (the indicative of what God has done for us in Jesus Christ). It is the hallmark of Protestant liberalism to invert these two categories. The result is that the church ceases to be the church and becomes instead an institution fundamentally driven by the attempt to solve the ills of society. To be sure, the church *must* do—in the power of the Holy Spirit—all it can to address ever-present social malaise. But if there is no gospel in the endeavor, the institution cannot be called a church. For the church is first and foremost the spokesperson of the gospel. One then may ask, What *is* the gospel? This is precisely what Paul expounds in 1 Timothy 3:16.

To explain 1 Timothy 3:16 at least the following two observations must be made. First, the form of the verse is given in a confessional formula.[33] We are likely dealing with what was a hymn or a liturgical piece of the early church. Perhaps Paul himself had a hand in its original composition. Whatever the case, as the hymn stands in 1 Timothy 3:16 it has Paul as its final author. The second observation to be made is that in this poetic rendition of the gospel all three members of the Trinity are present. The one who *was revealed in the flesh* is the incarnate Christ. Putting the incarnation in this form implies the preexistence of Christ and therefore his divinity. The hymn continues with the work of the Spirit: Jesus Christ *was vindicated in the Spirit*. In context the sense is that the Spirit raised Jesus from the dead. Given the shameful death by crucifixion which Jesus endured—and which was reserved for the worst of criminals—it might have been easy to conclude that Jesus was not the Messiah but a revolutionary impostor. Paul's words in 1 Corinthians 1:18-25 suggest that this was a stumbling block for the reception of the gospel by both Gentiles and Jews. And outside the Bible, in material that probably goes back to the New Testament period, we read of Jewish polemic against Jesus: he was rightly hung to death on a tree because he was a false prophet and magician (*b. Sanh.* 43a). But the glorious resurrection by the power of the Spirit (see also Rom 1:4) and the will of the Father (see Acts 2:32) demonstrated (for those with eyes to see!) that Jesus truly was the Messiah and king, and the Lord of Lords. Last, we can point to the work of the Father, who took up Jesus *in glory* (cf. also Acts 2:33). Augustine's *theologoumenon* (i.e., theological statement that has gained authority in the church), *opera trinitatis ad extra indivisa sunt* ("the works of the Trinity outside itself are indivisible") is not some fancy theological speculation; it is anchored in a number of scriptural texts, including this one. Theologically speaking, therefore, we can say that the gospel is trinitarian in nature.

Application. ¡Música, maestro! Hispanics love music. All cultures love music. In fact, a particular type of music may be the only thing someone may know of a country. Perhaps you know little of Brazil, but when you hear bossa nova you know it comes from Brazil. Music is

[33]M. Dibelius and H. Conzelmann, *The Pastoral Epistles*, trans. Philip Buttolph and Adela Yarbro (Philadelphia: Fortress Press, 1972), 61, and most commentators.

beautiful. It is a gift from our beautiful God that often helps speak what the tongue is incapable of articulating. It should thus not be surprising that the Bible is full of musical elements and songs. With music we praise God. Furthermore, as Paul says in Colossians 3:16, we learn the word of God "through psalms, hymns, and songs from the Spirit" (NIV). Although it is difficult to differentiate between these three categories, it is likely that the third refers to shorter, more spontaneous songs that may lack the sophisticated arrangement that one discovers in psalms and hymns. Now, my non-Hispanic readers must understand that, relatively speaking, Protestantism is new for us. As a result, we lack in our Protestant churches the large volume of sophisticated hymnody found in, say, German Protestant churches. On the other hand, we do have hundreds of the shorter "spiritual songs." Whenever I visit my mother in the south of Florida I often hear her, as she works around the house, worshiping by singing these "spiritual songs," which tend to be christological in content. I quietly join her from another part of the house and so we worship the Lord together. This is good and should be cherished. On the other hand, I have sometimes found that these "spiritual songs," while catchy and full of rhythm, are deficient—not to say heretical!—in their theology. I would like to encourage my non-Hispanic sisters and brothers who are musically talented to compose and write beautiful music for the Lord! But also they should take this opportunity to teach the church sound and rich theology—rather like Paul in this text, where he instructs us on the trinitarian nature of the gospel.

1 TIMOTHY: PART TWO

Theological affirmations and pastoral instructions (1 Timothy 4:1-16). In this section Paul returns to warnings and commands, somewhat ad hoc. If there is a unifying theme in the section it is the statement that Timothy will be a good "servant" (*diakonos*, see 1 Tim 3:8) of Jesus Christ if he courageously teaches what Paul is passing down to him. The primary subject of 1 Timothy 4:1-16 is the conduct and teaching of the false teachers in the "later times." In biblical studies and eschatology we normally call these "later" or "last" days *eschatology*. The concept, which is central to the Scriptures but is also found in those Jewish books that were written between the Old Testament and the New (we call this period the "Second Temple" period), consists of the idea that God is driving the world and humanity to a specific "end" of which he is totally in control. Both Jews and Christians believed that this would be a time when the Messiah would be present and play a central role. The Christians believed that in Jesus Christ eschatology or the "last days" had already started, the last days, when the kingdom of God would be here, had already been inaugurated with the coming of Jesus and the pouring out of the Holy Spirit. But the Jews rejected this, in large part because they could not conceive of a Jewish Messiah who would die by crucifixion and abandon their nation to a foreign power. Both the Jews and the Christians believed that eschatology would be a period ripe with false teaching, sometimes coming from supernatural powers like demons. It is not surprising, therefore, that when Paul speaks about the last days in this section he spends time describing the content of the teachers and their false teaching, for the early Christians believed that the last days were *already* here, alongside the kingdom of God. What did the false teaching consist of?

First, in 1 Timothy 4:3-4 Paul highlights the false teachers' understanding of the material world. In a few words, the false teachers viewed the world, at least indirectly, in a negative manner. Later in the century, and then specially in the second century, there would be a group of false teachers that we call Gnostics. They would reject the teaching of the Bible that God was the creator of all things, "visible and invisible." They were destructive of Christianity, particularly of the incarnation. This antimaterial philosophy was not original with the Gnostics, for we know that there was a fundamental plank in Greek thought (see Plato in particular) that viewed the material as degradant and inferior, while the immaterial as generally good. This kind of thought, although not in full flower, was already present in the first century, and Paul encountered it in many of the Gentile folks he ministered to; which is not surprising, since he was ministering primarily to Gentiles. Note the wonderful material things that these false teachers were prohibiting: "they forbid marriage and abstain from certain foods, which God created to be received with thanksgiving by those who believe and know the truth" (1 Tim 4:3). Paul makes it clear that these are good things precisely because, who is essentially good—or is goodness itself—created them. The Christians know this, and so they should not reject any of these heretically inspired prohibitions.

Second, in 1 Timothy 4:6-10 Paul is a bit more direct in what Timothy is to teach the believers. The language of *training* and *exercise* are juxtaposed in these verses with the language of *instructions* and *sound teaching*. Paul is not saying that exercise is bad. On the contrary, he says that *physical training is of some value* (1 Tim 4:8). But the readers must remember that the Greeks were truly obsessed with exercise; it was one of the fundamental values of Greek or Hellenistic thought. So Paul is not so much discoursing on how much exercise one should do as much as he is reminding his readers that there is a different type of exercise, *godliness*, that is superior, because it holds "promise for both the present life and the life to come" (1 Tim 4:8). The point is not primarily chronological, as if Paul were saying that *godliness* leads to unending life but physical exercise does not. Living forever is not what the Bible is getting at when it talks about eternal life. In fact, I know many people who are terrified at the idea of living forever. The biblical understanding of eternal life is existence with and in God forever, who is pure joy. The gospel promises *this* life, which exercise, as good as it is, cannot promise or deliver.

Third, Paul gives Timothy a number of ad hoc instructions, one of them being not to allow his youth to be a reason for contempt. As Paul puts it, "Let no one despise your youth." In Greco-Roman and Jewish culture, it was the men with gray hairs who were thought best to lead. Ironically, there is much literature (especially in Aristotle) and epigraphic evidence that despised old age in both men and women. Paul is clear that in Christian leadership age is not the primary factor; what matters is character: "set the believers an example in speech and conduct, in love, in faith, in purity."

Application. In Hispanic culture, as well as in most other cultures, youth is not a time for leadership. The Bible itself, in distilling its wisdom, reminds us that youth tends to be a time of rash living, which disqualifies a young man or woman from leading. Yet, there are examples of youth, like David, who could be the leaders of a nation while being young. And although the Lord Jesus Christ may not have been considered young in some cultures, he was not elderly when he began and completed his ministry. At the end of the day, what matters is godliness with sound doctrine and sound doctrine with godliness. If you are young, show humility to the elders in your church. But if the Spirit of the Lord comes on you to lead, do not back down. Give an example of godliness and lead with freedom!

Managing well the household of God (1 Timothy 5:1–6:2). It was common among moral philosophers of the period of Paul to address a group of people in accordance with the stations of life in which they found themselves at that time. Although not quite a household code (see under Titus 2:1-10), the exhortation visible here is similar to it in that the pattern of the family is employed. Thus in 1 Timothy 5:1-2 Paul addresses older men, older women, young men, and young women. In 1 Timothy 5:3-16 there is a long section on the treatment of widows. In 1 Timothy 5:17-25 the elders are treated, but not as an age group (although, to be sure, some of the elders treated here may have been older biologically) but as an honorable group that that were quite influential in the church. Last, in 1 Timothy 6:1-2 Paul gives commands regarding household slaves, a situation that would have been very common in the Greco-Roman world. Like a household, the church is a family, where we must treat one another in a way that is becoming to the gospel.

First, Paul commands that older men and women should be treated as if they were our own fathers and mothers. The term "harshly," used to describe how older men should *not* be treated was very common in these types of codes. Second, Paul commands that as a young man Timothy should treat men his age "as brothers." For the young women, Paul adds that they should be treated "as sisters—with absolute purity." The prepositional phrase after the dash highlights the importance of sexual purity. This is underlined because the general belief in the culture was that the least controllable urge in young men was sexual in nature (see Philo, *Abr.* 98).

The third section, dealing with widows, is the longest. Is there a particular reason why widows receive the longest amount of commands? There are a number of possibilities.[34] The view of this commentator is that as a matter of fact there were many widows in society as a whole and many widows converted to the gospel. Furthermore, the churches had limited funds, so the leaders had to put together a list of what constituted a real widow who could receive financial help. Remember, this is the first century AD, where such things as social security or pensions did not exist! In fact, in most poor countries of the world there are no such "safety nets," and if there are, they tend to be very thin. The church, therefore, must care for the widows in its society, especially those who are "of faith" (Gal 6:10). Below I provide my understanding of the list of what comprises a true widow.

1. *The widow must be sixty or older.* For Greco-Roman standards, this was a very advanced age. We should contextualize this age according to what is considered old in our culture. Why does Paul give the age of sixty or older? In 1 Timothy 5:6-8, 11-15 he gives some reasons. Younger widows may be moved by sexual desires in such a strong way that they are willing to marry, and to marry even unbelievers. This would have meant taking on the gods of this new husband (if the husband was a Gentile). In fact, therefore, by doing this they would have "violated their first pledge" (1 Tim 5:12), that is, turn their back on their conversion to Christ. Furthermore, without children to occupy themselves and while still possessing the energy of a younger woman, these widows below sixty would make it their habits to go around and spread false doctrine.

---

[34]See Marshall, *Pastoral Epistles*, 574-81.

In fact, some of them are already doing this (1 Tim 5:15).

2. The widow must have been faithful to her deceased husband. There is little question that Paul is here alluding to the Roman virtue of the *univira*. In what follows I give an explanation from my Pastoral Epistles commentary:[35]

> Literally, the phrase is "a one-man woman." It is quite likely that Paul is referring to the *univira*, i.e., a widow who, having been widowed, took a vow never to remarry so as to honor the memory of her deceased husband. The *univira* was praised in the Roman world for what seemed in the sight of many to be a virtuous mindset.[36] It should be noted that in many countries of Latin America this is also viewed as virtuous. One of the reasons is that remarrying is considered a dishonor to the dead husband. This attitude is common of patriarchal societies that value more the honor of the dead male than the possibility of the widow having funds to survive in the present! Is Paul capitulating to the Greco-Roman patriarchal culture in which he lived when he makes it a condition of receiving funds that the widow should be a *univira*? This is unlikely. It is more probable that Paul is thinking in practical terms. For a widow who was already sixty *and* had married only once was less likely to have many children who could care for her. Given the limited funds of the church, Paul had to think of those widows who were most vulnerable: the *univira* would have been such. Thus, the qualification here is not a matter of virtue but of the harsh realities of poverty and being an older woman in the ancient world.

3. The widow must be dedicated to good works. Paul describes these in 1 Timothy 5:5, 9-10. The virtue of bringing up children may refer to caring for orphans.[37]

The fourth section of this text deals with *elders*. Under Titus 1:5-10 I will argue that this is not an office, as the overseer and deacon. For now, the following can be said.[38] The title is found in the Septuagint to refer to rulers of Israel (e.g., Ex. 3:16, 18; Lev 4:15; Num 11:16; Josh 7:6; 8:10). In the Greco-Roman contexts elders could refer to leaders in a number of contexts (e.g., city leaders: Diodorus Siculus, *Hist.* 21.18.1; Aristotle, *Pol.* 1272A).[39] The *presbyteroi* were likely an important group of leaders of the congregations. We should think of the elders as a collective term for a group of leaders, not necessarily an office.[40] For the option that elders are synonymous to overseers, see under Titus 1:5-9. Paul completes the section by instructing Timothy on how to deal with elders who fall into sin.

The last section has to do with the attitudes and actions of slaves. Slavery was common in the Greco-Roman world. Slavery then, unlike the modern Caribbean and southern United States, was not based on the color of one's skin, lack of education, poverty, and so on. Most people were slaves because they were children of slaves (which automatically made you a slave), because of being on the losing end of a war, piracy, and brigandry. Slaves who labored in the homes of the wealthy were in the least bad position, in contrast to slaves who worked in the mines or the brothels. Paul is clear that

[35]Padilla, *Pastoral Epistles*, 128.

[36]See G. Clark, *OCD*, 1573; M. Lightman and W. Zeisel, "'*Univira*:' An Example of Continuity and Change in Roman Society," *CH* 46 (1977): 19–32; A. Malherbe, *Light from the Gentiles: Hellenistic Philosophy and Early Christianity; Collected Essays*, 2 vols. (Leiden: Brill, 2014), 1:491-92.

[37]Marshall, *Pastoral Epistles*, 595.

[38]For what follows, see Padilla, *Pastoral Epistles*, 238-46.

[39]I am indebted to Craig Keener, *1 Peter: A Commentary* (Grand Rapids, MI: Baker Academic, 2021), 355-59 for many of these sources.

[40]A. D. Clarke, *A Pauline Theology of Church Leadership*, LNTS (London: T&T Clark, 2008), 56: "Accordingly, 'eldership' is not an individual office, but an honoured status, bringing with it membership of an influential and respected body."

slavery was evil. He calls it *the yoke of slavery* (1 Tim 6:1). So why did he not do away with it? In fact, he was attempting to do this (see the Letter to Philemon). But the Roman empire was not a democracy! Paul and the Christians could not simply march in front of the forum in Rome! They would have been imprisoned or killed and things might have gone bad for other Christian slaves. Paul's strategy was more subtle: he desired that Christians who owned slaves would either treat those slaves like brothers and thereby free them! Or, if they continued to own them as slaves, the owners should have remembered that God would judge them on the last day (see Col 4:1). The Christian slaves should behave with great respect, not stealing or gossiping about their owners. It is to be remembered that slaves who behaved well could thereby earn their freedom.

Application: Familia! Paul wanted the church to view itself as a family. There is much here that our Hispanic brothers and sisters, especially from poor socioeconomic backgrounds, could teach us. These Christians understand that the church family is even more sacred than blood family. They depend (*must* depend) on one another to meet each other's needs, for they are often poor. They seek reconciliation quickly once there has been an offense. Of course, things are far from perfect! But because these Hispanic believers already view the blood family as central to their existence, they view the Christian family as even more sacred and delicate.

False teaching, wealth, and final exhortation (1 Timothy 6:2-21). The two main themes of this section are the following: a continuation of exhortations to continue teaching sound doctrine and a warning about false teaching being motivated by love of money.

First, in 1 Timothy 6:2-10 there is a catalog of vices to describe those who reject sound teaching: "Whoever teaches otherwise and does not agree with the sound words of our Lord Jesus Christ and the teaching that is in accordance with godliness is conceited, understanding nothing, and has a morbid craving for controversy and for disputes about words. From these come envy, dissension, slander, base suspicions, and wrangling among those who are depraved in mind and bereft of the truth, imagining that godliness is a means of gain."

To be sure, Paul clarifies that there is actually great gain when godliness is accompanied by *contentment* (*autarkeia*, 1 Tim 6:6). This last term was very common among moral philosophers such as Stoics and Cynics.[41] They taught that living well was an art that included *auterkeia*. Of course, the concept of being content with God's provision is already found in the Old Testament. One clear example is Proverbs 30:8-9: "Give me neither poverty nor riches; feed me with the food that I need." And in Philippians 4:10-13 Paul had expressed that he had learned to be content whatever his circumstances (*auterkeia*, Phil 4:11). To provide grounding for the statement above, that godliness with contentment is great gain, Paul provides proverb-like statements in 1 Timothy 6:7-8: "For we brought nothing into the world, so that we can take nothing out of it, but if we have food and clothing, we will be content with these." Paul adds in 1 Timothy 6:10: "For the love of money is a root of all kinds of evil, and in their eagerness to be rich some have wandered away from the faith and pierced themselves with many pains."

Second, in 1 Timothy 6:11-19 there is another catalog of virtues for Timothy to follow. 1 Timothy 6:17-19 constitute words of exhortation for the rich in the communities at Ephesus. We can summarize Paul's teaching in

[41]Dibelius and Conzelmann, *Pastoral Epistles*, 84.

two ways. First, he exhorts the rich not to put their hope in money, which is uncertain. Second, he exhorts the rich to share with those who are not rich. In fact, the concept is that God's rich provision is ineluctably tied to sharing with those who lack.

Paul concludes the letter by reminding Timothy to "guard what has been entrusted" (1 Tim 6:20 NIV), that is, the gospel, and to avoid false teaching. In this way he closes the letter the same way he began it.

Application. Money situations vary tremendously depending on what part of Latin America or the United States a Hispanic individual resides. As a whole, however, Hispanics do not belong to the upper socioeconomic stratum of North American culture. This is another way of saying that there is more pronounced poverty among Hispanics than in other people's group. Many Hispanic church members have therefore learned to lean on one another as well as the church in its official capacity to help meet the basic necessities of life. When we as Hispanics (as well as other racial minorities) read those biblical texts that speak about poverty, we listen very carefully, because we know they address us! The Bible is full of statements of God's deep care for the poor and vulnerable. There is no such thing as a Christianity without care for the poor. In fact, I would go so far as to say—and here the book of James backs me up—that caring for the unfortunate is part of Christian orthodoxy.

2 TIMOTHY

Salutation (2 Timothy 1:1-2)

On Paul's salutations to Timothy, refer to 1 Timothy 1:1-2.

Persevere in guarding the gospel (2 Timothy 1:3–2:13)

In this first main section of the letter the apostle Paul encourages Timothy to persevere in the gospel that has been entrusted to him (see 1 Tim 6:20). Paul will provide Timothy with *four* broad bases to help the latter persevere.

First, in 2 Timothy 1:3-5 Paul reminds Timothy of his faith pedigree. Timothy learned the faith from his grandmother Lois and his mother Eunice. Just as Paul speaks of his "ancestors" in 2 Timothy 1:3, so he reminds Timothy that *his* ancestors (grandmother and mother) taught him a sound and strong faith. Who says that the Christian faith is mostly a masculine faith? Many great saints (think of Augustine) have learned the faith through their mothers and grandmothers. Furthermore, the church today is coming to recognize more and more that God's call to minister for the church is based on being baptized by the Holy Spirit, not on the basis of one's gender.

Second, from 2 Timothy 1:6-14 Paul places emphasis on the Holy Spirit as the one who will help Timothy persevere. Although Paul uses various terminology, ultimately the reference is to the Holy Spirit, and this reference occurs five times (2 Tim 1:6, 7 [twice], 8, 12 and 14). In 2 Timothy 1:6 Paul reminds Timothy "to rekindle the gift of God that is within you through the laying on of my hands." Often in the Bible the Holy Spirit is analogized with fire in order to highlight his purity, his cleansing power, and the judgment that he brings (see e.g., Mt 3:7-12). Timothy is to remain in step with the Spirit in order to carry out his ministry. In 2 Timothy 1:7 Paul speaks of God "giv[ing] us . . . a spirit of power and of love and of self-discipline." That is, the Holy Spirit gives us the strength to live godly lives of ministry and virtuous existence. Paul asks Timothy in 2 Timothy 1:8 to join him in suffering "in the power of God," yet another reference to the Holy Spirit. In 2 Timothy 1:12, 14 Paul reminds Timothy that they will be able to preserve the gospel because of the powerful

Spirit that has been given to them. To summarize: faithful ministry is impossible without the power of the Holy Spirit, on whom we must depend completely.

Third, Paul gives Timothy the example of Onesiphorus (2 Tim 1:15-18). Paul reminds Timothy that on his trial at Rome the believers from Asia, but especially Phygelus and Hermogenes, abandoned him. Given the honor/shame culture of the Greco-Roman world, it is easy to imagine Paul's "friends" turning their backs on him because of his status as a prisoner. There was one exception, however: Onesiphorus! He traveled to Rome (already densely populated), found Paul, and encouraged him both physically and emotionally constantly. Timothy is to imitate the brave example and friendship of Onesiphorus to preserve the gospel.

Fourth, Paul reminds Timothy of the example of Jesus Christ himself (2 Tim 2:1-13). Before that, however, he gives three exempla that would have been well-known in their culture: the professional soldier, the athlete, and the farmer (2 Tim 2:4-7). All three vocations called for sacrifice, hard work, and commitment. The most powerful exemplum of all, however, is introduced in 2 Timothy 2:8: "Remember Jesus Christ, raised from the dead, a descendant of David—that is my gospel." Jesus Christ was the ultimate faithful witness (Rev 1:5). In calling Jesus the *Christ*, Paul is highlighting the title of Jesus as the Messiah. It would appear, however, that Jesus was anything but a messiah, given his execution by crucifixion! But Paul adds about Jesus, "raised from the dead," a statement that points to a reality that demonstrates that Jesus *was* the Messiah: God raising him from the dead *vindicated* Jesus' identity: he truly was the Messiah of Israel, the Son of David (see Rom 1:4). This constitutes Paul's gospel, the good news that in Jesus Christ the kingdom of God had been inaugurated.

In 2 Timothy 2:9-13 Paul implies that he too has suffered like Jesus, "like a criminal." Yet, because "the word of God is not chained," Paul continues suffering for the sake of those who presently believe and who will believe in the future, through the agency of the gospel. Paul concludes the section with an encouraging word for Timothy: even if, in times of hardship, he should prove unfaithful to the Lord, God will not abandon him and the gospel will continue. Why? Because God "remains faithful—for he cannot deny himself."

Application. Although Paul mentioned his ancestors as well as Timothy's, we would get the wrong idea were we to conclude that ministry and ministerial capacity are ultimately matters of family lines. Here I must offer a critique to a practice that I see in churches around the world, but perhaps especially those of minorities in the United States (although I have seen this happen in enough Anglo-Saxon settings to recognize that it plagues everyone). I am referring to the passing down of pastoral offices on the basis of family name. For example, although the son of the current pastor may not have gifting or calling to the ministry, he is installed as the new pastor simply because his father was the previous pastor. To be sure, there may be cases where passing down the pastorate is a legitimate activity. But we must never ordain or give an ecclesial position to someone just because of their last name.

Ministerial call and capacity are works of the Holy Spirit, not family connections. It is the Spirit, who most powerfully worked in raising the Messiah Jesus from the dead, who leads those who will care for the sheep.

Do's and don'ts of a minister of the gospel (2 Timothy 2:14-3:9). This is the second main section of 2 Timothy. The first part of this section runs until 2 Timothy 3:9. There are three main themes in this part, which primarily have to do with conduct.

First, Paul reminds Timothy that the latter's work is being observed by God and will be judged by God. This is not just about what other people think about Timothy; his ministry is "before God" (2 Tim 2:14). This should make a great difference in Timothy's attitude and work in the ministry.

Second, Paul highlights "the word of God," both its right use and its misuse by false teachers (see 2 Tim 2:15, 17, 18). In 2 Timothy 2:15 he speaks about a servant who is "rightly explaining the word of truth." The KJV translates "rightly explaining" as "divide." This translation may be closer to the original way the verb (*orthotomeō*) was employed as a medical metaphor by moral philosophers. In this context, the "word" referred to the "rational word," which was likened to a scalpel that helped cut with precision to help perform "surgery" and help the individual lead an existence of virtue. It would appear that Paul is encouraging Timothy to use God's word well, with precision, in order to lead the believers in right living and rebuking the false teachers.

The third theme of this section is a warning against false teachers. While in 2 Timothy 2:20-26 Paul gives a catalog of *virtues* that Timothy is to follow, in 2 Timothy 3:1-5 he gives a catalog of *vices* that unmask the false teachers. Paul provides basic New Testament teaching when he says that in the "last days," that is, the time from the advent of the Messiah to the consummation of the present age, deceiving teachers will abound (see, e.g., Mt 24:5-14). The teachers that are attempting to deceive the congregations where Timothy is ministering are precisely these teachers.

In describing these teachers Paul highlights the following. First, the sin that is at the root of their vices is translated as "lovers of themselves" (*philautoi*). This is the first vice listed (2 Tim 3:2). The last vice listed in 2 Timothy 3:4 repeats in a slightly different way the first one: "lovers of pleasure rather than lovers of God." Thus, this evil of self-loving over love of God and neighbor serves as a bookend, highlighting what is motivating the false teachers. Second, in 2 Timothy 3:5 Paul affirms that these teachers give the outer impression that they are godly; but a closer look at their lives makes it apparent that this is a false impression. In reality, they do not possess the power of the Holy Spirit, the only one who can change us (compare this to 2 Tim 1:6-14, where the Spirit is the one who empowers Paul and Timothy to carry out their ministries). In order to illustrate the deception of these teachers, Paul refers in 2 Timothy 3:6-7 to a common phenomenon of the period. Often, so-called philosophers would be hired by wealthy husbands so that they would teach philosophy to their wives.[42] But often these philosophers ended up seducing the wives, even taking them away.[43] These were not real philosophers—and neither are those that Paul is warning Timothy about. In fact, they are no better than charlatan magicians, like Jannes and Jambres, referred to simply as magicians in Exodus 7:10-12, who were known even beyond the Jewish world (see Pliny the Elder, *Natural History* 30.11).

Application. Magic is very common from the part of the Caribbean where I come from. The type of magic practiced there is often called *Santería*. This involves the sacrifice of animals, demon possession, lighting of candles,

[42]The reader should not think that the goal of teaching the wives was so that they could learn to reason with men. Rather, the goal of the philosopher was to educate the women to be the best wives possible: see Annette Huizenga, *Moral Education for Women in the Pastoral and Pythagorean Letters*, NovTSup147 (Leiden: Brill, 2013), and the example of Musonius Rufus.

[43]For the primary sources, see Padilla, *The Pastoral Epistles*, 195-97.

communicating with the dead, and so on. One of the fascinating aspects of Santería is that almost all the practitioners—by which I mean the so-called magicians—invoke some form of Christianity as they are performing their rituals. The rooms where Santería is done have paintings of Jesus Christ (usually blond and with sparkling blue eyes!) hanging on the walls, Bibles opened to particular texts and other religious paraphernalia. The magicians want their customers to believe that they (the magicians) are pious men (and sometimes women). But of course this is not true. Not only are they practicing syncretism; but many of them lead immoral lives, especially once they switch back to their "normal" state. The "piety" they paraded with such seriousness when they practiced magic is shown to be just a mask for which the goal was to charge expensive fees.

It is unlikely that one will find this type of "raw" magic in most places of North America. However, it is very common to encounter religious leaders who seek to lead large congregations. They will often use the language of Christianity, and thereby persuade many. However, a closer look at their lives, especially what turns out to be ravenous greed and lust, demonstrate that they are not really servants of Christ.

Resisting godlessness (2 Timothy 3:10-17). How can Timothy—and other Christian leaders—resist these temptations that may come with ministry? In this short section Paul provides two antidotes. First, Paul encourages Timothy to pay close attention to the *example* of godly Christians. Here he mentions his own sufferings as an apostle and also speaks of those "from whom you learned" (2 Tim 3:14) since childhood. As we saw in 2 Timothy 1:5, Timothy's early teachers were his mother and grandmother. There is a second way to resist—and that is by Timothy committing himself to the "sacred writings" (2 Tim 3:15).[44] Paul further describes these writings by speaking of their nature: "All scripture is inspired by God. . . ." The phrase gives the sense of the Scripture being "breathed out" by God himself. Paul is not interested in *how* God gives his people the Scriptures (i.e., the *manner* of inspiration) but *what* the Scriptures are and what their functions are in the church.[45] But we must make clear the logic of this passage (something that many commentators do not): the Scriptures are able to lead us in virtue *precisely* because they are inspired by God. Surely one can learn great lessons for life by reading written material, say, the novels of Dostoyevsky. But for Christians Dostoyevsky does not have the *authority* of the Bible because his writings are not "breathed out" by God. The nature or ontology of the Bible matters.

Application. The Bible is revered and respected in Latin America, even by those who do not confess the Christian faith. Christians, of course, also revere it; and are taught from very early that "this book is sacred." Sometimes, however, especially among evangelical Christians, the Bible becomes a transcendent object with almost the same sacredness as God. Thus, for example, you may be reproved for setting the Bible on the floor during a church meeting; or you may be asked to stand every time the Bible is read; or you may be told that only one translation can be read. It is as if the black (or red!) signs of ink that make up the words of the Bible are themselves inspired. But this would be a magical view of the Bible! The signs of ink in our Bibles are not themselves transcendent.

[44]This is probably a reference to the Old Testament and perhaps very early sections of what became the New Testament.

[45]Many Christians simplify what is undoubtedly a mysterious event. One sign of this simplification is the preference to use the prophetic manner ("thus says the Lord") as the dominant manner of how God inspired the Bible. We must be wary of this simplification. Large portions of the Bible are inspired in ways that remain mysterious to us (e.g., the Psalms).

God, through his Spirit, speaks to us through the Bible without becoming objectified with the material books of leather and paper that we call the Bible. Because ultimately it is not the Bible that "speaks" to us but God himself, the living Word who meets us as he promised he would. Evangelical Christians in North America, especially those who have been raised in churches that lean toward fundamentalism, must be careful not to make the mistake that many believers in Latin America fall into.

Final exhortations, Paul's situation, and greetings (2 Timothy 4:1-22). The logic of this final section of the epistle can be expressed in the following manner: since Timothy was living in the final eschatological season, and since Paul was about to depart this world, Timothy must understand the urgency of the moment and proclaim the sound doctrine whatever circumstances he was facing.

Paul begins with exalted and likely creedal language of the early church when he tells Timothy that what he (Paul) is about to command is something being witnessed by God: "In the presence of God and of Christ Jesus, who is to judge the living and the dead, and in view of his appearing and his kingdom, I solemnly urge you." Timothy was probably gripped by such language! To note also is that God and the Messiah Jesus are in a sense identified as one, for their activities are joined, especially at the beginning of the verse. Christ Jesus is to be the judge of the living and the dead. In light of the Old Testament, it is clear that this is a prerogative that belongs to God alone. And yet it is "God and Christ Jesus" who will judge all. As we shall observe in Titus, Paul makes it clear that Jesus Christ is identified as one with the God of Israel.

Having caught the attention of Timothy, Paul gives a command that is then developed in the rest of 2 Timothy 4:2: "Proclaim the message." The language employed by Paul that is translated as "proclaim" (*keryssō*) by the NRSV is traditional language of the early church for the proclamation of the kingdom of God and the gospel (e.g., Mk 1:14; Rom 10:8-9; 1 Cor 1:23; 15:11-12; 2 Cor 4:5; Gal 2:2; Phil 1:15; 1 Thess 2:9). Along with the command in 2 Timothy 4:5, namely, "do the work of an evangelist," it is clear that Timothy's preaching is not just for those who have already experienced conversion but also for unbelievers. Furthermore, Timothy is to proclaim the gospel message "whether the time is favorable or unfavorable." It is likely that by using this phrase Paul is evoking for Timothy one of the questions constantly asked by moral philosophers and rhetoricians of the period: What are the times when it is inappropriate (from the point of view of the hearers) to speak with frankness?[46] In light of the coming period (which for Paul is already present), when hearers will refuse the sound doctrine in preference for novelties of "itchy ears," Timothy must *always* proclaim the message. The situation is so dire that it requires constant proclamation (2 Tim 4:3-4).

There is a second reason for why Timothy must constantly preach the gospel message: Paul's time of departure from life is near. He states in 2 Timothy 4:6: "As for me, I am already being poured out as a libation, and the time of my departure has come." In contrast to Philippians 1:19-26, where an imprisoned Paul knows (by the witness of the Spirit?) that he will be released from prison and remain alive, the Paul of 2 Timothy knows that he is about to die. To speak of his death Paul uses two metaphors. First, he says that he is being "poured out as a libation." The metaphor is that of a sacrificial offering. This metaphor could convey many different meanings; such is the

[46]See Padilla, *Pastoral Epistles*, 211.

way of metaphors. Speaking existentially, the metaphor suggests that Paul did not view his death as just another step in the inexorable succession of human, biological existence (step by step from birth to death). No, his death has *meaning*. It is offered to God so that it would bless those believers who are coming after him. The second metaphor Paul uses to explain his death comes from the world of athletics (hugely popular in the Greco-Roman world), specifically running, although wrestling could also be in view. The words of Towner are helpful: "Keeping Pauline usage in mind, the application here is necessarily broad, viewing the whole of life as an intense struggle against an opposition in which spiritual power must be matched by personal commitment and resolve to endure to the end of the contest."[47] Because, by God's grace, Paul has kept the faith until the end, he will receive from the Lord "the crown of righteousness" on the day of judgment. This calls to mind the crowns that athletes of the period received when they were victorious. The crowns were made of a wreath of ivy or celery leaves.

Having exhorted Timothy in 2 Timothy 4:1-8, Paul now moves in 2 Timothy 4:9-18 to provide him with details of his present situation in prison. To make sense of this section it is crucial that the modern reader understand that in the Roman system imprisonment was not as such a punishment in the way that it is in the present in most parts of the world. Punishment for crimes, depending on the severity of the crime, rather consisted in fines, corporal punishment, exile and execution. It is likely that Paul had probably received the first of two possible hearings in the judicial process. He was now awaiting the second hearing (*apud iudicem*, "before the judge"). Paul expected (again, by promptings from the Spirit?) that this second hearing would lead to his execution.

Paul, then, provides Timothy with the latest about his situation. As I have noted elsewhere, Paul uses the language of martyrdom, primarily from Psalm 22, to speak of the adversarial situation in which he found himself.[48] Paul provides information on a number of individuals: Demas, who has forsaken him; Crescens and Titus, whom he sent to Galatia and Dalmatia, respectively; Luke is with him; Mark should come with Timothy soon to see Paul; and Tychicus he sent to Ephesus. Paul mentions Alexander "the coppersmith" (see 1 Tim 1:20), who hurt Paul's case by probably bearing false witness against him (2 Tim 4:14-15). Practically, Paul asks Timothy to bring him his cloak and the books and parchments that he had left in Troas. The cloak was a poncho-like piece to protect from the cold. The books and parchments could be anything from books of the Old Testament to personal documents and letters. Last, in 2 Timothy 4:16-18 Paul gives Timothy information of his first judicial hearing. Although no human friends stood by his side, the Lord certainly did. He empowered Paul to preach the gospel even in this situation so that the Gentiles, to whom Paul had been sent to preach the good news, would hear the gospel: in this way Paul completed his task (cf. Acts 26:1-23). Paul concludes on a victorious note. By not being executed after his first hearing, Paul was delivered from "the lion's mouth" (see Ps 22:13, 21). In fact, the Lord will deliver Paul from the ultimate evil, namely death, by raising him from the dead (2 Tim 4:18).

Paul closes the letter with greetings and a blessing (2 Tim 4:19-22). He mentions a number of saints who have been his coworkers in the gospel for many years. The main

[47]Philip Towner, *The Letters to Timothy and Titus*, NICNT (Grand Rapids, MI: Eerdmans, 2006), 612.
[48]Padilla, *The Pastoral Epistles*, 219-20.

example is Priscilla and Aquila. The Linus of 2 Timothy 4:21 is likely a reference to the first bishop of the churches of Rome after the death of the apostles (see Irenaeus, *A. H.* III.3.3).

Application. Media vita in morte sumus: "In the midst of life we are in death" (Book of Common Prayer, Burial I). Death comes to all, no matter the color of our skin. Different cultures deal with death in different ways. It is impossible to say that there is *one* dominant manner of dealing with death in North America. We come from too many different places for there to be one standard. However, in those contexts that are dominated by a view of life that is purely scientific, there is currently a tendency to view—to accept—death as the final phase. Like the rest of nature (plants and animals), we too come to death. And that is the end. And we should learn not only to accept this view of things but to embrace them with (almost religious!) joy, for this is natural, and the best way to exist and die is with the rhythms of nature.

Whatever be our view of the possibility of death before or after the fall, as things stand now (and have for a long time!), death is part of the pattern of human existence. And yet, for those whose lives are united to Jesus Christ, there is another rhythm of existence. After Good Friday comes Resurrection Sunday; the darkness of Good Friday and Holy Saturday is pierced and overcome by the glorious light of Resurrection Sunday. To be sure, there is a sort of rebirth in nature as well: winter gives over to spring, when all that was brown and dead returns in bright green. But spring ends and all dies again in fall and winter. The Christian pattern shares the pattern of creation, but through Jesus Christ something fundamental is added: we are born, die and rise again, *never to experience death again*. The cycle ends when our bodies are raised immortal, similar to the body of Jesus post resurrection. This glorious, incorruptible body (see 1 Cor 15:42-49) will be in perfect communion with the Father the Son and the Holy Spirit and with all the saints past, present, and future.

It is because Paul believed this that, although somewhat sad and lonely in a Roman prison (2 Tim 4:9, 16), he could nevertheless rejoice instead of being swallowed by hopelessness.

TITUS: PART ONE

Salutation (Titus 1:1-4). In many ways the salutation to Titus is almost identical to those of 1–2 Timothy. However, Paul lengthens the salutation, as can be seen from the fact that in 1–2 Timothy it is only two verses long while here it is four verses long. Why precisely Paul has written a longer introduction in his letter to Titus we cannot answer with certainty. One thing is clear, however, and that is that in this introduction he mentions a number of themes that will be developed in the rest of Titus or that have been developed in 1–2 Timothy.[49] Some examples include the following: "faith" (Titus 1:4, 13; 2:2, 10; 3:15); "knowledge of the truth" (Titus 1:14; 1 Tim 4:3; 2 Tim 2:25; 3:7), and "sound," as something that is healthy (Titus 1:9, 13; 2:1, 2, 8). As a good rhetorician or speaker of the period, Paul introduces key themes in the *exordium* or introduction of the letter or speech.

One aspect that stands out in the use of these terms is their *objective* sense. That is, in speaking of faith, truth, and soundness of faith Paul is referring to the *content* of the gospel, the sound apostolic doctrine that is contrasted to false teaching. This comes out particularly in Titus 1:4, where Paul speaks of the "common

[49]This statement is not meant to be taken as an answer to the order in which the letters were written. Some commentators believe that Titus was the first written Pastoral Letter, even though it is the third in our modern Bibles.

faith" (*koinēn pistin*) to which Titus adheres (see the similar expression in Jude 3). To summarize, we can say that Paul emphasizes in the introduction *fides quae* (that in which one believes). To be sure, Paul will also speak of faith as an act of trusting God (*fides qua*) and as *habitus*, a way of living that is faithful to the commands of the Lord. But in this introduction, the objective, universal apostolic faith to which there must be ascent is what is being highlighted.

Instructions for the life of the church (Titus 1:5–3:11)

Instructions for the placing of leaders in the churches at Crete (Titus 1:5-9). Already in the Pastoral Epistles we have seen Paul instruct his coworkers on the importance and setting-up of leaders in the church (see under 1 Tim 3:1-13; 5:17-25). In these verses we have a third set of instructions. We will focus our exposition on two aspects that are particularly important to understanding this section. First, there is a juxtaposition between elders and overseer. That is, Paul begins by speaking of the virtues necessary for elders in Titus 1:5-6: they must be "blameless, married only once" and so on. This is said of the *elders*. But in Titus 1:7 Paul switches to virtues that the *overseer* must possess: "must be blameless; he must not be arrogant or quick-tempered" and so on. How do we explain the switch from *elders* to *overseer*?[50]

The view taken by this author is the following. The term *elder(s)* is a collective, honorary term, not an office. In his authoritative work on elders, Campbell put it this way: the terminology *elder* is "*more a way of speaking about leaders, than an office of leadership itself*."[51] Clarke, a few years later, observes in light of both Jewish and Greco-Roman sources, "the concept of council of elders was widespread in ancient society"[52] Therefore, it is likely that in the early stages of the church, where Christians mostly met at homes, elders were a group of respected men who provided leadership to the churches. Those elders who "labored" (perhaps meaning who went beyond their normal responsibilities) well in leading and teaching were to receive material compensation for their labor (1 Tim 5:17-18). With this in mind, we are in a better position to explain the juxtaposition between elders and overseer in Titus 1:5-9. I suggest that the overseer likely came out of the council of elders. He was someone who desired the office of overseer (1 Tim 3:1) and possessed the virtues and gifting to carry out the work of this office. But since he worked with the elders, it would have been easy to switch from elder to overseer as Paul does in Titus 1:7. To conclude: an overseer could have belonged to the council of elders but an elder did not necessarily occupy the office of overseer.

The second observation to be made is the concept of leadership presented in this text. In particular, in Titus 1:7 Paul states that the overseer is "God's steward" (*oikonomos*). This taps into the discourse of *oikonomia* or stewardship that was so popular among moral philosophers of the period. Basically, an *oikonomos* was someone who was under the owner of the household and took care of it. A good *oikonomos* kept the garden and all other parts of the home in good shape. There are a number of texts where an *oikonomos* was also presented as someone who provided care to those in need. One example is that of the *oikonomos* visiting and taking care of the sick.

[50]For an extensive report of scholarship (as of 1999) as well as possible solutions, the reader is directed to Marshall, *The Pastoral Epistles*, 170-81.

[51]R. A. Campbell, *The Elders: Seniority Within Earliest Christianity*, SNTW (Edinburgh: T&T Clark, 1994), 140, italics original.

[52]Clarke, *A Pauline Theology*, 56.

Since Paul viewed the church as the household of God (1 Tim 3:15), it was natural to use this type of language to explain the fundamental attitude that the overseer should have toward the church.

Application. In much of North American, evangelical culture, the pastor (whether called minister, priest, reverend), especially in larger churches, is viewed primarily through the prism of *public speaking* or *preaching*. A true pastor (and therefore leader of the church) is someone who can deliver a well-crafted sermon Sunday morning after Sunday morning. To the extent that we can actualize the Pastoral Epistles' presentation of the overseer to the modern pastor (not a straightforward application!), there is in the contemporary church a significant gap. For if the pastor of the church is an *oikonomos*, his or her duty goes well beyond just preaching a mighty sermon on Sunday morning. To be sure, preaching and teaching are crucial to lead the church. However, a true *oikonomos* is also someone who cares deeply and personally for the members of the church. As *oikonomos*, the pastor needs to put as much effort in visiting the sick, comforting the afflicted of soul, buying groceries for those homes where the paycheck is not sufficient, and so on. This is in fact what many pastors do in other parts of the world where a "normal" church is no larger than twenty people. We in North America stand to learn much from them.

The identity of the false teachers and exhortations (Titus 1:10-16). Paul clearly links the previous paragraph to this one with the Greek word *gar* ("for, because") used in Titus 1:10 but left untranslated by the NRSV. The implication is that Titus must place godly leaders in the different churches of Crete because false teachers are out to pervert the gospel.

Who are these false teachers? The language is very similar to 1 Timothy 1:3-6; but here Paul makes it even clearer that the false teachers are Jewish Christians. Paul speaks of them as "those of the circumcision" (see also Acts 10:45; 11:2; Rom 4:12; Gal 2:12; Col 4:11). It is almost certain that these were Jews who taught that in order to be saved it was not sufficient to believe in Jesus; one first had to become a Jew, which in the case of males demanded circumcision. Furthermore, Paul makes it clear that these false teachers are not only doctrinally deficient. At the end of Titus 1:11 he adds that they teach "for sordid gain." It was a common part of polemics in ancient moral philosophy to accuse other philosophers of instructing solely for the sake of money. This accusation also serves as a transition to the statement about the Cretans, since Cretans were often portrayed as hungry for ill gained money (see Polybius 6.46).

Paul quotes in Titus 1:12 a popular saying about the Cretans that goes back originally to Epimenides in the seventh century BC and was elaborated on by Callimachus of Cyrene in the third century BC: "Cretans are always liars, vicious brutes, lazy gluttons."[53] Some readers find Paul's approving quotation about the Cretans offensive. We do well to remember, however, that there is clearly hyperbole in this quotation. Furthermore, this type of jabbing was common in the ancient world and was taken less seriously than we may in the Western world today. On the other hand, we should recognize that Paul is giving the Cretan believers a strong warning. In light of the moral problems of Cretan culture (in which the Jewish false teachers apparently participated), Titus must "rebuke them sharply, so that they may become sound in the faith" (Titus 1:13). This translation from the NRSV might be read as suggesting that the faith of the Cretan believers was not sound. It is better to

[53]See also Diodorus Siculus 31.45; Plutarch, *Phil.* 13.8, among many other texts.

understand the Greek as meaning that they should be careful in continuing to be sound in the faith. On the language of Titus 1:14-16, see under 1 Timothy 1:3-7.

Behavior in the household (Titus 2:1-10). In this section Paul uses what is clearly a household code (*Haustafeln*, German plural). The literature of the Greco-Roman period makes it clear that moral philosophers provided for the fathers of the household a manual on how to care for their respective families. We find *Haustafeln* from the time of Aristotle (*Pol.* 1.2.1-1.5.12), although they may come from before him, if *Haustafeln* were linked to the literature on *oikonomia*.[54] In Aristotle *Haustafeln* are somewhat rigid in its pairing format, with the father clearly being the main person addressed. Thus, the order was as follows: fathers-sons; fathers-wives; fathers-slaves. As time passed, the format—but not the spirit—changed somewhat.[55] When we look at authors like Epictetus, for example, we see flexibility in format (e.g., *Ench.* 30; *Diss.* 2.30-33). But again, it is assumed that the father of the house ruled in ancient patriarchal fashion.

Since Paul was a Hellenistic-Jew, it may be helpful to examine how Hellenistic Jews used the *Haustafel*, since they may provide a historical bridge to Paul's use of the code and also help in clarification as to why Paul used it. Here is an example from Philo of Alexandria that is clearly inspired by the code. I quote the statement in full:

> In the fifth commandment on honouring parents we have a suggestion of many necessary laws drawn up to deal with the relations of old to young, rulers to subjects, benefactors to benefited, slaves to masters. For parents belong to the superior class of the above-mentioned pairs, that which comprises seniors, rulers, benefactors and masters, while children occupy the lower position with juniors, subjects, receivers of benefits and slaves. And there are many other instructions given, to the young on courtesy to the old, to the old on taking care of the young, to subjects on obeying their rulers, to rulers on promoting the welfare of their subjects . . . to servants on rendering an affectionate loyalty to their masters, to masters on showing the gentleness and kindness by which inequality is equalized. (Philo, *The Decalogue* 165-67, translation from LCL)

Another fascinating example can be found in Josephus, who in at least two places uses the code and spirit of the *Haustafel* as an apologetic against charges that the Jews were impious.[56] Josephus insists, at times by using the testimony of others, that the Jews practice *pietas* (godliness) as much as the best of the Greeks and even better.

It is likely that a similar reason animates Paul's use of the *Haustafel* in Titus 2:1-10.[57] The *Christianoi* were likely viewed as another sect from the East (many came from Egypt). The Greco-Roman literature of the period shows the suspicion and great antagonism which new religions from the east raised in the more traditional Greek city-states. There is enough evidence in Titus 2:1-10 that Paul's use of the *Haustafel* was apologetic in nature. That is, he wanted the believers in Crete to be pious—for in fact there was much overlap in what constituted pious behavior in both the Greek cities and the church. Furthermore, Paul states in Titus 2:10 that the believers' behavior should be "an ornament to the teaching of God our Savior."

[54]See Petr Pokorný, *Colossians: A Commentary*, trans. Siegfried S. Schatzmann (Peabody, MA: Hendrickson, 1991), 176.
[55]But see Seneca, *Ep.* 94.1, which looks close to the Aristotelian model.
[56]See Josephus, *Ag. Ap.* 1.199-205; 2.220-276.
[57]For similar conclusions, see Pokorný, *Colossians*, 176-78.

This statement assumes that the Christians spoke to others about their faith; but that was not enough. They had to show how good and beautiful Christian doctrine was by simultaneous good and beautiful lives. In short, the *Haustafel* would have had a *missional* end in the existence of the church.

This, however, has not been the view of many Protestant scholars. The influential commentary by Dibelius/Conzelmann views the "family ethic" of the city presented in the Pastorals as in conflict with Paul's life of conflict, which apparently arose in part because he did not want to be like the world and because of his fervent expectation of an immediate parousia.[58] These authors (and others) conveniently pass over texts like Romans 13:1-7, where Paul calls for obedience to the authorities. In any case, Dibelius/Conzelmann say that "the author of the Pastorals seeks to build the possibility of a life in this world, although on the basis of Christian principles. He wishes to become part of the world."[59] Others have picked up these ideas and have concluded that either Paul did not write the Pastorals (how could he, they say, in light of the radical equality found in Gal 3:26-29?); or that in Paul's later years he had capitulated to a bourgeois Christianity that had lost the edge of the first decades; or a combination of both. For the commands of Titus 2:1-10 emphasize the submission of the wife to the husband (Titus 2:4-5) and the continuation of slavery (Titus 2:9-10) *simpliciter*. But this view tends itself to be simplistic. It stems (in part) from the idea that Paul (or whoever wrote the Pastorals) that the only form of Christian existence in the present is radical separation or protestation. I do not disagree that Christians should protest abuses of the state or the culture. But this must be done wisely. Paul did not live in a democracy! He lived under a ruthless empire that would not permit views that strongly challenged its values (despite the Roman propaganda that Octavian had brought peace to the world!). Paul could not simply march before the Forum and protest slavery. He would have been apprehended and killed. Paul's strategy, especially as seen in Romans 14–15, Gal 3:26-29, and the Epistle to Philemon, was to encourage the believers to practice in the *ecclesia* the freedom-in-love that would negate slavery and treat women as equal partners in the work of the kingdom. Sometimes this backfired (see 1 Cor 11:2-16 and 1 Tim 2:9-15!). At the same time, Paul's strategy was to win unbelievers to the faith by living out pious behavior. As I have said elsewhere, winning friends to the faith who are suspicious of the gospel (or "religion") is often done by being a truthful friend, by being good parents, by being honest and hard-working, by being a good neighbor.[60] These actions, which often take a very long time depending on the culture, are motivated and accompanied by the preaching of the gospel and bring down abusive governments and even empires. Paul believed that only the gospel could change the world. Do we?

Application. Some North Americans, especially those from the United States, have a conception of freedom that is used as a lens to read the Bible. Texts like Titus 2:1-10 cause great distress when read through that lens. The reason is that the text seems to stifle freedom, not only because slaves are told to be the best slaves but also because there seems to be a dictated niche for each person of the family. Many in the United States react negatively to this text,

[58]See esp. Dibelius and Conzelmann, *Pastoral Epistles*, 39-40.
[59]Dibelius and Conzelmann, *Pastoral Epistles*, 39.
[60]See Padilla, *The Pastoral Epistles*, 261-62.

especially its author, for the latter seems to perpetuate repression and slavery. Reading this text in a culture that believes anything can be changed if we hold hands and protest, the Bible appears to be a cowardly (at best) and a hateful (at worst) book that, if taken *au pied de la lettre*, can (and *has*) caused oppression of the worst type. These are serious statements that require careful answers: and it just may be that reading the New Testament from another culture may shed some light.

I am from the Dominican Republic, which I left when I was thirteen years old. When I left my country, it was a firmly democratic nation, albeit with a lot of corruption. Yet, as a whole, there was freedom and democracy. But that was not always the case. A previous generation, the generation of my parents, had lived for thirty-one years of brutal oppression under the dictatorship of Rafael Leonidas Trujillo, one of the bloodiest and most evil dictators in the history of Latin America. When I ask my parents how life was during this period, they give me troubled looks. They tell me that speech was always monitored: you had to be careful in what you said even to "friends," for they might report you to the authorities. The lights in your home had to be shut off by a certain time. You needed to have a portrait of Trujillo visible in the home; under the portrait the following words were inscribed: "God in heaven and Trujillo on earth." If you were considered an "attractive" young woman, you lived in fear of being given (by your parents at times!) or taken to be sexually abused by Trujillo and his family and friends. Protest was not permitted. If a group of people tried to march in front of the Supreme Court buildings they would have been "disappeared"—literally. If Trujillo took a fancy to your home, he could "buy" it from you. Demonstrations were not allowed: you would be killed, perhaps along with the rest of your family. When I ask my parents about how change could have been accomplished under this dictatorship, they have a very difficult time answering. Now that they are Christians, they are still not sure. But they do believe strongly that a humble Christian testimony (which perhaps might have led to martyrdom) was the only Christian way to bring an end to the diabolical oppression they experienced.

I want to state as strongly as possible that this is the type of government and dictatorship under which Paul lived in the Roman empire—only even more brutal. Many Americans, especially in elite educational institutions, are critical of Paul (or the author of the Pastoral Epistles if they do not believe in Pauline authorship). But I wonder if they would be as critical if they had lived during the Roman empire or in contemporary dictatorships. Paul could not destroy slavery and the maltreatment of women, children, and the elderly by unity and sheer willpower. He could not bring freedom to slaves by "democratic arguments" and votes. He could not march before the Roman Forum. It seems to me that for Paul freedom could be experienced even in the midst of a patriarchal culture and slavery (see Gal 5:13-6:2). In fact, freedom was already being experienced in the *ecclesia*, where what counted was being birthed by the Holy Spirit and serving one another as sisters and brothers in Christ. Perhaps this is what the following collect from the Book of Common Prayer is asking us to pray and reflect: "O God, who art the author of peace and lover of concord . . . whose service is perfect freedom: Defend us, thy humble servants, in all assaults of our enemies" (BCP).

Let us not be mistaken: domination of women by men as often happens in patriarchal societies and slavery are evil. If we live in a nation that permits protestation against these evils, we should take full advantage to fulminate such evils. Paul too wanted oppression to finish. But he did not live in a democratic country. His approach was *missional.* And this meant living in a godly manner in difficult stations of life, where the gospel could be preached with deeds and words. For the gospel alone can bring genuine change and freedom. Paul was martyred for this gospel.

Salvation as the basis of missional behavior (Titus 2:11-15). Paul finished Titus 2:10 by speaking of "the teaching of God our *Savior* [*sōtēr*]." He connects that previous section with the current one by using a cognate of *sōtēr* to begin Titus 2:11: "For the grace of God has appeared, bringing salvation [*sōtērios*] to all." The term for "appeared" (*epiphanē*) is mostly encountered in the New Testament in the Pastoral Epistles. The word elevates the prose, for the verb or noun (*epiphania*) is often used in the LXX to underline the transcendence of God as he comes down to deliver his people. In much Hellenistic literature the word can refer to the *epiphania* of a king to fight for his people. Paul's truth claim here is that God himself has appeared to bring salvation (for what is salvation if not God himself in his act of deliverance).[61] Since the referent of "God" in Titus 2:11 is Jesus Christ, Paul is presenting the Messiah as God himself coming to earth to save all. In fact, in Titus 2:13 Paul states the following concerning the nature of Jesus Christ: "While we wait for the blessed hope and the manifestation [*epiphania*] of the glory of our great God and Savior, Jesus Christ." Along with texts like John 1:1; Romans 9:5; Philippians 2:6-11; Hebrews 1:8 and 2 Peter 1:1, this is one of the clearest verses in the New Testament that affirms that Jesus Christ is God in the flesh (see further our discussion of Titus 3:3-7).

What does salvation mean? And what does it have to do with the conduct that believers should display as described in Titus 2:1-10? Salvation is *transformative* of our existence: "training us to renounce impiety and worldly passions and in the present age to live lives that are self-controlled, upright, and godly, while we wait for the blessed hope." Notice that salvation encompasses all tenses: God has appeared (past), and is training us (present) while we wait for his future return (future).

Paul could have finished his thought with what is in our modern Bibles Titus 2:13. Nevertheless, probably using a creedal statement of the church (to which Paul himself might have contributed!), he will go deeper into what Christ has done to save us.[62] The statement that follows stems from Jesus himself (see Mk 10:45; Lk 22:19); then it was developed further (e.g., Gal 1:4; 2:20; 1 Pet 2:21-23). This formula-like statement has the following two components: (1) the language of *giving*: "He it is who gave [*didōmi*] himself." (2) The language of *vicariousness*: "for [*hyper*] us." Jesus Christ, the great God and Savior, has assumed humanity and has given himself (both in his life and crucifixion) for us. That is, he has taken our place to suffer for our sins *instead* of us taking that place. For Paul, there is no contradiction between the majesty of Christ and the humiliation of Christ. In some ways the latter defines the former: "When the crucified Jesus is called 'the image of the invisible God,' the meaning is that *this* is God, and God is like *this.* God is not greater than he is in his humiliation. God is no more glorious than he is in this self-surrender."[63]

[61]See helpfully Karl Barth, *Church Dogmatics*, ed. G. W. Bromiley and T. F. Torrance, trans. G. W. Bromiley et al., study edition, 31 vols. (London: T&T Clark, 2010), II.1, 356.

[62]For what follows, cf. Padilla, *Pastoral Epistles*, 267-68.

[63]Jürgen Moltmann, *The Crucified God: The Cross of Christ as the Foundation and Criticism of Christian Theology*, trans. R. J. Wilson and J. Bowden (New York: Harper & Row, 1974), 295.

At the end of Titus 2:14 Paul gives more precision to the previous statement by speaking of the purpose of the self-giving of Jesus: "That he might redeem us from all iniquity and purify for himself a people of his own who are zealous for good deeds." The two key thoughts are those of redemption and purification. In the LXX, redemption often conveys the sense of rescuing or freeing (see GELS, 436). In fact, Paul's statement here is almost a quotation of Psalm 130:8 (129:8 LXX): "It is he [the Lord] who will redeem Israel from all its iniquities." Christologically speaking, it is essential that we notice that what Yahweh promised to do in the Old Testament is what Jesus accomplishes in the New Testament, for Jesus Christ is in fact the God of Israel. It is also worth noting that with the language of rescuing and freeing the exodus from Egypt is evoked. This is not surprising, since this event is the biblical paradigm for God's work of deliverance. The other side of the coin of Jesus' self-surrender is that of *purification*. The language here is cultic, reminding us of the purification from sin of the sacrifices and offerings of the Old Testament.

To sum up this section, the logic is that we can only become and behave like the people of God because God himself has made us his people by the vicarious giving of Jesus Christ. God saves us, that is, frees us from our enslaving iniquities and cleanses our shameful sins. This work of God enables us to behave missionally (Titus 2:1-10).

The "then" and "now" of Christians and its relationship to the state (Titus 3:1-11). With this section we come to the end of part one of the Epistle to Titus. Titus 3:1-2 speaks of the behavior of Christians to the state and society in general. We may summarize this relationship as one of *respect, wisdom* and *gentleness*. The basis or capacity to behave in this manner is the fundamental change that has occurred in the lives of Christians. Paul explains this change by a "then" and "now" structure (see also Eph 2:1-10) as well as a trinitarian configuration that is perhaps the clearest in the letters of Paul.

Paul presents a catalog of vices (see also 1 Tim 6:3-6) to describe the type of existence we led prior to conversion. The climax (or bottom!) of this former life is given at the end of Titus 3:3 with the phrase "hating one another." This is breaking the second fundamental command of the Shema, namely, to love our neighbors as ourselves. In other words, what animates the terrible behavior described in Titus 3:1-2 is ultimately hate for others, which necessarily means that we also hate God.

But this very God intervened powerfully to redeem us and transform us from this type of life. In a beautiful periodic sentence that covers Titus 3:4-6, Paul provides a deep explanation of the united work of our Triune God for the salvation of humanity. My theological commitment from the North African theologian St. Augustine in part guides my interpretation: *omnia opera Trinitatis ad extra indivisa sunt*: All the works of the Trinity ad extra are indivisible. For this reason, there will be times in the following where it is not necessary to have a perfect answer of the referent of the word *God* (i.e., is God here referring to the Father or the Son?). In other contexts, of course, this would be crucial.

First, we hear the following: "But when the goodness and loving kindness of God our Savior appeared . . . he saved us." I take this to be a reference to the Father; but given the use of the word *Savior*, it may refer to the Father and the Son. God saved us on the basis of his own mercy, not anything would have accomplished salvation. Second, we hear of the work of the Spirit: "Through the water of rebirth and renewal by the Holy Spirit." Similar to texts like

John 3:6, the affirmation is that salvation includes regeneration, a new birth for the one who believes. In the New Testament, baptism is the locus of this action, although of course it is not some magical power of the water. Third, we are told that it is Jesus Christ who pours the Holy Spirit on us richly (cf. Acts 2:32-33). This pouring of the Spirit leads to our justification (Titus 3:7). The logic may be that through new birth by the Spirit we are united to Christ and thereby justified or acquitted from the guilt and penalty of our sins.

Application. The New Testament in Color primarily works with the reality that we read the Scriptures from a particular place: there is no such thing as "the view from nowhere" that modernity searched after. The particular place from which we have focused is the ethnic one, which of course is weaved together with many other aspects of who we are as persons. At times we have suggested that practices from our own ethnicity can tend to be harmful to the church. At other times we have suggested that our ethnicity may provide a lens that can protect us from distorting God's Word and therefore ungodly living. In the final application of this particular commentary my observation (and complaint) is more toward a period or age than ethnic identities, although the problem is mostly Western European. To put it in a nutshell, the problem I am referring to is the idea that the work of the New Testament scholar is primarily descriptive and historical, not theological. To tell the story of how this came about would require another volume(s)! Nevertheless, we have enough space here to say that this mentality began with the Enlightenment, first in the realm of rationalism (think G. E. Lessing), and continued with the growth of historicism (e.g., J. P. Gabler).[64] The manner of thinking that emerged from this period was one of compartmentalization: biblical scholars on one side of the building; theologians on another side of the building. The sad, even tragic, truth is that in our generation the majority of evangelical biblical scholars operate within this schema. To take the example of my trinitarian reading of Titus 3 above, I have been told by other New Testament scholars that I am reading later doctrine of the church into the biblical text (without knowing it, they are agreeing with Adolf von Harnack!). In particular, I am told that the word *Trinity* does not appear in the New Testament (at least in the best manuscripts). But this way of thinking assumes that for something to be real it must have a label or name. If my best friend tells me that he is always sad, cannot get out of bed, has lost all appetite, and cannot cease from crying, I do not need to use the word *depression* to make his symptoms worthy of being called depression. Equally, the New Testament does not use the word *Trinity*, but the New Testament *shows* us the Trinity—and from very early on, namely, the baptism of Jesus.

My hope is that *The New Testament in Color* will inspire readers to break away from this Enlightenment-based reading of the Bible to a more theological one.

TITUS: PART TWO

Final greetings and exhortations (Titus 3:12-15)

Instructions (Titus 3:12-15). Much like 2 Timothy, Titus ends with Paul giving ministry traveling directions to his coworkers in the gospel. Familiar names like Tychicus and Apollos are mentioned. Perhaps the most important part of this final section is Paul's

[64]For those with German, I recommend the trenchant critique of Ulrich Wilckens's *Theologie des Neuen Testaments*, 7 vols. (Göttingen: Neukirchener/Vandenhoeck & Ruprecht, 2002–2017). A penetrating account of the period as a whole is found in Karl Barth, *Protestant Theology in the Nineteenth Century*, new ed., trans. B. Cozens and J. Bowden (Grand Rapids, MI: Eerdmans, 2002).

closing exhortation that the Christians "learn to devote themselves to good works . . ." This has been a dominant motif in the Pastoral Epistles. It is also encouraging to hear that the doing of good works is something that takes time, that must be learned. Perhaps this can help us be more patient with one another.

BIBLIOGRAPHY

Ascough, Richard, et al. *Associations in the Greco-Roman World: A Sourcebook*. Waco, TX: Baylor University Press, 2012.

Barclay, John M. G. *Paul and the Gift*. Grand Rapids, MI: Eerdmans, 2015.

Barth, Karl. *Church Dogmatics*. Edited by G. W. Bromiley and T. F. Torrance. Translated by G. W. Bromiley et al. Study ed. 31 vols. London: T&T Clark, 2010.

———. *Protestant Theology in the Nineteenth Century: Its Background and History*. New ed. Introduction by Colin Gunton. Translated by Brian Cozens and John Bowden. Grand Rapids, MI: Eerdmans, 2002.

Baum, Armin. *Pseudepigraphie und literarische Fälschung im frühen Christentum: mit ausgewählten Quellentexten samt deutscher Übersetzung*. Tübingen: Mohr Siebeck, 2001.

Campbell, R. A. *The Elders: Seniority Within Earliest Christianity*. Edinburgh: T&T Clark.

Clarke, Andrew D. *A Pauline Theology of Church Leadership*. London: T&T Clark.

Dibelius, M., and H. Conzelmann. *The Pastoral Epistles*. Translated by Philip Buttolph and Adela Yarbro. Philadelphia: Fortress Press, 1972.

Gathercole, Simon. *The Gospel and the Gospels*. Grand Rapids, MI: Eerdmans, 2022.

Hengel, Martin. *Judaism and Hellenism: Studies in Their Encounter in Palestine During the Early Hellenistic Period*. Translated by J. Bowden. 2 vols. Philadelphia: Fortress Press, 1974.

Huizenga, Annette. *Moral Education for Women in the Pastoral and Pythagorean Letters*. Leiden: Brill, 2013.

Johnson, Luke Timothy. *The First and Second Letters to Timothy: With Introduction and Commentary*. New Haven, CT: Yale University Press, 2001.

Keener, Craig. *1 Peter: A Commentary*. Grand Rapids, MI: Baker Academic, 2021.

Kidson, Lyn M. *Persuading Shipwrecked Men: The Rhetorical Strategies of 1 Timothy 1*. Tübingen: Mohr Siebeck, 2020.

Kloppenborg, John S. *Christ's Associations: Connecting and Belonging in the Ancient City*. New Haven, CT: Yale University Press, 2019.

Lightman, Marjorie, and William Zeisel. "*Univira*: An Example of Continuity and Change in Roman Society." *CH* 46 (1997): 19-32.

Malherbe, Abraham. *Light from the Gentiles: Hellenistic Philosophy and Early Christianity; Collected Essays: 1959–2012 by Abraham Malherbe*. 2 vols. Edited Carl Holladay et al. Leiden: Brill, 2014.

Marshall, I. Howard. *The Pastoral Epistles*. Edinburgh: T&T Clark, 1999.

Moltmann, Jürgen. *The Crucified God: The Cross of Christ as the Foundation and Criticism of Christian Theology*. Translated by R. J. Wilson and J. Bowden. New York: Harper & Row, 1974.

Morgan, Teresa. *Roman Faith and Christian Faith:* Pistis *and* Fides *in the Early Roman Empire and Early Churches*. Oxford: Oxford University Press, 2015.

Mutschler, Bernhard. *Glaube in den Pastoralbriefen:* Pistis *als Mitte christlicher Existenz*. Tübingen: Mohr Siebeck, 2010.

Padilla, Osvaldo. *The Pastoral Epistles*. TNTC. Downers Grove, IL: InterVarsity Press, 2022.

Pokorný, Petr. *Colossians: A Commentary*. Translated by Siegfried S. Schatzmann. Peabody, MA: 1991.

Porter, Stanley, and G. P. Fewster. *Paul and Pseudepigraphy*. Leiden: Brill, 2013.

Rajak, Tessa. "Was There a Roman Charter for the Jews?" In *The Jewish Dialogue with Greece and Rome: Studies in Cultural and Social Interaction*, 301-33. Leiden: Brill, 2001.

Roloff, Jürgen. *Der erste Brief an Timotheus*. Neukirchen/Vluyn: Neukirchener, 1988.

Stanton, Graham. *Jesus of Nazareth in New Testament Preaching*. Cambridge: Cambridge University Press, 1975.

Towner, Philip. *The Letters to Timothy and Titus*. Grand Rapids, MI: Eerdmans, 2006.

van Nes, Jermo. *Pauline Language and the Pastoral Epistles: A Study of Linguistic Variation in the* Corpus Paulinum. Leiden: Brill, 2018.

White, Benjamin L. *Remembering Paul: Ancient and Modern Contests over the Image of the Apostle*. Oxford: Oxford University Press, 2014.

Wilckens, Ulrich. *Theologie des Neuen Testaments*. 7 vols. Göttingen: Neukirchener/Vandenhoeck & Ruprecht, 2002-2017.

LETTER TO PHILEMON

Dennis R. Edwards

As with Colossians, slavery complicates the message of Philemon for African Americans.[1] While slavery is not the main point of the letter—fellowship (*koinōnia*) is—African Americans do not have the luxury of ignoring the social situation of Onesimus or that of our ancestors. Some interpreters read Philemon without the legacy of slavery in Europe and the New World at the forefront. For example, John G. Nordling complains

> [We] cannot adapt (distort) the teaching of St. Paul on slavery to suit the demands of certain voices of today, each stridently insisting on being "heard" at the dawn of the third millennium C.E. No, faith submits to what the Word of God has always said through the passing of the ages and does not gladly suffer the plain meaning of Scripture to be twisted to suit constantly changing societal norms—a particular American "mentality" for example.[2]

Without trying to unpack Nordling's loaded expression, "the plain meaning of Scripture," we should be wary of the perspectives of scholars who minimize or dismiss the analyses of those harmed by the application of biblical texts. These scholars, in the words of Demetrius K. Williams, have "consecrated the status quo instead of speaking prophetically to it."[3] Nordling, and countless other White scholars, are able to distance their reading of Philemon from slavery in Europe and the New World by finding ways to separate their peoples' practices from the slavery of Paul's time. However, it was the slavery of Paul's time, and the New Testament's instructions directed to ancient slaves, that became part of the religious justification for enslaving Africans. Greco-Roman slavery is intertwined with slavery in Europe and the Americas because of the role the Bible played. Williams recognizes that the Scriptures do not condemn slavery outright and comments:

> To be sure, this "silence" of the New Testament writers and later Christian writers in particular on the moral question and challenge against the institution of slavery provided the seedbed for supporting its social and economic resurgence in the early modern period in Europe and the Americas. Protestant denominations in America used Philemon and other passages in the Bible to debate the church's position in slaveholding. Philemon in particular was considered a ready resource in particular for the American Protestant church's response to the Fugitive Slave law of 1850, because they read the letter as a depiction of their own historical and

[1]Lloyd A. Lewis, "Philemon," in *True to Our Native Land: An African American New Testament Commentary*, ed. Brian K. Blount, Cain Hope Felder, Clarice J. Martin, and Emerson B. Powery (Minneapolis: Fortress Press, 2007), 437.

[2]John G. Nordling, *Philemon* (Saint Louis: Concordia, 2004), 68-69, quoted in Demetrius K. Williams, "No Longer as a Slave: Reading the Interpretation History of Paul's Epistle to Philemon," in *Onesimus, Our Brother: Reading Religion, Race, and Culture in Philemon*, ed. Matthew V. Johnson, James A. Noel, and Demetrius K. Williams, Paul in Critical Contexts (Minneapolis: Fortress Press, 2012), 43.

[3]Williams, "No Longer as a Slave," 44.

> judicial situation: Paul was returning a fugitive/runaway slave to a Christian slave master.[4]

Proslavery advocates in Europe and the Americas relied on the words of Paul to assuage their consciences, and Philemon played a key part in justifying the actions of slaveholders as Christians used the letter to support the capture and return of runaway slaves, notably in the 1850 Fugitive Slave Act.[5]

There are, however, scholars who see Philemon as relevant to the plight of African Americans and anyone else who struggles to reconcile their faith in Jesus with the legacy of slavery. Many of these scholars are African American, but not all. For example, Scot McKnight tackles the issue of slavery head-on in his commentary on Philemon, devoting several pages not only to the slavery of Greco-Roman times, but also to practices in the New World and today.[6] Cain Hope Felder acknowledges that those who defended the European and American slave trade appealed to Philemon to justify their actions, but also observes, "The central meaning and purpose of the Letter to Philemon concern the difference the transforming power of the gospel can make in the lives and relationships of believers, regardless of class or other distinctions."[7] This transforming power can turn enemies into friends and slaveholders into siblings of those who have been enslaved (Philem 16).

AUTHORSHIP AND DATE

Scholars generally agree that the apostle Paul wrote Philemon from prison, likely sent in the early to mid-AD 50s from a prison in Ephesus.[8] If Paul wrote Colossians, then the letters were either sent together or close in time to each other.

SETTING

Because Philemon and Colossians may have been written around the same time from the same place, their interpretations often appear together. Both letters list several of the same names (Timothy, Archippus, Aristarchus, Onesimus, Epaphras, Mark, Luke, Demas). The letter to Philemon is chiefly Paul's plea for his friend and partner (Philem 1) to welcome Onesimus, who was apparently Philemon's slave and became a disciple of Jesus under Paul's influence (Philem 10).[9] However, the letter lacks details, inviting interpreters not only to theorize concerning the location of Paul's incarceration, but also about Onesimus's backstory. Was Onesimus a fugitive? Had he stolen from Philemon (Philem 18)? Did he deliberately seek out Paul, or find him providentially? Did Philemon send Onesimus to Paul?

African American interpreters generally reject the notion that Onesimus was a fugitive. The letter never depicts Onesimus as a runaway, and seeing him as such may reflect the biases brought to the text. Another theory

---

[4]Williams, "No Longer as a Slave," 33 (emphasis original).

[5]Lewis Brogdon, *A Companion to Philemon*, Cascade Companions (Eugene, OR: Cascade Books, 2018), 12-14.

[6]Scot McKnight, *The Letter to Philemon*, NICNT (Grand Rapids, MI: Eerdmans, 2017), 1-36. See also Thompson, *Colossians and Philemon*, 193-94.

[7]Cain Hope Felder, "The Letter to Philemon: Introduction, Commentary, and Reflections," in Second Corinthians to Philemon, vol. 11, *The New Interpreter's Bible*, ed. Leander Keck (Nashville: Abingdon, 2000), 885.

[8]See the exegetical commentaries (such as those cited in notes 5-7) for the options. One key issue is the geographic proximity of Colossae to Ephesus in contrast to Rome as it relates to Onesimus's journey to Paul and Paul's anticipated visit (Philem 22).

[9]Virtually all commentators understand Onesimus to have been Philemon's slave with the notable exception of Allen Dwight Callahan (and some who followed Callahan's argument). Callahan argues that Onesimus was Philemon's estranged biological brother. See Allen Dwight Callahan, "Paul's Epistle to Philemon: Toward an Alternative *Argumentum*," *HTR* 86, no. 4 (1993): 357-76; Callahan, *Embassy of Onesimus: The Letter of Paul to Philemon*, New Testament in Context (Valley Forge, PA: Trinity Press International, 1997).

is that Onesimus knew Paul to be *amicus domini*, a friend of his master, and purposely appealed to Paul.[10] Enslaved people in the Roman Empire appealed to the *amicus domini* when they were treated unjustly by their masters. We noted that Colossians 4:1 (above), which may have been addressed to the church in Philemon's home, instructs slaveholders to treat slaves justly and equitably. If Onesimus was not being treated fairly, he may have sought out Paul to voice his complaint. Even though we are not told of any explicit action of Philemon against Onesimus, neither are we given any explicit details regarding Onesimus's behavior. It is possible that Onesimus witnessed the loving community within Philemon's household and wondered why he was not invited into it. Perhaps he sought out Paul to understand the faith that Philemon should have explained to him. Another possibility is that Philemon sent Onesimus to minister to Paul.[11] We do not know how or why Onesimus made contact with Paul, so we do not need to assume that he was a thieving runaway who had shirked responsibility, which is how some scholars (such as Nordling noted above) depict Onesimus.

In addition to questions about Onesimus's past, there are also questions about his future. We do not know if Philemon acquiesced. However, some have attempted to connect Onesimus to a bishop of Ephesus mentioned by Ignatius of Antioch in the early second century.[12] Furthermore, we do not know how Philemon treated Onesimus upon his return or how Paul's letter impacted the lives of any other enslaved people.

THEMATIC OUTLINE

Philemon, like Colossians, is pastoral communication that conforms to the typical pattern of ancient Greco-Roman letters.

Letter opening: Paul's pastoral appreciation and intercessory prayer (Philem 1-7)

- Opening greetings from Paul and Timothy (Philem 1-3)
- Paul's prayer for Philemon (Philem 4-7)

Main body of the letter: Paul's threefold appeal to Philemon on behalf of Onesimus (Philem 8-21)[13]

- The first appeal based on love and Onesimus's conversion (Philem 8-11)
- The second appeal based on Philemon's good will and Onesimus's good work (Philem 12-16)
- The third appeal based on Paul and Philemon's partnership (Philem 17-21)

Letter Closing: Gracious restoration, association, and consolation (Philem 22-25)

- Preparing for Paul to be graciously restored (Philem 22)
- Greetings from fellow prisoners and workers (Philem 23-24)
- Benediction (Philem 25)

INTRODUCTION

Paul, the pastor, applies cleverly nuanced pressure for Philemon to demonstrate Christian fellowship.[14] For example, Paul claims not to appeal to his apostolic authority to command Philemon

---

[10]Fitzmyer, *Philemon*, 18-23.

[11]See Stephen E. Young, *Our Brother Beloved: Purpose and Community in Paul's Letter to Philemon* (Waco, TX: Baylor University Press, 2021), 43-47.

[12]Ignatius of Antioch ca. 110 CE (*Eph* 1-3) mentions an Onesimus as bishop of Ephesus. Fitzmyer, *Philemon*, 15, notes the "possibility" of Paul and Ignatius referring to the same person, and Brogdon, *Philemon*, 53-54, views the connection as likely within a discussion of Philemon's status in the New Testament canon.

[13]Part two of my outline varies slightly from that of McKnight, *Philemon*, 46.

[14]See Brogdon, *Philemon*, xxi-xxii for a table juxtaposing Paul's "wordplays," with "subtle yet overt statements," along with "loaded/bold statements."

(Philem 8) and instead bases his appeal on love (Philem 9), on Philemon's good will (Philem 14), and on the partnership the two men have (Philem 1, 17). Philemon likely knew he needed to comply with Paul's request because Paul highlights Philemon's indebtedness (Philem 19) and also requests hospitality (Philem 22), suggesting he will visit and check for himself if Philemon followed through, The fellowship that Paul expects is not only that between him and Philemon but between Philemon and Onesimus. Key to the letter is Paul's appeal that Onesimus return "no longer as a slave, but more than a slave, a beloved brother" (Philem 16). African Americans generally have our people's history in mind when reading that verse. Paul's admonition means a change of status for Onesimus within Philemon's household based on the three men (i.e., Paul, Philemon, and Onesimus) having a relationship with Jesus. On the one hand, the letter to Philemon has been used to bolster slavery, condemning enslaved African Americans who sought to escape. Yet, on the other hand, the letter opened the door to expose slavery as antithetical to Christian sisterhood and brotherhood.

LETTER OPENING: PAUL'S PASTORAL APPRECIATION AND INTERCESSORY PRAYER (PHILEMON 1-7)

Opening greetings from Paul and Timothy (Philemon 1-3). Colossians opened with Paul identifying himself as apostle (Col 1:1), and ended with a reminder of his imprisonment (Col 4:18). Philemon, however, opens with the only time Paul addresses a letter as "prisoner of Jesus Christ." "Prisoner" serves as a double entendre: Paul is literally bound in a Roman prison, and also spiritually bound in service to Christ Jesus. Timothy, as in Colossians, is Paul's coauthor. Even though Paul also addresses the letter to Apphia (the only woman addressee of a New Testament letter), Archippus, and the entire church in Philemon's house, the focus is on Philemon, demonstrated in the use of second-person-singular constructions throughout much of the letter.

Paul's prayer for Philemon (Philemon 4-7). Paul thanks God for Philemon's love and faith in Jesus Christ, which also is a cause for the apostle's joy (Philem 7). Paul's prayer deftly challenges Philemon. The apostle includes a wish for Philemon's partnership, or sharing (*koinōnia*) of his faith to be effective (Philem 6).[15] Reminiscent of the Pastoral Epistles, Paul expects Philemon, as a leader, to set an example for others (e.g., 2 Tim 2:2). When Philemon's participation in the faith is active, or effective, it will bring knowledge of all the good that we have in Christ.[16] Philemon's knowledge includes seeing Onesimus in a better light (Philem 16). The good (see Philem 14) found in Christ indicates the new and improved relationship Philemon is to have with Onesimus.

Without a better relationship with Onesimus, Philemon's partnership in the faith is not fully active in meeting the goal of genuine solidarity. To be clear, the leader, who is a slaveholder, is deficient in his understanding of what is morally upright ("good") without a new relationship with an enslaved member of his household. Although Onesimus is silent throughout the letter, Philemon needs him. Philemon will not fully understand the fellowship of faith without Onesimus. Likewise, Christians of European descent in the New World largely failed to understand how they needed Native Americans, Africans, and other non-Europeans in order for the fellowship of faith to be fully energized. This is to say that being fully

[15]Fitzmyer, *Philemon*, 97, claims Philem 6 "is the most difficult one to understand in the whole letter."

[16]See the technical commentaries for discussions of the textual variant (*hēmin*, "us" versus *hymin* "you all") and various ways to render *eis Christon*).

human—which includes loving in the robust manner demonstrated by Jesus—requires humanity to be in solidarity with others, including those of diverse backgrounds.

MAIN BODY OF THE LETTER: PAUL'S THREEFOLD APPEAL TO PHILEMON ON BEHALF OF ONESIMUS (PHILEMON 8-21)

The first appeal based on love and Onesimus's conversion (Philemon 8-11). Paul emphasizes love in his first appeal to Philemon (Philem 9). Love is supreme to Paul (1 Cor 13:1-13) and he views it as the practical outworking of faith, as in Galatians 5:6, "the only thing that counts is faith working through love." Ironically, it is Paul's faith in Jesus that has landed him in prison. Furthermore, there is no shame in Paul's imprisonment; he acknowledges it at least five times in this brief letter (Philem 1, 9, 10, 13, 23). Paul refers to himself as a prisoner the same way he calls himself a slave. Both terms provoke a range of emotions for some African Americans. We've already seen how the New Testament's references to slavery and failure to denounce it create difficult issues in light of the Transatlantic slave trade. Likewise, the criminal justice system in the United States, including mass incarceration, appears to target Black and brown bodies.[17] We are reluctant, therefore, to minimize or overlook Paul's self-designation as prisoner or as slave. Instead, we celebrate how the enslaved and prisoners, who are ordinarily demonized in society, demonstrate the character of Jesus Christ.

Onesimus is first mentioned in Philemon 10. Without sharing details, Paul uses familial language to make clear that Onesimus has become a fellow follower of Jesus Christ under Paul's guidance. It is because the name Onesimus means "useful," and was a common name for slaves, as well as the phrase "no longer a slave" in Philemon 16, that we surmise that Onesimus was a slave in Philemon's household. However, it is the stereotype of enslaved people being shiftless, lazy, and thieving that define our understanding of "useless" in Philemon 11. White people have often caricatured enslaved Africans in the Americas as shiftless, lazy, and thieving, despite the reality that enslaved people performed backbreaking labor to advance the country's economy, while simultaneously strategizing for survival and resistance, creating a new indigenous culture along the way. Beyond Paul's wordplay on Onesimus's name are our assumptions regarding the character of this slave. Paul does not impugn Onesimus's integrity; instead, he praises Onesimus's ability to serve as a Christian believer (Philem 13). Paul commends Onesimus as having become useful in light of his conversion. Paul indicates that before his conversion, Onesimus was not useful in ministry but now he is (Philem 13). In 1 Timothy 4:11, Paul uses the same vocabulary in his request for Mark's presence because "he is useful in my ministry." Paul wants Philemon to know that an enslaved person can perform Christian ministry.

Since Onesimus was not converted while in Philemon's house, it may be that Paul offers a subtle rebuke to the leader. Robert H. Van Dyke observes, "It could well be that Paul's appeal on behalf of Onesimus was a wake-up call to Philemon and others at the house (which was their church) about what they were doing. The question that screams at me is: 'How did they have a practicing Christian household, doing what they were supposed to be doing and teaching, and living into the faith while neglecting to spend the effort to convert their

[17]See Michelle Alexander, *The New Jim Crow: Mass Incarceration in the Age of Colorblindness* (New York: New Press, 2012), and Dominique DuBois Gilliard, *Rethinking Incarceration: Advocating for Justice That Restores* (Downers Grove, IL: InterVarsity Press, 2018).

servants? Why did Paul have to convert Onesimus?'"[18] Philemon needs to know that Onesimus the slave has a relationship with Jesus Christ in the same way that his earthly master does, and can do ministry, even providing valuable assistance to the apostle Paul. There is no way to know why Onesimus was not converted in Philemon's household. It does, however, provoke questions concerning Philemon's attitude toward enslaved people and if he could accept the implications of a converted servant. The conversion of Onesimus communicates how those once considered useless—for whatever reasons—can indeed be useful in Christian service.

The second appeal based on Philemon's good will and Onesimus's good work (Philemon 12-16). Paul continues with his praise of Onesimus in Philemon 12-13, placing him on equal footing as the master: Paul comments that Onesimus is providing ministry that Philemon could do (Philem 13). Paul deftly encourages Philemon to do the right thing, appealing to the church leader's good will rather than applying overt pressure (Philem 14). Paul even speculates that the absence of Onesimus providentially created the occasion for a better, nontransactional, egalitarian, eternal relationship between a slaveholder and an enslaved fellow Christian (Philem 15).

Philemon is to receive Onesimus no longer as a slave, but more than (*hyper*) a slave, and as a Christian brother. Onesimus is a beloved brother to Paul and to Philemon, spiritually ("in the Lord"), and also in the context of physical, daily interactions ("in the flesh"). Earlier discussion (particularly of household codes) pointed out that New Testament writers, including Paul, never outrightly condemned slavery. Therefore, some scholars believe it is unlikely that Paul encouraged the manumission of Onesimus.[19] As Lewis Brogdon stresses, "Paul is trying to change the fundamental nature of their relationship as master and slave, without which, manumission would not make a difference. . . . Paul is saying, in effect that Philemon's relationship with Onesimus can no longer be dictated by a legal relationship (master-slave) but by a spiritual relationship (brothers)."[20] African Americans know that even with President Abraham Lincoln's Emancipation Proclamation executive order, our status in the eyes of many White people did not change. The country found new ways to dehumanize us. This is not to say that manumission is unnecessary, and it may be that Paul is requesting Philemon to free Onesimus.[21] What is clear, however, is that Paul focused on the Christian fellowship Onesimus and Philemon should have. Regarding Onesimus, McKnight argues that "in the house of his master he was family and therefore no longer a slave deprived of status and power."[22] African Americans are not subordinate to Whites. We know this not only because the law of the land grants us equality, but because God made all humans in God's image (Gen 1:26, 27) and declares all who are in Christ to be equal (Gal 3:28; Col 3:11).

The third appeal based on Paul and Philemon's partnership (Philemon 17-21). Paul continues to affirm Onesimus's dignity by requesting that Philemon welcome Onesimus back in the same way that Paul would be welcomed (Philem 17). Paul connects his status as a fellow believer and as an apostle, to that of

---

[18]Robert H. Van Dyke, "Paul's Letter to Philemon: An Appeal Above and Beyond the Law," *Sewanee Theological Review* 41, no. 4 (1998): 391.

[19]See 1 Cor 7:21-24 and the treatment of that passage by McCaulley, *Reading While Black*, 151-59.

[20]Brogdon, *Philemon*, 78-79.

[21]Young, *Our Brother Beloved*, 167-205, makes a case for Paul requesting that Philemon free Onesimus.

[22]McKnight, *Philemon*, 98 (emphasis his).

Onesimus. Paul returns to the language of *koinōnia,* fellowship (see Philem 6). Philemon's *koinōnia* will be active, or effective, when he receives Onesimus as a fellow believer. Paul vouches for Onesimus in the same way that Barnabas vouched for him in Acts 9:27. The apostle also agrees to make restitution for any losses that Philemon may have accrued because Onesimus left. Most commentators assume that Onesimus robbed Philemon, because there are ancient accounts of enslaved people stealing from their masters. As observed earlier, attitudes toward enslaved African Americans also factor into the depiction of Onesimus as a thief. There is no mention of robbery within the letter. Also, one might expect Paul to mention the converted Onesimus's sorrow if he stole something. Arguments from silence are of limited value, so we cannot conclude whether or not Onesimus was a thief. It is likely, however, that Onesimus's absence did result in financial losses for Philemon, in the form of lost labor, causing him to feel wronged. Perhaps Paul is offering to remunerate Philemon for those losses.

Paul's eagerness in vouching for Onesimus in this section communicates how important reconciliation and fellowship are to him. It also suggests how those in relative positions of power have a responsibility to address the situation of those in vulnerable positions. Missing the voice of Onesimus is problematic. However, seeing a Roman citizen (Paul), advocate for an enslaved person's status can provide some guidance for us. Oftentimes White people have minimized the voices of those on the margins, but perhaps they can receive challenging admonitions from those with similar privilege.

Paul's emotional appeal in Philemon 17-21 include his expectation that Philemon will go beyond Paul's request. Once again, we are not sure what Paul means, although, as mentioned above, manumission is a possibility. Perhaps Philemon can turn his attention to other enslaved people if there are others in his household. Bearing in mind Paul's words in Galatians 6:10, "So then, whenever we have an opportunity, let us work for the good of all and especially for those of the family of faith," it is fair to imagine Paul wanting Philemon to look beyond the Onesimus situation and treat any other enslaved people as Christian siblings.

LETTER CLOSING: GRACIOUS RESTORATION, ASSOCIATION, AND CONSOLATION (PHILEMON 22-25)

Preparing for Paul to be graciously restored (Philemon 22). Paul requests hospitality with hopes that he will be released from prison and make a visit to Colossae. Through the prayers of the community (the "your" is plural), Paul writes that "I will be graciously given to you all." Our society has been notorious for disrespecting formerly incarcerated people, and African Americans, along with Latino/a people, make up disproportionately high percentages of those in the penal system. Those released from prison typically face obstacles in employment, housing, voting, and other areas, not to mention the pervasive stigma that perpetually marks them as outcasts.[23] Much of the treatment of the formerly incarcerated stands in stark contrasts to the picture in Philemon 22, where Paul expects hospitality and warm welcome from a prayerful community.

Greetings from fellow prisoners and workers (Philemon 23-24). We met Epaphras in Colossians 1:7; 4:12, and with the designation "fellow prisoner" here in Philemon 23, Paul

[23] I draw attention again to Alexander, *New Jim Crow*, and Gilliard, *Rethinking Incarceration*, for their hefty discussions of mass incarceration. Another helpful and engaging work that discusses some of the problems formerly incarcerated people face is Bryan Stevenson, *Just Mercy: A Story of Justice and Redemption* (New York: Spiegel & Grau, 2014).

reminds readers one last time of his imprisonment. Paul's frequent references to his imprisonment highlight his marginal status as a prisoner, although he may have enjoyed relative privilege as a citizen. With respect to his imprisonment, Paul has some degree of "social proximity to Onesimus."[24] Additionally, the greetings from Mark and Aristarchus (Col 4:10), and Demas and Luke (Col 4:14), serve as subtle pressure on Philemon to acquiesce to Paul's requests. These "fellow workers" know the contents of the letter and share Paul's perspective that Onesimus be treated as a fellow Christian. If Paul indeed wrote Colossians, then likely Brother Onesimus (Col 4:9) will return with both letters.

Benediction (Philemon 25). Grace, one of Paul's favorite terms, is a gift that comes from the Lord Jesus Christ and is meant as consolation for the entire community ("your" in Philem 25 is plural). One might imagine Paul anticipates Philemon's agitation, which others in the church might sense when Onesimus arrives bearing the letter. Grace is always needed in the work of reconciliation, especially when the life, or at least living conditions, of those with relatively little power in society is largely determined by those with privilege. Because God opposes the proud but gives grace to the humble (cf. Jas 4:6; 1 Pet 5:5), the privileged of society may face divine opposition if they fail to treat the marginalized as full siblings in Christ. Yet they can find grace when they humble themselves and treat others as equals.

BIBLIOGRAPHY

Alexander, Michelle. *The New Jim Crow: Mass Incarceration in the Age of Colorblindness*. New York: New Press, 2012.

Bevere, Allan R. "Colossians and the Rhetoric of Empire: A New Battle Zone." In *Jesus Is Lord, Caesar Is Not: Evaluating Empire in New Testament Studies*, edited by Scot McKnight and Joseph B. Modica, 183-96. Downers Grove: IVP Academic, 2013.

Blount, Brian K. *Then the Whisper Put On Flesh: New Testament Ethics in an African American Context*. Nashville: Abingdon Press, 2001.

Bowens, Lisa M. *African American Readings of Paul: Reception, Resistance, and Transformation*. Grand Rapids, MI: Eerdmans, 2020.

———. "Liberating Paul: African Americans' Use of Paul in Resistance and Protest." In *Practicing with Paul: Reflections on Paul and the Practices of Ministry in Honor of Susan G. Eastman*, edited by Presian Burroughs, 57-73. Eugene, OR: Cascade, 2018.

Bradley, K. R. *Slaves and Masters in the Roman Empire: A Study in Social Control*. New York: Oxford University Press, 1987.

Brogdon, Lewis. *A Companion to Philemon*. Cascade Companions. Eugene, OR: Cascade Books, 2018.

Byron, Gay L. *Symbolic Blackness and Ethnic Difference in Early Christian Literature*. London: Routledge, 2002.

Byron, John. *Recent Research on Paul and Slavery*. Recent Research in Biblical Studies 3. Sheffield, UK: Sheffield Phoenix Press, 2008.

Callahan, Allen Dwight. *Embassy of Onesimus: The Letter of Paul to Philemon*. New Testament in Context. Valley Forge, PA: Trinity Press International, 1997.

———. "Paul's Epistle to Philemon: Toward an Alternative Argumentum," *HTR* 86, no. 4 (1993): 357-76.

———. *The Talking Book: African Americans and the Bible*. New Haven, CT: Yale University Press, 2008.

deSilva, David A. *An Introduction to the New Testament: Contexts, Methods and Ministry Formation*. Downers Grove: IVP Academic, 2018.

De Vos, Craig Steven. "Once a Slave, Always a Slave? Slavery, Manumission and Relational

[24]McKnight, *Philemon*, 110.

Patterns in Paul's Letter to Philemon." *JSNT* 23, no. 82 (July 2001): 89-105.

DiAngelo, Robin J. *White Fragility: Why It's So Hard for White People to Talk About Racism.* Boston: Beacon Press, 2018.

Edwards, Dennis R. "Hermeneutics and Exegesis." In *The State of New Testament Studies: A Survey of Recent Research*, edited by Scot McKnight and Nijay Gupta, 63-82. Grand Rapids, MI: Baker Academic, 2019.

Emerson, Michael O., and Christian Smith. *Divided by Faith: Evangelical Religion and the Problem of Race in America.* New York: Oxford University Press, 2000.

Felder, Cain Hope. "The Letter to Philemon: Introduction, Commentary, and Reflections." In Second Corinthians to Philemon, vol. 11, *New Interpreter's Bible*, edited by Leander Keck 881-905. Nashville: Abingdon, 2000.

Fitzmyer, Joseph A. *The Letter to Philemon: A New Translation with Introduction and Commentary.* AB 34C. New York: Doubleday, 2000.

Foster, Paul. *Colossians.* BNTC. New York: Bloomsbury T&T Clark, 2016.

Gilbreath, Edward. *Birmingham Revolution: Martin Luther King Jr.'s Epic Challenge to the Church.* Downers Grove, IL: InterVarsity Press, 2013.

Gilliard, Dominique DuBois. *Rethinking Incarceration: Advocating for Justice That Restores.* Downers Grove, IL: InterVarsity Press, 2018.

Gupta, Nijay K. *Colossians.* Smyth & Helwys Bible Commentary. Macon, GA: Smyth & Helwys, 2013.

Holt, Thomas C. *Children of Fire: A History of African Americans.* New York: Hill and Wang, 2010.

Hooker, Morna D. "Colossians." In *Eerdmans Dictionary of the Bible*, edited by David Noel Freedman, Allen C. Myers, and Astrid B. Beck, 1404-12. Grand Rapids, MI: Eerdmans, 2000.

Johnson, Matthew V., James A. Noel, and Demetrius K. Williams, eds. *Onesimus, Our Brother: Reading Religion, Race, and Culture in Philemon.* Paul in Critical Contexts. Minneapolis: Fortress Press, 2012.

Lewis, Lloyd A. "Colossians." In *True to Our Native Land: An African American New Testament Commentary*, edited by Brian K. Blount, Cain Hope Felder, Clarice J. Martin, and Emerson B. Powery, 380-88. Minneapolis: Fortress Press, 2007.

———. "Philemon." In *True to Our Native Land: An African American New Testament Commentary*, edited by Brian K. Blount, Cain Hope Felder, Clarice J. Martin, and Emerson B. Powery, 437-43. Minneapolis: Fortress Press, 2007.

Maier, Harry O. *Picturing Paul in Empire: Imperial Image, Text and Persuasion in Colossians, Ephesians and the Pastoral Epistles.* New York: Bloomsbury, 2013.

———. "A Sly Civility: Colossians and Empire." *JSNT* 27, no. 3 (2005): 323-49.

Martin, Clarice J. "The Haustafeln (Household Codes) in African American Interpretation: 'Free Slaves' and 'Subordinate Women.'" In *Stony the Road We Trod: African American Biblical Interpretation*, edited by Cain Hope Felder, 206-31. Minneapolis: Fortress, 1991.

Maynard-Reid, Pedrito U. *Diverse Worship: African-American, Caribbean and Hispanic Perspectives.* Downers Grove, IL: InterVarsity Press, 2000.

McKnight, Scot. *A Fellowship of Differents: Showing the World God's Design for Life Together.* Grand Rapids, MI: Zondervan, 2015.

———. *The Letter to the Colossians.* NICNT. Grand Rapids, MI: Eerdmans, 2018.

———. *The Letter to Philemon.* NICNT. Grand Rapids, MI: Eerdmans, 2017.

Pokorný, Petr. *Colossians: A Commentary.* Peabody, MA: Hendrickson, 1991.

Raboteau, Albert J. *Slave Religion: The "Invisible Institution" in the Antebellum South.* New York: Oxford University Press, 1978.

Smith, Abraham. "Paul and African American Biblical Interpretation." In *True to Our Native Land: An African American New Testament Commentary*, edited by Brian K. Blount, Cain Hope Felder, Clarice J. Martin, and

Emerson B. Powery, 31-42. Minneapolis: Fortress Press, 2007.

Smith, Mitzi J. "Slavery in the Early Church." In *True to Our Native Land: An African American New Testament Commentary*, edited by Brian K. Blount, Cain Hope Felder, Clarice J. Martin, and Emerson B. Powery, 11-22. Minneapolis: Fortress Press, 2007.

Stevenson, Bryan. *Just Mercy: A Story of Justice and Redemption*. New York: Spiegel & Grau, 2014.

Thompson, Marianne Meye. *Colossians and Philemon*. The Two Horizons New Testament Commentary. Grand Rapids, MI: Eerdmans, 2005.

Thurman, Howard. *Jesus and the Disinherited*. Boston: Beacon Press, 1976.

Tinsley, Annie. *A Postcolonial African American Re-reading of Colossians: Identity, Reception, and Interpretation Under the Gaze of Empire*. New York: Palgrave Macmillan, 2013.

Tisby, Jemar. *The Color of Compromise: The Truth About the American Church's Complicity in Racism*. Grand Rapids, MI: Zondervan, 2019.

Van Dyke, Robert H. "Paul's Letter to Philemon: An Appeal Above and Beyond the Law." *Sewanee Theological Review* 41, no. 4 (1998): 384-98.

Volf, Miroslav. *The End of Memory: Remembering Rightly in a Violent World*. Grand Rapids, MI: Eerdmans, 2006.

Walsh, Brian J., and Sylvia C. Keesmaat. *Colossians Remixed: Subverting the Empire*. Downers Grove, IL: InterVarsity Press, 2004.

Weima, Jeffrey A. D. *Neglected Endings: The Significance of the Pauline Letter Closings*. JSNT 101. Sheffield, UK: JSOT Press, 1994.

Whelchel, L. H. *The History and Heritage of African-American Churches: A Way out of No Way*. St. Paul, MN: Paragon House, 2011.

Wilkerson, Isabel. *The Warmth of Other Suns: The Epic Story of America's Great Migration*. New York: Random House, 2010.

Wimbush, Vincent L. *The Bible and African Americans: A Brief History*. Facets. Minneapolis: Fortress, 2003.

Yamauchi, Edwin M. *Africa and the Bible*. Grand Rapids, MI: Baker Academic, 2004.

Young, Stephen E. *Our Brother Beloved: Purpose and Community in Paul's Letter to Philemon*. Waco, TX: Baylor University Press, 2021.

LETTER TO THE HEBREWS

Madison N. Pierce

INTRODUCTION

The twenty-first century has a fascination with origin stories.[1] What happened *before* the hero wore a cape? How was that leader shaped *before* she took power? Prequels abound. Biblical interpreters share this interest; the social situation of the implied author as well as the audience assists them in interpreting the text well. But for one New Testament book in particular, the Epistle to the Hebrews, this story remains largely unknown. Almost every element of its background is contested, and the anonymity of the author generates an ongoing fascination among its readers. This introduction provides the most prominent positions.

Author. Rather than making a firm determination about the identity of the epistle's author, in more recent years the trend has been to develop an author profile. Based primarily on evidence found within Hebrews, we see that the author has a command of Greco-Roman rhetoric and knowledge of contemporary philosophical traditions. The composition contains over thirty quotations and innumerable allusions to Jewish scripture. The author of Hebrews interprets Scripture in ways that resemble other contemporary extrabiblical traditions, suggesting that he is likewise familiar with broader interpretive trends in both early Jewish and Christian literature.[2] Many conclude from these characteristics that the author is from Alexandria. Further, the reference to Timothy in particular (Heb 13:23) has led most to conclude that the author is associated with the apostle Paul in some way. This profile illuminates why interpreters have proposed certain individuals as possible authors. Among those with extant writings are Paul, Luke, and Clement of Rome. The work of each of these writers has been analyzed in comparison with Hebrews. The majority has concluded that their work is not a "match." Among those without extant writings are Apollos, Prisca, and Barnabas.[3] These writers fit the "profile," but no additional analysis is available.

Even though few today conclude that he is the author, the association between Hebrews and Paul must be addressed since Hebrews circulated within the Pauline letter collection early on. In P46, a very important manuscript, for example, Hebrews is found directly between Romans and 1 Corinthians. Further, although a number of early Christian interpreters (esp. in the West) raised considerable doubts about Pauline authorship, the apostle was the starting point for their inquiry. In other words, for the most part, Hebrews was Pauline until able to be proven otherwise.

[1]Many thanks are due to Ross Neir and Lauren Januzik for their exceptional feedback on this commentary.

[2]Take, for example, the appeal to Melchizedek (see below). This priest-king attains legendary status in Second Temple literature (see, e.g., 11QMelch), and it seems very likely that this is the backdrop for the author's appeal.

[3]Barnabas was proposed by Tertullian—at almost the same time that Pantaenus and Clement of Alexandria first proposed Paul. Apollos was not proposed until Martin Luther, and Prisca was not proposed until Adolf von Harnack.

Further, Hebrews was "Pauline" in a broader sense because a number of early interpreters considered Hebrews to be representative of Paul's teachings or one of his sermons, but proposed that someone else, such as Luke or Clement, had written down his content or translated it.[4] Beyond this, however, there is no further consensus on authorship.

Implied audience. The group addressed by the epistle is likewise unknown. Traditionally, Hebrews was thought to be written to a Jewish audience contemplating a return to Jewish religion; however, this view draws significantly on outdated assumptions about Jewish practice. Thus, it seems more likely, historically, that the audience was a diverse congregation. They were a group from various backgrounds who needed the same push: continue on and draw near despite the suffering that they were experiencing. As for their physical location, while Jerusalem and other options have been put forward, the prevailing opinion is that this letter was written to a group in or around Rome. Moving beyond the historical reality of this audience, however, the title of the book "To the Hebrews" reflects what we see in the pages to follow. The author invites his readers, Jew or Gentile, to enter the story of the people of God.[5] Nevertheless, it must be said that the author *never* asks the readers to relinquish their distinctives. Further, the author of Hebrews is not likely the one who assigned its title. This is an important point for our purposes because the title employs an ethnic designation, but the rest of the letter calls them to identify with a *family* (see, e.g., the language of "ancestors" in Heb 1:1; 2:16; 3:9; 8:9),[6] and it is a family with adopted children, whose skin, eye, and hair color do not have to match.

Date. Hebrews was likely written between 60 and 90 CE.[7] The two main reasons for this starting date are (1) the likely indications that the audience consists of second-generation Christians (e.g., Heb 2:3) and (2) the references to increasing levels of persecution (e.g., Heb 10:32-34; 12:4). The end point for this range (1) assumes that the composition is referenced in 1 Clement, often dated to the mid-90s, and (2) allows for a genuine reference to Timothy, who according to tradition was martyred in Ephesus in 97 CE.[8] As with a number of first-century compositions, the key question is whether Hebrews should be dated before or after the destruction of the temple (70 CE). Evidence does not allow for a firm conclusion to this end, though consensus among contemporary English-language commentaries appears to be pre-70 and among contemporary German-language commentaries to be post-70.[9]

---

[4]Among those who propose this "collaborative" view are Clement of Alexandria (and possibly his mentor Pantaenus), Origen, and Ephrem the Cyrian.

[5]Robert W. Wall states this rather strongly: "Surely the intention of the canonizing community in giving this letter that title was not to identify its first readers as Christian Jews; rather, its purpose was to reimagine the identity of its current Christian readers as the current generation of 'the Hebrews,' characters of a biblically shaped story of the Hebrews [*sic*] exodus out of Pharaoh's Egypt to God's promised land." See Robert W. Wall, "Epilogue: A Reflection," in *Muted Voices of the New Testament: Readings in the Catholic Epistles and Hebrews*, ed. Katherine M. Hockey, Madison N. Pierce, and Francis Watson, LNTS 565 (London: T&T Clark, 2017), 199-209.

[6]There are two notable exceptions to my claim. (1) The new covenant is with the "house of Israel" and "house of Judah" (Heb 8:8, 10, quoting Jer 31). (2) The people are described as the "offspring of Abraham" in Heb 2:16. The latter, however, from my perspective still highlights the familial quality of the connection.

[7]Craig R. Koester, *Hebrews*, AB 36 (New York: Doubleday, 2001), 50. Other broad ranges are put forward, such as 60–100 CE (Harold W. Attridge, *Hebrews*, Hermeneia [Philadelphia: Fortress Press, 1989], 6-8); as well as 50–90 CE (Gareth Lee Cockerill, *The Epistle to the Hebrews*, NICNT [Grand Rapids, MI: Eerdmans, 2012], 41).

[8]This is found in the apocryphal Acts of Timothy. I am not aware of any alternative traditions.

[9]This author has a slight preference for a pre-70 date, though she acknowledges that this might be the influence of her tradition.

Outline

The Household of God (Heb 1:1–4:16)

[Hinge Section: Heb 4:11-16]

The Tabernacle of God (Heb 4:11–10:25)

[Hinge Section: Heb 10:19-25]

The City of God (Heb 10:19–13:25)

This outline is organized around the spaces or spheres that are prominent in each section. As we shall see, when each section is introduced, the author moves from categories and relational designations associated with the home to the tabernacle to the city.[10] Drawing on the work of Cynthia Long Westfall, I have indicated two hinges between the three major sections. These hinges summarize what precedes them and also introduce the themes that follow.[11] Further, there are striking parallels between these two sections, which both contain a series of three hortatory subjunctives (more below).

THE HOUSEHOLD OF GOD (HEBREWS 1:1–4:16)

The primary sphere for the first major section of Hebrews is the home. First, we are told God's mode of speech with our ancestors (Heb 1:1; cf. 3:9). Then, we witness a dialogue between the "Father" and "Son" in Hebrews 1. We learn that the Son has "brothers and sisters" in Hebrews 2. They are the "children" whom God has given him. Finally, in Hebrews 3, the author says that we are his "house," or better his "household" (*oikos*), if we hold fast. Although the author of Hebrews does not *explicitly* extend these relational designations to "sisters" and "daughters," the primacy of this familial imagery and the focus on the "household" welcomes the inclusion of women. In the first century, for the typical woman, this was her space.

The Son of God (Hebrews 1:1-14). The author of Hebrews opens his epistle with a reminder of how God has interacted with his people for all time. He spoke to their ancestors—"long ago . . . in many and various ways" (Heb 1:1); now he speaks to us through his Son (Heb 1:2). Although it is common to focus on the many contrasts that we find in Hebrews, the comparisons are just as important. God has always been a speaking God.[12] The Son, like the prophets before him, is another mode of God's communication. But he is by no means just another messenger; in addition to being a part of God's creative work, he is heir of all things (Heb 1:2). This Son radiates the glory of God. Early Christian authors, such as Athanasius, understand this to be an image of mutuality (*C. Ar.* 1.4.12). Could we conceive of the sun without the light that it emits? This is fitting in this chapter in Hebrews 1 with its Father-Son imagery, since we likewise cannot have a parent without a corresponding child. The author of Hebrews then moves from the image of the Son radiating the glory of God to another metaphor. He has God's likeness

[10]This is less true of the third section, but there the city (Heb 11:10, 16; 12:22; 13:14) or mountain (Heb 12:22) or even "kingdom" (Heb 12:28) is mentioned consistently as their destination or goal. City is merely representative.

[11]Cynthia Long Westfall, *A Discourse Analysis of the Letter to the Hebrews: The Relationship Between Form and Meaning*, LNTS 297 (London: Bloomsbury, 2006), 136–37. The first major proponent of a tripartite structure for Hebrews (and the first to notice some striking parallels between these verses) was Wolfgang Nauck. See Wolfgang Nauck, "Zum Aufbau des Hebräerbriefes," in *Judentum, Urchristentum, Kirche: Festschrift für Joachim Jeremias*, ed. Walther Eltester, BZNW 26 (Berlin: Töpelmann, 1960), 199–206. More recent proponents are: Cockerill, *Epistle to the Hebrews*; William L. Lane, *Hebrews 1-8*, WBC 47a (Dallas, TX: Word, 1991); James W. Thompson, *Hebrews*, Paideia (Grand Rapids, MI: Baker Academic, 2008); Hans-Friedrich Weiß, *Der Brief an die Hebräer*, KEK 13 (Göttingen: Vandenhoeck & Ruprecht, 1991).

[12]For more on continuity and God's speech in Hebrews, see Madison N. Pierce, *Divine Discourse in the Epistle to the Hebrews: The Recontextualization of Spoken Quotations of Scripture*, SNTSMS 178 (Cambridge: Cambridge University Press, 2020).

stamped on him like a coin.[13] The Son reveals the Father, and he bears or "sustains" all things by the powerful word of God (Heb 1:3).[14]

Up until now, the author has described the Son of God in terms of his very nature. These things are always true of the Son. But in Hebrews 1:3, once we finally reach the main verb of this long Greek sentence, we see a preview of what is to come. The Son, at a particular point in time, provided purification for sins, and after doing so, he sat down at the right hand of the Majesty in heaven (Heb 1:3); through this series of actions, only represented in part here, the Son is exalted above the angels, and his exaltation fits with the name that he has inherited (Heb 1:4).[15] We inherit name and status from our family—*if* our family has it to offer.

Shortly after I was born, my family was transplanted to a small town in Texas. For most of my life, I was in predominantly White schools, which meant my socioeconomic status and class mattered quite a bit. The parents and grandparents of my peers knew each other, went to school together, or played golf together. The children in my class were from prominent families in the community and had their names—their family names—on billboards and offices for doctors and lawyers. In contrast, my family's name was unknown. In that context, I had little to inherit from my name. But when I got to high school, my school was no longer predominantly White, and I suddenly had more than enough. I was rich with privilege, not because of my name, but because of my race. What we inherit must come from our parents, and when one becomes incorporated into the family of God, God the Father has much, actually *all things*, to offer.

In Hebrews 1:5, now expanding on the superior name inherited by the Son, the author introduces a dialogue. This conversation is primarily between the Father and the Son, but others play a significant role—the angels. This conversation consists of the Father speaking seven things that previously appeared within a different context in scripture. In each quotation, the Father speaks to or about him. In the first two, the angels are those that the Father does not call "son"; he does not declare himself *their* father (Heb 1:5; quoting Ps 2:7 and 2 Sam 7:14).[16] Instead, he exhorts them to worship the firstborn (Heb 1:6; quoting Deut 32:43). The introductory formula here, "when he brings the firstborn into the world," alludes to Psalm 89, and it rightly implies that this son has siblings.[17]

Hebrews 1:7 continues to speak about the angels. Here the Father says that the Son

---

[13]Michael P. Theophilus, "The Numismatic Background of Χαρακτήρ in Hebrews 1.3," *Australian Biblical Review* 64 (2016): 69-80. For more on how this relates to the familial imagery, see David A. deSilva, *Perseverance in Gratitude: A Socio-rhetorical Commentary on the Epistle to the Hebrews* (Grand Rapids, MI: Eerdmans, 2000), 89; Amy L. B. Peeler, *You Are My Son: The Family of God in the Epistle to the Hebrews*, LNTS 486 (London: T&T Clark, 2014), 17.

[14]Peeler, *You Are My Son*, 17-18.

[15]Although a majority of scholars think the name is "Son," it seems more likely to me that the name that he inherits is YHWH. So also Richard Bauckham, "The Divinity of Jesus Christ in the Epistle to the Hebrews," in *The Epistle to the Hebrews and Christian Theology*, ed. Richard Bauckham et al. (Grand Rapids, MI: Eerdmans, 2009), 21-22; Peeler, *You Are My Son*, 59-61; Jarl Henning Ulrichsen, "Διαφορώτερον ὄνομα in Hebr. 1,4 Christus als Träger des Gottesnamens," *Studia theologica* 38, no. 1 (2008): 65-75; John Webster, "One Who Is Son: Theological Reflections on the Exordium to the Epistle to the Hebrews," in *The Epistle to the Hebrews and Christian Theology*, ed. Richard Bauckham et al. (Grand Rapids, MI: Eerdmans, 2009), 93.

[16]Here and throughout this commentary, I assume that the author is drawing upon a Greek version of Jewish Scripture, though the English numeration will be used. For more on the author's use of Scripture, see Susan E. Docherty, *The Use of the Old Testament in Hebrews: A Case Study in Early Jewish Bible Interpretation*, WUNT II 260 (Tübingen: Mohr Siebeck, 2009).

[17]For more on this allusion and the reference for the quotation, see esp. Cockerill, *Epistle to the Hebrews*, 105-8; cf. Gareth Lee Cockerill, "Hebrews 1:6: Source and Significance," *Bulletin for Biblical Research* 9 (1999): 51-64.

"makes his angels winds and his servants flames of fire" (quoting Ps 104:4).[18] The angels are created, unlike the Son, who is Creator. The next quotation spoken by God, found in Hebrews 1:8-9, is spoken to the Son again. With these words from Psalm 45:6-7, the Father refers to the Son as "God" (*ho theos*) and says that his "throne will last forever." His kingdom is characterized by justice and a love of righteousness. In this way, the Son is like his Father, certainly, but the focus rests on the fact that he is faithful to his Father. This faithfulness seen in his love for righteousness and hatred of wickedness is what sets him apart from his "companions," his human siblings (Heb 1:9).[19] In this quotation, we see the author oscillate between the Son's relationship with humanity and his relationship with his Father. The latter is without true parallel, yet this web of relationships produces dynamics similar to those in human families. I have siblings, and while I had several years with my parents before my younger brother was born, most of my time with my parents has been shaped by my siblings' presence. My parents are *our* parents. In the same way, although the analogy breaks down, when we think of the Son's mission on our behalf, we realize that his entrance into this world—analogous to his own eternal generation—characterizes the Son in a significant way. Nevertheless, this chapter of Hebrews focuses on the Son's likeness to his Father, and that is certainly clear in the next quotation from Psalm 102:25-27. With it, the Father calls the Son "Lord" (*kyrie*), and he attributes the creation of the foundations of the earth and the heavens to the Son (Heb 1:10). Further, he says that the Son, who by virtue of creating these things preexisted them, will also endure them. He will remain the same, even when they disappear (Heb 1:11-12; cf. 13:8).

The author ends this series of quotations in the same way that he began—with a rhetorical question: "to which of the angels has he ever said." This question introduces his final quotation from Psalm 110:1 in which the Father says to the Son, "Sit at my right hand until I make your enemies a footstool." In its original context, this quotation is introduced with "The Lord said to my Lord. . . ." Although it does not appear in Hebrews, this formula is likely operative here as well. We know from the quotation in Hebrews 1:10-12 that the Father calls the Son "Lord." The Father promises the Son dominion. Someday all things will be placed in submission. But what about the angels? And what about the Son's companions? In his concluding comment, the author begins to answer these questions: "Are not all angels spirits in the divine service, sent to serve for the sake of those who are to inherit salvation?" Those who will inherit salvation are the humans, and the angels serve them. This description of the angels as "spirits in the divine service" likely parallels the language from the author's quotation of Psalm 104:4 in Hebrews 1:7. It not only provides a useful transition into the author's discussion of the Son's connection with humanity in Hebrews 2, but also underscores the main point, namely, that the Son is greater than the angels.

The Son and his siblings (Hebrews 2:1-18). A comparison between the Son and the angels is also present in Hebrews 2, and Hebrews 2:1-4

[18]Many say that "God"—presumably the Father—is *ho poiōn*. This is possible; however, this would render this the sole quotation that does not identify the Son as a subject or addressee in this series (so also John P. Meier, "Symmetry and Theology in the Old Testament Citations of Heb 1,5-14," *Biblica* 66, no. 4 [1985]: 504-33). Additionally, in Heb 1:10-12, the Son is portrayed as a primary agent in creation, which allows for that possibility here.

[19]Cockerill, *Epistle to the Hebrews*, 111; Koester, *Hebrews*, 195; Dana M. Harris, *Hebrews*, Exegetical Guide to the Greek New Testament (Nashville: B&H Academic, 2019), 29.

provides a bridge between it and Hebrews 1. The author indicates its connection to the previous section with *dia touto* ("for this reason") in Hebrews 2:1. This likely refers to the overall message of Hebrews 1—that the Son is commended by the Father to be superior to the angels. It is for this reason that "we must pay greater attention to what we have heard, so that we do not drift away" (Heb 2:1) because, as the author says, if God expected his people to obey the message he delivered through angels, then he certainly expects them to obey the message from his Son. But it is not just the messenger that separates these messages. The Son's—here the "Lord's"—testimony is accompanied by "signs and wonders and various miracles and by gifts of the Holy Spirit, distributed according to [God's] will" (Heb 2:4).[20] This is one of five passages in Hebrews where we see the author turn toward the audience and warn them to continue in light of the tremendous gifts of God.[21]

Hebrews 2:5 provides the reason that God has been so generous with humanity. With a similar rhetorical strategy to what we saw in Hebrews 1, he says, "Now God did not subject the coming world, about which we are speaking, to angels." Further, because the angels serve us, the world to come will be subjected to us as well. The author then offers proof from Scripture, here spoken by "someone somewhere." Various explanations for this curious citation formula have been given, but unfortunately, the author's rationale stands beyond our grasp. Even so the *effect* remains: this quotation is not tied to a person from a particular background, ethnicity, gender, or socioeconomic status. This word, in the spirit of so many other recontextualized quotations in Hebrews, could have been spoken by anyone. By any of us. Moreover, this passage speaks on behalf of all of us. Although this passage uses masculine pronouns to refer to the "person" whom God remembers and cares for, this is merely grammatical; all genders are in view. I highlight this because it is notoriously difficult to translate for those among us with strong convictions about inclusive language. How do we communicate that Psalm 8 is a message of hope for all? This is particularly troublesome in Hebrews where the author introduces some double meaning, which English cannot convey as well as Greek. There *anthrōpos* can refer to "humanity" and to a single man. This works because our perfect human representative was male, and sadly, due to persistent bias, it is unlikely that this representative at any time in human history thus far could have been female. Further, his representation of women has been diminished through the ages when we have not been considered as full image-bearers. But Psalm 8 alludes to Genesis 1:27-28, where we learn that humanity is in the image of God. The woman and the man both receive the clear directive: "Be fruitful and increase in number; fill the earth and subdue it" (NIV).

The Messiah also was not born with my ethnicity, but because White voices have been dominant in my own contexts, Jesus as a representative for *my* ethnicity is easier for me to accept. But it shouldn't be. Jesus was not "White"—neither in melanin nor in his political or social situatedness, his interaction with power. Jesus suffers death on our behalf

[20]English versions usually translate *pneumatos agiou merismois* as "gifts of the Holy Spirit" (KJV, NASB, NKJV, NLT) or "gifts of the Holy Spirit distributed" (ESV, NET, NIV, NRSV; cf. CSB). For a convincing case against this interpretation, which likely harmonizes Hebrews with Paul's "spiritual gifts" passages (e.g., Rom 12; 1 Cor 12), see David M. Allen, "The Holy Spirit as Gift or Giver? Retaining the Pentecostal Dimension of Hebrews 2.4," *Bible Translator* 59, no. 3 (2008): 151-58.

[21]For a more thorough introduction to these "warning passages," see Scot McKnight, "The Warning Passages of Hebrews: A Formal Analysis and Theological Conclusions," *Trinity Journal* 13, no. 1 (1992): 21-59.

so that we might *share* in his dominion—that we might be crowned with glory and honor too (Heb 2:10). He did not consider our honor and glory as a threat to his own; he knew that his power could not be diminished. Jesus actively sought the release of his sisters and brothers (Heb 2:14-15). He did not acknowledge their equality while continuing to ignore their pain.[22] He did not declare them "separate, but equal." In most contexts throughout history, especially in North American evangelicalism, White Christians at worst relish their power, and at best fail to extend power and space to our minoritized brothers and sisters. "We do not see all things in subjection to [Jesus]." Instead, we see things in subjection to sin, served by hatred and bias and ignorance. We see our minoritized brothers and sisters subject to another law—one set in place to control them. It demands they do everything in their power not to "startle" the majority, simply by being present. They are still subject to our bias.[23]

But we do see Jesus crowned with glory and honor.

In Hebrews 2, it is not just Jesus' representation that makes us heirs. We are his siblings, and our older brother is not ashamed of us—despite the fact that he is God and Lord and Firstborn. Rather than being ashamed, he acknowledges us; he sings with us in the assembly (Heb 2:12). He also models faith in the Father (first half of Heb 2:13 quoting Is 8:17) and presents us as those whom the Father has put in his care (second half of Heb 2:13 quoting Is 8:18). Further, "since . . . the children share flesh and blood," he shares in humanity as well. Although the theological complexities of this are beyond our scope, the author states that Jesus is made "like his brothers and sisters in every respect, so that he might become a merciful and faithful high priest" (Heb 2:17). Jesus is a perfect representative of every individual person, not just every category of person.

The call to hear his voice (Hebrews 3:1-19). As this section begins, the author calls his audience "brothers and sisters, holy" (*adelphoi hagioi*). Although this form of address is common in the New Testament, this is the first time that the author of Hebrews uses it. It seems likely, given the proximity, that the author develops his previous argument that women and men are the sisters and brothers of Christ.[24] These holy siblings are those who are "holy . . . partners in a heavenly calling" (Heb 3:1). This verse is a great encouragement to those who wrestle with their vocation—or those whose vocation has been called into question—because we share a calling that transcends our individual calls to particular ministries. This "heavenly calling" is "an invitation to and from heaven. God's people are invited to enter the heavenly Most Holy Place (4:14-16; 10:19-25)."[25] In Hebrews 3:2, the author introduces a comparison with Moses. Moses was faithful in God's house (Heb 3:2, 5), "to testify to the things that would be spoken later" (Heb 3:5). This latter commendation of Moses fits well with the series in Hebrews 11. As we shall see, Moses is praised for bearing witness to a reality that extends beyond his own

---

[22]He also did not actively argue against their equality as my White brothers and sisters have.

[23]In "Letter from a Birmingham Jail" (April 16, 1963), Martin Luther King Jr. said, "I have almost reached the regrettable conclusion that the Negro's great stumbling block in the stride toward freedom is not the White Citizen's Council-er or the Ku Klux Klanner, but the white moderate who is more devoted to 'order' than to justice; who prefers a negative peace which is the absence of tension to a positive peace which is the presence of justice; who constantly says 'I agree with you in the goal you seek, but I can't agree with your methods of direct action.'"

[24]Cockerill, *Epistle to the Hebrews*, 159; Harris, *Hebrews*, 68; Luke Timothy Johnson, *Hebrews: A Commentary*, NTL (Louisville, KY: Westminster John Knox, 2006), 105; Koester, *Hebrews*, 242.

[25]Cockerill, *Epistle to the Hebrews*, 158.

experiences. The faithfulness or trustworthiness of Moses is attested in Numbers 12:7: "He is faithful in all my house" (*en holō tō oikō mou pistos estin*). There Aaron and Miriam criticized Moses for marrying a Cushite (or "Ethiopian"; LXX) woman,[26] and God speaks on his behalf. The Lord descends in the pillar and addresses them directly explaining that prophets receive his words in visions and dreams, but Moses hears from him directly, plainly. "[Moses] beholds the form of the Lord" (Num 12:8). Moses was able to approach God. In Moses' day, this was exceptional, but the author of Hebrews will soon encourage each and every one of us to draw near.

But Moses is introduced in comparison with Jesus. Moses is faithful as a "servant," or better a "steward" (*therapōn*; cf. Ex 14:31);[27] Jesus is faithful as a Son *over* God's house. In other words, he is not a hired worker or a tenant; the house is his inheritance. This comparison continues into the next section. Even though all God's people are imagined as those on the same journey through the wilderness, some generations were not able to reach God's promised rest. This is particularly true of Moses' generation. At the end of this comparison, where various relationships are articulated, "we" are told our place in the schema: "we are his house[hold?] [*oikos*] if we hold firm the boldness and the pride inspired by hope" (Heb 3:6). Within this passage, *oikos* clearly refers to a "house" that has been constructed by the "builder of all things" (*o panta kataskeuasas*, Heb 3:4), but it could also refer to a "household" since family language has been so prevalent to this point.[28] Nevertheless, we are a part of this entity, "if we hold firm the boldness and the pride inspired by hope" (Heb 3:6).

Our conditional inclusion in the *oikos* of God is supported through a quotation from Scripture, specifically from Psalm 95:7-11 (Ψ Ps 94:7-11). Here the author uses a distinctive introductory formula: "Therefore [*dio*], as the Holy Spirit says." As we have seen, it is not unusual for the author of Hebrews to introduce a quotation as the speech of God (Heb 1:5-13; 2:12-13). Both the Father and Son have spoken, which happens elsewhere in the New Testament (see, e.g., Rom 10:18-21); however, the Holy Spirit only speaks Scripture in two places in the New Testament—here and Hebrews 10:16-17.

The lengthy quotation serves the author's warning to the present audience to continue faithfully, heeding the words of the Spirit of God, who is envisioned as the one who journeys with them in the wilderness, perhaps as the pillar of cloud and fire.[29] In the Spirit's speech, we find that the *Spirit* was the one tested by the ancestors, so he became angry and prohibited them from entering into *his* rest. Although this is not explicit in Hebrews, the combination of rest, testing, and the wilderness likely evokes additional intertextual allusions to Isaiah 63, where the wilderness generation rebels against the Holy Spirit

[26]Much could be said about the narrative in Num 12, but here I acknowledge that the curse pronounced upon Miriam is that her skin becomes white with lepra.

[27]Cockerill, *Epistle to the Hebrews*, 167-68.

[28]James Earl Massey, "Hebrews," in *True to Our Native Land: An African American New Testament Commentary*, ed. Brian K. Blount et al. (Minneapolis: Fortress Press, 2007), 449. This mixed use of the metaphor also appears in Eph 2:19-22. There we are "members of the household of God" built into a "dwelling place for God."

[29]The argument in this section is built upon many claims that cannot be established in full here. But in short, I assume that the so-called pilgrimage (I prefer "journeying") motif is operative in Hebrews, esp. in Heb 3–4, and I assume that the Spirit is the primary divine agent throughout this section. For more, see Pierce, *Divine Discourse in Hebrews*, chap. 4. See also Jennifer T. Kaalund, *Reading Hebrews and 1 Peter with the African American Great Migration: Diaspora, Place and Identity*, LNTS 598 (London: Bloomsbury T&T Clark, 2018), chap. 4.

(Is 63:10), who gave them rest (Is 63:14). This also connects with traditions about Sophia in Wisdom of Solomon and Sirach, where Sophia leads the Israelites (Wis 10:17) and offers them rest (Wis 8:16; Sir 6:28). Some contemporary authors, especially Philo,[30] moved away from depicting Wisdom as Sophia, a woman who acts on God's behalf, but not the author of Wisdom of Solomon, who portrays Sophia as a woman leading the Israelites and protecting them from enemies. Sophia is a female personification that early Christian writers often parallel with both Jesus and the Spirit. The author of Hebrews draws parallels between Sophia and Jesus in Hebrews 1, and here he draws parallels between Sophia and the Spirit.

At the end of the author's quotation from Psalm 95:7-11, he turns toward a more targeted exhortation (Heb 3:12-14). What is important to note here, in the midst of this second "warning passage," is that this passage is focused on caring for those within one's community, not caring for oneself (paraphrasing): "Make sure no one is falling behind and encourage one another because we are partakers of Christ—if we persevere."

On this journey, some will grow weary, and they will need help. But of course, malaise is not the only problem. Those whom the author addresses are willingly stopping their journey. They are "[turn] away from the living God" (Heb 3:12)—leaving the clearly marked path. Those hearing these words from the author of Hebrews might say, "That would *never* happen to me"; however, if it can happen to the wilderness generation, it can happen to anyone.[31]

The promise of Rest (Hebrews 4:1-11). Even though Hebrews 3:7-19 uses Psalm 95 to *warn* the audience not to repeat the sins of their ancestors, the author of Hebrews has not exhausted his application of this passage. Hebrews 4:1-11 now uses the psalm to encourage them. The failure of our ancestors to "enter" (Heb 3:19) means that promise still stands (Heb 4:1). Like the exhortation in Hebrews 3:12-14, here the author's exhortation focuses on their role within the community. They are to "take care that none of [them] should seem to have failed to reach it" (Heb 4:1). Then the author highlights the continuity between the two generations (past and present): both heard the "good news" (*euēngelismenoi*) of the promised rest. But the previous generation did not "benefit" from what they heard "because they were not united by faith with those who listened" (Heb 4:2).[32]

They "[enter] that rest, just as God has said. . . ." The author again quotes Psalm 95:11, citing particular verses to support different parts of his argument as it develops. Then he introduces another passage to serve his point—Genesis 2:2 (Heb 4:4). By linking the promised rest proclaimed by the Spirit ("my" rest) in Psalm 95 with God's rest at creation, the author clarifies that God is inviting humanity into the rest that he has enjoyed since the seventh day of creation when his works were completed; God has been resting since "the foundation of the world" (Heb 4:3). This is a promise for

---

[30]It is often suggested that this is due to Sophia's gender (e.g., Joseph R. Dodson, *The "Powers" of Personification: Rhetorical Purpose in the Book of Wisdom and the Letter to the Romans*, BZNW 161 [Berlin: de Gruyter, 2008], 87). To this end, in *Fug.* 51, Philo argues that, though her name is female, she is clearly male.

[31]Likewise, the quotation of Ps 95:7-11 in Hebrews has a *dio* inserted at the beginning of Heb 3:10. This reading, unlike others, describes a forty-year period of God's works, rather than a forty-year period of God's anger. Both are found in the Pentateuch, where the wilderness is a place where God provides abundantly for the Israelites for forty years (Deut 2:7; 8:4; 29:4; cf. Amos 2:10), but he is angry for that long also (Num 14:33, 34; 32:13). Even though here in the quotation God's works last for forty years, the author of Hebrews also attests to his anger lasting this long in his series of rhetorical questions (Heb 3:17).

[32]For this interpretation of Heb 4:2, see Cockerill, *Epistle to the Hebrews*, 203; so also Harris, *Hebrews*, 94.

every person to enter this space where God has been all along.

The possibility to enter that rest remains because the previous generation did not do so. To demonstrate that this promise is available for the audience, the author returns to Psalm 95 again. This time he highlights a single word: "today." That is the day that rest is available to those who hear God's voice. This is what was declared when God spoke in the psalms. But what is this "rest"? It is *not* the promised land of Canaan. If it were, then rest would not be available for us because "if Joshua had given them rest [by bringing them into the land], God would not speak later about another day" (Heb 4:8). Again, the author reminds his audience that *rest remains* available (Heb 4:9).[33] The author communicates more about the implications of this rest in Hebrews 4:10, as someone has already reached it. "For the one who entered into [his] rest has himself also rested from his works just as God did from his."[34] Christ, as our forerunner, has gone before us into this rest. "Let us therefore make every effort to enter that rest, so that no one may fall through such disobedience as theirs." We strive to be faithful and to ensure that no one fails to enter the promised rest.

THE TABERNACLE OF GOD (HEBREWS 4:11–10:25)

The great high priest (Hinge: Hebrews 4:11-16). The final exhortation of the previous section also technically falls within the first major hinge for the Epistle to the Hebrews. As mentioned in the "Structure" section above, the three major sections of Hebrews are separated by two transitional sections that summarize the section before and preview the section after.[35] The two hinges have not only similar rhetorical functions, but also structure and language:

Both hinges contain three hortatory subjunctives and appear to mirror one another, resulting in an A-B-C-C'-B'-A' pattern.

As for the content of Hebrews 4:11-16 itself, as well as its relationship to the surrounding material, this section summarizes several elements from Hebrews 1:1–4:11. First, of course, is the reference to the immediately preceding section in Hebrews 4:11. Next, the author turns toward the "word of God." Many see this as a reference to the Word of God generally, or the word of God that has come through Psalm 95 specifically; however, if this section provides a recapitulation of the argument of Hebrews thus far, the "word of God" likely also refers to the speech of "God" (Father, Son, and Spirit)

Table 22.1. Hebrews 4 and Hebrews 10

Hebrews 4	Hebrews 10
Hebrews 4:11—Let us make therefore make every effort [*Spoudasōmen*] to enter that rest.	**Hebrews 10:22**—Let us approach [*proserchōmetha*] with a true heart.
Hebrews 4:14—Let us hold fast [*kratōmen*] to our confession.	**Hebrews 10:23**—Let us hold fast [*katechōmen*] to the confession of our hope without wavering.
Hebrews 4:16—Let us approach [*proserchōmetha*] the throne of grace with boldness . . .	**Hebrews 10:24**—Let us consider [*katanoōmen*] how to provoke one another to love and good deeds.

[33]Here *sabbatismos* rather than *katapausis* is used. "The [choice of *sabbatismos*], at the very least, indicates that the promise offered to God's people now is no longer that of a material possession, but of a participation in the divine life." See Johnson, *Hebrews*, 129.

[34]For this translation and more on this christological interpretation of Heb 4:10, see Nicholas J. Moore, "Jesus as 'the One Who Entered His Rest': The Christological Reading of Hebrews 4.10," *Journal for the Study of the New Testament* 36, no. 4 (2014): 383-400.

[35]For a more thorough development of this proposal, see Westfall, *Discourse Analysis of the Letter to the Hebrews*, 136-37.

thus far in Hebrews, as well as references to God speaking throughout history and "in these last days" (Heb 1:1-2). The description of the "word" that comes next corresponds best with the warning from the Spirit in Hebrews 3–4, since it "separates" those who are faithful and unfaithful with its sharp sword. Still, it is likely that the recipients' "thoughts and attitudes" (*enthymēseōn kai ennoiōn*) toward the Father's commendation of the Son as God and Lord (Heb 1:5-14) and the Son's faithful trust in the Father (Heb 2:12-13) are also in view. Hebrews 4:14-16 shifts toward a more overt discussion of Jesus as our great high priest. This section also has connections with what precedes. For example, Jesus is explicitly referred to as "Son of God" (Heb 4:14), which connects with the author's discussion in Hebrews 1. Hebrews 4:15 describes the empathy of Jesus, who was tested in every way. This verse emphasizes the extent of Jesus' humanity—his solidarity with his brothers and sisters, which was the author's main point in Hebrews 2.[36]

The author also previews what is to come, and some of the author's summary of his previous material pivots in a way that foreshadows how it will be developed in the next section. For example, the testing of Jesus, here, is proof that our great high priest is able to empathize with us. As we shall see, that language will appear again very soon in the author's discussion of why priests must be "from among mortals" (Heb 5:1). Moreover, the language of "entering rest" (Heb 4:11) develops as hints of the heavenly tabernacle emerge in the author's language of his sacrifice and approaching God's throne of grace (Heb 4:16).

The Son and the Levites (Hebrews 5:1-10). Although many consider Hebrews 5 a contrast between Jesus and the Levitical priests, the author's primary aim is to present Jesus as a *high* priest. He does this by comparing, not contrasting, Jesus with other high priests.[37] Like them, he is human and able to serve on behalf of humanity—"represent them" (Heb 5:1), and he can "deal gently" with humanity because he also is subject to weakness (Heb 5:2). This is why, if/when the high priest sins, an offering is prescribed for him, one that corresponds to the offering that he makes on behalf of the people (Heb 5:3).[38] No (legitimate) high priest in human history was able to choose to be a high priest—to choose to be born in the line of Levi within the line of Aaron and then to be selected. Instead, God ordains him; he calls him, just as he did with Aaron (Heb 5:4). The Levitical high priests were born into a place of privilege, given opportunities that others were not, and at least once, with Korah and those whom he led in rebellion (Num 16), this caused a significant rift among the people of God. The cry of Korah was (Num 16:3): "All the congregation are holy, every one of them, and the Lord is among them. So why then do you exalt yourselves above the assembly of the Lord?" Korah questioned the special calling of the sons of Aaron. He and his family were Levites too, Kohathites, but they carried the items from the tabernacle while the people of God were in transit. They were only permitted to touch them once the priests had wrapped them up. If they did not follow these instructions, they would die (see Num 4). Korah insists that the

[36]Additionally, the author entreats them to "hold fast to [our] confession," which connects with Heb 3:1, where Jesus is the "apostle and high priest of our confession."

[37]He begins, "Every high priest . . ." (Heb 5:1). Hebrews 8:3 has the same language and more clearly has Jesus in view. A similar claim is made by Bryan R. Dyer, "'One Does Not Presume to Take This Honor': The Development of the High Priestly Appointment and Its Significance for Hebrews 5:4," *Conversations with the Biblical World* 33 (2013): 125-46.

[38]This does not imply that Jesus sinned, only that, *if* he sinned, he too would need to make an offering.

high priests "set themselves above" the rest, but as Hebrews says, they received this privilege from God (Heb 5:4). This is not true for many privileged groups today, especially my own. God did not call White people to privilege; we took it. We are not like these high priests who were called to a distinguished position of service. Their lives were not easier because they were high priests; they depended on the gifts of others for their well-being (Num 18:28, 30-31) and received no inheritance of their own (Num 18:23). We, on the other hand, even if we do not actively *pursue* benefits that come from our "race" and ethnicity, we receive them nonetheless.

Jesus did not glorify himself (Heb 5:5), nor elevate himself to a place of privilege. He did not choose to be a priest, but as we shall see (e.g., in Heb 10:5-7), he did choose to become human and to be "made lower than the angels" (Heb 2:7). But God *did* glorify him, when he said, "You are my Son" (Heb 5:5), and "You are a priest forever" (Heb 5:6). These quotations likely point back to the series in Hebrews 1:5-14, since that catena opens with Psalm 2:7 and ends with Psalm 110:1. The author points backward to remind his readers what he established through those quotations, but by quoting Psalm 110:4 here, he also adds to our portrait of the Son. He is a Son, and he is a (high) priest.[39]

Nevertheless, stating that God appointed Jesus to be high priest raises the question: When? At what point does Jesus begin to serve in this capacity? This is an important question for Hebrews. Although many would assert that Jesus served as a priest on earth, and by extension that his "offering" took place on the cross, a growing number would argue that the author of Hebrews presents Jesus becoming qualified to serve as priest upon his resurrection.[40] Hebrews 5:7-10 is one of the key passages to support that claim. When Jesus was on earth, he "offered" prayers, petitions, loud cries, and tears to the one who could save him "out of death" (*ek thanatou*).[41] Jesus was "heard because of his reverent submission" (Heb 5:7). Through "what he suffered" (*aph' ōn epathen*), he "learned obedience" (*emathen tēn hypakoēn*; Heb 5:8), and then "*having been made perfect*, he became the source of eternal salvation for all who obey him, having been designated by God a high priest according to the order of Melchizedek" (Heb 5:9-10, emphasis mine).[42] No matter where one lands on that interpretive issue, the portrait of Jesus here is one of submission to the Father, even at his death.

The need for maturity (Hebrews 5:11–6:12). At Hebrews 5:11, the author stops and expresses his desire that the audience be able to hear more of what he has to say. They are, effectively, infants (Heb 5:12-13), who should be teachers but are not mature enough to partake of "solid food" (Heb 5:12, 14). But then the author calls them to move beyond the "basic elements," some of which he mentions (Heb 6:1-3), and soon returns to his discussion of Melchizedek

[39]For more on the connection between sonship and priesthood, see Amy L. B. Peeler, "If Son, Then Priest: The Filial Foundation of Ordination in Hebrews and Other New Testament Texts," in *Listen, Understand, Obey: Essays in Honor of Gareth Lee Cockerill*, ed. Caleb T Friedeman (Eugene, OR: Pickwick, 2017), 95-115. There Peeler also develops an argument for something akin to the "priesthood of all believers," which fits well with the present emphasis on the connection between Jesus' humanity and his priesthood.

[40]See, especially, David M. Moffitt, *Atonement and the Logic of Resurrection in the Epistle to the Hebrews*, NovTSup 141 (Leiden: Brill, 2011). See also R. B. Jamieson, *Jesus' Death and Heavenly Offering in Hebrews*, SNTSMS 172 (New York: Cambridge University Press, 2019), 23-35.

[41]Moffitt, *Atonement and the Logic*, 191-92.

[42]For a more thorough discussion of perfection and this passage, which largely follows Moffitt, see Pierce, *Divine Discourse in Hebrews*, 129-33.

at Hebrews 6:13. What stands between is another exhortation they persevere.

Hebrews 5:11–6:12 is considered one of the "warning passages," as well as a "digression"; however, a key point in the argument of Hebrews continues to develop: the gifts of this covenant are better, while the punishments are harsher. The gifts for those who partake of the new covenant, from my perspective, are those outlined in Hebrews 6:4-5. Believers have been "enlightened and have tasted the heavenly gift and have shared in the Holy Spirit and have tasted the good word of God and the powers of the age to come."[43] They have experienced God—Father, Son, and Spirit. If the ones who experience God in this way fail to complete their journey, to enter the promised rest, then it is "impossible" for them to be restored. Christ's once for all work is sufficient for all and cannot be repeated (Heb 6:6). As the author says, the grace of God is extended to all, like rain on the ground, and yet the rain has not failed if the ground produces thorns and thistles (Heb 6:7-8). The author offers this harsh warning, but also encourages them, saying he is "confident of better things in [their] case" (Heb 6:9). God will reward them if they persist and imitate those who will inherit (6:10-12).

The oath (Hebrews 6:13-20). Although this commentary follows many others that present a break in the text before Hebrews 6:13, the transition is not as stark as some scholars suggest. The exhortation in the previous section ends with the call to be "imitators of those who through faith *and patience* inherit the promises" (Heb 6:12, emphasis mine). In Hebrews 11, the author reveals the identity of some of these heirs—"those who inherit." They are those who acted "by faith" (*pistei*). Yet "did not receive what was promised" (Heb 11:39). For generations, they have waited.

What if they are waiting for nothing? What if *we* are waiting for nothing?

Turning back to Hebrews 6:13-20, the author assures his readers with a reminder about the certainty of God's Word. He begins with an example—the promise to Abraham in Genesis 22:17, which comes after he demonstrates that he is willing to sacrifice Isaac (Heb 6:13-14). This is the first time that God "swears" (from *omnymi* or *šb*ʿ) something; he swears "by himself" (Heb 6:13); and this is the final iteration of the promise to Abraham (cf. Gen 12:2; 15:5). After being "patient," Abraham received what was promised (Heb 6:15). The author of Hebrews presents this as evidence for the argument that follows about the certainty of the oath that God has sworn to all the heirs. God swore, not because God needs to swear to fulfill his word; he swears because he "desired to show even more clearly" the "unchangeable character of his purpose" (Heb 6:17). He did this "we who have taken refuge might be strongly encouraged to seize the hope set before us" (Heb 6:18). That hope is an anchor, something that keeps our souls firmly in place and enters the inner sanctuary, joining our forerunner, Jesus, the priest in the likeness of Melchizedek.

The One like Melchizedek (Hebrews 7:1-28). Seamlessly, the author turns back to the priesthood of Jesus, but before the author can say too much, he must explain who this "Melchizedek" is. In Hebrews 7:1-2, the author of Hebrews begins by telling us that Melchizedek was a "King Melchizedek of Salem . . . priest of the Most High God" (Gen 14:18) who met Abraham after his defeat of many kings (Gen 14:17) and who blessed Abraham

[43]For other views on this passage, see Herbert Bateman IV, ed., *Four Views on the Warning Passages in Hebrews* (Grand Rapids, MI: Kregel Academic, 2007).

(Gen 14:19). Then the author of Hebrews proceeds to an explanation of the Hebrew: "Melchizedek" means "righteous king," and "salem" means "peace." To this point, the portrait of Melchizedek in Hebrews is consistent with the one in Genesis; however, at Hebrews 7:3, a divergence occurs: "Without father, without mother, without genealogy, having neither beginning of days nor end of life but resembling the Son of God, [Melchizedek] remains a priest forever."

The basis for this claim from the author is disputed. For example, some think he is exploiting the lack of details in the Abraham narrative, since the birth, death, and lineage of Melchizedek is not mentioned.[44] But Scripture later does speak about this priest's perpetuity (Ps 110:4). Moreover, in extrabiblical literature, Melchizedek is a legendary figure who is presented in parallel with Michael the archangel (4Q544 3 IV, 2-3), one who serves as a priest (4Q401 11 I, 1-2), and one who brings eschatological judgment (11QMelch II, 23-25).[45] The author of Hebrews introduces none of those extrabiblical details explicitly; thus, no literary dependence can be established, yet the lore it represents appears to be operative here.

In Hebrews 7:4, the author substantiates his preeminence in another way—Abraham himself pays him a tenth of his spoils! Even though he is not a Levite, he still receives this priestly benefit (Heb 7:6). Additionally, he blesses Abraham (Heb 7:7), and Melchizedek *lives* (Heb 7:8). Both of these things are offered by the author of Hebrews as evidence of Melchizedek's superiority, and the author makes one final suggestion. The presence of Levi in the "loins" of Abraham—his genealogy—might serve as evidence that Melchizedek is greater than the Levitical priests. But this is not the end of the comparison.

Hebrews 7:11 introduces the necessity for another priesthood. The first did not offer perfection. In fact, the mere presence of the other priesthood calls for the first's evaluation: "Now if perfection had been attainable through the Levitical priesthood . . . what further need would there have been to speak of another priest arising according to the order of Melchizedek rather than one according to the order of Aaron?" Insufficient or not, the Levitical priesthood was legislated, and the other must be too. The author goes on to remind his readers that this priesthood is not different in name only. Jesus is not qualified to be a "Levitical" priest because he is not a Levite. He was not born into that particular position. Instead, "it is evident," says the author, "that our Lord was descended from Judah" (Heb 7:14). God overturns the priestly establishment—opting instead for a line that began with the youngest son of a shepherd. Torah says nothing legislating a priest from the line of Judah (Heb 7:14), but such a priest appears! Nevertheless, unlike the Levitical priests, he is not qualified to serve "not through a legal requirement concerning physical descent but through the power of an indestructible life" (Heb 7:16).[46] An indestructible

[44]Many refer specifically to the rabbinic principle *quod non in thora non in mundo* ("what is not in Torah is not in the world"). See, for example, Joseph A. Fitzmyer, "'Now This Melchizedek' (Heb 7:1)," *Catholic Biblical Quarterly* 25, no. 3 (1963): 305-21; Joseph A. Fitzmyer, "Further Light on Melchizedek from Qumran Cave 11," *Journal of Biblical Literature* 86, no. 1 (1967): 25-41; Fred L. Horton Jr., *The Melchizedek Tradition: A Critical Examination of the Sources to the Fifth Century AD and in the Epistle to the Hebrews* (Cambridge: Cambridge University Press, 1976).

[45]For more on the presentation of Melchizedek in these texts, see Eric F. Mason, *"You Are a Priest Forever": Second Temple Jewish Messianism and the Priestly Christology of the Epistle to the Hebrews* (Leiden: Brill, 2008).

[46]Hebrews 7:3 is sometimes read as describing both Melchizedek and Jesus; however, Jesus "clearly" has a genealogy (Heb 7:16), whereas Melchizedek has none. This priesthood is *not* on the basis of genealogy—or a lack thereof. For more, see Pierce, *Divine Discourse in Hebrews*, 72-73.

life that qualifies him to serve as a priest "forever" (Heb 7:17, quoting Ps 110:4). The former, as the author has said (Heb 7:11), does not offer perfection, and thus, it has been set aside, making way for the hope "through which we approach God" (Heb 7:19).

This hope is certain because it comes through an oath (cf. Heb 6:13-20). Lest someone question whether God might decide to install yet another priest, the author reminds his readers that this priest, who serves forever, became a priest through an oath. In Hebrews 7:21, the author of Hebrews quotes Psalm 110:4 for the third time (in addition to clear allusions), and for the first time, he introduces the speech with the quotation formula from the psalm: "The Lord has sworn and will not change his mind." God who cannot lie and whose word is true has installed this perpetual priest. This is wholly different from what people have experienced before. Every other priest has died (Heb 7:23-24), and thus, their intercession was bounded (Heb 7:25). But this high priest lives forever (Heb 7:24). Further, he is "holy, blameless, undefiled, separated from sinners, and exalted above the heavens" (Heb 7:26). His ministry is not hurried, nor is it on his own behalf (Heb 7:27). He made the self-offering once because he has been made perfect forever (Heb 7:28).

The new covenant (Hebrews 8:1-13). After concluding his discussion of Jesus as a priest in the likeness of Melchizedek, the author of Hebrews (again) connects what he has just said to the main points of his argument to follow. Most importantly, he makes clear that the high priest that he just described—the one who is blameless, appointed with an oath, and enduring—is *our* priest (Heb 8:1), and this priest serves in a heavenly space, set up by the Lord (Heb 8:2).

The author develops his argument in a way that parallels Hebrews 5. There, he begins, "Every priest . . ."; here, it is "every high priest. . ." The ministry of Jesus is consistently brought into parallel with the established ministry of the earthly priests. Every high priest makes offerings (Heb 8:3). Earthly offerings are prescribed by Torah, which installs *Levitical* priests (Heb 8:4). This supports the author's argument that this high priest does not serve in the earthly tabernacle. That tabernacle was constructed to serve as a "sketch" or "copy" or "shadow" of the one in heaven. Since it pointed toward that heavenly reality, its specifications were of the utmost importance (Heb 8:5). Jesus does not make "earthly" offerings or serve in the earthly tabernacle. Instead, he offers something "better": "has now obtained a more excellent ministry, and to that degree he is the mediator of a better covenant, which has been enacted through better promises" (Heb 8:6-7). Those "better promises" are likely the oaths and declarations that God has spoken thus far (e.g., Heb 5:5-6, esp. Ps 110:4).[47] These enduring commitments from God install a perpetual priest, who mediates a superior covenant, one that God declared upon finding fault with the prior priests.

But what is "new" about this covenant? And when is it "coming"? The latter question is easier to answer; the inauguration or "coming" of this covenant is likely at Jesus' death.[48] It is essential for atonement in Hebrews, even

[47]Moffitt argues that these promises are those contained within the quotation itself. See Moffitt, *Atonement and the Logic*, 232-33. This is a possibility, but it would seem that rather than being the "promises" on which the covenant is "established" or "legislated" that these promises from Jeremiah are instead the benefits. Certainty is not possible on this point, however, because the author of Hebrews uses "promise(s)" in many ways.

[48]David M. Moffitt, "Wilderness Identity and Pentateuchal Narrative: Distinguishing Between Jesus' Inauguration and Maintenance of the New Covenant in Hebrews," in *Muted Voices of the New Testament: Readings in the Catholic Epistles and Hebrews*, ed. Katherine M. Hockey, Madison N. Pierce, and Francis Watson, LNTS 565 (London: T&T Clark, 2017), 153-71.

though Jesus' once-for-all offering takes place in the heavenly tabernacle.[49] The degree to which this covenant is "new" proves to be a more complicated question, and yet it is of utmost importance for understanding Hebrews as a whole. At the conclusion of this quotation, the author says, "In speaking of a new covenant, he has made the first one obsolete, and what is obsolete and growing old will soon disappear" (Heb 8:13). If the author of Hebrews simply regards the first covenant to be defunct and flawed, then he could be accused of advocating for a harsh supersessionist or even anti-Jewish reading of Jeremiah 31, a text that promises restoration for God's people, specifically those identified as the "house of Judah" and "house of Israel." But rather than being a covenant that is wholly "new," this is a covenant that is "renewed," though enhanced at its renewal. Now the laws will be written on their hearts *by God* (Jer 31:33). All will know the Lord. Further, God will no longer remember their sins as they have been forgiven (Jer 31:34). The author of Hebrews introduces a distinct mediator, Jesus, but his description of the new covenant comes from Jeremiah. This is, therefore, a christological reading of Jeremiah, but not the author "[using] the Old Testament against [itself]."[50] The promised covenant is not taken from Israel and Judah, but its benefits are extended to the readers, whatever their ethnic background. Here again, we see that the gifts of God are not a "zero sum" game.

The tabernacles (Hebrews 9:1-10). After his brief (one-verse) explanation of Jeremiah 31, the author turns to describing regulations regarding the spaces where the covenants will be administered—the two tabernacles. He begins with the "earthly" or "worldly" (*kosmikos*). The tent is "built" (*kataskeuazō*)[51] and has a "first" and a "second" room.[52] The first, likely the Holy Place, contains the golden lampstand, a table, and the "presentation of breads" (*ē prothesis tōn argōn*).[53] The most holy place, in Hebrews' presentation, contains the altar of incense and the ark of the covenant, which contained the jar of manna, staff of Aaron, and tablets of the covenant. As Gary A. Anderson argues, the tabernacle *and* its furniture signify the presence of God, which provides an important analogy for the incarnation.[54] In Hebrews 9, the author names a number of items that would have rich significance for his readers. This furniture and the tabernacle, where the presence of God was thick like the smoke from the altar, offered priests their most "real" encounter with YHWH. Each element has its own distinctive significance, but since their mere mention is likely enough for his main point, the author does not need, nor does he desire, to "speak now in detail" (Heb 9:5).

Remembering that the author portrays his readers in the wilderness with their ancestors

[49]Moffitt, *Atonement and the Logic*. For another proposal that places much more emphasis on the death of Jesus, see Jamieson, *Jesus' Death and Heavenly Offering in Hebrews*.

[50]Walter Brueggemann, *The Theology of the Book of Jeremiah*, Old Testament Theology (New York: Cambridge University Press, 2006), 191.

[51]The occurrence of *kataskeuazō* prior to this is in Heb 3:4 (author translation) where the author declares, "God is the one who builds everything."

[52]In Heb 9:2-3, the author explicitly refers to these as the "first tent" (*skenē . . . ē prōtē*) and "second veil" (*to deuteron katapetasma*). The terminology and background for this section is complex and disputed. For a recent overview, see Benjamin J. Ribbens, *Levitical Sacrifice and Heavenly Cult in Hebrews*, BZNW 222 (Berlin: Walter de Gruyter, 2016), 102-13.

[53]Translation via Attridge, *Hebrews*, 233.

[54]Early Jewish authors argue that these items also had cosmological significance. "The four colors on the curtain recalled the four elements, the seven branches of the lampstand symbolized the seven 'planets,' the twelve loaves stood for the twelve months, and the incense altar indicated thanksgiving for the elements." For this and more, see Koester, *Hebrews*, 401-2.

(see above), it makes sense that he would move from the necessity of setting up the tent to the ministry contained therein. He describes the roles of its ministers next. The priests, a limited group, entered the outer room to complete their ministry (Heb 9:6). Further, the high priest, a single person, entered the inner room, the most holy place, but only once a year with the sole purpose of making the prescribed offering (Heb 9:7). "By this the Holy Spirit indicates that the way into the sanctuary has not yet been disclosed as long as the first tent is still standing" (Heb 9:8). The current tent obstructs one's view of the most holy place, and yet by the Spirit, they see that there is more. The location of this "most holy place" is unclear. On the one hand, the earthly tabernacle has been the focus thus far (Heb 9:1-7), but on the other, readers are anticipating the comparison with the heavenly, which provided the plans for the earthly.[55] Given the focus on "access" as well as the following comment about the limitations of the earthly offerings (Heb 9:9-10), it seems likely that the heavenly tabernacle is in view.[56] Thus, through the limitations of the first covenant in terms of access as well as the necessity for repeated offerings (that still did not cleanse the conscience), the Holy Spirit showed that the way into the holiest of all holy places, the most holy place in the heavenly tabernacle, had not been revealed.[57] This highlights the didactic function of the earthly system that comes through its "confessed inadequacy."[58] Some Jewish literature from this time period suggests that people looked forward to access—not just to the earthly tabernacle—but to the heavenly space as well. The message of Hebrews is not to wait, but to enter that space *now*.[59]

Nevertheless, the space is not the only contrast. The author is not making the point that just the high priests or just the priests or just the Levites have access to the holy space. The heavenly tabernacle—the holiest of all spaces—is for everyone. Therefore, this is a space for *us*. Historic divisions among the people of God are eliminated. Further, this privileged place of priestly service is not restricted to a particular class, a particular ethnicity, or a particular gender. Those who have been asked to "remain silent in the churches," and those who have been seated in their own sections, the balconies, or sent to their "own" churches across town, they enter the holiest space with every benefit of God's promise.

The ministries (Hebrews 9:11-28). Hebrews 9:11 marks a clear shift to the ministry of Christ in contrast to the ministries of the priests and high priests of the earthly covenant. When he "came" (cf. Heb 10:5) as the high priest of the "good things that are coming" (au. trans.),[60] he

---

[55]Cockerill, *Epistle to the Hebrews*, 381-82.

[56]Félix H. Cortez, *Within the Veil: The Ascension of the Son in the Letter to the Hebrews*, Studies in Jewish and Christian Literature (Dallas: Fontes Press, 2021), 229-33.

[57]"Understood in this sense, 9.8 indicates that just as the most holy place cannot be seen because of the outer tent, so also the *true* or *heavenly* most holy place could not be seen while the first tent (i.e. the whole tabernacle system) existed." See Nicholas J. Moore, *Repetition in Hebrews: Plurality and Singularity in the Letter to the Hebrews, Its Ancient Context, and the Early Church*, WUNT II 388 (Tübingen: Mohr Siebeck, 2015), 183.

[58]George B. Caird, "Exegetical Method of the Epistle to the Hebrews," *Canadian Journal of Theology* 5, no. 1 (1959): 47.

[59]For more on the heavenly temple and tabernacle in Jewish literature and Hebrews, see Philip Church, *Hebrews and the Temple: Attitudes to the Temple in Second Temple Judaism and in Hebrews*, NovTSup 171 (Leiden: Brill, 2017); Benjamin J. Ribbens, *Levitical Sacrifice and Heavenly Cult in Hebrews*, BZNW 222 (Berlin: Walter de Gruyter, 2016).

[60]NA28 reads *genomenōn*, found in P46 B D*, rather than *mellontōn*, found in ℵ A D^2 I^{vid}. The latter could easily be explained by assimilation to Hebrews 10:1, and thus the decision of NA28 seems reasonable. Nevertheless, my translation "coming" fits with either reading and allows that *genomenōn* could be a stylistic variation on *mellontōn* (or vice versa—though the author uses *mellontōn* far more) or inceptive with more focus on what has "come" in addition to the expectation that more is coming. For the latter, see, e.g., Harris, *Hebrews*, 222; William L. Lane, *Hebrews 9–13*, WBC 47b (Dallas: Word, 1991), 229.

passed through the "greater perfect tent (not made with hands)" (Heb 9:11), entering "once for all" (Heb 9:12). The contrast continues as the author highlights his *self*-offering. He does not bring animal blood, but carries his own blood to the altar, "obtaining eternal redemption" (*eis ta hagia aiōnian lytrōsin heuramenos*, Heb 9:12). For if the blood of bulls and goats was able to sanctify them in part, then how much more will this perfect, willing self-offering accomplish? This offering is given to God through the eternal Spirit (Heb 9:14).[61]

Christ's ability to cleanse the people effectively is the reason that he has been designated the "mediator" of this new covenant. His death inaugurates the covenant and sets humanity free "from the transgressions under the first covenant" (Heb 9:15).[62] In Hebrews 9:16-18, the author introduces some wordplay. The Greek word for "covenant" (*diathēkē*) can also be used to refer to a "will" or "testament," which offers rights to one's designated heir(s).[63] Although to this point, he has used this Greek word to refer to covenants, in this section, he moves "from the conceptual world of Jewish sacrifice and covenants toward the conceptual world of last wills and testaments."[64] It is here that the author argues that death and sacrifice are a necessary part of Christ's work since blood cleanses. "Indeed, under the law almost everything is purified with blood, and without the shedding of blood there is no forgiveness" (Heb 9:22). All things, heavenly and earthly, required cleansing. The earthly things were cleansed by the earthly sacrifices, and the heavenly things by the once for all sacrifice of Christ.[65] He entered the heavenly tabernacle to appear before God "on our behalf" (*hyper hēmōn*). He did not offer the blood of animals, and he did not offer it time after time (Heb 9:25). He appears once to make one efficacious self-offering. And though he now lives, he died but once. When he returns, it will yet again be on our behalf (Heb 9:28).

The offerings (Hebrews 10:1-10). The author continues to build his contrast between the offering of Christ and those of the other high priests in Hebrews 10. Having made a case for why another *priest* was needed in Hebrews 7, here the author makes a case for another *offering*. To do this, he substantiates and develops what he has said about the work of Christ in Hebrews 9:23-28. But he begins with the law, which he says has a "shadow" (*skia*) of what is coming. For us, the word "shadow" can evoke thoughts of darkness, but this might not be what the author intends here. Shadows can cause fear, for example, when a tree outside one's window becomes a frightening monster. But shadows also can show the shape of real things. We find an implicit contrast in the author's imagery here. In Hebrews 1:3, the Son

---

[61]Although some connect this spirit with Christ in some way (e.g., Attridge, *Hebrews*, 251; David A. deSilva, *Perseverance in Gratitude*, 306), most favor the identification of the "eternal Spirit" with the "Holy Spirit" (e.g., Albert Vanhoye, "Esprit éternel et feu du sacrifice en He 9,14," *Biblica* 64, no. 2 [1983]: 263-74; cf. Cockerill, *Epistle to the Hebrews*, 398; Paul Ellingworth, *The Epistle to the Hebrews*, NIGTC [Grand Rapids, MI: Eerdmans, 1993], 457; Koester, *Hebrews*, 410-11; Lane, *Hebrews 9-13*, 240).

[62]Jamieson, *Jesus' Death and Heavenly Offering in Hebrews*, 116-26; cf. Moffitt, "Wilderness Identity and Pentateuchal Narrative."

[63]So also Moffitt, *Atonement and the Logic*, 291-92. Contra, e.g., S. W. Hahn, "A Broken Covenant and the Curse of Death: A Study of Hebrews 9:15-22," *Catholic Biblical Quarterly* 66, no. 3 (2004): 416-36.

[64]Moffitt, *Atonement and the Logic*, 291.

[65]Hebrews 9:23 refers to "sacrifices" (plural), which might cause confusion given the author's argument about Christ's one sacrifice. Rather than describing what must take or has taken place, the author offers this statement to present the logic of the heavenly sacrifices, which theoretically could have been plural, but due to the sufficiency of Christ's sacrifice were not. The author uses a plural form because this is part of a "general principle." See Attridge, *Hebrews*, 261; Cockerill, *Epistle to the Hebrews*, 416.

radiates the glory of God and is an imprint of his being; he reveals the Father. Here in Hebrews 10, the sacrifices revealed in the law do not radiate the glory of God—they do not reveal God themselves—but they do *imply* the glory. A shadow must be cast by something.

These sacrifices offered every year "can never . . . make perfect those who approach" (Heb 10:1).[66] If they had, then they would have ceased. Moreover, the worshipers would no longer have "consciousness of sin" (*syneidēsin hamartiōn*, Heb 10:2). With the earthly sacrifices, they have a "reminder of sin year after year" (*anamnēsis hamartiōn kat' eniauton*, Heb 10:3). This introduces an additional existential benefit for the worshiper. Purification, access, and inclusion in the family of God (among other things) is accompanied by freedom from guilt. The blood of bulls and goats simply cannot do that (Heb 10:4), especially when the offering is offered hypocritically.[67] "Consequently," the author tells us, Christ spoke these words when he entered the world (Heb 10:5):

> Sacrifices and offerings you have not desired,
> but a body you have prepared for me;
> in burnt offerings and sin offerings
> you have taken no pleasure.
> Then I said, "See, I have come to do your will, O God"
> (in the scroll of the book it is written of me). (Heb 10:5-7)

With this quotation of Psalm 40:6-8, Christ enters the world, to offer the body prepared for him, and he comes "to do [God's] will." Here again, the author uses the words of Jesus to depict him as one who is wholly faithful to the Father, modeling trust to his brothers and sisters (cf. Heb 2:12-13). In his commentary on the text (Heb 10:8-10), the author presents the quotation as representative of the two covenants. Hebrews 10:5-6 (Ps 40:6-7) refer to the offerings of the first covenant—offered "according to the law" (*kata nomon*), and Hebrews 10:7 refers to those from the second covenant. By the second, by the will of God, "we have been sanctified through the offering of the body of Jesus Christ once for all" (Heb 10:10).

At Hebrews 10:11, the author returns to a contrast between the priests and Jesus. They stood, making offerings each day that consisted of the same sacrifices—which could not remove sins (Heb 10:11). Jesus (here "this one") made one offering and sat down forever (Heb 10:12),[68] waiting for his enemies to be put under his feet (Heb 10:13). This allusion to Psalm 110, as well as the others, offers another portrait of solidarity between Jesus and his siblings. Justice often does not seem to be served. We see evil at work in individuals and in systems, left unchecked over and over again. We wait for those things to be trampled underfoot, and yet Jesus awaits the subjection of all things too. Even so, as he waits, "by a single offering he has perfected for all time those who are sanctified" (Heb 10:14). The Spirit bears witness to this. The author again quotes from Jeremiah 31, but this time the Spirit speaks a shorter section of the text. Given the way the quotation is introduced, "for after saying," Jeremiah 31:34 (in Heb 10:17) appears to be the focus for this quotation: "I will

[66]"The verb *proserchesthai* was used primarily for the priests who 'draw near' the altar (Lev 9:7-8; 21:17, 21; Num 4:19), but it was also used for all worshipers (Lev 9:5; Num 10:3-4)." See Koester, *Hebrews*, 431.

[67]Justin Duff argues that "bulls and goats" introduces an allusion to Is 1:11, which criticizes offerings by those who are "unfaithful." See Justin Harrison Duff, "The Blood of Goats and Calves . . . and Bulls? An Allusion to Isaiah 1:11 LXX in Hebrews 10:4," *Journal of Biblical Literature* 137, no. 3 (2018): 765-83.

[68]Cockerill, *Epistle to the Hebrews*, 449.

remember their sins and their lawless deeds no more." This signifies true forgiveness for the author (Heb 10:18).

THE CITY OF GOD (HEBREWS 10:19-13:25)

The heavenly sanctuary (Hinge: Hebrews 10:19-25). Hebrews 10:19-25 marks the transition between the second and third major sections of Hebrews. As noted above, like the hinge in Hebrews 4:11-16, this section summarizes the previous section and also introduces some of the themes that will be discussed in the next and is built around three hortatory subjunctives: Let us draw near (Heb 10:22), hold fast (Heb 10:23), and consider how we may spur one another on (Heb 10:24). In the section just prior, the author contrasts their offerings with the single offering of Christ. Nevertheless, after establishing the effectiveness of Christ's offering, he did not extend his argument to show how we now have access to the heavenly sanctuary. He assumes that the readers would be "confident" to enter (Heb 10:19). This points back to the first hinge. There, on the basis of our empathetic high priest, who offers mercy and grace, the author of Hebrews exhorts his readers to "approach the throne of grace with boldness" (Heb 4:16). He encourages them to enter into the heavenly sanctuary first, which allows his readers to consider the limitations of the first covenant in light of their own tremendous gifts, as he develops his argument in Hebrews 5:1-10:18. In Hebrews 10:19, he encourages them again, now grounding his assertion in Christ's offering of his own body (cf. Heb 10:5-7). We have a "new and living way" through the curtain, opened through his body (Heb 10:20).[69] Through the body of Christ, they can draw near to God, thoroughly cleansed outwardly *and* inwardly (Heb 10:22; cf. 9:9-10; 10:1-4, 11-14). The author encourages "us" to "hold fast to the confession of our hope" (Heb 10:23), which connects to the certainty of God's promises and the hope derived from it (cf. esp. Heb 6:16-20). The connections to the next section are less explicit, but the author encourages them to "approach . . . in full assurance of faith" (Heb 10:22) in advance of his presentation in Hebrews 11 of their ancestors who have done just that. The third section of Hebrews moves from an explicit presentation on the work of Christ to an extended exhortation for the readers to respond appropriately—to live in light of the cleansing and forgiveness that they have received. They are to remain in community, spurring one another on to love and good works (Heb 10:24-25).

The call to continue (Hebrews 10:26-39). The next section offers the reverse—what will happen if, rather than approaching God confidently and holding fast to their hope, instead they sin intentionally. No sacrifice remains for that sin. The author of Hebrews is likely offering a parallel between the first and second covenants again, first, through the distinction between intentional and unintentional sins (Num 15:22-31) and, second, through the harsh penalties prescribed for those who reject God (Deut 16:21-17:7).[70] The main point of the section is that one cannot reject the covenant (intentionally) and still reap its benefits (Heb 10:26-30). This tramples the Son of God underfoot, profanes his blood, and outrages the

[69]Hebrews 10:20 is notoriously difficult. Many think it equates the "veil" with Jesus' "body" (see, e.g., major English translations). But this does not fit with the rest of Hebrews where the heavenly tabernacle (as well as the veil) is a space that Jesus occupies or passes through. For a summary of positions and an argument for my interpretation, represented in the main text, see Jamieson, *Jesus' Death and Heavenly Offering in Hebrews*, 86-91.

[70]Rather than persistent or ongoing sinful behavior, the author's appeal to Deut 16–17, especially when paired with other warnings, suggests the "sin" in view is apostasy. See Johnson, *Hebrews*, 263-67.

Spirit. The punishment is certain, as God himself has said.[71]

In Hebrews 10:32-35, the author implies that he knows the addressees, especially as he comments on the manner by which they endured persecution (e.g., Heb 10:34). These Christians have endured despite a "hard struggle" (Heb 10:32), in which they were insulted, persecuted publicly (Heb 10:33), and lost their possessions (Heb 10:34). They also "suffered alongside" others who experienced these things as well as imprisonment. The author interprets this as "boldness," which will be rewarded if they persist. In this section, the author praises his readers for their persistence in the midst of their own personal sufferings, as well as their support of others who were suffering. Here again we see a focus on maintaining community and caring for one another. But this does not stop at encouragement. These Christians "stood side by side" and "suffered alongside" other Christians who were being persecuted.

For those among us who are not currently facing discrimination or mistreatment, the example of these Christians would serve us well. In my own social location, Christians do not face this sort of harsh treatment for being Christians; in fact, growing up in the American South, I assumed that someone was a Christian and generally held to the same broad moral framework, unless I was told otherwise.[72] But what I could have done better is stand alongside my Black brothers and sisters who were suffering, especially those whose religious devotion was mocked by the White majority in my context. My Black brothers and sisters were mocked because we—White Christians—did not understand the style of their preaching or the length of their services or the passion of their worship. It was different, and so we assumed it was defunct. We were wrong, and we lost our opportunity to learn from their diverse expressions of faithfulness. In the United States and Canada, Christians are not suffering for being Christians (on the whole), but Christians in minoritized groups *are* suffering, and we *must* stand with them.

As for the original addressees of Hebrews, the author encourages them to persist (Heb 10:36). If they do, they will receive what God has promised. The author grounds this in a quotation from Habakkuk 2:3-4,[73] which communicates two things: One is coming, and they cannot "shrink back." The author ends this section with a note of encouragement: "But we are not among those who shrink back and so are lost but among those who have faith and so preserve our souls" (Heb 10:39, *hēmeis de ouk esmen hypostolēs eis apōleian alla pisteōs eis peripoiēsin psychēs*). He warns them alongside his sincere hope that they will persevere.

The faith of our ancestors (Hebrews 11:1-40). With the Habakkuk quotation, the author brings "faith" to the forefront. The addressees should "live by faith." But what does this entail? "Now faith is the assurance of things hoped for, the conviction of things not seen" (Heb 11:1). Faith offers certainty about what is promised, even without tangible evidence. The ancestors exhibited this, and they were commended (Heb 11:2). But the first act of faith is "ours." The author says, "By faith we understand that the worlds [*tous aiōnas*] were prepared by the word [*rhēmati*] of God"

[71]Here the author quotes Deut 32:35-36. Given the proximity of this speech to the reference to the Spirit and its fit with other speeches by the Spirit in Hebrews, he is the most likely speaker. See Pierce, *Divine Discourse in Hebrews*, 182-85.

[72]This is not to say that everyone was a Christian, but to say that Christian values shaped that culture.

[73]Susan E. Docherty, "Composite Citations and Conflation of Scriptural Narratives in Hebrews," in *Composite Citations in Antiquity*, vol. 2, *New Testament Uses*, ed. Sean A. Adams and Seth Ehorn, LNTS 593 (London: T&T Clark, 2018), 190-208.

(Heb 11:3). This act of faith is different from those that follow in two key ways: (1) the inclusion of the addressees or contemporary audience, and (2) faith is not in the end but in the means. The addressees are not commended for believing that the universe exists, but for believing that the universe was made through the "word of God." From this point, however, each person mentioned trusts in something future.

Like their ancestors, the addressees are foreigners or sojourners. The author of Hebrews presents the faith of our ancestors from the expulsion from Eden up until the entrance in the land of Canaan. The author's metaphorical depiction of this group as those journeying through the wilderness is apt (Heb 3–4). If the author is writing to Rome, many of these Christians were displaced during the Edict of Claudius (49 CE), expelled from their homes, and made to wander. Some of God's people have been powerful, but that is not found in their depictions in Hebrews 11. Instead, the author focuses on their rise (e.g., Abraham in Heb 11:8-10) or their fall (e.g., Moses in Heb 11:24-26).

Nevertheless, other threads emerge in this series of exemplary works, such as trust in something unseen or future. For example, Abel, born in exile, offers something pleasing to God. This is likely due to the pattern of his offering, which resembled the offering of Christ more than Cain's offering.[74] He also is commended for speaking, even though he is dead (Heb 11:4). In the next example, by faith, Enoch was "taken" and never experienced death (Heb 11:5). Presumably, this is because he "pleased" God, trusting "that he exists" and that he "rewards those who seek him" (Heb 11:6). Enoch trusting that God would reward him in the future saves him from the sting of death. The next example is Noah. He was warned about things "not yet seen" and trusted the warning enough to build an ark. According to extrabiblical traditions, Noah attempted to warn others also, but they did not believe him. Thus, his abundant faith "judged" their lack (Heb 11:7).

By faith, Abraham left his home when he was called (Heb 11:8). He "stayed for a time [*parōkēsen*] in the land he had been promised, as in a foreign land, living in tents, as did Isaac and Jacob, who were heirs with him of the same promise" (Heb 11:9). Typically, English translations downplay Abraham's experience as an immigrant. He is not "like a stranger"; he *is* a stranger, one who travels to a better place for his family. He looked forward to a city built by God, another act of trust (Heb 11:10), but he never resided there. Sarah also acts in faith. Even though previously she was unable to have children and now was past menopause, she trusted that God was faithful (Heb 11:11). This couple, by faith, had many descendants. They trusted that God could bring life out of what was considered dead (Heb 11:12).

Hebrews 11:13 is jarring: "All of these died in faith." The ancestors trusted in something that they never fully experienced themselves. They "saw" and "greeted" the promises, but at a distance. They considered themselves "strangers and foreigners" (Heb 11:13),[75] which demonstrates that the place that they considered home was not on earth (Heb 11:14-15). "But as it is, they desire a better homeland, that is, a heavenly one" (Heb 11:16). The ancestors did not seek an idealized, fictitious home; they looked forward to the place that God had prepared for them.

---

[74]This could be because it was the firstborn and/or an animal offering or because of the attitude of Abel.

[75]See, e.g., Gen 23:4; cf. Lev 25:23.

Abraham, still in view in Hebrews 11:17-19, acts in faith once more. Abraham offers his one and only son, even though he knew the promise would be fulfilled through him (Heb 11:17-18). Abraham "considered the fact that God is able even to raise someone from the dead—and, figuratively speaking, he did receive him back" (Heb 11:19).[76] Isaac and Jacob receive little attention compared to their father. Both are commended for the blessings that they offer their sons (Heb 11:20-21). Joseph anticipated God's deliverance from Egypt asking to have his bones taken to the Promised Land (Heb 11:20).

By faith, Moses' parents knew their child was "handsome" or "good" (*asteios*), so they protected him from the Pharoah (Heb 11:23). When he grew up, he relinquished his position, set aside his privilege, and chose to be mistreated alongside his Hebrew brothers and sisters (Heb 11:24-25). This description of Moses as one who chose "ill-treatment" (Heb 11:25) and "considered abuse . . . to be greater wealth" (Heb 11:26) is similar to the author's description of Jesus in Hebrews 12:2: "for the sake of the joy that was set before him endured the cross, disregarding its shame, and has taken his seat at the right hand of the throne of God." Moses was willing to suffer, waiting and trusting that something better would come. Also by faith, he left Egypt and kept the Passover (Heb 11:27-28).

In addition to Moses' parents (Heb 11:23), the next three examples are reminders that this chapter is not merely concerned with patriarchs—and Sarah. Again, these acts of faith do not come through worldly power. They are the work of migrants and refugees and exiles. Among them are the people of Israel, who acted in faith when they crossed the Red Sea (Heb 11:29). In Hebrews 11:30, it is the "walls of Jericho" that fall by faith. Finally, Rahab did not perish because she welcomed the scouts (Heb 11:31).

Rahab is the last to be commended. The author mentions a number of other individuals, who might be discussed for their acts of faith, and yet "time would fail [him]." These characters range in significance as well as character. For some, it is surprising that they were included even in this "afterthought" (e.g., Jephthah), while others (e.g., David) surely would warrant more attention (Heb 11:32). No matter their reception, all those referenced here are rejected by the people around them, to the point of physical harm (Heb 11:32-37). The author of Hebrews appeals to specific stories but generalizes to allow his readers to identify with them. They endured physical harm and wandered so that they might receive something better (Heb 11:38).

These were all commended for their faith, yet none of them received what had been promised, since God had planned something better for us so that only together with us would they be made perfect (Heb 11:39-40).

They died in faith, and they are still waiting to receive the promise with us.

The training (Hebrews 12:1-17). For the ancestors to receive the promise or to be made perfect (Heb 11:40), the addressees must persevere. The author uses athletic imagery to support this point, first running and then wrestling.[77] Their journey through the wilderness is now a "race" (Heb 12:1, *agōn*) that they must run. Like a first-century runner would shed clothing, they must shed anything that would slow them down or obstruct them,

[76]For more on this reading of Heb 11:17-19, as well as this translation of *en parabolē*, see Pierce, *Divine Discourse in Hebrews*, 131n113.

[77]deSilva, *Perseverance in Gratitude*, 425-38.

such as sin (Heb 12:1). While they run, a great "cloud of witnesses" stands to the side, cheering, and Jesus stands ahead. Their "pioneer and perfecter" has forged their path and completed the race (Heb 12:2). Jesus likewise had a prize set before him—joy. For that prize, he endured the cross and ignored the public disgrace that came from it (Heb 12:2). This provides an example for those who are currently suffering. Consider the race run by Jesus, so you might endure (Heb 12:3). Although elsewhere the author has emphasized the pain of the present community, here he reminds them that, unlike Jesus, they have not shed blood in their struggle against sin (Heb 12:4).[78]

The author underscores his point with a quotation from Proverbs 3:11-12. The introductory formula here is exceptional. Rather than presenting this quotation as something spoken by God, here it is an "exhortation that addresses you as children." The proverb says that they are instructed and punished (perhaps even "whipped")[79] because they are loved. The author summarizes the message as, "Endure [your situation] for the sake of discipline" (Heb 12:7, *eis paideian hypomenete*).[80] He says this is a sign that "we" are legitimate children, truly considered heirs, because God concerns himself with our "education" or "discipline" (*paideia*).[81] In that cultural context, this is good news, even if corporal punishment is in view. All are full recipients of God's training and inheritance (Heb 12:8).[82] This passage appeals to some elements of first-century culture that might cause us difficulty. For example, this acknowledges the distinction between "legitimate" and "illegitimate" children that permitted wealthy men to abuse their slaves sexually and never share their wealth with the women or the offspring that resulted from that union. This passage raises questions regarding the position of daughters in the first century, whose education and inheritance was completely contingent on their fathers' choices. Finally, this passage reminds readers of the consistent use of corporal punishment in the ancient world, which could be very harsh.[83]

After this discussion of discipline, the author returns to athletic imagery: "Therefore lift your drooping hands and strengthen your weak knees" (Heb 12:12) and more specific moral instruction. Among this instruction is the call to avoid the example of Esau, who not only was sexually immoral but lost interest in his divine blessing. The latter is evidenced by his willingness to forsake his inheritance for "a single meal" (Heb 12:16). This was a mistake that left no occasion for repentance (Heb 12:17).

[78]N. Clayton Croy (*Endurance in Suffering: Hebrews 12:1-13 in Its Rhetorical, Religious, and Philosophical Context*, SNTSMS 98 [Cambridge: Cambridge University Press, 1998], 194) argues that "sin" is personified here and that this reference in Heb 12:4 refers to the "sinners" (*hamartōloi*) from Heb 12:3. He considers it unlikely that this refers to a struggle "against one's own inner desires" (citing Lane, *Hebrews 9-13*, 418). Yet Croy does not establish his own position sufficiently. Rather than a reference to the "sinners," it would seem that this *is* a personification of Sin, but a personification that presents Sin as a power who is the opponent against whom the readers "wrestle."

[79]This verb (*mastigoō*) is used to describe Jesus' own torture in the Gospels (Jn 19:1; cf. Mt 20:19; Mk 10:34; Lk 18:33) as well as the subsequent persecution of the disciples (Mt 10:17).

[80]Translation via Peeler, *You Are My Son*, 157.

[81]Many discuss whether Heb 12 is "punitive" or "nonpunitive." For a comprehensive defense of each, see (respectively) Phillip A. Davis Jr., *The Place of Paideia in Hebrews' Moral Thought* (Tübingen: Mohr Siebeck, 2018); Croy, *Endurance in Suffering*.

[82]For resources on the education of women that also discuss wealth inequality and slavery, see Craig Keener, "Women's Education and Public Speech in Antiquity," *Journal of the Evangelical Theological Society* 50, no. 4 (2007): 747; Lynn H. Cohick, *Women in the World of the Earliest Christians: Illuminating Ancient Ways of Life* (Grand Rapids, MI: Baker Academic, 2009), 225-55; Susan E. Hylen, *Women in the New Testament World*, Essentials of Biblical Studies (New York: Oxford University Press, 2018), esp. 119-20.

[83]Davis, *The Place of Paideia in Hebrews' Moral Thought*, 120-25.

The main message of the author's exhortation in Hebrews 12:12-17 is to prepare and persevere. The example of Esau demonstrates the peril that might come if they do not. But as he continues, the author anticipates another concern from his readers: What if they do persevere? What if they do approach God? The wilderness generation met God at Sinai, and it was harrowing. They came to a mountain that burned; they saw thunder and lightning and darkness (Heb 12:18). They also heard the voice of God, but what they heard terrified them, even for Moses (Heb 12:19-21).

That is not the destination for these Christians. They are not headed for Sinai, but for Zion,[84] which is a place for celebration! The author elaborates with great detail about what they will encounter:

> But you have come to Mount Zion and to the city of the living God, the heavenly Jerusalem, and to innumerable angels in festal gathering, and to the assembly of the firstborn who are enrolled in heaven, and to God the judge of all, and to the spirits of the righteous made perfect, and to Jesus, the mediator of a new covenant, and to the sprinkled blood that speaks a better word than the blood of Abel. (Heb 12:22-24).

Their destination, the promised rest, takes on additional imagery. It is the city that Abraham saw (Heb 11:9), the homeland that all the ancestors sought (Heb 11:16). This is a mountain where the people join the angels in song (Heb 12:22) and where they are not just "children," but all are "firstborn"[85]—heirs of "a kingdom that cannot be shaken" (Heb 12:28). Nevertheless, they must persevere and heed the voice that warns them. The wilderness generation was afraid when they heard God's warning, and the addressees cannot turn away (Heb 12:25). The message is that all things will be "shaken" (via Hag 2:6), the earth and the heavens, and this will reveal the kingdom of God (Heb 12:27). With this description of the "shaking" of the universe and the description from Deuteronomy that God is a "devouring fire" (Deut 4:24), the author highlights continuity in his portrait of God. God is still "scary," but if they remain faithful, they have no reason to fear.

The love (Hebrews 13:1-19). The transition from Hebrews 12:29 to Hebrews 13:1 is abrupt. The author uses no conjunctions as he moves from "Our God is a consuming fire" to "Let mutual love continue."[86] This chapter is markedly different from those before it; however, clear connections are present. For example, this opening exhortation extends the author's presentation of the readers as children of God as well as siblings of Jesus and one another. He then proceeds to "concrete expressions" of mutual love. First, he calls for their hospitality—drawing on the example of Abraham yet again with his allusion to Genesis 18–19.[87] Then he encourages them toward continued empathy for those in prison or suffering (cf. Heb 10:32-36). The author's next exhortations—to sexual purity and to avoid a "love of money"—also serve his call to "mutual love." Sexual immorality affects the church

---

[84]Hebrews says that they "have come to Mount Zion," which would mean that their journey is over (Heb 12:22); however, as Michael Kibbe says, "both [the authors of Deuteronomy and Hebrews] position their audiences at the threshold of the promised land and yet simultaneously on the mountain." For this as well as more on the influence of Deuteronomy and Exodus on this passage (and Hebrews more broadly), see Michael Kibbe, *Godly Fear or Ungodly Failure? Hebrews 12 and the Sinai Theophanies*, BNZW 216 (Berlin: De Gruyter, 2016), here 185.

[85]Peeler, *You Are My Son*, 170.

[86]The translation of *hē philadelphia* as "mutual love," rather than the typical "brotherly love," is influenced by Johnson, *Hebrews*, 339.

[87]Johnson, 339-40.

(1 Cor 6:18-20), and greed keeps us from caring for others materially. Greed also portrays a lack of trust in God. To assure his readers, the author encourages them with a final quotation spoken by God: "I will never leave you or forsake you."[88] This quotation varies from the author's previous pattern, as this is the first time that a divine character other than the Spirit has addressed the readers directly. This speech serves the author's singular point about money, and yet also offers a capstone to the speech of God presented thus far, especially when paired with the next quotation from Psalm 118:6-7. This is the first time that "we" join God in speaking Scripture:[89]

> The Lord is my helper;
>   I will not be afraid.
> What can anyone do to me?

The author presents this as something that "we" say, and yet it is in first-person singular language. Each of us confesses trust in God, but we do so in unison—a concise representation of the author's ecclesiology. We are personally responsible, and yet we need each other.

After this quotation, the author resumes his series of exhortations, that run one after another still with no conjunctions. In Hebrews 13:7, they are to remember their leaders and imitate them. The next exhortation is to resist being "carried away" by strange teachings in Hebrews 13:9. Between these two imperatives, the author says, "Jesus Christ is the same yesterday and today and forever" (Heb 13:8). Like their leaders and unlike these enticing teachings, Jesus is consistent and endures. Here the author introduces a final contrast between the first and second covenants. They are not to be strengthened by empty ritual, but by grace. It is important to note that the author of Hebrews is not dismissing ritual completely. In fact, quite the opposite is true. Here in Hebrews 13 the author's contrast is not limited to the Levitical priests and Jesus; the readers are called to offer a sacrifice of praise continually (Heb 13:15). Just as the sacrifices for sin were accompanied by various offerings (Lev 6), the sacrifice of Christ for sins is accompanied by ongoing worship through praise and thanksgiving (Heb 13:15) and fellowship (Heb 13:16). Throughout Hebrews, the readers are called to "draw near" and to "enter" the holiest place in heaven and earth, and they are called to offer sacrifices and eat from the altar (Heb 13:10). They are priests, serving in a role previously reserved for those in the line of Aaron. In Hebrews, we see that every person who approaches God with confidence serves at the altar alongside the high priest in the likeness of Melchizedek. This is a message of hope and honor to all those who have been stripped of dignity in the earthly sanctuary.[90]

But suffering and death often accompany honor and glory in Hebrews. This is no exception. In the new covenant, the High Priest is both priest *and* offering. Like the animals offered in the first covenant, Jesus was taken outside the camp to die (Heb 13:11-12), and the author calls them to go and join him, bearing his disgrace (Heb 13:13).

The blessing (Hebrews 13:20-25). After some final instructions, including a request for prayer on his behalf (Heb 13:18-19), the author ends his letter with some final greetings (Heb 13:22-25) and this benediction (Heb 13:20-21):

> Now may the God of peace, who brought back from the dead our Lord Jesus, the great

[88]This could be a quotation of Deut 31:6 or Gen 28:15. I think the latter is more likely given its context. There Jacob is promised something that will take generations to accomplish, but he must trust God nevertheless.

[89]Moses speaks in Hebrews, but at distinct moments in history (Heb 9:20; 12:21).

[90]For more on the priesthood of the audience, see Peeler, "If Son, Then Priest," 101-5.

shepherd of the sheep, by the blood of the eternal covenant, make you complete in everything good so that you may do his will, as he works among us that which is pleasing in his sight, through Jesus Christ, to whom be the glory forever. Amen.

He blesses them with the promise that they will have everything they need to persevere. In his final greetings, the author asks them to "bear with" his "word of exhortation," which he considers brief (Heb 13:22). He mentions that Timothy will visit soon, now that he has been released from prison (Heb 13:23), and sends greetings from some from Italy (perhaps Prisca and Aquila; Heb 13:24).

CONCLUSION

The author of the Epistle to the "Hebrews" calls his readers to persevere. He asks them to think of themselves as those whose ancestors left Egypt with Moses. He also establishes that they are sons and daughters of God. Their status is not determined by their blood or skin or hair; legitimate children are those whom God disciplines in love. The author portrays these children—alongside their faithful brother and representative, Jesus—journeying from the wilderness to Mount Zion. All the while, the author tells them of the immeasurable honor of their brother. He is one exalted above the angels. He is the pioneer or originator of their faith, as well as its perfecter. He is the firstborn Son of God, and he is a high priest in the likeness of Melchizedek. He offers himself once, willingly, in the heavenly tabernacle and is seated at God's right hand.

The author of Hebrews imagines the people of God as a family, one knit together by faith. This family is not without suffering. They are mocked, imprisoned, and attacked; they do not see all things in subjection to Jesus—yet. But they stand together. They ensure that no one fails to enter rest. They continue meeting together in order to care for their brothers and sisters. For White Christians who read Hebrews, we must take seriously the author's call to stand alongside our minoritized brothers and sisters in their pain. To support them well, we must be in community *with* them. We must hear *their* voices and not harden our hearts.

BIBLIOGRAPHY

Allen, David M. "The Holy Spirit as Gift or Giver? Retaining the Pentecostal Dimension of Hebrews 2.4." *Bible Translator* 59, no. 3 (2008): 151-58.

Attridge, Harold W. *Hebrews*. Hermeneia. Philadelphia: Fortress Press, 1989.

Bateman, Herbert, IV, ed. *Four Views on the Warning Passages in Hebrews*. Grand Rapids, MI: Kregel Academic, 2007.

Bauckham, Richard. "The Divinity of Jesus Christ in the Epistle to the Hebrews." In *The Epistle to the Hebrews and Christian Theology*, edited by Richard Bauckham, Daniel R. Driver, Trevor A. Hart, and Nathan MacDonald, 15-36. Grand Rapids, MI: Eerdmans, 2009.

Brueggemann, Walter. *The Theology of the Book of Jeremiah*. Old Testament Theology. New York: Cambridge University Press, 2006.

Caird, George B. "Exegetical Method of the Epistle to the Hebrews." *Canadian Journal of Theology* 5, no. 1 (1959): 44-51.

Church, Philip. *Hebrews and the Temple: Attitudes to the Temple in Second Temple Judaism and in Hebrews*. NovTSup 171. Leiden: Brill, 2017.

Cockerill, Gareth Lee. *The Epistle to the Hebrews*. NICNT. Grand Rapids, MI: Eerdmans, 2012.

———. "Hebrews 1:6: Source and Significance." *Bulletin for Biblical Research* 9 (1999): 51-64.

Cohick, Lynn H. *Women in the World of the Earliest Christians: Illuminating Ancient Ways of Life*. Grand Rapids, MI: Baker Academic, 2009.

Cortez, Félix H. *Within the Veil: The Ascension of the Son in the Letter to the Hebrews*. Studies in

Jewish and Christian Literature. Dallas: Fontes Press, 2021.

Croy, N. Clayton. *Endurance in Suffering: Hebrews 12:1-13 in Its Rhetorical, Religious, and Philosophical Context*. SNTSMS 98. Cambridge: Cambridge University Press, 1998.

Davis, Phillip A., Jr. *The Place of Paideia in Hebrews' Moral Thought*. Tübingen: Mohr Siebeck, 2018.

deSilva, David A. *Perseverance in Gratitude: A Socio-rhetorical Commentary on the Epistle to the Hebrews*. Grand Rapids, MI: Eerdmans, 2000.

Docherty, Susan E. "Composite Citations and Conflation of Scriptural Narratives in Hebrews." In *Composite Citations in Antiquity*. Vol. 2, *New Testament Uses*, edited by Sean A. Adams and Seth Ehorn, 190-208. LNTS 593. London: T&T Clark, 2018.

———. *The Use of the Old Testament in Hebrews: A Case Study in Early Jewish Bible Interpretation*. WUNT II 260. Tübingen: Mohr Siebeck, 2009.

Dodson, Joseph R. *The "Powers" of Personification: Rhetorical Purpose in the Book of Wisdom and the Letter to the Romans*. BZNW 161. Berlin: de Gruyter, 2008.

Duff, Justin Harrison. "The Blood of Goats and Calves . . . and Bulls? An Allusion to Isaiah 1:11 LXX in Hebrews 10:4." *Journal of Biblical Literature* 137, no. 3 (2018): 765-83.

Dyer, Bryan R. "'One Does Not Presume to Take This Honor': The Development of the High Priestly Appointment and Its Significance for Hebrews 5:4." *Conversations with the Biblical World* 33 (2013): 125-46.

Ellingworth, Paul. *The Epistle to the Hebrews*. NIGTC. Grand Rapids, MI: Eerdmans, 1993.

Fitzmyer, Joseph A. "Further Light on Melchizedek from Qumran Cave 11." *Journal of Biblical Literature* 86, no. 1 (1967): 25-41.

———. "'Now This Melchizedek' (Heb 7:1)." *Catholic Biblical Quarterly* 25, no. 3 (1963): 305-21.

Hahn, S. W. "A Broken Covenant and the Curse of Death: A Study of Hebrews 9:15-22." *Catholic Biblical Quarterly* 66, no. 3 (2004): 416-36.

Harris, Dana M. *Hebrews*. Exegetical Guide to the Greek New Testament. Nashville: B&H Academic, 2019.

Horton, Fred L., Jr. *The Melchizedek Tradition: A Critical Examination of the Sources to the Fifth Century AD and in the Epistle to the Hebrews*. Cambridge: Cambridge University Press, 1976.

Hylen, Susan E. *Women in the New Testament World*. Essentials of Biblical Studies. New York: Oxford University Press, 2018.

Jamieson, R. B. *Jesus' Death and Heavenly Offering in Hebrews*. SNTSMS 172. New York: Cambridge University Press, 2019.

Johnson, Luke Timothy. *Hebrews: A Commentary*. NTL. Louisville, KY: Westminster John Knox, 2006.

Kaalund, Jennifer T. *Reading Hebrews and 1 Peter with the African American Great Migration: Diaspora, Place and Identity*. LNTS 598. London: Bloomsbury T&T Clark, 2018.

Keener, Craig. "Women's Education and Public Speech in Antiquity." *Journal of the Evangelical Theological Society* 50, no. 4 (2007): 747.

Kibbe, Michael. *Godly Fear or Ungodly Failure? Hebrews 12 and the Sinai Theophanies*. BNZW 216. Berlin: De Gruyter, 2016.

Koester, Craig R. *Hebrews*. AB 36. New York: Doubleday, 2001.

Lane, William L. *Hebrews 1–8*. WBC 47a. Dallas: Word, 1991.

———. *Hebrews 9–13*. WBC 47b. Dallas: Word, 1991.

Mason, Eric F. *"You Are a Priest Forever": Second Temple Jewish Messianism and the Priestly Christology of the Epistle to the Hebrews*. Leiden: Brill, 2008.

Massey, James Earl. "Hebrews." In *True to Our Native Land: An African American New Testament Commentary*, edited by Brian K. Blount, Cain Hope Felder, Clarice J. Martin, and Emerson B. Powery, 444-60. Minneapolis: Fortress Press, 2007.

McKnight, Scot. "The Warning Passages of Hebrews: A Formal Analysis and Theological Conclusions." *Trinity Journal* 13, no. 1 (1992): 21-59.

Meier, John P. "Symmetry and Theology in the Old Testament Citations of Heb 1,5-14." *Biblica* 66, no. 4 (1985): 504-33.

Moffitt, David M. *Atonement and the Logic of Resurrection in the Epistle to the Hebrews.* NovTSup 141. Leiden: Brill, 2011.

———. "Wilderness Identity and Pentateuchal Narrative: Distinguishing between Jesus' Inauguration and Maintenance of the New Covenant in Hebrews." In *Muted Voices of the New Testament: Readings in the Catholic Epistles and Hebrews*, edited by Katherine M. Hockey, Madison N. Pierce, and Francis Watson, 153-71. LNTS 565. London: T&T Clark, 2017.

Moore, Nicholas J. "Jesus as 'the One Who Entered His Rest': The Christological Reading of Hebrews 4.10." *Journal for the Study of the New Testament* 36, no. 4 (2014): 383-400.

———. *Repetition in Hebrews: Plurality and Singularity in the Letter to the Hebrews, Its Ancient Context, and the Early Church.* WUNT II 388. Tübingen: Mohr Siebeck, 2015.

Nauck, Wolfgang. "Zum Aufbau des Hebräerbriefes." In *Judentum, Urchristentum, Kirche: Festschrift für Joachim Jeremias*, edited by Walther Eltester, 199-206. BZNW 26. Berlin: Töpelmann, 1960.

Peeler, Amy L. B. "If Son, Then Priest: The Filial Foundation of Ordination in Hebrews and Other New Testament Texts." In *Listen, Understand, Obey: Essays in Honor of Gareth Lee Cockerill*, edited by Caleb T. Friedeman, 95-115. Eugene, OR: Pickwick, 2017.

———. *You Are My Son: The Family of God in the Epistle to the Hebrews.* LNTS 486. London: T&T Clark, 2014.

Pierce, Madison N. *Divine Discourse in the Epistle to the Hebrews: The Recontextualization of Spoken Quotations of Scripture.* SNTSMS 178. Cambridge: Cambridge University Press, 2020.

Ribbens, Benjamin J. *Levitical Sacrifice and Heavenly Cult in Hebrews.* BZNW 222. Berlin: Walter de Gruyter, 2016.

Theophilus, Michael P. "The Numismatic Background of Χαρακτήρ in Hebrews 1.3." *Australian Biblical Review* 64 (2016): 69-80.

Thompson, James W. *Hebrews.* Paideia. Grand Rapids, MI: Baker Academic, 2008.

Ulrichsen, Jarl Henning. "Διαφορώτερον ὄνομα in Hebr. 1,4 Christus als Träger des Gottesnamens." *Studia theologica* 38, no. 1 (2008): 65-75.

Vanhoye, Albert. "Esprit éternel et feu du sacrifice en He 9,14." *Biblica* 64, no. 2 (1983): 263-74.

Wall, Robert W. "Epilogue: A Reflection." In *Muted Voices of the New Testament: Readings in the Catholic Epistles and Hebrews*, edited by Katherine M. Hockey, Madison N. Pierce, and Francis Watson, 199-209. LNTS 565. London: T&T Clark, 2017.

Webster, John. "One Who Is Son: Theological Reflections on the Exordium to the Epistle to the Hebrews." In *The Epistle to the Hebrews and Christian Theology*, edited by Richard Bauckham, Daniel R. Driver, Trevor A. Hart, and Nathan MacDonald, 69-94. Grand Rapids, MI: Eerdmans, 2009.

Weiß, Hans-Friedrich. *Der Brief an die Hebräer.* KEK 13. Göttingen: Vandenhoeck & Ruprecht, 1991.

Westfall, Cynthia Long. *A Discourse Analysis of the Letter to the Hebrews: The Relationship Between Form and Meaning.* LNTS 297. London: Bloomsbury, 2006.

RESOURCES FOR THE MENTAL HEALTH OF THE OPPRESSED IN THE NEW TESTAMENT

A CONTEMPORARY READING OF ANCIENT TEACHINGS

CHRISTIN J. FORT

APPROACHING THE TEXT

Exploring the richness of God's Word is an ongoing, transformative process that offers life and nourishment to those who encounter it. This *New Testament in Color* volume is intended to offer resources for the people of God that are based on the prayerful insights and careful study of an ethnically diverse group of scholars and practitioners who draw on their own training and embodied experiences as they engage the text of Scripture. The ultimate aim of each of these chapters is to edify and exhort Christ's body. I wrote this particular chapter to help the reader develop faithful interpretive resources that enhance psychological well-being.

As we begin this explorative journey, note that the New Testament is filled with commands, callings, and invitations pertaining to emotional health and well-being: "do not be anxious about anything" (Phil 4:6); "my brothers and sisters, whenever you face various trials, consider it all joy," (Jas 1:2); "rejoice in the Lord always; again I will say, Rejoice" (Phil 4:4); "be angry but do not sin" (Eph 4:26), to name just a few.

At first glance, the list of psychological "dos and don'ts" of the New Testament seems simple. But reading such texts with both an eye to the original audience and an ear to the ways that contemporary readers are likely to understand them is challenging. Discerning how to apply these admonitions in today's emotionally turbulent world can be completely overwhelming—especially for historically marginalized communities and individuals who live with mental-health diagnoses. Although space does not permit diving into great detail about how to interpret each of these individual passages, there are several important principles of integrative interpretation to explore—particularly as we seek to make meaning of psychologically oriented biblical texts.

PRINCIPLES TO GUIDE OUR ENGAGEMENT WITH THE TEXT

First, *the Bible was written for us, but not to us. Therefore, we should avoid anachronistic assumptions of the text.* Anachronistic assumptions are assumptions that are historically inconsistent with the time period in question. So, for example, the Old Testament speaks a great deal about "fear," and the New Testament speaks a great deal about "anxiety." While we believe that the biblical truths in these passages always have important insights for us to glean as modern readers, it is essential that we do not assume that the first hearers of these words would have understood "fear" and "anxiety" in exactly the same way that we do.

This principle is especially important for us to acknowledge as we seek to ascertain wisdom from the Scriptures regarding mental health. For many early Christians, the New Testament text would have been read against the backdrop of the ancient Greco-Roman world—a world in which perspectives on emotions were heavily influenced by Stoic philosophers and other Greek thinkers.[1] For those early Christians who were also Jewish, these interpretations were layered on top of their understandings of the Hebrew Bible, or Old Testament, texts as well. Thus, when Paul speaks of "anxiety," we cannot automatically assume that the construct that he has in mind automatically maps onto our understanding of clinical and nonclinical definitions of that term. Undoubtedly God's Word remains as true for us as it did for the first-century hearers, but what that truth is will require some digging. Faithful digging often requires cross-disciplinary study in order to understand the ways that the biblical author would have understood the concepts and the ways that contemporary scholars have helped us understand the concept in more detail as well.

For example, psychologists, neurologists, and other scientists have done a great deal of work to understand the difference between temporary and long-lasting emotional experiences. These distinctions are often categorized as emotional *states* and emotional *traits* based on the frequency and duration that someone might have a particular experience.[2] For example, everyone experiences temporary periods of the *state* of anxiety. These are moments of intense stress that ebb and flow depending on the situation. Others of us, however, have *long-term* experiences of anxiety that affect us in ways that are largely outside our immediate control and that many others have never experienced. These chronic, clinical types of anxiety are qualitatively different from the more temporary experiences of anxiety.

Understanding that Paul likely had little exposure to the type of gripping clinical anxiety that has become a more common experience in the twenty-first century should inform our exegetical work and make us especially careful to allow contemporary scholarship on a topic (such as anxiety) to complement what we understand of the biblical witness. Failure to do so often leads to poor exegesis and deeply damaging pastoral exhortations that drive the one who is living with a chronic diagnosis to experience a depth of shame for their experiences that was never intended by the biblical text. Thus, careful biblical scholarship ought also to be in conversation with contemporary scholarship on a host of issues so that God's Word may be understood more completely and applied more faithfully.

Embracing this call to a more holistic view of biblical interpretation leads to our second principle of exegesis: *avoid eisegesis during the exegetical process*. Put simply, biblical eisegesis is the process of projecting one's own ideas about a topic onto the biblical text. For those who have been diligent in seeking to understand the psychological landscape of the twenty-first-century church, it can be very difficult to read a text that is directly addressing

[1]For a more robust review of potential implications of these Greco-Roman perspectives on early Christian doctrine, see Richard J. Bauckham, "Only the Suffering God Can Help: Divine Passibility in Modern Theology," *Themelios* 9, no. 3 (1984), https://theologicalstudies.org.uk/article_god_bauckham.html.

[2]For a more thorough review of the physiological distinctions between the state and the trait of anxiety, see Francesca Saviola et al., "Trait and State Anxiety Are Mapped Differently in the Human Brain," *Scientific Reports* 10, no. 1 (2020), https://doi.org/10.1038/s41598-020-68008-z.

an emotional topic (e.g., fear, joy, sadness, anxiety) without jumping to certain conclusions. However, wise and careful students of the Word will be prayerful and intentional in approaching the text with an eye to holding our assumptions about the text and the application of the text loosely. This does not mean that we simply ignore our perceptions and experiences and how they might inform our view of the text. But it does mean that we seek to be conscientious about the ways that our experiences may narrow or expand our view of the text, and we pursue checks and balances to help (e.g., reading the Scriptures in diverse community; listening to the wisdom of the global church).

In order to honor the aforementioned principles of exegesis and approach the text honestly, it is necessary to *acknowledge the unique subjective perspectives that each of us bring to the text.* This is the third principle of biblical exegesis, and it is one that we are especially prone to forget (and sometimes actively avoid) in biblical and theological scholarship. We simply cannot escape the reality that our lived experiences always inform our reading of the text. So, what do we do about this fact?

For many, it can feel frightening to acknowledge our subjectivity when approaching the text of Scripture. We would like to believe that we can approach the "objective truth" of God's Word from an "objective" standpoint. However, little could be further from the truth. Our best efforts to ignore our cultural backgrounds and belief systems can never fully mitigate the impact of our subjective perceptions. One might argue, as I do, that simply ignoring our backgrounds might actually inhibit us from fully engaging the text as honestly and humbly as we ought.

Rather than ignoring, minimizing, or consciously dismissing our social location, perhaps a more faithful reading of the text will be found when we acknowledge the sociocultural contexts, academic or professional training, and personal experiences that shape our perceptions and humbly bring these perspectives to the interpretive community of faith as we engage with the sacred text. Together we may discern the significance of our individual and collective theological insights. Perhaps this is part of what it means to be "one body" with "many members" (1 Cor 12:12).

The rationale for acknowledging our social location is grounded in the conviction that our familial, cultural, national, and historical contexts are not incidental to God. God was intentional in the details of our individual formation in the womb (Ps 139:13) as well as with the family and community into which we were born (Acts 17:26). Since these realities are not accidents, I believe that choosing to acknowledge, and even embrace, the contextual realities that shape us will actually empower us to observe, interpret, and apply the text with greater clarity and humility.

With this assertion in mind, I will turn to an example of my own contextual background that shapes the framework within which I approach God's word.

ACKNOWLEDGING THE INTERSECTIONAL IDENTITIES OF THE INTERPRETER

I am an African American female psychologist and integrative scholar. I have chosen to embrace what many today would call a high view of Scripture. For me this means that I engage with the biblical witness in full trust that all Scriptures are "God-breathed" (2 Tim 3:16 NIV), that Jesus is "the image of the invisible God" (Col 1:15), and that the Holy Spirit reminds us of the words of Christ (Jn 14:26).

As an African American born in the lineage of enslaved people in the United States, I am very aware of the fact that the history of my people's continued oppression shapes the ways that I encounter the Scriptures today. Just as my enslaved ancestors approached the Scriptures (and God) fully acknowledging their suffering, crying out against injustice and pleading for divine intervention, I too approach the Word in a similar manner as I have been trained to do. *My faith is strengthened in the face of despair when I recall and emulate the faith of my ancestors.*

As a woman, particularly a racialized minority woman in the United States, the *stories* of women, the *silence* of women, and the *silencing* of women within the corpus of Scripture has always stood out to me. This was true even as I meditated on the Scriptures as a very young girl. I recall my questions in middle school as I read through Leviticus and wondered why women were literally worth less than men from an economic standpoint (e.g., Lev 27) and when I wrestled with the similarities and differences between the various forms of slavery mentioned in the Scriptures (e.g., Onesimus's story in the book of Philemon) and the horrifying accounts of the chattel slavery of my African American ancestors.[3]

As a psychologist trained at the doctoral level to engage with both clinical psychology and biblical theology, I seek to approach the text with humility and confidence. These characteristics are born out of an acknowledgment of the educational privileges that allow me to engage with my two favorite subjects, God and people, in such an integrated fashion. Rather than seeking to *mute* these realities or *minimize* them (both psychological coping mechanisms we often gravitate toward when we feel anxious, confused, and/or overwhelmed), I embrace these embodied, intersectional experiences that shape my perspectives as worthy of careful attention even, and perhaps especially, as I engage in biblical interpretation.[4]

Knowing that I bring these interpretive lenses to the texts empowers me to intentionally locate my perspectives in their sociohistorical contexts. This intentional *acknowledgment of my own subjectivity* serves as one of many safeguards against *anachronistic* and *eisegetical* readings of the text. As I acknowledge my subjectivity, I must also allow my perspectives to be refined within the context of communal biblical inquiry in order to engage with the texts as holistically as possible.

"CAST ALL OF YOUR CARES ON HIM"

In light of these general principles for biblical interpretation, we will now direct our attention to the practical aspects of our exploration together: What do we do with the pain that marks the lives of those who are oppressed? I believe that we have received a divine invitation to bring our pain and sorrow (whether personal or communal, historical or contemporary) to God and to trusted others in order to pursue healing and wholeness.

There are several biblical truths that can frame how we might understand the winding path toward health and healing in the midst of pain and suffering. I will make three observations about the ways that God engages with the deep distress of the oppressed in the Scriptures.

[3]This posture of embrace is in keeping with the womanist, *mujerista*, and Asian (American) feminist interpretive traditions. For a more robust review of this hermeneutical framework, see Charlene Jin Lee, "I Come from a Place: Reflections on Katie Cannon's Womanist Classroom." *Interpretation* 74, no. 1 (2020), https://doi.org/10.1177/0020964319876579.

[4]For a more thorough review of the value of intersectionality theory in the interdisciplinary work of scholars who integrate psychology and theology, see Christin J. Fort and Terri S. Watson, "Journeying Toward a More Inclusive Integrative Endeavor: Fostering Integrative Leadership Through an Intentional Focus on Intersectionality, Mutuality and Empowerment," *Journal of Psychology and Christianity* 40, no. 1 (2021): 40-54.

We will focus the majority of our attention on our final observation.

First, it is essential that we see that *God is attentive to the experiences and needs of the marginalized.* From God's attunement to the needs of Hagar, the Egyptian slave who had been physically and psychologically abused by her master and mistress (Gen 16), to the tenacious advocacy of the Syrophoenician woman on behalf of herself, her daughter, and her people (Mk 7:24-30), we see a God who is mindful of those who have been purposefully pushed to the margins of society. God's emotional attunement is evidenced over and over again in Scripture, and it is encapsulated beautifully in the image of God stooping down to wipe every tear from our eyes (Rev 7:17) and bottling up each of those tears (Ps 56:8)—demonstrating how sacred they are to God. God's attunement to the needs of God's people is a model for us to do the same.

Second, even though God knows what we need even before we ask (Ps 139:4), *we are exhorted to tell God our needs and our desires anyway* (Mt 7:7; Jn 14:13). God's receptivity to the cries of the oppressed for divine intervention is repeated throughout the Scriptures. A prime example of this Old Testament theme that is echoed in the New Testament is seen in the life and death of Jesus. As he takes his final breaths while hanging on the cross, Jesus echoes the desperate words of the psalmist: "My God, my God, why have you forsaken me?" (Ps 22:1; Mt 27:46). In this passage, Jesus models a level of authenticity in the midst of his grief and pain that all of the people of God—particularly those who have been oppressed, abused, and mistreated by the governing authorities—are invited to emulate. Rather than hiding the depth of our confusion, fear, anxiety, trauma, depression, or any painful experience, we are invited to bring our requests before the Lord (Mt 11:28) so that we might receive mercy in our time of need (Heb 4:16).

For many, however, this invitation to such painful honesty with the Lord seems like a foreign concept, and it is often perceived to be sacrilegious. Can you really tell God how angry you are? Is it OK to voice your fear that you have been forsaken?[5] For so many people, especially women and historically marginalized communities, unmasking our distress and making a bold request for what we need or desire seems wrong.

When we encounter such internal hesitancy to authentic engagement with God and others, we need to ask ourselves whether our belief system about what is acceptable or unacceptable to express to the Lord is *rooted in the Scriptures* or, rather, in a portion of *church tradition* that may not be fully grounded in biblical truth. It can be surprising to discover that the Scriptures make clear that we do not have to be ashamed to acknowledge that we are in need and to receive support not only from God but from others as well (Acts 4:34; Gal 6:2).

These reflections lead to our third and final observation of divine engagement with pain and suffering. The perfect example of this can be seen in Jesus on the night that he was arrested (Mt 26:36-56; Mk 14:32-52; Lk 22:39-53; Jn 18:1-12). The image we see of Jesus in the garden of Gethsemane is one of the most intimate snapshots of the emotional life of the Son of God.

From a psychological point of view, the intensity of this night cannot be overestimated.

[5]For a more robust and integrative, or interdisciplinary, review of the psychological value of this type of disclosure with God, see Julie J. Exline, Kalman J. Kaplan, and Joshua B. Grubbs, "Anger, Exit, and Assertion: Do People See Protest Toward God as Morally Acceptable?," *Psychology of Religion and Spirituality* 4, no. 4 (2012), https://doi.org/10.1037/a0027667.

In one evening Jesus experienced a series of traumatic events: acute psychological distress as he anticipated what was to come, relational betrayal, false accusations about who he was and what he did, a government-sanctioned arrest, a judicial sentencing that placed him on death row, and a painful beating that left his sleep-deprived body raw and mangled. The trauma of that night was unspeakable. But rarely do we attend to the impact of this trauma on Christ.

The importance of this night, and the events that follow, is so essential to the faith that *all four of the Gospel writers take note of it.* We often jump to the scenes that take place later, when Jesus stands trial and is crucified. But the details of Maundy Thursday pull back the curtain to grant us a precious view into the life of God that foreshadows all that was to come. Together, the Gospel writers paint an intimate picture of the anguish of the Son of God during the most vulnerable time of his life on earth.[6]

Specifically, the Gospels of Mark and Luke paint a vivid image of the weary Son of Man who was eager to be upheld by the Father and supported by his friends in his hour of need. The intensity of the moment that Jesus is facing is highlighted by the physical, psychological, and spiritual nature of his experience—each of which is highlighted in the text. We will turn our attention to this narrative in detail in the hope that offering an interdisciplinary perspective of this painful night in Jesus' life may help us to navigate our own pain and suffering in a more holistic manner.

According to the Synoptic Gospel accounts, upon entering the garden of Gethsemane Jesus immediately asks his disciples to stay on high alert—both spiritually and physically—as he prompts them to "keep awake" (Mk 14:34) and to "pray" (Lk 22:46)."[7] Luke tells us that Jesus was in such deep anguish that he began to sweat uncontrollably. (Anyone who has ever experienced severe anxiety will recall the visceral sensations that humans experience when we feel deeply overwhelmed.)

In Jesus' case, the magnitude of the stress that he is facing results in a rare but well-documented medical issue known as *hematohidrosis*, in which his sweat was like great drops of blood (Lk 22:44). Medical doctors have studied these types of physiological conditions for years, and it is well-known that one of the major causes of this type of condition is severe psychological stress.[8] It comes as no surprise, then, that Luke—the resident physician among the early church—would be the clinician to document this important detail.

Notably, this type of physical condition is also of interest to clinical psychologists because it is considered a *psychosomatic* illness—a condition in which the experience of psychological stress is correlated with a physical health concern.[9] Jesus experienced psychological distress and spiritual weightiness that manifested itself in his physical body. The weight he carried was so overwhelming that he knew he needed support—and he sought it out.

As Jesus attempts to make meaning of the crushing weight he feels inside, he voices these words: "My soul is overwhelmed with sorrow to the point of death" (Mk 14:34 NIV). Sorrow to the point of death. Lest anyone wonder whether God is able to understand the depth

[6]Parallel accounts of this night can be found in Mt 26:36-50; Mk 14:32-46; Lk 22:39-40; Jn 18:1.

[7]Anyone who has experienced a severe trauma may easily empathize with Jesus' felt need to be hypervigilant in anticipation of a frightening night ahead.

[8]For a medical review of hematohidrosis, see Saugato Biswas, Trupti Surana, Abhishek De, and Falguni Nag, "A Curious Case of Sweating Blood," *Indian Journal of Dermatology* 58, no. 6 (2013), https://doi.org/10.4103/0019-5154.119964.

[9]The importance of psychosomatic experiences has garnered enough attention that interdisciplinary researchers have devoted entire academic journals to such issues (e.g., *Journal of Psychosomatic Research*).

of human pain, Jesus articulated his own experience, proclaiming that he knows what it means to be pressed to the point of death.

If we step back to see Jesus' words in biblical context, we will recall the words of the prophet Isaiah foretelling that the Son of God would also be "a man of suffering, and familiar with pain" (Is 53:3 NIV). Pain was a familiar companion to Jesus. This moment in the garden was surely not his first encounter with pain (see Jn 11:35). But it was the most all-consuming up until that point.

The writer of Hebrews echoes Isaiah's affirmation of Christ's own experience of vulnerability when writing, "For we do not have a high priest who is unable to empathize with our weaknesses" (Heb 4:15 NIV). Put simply: we have a high priest who is more than able to empathize with our weakness. This empathy denotes a type of *experiential knowledge* that is more substantive than mere intellectual awareness. Jesus *knows* what pain is—physical pain and psychological pain.

Returning to Jesus' experience in Gethsemane, we are reminded that this experience of great anguish drove Jesus to reach out for support. He asks his disciples to stay alert with him. And he asks his Father whether there is any way to avoid the pain that is coming.

As we think of Jesus' prayer in the garden, we often skip to the end, recalling only the final sentence of a longer divine exchange: "Yet, not what I want, but what you want" (Mk 14:36). These words are powerful—and they are words for us to pray as well. But we completely forget the urgency and anxiety that marked the journey that led Jesus to those words. Moreover, we miss the profound fact that Jesus—the second member of the Godhead—voiced a desire that was other than the eventual outcome that he would experience: he told the Father, point blank, that he would rather have it another way.

The confidence and clarity with which Jesus approached the Father with his request is riveting. Jesus does not seem to be ashamed in the least. He asks for his heart's desire. May it not be lost on us that the Father's decision *not* to honor the Son's request by granting his desire did not dissuade the Son from asking—repeatedly—for what he longed for. We are invited to ask.

"BE IMITATORS OF GOD"

What, then, does it mean for us to be "imitators of God" (Eph 5:1) in light of what we see of Jesus in the garden? Perhaps it means that we are honest with ourselves, with God, and with others about our own pains and griefs. Perhaps it means that we acknowledge the histories and legacies that have perpetuated inequity and intergenerational trauma that have led to symptoms of post-traumatic stress disorder, generalized anxiety disorder, substance abuse disorder, and major depressive disorder for so many racialized minority and/or impoverished communities.

Perhaps it means that we take stock of the histories of patriarchy, misogyny, and sexism that have created cultures of underreporting sexual violence that devolve into communities of complicity and shame that perpetuate these same cycles within the church. Perhaps it means that we acknowledge that the homophobia and heteronormativity that are the hallmark of so many Christians are too often correlated with an incomplete view of the *imago Dei* of every human and an inadequate understanding of the unconditional love of God.

The list of pains and griefs we experience as individuals and as communities is long. Acknowledging these pains feels weighty and costly in its own right. But the depth of divine empathy and unconditional love that we are invited to draw from is limitless. These divine resources are extended to us—validating, healing, and restoring us to holistic health. These resources are also for others—equipping us to be the hands and feet of Christ to those around us. It is only as we come to realize the weight of all that Jesus carried on our behalf—the spiritual, physical, and psychological weight—that we can begin to understand the fullness of the freedom from all forms of oppression that Christ has come to bring. As we understand that freedom, we will be liberated to advocate for that freedom for all around us and to take full advantage of these limitless divine resources that were intended for us all.

MULTILINGUALISM IN THE NEW TESTAMENT

Ekaputra Tupamahu

In an op-ed published in early December 2022, sociologist Nancy Wang Yuen reflects on how strange Christmas was to her when she came to the United States as an immigrant from Taiwan. A phrase in the middle of this article caught my eye. She writes, "As a kid who got bullied at school for not speaking English . . ."[1] That she recounts this in an op-ed that has nothing to do with language demonstrates that this experience left a mark and that language difference can become a site of discrimination and social exclusion. Especially in the United States, racialization is not just about one's skin color but also about one's language. Being able to speak English can be an act of performing whiteness.[2] Nowadays, not only in the United States but worldwide, the inability to speak English can have a serious negative effect on one's social and professional life.

When language contact happens, often through immigration and colonialization, the linguistic struggle is almost inevitable. Language is always politically contested. English has become the international language it is today not because it is better than other languages but rather because English is supported by a colonial power that has expanded its territory far beyond its original site in Europe. In other words, colonization and the expansion of language use go hand in hand.

Paul seems to be aware of this multiplicity of languages around him. His statement in 1 Corinthians 14:10 reveals his basic convictions about the multiplicity of languages in the world, namely that "there are doubtless many different kinds of sounds in the world, and nothing is without sound." The word *phōnē* in Greek means "sound" or "voice" but is very often used for language (as in *phonetics*, for example). Rather than one word for "language" in Greek, instead words such as "tongue" (*glōssa*) and "voice" (*phōnē*) are used—as they still are in English too. Someone who speaks French, for instance, is a Franco*phone*, and an English-speaking person is an Anglo*phone*. *Phōnē* means "language." So, when Paul says that "there are many different kinds of *sounds* in the world," he is acknowledging that the world is filled with many languages. The second phrase, "nothing is without sound," can also be translated, "nobody is without language." To exist means to live in a world created by language, and everyone has language to

[1]Nancy Wang Yuen, "As an Immigrant Kid, I Learned About Christmas from TV—And It Nearly Broke My Heart," Today.com, December 6, 2022, www.today.com/popculture/essay/immigrant-kid-learned-christmas-tv-rcna60163.

[2]I've explained this historical connection in Ekaputra Tupamahu, "'I Don't Want to Hear Your Language!' White Social Imagination and the Demography of Roman Corinth," *The Bible and Critical Theory* 16, no. 1 (2020): 64-91. On raciolinguistic theory, see H. Samy Alim, "Introducing Raciolinguistics: Racing Language and Languaging Race in Hyperracial Times," in *Raciolinguistics: How Language Shapes Our Ideas About Race*, ed. H. Samy Alim, John R. Rickford, and Arnetha F. Ball (New York: Oxford University Press, 2016), 1-30.

speak. Like us, people in the New Testament were aware of the multiplicity of languages.

When Jesus was crucified, Pilate ordered an inscription to be written and attached to the cross. According to John 19:20, the inscription was written in three languages: Hebrew/Aramaic, Latin, and Greek (*Hebraisti, Rhōmaisti, Hellēnisti*).[3] The other Gospels do not have this extra information—although the Vulgate version of Luke 23:38 does.[4] These three languages were the main languages of the people in Palestine at the time of Jesus.[5] Though we do not have the actual inscription that Pilate placed on the cross, only the record from the Gospel of John, trilingual inscriptions were quite rare in the Greco-Roman world. When they occurred, they usually represented the languages spoken by the people so that people from different linguistic groups could read them.

With regards to the languages in Palestine during the times of Jesus and his early followers, we can say that Aramaic was widely used because it was the language of the Persian Empire. Some scholars even argue that Aramaic was the mother tongue or the first language of Jesus and many Jews in the first century.[6] Some parts of the Old Testament are written in Aramaic (Dan 2:4-7; Ezra 4:8–6:18; 7:12-26, for instance).[7] Because of the widespread rule of the Persian Empire, the imperial Aramaic was understandably the lingua franca at that time, particularly in the eastern part of

[3]The exact meaning of the Greek word *Hebraisti* is debatable. Joseph Fitzmyer argues that this word was used in the first century to "refer to the native Semitic language of Palestine." It does not have to mean "Hebrew" because in many instances of its occurrences in the NT, the words are Aramaic. For example, in Jn 19:13, the word *Gabbatha* is "a Grecized form of the Aramaic word *gabbetä*, 'raised place.'" In the later period, however, the word *syristi* or *syriakē* is used specifically to refer to Aramaic. See Joseph A. Fitzmyer, *A Wandering Aramaean: Collected Aramaic Essays* (Chico, CA: Scholars Press, 1979), 43. Randall Buth and Chad Pierce have challenged this proposal. For them, this word can only mean "Hebrew." Their argument is mainly based on the reading of Acts 22:2. If *Hebraidi* in this passage refers to Aramaic, the idea the crowd was surprised does not make any sense because Aramaic was a common language and widely used. They also trace the use of this word in other literature from the Septuagint to rabbinic and patristic texts. Regarding the word *Gabbatha* that Fitzmyer uses to build his case, they argue, "Even if the etymology were Aramaic, it would still be the name in use in Hebrew, just like Californians call their two biggest cities San Francisco and Los Angeles in English." See Randall Buth and Chad Pierce, "Hebraisti in Ancient Texts: Does Ἑβραϊστί Ever Mean 'Aramaic'?," in *The Language Environment of First Century Judaea*, ed. Ruth Randall and Chad Pierce (Leiden: Brill, 2014), 66-109. Cf. Ken M. Penner, "Ancient Names for Hebrew and Aramaic: A Case for Lexical Revision," *NTS* 65, no. 3 (July 2019): 412-23.

[4]See the discussion on this Latin version of Luke in Shmuel Safrai, "Spoken and Literary Languages in the Time of Jesus," in *Jesus' Last Week: Jerusalem Studies in the Synoptic Gospel*, vol. 1, ed. R. Steven Notley, Marc Turnage, and Brian Becker, Jewish and Christian Perspectives 11 (Leiden: Brill, 2006); Sabrina Longland, "Pilate Answered: What I Have Written I Have Written," *The Metropolitan Museum of Art Bulletin* 26, no. 10 (1968): 410-29.

[5]A collection of Aramaic texts and inscriptions can be seen in Joseph A. Fitzmyer and Daniel J. Harrington, eds., *A Manual of Palestinian Aramaic Texts: (Second Century B.C.-Second Century A.D.)* (Rome: Biblical Institute Press, 1978).

[6]This idea was first introduced by Arnold Meyer in 1896. Although some other German scholars, such as Julius Wellhausen and Eberhard Nestle, had talked about this, it was Meyer's monograph that provided a full-scale argument for Aramaic as the first language of the Jewish community in the first century. See Meyer, *Jesu Muttersprache; das galiläische Aramaisch in seiner Bedeutung für die Erklärung der Reden Jesu und der Evangelien überhaupt* (Leipzig: Mohr, 1896). A few years after the publication of *Jesu Muttersprache*, Gustaf Dalman published his *Die Worte Jesu* (first published in 1898, later translated and published in English in 1902), in which he argues that Aramaic was the spoken language and Hebrew appears mainly in literary uses. In this book he also challenges the idea that Hebrew was the mother tongue of Jesus and follows Meyer's conclusion that it was in fact Aramaic. See Gustaf Dalman and David Miller Kay, *The Words of Jesus Considered in the Light of Post-biblical Jewish Writings and the Aramaic Language* (Edinburgh: T&T Clark, 1902). For the history of this discussion, see Steven E. Fassberg, "Which Semitic Language Did Jesus and Other Contemporary Jews Speak?," *CBQ* 74, no. 2 (2012): 264-67. More recent scholars generally agree with this assertion. See Samuel W. Patterson, "What Language Did Jesus Speak?," *The Classical Outlook* 23, no. 7 (1946): 65. Maurice Casey, *Aramaic Sources of Mark's Gospel*, SNTSMS 102 (Cambridge: Cambridge University Press, 1999), 79.

[7]Daniel 2:4 reads, "The Chaldeans said to the king (in Aramaic)" (*waydabru hachasdim lamelech 'aramit*). This is the beginning of the Aramaic section (until Dan 7) in the book of Daniel.

the Mediterranean and over to Pakistan.[8] Many inscriptions discovered in Palestine (particularly on ossuaries), some Aramaic scrolls in Qumran, and the appearance of Aramaic words in the New Testament confirm the use of Aramaic in the first century.[9]

Hebrew, the language of most of the books in the Old Testament, was still used in the first century, but in a very limited way.[10] Joseph Fitzmyer notes, "There are clear indications, both epigraphic and literary, that Hebrew continued in use in certain social strata of the people and perhaps also in certain geographical areas. The evidence, however, is not as abundant as it is for Aramaic."[11] Scholars often use Charles Ferguson's theory of diglossia to explain the link between Hebrew and Aramaic in their complex social relationship.[12] Besides Hebrew and Aramaic, Greek was the language of the Hellenistic Empire. Since the reign of Alexander the Great, Greek quickly became the dominant language in the eastern Mediterranean world. It is no surprise that the entire New Testament is written in Greek. There are debates among scholars on whether Jesus was able to speak Greek. Some argue that Jesus' knowledge of Greek was sufficient to even teach in Greek, others that he mainly spoke Aramaic.[13] The arguments are mainly concentrated on how scholars understand the epigraphic and other written evidence available. Mark Chancey, for instance, argues that there is insufficient evidence to prove that Greek was commonly spoken in Galilee in the first century.[14] Yet that does not mean that people did not know Greek at all—although the level of their knowledge of Greek is highly debatable. What we do know is that

> a Jewish resident of first-century Palestine (Josephus is again an instructive example) could write a marriage contract in Aramaic; complete a financial transaction with a bill of sale in Greek, to make it enforceable in a Roman court; write his brother's epitaph in Greek, Hebrew or Aramaic, according to his own abilities, his brother's wishes and the expected audience; record his contribution to the repairs of a synagogue in Aramaic, Hebrew or Greek, according to the

[8]See Joseph A. Fitzmyer, "Presidential Address: The Languages of Palestine in the First Century A.D.," *CBQ* 32, no. 4 (1970): 502.

[9]See Hannah M. Cotton et al., eds., *Corpus Inscriptionum Iudaeae/Palaestinae*, vol. 1, *Jerusalem; Part 1: 1-704* (Berlin: de Gruyter, 2010).

[10]Klaus Breyer suspects that Hebrew was not used anymore in Palestine after 400 BCE. See Klaus Beyer, *The Aramaic Language: Its Distribution and Subdivisions*, trans. John F. Healey (Göttingen: Vandenhoeck & Ruprecht, 1986).

[11]Fitzmyer, "Presidential Address," 528.

[12]Charles A. Ferguson, "Diglossia," *WORD* 15, no. 2 (1959): 325-40; Pinchas Lapide, "Insights from Qumran into the Languages of Jesus," *Revue de Qumrân* 8, no. 4 (1975): 483-501; Hughson T. Ong, "Ancient Palestine Is Multilingual and Diglossic: Introducing Multilingualism Theories to New Testament Studies," *CurBR* 13, no. 3 (2015): 330-50; Jonathan M. Watt, "The Current Landscape of Diglossia Studies: The Diglossic Continuum in First-Century Palestine," in *Diglossia and Other Topics in New Testament Linguistics*, ed. Stanley E. Porter (Sheffield: Sheffield Academic Press, 2000), 18-36. Steven Fraade calls this phenomenon "internal Jewish bilingualism." See Fraade, "Language Mix and Multilingualism in Ancient Palestine: Literary and Inscriptional Evidence," *Jewish Studies* 48 (2012): 6. For a critical response to the application of diglossia, see Mark Janse, "Bilingualism, Diglossia and Literacy in Jewish Palestine," in *Encyclopedia of Ancient Greek Language and Linguistics*, ed. Giorgios K. Giannakis (Leiden: Brill, 2014), 238-41.

[13]Stanley E. Porter, "Did Jesus Ever Teach in Greek?," *TynBul* 44, no. 2 (1993); G. Scott Gleaves, *Did Jesus Speak Greek?: The Emerging Evidence of Greek Dominance in First-Century Palestine* (Eugene, OR: Pickwick, 2015); Maurice Casey, "In Which Language Did Jesus Teach?," *The Expository Times* 108, no. 11 (August 1997): 326-28. Casey launches a strong attack on Stanley Porter's argument that Jesus was able to teach in Greek. Of all his arguments, the most devastating one is that "This [Porter's argument] is a fundamentalist dream, and ultra conservative assumptions are required to carry it through." See also Porter's response in Stanley E. Porter, "Jesus and the Use of Greek: A Response to Maurice Casey," *BBR* 10, no. 1 (2000): 71-87.

[14]Mark A. Chancey, *Greco-Roman Culture and the Galilee of Jesus*, SNTSMS 134 (Cambridge: Cambridge University Press, 2005), chap. 5.

> epigraphic custom and idiom of the building, the expected audience and even the size of the contribution; or write a letter to his children in a language he taught them to read and write but not necessarily the language they spoke at home (literally, their mother-tongue).[15]

Though the debate continues about whether Greek was commonly used in Galilee, throughout the Mediterranean world Greek was a lingua franca. In the eastern Mediterranean, Greek remained the dominant language, while the Romans used Latin for their administrative purposes. However, local languages were still very much used in many areas, and so it is no surprise that bilingualism was quite common in the first century.[16] When an imperial language invades a space, people do not just give up their language and embrace the language of the colonizer. In other words, language change does not happen easily and voluntarily. People often maintain their local language as an act of resistance against the colonial rule.

The book of 2 Maccabees recounts an interesting story that illustrates this situation. When Antiochus IV Epiphanes and his troops attempted to force the Jewish people to abandon their culture and embrace the Hellenistic culture, they did it in a violent way. The temple in Jerusalem was called "the temple of Olympian Zeus" (2 Macc 6:2). There they were required to celebrate the festival of Dionysus. As part of that celebration, Eleazar "was being forced to open his month to eat pig's flesh" (2 Macc 6:18). He chose to die as a martyr instead of eating pork. In 2 Maccabees 7, however, the story is about the death of seven brothers and their mother. To make a long story short, these brothers are called one by one and asked to abandon their tradition, culture, and religion. After the first brother is killed, the second brother is asked to eat swine's flesh, just like Eleazer. He refuses by saying no in the language of his ancestors, likely Hebrew/Aramaic (2 Macc 7:8). One by one, Antiochus kills all the brothers. The story describes what the mother does: "The mother was especially admirable and worthy of honorable memory. Although she saw her seven sons perish within a single day, she bore it with good courage because of her hope in the Lord. She encouraged each of them in the language of their ancestors" (2 Macc 7:20-21). By the end of the story, all seven brothers and their mother have been slaughtered. They used their mother tongue, that is, the language of their ancestors, as a way to resist the colonial cultural imposition.

In a multilingual society like that one and like many of ours today, people commonly code-switch from one language to another. Sociolinguists often use the concepts of domains or network to explain both social spaces where people use a specific language and why they code-switch.[17] In Acts 21, for instance, when Paul defends himself in front of the Roman tribune, the tribune asks Paul, "Do you know Greek?" (Acts 21:37). This question seems to be a test of whether Paul is the Egyptian who revolted against the Romans (Acts 21:38). Right after telling the tribune who he is, Paul then asks permission to speak to the people (Acts 21:39). Paul speaks to them in the Hebrew/Aramaic language (Acts 21:40). In

[15]Jonathan J Price, "The Languages of the Jews in Roman Palestine: The Evidence of Inscriptions (TAB. I-II)," *Orientalia* 89, no. 1 (2020): 116.

[16]See J. N. Adams, M. Janse, and S. Swain, eds., *Bilingualism in Ancient Society: Language Contact and the Written Word* (Oxford: Oxford University Press, 2003); J. N. Adams, *Bilingualism and the Latin Language* (New York: Cambridge University Press, 2003).

[17]See Joshua A. Fishman, "Who Speaks What Language to Whom and When?," *La Linguistique* 1, no. 2 (1965): 67-88.

other words, Paul immediately code-switches from Greek to Hebrew/Aramaic.[18] Now, of course it is much easier to conduct such domain analysis study when the languages are still alive and spoken, but it is almost impossible to do for people in the first century. Some scholars have tried, but since they can rely only on written materials, their conclusions are highly speculative for the obvious reason that written materials do not fully represent the actual life of language.[19]

However, there are records of how early followers of Jesus wrestled with the linguistic differences around them. What language should be used in their gatherings, especially when people came from different linguistic backgrounds? This question gets to the heart of the politics of language. In Corinth, for instance, Greek was the principal language on the street, while Latin inscriptions can be found where administrative buildings were located.[20] This, however, does not mean that other languages did not exist in Corinth. As a city that received many immigrants from other places, Corinth was likely also a multilingual city.[21] So although inscriptions in Corinth are mainly written in Greek and Latin, that does not necessarily mean that everyone spoke only Greek or Latin. Immigrants often have to operate in the dominant language and speak their native language at home with those who come from the same linguistic background. In other words, code-switching and being multilingual are almost inevitable for immigrants.

Josephus is a good example to illustrate this discrepancy between writing and speech. When he was dislocated to Rome, interestingly, he used mainly Greek. He might have had some knowledge of Latin, but all his multivolume writings are in Greek. Writing in Greek, of course, was not easy at all. So, Vespasian and Titus gave him "assistants" (*synergoi*) to help with his Greek (Josephus, *Ag. Ap.* 1.50). He also acknowledges that he has a hard time acquiring precision in the pronunciation of Greek because of the habit of his mother tongue (Josephus, *Ant.* 20.263-264). All this to say that even when he was able to write in Greek (with the help of assistants), he kept his mother tongue. This is a typical struggle of many immigrants, especially of first-generation immigrants. Speaking a colonial language does not mean that one gives up one's mother tongue.

In Corinth, too, when people moved to this city from other places, they did not give up their native languages. So, although most of the inscriptions are in Greek and Latin, that does not necessarily mean that the other, minoritized languages did not exist there. Evidence for this dynamic of multilingualism in the city of Corinth can be found in 1 Corinthians in Paul's discussion on speaking in tongues. Scholars debate the exact nature of this phenomenon. The dominant view today is

[18]See Hughson T. Ong, "Sociolinguistics and New Testament Exegesis: Three Approaches to Discourse Analysis Using Acts 21:27–22:5 as a Test Case," *Biblical and Ancient Greek Linguistics* 4 (2015): 49-84.

[19]The latest attempt to do this is by Hughson Ong. Ong attempts to map out the languages that Jesus *might have used* in different domains or social networks in the Gospel of Matthew. See Hughson T. Ong, *The Multilingual Jesus and the Sociolinguistic World of the New Testament* (Leiden: Brill, 2015).

[20]See Benjamin W. Millis, "The Social and Ethnic Origins of the Colonists in Early Roman Corinth," in *Corinth in Context: Comparative Studies on Religion and Society*, ed. Steven J. Friesen, Daniel N. Schowalter, and James C. Walters (Leiden: Brill, 2010), 13-35. See also Cavan W. Concannon, *"When You Were Gentiles": Specters of Ethnicity in Roman Corinth and Paul's Corinthian Correspondence*, Synkrisis: Comparative Approaches to Early Christianity in Greco-Roman Culture (New Haven, CT: Yale University Press, 2014).

[21]See my discussion in Ekaputra Tupamahu, *Contesting Languages: Heteroglossia and the Politics of Language in the Early Church* (New York: Oxford University Press, 2022), chap. 3.

that tongues is an unintelligible ecstatic experience. This interpretation, however, is quite new in history. As I have discussed elsewhere, it came out of eighteenth- and nineteenth-century German scholarship, influenced by the rise of German nationalism and Romantic philosophy.[22] Prior to then, almost everyone, if not all, saw this phenomenon as a linguistic one. Why? The word "tongue" (*glōssa*) is a common word for "language." We still use this word for language today. For instance, a mother *tongue* means one's native *language*. In this sense, Paul's discourse on speaking in tongues in 1 Corinthians 14 is a regulation of language in the gatherings of early followers of Jesus. When people began to follow the Jesus movement in the first century, they would get together and speak or pray in their own (various) languages. This multilingual situation felt very chaotic to Paul, and so he demands there be translation (1 Cor 14:13, 27). And in those instances in which no one was available to provide it, Paul silences these languages altogether (1 Cor 14:28). In other words, Paul tells the Corinthians that if they want to use their native languages, they can only do it when accompanied by translation. If no one translates their language, then they can only use it for themselves and to speak to God.[23] In short, Paul wants to regulate the use of languages in Corinth through a monolingual structure. Only the dominant language can be useful for building the church, Paul insists in 1 Corinthians 14:14.

Paul's monolingual imagination is quite different from what we see in the book of Revelation. In Revelation 7, in his depiction of the cosmic drama in which the Lamb is the main protagonist of the story, John says that he saw a multitude "from every nation, from all tribes and peoples and languages [*glōssōn*], standing before the throne and before the Lamb" (Rev 7:9). The Lamb throughout the story of Revelation symbolizes Christ (see Rev 5:6). So, this great multitude is those who follow the Lamb, that is, the followers of Christ. Those who are ransomed by the blood of the Lamb, John declares, are "saints from every tribe and language and people and nation" (Rev 5:9). Here is a somewhat different picture of how the early followers of Jesus saw themselves in light of the multilingual world around them. If Paul pushes for a monolingual order, the book of Revelation sees many languages as one of the markers of the followers of the Lamb. In other words, linguistic differences are not erased. While Paul regards tongues or languages as a source of chaos by which the church is not built up, Revelation regards tongues as ingrained in the very identity of the followers of Christ. The vision of multilingual followers of Christ in Revelation is parallel to what is present in Acts 2. The outpouring of the Spirit on the day of Pentecost is marked by the opening of social spaces to many languages.

Just as many of us today struggle with linguistic differences, so too did the early followers of Jesus in the first century. Thanks to colonial political powers, colonial languages tend to impose themselves on the colonized world. Greek and Latin in the first century, and now English, Spanish, and French, are languages of the colonizers. They are international languages not because they are better than other languages but because they are sustained by colonial powers. Musa Dube points out:

> Because colonizers tend to install their languages among the colonized, thus displacing the local ones, the subject of language is

[22]Tupamahu, *Contesting Languages*, chap. 1.

[23]See Tupamahu, *Contesting Languages*, chap. 5.

> central to postcolonial debates. Questions such as why do the colonizers give their languages to their subjects? What happens to the languages of the colonized? What exactly is lost when the colonized begin to speak, read and write in the colonizer's language and neglect their own languages? The question, What strategies are adopted by the colonized to resist the imposition of the colonizer's languages? remain central to postcolonial debates.[24]

Dube's point is clear: if one wants to talk about the cultural effects of colonialism, one should not disregard linguistic struggles. Reading the New Testament from a marginalized linguistic point of view should bring the politics of language to the surface.

Many churches today call themselves multiethnic. What do we mean by that term? Have we seen churches open to a multilingual liturgy? Can people express themselves in their own language in the church gathering? Yes, eleven o'clock on Sunday morning is still the most segregated hour in America.[25] It is not only a racial segregation but also linguistic segregation. Korean, Indonesian, Urdu, Spanish, and English congregations, and so on, worship in different spaces. Linguistic integration is almost unthinkable. Can the church become a space of linguistic hospitality in which all languages are welcomed and accepted, instead of subjugated and silenced under the power of a colonizing language?

---

[24]Musa W. Dube, "Consuming a Colonial Cultural Bomb: Translating Badimo into 'Demons' in the Setswana Bible (Matthew 8.28-34; 15.22; 10.8)," *JSNT* 21, no. 73 (1999): 33-34.

[25]Martin Luther King Jr., "The Most Segregated Hour in America," April 17, 1960, www.youtube.com/watch?v=1q881g1L_d8.

IMMIGRANTS AND THE KINGDOM OF GOD

DO THEY HAVE A HOME IN GOD'S CITY?

Rodolfo Galvan Estrada III

Talking about immigration within our contemporary context can sometimes lead the conversation to solely focus on the loudest and extreme voices on the debate, those who champion open borders or those who advocate for the building of a wall. For many who live in the US borderlands, the topic is personal especially when many immigrants share our Christian faith.[1] Immigration, however, is a global issue. It is not limited to the United States. Migration occurs in Syria, South and West Asia, and within Africa. We hear about immigration challenges from the United States and Latin American perspective, especially when politicians utilize news media reports on migrants to stoke fears of foreigners in "caravans" and justify cruel child-separation policies.[2] But, as Daniel Carroll states, "Immigration is neither a new phenomenon nor a recent political concern. It has been a topic of national interest since the colonial era."[3]

It is tempting to think that immigrants come to the United States solely for better economic opportunities. The reality is a bit more complicated. Miguel De La Torre points out that US foreign policies are responsible for Latin American migration. The influence of US foreign policy on immigration can be seen, for example, in the doctrine of Manifest Destiny that justified violence and seizure of Mexican land and the NAFTA trade deal that enriched many US farmers at the cost of impoverishing many Latin American farmers.[4] The US created such policies, often with the sanction of the church, in order to justify nationalism, military interventions, and the removal of indigenous and Mexican people from their land.[5] In addition, US imperialism in Latin American countries during the twentieth century led to the removal of many democratically elected leaders.[6] De La Torre thus insists that it is erroneous to believe that immigrants come to take away American jobs, use up social resources, or come in search of the American dream. Instead, US imperialism and interventionism have led to the social and

[1]Gregory Lee Cuéllar, "Channeling the Biblical Exile as an Art Task for Central American Refugee Children on the Texas–Mexico Border," in *Latinxs, the Bible, and Migration*, ed. Efraín Agosto and Jacqueline Hidalgo (Cham, Switzerland: Palgrave, 2018), 67-88.

[2]D'Vera Cohn, Jeffrey S. Passel and Ana Gonzalez-Barrera, "Rise in U.S. Immigrants From El Salvador, Guatemala and Honduras Outpaces Growth from Elsewhere," Pew Research Center, Washington DC, December 7, 2017, accessed May 30, 2020, www.pewresearch.org/hispanic/2017/12/07/rise-in-u-s-immigrants-from-el-salvador-guatemala-and-honduras-outpaces-growth-from-elsewhere/.

[3]Daniel Carroll, *Christians at the Border: Immigration, the Church, and the Bible* (Grand Rapids, MI: Brazos, 2013), 5.

[4]Miguel De La Torre, *The U.S. Immigration Crisis: Toward an Ethics of Place* (Eugene, OR: Cascade, 2016), 13-18.

[5]Robert Chao Romero, *Brown Church: Five Centuries of Latina/a Social Justice, Theology, and Identity* (Downers Grove, IL: InterVarsity Press, 2020), 99-119.

[6]De La Torre, *Immigration,* 69-70.

economic conditions in Latin America.[7] Certainly, other factors contribute to immigration such as ecological devastations and climate change.[8] However, we cannot ignore the role and unintended consequences that US imperialism has on the lives of many foreigners. This leads us to recognize that asking why migrants would leave their country, risk their lives, and traverse dangerous regions in order to live in the US is the wrong question. We cannot explore the topic of immigration isolated from imperialism because no empire exists apart from the acquisition and military intervention on indigenous land.

Given these relations between immigration and the empire, we now see why it is necessary to discuss these aspects in light of God's kingdom. It is George Eldon Ladd who defines the kingdom as God's kingly rule that is both a reign in the future and present reality that "came into history in the person and mission of Jesus."[9] Since the kingdom is about God's rule, he suggests that "every aspect of the kingdom must be derived from the character and action of God."[10] But one aspect that Ladd does not discuss deserves our attention. Although his exploration insists that God is a seeking God, he does not sufficiently elaborate on its implications for foreigners, immigrants, or the kingdom of Rome.[11] This chapter seeks to fill in that void by explicitly focusing on how the kingdom of God shapes our views of the immigrant—those who are strangers and foreigners. In order to do so, I first situate our understanding of the kingdom in light of the Roman Empire's view and relationship with foreigners. I then demonstrate that while there is not an equivalency between immigration today and immigration in the ancient world, there are points of contact between the way that empires view and treat foreigners. Last, I argue that our posture toward immigrants is not just a political issue. How we view the immigrant also reflects which kingdom values and practices we have embraced, either from the kingdom of Rome or from the kingdom of God.

THE KINGDOM OF ROME AND THE FOREIGNER

The early Christians knew of only one earthly kingdom—the empire of Rome. We may assume that the conquest of various regions throughout the Mediterranean world ushered a period of peace for all people, also known as the *Pax Romana*. But this was more of an ideal than a reality. Peace according to Emperor Caesar Augustus meant that foreigners were no longer in a position to threaten Rome.[12] Indeed, the Roman poet Virgil, who was commissioned to write the *Aeneid* by the emperor, states it well: "You, Roman, remember to rule nations with your command, these will be your arts, to stamp peace with men's practice, to spare the humble and to crush the proud."[13] How did foreigners lose this ability to threaten Rome and become pacified? How did Rome "crush the proud" as Virgil describes? Conquest.

The Romans were known for conquering a region by totally defeating their enemies in

[7]De La Torre, *Immigration*, 151.

[8]Guy Abel, Michael Brottrager, Jesus Cuaresma, and Raya Muttarak, "Climate, Conflict and Forced Migration," *Global Environmental Change* 54 (2019): 239-49.

[9]George Ladd, *A Theology of the New Testament* (Grand Rapids, MI: Eerdmans, 1993), 65-67.

[10]Ladd, *Theology*, 79.

[11]Ladd, *Theology*, 82-85,

[12]*Res gest. divi Aug.* 3.

[13]Virgil, *Aen.* 6.851-3 (Fairclough, LCL).

order to bring fear to those who remained.[14] This practice occurred since the period of the Roman Republic. Polybius recounts Roman conquest in Carthago Nova (Spain) where all the inhabitants, including animals, were massacred by the Roman armies.[15] Likewise, when the Gauls (modern-day France and Belgium) revolted "the Romans no longer made war on them for the sake of supremacy and sovereignty, but with a view to their total expulsion and extermination."[16] Others such as Velleius Paterculus narrate how the Romans exterminated the Teutons, a Germanic tribe.[17] We also have firsthand accounts by Julius Caesar, who mentions that the Nerviii people, a Belgic tribe from northern Gaul, were almost annihilated.[18] In addition, when the Britons (modern-day United Kingdom) desired to reclaim their freedom, thousands died, including women and animals.[19] Tacitus records the speech of Calgacus, a leader of a Brittonic tribe, who states,

> Terrible Romans, from whose oppression escape is vainly sought by obedience and submission. Robbers of the world, having by their universal plunder exhausted the land, they rifle the deep. If the enemy be rich, they are rapacious; if he be poor, they lust for dominion; neither the east nor the west has been able to satisfy them. Alone among men they covet with equal eagerness poverty and riches. To robbery, slaughter, plunder, they give the lying name of empire; they make a solitude and call it peace. (*Agr.* 30.4-6 [Peterson, LCL])

Last, the Jewish rebellion against the Romans in 66–70 CE was not any different. Josephus mentions that at one point there were hundreds of Jewish people who were daily captured trying to escape Jerusalem. The Roman General Titus ordered that they should be crucified in front of the wall in order to instill fear on those who resisted. It was a mass crucifixion to the point that "space could not be found for the crosses nor crosses for the bodies."[20]

The Romans did not bring "peace" to those who resisted their rule. They brought death, slavery, or submission. However, the most striking thing about Roman expansion was the persistent phenomenon of native resistance and revolt in various places which demonstrates that not all were content with their colonizers.[21] We cannot fail to ignore that Roman expansion into foreign regions suggests that there is the acquisition of land and resources from the "other." Their extension of "peace" included death to indigenous people who resisted. Of course, the Romans did not always need to overtake a region through violence. They installed puppet leaders—client kings and aristocrats, the local elite, and influential people to rule on their behalf.[22] This familiar face made it possible to keep foreigners and their resistance at bay. But managing the empire was difficult. Cassius Dio admits that the Romans "[embraced] every variety of mankind in terms of both race and character" but "these evils have gone so far that they can only be controlled with great difficulty."[23] What

[14]Tacitus, *Ann.* 12.33.
[15]Polybius, 10.15.4-5.
[16]Polybius, 2.21.9 (Paton, LCL).
[17]Velleius, 2.12.4.
[18]Julius Caesar, *Bell. Gall.* 2.28.
[19]Tacitus, *Ann.* 14.37.
[20]Josephus, *J.W.* 5.449-51 (Thackeray, LCL).
[21]Stephen Dyson, "Native Revolts in the Roman Empire," *Historia* (1971): 239-74.
[22]Neville Morley, *The Roman Empire: Roots of Imperialism* (New York: Pluto, 2010), 38.
[23]Cassius Dio, *Rom his.* 52.15 (Cary, LCL).

are these evils that Dio refers too? Is it ruling over others or the diversity of humanity that resists Roman rule? It is likely the latter based on the fact that Dio regularly turns to Augustus's desire that his successors should manage the empire and expand it no further.[24]

The kingdom of Rome justified this colonial enterprise on the belief that the foreigners were uncivilized and needed to be made more human, or at least, more Roman. The Romans believed that their rule was in the best interest of the conquered. Whatever use of force, the kingdom of Rome was always in the "right" given the many benefits it provides. In fact, Pliny describes Rome as chosen by the gods to

> unite the scattered empires of the earth, bestow a polish upon [humanity's] manners, unite the discordant and uncouth dialects of so many different nations by the powerful ties of one common language, confer the enjoyments of discourse and of civilization upon mankind, to become . . . the mother-country of all nations of the earth. (*Nat.* 3.6; trans. John Bostock, et. al. [London: Taylor and Francis, 1855])

The Romans presumed that they were chosen by the gods to rule over all foreigners. They believed that civilization was being extended to all. As Benjamin Isaac also finds, Roman writers such as Pliny would describe foreigners in manners that would justify conquest, especially when it was believed that foreigners could be turned into regular human beings.[25]

There is also another way of looking at the relationship between imperialism and foreigners. Roman conquest was also fueled by racial ideologies that presumed foreigners were incapable of matching Roman might. Since the Romans assumed to be geographically positioned in the center of the world, this meant that all others would be inferior in some fashion.[26] This racial ideology was not a novel idea. It was early Greek racial theories that first perpetuated a correlation between the geography and climate of various regions and the physical appearances and characters of people. Hippocrates judged the people of Asia as "less warlike than the people of 'our' part of the world." They were in a sense "feeble" because of their climate and thus only capable of living under despots.[27] Aristotle also claims that people who live in cold climates, Europe, and Asia may have freedom, but they lack intelligence and political organization.[28] Since "the Greeks are geographically in between Asia and Europe" they are "continually free, have the best political system, and the ability to rule over others."[29] The Greeks, however, never extended their rule or created an empire parallel to the Romans. But what Aristotle and early Greek writers racially conceived about "others" became a reality for the Romans. Pliny admits that empires never rise from "remote races." It is those who live in the middle regions who have "gentle customs, clear thoughts, and temperaments open and capable of understanding all nature."[30] In other words, it is the "civilized" who live in a balanced climate, which so happens to include the Romans.[31]

[24]Cassius Dio, *Rom his.* 53.10; 56.33.3-5; 56.41.7.

[25]Benjamin Isaac, *Invention of Racism in Classical Antiquity* (Princeton, NJ: Princeton University Press, 2004), 214-15.

[26]Vitruvius, *On Architecture*, 6.1.4; 6.1.10-11.

[27]Hippocrates, *Aer.* 16 (Jones, LCL); See also Herodotus, *Hist.* 9.122.

[28]Aristotle, *Pol.* 7.5.6.

[29]Aristotle, *Pol.* 7.5.6 (Rebecca Kennedy et al., *Race and Ethnicity in the Classical World: An Anthology of Primary Sources in Translation* [Indianapolis: Hackett, 2013], 44).

[30]Pliny, *Nat.* 2.80.

[31]Ptolemy, *Tetra.* 2.2.

While Rome was indeed a powerful empire, it was also one that justified its domination over foreigners by appealing to their mission to civilize the world. By extending the Roman kingdom over others, it also brought conquest, dehumanization, and subjugation of indigenous people. As Edward Said explains, imperialism is not just about the control of distant lands but also about the rhetoric, attitudes, and ideologies that undergird that control and conquest.[32] The belief that a land is geographically positioned in the center of the world with the most superior people lends itself to imperial expansion. Even more, since the conquest of the Mediterranean world was divinely foretold in Virgil's *Aeneid* and believed to be for the betterment of humanity, the subjugation of foreigners would have been a natural imperial outcome.

FOREIGNERS IN ROME AND IMMIGRANTS TODAY

What then are the points of contact between immigration today and the presence of foreigners in the Roman age? We have already reviewed how imperial and racial ideologies facilitated the belief that Rome ought to have dominion over foreigners. But at the same time, we must also notice that there were some drawbacks. Absorbing all these foreigners were also perceived as leading to the corruption of Rome.[33] Juvenal's *Satires* also provides further evidence of the perception of foreign influence and corruption. He describes various immigrants from Syria and Anatolia who bring their customs, language, music, habits, and women in order to "worm their way into the houses of the great and become their masters."[34] Denise McCoskey notices that Juvenal's critiques sound similar to "modern laments about immigration, namely that Rome was being overrun by foreigners."[35] This leads us to recognize that although Rome was an expanding empire that would absorb and include various people from diverse backgrounds, this does not mean that they were motivated by a utopian ideal to build an empire that united all people in peace and harmony. There were limitations to the tolerance of Rome, especially toward foreigners and their cultures. Foreigners were certainly absorbed, but if their foreign presence occluded the Roman identity, they were deported. This is most notable in the significant amount of foreign expulsion from the city of Rome since the late Republic.

This power to exile people, and thus create immigrants, is a form of punishment for those who found themselves in precarious political and legal situations.[36] Sedition, or committing a political or moral crime, was not the only reason for being exiled. Augustus had also exiled people who did not commit any crimes except for being a perceived burden to Roman society. Suetonius remarks that during a time of grain scarcity that Augustus "expelled from the city the slaves that were for sale, as well as the schools of gladiators, all foreigners with the exception of physicians and teachers, and a part of the household slaves."[37] Likewise, the Emperor Tiberius also abolished foreign cults, especially Egyptian and Jewish rites, and exiled Jews and others who had similar beliefs. This

[32]Edward Said, *Culture and Imperialism* (New York: Vintage, 1994), 78.

[33]See for example Pliny's (*Nat.* 24.1) and Seneca's critique of foreigners (Augustine, *Civ.* 6.11).

[34]Juvenal, *Satires*, 3.60-72 (Braund, LCL).

[35]Denise McCoskey, *Race: Antiquity and its Legacy* (New York: Oxford, 2012), 119.

[36]Jo-Marie Claassen, *Displaced Persons: The Literature of Exile from Cicero to Boethius* (Madison: University of Wisconsin, 1999), 9-11; Gordon Kelly, *A History of Exile in the Roman Republic* (New York: Cambridge University Press, 2006), 5; See also Cicero, *De dom. su.* 27; *Pro rab.* 15-16; *Pro Cae.* 100.

[37]Suetonius, *Aug.* 42 (Rolfe, LCL).

exile came with a threat. Tiberius warned foreigners that if they would not leave Rome they would be sold into slavery.[38] Indeed, Laurens Tacoma notes that exile was "clearly symbolically charged" and regarded as a way of establishing the boundaries of the community by defining who did not belong to it.[39] It was a form of "immigration control" and thus viewed as a cleansing of the Roman community by ridding unwanted people.[40]

When we compare the power to exile people to the forms of immigration control within a US context, there are some notable similarities and differences. Most certainly, Rome during the late republic and early imperial age did not have a bureaucratic system akin to the Department of Homeland Security of the United States. Roman soldiers were not border patrol agents who checked the immigration status of individuals within Rome's borders. This is one of the most obvious differences. This does not mean that Rome did not care about the residency status of people or groups of people within its boundaries. Rome did deport people, and this is perhaps the major similarity with US immigration control that we have today. Like the US government, the Roman government also had the power to grant residency permission and deport people who were considered unsuitable residents of Rome.[41] As the Roman Empire expanded and absorbed various people, foreigners, their customs, arts, and cultures, it was later perceived to have a corrupting influence on the very identity of the Roman people. These sentiments from various Roman writers, including Juvenal, echo a desire to make Rome great again. They were fearful that the very people Rome conquered were now conquering them. In a sense, they believe that the empire was crumbling from within because of immigrants. This helps explain the numerous deportations of foreigners who resided in Rome. But it is important to also recognize that not everyone who was expelled during the Roman Empire committed a crime nor was a foreigner. Some foreigners were expelled simply to alleviate social pressure during periods of agricultural scarcity. Rome may have targeted foreigners and expelled them, but Rome did not utilize this tool simply against foreigners. Rome had a tendency of also expelling its own citizens, those who considered undesirable and had forfeited their right to live on the land. This is something that we do not have today. Citizens of the US who commit crimes may be incarcerated, but they are incarcerated on US territory and not banished to some distant land outside of Rome.

THE KINGDOM OF GOD AND THE IMMIGRANT

How would the New Testament's description of the kingdom of God and its relationship to foreigners resonate in light of the Roman Empire? Is the kingdom of God another imperialistic kingdom that comes to steal land, make immigrants, and exile people who are undesirable? Similar to Ladd's interpretation, the kingdom of God is the political reign and rule of God that was inaugurated with Jesus' mission and ministry. But Leonardo Boff and Clodovis Boff also remark that it includes a "full and total liberation of all creation" which

[38]Suetonius, *Tib.* 36.

[39]Laurens Tacoma, *Moving Romans: Migration to Rome in the Principate* (New York: Oxford, 2016), 97, 102.

[40]Tacoma, *Moving Romans*, 103.

[41]Reversing one's exile status is most evident in the *Laudatio Turiae*, a funerary inscription written by a husband for his wife who had deceased. See "A Funeral Eulogy," in *Women's Life in Greece and Rome: A Source Book in Translation*, ed. Mary Lefkowitz and Maureen Fant (Baltimore: John Hopkins University, 2016), 166.

will be "purified of all that oppresses it."[42] In other words, the kingdom is not indifferent to the plight of the immigrants. As they insist, "the kingdom of God is always present where persons bring about justice, seek comradeship, forgive each other, and promote life."[43] It brings both a liberation from sin and a transformation of the social and structural sin of oppression and injustice.[44]

This all-encompassing presence of God's kingdom is in contrast to Rome's reign, perception of foreigners, and unjust acquisition of indigenous land. God's kingdom does not seek to pillage the land, justify violence, or presume foreigners will lead to the deterioration of the kingdom. We find portraits of God's kingdom in Jesus' parables.[45] Jesus compares the kingdom of God to a mustard seed, which he describes as the smallest of all seeds that will grow tall and attract birds. This suggests that God's kingdom will eventually grow without force or violence. Its natural growth will not only be magnificent for all to see, but a place of rest for the weary and those who, like birds, may be seen as enemies (Mt 13:31-32).[46] Another parable portrays the kingdom expanding without human intervention. The kingdom is like a seed buried in the soil by a farmer (Mk 4:26-29). It may be hidden from sight, but it is presently growing. Jesus also compares the kingdom to leaven that a woman mixes with the dough until it is spread to every part (Lk 13:20-21). Like leaven in bread, God's kingdom aims to spread throughout the world—in a manner that will make everything it touches more bountiful, tasteful, and nurturing for all.

Jesus' teaching on the coming kingdom was not an announcement of conquest. Rather, it includes the invitation to join by changing one's sinful ways, behaviors, attitudes, and actions toward others. His first words in the Gospels include the message, "Repent, for the kingdom of heaven has come near" (Mt 4:17; Mk 1:15). This kingdom that Jesus preached was based on different political values of redemption and salvation. It required one to live a life of love and forgiveness toward one another, including the foreigner. But he also warned that "not everyone who says to me, 'Lord, Lord,' will enter the kingdom of heaven, but only the one who does the will of my Father " (Mt 7:21). What is the will of the Father? What are the political values that God as King requires of his people who have politically aligned themselves with the divine kingdom?

Matthew 25:31-46 provides a portrait of the kingdom's political values. Jesus states that at the end of the age, when all the nations are gathered before the throne, those who enter the kingdom of God are the ones who fed the hungry, clothed the naked, visited the sick and imprisoned, and welcomed the "stranger." The word for "stranger" is the Greek term *xenos*, which can also be translated as "alien," or "foreigner." It appears also in Ephesians 2:12-19 when Paul describes the Gentiles as people who were once "strangers" to the covenant of God but now made fellow members of God's household. The term also emerges in Hebrews 11:13 to describe the heroes of the faith who died as "strangers and foreigners" on earth. What is remarkable with Matthew's use is not only that the people who enter the kingdom of God were hospitable to foreigners, but by doing so they were welcoming the king. On the other hand, those who did not inherit

[42]Leonardo Boff and Clodovis Boff, *Introducing Liberation Theology* (Maryknoll, NY: Orbis, 1997), 52.
[43]Boff and Boff, *Liberation*, 53.
[44]Boff and Boff, *Liberation*, 54-55.
[45]Mt 13:1-52; 18:23-35; 20:1-16; 22:2-14; 25:1-13; Mk 4:11; 4:26-34; Lk 8:4-15; 13:18-19, 20-21.
[46]Joachim Jeremias, *Jesus' Promise to the Nations* (Philadelphia: Fortress, 1982), 69.

the kingdom protested that they did not have the opportunity to perform such deeds. They ask, "Lord, when was it that we saw you hungry or thirsty or a stranger or naked or sick or in prison and did not take care of you?" (Mt 25:44). The king replies, "Just as you did not do it to one of the least of these, you did not do it to me" (Mt 25:45). In this teaching, God as the king is associated with the foreigner. To be welcoming and hospitable to the foreigner is to do so with God. Or said another way, the people of the kingdom are those who can see the face of God on the face of the foreigner. We must recall that earlier in the Gospel Jesus was also a foreigner when he migrated to Egypt as a child (Mt 2:1-23). Only Matthew records this migration and refugee status of Jesus and his family. In fact, Carroll states, "The migration of [Jesus'] family locates the Jesus story within a movement that spans history, of people desiring a better life or escaping the threat of death."[47] Like many other immigrants who leave their country and come to the United States, Jesus and his family do so not because they want to be here, but due to the violence and foreign policies that make their own country oppressive. As Matthew 25 teaches, what we do on earth and how we act toward immigrants will have implications for how we are received when God's kingdom is manifested in the future.

There are differences in the practices and values between the kingdom of Rome and the kingdom of God. That is, instead of robbing people's land like the kingdom of Rome, the kingdom of God is a home for the migrant and landless who flee oppressive empires. Instead of justifying cruelty and massacring foreigners who resist the kingdom of Rome, the kingdom of God gives nourishment and healing to all people who accept the invitation. Instead of lamenting that the absorption of foreigners has corrupted the kingdom of Rome, in God's kingdom the embrace of foreigners has led to its beautification. The kingdom of God is not the place for the rich, proud, or arrogant. The kingdom of God is a home for the "least of these," the poor, children, the humble, tax collectors, and prostitutes.[48] And most importantly, the kingdom will include a home for foreigners and immigrants. Jesus remarks that "many will come from east and west and will take their places at the banquet with Abraham and Isaac and Jacob in the kingdom" (Mt 8:11). Those whom Rome may see as inferior because of the geographical region in which they reside are actually God's guests in the kingdom. Foreigners will come from various parts of the world to take their seats because it belongs to them just as much as it belongs to us. In Revelation 5:9-10 we hear a declaration in heaven that praises the Lamb because he has gathered people from "every tribe and language and people and nation" to be "a kingdom and priests serving our God" who will also "reign on earth." From this perspective, the kingdom of God is the home for all people, including those who are currently migrating and fleeing political oppression.

CONCLUSION

How then should the church respond today to immigrants? While this chapter does not aim to solve the immigration debate, it does propose that we view the immigrant and foreigner among us from a different lens. Although the imperial policies of Rome may oppress the foreigner, this is not so in God's kingdom. In God's kingdom all people, including the foreigner and immigrant have an

[47]Carroll, *Border*, 106.

[48]Mt 18:1-4; 19:13-15, 23-24; 21:31, 43; Mk 10:14-16, 23-25; Lk 6:20.

eternal home. But this kingdom was not solely a heavenly reality. It has political implications on earth. The political values of those who will inherit the kingdom are those who have a concern for the "other," the less fortunate, victims of injustice, and landless immigrant. Since the preaching of Jesus, the kingdom of God has been inaugurated on earth and we are invited to reject earthly social and structural sins of oppression toward the immigrant. This also suggests that instead of appealing to current political views and ideologies about nation-states, we need to allow the values of the kingdom of God to shape and influence our views of the immigrant. If it is inconceivable that Jesus' followers would align themselves with the Romans who upheld racial ideologies that dehumanized foreigners, why would Christians today align themselves with political ideologies, policies, or agendas that adopt such views toward immigrants? If Jesus describes his miracles of healing and exorcisms as the inbreaking presence of the kingdom, how much more would the inclusion of foreigners and immigrants also testify of God's kingdom on earth?[49] As we have come to notice, the kingdom of God is not just an ethereal place where God rules. It has implications to how we live here and now. The kingdom of God is a home for the foreigners and migrants among us. It is the home of the refugee, the foreigner, the expelled, especially those under the threat of imperial violence. We must always continually ask ourselves if our views of the immigrants are reflective of Roman imperial values or God's kingdom. And most importantly, we must also continue to live in such a manner that our views of the immigrant and actions toward them will testify that we are members of God's kingdom.

[49]Mt 4:23; 9:35; 10:7-8; 12:28; 16:19; Lk 9:2, 11; 10:9; 11:20.

LETTER OF JAMES

Daniel K. Eng

INTRODUCTION

Author. The author identifies himself as James in the first verse of the epistle. This James is most likely the half brother of Jesus, the son of Joseph or Mary. While James (Jacob) was a common name in this context, the fact that the author does not give any qualifications in an imperative-filled letter suggests that this James is prominent. There are two prominent New Testament figures with this name: (1) the son of Zebedee and brother of John, one of the Twelve, also called James the Great, and (2) the brother of Jesus, son of Joseph, also called James the Just or *Adelphotheos*. The early martyrdom of James the son of Zebedee (by AD 44, see Acts 12:2) leaves us with the second option.[1] Therefore, the most likely author of this letter is James the Just, an attribution that is corroborated by early church tradition, especially in the writings of Eusebius, Jerome, and Origen.

James the Just played an authoritative role in early Christianity. Paul identified James as an eyewitness of the resurrected Christ (1 Cor 15:7) and as one of the "pillars" of the church (Gal 2:9). It was he, not one of the Twelve, who presided over the Jerusalem Council (Acts 15:13-21). As a leader of the Jerusalem church, his words would hold considerable influence over the early Christians, especially with Jewish believers both in and outside their ancestral land.

Date. Several factors point to a relatively early date for the Epistle of James. First, given that James the Just is the author of the epistle, it follows that its dating must be before his martyrdom in AD 62.[2] Second, the lack of content about circumcision and the inclusion of the Gentiles into the church suggests a date before AD 49, the approximate date of the Jerusalem Council. Third, while James 2:14-26 shares key terms with the apostle Paul's teaching on justification in Romans and Galatians, the terms are used differently and address a different concern in the church. If the teachings characteristic of Romans and Galatians were already circulating, one might expect James to use different terminology or qualify his teaching to prevent the misunderstanding that his letter is associated with Paul's letters. The similar terms used in a different context suggest that James is not directly interacting with Paul. The discrepancy points to a date (1) before Paul's second missionary journey and (2) before the first significant meeting between Paul and James, at the time of the Jerusalem Council. With these factors in view, we date James in the mid- or late 40s, which would make it one of the earliest New Testament documents.[3]

---

[1]For a survey of the views regarding the authorship of James, including the view that the letter is a pseudepigraphon, see Alicia J. Batten, *What Are They Saying About the Letter of James?* (Mahwah, NJ: Paulist Press, 2009), 28-43.

[2]See Josephus, *Ant.* 20.9.

[3]For a more thorough argument for dating James in the mid- to late 40s, see Douglas J. Moo, *The Letter of James*, 2nd ed., PNTC (Grand Rapids, MI: Eerdmans, 2021), 30-32.

Setting. As a *general* or *catholic* epistle, James does not address a particular person or church, with the address "to the twelve tribes in the Dispersion" (Jas 1:1). The term *diaspora* or "dispersion" refers to Jews living outside the ancestral land. While some view the reference to the diaspora as a metaphor for Christians everywhere,[4] the qualification of "the twelve tribes" suggests that the epistle's intended hearers are indeed Jews. Also, the allusions or quotations of Old Testament sayings (e.g., Lev 19:18 in Jas 2:8, or Prov 3:34 in Jas 4:6) and the mention of a synagogue (Jas 2:2) add support to this view. Notably, the call to care for orphans and widows in James 1:27 repeats a familiar Old Testament refrain (e.g., Ex 22:21-22; Deut 10:18; 14:29; 16:11,14; 24:19-21; 26:12-13; Jer 7:6; 22:3; Zech 7:10; Mal 3:5). This repeated Old Testament command usually includes the stranger or alien. James's omission of the alien suggests that the primary hearers of the epistle are themselves strangers outside their homeland.

Also, the references to Jesus Christ (Jas 1:1; 2:1) indicate a Christian message. James is thus writing to Jews everywhere who have professed faith in Jesus Christ. Also, the letter shows a high affinity with the teachings of Jesus, with more connections than any other New Testament writing.[5] These connections include an eschatological reversal, concern for the marginalized, rejoicing in trials, and exhortations to lowliness.

Major themes and outline. The unifying theme in James is a *future reward for those who persevere in faithfulness to God.* James calls his diaspora hearers to obedience and loyalty to God, looking forward to future judgment and reward. This theme is summed up in James 1:12, which serves a pivotal purpose in the epistle's opening content, "Blessed is the one who endures temptation. Such a one who, after having stood the test, will receive the crown of life which the Lord has promised to those who love him" (my translation).

James features an introductory prologue that previews the major themes of the letter. Themes like *eschatology, rich and poor, use of the tongue, wisdom,* and being a *doer of the law* are introduced in James 1. The repeated terms like *endurance, trial,* and *blessing* occur at the beginning (Jas 1:2-3), middle (Jas 1:12), and end (Jas 1:25) of the introductory prologue, pointing to the pivotal saying in James 1:12 and summarizing the introduction. *Blessing* and *endurance* are repeated at the end of the body in James 5:11, which creates brackets (an *inclusio*) that frame the entire letter.

The rest of the epistle presents ways to receive a future reward by *persevering* in obedience to God. Woven throughout the letter are references to God being the one who will *judge* in the end (Jas 2:12-13; 3:1; 4:12; 5:9, 12). The bulk of the epistle is framed by another *inclusio* marked by the clustering of *doing, acting, judgment,* and *the law* (Jas 2:12-13; 4:11-12). If they remain in obedient loyalty to God, the hearers will receive a favorable judgment in the end.

Also, the many imperatives issued by James are largely lived out in the *community.* James displays constant concern about how the hearers of the letter treat one another. Obedience to God, as James explains, becomes the basis of judgment from God in the end. Those who persevere in their loyalty to God, obeying his commands, will be rewarded in the end.

James can be outlined as follows:

Introductory Prologue (Jas 1:1–27)
- Salutation (Jas 1:1)
- Joy in Trials (Jas 1:2-4)
- Asking God for Wisdom (Jas 1:5-8)

[4]This is likely the connotation of diaspora in 1 Pet 1:1, which does not include the twelve tribes.

[5]Patrick J. Hartin, *A Spirituality of Perfection: Faith in Action in the Letter of James* (Collegeville, MN: Liturgical Press, 1999), 2.

Lowly and Rich (Jas 1:9-11)
Blessing and Reward for Perseverance (Jas 1:12)
Temptation Leads to Death (Jas 1:13-15)
The Generosity of God (Jas 1:16-18)
Listening and Doing (Jas 1:19-25)
Preview of the Body: Statements about Religion (Jas 1:26-27)

Favoritism Forbidden: An Example of Obedience (Jas 2:1-13)

Faith and Deeds (Jas 2:14-26)

Taming the Tongue (Jas 3:1-12)

Having the Right Kind of Wisdom (Jas 3:13-18)

Submitting to God (Jas 4:1-10)

Summary and Transition Statements: Only God is Judge (Jas 4:11-12)

Apostrophe: Addressing Those Outside the Hearers (Jas 4:13–5:6)
Arrogant Merchants (Jas 4:13-17)
Oppressive Rich (Jas 5:1-6)

Two-Part Conclusion
Conclusion to the Body: The Coming of the Lord (Jas 5:7-11)
Final Exhortations (Jas 5:12-20)

INTRODUCTORY PROLOGUE (JAMES 1:1-27)

Salutation (James 1:1). Like other ancient Greek letters, James begins like many other letters at the time, identifying the sender and recipients. James identifies himself as a *slave* of God and the Lord Jesus Christ. For the Jewish first-century hearers of James, this term evokes their ancestral history of slavery in Egypt. Likewise, slavery carries significant weight for a modern American reader, especially for African Americans. Like American slavery, Greco-Roman slavery involved slaves being viewed as the property of their owners. Slaves did not have rights; they identified themselves by their "vertical" relationship with their masters. Likewise, James identifies himself by his relation to God and the Lord Jesus Christ. He expresses loyalty to his master and fulfills his duty of obedience. Even so, his identification possibly carries an honorific nature, since *servant of God* was a title for revered figures in Israel's history (e.g., Gen 26:24; Deut 34:5; Judg 2:8; Ps 36:1).

The identification of the hearers as the "twelve tribes in the Dispersion" emphasizes that they are Jews outside their homeland. Some migrated out of their native land, and others were forced out. Much like many modern immigrants and refugees, these Jews are unfamiliar people in an unfamiliar place. Even while settled in a new home, they retained their ethnic identity, remembering their heritage with the nation of Israel. Jews in the diaspora had some rights, but never collectively had the full rights of Greek citizenship.[6] The designation of the diaspora brings to mind the experiences of minority Americans, including liminality and marginalization.

They likely faced discrimination, first because they were minority Jews, and second because they were Christians. They were strangers in their new home, never fully belonging.

Joy in trials (James 1:2-4). James calls his addressees "my brothers," a common address in the New Testament that is inclusive of both men and women. By using familial language, James intimately identifies himself with the recipients of the epistle. Despite the authoritative tone of the letter, James uses this address fifteen times,

[6]For a description of the experience in the diaspora, see David A. deSilva, "Jews in the Diaspora," in *The World of the New Testament: Cultural, Social, and Historical Contexts*, ed. Joel B. Green and Lee Martin McDonald (Grand Rapids, MI: Baker Academic, 2013), 272-90.

sometimes adding the qualifier *beloved*. He affirms that they are all in the same family.

The first exhortation of the letter is remarkable, as it calls for a response of rejoicing amid "trials of any kind." The language conveys that these tough times serve as a test for them. While there is a temptation for these marginalized minority Jews to escape trial or complain about the testings, James urges his hearers to have joy and persevere through them.[7]

This command serves the hearers as a theodicy: a defense of God's good intentions amid difficulty. Instead of questioning God or viewing the trials as a punishment for sin, they are to rejoice; the tests will result in their good. James affirms that the "testing of your faith" will build "endurance." He urges them to let this perseverance finish its work, with the result that these marginalized Christian hearers will be "mature" and "complete."

We must note that, while difficulties serve a good purpose in the lives of God's people, James does not condone the oppression and mistreatment of others. He addresses the recipients of difficulties here, but elsewhere in the letter he condemns those who mistreat others (Jas 2:6-7; 5:1-6).

For those facing difficulties, the building of perseverance does not occur instantaneously but over time. The reference to many or diverse trials indicates that James does not have specific difficulties in mind, but that this is a repeated process. The Christian life is full of difficulty, suffering, and persecution (Mt 5:11; Jn 15:20; 16:33; Gal 3:4; 2 Tim 3:12), but James affirms that the process of these repeated trials serves as a test of faith. Just like a precious metal becomes increasingly refined as it is repeatedly placed into the fire, the Christian gets closer and closer to maturity and full development with each trial.

The term for "mature" here (*teleioi*) does not mean sinlessness but conveys full development and integrity. It is the term used in Matthew 5:48 and 19:21, as Jesus teaches his hearers at the Sermon on the Mount or the rich man about being perfect. It often corresponds with the Hebrew *tāmîm* (see Deut 18:13), which also indicates maturity and completeness. At the end of the process of testing and trial, those who follow Christ will have fully developed character, "lacking in nothing."

Asking God for wisdom (James 1:5-8). With the previous saying as a springboard, James then launches into a section about receiving wisdom from God. Wisdom is a necessary part of being mature (Jas 1:4), and it helps those undergoing testing (Jas 1:2). James later writes an extended section about wisdom in the body of the epistle (Jas 3:1-12).

James affirms that God is the source of wisdom, and encourages his hearers to request it from him. James introduces the attribute of God as one who gives, which is revisited in James 1:17-18 (cf. Jas 1:12; 2:5). Also, God's giving is impartial, a theme that will occur again in James 2:1-9. He gives to all without reproaching or finding fault. This impartiality would resonate deeply with the marginalized minority hearers of James, for they are likely facing discrimination around them.

For many Asian Americans, the affirmation that God gives without demeaning someone can be profound. Asian Americans have carried the reputation of being the *model minority*, with the perception that we have "succeeded" in America without making waves. The designation ends up being harmful: it serves as a veiled attempt to demean all

[7]Note that James is addressing the marginalized here, not any perpetrators of injustice. Later in the letter, he will condemn those who do the oppressing (see Jas 2:6; 5:4-6).

minorities for speaking out about injustice. In James 1:5, God does not demean his people for requesting wisdom. Despite the stigma we might face in society for speaking up, we do not have to be reluctant to ask God.

In James 1:6, James proceeds to give a condition for asking God for wisdom: ask in faith(fulness), not "disputing" (my trans.). The word here for *disputing* (*diakrinomenos*) is often rendered *doubting*.[8] However, one may misconstrue doubting as referring to the perception of the unlikelihood of an event. In this passage, with the context of God's generosity and the contrast with faithfulness, a better translation is *disputing*. Asking "in faith" refers to a commitment to God, having a trajectory of trust and allegiance to him. One who *disputes* does not give full allegiance to God. This rendering is corroborated by James 1:6-8, which vividly describes the *disputing* person like a wave of the sea, being unstable and double-minded. James calls for his hearers to be singly committed to God alone; God gives wisdom generously to his singularly-devoted people.

Lowly and rich (James 1:9-11). In this subsection of the introductory prologue, James discusses the rich and the lowly, a motif that will frequently appear in the epistle. Here, the modern reader hears more about the plight of the marginalized minority Jewish Christians. While the terms *rich* and *lowly* include a connotation about monetary resources, one must also read the references to *rich*, *lowly*, and *poor* in terms of socioeconomic status as well. The dynamics of class, influence, and privilege were prevalent in the ancient world, just like they are today. The rich not only had money, but they also had political power (see Jas 2:6).

Conversely, the poor did not just suffer from a lack of monetary resources; they were socially marginalized as well. These people were often oppressed (Jas 2:6), at the mercy of others (Jas 2:15), and cheated (Jas 5:4). With this status in view, it is unsurprising that the contrast to the rich in this passage is "lowly." The rich have power, and the lowly do not.

While it is not explicit in this passage, the Jewish Christian hearers of James were most likely identified with the lowly here. Because they had minority status, experienced discrimination, and had little political power, it would be difficult for a marginalized diaspora Jew to gain wealth and power. Thus, the encouragement for the lowly would most likely apply to the primary audience of James.

In this passage, James gives parallel exhortations for both the lowly and the rich to glory or "boast" in their respective positions. The basis of this boasting is a hope set in the future. In view here is the "great reversal"—the expectation that there will be a reversal of status in the end times (see Mt 19:30; 23:12; Lk 13:30). While the rich are powerful and oppress others now (Jas 2:1-6; 5:1-6), they will be "brought low" when the end times come. Likewise, the lowly, while presently marginalized in society, will be exalted.[9] For these marginalized lowly believers, James calls them to place their hope in the Lord, giving them an elevated position when the end comes.

It is unclear whether the rich person in James 1:10-11 is part of the audience. On the one hand, the rich person is not called a *brother*, and it seems farfetched that there would be an exhortation for someone to "boast" in a low end-times status and the fleeting nature of life. It is also difficult to envision the

[8]See the same term used in Mk 11:23 and Rom 4:20.

[9]The exaltation of the lowly is a prominent theme in Mary's Magnificat (Lk 1:46-55), which is notable if Mary is indeed the mother of this epistle's author.

other usages of "rich" in James (Jas 2:6-7; 5:1-6) referring to Christians. On the other hand, the parallelism between James 1:9 and James 1:10 suggests continuity, and James uses two faithful wealthy men as examples to his hearers: Abraham (Jas 2:21-23) and Job (Jas 5:11). Also, this passage may be an echo of Jeremiah 9:23-24, which urges the wise and rich among God's people not to boast in their assets, but in knowing the Lord.

Whether or not the rich person in James 1:10-11 is a believer, the passage as a whole communicates a faithful attitude toward riches and status in this world. After the value of godly wisdom is affirmed in James 1:5-8, wisdom is applied to one's socioeconomic status in James 1:9-11. Both riches and lowliness can serve as a trial (Jas 1:2-4): one can either (1) submit to God by living in obedience to him, or (2) turn away from God by cursing him or oppressing others. James exhorts his hearers to have the proper perspective: their status is not permanent. The poor are called to celebrate their position of being part of God's family.[10] The rich are called to humble themselves before God. This perspective comes from godly wisdom.

Blessing and reward for perseverance (James 1:12). The saying in James 1:12 serves as the thesis statement for the epistle of James. It serves as a "hinge" verse for the introductory prologue; it has connections with the content before and after it. It has a strong connection with the opening command, with the language of endurance and trial. James 1:12 also has a strong connection with James 1:25, another statement of blessing about one who perseveres. Its main ideas are also reprised at the conclusion to the main body of James, with the description of Job as the example of receiving blessing after perseverance (Jas 5:11). With content about *God's judgment* (e.g., Jas 2:12-13; 3:1; 4:12; 5:9, 12) and descriptions of *end-time blessing* (e.g., Jas 1:9; 2:5, 14; 3:18; 4:6-10; 5:7-11) permeating the epistle, James 1:12 is a representative statement. It communicates that those who endure in obedience to God will receive a favorable judgment.

The statement of blessing is a *macarism*, or beatitude saying. Following the same formula found in sayings of Jesus in the Sermon on the Mount (Mt 5:3-12) and Sermon on the Plain (Lk 6:20-23), it declares that a particular group is *blessed*, or fortunate, along with a description of their future reward or favorable state. In this statement in James 1:12, it is the person who "endures" or "has stood the test" who is favored. This person will receive a future reward, the "crown of life."

Trials serve as tests, and they give people an opportunity to either (1) persevere and remain faithful to God or (2) turn away from him. Poverty, hunger, opposition, persecution, discrimination, and natural disasters all qualify as trials, and James affirms those who remain steadfast with God, not taking the opportunity to turn away. With all the social difficulties faced by the recipients of this letter, they are assured that their perseverance will be rewarded; they can look forward to the crown of life.

Note that James is not addressing an acceptance or a fight against oppression or discrimination here. Again, he will address that later in the letter (see, for example, Jas 2:1-7 and 5:4-6). The dichotomic choice presented in this portion of James is between being faithful to God or turning away from him.

[10]James addresses the poor themselves here. As the epistle unfolds, he repeatedly addresses his hearers in general about caring for the less fortunate. James also condemns those who unjustly oppress the less fortunate. See, for example, the commentary below on Jas 1:27; 2:3-4, 15-16; 5:4-6.

This beatitude introduces a theme that recurs throughout James: *evaluation* or *judgment*. Those who persevere under trial will be evaluated. Once people are *approved*—or *tested and proven*—then they will receive their reward. This term for *approved* is *dokimos*, which is used in the Greek translation of the Hebrew Scriptures to refer to pure and refined precious metal (e.g., 1 Kings 10:18; 2 Chron 9:17) and elsewhere in the New Testament to describe those tested and proven to be esteemed (e.g., 2 Cor 10:18; 2 Tim 2:15). The implied evaluator is God; he is the one who will approve those who persevere.

The reward for those who persevere is "the crown of life." The term for "crown" here is *stephanos*, an adornment worn by someone of high esteem, often as a prize for an achievement. Much like the exaltation of the lowly in James 1:9, the one persevering through trial without turning away is rewarded with public honor. The qualifier "of life" probably indicates the nature of the crown itself; in other words, the "crown that is life." Eternal life is the reward awaiting those who persevere (cf. 1 Pet 5:14; Jude 21; Rev 2:10).

The crown has another qualifier, specifying its intended recipient: "that the Lord has promised to those who love him." God, the implied subject of the promise, will give this reward to those who love him. The association of *perseverance under trial* with *loving God* is fitting because the alternative to perseverance is turning away from him. Through this beatitude, James exhorts his hearers to persevere in their difficulties as an expression of love for God. The crown is a promise of reward in the end times for those who are faithful.

This saying in James 1:12 introduces several themes that will recur throughout James. First, it introduces the concept of end-time judgment and reward. God will be the one to evaluate someone and *approve* him or her (see Jas 2:12; 4:12; 5:9, 12), and there will be future rewards for those who are approved (see Jas 2:5; 3:18; 4:10; 5:7, 11, 20). Second, it introduces the concept that endurance (see Jas 1:3-4) and loving God will result in favor from God in the end (see Jas 1:25; 2:5; 4:4-10).

Temptation leads to death (James 1:13-15). Like the epistle's first command (Jas 1:2-4), James begins the second half of the introductory prologue with content about *testing*. This time, however, James writes about a particular kind of testing, the intention for which is that someone might turn away from God and sin (see Mt 4:1; Mk 1:13; Heb 4:15). For this particular kind of testing, we can use our modern English term *temptation*.

Again, much like the opening command, temptation raises an occasion for a theodicy: James defends God's reputation. While the Old Testament does indicate that God *tested* his people (e.g., Gen 22:1; Ex 15:25; Deut 13:3), those tests did not come to them in the manner described in this passage; God did not entice them to sin. James insists that God never tries to get people to abandon him.

Through this point-counterpoint expression, James explains to his marginalized hearers that the source of temptation to sin is not God, but the *desire* that is inside a person. Desire drags someone away, tempting them to do evil. Notably, a person does not get *pushed* toward sin but gets *lured* toward it because of his or her longing. Even though the marginalized hearers of James face discrimination and disadvantage with their minority status, they are responsible for how they respond to their difficulties.

James then introduces the life cycle of sin in James 1:15, using imagery of pregnancy and birthing to portray the process. When evil desire (perhaps we can even call it *lust*) has conceived, it gives birth to a child, sin. The latter part of the verse reveals the result of sin—when sin "is fully grown," it gives birth to "death." We see three generations of this tragic lineage: desire, sin, and death. God does not desire for this death to be birthed.

The generosity of God (James 1:16-18). James continues his defense of God's reputation, this time in a positive way, rather than refuting an accusation (Jas 1:13). In an affirmation much like James 1:5, James declares that God is the source of good things. Using language that possibly appeals to the Roman phenomenon of benefactors,[11] he affirms that every "generous act of giving" and "perfect gift" comes from God.

In James 1:17, James describes God in two connected ways. First, God is the "father of lights" here, a title that emphasizes his role and status as the Creator of the sun, moon, and stars.[12] Fittingly, the gifts mentioned in James 1:17 come down from him, perhaps suggesting the imagery of rain as a gift to those who need it. Second, James asserts that God is not subject to variation, which describes shadows and perhaps the heavenly lights. Unlike creation, which changes, God is unchanging. The point of this description is that God is invariably generous. Not capricious, he only gives good things and never evil.

James continues (Jas 1:18) his affirmation of God's generous character by describing how his generosity has already benefited him and his Jewish Christian hearers. Using language that echoes the birthing imagery found in James 1:15, James teaches that the Father of creation decreed that he would birth us through the word of truth. While it is possible that the birthing by the word here refers to the initial creation of humanity,[13] the language of God's will (his choice) and the concepts of "first fruits"[14] here point to his redemption of already-created people, that is, rebirth through the gospel. The Father of lights, having created all things, now "adds saved human beings into his eternal family."[15] The "word of truth" here indicates how God does the birthing; it is through his word, which includes the message of the gospel of Jesus Christ. God's word is reliable and powerful. It makes James and his hearers into first fruits, set apart as special for God.

To whom does James 1:18 apply? On the one hand, James appeals to his hearers' ethnic identity using the language of God's sovereign will that echoes the election of Israel in the Old Testament. James and his Jewish Christian hearers are set apart for God. On the other hand, the words here leave open the possibility that others beyond Israel can be included in the family of the Father of lights. The "word of truth," which includes the gospel, is for all people. In the end, this saying focuses on God: the divine will, the divine word, and the first fruits that belong to God. There is no room for ethnocentrism here, no room to reject those whom God might call.

Listening and doing (James 1:19-25). James continues by offering a three-part exhortation: "let everyone be quick to listen, slow to speak, slow to anger." This saying introduces themes of this section as well as themes in the rest of the epistle.

The third part of the exhortation, being "slow to anger," receives development immediately in

[11]See Alicia J. Batten, *Friendship and Benefaction in James*, Emory Studies in Early Christianity 15 (Dorset, UK: Deo, 2010), 68-75, 116-19.

[12]For a discussion of this title, which is not found in the Old Testament, and its possible connection with Ps 136, see Esther Yue L. Ng, "Father-God Language and Old Testament Allusions in James," *Tyndale Bulletin* 54 (2003): 43-48.

[13]E.g. see L. E. Elliott-Binns, "James I. 18: Creation or Redemption?," *New Testament Studies* 3 (1957): 148-61.

[14]First fruits elsewhere in the New Testament describes converts. See Rom 16:5; 1 Cor 16:15; Rev 14:4.

[15]Craig L. Blomberg and Mariam J. Kamell, *James*, ZECNT (Grand Rapids, MI: Zondervan, 2008), 75.

James 1:20. It echoes Jewish wisdom tradition (e.g., Prov 14:29; 19:11; Eccles 7:9) that a righteous person is slow to become angry. Indeed, James affirms that human anger does not produce "God's righteousness." This latter concept most likely refers to actions that reflect God's standard.[16] This topic will be addressed again later in the epistle (see Jas 3:16; 4:1-4, 11-12; 5:9).

In James 1:21, James builds on his exhortation. Given the priority to live within God's standards (Jas 1:20), James gives a two-part, progressive command here: (1) what to *remove* and (2) what to *receive*. To receive, one first has to remove *filth* and *wickedness*, or the grime of sinful deeds. The term used here for removing (*apotithēmi*) indicates a *laying aside* or *abandoning*, also used elsewhere in the NT to refer to removing wicked behavior (see Rom 13:12; Heb 12:1; Eph 4:22, 25; 1 Pet 2:1). Wickedness described as filth here continues an Old Testament image (e.g., Ps 24:4; 51:2; Is 1:16; 64:6; Ezek 22:15) and will recur later in the epistle (Jas 4:8). In the place of the filth, James urges his hearers to "welcome with meekness the implanted word." This concept of an innate or inborn gift from God fits with the imagery of James 1:18, as the word that God used to birth them is now a part of them.[17] James clarifies that the word "has the power to save your souls," a reference to its ability to bring its recipients to final salvation at the eschaton. They are to receive this word with *humility*, or "meekness," an attitude of gentleness and submission to God and his ways (see Jas 3:13).

In James 1:22-25, James takes the command to be "quick to hear" further: do not just be a *hearer* but also be a *doer* of the word. The motif of self-deception (see Jas 1:16) continues here, as James says that being just a hearer without doing God's word is *deceiving yourselves*. One who does not carry out the commands is cutting off the process that produces righteousness and brings salvation (Jas 1:20-21). James illustrates the insufficient process with the image of an individual looking at a mirror (Jas 1:23-24), which he contrasts with someone who looks into the perfect law (Jas 1:25). The point of this contrast is to show two different responses to hearing the word, or perfect law, of God. One can look intently at it, studying it and pouring over its details, but this act of looking must change one's behavior. Hearing without doing is like studying oneself in a mirror and then walking away and forgetting the image: all that time and intent amounted to nothing. James calls his hearers to be like the one in James 1:25, persevering with the law, and being a doer, an executor of God's will. This topic will be developed later in the epistle (Jas 2:8-26; 4:11).

James 1:25 contains a statement that echoes the hinge saying in James 1:12. Just like the one who perseveres through trial and loves God is blessed (Jas 1:12), the doer of the word who perseveres, or continues in the law, is also blessed (Jas 1:25).

Preview of the body: Statements about religion (James 1:26-27). Two statements describing "religion" occur at the end of James 1. The terms *religious* and *religion* in these two verses convey *piety* or *devotion to God*. The two statements describe a contrast between worthless religion and acceptable religion in the sight of God.

In James 1:26, James convicts someone who claims devotion to God yet does not bridle his or her tongue. Today, sins of speech like lying, gossip, swearing, cursing, and verbal abuse are

[16]Peter H. Davids, *The Epistle of James*, NIGTC (Grand Rapids, MI: Eerdmans, 1982), 93.

[17]George H. Guthrie, "James," in *The Expositor's Bible Commentary*, *Hebrews–Revelation*, ed. Tremper Longman and David E. Garland, rev. ed. (Grand Rapids, MI: Zondervan, 2006), 226.

often tolerated and treated as excusable, especially in social media. But James makes it clear that keeping words unbridled reveals the worthlessness of one's religion in the eyes of God.

In James 1:27, James moves to positive exhortation, describing worthy acts of devotion. In using terms like *pure, undefiled,* and *unstained,* James applies concepts of "ritual worship . . . to moral purity,"[18] associating ethics with ritual preparation. One who claims piety should demonstrate it with acts of mercy: caring for orphans and widows. James affirms that sincere devotion to God manifests through showing mercy.

While James does not claim to be describing all the requirements of devotion to God here, note that he explains what piety must include. His emphasis on doing the word (Jas 1:22-25) continues here in two areas of life: "to care for orphans and widows" and "to keep oneself unstained from the world."

First, in calling the marginalized hearers to care for the less fortunate, James states that *social concern* is evidence of true piety. If they claim faithfulness, they must show mercy. Jesus is known for condemning the Pharisees for their fastidious expressions of personal piety but not showing mercy to others (Mt 23:23). Despite the discrimination they face as minorities, the hearers of James must care for the helpless. In doing so, they imitate the character of God and fulfill the Old Testament mandate (Ex 22:21; Deut 10:17-18; Ps 68:5; Is 1:16-17). Today, we see those homeless, hungry, abused, displaced, and oppressed around us facing the same plight as the fatherless and the widow. In caring for them, we imitate the character of our heavenly Father and show ourselves to be followers of Christ.

While James declares that showing mercy is a mark of piety, some American Christians are often slow to engage in this. Many Asian Americans have kept their heads down and remained industrious, not making waves when facing discrimination and inequality. The reluctance to receive a handout from others often makes one likewise reluctant to help others in need, especially in light of the hardship one has faced. These marginalized minority believers may have faced similar struggles that Asian Americans face, yet James calls them to show compassion for the less fortunate.

Second, in declaring that piety involves keeping oneself unstained from the world, James urges *ethical purity*, which repeats the theme from James 1:21. The societies of the original hearers of James held values opposed to the values of Christ. These believers were in danger of being influenced by the beliefs and practices around them.

James 1:26-27 has two functions: it (1) closes the introductory prologue, and (2) introduces the content that follows. The next several sections of James involve the treatment of the less fortunate (Jas 2:5, 15-16), the expression of faith through deeds (Jas 2:14-26), the bridling of the tongue (Jas 3:1-12), and the opposition of the worldly and spiritual (Jas 3:15-18; 4:4), among other themes. These exhortations are developments of the thesis statement (Jas 1:12) that one who remains faithful will be rewarded in the end.

FAVORITISM FORBIDDEN: AN EXAMPLE OF OBEDIENCE (JAMES 2:1-13)

In this section, James moves from a specific exhortation to a general principle that the marginalized hearers are to follow. He urges them not to show "favoritism" to the rich, which reinforces the marginalization of the poor (Jas 2:1-7). Then, building from this command, James urges obedience to the whole law rather than a part of it, knowing that they will face judgment under this law (Jas 2:8-13). As we

[18]Blomberg and Kamell, *James*, 94.

will see, this section develops the thesis statement (Jas 1:12) that the hearers adhere to God's ways so that they can be judged favorably in the end.

The hypothetical scenario described in James 2:1-4 likely involves the related dynamics of *reciprocity* and *patronage*. In Greco-Roman culture, patronal relationships were prevalent, making up the fabric of society. If one had low status and influence, one could seek the favor of someone with higher status and influence for goods and services. The exchange entered two parties into a relationship where the higher status, the patron, would open opportunities for those of lower status, the clients. Those in political offices, like senators or regent-kings, commonly had clients. Patronal relationships were held together by *reciprocity*. While not upheld by law, they were held by mutual obligation. Clients pledged loyalty to their high-status patrons, promising future support when a future opportunity arose, often for political influence.[19]

The principle of reciprocity is familiar to many Americans of East Asian descent. Mutual obligation often influences decision-making. For example, many Asian Americans feel obligated to bring a gift to a host when visiting someone in their home. In turn, the host offers hospitality. With higher stakes involved, reciprocity is often displayed in the exchange of political favors, loyalty, and access to opportunity.

The scenario here in the first part of James 2 implies a certain kind of reciprocity. The hearers of James, having little privilege and access to goods and services, would be tempted to show favoritism to a rich person of high class to procure favor in a relationship of reciprocity. The hypothetical scenario also involves degrading the poor man who walks into their assembly, relegating him to sit on the floor.

James gives a list of reasons why he forbids such partiality to the rich. First, doing so makes James's hearers like "judges with evil thoughts" (Jas 2:4), showing corruption and injustice. Judges are expected to show impartiality, and one with evil thoughts is condemned (see Lev 19:15). Such favoritism perpetuates the injustice faced by those marginalized in society: the poor, the weak, and minorities.

Second, James declares that one should not show favoritism to the rich because God has chosen the poor to be "rich in faith and to be heirs of the kingdom." James makes sure to qualify the term *poor* with the phrase "in the world," pointing to those who are materially poor and socially marginalized in contrast to the rich in James 2:6. A repeated Old Testament concept is that God has a predilection for the poor (e.g., 2 Sam 22:28; Ps 9:19; 34:10; Job 34:28). The people were taught to care for the poor (Ex 23:11; Lev 19:10; Deut 24:19), and God favors those who help the poor (Ps 40:2; Prov 14:21; 22:9; Is 58:8). The poor are dependent on God, waiting for him to act to provide and vindicate them (Ps 9:35; 13:6; 101:1). In several psalms, David describes himself as poor, associating the term with neediness and dependence on God (Ps 24:16, 39:18; 68:30; 69:6; 85:1; 108:22).

However, James does not state that God chooses the poor without distinction, as the end of James 2:5 qualifies the saying: "those who love him." It is the poor who love God, the ones with few resources and influence in society, who are chosen by him. They are needy and depend on him, showing themselves to be favored by

[19]For a primer on patronage and the New Testament, see David A. deSilva, *Honor, Patronage, Kinship and Purity: Unlocking New Testament Culture* (Downers Grove, IL: IVP Academic, 2000), 95-156.

God. They can expect two rewards. They are chosen to be "rich in faith." While they are poor in the world, they are rich in the realm of faith, or rich when "judged by God's standards."[20] They are also "heirs of the kingdom." They can look forward to God's rule and will be part of the kingdom in the future, associated with eternal life, just as Jesus teaches (Mt 19:29; 25:46; Mk 10:30; Lk 18:29-30). Also, the designation of "heirs to the kingdom" recalls the repeated language of Israel inheriting the land (Ex 15:17; Lev 20:24; Num 14:31; Deut 1:8; 8:1). For these marginalized Jewish believers far away from the land they identify with, this designation of "heirs" is significant. If they, like the poor, depend on God rather than their judgment, they show their love for God and can hope in the promise given to the poor in James 2:5. They, longing for a place to belong where they are not oppressed and marginalized, can place their hope in the inheritance of the land from which they are alienated. This inheritance is the eschatological reward for the faithful, just like the crown of life in the parallel saying in James 1:12.

Third, James warns the hearers of the epistle not to favor the rich, because the rich are the ones who often oppress them (Jas 2:6). These marginalized minority believers experience discrimination and oppression, with little influence and few rights. While James does not elaborate on this oppression, one suspects that the rich have the social influence to receive legal verdicts in their favor, perhaps even unjustly. This would especially work to the disadvantage of those whom they "drag into the courts." Likewise, today's wealthy have the means to hire the most qualified attorneys and the social clout to maintain an advantage in legal matters.

Fourth, the rich blaspheme the name of Christ, dishonoring his reputation (Jas 2:7). James does not specify how the rich blaspheme or slander the name of Christ, but he reminds the hearers that they identify with Christ's very name. The "excellent name that was invoked over you," that of Christ, is what gives believers their identity. Just like these minority hearers have a sense of identity with their Jewish roots and the land, they also identify with Christ, bearing that name—they are *Christians*. The rich have dishonored Christ, and James warns against showing them favoritism.

James goes on to expand the exhortation to a general call to obey the law. He states that those who show favoritism to the rich are "transgressors" (Jas 2:9). They do not just break the law but carry the *identity* of ones who rebel against God, a strong directive for those who identify with minority status. James shows an all-or-nothing approach to obedience: breaking one command, even while keeping the rest, renders someone to be a transgressor, accountable for all of it (Jas 2:10-11). One cannot follow Jesus half-heartedly: it requires full commitment.

In the sayings in James 2:12-13, the author concludes the current section and sets up the next few movements of the epistle. These sayings also mark the opening of an *inclusio* along with James 4:11-12, framing the intervening content around the theme of *doing* and *acting* in accordance with the law. James reminds the hearers of judgment and the end times, which appear in the opening verses (Jas 1:3, 12) as a central motivation for the commands in the epistle. By listing both *speak* and *act* in this context, James connects both actions and words to divine judgment, as he did in the opening chapter (Jas 1:22-27). The twofold command to speak and act in light of future judgment sets up the next two sections: pairing action with faith (Jas 2:14-26) and keeping a bridle on the tongue (Jas 3:1-12).

[20]James Hardy Ropes, *A Critical and Exegetical Commentary on the Epistle of St. James*, ICC (Edinburgh: T&T Clark, 1916), 194.

FAITH AND DEEDS (JAMES 2:14-26)

After James's reminder that the hearers will face judgment for what they speak and do (Jas 2:12-13), he launches into a section that discusses the latter, their actions. The focus of this unit is the relationship between faith and deeds. In what follows, we will use the terms *works* and *deeds* interchangeably, but some may prefer the latter term for James's context.

This section has thematic continuity with James 2:1-7, as it discusses the treatment of someone less fortunate. We will see in this section that James teaches that the kind of faith that has worth is paired with good deeds. This section is a further development of the thesis statement in James 1:12, offering a view into faithfulness to God.

This section of James's is often put into a conversation with apostle Paul's teaching about faith, deeds, and justification, especially in Romans and Galatians. After all, they use the same terminology: "faith" (*pistis*), "deeds" (*erga*), and "justify" (*dikaioō*). The following two sayings epitomize the teachings of the two biblical authors:

> We have come to believe in Christ Jesus, so that we might be justified by the faith of Christ and not by doing the works of the law, because no one will be justified by the works of the law. (Gal 2:16)

> You see that a person is justified by works and not by faith alone. (Jas 2:24)

As we examine both the teaching of Paul and the teaching of James, we face the challenge: *Do James and Paul contradict each other?* We will address this question as we approach the passage in James.

James starts with two rhetorical questions in James 2:14. In the first, he teaches by implication that a profession of faith (*pistis*), when not accompanied by works (*erga*), is worthless. In the second, he teaches by implication that the particular faith, namely the one without works, will not save the person who makes that profession.

In James 2:15-16, the author gives an illustration of the uselessness of a profession of faith without deeds. In a hypothetical scenario of which the format is reminiscent of the situation posed in James 2:2-4, a poor brother or sister without food and clothing represents an opportunity to act, not just profess. The speaking of "Go in peace; keep warm and eat your fill" is of no use unless accompanied by appropriate deeds. James reiterates the point: a profession of faith—speaking about having faith—is useless without accompanying deeds that show that faith (Jas 2:17). Using concepts that remind the hearer of the earlier exhortation to be a doer of the word (Jas 1:19, 22, 25), James urges the hearers to show that they have the type of faith that saves—the type accompanied by acts.

James 2:18 unfolds in the diatribe style, an extended discourse in which a speaker addresses a hypothetical opponent. This verse carries a bit of controversy, chiefly because the roles of the ones doing the speaking are unclear, as well as which words belong to which voice.[21] However, the point in James 2:14-17 is clear—reiterated in James 2:19-26—namely that the faith that is accompanied by good works is the kind that saves someone.

James 2:19 gives an example of *faith without deeds* to reinforce the point that such faith is useless. Just like someone who professes faith, the demons also believe. James reveals how he defines faith in this context: *belief in one God.* This belief is the kind of faith that the demons have, and they tremble. However, this "faith" is not good enough for salvation because it is not

[21]For a helpful delineation of the different views, see Blomberg and Kamell, *James*, 132-34.

accompanied by works of obedience or fulfilling God's will.

After the negative example of the demons, who have faith but no works, James gives two positive examples that illustrate *faith along with deeds*. He introduces these two examples with a question: "Do you want to be shown . . . that faith apart from works is worthless?" In the question, James calls his interlocutor a foolish, "senseless person" (*kene*—"empty"). With the hearers' best interest in mind, he uses the jarring language to indicate that he is serious—the notion that faith without deeds is disgraceful. James gets his hearers' attention and points to the two examples: Abraham and Rahab (Jas 2:21-25).

James's choice of these two examples from the Old Testament is strategic in reinforcing the importance of faith accompanied by deeds. The inclusion of both Abraham and Rahab in parallel statements sends a clear message to these hearers who strongly identify with their ethnic heritage: *the criteria for justification are the same for everyone*. First, James cites the example of Abraham (Jas 2:21-23). The diaspora Jewish hearers of James identify strongly with their roots, especially with their marginalized and minority experience strengthening their ethnic identity. Abraham is the figure that represents their people as their celebrated patriarch (see Lk 1:55; 13:16; 19:9; Jn 8:33). Second, James cites the example of Rahab, the prostitute who assisted the Israelite spies at Jericho (see Josh 2). While Abraham is the esteemed father of Israel, the Canaanite harlot has several characteristics that make her marginalized: her ethnicity, gender, and profession. She is, in more than one way, unlikely to be honored by the Jews. Yet Rahab displays faith accompanied by deeds the same way the patriarch does, and she is justified. For diaspora Jews who might feel the stigma of being "bad Jews"—far from their sacred land—the impact of describing Rahab's justification cannot be underestimated. The standard is the same for all.

In examining James 2:21-25, we can determine that James uses the term *justified* to refer to *one's righteousness being vindicated*. The term occurs three times in this passage. It describes Abraham as a result of his offering up Isaac (Jas 2:21); Abraham's actions demonstrated a living faith. The term also applies to Rahab as a result of her actions in receiving and sending out the spies safely (Jas 2:25); Rahab's actions demonstrated her faith. The examples of Abraham and Rahab indicate how James uses the term *justified* in the pithy, general statement that "a person is justified by works and not by faith alone" (Jas 2:24). We can observe this usage of the term *justified* in the words of Jesus (see Mt 12:37; Lk 18:14), and even from Paul (see Rom 3:4). Thus, for James, for a person's righteousness to be vindicated, one needs to profess *belief* in one God (Jas 2:19) but also display *deeds* that demonstrate that belief.

We can reconcile the teachings of James 2:14-26 with Paul's teaching on justification in passages like Romans 3:21-31 and Galatians 2:15-16 by acknowledging that the two authors are in different contexts and using the terms differently. While Paul writes to correct people who look at their works of the law as a way to gain salvation, James writes to correct people who claim that their faith is a license to *not* engage in good deeds. While Paul uses faith to describe trust in Jesus Christ, James uses faith to describe a profession that there is one God. Ultimately, while Paul is concerned with the *initial entry* into a relationship with God, James is concerned with an *end-time judgment* that vindicates saving faith. James would agree with Paul about being saved by faith. He affirms by implication that a person is saved by faith (Jas 2:14), a certain kind of faith: one that *works together* with deeds (Jas 2:22). Paul would agree with James that what matters is not circumcision (a work of the law), but faith working through love (Gal 5:6). Our association with Christ is by grace, but for good works (Eph 2:8-10).

James ends this section on faith and deeds by reiterating the opening statement (Jas 2:14) that faith without deeds is useless. Just like a body without the invigoration of the spirit is dead, faith without the invigoration of deeds is also dead (Jas 2:26). The kind of faith that saves is a living faith, one that is expressed and vindicated by works.

TAMING THE TONGUE (JAMES 3:1-12)

In this second section, after the call to purposefully *speak* and *act* (Jas 2:12-13), James now addresses the former: how they speak. This section offers another view into what remaining faithful to God looks like (Jas 1:12). The use of the tongue unites this entire section, which can be segmented into several subsections.

First, James introduces the topic of the ethics of speech by offering *a specific application* of a general principle that will be introduced afterward. He discourages the hearers from becoming teachers (Jas 3:1-2). In the world of the hearers of James, a teacher held high esteem (see Mt 10:24; Jn 13:13); *Rabbi* was an honorific title (see Mt 23:6-8). One could imagine that the marginalized hearers of James would desire some kind of honor in the diaspora, much like minority immigrants in America strive for educational credentials and marketplace success today. But James urges his hearers that "not many" should become teachers. The basis of this is that "we who teach will face stricter judgment." James includes himself ("we") in those receiving this greater judgment. It follows that teachers in their communities had influence over others and would be held to a higher standard for what they teach, that is, *how they use their mouths.* He supports the exhortation against many becoming teachers by acknowledging how common it is for all to stumble in what they say. Not only do all stumble, but all stumble many times and in many ways (Jas 3:2).[22] A Chinese proverb has a similar message: *In a group of many words, there is bound to be a mistake.* Once again, James shows that one of his chief concerns is for his hearers to receive a favorable verdict in the end. He warns them against being teachers because of how common it is to stumble, falling short of the higher standard set for teachers.

From the specific application for teachers, James expands the discussion to include the need to control the tongue. Using vivid imagery of a bit in a horse's mouth and the rudder of a large ship, James teaches that the tongue, while a small part of the body, controls the very direction of the entire person. The intent of the person, illustrated by the horse's rider or ship's pilot, is expressed by the tongue. Controlling the tongue amounts to controlling the whole body.

James supports his charge to control the tongue by discussing the devastation the tongue can cause (Jas 3:5-6). Like a small fire can destroy an entire forest, the tongue has the potential to destroy the entire course of life. The reference to *hell* in James 3:6 is likely an indication that the tongue, which causes so much destruction, will be set on fire in the end as an eschatological punishment; there are eternal ramifications for an unbridled tongue.[23]

The author continues this section by affirming the difficulty of training the tongue. In an agrarian society, the hearers of James would agree that humans have been able to tame the

[22]Davids, *Epistle of James*, 137.

[23]Richard Bauckham, *James: Wisdom of James, Disciple of Jesus the Sage* (London: Routledge, 1999), 45, 213.

animals (Jas 3:7). In modern developed societies, we have pets and zoos to demonstrate our ability to harness the animal kingdom. However, James laments that humans cannot control the tongue (Jas 3:8). This lament is not a defeatist statement, for the next section describes that one with wisdom from above can produce good fruit in the community (Jas 3:17). Ultimately, James describes the tongue as a restless evil with great destructive potential.

James completes this section with a call for his hearers to have singular use of the tongue (Jas 3:9-12) for good. He illustrates the problem first, like the double-minded man in James 1:8, we often use our tongues for both good and evil. We bless God, but turn around and curse other people. This duplicity, according to James, should not happen (Jas 3:10). He continues by urging his hearers who identify with Jesus to produce only one kind of fruit. The images of the spring, fig tree, grapevine, and salty pond illustrate that a certain sort of source only has a single sort of produce. Likewise, a person who professes loyalty to Jesus should only use the tongue for beneficial use.

HAVING THE RIGHT KIND OF WISDOM (JAMES 3:13-18)

James 3:13-18 serves as a bridge between the content about the tongue and the content in James 4 about harmony in the community. After the call to only use the tongue for good, James describes the source of good fruit: "wisdom that comes down from above." Here, James presents the contrast between the ways of the world and the ways of God, calling his hearers to choose faithfulness to God (see Jas 1:12).

James 3:13-18 addresses wisdom, which he introduced in the prologue in James 1:5. In another "show me" statement (see Jas 2:18), he challenges anyone who identifies as wise to demonstrate it with good deeds that come from wisdom (Jas 3:13). This passage confronts the hearers with a dichotomy: *earthliness* and *wisdom from above*. The mindset of earthliness is fleshly and characterizes the demons (Jas 3:15). The intentions of envy and selfish ambition, which are evidence of the earthly mindset, manifest themselves in evil deeds (Jas 3:14, 16).

In contrast to what is earthly, James describes the wisdom from above (Jas 3:17). He describes it as "pure," which recalls the kind of religion that is undefiled before God (Jas 1:27). He also describes it as "peaceable" or peace-loving, which sums up the rest of the descriptors: "gentle," "willing to yield," "full of mercy and good fruits," "without a trace of partiality or hypocrisy." The mindset that encourages peace is demonstrated in actions, especially concerning God and other people.

James 1:17 teaches that heavenly wisdom is manifested in the good of the community. This priority of the collective has an affinity with East Asian cultures. In such collectivistic cultures, the actions of the individual impact the honor of the collective. While many Eastern cultures consider it one's duty to place the community first for the sake of harmony, James has a different reason for putting the community first: *pleasing God.*

Much like previous sections of James (e.g., Jas 2:13; 2:26; 3:12), this section ends with a wise and timeless saying in James 3:18: those who make peace sow the fruit of righteousness. In light of James's repeated concept that one's current actions are evaluated and will have eternal consequences (especially the thesis statement in Jas 1:12), this saying likely points to an eschatological reward. As James's hearers have godly wisdom and display righteous deeds that are pleasing to God, they can look forward to a harvest of reward in the end.

SUBMITTING TO GOD (JAMES 4:1-10)

In this section, James's exhortation reaches its climax.[24] Building on his declaration that godly wisdom is peaceable (Jas 3:17) and his urging for the tongue to only be used for blessing (Jas 3:10), James confronts his hearers who engage in quarrels and fights in their communities (Jas 4:1). He condemns them for not remaining faithful to God (see Jas 4:4), keeping the theme presented in James 1:12. Again, he connects outward actions with one's inner state: waging war with others comes from the war going on inside (Jas 4:1). James attributes the fighting and quarreling with selfish and unfulfilled desires (Jas 4:2-3).

Just like he did in James 2:20, James uses a jarring label; his passion has boiled over. He calls his hearers *adulteresses*. It is notable that the term is feminine and describes a woman unfaithful to her husband. This attention-getting designation echoes the Old Testament imagery of adultery representing the people's unfaithfulness to God (e.g., Ezek 23:37; Ps 73:27; Jer 3:6-10; Hos 4:12-14). James denounces those who are controlled by their selfish, worldly desires. The accusation is apt: they follow the ways of the world rather than the ways of God; they have cheated on God.

James uses the jarring label of *adulteresses* in James 4:4 to motivate his hearers to repent. While many Americans might be shocked to hear this kind of strong language from their pastor, James does this to shame those to whom he ministers. This approach is similar to the manner Asian parents call their children *useless* or *lazy* as a means of motivation. Unlike the cursing described in James 3:10, this strong language is delivered out of loving concern, not malice. James is deeply troubled by their quarrels and selfishness, and he writes with a sense of urgency.

The dichotomy in James 4:4 is clear: choose God or choose the world. This concept may be an echo of the challenge to the people to *choose life* by obeying God rather than death through disobedience in Deuteronomy 30:15-20. It also resembles the teaching of Jesus: "No one can serve two masters" (Mt 6:24; Lk 16:13). Choosing to be a friend of the world means choosing enmity with God.

The "all-or-nothing" paradigm in James 4:4, which is reflected in other places in James (e.g., Jas 2:10), would likely stand out to these minority hearers. Feeling the pressure to assimilate into Hellenistic or other majority cultures, these Jews in the diaspora constantly occupied two worlds, even adopting the names and customs of those around them.[25] They kept their Jewish identity while assimilating to their environments. However, regarding loyalty to God, they cannot occupy both worlds—they must choose one or the other.

James 4:5 is a source of controversy. The NRSV renders this, "Or do you suppose that it is for nothing that the scripture says, 'God yearns jealously for the spirit that he has made to dwell in us'?" However, it is unclear from which "scripture" or "writing" the saying comes. Another question is whether the spirit is the subject or object of this sentence, as the Greek is ambiguous. Also, it is unclear if the spirit is the human life force, the Holy Spirit, or something else. The Old Testament language of God being jealous for Israel (see Ex 20:5) favors the interpretation that it is God who is jealous for the human spirit, especially given the adultery imagery in James 4:4.

---

[24]See William Varner's designation of Jas 4:1-10 as the hortatory peak in James. William C. Varner, *James: A Commentary on the Greek Text* (Lexington, KY: Fontes, 2017), 39, 269-305.

[25]deSilva, "Diaspora," 281-83.

James 4:6, however, clearly is a quotation of Proverbs 3:34: "God opposes the proud, but gives grace to the humble." Having urged his hearers to choose alignment with God rather than the world, James reminds them of the generous God (cf. Jas 1:5, 17) who grants favor to those who are lowly. Rather than looking for their selfish needs, the hearers of James are to be lowly like the poor in James 2:5. Just like God favors the poor, he favors those who display humility and repentance.

In James 4:7-10, James prescribes the response to the principle that "God . . . gives grace to the humble." The first command, "submit yourselves therefore to God," likely acts as a larger category under which the next several commands fit. The act of submitting, or being subject to God, involves allegiance to him as master and obeying his authority. Submission to God involves "resist[ing] the devil." Just like God opposes the proud (Jas 4:6), James calls the hearers to stand in opposition to the devil, who is associated with the ways of the world (Jas 4:4). Next, James calls his hearers to "draw near to God," building their relationship with him. This language is reminiscent of priests approaching God (e.g., Ex 19:22) and how believers can come near because of Christ's sacrifice (Heb 10:22).

The call to draw near resonates deeply with these diaspora hearers since they profoundly feel their distance from the land of their heritage, the center of their faith. It is striking that they can be *near* to God. Like modern-day refugees and immigrants, they constantly face the stigma of being far away. James 4:8 teaches the minority hearers of James that they do not need to be ashamed before God because of their distance from their land and people; they can have intimacy with him.

The results of resisting the devil and approaching God are parallel: the devil "will flee from you," *and* God "will draw near to you." After that, James calls his hearers to "cleanse your hands" and "purify your hearts," using language found in Psalm 24:3-4 for someone who is acceptable to God and can approach him. James calls his hearers "double-minded," a term used in James 1:8 to refer to the unstable person who wavers in his or her allegiance to God. The double-minded hearers of James need to be singly loyal to God, and they need purification. Again, James uses shame to motivate the diaspora hearers. If they repent, they can still be acceptable to God despite their migrant status.

In James 4:9, James calls his hearers to "lament and mourn and weep," terms that recall the outward display of repentance in the Old Testament (Joel 2:12-17; Jon 3:5-10; Amos 8:10). Finally, James closes this section (Jas 4:10), reiterating the principle of Proverbs 3:34, calling his hearers to be humble before God. The result of this humbling is declared here: "he will exalt you." The exaltation of those who humble themselves before God is found in Jesus' teaching (Lk 14:11; Mt 23:12).

The call to humility in James 4 differs from the virtue of modesty in East Asian cultures. Confucius wrote that "a superior man is modest in his speech, but exceeds in his actions." Likewise, a Japanese proverb reads, "The nail that sticks out will be hammered down." However, James's call is not a simple self-lowering. The command is to humble themselves *before God*, recognizing that the divine will is the one to obey. It is God who will exalt those who submit to him.

SUMMARY AND TRANSITION STATEMENTS: ONLY GOD IS JUDGE (JAMES 4:11-12)

The warning in James 4:11-12 likely serves as a summary, having connections with much of the epistle's previous content. It also marks the end of an *inclusio* that discusses speaking and acting in submission to future judgment (Jas 2:12). James 4:11-12 revisit the calls to be peaceable (Jas 3:16-17), to have singularly beneficial use of the tongue (Jas 3:9-12), to uphold the law (Jas 2:8-11). Here, James makes a close association between *speaking evil against* a fellow Jesus-follower and *judging* that person. The prohibition of *slandering* a *neighbor* is a familiar one to these Jewish hearers, found in Leviticus 19:16.

James supports his warning by stating that one who speaks evil against another person sets him or herself up as a judge over the law. This person ends up being a judge, not obeying the call to be a doer of the law (Jas 1:25). In James 4:12, he affirms that there is only one Judge, the one who gave the law. God is the only one who saves and destroys. We cannot usurp God's role as the judge.

APOSTROPHE: ADDRESSING THOSE OUTSIDE THE HEARERS (JAMES 4:13-5:6)

Both James 4:13-17 and James 5:1-6 likely function as *apostrophe*: a literary device addressing those outside the audience to benefit those who are hearing.[26] In other words, he "talks over their shoulders," not expecting the merchants or oppressive rich to hear, but for the benefit of his audience.

Several factors support the view that these sections function as apostrophe. First, the two passages are linked by the call "come now," which occurs nowhere else in the epistle. Second, the two sections lack the familiar address *adelphoi* ("brothers and sisters," occurring fifteen times in James in the vocative case) or "among you" (five times) that indicates James's audience. Furthermore, the sayings immediately after these two, James 5:7-10, contain the highest concentration of the address *adelphoi* (three times in a short span), indicating that James has returned to addressing his audience. Third, the content shifts from pastoral exhortation to a pessimistic tone, with no indicated urge for the two groups to repent from their sin. Fourth, aside from the formulaic "come now" and the call for the rich to weep (Jas 5:1), there is a notable lack of imperatives in these two passages, which makes these passages stand out in the New Testament document with the highest frequency of imperative forms.[27]

Finally, while some diaspora Jews could have been traveling merchants (Jas 4:13-17) or wealthy landowners (Jas 5:1-6), the disadvantages and discrimination they faced would make such cases rare. It is more likely that, given their marginalized minority status, the hearers of James would not have the means to fall into either of these categories.

In both texts, James offers his hearers a view into the lives and fates of those who are not faithful to God. Further developing the thesis statement found in James 1:12, he shows how the two groups do not recognize God and will reach their demise. These sections serve the purpose of reinforcing the call to remain faithful to God.

Arrogant merchants (James 4:13-17). With the first instance of "come now," James addresses traveling merchants who engage in business in different towns. His warning is not against planning per se but against assuming that they are in control of their future. They presume about their business and their profits. They do not submit to God or his will. James calls this "boast[ing] in arrogance," and it is "evil" (Jas 4:16).

This passage echoes Jesus' parable of the rich fool who builds bigger barns for his plentiful crop: "You fool! This very night your life

[26]Old Testament examples of apostrophe include Jer 5:10, where the prophet "addresses" the enemy who will destroy much of the land, or Is 44:23, where the prophet turns to address the heavens.

[27]See Varner's graph of the ratio of imperatives to total words in each New Testament book, with James having 3.387 percent, in Varner, *James*, 22.

is being demanded of you. And the things you have prepared, whose will they be?" (Lk 12:20). Likewise, the arrogant merchants could lose their lives tomorrow (Jas 4:14).

James gives an alternative for his actual hearers to follow: they ought to submit the future to God: "If the Lord wishes, we will live and do this or that" (Jas 4:15). Often called the *Conditio Jacobaea,* the phrase "Lord willing" conveys an attitude of submission to God's will. It is meant to recognize the sovereignty of God, reflecting a way to live out the command of James 4:7.

In James 4:17, the author expands this command into a more general one: a warning to those who know the commands of God but do not obey them. The hearers of James know the command to be humble and submit to God's will, but it must not end there. One who knows but does not obey commits sins of omission. Once again, they are called not just to be hearers, but doers (Jas 1:22-25).

Oppressive rich (James 5:1-6). In James 5:1-6, the second call to "come now" addresses rich landowners who oppress their workers. After the warning against presumption about gaining wealth (Jas 4:13-17), there is now a pronouncement of condemnation on those who have much wealth and cheat others.

Much like the Old Testament prophets pronouncing judgment (e.g., Is 13:6; Amos 8:3; Zech 11:2), James calls the oppressive rich to "weep and wail." While they are enjoying themselves now, they will have misery when the end comes. The images of rotting wealth, moth-eaten clothes, and rusted gold (Jas 5:2-3) indicate that their wealth will be worthless in the end. The corrosion of gold and silver is especially poignant. Since these precious metals do not rust corrosion indicates false precious metals. The imagery of false gold and silver may have a connection to the language in James 1:2-4, 12 that is reminiscent of a metalworker testing metal for purity. Their worthless riches and the graphic imagery of these rich being fattened for slaughter (Jas 5:6) confirm that they will not remain when the end comes.

The reminders of impending judgment (Jas 4:12; 5:9) surrounding these two sections of apostrophe confirm to the hearers of James that justice will come against the wicked rich. The withheld wages and cries of the workers both act as evidence against these oppressive landowners (Jas 5:4). The title "Lord of hosts" reminds the hearers that God commands powerful armies and will take vengeance on the wicked. These rich have an indulgent lifestyle at others' expense, but they will justly receive their misery.

Economic disparity existed during the time of James, and it continues today. James teaches that the rich will be judged according to how they use their wealth. Those who abuse their privilege and cheat others to their advantage will receive condemnation.

TWO-PART CONCLUSION (JAMES 5:7-11, 12-20)

The closing content of James can be delineated as two movements: (1) a conclusion to the main body, which revisits the main themes of James, and (2) closing exhortations, which bring the letter to an end.

Conclusion to the body: The coming of the Lord (James 5:7-11). As the body of the letter closes, the content about the eschaton reaches a crescendo. James returns to his familiar address of *adelphoi* (brothers and sisters) in James 5:7, as he encourages his hearers to be patient and persevere. The imagery of a farmer in James 5:7 stands in contrast to the traveling merchants and wealthy landowners in the previous two sections; this is a man who remains dependent on God to provide rain for his livelihood. Just like the farmer waits for the rain, the hearers of James are urged to wait for the Lord to come (Jas 5:8). Remarkably, James's imagery appears to treat the rain as a foregone conclusion; he knows it will arrive. For the hearers of James, the coming of the Lord is a foregone conclusion, the variable is not *if*, but *when* the Lord will arrive. Furthermore, there is no question of whether the coming of the Lord will bring favor for the hearers; they are to place their hope in the *parousia*.

The diaspora hearers of James occupied a unique temporal space. They looked to the *past*—their homeland of Israel, the center of their identity. While James does not teach them to forget about the past, he urges them to place their hope in the *future*—the coming of the Lord. Likewise, refugees and immigrants in modern North America often identify with the *past*—their places of origin. Their God-given heritage gives them a strong identity, with traditions and customs to celebrate. At the same time, the message in James encourages the modern reader to also look forward to a favorable future. Inclusion in Christ is our hope, and his return will benefit many distinctive people groups.

Even with the hope set in the future, James issues a warning that his hearers must be careful how they act toward one another in this waiting period. The warning to refrain from "grumbling" against one another in James 5:9 returns to the theme of divisiveness in the community (see Jas 3:16; 4:1-4, 11). It also picks up the theme of proper use of the tongue (Jas 1:26; 3:1-12). Those who do grumble against others will face judgment when the Lord returns. He is called the "Judge" in Jas 5:9, and his arrival is imminent—"at the doors." The references to judgment in James (e.g., Jas 2:12-13; 3:1; 4:12) point to the Lord as the judge, and his imminent return motivates present behavior.

After the warning against grumbling, James returns to encouraging his hearers to be patient. This time, however, he acknowledges that waiting comes with suffering (Jas 5:11). James calls them to look to the suffering and patience of the Old Testament prophets as an example during this challenging time. While he does not name specific prophets, prophets like Jeremiah and Elijah come to mind—faithful men who suffered injustice. They continued to speak in the name of the Lord despite their suffering.

North American minorities, like the minority hearers of James, often look to past figures as examples of faithfulness in the face of injustice. For example, Harriet Tubman is often celebrated among African Americans, and César Chávez among Latino/a Americans. These figures persevered in their causes despite the suffering they faced. Similarly, the hearers of James, identifying with their heritage, are called to see the prophets as an example to them.

James 5:11 draws together several major themes in the epistle. First, the mention of Job continues the appeal to Old Testament exemplars not only found in the previous verse but also in James 2:21-25. Second, it reminds the hearers of the blessedness for those who endure, a theme found in the beginning (Jas 1:2-3), middle (Jas 1:12), and end (Jas 1:25) of the introductory prologue. Third, it encourages the hearers to look forward to a *future reward* from a compassionate and merciful God, which has been discussed throughout James (Jas 1:12; 2:5; 3:18; 4:6-10; 5:7).

This conclusion to the body in James 5:11 shows that the uniting motif in James is the future blessing for those who endure in faithfulness to God, epitomized by the saying in James 1:12. Throughout the epistle, James teaches his hearers what obedience and loyalty to God look like, from caring for the poor to having proper use of the tongue. James upholds Job as the example of perseverance—he suffered, but he did not sin in accusing God of wrongdoing (Job 1:22). At the end of the account of Job, we see God's compassion and mercy toward him (Job 42:10-17). James urges his hearers to persevere like Job and place their hope in God's compassion and mercy as well.

Final exhortations (James 5:12-20). The closing content of James contains a list of commands. While they might seem disjointed, these sayings contain elements consistent with the endings of other ancient Greek letters: the phrase "above all" (Jas 5:12), content about oaths (Jas 5:12), a wish for good health (Jas 5:13-15), and content about prayer (Jas 5:14-18).[28] By using these elements, James signals the end of his letter.

James 5:12 exhorts his hearers not to swear. Instead of making an oath, which is a convention of the ending of ancient Greek letters, he prohibits them. This command recalls the teaching of Jesus in the Sermon on the Mount (Mt 5:33-37). In accordance with his teaching about the use of the tongue (Jas 1:19, 26; 3:1-12; 4:11, 5:9), James urges his hearers always to be truthful: "let your 'Yes' be yes and your 'No' be no." Having a reputation for having honesty eliminates the need to make an oath. The appeal to God's judgment revisits a theme frequently found in the epistle (Jas 2:12-13; 3:1; 4:12; 5:9).

Much like the endings of other New Testament letters (e.g., Rom 15:30-32; 1 Thess 5:16-18; Philem 22; Jude 20), James 5:13-18 contains some content about prayer. First, James teaches that communication with God is appropriate in any circumstance: if someone is "suffering," "cheerful," or "sick" (Jas 5:13-14).

Next, James encourages prayer for one another as well, having elders of the church pray over the sick (Jas 5:14) and praying for one another's sins (Jas 5:16). With the former, James offers the outcomes of prayer for the sick: restoration, raising (probably from the sickbed), and forgiveness of his sins (Jas 5:15). With the latter, James urges his hearers to intercede in prayer for one another as they "confess your sins to one another" (Jas 5:16). The healing in view could be physical (if connected with Jas 5:14-15), spiritual (if the focus is on the sin's effect on the individual), or social (if the focus is on the impact on the community). It could refer to all three dimensions, as sin has far-reaching consequences. If all three were in view, their intertwining would resonate with many Asian cultures, which hold a holistic view of how one's decisions affect the mind, body, spirit, and relationships.

James then appeals to another Old Testament example, the prophet Elijah. The example of Elijah's prayer regarding rain suggests that James has something more specific in mind than just the power of prayer in general. After all, he could have chosen a different event from Elijah's life.[29] Since the context of Elijah's prayer was the apostasy of the king and the people (see 1 Kings 16:29–18:46), James is likely applying Elijah's example to the confession of sins in James 5:16 and the restoration of a wanderer in James 5:19-20. Thus, he calls for his hearers to repent from their sins, praying for restoration as Elijah did.

Fittingly, James returns to an explicit discussion of the eternal fate of those in the Christian community in James 5:19-20. After

[28]For a detailed discussion on Greek letter-endings and other conventions, see Francis Xavier J. Exler, "The Form of the Ancient Greek Letter: A Study in Greek Epistolography" (PhD diss., Catholic University of America, 1923); Stanley Kent Stowers, *Letter Writing in Greco-Roman Antiquity*, LEC 5 (Philadelphia: Westminster, 1986).

[29]See Blomberg and Kamell, *James*, 246-47.

warning his audience against being deceived (Jas 1:16, 22, 26), he now addresses the issue of those who wander "from *the* truth." Within the context of James's repeated emphasis on action, the truth probably refers to the "right" way of behaving. The exhortation in James 5:19 is not for those who wander, but for those who bring back a wanderer.

James 5:20 reveals the twofold result of the restoration of a sinner: (1) "saving his soul from death" (au. trans.) and (2) "cover[ing] a multitude of sins." Whose soul is being saved and whose sins are covered? While a case can be made that the benefits are for the restorer. However, the most straightforward reading of these sayings keeps the same antecedent for "him" in James 5:19 and "his" in James 5:20, and the parallel expressions in James 5:20 suggest that they refer to the same person as well. Consequently, it is the one restored whose soul is saved and whose sins are covered.

The calls to restore a wanderer in James 5:19-20 would likely resonate with the marginalized minority hearers of James. Like many diaspora communities today, they probably placed a high value on inclusion in the community. These marginalized Jews are assured that their distance from their homeland does not disqualify them from salvation in the end. The letter concludes with a call for them to look after one another as they face their trials and await the coming of the Lord.

BIBLIOGRAPHY

Allison, Dale C., Jr. *James: A Critical and Exegetical Commentary*. ICC. New York: T&T Clark, 2013.

Batten, Alicia J. *Friendship and Benefaction in James*. Emory Studies in Early Christianity 15. Dorset, UK: Deo, 2010.

———. *What Are They Saying About the Letter of James?* Mahwah, NJ: Paulist Press, 2009.

Bauckham, Richard. *James: Wisdom of James, Disciple of Jesus the Sage*. London: Routledge, 1999.

Blomberg, Craig L., and Mariam J. Kamell. *James*. ZECNT. Grand Rapids, MI: Zondervan, 2008.

Cheung, Luke L., and Andrew B. Spurgeon. *James: A Pastoral and Contextual Commentary*. Asia Bible Commentary. Carlisle, UK: Langham Global Library, 2018.

Davids, Peter H. *The Epistle of James*. NIGTC. Grand Rapids, MI: Eerdmans, 1982.

Eng, Daniel K. "East Asian and Asian American Reflections on James." *Journal for Baptist Theology and Ministry* 19.2 (2022): 245-57.

———. *Eschatological Approval: The Structure and Unifying Motif of James*. New Testament Monographs. Sheffield: Sheffield Phoenix Press, 2022.

———. "'The Refining of Your Faith'?: Metallurgic Testing Imagery in James." *Bulletin for Biblical Research* 32.2 (2022): 182-201.

Francis, Fred O. "The Form and Function of the Opening and Closing Paragraphs of James and I John." *ZNW* 61 (1970): 110-25.

Moo, Douglas J. *The Letter of James*. 2nd ed. PNTC. Grand Rapids, MI: Eerdmans, 2021.

Ropes, James Hardy. *A Critical and Exegetical Commentary on the Epistle of St. James*. ICC. Edinburgh: T&T Clark, 1916.

Tamez, Elsa. "James: A Circular Letter for Immigrants." Translated by Gloria Kinsler. *RevExp* 108.3 (2011): 369-80.

Taylor, Mark Edward. *A Text-Linguistic Investigation into the Discourse Structure of James*. LNTS. London: T&T Clark, 2006.

Varner, William C. *James: A Commentary on the Greek Text*. Lexington, KY: Fontes, 2017.

FIRST LETTER OF PETER

Janette H. Ok

INTRODUCTION

The idea of being a Christian is often taken for granted for those who have grown up in the church or who have been believers for a long time. But how does one become a Christian? How do God's people live into the reality of what Christ has done for them? What is the process of identifying as a Christ-follower and as members of the household of God? And how do believers negotiate their precarious and often fraught relationships with their nonbelieving acquaintances and authority figures who are hostile to their new way of life? The letter of 1 Peter addresses such questions as it seeks to comfort, console, and exhort believers who are experiencing social alienation as a result of their conversion. It also presents a strategy for how to maintain peaceable relationships—insofar as it is possible—with nonbelievers and bear an ever-ready witness to Christ. In the midst of such precarity, the author encourages his readers to find solace, solidarity, and kinship among fellow believers. First Peter, in short, speaks to the difficult challenge of becoming Christian, embracing a voluntary exilic existence, and belonging to the household of God, while living holy lives among unbelievers who are hostile to the new Christ-follower identity.

The author identifies himself as "Peter, an apostle of Jesus Christ" in the opening line of the letter, and later as "a fellow elder and witness of the sufferings of Christ" (1 Pet 1:1; 5:1 ESV). For centuries before the advent of modern critical scholarship, readers took, at face value, the identification of Simon Peter as the author of 1 Peter. Interpreters who view 1 Peter as a letter written pseudonymously by a later Christian in Peter's name—that is, who do not think Simon Peter penned the letter—argue that what is known of Simon Peter based on the canonical Gospels, Acts, and Galatians does not accord well with the contents of the 1 Peter itself. How could an "uneducated" (Acts 4:13) Galilean fisherman whose mission focused on the Jews (Gal 2:9) write in the polished and sophisticated Greek used in 1 Peter? Interpreters who accept the letter's traditional authorship maintain that either the letter was written by Simon Peter with the help of Silvanus (1 Pet 5:12), his Greek-educated secretary (*amanuensis*), or that Simon Peter himself learned and gained mastery of Greek.[1]

The question of who authored 1 Peter relates directly to the dating of the letter. If Simon Peter penned it, or had it dictated before his death, then the letter dates to the reign of Nero (no later than the '60s CE). However, if the letter was written in the name of Simon Peter but was neither written or dictated by Peter himself, then the question of dating centers on internal

[1]As an example of an argument in favor of traditional Petrine authorship of 1 Peter, see Karen H. Jobes, *1 Peter*, 2nd ed., BECNT (Grand Rapids, MI: Baker Academic, 2022), 5-19.

features of the letter. For example, the author's veiled mention of "Babylon" in 1 Peter 5:13 may support a later dating because the reference functioned in some Jewish and Christian circles as a code name for Rome after the Romans destroyed Jerusalem in 70 CE (cf. Rev 17:5; 18:2, 10, 21). The use of the name *Christianos* (1 Pet 4:16) serves as one of the earliest recorded instances of the term in Christian literature, appearing only two other times in the New Testament (Acts 11:26; 26:28). The term seems to have been a stigmatizing label first used by outsiders (see, e.g., Tacitus, *Ann* 15.44, who refers to Nero's scapegoating of "Christians" for the fire that engulfed Rome in 64 CE). The fact that "Christians" does not appear in the Pauline letters or the Gospels suggests that it took some time for the term's derogatory use to go viral enough to become familiar to a large group of Christians.[2]

The anti-Christian social hostility and slander described in the letter (1 Pet 2:12; 3:14; 4:4, 12-13, 16) bear some resemblance to the state-sponsored persecution of Christians at the instigation of their neighbors described by Pliny in his letter to Emperor Trajan (*Ep.* 10.96) around 111–113 CE. Although 1 Peter does not refer explicitly to formal persecution, the letter speaks of the hostility, persecution, and suffering in the form of slander, ridicule, false accusation, stigmatization, and even possibly formal charges made against Christians by members of their communities, cities, or households (1 Pet 1:6; 2:12, 19, 21-25; 3:9, 14-16, 17; 4:1, 12-16; 5:8-10). The author offers an ambivalent view of the state while exhorting believers to accept the authority of the emperor and the governors sent by him (1 Pet 2:13-17; cf. Rom 13:1-7), making it plausible that the letter reflects the circumstances that *led up* to the situation of official persecution described by Pliny. Thus, in light of the letter's internal evidence, a possible date for the letter of 1 Peter lies sometime roughly between 70 and 95 CE.

While it is impossible to know the precise ethnic-religious makeup of the letter's original addressees, the author of 1 Peter writes to them as though they are Gentiles, referring frequently to their former way of life (e.g., 1 Pet 1:14; 18; 2:10). With a significant number of Jews living in Asia Minor, the presence of Jewish converts in these Christian communities was likely, with the majority being Gentile. The letter was intended to circulate among Christian communities scattered throughout the Roman provinces that make up the larger part of Asia Minor, modern-day Turkey (1 Pet 1:1; cf. Acts 15:23-29; Col 4:16). This is why readers often refer to 1 Peter as a Catholic or General Epistle or as a circular letter, along with James, 2 Peter, 1–3 John, and Jude. Rather than address specific congregations, the letter is written to Christians across a broader geographical area.

Thematic outline:

Letter's Opening (1 Pet 1:1-2)

Living as Foreign-Born People of God (1 Pet 1:3–2:10)

Living as Foreigners Among the Gentiles and as Family Within the Household of God (1 Pet 2:11–4:11)

Sharing in Christ's Suffering as "a Christian" and Maintaining the Unity of the Household of God Through Humility and Resistance (1 Pet 4:12–5:11)

Letter's Closing (1 Pet 5:12-14)

[2]David G. Horrell and Travis B. Williams, *1 Peter: A Critical and Exegetical Commentary*, vol. 1, *Chapters 1–2*, ICC (London: T&T Clark, 2023), 104-6.

LETTER'S OPENING (1 PETER 1:1-2)

From the opening lines of the letter, Peter[3] sets out to establish the identity of his letter's recipients: they are "the elect who are living as foreigners in the diaspora in Pontus, Galatia, Cappadocia, Asia, and Bithynia, according to the foreknowledge of God the Father" (1 Pet 1:1-2 my trans.).[4] God the Father chooses believers "as a result" of his foreknowledge (1 Pet 1:2). This divine choosing was not random or arbitrary, but rather the fulfillment of a divine plan. "Foreknowledge" (*prognōsis*) expresses God the Father's loving intentionality and eternal decision in choosing Christians to become his children (1 Pet 1:14), his household (1 Pet 2:5; 4:17), and his people (1 Pet 1:9-10).[5] A similar reference to the concept of divine foreknowledge can be found in Jeremiah 1:5, where the prophet understands God as the one who conceived, sanctified, and ordained him even prior to his conception and birth: "Before I formed you in the womb, I knew you, and before you came out of the womb, I sanctified you; I appointed you to be a prophet to the nations."

Holiness and obedience, as concepts, relate to each other in 1 Peter 1:2 (cf. 1 Pet 1:15, 22). It is through the "Spirit's sanctifying activity" that God's election of believers is accomplished (1 Pet 1:2).[6] And it is "because of the obedience and sprinkling of the blood of Jesus Christ" that the Spirit can make holy those whom God has chosen (1 Pet 1:1-2).[7] Peter uniquely embraces the exilic condition as one that results from God the Father's choosing of believers, whom God foreknew and the Spirit consecrated by the blood of Christ for obedience.

The image of diaspora permeates the letter of 1 Peter.[8] The term diaspora literally means the "scattering of seed" and came to denote the "dispersion" of the Jews among the Gentiles outside of the Holy Land as a result of involuntary and voluntary forces.[9] Biblical and early Hellenistic Jewish writers characterized diaspora in negative terms as an act from God meant to punish the people of Israel for their disobedience and call them to repentance.[10] God allowed Israel to experience the misfortunes of military defeat, foreign conquest, and geographical displacement. However, during the Second Temple period, between 516 BCE

---

[3]Throughout this study, I will use the traditional name when referring to the letter's author for the sake of convenience.

[4]Translation mine, unless otherwise noted.

[5]Cf. Jdt 9:6; 11:19; Acts 2:23. With J. Ramsey Michaels (*1 Peter*, WBC 49 [Waco, TX: Word, 1988], 10-11) and Leonhard Goppelt (*A Commentary on I Peter*, ed. Ferdinand Hahn, trans. John E. Alsup [Grand Rapids, MI: Eerdmans, 1993], 72-73). Goppelt understands *prognōsis* as divine predetermination that is "as effective as election" (73). Michaels sees *prognōsis* as "synonymous with what Peter five times refers to as being 'called' (1:15; 2:9, 21; 3:9; 5:10)" (*1 Peter*, 10).

[6]Paul J. Achtemeier, *1 Peter: A Commentary on First Peter*, Hermeneia (Minneapolis: Augsburg Fortress, 1996), 87; Charles A. Bigg, *Critical and Exegetical Commentary on the Epistles of St. Peter and St. Jude*, ICC (New York: Scribner's, 1901), 92. Cf. 2 Thess 2:13, which employs the same phrase (*en hagiasmō pneumatos*) in order to convey a very similar thought: "God chose you as the first fruits for the purpose of salvation *by means of the Spirit's sanctifying activity* and belief in the truth" (italics mine). See J. N. D. Kelly, *A Commentary on the Epistles of Peter and of Jude* (New York: Harper & Row, 1969), 43.

[7]Francis H. Agnew, "1 Peter 1:2—An Alternative Translation," *CBQ* 45 (1983): 68-73. For a closer analysis of the difficulties of Agnew's proposal, see Sydney H. T. Page, "Obedience and Blood-Sprinkling in 1 Peter 1:2," *WTJ* 72, no. 2 (2010): 291-98. Agnew's reading has been adopted by John H. Elliott, *1 Peter: A New Translation with Introduction and Commentary*, AB 37B (New York: Doubleday, 2000), 319; Earl J. Richard, *Reading 1 Peter, Jude, and 2 Peter: A Literary and Theological Commentary* (Macon, GA: Smyth & Helwys, 2000), 32; Joel B. Green, *1 Peter*, THNTC (Grand Rapids, MI: Eerdmans, 2007), 20.

[8]Troy W. Martin, *Metaphor and Composition in 1 Peter*, SBLDS 131 (Atlanta: Scholars Press, 1992). 144-267; Shively T. J. Smith, *Strangers to Family, Diaspora and 1 Peter's Invention of God's Household* (Waco, TX: Baylor University Press, 2016), 15-83.

[9]See, e.g., Deut 28:25; 30:4; Jer 15:7; LXX Jer 41:17; *Pss. Sol.* 8:28; 9:2; *T. Ash.* 7:2.

[10]Harold W. Attridge, review of *Das Selbstverständnis der jüdischen Diaspora in der hellenistisch-römischen Zeit*, by Willem Cornelis Van Unnik, *JAOS* 115, no. 2 (1995): 323-24 (324); Smith, *Strangers to Family*, 35.

and 70 CE, a change in the Jewish understanding of exile took place, as diaspora came to signify marginalization that went beyond forced migration and geographical displacement and encompassed various forms of alienations.[11]

In 1 Peter 1:1, "diaspora" refers to those who have voluntarily taken on a new religious and social identity as Christians. When taken metaphorically and in relation to their "chosen" status, the phrase "to the exiles of the diaspora" offers a glimpse of the social alienation and marginalization experienced by believers *as a result* of their divinely chosen status. God the Father's election of believers places them within a Jewish past, and, at the same time, displaces them within the Roman imperial structure.[12] Their spiritual status as members of the people and household of God (1 Pet 2:5, 10; 4:17), and their faithful response and embrace of God's action through Christ,[13] puts them at odds with the values, practices, and culture among the people they once found so familiar. Thus, Peter's addressees are not literal exiles but rather religious exiles who find themselves no longer at home in the dominant culture because of their conversion. Believers can embrace their exilic condition because their past election and future hope put their present hardships in temporal perspective as they "live in fear during the time of [their] exile" (1 Pet 1:17 NRSV).

Peter thus makes reference to five Roman provinces in Asia Minor in 1 Peter 1:2 not as metaphorical geographical points but to present his addressees, who live in a vast geographical area (roughly a little smaller than the square mileage of the state of California),[14] as members of a divinely scattered yet cohesive people group. He situates his audience's social locatedness in God's primordial and eschatological plan over their lives. Doing so enables them to see their present sufferings from the perspective of their past, that is, God's election (1 Pet 1:1-2), and future, that is, God's promise of a heavenly inheritance (1 Pet 1:4-5). Christians are to voluntarily enter into and endure exile as a real but protracted reality.[15] They must learn how to navigate living as elect foreigners in a familiar land and sociopolitical structure. Such social-political displacement leads to the creation of a spiritual household that is characterized by eschatological hope and familial love, and makes it easier for believers to disidentify with their former way of life.

Acclaimed author Viet Thanh Nguyen explains how the universal preoccupation with home becomes "particularly dire for those whose identities make them vulnerable to the threat of never belonging. This has certainly been the case for Asian Americans, whose experience with racism in the United States has oftentimes occurred through being painted as the perpetual foreigner, the yellow peril or brown terror, with unbreakable ties to a land of origin or ancestry."[16]

Foreigners have a fraught and precarious relationship with home. The experience and accusation of being a foreigner is often imbued with negative associations. Racially-fueled demands like "Go home!" or "Go back to where

[11]Martien Halvorson-Taylor, *Enduring Exile: The Metaphorization of Exile in the Hebrew Bible* (Leiden: Brill, 2011), 1.

[12]Jennifer T. Kaalund, *Reading Hebrews and 1 Peter with the African American Great Migration: Diaspora, Place, and Identity*, LNTS (London: Bloomsbury T&T Clark, 2019), 116.

[13]Smith, *Strangers to Family*, 21.

[14]Jobes, *1 Peter*, 19.

[15]See Halvorson-Taylor, *Enduring Exile*, 8, who uses the language of "enduring exile" in her study of exile in Second Temple literature.

[16]Viet Thanh Nguyen, "Forward," in *Go Home!*, ed. Rowan Hisayo Buchanan (New York: Feminist Press, 2018), xvi.

you came from," can provoke visceral fear and ambivalence among those who are viewed as foreigners in a context they consider home or seek to establish as home.

In everyday life, home is where one leaves and returns to. For those living in diaspora, home is more elusive. Exiles—whether by force, choice, or both—have left their homes with the prospect of never returning. Thus, exiles and immigrants forge new homes in places where they may never quite feel at home. Home stands at the heart of the exilic condition, whether literal or figurative. In the letter of 1 Peter, the exilic condition stands at the heart of Christian experience.

LIVING AS FOREIGN-BORN PEOPLE OF GOD (1 PETER 1:3–2:10)

1 Peter 1:3-9. This section begins with resounding praise for God the Father, who makes salvation and new birth possible through Jesus, and ends with joy-filled astonishment at the salvation in Christ that angels eagerly investigate. Plenitude punctuates 1 Peter 1:3-4, as Peter speaks of the abundance of God's mercy in the past, present, and future, as if to remind readers that divine mercy is not on short supply and to infuse them with confidence.

Peter directs worship to God in his role as Father of Jesus Christ. The loving intentionality by which God the Father chooses believers manifests itself in God's merciful role as the Begetter. The elect exiles of the diaspora have been "born anew to a living hope through the resurrection of Jesus Christ from the dead" (1 Pet 1:3). The language of new birth (*anagennaō*) appears only twice in the New Testament, both times in 1 Peter (1 Pet 1:3; 23). In 1 Peter 1:3, Peter (using the aorist active participle) puts the emphasis on God the Father as the active agent of rebegetting, such that God could be given here a virtual title, "the Begetter," "the Progenitor," or "the Parent."[17] Through spiritual regeneration, not by physical birth, believers have become children of God. However, it is in Jesus Christ's physical resurrection from the dead that they experience this radically new existence. Peter explicitly declares God as the father of Jesus Christ in 1 Peter 1:3 to make clear that believers are brought into a new patrilineage or family line through God's relationship with Jesus Christ. It is through God's relationship with Jesus Christ that Gentile Christians can have a relationship with God as Father and a new status as God's people (1 Pet 2:9-10). Peter puts the emphasis on God the Father's great mercy and action.

New birth thus leads to what Joel B. Green refers to a "conversion of the imagination," as believers live out a radically transformed existence in view of God's mercy and by means of Jesus' resurrection.[18] This transformation, while decisive through the ransoming blood of Jesus Christ (see 1 Pet 1:18-19), is an ongoing process of resocialization, reconstruction, and redefinition as God's children (1 Pet 1:3, 14) and members of God's household (1 Pet 2:5; 4:17). The phrase "living hope" is unique to the New Testament. Those chosen and born anew now have a "living hope" that is a dynamic, anticipation-filled expectation made possible through the resurrection of Jesus Christ from the dead.

It is implied in 1 Peter 1:4 that believers face challenging circumstances as Peter frames their present reality in eschatological perspective. He assures them that God has "kept in heaven for you [plural]" an inheritance that will not be affected by the precarious busts and booms of

---

[17]Michaels, *1 Peter*, 18. Michaels suggests *ton gennēsanta*, "the parent," as a possible New Testament equivalent (1 Jn 5:1; cf. LXX Deut 32:18).

[18]Green, *1 Peter*, 26.

their present-day circumstances (1 Pet 1:4).[19] In the perfect tense, the participle *tetērēmenēn* ("kept" or "protected") conveys unbreakable security as God guards their future inheritance. The phrase "for you" (*eis hymas*), which appears multiple times throughout the rest of the letter, emphasizes here the "for-you-ness" of God's saving action.[20] Peter adds another level of assurance when he employs military language in 1 Peter 1:5 to describe how God "protects" (*phroureō*), similar to the way a military sentinel keeps watch over a fort.

The three adjectives Peter uses to describe believers' inheritance in 1 Peter 1:4—"imperishable, undefiled, and unfading" (NRSV)—refer to an eschatological promise that will be fully realized at the final revelation of Jesus Christ (1 Pet 1:5, 7). Commensurate to such a promise is a resilient and thriving hope and genuine faith made manifest in the lives of believers in the present (1 Pet 1:4, 7). In 1 Peter 1:5, Peter links God's protecting power to their imminent salvation. Faith (*pistis*) appears three times in this section (1 Pet 1:5, 7, and 9) in reference to believers' enduring trust in God's power to save (1 Pet 1:7, 9, 21). Faith bears witness to God's protection (*dia pisteōs*) in the sense that such hope-filled confidence on the part of believers bears witness to the reality of God's saving power that guards them even now.[21] Hope continues to live because God's protecting power is active and unceasing. The reason why Peter emphasizes God's protecting power becomes clearer in 1 Peter 1:6, when he alludes to the clear and present difficulties faced by his addressees.

In 1 Peter 1:6-8, Peter brings together two seemingly incongruous concepts: suffering and joy. The antecedent for "in this you rejoice" (*en hō agalliasthe*) most likely refers to the whole subject of living hope in 1 Peter 1:3-5. Believers have every reason to rejoice even when they suffer various trials, because they have a secure heavenly inheritance that will not be affected by the precarious busts and booms of their present-day circumstances.

Present joy that is rooted in eschatological hope enables believers to endure various "trials" (*peirasmois*; cf. Mt 6:13). Although the temporary nature of such trials makes them easier to endure, the author also sees trials as having a purpose: they test and prove the genuineness of faith (*pistis*). God finds genuine faith, in other words, that which has been tested by trials, "more valuable" than tempered gold (1 Pet 1:7). Faith makes it possible for Christians to "love" (*agapaō*, cf. 1 Pet 2:17) Jesus, whom they have never "seen" and do not "see" now but in whom they "trust" and "rejoice" (1 Pet 1:8). Peter's double emphasis on *not* "seeing" (*horaō*) reminds believers that seeing is not believing: one can love, trust (*pisteuō*), and rejoice (*agalliaō*) in Jesus without having ever physically seen or encountered him.[22] One can bear witness to Jesus without being an eyewitness to Jesus. Suffering, though not a precondition for faith, creates opportunities for faith to be tested and proven genuine (cf. 1 Pet 5:9). Suffering also poses no threat to salvation (*sōtēria*), which is the outcome (*telos*) of faith (1 Pet 1:9).

Christians thus have an entirely new life expectancy resulting from their eschatological

---

[19]For other examples of texts that attest to the idea of a heavenly inheritance that awaits God's children, see Ps 16:6; *1 En.* 11:1; 2 Bar 4:6, Rom 8:17; Gal 4:7.

[20]Elliott, *1 Peter*, 336.

[21]Achtemeier, *1 Peter*, 97. The description of faith in Heb 11:1 as "the assurance of things hoped for, the conviction of things not seen" conveys this similar idea.

[22]Elliott, *1 Peter*, 342.

perspective on their present circumstances. "Living hope" (1 Pet 1:3) manifests in an anticipation-filled life that gives believers every reason to rejoice, even as they suffer various trials (1 Pet 1:6).

A life transformed by Christ not only reframes suffering as a result of one's following in the way of Christ but also brings about more suffering because the way of Christ is so contrary to the ways of the world. Being elect exiles who are born anew to a living hope does not guarantee a home that accrues equity, a high-powered, socially respectable job, marriage, children, and the capitalistic notion of the pursuit of happiness. But it does result in life-giving, hope-filled instability—the kind that results in a resounding, abundant, paradoxical, unexpected, peculiar, and abundant joy.

1 Peter 1:10-12. Peter places salvation along the continuum of what God has already been doing through ancient Israel when he speaks of the prophets in the past who witnessed to his addressees' salvation.[23] The newness of life brought about by the resurrection of Jesus Christ from the dead does not mean Peter's addressees are to understand themselves as belonging to a new religion severed from God's people, Israel. Rather, as Gentile believers await their salvation, they can take comfort and confidence in the fact that they stand in solidarity with God's ancient people, that they are "coparticipants" in God's one cosmic redemptive plan.[24] The repeated use of the second-person pronoun (1 Pet 1:10, 12, 20) reinforces the point Peter has already made in 1 Peter 1:2, that God's election of Christ and election of Christians was not a divine afterthought or an arbitrary decision. Rather, it was a carefully planned and much-anticipated choice of a loving, caring, and gracious father on behalf of the estranged and persecuted Christians addressed in the letter.[25]

1 Peter 1:13-21. The emphasis in 1 Peter 1:13-21 on disidentifying with their past underscores how the author perceives his audience as comprising Gentile converts. Peter does not tell his addressees to keep the commands or laws of God. Rather, he urges them to "no longer be shaped by the evil desires that characterized your former time of ignorance" (1 Pet 1:14), and to resist the fleshly cravings and futile way of life from which Christ has liberated them (1 Pet 1:18-19). Such "desires" (*epithymiai*) and behavior have no place in the present and future life of God's "obedient children" (1 Pet 1:13).

In Greco-Roman society, children were expected to obey their fathers. Peter has similar expectations of God's children. However, rather than tell them to do whatever God tells them, Peter offers a theological basis for his ethical exhortations that are based largely on Leviticus 19: God's children need to know their Father's character because who God is shapes how they live. God the Father is holy, and so God's obedient children must also be holy.[26]

The holy one who called believers (1 Pet 1:15) is the same God whom believers can call "Father" (1 Pet 1:17). All of God's children have one Father and belong to one family because of their relationship to the Son. But God the Father is also an impartial judge. So, God's children are to live "in reverent fear" of their benevolent Father, who will judge all people according to their deeds, beginning with the household of God (1 Pet 1:17; 4:17). This

---

[23]Jobes, *1 Peter*, 101.

[24]Michaels, *1 Peter*, 39.

[25]Janette H. Ok, *Constructing Ethnic Identity in 1 Peter: Who You Are No Longer*, LNTS (London: T&T Clark, 2021), 38.

[26]Ok, "Commentary on 1 Peter 1:17-23," *Working Preacher*, April 26, 2020, www.workingpreacher.org/commentaries/revised-common-lectionary/third-sunday-of-easter/commentary-on-1-peter-117-23-3.

reverence for God "during the time of your exile" means that Christians voluntarily embrace an exilic orientation toward the world in ways that make the strange familiar and the familiar strange. This is a particularly important call for believers who feel very much at home in the dominant culture.

As chosen exiles, believers must disidentify not only with values of the dominant culture, but also with the values of their ancestors, if those values are contrary to God's will. Believers have been "ransomed from the profitless way of life inherited from the fathers" (1 Pet 1:18). The Greek adjective for "inherited from the fathers" (*patroparadotos*) appears nowhere else in the New Testament and Greek Old Testament (LXX). When it does occur in Hellenistic literature, it has a positive connotation. Peter, however, dismisses as "futile" or "dead-end" (*mataias*) the entire way of life handed down from the fathers. In doing so, he rejects the very values, commitments, and norms that gave them meaning and coherence.

The focus of Christ's redemption in 1 Peter 1:18-19 is not on individual sins but rather on corporate sins. God's children do not just sin because of their personal decisions but also because of broader, cultural, familial, systemic conditions. They sin also because of the inculcated, deep-seated, systemic sins perpetuated in their histories, passed down from their forefathers and ancestors, and still impacting and influencing them in the present.

In light of the United States' colonial past and the undeniable racial underpinnings that appeals to the greatness of America's past, the idea of being ransomed from the ways of one's ancestors seems more applicable to "heathen" foreign nations who hold un-American values, commitments, and norms than it does to White American Christians who determine what it looks like to be a nation under God. However, those who have been dispossessed of their lands, oppressed by colonial forces, marginalized by White Christian nationalist narratives, or who are among minoritized and dominated classes may have the interpretive edge in understanding 1 Peter's message. This is because the letter is addressed primarily to the subaltern, that is, people in subordinated classes or dominated members of the household with little to no means for social mobility. Such readers in similar subaltern conditions also have the interpretive challenge of reading 1 Peter 1:18-19 not as a further degradation and disavowal of the ways of their ancestors, but as a reminder that while there is good in every culture that can be promoted, there is no single culture, ethnicity, race, or nation that can be equated with the kingdom of God. While some governments serve law and order better than others, all governing authorities are subject to corruption and the abuse of power. All Christians have "sins of the fathers" to confess, disinherit, and be ransomed from. However, Christians from the dominant classes, the majority race or ethnicity, and/or imperializing nations should take greater caution not to conflate their social privileges and powers with their identity as a "holy nation, chosen race, royal priesthood, people of God's possession" (1 Pet 2:9).

1 Peter 1:22-25. Peter picks up on the language used in 1 Peter 1:3-4 and associates them with other concepts in 1 Pet 1:23-25. Believers are "born anew" through the "living word." Not only do believers possess an "imperishable inheritance," but they have been "born anew . . . of imperishable seed through the living and enduring word of God." Obedience on the part of God's children is not blind allegiance, but an intentional patterning one's life after "the truth" (*tēs alētheias*). Although it is not entirely clear what "truth" refers to in 1 Peter 1:22, the term stands in stark contrast to actions that are disingenuous, hypocritical, deceitful (see 1 Pet 2:1) and most likely refers to faith in Christ or the truth of the gospel. By means of their obedience to the truth, believers have already purified their souls, as the perfect tense of the verb *hēgnikotes* indicates (1 Pet 1:2). "Obedience" (*hypakoē*) has already been mentioned several times in reference to the obedience of Jesus Christ (1 Pet 1:2) and the letter's addressees (1 Pet 1:14) and relates closely to the idea of holiness. Holiness is what Peter most likely means when he speaks of purification in 1 Peter 1:22. Just as faith on the part of a Christian activates God's protection, so obedience to truth enables Christians to be morally pure. Such purity of heart has communal purpose and impact as it enables Christians to love one another with "genuine mutual love" or more literally with "unhypocritical brotherly [and sisterly] love" (1 Pet 1:22).

In 1 Peter 1:22, Peter describes "love" (*philadelphia*) among the community of believers not as a compulsory obligation, but as a sticky, enduring commitment to strangers who have become family because of Christ. The word *ektenōs* can convey the warmth and intensity of love, as we see with the translation "deeply" (NRSV, NIV) or "earnestly" (ESV, NET). It can also be more literally rendered "constantly,"[27] or "unremittingly,"[28] in order to express the persistent, persevering nature of love in the face of adversity. The first rendering of *ektenōs* speaks to love's affect and the second to love's effect. That is, believers express love for one another through their emotions and actions. In context, both translations seem to convey the kind of earnest and resilient love that binds a community together toward a common purpose.

The Korean concept of *jeong* helps convey both the affective and effective dimensions of Christian love in 1 Peter 1:22. Sue Kim Park describes *jeong* as deep and active love and affection that leads to solidarity among people: "Jeong intricately weaves human strength to birth resilience in the face of trials by activating and connecting shared love and affection in human beings. This love is fierce and does not relent. . . . Jeong as love generates freedom and contagiously compels others to do the same, creating space for solidarity."[29] For Peter, love among members of God's household is characterized by resilient fervor and affection that promotes mutual thriving and solidarity, even in the midst of forces that work to dissolve such bonds of intimacy.

1 Peter 2:1-3. While Peter has alluded to the external forces challenging the Christian community (1 Pet 1:6), he also addresses the internal forces at work to dissolve and destroy solidarity in 1 Peter 2:1: "malice," "deceit," "hypocrisies," "envies," and "slanders."[30] Believers must "get rid" of "all" such relationally and communally destructive vices. They must also develop new taste buds for "the Lord," whom Peter understands as referring to Jesus Christ (1 Pet 2:3; Ps 33:9 [34:8 LXX]). Hence Peter commands them to "long for the pure, spiritual milk" (1 Pet 2:2). The NRSV and NIV translate the Greek adjective *logikos* as "spiritual," but other translations directly relate it to the word (*logos* in 1 Pet 1:23), as conveyed by

---

[27]So Elliott, *1 Peter*, 387.

[28]So Michaels, *1 Peter* 76.

[29]Sue Kim Park, "Jeong: A Practical Theology of Postcolonial Interfaith Relations," *Religions* 11, no. 10 (2020): 515. https://doi.org/10.3390/rel11100515.

[30]James 1:21 appears to be the closest parallel (so Michaels, *1 Peter*, 84), although similar vice lists appear in the Pauline tradition (see, e.g., Rom 1:29-31; 1 Cor 5:10-11; Gal 5:19-21; Eph 4:31; Col 3:5) and in the Dead Sea Scrolls (e.g., 1QS 4.9-11; 10.21-23; so Jobes, *1 Peter*, 132-33).

the CEB: "milk of the word."[31] In reference to the metaphor of a newborn babe, milk, and the idea of growing up into salvation, *logikos* seems best to refer to the need for Christians to grow spiritually akin to the way infants need to grow physically. The phrase "as newborn infants" in 1 Peter 2:2 draws on the cognate verb for "born anew" (1 Pet 1:23; cf. 1 Pet 1:3), functioning as a metaphor similar to "as obedient children" in 1 Peter 1:14. Peter associates the longing for spiritual milk with maturity, whereas Paul associates milk with immaturity (cf. 1 Cor 3:2). Just as newborns have the instinctual and insatiable desire for a mother's milk, believers at every stage of maturity are to crave that which nourishes and sustains faithful obedience, communal love, and growing toward God's salvation (cf. 1 Pet 1:5, 9). Reference to infants in 1 Peter 2:2 also relates to the theme of newness in the letter and Peter's emphasis on his recipients being God's new people.[32]

1 Peter 2:4-8. In 1 Peter 2:4, Peter shifts from the metaphor of newborn babes to that of living stones, and from the idea of craving spiritual milk to being built up into a spiritual house. The image for Jesus Christ also changes, as Peter goes from describing him as life-giving milk to a "living stone." Just as believers are to crave spiritual milk, they are to come to Jesus, who though "rejected by humans" is "chosen, precious in God's sight" (cf. 1 Pet 1:1, 7, 19). The participle "living" (*zōnta*) links Jesus even more explicitly with "living hope" (1 Pet 1:3) and the "living word" (1 Pet 1:23).

The main verb in 1 Peter 2:5, *oikodomeisthe*, can be taken as an imperative, "be built" (NRSV) or as a statement of reality, "being built" (NIV). The latter translation puts the emphasis on God's action. In coming to Jesus, a living stone, believers are being built into a spiritual house to be a holy priesthood that offers spiritual sacrifices. The point of Peter's mixing of architectural and cultic images becomes clearer in 1 Peter 2:6, when he alludes to Isaiah 28:16. As Christians come to Jesus, "a cornerstone chosen and precious," God incorporates them into his household, where Christ serves as the foundation and blueprint. Christians become the household of God, not only to be in loving solidarity with one another, but to lead lives of worshipful holiness. After all, they are the holy priesthood of a holy God (cf. 1 Pet 1:15-16; 2:9).

In contrast to believers for whom Jesus is precious, unbelievers reject Jesus as the foundation and blueprint of their lives. Peter frames their rejection as part of God's sovereign plan, while also making a strong connection between belief and destiny. Whereas those who believe have been chosen for the purpose of obedience (1 Pet 1:1, 14), those who do not believe disobey the word because "for this purpose they were destined" (1 Pet 2:8). Despite this stark contrast between those who believe and obey and those who do not believe and disobey, Peter maintains that God will judge both those within and outside of his household (1 Pet 4:17).

1 Peter 2:9-10. The two verses in 1 Peter 2:9-10 burst with identity-forming language, as Peter expresses his addressees' election in explicitly ethnic and religious terms.[33] Christians are *eklekton* in the sense that they are "chosen" by God to live a life set apart for God among the nations, the races, and the people (1 Pet 2:9-10), just as God selected and gathered Israel

[31]*Logikos* occurs in only one other instance in the New Testament in Rom 12:1, which the NRSV translates as "spiritual" and the NIV translates "true and proper."

[32]Paul J. Achtemeier, "Newborn Babes and Living Stones: Literal and Figurative in 1 Peter," in *To Touch the Text: Biblical and Related Studies in Honor of Joseph Fitzmyer, S.J.*, ed. Maurya P. Horgan and Paul J. Kobelski (New York: Crossroad, 1989), 207-36.

[33]For a full-length study on Peter's construction of ethnic identity in 1 Peter, see Ok, *Constructing Ethnic Identity*.

of old from among all the races, nations, and people of the earth.[34] The fact that he utilizes Israel's identity-forming terminology, which is both ethnic and religious in meaning, demonstrates that he finds ethnoreligious categories helpful and important for shaping Christian self-understanding.

Peter builds up to the biggest antithesis in the letter: between believers and their former selves. He first describes believers as those whom God "has called out of darkness and into his marvelous light;" who were "once not a people but now are God's people"; and who "had not received mercy but now have received mercy."[35] Here, Peter reiterates the theme of God the Father's merciful act of rebegetting believers (1 Pet 1:3). Peter also builds on the contrast he started to draw between their new identity as God's obedient, holy, reverent, and ransomed children and their former identity as ignorant people living according to their fleshly desires. They should no longer live according to the conduct they have inherited from their ancestors (1 Pet 1:14-19).

Christians are "now people of God" in contrast to their "former" existence as a "people *not* of God." By "not a people" (*ou laos*), Peter means that, prior to their conversion, believers did not possess a shared communal identity. But now, they can overcome any overt difference among them, such as bloodlines, class, status, gender, and racial-ethnic identity that would have previously prevented them from seeing each other as belonging to the same people group, family, and household (1 Pet 2:5, 17; 3:8; 4:8-10).[36]

The major comparison operating in 1 Peter is that between the people of God and the people not of God.[37] Peter does not make a Jew/Gentile dichotomy in the letter, but rather broadens the identification of Israel to include his Gentile Christian addressees. He then contrasts this exceptional and holy people with the "Gentiles" (*ta ethnē*), that is, the people *not* of God (1 Pet 2:12). Peter draws from the Jewish Scriptures (Ex 19:6 and Is 43:20-21) when circumscribing his audience with the community- and ethnic-identity forging titles and dignities of Israel. In doing so, he does not attempt to replace Israel as the "people of God" (1 Pet 2:10), or transpose the status and identity of Israel unto the Church.[38] Rather, as David Horrell explains, Peter draws on the specific traditions of Judaism because they are "a form of ethnic identity with religio-cultural practices at its heart"[39] that make it possible for him to construct the same form of identity for his addressees "without recourse to a specific territorial attachment or to biological (human) kinship links."[40]

A challenge Asian American Christians face is recognizing that our identity as exceptional does not come from our supposed genetic academic superiority, or from meeting the certain expectations and stereotypes that we are all well-educated, successful professionals, straight-A students, and born and bred for certain types

[34]See 1 Chron 16:13; Ps 88:4; 104:6, 43; Is 65:9, 15, 23 for examples of God's choosing of Israel. For examples of Israel described as a particular *genos*, see Ex 1:9; Josh 4:14; 11:21; Esth 2:10. For examples of Israel as an *ethnos* among *ethnē*, see Gen 12:2; 18:18; Ex 19:5-6; Lev 20:26; Deut 7:6-7; 10:15; 14:2; 26:19. For examples of Israel as God's *laos*, see Ex 6:7; 7:4; 7:16; Deut 9:26, 29; 14:2, 21; 26:15.

[35]Hos 2:23 (2:25 LXX).

[36]Ok, *Constructing Ethnic Identity*, 65.

[37]Ok, *Constructing Ethnic Identity*, 11.

[38]Ok, *Constructing Ethnic Identity*, 60

[39]David G. Horrell, *Becoming Christian: Essays on 1 Peter and the Making of Christian Identity*, LNTS 394 (London: Bloomsbury T&T Clark, 2013), 161.

[40]Horrell, *Becoming Christian*, 161.

of careers.[41] The model minority stereotype praises Asian Americans, not for who we are, but for who we are not, as it inherently pits Asian Americans against other people of color by comparing us to other racial minorities and valorizing us relative to Whites, who continue to be the standard bearers for mainstream success.[42] For Christians of every race and ethnicity, our exceptional or "chosen" status comes from our identity in Christ. When we quietly accept rather than vocally contest the model minority myth, we end up identifying more with privileged members of the dominant culture rather than the less privileged members of our own ascribed communities. That said, debunking the model minority stereotype does not do away with our unique differences and contributions. There are many ways of being Asian American, just as there are many expressions of being Christian.[43]

LIVING AS FOREIGNERS AMONG THE GENTILES AND AS FAMILY WITHIN THE HOUSEHOLD OF GOD (1 PETER 2:11–4:19)

1 Peter 2:11-12. The stark contrast between those who believe and those who do not believe functions to distinguish his readers' past as nonbelievers from their present as believers, as Peter urgently and affectionately pleads in 1 Peter 2:11, "Beloved, I exhort [you], as resident aliens and foreigners [*paroikoi* and *parepidēmoi*], to disengage [*apechō*] from the desires of the surrounding culture, which wage war against [your] life." The verb *apechō*,[44] literally "hold oneself" (*echō*) "apart from" (*apo*), when combined with the direct object *epithymia*,[45] conveys the sense of "stay clear away from," "deliberately avoid." The fact that this admonition comes immediately after Peter has spelled out in rich ethnic language who his readers are (1 Pet 2:9-10) reveals that their Gentile past continues to trouble them in the present.

Peter makes use of the military term *strateuomai* ("wage war") to convey the assault that Gentile-like desires have on believers' identity. Peter has already spoken of *epithymiai* in 1 Peter 1:14 as the cravings of their former ignorance and describes them in 1 Peter 2:11 as "resident aliens and foreigners" within society. Thus, to render *apechesthai* as "to disengage" serves to underscore how believers must actively stop behaving in ways that are antithetical to their new life in Christ.

Engaging in "honorable conduct" (*anastrophēn . . . kalēn*) does not guarantee that Christians experience a less conflictual existence. Nor does it mean their "good works" (*kalōn ergōn*) will necessarily correspond to the values of the dominant culture.[46] In the present, Gentiles may still condemn them as "evildoers" (*kakopoiōn*). Christians then are to do what is right in God's sight with the assurance that on the eschatological "day of visitation," those who condemn them will glorify God. To glorify God in 1 Peter 2:12 does not mean detractors necessarily became converts but that they will rightly recognize as good that which God has approved.

1 Peter 2:13-17. Christians set themselves apart by choosing to live an exilic existence. Their new identity as God's chosen people, however, does not give them license to reject

---

[41]Ok, "The Myth of Model Minority," in *Intersecting Realities: Race, Identity, and Culture in the Spiritual-Moral Life of Young Asian Americans*, ed. Hak Joon Lee (Eugene, OR: Cascade, 2018), 121-33.

[42]Ok, "The Myth of Model Minority," 122-23.

[43]Ok, "The Myth of Model Minority," 131-32.

[44]See, e.g., Acts 15:20, 29; 1 Thess 4:3; 5:22 for a similar use of *apechesthai*.

[45]Elliott, *1 Peter*, 462.

[46]Travis B. Williams, *Good Works in 1 Peter: Negotiating Social Conflict and Christian Identity in the Greco-Roman World* (Tübingen: Mohr Siebeck, 2014), 168; Ok, *Constructing Ethnic Identity*, 68.

wholesale the sociopolitical authorities and laws of the land. Christians are to "subordinate" themselves "for the Lord's sake to every human authority whether to the emperor, as the supreme authority, or to governors, who are sent by him to punish those who do wrong and to commend those who do right" (1 Pet 2:13-14). Translating the verb *hypotagēte* as "subordinate," rather than "submit" or "obey," helps convey a positional sense of obedience. Rather than demand unconditional obedience to civil authority, masters, and husbands, Peter advocates for a more nuanced approach in which they find their proper place of subordination in the social order and household and act accordingly.[47]

The phrase *anthrōpinē ktisei* in 1 Peter 2:13 is often translated "every human institution" (NASB, ESV), while other renderings maintain its literal meaning as "every human creature."[48] The latter more clearly conveys the common humanity emphasized by the inclusio-forming imperatives *hypotagēte* ("be subordinate") in 1 Peter 2:13 and *timēsate* ("honor") in 1 Peter 2:17. The humanizing language limits and relativizes the authority bestowed on the emperor, who in the Roman social order was superordinate to all, but who is no more worthy of honor than other human beings.

The Roman Empire was socially and economically hierarchical, in which a very small ruling elite held great power, wealth, and status.[49] The emperor controlled all the land, which served as the basis of wealth. He also had command over the sea and claimed a share of all produce grown on the land, such as crops and livestock, as we see in the parables of Jesus (cf. Mk 12:1-12; Mt 20:1-16). While most of the population was to varying degrees poor, the Roman economy, which depended on land and trade, favored ruling elites. The empire's tributary economy required people to pay taxes and tributes in the form of goods. This system placed onerous financial burdens on poorer folks like farmers, who paid taxes and rents to imperial, regional, and local authorities.[50] Most members of society lived below or right at subsistence levels and struggled to make ends meet.

Peter's admonition to behave in a manner that shuts up their detractors in 1 Peter 2:15 means that they are not to be quiescent, invisible members of society.[51] Rather, their nonconformity to the values of the dominant culture that are at odds with their obedience to God puts them at greater odds with outsiders. Silencing one's slanderers does not equate to converting them or even changing their minds, as Peter refers to such slander as "the ignorant talk of foolish people" (CEB). This is why Peter is at pains to strengthen his readers' sense of communal identity, since their decision to become Christians has resulted in increased social hostility, disadvantage, and marginalization. Peter's exhortation in 1 Peter 2:16 to live as "free people" (*eleutheroi*) suggests that he thought of his readers in this way,[52] and that his primary concern is to help them understand their identity as people of God in the face of external scrutiny, criticism, stereotyping, and persecution.

Asian Americans have long been invisible and excluded from mainstream discussions of

---

[47]Achtemeier, *1 Peter*, 182.

[48]So Elliott, *1 Peter,* 484, 496; Achtemeier, *1 Peter*, 179-80.

[49]Warren Carter, "Economic Justice and the Roman Empire," *Bible Odyssey*, n.d., www.bibleodyssey.org/passages/related-articles/economic-justice-and-the-roman-empire.

[50]Carter, "Economic Justice and the Roman Empire."

[51]Layang Seng Ja, "The Letters of Peter," in *An Asian Introduction to the New Testament*, ed. Johnson Thomaskutty (Minneapolis: Fortress, 2022), 474.

[52]Michaels, *1 Peter,* 64.

race in the United States. The dominant culture often treats Asian Americans as honorary Whites, model minorities, and perpetual foreigners, but rarely understands them on their own terms and in light of their shared and distinct histories and complex diversity and heterogeneity. This stereotype of the perpetual foreigner interrogates the identity of those who understand themselves to be as American as their European and African American counterparts, but who are perceived by both Black and White Americans as less American.[53] Like the model minority stereotype, it makes Asian Americans stand out in exoticized, foreignized, and racialized ways while disregarding the ways they have experienced racism, hostility, and violence. It ignores how they have been an integral and vital part of the national identity. Studies show how being perceived as and treated as perpetual foreigners may lead to depressive symptoms, a decreased sense of hope and life satisfaction, and a lower level of civic participation among Asian Americans relative to White Americans.[54]

It is important as Christians not to fall prey to "the ignorant talk of foolish people" and perpetuate stereotypes about Asian Americans. One way to do this is by educating yourself about the unconscious biases, common stereotypes, and microaggressions that you or those around you may unwittingly harbor. Speak up, step in, or advocate when you see and hear people acting on ignorant assumptions. Learn about the varied histories and experiences of Asian American Pacific Islanders while being careful not to dismiss the unique lived experiences of individual Asian Americans.

1 Peter 2:18-25. In the letter's section known as the *Haustafel* or household code (1 Pet 2:18-3:7), Peter addresses appropriate relationships between slaves and masters, wives and husbands, and husbands and wives. According to Roman writers, the ideal household served as a microcosm of the intensely hierarchical structure of society in which the emperor reigned supreme, while all others held lower status positions largely determined by their birth and gender. Thus, in the Roman household, the paterfamilias—usually a free male and the oldest living male in a household—ruled over all subordinate members. The household also served as the site of religious activity where members, which might extend to family members, slaves, employees, and other dependents, worshiped the gods of the paterfamilias.[55] Although masters or husbands usually presided over the domestic cult, slaves and wives often had the role of preparing and carrying out cultic rituals in the household.[56]

This section reveals details about the socioeconomic makeup of the letter's recipients. Shively Smith notes the striking fact that Peter does not address the master class at all and that most of his addressees likely were composed of the servant class, or were subordinates in a household.[57] It is also possible, as Horrell suggests, that Peter focuses on "weaker" members of the household because they were most likely to face negative consequences if perceived as deviating from social and

[53]Ok, "Always Ethnic, Never 'American': Reading 1 Peter Through the Lens of the 'Perpetual Foreigner' Stereotype," in *T&T Clark Handbook to Asian American Biblical Hermeneutics*, ed. Seung Ai Yang and Uriah Y. Kim (New York: T&T Clark, 2019), 417-26.

[54]Ok, "Always Ethnic, Never 'American,'" 420-21.

[55]Caroline E. Johnson Hodge, "'Holy Wives' in Roman Households: 1 Peter 3:1-6," *Women and Spirituality* 4, no. 1 (2010): 1-24, esp. 5-7.

[56]Johnson Hodge, "'Holy Wives' in Roman Households," 7-8.

[57]Smith, *Strangers to Family*, 72.

religious expectations.[58] Peter takes for granted that most of those in sociopolitical and domestic positions of authority over Christians are unbelievers (1 Pet 2:13–3:6; cf. 3:7). While he uses the same verb, *hypotassō*, to exhort all believers to subordinate themselves (1 Pet 2:13, 18; 3:1), he singles out two particular groups, slaves and wives. Most Greek moral philosophers referred to slaves and wives without addressing them directly, and did not attribute either group as having much moral and personal agency. However, Peter directly addresses slaves and wives. He assumes that Christians, slave or free, possess the moral discernment and agency to do what is right, and endure unjust suffering as a result. Christians may not be able to change their social circumstances or subordinated positions, but they can change the way they perceive their situation and conceive of God. The emphasis in 1 Peter 2:19-20 is thus not how slaves might appease their masters, but on how they can gain God's "approval" (*charis*) by doing what is commendable in God's sight.

What pleases God may not always please one's master. Thus, Peter encourages slaves to endure with patience the pain ("beating") that results from righteousness' sake, not from their own mistakes (1 Pet 2:20). Peter distinguishes between deserved and undeserved suffering in 1 Peter 2:19-20 to caution Christians against being hotheads who go out of their way to suffer unnecessarily, since by doing what is right by God, they may be maligned as being evildoers and suffer undeservedly at the hand of their master.

Suffering in 1 Peter is the inevitable result of a transformed Christian life that is holy and obedient to God in a world that is hostile to the Christian way of life (1 Pet 1:6; 2:12; 3:14-17; 4:12, 16; 5:9-10). Slaves had little sociopolitical power, bearing the brunt of undeserved suffering in the Roman household. And this is perhaps the reason why Peter addresses them first in the household code. The Christian slave's response to affliction is instructive for all members of God's household, who must also find the courage to remain faithful to God even if they are abused for it (1 Pet 3:9, 16-17).[59]

The clause "for to this you have been called" in 1 Peter 2:21 connects appropriate behavior to its christological motivation: Christians are called to suffer for doing good in order to gain God's approval "because Christ also suffered for you, leaving you an example, so that you should follow in his steps" (1 Pet 2L21). The language of "example" or "pattern" (*hypogrammos*) paints a tangible picture of discipleship. Christ leaves his followers with a moral paradigm and a previously trodden path to take that will not lead them astray (1 Pet 2:25), although it may put them in harm's way.

Drawing from Isaiah 53, Peter identifies Jesus as the Suffering Servant to show how the Messiah models innocent suffering in ways that are both paradigmatic (1 Pet 2:22-24) and atoning (1 Pet 2:24-25; 3:18). Peter focuses on the verbal aspect of Jesus' exemplary suffering (1 Pet 2:22-23). Christ did not commit sin or speak deceitfully; he did not return insult or suffering with insult or threat. Rather, he entrusted himself to God who judges justly. For Peter, this strategy is one of resistance, not passive resignation or suppressed indignation. Resistance to sin and enduring trust in God is possible because of Christ's redemptive work on the cross (1 Pet 2:24-25). Although disciples are not capable of emulating Christ's suffering when he "bore our sins in his body on the cross," his atoning activity enables believers to

[58]David G. Horrell, *1 Peter*, NTG (London: T&T Clark, 2008), 83.
[59]See Elliott, *1 Peter*, 540-43.

bear the wrongs done against them in ways that please God, if not those with political and socioeconomic power over them.

Peter's injunctions to slaves in 1 Peter 2:18-21 carries over to wives in 1 Peter 3:1-6. The parallel New Testament household codes address both husbands and wives in Christian marriages (Col 3:18-19; Eph 5:21-33; cf. Titus 2:3-5). However, the advice Peter offers wives applies specifically to Christian women married to nonbelievers.

1 Peter 3:1-7. Peter's plea that women subordinate themselves to their nonbelieving husbands corresponds to the prevailing norms, expectations, and values concerning the roles and interactions of husbands and wives in the Greco-Roman domestic context. It was expected that a submissive and deferential wife wholeheartedly accept the religion of her husband. The influential first-century Greek writer and scholar Plutarch warns, "[a] married woman should therefore worship and recognize the gods whom her husband holds dear, and these alone. The door must be closed to strange cults and foreign superstitions. No god takes pleasure in cult performed furtively by a woman."[60] From the perspective of their nonbelieving husbands, Christian wives worshiped and recognized a "foreign" deity of a strange, new cult known as "the Christians."[61] The fact that in 1 Peter 3:1 Peter suggests the possibility of husbands adopting the religion of their wives is remarkable.

The phrase "free from all fear" in 1 Peter 3:6 implies that wives have something to be terrified about and are vulnerable to the possible threat of violence. Throughout the letter, Peter gives multiple references to the negative attitudes toward Christians harbored by non-Christians (e.g., 1 Pet 2:12; 3:13-14, 16; 4:4, 14-16) and identifies his audience as "resident aliens and foreigners" (1 Pet 2:11). In some households, unbelieving husbands would likely have become antagonistic toward their wives because of their new beliefs and odd activities. Although wives were not in a position of power to not accept the authority of their husbands, Peter's injunctions do not leave them powerless or encourage complete passivity. Rather, believers are to take risks for "doing what is right" (1 Pet 2:12; 3:6, 14). So, a wife's reverent and chaste behavior may please or even convert her husband, but it may also put her in conflict with him.

Peter offers a less potentially devastating and more realistic approach to navigating marriage in non-Christian households. He does this by not equating faithfulness to God with wholesale submission to their unbelieving husbands nor with outright resistance to their authority.[62] Rather, he seeks to engender in Christian wives a resilient sense of their chosen status not as wives or mothers but as children endowed with a spiritual heritage that cannot be taken away from them.[63] Peter's concern is on wives' identity formation, rather than on wifely submission, or even with the conversion of unbelieving spouses. This is why he appeals to "holy wives" in 1 Peter 3:5. In doing so, he offers Christian wives the honorary status as Sarah's children in 1 Peter 3:6.[64]

---

[60]Sarah B. Pomeroy, ed., *Plutarch's Advice to the Bride and Groom and a Consolation to His Wife: English Translations, Commentary, Interpretive Essays, and Bibliography* (Oxford: Oxford University Press, 1999), 7.

[61]Johnson Hodge, "'Holy Wives' in Roman Households," 9.

[62]James W. Aageson, "1 Peter 2.11–3:7: Slaves, Wives, and the Complexities of Interpretation," in *A Feminist Companion to the Catholic Epistles and Hebrews*, ed. Amy-Jill Levine with Maria Mayo Robbins (London: T&T Clark, 2004), 34-49, 44.

[63]Ok, "'You Have Become Children of Sarah': Reading 1 Peter 3:1-6 Through the Intersectionality of Asian Immigrant Wives, Patriarchy, and Honorary Whiteness," in *Minoritized Women Reading Race and Ethnicity: Intersectional Approaches to Constructed Identity and Early Christian Texts*, ed. Mitzi J. Smith and Jin Young Choi (Lanham, MD: Lexington Books, 2020), 124.

[64]Ok, "You Have Become Children of Sarah," 117-19.

By identifying Christian wives as children of Sarah, Peter imbues them with an honored status before God as children of obedience, regardless of how others view or treat them. The fact that Peter offers only one brief exhortation to believing husbands in 1 Peter 3:7, strongly suggests that among his addressees, marriages between believers was the exception, not the rule. Like Christian wives, Christian husbands must also bear witness to their spouses, as indicated by the use of the adverb "in the same way" (*homoiōs*) in 1 Peter 3:7. This word connects Peter's exhortation to slaves (1 Pet 2:18-25) with his exhortations to wives (1 Pet 3:1-7), such that "Christian husbands are to take their behavioral cues from wives, who in turn take *their* cues from slaves."[65] Unlike Christian wives, however, Christian husbands have the authority to impact the way their wives are regarded and treated within their own households.

Men were generally more honored than women, but Peter here offers a particular expression of what it means to honor "all" and love members of their spiritual family (1 Pet 2:17). The rationale in 1 Peter 3:7 that Peter gives to the Christian husband to encourage the honorable treatment of his wife is that the latter is the "weaker vessel."[66] The word "vessel" (*skeuos*) has various biblical meanings, such as an ordinary utensil (1 Sam 21:5); a holy utensil (Ezra 8:28); a container like a jar or pot (Is 30:14); a human body (1 Thess 4:4); and a person serving as a divine instrument (Acts 9:15; 2 Cor 4:7). While Peter may have in mind a situation where a Christian husband lives with a reluctant, unbelieving wife,[67] it is more likely that he addresses husbands married to believing wives. Peter describes these wives as "coheirs (*sygklēronomos*) of the grace of life," an expression recalling the eschatological "inheritance" that God has secured for all believers (1 Pet 1:4; 3:9).[68] Thus, wives are to be understood and cared for as members of the household of God—not just a husband's domestic household.

By referring to wives as the "weaker vessel" Peter could be subscribing to ancient views of women as physically, emotionally, intellectually, or socially weaker.[69] It is likely that Peter expects Christian husbands to show preference or consideration for wives, who occupy more vulnerable social positions.[70] Prior to this, Peter has shown an awareness of the power difference between slaves and masters (1 Pet 3:18-20), and wives and husbands (1 Pet 3:1-6). Thus, Peter's exhortation to husbands in 1 Peter 3:7 reflects a concern with the proper treatment and view of women, who are the more socially vulnerable but not spiritually inferior members of God's household.

Peter's words to husbands have relevance today for all Christians in positions of authority and with the social capital to shape the culture and practices of their households, communities, churches, and workplaces. Christian leaders should not read 1 Peter as justification to tolerate or perpetuate the mistreatment or abuse of women, children, those with special needs, and elderly folks, and other socially marginalized and vulnerable people within or outside of the church. Rather, the onus is on believers who have greater social status to promote the honored status and treatment of those with less.

---

[65]Dennis R. Edwards, *1 Peter*, SGBC (Grand Rapids, MI: Zondervan, 2017), 133.
[66]Or "weaker partner" (CEB, NIV).
[67]Jobes, *1 Peter*, 208.
[68]Elliott, *1 Peter*, 580; Craig S. Keener, *1 Peter: A Commentary* (Grand Rapids, MI: Baker Academic, 2021), 251.
[69]For examples of ancient sources espousing each of these views respectively, see Keener, *1 Peter*, 246-47.
[70]Keener, *1 Peter*, 245.

1 Peter 3:8-12. Peter returns his attention "finally" to "all" Christians—regardless of position in life (cf. 1 Pet 5:5). While it is uncommon for household codes to end with general exhortations like the ones found in 1 Peter 3:8-12, it is not surprising that Peter's distinct adaptation of the codes, which begins with relational advice directed to "all" believers in 1 Peter 2:17, should end with an exhortation to that same audience in 1 Peter 3:8.[71] The following outline by Green highlights the chiastic structure of Peter's admonitions to all believers, to specific believers navigating particular domestic power dynamics, and returning back to all believers, whether slave or free, man or woman. At the center of this inverted parallelism is Christ's example:

1 Peter 2:13-17: instruction for everyone
  1 Peter 2:18-20: instruction for slaves
    1 Peter 2:21-25: the example of Christ
  1 Peter 3:1-7: instruction for wives (and husbands)
1 Peter 3:8-12: instruction for everyone[72]

While the instructions in 1 Peter 3:8 address everyone, Peter's focus is on fostering unity and solidarity among believers. The internal cohesion, tender affection, and mutual humility that Peter seeks to cultivate find their expression in a list of peculiar and interrelated adjectives: "like minded (*homophrones*), sympathetic (*sympatheis*), familial in affection (*philadelphoi*), big-hearted (*eusplagchnoi*), and humble in thinking (*tapeinophrones*)."[73] A posture that runs throughout these qualities is that of subordination. Whereas slaves and wives are to subordinate themselves to their non-Christian masters or husbands, respectively, now Peter exhorts all believers to humble themselves and submit to one another in the best interests of the entire community. Thus, subordination within the household of God is not a matter of Christian witness and strategic survival under the precarious authority of nonbelievers, but rather is an ethic that "grows out of the heart of the Christian faith,"[74] and is patterned after the example of Christ.

Christians respond to outside hostility by doing what is good in the sight of God, which includes repaying evil and insult with a "blessing" (*eulogia*; 1 Pet 3:9). While the word *eulogia*, from which we get "eulogy," means "to speak well of," in the LXX and New Testament, it often has a religious meaning of, "calling down or bestowing God's favor upon others"—in this case, one's oppressors. The ethic of nonretaliation is thus not passive but active. It is consistent with Jesus' example (1 Pet 2:21-25) and teaching (Mt 5:39; Lk 6:28-29; see also 1 Cor 4:12; Rom 12:14; cf. Jas 3:6). Just as slaves are "called" (*kaleō*) to endure unjust suffering by doing what is right (1 Pet 2:21), so all believers are "called" (*kaleō*) to respond righteously to unjust suffering (cf. 1 Pet 1:15). In doing so, they will "inherit blessing" (cf. Heb 12:17).

In 1 Peter 3:10-12, Peter cites and adapts a segment of LXX Psalm 33:13-17 (Ps 34:12-16) to provide support for his teaching. Much of LXX Psalm 33 aptly befits the context of 1 Peter with its shared concepts and language, such as the suffering of the righteous (Ps 33:7, 18, 29), "resident aliens" (Ps 33:5), "reverence" for the Lord (Ps 33:8, 9, 10, 12), "hope" (Ps 33:8, 23), and blessing for the

---

[71]Michaels, *1 Peter*, 172.

[72]Green, *1 Peter*, 72.

[73]Four of the five adjectives listed in 1 Pet 3:8 are *hapaxes*, occurring nowhere else in the New Testament (Elliott, *1 Peter*, 600). Peter's unusual word choice may reflect his effort to speak in fresh ways of what was already esteemed Christian qualities (Achtemeier, *1 Peter*, 223n45, citing Karl Phillips, *Kirche in der Gesellschaft nach dem 1. Petrusbrief* [Gütersloh: Gütersloher Verlagshaus-Gerd Mohn, 1971]).

[74]Achtemeier, *1 Peter*, 223.

"just" (Ps 33:16, 18, 20, 22).[75] The psalm's imperatives in Psalm 33:13-17 correspond to the response Peter asks of his readers: to restrain the tongue (1 Pet 3:10), do what is right (1 Pet 3:11), and seek and pursue peace (1 Pet 3:11). Peter's repetition of "from evil" (*apo kakos*) reinforces for those born anew to a living hope how appropriate speech and action are inseparable and go hand in hand. Believers must keep their tongue from evil (1 Pet 3:10), and turn their conduct away from evil (1 Pet 3:11; cf. 1 Pet 2:14, 15, 20; 3:6, 17; 4:19).[76] The theological and eschatological basis for these exhortations lies in the assurance of God's attentive and just judgment. God hears and sees his children, their actions and prayers and the wrongs done to them. God favors the "righteous," but opposes "those who do what is wrong" (1 Pet 3:12; cf. 1 Pet 4:17-19).

In today's political and religious climate in the United States, Christians are often the initiators of slander against fellow Christians and non-Christian alike. The unifying bonds of Christ's ransoming blood do not seem to lead to like-mindedness, sympathy, familial affection, generosity in spirit, and mutual humility across the aisle among believers who bear different political and theological stripes. For Peter, to dissolve or destroy the unity and witness of God's people in Christ's name through slander and malicious speech is evil.

1 Peter 3:13-17. This section begins with a rhetorical question, "Who, then, will harm you if you become zealous to do good?" (1 Pet 3:13), to which the implied answer is "No one!" Peter suggests that, similar to provincial governors in 1 Peter 2:14, unbelievers are capable of recognizing honorable conduct when they see it. However, Peter points to the capricious nature of public opinion when speaking of the sobering possibility that Christians may indeed suffer "because of righteousness" (*dia dikaiosynē*) in 1 Peter 3:14 and for their "good behavior" in 1 Peter 3:16.[77] Peter both consoles and assures readers in 1 Peter 3:14 that "if" they should suffer despite their innocence, they are "blessed" (*makarioi*), echoing Jesus' teaching found in Matthew 5:10 (and Lk 6:22).

Peter thus circles back to the question raised in 1 Peter 3:13 with the eschatological understanding that those who suffer because of their devotion to God's will (1 Pet 2:15) ultimately cannot be harmed, because they are in right standing with God, in contrast to the wicked (1 Pet 3:12, 17). To further alleviate fear and instill confidence in his readers, Peter draws on and slightly modifies the language of LXX Isaiah 8:12: "Have no fear of them and do not be troubled." Here, he applies Isaiah's words to their present hardships, reminding them that they too belong to the story of God's people who under enemy threat have the assurance that "God is with us" (LXX Is 8:10).

Peter understands *kyrios* as a primary designation for Jesus. This is evident in the way he identifies the "Lord" YHWH of LXX Isaiah 8:13 as "the Christ" in 1 Peter 3:15. In doing so, he equates Christ with the God of the Old Testament, reinforcing the connection between his audience and God's people Israel through Jesus Christ.[78] The confession of

[75]Elliott, *1 Peter*, 611.

[76]Michaels, *1 Peter*, 180.

[77]Peter speaks elsewhere about the suffering inflicted on Christians for doing what is right in, e.g., 1 Pet 2:20; 3:9, 10-11, 4:15-16. The conditional particle *ei* ("if") coupled with Peter's use of the optative mood of the verb *paschoite* ("if it happens that you should suffer") expresses the plausibility that Christians may experience unjust suffering (Elliott, *1 Peter*, 621; Green, *1 Peter*, 114). See 1 Pet 1:6; 2:19-20; 3:17 for similar conditional formulations.

[78]Peter has previously identified Jesus as "Lord" through his modification of Old Testament sources in 1 Pet 1:25 (Is 40:8) and 1 Pet 2:3 (Ps 33:9). For other instances in the New Testament when the designation *kyrios* is applied to Christ as a way to equate him with YHWH, see, e.g., Phil 2:11; 1 Cor 8:6; Acts 2:36.

Christ as Lord begins not with one's words but one's interior attitude and disposition toward God, as with Christian wives in 1 Peter 3:4. Peter exhorts believers to "sanctify" (*hagiasate*) or acknowledge the holiness of Christ the Lord (cf. Mt 6:9 // Lk 11:2), adding to Isaiah's statement the phrase "in your hearts" (cf. Lk 21:14). In ancient Greco-Roman thought, the heart (*kardia*) served as the organ or seat of physical, spiritual, and mental life. Holy and hidden reverence for Christ pleases God who sees "the hidden person of the heart" (1 Pet 3:4 RSV). "Holy fear" also "drives out other fears" and makes it possible for believers to respond readily to interrogations about their Christian hope with an appropriate "defense" (*apologia*) and a "good conscience" (*syneidēsis agatha*).[79] With his additional emphasis on "gentleness and reverence" in 1 Peter 3:16, Peter shows his concern lies more with the "motivation and manner" in which their defense is made than with the specific content of their arguments.[80]

What Peter means then by "good" becomes clearer in 1 Peter 3:16 as he connects "good behavior" to Christ, thereby defining "good" in Christian, not cultural terms.[81] Again, Peter takes for granted that "good behavior in Christ" may incite contempt from unbelievers, and thus offers the vindicating consolation that those who deride them "may be put to shame." While the verb *kataischynō* (an aor. pass. subj.) could refer to an immediate social shaming, it most likely functions similar to its usage in 1 Peter 2:6, referring to an eschatological shaming of nonbelievers at the final judgment (see 1 Pet 2:12).

Peter puts suffering in Christian context, as he did with "good behavior" in 1 Peter 3:16: If one suffers at all, let it be for the right reasons and in the right way (1 Pet 2:19-20; 4:15-16). Peter does not idealize suffering or describe its benefits (cf. Rom 5:3-5). Rather, he reminds his beleaguered addressees that suffering for what is right can be "the will of God" in that their obedience to God's will may result in their mistreatment (1 Pet 4:19). The innocent can endure unjust suffering knowing that they possess God's favor and care (1 Pet 2:20; 5:6-7), and that God will vindicate them (1 Pet 3:16; 5:10).[82]

1 Peter 3:18-22. This section contains some of the most difficult verses in the letter. For all of its perplexing aspects, Peter makes it clear in 1 Peter 3:18 that the motivation for doing what is right even if it leads to mistreatment and hardship is christological. The two other major christological texts, 1 Peter 1:18-21; 2:21-25, focus on Jesus' passion and sacrificial death. In both 1 Peter 2:21-25, Peter brings Jesus in solidarity with believers who suffer unjustly, "for Christ also" (*hoti kai Christos*) suffered in this way (1 Pet 2:21, 3:18).[83] Peter presents Jesus as the paragon of righteous suffering. Furthermore, Jesus' redemptive work makes it possible for believers to follow in his steps and suffer in the right way and for the right reasons. Peter describes Jesus' suffering as vicarious ("for the unrighteous ones," cf. 1 Pet 2:21) and "atoning" ("for sins," cf. 1 Pet 2:24). However, he goes even further in 1 Peter 3:18-22, to emphasize the singularity of Christ's "once-for-all" suffering,

[79]Michaels, *1 Peter*, 187

[80]Edwards, *1 Peter*, 152.

[81]Achtemeier, *1 Peter*, 236.

[82]Cf. Mt 10:28-30 // Lk 12:4-7.

[83]The CEB renders *sarki* ("in the flesh") in 1 Pet 3:18 "as a human," which helps emphasize that Jesus died a physical death and was a real human being. The juxtaposition of "in the flesh" and "in the Spirit" helps underscore that Jesus was not only "put to death" (Mk 14:55) but brought back to life (1 Pet 1:3; Jn 10:18).

the cosmic scope of his action,[84] and the totality of his vindication.[85]

The passive form *hypotassō* ("to subject" or "to subordinate") in 1 Peter 3:22 reminds readers that the spiritual powers behind earthly authorities have already been subordinated to Christ.[86] In emphasizing Christ's cosmic action, which reaches to the spirits in prison at the time of Noah and to the heavens, where Christ sits enthroned in heaven at the right hand of God, the author reveals what Horrell and Wan call his "eschatological Christology."[87] That is, Peter attempts to narrate how "the whole sweep of time from the beginning to its imminent end—is found in Christ, whose authority is above all others, since 'angels, authorities, and powers' have all been subjected to him (3.22)."[88] Thus, in a section that remains opaque about what Christ preached to the spirits in prison, who are the spirits, when and where this proclamation took place, and the role of baptism in all of this, Peter makes it clear that the suffering and resurrection of Christ results in his triumph after death. He puts innocent suffering and also earthly time and authority in proper Christological perspective.

1 Peter 4:1-6. The reality of Christ's earthly suffering and heavenly vindication (1 Pet 3:18-22) should strengthen the "resolve" (*ennoia*; cf. Heb 4:12) of believers to act in ways that please God, irrespective of how nonbelievers react to them. In the previous section, Peter emphasizes Christ's solidarity with suffering believers. In 1 Peter 4:1, he encourages Christians to be in solidarity with Christ ("you also," *kai hymeis*).[89] The imperative "arm yourselves" (*hoplizō*) conveys the military image of going to battle (cf. 1 Pet 2:11), and thus speaks to the mental fortitude and readiness needed to resist the evil desires of the flesh (1 Pet 1:13). It also implies that Christians experience belligerent hostility from their non-Christian contemporaries.

Peter's audience also face internal battles in their struggle to disidentify with their former way of life. This is why he urges them to put a hard stop to succumbing to the "human desires" that fueled the behaviors of their not-so-distant Gentile past. As in 1 Peter 1:14, Peter, imbues the term "desire" in 1 Peter 4:2 with pejorative meaning by associating it with "unrestrained immorality and lust, their drunkenness and excessive feasting and wild parties, and their forbidden worship of idols" (1 Pet 4:3, CEB). In order to convince his readers that they "have already spent enough time doing what the Gentiles like to do" (1 Pet 4:3), Peter presents their former way of life as utterly incompatible with their new identity as Christians. What baffles or surprises (*xenizō*) unbelievers is not what Christians do, but what they refuse to do (1 Pet 4:4). By refusing to participate in the "same flood of unrestrained wickedness," Christians risk offending their former Gentile party companions, who interpret their abstinence as antisocial, judgmental, and offensive. Thus, Gentiles ironically speak evil (*blasphēmeō*) of Christians, even though they are the ones engaging in sinful activities (1 Pet 4:4).

In 1 Peter 4:5-6, Peter returns to the theme of divine judgment (see 1 Pet 1:17; 2:12, 23; 4:17)

---

[84]Elliott, *1 Peter*, 639-40.

[85]Michaels, *1 Peter*, 221.

[86]Keener, *1 Peter*, 283.

[87]David G. Horrell and Wei Hsein Wan, "Christology, Eschatology and the Politics of Time in 1 Peter" *JSNT* 38, no. 3 (2016): 263-76.

[88]Horrell and Wan, "Christology, Eschatology and the Politics of Time," 272-73. On the language and meaning of "powers" in 1 Peter and in the New Testament, see Green, *1 Peter*, 124-25, 267.

[89]Edwards, *1 Peter*, 169.

and again makes a distinction between the past, present, and future (see 1 Pet 1:5, 7, 13; 4:2-3, 13, 17; 5:4). In the present, Gentiles may misjudge and malign believers for their faithfulness. However, in the imminent future, these same people will have to answer to God, who will judge everyone, both "living and dead." That fact that God judges the dead (1 Pet 3:19) serves as a warning to unbelievers and a consolation to believers. For as Jobes explains, "the efficacy of the gospel continues after physical death to be the basis for God's judgment, and therefore a decision to live for Christ in this life is truly the right decision, even despite appearances to the contrary as judged by the world's reasoning."[90]

1 Peter 4:7-11. The eschatological momentum reaches its climax in 1 Peter 4:7 with the declaration, "the end [*telos*] of all things is near" (1 Pet 1:9; 4:17). The closeness of God's judgment should compel the beleaguered to be "clear-headed and on the alert" (*sōphronēsate kai nēpsate*; 1 Pet 1:13; 5:8). Sound mindedness and vigilance are needed not only to resist temptation but for Christian formation—"for the purpose of prayer."[91] Rather than thoughtlessly pattern their actions according to the desires and values of the prevailing culture, Christians must sculpt their thought patterns according to the reality of Jesus' redemptive suffering (1 Pet 4:1) and structure their lives around the will of God (1 Pet 4:2).[92] They do this through the practice of prayer and intentional cultivation of community-forming, *jeong*-permeated love (1 Pet 4:7-8; see comment on *jeong* in 1 Pet 1:22).

Wohnee Anne Joh offers a theological understanding of the Korean concept of *jeong* when she describes it as "the power embodied in redemptive relationships."[93] Jesus embodied redemptive *jeong* in his connectedness with other people and his cleaving to us on the cross, and those redeemed by Christ embody his *jeong* through their resilient, earnest love. This kind of love "covers a multitude of sins" (1 Pet 4:8) not by making excuses for the wrongdoings and offenses of others. Rather the redemptive love Peter envisions in 1 Peter 4:8 does not displace or disavow its members or tell them to go "back to their place" of foreignness. Rather, it is a love that perpetuates residence within the community of believers without threat or fear of rejection. It is a love that is hospitable (1 Pet 4:9), not hostile, and that embraces the manifold grace of God and manifold gifts and differences among God's people. It is a love that uses words to build up one's Christian identity, not diminish it (1 Pet 4:11).

Asian Americans often experience a greater sense of "cultural homelessness" and conflict about their national identity because they are frequently perceived as foreigners and denied their in-group status.[94] Peter in effect encourages his addressees to perceive themselves as perpetual foreigners and to not feel at home in the dominant culture through his sharp contrasts between the exceptional and holy people of God and "the Gentiles" (1 Pet 2:12; 4:3). By being "built into a spiritual house" and constituting the household of God" (1 Pet 2:5; 4:17), believers can experience "at-home-ness"[95] among fellow believers and no longer feel at home among the Gentiles. Such chosen foreignness however can be painfully alienating. Peter's emphasis on Christian communal

[90]Jobes, *1 Peter*, 267-68.

[91]Achtemeier, *1 Peter*, 292; Green, *1 Peter*, 143. See Mt 26:41/Mk 14:28; Lk 21:36; Col 4:2; 1 Thess 5:8, 17 for other New Testament examples that associate sound judgment with prayer in light of the eschatological hour (Elliott, *1 Peter*, 749).

[92]Green, *1 Peter*, 143.

[93]Wonhee Anne Joh, *Heart of the Cross: A Postcolonial Christology* (Louisville, KY: Westminster John Knox, 2006), xxi.

[94]Ok, "Always Ethnic, Never 'American,'" 417.

[95]Elliott, *Conflict, Community, and Honor: 1 Peter in Social-Scientific Perspective* (Eugene, OR: Cascade, 2007), 14.

identity formation and hospitality is thus vital for enduring faithfulness and togetherness in a hostile, inhospitable environment.

SHARING IN CHRIST'S SUFFERING AS "A CHRISTIAN" AND MAINTAINING THE UNITY OF THE HOUSEHOLD OF GOD THROUGH HUMILITY AND RESISTANCE (1 PETER 4:12–5:11)

1 Peter 4:12-19. Continuing the theme of love and at-home-ness among the Christian community, Peter refers to his hearers with the direct and intimate address "beloved" (*agapētos*; 1 Pet 2:11). In doing so, he also marks a transition in his teaching. Many of the themes found in 1 Peter 4:12–5:11 have already appeared in the letter, though here they are expanded and intensified, with the subsection 1 Peter 4:12-19 that presents suffering for being Christian as an inevitable and unsurprising part of life.[96] In 1 Peter 4:12, Peter fleshes out the images and ideas in 1 Peter 1:6-8 with his reference to "fiery trial[s]," which the present particle *ginomai* ("taking place") indicates they are facing in real time. Peter puts suffering and joy in eschatological perspective. Through suffering, Christians "share" (*koinōneō*) in Christ's sufferings (cf. 1 Cor 10:16; Phil 3:10), which gives them reason to rejoice now and overwhelmingly more when his glory is revealed (1 Pet 4:13). At present, joy and suffering intermingle, but when Christ returns, only joy will remain.[97]

Peter's use of the label "Christian" (*Christianos*) in 1 Peter 4:16 gives us a glimpse into the way the term emerged out of the difficult encounter between Christians and non-Christians. Christians had to negotiate their relationship to the larger society, as they faced both formal and informal hostility.[98] David Horrell explains the label as used in this passage serves as the "earliest witness to the crucial process whereby the term was transformed from a hostile label applied by outsiders to a self-designation borne with honor."[99]

If Gentile unbelievers criticize and harass believers for their association with the contemptuous name "Christian" (1 Pet 4:14, 16), those who suffer innocently should not feel embarrassed or ashamed but rather "blessed" because their suffering is a means to glorify God (1 Pet 4:16; 3:14).[100] So, it is not *that* Christians will suffer but *how* and *why* Christians suffer that will surprise those who slander and mistreat them. Christians are to respond with irreproachable and honorable conduct.[101] Because the term *Christian* is so closely associated with criminality,[102] Peter wants his audience to give no just cause for their critics to condemn them.

The logic the author offers for why Christians can rejoice and take courage in being reviled for the "name of Christ" (1 Pet 4:14) is expressed by Mahatma Gandhi when he says, "Truth never damages a cause that is just." So those who live in reverence and obedience to God don't have to live in fear that their cause is futile or vain. God sees, God cares, God will judge both the righteous and the unrighteous (1 Pet 4:19).

---

[96]David L. Bartlett, "The First Letter of Peter: Introduction, Commentary, and Reflections," in *NIB*, vol. 12, ed. Leander E. Keck (Nashville: Abingdon, 1998), 227-319, 308.

[97]Bartlett, "The First Letter of Peter," 310.

[98]Horrell, "The Label Χριστιανός (1 Peter 4:16): Suffering, Conflict, and the Making of Christian Identity," in *Becoming Christian*, 176, 209-10.

[99]Horrell, "The Label Χριστιανός," 165.

[100]Elliott, *Conflict, Community, and Honor*, 72.

[101]Elliott, *Conflict, Community, and Honor*, 73.

[102]Kaalund, *Reading Hebrews and 1 Peter*, 25.

God's judgment will begin with the household of God but will end with those who do not obey the gospel of God. Unjust suffering should be experienced and understood in light of the reality that God's righteous judgment is impending for both believers and unbelievers. This, the author speaks to bring comfort, not anxiety to God's people. Suffering for doing what is right—for bearing the difficult name of Christ and being slandered as Christians—is not the result of God's discipline or retribution. It is the result of bearing the name and living in the way of the One who is foreign, alien to the dominant culture. It puts them in sanctifying solidarity with their Lord and with fellow members of God's household.

For Peter, moral courage and ethical integrity are required of those who bear the name of Christ. Christians share in the sufferings of Christ and in solidarity with suffering believers. However, in the United States, "Christian" has become a dog whistle, a rallying cry, an assemblage of symbols, flags, myths and a religious guise for White nationalism. Rather than a difficult, contemptuous, and costly name it has become for many a household name, used to show contempt for justice, mercy, and the marginalized. Neither Peter nor Jesus would recognize nor condone such usage.

1 Peter 5:1-11. 1 Peter 5:1-5 contains the letter's final teachings and begins with a focus on Christian leadership. In 1 Peter 5:1-4, Peter addresses the responsibilities of three groups: "elders" (*presbyteroi*) in 1 Peter 5:1-4, "younger persons" (*neōteroi*), and "all" in 1 Peter 5:5 (cf. 1 Jn 2:12-14). With external pressures threatening to disintegrate in-group cohesion, Peter includes between 1 Peter 4:12-19 and 1 Peter 5:6-11 (which focus on suffering) his vision for Christian leadership and relational dynamics because intrachurch solidarity amid persecution depends on Christlike shepherding of the flock.[103] The term *elder* does not necessarily refer to a formal leadership role but rather designates Christians who are older in age and possibly older in the faith.[104] Peter uses pastoral imagery to describe the Christian community and the task of the elders in 1 Peter 5:2. Elders are to "shepherd the flock of God among you, exercising oversight" (*episkopountes*). Because Christ is the "chief shepherd" (1 Pet 5:4; cf. Jn 10:11, 14) and the "guardian (*episkopos*) of your souls" (1 Pet 2:24) elders function like undershepherds who ungrudgingly and willingly guard and serve the best interests of the sheep without being domineering (*katakyrieuontes*; 1 Pet 5:3).[105]

"In the same way," younger persons are to show mutual respect and "accept the authority of the elders" (1 Pet 5:5, NRSV). Peter uses the same verb *hypotassō* used in 1 Peter 2:13, 18; 3:1, 5, 22 and keeps his comments to youth brief. In the Roman Empire at large and the pagan household (or the empire writ small), submission is necessary to negotiate precarious and potentially hazardous power dynamics and relationships. In the household of God, however, submission is the result of mutual and sincere respect, love, and care between members of the Christian community (1 Pet 1:22; 3:8). Christlike leadership and submission both require humility. Thus "all" must have a deferential attitude to one another and humble postures before God, who "opposes the proud but gives grace to the humble." Peter's citation of LXX Proverbs 3:34 grounds the call to humility in the intention of God.[106]

[103]Peter H. Davids, *The First Epistle of Peter* (Grand Rapids, MI: Eerdmans, 1990), 174.

[104]Jennifer Strawbridge, ed., *The First Letter of Peter: A Global Commentary*, Lambeth Conference (London: SMC Press, 2020), "Authority in Christ" (1 Peter 5), eBook.

[105]Elliott, "Elders as Leaders in 1 Peter and the Early Church," *Currents in Theology and Mission* 28, no. 6 (2001): 549-59.

[106]Bartlett, "The First Letter of Peter," 316.

When Christians humble themselves "under the mighty hand of God," they entrust themselves in God's care (1 Pet 5:6-7). Here, Peter gives a positive sense to psalmist's negative expression "they were humbled under their hands" (LXX Ps 105:42) and adopts the biblical imagery of God's "mighty hand," which recalls God's deliverance of Israel from slavery in Egypt (see, e.g., Ex 3:19; Deut 3:24).[107] The same mighty hand that humbles Christians also comforts them,[108] which is why they can "throw all [their] anxieties" on God (1 Pet 5:7; cf. Phil 4:6).

Peter returns to the theme of sobriety and vigilance (1 Pet 1:13; 4:7) when he explains, "Be on the alert! Wake up!" However, rather than point to God's judgment as the primary motivation, he warns, "Your adversary [*antidikos*], the devil [*diabolos*], is on the prowl like a roaring lion ready to devour [its prey]" (1 Pet 5:8; cf. Mk 13:33; 1 Thess 5:6). The battle against the desires of the flesh now takes on a named, personified foe. Peter does not launch a full-scale attack against the devil, but rather urges his hearers to "resist" (*anthistēmi*) the devil's attacks by standing "firm in faith" and in solidarity with fellow believers experiencing "the same suffering throughout the world" (1 Pet 5:9). Faith and solidarity reinforce each other to form an effective means of resistance. Faith brings into larger focus the glory soon to come and puts in eternal perspective the temporary duration of their sufferings. Christian unity builds a stronger defense against the enemy, who is one, while they are many. In 1 Peter 5:10, Peter reminds them that their greatest defense and source of comfort is God, who will "restore, support, strengthen, and establish" them (NRSV).

LETTER'S CLOSING (1 PETER 5:12-14)

The letter closes with a final greeting that refers to Silvanus, whom Peter identifies as "the faithful brother." While Silvanus's exact role in the writing of the letter remains uncertain, Peter offers a clear purpose for why he has written the letter—to "encourage" and "testify" (1 Pet 5:12), which he has done primarily in the form of instruction. Peter leaves his addressees with one final imperative: "Stand firm [*histēmi*] in [the grace of God]." Such steadfastness helps them not only resist the adversary (1 Pet 5:9) but remain faithful while in "Babylon" (1 Pet 5:13), a term most commentators understand as a coded reference to Rome.[109] The language of "brother," and "son" (1 Pet 5:13) reiterate the familial affection and bonds characteristic of God's household. Their "coelect" (*syneklektos*) status reminds believers that God has chosen them in community for community.

BIBLIOGRAPHY

Aaegeson, James W. "1 Peter 2.11–3:7: Slaves, Wives, and the Complexities of Interpretation." In *A Feminist Companion to the Catholic Epistles and Hebrews*, edited by Amy-Jill Levine with Maria Mayo Robbins, 34-49. London: T&T Clark, 2004.

Achtemeier, Paul J. *1 Peter: A Commentary on First Peter*. Hermeneia. Minneapolis: Augsburg Fortress, 1996.

———. "Newborn Babes and Living Stones: Literal and Figurative in 1 Peter." In *To Touch the Text: Biblical and Related Studies in Honor of Joseph Fitzmyer, S.J.*, edited by Maurya P. Horgan and Paul J. Kobelski, 207-36. New York: Crossroad, 1989.

[107]Michaels, *1 Peter*, 295.

[108]Bartlett, "The First Letter of Peter," 316.

[109]E.g., Claus-Hunno Hunzinger, "Babylon als Deckname für Rom und die Datierung des 1. Petrusbriefs," in *Gottes Wort und Gottes Land: Hans Wilhelm Hertzberg zum 70*, ed. Henning Graf Reventlow, (Göttingen: Vandenhoeck & Ruprecht, 1965), 67-77; Elliott, *1 Peter*, 882–86; Green, *1 Peter*, 183-84; Horrell, *1 Peter*, 23-25; Keener, *1 Peter*, 404. On the set of terms "refugees, Diaspora, and Babylon" as identifying Rome as the center of imperial power akin to Israel's experience of oppression under Babylon, see Horrell, *1 Peter*, 85-91.

Agnew, Frances H. "1 Peter 1:2—An Alternative Translation." *CBQ* 45 (1983): 68-73.

Attridge, Harold W. Review of *Das Selbstverständnis der jüdischen Diaspora in der hellenistisch-römischen Zeit*, by Willem Cornelis Van Unnik. *JAOS* 115, no. 2 (1995): 323-24.

Bartlett, David L. "The First Letter of Peter: Introduction, Commentary, and Reflections." *NIB*. Vol. 12. Edited by Leander E. Keck, 227-319. Nashville: Abingdon, 1998.

Bigg, Charles A. *Critical and Exegetical Commentary on the Epistles of St. Peter and St. Jude*. ICC. New York: Scribner's, 1901.

Carter, Warren. "Economic Justice and the Roman Empire." *Bible Odyssey*, n.d. www.bibleodyssey.org/articles/economic-justice-and-the-roman-empire/.

Davids, Peter H. *The First Epistle of Peter.* Grand Rapids, MI: Eerdmans, 1990.

Edwards, Dennis R. *1 Peter*. SGBC. Grand Rapids, MI: Zondervan, 2017.

Elliott, John H. *Conflict, Community, and Honor: 1 Peter in Social-Scientific Perspective*. Eugene, OR: Cascade, 2007).

———. "Elders as Leaders in 1 Peter and the Early Church." *Currents in Theology and Mission* 28, no. 6 (2001): 549-59.

———. *1 Peter: A New Translation with Introduction and Commentary*. AB 37B. New York: Anchor Bible, 2000.

Goppelt, Leonhard. *A Commentary on I Peter*. Edited by Ferdinand Hahn. Translated by John E. Alsup. Grand Rapids, MI: Eerdmans, 1993.

Green, Joel B. *1 Peter*. THNTC. Grand Rapids, MI: Eerdmans, 2007.

Halvorson-Taylor, Martien. *Enduring Exile: The Metaphorization of Exile in the Hebrew Bible*. Leiden: Brill, 2011.

Horrell, David G. *Becoming Christian: Essays on 1 Peter and the Making of Christian Identity*. LNTS 394. London: Bloomsbury T&T Clark, 2013.

———. *1 Peter*. NTG. London: T&T Clark, 2008.

Horrell, David G., and Travis B. Williams. *1 Peter: A Critical and Exegetical Commentary*. Vol. 1, *Chapters 1–2*. ICC. London: T&T Clark, 2023.

Horrell, David G., and Wei Hsien Wan. "Christology, Eschatology and the Politics of Time in 1 Peter." *JSNT* 38, no. 3 (2016): 263-76.

Hunzinger, Claus-Hunno. "Babylon als Deckname für Rom und die Datierung des 1. Petrusbriefs." In *Gottes Wort und Gottes Land: Hans Wilhelm Hertzberg zum 70*, edited by Henning Graf Reventlow, 67–77. Göttingen: Vandenhoeck & Ruprecht, 1965.

Jobes, Karen H. *1 Peter*. BECNT. 2nd ed. Grand Rapids, MI: Baker Academic, 2022.

Johnson Hodge, Caroline E. "'Holy Wives' in Roman Households: 1 Peter 3:1-6." *Women and Spirituality* 4, no. 1 (2010): 1-24.

Kaalund, Jennifer T. *Reading Hebrews and 1 Peter with the African American Great Migration: Diaspora, Place, and Identity*. LNTS. London: Bloomsbury T&T Clark, 2019.

Keener, Craig S. *1 Peter: A Commentary*. Grand Rapids, MI: Baker Academic, 2021.

Kelly, J. N. D. *A Commentary on the Epistles of Peter and of Jude*. New York: Harper & Row, 1969.

Layang, Seng Ja. "The Letters of Peter." In *An Asian Introduction to the New Testament*, edited by Johnson Thomaskutty, 467-93. Minneapolis: Fortress, 2022.

Martin, Troy W. *Metaphor and Composition in 1 Peter*. SBLDS 131. Atlanta: Scholars Press, 1992.

Michaels, J. Ramsey. *1 Peter*. WBC 49. Waco, TX: Word, 1988.

Nguyen, Viet Thanh. "Forward." In *Go Home!*, edited by Rowan Hisayo Buchanan, xii-xviii. New York: Feminist Press: 2018.

Ok, Janette H. "Always Ethnic, Never 'American': Reading 1 Peter Through the Lens of the 'Perpetual Foreigner' Stereotype." In *T&T Clark Handbook to Asian American Biblical Hermeneutics*, edited by Seung Ai Yang and Uriah Y. Kim, 417-26. New York: T&T Clark, 2019.

———. "Commentary on 1 Peter 1:17-23." *Working Preacher*. April 26, 2020. www.workingpreacher.org/commentaries/revised-common-lectionary

/third-sunday-of-easter/commentary-on-1-peter-117-23-3.

———. *Constructing Ethnic Identity in 1 Peter: Who You Are No Longer*. LNTS. London: T&T Clark, 2021.

———. "The Myth of Model Minority." In *Intersecting Realities: Race, Identity, and Culture in the Spiritual-Moral Life of Young Asian Americans*, edited by Hak Joon Lee, 121-33. Eugene, OR: Cascade, 2018.

———."'You Have Become Children of Sarah': Reading 1 Peter 3:1 6 Through the Intersectionality of Asian Immigrant Wives, Patriarchy, and Honorary Whiteness." In *Minoritized Women Reading Race and Ethnicity Intersectional Approaches to Constructed Identity and Early Christian Texts*, edited by Mitzi J. Smith and Jin Young Choi, 111-25. Lanham, MD: Lexington Books, 2020.

Page, Sydney H. T. "Obedience and Blood-Sprinkling in 1 Peter 1:2." *WTJ* 72, no. 2 (2010): 291-98.

Park, Sue Kim. "Jeong: A Practical Theology of Postcolonial Interfaith Relations." *Religions* 11, no. 10 (2020). https://doi.org/10.3390/rel11100515.

Phillips, Karl. *Kirche in der Gesellschaft nach de 1. Petrusbrief*. Gütersloh: Gütersloher Verlagshaus-Gerd Mohn, 1971.

Pomeroy, Sarah B., ed. *Plutarch's Advice to the Bride and Groom and A Consolation to His Wife: English Translations, Commentary, Interpretive Essays and Bibliography*. Oxford: Oxford University Press, 1999.

Richard, Earl J. *Reading 1 Peter, Jude, and 2 Peter: A Literary and Theological Commentary* . Macon, GA: Smyth & Helwys, 2000.

Smith, Shively T. J. *Strangers to Family: Diaspora and 1 Peter's Invention of God's Household*. Waco, TX: Baylor University Press, 2016.

Strawbridge, Jennifer. "Authority in Christ" (1 Peter 5). In *The First Letter of Peter: A Global Commentary*. Edited by Jennifer Strawbridge. London: SMC Press, 2020. eBook.

Williams, Travis B. *Good Works in 1 Peter: Negotiating Social Conflict and Christian Identity in the Greco-Roman World*. Tübingen: Mohr Siebeck, 2014.

THE SIMILARITIES BETWEEN 2 PETER AND JUDE

Standing perhaps as the most neglected of the New Testament writings, the Second Letter of Peter and the Letter of Jude deal with the spreading of false teaching and malicious behavior in Christian communities during the initial stages of the movement. The concern is for the integrity of the church, both in terms of doctrine and, most importantly, behavior. The writings remind Christian communities in every space and time of the danger of allowing harmful patterns of thought and action to affect their identity and calling. Their message is as important today as it was at the time they were written—a message which Christians cannot afford to overlook.

Readers familiar with the canonical order of the New Testament will perhaps find puzzling that commentaries usually treat 2 Peter and Jude side by side. The reason is the remarkable degree of similarity—literary and theological—between these writings. In fact, no other two writings of the New Testament are as alike.

The similarities are perceived, first of all, on a lexical and thematic level, with 48 percent of the verbs, nouns, and adjectives used in Jude being found in 2 Peter. More significantly, the shared vocabulary is largely employed in similar literary and theological contexts.[110]

The letters also have very similar structures, as seen in table 30.1.

Table 29.1. Structure of Jude and of 2 Peter

Structure of Jude	Structure of 2 Peter
Opening and Salutation (Jude 1-2)	Opening and Salutation (2 Pet 1:1-2)
Introduction: Statement of Purpose (Jude 3-4)	Introduction: A Virtuous Life According to our Calling and Election (2 Pet 1:3-11)
Marker: "Now I desire to remind you. . ." (Jude 5)	***Marker: "Therefore I intend to keep on reminding you. . ." (2 Pet 1:12)***
Exposing the Opponents (Jude 5-16)	Exposing the False Teachers (2 Pet 1:12–2:22)
Marker: "But you, beloved, must remember. . ." (Jude 17)	***Marker: "I am trying to arouse your sincere intention by reminding you" (2 Pet 3:1)***
Admonitions to the Church (Jude 17-33)	Instructions and Admonitions Concerning the Day of the Lord (2 Pet 3:1-18)
First Admonition: Remember the Word Prophesied by the Apostles (Jude 17-19)	The Certain Coming of the Day of the Lord (2 Pet 3:1-13)
Second Admonition: Build Yourselves in Faith, Keep Yourselves in Love (Jude 20-23)	Final Admonitions (2 Pet 3:14-18)
Doxology (Jude 24-25)	Doxology (2 Pet 3:18)

The case for literary dependence is strong. While we cannot provide a detailed analysis of the various proposals to explain this dependence, it is worth pointing out that there are instances in which it makes more sense to explain the similarities and differences as an appropriation of Jude by the author of 2 Peter.[111] However, given that the other hypotheses are also reasonably coherent, no definitive case can be made.

More importantly, despite the similarities, it is clear that 2 Peter and Jude use their shared language for individual purposes. The larger intent is the same—to warn the church about malicious individuals who were infiltrating the communities—but the authors go in distinct directions with their arguments. 2 Peter puts more emphasis on false teaching, highlighting the reality of eschatological judgment related to the coming of Christ, while Jude focuses on the behavior of certain individuals, who were causing divisions in the church. For this reason, we should consider each letter on its own terms.

[110]Examples include: 2 Pet 2:1-3/Jude 4; 2 Pet 1:12/Jude 5; 2 Pet 2:4/Jude 6; 2 Pet 2:6/Jude 7; 2 Pet 2:10/Jude 8; 2 Pet 2:11/Jude 9; 2 Pet 2:12/Jude 10; 2 Pet 2:15/Jude 11; 2 Pet 2:13, 17/ Jude 12; 2 Pet 3:2-3/Jude 16-17.

[111]The most telling cases are 2 Pet 2:1-3/Jude 4; 2 Pet 2:4/Jude 6; and 2 Pet 2:6/Jude 7. In these instances, there seem to be explanatory expansions in 2 Peter. For an extended discussion of the different hypotheses see Richard Bauckham, *Jude, 2 Peter*, Word Biblical Commentary (Grand Rapids, MI: Zondervan, 1983), 141-43; Douglas J. Moo, *2 Peter and Jude: From Biblical Text—to Contemporary Life* (Grand Rapids, MI: Zondervan, 1996), 16-18.

SECOND LETTER OF PETER

Mateus F. de Campos

AUTHORSHIP AND DATE

The letter known as 2 Peter is attributed to Simon Peter, the most prominent of Jesus' disciples. The author identifies himself as *Symeōn Petros*, utilizing a Greek transliteration of the Hebrew name *Shimeon*, which is how Peter would have been known among his family and kinsmen of Palestinian origin (cf. Acts 15:14). That the name refers to the renowned apostle is made clear by the allusion to the transfiguration, with which Peter is famously associated (2 Pet 1:17-18; cf. Mk 9:2-8). The author's status as an eyewitness of the event is the basis of his authoritative status, and the audience would have promptly acknowledged the claim of apostolic authority of the letter.

The author also identifies himself as a "servant and apostle of Jesus Christ" and refers to the knowledge of his impending death as the reason for his writing (2 Pet 1:13-15). Furthermore, he frequently employs the first-person plural—probably an indication of his role as representative of an apostolic group (2 Pet 1:1, 16, 18, 19). The author, therefore, intends his message to be received as legitimate and authoritative apostolic teaching.

Despite these indications, the authorship of 2 Peter has been subject to intense scrutiny, with the majority of modern scholars arguing against its authenticity. While Petrine authorship cannot be proven beyond doubt on the basis of the internal evidence, a case against it also falls short of conclusive arguments.[1] What one has to consider then is the authoritative claims of the letter. If, as suggested above, the references to Peter were meant to establish the apostolic authority of the letter, and if there were sufficient grounds for some of the original readers to consider it a letter by Peter himself, a pseudonymous 2 Peter would have been potentially deceitful to such readers, whether intentionally or unintentionally. This would have been ironic for a letter whose main purpose is to combat false teaching. The fact remains that, despite the initial hesitance in relation to the letter in the second century, 2 Peter was accepted as legitimate apostolic teaching in several regions where Christianity had spread and eventually made its way to the canon as one of Peter's letters.

From an interpretive standpoint, the argument of the letter creates a scenario in which the apostle Peter speaks directly to his audience. For this reason the present commentary takes the position that such a scenario is the de facto operative context of the letter. Therefore, our interpretation will assume Petrine authorship.

---

[1]The most accepted pseudonymity hypothesis was proposed by Richard Bauckham, *Jude, 2 Peter*, Word Biblical Commentary (Grand Rapids, MI: Zondervan, 1983), 131. For a thorough critique of Bauckham, see Thomas R. Schreiner, *1, 2 Peter, Jude*, New American Commentary 37 (Nashville: Broadman and Holman, 2003), 274-76. A robust assessment of authorship can be found in Gene Green, *Jude and 2 Peter*, Baker Exegetical Commentary on the New Testament (Grand Rapids, MI: Baker Academic, 2008), 139-50.

An assessment of the date is largely dependent on issues of authorship, with a possible range from AD 64–110. If by Peter, the letter should be dated between AD 64 and 65, prior to the traditional date for Peter's martyrdom.

AUDIENCE, PURPOSE, AND OCCASION

The audience is identified only in general terms (2 Pet 1:1). The situation envisioned seems to be related to a particular set of circumstances, which suggests a local audience, the most common scholarly suggestion being Asia Minor, largely because of 1 Peter 1:1. The audience is most likely Gentile (2 Pet 1:4). It is a well-established community (2 Pet 1:12), which is nonetheless in need of an apostolic reminder (2 Pet 1:13). Peter seems to have had some role in preaching the gospel to them (2 Pet 1:16) and had written them a previous letter of admonition (2 Pet 3:1). They had also received a letter from Paul (2 Pet 3:15).

The purpose of 2 Peter is clearly stated as "reminding" the church of the virtues they need to nurture to avoid being unfruitful and falling away as well as reminding them of the apostolic warnings about the emergence of false teachers in the last days (2 Pet 1:12-15; 3:1-3). Judging from these admonitions, the church seems to be at risk of adopting the doctrine and lifestyle of the false teachers who had already infiltrated the community, including their meal gatherings (2 Pet 2:13).

The false teachers, identified as the "ungodly" or "wicked" (2 Pet 2:5-7, 9; 3:7), were people who formerly professed an orthodox faith (2 Pet 2:20-21) but were now stirring up trouble in the church both by questioning essential doctrines and by enticing others to live in a libertine way. Doctrinally, their main contention was with the teaching of the parousia, the return of Christ. They ridiculed the idea of eschatological judgment (2 Pet 3:3-4), which led to a libertine lifestyle characterized by different forms of sexual sin (2 Pet 2:2, 7, 10, 14, 18), greed (2 Pet 2:14-15), and self-indulgence and hedonism (2 Pet 2:13), and fostered by an antinomian, twisted view of human freedom (2 Pet 2:19). They also despised authority and blasphemed against the apostles and their teaching (2 Pet 2:2, 10-12). Peter, therefore, has the challenging task of reminding his audience of essential doctrinal and ethical truths while they are under growing pressure from the false teachers.

False or unorthodox teaching remains a problem for the modern church in various parts of the globe. Eschatology is often a critical issue, with some leaning toward an alarmist posture, and others toward a more pragmatic sort of faith devoid of any serious embracing of eschatological promises. Both postures overlook the genuine effect of the Christian hope. Peter's reminders are, therefore, still tremendously relevant today.

STRUCTURE

The letter is structured around two main blocks of arguments (2 Pet 1:12–2:22; 3:1-13) marked off by the author's purpose statements (2 Pet 1:12; 3:1).

Opening and Salutation (2 Pet 1:1-2)

Introduction: A Virtuous Life According to Our Calling and Election (2 Pet 1:3-11)

Marker ["Therefore I intend to keep on reminding you" (2 Pet 1:12)]

Exposing the False Teachers (2 Pet 1:12–2:22)

- The Trustworthiness of the Apostles' Teaching (2 Pet 1:12-21)
- The Deceit of the False Teachers (2 Pet 2:1-22)

Marker ["I am trying to arouse your sincere intention by reminding you" (2 Pet 3:1)]

2 PETER 1:1-2

As is customary in apostolic writings, Peter opens his letter with an expanded version of the standard epistolary salutation, conveying important truths about himself, the recipients, and Jesus Christ. He identifies himself as "a slave and apostle of Jesus Christ" (au. trans.) combining two important aspects of his identity and status. The word *doulos* can be translated as "slave" or "servant" and connotes both the honored status of a "servant of God" and the status of "belonging to Christ" as a slave to his owner (cf. Rom 6:16; 1 Cor 7:23; Gal 1:10). The language would likely have been perceived as a title of honor among Christians, as is the case in most modern contexts in Latin America, but the social significance of the word as referring to a lowly position would hardly have been lost on a Gentile audience familiar with the dynamics of slavery in the Roman Empire.

Although not to be mistaken for the racially based modern practice of slavery that drastically marred the history of many countries, slavery in the ancient world was still a harsh system. Some slaves owned by good masters would have had a better life than some free persons living in an unjust society. However, a slave was still considered the least in the social order, regarded as property and often terribly mistreated. In such a context, an apostle identifying himself as a slave was certainly noteworthy. The phrase "slave and apostle" creates an important juxtaposition of service and authority. Peter is both the slave, whose status as one who belongs to Jesus informs his call to serve, and the apostle, whose authority is given to him by Jesus Christ. In a context where honor and shame were the dominant paradigms of social validation, such identification coming from someone like Peter would have elevated the slaves in the perception of the community.

This humble awareness likely informed Peter's address to his recipients. They are "those who have received a faith equally precious as ours." The comparison is likely between the apostolic group, of which Peter is a main representative, and the audience. Peter makes sure the recipients understand that theirs is a common faith they share with the apostles. Ultimately, for both the apostles and the church, their sense of identity and worth comes from the common faith they received from their Lord.

The Greek term for "received" has the sense of "obtaining by lot" and relates to a privilege that comes with "being chosen."[2] The verb implicitly describes faith as the result of God's election (cf. 2 Pet 1:10). Typically in the New Testament, faith is not described as something received but rather as the means by which something else (e.g., promise, inheritance) is received (cf. Acts 26:18; Gal 3:2, 14; Heb 11:8, 11, 39). For this reason, it is best to interpret "faith" here not as the act of believing but as the truth of the gospel—a shared portion between the apostles and the church and obtained solely by God's favor.[3] The reference to "a faith received" points at the same time to the privilege and duty the apostles and the church share in relation to the truth of the gospel.

[2]Cf. Lk 1:9; Jn 19:24; Acts 1:17.

[3]A similar idea can be found in Paul's instructions to the Philippians (Phil 1:27). See also Jude 1:3. Other instances of the term being used in this way include Acts 6:7; 14:22; 1 Cor 16:13; 2 Cor 13:5; Eph 4:5.

The agency of Christ is fundamental in the letter and highlighted in the opening. The title "our God and Savior Jesus Christ" conveys the divine identity of Jesus. Grammatically, the coordination of the nouns "God" and "Savior" suggests that both nouns refer to Christ. That Peter sees Jesus as God is clear from his formulaic use of the title Lord (2 Pet 1:8, 11, 14, 16; 2:20; 3:18), which is the word used in the LXX to refer to the name of YHWH. The title expresses the divine identity of Jesus, who stands as a central focus of the letter.

Christ's central role is also emphasized in the phrases "the righteousness of . . . Jesus Christ" and "the knowledge of . . . Jesus our Lord." Peter uses the term "righteousness" three more times in his letter in an ethical sense (2 Pet 2:5, 21; 3:13). Accordingly, faith here is said to be granted on the righteous merits of Jesus Christ, and by implication, not by one's own virtues. This affirmation comes as an important preface to the pervasive ethical instructions of the next section of the discourse (2 Pet 1:3-12). In the same manner "the knowledge of God and of Jesus our Lord," namely, the recognition that comes with one's conversion and is ultimately reflected in one's way of living,[4] is the source of virtue and the very basis of the ethical transformation Peter is about to explain (cf. 2 Pet 1:3; 2:20; 3:18).

Peter's opening is purposeful. He has before him the difficult task of reminding the church of their identity, appealing strongly for a virtuous and ethical life in opposition to the libertine lifestyle of the false teachers. To do so, he has to rely quite heavily on his apostolic credentials. However, while asserting himself in an authoritative manner, Peter positions himself as a servant, sharing a common faith with the church. It is out of this place of authority, humility, and fellowship that he will speak into their lives. Moreover, given the strong emphasis on virtue and ethics, the apostle makes sure to affirm the true source of virtue. If they are to "make every effort" (2 Pet 1:5) to develop a virtuous life, they should first be reminded that this life is grounded in the righteousness of Christ and in the knowledge of God and Christ.

In some cultures, with a heightened awareness of hierarchical authority, ethics can often be communicated as top-down prescriptive commands, based on a sometimes unhealthy notion of authority. In other cultures, where authority is much less emphasized and the dynamics are much less hierarchical, to make an appeal to a virtuous and moral life is often taken as forceful and patronizing. Peter provides us with a helpful pastoral model to follow when dealing with difficult issues—one that balances authority and humility, ultimately grounding the ethical imperatives in the actions of God in Christ.

2 PETER 1:3-4

The section of 2 Peter 1:3-12 serves as a foundational introduction to the entire argument of the letter. Before confronting the false teaching and unethical conduct of the opponents, Peter describes what a virtuous life looks like. The list of virtues, which constitutes the core of these verses, stands as a foil to the description of the false teachers (2 Pet 2:1-22).

2 Peter 1:3-4 establishes the basis for the admonition to a virtuous life. A virtuous life does not stem from mere self-generated moral actions but from a sense of calling, grounded in the believers' understanding of their participation in the divine nature. The paragraph is punctuated with benefaction language.[5] The mention of "the divine power," the verb "to

[4]See Bultmann, "γινώσκω," *TDNT*, 1:707.

[5]See Frederick W. Danker, "2 Peter 1: A Solemn Decree," *The Catholic Biblical Quarterly* 40, no. 1 (1978): 64-82.

bestow" (2x), the emphasis on God's "*own* glory and virtue," and the mention of participation point to the Greco-Roman notions of benefaction and reciprocity.

The Greco-Roman society was structured hierarchically. Those in power were regarded as patrons of society, bestowing benefits on those who were loyal to them and dependent on such generous gifts. Given the honor and power of the benefactors, their acts of benefaction were regarded as gratuitous and could not be repaid. However, they were to be met with appropriate response, which often meant actions by the clients that would render honor to the patron. Second Peter 1:3-4 employs benefaction language to describe Christ's action toward the believers, while 2 Peter 1:5-11 corresponds to the appropriate response expected.

The pronoun "his" identifying the benefactor could refer to God or Christ, an ambiguity that might have been intentional. Christ's divine power, the power he shares with God himself, is the source of the gift bestowed on believers—namely, "everything needed for life and godliness." "All things" appears with emphasis in the Greek text, highlighting the all-encompassing nature of the benefaction. The verb for "bestowing" is in the perfect tense, indicating a complete act with ongoing effects. Believers have been granted everything they need to live in a godly way.

The means by which the benefaction is granted is "the knowledge of him who called us by his own glory and virtue" (au. trans.). The word for "virtue," here associated with "glory," was a common term employed to discuss morality and character in the Greco-Roman world and has the connotation of moral excellence. These attributes are emphasized as pertaining to God himself (i.e., "his *own*"). In other words, the gifts for a godly life are the result of God's calling, which is predicated on his own moral excellence. But while Peter uses Hellenistic terminology to introduce the issue of moral virtue, the associated ideas of election and moral excellence are very much part of the Hebrew understanding of God's election of the people of Israel (Ex 19:6; Deut 7:6; Lev 19:2; 20:7, 26)—a concept that was appropriated in the early Christian understanding of election (cf. 1 Pet 1:14-16; 2:9). A virtuous and godly life is predicated on God's own character and on his formative action of calling a people for himself.

This leads us to the key statement of the passage: "so that through them [these promises] you may . . . become participants of the divine nature" (2 Pet 1:4). Being participants of the divine nature is the ultimate benefaction, whereby the benefactor shares with the believer something of his own nature. But what does "divine nature" refer to?

Commentators often allude to the Platonic concept of *theosis* or deification as a background for the phrase.[6] Plato understood material existence as a prison from which one has to escape; and that "to escape is to become like God . . . to become righteous and holy and wise."[7] This is achieved by one's effort to develop moral virtues and avoid vices, which would lead one to conform to a divine pattern. Similarly, in Hellenistic Jewish thought, sharing in the divine nature entails issues of virtue and character.[8] Even though the concept of sharing in the divine nature may have

[6]Peter H. Davids, *The Letters of 2 Peter and Jude*, Pillar New Testament Commentary (Grand Rapids, MI: Eerdmans, 2006), 172-73.

[7]Plat. Theaet. 176. *Plato. Plato in Twelve Volumes*, vol. 12, translated by Harold N. Fowler. (Cambridge, MA: Harvard University Press, 1921). Cf. also Plut. Arist. 6:3.

[8]James M Starr, *Sharers in Divine Nature: 2 Peter 1:4 in Its Hellenistic Context* (Stockholm: Almqvist & Wiksell, 2000), 234. Josephus speaks of wisdom and knowledge as marks of partaking the divine nature (*Ag. Ap.* 1.26: 232).

multiple nuances, the idea is not primarily one of divinity—as if one would become a divine being—but of sharing in some qualities pertaining to God, such as immortality and moral excellence. In 2 Peter, the emphasis falls heavily on moral virtue. Becoming partakers of the divine nature is explained in terms of having "escape[d] from the corruption that is in the world because of lust," a reference to the corrupt system of values governed by and expressed in the human fallen nature.

The important emphasis is that virtue is the product of divine benefaction. It is God and Christ, solely through divine power, who provide everything the believer needs to live a virtuous life according to God's calling. In the sequence, Peter will use the language of effort when speaking about the nurturing of virtues, but that effort is no more than a fitting response to God's generous benefaction. Because he has given all that is needed for a godly life, believers are now called to pursue a virtuous life and therefore confirm their calling and election (2 Pet 1:10).

2 PETER 1:5-11

Having established that a godly life is provided by divine benefaction, Peter now goes on to call his readers to pursue actively the specific qualities that characterize such a life. The passage begins with a linking inference—"for this very reason." Therefore, the appeal to "make every effort" is already grounded in what has been richly provided by God (2 Pet 1:3). Furthermore, four of the eight qualities prescribed (faith, virtue, knowledge, and godliness) have been mentioned in 2 Peter 1:1-4 in reference to God and Christ. Hence, the qualities that are to be pursued have their ultimate source in the divine nature in which the believers are called to participate.

Nevertheless, believers are called to pursue these qualities intentionally and diligently. The language of effort employed here is found in contexts of benefaction or service, in which someone "employs all effort" to provide what is needed for a given task.[9] Therefore, although what is necessary for a godly life has been amply provided by divine benefaction, developing those qualities is also a matter of active engagement. For Peter, there is no tension between God's gracious provision and the believer's intentional effort. Being a participant in the divine nature is a call to apply oneself diligently to act in accordance with that nature. It entails aligning oneself with God's will in response to his gracious provision.

The list of virtues comprises eight items (faith, virtue, knowledge, self-control, endurance, godliness, brotherly love, and love) follows the genre of a *sorites*, a list with a progressive nature leading up to a climax.[10] Virtue lists are commonly found in Christian and non-Christian writings.[11] Aside from faith and love, all qualities are also found in contemporary pagan virtue lists. The lists are part of philosophical ethical discussions in the Greco-Roman world, particularly within Stoicism.

For the Stoics, one should make moral progress through the pursuit of virtue a primary goal in life. The reason for this pursuit was to align oneself with "nature," the cosmic principle governing the universe, which the Stoics saw as reflecting perfect reason. Human nature is special because, through rationality, humans can participate in the nature of the universe. When humans are aligned with that nature, they find the purpose of life. Therefore, the human task is

---

[9]*Ant.* 6:34; 11:324; 20:204; Philo. *Mos.* 2:136; Polybius 21.29.12.

[10]Cf. J. Daryl Charles, "The Language and Logic of Virtue in 2 Peter 1:5-7," *Bulletin for Biblical Research* 8 (1998): 55-73.

[11]Cf. Gal 5:22-23; 2 Cor 6:6-7; Eph 6:14-17; Phil 4:8; Col 3:12-14; 1 Tim 6:11; Jas 3:17; *Barn.* 2:2-4; *1 Clem.* 62:2.

"to live according to nature," which is essentially attained by seeking a virtuous life through reason.[12] Because humans are prone to be distracted by appearances and desires, developing a virtuous life is a matter of strenuous effort and discipline. Therefore, virtue is nurtured.

Second Peter 1:3-11 fits well with this discussion. Speaking about divine "nature" and "exerting effort" to develop virtue, the letter employs language that would sound familiar to those aware of the Stoic ethical instructions. But a few important differences suggest that the argument of 2 Peter proposes a very different idea.

First, for Peter, a virtuous life stems from one's alignment with the divine nature. Although this might sound similar to what Stoics affirmed, a fundamental difference is that by "divine power and nature" Peter does not mean the impersonal cosmos governing through reason but the personal God and Lord Jesus Christ—the one who calls, blesses, and can be known by his people. Furthermore, for Peter, the cosmos is not reflective of a perfect nature; rather, it is the context of corruption from which believers are urged to escape (2 Pet 1:4). Therefore, a virtuous life is not obtained by aligning oneself with the cosmos but by rejecting the corruption of the cosmos and human desire in order to align oneself with the divine nature.

Second, the list begins with faith, which is the foundation on which all other virtues are built. Interestingly, knowledge, which would be the essential value for the Stoics because of reason, is the third element. The virtuous life is not obtained on the basis of a personal rational exercise but built on faith.

Third, the list—although mentioning several qualities that would be recognized as valuable by the Stoics, such as virtue, self-control, and godliness—has as its final climactic element love. Therefore, the list has a typical Christian orientation, beginning with faith and culminating with love. That, one might say, is the whole direction of Christian spirituality—one that is grounded in faith and ultimately expressed in love.

Finally, Peter's ethical instruction is eschatologically oriented. While Stoic ethics presupposed an unchanging universe, Peter ties his ethical instructions to an eschatological hope (2 Pet 1:11): entrance into the kingdom will be richly "provided." Here we find an important dynamic between ethics and eschatology that underlies the entire letter. While Peter's main concern is ethical admonition, that purpose is not self-standing but theologically driven by a fundamental hope. It is precisely because God is at work in the history of the world, leading it to its climax in the return of Christ and the realization of his kingdom, that people are called to conduct themselves in a virtuous manner. The flip side of that is that the false teachers, denying an eschatological hope, exhibit libertine conduct. Eschatological hope is essential not only because of its future implications but because of its present effects.

In this framework, the virtues are of crucial importance. They are that which prevent an unfruitful and ineffective life (2 Pet 1:9). Those who lack them are nearsighted to the point of being blind. Lacking a "long-distance" perception of both past forgiveness and future redemption, they behave as if they have never been cleansed (2 Pet 1:9). In light of this dreadful scenario, Peter utters a final command. Repeating the language of effort ("apply yourselves," 2 Pet 1:10, au. trans.), the apostle urges the audience to "confirm your call and election." God's election is not a subjective call; it is expressed concretely in the virtuous life of the believer.

---

[12]On the role of reason in the pursuit of virtue in Stoicism, see J. Daryl Charles, *Virtue Amidst Vice: The Catalog of Virtues in 2 Peter 1* (Sheffield, UK: Sheffield Academic Press, 1997), 99-105.

Peter tells us that an ethical and moral life is expected of those who are called by Jesus. These virtues, of course, are not an end in themselves, but they are inevitable manifestations of one's alignment with the divine nature. Obviously, some of these qualities were not exclusively affirmed by Christians. Certainly there were non-Christians in society who could be described as ethical and virtuous people. But Christians should see these qualities as a matter of identity, emanating from a profound awareness of God's gracious actions that provided them with the resources to live a godly life, and deriving their thrust from the hope of God's final installation of his kingdom.

It is common to fall into the extremes of deemphasizing ethics for fear of a "works righteousness" mentality, or superemphasizing it, as if being a Christian were simply a matter of morality. In a world where promiscuity, corruption, and licentiousness are ingrained in the culture, Christians often define themselves in opposition to these sinful practices. Yet, Peter reminds us that the call of the gospel is to understand our identity in Christ and live according to the divine nature. It is a call to pursue virtue because of God's actions on our behalf. And it is a call to align ourselves with God's will and his character. For the Christian, virtue is not defined simply based on a "natural" moral standard. It is defined based on God's own virtue and holiness and on his provision and call for us to participate in the divine nature.

2 PETER 1:12-15

After the introduction, we find the first of the two literary markers initiating the two main blocks of discourse (2 Pet 1:12–2:22; 3:1-13). Both markers use the language of "reminding" to indicate the purpose of the letter. Reminding was a common pastoral strategy (cf. Rom 15:15; 1 Cor 4:17; 15:1; 2 Tim 1:6; 2:14; Titus 3:1; Jude 1:5). Peter's language of "awakening by way of reminder" indicates that even though his admonitions are not new to this well-established church, his words are intended to confront their complacency.

The speech contemplates the apostle's impending death. It is not clear whether some form of persecution is in view, but Peter is convinced that his death is near, a knowledge confirmed by the fact that "our Lord Jesus Christ has made [it] clear to me" (cf. Jn 21:18-19). Peter's letter, therefore, comes as an urgent awakening appeal, meant to stir people back to the pursuit of a meaningful virtuous life. The letter is part of his legacy—a way for his voice to keep reverberating in their ears as a constant reminder of his teaching.

2 PETER 1:16-18

Following his weighty purpose statement, Peter now offers the reasons for his teaching to be taken as trustworthy, which paves the way for his exposure of the false teachers (2 Pet 2:1-22; 3:1-13). He offers two main reasons: the historical events witnessed by the apostles (2 Pet 1:16-18) and the prophetic word affirmed by the apostles (2 Pet 1:19-21).

Addressing potential accusations that the teaching of the apostles rested on baseless myths (2 Pet 1:16), Peter alludes to their experience with the historical Jesus. Historical testimony was of crucial importance in the apostolic proclamation (cf. 1 Cor 15:1-8; 1 Jn 1:1-4). Interestingly, however, Peter makes use of the historical reliability of his testimony to corroborate his teaching regarding a future event—the "power and coming [*parousia*] of our Lord Jesus Christ" (2 Pet 1:16). The word *parousia* was often used to describe the momentous arrival of kings and dignitaries to a city.[13] In Christian tradition, it was used to refer to the

[13]3 Macc 3:17-18. Cf. Oepke, "παρουσία, πάρειμι," *TDNT*, 5:859.

eschatological coming of Christ (cf. Mt 24:3; 1 Thess 2:19; 2 Thess 2:1, 8; Jas. 5:8) and was an integral part of the apostolic proclamation, along with Christ's death and resurrection (cf. 1 Cor 15:20-25). It was the climactic event for which Christians should live.

The certainty of the future manifestation of Christ is grounded in his historical manifestation, witnessed by the apostles. Positioning himself as one among the apostles, Peter opts for the term *epoptēs* to describe his eyewitness experience. The term means "watcher" or "observer" and has in its root a sensory idea. It is the credibility of the apostle's witness of a historical event, when the glory of Jesus was manifested before his eyes, that grants trustworthiness to his teaching about the Lord's coming.

As important as what the apostle has seen is what he has heard. Referring to the transfiguration event (Mk 9:2-9), Peter recalls the words of the voice from heaven attesting Jesus' divine sonship. The words and phrases "majesty," "honor and glory," and "majestic glory," along with the mention of "God the Father" as the one who affirms his dignity, emphasize Jesus' exalted status. In the New Testament, "glory" often establishes a connection between the transfiguration event and the second coming of Christ (Mk 8:38; 13:26; Mt 16:27). In both events, the glory of Jesus as the vindicated Son of God was and will be made evident. Hence, as one who has been an eyewitness of the first event, Peter's proclamation of the second is trustworthy.

2 PETER 1:19-21

The second corroboration Peter offers for his teaching is the apostles' reliance on inspired Scripture. The apostles not only heard the voice from heaven, but they also rely on the testimony of Scripture, which is, in a very real sense, the voice of God, since he inspired it. Peter, therefore, establishes continuity between their historical testimony and the testimony of Scripture.

The use of the phrase "prophetic word" and similar expressions to refer to Scripture is common enough (cf. Rom 16:26; Philo *Leg.* 3:43; *Plant.* 1:117, *Sobr.* 1:68; *2 Clem.* 11:2). However, since later Peter talks about the predictions of the "holy prophets" in equal standing with "the commandment of the Lord and Savior spoken through your apostles" (2 Pet 3:2) and speaks of Paul's writings as "Scriptures" (2 Pet 3:16), it is likely that "prophetic word" includes the writings by the apostles themselves, which he held as inspired.

Peter responds to the attacks from the false teachers who not only were discrediting the apostolic teaching as based on "myths" but were also disparaging Scripture as the product of human imagination. Just as Peter defended the apostolic proclamation based on the historical experience of the transfiguration, he now defends the trustworthiness of the prophetic word on the basis of divine inspiration. Scripture is not the result of "one's own interpretation," namely, it is not fabricated by fanciful human interpretation of divine oracles, but came through an act of divine communication by the Spirit. Peter repeats a key verb to make his argument clear: "prophecy was never *carried out* by the will of man, but men *carried along* by the Spirit spoke from God" (au. trans.) Humans are not the agents of prophecy, but participate in God's communicative act.[14] It is significant that Peter repeats the word "men" (2 Pet 1:21) to emphasize the human element.[15] Human participation does not compromise the credibility of

[14]The role of the Spirit in inspiring prophecy is well-attested in the Hebrew Bible and the New Testament. See Green, *Jude and 2 Peter*, 233.

[15]The emphasis here is on the humanity of the agents, not on their gender. The NRSV translation "men and women" is appropriate to reflect God's inspiration of both men and women.

the divine communication; rather, humans are mysteriously incorporated in God's revelation. When the glory of God was revealed in Jesus in the transfiguration, it was witnessed and testified by humans. Likewise, the communication of the truth of Scripture also includes human participation. This dynamic ties Peter's argument together. It is precisely because God revealed his glory and his prophecies to the apostles that he can affirm with certainty the promise of the coming of the Lord.

The eschatological hope of the coming of Christ is of fundamental importance for the apostle. He puts the full weight of his view of Scripture (2 Pet 1:19-21), his experience with the historical Jesus (2 Pet 1:16-18), and the knowledge of his imminent death (2 Pet 1:12-15) behind this important proclamation. The degree to which the coming of Christ is emphasized in modern global Christianity varies sometimes according to different contexts. It is not uncommon for Christian communities in the Global South that experience certain socioeconomic difficulties to speak more enthusiastically about Christ's return. Similarly, at certain points in history when there has been considerable tension and uncertainty about the stability of the world, Christians have often availed themselves of eschatology in search of meaning and hope, only to revert to a more existential kind of Christianity when things get back to "normal." Second Peter shows us that the coming of Christ is integral to gospel preaching, not an afterthought. The coming of Christ is not an accessory doctrine to be used at the convenience of believers. The Christian faith is essentially eschatological in its orientation, and retaining this emphasis is imperative for Christianity not to lose its fundamental character.

2 PETER 2:1-3

Peter's defense of the apostolic teaching paves the way for his exposure of the false teachers. Given the length of 2 Peter 2:1-22, it is clear that the attack on the false teachers is the primary focus of the author. The section is centered around examples taken from Jewish traditional reflections on the rebellion of certain groups and individuals who function as archetypes of error and serve as a frame of evaluation for the attitudes and destiny of the false teachers.

Second Peter 2:1-3 is Peter's formal introduction of the opponents. His criticism flows smoothly from his previous argument on prophecy, now alluding to the false prophets in the history of Israel. The allusion is meant to foster a comparison: just as in the past there was the need to distinguish inspired from false prophecy, now there is the need to distinguish between legitimate apostolic teaching and false teaching in the church.

Peter uses the paradigm of the "false prophets" of the past as a frame of evaluation of the "false teachers" of his day. The reference to "false prophets" might carry the nuance of the term as it is used in the LXX, particularly in Jeremiah (LXX Jer 33:7-8, 11; 34:9; 35:1; 36:1, 8; cf. Zech 13:2).[16] In that context, while Jeremiah prophesied the captivity of Judah as divine judgment, these false prophets insisted that such a captivity would never take place, leading the people astray (cf. LXX Jer 27:8-11). Therefore, what is false about the prophets in that context is both their deceitful prophecies and their opposition to legitimate prophecy. Peter might be seeing a similar opposition in the false teachers. They are false because of their destructive teaching, which denies the reality of God's judgment, but also because

[16]Similar treatments of false prophets can also be found in Philo (*Spec.* 4:50-51) and the Apostolic Fathers (*Did.* 11:5-6, 8-10; 16:3; Herm. *Mand.* 11:1-16).

they oppose the legitimately inspired prophetic warning issued by the apostles.

Despite their similarity to the false prophets, the label "false teachers" is the main descriptor of the opponents. Their teaching is identified as "destructive opinions." The term is sometimes translated as "heresies," but it is unlikely that it had acquired such a technical sense at the time. Rather, it denotes a way of thinking, characterized by particular opinions, and also a way of living (cf. Acts 24:14; 26:5).

Their destructive teaching is tantamount to "denying" Christ. The verb "to deny" is sometimes used to describe the open rejection of Christ (Mt 10:33; Mk 14:68, 70) but can also refer to actions that are inconsistent with faith and entail the rejection of Christ (1 Tim 5:8; 2 Tim 3:5; Titus 1:16). It is in this latter sense that the false teachers deny Jesus. Their false teaching and their condemnable behavior are equivalent to an attitude of rebellion. They deny Jesus as their "Master who bought them," which projects the context of slave ownership as a framework (cf. 1 Tim 6:1-2; 2 Tim 2:21; Titus 2:9; 1 Pet 2:18). The idea of purchase is used elsewhere in the New Testament to talk about the redemption of believers (1 Cor 7:21-24). Therefore, we learn something important about the false teachers: they were at one point believers.

The language of slavery is significant in the context of the letter. Later, Peter will condemn the false teachers as people who "promise them freedom" but are "slaves of corruption" (2 Pet 2:19). The fact that Peter utilizes slavery as a metaphor does not mean he supports the institution of slavery. Rather, given its ubiquitous nature, Peter employs the language to illustrate the contrast between slavery to corruption and loyalty to God, in the strongest possible terms. The opponents' rebellious desire to "gain freedom" from their Master led them to a state of slavery to corruption and a complete obliviousness to what freedom really means.

Second Peter 2:2-3 spell out the effect of their rebellious teaching in the lives of others. First, "many will follow their debaucheries." So great was their departure from faith that they were practicing promiscuous acts and leading others to a sinful lifestyle. Second, "the way of truth will be maligned."[17] Since they prove to be as corrupt as the pagans around them, their actions affect the reputation of the entire community and indeed the gospel itself. Finally, in their greed, they "exploited" the community, likely charging fees and raising money among the congregation, and doing so with their "deceptive words." Peter uses language reminiscent of the charge of the opponents against the apostles in 2 Peter 1:16, turning it against them.[18] They are the ones who use fabricated words devoid of truth. The description ends with an affirmation of certain destruction. God's judgment is not idle.

2 PETER 2:4-10

Before exposing the behavior of the false teachers, Peter frames his confrontation in the context of God's past judgment actions. The apostle offers three examples (2 Pet 2:4-8) followed by an application (2 Pet 2:9-10). As he develops the idea of judgment, he also emphasizes God's preservation of the righteous. God's eschatological intervention, after all, always entails salvation and judgment.

Rhetorically, the segment progresses gradually. We find three parallel examples of divine judgment involving the fallen angels (2 Pet 2:4), the ancient world (2 Pet 2:5), and Sodom and Gomorrah (2 Pet 2:6). The first example focuses solely on judgment, while the second and third contrast God's judgment of the

[17]This likely echoes Is 52:5.

[18]Philo often uses the concept of fabrication to refer to fictional stories or myths (*Opif.* 1:157; *Det.* 1:125; *Congr.* 1:61; *Abr.* 1:243).

wicked with the preservation of the righteous, Noah (2 Pet 2:5) and Lot (2 Pet 2:7). The example of Lot, in its turn, becomes the central focus, with an added expansion on his conduct in the midst of the wicked (2 Pet 2:8).

In the example of the fallen angels, the focus is exclusively on their punishment. Peter draws from a tradition reflected in extracanonical texts that advanced a particular interpretation of Genesis 6:1-3.[19] In Genesis, the "sons of God" took the "daughters of men" for their wives, which caused YHWH to limit the numbers of days of humankind. Jewish writings during the Second Temple period understood the "sons of God" to be fallen angels, also called watchers or giants. In these expansions of Genesis, which informed Peter's argument, the sin and judgment of these fallen beings are highlighted.

Peter does not specify the sins in view, but there are at least two connections between the sins of the watchers and the sins of the false teachers: immorality and rebellion against God's authority. Both sins are mentioned in 2 Peter 2:10 in Peter's injunction against the false teachers. The most direct connection, however, is the reality of impending judgment itself: just as the angels are "being kept" for judgment, the punishment of the opponents is certain.

The second example contrasts the judgment of the wicked and the preservation of the righteous, with the latter more vividly in focus. Noah is contrasted with the wicked of the ancient world, who were not spared by God. Once again, we are not told explicitly what the sins of the wicked were. Instead, there is an emphasis on Noah's righteousness (cf. Gen. 6:9; Ezek 14:14, 20). Righteousness is contrasted with godlessness and in context is to be understood in moral terms. Jewish reflections on Noah's righteousness often highlight his obedience (Gen 6:22; *Jub.* 5:19, 22), his moral conduct (cf. *Jub.* 7:20), and his attempt to persuade the wicked to change their ways (*Ant.* 1:74; cf. *Sib. Or.* 1:128-129), which probably stands behind Peter's use of the epithet "herald of righteousness."

The final example is the most elaborate, with detailed descriptions of the wickedness of Sodom and Gomorrah and the righteousness of Lot. There is an escalation in the depiction of judgment, and the wicked cities are clearly identified as "an example" of the coming judgment to befall the ungodly. However, the emphasis quickly turns to the preservation of Lot, whose righteousness is mentioned three times. For those familiar with Lot's story (Gen 19), the references to his righteousness may seem surprising.[20] The account in Genesis leaves room for diverging interpretations. On the one hand, Lot offers generous hospitality to the messengers of YHWH (Gen 19:1-3) and puts his own life in danger to protect them (Gen 19:9-10). On the other hand, Lot outrageously offers his daughters to the men of Sodom (Gen 19:8). Lot and his family are later spared from God's judgment in response to Abraham's pleading that God would spare the righteous before overthrowing the cities (Gen 18:16-33). Therefore, according to the narrative's own implicit evaluation, despite his obvious flaws, Lot is eventually found to be righteous.

For Peter, however, what makes Lot righteous is the fact that he endured while "being oppressed" (au. trans.) by the sexual immorality of the wicked. The word for "oppressed" is rare (cf. Acts 7:24; 3 Macc 2:2, 13) and denotes the idea of suffering, including both physical and psychological distress. The psychological aspect is emphasized in the following description that Lot "was tormented in

[19]Cf. *1 En.* 6-19; 3 Macc 2:4-8; *T. Naph.* 3:4-5; CD 2:16-3:1; *Jub.* 5:1-2; *2 Bar.* 56; *Ant.* 1:73.

[20]Although cf. Wis 10:6, *1 Clem.* 11:1.

his righteous soul" with the lawless things he saw and heard while living among the wicked (2 Pet 2:8). Peter stresses the fact that Lot was tremendously afflicted by the sinful environment in which he lived, which should be the experience of his audience amid the lawlessness in their own social context.

Peter makes his point clear in his application: "The Lord knows how to rescue the godly from trial and to keep the unrighteous until the day of judgment, when they will be punished." Like the righteous Noah and Lot, the godly will be delivered. Like the fallen angels and the wicked in the days of Noah and Lot, the ungodly will be judged. Peter then clarifies the target of his injunction: "those who indulge their flesh in depraved lust and who despise authority" (2 Pet 2:10), which entails rebellion against the Lord (cf. 2 Pet 2:9).

Peter's point in the passage can be summarized thus: the righteous are afflicted by the surrounding godlessness, but the Lord's deliverance is certain, as is the punishment of the ungodly. When godlessness abounds, it is not uncommon for the soul to become numb, either accustomed to the surrounding expressions of sin and evil or hopeless in relation to the possibility of change. The expected attitude of the righteous, however, cannot be fatalism or complacency. Rather, the righteous nurture growing restlessness and discontent, a posture that does not go unnoticed by God. In fact, God's judgment of the wicked and the preservation and vindication of the righteous at the final day will be a response to this righteous discontent.

2 PETER 2:10-22

With the background portrayals of judgment installed, Peter now moves to a lengthy denunciation of the false teachers. The denunciation follows the genre of *vituperatio,* the Greco-Roman rhetorical strategy designed to expose and confront opposing ideas and, in the process, persuade the readers of the writer's positions.[21] The sequence reflects one of the author's central concerns: to make the wickedness of the false teachers plainly visible so that the community will be emboldened to reject their influence. Although their faulty worldview and theology were the source of the problem—an issue Peter will tackle soon—it is their seriously reproachable conduct that first receives attention.

The first denunciation is regarding the opponents' arrogance. They are "arrogant audacious people" who "do not tremble while blaspheming [the] glories" (2 Pet 2:10, au. trans.). Their attitude is contrasted with that of angels who "do not bring against them a slanderous judgment from the Lord" (2 Pet 2:11). The passage is muddled by several ambiguities, and different interpretations have been suggested as to whom the "glories" refer. Most commentators agree that the term refers to angels, but there is no consensus as to whether the angels in view are good or evil. It is worth noticing that the overall injunction is against an attitude of rebellion against God. If the mention of "angels" recalls the example of fallen angels in 2 Peter 2:4, then the sin in view is their rebellion against God, which likely influenced Peter's comment in 2 Peter 2:10 about the opponents despising authority. Similarly in our passage, the focus is on the opponents' arrogance (cf. NRSV "bold and willful") that leads to rebellion, a theme that has already been introduced in 2 Peter 2:1 with the teachers' denial of "the Master who bought them."

Furthermore, the word "blaspheming" is often used in the New Testament to refer to slander against God, his Spirit, and his word

[21]Green, *Jude and 2 Peter*, 20-22. Andreas B. Du Toit, "Vilification as a Pragmatic Device in Early Christian Epistolography" *Biblica* 75, no. 3 (1994): 411.

(Mk 2:7; 3:29; Jn 10:36; Rom 2:24; 1 Tim 1:20; 6:1; Titus 2:5; Jas 2:7; 2 Pet 2:2). Finally, the word "glory" in the overwhelming majority of occurrences in the New Testament refers to God or Christ.[22] In 2 Peter itself, the word is used in 2 Peter 1:17 as a divine title. Hence, it is likely that "blaspheming glories" relates to an arrogant contempt for divine authority, which connects seamlessly with "despising [divine] authority" in 2 Peter 2:10.

Therefore, the criticism is that the false teachers in their arrogance do not tremble when reviling God's authority, which may include the angels as representatives but ultimately entails opposition to God himself.[23] In contrast, the angels, who are exceedingly more powerful, do not dare to utter a blasphemy against them before the Lord, despite how reproachable they are. The point of the contrast is to highlight the irrational nature of the opponents' arrogance.

Their arrogance stems from their ignorance, which is highlighted in the description of the opponents as "irrational animals" (2 Pet 2:12). The rhetoric is strong. It suggests that this kind of active opposition to God reflects a dehumanized state in which the teachers react out of animal instinct, deprived of the basic faculties of rationality.

The next block of denunciations has to do with the sins of self-indulgence (2 Pet 2:13-14): "they consider daytime self-indulgence a pleasure" (au. trans.). The word for "self-indulgence" here relates to activities associated with extravagant parties, often marked by drunkenness and immoral practices, which were common in certain Greco-Roman circles. Given the nature of these activities, they were normally conducted at night, which made daytime self-indulgence even more reprehensible (cf. Rom 13:13; Is 5:11). Pleasure was an important topic in ancient philosophical debate, with some groups condemning the lack of self-control reflected in such practices and others advocating for unrestrained pleasure, a notion that was to a large extent based on the idea of the gods' obliviousness to humankind.[24] The opponents seem aligned with this line of thinking. Considering eschatological judgment a myth, they became reckless in their lifestyle, also enticing the impressionable (2 Pet 2:13-14). "Reveling in their pleasures," these false teachers would violate even the sacred fellowship meal to lead people astray.

The next block (2 Pet 2:14-16), introduced by the label "accursed children," reflects on the motivation of the group by appealing to the well-known story of Balaam (Num 22–24). Balaam was perceived as an archetype of error, especially because of his role in leading Israel into idolatry (cf. Num 31:16). In the comparison, Peter underscores Balaam's greed, suggesting that the opponents sought profit by manipulating people. Ultimately, however, it is Balaam's madness, reflected in his being rebuked by a donkey, that fosters Peter's exposure of the teachers as objects of ridicule. As in the case of Balaam, their greed reflects their madness.

Rhetorically, the final section of denunciations (2 Pet 2:17-22) represents a climax in the *vituperatio*. The metaphors "waterless spring" and "mists driven by a storm" allude to the teachers' empty promises. A fountain without water is a tremendous disappointment, especially in warmer areas; as is a mist, which in warm regions brings refreshment in a hot day,

---

[22]The plural form is rare. Aside from 2 Pet 2:10 and Jude 9, it appears in the New Testament only in 1 Pet 1:11 and three times in the LXX canonical books (Ex 15:11; 33:5; Hos 9:11) but with other connotations.

[23]Also notice that trembling is normally a sign of reverence toward God (cf. Ps 104:32; Is 66:2, 5; Dan 10:11).

[24]This notion may have been derived from the popular hedonistic views of Epicurus, although the philosopher himself did not necessarily advocate for debauchery. See Green, *Jude and 2 Peter*, 278-79.

only to be quickly swept away by the wind. Both the spring and mist would be initially promising but incapable of delivering on their promise, which is what Peter subsequently says about the false teachers' empty promises of freedom (2 Pet 2:19). But the problem is not only their empty promises but also that they entice others to err. Peter uses a fishing metaphor to describe their strategy to "entice" immature Christians with the promise of "freedom," which, in context, relates to their promoting of a libertine lifestyle, "free" from the fear of judgment.[25] Although it might seem strange that a Christian community would tolerate such libertine behavior, as Gentiles, licentiousness was not at all uncommon in their social environment, which, associated with a distortion of Christian teaching, could easily confuse the weak. Error gradually infiltrates the community which is not sufficiently grounded in the truth, especially if the error finds precedent and support in social practice.

The irony is that the empty promises of freedom actually reveal their slavery to corruption (2 Pet 2:19). The language draws on the social contrast between slaves and free citizens in the Roman Empire and evokes 2 Peter 2:1. In their attempt to gain freedom from their generous Master and benefactor, they find themselves in a true state of slavery.

Peter's description of the false teachers is meant to contrast with his description of the godly life in the beginning of the letter. In 2 Peter 1:3-4 God's divine power grants the believer everything pertaining to life and godliness, through the knowledge (*epignōseōs*) of the one who called them and granted them his great promises (*epaggelmata*), which allowed them to escape (*apophygontes*) lustful (*en epithymia*) corruption (*phthoras*). In 2 Peter 2:17-22 the teachers, after having escaped (*apophygontes*) the worldly defilements through the knowledge (*epignōsei*) of Christ, not only become slaves of corruption (*phthoras*) but also entice the weak with the lust (*en epithymiais*) of the flesh, promising them (*epaggellomenoi*) false freedom. The contrast is intentional. The false teachers were once believers who at one point apostatized. They once had known Jesus as their "Lord" and "Savior" (2 Pet 2:20) as well as the way of righteousness (2 Pet 2:21).[26] They were entrusted with the holy commandments (2 Pet 2:21) and had escaped the defilements of the world. But they got entangled once again and were overcome by them (2 Pet 2:20).

Peter condemns the apostates with harshness. First, likely citing Jesus' saying in Matthew 12:45, Peter declares that their state of apostasy is worse than the first state of ignorance (2 Pet 2:20-21). Second, citing well-known proverbs, he likens them to unclean animals according to Jewish understanding—a dog going back to its vomit (cf. Prov 26:11)—and a washed pig who returns to the mire. The images are strong and meant to evoke disgust.

Peter's open defamation of the opponents might be considered socially offensive according to modern notions of politeness. It is easy to credit passages like these to foreign and perhaps antiquated cultural norms and expectations. Some cultures, like my own Brazilian culture, are less apologetic about confronting these issues in preaching. But one's cultural sensitivities should not obfuscate the thrust of the passage. The harshness of the denunciations are grounded in a serious confrontation of sin and in the need to warn those who are on the verge of falling away. Living in a context marked by licentious hedonism, the community that does not take seriously the influence of such harmful

[25]This is likely related to some misappropriations of Paul's gospel of grace, as indicated in 2 Pet 3:15-16.

[26]Knowledge in 2 Peter always refers to the experience of the believer (2 Pet 1:2-3, 5-6, 8, 12).

patterns of behavior will find itself hosting them. Therefore, sin must be confronted, lest the damage be too great. Peter's injunction fulfills two simultaneous purposes: it denounces the opponents' wrongdoing so that it may be identified and shunned while at the same time warning his audience in no uncertain terms about the danger of apostatizing and its catastrophic results.[27]

2 PETER 3:1-7

Peter now begins the final section of his argument (2 Pet 3:1-18), marked by instructions and admonitions to the church. The section still deals with the opponents, but the focus now turns from their ethical misconduct to their faulty theology and worldview, which allows the apostle to teach his audience about eschatological events. By moving from ethics to theology, Peter indicates that as important as it is to confront sinful behavior, the issue is not only an ethical one. Rather, the origins and the internal logic of such misconduct lie in a deeper distortion of fundamental tenets of faith. Bad theology leads to bad behavior.

Peter situates his confrontation within the context of prior and ongoing revelation—the words of the prophets and the apostolic commandment. His task is not merely to prescribe personal opinions but to remind the audience of what has been announced by the prophets and apostles (cf. Eph 2:20; 3:5; cf. Lk 11:49). Warnings against the emergence of false teachers were part of both prophetic and apostolic discourse (Amos 9:10; Mal 2:17; Acts 20:29-31; 1 Jn 2:18; 2 Tim 3:1-9). The continuity between prophetic and apostolic warnings reflects the continuity of revelation in the old and new covenants. Therefore, Peter's warning comes with the backing of God's revelation throughout history.

The opponents' appearance is part of the eschatological time—"the last days" (2 Pet 3:3)—which in the understanding of the apostles has already begun (cf. 1 Cor 7:31; 10:11; 2 Cor 5:17). Before confronting their faulty theology, Peter once again emphasizes their sinful conduct: they will come "scoffing and indulging their own lusts" (cf. 2 Pet 2:10, 18). Their moral corruption is projected again as the backdrop of their erroneous worldview. What they think and how they act are codependent aspects of their corruption.

We are then told about the teachers' objection in their own voice, so to speak, as Peter quotes them: "Where is the promise of his coming?" (2 Pet 3:4). The teachers' ground for the objection is the apparent immutability of things. According to them, all things remain the same as they were since "the beginning of creation" (2 Pet 3:4).[28] The objection participates in the philosophical discussions regarding cosmology. The prevailing notion in Hellenism was that the cosmos remained unchanged. Stoics believed that the cosmos went through cycles of regeneration, always coming to its original form after a conflagration. Epicureans, in general, argued for the complete unchangeability in the universe.[29] The false teachers probably drew on these philosophical ideas but directed them more explicitly toward a denial of divine

---

[27]Despite the theological debate among different Christian traditions regarding the possibility of apostasy, from an exegetical standpoint, 2 Peter leaves no room for apostasy to be seen as hypothetical or phenomenological (contra Schreiner, *1, 2 Peter, Jude*, 364.) On the issue of predestination and apostasy in 2 Peter, see Charles, *Virtue Amidst Vice*, 159-74. Cf. also I. Howard Marshall, *Kept by the Power of God* (London: Epworth Press, 1969).

[28]The "fathers" mentioned in the passage is a typical way to refer to ancestors (Mt 23:30, 32; Lk 1:55, 72; 11:47; Jn 4:20; Acts 3:13; 5:30). Cf. Green, *Jude and 2 Peter*, 317-18.

[29]Green, *Jude and 2 Peter*, 318. For a similar idea within Hellenistic Judaism, see Philo *Aet.* 1:93.

intervention and judgment.[30] The irony, however, is that by acknowledging creation as the starting point of the universe, they conceded that divine action was effective at least in the origins of the cosmos.[31]

Peter builds on that premise to expose their flawed logic. Since they grant that creation was the starting point, Peter situates his cosmology in the account of Genesis, pointing out two elements as instrumental in the creation of the cosmos: the word of God and water. Both feature in Genesis, where creation is portrayed as the result of God's speech and his separation of the waters to reveal the dry land and the firmament (Gen 1:6-10). In the sequence, Peter again emphasizes the two elements, but now as the instruments of judgment against the ancient world in the deluge (2 Pet 3:6). The point of the repetition is to identify God's intervention in both creation and judgment. God, who created the world by his word and by water, exercised judgment over it by the very same means.

The climax of the refutation then comes in 2 Peter 3:7, in the announcement of final judgment. Now, water is substituted by fire as the main instrument of judgment, while the reference to the word of God is retained—heaven and earth are "reserved for fire" by "the same word." The idea of something being "reserved" denotes the preservation or saving of something for a future purpose (cf. Mt 6:19-20; 1 Cor 16:2) but is also used in the New Testament to refer to eschatological judgment (cf. Rom 2:5). The image reflects the concept of divine forbearance (cf. 2 Pet 3:8-10). God is not oblivious. His judgment will certainly be carried out, just as it was in prior stages of the history of the cosmos. The reason his judgment has not yet been manifested is his merciful patience.

Although cosmic conflagration is very much in view, the judgment of the cosmos is articulated in relation to God's judgment of the wicked (2 Pet 3:7). The ultimate focus is not on the utter destruction of creation itself but on the judgment of the ungodly, a thoroughly Jewish notion (Is 30:30; 66:15-16; Amos 7:4).[32] The reason Peter develops the idea of cosmic conflagration is precisely to refute the false teachers' logic of immutability. Their rationale is based on cosmology, and so Peter refutes their argument on their own terms. The word of God—which remains active throughout the different stages of the history of the cosmos—is bringing history to its climax. Therefore judgment, even from a cosmic perspective, is certain.

2 PETER 3:8-13

Since Peter's counterargument is that the very history of God's actions in the cosmos points to his final eschatological judgment, he has to address the apparent lack of signs of divine intervention. To do so, Peter reflects on God's perspective on time, an idea he derives from Psalm 90:4. The psalm reflects on the fact that in God's sight a thousand years are like a night watch, and both creation and human existence are but a transitory interval in comparison to God's eternity (Ps 90:2-6). The God of the psalmist is eternal, but his eternity does not mean he is aloof or uninvolved. On the contrary, the psalm goes on to affirm God's wrath toward and judgment on wickedness (Ps 90:7-11). The claims of the opponents in 2 Peter is a reversal of these truths. For them, the world is unchanging, and God's judgment is but a fable. Peter then deploys the psalm in a

---

[30]Jörg Frey, *The Letter of Jude and the Second Letter of Peter: A Theological Commentary* (Waco, TX: Baylor University Press, 2018), 384.

[31]A point rightly emphasized by Schreiner (*1, 2 Peter, Jude*, 374-76).

[32]Bauckham, *Jude, 2 Peter*, 299-301.

creative way, highlighting God's relationship with time to affirm the certainty of judgment.

In light of God's supremacy over time, a new perspective is required. What some count as "slowness"—a passive lack of response (cf. Lk 24:25; Jas 1:19)—is in fact God's "patience"—an active and intentional response by which God mercifully withholds his judgment in order to give people the opportunity to repent.[33] Although 2 Peter 3:9 often features in discussions regarding universalism, it is clear that Peter's statement has his particular audience in view—God is patient "with you"—and therefore assumes their status as believers. The emphasis falls on human response: God's desire is that "all to come to repentance." In his mercy, God keeps on exercising his patience so that people will respond to him. Thus, the emphasis on God's will to save is not a blanket statement about an unqualified universal salvation but a reflection on God's desire that those "who have received a faith" (2 Pet 1:1) will respond to him in faith.

Having established God's mercy, Peter goes back to God's judgment. In contrast to his patience, the day of the Lord will come suddenly, as a thief (2 Pet 3:10).[34] What follows is a vivid depiction of judgment that will involve various elements of the cosmos. The picture relies on the Hebrew cosmology derived from Genesis, where the Creator God puts order into the chaotic reality of the cosmos. He does that first by separating the waters and creating the expanse—a sort of structure around the earth to prevent the waters above from collapsing on the earth below, which God calls "Heaven" (Gen 1:6-8). Second, he gathers the waters below the heavens to form dry land, which God calls "Earth" (Gen 1:10). Later, in the fourth day, God puts luminaries in the expanse to rule over day and night (Gen 1:14-19).

Second Peter's apocalyptic scene engages the imagination by working with this fundamental cosmology. God's judgment unfolds in three stages. First, "the heavens will pass away with a roar" (au. trans.). The verb for "passing away" is often used in the New Testament to refer to the transitoriness of things, including "heaven and earth" (Mt 5:18; 24:34-35; Mk 13:30-31; cf. 2 Cor 5:17). With the onomatopoeic word "roar" (*rhoizēdon*), Peter paints a picture of a thunderous divine action that precipitates the dissipation of heaven.[35]

The next stage is the burning and destruction of the "heavenly bodies" (au. trans.). The meaning of the word for "heavenly bodies" is a subject of debate. Some interpreters point to the primordial elements—water, air, fire, and earth—which, according to ancient Greek cosmogony, constituted the universe.[36] This notion played an important part in the Stoic view of cosmic conflagration, whereby the universe would be dissolved in fire (the primal element) and reemerge in a recycled form. Alternatively, those who prioritize the Jewish apocalyptic background of 2 Peter see the term as a reference to the heavenly bodies, namely, the sun, moon, and stars.[37] As J. Dennis points out, it is possible that 2 Peter assumes the audience's familiarity with the popular Stoic cosmogony and may have used such a framework to communicate with them. However, the cataclysmic orientation of the scene emphasizing a climactic judgment and the creation of new heavens and

[33]The theme of divine forbearance can be found in texts like Ex 34:6; Neh 9:17; Joel 2:13.

[34]The reference follows the traditional sayings of Jesus (Mt 24:43-44; Lk 12:39-40; cf. 1 Thess 5:2; Rev 3:3; 16:15).

[35]Bauckham, *Jude, 2 Peter*, 315.

[36]Edward Adams, *The Stars Will Fall from Heaven: Cosmic Catastrophe in the New Testament and Its World*, Library of New Testament Studies 347 (London: T&T Clark, 2007), 216-20.

[37]The dissolution of the hosts of heaven in Is 34:4 is a possible source for this imagery. See Bauckham, *Jude, 2 Peter*, 316.

new earth is more clearly Jewish and is at odds with the Stoic idea of cyclical renewal of the world.[38] Therefore, the burning and destruction of the "heavenly bodies" is most likely in view.

The third stage is the exposure of "earth and everything that is done on it." The idea is conveyed through the verb translated as "will be found" (au. trans.). The interpretation of the word is notoriously difficult, which is reflected in the early scribal attempts to provide a more coherent alternative for it.[39] The word likely functions as a synonym for "being made manifest" (cf. 1 Cor 3:12-15).[40] The scene in 2 Peter describes a divine act of judgment that undoes the cosmic structures to expose the sinful works of the wicked on earth. Although cosmic dissolution is the means of judgment, the emphasis falls on the exposure of the works of men. The entire dissolution of the elements has as its purpose the judgment of the wicked. This judgment fosters Peter's appeal for his audience to live holy and godly lives (2 Pet 3:11). The pursuit of godliness emphasized in the beginning of the letter (2 Pet 1:3, 6-7) is now situated within the eschatological framework. A virtuous life in Peter's theological schema is fueled by the reality of God's intervention at the end times.

It is significant that Peter uses the negative concept of judgment to encourage the positive pursuit of holiness and godliness. In a culture that abhors the idea of hell and punishment, this sounds very counterintuitive to the modern ear. We much rather speak of love and grace as motivators for a godly life; and they certainly are. In fact, Peter has already reminded us that a virtuous life flows out of God's gracious benefaction (see commentary on 2 Pet 1:3-4). But for Peter, it is not incongruous to speak of gracious provision alongside eschatological judgment. The apostle reminds his readers that the reality of judgment exists in complete harmony with God's merciful character. God's forbearance is precisely the point at which his mercy and the inevitable reality of judgment meet. God is patient toward us to allow us to arrive at the place of repentance. But judgment tells us as much about the character of God as does his mercy. God is committed to bringing the created universe to a restored reality. And that certainly propels us to pursue a life that reflects his character.

In light of this, Peter encourages the faithful to be "waiting for and hastening" the day of the Lord (2 Pet 3:12). "Waiting" denotes eager expectation (Mt 11:3; Lk 1:21; 3:15; 12:46; Acts 3:5). The believers' posture in relation to the eschatological future is not passive but a pregnant anticipation for the future that informs the present. The idea of "hastening" the day works with the theme of God's forbearance in dynamic relationship. God patiently gives opportunity for repentance while the faithful hasten his return with their hope-filled godly living, all of which works together within God's sovereign timeline (cf. 2 Pet 3:8). Therefore, the posture of the church while Christ does not return is not at all passive; rather, it is one of meaningful expectancy and godly living

[38]John Dennis, "Cosmology in the Petrine Literature and Jude," in *Cosmology and New Testament Theology*, edited by Jonathan T. Pennington and Sean M. McDonough, Library of New Testament Studies 355 (London: T&T Clark, 2008), 175-76.

[39]Alternatives include "will not be found," "will be found when they are destroyed," "will disappear," and "will be consumed." The reading "will be found" has better witnesses supporting it and is also the variant that most easily explains the origins of the others. See Bruce M. Metzger, *A Textual Commentary on the Greek New Testament: A Companion Volume to the United Bible Societies' Greek New Testament*, 2nd ed. (London: United Bible Societies, 1971), 636.

[40]Cf. Mk 4:22; Jn 3:21. The second century document *2 Clement*, which seems to refer to 2 Peter or at least to a common tradition, substitutes the verb with "to appear" (*2 Clem.* 16:3). Wenham suggests that the idea of exposure stems from Jesus' eschatological teaching, when the Lord would return and "find" his servants (Mt 24:46; Mk 13:36; Lk 12:37-38). See David Wenham, "Being 'Found' on the Last Day: New Light on 2 Peter 3:10 and 2 Corinthians 5:3," *New Testament Studies* 33, no. 3 [1987]: 477-79.

which rest in the confidence of God's promise. The final scene in 2 Peter's apocalyptic drama does not disappoint. The promise will be fulfilled: a new heaven and new earth will inaugurate a new reality, and righteousness will overtake ungodliness (2 Pet 3:13).[41]

Waiting and hastening the day of the Lord reflects an eschatologically oriented lifestyle. In a complacent modern society, people often adopt a functionally cyclical worldview ("Things are always the same"; "What's the point?"). However, believers are to be infused with the hope that comes with the promise of Christ's return. This hope is the driving force behind ethical living and the pursuit of virtue. In the Brazilian charismatic context in which I grew up, the return of Christ has always been a central theological truth that encourages and motivates the Christian life. While this can sometimes develop into an unhealthy fearful spirituality, when biblically grounded, it does justice to the kind of biblical admonition we see in this text. In an important way, the godly life is grounded in the firm conviction that God will again intervene by judging the ungodly and restoring righteousness in the cosmos. We see, therefore, the paramount importance of eschatology. Far from a mere doctrine concerning the future, it infuses the present with meaning. It is a doctrine that the believers cannot afford to overlook; for without it, the church falls prey to erroneous thinking and ungodly living.

2 PETER 3:14-18

Closing the denunciation of the false teachers and also the letter as a whole, Peter offers his final remarks. The closing brings an appeal to holiness (2 Pet 3:14), a final warning about the error of the false teachers (2 Pet 3:15-18), and a doxology (2 Pet 3:18).

The appeal to holiness repeats the language of the previous section. In light of their eager expectation for the new heavens and new earth the believers are commanded to employ every effort "to be found . . . without spot or blemish." An obvious contrast is established with the opponents, who are "spots" and "blemishes" (2 Pet 2:13) and whose works will "be found" in judgment (2 Pet 3:10). As Peter already indicated (2 Pet 2:4-10), the judgment of the wicked and the preservation of the righteous are two complementary sides of the coming of Christ.

The believers are also to "regard the patience of our Lord as salvation" (2 Pet 3:15), recalling the theme of divine forbearance. The admonition comes substantiated by a reference to Paul's writings. The parenthetical comment has the twofold function of corroborating Peter's own teaching and exposing once again the false teachers, who employ erroneous interpretations of Paul's writings to support their views. Peter may be alluding to Paul's teaching on divine forbearance (cf. Rom 2:4; 9:22) to support his own. His mention of Paul, however, leads him to a broader comment on the relative complexity of Paul's writings, of which the opponents take advantage to lead others astray. Here, Peter must be thinking of Paul's teaching on grace, which was often twisted to support antinomian views and licentious living—a distortion that Paul himself sought to confront (cf. 1 Cor 6:9-20). The opponents are described as ignorant and unstable but also as lawless, which highlights their willfulness. In line with his condemnation of these attitudes previously in the letter, Peter restates that their actions will lead to their own destruction (2 Pet 3:16).

The audience is, therefore, alerted against their error and told instead to "grow in the

[41]On the permanence of the new reality after judgment is done, see Frey, *The Letter of Jude*, 418.

grace and knowledge of our Lord and Savior Jesus Christ" (2 Pet 3:18). The final instruction forms a neat *inclusio* with 2 Peter 1:1-2, where Peter's opening and salutation uses a similar Christological formula and affirms grace and peace being multiplied in the knowledge of Christ.

The letter then ends with a fitting doxology with an eschatological emphasis: "To him be the glory both now and to the day of eternity. Amen" (2 Pet 3:18). Throughout the letter, believers are called to live godly lives in the present, with awareness and expectation for the eschatological manifestation of Christ on the last day. Therefore appropriately, God is to be glorified both now in the godly living of his people and to the day of eternity, when he manifests his judgment and salvation.

BIBLIOGRAPHY

Adams, Edward. *The Stars Will Fall from Heaven: Cosmic Catastrophe in the New Testament and Its World.* Library of New Testament Studies 347. London: T&T Clark, 2007.

Bauckham, Richard. *Jude, 2 Peter.* Word Biblical Commentary. Grand Rapids, MI: Zondervan, 1983.

Charles, J. Daryl. "On Angels and Asses: The Moral Paradigm in 2 Peter 2." *Proceedings* 21 (2001): 1-12.

———. "The Language and Logic of Virtue in 2 Peter 1:5-7." *Bulletin for Biblical Research* 8 (1998): 55-73.

———. *Virtue Amidst Vice: The Catalog of Virtues in 2 Peter 1.* Sheffield, UK: Sheffield Academic Press, 1997.

Danker, Frederick W. "2 Peter 1: A Solemn Decree." *The Catholic Biblical Quarterly* 40, no. 1: 64-82.

Davids, Peter H. *The Letters of 2 Peter and Jude.* Pillar New Testament Commentary. Grand Rapids, MI: Eerdmans, 2006.

Dennis, John. "Cosmology in the Petrine Literature and Jude." In *Cosmology and New Testament Theology*, edited by Jonathan T. Pennington and Sean M. McDonough, 157-77. Library of New Testament Studies 355. London: T&T Clark, 2008.

Du Toit, Andreas B. "Vilification as a Pragmatic Device in Early Christian Epistolography." *Biblica* 75, no. 3 (1994): 403-12.

Frey, Jörg. *The Letter of Jude and the Second Letter of Peter: A Theological Commentary.* Waco, TX: Baylor University Press, 2018.

Green, Gene. *Jude and 2 Peter.* Baker Exegetical Commentary on the New Testament. Grand Rapids, MI: Baker, 2008.

Green, Michael. *Second Peter and Jude.* Tyndale New Testament Commentaries. Grand Rapids, MI: Eerdmans, 1987.

Marshall, I. Howard. *Kept by the Power of God.* London: Epworth Press, 1969.

Metzger, Bruce M. *A Textual Commentary on the Greek New Testament: A Companion Volume to the United Bible Societies' Greek New Testament.* 2nd ed. London: United Bible Societies, 1971.

Moo, Douglas J. *2 Peter, and Jude: From Biblical Text—to Contemporary Life.* Grand Rapids, MI: Zondervan, 1996.

Schreiner, Thomas R. *1, 2 Peter, Jude.* New American Commentary 37. Nashville: Broadman and Holman, 2003.

Starr, James M. *Sharers in Divine Nature: 2 Peter 1:4 in Its Hellenistic Context.* Stockholm: Almqvist & Wiksell, 2000.

Wenham, David. "Being 'Found' on the Last Day: New Light on 2 Peter 3:10 and 2 Corinthians 5:3." *New Testament Studies* 33, no. 3 (1987): 477-79.

LETTERS OF JOHN

Miguel G. Echevarría

INTRODUCTION

Church tradition has commonly attributed the short letters 1, 2, and 3 John to John the beloved disciple and brother of James (cf. Mk 1:19-20).[1] He is the same person credited with authoring the Gospel of John and Revelation. Over the past two centuries, however, scholars have questioned the authenticity of the letters and books ascribed to him, including the Johannine epistles.

The problem with accepting Johannine authorship of 1, 2, and 3 John is that the letters do not identify the author. The clearest evidence for authorship is the title "elder" assigned to the writer of 2 and 3 John. Though the letters are technically anonymous, early recipients of 1, 2, and 3 John likely knew John was the author. They were either acquainted with John personally or trusted witnesses who ascribed the letters to the beloved disciple.[2] That was enough for them. And it was enough for the majority of Christians until the rise of modernity.

Questions about the authenticity of John's epistles are not matters that most Latino/a readers wonder about. We usually don't open the Bible and ask questions about authorship, the kind associated with historical criticism.[3] We are more concerned about how God will use the text to speak into our daily struggles. So, we look to the Bible for hope, comfort, and guidance. Disputes about authorship are simply not a priority.

The matter is much different in the West, where historical criticism has had a heavy influence on how Christians approach the Scriptures. Even in evangelical circles there is the temptation to spend more time "behind the text," addressing critical issues of authorship and historical context, than devoting time to what the text actually says and how it speaks to readers. But we must concede that the influence of historical criticism has not remained isolated to places like Germany, England, and the United States—it has made inroads into Catholic and Protestant universities and seminaries in Latin America. Nevertheless, the influence on the region's general Christian population has been minimal.

For the sake of those who bring more critical questions to the text, we will address matters of authorship, dating, and historical setting.

Authorship. Some contend that one of John's pupils wrote the letters, or that a

[1]Colin G. Kruse, *Letters of John*, The Pillar New Testament Commentary (Grand Rapids, MI: Eerdmans, 2000), 14. Of the Johannine letters, the most disputed have been 2 and 3 John. One of the few resources that deals solely with the issues associated with these letters is Judith M. Lieu, *The Second and Third Epistles of John: History and Background* (Edinburgh: T&T Clark, 1986).

[2]Karen Jobes, *1, 2, and 3 John*, Exegetical Commentary on the New Testament (Grand Rapids, MI: Zondervan, 2016), 22.

[3]Samuel Escobar describes Latin America as a context that "never really doubted the authority of the word of God!" (David C. Kirkpatrick, *A Gospel for the Poor: Global Social Christianity and the Evangelical Left* [Philadelphia: University of Pennsylvania Press, 2019], 81.)

Johannine school wrote them,[4] or that the author resists identification, choosing the literary technique of anonymity.[5] While each of these theories has its own appeal, the following shows there is no convincing reason to question the authenticity of John's epistles.

First, the Johannine epistles bear many similarities to John's Gospel, such as the theme of "truth" (1 Jn 1:6; 2 Jn 4; 3 Jn 3; cf. Jn 3:21), the command to "love" (1 Jn 3:23; 2 Jn 5; cf. Jn 15:12), and eyewitness testimony about the "word" (1 Jn 1; cf. Jn 1:1, 14; 15:26, 27).[6] The similarities point to the common authorship of the Johannine epistles and the Gospel of John.

Second, all manuscripts assign authorship to John.[7] For those who doubt the importance of the manuscript evidence, Yarbrough argues, "If for some considerable period of time no one really knew, really, who wrote these letters as they circulated, and John represents a later guess, how likely is it that hundreds of copies, or at least the numerous lines of manuscript transmission that are reflected in the extant copies, all guessed the same person for just these three particular documents?"[8]

Third, Polycarp and his second-century contemporary Papias attest that John wrote the letters and Gospel bearing his name.[9] It is also significant that, as Jobes observes, "Polycarp and Papias lived in the greater vicinity in Ephesus in western Asia Minor, the location to which the apostle John is said to have fled at about the time when the Romans destroyed the Temple in Jerusalem, taking Mary the Mother of Jesus with him. There he presumably lived for the rest of his life."[10] Their proximity to John's home adds weight to their testimony.

Fourth, the Muratorian Canon (ca. 170–215 CE) notes John's authorship of the Gospel and letters attributed to him. As soon as the late second century, then, shortly after their composition, an early canon list recognizes the authenticity of these writings.

With these things in mind, we have reason to believe that John the beloved disciple wrote 1, 2, and 3 John. He is the same eyewitness to the ministry of Jesus who penned the Gospel of John and the elder mentioned in 2 and 3 John. Thus, I will refer to John as the author of the Johannine epistles—which is what the church has said all along, and Latino/a Christians have never really questioned.

Date. John's epistles were written between the years 90 and 100 CE,[11] following the composition of the Gospel of John. The readers of 1, 2, and 3 John would have been familiar with John's Gospel and would have heard echoes of his earlier work. In his letters, John could be more succinct with ideas that he expounds on in his earlier work, expecting that his audience would be familiar with them. Under that assumption, we will appeal to John's Gospel to bring clarity to select themes in his letters.[12]

[4]See discussions in Constantine R. Campbell, *1, 2, and 3 John*, Story of God Bible Commentary (Grand Rapids, MI: Zondervan, 2017), 4; Charles E. Hill, "1–3 John," in *A Biblical-Theological Introduction to the New Testament* (Wheaton, IL: Crossway, 2016), 486.

[5]Judith M. Lieu, *I, II, and III John: A Commentary*, The New Testament Library (Louisville, KY: Westminster John Knox, 2008), 6-9.

[6]Jobes provides a helpful chart of the similarities between the Gospel of John and 1 John (*1, 2, and 3 John*, 25-27).

[7]Robert W. Yarbrough, *1–3 John*, Baker Exegetical Commentary on the New Testament (Grand Rapids, MI: Baker Academic, 2008), 12.

[8]Yarbrough, *1–3 John*, 12.

[9]Papias's writings survive only in the works of Irenaeus and Eusebius.

[10]Jobes, *1, 2, and 3 John*, 22.

[11]Marianne Meye Thompson, *1–3 John*, The IVP New Testament Commentary Series (Downers Grove, IL: InterVarsity Press, 1992), 20-21.

[12]My methodology assumes that John's Gospel was written first, likely between 80–90 CE. John wrote 1, 2, and 3 John thereafter. That would allow him to allude to earlier material in his Gospel. For a discussion of the dating of the Gospel of John,

Historical setting. John spent his later years in Ephesus and likely ministered to the churches in the area.[13] Irenaeus (*Haer.* 3.1.1) and Eusebius (*Hist. eccl.* 3.23.1-4) note that John published his Gospel while a resident in Ephesus.[14] It is probable that he also wrote his letters there.[15]

With that in mind, some argue that 1, 2, and 3 John were written to combat the influences of Docetism or Gnosticism in Ephesus.[16] Both of these heresies share the error of devaluing the body or flesh, which was common among Hellenistic philosophies such as Platonism and Stoicism. But it is doubtful that full blown Docetism or Gnosticism were present in Asia Minor at the end of the first century. We should therefore read John's letters as an attempt to shepherd saints to stay within the bounds of orthodoxy rather than confront specific heresies.[17] This approach frees us to focus on how John describes sound teaching, which applies to all Christians throughout history, including modern readers, rather than reconstructing potential heresies that may (or may not) have threatened the churches to whom John ministered.

1 JOHN

In his first epistle, John instructs us about the importance of truth, love, and identifying false teachers. Of these, he spends the majority of the letter on love, encouraging believers to love God and neighbor. This is nothing new, of course. It's what Moses expected of God's people (Ex 20). What is new is that believers now have the promised Spirit, as the prophets anticipated, spurring us on to loving obedience.

Prologue (1 John 1:1-4). John opens his first letter by appealing to "what was from the beginning" (1 Jn 1:1). The referent for the pronoun "what" is not apparent in the immediate context. We must look to the prologue in John's Gospel, which begins with the similar phrase "in the beginning," clarifying that the referent is Jesus Christ (Jn 1:1-5).[18] The mention of the "beginning," found in both prologues, alludes to the creation account in Genesis 1. So, when mentioning the "word of life," John expects us to envision that Jesus is the creative agent with the Father, the one who brought all things into existence (1 Jn 1:1; cf. Gen 1:3, 6, 9, 11, etc.). This is the one whom John and his fellow apostles heard, saw, and touched (1 Jn 1:1).[19]

---

see D. A. Carson, *The Gospel According to John*, The Pillar New Testament Commentary (Grand Rapids, MI: Eerdmans, 1991), 81-86.

[13]Campbell, *1, 2, and 3 John*, 19.

[14]Jan van der Watt, *An Introduction to the Johannine Gospel and Letters* (London: T&T Clark, 2007), 124.

[15]Daniel Akin, *1, 2, 3 John*, The New American Commentary, vol. 38 (Nashville: Broadman & Holman, 2001), 27.

[16]Rudolph Bultmann's *The Johannine Epistles: A Commentary on the Johannine Epistles*, Hermeneia—A Critical and Historical Commentary on the Bible (Philadelphia: Fortress, 1973) is a prominent example of a work that argues that the Johannine epistles oppose Gnosticism.

[17]Jobes, *1, 2, and 3 John*, 24. The idea of a Johannine community behind 1, 2, 3 John, which has been proposed by Raymond E. Brown (*The Epistles of John*, AB 30 [New York: Doubleday, 1982], 3-146) and Wayne A Meeks, "The Man from Heaven in Johannine Sectarianism," *JBL* 91 [1972]: 44-72), has come under serious scrutiny. Whoever John's original readers were, it is not possible to reconstruct these churches with any degree of certainty, or limit them to one particular area, such as Ephesus. John may have intended his letters to be read beyond the area in which he ministered. We just don't know. This is another reason why my commentary focuses on John's description of orthodoxy, rather than attempting to reconstruct a message for a hypothetical original audience. See the helpful discussion in Toan Do, "The Epistles of John," in *The State of New Testament Studies*, ed. Scott McKnight and Nijay K. Gupta (Grand Rapids, MI: Baker Academic, 2019), 444-58.

[18]Campbell, *1, 2, and 3 John*, 22.

[19]John commonly uses the pronoun "we" to refer to apostolic testimony. Gary W. Derickson, *1, 2, and 3 John*, Evangelical Exegetical Commentary (Bellingham, WA: Lexham, 2014), 49-50.

John witnesses to the incarnation and resurrection of Jesus (1 Jn 1:2; cf. Jn 20).[20] John discloses this testimony so that we may have fellowship with the Father and the Son (1 Jn 1:3). By calling Jesus the Son, John brings to mind messianic expectations associated with 2 Samuel 7 and Psalm 2.[21] Having fellowship with the Son means we have the privilege of knowing the one who reigns over the cosmos. It would bring John great joy for us to accept his testimony, so that we might enjoy fellowship with the creator and lord of the universe (1 Jn 1:4).

But many Westerners tend to be critical of testimony. They want to see and touch things for themselves, lest they refuse to believe. This is typical of a scientific worldview. For my Cuban family, however, the testimony of our elders was not questioned. They had left Cuba and learned to thrive in the strange land of the United States. What they saw and experienced gave them credibility. So, when our elders spoke, we listened. I believe John expects the same posture from his readers. He is, after all, our "elder" (2 Jn 1), who has seen the very Son of God.

God as light (1 John 1:5). After establishing his credibility, John presents the fundamental statement on which he bases his instruction: "God is light and in him there is no darkness at all" (1 Jn 1:5). Though there are parallels with Qumran thought, John's Jewish heritage suggests that his primary source for understanding God as "light" is the Old Testament.[22] David, for instance, notes that God's spiritual light removes darkness (2 Sam 22:9). Job often compares God's light to darkness (Job 22:8; 29:3). Micah confesses that though "I sit in darkness, the Lord will be a light" (Mic 7:8). Like these, there are scores of other examples throughout the Old Testament, such as the Psalms, Proverbs, and Isaiah, which describe God as light in comparison to darkness. What is common among them is that light is associated with God as the epitome of truth and holiness.

John's Gospel shifts the spotlight on Jesus, identifying him as the light, often in contrast to darkness.[23] For instance, in John 8:12 Jesus says, "I am the light of the world. Whoever follows me will never walk in darkness but will have the light of life." And in John 12:35, he says, "The light is in you for a little longer. Walk while you have the light, so that the darkness may not overtake you. If you walk in the darkness, you do not know where you are going." As the one sent into the world, Jesus is the representation of the Father (Jn 4:14; 8:19; 12:45). So, it is through Jesus that we come to know God as "light."

John's use of light sets the standard for truth for the remainder of the epistle. What we know about orthodoxy has its basis in the fact that "God is light," a truth we have come to know through Jesus Christ.

---

[20]Bruce G. Schuchard, *1-3 John*, Concordia Commentary (Saint Louis: Concordia, 2012), 89; Stephen S. Smalley, *1, 2, and 3 John*, Word Biblical Commentary 51 (Waco, TX: Word, 1984), 19. Matthew D. Jenson, *Affirming the Resurrection of the Risen Christ*, Society for New Testament Monograph Series 153 (Cambridge: Cambridge University, 2012), 25.

[21]Jobes, *1, 2, and 3 John*, 53.

[22]The vocabulary of "light" and "darkness" is common enough in DSS documents such as 1QM 1:5; 13:1-5. The vocabulary of "doing the truth" in 1 Jn 1:6 is similar to 1QS 1:5, 5:3, 8:2. Bultmann connects the Johannine vocabulary of "light," "darkness," and "truth" to Gnosticism. "This was understandable," as Smith argues, "since many terms common in the Gospel and Epistle of John were used by gnostic Christians—not only 'word,' 'truth,' and 'life,' but 'light,' 'darkness,' and 'world,' not to mention the verb 'to know,' *ginōskein*, from which gnosticism is derived (*First, Second, and Third John*, Interpretation [Louisville, KY: John Knox, 1991], 49). See Bultmann, *The Johannine Epistles*; "γινώσκω," in *TDNT*, ed. Gerhard Kittel, trans. Geoffrey Bromiley (Grand Rapids, MI: Eerdmans, 1967), 1:689-719. See also his discussion of Gnosticism in relation to John's Gospel in *The Gospel of John: A Commentary*, trans. G. R. Beasley-Murray, The Johannine Monograph Series (Eugene, OR: Wipf & Stock, 2014), 7-9. Yarbrough notes God's association with "light" in the Old Testament (*1–3 John*, 48-49).

[23]The Gospel of John identifies Jesus as light on twenty-three occasions.

Light and darkness (1 John 1:6-10). John now informs us about the characteristics of those who live in "darkness" and those who live in the "light" (1 Jn 1:6-10). The former claim to "have fellowship" with God but are "liars" who live out of step with the "truth" (1 Jn 1:6). Even more audacious is that they claim to have no sin (1 Jn 1:8). By denying the need for forgiveness of sin, they make God out to be a liar, for they reject the very reason why he sent Jesus into the world (1 Jn 1:10; cf. Jn 3:16; Rom 5:8; Gal 1:4; 1 Pet 2:24). If we believe this error, then John speaks of us—we are those who do not know the truth of God's word (1 Jn 1:10).[24]

Those living in the light, on the other hand, have fellowship with God and other believers (1 Jn 1:7). They understand that they need to be cleansed of their sins through the blood of Jesus Christ, God's very Son (1 Jn 1:7). And they confess their sins and find that God is righteous to forgive them (1 Jn 1:9). God's people, of course, have always seen their need for forgiveness through the shedding of blood (Heb 9:22). Under the old covenant, believers' sins were cleansed through the blood of a chosen sacrifice (Ex 30:10; Lev 16:15-19). Now under the new covenant, the blood of Jesus removes the guilt and penalty of our sins once and for all, assuring that we will dwell in God's marvelous light.[25]

Those living in "darkness" do not understand this truth. Perhaps they would benefit from a trip to Latin American countries like Cuba and Venezuela, where power outages, and thereby darkness, are a part of life. People in these countries know that darkness hinders them from seeing where they are going, like when the city lights go out as they are driving, and everything is suddenly pitch dark. It becomes difficult to discern where they are headed, endangering their lives. So, they appreciate the light. In like manner, the darkness blinds us to the fact that we are headed toward destruction, only of a more permanent kind. What we need is the light of God's truth, which illumines our way, revealing our need for forgiveness.

Jesus' death for (all) sinners (1 John 2:1-2). Addressing the realities of sin may have a bludgeoning effect on readers. So, John shifts his tone, addressing us with the affectionate designation "my little children" as he prepares to mention a major purpose for his instruction: "that you may not sin" (1 Jn 2:1). This includes all the ways that sin is possible, such as denying the need for forgiveness.[26]

Although disobedience is never condoned, John understands the reality of living in a sinful world—we will be tempted to sin. And when we do, we have the assurance that Jesus is our "advocate" (*paraclete*) before the Father (1 Jn 2:1).[27] In John's Gospel, *paraclete* refers to the Holy Spirit, who "helps" and is "with" believers (Jn 14:6; cf. Jn 15:26; 16:7-11). In 1 John 2:2, the term applies to Jesus. Jobes remarks, "Although the Spirit is also a paraclete, it is the unique status of Jesus as the atoning sacrifice for sin (see 2:2) that is the basis of his advocacy for sinners, which therefore provides consolation for anyone who sins."[28]

In addition to his role as *paraclete*, Jesus is also the *hilasmos* for our sins (1 Jn 2:2). Interpreters argue whether to translate *hilasmos* as "propitiation" or "expiation." Campbell provides

[24]Jobes, *1, 2, and 3 John*, 72.

[25]See discussion in Campbell, *1, 2, and 3 John*, 38-39.

[26]Jobes, *1, 2, and 3 John*, 77.

[27]In other places in the letter, John uses "we" for apostolic witness (1 Jn 1:4). His use of the pronoun in 1 Jn 2:1 includes himself in the Christian body as a beneficiary of Jesus' advocacy before the Father.

[28]Jobes, *1, 2, and 3 John*, 79.

helpful definitions for these terms: "*Propitiation* refers to the aversion of wrath such that God's wrath is redirected *away* from sinful humanity and *toward* a sacrificial victim. *Expiation* is the removal of guilt so that the offense of humanity's guilt is expunged."[29] But do we really have to choose one or the other? Could *hilasmos* communicate both propitiation and expiation?

Perhaps the confusion lies in that most commentaries have been written from a post-Enlightenment Western European/North American approach to the Scriptures, which often forces the reader into a false "either-or" binary.[30] Written from this perspective, commentators work under the assumption that *hilasmos* must mean either propitiation or expiation. But John is not a Western scholar, nor is he writing after the Enlightenment—he is a first-century Jew whose worldview is flexible enough to handle how God can use words to signify more than one thing. We have already seen how elastically he uses "what was from the beginning" to bring to mind both John 1 and Genesis 1 (1 Jn 1). So, let's not impose a binary that would have been foreign to John. We should envision that he uses *hilasmos* to signify that Jesus is the sacrifice that averts God's wrath away from us and toward him (propitiation) and also removes our guilt (expiation).

Although arguments for limited atonement restrict Jesus' *hilasmos* to the elect, we should note that this does not square with the assertion that Jesus' death was "of the whole world [*kosmos*]" (1 Jn 2:2). John's use of the word *kosmos* lends itself to a cosmic view of the atonement.[31] So what he argues is that no one in the entire world, regardless of their ethnicity, language, or culture, is beyond the scope of Jesus' propitiatory and expiatory death.

Keeping the commands (1 John 2:3-6). After all the talk of atonement, we would anticipate John saying that our status before God rests on nothing but Jesus. But he doesn't. He says it depends on keeping God's "commands" (1 Jn 2:3), which is synonymous with keeping his "word" (1 Jn 2:5; cf. Jn 14:21-24).[32] First John 3:23 provides an initial explanation of what John means by "commands." In this verse, he clarifies that keeping God's commands is equivalent to "believing in the name of the Son Jesus Christ" and "loving one another."[33] John grounds our assurance in the twofold obedience that prophets like Ezekiel and Jeremiah expected of God's people (Ezek 36–37; Jer 31), which fulfills the Mosaic law (Ex 20; cf. Gal 5:14).

While he affirms that believing in Jesus fulfills the command to love God, we should keep in mind that John's reference to the "commands" also includes loving fellow believers (1 Jn 3:23). So, our confidence before God not only depends on believing all the right things about Jesus, like his death for sinners. It also involves loving fellow brothers and sisters. That's the true test of whether we really know God or are lying about our faith (1 Jn 2:4).

Commands old and new (1 John 2:7-11). John puts to rest any doubts about the authority of his instruction in 1 John 2:3-6, arguing that it

---

[29]Campbell, *1, 2, and 3 John*, 50. Moisés Silva summarizes, "In short, propitiation appeases the offended person, whereas expiation is concerned with nullifying the offensive act" ("ἱλάσκομαι," in *NIDNTTE* [Grand Rapids, MI: Zondervan, 2014], 2:534).

[30]Thomas B. Slater, "1–3 John," in *True to Our Native Land: An African American New Testament Commentary*, ed. Brian K. Blount (Minneapolis: Fortress, 2007), 503.

[31]To argue that *kosmos* refers to a particular group of people is outside the semantic use of the word. BDAG restricts the relevant uses of *kosmos* to (1) "the world, the orderly universe"; (2) "the sum total of all beings above the level of animals, the world"; (3) "planet earth as a place of inhabitation, the world"; (4) "humanity in general, the world"; (5) "the system of human existence in its many aspects, the world"; (6) "collective aspect of an entity, totality, sum total" (561-63). Consequently, the argument for limited atonement must come from outside this passage.

[32]See Smalley, *1, 2, 3 John*, 48.

[33]Lieu, *I, II, and III John*, 69; Jobes, *1, 2, and 3 John*, 83.

is based on "an old commandment" that believers "have had from the beginning" (1 Jn 2:7). The "old commandment" refers to the exhortation to love God and neighbor in the Ten Words or Ten Commands God gave to Moses (Ex 34:28; Deut 10:4).[34] These are the central mandates under the Old Covenant (Deut 6:5).[35]

His instruction, though, is also based on "a new commandment" (1 Jn 2:8). We should not think it strange that John's teaching is both old and new, as if he must choose one or the other. John does not operate in the world of neat binaries. So, he grounds his teaching in what is old, in the sense that it is rooted in the old covenant, and what is new, in the sense that it is rooted in the arrival of Jesus.[36] While there is continuity with God's revelation to Israel, John's apostolic instruction marks a shift to the new covenant age associated with the light, which causes the previous age of darkness to pass away (1 Jn 2:8). Although Israel failed to keep the commands, we have the clear example of Jesus, who modeled what it means to "Love the Lord your God with all your heart. . . . Love your neighbor as yourself" (Mt 22:37-40).

John also teaches that those who claim to be "in the light" but "hate" other believers live "in the darkness" (1 Jn 2:9-11). On this topic, John has no room for both/and reasoning. He's very direct: we live either in light or darkness. We cannot abide in both realms. The test of whether we dwell in the light is whether we love other believers. If we don't, we dwell in darkness.

John's use of "hate" demands our added attention. Christians who practice hate toward other believers contradict the very faith they claim to practice, the one that calls us to love those we deem (for whatever reason) unlovable. Perhaps we struggle to love believers of different races and ethnicities. Perhaps we struggle to love believers of different theological persuasions. Maybe we have trouble loving believers of different political parties. Whatever our reasons for holding on to hate, the moment we trust in Jesus, we now step into the light that reveals we are to express the love that people such as Moses and John expected of God's people (cf. Lev 19:17; Jas 2). Consequently, we must put away all our former excuses for hating others, which are uncharacteristic of Jesus' followers. If we fail to do so, despite how difficult it may be to put aside long seeded resentment, we must come to grips with the possibility that we may reside in the realm of darkness.

Victory over the world (1 John 2:12-17). With hate so prevalent, it is difficult to envision that the present age is passing away. Yet John reassures us of our victory over sin and the evil one, Satan (1 Jn 2:13). We indeed know the Father and his "word," which calls us to love God and others (1 Jn 2:14). So, our victory is secure.

As we await our triumph, we are not to love this fleeting world (1 Jn 2:15-17). John uses "world" to refer to "sinful humanity in opposition to God." He uses it similarly in his farewell discourse, where he recognizes the world's hostility toward him and his followers (Jn 14:1-17:26).[37] Those who belong to the world are dominated by sinful urges such as the "desire of the flesh," the "desire of the eyes," and the "pride in riches" (1 Jn 2:16).[38] If we are

[34]Jobes, *1, 2, and 3 John*, 95.

[35]Peter Leithart's *The Ten Commandments: A Guide to the Perfect Law of Liberty*, Christian Essentials (Bellingham, WA: Lexham, 2020) provides an exemplary Christian reading of the Ten Commandments.

[36]Jobes, *1, 2, and 3 John*, 95.

[37]Campbell, *1, 2, and 3 John*, 82; N. H. Cassem, "A Grammatical and Contextual Inventory of the Use of κόσμος in the Johannine Corpus with Some Implications for Johannine Cosmic Theology," *NTS* 19 (1972): 91.

[38]George Strecker, *The Johannine Letters: A Commentary on 1, 2, and 3 John*, Hermeneia—A Critical and Historical Commentary on the Bible (Minneapolis: Fortress, 1996), 58-59.

known by such vices, we show that we are being overcome by the world. As believers, we should always be recognized by our love for God and others—displaying the values that will outlive the present age (1 Jn 2:17).

Beware of antichrists (1 John 2:18-27). John begins a new section by addressing us as "children" (1 Jn 2:18; cf. 2:1). Since this is the second time he addresses us as such, we should note the way persons of color feel when the term is spoken in their direction—it reeks of paternalism. We catch a whiff of this odor even when others think there is nothing in the air. It carries the scent of condescension and superiority. We have to remind ourselves that this is not John's intention. He uses the term positively, calling us "children" in the sense that we are "open to instruction" (cf. Mt 18:3).[39]

With that settled, we can once more listen to John's teaching. He warns us that it is the "last hour" (1 Jn 2:18), which is parallel to saying it is the "last days."[40] This period describes the current, temporal situation of believers—we live in between the passing of the old age of darkness and the arrival of the new age of light. With every second, the old age is one step closer to fading away.

Yet we still feel the effects of darkness in this "last hour." Daniel envisions the "last hour" as a time the evil one will attempt to deceive God's people (e.g., Dan 11).[41] His expectation is coming to fruition in John's warning that antichrists are present in the church (1 Jn 2:18). While popular books and movies point to a singular figure, John acknowledges that there are "many antichrists" who have departed from the faithful (1 Jn 2:18-19). These persons make it their aim to deceive believers, denying that Jesus is the Christ, the Son of God (1 Jn 2:22, 23, 26).

Their denial is akin to the ancient heresy called Docetism, which is associated with Gnosticism and holds that Jesus only seemed to be human but never put on flesh.[42] And if he was not human, he is not David's physical descendant and cannot be the promised Messiah and God's Son (2 Sam 7; Ps 2). Promoting a disembodied Jesus is tantamount to rejecting him, which is also a rejection of the Father, placing antichrists outside the community of believers (1 Jn 2:23). Though they were once part of the church, their departure from orthodoxy reveals that they were never really among the faithful (1 Jn 2:19).

Despite the false teachings of antichrists, Jesus' followers accept his humanity—because we have the "anointing" from the Holy One, which "remains" in us and "teaches" us (1 Jn 2:20, 27). The farewell discourse in John's Gospel discloses that the anointing is the "Holy Spirit," who teaches his followers "all things," protecting us from deception (Jn 14:25-26).[43] In the case of 1 John, the Holy Spirit protects us from succumbing to the false teachings of antichrists, who deny Jesus' humanity.

Thus far, 1 John 1–2 has warned us about the consequences of hating brothers and sisters and denying the physical nature of Jesus. As I see it, the problem stems from a worldview that values what is spiritual over what is bodily (or physical). When we abandon the importance of the body, especially the incarnation of

---

[39]See BDAG, "παιδίον," 749.

[40]John uses "last day" in his Gospel (Jn 6:39-40, 44, 54; etc.). "Last days" is found in Acts 2:17; 2 Tim 3:1; Heb 1:2; Jas 5:3; 2 Pet 3:3.

[41]G. K. Beale, "The Old Testament Background of the 'Last Hour,' in John 2,18," *Bib* 92 (2009): 254.

[42]Smith, *First, Second, and Third John*, 74.

[43]Slater, "1–3 John," 507. D. A. Carson, "1 John," in *Commentary on the New Testament Use of the Old Testament*, ed. G. K. Beale and D. A. Carson (Grand Rapids, MI: Baker, 2007), 1065-67, argues that the anointing of the Holy Spirit is a fulfillment of the new covenant promise of Jer 31.

Jesus, we lose the importance of ethics.[44] If a soul or spirit is all that matters, then there is no reason to treat flesh and blood brothers and sisters with the respect and dignity they deserve. Though John does not address a particular heresy, the ideas he opposes were the seedbed of post-second century Gnosticism—which denies the importance of embodiment and, as a result, has no reason for treating others ethically.

And if we haven't noticed, Gnosticism has not gone anywhere. We hear it on the lips of people who claim that Jesus only came to save souls into heaven—with no regard for how salvation effects embodied lives in the present. Or those who say, "Just preach the gospel!"—as if the good news encompassed no social concern. Latino theologians such as C. René Padilla and Samuel Escobar have long argued against such a disembodied gospel, contending that the preaching of Jesus provides hope for the poor and oppressed (Mt 5:5; Lk 4:18-19).[45]

And since the arrival of Jesus marks the inbreaking of the coming age, the Spirit is the one who influences believers to love others tangibly, which includes things such as standing against racism, treating immigrants with dignity, and protecting women and children from abuse (1 Jn 2:8, 20, 27). We cannot reduce the preaching of Jesus to the deliverance of souls into a future spiritual realm. Jesus cares about more than that—he cares about seeing whole people, body and soul, experience love and acceptance in the here and now, even as the darkness has not yet faded away. Having the anointing of the Spirit compels us to follow the example of our savior, who ministered in full humanity, fulfilling what it means to love God and neighbor.

Evidence of new birth (1 John 2:28–3:10). In this new section, John exhorts us to "abide in him," so as to have "confidence" and not be "put to shame" at Jesus' coming (1 Jn 2:28).[46] As he promises in his farewell discourse, Jesus will return for his people (Jn 14:18). If we "abide in him," continuing in our love for God and others, we will rejoice to see our savior (1 Jn 2:28).

Living this way displays that we have been "born of God" (1 Jn 2:29). The metaphor of new birth alludes to John's Gospel, where Jesus instructs Nicodemus to be "born again," that is, to experience spiritual rebirth (1 Jn 3:1-8).[47] This account, in turn, alludes to Ezekiel's promise that God will place his Spirit within his people, cleansing them of their sins and enabling them to obey his commands (Ezek 36:25-27). These intertextual connections shed light on the significance of being "born of God": that the Spirit gives us new life and enables us to live righteously in lieu of Christ's return (cf. 1 Jn 2:20, 27).

But we should not think that our righteous living will lead to acceptance from a world that

[44]Although he focuses on Paul, Douglas A. Campbell provides a helpful, albeit brief, discussion on the connection between disembodiment and loss of ethics (*Pauline Dogmatics: The Triumph of God's Love* [Grand Rapids, MI: Eerdmans, 2020], 585).

[45]See, for instance, C. René Padilla, *Misión integral: Ensayos sobre la iglesia y el reino* (Grand Rapids, MI: Eerdmans, 1986). The English version is available under the title *Mission Between the Times: Essays on the Kingdom* (Grand Rapids, MI: Eerdmans, 1985). See also Samuel Escobar's *In Search of Christ in Latin America: From Colonial Image to Liberating Savior* (Downers Grove, IL: InterVarsity Press, 2019). This work discusses his views on the work of Christ as well as other prominent Latin American voices. Kirkpatrick's *Gospel for the Poor* makes the case that, since the 1960s and 1970s, prominent Latino/a theologians have been advocating a gospel that includes social concern for the poor and oppressed, despite the fact that many North American pastors and theologians dismissed their teachings.

[46]Several commentators, such as Lieu (*I, II, and III John*, 112-16) and Jobes (*1, 2, and 3 John*, 132-33), take 1 Jn 2:28 as the concluding statement of the previous section. I see 1 Jn 2:28 as the start of a new section, which is consistent with the way John uses vocatives, in this case *teknia*, to begin new, but related, instruction (cf. 1 Jn 2:1, 7, 18, etc.).

[47]Campbell, *1, 2, and 3 John*, 101.

does not know God, that is, one that has not been reborn (1 Jn 3:1). We should expect that their "rejection of God will result in a rejection of his disciples,"[48] which is a consistent message in John's writings (Jn 15:18–16:4). We are to fix our eyes on Jesus, not the world's approval, anticipating the time when we are "made like him" (1 Jn 3:2). When this happens, we will bear the character of our heavenly Father.[49] This eschatological hope should motivate us to live holy lives in the present (i.e., "sanctify ourselves"; 1 Jn 3:3).

If our lives are characterized by "sin," we instead reveal our affinity for "lawlessness" (1 Jn 3:4). Jobes argues that "lawlessness" should be understood in view of covenant passages such as Leviticus 26:42, which reveal a disdain for "the very idea of a law to which one must submit."[50] To sin, then, reveals a disdain for God's commandments. We should never be known for what Jesus died to take away (1 Jn 3:5; cf. Is 53). If we are, we reveal that we really "do not know" God (1 Jn 3:6) and are worthy of eschatological punishment (1 Jn 2:28).[51]

John leaves no middle ground: We either belong to God or the devil (1 Jn 3:7-10). The litmus test for whether we belong to God's family is whether we love both God and neighbor. So, if we claim to love Jesus but are in the habit of telling people from places like Mexico, Guatemala, and Syria to "go home," despite that many of them are faithful followers of Jesus, we should examine our familial allegiance.

Loving everyone (1 John 3:11-19). John contends that the person who lacks love is nothing short of evil. He uses the example of Cain, who resented his brother's righteous deeds and murdered him (1 Jn 3:12). Hence, our actions demonstrate our true nature.

Believers are not like Cain. We are like righteous Abel. So, we should not be surprised when the world hates us—as Cain hated Abel (1 Jn 3:12-13). But we cannot let this deter us from loving those who treat us with contempt. Even unbelievers love those who love them (Lk 6:32-38). The true test of whether we have crossed from "death to life" is how well we love even the most difficult people (1 Jn 3:14).

I can speak of how difficult this is for many Christians of color. We are sometimes taken aback when a person quotes doctrinal statements like the Westminster Shorter Catechism and the 1689 London Baptist Confession but slander us for promoting racial reconciliation and social justice, accusing us of teaching critical theories or cultural Marxism. If they honestly evaluated our works, they would know that we are trying to obey Scripture's call to love our neighbor—which is the very thing John expects of us. Our social concern is rooted in the Bible, not secular teachings.[52] While it is difficult to love those who malign us, we must not succumb to hate. We must ask the Spirit to empower us to follow the example of Jesus, who showed us what true love looks like in "laying down his life" (1 Jn 3:16; Jn 10:11, 15, 18).[53]

Lieu gives us some clarity on what it means to "lay down our lives." She argues that this phrase is used in Greek literature to mean "to take a risk, to hazard one's life rather than

[48]Smalley, *1, 2, 3 John*, 142.

[49]See Jobes, *1, 2, and 3 John*, 142.

[50]Jobes, *1, 2, and 3 John*, 143.

[51]Yarbrough (*1-3 John*, 181), Lieu (*I, II, and III John*, 128), and Strecker (*Johannine Letters*, 94-95) also note that eschatological punishment is in view.

[52]I am not arguing that Christians should not interact with critical theories. I am simply saying that, for many minorities, myself included, the concern for racial justice and reconciliation is rooted in the Bible.

[53]This does not mean that we condone abuse or racist remarks. The context will clarify what our love should resemble.

actually sacrifice it: to put oneself on the line."[54] And this is exactly what believers do—we risk what we possess to provide for others (1 Jn 3:17). This expectation is grounded in the Old Covenant's call to provide for destitute community members (Lev 23:22; 25:35).[55] As Jesus gave his life for us, we should be prepared to do the same for others. Watching someone die for lack of food, shelter, or clothing—and offering no assistance from our supply—is tantamount to committing murder; it means we are no different from Cain (1 Jn 3:15).[56] And what better testimony to God's love than when we do this for someone who has maligned us. Is this not what Jesus did, when he gave his life for his enemies (Rom 5:8)? While it goes against the world's expectations, it is "in this" that we reveal we are "from the truth," which is another way of saying that we are "from God" (1 Jn 3:19).[57]

Assurance for our doubt (1 John 3:19-24). Despite their love for others, some Christians doubt their standing before God, experiencing "condemnation" in their "hearts" (1 Jn 3:20).[58] This is a constant danger for believers who take seriously the call to love our brothers and sisters. What we soon discover is that we can never help enough—there is always one more hungry mouth, one more person who needs employment, and one more single mother who needs help paying bills. Believers may feel convicted of their inadequacy to meet every need and are weighed down with guilt.

When we sense such conviction, John assures us that "God is greater" than our condemnation and "knows everything" (1 Jn 3:20). He knows that our obedience comes from a regenerate heart, seeking to love others as Jesus has loved us (1 Jn 2:16). And he knows that only he can supply every need. So, we seek to love others, as best as we can, knowing that God is more than capable of providing for our struggling neighbors.

Some Christians love their neighbors as they are able, but their "hearts do not condemn" them and have "boldness" of their standing "before God" (1 Jn 3:21). And that's just fine. But for those who struggle with guilt, we should pray that the Spirit might flood our minds with the truth. No sense of doubt can change the fact that we are God's children.

Since our status is secure, we can approach God in prayer, confident that we will receive "whatever we ask" (1 Jn 3:22; cf. Jn 14:14; 15:16; 16:23). John does not insinuate that God will grant our every wish. In 1 John 5:14, he explains that believers will receive "whatever is in accordance with his will." And in the remainder of 1 John 3:22, he clarifies why we

---

[54]Lieu, *I, II, and III John*, 149.

[55]J. Richard Middleton, *A New Heaven and a New Earth: Reclaiming Biblical Eschatology* (Grand Rapids, MI: Baker Academic, 2014), 88.

[56]Jobes, *1, 2, and 3 John*, 159.

[57]The phrase *kai en toutō* ("and in this") could refer to what precedes or what follows. Taking the phrase with what follows disconnects 1 Jn 3:18 from the previous context, which seems unlikely, given that καί marks a connection between the closely related contexts in 1 Jn 3:13-18 and 1 Jn 3:19-21. See Steven Runge, *A Discourse Grammar of the Greek New Testament: A Practical Guide for Teaching and Exegesis*, Lexham Bible Reference Series (Bellingham, WA: Lexham, 2010), 24-26.

[58]Jobes (*1, 2, and 3 John*, 166-67) is right to point out the difficulty in making sense of the *hoti* at the beginning of 1 Jn 3:20. Was it originally intended as two words (*ho ti*, "in that which") or as it reads in the NA28 and UBS5 (*hoti*, "for")? The problem is compounded by the fact that the *hoti* at the inception of the second clause seems grammatically unnecessary if we take the second option. Perhaps for this reason Codex A and several minuscules (33. 436. 642. 234) omit the second *hoti*. If we choose the first option, we can render 1 Jn 3:19-20 as "and we put our hearts at ease before him *in that which* our hearts convicts us, *for* God is greater than our heart and knows all things." If we choose the second option, we can translate the verses as "and we put our hearts at ease before him, *for* whenever our hearts convict us, we know that God is greater than our heart and knows all things." The confusion is evidenced in some of the major translations such as the NIV, ESV, and NRSV. Regardless of our choice, the main idea is still clear: God knows how much we love our brothers and sisters, so we can stand before him with confidence.

have such confidence: "for we keep God's commands and do what is pleasing before him" (au. trans.).[59] We can argue, then, that God grants "whatever we ask" in keeping with his "will," which is summed up in the commands to which John has already referred: love of God and neighbor (1 Jn 2:7-11; 3:13-19).

These commands reappear in 1 John 3:23, where John mentions the command to "believe in the name of his Son Jesus Christ and love one another." Where we would normally expect "God," John supplies the name of Jesus (cf. Deut 6:4; Ex 20). This move reflects the high Christology throughout John's writings, which communicate the importance of worshiping Jesus as God (e.g., Jn 1:1-4; 1 Jn 1:1-4; Rev 5:1-14; 19:1-8).

John now initiates a transition to the following chapters, arguing that the Spirit enables us to "obey his commandments" (1 Jn 3:24). We must keep in mind that the commands emphasize right belief and right practice, that is, orthodoxy and orthopraxy. What we believe about Jesus will coincide with how we treat others—they are like two sides of the same coin. John expounds further on the Spirit's relationship to the "commands" in the remaining chapters.

Testing the Spirits (1 John 4:1-6). John notes that the Spirit influences what we proclaim about Jesus. In Latino/a congregations, the Spirit plays a vital role, especially in Pentecostal and Charismatic contexts. Congregants depend on the Spirit to provide for the needs of the church, to supply a word of prophecy, and to heal the sick, not unlike what we see in Acts. Yet, some ministers invoke the Spirit's name so that no one may question their "inspired speech," which is sometimes nothing more than false teaching about Jesus. While the reliance on the Spirit is healthy, we must be aware of abuses. That's why John calls us to "test the spirits [*pneumata*]" (1 Jn 4:1).

John's use of the plural *pneumata* is significant. He could have used the singular form *pneuma*, which may refer to "wind," "life-giving breath," "human personality," "human spirit," or "Holy Spirit."[60] That he uses the plural suggests he has "angels" or "demons" in mind.[61] Of the possible referents, demons are most likely the spirits mentioned here.[62] Thus, some who claim to speak from the Holy Spirit actually speak from demonic spirits. These are "false prophets [who] have gone out into the world" to deceive us into believing heterodox teachings about Jesus Christ (1 Jn 4:1).

We know that a person's teaching is sourced in "the Spirit of God" if they confess "that Jesus Christ has come in the flesh" (1 Jn 4:2). This is like the earlier emphasis on believing that Jesus is the Christ, the promised physical descendant of David (1 Jn 2:22; cf. 2 Sam 7; Ps 2). Someone who truly speaks from the Spirit confesses that Jesus took on full humanity—performing genuine miracles, making atonement for sins, and rising bodily from the grave.[63] The Holy Spirit would never lead someone to say that Jesus is not human. That teaching comes from the evil spirit of the antichrist, who tries to fool people into believing that Jesus only seemed to be human, like some kind of phantasm (1 Jn 4:3).[64]

---

[59]The *hoti* in 1 Jn 3:22 carries a causal sense. Hence the translation "for."

[60]See BDAG, 832-836.

[61]Lieu (*I, II, and III John*, 163) and Jobes (*1, 2, and 3 John*, 176) mention these possible translations.

[62]Jobes, *1, 2, and 3 John*, 176.

[63]Martinus de Boer, "The Death of Jesus Christ and His Coming in the Flesh (1 Jn 4:2)," *NovT* 33 (1991): 336-37.

[64]In 1 Jn 4:3, John says, "every spirit that does not confess Jesus." When considering the context of the passage, this is simply a shorthand way of saying what he already makes explicit in 1 Jn 4:2: "every spirit that does not confess Jesus [has come in the flesh]." Sinaiticus (א) includes the implied words *en sarki elēlythota*.

Despite the pressures to succumb to false teaching, John assures us that we are "from God" and have "conquered them, for the one who is in you is greater than the one who is in the world" (1 Jn 4:4). The "one in us" is the Holy Spirit, whom the Father has sent to his disciples to teach us all truth (Jn 14:26). Through him, we understand John's instruction about Jesus—that he came in the flesh to redeem humanity from darkness and bring us into the light (1 Jn 4:5-6). Those who reject his teaching, and proclaim another Jesus, are influenced by the "spirit of error," which is one and the same with the spirit of the antichrist (1 Jn 4:6).

We must not be deceived by those who appeal to the Holy Spirit to peddle their false teachings. This does not mean that we downplay the work of the Spirit. On the contrary, we rely on the Spirit to discern truth from error (1 Jn 4:6).

Revisiting important matters (1 John 4:7-12). At this point in the letter, we have witnessed John repeat several themes. As modern readers, we may think this is redundant or unnecessary. John does not think this way. He uses repetition to emphasize important ideas, like the exhortation to "love one another" (1 Jn 4:7). Obeying this command, as John has already suggested, reveals we have been "born of God" (1 Jn 4:7; cf. 1 Jn 2:3), which is the same as experiencing new birth (Jn 3:1-18; 1 Jn 2:20, 27; cf. Ezek 36:25-27). That John connects "loving one another" with being "born of God" affirms that only the Spirit enables us to love our neighbor, fulfilling what prophets like Ezekiel and Jeremiah envisioned would be true of new covenant people.

Another repeated theme is that failing to love others means we do not know God (1 Jn 4:8; cf. 1 Jn 3:10). If we knew him, we would share his love with others. His love, of course, was on full display when he sent his "unique Son into the world" (1 Jn 4:9 au. trans.) as the "*hilasmos* for our sins" (1 Jn 4:10 au. trans.; cf. Jn 3:16-17).[65] Earlier, John used *hilasmos* to encompass both propitiation and expiation (1 Jn 2:2). He uses the word in the same manner in 1 John 4:10: to remind us that God sent Jesus to be the sacrifice that averts his wrath away from us and toward his Son (propitiation) and removes our guilt (expiation). The world has never witnessed a greater act of love.

We who have experienced new birth are to love others in the same way that God has loved us (1 Jn 4:11). As we witnessed earlier, this means we should be willing to risk all we possess—our very lives, just like Jesus—to provide for those in need (1 Jn 2:16). Yarbrough puts it well: "Christ's costly propitiatory atonement uncaps an artesian well of selflessness in which believers find resources for sacrificial care for each other."[66] Such care fulfills the law's call to provide basic necessities for struggling brothers and sisters (Lev 23:22; 25:35). Like Padilla and Escobar, Latino theologians Orlando Costas and Justo González stress social concern as an important element of the gospel.[67] Reading such Latino theologians may just help us grasp John's emphasis on loving God and neighbor.

---

[65]The word *monogenēs* has often been translated as "only begotten." A better translation emphasizes his unique status among God's many children. Jobes explains: "God has many children, both sons and daughters throughout history, but Jesus is not just one of them. He is unique, the *monogenes* Son, who was with God and was God (John 1:1)" (*1, 2, and 3 John*, 192).

[66]Yarbrough, *1–3 John*, 240.

[67]See, for example, Orlando Costas, *Liberating News! A Theology of Contextual Evangelization* (Grand Rapids, MI: Eerdmans, 1989). Many American evangelicals mainly know Justo González from his two-volume *The Story of Christianity* (San Francisco: HarperOne, 2014) but, for the most part, are unaware of his works on theology, such as *Mañana: Christian Theology from a Hispanic Perspective* (Nashville: Abingdon, 1990) and *Santa Biblia: The Bible Through Hispanic Eyes* (Nashville: Abingdon, 1996).

If this advice comes as a shock, we should consider that the statement "no one has ever seen God" (1 Jn 4:12) would have led first-century readers to recall the old covenant community's writings, particularly Exodus 33:20 ("You cannot see my face, for no one shall see me and live") to discern John's message.[68] The Scriptures themselves, then, encourage us to turn to people from different contexts for interpretive insight. The Spirit may even use different communities to expose our interpretive blind spots. For too long, a major flaw among North American Christians has been the emphasis on sound doctrine with little concern for neighbor. John knows nothing of this kind of Christianity. Nor do most communities of color, such as Blacks and Latinos/as, who have borne the consistent burden of encouraging the church to carry out the duty to love both God and neighbor.

Loving the easy way (1 John 4:12b-21). Although no one has seen him, God's character is revealed when we "love one another" (1 Jn 4:12).[69] When those living in darkness gaze at the church, they should see a community fulfilling the call to love their neighbor, which in turn testifies to God's love in sending Jesus to die for our sins.[70] This is akin to the way Israel's obedience to the Torah was to draw the nations to worship Yahweh. Although Israel failed at their vocation, new covenant believers have the promised Spirit, enabling us to fulfill the second of the greatest commands (Mt 22:36-40; Mk 12:31). Our hope is that unbelievers may be drawn to worship the God who sent his Son to redeem us from darkness and into his marvelous light (cf. 1 Pet 2:9).

The Spirit also assures us of God's indwelling presence and enables us to trust that God has sent Jesus, God's Son, to be "the Savior of the world" (*kosmos*; 1 Jn 4:13-16).[71] As in 1 John 2:2, John uses the word *kosmos* to convey a cosmic view of salvation: that God has sent his Son into the world to redeem all people. No ethnicity, culture, or language is outside of his saving mercy. If we remain in Jesus' love—epitomized by the way he gave his life for the world—we will have confidence in the day of judgment, and we will have no reason to fear God's wrath (1 Jn 4:16-19). John calls this "fulfilled love"—it's love that is directed toward others (1 Jn 4:12, 17, 18).[72] Those who claim to have received God's love, but never share it with others, show that they still live in darkness, and have reason to fear God's judgment.

John now reminds us that those who claim to "love God" and "hate their brothers or sisters" are "liars" (1 Jn 4:19). Consequently, our profession of faith is not enough. We may claim to love God with all of our heart, believing all the right historic confessions and doctrines, even teaching about him in a Sunday school class or from a pulpit; but if we do not love fellow believers, like the poor, the marginalized, and the immigrant, we reveal the unregenerate state of our hearts. John uses a suitable analogy: if a person "do[es] not love a brother or sister, whom [he has] seen," he "cannot love God whom [he has] not seen" (1 Jn 4:20). In other words, a "person who does not show love

---

[68]Strecker also notes a possible allusion to Greek tradition where "as early as Homer . . . invisibility is proper to the deity" (*The Johannine Letters*, 156).

[69]John's Gospel says that God is also revealed in Jesus (Jn 1:18; 5:37; 6:46).

[70]Lieu argues, "The author is not asserting that God's presence will be a reward for love or even its consequence but that it *is* a present reality when those who are loved love one another" (*I, II, and III John*, 185).

[71]The prepositional phrase *ek tou pneumatos* ("from the Spirit") clarifies that the Holy Spirit is the "source" of our assurance.

[72]Translations often render *teteleiōtai hē agapē* as "perfected love." Since John consistently alludes to the commands to love God and neighbor, which the church is called to fulfill, we should translate this phrase as "fulfilled love."

the easier way (toward people they can see) will not be able to love others the harder way (toward God, whom they cannot see)" (au. trans.).[73] If that describes us, then we should consider Jesus' advice to Nicodemus—we must be born again (Jn 3:7).

Believing in Jesus and loving neighbor (1 John 5:1-5). John now describes the relationship between the commands to believe in Jesus and love our neighbor. He addresses the latter in affirming that everyone who trusts that "Jesus is the Christ" has experienced new birth (1 Jn 5:1; cf. 1 Jn 2:22).[74] Confessing "Jesus is the Christ" is of a piece with saying "Jesus is Lord" (Lk 2:11; 1 Cor 8:6; 12:3; 2 Cor 4:5; Phil 2:9-11; Rev 17:4). This confession has historically united Christians across denominational and ethnic boundaries, testifying to the universal reign of Jesus.

Additionally, John contends that "everyone who loves the one who begets loves also the one born of him" (1 Jn 5:1 au. trans.). The "one who begets" is God the Father. If we claim to love him, we will also love those who have been "born of him," fulfilling the commands to love God and neighbor (1 Jn 5:2).[75] That's the inclination of those who have experienced new birth—for the Spirit compels us to love others, despite the things that would normally divide us, like race, class, gender, and nationality. What better way to testify to the lordship and messianic identity of Jesus than by mirroring the kind of unconditional love that we will experience when Jesus returns to reign over the earth.

Many minorities in the United States understand that we are far from achieving this vision. We recognize, for instance, that there is still far too much partiality in our evangelical colleges and seminaries. Other than diversity positions, most evangelical institutions do not have sufficient people of color in leadership positions such as dean and vice president. Why would a dark world be impressed with us? Why would they want to worship alongside people who fail to love those who believe the same things about Jesus but happen to be of different ethnic groups and nationalities?

We should take seriously that our "love for God" (au. trans.)[76] will be manifested in "obey[ing] his commandments" (1 Jn 5:3).[77] If we really love God, then we have the Spirit; therefore, for example, diversifying leadership, which shows love for different brothers and sisters, should not be "burdensome" (1 John 5:3). It should be something we do willingly.

Though we still struggle with these matters, we have confidence that we overcome the world, so long as we continue to exercise faith in Jesus (1 Jn 5:4). And when we are finally victorious, we will live in a place where the light of Jesus will lead us to appreciate our differences. In the meantime, we should be on guard against those who preach the need for faith in Jesus but have no concern for loving their neighbor.

The witness of the Spirit (1 John 5:6-12). While not negating our diversity, Christians find their unity in what we believe about Jesus, like his full humanity. John expounds on the

[73]Campbell (*1, 2, and 3 John*, 148) cites Smalley (*1, 2, 3 John*, 251). Smith (*First, Second, and Third John*, 121) notes, "The gospel cannot be reduced to a kind of benign humanism with a horizontal, but no vertical, dimension. Our love for each other is beautiful, ennobling, but tinged with sadness and ultimately tragic apart from the love of God."

[74]I agree with Campbell (*1, 2, and 3 John*, 154) that arguing for an *ordo salutis* in 1 Jn 5:1 misses the point; *contra* Matthew Barrett, "Does Regeneration Precede Faith in 1 John?," *Mid-America Journal of Theology* 23 (2012): 5-18.

[75]The plural "commandments" point to exhortations such as "You shall not murder," "You shall not bear false witness," etc., in the Ten Words (Ex 20:1-17; Deut 5:6-21). See Jobes, *1, 2, and 3 John*, 210.

[76]*hē agapē tou theou* is an objective genitive construction, hence my translation "love for God."

[77]Thompson, *1–3 John*, 131-32; Campbell, *1, 2, and 3 John*, 155.

importance of what Jesus accomplished in his humanity, saying that he "came by water and blood" (1 Jn 5:6). I propose two possible readings for water and blood.[78] First, water refers to Jesus' baptism and blood points to his atoning death.[79] Second, water and blood allude to Jesus' death, a metaphor that recalls the presentation of Jesus' sacrifice in John's Gospel, where water and blood flow from Jesus' side (Jn 19:34-35).[80] Of these, the first coheres with the context of 1 John 5:6-9 and John's Gospel, for the remainder of 1 John 5:6 notes that "the Spirit is one that testifies" to Jesus coming in water and blood, and John's Gospel testifies to the Spirit descending on Jesus at his baptism (Jn 1:29-34).[81] Campbell rightly argues, "The baptism is also a testimony of the Spirit, since he descended on Jesus and remained on him. In this sense, Jesus' baptism represents a clear moment of 'testimony,' which fits the context of 1 John 5:6-9 very well."[82] Thus, the Spirit witnesses that in his baptism (to which John alludes with the term water) Jesus is confirmed as God's Son, an event which begins an earthly ministry that would culminate in his atoning death for sinners (to which John alludes with the word blood). The one who believes the Spirit's testimony about Jesus has eternal life (1 Jn 5:10-12).

Petitions according to God's will (1 John 5:13-14). As he winds down his letter, John once more assures us that those who "believe in the name of the Son of God" have eternal life (1 Jn 5:13). This status entitles us to request of God "anything according to his will" (1 Jn 5:14). In keeping with the instruction in 1 John 3:22-23, petitions according to God's will promote love for God and neighbor. We have the confidence that God hears whatever is in keeping with these two great commands (1 Jn 5:15).

John's teaching serves as a warning against false teachings such as the prosperity gospel. Regrettably, this movement is very popular in Latin America. Millions of people live in poverty or in environments where there is little hope for social advancement, so they are vulnerable to false prophets who encourage them to name and claim God's material blessings. Now there is nothing wrong with asking God to provide for our needs. Nor is there anything wrong with asking God to supply us with abundant resources. The problem is when we make self-centered petitions, intending to exhaust God's goodness on our own selfish desires, such as expensive cars and lavish homes (cf. Jas 4:3). When requesting God's blessings, we must be sure that our petitions are in accordance with love of God and neighbor, like asking for plentiful resources that will supply our needs and those of others. These are the kinds of petitions God is delighted to answer.

Two kinds of sins (1 John 5:15-17). As recipients of eternal life, we should also heed John's instruction about "what is not a deadly sin" and "a sin that is deadly" (1 Jn 5:16-17). The latter is the most puzzling. Does God not forgive all sins? What, then, is the sin that leads to death? Fortunately, John has left a clue. He has already explained that faith in Jesus, which leads to new life, fulfills the command to love

[78]For a more extensive discussion of the options, see A. E. Brooke, *1, 2, 3 John*, A Critical and Exegetical Commentary on the Johannine Epistles (Edinburg: T&T Clark, 1948), 132-37; Smalley, *1, 2, 3 John*, 277-80; Tom Thatcher, "'Water and Blood' in Antichrist Christianity (1 Jn 5:6)," *SCJ* 4 (2001): 235-48.

[79]Smith, *First, Second, and Third John*, 123; Campbell, *1, 2, and 3 John*, 156-58.

[80]John Calvin, *Commentaries on the First Epistle of John*, Calvin's Commentaries, vol. 22 (Grand Rapids, MI: Michigan, 1993), 256-57.

[81]While John does not specifically mention Jesus' baptism, the scene refers to the event recorded in Mt 3:13-17; Mk 1:9-11; and Lk 3:21-22.

[82]Campbell, *1, 2, and 3 John*, 158.

God (1 Jn 3:22-23). Consequently, a "sin that is deadly" is failing to believe that God's Son was sent into the world to save sinners—for there is no forgiveness outside of his sacrificial death.[83] Since a "sin that is deadly" brings to mind the greatest command, it is likely that "what is not a deadly sin" refers to the complementary command to love one's neighbor. So, we should pray for brothers and sisters who struggle with loving others. We should pray that God would lead them to repent of their sin and embrace those whom they have shunned. What's more, and perhaps closer to the heart of the issue, we should pray that the Holy Spirit would open their eyes to the whole gospel, which encompasses love for God and neighbor.

Assurance of eternal life (1 John 5:17-20). John returns to a familiar claim: "Those who are born of God do not sin" (1 Jn 5:18; cf. 1 Jn 3:9). As in 1 John 3:9, practicing sin is antithetical to the character of the believer—particularly the sin of hating fellow Christians. Our lives should be characterized by love for others. But since we still struggle with darkness, there are times we sin against believers, even practicing the very partiality we despise. When this happens, God is gracious to lead us to repentance (cf. 1 John 1:6-10). There is no way that "the evil one" can bring us back under the power in which the whole world lies, which fosters hate for others rather than love (1 Jn 5:18-19).

It's understandable, though, that our sin against fellow saints, even though we seek forgiveness, may cause us to question our born-again status. If this happens, we should consider John's instruction: our new life rests not in our ability to love perfectly, as much as we strive for this, but on the fact that "the Son of God has come" to redeem sinners (1 Jn 5:20). If that were not enough, Jesus has even given us "insight" (*dianoia*) into the significance of his life and death (1 Jn 5:20).[84] Jesus uses the word *dianoia* when he sums up the greatest command: "Love the Lord your God with all your heart and with all your soul and with all your mind [*dianoia*]" (Mt 22:37; cf. Mk 12:30; Lk 10:7).[85] Two verses later, Jesus also mentions the second of the greatest commands (Mt 22:39). Jesus' reference to these commands coheres with 1 John's focus on loving God and neighbor. Jeremiah 31:33 (38:33 LXX) also uses the word *dianoia*: "This is the covenant I will make with the people Israel. . . . I will put my law in their minds [*dianoia*] and write it on their hearts."[86] These canonical connections provide us with a more robust understanding of 1 John 5:20: that the Son of God has given us insight into the fact that his coming is a fulfillment of the new covenant promises (1 Jn 5:20). By trusting in him, we can rest assured that we know God and have eternal life (1 Jn 5:20).

Staying away from idols (1 John 5:21). For the final time in the letter, John addresses us as "children" (cf. 1 Jn 2:1, 12, 28; 3:7, 18; 4:4). He is giving us one final point of instruction: "Keep yourselves from idols!" Jobes remarks that "the original recipients would most likely have seen this 'punchline' as a rhetorically powerful ending that demanded a response to the implied question, 'Whom will you serve? The one true God or idols?'"[87] Some argue that the idols are pagan deities of wood and stone common

[83]For a discussion of the interpretive options regarding a "sin leading to death," see Akin, *1, 2, 3 John*, 208-210; Kruse, *Letters of John*, 193-94.

[84]The term *dianoia* only occurs here in John's writings. BDAG (234) argues that the word refers to the "insight" given to believers.

[85]Jobes, *1, 2, and 3 John*, 241.

[86]Jobes, *1, 2, and 3 John*, 241.

[87]Jobes, *1, 2, and 3 John*, 241.

in the first century.[88] But John has yet to mention literal idols, so it seems unwarranted for him to do so at the end of the letter. It is more likely that he uses the term idols to refer to false beliefs about Jesus, like the notion that Jesus did not really have a body, which is comparable to fashioning a false god (1 Jn 2:22, 23, 26).[89] And if embodiment is unimportant, ethics goes out the window—there is no reason to love flesh and blood people.

We should note that the Old Testament associates the worship of false gods with a life characterized by injustice (Deut 12:30-32; Is 1:16-20; Jer 10:2-5).[90] John's letter does something similar, linking the denial that Jesus took on flesh with a failure to love others (cf. 1 John 1–2). A false god who does not value the physical body, like that of Jesus, can justify all kinds of injustices. Slaveowners in the antebellum South, for instance, preached a god who came to save peoples souls but left them in chains. The Spaniards converted (in many cases by force) indigenous peoples but stole their land and raped women and children. This is not the God of the Bible, who poured out his Spirit on the earth to enable us to love one another. This is a false god who wants to deceive us into thinking that saving souls is all that matters. This is the god of the Gnostics. He has been around a long time. So, we need to make sure that we can differentiate between him and the God who humbled himself and took on flesh. If we have listened to the wisdom of 1 John, we know the identity of the true God. But we must still ask ourselves: Whom will we serve? The true God or an idol?

2 JOHN

This short epistle repackages matters discussed at length in 1 John, such as truth, love, and warnings against false teachers, into more concise arguments. Second John is more than just a summary, though, as it applies these themes with a focus on hospitality. Aside from the added emphasis, the similarities with 1 John, which summarize essential content, lead many to assume that 2 John circulated as a cover letter for 1 John.[91]

Listening to the elder (2 John 1-3). Though 2 John is technically anonymous, the introductory greeting identifies the author as the "elder" (2 Jn 1). This title implies that the author holds a position of ecclesial authority over his readers. While modern scholarship doubts Johannine authorship, church tradition holds that the apostle John penned the letter.[92]

In our discussion of 1 John 1:1-4, I mentioned how my Cuban heritage cultivates a respect for our elders. I think we can apply a similar analogy to our reading of 2 John 1. When recalling my grandparents, for instance, my sister and I never questioned their authority. So, when they told stories, we listened closely. This may be nostalgia speaking, but I remember their stories having a sermonic quality, full of the fruit of age and wisdom, of a life well lived. I think this is a helpful way to approach 2 John. As our elder, we should not spend time doubting John's right to speak into our lives. Rather, we should hang on to all he says about truth, love, and false teachers.

John's addressees, whom he addresses as "the elect lady and her children," is another matter worthy of our attention (2 Jn 1).

---

[88]For a fuller discussion of the options, see Kruse, *Letters of John*, 200-202.

[89]Bultmann (*Johannine Epistles*, 90) makes the connection between false teaching, which the author calls idols, and the "sin unto death" in 1 Jn 5:16.

[90]Middleton, *A New Heaven and a New Earth*, 103.

[91]Similarly, Thompson, *1–3 John*, 150.

[92]See my earlier discussion on the authorship of John's epistles.

Although "the elect lady" may refer to a specific person, John has the church in view. His use of this designation is in keeping with "the biblical personification of Israel as a woman, or Jerusalem as the 'mother' of Israel (cf. Is 54:1-8; Gal 4:25; Rev 12:17; 21:2), and the NT picture of the church as the 'bride' of Christ (cf. 2 Cor 11:2; Eph 5:22-32)."[93] "Elect lady and her children," then, is an acceptable way to address the people of God, which includes all believers throughout redemptive history.

Walking in the truth (2 John 4-6). With that settled, we should turn our attention to John's first observation: that "some" of the elect lady's children "are walking in the truth" (2 Jn 4).[94] Not all are obeying what is "commanded by the Father" (2 Jn 4), which John identifies in his previous epistle as the command to "believe in the name of his Son Jesus Christ and love one another" (1 Jn 3:23; cf. 1 Jn 1:1; 2:7, 13-14, 24; 3:8, 11). These are covenant obligations for believers that go back to the "beginning," when God gave the law to Moses (1 Jn 5–6; cf. Ex 20; Mt 22:40). Since John is not imposing a new expectation, why are some not "walking according to [God's] commandments" (2 Jn 4-5)? In other words, why are some people still claiming to believe in Jesus but not loving their brothers and sisters? Could it be that they really don't have the anointing of the Spirit (1 Jn 2:20), which prophets like Ezekiel and Joel said would lead to the kind of obedience the old covenant saints found so difficult to live out? We should recall one of John's previous assertions: "Those who say, 'I love God,' and hate a brother or sister are liars" (1 Jn 4:20).

While only God knows a person's heart, Black and brown people can affirm that they have all too often experienced hate from fellow Christians. We can certainly point to overt acts of exclusion. But there are more subtle ones. Latinos/as in ecclesial settings, for example, are sometimes complimented on how well we speak English or how intelligent we are. While these remarks seem innocent enough, they communicate people's biases: they don't expect Latinos and Latinas to speak good English or to be intelligent. I wish I could take some folks to my hometown of Miami, where they would meet Cubans, Venezuelans, and Colombians who would alter their preconceptions of Latinos/as and other minority groups. Before we speak, love would compel us to examine our stereotypes or perhaps do a little research about people.

More antichrists (2 John 7-11). John begins 2 John 7 with the conjunction "for" (au. trans.) to link those who do not love others (2 Jn 6) to those who claim that Jesus Christ did not "come in the flesh," that is, that he did not act in human history to redeem sinful humanity. John warns us to stay clear of such people, whom he associates with the "deceiver" and the "antichrist" (2 Jn 7). If we do not take John's admonition seriously, we are in danger of succumbing to false teaching and losing our eschatological "reward" (2 Jn 7-8; cf. Mt 5:12; Mk 9:41; Rev 11:18; 22:12).[95]

As in 1 John, we can argue that a failure to love brothers and sisters arises from a false Christology which does not envision a human Jesus acting in history. And if he did not condescend to putting on flesh and blood, Jesus did not die to redeem people from the sinful effects of the curse, like racism and poverty. All that matters is what he possessed: a spiritual nature. As we have argued, those who preach a Jesus who only came to save souls are more

---

[93]Smalley, *1, 2, 3 John*, 318.

[94]The prepositional phrase *ek tōn teknōn sou* is partitive, meaning that only a portion of the church is living in obedience.

[95]Yarbrough, *1–3 John*, 345; Jobes, *1, 2, and 3 John*, 265.

influenced by Gnosticism than orthodox Christology. John warns us about this kind of teaching, the kind that means we have no fellowship with the true God (2 Jn 10). We must even be careful about showing hospitality to these teachers, for fear of sharing in their evil, which shows no concern for the real Jesus nor the people for whom he died (2 Jn 11).

Closing (2 John 12-13). John has more to write, but he would rather tell us in person. As modern readers, we won't have this privilege until we meet him in the new heavens and new earth. Until then, we can be assured that John's instruction is meant for the well-being of the church. He truly desires that we have real fellowship with the true God and love our neighbors. What he desires is no different from what Moses or Jesus desired for God's people (Ex 20; Mt 22). What is different is that new covenant believers have the promised Spirit, which enables us to do what was so difficult for old covenant saints: love God and others from the heart.

3 JOHN

Third John has the distinction of being the shortest book in the Bible. Its small size, however, is not a sign of insignificance. Like the other Johannine epistles, 3 John speaks on important matters such as truth and love. We would all benefit from reading this little, yet significant, letter.

The example of Gaius (3 John 1-4). The author of 3 John identifies himself as "the elder," whom we have already acknowledged as John (3 Jn 1; cf. 2 Jn 1).[96] Unlike in 1 and 2 John, John addresses this letter to an individual named "Gaius," rather than the church (3 Jn 1). This may be the Gaius whom the apostle John installed as bishop of Pergamum in Asia minor (Acts 20:4)—but it is difficult to say for certain.[97] What we know for sure is that 3 John is in the Christian canon—so its instructions extend beyond its original, mysterious recipient to include all Christians throughout history.

John then mentions that fellow Christians have reported to him that Gaius (whoever he was) is "walk[ing] in the truth" (3 Jn 3). This Gaius has a good testimony among believers, for he lives consistent with the truth of Jesus Christ who, in his death for sinners, exemplified love for God and neighbor. John rejoices when he hears such reports about his spiritual children (3 Jn 4). As he would also rejoice in us, if he knew we were following Gaius's example.

Showing hospitality (3 John 5-8). Next, John commends Gaius for showing hospitality to fellow Christians (3 Jn 5). We should note that these were not personal acquaintances—they were "strangers" (*xenous*).[98] Jesus also uses the word *xenos* in his Olivet Discourse, when he says, "I was a stranger [*xenos*] and you welcomed me" (Mt 25:35).[99] And that's what Gaius does—he welcomes those with whom he was unfamiliar, perhaps those on the margins of society. His kindness is magnified when we consider that, in the ancient world, extending hospitality to someone meant that they were accepted as members of the community.[100] When taking this into consideration, in actuality John commends Gaius for welcoming strangers into the community of believers.

---

[96]See my earlier section on the authorship of the Johannine epistles.

[97]Campbell, *1, 2, and 3 John*, 214; Jobes, *1, 2, and 3 John*, 289-90.

[98]The final phrase (*eis tous adelphuos kai touto xenous*) is not read without difficulty. I argue that *xenous* clarifies that the *adelphous* are "strangers." Yarbrough reads the phrases similarly (*1-3 John*, 371). Daniel B. Wallace calls this kind of construction a "second group subset of the first" (*Greek Grammar Beyond the Basics: An Exegetical Syntax of the New Testament* [Grand Rapids, MI: Zondervan, 1996], 281).

[99]Yarbrough, *1-3 John*, 371.

[100]Bruce J. Malina, "The Received View and What It Cannot Do: III John and Hospitality," *Semeia* 36 (1986): 181-83.

And his only criteria for doing so is that they are Christians. Nothing else mattered.

What if contemporary Christians extended this kind of hospitality? The kind that welcomes immigrants, people of different ethnicities, and the homeless into our churches? Would this not be a vivid picture of the kind of acceptance that Jesus offers a broken world? Is this not what we are called to do, as participants of the truth of Jesus Christ (3 Jn 7-8)?

The example of Diotrephes (3 John 9-12). But for every Gaius there is also a Diotrephes (3 Jn 9). Diotrephes was a real, historical person. We just don't know his true identity beyond his name. Whoever he was, he had enough power to refuse hospitality to John and his associates (3 Jn 9-10). He even went so far as to forbid believers from extending hospitality to outsiders, threatening to "[expel] them from the church" (3 Jn 10). As Gaius is not to follow his example, neither are we (3 Jn 11). We are, instead, to make a habit out of welcoming all brothers and sisters.

When we follow the example of Gaius, we show that we really do belong to God (3 Jn 11). But if we follow the example of Diotrephes, excluding people from the community of believers, we reveal that we have never really "seen God" (3 Jn 11), which is another way of saying we don't know him (cf. Jn 14:7-9). And in case we have forgotten, welcoming someone into the church means they are (fully) included in the life of the congregation. They are not separated into their own ethnic group, away from the rest of the body, as happens to Hispanics and Asians, often under the guise of ethnic ministry. Rather, they are to be integrated into the life of the church. That's the kind of hospitality that genuine believers, like John, affirm (3 Jn 12). Anything less is not in keeping with the inclusive truth of the gospel (3 Jn 12).

Closing (3 John 13-15). As in his previous letter, John has more to write, but he would rather communicate in person (3 Jn 13-14). In the meantime, the elder wishes Gaius "peace" (3 Jn 15). This peace also extends to us, as we offer hospitality to those excluded from full fellowship in communities modeled after Diotrephes. This is an appropriate end to a group of epistles that expects God's people to model the kind of love that Jesus unconditionally extended to humanity, when he gave his life for all (1 Jn 2:2). What John's epistles expect of us, then, is nothing more than being like Jesus in the way we love God and others, fulfilling the commands that everyone from Moses to John has expected of God's people.

BIBLIOGRAPHY

Akin, Daniel. *1, 2, 3 John*. Nashville: Broadman & Holman, 2001.

Barrett, Matthew. "Does Regeneration Precede Faith in 1 John?" *Mid-America Journal of Theology* 23 (2012): 5-18.

Beale, G. K. "The Old Testament Background of the 'Last Hour,' in John 2,18." *Bib* 92 (2009): 231-54.

Brooke, A. E. *1, 2, 3 John: A Critical and Exegetical Commentary on the Johannine Epistles*. Edinburgh: T&T Clark, 1948.

Brown, Raymond E. *The Epistles of John*. New York: Doubleday, 1982.

Bultmann, Rudolf. *The Johannine Epistles: A Commentary on the Johannine Epistles*. Philadelphia: Fortress, 1973.

Calvin, John. *Commentaries on the First Epistle of John*. Calvin's Commentaries. Vol. 22. Grand Rapids, MI: Michigan, 1993.

Campbell, Constantine R. *1, 2, and 3 John*. Grand Rapids, MI: Zondervan, 2017.

Campbell, Douglas A. *Pauline Dogmatics: The Triumph of God's Love*. Grand Rapids, MI: Eerdmans, 2020.

Carson, D. A. *The Gospel According to John*. Grand Rapids, MI: Eerdmans, 1991.

———. "1–3 John." In *Commentary on the New Testament Use of the Old Testament*, edited by

G. K. Beale and D. A. Carson, 1063-68. Grand Rapids, MI: Baker, 2007.

Cassen, N. H. "A Grammatical and Contextual Inventory of the Use of κόσμος in the Johannine Corpus with Some Implications for Johannine Cosmic Theology." *NTS* 19 (1972): 81-91.

Costas, Orlando. *Liberating News! A Theology of Contextual Evangelization*. Grand Rapids, MI: Eerdmans, 1989.

de Boer, Martinus. "The Death of Jesus Christ and His Coming in the Flesh (1 Jn 4:2)." *NovT* 33 (1991): 326-46.

Derickson, Gary W. *1, 2, and 3 John*. Bellingham, WA: Lexham, 2014.

Do, Toan. "The Epistles of John." In *The State of New Testament Studies*, edited by Scott McKnight and Nijay K. Gupta, 444-58. Grand Rapids, MI: Baker Academic, 2019.

Escobar, Samuel. *In Search of Christ in Latin America: From Colonial Image to Liberating Savior*. Downers Grove, IL: InterVarsity Press, 2019.

González, Justo. *Mañana: Christian Theology from a Hispanic Perspective*. Nashville: Abingdon, 1990.

———. *Santa Biblia: The Bible Through Hispanic Eyes*. Nashville: Abingdon, 1996.

———. *The Story of Christianity*. San Francisco: HarperOne, 2014.

Hill, Charles. "1–3 John." In *A Biblical-Theological Introduction to the New Testament*, edited by Michael Kruger, 483-508. Wheaton, IL: Crossway, 2016.

Jenson, Matthew D. *Affirming the Resurrection of the Risen Christ*. Cambridge: Cambridge University Press, 2012.

Jobes, Karen. *1, 2, 3 John*. Grand Rapids, MI: Zondervan, 2016.

Kirkpatrick, David. *A Gospel for the Poor: Global Social Christianity and the Evangelical Left*. Philadelphia: University of Pennsylvania, 2019.

Kruse, Colin. *Letters of John*. Grand Rapids, MI: Eerdmans, 2000.

Liethart, Peter. *The Ten Commandments: A Guide to the Perfect Law of Liberty*. Bellingham, WA: Lexham, 2020.

Lieu, Judith M. *The Second and Third Epistles of John: History and Background*. Edinburgh: T&T Clark, 1986.

———. *I, II, and III John: A Commentary*. Louisville, KY: Westminster John Knox Press, 2008.

Malina, Bruce. "The Received View and What It Cannot Do: III John and Hospitality." *Semeia* 36 (1986): 171-94.

Meeks, Wayne. "The Man from Heaven in Johannine Sectarianism." *JBL* 91 (1972): 44-72.

Middleton, Richard J. *A New Heaven and a New Earth: Reclaiming Biblical Eschatology*. Grand Rapids, MI: Baker Academic, 2014.

Padilla, René. *Misión integral: Ensayos sobre la iglesia y el reino*. Grand Rapids, MI: Eerdmans, 1986.

Runge, Steven. *A Discourse Grammar of the Greek New Testament: A Practical Guide for Teaching and Exegesis*. Bellingham, WA: Lexham, 2010.

Schuchard, Bruce G. *1-3 John*. Saint Louis: Concordia, 2012.

Smalley, Stephen. *1, 2, 3 John*. Rev. ed. Nashville: Nelson, 2007.

Slater, Thomas B. "1–3 John." In *True to Our Native Land: An African American New Testament Commentary*, edited by Brian K. Blount. Minneapolis: Fortress, 2007.

Strecker, G. *The Johannine Letters: A Commentary*, translated by L. M. Maloney. Minneapolis: Fortress Press, 1996.

Thatcher, Tom. "'Water and Blood' in Antichrist Christianity (1 Jn 5:6)." *SCJ* 4 (2001): 235-48.

Wallace, Daniel. *Greek Grammar Beyond the Basics: An Exegetical Syntax of the New Testament*. Grand Rapids, MI: Zondervan, 1996.

van der Watt, Jan. *An Introduction to the Johannine Gospel and Letters*. London: T&T Clark, 2007.

Yarbrough, Robert. *1–3 John*. Grand Rapids, MI: Baker Academic, 2008.

LETTER OF JUDE

Mateus F. de Campos

AUTHORSHIP AND DATE

The author of Jude identifies himself by the Jewish name *Ioudas,* which can be translated Judah, Judas, or Jude in English.[1] The name was fairly common in Palestinian circles, primarily because of Judah, son of Jacob (Gen 29:35). In the New Testament, several individuals bearing the name Judas are mentioned (cf. Mt 10:4; Mk 6:3/par.; Lk 6:16; Acts 1:13; 5:37; 15:22). The author of our letter identifies himself as the brother of James, most likely a reference to the half brother of Jesus and prominent leader of the church in Jerusalem (Acts 15:13). This almost certainly makes the author of the letter one of the half brothers of Jesus mentioned in Mark 6:3/par.,[2] who, along with the rest of his family, had difficulties accepting Jesus' early ministry (cf. Mk 3:20-21) but became a believer after the resurrection (cf. Acts 1:14) and subsequently a prominent leader in the church in Jerusalem.

The polished nature of the Greek, along with some elements that have been understood as indicators of a second century setting, has led some to question the traditional authorship of the letter. In our estimation, these arguments are not convincing. Given the intense missionary activity of the early church, it is not unlikely that Jude would have been engaged in such activity (cf. 1 Cor 9:5) and that his possibly basic knowledge of Greek would have improved as a result. Furthermore, the elements typically cited as markers of a late composition cannot be unequivocally traced back to a second century setting.[3]

Jude's use of the Old Testament (Jude 5-7) and particularly of extracanonical writings such as *Assumption of Moses* and *1 Enoch* (Jude 9), along with the use of Semitisms, points to a Palestinian origin. The author does not identify himself as an apostle (Jude 17-18) but makes use of apostolic language (cf. "slave of Jesus Christ" [Jude 1 au. trans.], and the doxology [Jude 24-25]). He seems to be somewhat familiar with the audience and would likely have been recognized as someone with authority.

Assuming that the author is indeed Jude, brother of James, the letter should be dated sometime between AD 40 and 80. If it is assumed that 2 Peter is dependent on Jude (see comments above) and written by the apostle Peter, then the latest possible date for Jude would be sometime before AD 64.

---

[1]On the relationship between Jude and 2 Peter, see sidebar above in commentary on 2 Peter, "The Similarities Between 2 Peter and Jude." The commentary on 2 Peter above also contains content relevant to the book of Jude.

[2]There was considerable confusion regarding the identity of this individual in the postapostolic period. Nevertheless, the authenticity of Jude was attested by prominent figures such as Jerome, Tertullian, Athanasius, and Augustine. See Gene Green, *Jude and 2 Peter*, Baker Exegetical Commentary on the New Testament (Grand Rapids, MI: Baker Academic, 2008), 1-8.

[3]Peter H. Davids, *The Letters of 2 Peter and Jude*, Pillar New Testament Commentary (Grand Rapids, MI: Eerdmans, 2006), 16.

AUDIENCE, PURPOSE, OCCASION

There is no clear indication of the audience's location or ethnicity. However, in light of the elegant Greek, the use of the Hebrew Bible and portions of the Pseudepigrapha, and the references to licentiousness (Jude 4, 7-8), a reasonable suggestion is that the audience is a group of competent Greek-speaking Jews living in a predominantly Gentile setting where immoral practices were more pervasive. The most common suggestions are Egypt, Syria, or Asia Minor, all of which had a considerably large Jewish population.

Jude expresses his intent very clearly in Jude 3. The language implies that a strong conflict was threatening the community. The source of the conflict was certain individuals who had infiltrated the church (Jude 4). These opponents—designated "ungodly" (Jude 4, 15)—were recognized by members of the community as believers, even participating in their feasts (Jude 12). They were guilty of sexual immorality (Jude 3, 7-8) and self-serving arrogance and rebelliousness (Jude 8, 16). They infiltrated the church to cause divisions (Jude 19) by instigating discontent (Jude 16), opposing the authoritative leadership (Jude 8), and leading some astray (Jude 22-23). In order to influence people, they relied on their notions of prophetic dreams (Jude 8), claiming to be inspired by the Spirit (Jude 19).

The picture, in general, is similar to 2 Peter, and it is clear that both authors use shared language to describe their opponents. However, while Peter focuses most of his attack on the opponents' teaching regarding Christ's return, it is noticeable that Jude never clearly identifies his opponents as false teachers. Rather, his emphasis is on their behavior. To be sure, they are "pervert[ing] the grace of our God into debauchery" (Jude 4), which most likely includes some theological justification for their practices, but different from 2 Peter, Jude does not elaborate much on doctrine—christological, eschatological, or otherwise. It is the opponents' practices that lead Jude to write his admonition.

In light of this picture, Jude's purpose is twofold. The first, more negatively, is to expose the behavior of these opponents and their potential harm to the church. The second, more positively, is to urge the community to keep their faith (Jude 20-21) and to be proactive in rescuing some who are dangerously close to losing it (Jude 22-23). Jude employs a "you-versus-them" rhetoric to make his point. The opponents are "they" or "these people" (Jude 8-12, 14, 16), while the church is addressed with the contrastive "but you, beloved" (Jude 17, 20, cf. also Jude 18, 24). The discourse intentionally demarcates the boundaries between the two groups. The believers are to dissociate themselves completely from the opponents. They must protect themselves, snatching back those who are being lured and clearly avoiding any interaction that could compromise their integrity (Jude 23). The letter, therefore, fosters a defensive posture. Their faith is under attack, and they must contend for it.

STRUCTURE

As we pointed out, 2 Peter and Jude present a remarkably similar macrostructure. However, Jude's central section (Jude 5-16) is a lot more intentionally arranged, with a precise alternation between scriptural basis and the denunciation of the opponents. This pattern is typically understood against the background of midrash, an ancient Jewish interpretation technique similar to the ones present in texts like the Qumran *pesharim* and the rabbinic writings, which corroborates the theory about the author's Palestinian origins.

Opening and Salutation (Jude 1-2)

Introduction: Statement of Purpose (Jude 3-4)

Marker ["Now I desire to remind you" (Jude 5)]

Exposing the Opponents (Jude 5-16)

- Scriptural Examples: Israel, Angels, Sodom and Gomorrah (Jude 5-7)
- First Denunciation: Their Rebellious Arrogance and Ignorance (Jude 8-10)
- Scriptural Examples: Cain, Balaam, Korah (Jude 11)
- Second Denunciation: Their Rebellious Self-Serving Attitude and Futility (Jude 12-13)
- Prophecy: The Prophecy of Enoch (Jude 14-15)
- Third Denunciation: Their Rebellious Speech (Jude 16)

Marker: ["But you, beloved, must remember" (Jude 17)]

Admonition to the Church (Jude 17-23)

- First Admonition: Remember the Word Prophesied by the Apostles (Jude 17-19)
- Second Admonition: Build Yourselves in Faith, Keep Yourselves in Love (Jude 20-23)

Doxology (Jude 24-25)

Jude 3-4 and 17-23 seem to be arranged in parallel, with several common elements, such as the vocative "beloved" (Jude 3, 17, 20); the mention of faith (Jude 3, 20); the mention of the ungodly (Jude 4, 18); the reference to prediction (Jude 4, 17); and the title Lord Jesus Christ (Jude 4, 21). Taking these similarities in consideration, the argument can be alternatively arranged in a chiastic structure:

A: Opening and Salutation (Jude 1-2)
    B: Introduction: Statement of Purpose (Jude 3-4)
        Marker ["Now I desire to remind you"(Jude 5)]
        C: Exposing the Opponents (Jude 5-16)
        Marker ["But you, beloved, must remember" (Jude 17)]
    B′: Admonition to the Church (Jude 17-23)
A′: Doxology (Jude 24-25)

According to this structure, the center of the letter is the indictment against the opponents (Jude 5-16), which serves as a foil to the positive admonition to the church. Jude develops his letter using a rhetoric of contrast, meant to highlight the distinction between the groups.

JUDE 1-2

The two epithets employed by the author to identify himself are especially significant if he is indeed the half brother of Jesus. The first—"slave of Jesus Christ" (au. trans.; see commentary on 2 Pet 1:1)—represents a remarkable shift in the way Jude relates to his older brother. Jude was probably the youngest of the brothers (Mt 13:55) and, like his siblings, he initially resisted Jesus' ministry in Galilee (Jn 7:3), even questioning Jesus' sanity (Mk 3:21). In an honor-shame culture, the shameful actions of one family member would affect the entire family. Thus Jude, who along with his brothers once resisted Jesus' ministry to protect the honor of his family, now calls himself a "slave" of Jesus, attributing to him ultimate reverence.

Also significant is the fact that Jude identifies himself as "brother of James," when the more honorific title "brother of the Lord" was commonly used to refer to Jesus' siblings (cf. 1 Cor 9:5; Gal 1:19). Jude seems to avoid using his familial ties with Jesus to assert his authority, identifying himself instead in relation to James, the prominent leader of the church in Jerusalem. Mentioning his connection to James is as far as Jude goes to assert his credentials, even mentioning the apostles' authority as separate from his own (Jude 17-18). His ministry, however, bears the marks of an apostolic one. He is a teacher and a pastor, leading the church in its struggle for the sake of the faith delivered to the saints.

Jude addresses his audience with a meaningful theological statement. The adjective "called" denotes election, which is established on the basis of God's love and his keeping of the saints for the day of Jesus Christ. The implicit agent is God the Father, since the activity of "calling" is typically attributed to God in the New Testament (Rom 1:7; 8:28, 30; 1 Cor 1:9; 1 Pet 2:9). Jude uses the *agapē* word group with relative frequency in the letter, with the term "beloved" being his favorite form of address to the audience. For him, "being loved by God" is the essential quality of their identity.

They are also "kept"—a verb that denotes the preservation of the saints for the eschatological future. Once again, God is the agent, and Christ is the one for whom the believers are being kept. The sense of preservation is the same one present in Jude's doxology (Jude 24), although with a different verb. Jude, therefore, begins and ends with a statement of assurance, which is paramount in light of the overall atmosphere of the letter. Their faith is under attack, but they can trust that their identity is guaranteed by God's sovereign call, love, and keeping.

Instead of the more typical apostolic greeting "grace and peace," Jude offers a somewhat unique triad—mercy, peace, and love—a fitting combination in light of his purpose. The atmosphere is one of contention and division. Although it is clear that the opponents are harmful infiltrators, it is likely that some in the congregation had not perceived them as such. In this context, Jude's letter would cause no small commotion, as he outspokenly exposes and condemns these individuals (Jude 23). However, the spirit in which they are to deal with these issues is one of mercy, peace, and love—qualities that are not self-produced but furnished and multiplied by God.

JUDE 3-4

The letter Jude writes is prompted by a sense of urgency. While writing a more comprehensive account of "our common salvation," Jude was prompted to write a more direct admonition to address the pressing issues of his audience. We are not told exactly what prompts his change of heart, but it is possible that the author received some report of the opponents' activity in the church, which required immediate response. In this case, therefore, admonition takes precedence over instruction. If the immediate error was not promptly combated, any attempt to provide a more comprehensive doctrinal teaching would be useless.

Jude writes "to urge" the audience "to contend for the faith that was and once for all handed on to the saints." Faith here functions as a shorthand for the truth of the gospel, and would encompass doctrinal faith claims, but also the faithful way of living expected of those who professed to believe. The language of being "entrusted" refers to apostolic tradition (*paradosis,* cf. Mt 15:2; 1 Cor 11:2; 2 Thess 2:15; 3:6)—a body of teaching, both doctrinal and ethical, that was passed on by authorized teachers and served as authoritative guidelines by which believers were supposed to live. The fact that it has been delivered "once" speaks to the fixity of the tradition.[4] The adverb often indicates the definitive character of something (e.g., Christ's atoning sacrifice, cf. Heb 9:28; 1 Pet 3:18) and here highlights that this "faith" is not to be tampered with or subject to the innovative interpretations of the day. The recipients of this faith are "the saints." Therefore, not only Jude's audience, but all those who identify with the gospel have been given this treasured tradition and are responsible for its protection.

The verb "to contend," used to describe the combative posture of the church, denotes athletic effort, often related to ancient fighting competitions. The public nature of these competitions perhaps informs Jude's encouragement to the church and his own public invective against the opponents. Their confrontation of error should be an active engagement, which inevitably entails conflict. Having set up the contentious atmosphere, Jude goes on to identify the opponents, referring to them as "certain intruders." The indefinite language could suggest either that Jude does not know the troublemakers personally, or, more likely, that he deliberately wants to present them as "shadowy characters."[5]

The negative characterization achieves full force in the label "ungodly." In the Greco-Roman context, the word is used mostly in a religious sense, indicating one's lack of allegiance to the gods and refusal to participate in the cult. Foerster points out that in Hellenistic Judaism "ungodliness" always relates to conduct and not merely an attitude or disposition.[6] This seems also to be the case in the New Testament, where the term appears associated with sinful practices, often paired with unrighteousness and sin (Rom 1:18; 2 Tim 2:16; Titus 2:12; 1 Pet 4:18). In fact, Jude himself speaks later of "deeds of ungodliness" (15), focusing on evil actions, which, as we will soon be told, constitute a rejection of Christ.

The description of the opponents' secretive intrusion connotes the idea of "undercover agents" and heightens the sense of alert in the speech.[7] Apparently, they are already in their midst but many in the congregation have not noticed them; hence the author's need to expose them. This covert nature of their incursion contrasts with their clearly sinful actions ("pervert the grace . . . into debauchery . . . deny our only Master . . ."), which begs the question: How can such blatantly sinful behavior creep in unnoticed in the church?

The answer, likely, is that their actions were not promptly perceived by the community as Jude describes them. The fact that they "pervert the grace of our God into debauchery" probably includes some sort of theological or philosophical justification for their actions. This could be a version of Platonic dualism, in which they advocated for a complete separation between the realms of the flesh and the spirit, or, more likely, an antinomian misappropriation of Paul's teaching on grace and Christian freedom. Whatever the justification, some seem to have accepted it (cf. Jude 22-23), and for Jude, their actions have to be exposed for what they are: licentiousness—an unrestrained and impious self-indulgence, which is tantamount to denying Jesus. Although they probably did not go so far as to curse openly the name of Jesus, their behavior was tantamount to a denial of his Lordship. One does not have to express openly their rebellion

---

[4]This does not necessarily require a later date, since Paul in his earliest letters already could speak of a traditional apostolic teaching on which he relied (1 Cor 11:2, 23).

[5]Andreas B. Du Toit, "Vilification as a Pragmatic Device in Early Christian Epistolography," *Biblica* 75, no. 3 (1994): 406-7.

[6]Foerster, "σέβομαι," *TDNT*, 7:187.

[7]Du Toit, "Vilification," 406.

against Jesus to deny him; the conscious refusal to live according to his commandments is just as condemnable.

Jude sets up a confrontational mood for his letter. The faith once delivered to the saints is now under attack by godless infiltrators who are creeping in unnoticed among the believers. The rhetoric is charged and might seem exaggerated to modern sensitivities. Is the church really supposed to live with such a heightened awareness of the dangerous influence of malicious behavior? For Jude, the answer is a resounding yes. First, the inestimable value of the gospel makes it necessary for those who have been entrusted with it to contend for its preservation. Second, and most importantly, error creeps in unnoticed, and, when left unchecked, has the potential to lure and destroy.

As someone who grew up in Brazil and lived in North America and England, it is interesting to observe how Christians in different places relate differently to the task of confronting sin. Some Western cultures are profoundly apologetic, seeking to avoid conflict, while South American culture is in general more explicit about this sort of confrontation. While cultural sensitivities have to be taken into consideration, Christians have to pay attention to this sort of open defense of the gospel and confrontation of sin observed in Scripture.

JUDE 5-7

Jude's denunciation of the opponents (Jude 5-16), like its counterpart in 2 Peter, can largely be classified as *vituperatio*.[8] Jude's *vituperatio*, however, is shaped by Jewish ideas and arranged in midrashic fashion. Similar to the teachers in Qumran, Jude alternates scriptural references with expanded denunciations based on the references. His denunciation is, therefore, scripturally shaped and would have been especially meaningful to a largely Hellenistic Jewish audience. Jude begins his denunciation with a nod to the audience. Using the language of "reminding"[9] and mentioning how "you are fully informed" (Jude 5), he subtly charges his audience with the responsibility to deal with the malicious influence.

In the first segment, Jude puts together three scriptural examples as a background for the exposure of the opponents: the wilderness generation (Jude 5), the fallen angels (Jude 6), and Sodom and Gomorrah (Jude 7). The examples feature prominently in Jewish writings, usually with an organizing theme binding them together, such as a warning against rebellion (*T. Naph.* 3:4-5; CD 2:17–3:12) or a description of divine judgment (3 Macc 2:4-8; Sir 16:7-10; 2 Pet 2:4-10). Jude's examples, at first, seem to have independent subjects: unbelief (Jude 5), trespassing one's proper position (Jude 6), and sexual immorality (Jude 7). However, since Jude does not follow a chronological arrangement, it is likely that the examples share a common theme. Furthermore, Jude uses the examples in his invective against the opponents, which implies that they are somehow collectively reflected in their attitudes. Therefore, identifying Jude's logic in employing the examples is crucial to understand the nature of his confrontation.

Jude's first example (Jude 5) follows the early Christian trend to reflect on Israel's failures in the exodus-conquest tradition to issue warnings to believers (cf. 1 Cor 10:1-11; Heb 3:7-13). Jude's evaluation is dependent on the narratives regarding the first generation of Israelites to leave Egypt—particularly their failure to keep YHWH's covenant, which led to their perishing before entering the promised land. Several

[8]Green, *Jude and 2 Peter*, 20-22.

[9]See commentary on 2 Pet 1:12-15.

events contributed to their demise (cf. Ex 17:1-7; Num 14:1-45; 16:1-35; 20:1-13; 21:4-9; 25:1-13). Which event does Jude have in mind and how does it relate to the opponents?

The language of unbelief and destruction is present in Numbers 14:11-12, which makes it possible that Jude has in mind the failure of the Israelites to trust YHWH to bring them into the land. Another possibility is the account of the immorality of the Israelites in Numbers 25:1-13. Jude's argument will climax with a reference to sexual immorality (Jude 7), where he uses the word *ekporneuō* to describe the immorality of Sodom and Gomorrah, a word used extensively in the LXX to identify promiscuous practices, including the incident of Numbers 25:1-13. Since Jude does not specify the event in question, it is likely that he has the overall rebellion of the Israelites in mind. In fact, given Jude's allusion to Balaam and Korah in Jude 11 (cf. Num 16:1-35; 22:1–24:25), it is possible that Jude's evaluation is reliant on the book of Numbers more generally. The point in these stories is that a generation of people saved by YHWH were disloyal and apostatized, consequently facing judgment. Therefore, Jude's picture of the opponents begins to form against the backdrop of the wilderness generation. Like the rebels, the opponents cannot rely on their supposed status as believers because in fact they are not. Accordingly, God's historical punishment of the covenant-breakers among his people constitutes an ominous threat.

The second example, concerning the fallen angels, is derived from Genesis 6:1-3 and subsequent traditional elaborations on it. More specifically, Jude seems to draw on 1 Enoch 15–16, where the angels are confronted for leaving their dwellings as spiritual beings and taking wives among the daughters of men, defiling themselves (*1 En.* 15:3-10). Their promiscuity is associated with their abandonment of their original heavenly positions. For that reason they are kept "until the great day of judgment" (*1 En.* 19:1)—language similar to Jude's. As mentioned above (see commentary on 2 Pet 2:4-10) the angels in the tradition are guilty of rebellion against God's authority, which in *1 Enoch* begins with their abandonment of their heavenly dwellings. Originally created as spiritual beings to live "an eternal, immortal life" (*1 En.* 15:6), the angels were consumed by lust and left their privileged status, going against God's created order. This rebellion is the central focus of Jude's account, but the angels' sexual immorality looms large in his interpretive horizon, which becomes clear in his third example.

The third example is Sodom and Gomorrah, a well-known paradigm in Jewish tradition. The cities feature prominently in canonical and noncanonical writings, typically employed in two ways.[10] First, they constitute a paradigm of sin. The sins of the cities are variously depicted, but some form of sexual immorality is frequently mentioned, such as adultery (Jer 23:14), the practice of "abominations" (Ezek 16:50), and following "unnatural desires" (Philo *Flight* 1:144; *Abr.* 1:135-141; *T. Naph.* 3:4-5). Second, the cities are brought up as examples of God's devastating judgment, which stands as a historical warning to sinners.

Jude focuses on sexual immorality. The word specifies unlawful sexual relations, normally between a man and a woman in the context of adultery or prostitution. Male engagement in prostitution was permitted in Greco-Roman settings, as long as it did not socially compromise the civil marriage.[11] Among Jews and Christians, however, the

[10]Cf. Is 1:9; 13:19; Jer 23:14; Lam 4:6; Ezek 16:49-50; Amos 4:11; *Jub.* 16:5; 2 Esd 2:8-9; Sir 16:7-10; 3 Macc 2:4-8; *m. Sanh.* 10:3; *T. Naph.* 3:4-5; 2 Pet 2:4-10; cf. also Philo *Abr.* 1:135-141.

[11]See Hauck and Schulz, "πόρνη," *TDNT*, 6:582.

practice was seriously denounced (Lev 19:29; 21:9; Jer 3:1; Hos 4:13; Mt 15:19; 1 Cor 5:1; 6:13-18; 10:8). According to Jude, the cities engaged in sexual immorality by "going after a different flesh" (au. trans.). Although somewhat elusive, the phrase is likely a reference to the attempt by the Sodomites to have sexual relations with the angels (Gen 19:4-5).[12] This creates a link with the aforementioned example of the angels, which is established by the comparative language. In the same manner as the angels left their dwellings and, according to the Enochic tradition Jude relies on, lusted after the daughters of men, the inhabitants of the cities "went after the flesh" of angels. The obvious interpretive problem is this: if Jude uses the examples as a paradigm for exposing the opponents, how can such a unique kind of sexual immorality be applicable to them?

At this point it is profitable to zoom out and look again at the underlying argument in Jude's examples. Jude builds his argument as a crescendo, with one example preparing the way for the next. He begins with the example of Israel in the wilderness. It is likely that early Christians, particularly Jewish Christians, would have seen themselves as an extension of the people of Israel.[13] Hence, the emphasis is on apostasy and covenant disloyalty. The contrast with the Lord's saving act intensifies their negative evaluation. Even some among those who were saved from Egypt fell into unbelief and were destroyed. This shocking apostasy then leads to the second example.[14] Angels, created for the heavenly dwellings, abandoned their positions of glory to lust after the daughters of men. The emphasis on lust is absent in Jude but surfaces in his comparative clause introducing the next and climactic example. Like the angels, the inhabitants of the cities engaged in immorality, also going against God's created order to follow after their desires. The big picture emerging out of the three examples is, therefore, of a defiant rebellion against God, which is reflected in the abandonment of his created order to pursue immoral desires. The most explicit expression of sin in the sequence is sexual immorality, but Jude condemns it not as a mere pursuit of sinful impulses but as the ultimate expression of unbelief and rebellion against God.

All examples are met with definitive judgment. The Israelites were destroyed; the angels were kept under chains for judgment; and the cities suffered punishment of eternal fire. The picture is gloomy, especially because of what it really means: the opponents are under the same judgment.

Jude takes sin very seriously. His focus on the sinful behavior of the opponents is meant to expose them and cause the audience to see their actions for what they are. The fact that Jude's argument lands on sexual immorality makes it a particularly relevant warning to modern believers. Sexual immorality often occupies a place of prominence in modern Christian discussions of sin, and that is for good reason. Most of us live in contexts where sex is absolutized in a hedonistic way. But Jude reminds us that sexual immorality is

[12]Some translations (e.g., ESV, NRSV) emphasize the unnatural aspect of the act, and some commentators interpret it as a reference to homosexuality (cf. Douglas J. Moo, *2 Peter and Jude*, NIVAC [Grand Rapids, MI: Zondervan, 1996], 242). Although homosexual practice is sometimes referred to as "against nature" and openly condemned in Scripture (cf. Rom 1:26-27; Philo *Abr.* 1:135-141), the language in Jude is better understood as a reference to the events described in Gen 19:4-5, since the angels can be understood quite literally as "a different flesh."

[13]Michael Green, *Second Peter and Jude*, Tyndale New Testament Commentaries (Downers Grove, IL: InterVarsity Press, 1987), 178.

[14]Charles rightly points out the fact that both Israel and the angels lose positions of privilege. See J. Daryl Charles, "'Those' and 'These': The Use of the Old Testament in the Epistle of Jude," *Journal for the Study of the New Testament* 12, no. 38 (1990): 114.

more than a matter of an improper view of pleasure and certainly more than a mere ethical issue. It ultimately reflects rebellion against God, and as such, it is met with the harshest of punishments.

JUDE 8-10

After presenting the emblematic examples, Jude moves on to his direct denunciation of the opponents, homing in on a particular issue, namely, blasphemy. Through the conjunction "yet," Jude underscores the shocking nature of the opponents' arrogant behavior in light of God's historical judgment on such attitudes. God's punishment against godless acts is patently demonstrated in history, yet some still defy him.

The reason behind their shameful practices is their arrogance and ignorance. They reject the authority of God and, relying on their own dreams, they blaspheme against things they do not understand. Having introduced the opponents with an indefinite pronoun ("certain intruders") in Jude 4, he now starts using the demonstrative ("these") to denounce them. The shift is appropriate since he now becomes more descriptive about and confrontational toward them. Following Jude's penchant for threes, the opponents' actions are described with a triad of independent verbs modified by a temporal participle—they "defile the flesh," "reject authority," and "blaspheme the glories" (au. trans.) as "dreamers."

The term for "dreamers" is used to describe the opponents' reliance on supposedly revelatory experiences to justify their actions (cf. Gen. 28:12; 37:5; Deut 13:2). The criticism is against attitudes sponsored by so-called dreams that are in fact contrary to the "faith that was once for all handed on to the saints" (Jude 3).[15] The contrast in the letter between the reliable tradition "entrusted" and the unreliable self-validating experience of the dreamers is noticeable.[16] Those who go against the faith elevate their own experiences over legitimate apostolic teaching, which manifests itself in error, arrogance, and ignorance.

The first two descriptions of their attitudes are loosely connected to the previous examples. Like the Sodomites and the angels, the opponents "defile the flesh" (cf. *1 En.* 15:3; *Jub.* 16:5-6). Like the wilderness generation and the angels, they despise lordship, likely a reference to the authority of the Lord (cf. Jude 4, 5).[17] The final element in the triad—blasphemy—is the center of gravity of Jude 8-10, with the *blasphēmeō* word group being used three times in the sequence. The repetition narrows the rebellion against authority down to a specific act of blasphemy. However, the expression "blaspheming the glories" is notoriously difficult. To whom or what is Jude referring?[18]

Jude uses a tradition found in the pseudepigrahical *Testament of Moses* to sharpen his denunciation of the opponents' blasphemy. In the story, which alludes to Zechariah 3:1-5, the archangel Michael disputes with the devil concerning the body of Moses. The story is elusive. Bauckham argues that the devil is accusing Moses for killing the Egyptian in order to deprive Moses' body of an honorable burial.[19] Nonetheless, Michael *refuses to accuse Satan of blasphemy* and relies on the authority of the Lord to rebuke him. Stokes, on the other hand,

---

[15]The criticism is not against spiritual revelation per se. Cf. Jude 20; Mt 1:20; Acts 2:17; 16:9-10; 1 Cor 14:26-33. Davids, *The Letters*, 54-55.

[16]Green, *Jude and 2 Peter*, 74-75.

[17]Schreiner, *1, 2 Peter, Jude*, 456.

[18]For interpretive options, see Bauckham, *Jude, 2 Peter*, 57-59.

[19]Bauckham, *Jude, 2 Peter*, 66.

suggests that the devil was intending to prevent Moses from ascending into God's presence and tried to execute him.[20] Michael, however, *refuses to blaspheme against Satan*, relying on the Lord's authority instead.

Jude's point in deploying the story is seen in his subsequent comparison of Michael's attitude with the opponents': "but these blaspheme that which they do not understand" (Jude 10 au. trans.). The opponents, relying on their so-called visionary experiences, developed an arrogant attitude, seeing themselves as superior even to heavenly beings; whereas even Michael, the archangel himself, did not rely on his own authority but on the authority of the Lord to deal with the devil. Using wordplay, Jude then contrasts what they "do not understand" with what they "understand" only "naturally," as "irrational animals"—a knowledge that leads them to destruction (Jude 10). In this context, "blaspheming glories" reflects an attitude of contempt toward heavenly realities—the things which the opponents do not understand. The contrast is between their instinctive arrogant "knowledge" and their ignorance of spiritual realities. Relying on their own mystical experiences, the opponents claimed to have superior knowledge—which in fact was but an instinctive, irrational understanding—and arrogantly defied the heavenly realities, thereby despising the authority of the Lord.

The manner in which they did this is not altogether clear. Although "blasphemy" typically suggests a verbal slander, it represents a deeper attitude of provocation. Since Jude speaks about the defilement of the flesh alongside the despising of authority, it is likely that he has in view the immoral acts themselves, which may have been accompanied by blasphemous words, and constituted an act of defiance against God.

The point of Jude's denunciation is to expose the arrogance and ignorance of people who rebel against God, using their so-called mystical experiences to justify their immoral actions. While the blatant immorality is the most visible expression of their sin, their arrogance and unruliness are at the heart of their error. Worse than the immoral is the immoral who is so blinded by their arrogance that they cannot understand the realities with which they are dealing. Arrogance, in fact, is the trademark of rebellion against God. In such cases of rebellion, all other manifestations of sin stem from a deep-seated contempt for God and a boastful attitude of superiority. This proud attitude in the end proves to be vain and fruitless, which is what Jude will address in the next section of his denunciation.

JUDE 11-13

Jude's next denunciation section follows the same rhetorical pattern of the first, now focusing on individuals as paradigms of error and judgment: Cain, Balaam, and Korah. The focus on individuals brings attention to the opponents' role as influencers.

As for the sins in view, the individuals have in common with the groups their rebelliousness against God. Cain, after having his offering rejected, was warned by the Lord about the danger of sin and yet killed his brother, being cursed and exiled as a result (Gen 4:1-16). Balaam, when asked by the king of Moab to curse the Israelites, heard from the Lord that he was not to curse them but still continued to try to appease the king, provoking the Lord's anger (Num 22–24). Finally, Korah rebelled against Moses and despised the Lord, being consumed by his wrath

[20]Ryan E. Stokes, "Not over Moses' Dead Body: Jude 9, 22-24 and the Assumption of Moses in Their Early Jewish Context," *Journal for the Study of the New Testament* 40, no. 2 (2017): 206.

(Num 16). Rebelliousness against God is that which connects the three examples and stands as Jude's primary charge. But the way he presents the examples adds further depth to the picture. The triad is arranged in parallelism (au. trans.):

They go	the way	of Cain
They gave themselves	to the error	of Balaam's wages
They were destroyed	in the contention	of Korah

The verbal progression creates a narrative that describes the gradual process of their apostasy. They walked, gave themselves, and were destroyed as a consequence. By using verbs in the aorist, Jude situates the opponents in the original setting of his examples, adding vividness to the portrayal. Whatever is true of the past examples is true of them.

Jude refers to the examples using three descriptors—way, error, and contention. Again, there is a sense of progression. The "way" typically reflects a teaching or philosophy (Mt 22:16; Acts 9:2; 1 Cor 4:17). The "error" denotes a specific deviation from the right path, typically associated with deceit (Rom 1:27; Eph 4:14; 1 Thess 2:3). The "contention" has a more poignant connotation of hostility and rebellion, characterized by strife and dispute (cf. Num 20:13; 27:14; Ps 55:9; Prov 17:11). The opponents' apostasy, therefore, has both a sense of passive acquiescence to a flawed way of thinking and living, and of an active rebellion which breeds division.

Finally, the genitives of possession—"of Cain," "of Balaam's wages," and "of Korah"—call attention to the agency and influence of these figures and consequently to the opponents' influence for evil. All three figures were understood in Judaism as responsible for steering others into error. Josephus describes Cain as "a teacher of wicked practices" (*Ant.* 1:61). Similarly, Balaam is said to have caused the people to act treacherously against the Lord (Num 31:16; *Ant.* 4:126-130). Jude's reference to the wages of Balaam emphasizes the opponents' greed as their motivation. Finally, Korah's role as the instigator of a group of 250 chiefs of Israel against Moses (Num 16:2) stands as the backdrop of his rebellion (cf. *Ant.* 4:15-24; *Num. Rab.* 18:2) and is probably employed to describe the opponents' rebellion against the church's established leadership.[21]

It is worth noticing that Jude never qualifies the opponents as "false teachers." His focus is not on the content of their teaching but their role as wicked influencers. While false doctrine is certainly a primary source of division and apostasy, it is not the only means by which a community is endangered. Rather, malicious talk, quarrelsome instigations, and wicked behavior coming from influential individuals can equally shipwreck an entire community.

Jude follows his scriptural picture with a series of direct denunciations of the opponents (Jude 12). They are "blemishes on your love-feasts, while they feast with you without fear." The early church practiced fellowship meals that usually included sharing in the Lord's Supper. In some cultures, meals carry very important purposes. They are opportunities for deep conversation, reconciliation, and bonding. But these are also informal situations, where harmful things can be suggested with subtlety and find their way into peoples' minds.

Next, Jude deploys a series of metaphors. First, they are "hidden reefs" (au. trans.).[22] The

[21]Green, *Second Peter*, 187-88.

[22]The word *spilades* is sometimes translated "blemishes" given its similarity to *spilos* (=spot, blemish)—the word used in 2 Pet 2:13. However, the words represent different lexemes and should not be conflated.

image of a sunken rock that goes unnoticed and damages the hull of ships is meant to reflect the covertness of the opponents' influence. Their real damaging potential lies beneath the surface and would have gone unnoticed by many in the congregation.

The second metaphor is of shepherds "feeding themselves," which comes from prophetic injunctions against self-serving leaders (Is 56:11; Jer 2:8; Ezek 34:2, 8, 10). The shepherd's primary characteristic is dedication to the welfare of the flock. Self-serving shepherds are guilty not only of ignoring the needs of the sheep but also of exploiting the flock for their own gain (cf. Ezek 34:3). The metaphor is the clearest indication that the opponents have a leadership role in the community and are held responsible for attending to the needs of the people. But instead, fueled by greed (like Balaam), they were exploiting the church.

The next four metaphors have a common emphasis: the opponents' futility. They are "waterless clouds," which although promising, have no substance and are carried away by the wind (cf. Prov 25:14). They are "autumn trees without fruit," frustrating to those who have waited until the last season to benefit from their fruit, but to no avail (cf. Mk 11:12-14). They are as disappointing as "wild waves of the sea" that foam up shame. Finally, they are as unreliable as "wandering stars"—likely a reference to planets, which in the ancient world were deemed unreliable for astronomical guidance due to their lack of a fixed course.[23]

The combined denunciation is ominous. The opponents, who have been exposed for their immorality, are now confronted for their malicious influence in the community. They are not only guilty of their own sin but also of frustrating and leading astray those who rely on them for guidance, for the sake of profit. The expected judgment is severe. Just as the angels in Jude 6, they are kept for "the deepest darkness."

The New Testament is very clear about the punishment reserved for those who lead people astray. Jesus himself warned that those who cause the little one to stumble are expected to receive the harshest of punishments (Mk 9:42-48). This should stand as a warning about the seriousness of one's influence as a leader, especially over those who are susceptible to falling away because of their weaknesses or naïveté. The Lord is on the side of the weak, who are to be snatched out of the fire (cf. Jude 23). But those who lead them astray are kept for eternal fiery judgment.

JUDE 14-16

Jude now arrives at his final denunciation of the opponents, still using the pattern of scriptural precedent (Jude 14-15) and direct denunciation (Jude 16). However, instead of allusions, Jude now for the first and only time quotes directly from a noncanonical text—*1 Enoch* 1:9—using a prophecy-fulfillment exegesis to present the opponents as the ones about whom Enoch prophesied.

The quote leads to the question about Jude's views on noncanonical material and their authority. Jude's use of the verb "to prophesy" to introduce the material makes it clear that he sees the text as legitimate prophecy. This, however, does not necessarily mean that he would have seen *1 Enoch* as canonical, not least because the canon of the Hebrew Bible was not formally established until much later.[24] There is little doubt, however, that he saw the prophecy in question as authoritative, which is corroborated by his description of

[23]Schreiner, *1, 2 Peter, Jude*, 467.
[24]See Schreiner, *1, 2 Peter, Jude*, 468-72.

Enoch as the seventh in Adam's genealogy (cf. Gen 5:3-19).[25]

Textually, the quote is very close to *1 Enoch* 1:9, with a few modifications to fit the author's purposes. In context, it is part of the introduction of a theophany whereby God (*1 En.* 1:4) comes to make peace with the righteous and exercise judgment on the ungodly (*1 En.* 1:8-9). Jude changes the subject of the verb to "Lord," whom he identified previously as Jesus (Jude 4, 25), attributing to him a role of judgment that only YHWH holds. The foci of judgment are the "deeds of ungodliness" and the "hardened words" (au. trans.) spoken "against him." Jesus is, therefore, also the one against whom the ungodly rebel.

Having spent considerable time denouncing the opponents' deeds, Jude now emphasizes the "things spoken" to denounce yet another expression of rebellion. The emphasis on speech is unpacked in three major elements. First, within the quote, the "hardened words" can refer to harsh or difficult things (cf. LXX Gen 42:7; Jn 6:60), but in light of the subsequent expansion in Jude 16, it is likely that he understood the term as related to the wilderness generation, with whom the terminology is frequently associated (cf. LXX Num 16:26; Deut 10:16; 31:27; 2 Chron 30:8; *1 En.* 5:4).[26] "Hardness" in this context denotes the idea of obduracy, the attitude that ultimately occasioned the wilderness generation's downfall (Ps 95:6-11).

Second, Jude describes the opponents as "grumblers"—a term often used to depict the rebellious complaining of the Israelites (cf. Ex 16:7-8; 17:3; Num 11:1; 14:27; 1 Cor 10:10). Jude further colors the description with (a) the word *mempsimoiroi*, which denotes an attitude of discontent with one's lot in life;[27] and (b) the description of them "indulg[ing] their lusts," which relates to their pursuit of self-centered passions.[28]

Third, Jude mentions their "arrogant words" (au. trans.) that they speak while "showing partiality for the sake of advantage" (au. trans.). The sentence is difficult to interpret, but in light of the connection with the quotation in Jude 15, Jude seems to be speaking of boastful utterances against Jesus, an idea similar to "despising Lordship" and "blaspheming the glories" in Jude 8.[29] This is accompanied by a deceitful show of deference—likely directed at influential members of the congregation—in order to obtain or preserve status. One possible scenario is that these ungodly leaders are saying very harmful things that are tantamount to rebellious speech but avoiding public reprimand by showing favoritism toward key individuals in the community.

Therefore, Jude combines the prophetic oracle of *1 Enoch* and the scriptural characterization of the wilderness generation to expose an attitude of ultimate rebellion against God, expressed in discontent, complaining, and self-indulgence. Jude's emphasis on speech is noticeable. Instead of emphasizing specific doctrinal teachings, he exposes the more subtle forms of harmful speech with which the opponents are undermining the community. Complaining, discontent, flattery, gossip, and things of the sort gradually erode the foundation of the congregation. Far from being some harmless "little sins," these things are

[25]Frey, *The Letter of Jude*, 119.
[26]Cf. Frey, *The Letter of Jude*, 129.
[27]Frey, *The Letter of Jude*, 130.
[28]Bauckham, *Jude, 2 Peter*, 98.
[29]Frey is probably right in saying that Jude positions the opponents alongside enemies of God, such as Pharaoh, Nebuchadnezzar, and Antiochus (Frey, *The Letter of Jude*, 131).

expressions of a rebellious disposition against the Lord, subject to judgment at the occasion of his coming.

JUDE 17-19

Having exposed the opponents, Jude now draws his attention back to the audience, admonishing them regarding the apostolic warnings (Jude 17-19) and need for self-edification (Jude 20-23). The emphatic second-person plural "you" and the vocative "beloved" trigger the rhetorical transition. To be sure, the admonitions still have the opponents very much in view, but now there is a stronger emphasis on the church's posture in relation to them.

The "you-versus-them" rhetoric, clearly seen in the contrast between "you" (Jude 17) and "these . . . people" (Jude 19), creates a stark distinction between the church and the opponents, which is reflected in a few different ways throughout the letter. The beloved are "kept safe for Jesus Christ" (Jude 1, 24), while the opponents are kept for judgment (Jude 6, 13). The beloved are to "build yourselves up in your most holy faith" and "pray in the Holy Spirit" (Jude 20), while the opponents are worldly people who rely on their own dreams and do not have the Spirit (Jude 8, 19). The contrast is intentional. Given the seriousness of their offense and their intent to influence the community, the opponents are to be seen as outsiders.

This may sound harsh, but the New Testament condemns this kind of harmful influence in very strong terms (cf. Phil 3:2-3, 17-21; 1 Tim 4:1-3; 2 Tim 3:1-9; 1 Jn 2:18-23). These "us/you-versus-them" texts are meant to expose the attempts to lead the people of God astray and preserve the integrity of the church. While fully engaged in its mission, the Christian community also needs to raise its awareness of harmful patterns of thought and behavior that may infiltrate the community and compromise its identity. Mission relies on identity, and identity safeguards the mission.

The first admonition features the first imperative of the letter—"remember." The first posture is one of remembrance of and reliance on apostolic teaching. The "predictions" of the apostles are part of the "faith that was once for all entrusted to the saints" (Jude 3). Jude's denunciations are not merely a rant against an isolated group but shed light on an eschatological event predicted by the apostles of the church.

After reemphasizing the scoffers' ungodly pursuit of sins of indulgence (cf. Jude 16), Jude adds two final items to his list. First, they are divisive. This rare word may refer to the opponents' elitism or to factious quarrels they were causing. Both issues are alluded to in the letter (cf. Jude 16). The example of Korah, who led a rebellious faction among the people of Israel, might still stand in the background. In any case, the effect of their actions is divisions in the community. Second, Jude describes them as "worldly people, devoid of the Spirit." The word for "worldly" functions effectively as the antonym of "spiritual." It may be, as some argue, that Jude is refuting a claim by the opponents that they were the spiritual ones, because of their "dreams" (cf. Jude 8).[30] The qualification expands on the label "the ones causing division." Therefore, the fact that they do not have the Spirit explains their divisive nature. The Spirit is the one who unifies the church (Rom 14:17; 1 Cor 12:13; Gal 5:22; Eph 4:3), and division is a clear sign of the absence of the Spirit.

[30]Although, as Frey alerts, some caution is probably necessary since the language may simply be Jude's own evaluation of the opponents. See Frey, *The Letter of Jude*, 138-39.

JUDE 20-23

In his final admonition, Jude turns his attention completely to the church. He spent most of the letter building a negative argument, exposing the opponents (Jude 5-16) and warning the congregation about them (Jude 17-18). Now he moves to a more positive admonition, a clear prescription of action.

The section has much in common with Jude's introduction (Jude 1-4). The words "mercy" and "love," with which Jude greets his audience, are now prescribed as objects of their actions. Similarly, those who are "beloved in God the Father and kept safe for Jesus" (Jude 1) are now to "keep yourselves in the love of God." Finally, the "faith handed on to the saints" is now the holy foundation on which they should build themselves (Jude 20). Significantly, what Jude has conveyed as facts about them in the beginning of the letter is now what they are supposed to pursue. The indicative leads to the imperative. What is already true of their existence is now prescribed as the basis from which they are to live.

The section is divided into two segments: the church's spiritual self-edification (Jude 20-21) and the church's attitude toward various groups (Jude 22-23). Three elements are part of the spiritual edification. First, they are to "build yourselves up on your most holy faith." The architectural language denotes the idea of building on a foundation, identified as "your most holy faith." Faith here, like in Jude 3, is the "faith handed on"—the faith of the apostles and the church. Facing the harmful influence of the opponents, the audience is called to strengthen themselves according to the unshakable foundation on which they are built.

The second element is a more practical admonition: "pray in the Holy Spirit." The expression might relate more generally to prayers that are guided by the Spirit (cf. Rom 8:26; Eph 6:18), or more specifically to praying in tongues, which Paul mentions as an instrument of self-edification in 1 Corinthians 14:1-4, 15. In any case, the expression denotes a spiritual practice, which distinguishes the believers from the "worldly," nonspiritual people in Jude 19.

The final element is "waiting for the mercy of our Lord Jesus Christ into eternal life" (au. trans.). Rhetorically speaking, the phrase appropriately brings the entire set of commandments to a climax. The verb for "waiting" denotes an active eschatological hope, which although forward looking, motivates one's life in the present (cf. Mk 15:43; Lk 2:25; Acts 24:15; Titus 2:13). Jude envisions eschatological redemption, eternal life, as the final goal of a Christian life in the same way that judgment is the final destiny of an ungodly life.

The three elements work together in a dynamic way, encompassing accomplished, ongoing, and future dimensions, and with human and divine actions propelling the believers' spiritual life. Firmly grounded and continuously building themselves on the foundation of faith, they should keep on living a life of prayer in the Spirit, looking forward to eternal life as their end goal. Significantly, this spiritual dynamic involves the activity of the triune God; the love of God, the mercy of the Lord Jesus, and the guidance of the Holy Spirit give shape to their spirituality. Therefore, when it comes to the spiritual life, there is a cooperation between the self-edification of the believer and the provision of the triune God. The foundation on which the believers build themselves is the faith delivered to them; the discipline of prayer is practiced "in the Holy Spirit"; and their active hope is grounded in the mercy of Christ. All these constitute the means by which they keep themselves in the love of God.

Having established how believers are to develop their own spiritual edification, Jude now turns to how they should deal with the opponents and those under their influence. Jude 20 has a complicated textual history, with high quality manuscripts attesting to different variants. Broadly speaking, there are two main options. Either Jude is referring to two or to three groups.[31] While the evidence does not allow for complete certainty, Jude's penchant for threes may be a good indication that the latter is the case.

According to this, Jude has three groups in mind. First, there are "those who dispute" (au. trans.).[32] He has just condemned the opponents' divisive nature (Jude 19), and now he calls the believers' attention to those who are caught up in their quarrels. The church is to approach this group with the same mercy they await from the Lord in the final day (Jude 21). Second, they are to "save others by snatching them out of the fire." Jude does not elaborate on who this group might be, but since he mentions judgment by fire when speaking about the punishment of the opponents (Jude 7), it is likely that this group is dangerously close to being persuaded by them.

Finally, he mentions another group on whom believers are supposed to exercise mercy, but with fear, being careful not to defile themselves. The mention of defilement of the body recalls the denunciation in Jude 8. Therefore, it is likely that Jude here refers to the opponents. While mercy should always characterize the believers' actions, their purity and integrity as the people of God remain the utmost priority. Therefore, they are to exercise caution in dealing with the opponents, avoiding any deeper relationship that might affect them.

In conclusion, in his last and climactic admonition, Jude clearly delineates the church's required posture in the troubled circumstances they are facing. It involves self-edification, reaching out to those who are led astray, and defense against ungodly influence. One might judge this a somewhat defensive, perhaps even withdrawn, position. Is not the church supposed to engage in missional proclamation, making disciples of all nations, as a church against whom the gates of hell should not prevail (Mt 16:18)? Should the church operate in such a defensive mode as Jude prescribes? We have to evaluate the admonition within its context. The community is under attack, and the integrity of their faith is at stake. The church is at risk of allowing their identity to be distorted by the ungodly behavior in their midst. Furthermore, the threat is not coming from pagans who are in need of the gospel. Rather, it comes from people who secretly infiltrate the church with the intent of undermining the gospel. Jude spares no adjective in exposing the dangerous nature of their influence. In this atmosphere, the community should be on alert, strengthening themselves, protecting the vulnerable, and contending for the faith. The church can only be successful in their mission as salt of the earth and light of the world when they are strongly grounded in their faith. Moreover, Jude calls attention to the seriousness of sin. Sinful behavior is not to be downplayed or ignored but exposed and confronted, particularly when it has the potential to spread and influence the minds of the most vulnerable. In this context, it is right and necessary for the church to focus on its own edification and protection.

JUDE 24-25

Jude ends his letter with a doxology, which appropriately brings the letter to a climax. The

[31]For a thorough discussion of the options, see Bruce M. Metzger, *A Textual Commentary on the Greek New Testament: A Companion Volume to the United Bible Societies' Greek New Testament*, 2nd ed. (London: United Bible Societies, 1971), 658-61.

[32]The word could also mean "to doubt," but since Jude uses it with a sense of "dispute" in Jude 9, the same meaning is preferred here.

tension created by the extensive denunciation of the opponents, along with the appeal for the church to edify and protect itself in the midst of such a harmful influence, now finds resolution in the assurance that God is able to watch over his church.

The doxology resolves the theme of "keeping" repeated throughout the letter. Here, however, instead of the verb *tēreō* which he employed previously, Jude uses the synonym *phylassō,* which has a more active sense of protection, rather than simple preservation.[33] The idea is therefore intensified: the God who preserves them for Jesus Christ (Jude 1) now is said to be able to protect them actively from falling. The word for "falling" renders the idea of being kept faultless before God. The verbal root of the word is sometimes used in the LXX to refer to being defeated in battle (1 Sam 4:2; 2 Kings 14:12; 1 Chron 19:19) but is also used in relation to falling in error or sin (Rom 11:11; Jas 2:10; 3:2; 2 Pet 1:10; see also Philo *Agr.* 1:177). Jude has painted a rather contentious scenario in his letter, with opponents threatening the faith of the community and the church snatching people from the fire and contending for the faith. In this context, the assurance that God is able to prevent them from falling comes as a great encouragement. They are not alone in their battle against sinful influence. God himself is the one who sustains them.

The assurance is complete with the image of the believers standing blamelessly and joyfully before God's glory. The ominous image is of God the Judge, whose glory reflects his holiness and power and before whom all will eventually stand. But Jude paints the picture of believers joyfully standing before the Lord. The verb "to stand" is used in a causative sense as an object of God's ability. Although a glorious judge, it is God himself who causes the believers to stand blamelessly before him. Jude then appropriately ends with attributing glory, majesty, dominion, and authority to God through Christ.

Jude's letter is a remarkable reminder to the believers. It reminds them that they live in a reality in which they have to engage actively in the defense of their faith. Ungodliness always looks for an opportunity to undermine the community, causing divisions, fostering wicked behavior, and preying on the most vulnerable. And it does so covertly, finding a place at their table and subtly exercising its malicious influence, sometimes even going undetected. Therefore, ungodly behavior has to be exposed so the community can take a stand against it and rescue those who waver. But most importantly, Jude reminds the church that they are beloved and kept. In the struggle for the faith, they do not contend on their own strength. God himself is actively involved in their strengthening and protection, and he will bring the church blameless before himself.

BIBLIOGRAPHY

Adams, Edward. *The Stars Will Fall from Heaven: Cosmic Catastrophe in the New Testament and Its World.* Library of New Testament Studies 347. London: T&T Clark, 2007.

Bauckham, Richard. *Jude, 2 Peter.* Word Biblical Commentary. Grand Rapids, MI: Zondervan, 1983.

———. "'Those' and 'These': The Use of the Old Testament in the Epistle of Jude." *Journal for the Study of the New Testament* 12, no. 38 (1990): 109-24.

———. *Virtue Amidst Vice: The Catalog of Virtues in 2 Peter 1.* Sheffield, UK: Sheffield Academic Press, 1997.

Davids, Peter H. *The Letters of 2 Peter and Jude.* Pillar New Testament Commentary. Grand Rapids, MI: Eerdmans, 2006.

[33]Bertram, "φυλάσσω," *TDNT,* 8:140.

Dennis, John. "Cosmology in the Petrine Literature and Jude." In *Cosmology and New Testament Theology*, edited by Jonathan T. Pennington and Sean M. McDonough, 157-77. Library of New Testament Studies 355. London: T&T Clark, 2008.

Du Toit, Andreas B. "Vilification as a Pragmatic Device in Early Christian Epistolography." *Biblica* 75, no. 3 (1994): 403-12.

Frey, Jörg. *The Letter of Jude and the Second Letter of Peter: A Theological Commentary*. Waco, TX: Baylor University Press, 2018.

Green, Gene. *Jude and 2 Peter*. Baker Exegetical Commentary on the New Testament. Grand Rapids, MI: Baker, 2008.

Green, Michael. *Second Peter and Jude*. Tyndale New Testament Commentaries. Grand Rapids, MI: Eerdmans, 1987.

Marshall, I. Howard. *Kept by the Power of God*. London: Epworth Press, 1969.

Metzger, Bruce M. *A Textual Commentary on the Greek New Testament: A Companion Volume to the United Bible Societies' Greek New Testament*. 2nd ed. London: United Bible Societies, 1971.

Moo, Douglas J. *2 Peter, and Jude*. NIV Application Commentary. Grand Rapids, MI: Zondervan, 1996.

Schreiner, Thomas R. *1, 2 Peter, Jude*. New American Commentary 37. Nashville: Broadman & Holman, 2003.

Stokes, Ryan E. "Not over Moses' Dead Body: Jude 9, 22-24 and the Assumption of Moses in Their Early Jewish Context." *Journal for the Study of the New Testament* 40, no. 2 (2017): 192-213.

REVELATION

Daniel I. Morrison

INTRODUCTION

The book of Revelation provides hope to victims of injustice at the margins of their societies. As a Black American, a member of an ethnic group that has traditionally experienced unjust discrimination in a North American context, my reading of the text provides insights regarding economic disparity, inequitable judicial treatment, and ecclesial alignment with the world's political systems. While the text addresses these and many other topics, they receive little attention in most studies or sermons. Exploration and embrace of Revelation's message demand the inclusion of these often overlooked themes.

Some Christians may argue that a socially located reading is dangerous and lacks respect for Scripture. Instead, such readings, when evidenced by the text, provide perspectives that may have yet to be considered. Such assertions fail to recognize that all readings of the Bible are socially located, whether from a majority or minority cultural context. Therefore, this reading should be acknowledged appropriately as *a* reading of the text. When considering the original audiences of the Apocalypse, such a reading would be no less absurd than an Ephesian or Philadelphian reading.

John sent his prophecy to the seven churches of Asia Minor. Though all the churches are within the same province of the Roman Empire and face the challenge of whether they will conform to the broader culture, each congregation has a unique experience unparalleled by the rest. The messages to these communities enable each group to hear Christ's address in their unique context. The diversity among the original congregations of Asia Minor permits each community to see how they operate within the context of Revelation. Contemporary audiences benefit from reading all the messages, enabling them to see how each one fits within its ancient context while understanding the diversity of meanings each of the original congregations could draw from the text as their community heard the remainder of the Apocalypse.

The book of Revelation spoke to John's original audiences and continues to speak to diverse audiences today. While not every reader will relate to the specific situations of those in the seven churches, they can aptly apply the text of Revelation to their lives. Christopher Rowland explains, "The visionary experience, while conditioned by life under Roman dominion, is not determined by it. It is the Beast and Babylon, not Rome and Caesar, which are the vehicles of John's message."[1] In other words, John's focus on the beast and Babylon demands that readers consider the beasts and Babylons in their lives and not restrict their focus to a distant sociopolitical context significantly different from their own. At the same time, the book of Revelation addresses various sociocultural issues that

[1]Christopher Rowland, *Revelation* (London: Epworth Press, 1993), 24.

directly impact people today. The text discusses power use, misuse, and abuse—all of which relate to justice. When reading the book with this in mind, one could say Revelation speaks to the diverse situations the global church faces in the twenty-first century just as well as it spoke to the circumstances the churches faced in Asia Minor during the first century.

This commentary hopes that those from different cultural backgrounds and social locations will come together and hear the multivalent voice of Scripture. Such variegated readings enable audiences of the Apocalypse to understand that no individual's or group's experiences serve as universal standards. Additionally, these readings challenge church members to listen to one another and gain an understanding of other people's experiences. This varied and reflective approach will allow the readers to "hear what the Spirit says to the churches."

Authorship. The authorship of the Apocalypse is one of the most debated aspects of the book. One of the earliest references to the book's authorship comes from Justin Martyr. He identified the author as the apostle John.[2] Irenaeus identified the author of the Apocalypse as the same person who authored the Gospel of John.[3] Tertullian advanced this position.[4] While significant external evidence appears in the testimony of the early church suggesting that the apostle John authored Revelation, David Aune, on the other hand, asserts that there is a lack of evidence to support this.[5] He explains that pseudonymity serves as a regular feature of Jewish and Christian apocalypses and notes the possibility that Revelation is pseudonymous.[6] J. Massyngberde Ford proposes that John the Baptist composed Revelation 4–11, while Revelation 12–22 comes from another individual, and Revelation 1–3 functions as a later Christian addition.[7] Interestingly, the section of the Apocalypse that Massyngberde Ford attributes to John the Baptist contains none of the self-attestations where the author identifies as John.

As can be seen, multiple theories exist regarding the authorship of Revelation. The diversity of thought reveals that an absolute determination of the author's identity "is a hopeless endeavour."[8] In light of the various suggestions regarding the book's authorship, it seems best to avoid attempts at narrowing the author to a "John" we already know. The text states that the author is "John," whom the original recipients of Revelation would have recognized as needing no further introduction.

Date. Closely connected to the discussion of authorship, the Apocalypse's composition date impacts our understanding of the book's interpretation. Adela Yarbro Collins explains that the sociopolitical nature of the topics the Apocalypse addresses demands precision in dating to avoid misinterpreting the text and missing Revelation's message.[9] The most popular and traditional position places the

[2]Justin Martyr, "Dialogue of Justin, Philosopher and Martyr, with Trypho, a Jew," in *The Ante-Nicene Fathers: Translations of the Writings of the Fathers Down to A.D. 325*, ed. Alexander Roberts and James Donaldson (Buffalo, NY: The Christian Literature Company, 1885), 240.

[3]Irenaeus, *Adversus haereses*, 4.20.11.

[4]Tertullian, *Adversus Marcionem*, 3.14.3.

[5]David E. Aune, *Revelation 1-5* (Dallas: Word Books, 1997), liii.

[6]Aune, *Revelation 1-5*, xlix.

[7]J. Massyngberde Ford, *Revelation: Introduction, Translation, and Commentary* (Garden City, NY: Doubleday & Company, 1975), 28-41.

[8]David Elton Graves, *The Seven Messages of Revelation and Vassal Treaties: Literary Genre, Structure, and Function* (Piscataway, NJ: Gorgias, 2009), 42.

[9]Adela Yarbro Collins, *Crisis and Catharsis: The Power of the Apocalypse* (Philadelphia: Westminster, 1984), 50.

composition of Revelation during the latter portion of Domitian's reign (81–96 CE). This position dates back to Irenaeus (ca. 180 CE).[10] It grew in popularity throughout the early church and maintains that prevalence. At the same time, a diversity of opinions exists regarding the composition date.

The mention of the temple and Jerusalem in Revelation 11 has been used to support a pre-70 date of composition. Because the second temple destruction did not occur until 70 CE, the mention of the temple has been interpreted by some to mean that the temple was still standing and functioning when John wrote Revelation. At the same time, readers must remember that not every aspect of Revelation, even in the vision of "what must take place" (Rev 4:1), speaks of future events. Events such as the birth of Christ (Rev 12:5), Christ's ascension (Rev 12:5), and Satan being cast to earth (Rev 12:9) are all depicted as completed events—not those occurring in the future.

The book's consistent reference to Babylon (Rev 14:8; 16:19; 17:5; 18:2, 10, 21), which refers to Rome, may suggest a post-70 CE composition date. The reference would seem appropriate in the post-70 context, given the parallel actions of Babylon and Rome in destroying the temple in Jerusalem.[11] Additionally, other Jewish writings composed after the temple's destruction refer to Rome as Babylon (E.g., *4 Ezra* 3:1-2, 28; 16:1; *2 Bar.* 11:1).

The association of persecution with the refusal to engage in emperor worship (Rev 13:4-10, 15-17) can support a later date for the composition of Revelation. Despite this possibility, Steven J. Friesen argues, "the date of Revelation should be established on other grounds" besides that of the imperial cult.[12] While widespread, government-sanctioned persecution of Christians is evidenced during the Trajanic period, the text of Revelation evidences a minority of the congregations experiencing persecution. In fact, John places the universal persecution in his future—not his present.[13]

While each position regarding the date of Revelation is plausible, this work embraces the stance that the book was composed toward the end of Domitian's reign, most likely in the mid-90s CE. This position aligns with the post-70 CE composition date while considering the external evidence of early church testimony. Such a position demands that readers of Revelation see the text challenging far more churches in their comfort than it consoles in their afflictions.

Setting. If the traditional scholarly position regarding the date of Revelation's composition is accurate (i.e., ca. 94–96 CE), it becomes essential to discuss the "settings" of Revelation. All the congregations were in areas under Roman rule. Though located in the same geographic region, the cities where each community resided had unique social circumstances. Similarly, writing to the seven churches in the United States, the seven assemblies in Alabama, or the seven parishes in Boston would require understanding each community's setting. During Domitian's reign, "the imperial cult was strongly promoted in the Roman provinces."[14] He also "demanded that

[10]Irenaeus, *Adversus haereses*, 5.30.3.

[11]Adela Yarbro Collins, *Crisis and Catharsis: The Power of the Apocalypse* (Philadelphia: Westminster, 1984), 58.

[12]Steven J. Friesen, *Imperial Cults and the Apocalypse of John: Reading Revelation in the Ruins* (Oxford: Oxford University, 2001), 150.

[13]David L. Mathewson, *Verbal Aspect in the Book of Revelation: The Function of Greek Verb Tenses in John's Apocalypse* (Leiden: Brill, 2010), 146-48.

[14]Elisabeth Schüssler Fiorenza, "The Followers of the Lamb: Visionary Rhetoric and Socio-political Situation," in *Early Christian Apocalypticism: Genre and Social Setting*, ed. Adela Yarbro Collins (Decatur, GA: Society of Biblical Literature, 1986), 136.

the populace acclaim him as 'Lord and God' and participate in his worship."[15]

Most congregations receiving the Apocalypse are in cities that promoted and advanced the imperial cult. The cult found a prosperous place for propagation in Ephesus, as the city had temples dedicated to various emperors. Smyrna, known as "an ally of Rome,"[16] was a provincial center for the imperial cult.[17] Pergamum served as the birthplace of the cult.[18] In Thyatira, "cultic propaganda went so far as to declare the Roman emperor to be the incarnation of Apollo and therefore a son of Zeus."[19]

The beginning of John's first vision highlights him as a brother and partner of those in the seven assemblies. The text continues by saying that he received a vision while on Patmos. Though Dwight Sheets asserts that John may have gone there "simply to write the Apocalypse,"[20] John notes that his presence on Patmos was "because of the word of God and the testimony of Jesus" (Rev 1:9). Throughout the book, he repeatedly mentions "the word of God" (Rev 6:9, 20:4) and testimony (Rev 6:9; 11:7; 12:11; 12:17; 19:10; 20:4) in direct connection to the suffering of the faithful. Like John, some congregations (Smyrna and Philadelphia) faced suffering, opposition, and persecution. John writes to these people, encouraging them to maintain their faithfulness to the kingdom. Other assemblies, like Ephesus, Thyatira, Sardis, and Laodicea, possess power but fail to use their authority in ways that reflect the teachings of Christ and the principles of his kingdom.[21] Instead, their activities parallel the systems of the worldly empire in which they live. The Christian community in Pergamum has already faced persecution at the hands of their local government when John writes to them (Rev 2:13). While some congregants remain faithful, others conform to the broader culture in light of the social and political pressures they face. John writes to these people and encourages them to do what today's church must do—unite and demonstrate the faith they previously professed.

Outline. The popular connection of Revelation with eschatology and attempts to determine the order of end-times events has significantly influenced how scholars, clergy, and laity classify the book's content. While the book of Revelation does not neatly fit into any chronological framework, it has a literary structure that guides readers through the text. Revelation begins with the prologue (Rev 1:1-8) that introduces the writing ("the revelation of Jesus Christ," Rev 1:1), author ("John," Rev 1:1, 4), and recipients of the text ("the seven churches that are in Asia," Rev 1:4). The references to John shifting from third-person singular (e.g., "he, him," Rev 1:1-2) to first-person singular ("I," Rev 1:9) signal the transition to the body of the text.

[15]Schüssler Fiorenza, "Followers of the Lamb," 136.

[16]Leon Morris, *Revelation: An Introduction and Commentary* (Downers Grove, IL: InterVarsity Press, 1987), 63.

[17]Giancarlo Biguzzi, "Ephesus, Its Artemision, Its Temple to the Flavian Emperors, and Idolatry in Revelation," *Novum Testamentum* 40, no. 3 (1998): 280-84.

[18]Friesen, *Imperial Cults and the Apocalypse*, 42.

[19]Brian K. Blount, *Revelation: A Commentary* (Louisville, KY: Westminster John Knox, 2009), 62.

[20]Dwight Sheets, "Something Old, Something New: Revelation and Empire," in *Jesus Is Lord, Caesar Is Not: Evaluating Empire in New Testament Studies Today*, ed. Scot McKnight and Joseph B. Modica (Downers Grove, IL: InterVarsity Press, 2013), 205.

[21]Karen Stanbridge and Howard Ramos, *Seeing Politics Differently: A Brief Introduction to Political Sociology* (New York: Oxford University Press, 2012), 3. While the Roman empire possesses power, that does not mean those under Roman domination lack power in all aspects of life. Stanbridge and Ramos explain that a person "possesses power only in relation to others." Therefore, while one person may possess more power than someone else, that same person with less power may have more than another individual. Even for a congregation like the one in Philadelphia that has "little power" (Rev 3:8), their resistance against the powerful functions as an exercise of power.

This central portion of the material consists of four distinct visions, initiated by a combination of three unique features: (1) an angel speaking to John (Rev 1:11; 4:1; 17:1; 21:9), (2) John receiving instructions related to the visionary experience he is about to have (Rev 1:11; 4:1; 17:1; 21:9), and (3) John's state of being "in the Spirit" (Rev 1:10; 4:2; 17:3; 21:10). Along with the instructions John receives regarding his visions, the angel usually provides him with an explanation of the vision. The second vision (Rev 4:1–16:21) predicts "what must take place after this" (Rev 4:1). The third vision (Rev 17:1–21:8) foretells "the judgment of the great whore" (Rev 17:1). The fourth vision (Rev 21:9–22:5) presents the bride (Rev 21:9). The first vision (Rev 1:9–3:22), unique from the others, portrays John—not an angel—noting that the vision is of one like a Son of Man amid seven golden lampstands (Rev 1:12-13). The book concludes with an epilogue (Rev 22:6-22) that recalls much of the language of the prologue and first vision. Thus, we have an inclusio, a bookend, encouraging recipients to heed what they have read and heard (Rev 1:3; 22:7, 9).

PROLOGUE AND EPISTOLARY GREETING (REVELATION 1:1-8)

Revelation's prologue (Rev 1:1-3) and epistolary greeting (Rev 1:4-8) emphasize the commonality shared by the book's recipients, who come from different social backgrounds. The prologue shows John and his recipients' shared status as Christ's slaves.[22] The epistolary greeting highlights how these varied communities share a common identity not only as Christ's slaves but as priests in God's kingdom because of Christ's redemptive work. It also provides a foundation for audiences to understand that Christ will abolish the systemic frameworks that oppress societal members. He will do this while manifesting his kingdom of righteousness and justice worldwide. This knowledge should guide those who have participated in the injustice of worldly kingdoms to forsake their participation in that which Christ will destroy.

Prologue (Revelation 1:1-3). John begins his work by highlighting that he and his recipients share the same status. The text opens by informing audiences that the content of the

Table 33.1. Visions of Revelation

Vision #	Angelic Identification	Content of the Vision	John "in the Spirit"
Vision 1	"I heard behind me a loud voice like a trumpet" (Rev 1:10, cf. Rev 1:1)	"I saw seven golden lampstands, and in the midst of the lampstands I saw one like the Son of Man" (Rev 1:12-13)	"I was in the spirit on the Lord's day" (Rev 1:10)
Vision 2	"And the first voice, which I had heard speaking to me like a trumpet" (Rev 4:1)	"I will show you what must take place after this" (Rev 4:1)	"At once I was in the spirit" (Rev 4:2)
Vision 3	"Then one of the seven angels who had the seven bowls came" (Rev 17:1)	"I will show you the judgment of the great whore" (Rev 17:1)	"So he carried me away in the spirit" (Rev 17:3)
Vision 4	"Then one of the seven angels who had the seven bowls full of the seven last plagues came" (Rev 21:9)	"I will show you the bride, the wife of the Lamb" (Rev 21:9)	"And in the spirit he carried me away" (Rev 21:10)

[22]Murray J. Harris, *Slave of Christ: A New Testament Metaphor for Total Devotion to Christ* (Downers Grove, IL: InterVarsity Press, 2001), 142-43. Harris acknowledges the negative aspects of slavery. He observes that the biblical writers utilize images of slavery both positively and negatively. They encourage slavery to Christ and strip this slavery of the negative images normally associated with it. As a result, he defines slavery as "someone whose person and service belong wholly to another." Based on this definition, all those whom Christ has redeemed should operate in service to him and therefore function as his slaves.

book is a "revelation of Jesus Christ," highlighting that the things they are about to read or hear did not originate with John but with God, who gave the revelation to Jesus "to show his slaves what must take place soon" (Rev 1:1 au. trans.). Reference to the recipients as slaves reinforces the understanding that these people have the same status and belong to God and Christ. Even as citizens of an earthly kingdom, they owe their utmost allegiance to the kingdom of God. Therefore, they should lean into their commonality and remain united while recognizing the diversity of their experiences. This means that whenever the practices and principles of an earthly kingdom conflict with the kingdom of God, the slaves of God and Christ should unite in submission to the will of their divine Masters—God and Christ.

The revelation begins with God, who gives it to Jesus, who reveals it to John via an angel. John identifies himself as a slave—the term he uses to describe his recipients. Many Bible translations render the term not as "slave" but as "servant." Given the history of the United States, many within the country may initially think of the horrors of the transatlantic slave trade that impacts the nation's present-day conditions. That is not the type of slavery of which John speaks. He notes that Christ "purchased" his slaves with his blood and made them "a kingdom and priests" to God, resulting in their royal participation in his kingdom. Regarding the horrible impacts of slavery, later parts of Revelation connect the judgment and condemnation of Babylon with the commodification of humans through the trading of enslaved people as nothing more than "cargo" (Rev 18:11-13). This acknowledgment of how people objectify others reveals that while slavery may have functioned as a normal part of the culture in the ancient world, God maintained concern then, as he does now, for those dehumanized through systems of slavery.

The text identifies John as a faithful witness to share his vision. This book's message is so significant that the implied author pronounces a blessing on those who read, hear the words of the prophecy, and keep the things written in it. The pronouncement of such a blessing informs the readers that if there are things they must "keep" (Rev 1:3, understood as "obey"),[23] they might have to change how they are living. This challenge remains for congregations that hear the words of Revelation today.

Epistolary greeting (Revelation 1:4-8). The epistolary greeting functions like the introduction of most of the letters in the New Testament, introducing the author and recipients. Generally, it also contains some form of declaration of grace and peace from God the Father and the Lord Jesus Christ. Like most New Testament epistles, John produces a similar greeting in the epistolary portion of his work. Considering the sociopolitical context of John and his recipients, the declaration of grace and peace may serve as more than an expressed desire for blessings on the recipients. John's epistolary greeting reveals the true source of grace and peace though he lives under an empire that claims to bring peace to its inhabitants.

John addresses his writing to "the seven assemblies" (Rev 1:4 au. trans.), referring to more than the worshiping community. Within the context of the New Testament, the term translated as "church" also refers to an "assembly of citizens, who gathered for deliberation."[24] John's language, therefore, highlights that the assemblies to which he writes consist of

[23]Craig R. Koester, *Revelation: A New Translation with Introduction and Commentary* (New Haven, CT: Yale University Press, 2014), 214.

[24]Koester, *Revelation*, 256. Acts 19 presents such an occurrence when a group that opposes the spread of the gospel comes together (Acts 19:32, 39, 40).

citizens of God's kingdom congregating in various geographic locations within Asia. This understanding reminds those in the churches that Christ's kingdom "is not of this world" (cf. Jn 18:36).

The salutation declaring the divine blessings of grace and peace reveals the promises of worldly governments as nothing more than a counterfeit or deficient sample of what God's kingdom offers. Grace and peace come from "him who is and who was and who is to come and from the seven spirits who are before his throne, and from Jesus Christ, the faithful witness, the firstborn of the dead, and the ruler of kings on earth" (Rev 1:4-5). Rome claimed to spread the *Pax Romana* (the Roman Peace), but this "peace" occurred through war, violence, bloodshed, and domination.[25] Instead of a false peace—or a selective peace for those favored by the empire—coming from Rome, John highlights the actual source of peace. The mention of a throne (Rev 1:4) announces the presence of an alternative kingdom to the worldly political kingdom under which John and his recipients lived. John declares that Jesus is "the ruler of the kings of the earth" (Rev 1:5) and that the power and authority of his kingdom supersede that of all world governments and their representatives. Such statements challenge readers of the Apocalypse to look to Christ and his kingdom—not the world's kingdoms—for solutions to their problems.

John follows his mention of Christ with a doxology, highlighting Jesus' work in giving John and his fellow servants another shared status. While these people are slaves, Christ makes them "a kingdom, priests" (Rev 1:6). The doxology speaks of deliverance from the bondage of sin. This language recalls the exodus, which recounts the story of God redeeming his people from the bondage of slavery in Egypt. In the exodus account, God overcomes one of the most powerful kingdoms in human history and frees his people from slavery. Later, he declares that he will make the Israelites a "kingdom of priests" (Ex 19:6). This reveals that Christ's deliverance is not simply spiritual but physical. Just as God delivered the children of Israel from the hands of the Egyptians, he can and does free the oppressed from the hands of their oppressors. Just as with the exodus, these acts of deliverance often occur through human agents who act according to God's will to see such liberation accomplished.

Though the people of God have experienced deliverance from the shackles of sin, some continue to experience physical oppression at the hands of others. John emphasizes the physical realities of oppression and deliverance through his appeals to Old Testament writings, particularly Daniel and Zechariah. Additionally, he utilizes language that also appears in Matthew. These texts highlight God's response to the injustice his people experience. He comes as the supreme Judge who rectifies the wrongs done in the world and acts especially on behalf of those who suffer for faithfully following him. Daniel mentions one like a Son of Man coming with the clouds. Zechariah discusses people mourning as they look at a figure they have pierced. Like Matthew, John conflates Daniel's and Zechariah's language into a single statement, suggesting the authors of these works maintain some shared understanding regarding divine judgment.

Despite the varying language among these writers, each text possesses a theme of divine judgment. Daniel has a vision of one like a

[25]Tacitus, *Agricola*, 30. David L. Mathewson, "Social Justice in the Book of Revelation: Reading Revelation from Above," in *The Bible and Social Justice: Old Testament and New Testament Foundations for the Church's Urgent Call*, ed. Cynthia Long Westfall and Bryan R. Dyer (Eugene, OR: Wipf and Stock, 2016), 181.

Son of Man coming "with the clouds" before the Ancient of Days, who sat on a throne. Daniel explicitly notes that "the court sat in judgment" (Dan 7:10). He discusses the abuse God's people experienced "until the Ancient One came; then judgment was given for the holy ones of the Most High, and the time arrived when the holy ones gained possession of the kingdom" (Dan 7:22). Daniel also notes that God judges the one who persecutes his people, takes away his power, and destroys him (Dan 7:26). Zechariah speaks of people mourning as they look on "the one whom they have pierced" (Zech 12:10). This occurs amid a series of oracles that speak of God's authority to judge the nations and those in covenant with him.[26] Matthew conflates the two prophetic writings. He places them in a context where "the kinds of disturbances in the heavens spoken of in Mt 24:29 accompany the herald of God's intervention and judgment."[27] While Zechariah seems to limit the framework of mourning to the people of Israel, Matthew universalizes it to all people. John engages in this same practice by declaring "every eye will see him" and noting the response of "all the tribes of the earth" (Rev 1:7). Additionally, John inaugurates his first vision by discussing his "persecution" (Rev 1:9), paralleling the language of the Matthean text (cf. Mt 24:9, 21, 29).

VISION 1: CONFRONTATION OF THE ASSEMBLIES (REVELATION 1:9–3:22)

John's first vision introduces one like a Son of Man—Jesus Christ—who evaluates the seven congregations regarding how they have functioned as citizens of the kingdom of God in the context of the earthly kingdoms in which they live. This figure confronts each congregation through communications resembling Roman imperial edicts.[28] The messages portray divine evaluations of each community that assess their faithfulness amid ever-present opportunities to conform to the surrounding culture. Just as these churches in the text receive evaluations, contemporary readers of the Apocalypse must recognize that God evaluates their faithfulness to him and will reward them accordingly.

In a world where sociopolitical disagreements divide the church, Christians should heed John's emphasis on the partnership in suffering that congregations are to share based on their identification as citizens of God's kingdom. He relates to his recipients by noting himself as a fellow participant in "the persecution and the kingdom and the endurance in Jesus" (Rev 1:9). This mention of tribulation parallels the Matthean material in signaling the coming of the Son of Man in judgment. For John, his tribulation occurs in his presence on Patmos "because of the word of God and the testimony of Jesus" (Rev 1:9). His experience embodies how prophetic voices often appear at the margins of society, where people experience suffering.

The churches do not need to hear John's opinions regarding their interactions or alignment with their government. They must listen to what Christ—the ultimate Judge and Ruler—says. The writing reiterates that John does not operate of his own accord. He is "in the spirit" (Rev 1:10). He writes to the churches based on instructions from an angel (Rev 1:10-11, cf. Rev 1:1) and Jesus Christ (Rev 1:19). The messages to the churches appear as the words of Christ, who is not distant from any of these

[26]Mark J. Boda, *The Book of Zechariah* (Grand Rapids, MI: Eerdmans, 2016), 694.

[27]John Nolland, *The Gospel of Matthew: A Commentary on the Greek Text* (Grand Rapids, MI: Eerdmans, 2005), 983.

[28]David E. Aune, "The Form and Function of the Proclamations to the Seven Churches (Revelation 2–3)," *New Testament Studies* 36, no. 2 (1990): 204.

communities. He is amid the seven lampstands (Rev 1:13), which are the seven churches (Rev 1:20). This introduction prepares the congregations to hear what their Judge has to say.

The presentation of one like a Son of Man portrays him as a Judge who exercises authority over creation. While interpreters offer various ideas regarding whether the depiction of the one like a Son of Man reflects a priestly role[29] or a social rank,[30] the imagery maintains many parallels with visions of Daniel 7 and Daniel 10. The similarities highlight the judicial authority of the one like a Son of Man. He begins by exercising this authority over the churches.

Evaluation and judgment of the assemblies (Revelation 2:1–3:22). Though all seven congregations are in Asia Minor, they appear in different social locations, resulting in differing experiences for each community. The community members' behaviors determine the message each group receives. The one like a Son of Man confronts each of the assemblies to which John addresses his writing.

Though John identifies Revelation's recipients as Christ's slaves, not all have obeyed their master. The groups at Ephesus, Pergamum, Sardis, and Thyatira receive both commendations and critiques. Christ only commends the communities in Smyrna and Philadelphia. The congregation at Laodicea receives only criticism. Despite the collective criticism of the community in Sardis, Jesus acknowledges the faithfulness of a few. These messages also impact how each assembly reads and understands the remainder of Revelation.

Revelation's readers must remember that the social locations of congregations and individuals do not determine Christ's commendations or critiques. Their collective and individual actions determine what Christ says to them. While believers from different social locations may disagree regarding the significance of their activity or inactivity, each community—and its members—must face the reality of Christ's evaluation no matter how well or poorly they believe they faithfully follow him.

Message to the church in Ephesus (Revelation 2:1-7). The message to the Ephesian church opens with praise for the congregation regarding their opposition toward evil. Their interactions with other people most clearly reflect this. They cannot stand evil people; they test self-proclaimed apostles and find them false. John's description of the congregation's attitude further demonstrates their opposition to evil. They exhibit patient endurance, bear up for Christ's name, and have not grown weary. Despite this praise, the congregation soon receives a critique regarding another aspect of their attitude.

While Jesus commends the community for their activities, he critiques them for the attitude behind their actions. They abandon a foundational principle of Jesus' teaching—love—to stand for him. In this instance, they seem to function as those who profess allegiance to Christ but fail to live according to his teachings consistently. Though he criticizes their lack of love, Christ commends them for their hate. The congregation hates the Nicolaitans' works—not the Nicolaitans themselves (Rev 2:6). This provides a biblical foundation for recognizing that one can hate a person's sins. Still, their hate for that sin does not legitimize hatred or mistreatment of the person.

In response to the church's lack of love, Jesus calls the congregation to repentance and notes that failure to repent will result in the

[29]Robert H. Mounce, *The Book of Revelation* (Grand Rapids, MI: Eerdmans, 1977), 57-58.
[30]David E. Aune, *Revelation 1–5* (Dallas: Word Books, 1997), 93.

removal of their lampstand (Rev 2:5). Since Jesus is "in the midst of the lampstands" (Rev 1:13), the removal of the lampstand constitutes the removal of this church from Christ's presence. Such a threat warns all Christians who attempt to act in Christ's name in an unloving manner that they are in danger of separation from him.

This first message, as do all of them, concludes with a call to hear what the Spirit says to the churches and a promise to the overcomer. In the first three messages, the call to hear precedes the promise. In the last four messages, the call to hear follows the promise. For those in the seven churches and the global church, people overcome by "remaining faithful, even to death in order to experience glorious, everlasting life with God, the Lamb, and all the redeemed in God's new heaven and earth."[31] The promise of access to the tree of life recalls the story of the creation and humanity's rebellion against God. With their rebellion, humans lost their access to the tree of life. It would seem that fulfillment of this promise results from demonstrating faithfulness to Christ amid an ungodly culture.

The message to the assembly in Ephesus encourages the congregation to maintain its standards in opposing evil and standing for righteousness but challenges them to do so in a loving manner. The history of the United States reveals that many people in North America who profess to follow Jesus have consistently taken it upon themselves to stand for Christ in ways that fail to reflect the love of Christ. Such attempts have resulted in church members compromising their faith and conforming to the broader culture, utilizing ungodly means to achieve what they perceive as godly goals.

Message to the church in Smyrna (Revelation 2:8-11). The city of Smyrna was known as an "ally of Rome" that possessed great wealth and served as a provincial center for the imperial court.[32] The church in Smyrna was no ally to their worldly government and suffered because of it. They did not possess the wealth of their surrounding community. They experienced tribulation and poverty, likely a result of their refusal to conform to the status quo of the broader culture.

Their poverty was the least of their worries. The slander they experienced from the "synagogue of Satan" only created more problems for this community. This "synagogue," likely comprised of individuals aligned with the Roman government,[33] brought accusations against those among them. Their slandering of the community would only create more problems for this group, resulting in increased poverty, imprisonment, and death.

Jesus, the one "who died" at the hands of the government under which he lived but "came to life" (Rev 2:8), warns the group of the future suffering they must face but encourages them not to fear. Though only "some" will experience imprisonment, this will negatively impact the entire community. Though this "tribulation" will occur for a limited time, it will likely result in the deaths of those imprisoned. Considering Jesus' death and resurrection, those in Smyrna are encouraged to remain faithful even if they face death. Such faithfulness will result in them receiving the crown of life.

With the call to hear the words of the Spirit comes the promise to the one who overcomes

[31]Michael J. Gorman, *Reading Revelation Responsibly: Uncivil Worship and Witness; Following the Lamb into the New Creation* (Eugene, OR: Cascade, 2011), 177.

[32]Mark R. J. Bredin, "The Synagogue of Satan Accusation in Revelation 2:9," *Biblical Theology Bulletin* 28, no. 4 (1998): 161; Koester, *Revelation*, 273–74.

[33]Richard Bauckham, *The Theology of the Book of Revelation* (Cambridge: Cambridge University, 1993), 124; Bredin, "The Synagogue of Satan Accusation in Revelation 2:9," 161.

that they "will not be harmed by the second death" (Rev 2:11). In other words, even if people die in this life because of their faithfulness to Jesus, they will never die again. The second death refers to the lake of fire, into which those who affiliate with the beast and his empire will be cast (cf. Rev 20:14).

The imprisonment of the faithful in the message to the congregation at Smyrna highlights the immoral use of the legal system under which the people lived. The lack of justice in the United States legal system has been a point of contention for many throughout its history. This is not to say that the country's legal systems are unjust in every situation. At the same time, they should not be unjust under any circumstances. Though not all who suffer at the hands of a prejudicial government are righteous before God, governments maintain a moral responsibility to act justly toward all people (cf. Rom 13). The message to the church in Smyrna promises that those faithful to Christ will receive the crown of life if they are "faithful until death." Readers of the Apocalypse in any era should understand that the resurrection of the righteous who die at the hands of an oppressive government serves as an indictment against world powers for their injustice. This should cause pause for those in positions of authority who enact such injustice and those who support such practices.

The message to the congregation in Smyrna encourages the community to remain faithful to Christ amid their experiences of legal and economic injustice. No matter how great civilizations have been, worldly governments' financial and legal systems possess some form of corruption. In the United States, people hear cries against systemic racism connected with concerns regarding economic opportunity and the country's legal system. While tools like affirmative action are said to bring equity within the job market, lending practices that charge ethnic minorities higher interest rates maintain and bolster economic inequity. The disproportionate sentencing of Black Americans and other minorities in the legal system continues to impact them negatively. During the era of the early Church, such discrimination existed against people of another ethnic group—Christians.[34]

Message to the church in Pergamum (Revelation 2:12-17). Pergamum was the first home of the imperial cult in the region, building a temple to Augustus while he was still alive.[35] The congregation in Pergamum faced opposition from the government for their faith. Their resistance to the government could result in death. Sadly, some within the church began to compromise on biblical standards and engage in practices such as idolatry and sexual immorality (Rev 2:14-15). The message to the church in Pergamum challenges the congregation to unite and stand against the pressures to conform to the customs of the secular culture.

The congregation lives where "Satan's throne is" (Rev 2:13). The presence of this throne shows that the assembly in Pergamum lives in a geographic location under the authority of a satanically-empowered worldly government that operates "in opposition to the kingdom of God."[36] Despite their environment, they had historically maintained their faith in Christ, even when it meant that Antipas, a Christian community member, was killed because of his faithfulness to Jesus (Rev 2:13). The mention of "the days of Antipas" seems to place his death at a time in the past, which suggests that things at the time of John's composition may not have

[34]Tertullian, *Ad Nationes*, 1.8. In this writing, Tertullian speaks regarding the derision and discrimination Christians face as a "third race" of people, highlighting the inferiority with which those outside the faith viewed them.

[35]Mounce, *The Book of Revelation*, 78-79.

[36]Laszlo Gallusz, *The Throne Motif in the Book of Revelation* (London: Bloomsbury T&T Clark, 2014), 205.

been as bad for the community as before, but that makes their situation no less significant.

Reference to the "throne of Satan" likely refers to the seat of the proconsul—an official empowered by the emperor to rule over the region and exercise the power of the sword in capital punishment.[37] No matter how intense things were or could get for the Christians in Pergamum, Jesus confronted this congregation because some had begun to compromise, capitulate to the culture, and "hold to the teaching of Balaam," likely to avoid persecution. They now engage in idolatry and sexually immoral acts in attempts at self-preservation. If they conform, they will not face the sword of the proconsul, but they will face another sword.

In response to the activities of some in this congregation, Jesus, the one "who has the sharp two-edged sword" (Rev 2:12), commands the assembly to repent. Such repentance would bring the church into a united resistance against the worldly government under which they live. For those in the community who fail to repent and continue to align with the broader culture, Jesus explains that they will face his sword. In Revelation 19:11-16, Christ fulfills this promise and appears as one who wages war with the sword from his mouth to strike down the nations. Considering this, Christ's threat to the impenitent of this community reveals that they will be identified with the unrighteous and suffer the same fate as they.

Those in the Pergamum assembly must determine before whom they will choose to stand guilty. Will they be guilty before the worldly government and suffer death in this life, or will they be innocent in the eyes of the world and face the sword of the supreme Judge? Contemporary Christians must answer the same questions as those in Pergamum did. While the temptations and practices may differ, they must decide whether they will unite with their brothers and sisters who continue to suffer under the oppressive hand of a tyrannical government and be found guilty with them or continue to align with prejudicial legal systems and stand guilty before Christ.

Like the congregation in Smyrna, the community in Pergamum experiences legal injustice but fails to remain united in their faithfulness to Christ. Unlike the churches in Ephesus and Smyrna, who were united in their activities, the church in Pergamum remained divided regarding their function amid their society. While the message begins with a favorable report of their faithfulness, "some" hold to aberrant teachings that likely reflected the practices and customs of the broader culture (Rev 2:14). It is against "them"—this impenitent subset of the community—that Christ will wage war (Rev 2:16).

In a similar fashion to the congregation in Pergamum, the cultural climate of the church in the United States reflects division on various topics. Though a diverse group of people marched with Dr. Martin Luther King Jr., some who professed to be of the same faith criticized his methods of resistance to the discrimination he and other Black Americans experienced.[38] The resurgence of discussions regarding racism in the United States during the 2010s has resulted in churches dividing over an issue on which they should stand in agreement.

Message to the Church in Thyatira (Revelation 2:18-29). The congregation in the city of

[37]Alan S. Bandy, "Patterns of Prophetic Lawsuits in the Oracles to the Seven Churches," *Neotestamentica* 45, no. 2 (2011): 197; Koester, *Revelation*, 93.

[38]Martin Luther King Jr., "Letter from a Birmingham Jail," in *Liberating Faith: Religious Voices for Justice, Peace, and Ecological Wisdom*, ed. Roger S. Gottlieb (Lanham, MD: Rowman & Littlefield, 2003), 177-87.

Thyatira sits at the opposite end of the spectrum from the church in Ephesus. This congregation possesses power but significantly differs in how it uses its authority. While the community in Ephesus stands against those who made false declarations, this assembly embraces the false teachings of those who come among them. The acceptance of false teaching results in infidelity to Christ, demonstrated by sexual immorality, idolatry, and division in the church. The message to the congregation in Thyatira opposes the community's welcome of worldly indoctrination in the church.

The community has numerous positive qualities, love being the first mentioned in the text. At the same time, the focus immediately shifts to their problem. They permit a woman John refers to as "Jezebel" to come into the community and spread her false teaching (Rev 2:20). This moniker recalls King Ahab's foreign wife—an outsider—who came in among the Israelites and led the king and the people, into idolatry (1 Kings 16:31).[39]

Jezebel being permitted to do these things reveals the community's active role in her presence among the congregation. The church not only fails to resist this imperial collaborator and her false teaching; they welcome her and her instruction. Jezebel's refusal to repent demands the execution of divine wrath on her and impenitent church members who align with her (Rev 2:22).

Some people within the church may suggest that God's grace will help people avoid such judgment and wrath. On the contrary, this text reveals that the grace of God is manifested in the opportunity for repentance and remains in effect for the penitent. The message eventually focuses on those who refuse the allure of imperial rhetoric. In contrast with Christ's actions of throwing Jezebel into bed and her adulterous partners into tribulation, he does not burden these faithful people. He calls them to maintain their position.

Many within the United States church have embraced and spread the political propaganda of their chosen party. They often do this to exercise political power. The message to the church in Thyatira reveals that this approach is not the way to achieve or exercise control. The evaluation concludes with a promise to the one who conquers and keeps Christ's works until the end. He promises to give the conqueror authority over the nations. Amid a group where people failed to exercise their power and stand against evil rightly but allowed it to infiltrate the congregation, those who refuse to conform to the ungodly standards of the world will receive authority. For those in the Christian community, their approaches to gaining political power in this life will determine their receipt of it in the coming age.

The message to the community in Thyatira challenges the congregation regarding their willful embrace and spread of the worldly empire's propaganda. History reveals that many church-going people engaged in and benefited from the transatlantic slave trade and Jim Crow segregation. These people professed to know Jesus but failed to follow his teachings. Contemporary discussions often excuse the behavior of these people by noting that their embrace of racism resulted from them being people of their time. Such responses acknowledge that those people welcomed the teachings and customs of their day and failed to conform to the teachings of Scripture and the practical outcomes of the faith they confessed. Such contemporary practices are like the congregation's at Thyatira in John's time.

[39]Sharon Betsworth, "The Child Snatched Away: Reading Revelation Through a Childist Lens," *Biblical Interpretation* 28, no. 5 (2020), 663.

Message to the church in Sardis (Revelation 3:1-6). The city of Sardis had a magnificent past, but its citizens failed to live in the present. They often relished in their historical reputation, demonstrated by the gathering of its elders in the palace of Croesus as a means of maintaining their city's history and reputation.[40] The location also served as a regional center for the Roman slave trade. Like the city, the church failed to live in the present but attempted to live on its reputation for being alive while exercising general inactivity. The message to the assembly in Sardis challenges this community's attempts at remaining neutral regarding life in the kingdom of God.

Though some may see the lack of activity in the community as the middle ground between the extremes of Thyatira and Ephesus, the community's apathy is a third immoral option. Unlike the assembly in Thyatira, which welcomes false prophets and their teaching, and the congregation in Ephesus, which violates biblical principles to oppose false teachings, the Christian community in Sardis does little. They have a reputation for being alive, but Christ describes them as "dead." The community is basically inactive, and Jesus declares their works incomplete before God.

While other communities' words and actions are evidence against them, this message challenges the community's silence and inactivity. Jesus commands them to "wake up and strengthen what remains and is on the point of death" (Rev 3:2). Like the congregation in Ephesus, this community receives a command to "remember" (Rev 3:3, cf. Rev 2:5). Their "name of being alive" had to have come from somewhere in their past. Like the conqueror in Thyatira, the congregation in Sardis is to "keep" what they "received and heard." This idea of keeping includes the concept of actively engaging in the practices associated with that which they were taught, much in the same way that a blessing is pronounced on those who "keep what is written" in the book. If the congregation does not wake up, Christ will come against them "like a thief" at an unexpected hour.

Like the churches in Pergamum and Thyatira, this community is divided. Similarly, many in the US church have remained silent regarding the abuse of ethnic minorities, but not all have. Jesus notes that "still a few" have not soiled their garments, signifying the righteous activities of those who have clean garments.[41] While most of the church is dead, some of the people in this assembly "will walk with [him], dressed in white, for they are worthy" (Rev 3:4). The conqueror receives a similar promise of being clothed in white garments but receives the additional assurances of their name remaining in the book of life, along with Jesus confessing that person's name before the "Father and before his angels." While earthly legal systems often fail to administer justice rightly, Christ's confession of the conqueror will bring eternal justice to them. This final part of the promise reveals that one's reputation and verbal confession of Jesus do not substantiate their status as the faithful. Christ's acknowledgment of that individual does.

The message to the assembly in Sardis confronts the church regarding its apathy and inactivity concerning righteous living. Under

---

[40]Koester, *Revelation*, 310.

[41]Clifford T. Winters, *Argument Is War: Relevance-Theoretic Comprehension of the Conceptual Metaphor of War in the Apocalypse* (Leiden: Brill, 2020), 77. Winters explains that in Revelation, "the righteous are dressed in bright and clean linens." Such imagery identifies them with the twenty-four elders (Rev 4:4), and those coming out of the great tribulation (Rev 7:13-14), the bride of the Lamb, which John identifies as "the righteous deeds of the saints" (Rev 19:8), and the armies of heaven (Rev 19:14).

normal circumstances, the dominant group often exercises power over the disadvantaged party in extreme ways when in conflict. At the same time, some attempt to remain inactive, silent, and neutral, hoping to avoid the tribulation they see others facing. Sometimes, this means being so different from the marginalized group that no one sees a connection with them. It also means being so much like the oppressive group that people assume participation and support. When speaking against racism in the United States, Martin Luther King Jr. explained, "It may well be that we will have to repent in this generation, not merely for the vitriolic words of the bad people and the violent actions of the bad people, but for the appalling silence and indifference of the good people."[42] This is because silence is not only perceived as a lack of care or concern for the plight of others. Some consider it support for the activities of others that bring about such difficulty. Those in the church must recognize that there is no neutrality in the kingdom of God.

Message to the church in Philadelphia (Revelation 3:7-13). Despite the status people share as human beings, in the United States and many other nations around the globe, people receive different treatment because of their social class, citizenship, gender, or ethnic group. Sometimes, multiple facets of a person's identity come together, resulting in how they are treated. The message to the congregation in Philadelphia encourages the community to remain faithful to Christ despite the disparate adverse treatment they experience compared to other members of the Jewish community in the area. The Roman government afforded Jewish people various "social privileges and protection . . . that were not granted to a Gentile Christian church."[43] While many Jewish people exercised those privileges, not all Jews experienced these liberties to the same degree. Those Jews—including ethnic Gentiles—who worshiped Jesus began to receive different treatment under the law and from their fellow Jews. Black Americans have also known the pains of disparity and unequal treatment. Just as Christian Jews had their identity brought into question, Black Americans had their identity as Americans questioned time and time again. In response to the treatment these Jewish people receive, Christ addresses the faithful and the issue of the closed door they face. Many pray that he will speedily do the same for Black Americans.

The text does not provide all the details regarding this congregation's societal restrictions. Despite this, Jesus would not need to provide open doors to the community if there were no doors closed to them. This community possesses little power. They have minimal capacity to resist the hostility from their opponents effectively. Despite their weakness, the Philadelphian Christians have remained steadfast in their commitments. In response to their faithfulness, Jesus demonstrates loyalty to them.

The community faces opposition from the same group as the Christians in Smyrna—the synagogue of Satan. While the Smyrnaean message mentions blasphemy, suggesting the slandering of the group by these self-professed Jews, the "synagogue" seems to have closed a door to the Philadelphian Christians. Though Ian Boxall mentions Paul's parallel language of an open door referring to an evangelistic

[42]Martin Luther King Jr., "MLK: The Other America," 1967, video recording, Stanford University, www.youtube.com/watch?v=dOWDtDUKz-U.

[43]Mikael Tellbe, "The Sociological Factors Behind Philippians 3.1-11 and the Conflict at Philippi," *Journal for the Study of the New Testament* 17, no. 55 (1995), 117.

opportunity,[44] it seems more likely that the door relates to the community's access to God amid their marginalization.[45] Since only Jewish people could exercise the aforementioned societal privileges, dissociating the Jesus-following Jews from the rest of the community would leave them unable to have the same privileges while stripping them of the only religious heritage they know as the people of God. For this reason, Jesus promises to make these people acknowledge this marginalized group as recipients of God's love. John's language recalls various texts in Isaiah (Is 60:14; 49:23; 43:4) but provides an ironic twist. While Isaiah portrays the opponents of the Jewish people as oppressors, John portrays these self-proclaimed Jews as the oppressors against God's faithful people.

Their faithfulness amid oppression leads Jesus to promise protection from a coming trial. The promise to keep them from "the hour of trial" reveals a season of universal turmoil that will affect a group known as the earth dwellers.[46] John later identifies these earth dwellers as those who, like the synagogue of Satan, aligned with their government, which oppressed and persecuted others in society. In light of the coming trial, Christ encourages this marginalized group by highlighting the immediacy of his coming. While Jesus' coming seems to have a negative association for some congregations, that is not the case for this community. Even as Jesus promises the overcomer in Smyrna the crown of life, he encourages the faithful people of Philadelphia to remain steadfast so they can keep their crowns.[47]

In the same way Black people in the United States have been told that they have no place in the country or have had doors shut to them because of who they are, those Christians in Philadelphia faced the same kinds of opposition. Despite the Jesus-worshiping community being ostracized and marginalized in Philadelphia, Jesus promises them a place of permanence in God's eschatological temple. If there was any doubt regarding their identity as God's people, the promise to the overcomer eradicates it. Jesus assures those who remain faithful an everlasting identity as the people of God. They will bear the names of God and Christ, along with the name of the new Jerusalem. These names not only identify them as God's people; they declare them citizens of his kingdom. No matter the opposition people face, no one individual or group possesses the power to bar the faithful from God's kingdom.

Message to the church in Laodicea (Revelation 3:14-22). The congregation in Laodicea receives a message that opposes their conformity to the broader culture for the sake of economic prosperity. The temptation to align with a worldly empire for personal gain is one of the most significant challenges to Christians living in a prosperous environment like the United States. Those who profess to follow Jesus must decide if they will be part of the world that revolves around money or if they will be willing to give up the economic power they acquire through their affiliation with worldly governments. The message to the congregation in Laodicea counsels the community to prepare to decide whether they will possess economic power at the cost of their soul or keep their soul at the expense of their power. This final message to the assembly stands in stark contrast to all the others, as neither the congregation nor any part

---

[44]Ian Boxall, *The Revelation of Saint John* (Peabody, MA: Hendrickson, 2006), 72.

[45]Koester, *Revelation*, 324.

[46]While some have taken Jesus' words in Rev 3:10 to support the belief in the rapture, later portions of Revelation reveal that the people of God are on earth throughout the book at the same time as the earth dwellers.

[47]This promise of the crown directly connects the suffering people of God.

of the group receives positive comments from Christ.

The negative evaluation of the congregation reveals just how much like the surrounding culture these people in the church have become. Jesus describes them as "neither cold nor hot" (Rev 3:15). These are relative terms. Something cold is distinct from that which surrounds it, just as something hot is distinct from that which surrounds it. In contrast with these two, that which is lukewarm has taken on the character of that which surrounds it. They have become so much like the surrounding culture that Jesus notes that he will separate them from him. This community's conformity to the surrounding culture results in Jesus promising to vomit the assembly out of his mouth.

Just as Laodicea possesses wealth, the speech of abundance reveals that the congregation also does. While they see themselves positively, Jesus points out that they are "wretched, pitiable, poor, blind, and naked" (Rev 3:17). Despite their state, Jesus provides them with counsel to help them rectify their problems. Ironically, Christ's counsel comes in the language of economic exchange. He recommends they buy gold to solve the problem of their poverty, white garments to fix their nakedness, and salve to recover from their blindness. Since they cannot make these purchases from Jesus with their money from the empire, these actions must represent repentance for their participation in the economic systems of the worldly empire.[48] Jesus' declaration of loving those he reproves and disciplines recalls the language of Proverbs 3:11-12. This passage discusses the Lord's discipline and follows the instruction to "honor the Lord with your substance" (Prov 3:9)—a lesson at which the congregation in Laodicea has miserably failed. In light of their failure, the community hears a call to "be zealous and repent."

Christ's comments regarding the congregation reveal their lack of relationship with him.[49] He is outside of the church—his church—knocking to get in. This depiction highlights the church's alignment with the empire to the point that even Christ is an outsider to this community. Though Jesus has threatened to vomit out this lukewarm congregation, this part of the message reveals the reality of the church's separation from him despite his desire to be with them.

For those in the congregation at Laodicea, dissociation from the broader culture and their fellowship with Jesus could potentially result in the loss of economic power. In light of this, Jesus offers authority to the one who conquers. He promises to share his throne with the conqueror. Just as alignment with the broader culture often results in possessing power in an earthly economic context, alignment with Christ and his kingdom will result in him granting power and authority to them. Those in the church today, just as those at Laodicea, must decide with which domain they will align.

Summary and conclusion. The varied social locations of each congregation highlight a reality that many in the church today miss. These communities were within a hundred-mile radius, yet each congregation had different societal experiences. While one community was rich, another was poor. Though one community had power, another experienced persecution. These distinctions among those who participated in some way in God's kingdom highlight that even for those believers living in the same country, the same state, or even the same city, their lived experiences can be vastly

[48]Robert W. Wall, *Revelation* (Peabody, MA: Hendrickson, 1991), 87.
[49]Craig Keener, *Revelation* (Grand Rapids, MI: Zondervan, 2000), 164.

different. John highlights those differences, allowing contemporary audiences to see the diverse backgrounds of each community and highlighting the potential for diverse experiences among Christians today.

VISION 2: JUDGMENT ON THOSE ALIGNED WITH UNJUST GOVERNMENTS (REVELATION 4:1–16:21)

Just as the seven assemblies have experienced judgment that began at the household of God, the recipients of Revelation now receive John's vision of "what will become of the ungodly and the sinners" (1 Pet 4:18). In a world of injustice, John communicates the authority of God and Christ—not only over the churches but—over all creation. The one seated on the throne judges rightly and does not conform to the frailties of earthly legal systems. This Judge cares for the marginalized and vindicates them against evildoers.

John's second vision consistently highlights the judgment of people based on their behavior. The depictions show no distinction between those who participate in the social institution of the Christian church and those who do not. The writing addressing the seven churches reinforces the understanding that people's church affiliation does not protect them from the wrath of God. Demonstrations of wrath are promised to the impenitent people who conform to the surrounding ungodly culture. In fact, John universalizes the experiences of all the churches, demonstrating that actions—not social location or affiliation—determine one's temporal and eternal state. People's repentance and faithfulness to the kingdom of God and Christ protect them from functioning as objects of wrath.

Entering the throne room (Revelation 4:1–5:14). Revelation 4–5 envisions a heavenly court scene.[50] This initial portion of the vision begins with John seeing a throne. While his mention of the throne inevitably recalls Satan's use of legal injustice (Rev 2:13), it also reminds audiences of the justice associated with the kingdom of God. John places the throne at the center of this scene and describes almost everything else in relation to it. The Lord is seated on the throne (Rev 4:2-3, 9-10; 5:1, 7, 13). A rainbow is around the throne (Rev 4:3). The twenty-four elders are around the throne (Rev 4:4). Flashes of lightning, rumblings, and peals of thunder come from the throne. The seven spirits and a sea of glass are before the throne (Rev 4:5-6). The four living creatures are around the throne, on each side of it (Rev 4:6). The elders cast their crowns before the throne (Rev 4:10). The sound of many angels surrounds the throne (Rev 5:11). The centrality of the throne highlights this portion of the Apocalypse as a throne room vision, which signifies forthcoming justice demonstrated through divine judgment (cf. *T. Lev.* 2:2-3; 4:1-2). Since "righteousness and justice are the foundation" of God's throne (Ps 89:14), this literary focus on the throne reassures audiences of the Apocalypse that what is issued from the throne is righteous and just (cf. Ps 9).

The hymnody of Revelation 4–5 reinforces the understanding that God and the Lamb judge in righteousness. The hymn of the four living creatures recalls the language of Isaiah 6:3, where the Lord functions as the supreme Judge.[51] The song of the twenty-four elders highlights God's role in creation (Rev 4:11). This reflects the language of Zechariah 12, which notes God's role as Creator and

[50]R. Dean Davis, *The Heavenly Court Judgment of Revelation 4–5* (Lanham, MD: University Press of America, 1992), 117-207.
[51]Gary V. Smith, *Isaiah 1–39* (Nashville: Broadman & Holman, 2007), 187-88.

establishes his right to judge his creation.[52] The "new song" of Revelation 5 recalls an Old Testament form of praise to God where he not only defeats an enemy but receives recognition as one who judges with equity (Ps 96:1, 10; 98:1, 9). Additionally, it notes the Lamb's role in the constitution of a new creation where he makes those he has redeemed into a kingdom and priests. The fourth hymn attributes many of the same characteristics to the Lamb as have already been attributed to the one on the throne (Rev 5:12; cf. Rev 4:11). The fifth hymn functions uniquely from the preceding ones, as it is to both the one on the throne and the Lamb (Rev 5:13).

The consistent reference to God's throne holds chapters four and five together. While the throne remains in the scene, Revelation 5 focuses on the scroll. The chapter begins with John seeing the scroll (Rev 5:1). An inquiry is made regarding someone being worthy to open the scroll (Rev 5:2), but no one is worthy to open the scroll or look at it (Rev 5:3-4). The Lion of the tribe of Judah is announced as worthy to open the scroll (Rev 5:5), but John sees a Lamb instead of a Lion. The Lamb stands, though it appears to have been slain, highlighting the victimhood of Christ as one killed at the hands of the Roman empire. This Lamb is worthy because of his death (Rev 5:9). The slain Lamb now judges all, including those who judged him.

A unique feature of the scroll is the writing on both sides. The description recalls the scroll Ezekiel saw with writing on the front and back (Rev 5:1; cf. Ezek 2:10). Since the words of Ezekiel's scroll would produce "lamentation and mourning and woe" (Ezek 2:10), one would expect John's scroll also to contain threats of divine judgment.[53] As opposed to the scroll that was open before Ezekiel, the scroll John sees is sealed with seven seals that prevent its contents from being revealed (Rev 5:1; cf. Ezek 2:10). That will change when the Lamb breaks the seals and opens the scroll.

Within a politically polarized society, many people have a vested interest in who sits in their government's seats of power. Such partisan extremism has led some in the church to attach spiritual value to the world's political power. Some go so far as to connect an ethical standard to political systems and parties. While their preferred pundits agree with the teaching of Scripture in one area, they often contradict Scripture in another. Such inconsistency demands that, first and foremost, those in the church maintain their focus on the politics of the kingdom of God and filter all their earthly political views through that framework.

The first six seals (Revelation 6). Multiple scholars have argued that breaking the seven seals is the first septet of demonstrations of divine wrath.[54] Commentators generally build their case based on the first four seals, which introduce the infamous "four horsemen of the Apocalypse." Despite the popularity of this position, the text provides different conclusions. Clifford T. Winters rightly asserts, "the seals are not judgments."[55] No demonstrations of divine wrath against humanity accompany the breaking of the seals. In fact, the last three seals

[52]Boda, *Zechariah*, 694.

[53]Walther Zimmerli, *Ezekiel 1: A Commentary on the Book of the Prophet Ezekiel, Chapters 1–24*, trans. Ronald E. Clements (Minneapolis: Fortress Press, 1979), 135.

[54]Blount, *Revelation*, 122; Mounce, *Book of Revelation*, 140; Grant R. Osborne, *Revelation* (Grand Rapids, MI: Baker Academic, 2002), 275. This appears to serve as the majority position among readers of Revelation.

[55]Winters, *Argument Is War*, 101. While Winters proceeds to argue, "The trumpets aren't judgments either," he seems to read an anticipation of coming judgment into Rev 11:18 that ignores the parallels between the trumpets and bowls of the Apocalypse.

testify against the position that the seals serve as judgments against humanity. The cry of the souls under the altar, which accompanies the breaking of the fifth seal, expresses a desire for judgment on those who dwell on the earth (Rev 6:10). Opening the sixth seal results in cosmic disturbances that incite fear among people but harm no one. Breaking the seventh seal results in the ability to open the scroll and initiates silence in heaven. Since the last three seals fail to function as demonstrations of divine wrath, readers must reconsider if the first four seals do.

While many scholars see these horsemen as agents of divine judgment on the earth, some rightly differ from this position. When discussing these seals, Elisabeth Schüssler Fiorenza explains, "The visions of the seals note the main characteristics of the final time—antichrist, war, hunger, and death."[56] These not only characterize the end; they highlight the injustice associated with worldly empires. Looking at the text in its historical context, she says that these horsemen "reveal and highlight the true nature of Roman power and rule."[57] David Mathewson explains that the first two seals portray Rome "as bent on violence and warfare."[58] Gordon Fee notes that the horsemen reflect "the obvious centuries of conquest by the earthly powers, with focus on the present one, Rome."[59] N. T. Wright explains that the horsemen depict "the basic ills which humans inflict upon one another."[60] This recognition of human—not divine—activities finds support in the parallels between Revelation 6 and Luke 21. In the Lukan passage, Jesus tells his followers about the time of the end of the age and the coming of the Son of Man. In each of these parallels, the passage describes human behaviors—not divine judgments.

The first rider comes on a white horse, holds a weapon of war (a bow), and possesses a crown. He represents the rise of counterfeit salvation through earthly political rule. The rider receiving a crown signifies political authority granted by another. No matter the source of the political power, the rider exercises it wrongly through military might to conquer and not care for others. Just as Jesus told his followers that there would be the rise of false messiahs (Lk 21:8), the political framework of Rome fulfilled a messianic expectation of bringing "peace" by conquering others. The empire's military propagates the "Roman Peace" by exercising injustice. Additionally, many of the empire's citizens worshiped the emperor as a deity. Just as Jesus warns against being led astray, John depicts this figure as a counterfeit Christ who conquers—not by giving his life like the Lamb but—through political power and military might.

While the first seal seems to reflect the political power of the worldly empire, the following three seals reveal the results of earthly rulers failing to exercise their authority in the way God intends. When people embrace the destructive patterns of the world's empires, it leads to further desolation. As Schüssler Fiorenza explains, "The second, third, and fourth seal visions symbolize the destructive powers of internal strife and civil war, inflation, and famine that devastate especially the poor. These visions also portray the destructive

[56]Elisabeth Schüssler Fiorenza, *The Book of Revelation: Justice and Judgment* (Minneapolis: Augsburg Fortress, 1998), 53.
[57]Elisabeth Schüssler Fiorenza, *Revelation: Vision of a Just World* (Minneapolis: Fortress Press, 1991), 63.
[58]Mathewson, "Social Justice in the Book of Revelation," 181.
[59]Gordon D. Fee, *Revelation* (Eugene: Cascade Books, 2011), 92.
[60]N. T. Wright, *Revelation for Everyone* (London: SPCK, 2011), 53.

powers of pestilence and death as the sum of all oppressive powers."[61]

The second rider comes on a red horse and is allowed "to take peace from the earth," resulting in people killing one another (Rev 6:4). Just as Jesus warned of wars and nations and kingdoms in conflict (Lk 21:9-10), John portrays people living in conflict and chaos. The third rider comes on a black horse and holds a pair of scales. The statement John hears speaks of a food shortage. The grain prices reveal the limited supply that can result from war and expose the harsh realities of economic inequities in many societies. Though Jesus declares that there will be famine (Lk 21:11), he does not state the cause of it. Despite this, the destruction of crops and the requisitioning of food and other military supplies served as methods for those engaged in warfare.[62] The fourth rider results from war and famine—Death, with Hades following. These two were given authority over a fourth of the earth, killing with the sword, famine, pestilence, and wild beasts. Luke also notes famines and pestilences as markers of what will occur (Lk 21:11). These things result from unrighteous imperial endeavors.

The fifth seal reveals the souls of those slain for their faithfulness. They ask how long it will be before the Lord judges and avenges their blood on the earth dwellers. John identifies these people with Christ by describing them in like manner—slain (Rev 6:9; cf. Rev 5:6).[63] Their deaths point to the injustice that pervades their legal system. Their suffering connects them with John, who perseveres on Patmos as a victim of legal injustice for the same reason they have been slain (Rev 6:9; cf. Rev 1:9). Their cry against the "inhabitants of the earth" (Rev 6:10), those who align with the unjust government, recalls Jesus' warning that family and friends would turn them over to religious and political leaders so they would be persecuted, and some killed (Lk 21:12, 16). These suffering souls refer to God using a political term—*despotēs* (Rev 6:10). While many translations render this term as "Sovereign Lord," John displays the faithful recognizing who indeed possesses political power. The additional description of God as "holy and true" recalls the message to the suffering assembly in Philadelphia, where the earth dwellers first receive attention (Rev 3:7, 10). It also contrasts the activity of unjust earthly rulers with the just judgment of the one who can judge and avenge rightly. The reception of white robes recalls the message to the community at Sardis (Rev 3:5) and suggests that these individuals clothed in white robes are those who have conquered, highlighting that the call to overcome includes the call to endure tribulation. Despite this, the Lord will bring judgment and avenge the righteous, but the time for judgment has not yet come (Rev 6:11).

The breaking of the sixth seal reveals a series of cosmic disturbances that result in trepidation from people in every sector of society. John's language parallels Luke 21:25-26, where the ungodly fear what will occur, but the faithful are encouraged because of their coming redemption. John's note that people from every sector of society respond in fear reinforces the understanding that while someone's faithfulness to God and Christ might determine their social location, one's social location does not determine their righteousness.

[61]Schüssler Fiorenza, *Revelation*, 62.

[62]Osborne, *Revelation*, 280.

[63]Though the breaking of the second seal results in people slaying one another, John's use of the perfect tense form, along with the passive voice in both Rev 5:6; 6:9, identifies this group with Christ, as opposed to a group of people who actively participate in slaying one another, as in Rev 6:4.

In this case, even those who are slaves have "seen the signs of God's coming judgment" and hide in fear.[64] The question that concludes the cry of these people reveals that they cannot stand, but, as will be revealed, the righteous can.

Interlude. John places an interlude between the sixth and seventh seals. This break amid the seals splits into two subsections, each depicting the faithful people of God. The first subsection portrays the people as those who have experienced marginalization. The second describes them as those who have endured tribulation. Both subsections of the interlude encourage all audiences to live as faithful citizens of the kingdom of God.

Sealing of the 144,000 (Revelation 7:1-8). Amid the breaking of the scroll's seals, this portion of the vision presents the sealing of individuals, protecting them from what will be unleashed with the unrolling of the scroll. While the souls under the altar in the fifth seal have been slain, their brothers and sisters on earth continue to endure but will receive protection from the wrath that God is about to execute. The sealing not only protects the faithful from the coming wrath, but it reminds those in Philadelphia that God keeps his promises. The faithful Philadelphians who have been ostracized see what will happen to them if they remain loyal. God will declare them among the tribes of Israel, highlighting their status as members of the kingdom of God. They will later discover that the seal contains the name of God and the Lamb (cf. Rev 14:1-5), part of the promise to the overcomer in Philadelphia (Rev 3:12).

*Innumerable multitude from every nation (Revelation 7:9-17)***.** In response to the question of "who is able to stand?" (Rev 6:17), John shares his vision of an innumerable crowd "standing before the throne and before the Lamb." This group, clothed in white robes, gives a cry of salvation that acknowledges the power of God and the Lamb in bringing about their redemption. In response to these people's worship, all the angels, as well as the living creatures and the elders, worship God and the Lamb for their exercise of power in the salvation of these people.

While John identifies this multitude as coming "from every nation, from all tribes and peoples and languages" (Rev 7:9), one of the elders asks John about their identity. John's response results in the elder explaining that these people have "come out of the great ordeal" (Rev 7:14). The whiteness of their robes comes from them washing their garments in the blood of the Lamb and highlights some form of active participation in the plan of God. For the church in Sardis, they discover that they must endure tribulation to obtain white robes. This portion of the vision also reveals that protection by God from his wrath does not mean protection from tribulation.

Silence in heaven and the power of prayer (Revelation 8:1-5). With the breaking of the seventh seal, the scroll's contents are revealed, and there is silence in heaven for a half hour. This silence prepares audiences for demonstrations of God's coming wrath. John aligns with the Old Testament prophetic tradition, which repeatedly connects silence with the judgment of the unrighteous (cf. Is 41:1; Hab 2:20; Zeph 1:7; Zech 2:13).[65] The specific mention of a half hour suggests the approach of God's wrath and the deliverance of his people from the oppression they face.[66]

In addition to the silence signaling the coming wrath, the trumpets prepare audiences

---

[64]Blount, *Revelation*, 139.

[65]Davis, *The Heavenly Court Judgment of Revelation 4–5*, 180.

[66]Ian Paul, *Revelation: An Introduction and Commentary* (Downers Grove, IL: IVP Academic, 2018), 165-66.

for what lies ahead. Even as Zephaniah 1:7 associates silence with judgment and wrath, the prophet reveals that the sound of the trumpet signals the coming day of the Lord (Zeph 1:15-16), a time when mighty cities will fall. If nothing else, the trumpets foreshadow the destruction that will come on Babylon (cf. Rev 18:10).

Additionally, another angel has a golden censer and receives much incense to offer with the prayers of all the saints (Rev 8:3). The incense, with the prayers, rises before God. While this is the second time the saints' prayers have received attention in Revelation, the angel now offers the prayers of *all* the saints (Rev 8:3). So far, audiences of the Apocalypse have heard only one prayer—the cry for divine judgment from the souls under the altar (cf. Rev 6:9-10). Despite this, it seems that the prayers of all the saints agree. Richard Bauckham explains that "to indicate that the prayers of the saints are answered by the eschatological judgment of God on the earth, the angel takes fire, symbolizing judgment, from the altar and throws it on the earth."[67] This initiates the episodes of divine wrath that occur in the blowing of the trumpets.

The seven trumpets (Revelation 8:6–11:19). The seven trumpets are the first septet of judgments in the book where angels administer divine wrath. While the execution of God's wrath demonstrates his divine justice, these manifestations recount biblical portrayals of God's judgment against world powers that have oppressed his people. While the first six trumpets recall judgments on Egypt,[68] the last trumpet draws on Old Testament language that discusses the fall of Babylon—the name John now gives to the oppressive government under which he lives.

While various aspects of creation suffer, the first six trumpets serve as judgments that result in restricted devastation. The first four trumpets repeatedly result in one-third of things being destroyed (Rev 8:7, 8-9, 10-11, 12). The fifth trumpet results in torment for five months. The sixth trumpet results in one-third of people dying. These limited judgments provide an opportunity for people to repent before total destruction comes (Rev 9:20-21). Additionally, the future framework of these judgments reminds many of the congregations of the call they received to repent and shows them what lies ahead for them if they fail to do so.

The first six trumpets (Revelation 8:6–9:21). The blowing of the first two trumpets recalls the sealing of the 144,000 in Revelation 7:1-8. The earth, sea, and trees were not to be harmed until after God's servants were sealed. Now, the earth, trees, and sea are negatively impacted. With the first trumpet, "hail and fire, mixed with blood," are thrown on the earth, resulting in a third of the earth and trees, along with all the grass, burning up. This hail and fire recall the seventh plague on Egypt, which consisted of hail and fire coming on the earth (Ex 9:23). The second trumpet results in what appears as a burning mountain being thrown into the sea, resulting in a third of the sea becoming blood, a third of the creatures in the sea dying, and a third of the ships being destroyed. The transformation of the sea to blood and the death of the sea creatures recall the first of the exodus plagues (Ex 7:17-18). For a region where people depended on seafood for a healthy portion of their diet, the death of the sea creatures would have negatively impacted the diets of many and would have had a negative economic

---

[67]Richard Bauckham, *The Climax of Prophecy: Studies on the Book of Revelation* (Edinburgh: T&T Clark, 1993), 82.

[68]G. K. Beale, "The Various Ways John Uses the Old Testament," in *John's Use of the Old Testament in Revelation*, ed. Stanley E. Porter (Sheffield, UK: Sheffield Academic, 1998), 78.

impact on those who sold sea creatures for food.[69] The destruction of the ships enhances the attack on the economics that uphold the unjust system.

Just as the second trumpet affects the sea, the third trumpet impacts the rivers and springs—sources of drinking water. A star falls from heaven onto one-third of these bodies of water. Though only one-third of these waters are affected, they have a horrible effect. Despite the medicinal uses of wormwood,[70] John sees it here as bitter and poisonous, resulting in many deaths.

The fourth trumpet recalls the ninth Egyptian plague, which brings darkness to the land (Ex 10:22). Additionally, darkness in the Old Testament signifies divine judgment. Isaiah 13:10, Amos 5:18, and Joel 2:2 all connect darkness with God's judgment. While Isaiah speaks of the judgment of Babylon, Amos and Joel talk about the judgment of those who are part of Israel. Ultimately, audiences once again receive a reminder that their participation in the churches does not preclude them from experiencing such judgments. Instead, it is faithfulness to Christ and his kingdom that does.

The fifth trumpet, with its locust-like creatures, seems to stand in contrast with the locust plague—the eighth plague on Egypt. In the plague on the Egyptians, the locusts left behind nothing green. In this judgment, the locusts do not negatively impact the vegetation. Instead, they torment the people for five months. In this situation, people desire to die but cannot.

Some of those who desire death due to the fifth trumpet find it because of the sixth. Here, one-third of humanity experiences death at the hands of the four angels bound at the Euphrates River. This language of angels bringing death to people recalls the destroyer of Exodus 12:23. This recollection of the tenth exodus plague reminds audiences of the Apocalypse that God can bring down powerful nations that seem indestructible. The text abruptly shifts to many troops who brought death and destruction. This vision of an army associated with the Euphrates—the empire's eastern border—would likely remind audiences of the Parthians, a people the Romans feared.[71] Audiences are left questioning whether they will align with what appears to be an unconquerable kingdom or the kingdom of God, which suffers at the hands of this world empire.

Interlude (Revelation 10:1–11:14). John's prophetic call sets a precedent for and models what it means to serve as a witness. The interlude between the sixth and seventh trumpets challenges those who identify as the people of God to speak to their culture. Additionally, the portrayal of the two witnesses informs the redeemed kingdom, priests that their participation in the church's prophetic role has the potential to cost their lives.

The angel and the little scroll (Revelation 10:1-11). This portion of the text reinforces John's status as a faithful witness.[72] Though John heard the instruction to write his visions and share them (Rev 1), he now receives a prophetic commission. A mighty angel with a little scroll descends from heaven to earth. This angel serves as a representative of God and Christ, noted by the rainbow above his head (Rev 10:1; cf. Rev 4:3), his face shining like the sun (Rev 10:1; cf. Rev 1:16), and his legs being like fiery pillars (Rev 10:1; cf. Rev 1:15).

---

[69]Paul, *Revelation*, 172.

[70]Koester, *Revelation*, 450.

[71]Mounce, *Book of Revelation*, 194.

[72]Peter S. Perry, *The Rhetoric of Digressions: Revelation 7:1–17 and 10:1–11:13 and Ancient Communication* (Tübingen: Mohr Siebeck, 2009), 105.

Even as the first mighty angel of Revelation is associated with a scroll (Rev 5:2), this angel is also (Rev 10:2). The act of setting his feet on the land and the sea signifies God's authority, as opposed to the authority of the Roman empire, over them. The angel swearing by God reinforces the understanding that God has power over all things, as he created all things (Rev 10:6; cf. Rev 4:11): heaven (to where the angel raises his right hand), earth (where he has placed his left foot), and the sea (where he has placed his right foot).

While the first scroll John sees had seven seals, this one does not. John receives instructions to behave in a similar manner as the Lamb—to take the scroll that is in the open hand of the angel (Rev 10:9; cf. Rev 5:7). The angel then tells John to eat the scroll but warns him that it will be sweet in his mouth but bitter in his stomach. After eating the scroll, the angel tells him what he must prophesy. The angel's mention of "peoples and nations and languages and kings" reveals John's task of prophetically addressing the sociopolitical climate in which he finds himself.[73]

The two witnesses (Revelation 11:1-14). The lives of the two witnesses tell what can happen when individuals do as they do and prophetically speak to their culture. While they experience protection for a significant amount of time, once their prophetic witness is complete, they die at the hands of their government. Instead of remaining silent regarding the wrong that is occurring in society or selectively addressing certain sins while excusing others, a biblically consistent lifestyle among the people of God challenging the wrongs done by people in power has the potential to result in death. Despite those aligned with the world government rejoicing over the bodies of the two witnesses, the vision demonstrates that God will raise the faithful who have consistently spoken to their cultures.

John's vision of the two witnesses encourages his audiences to follow his example and prophetically speak regarding the sociopolitical climates in which they find themselves. This image of how they are to function amid an ungodly society does not simply apply when the activities of the broader culture do not align with their political agendas. Instead, the text guides the people of God in consistently living according to the will of God and the guidance of the Holy Spirit. Strangely, many people in US churches, no matter their political affiliation, oppose some sins while embracing or excusing others. The activity of the two witnesses in Revelation 11 demonstrates that the people of God must consistently speak that which accords with God's Word.

Seventh trumpet (Revelation 11:15-19). Unlike the previous trumpets, the seventh trumpet brings no direct mention of destruction. At the same time, it comes with a declaration of defiance against Rome. John has already declared the heavenly reign of God and his creation of all things. The destructive, unjust practices of Rome have already been exposed. He notes that the heavenly kingdom of God and Christ has overcome the worldly kingdom. The Roman emperor no longer reigns. God and Christ reign forever. The worship from the twenty-four elders notes his exercise of power. The nations' rebellion against the rule of God and Christ (cf. Ps 2) precedes his wrath and judgment. Here, the text notes that judgment results in wrath against the rebellious and reward for the

[73]J. Massyngberde Ford, "The Christological Function of the Hymns in the Apocalypse of John," *Andrews University Seminary Studies* 36, no. 2 (1998): 226. Ford goes so far as to note that John receives a commission "to preach *against* nations and kings" (emphasis mine).

righteous. This refers to more than individuals; it includes economic and political systems. The destruction of those who destroy the earth (Rev 11:18) recalls the prophesied destruction of Babylon in Jeremiah 28:25 and foreshadows the future fall of Babylon, who corrupted the earth with her immorality (Rev 19:2).

The seven unnumbered scenes/signs in heaven and on earth (Revelation 12:1–15:8). Between the trumpets and the bowls appear a series of seven unnumbered scenes. Six of these scenes revisit the situations of the seven churches as they appear in the first vision (Rev 1:9–3:22). These scenes note what must take place by universalizing the situations of the congregations and placing them in a future context. This representation challenges the recipients of the Apocalypse to exhibit unyielding commitment to God and Christ while portraying what the faithful can expect to experience because of their loyalty to the kingdom of God.

The Woman and the dragon: The gospel's challenge to imperial propaganda (Revelation 12:1-17). The message to the church in Thyatira reveals that some in the community have embraced the worldly empire's propaganda instead of the gospel of Jesus Christ. The church in Thyatira permitted Jezebel to bring her teaching into their midst (Rev 2:20). This situation discloses that the congregation not only embraced but actively participated in the propagation of the empire's message. In this portion of the Apocalypse, John communicates that the gospel of Jesus Christ challenges propaganda purported as the good news of a world system.

Two portions of the text recall the message to the congregation in Thyatira. Mentioning that the child will "rule all the nations with a rod of iron" (Rev 12:5) recalls the promise to the overcomer (Rev 2:27). While Jezebel has deceived many in the Thyatiran community (Rev 2:20), John identifies Satan as "the deceiver of the whole world" (Rev 12:9). This common activity highlights the connection between Jezebel, Satan, and the empire.

Revelation 12 draws on the birth of Apollo—one of Rome's pieces of imperial propaganda. The Roman Empire thrived on the story for self-promotion and the encouragement of emperor worship.[74] The propaganda closely associated the reigning emperor with Apollo and supported the identification of the emperor as a son of god—Apollo incarnate.[75] In turn, John uses this popular narrative to advance an alternative polemic that identifies the incarnate Son of God, Jesus Christ, as the one who exercises universal rule over the nations.

Satan's throne and the first beast (Revelation 13:1-10). In the first part of Revelation 13, John points out the diabolical empowerment of the earthly government and the satanic manipulation of capital punishment for persecution. He reveals that the dragon transfers his power, throne, and authority to the beast (Rev 12:17; 13:2). This demonstrates that John sees the devil operating through worldly governments and the political figures who lead them.

The mention of the dragon's throne recalls the message to the assembly in Pergamum, where the community dwells in the same location as Satan's throne (cf. Rev 2:13). Just as the devil possessed the power to deceive, the beast now has that same ability. He does this through his appearance as one having a deadly wound that was healed. This description exposes him as an imitation of Christ, who experienced death and now lives (cf. Rev 2:8; 5:6). The people worshiped the beast and the dragon (Rev 13:3-4). Here, John discloses the danger of looking to earthly political figures as the

[74]Paul, *Revelation*, 214.

[75]Betsworth, "The Child Snatched Away," 663.

fulfillment of messianic hopes. This situation results in people engaging in idolatry, worshiping the devil and his satanically-empowered political leader, whom people see as incomparable and unconquerable (Rev 13:4).

The beast's activity shifts from speech and influence to actions against those who resist his political leadership and oppose his practices. Initially, the beast blasphemes God's name and people (Rev 13:6). Eventually, this verbal opposition against God and his people no longer suffices. The beast decides to wage war on the saints and overcome them (Rev 13:7). Despite the destructive behavior of the beast, all the earth dwellers worship it (Rev 13:8). The beast's worshipers do not suffer as political victims of their government. Therefore, they fail to identify with the slain Lamb and the people who suffer as he did. In typical governmental forms of oppression, such escalation is often normalized and accepted by those who are not victims of abuse.

The conclusion of this section also recalls the message to the community in Pergamum but speaks to all who face a similar situation as they do. The mention of the sword (Rev 13:10; cf. Rev 2:12, 16) comes to the forefront and encourages those who may identify with the Lamb through death at the hands of the empire. It also challenges those who would consider aligning with the empire that they will face a sword and suffer at the hands of Christ. As a result, John encourages the saints to remain steadfast in their faith.

Imperial worship and the economics of compromise (Revelation 13:11-18). John's third scene highlights the economic disparity and injustice related to alignment with and resistance against earthly political systems, particularly regarding the use of religion in support of political figures and structures. This scene recalls the circumstances of two communities—Smyrna and Laodicea—who experience poverty and wealth, respectively. Like these congregations, those who resist the earthly political systems experience poverty, economic injustice, and legal injustice, resulting in death. Those who align with the socioeconomic and political structures of the empire maintain the potential to prosper economically as participants in the systems at work in society.

John introduces this scene with another beast. While the first beast rises from the sea, this one emerges from the earth (Rev 13:11).[76] The disparity between the beast's appearance and speech underscores the potentially deceptive nature of religious integration with earthly political practices. Though the beast has some physical characteristics of a lamb, its true diabolical nature comes through its speech (Rev 13:11). The possession of the first beast's power only reinforces his connection with the dragon (cf. Rev 13:2). Here, John reveals that the acquisition of political power by religious groups can misguide people in viewing political leaders, even those empowered by evil, as messianic figures. For this reason, John warns against following signs that contradict the teachings and principles of the kingdom of God and Christ. This second beast engages in the deception of the earth dwellers (Rev 13:14), just like Jezebel deceives Christ's servants in Thyatira (Rev 2:20) and the dragon deceives the whole world (Rev 12:9).

The religious activity associated with the worldly empire affects every stratum of society (Rev 13:16). Only those who participate in the religious practices of the empire can economically advance. Therefore, those who

[76]Blount, *Revelation*, 242; Koester, *Revelation*, 532. The connection of these two beasts recalls the primeval myth of Leviathan and Behemoth, creatures that God separated from one another in creation as God brought order from chaos. The work of these two utilizing Satan's powers produces chaos for the people of God living under Babylon's rule.

oppose the unjust activities of their governments suffer economic disadvantages. For John and his audiences, the infamous "mark of the beast" reveals the economic benefits of acquiescence to ungodly practices and reveals to audiences—especially those in Laodicea—the spiritual dangers associated with economic prosperity in the context of the Roman empire. People cannot engage in monetary exchange unless they worship the beast's image and take his mark (Rev 13:15-17). The inability to participate in the commercial system without the beast's mark suggests that the mark is money. Like many countries today, the economic currency of John's day bears the image of the political leaders and their names. John explains that the mark is a name and provides a clue for his audiences to decipher the beast's identity, whose number is 666.

For a wealthy congregation like that in Laodicea, this portion of John's vision should challenge them regarding their faithfulness to Jesus versus their desire to maintain and grow their wealth. The poor community, like the one in Smyrna, receives encouragement to keep their distance from imperial compromise even when it means they will suffer economically and experience death. John points to a time when they must decide their ultimate allegiance. They must determine if they will possess economic strength at the cost of their soul or keep their soul at the price of their power.

God's people and political resistance (Revelation 14:1-5). For those in the worshiping community who experience marginalization because of their faithfulness to Jesus in both word and deed, John returns to the 144,000. While the group appeared in Revelation 7, this portion of the text most directly recalls the message to the congregation in Philadelphia where the one like a Son of Man promised the overcomer that he would write his father's name, the name of the holy city, and his name on him. Here, John contrasts those who follow the Lamb with those who follow the beast. The 144,000 are excluded from the economic systems like the faithful Philadelphians experienced marginalization. Despite this, the name of the Father and the Lamb on these people highlights their inclusion in God's kingdom.

For those who experience marginalization for faithfully following Christ, John reassures them of God's faithfulness. This group is on Mount Zion, the historically attested location of the temple and the place of messianic deliverance for the faithful.[77] This group is the only one that learns the "new song" of the heavenly chorus. For those who question the integrity of these people who note they are faithful to God, no lie appears in their mouths. They are blameless.

A call to resistance (Revelation 14:6-13). John's fifth scene denotes divergent outcomes for different groups based on their faithfulness to God and the Lamb or the beasts. While some may be tempted to assert that a lack of loyalty to either group constitutes some middle or neutral ground, the Apocalypse reveals that no neutral ground exists between these kingdoms. This scene recalls the message to the congregation in Sardis. This community has attempted to live on its reputation but engages in minimal activity. Their lack of resistance results in them failing to suffer at the hands of the empire. This portion of the text and the message to those in Sardis discuss eschatological outcomes in relation to angels. While Christ promises the conquerors that he will confess the names of the faithful before his Father and the angels of heaven, the current text notes the torment of the unfaithful before the holy angels.

[77]Osborne, *Revelation*, 525.

While this scene contains three angels making declarations, the only people who hear them beyond the world of the text are those in the seven congregations. The first angel instructs the earth dwellers to "fear God and give him glory" (Rev 14:7). The problem in many churches, like the one in Sardis, is that some people attempt to glorify God in their words but fail to do so through their deeds. Such an understanding also suggests that one's presence among the congregation does not prevent them from functioning as an earth dweller. The second angel declares the fall of Babylon and reveals the power of the empire that exercises authority over the nations and forces them to drink her wine and engage in sexual immorality (Rev 14:8). Babylon's action of "making" all the nations engage in such activity highlights the government's unjust exercise of power. Therefore, those in the churches receive a call to resist imbibing Babylon's intoxicating beverage. This abuse of political power demands the demonstration of divine wrath on the empire. God's wrath does not end there. A third angel proclaims that God will hold responsible for their actions the people who collaborate with and participate in ungodly imperial practices. Though Babylon forced them to drink, the people failed to resist. They have worshiped the beast and its image and received the beast's mark. Their activities—not the government's—will demand that they, along with Babylon, drink the wine of God's wrath (Rev 14:10). While those who die in Christ find rest (Rev 14:13; cf. Rev 6:11), these individuals do not (Rev 14:11). Instead of Christ confessing the name of the conqueror before his Father and his Father's angels, the individuals who fail to conquer will be tormented in the presence of the holy angels and the Lamb (Rev 14:10).

This portion of John's writing calls the saints to endure (Rev 14:12). He encourages the recipients of the Apocalypse to maintain an awareness that judgment is coming. Thus far, those in the churches engaged in ungodly alliances have an opportunity for repentance. That door of opportunity is quickly closing, and they do not want to be aligned with the worldly empire.

The harvests (Revelation 14:14-20). This sixth vision reinforces to those in the churches that the separation of the true and false, along with the eschatological outcome of each group, serves as an exercise of divine responsibility. Therefore, such a job is beyond the scope of those in the churches. Just as one like a Son of Man holds the seven stars in his hand when he confronts the congregation in Ephesus, he now has a sharp sickle in his hand. With this, he demonstrates that he and his heavenly agents effectively fulfill this duty in a righteous manner.

These harvests provide the recipients of the Apocalypse with the potential outcomes of their actions—salvation or wrath. Two harvests occur in this section. One like a Son of Man performs one (Rev 14:14-16) while an angel performs another (Rev 14:17-20). Recognizing the differences between the harvests becomes essential in understanding how those in the churches should respond to others. In this first harvest, one like a Son of Man puts out his sickle and reaps the earth. While some commentators express concern that the one like a Son of Man be understood as Christ because he receives a command, John focuses on the two harvests, not the receipt of a command.

In contrast with the first harvest, an angel performs the second. While the first harvest concludes by noting "the earth was reaped" (Rev 14:16), John draws on the imagery of Joel to reinforce the understanding that this second harvest leads to God's wrath.[78] If audiences fail to connect John's language to Joel, he explicitly notes that the angel throws that which he reaps into "the great winepress of the wrath of God" (Rev 14:19; cf. Joel 3:13). This foreshadows that which is to come as those who align with the politics of their empire will also "drink the wine of God's wrath" (Rev 14:10).

While those in the congregation at Ephesus attempted to decipher who was who in their church, they did so without love. Many in contemporary congregations do the same, trying to determine who belongs and who does not. People in today's contexts often attempt to determine this based on parallels in political ideology. Ultimately, such actions create ruptures in the body of Christ as many serve as collateral damage from the embrace of the world's practices. This scene highlights that the separation will occur according to God's will in the great harvest at the end of time.

The vision of the seven angels with the last seven plagues (Revelation 15:1-8). The last scene bridges these universal visions with what is to come—unlimited demonstrations of divine wrath. The universalized depictions of the situations in the churches precede unrestricted displays of punishment for the impenitent. The messages to the congregations reflect localized conditions while the trumpets resulted in limited demonstrations of divine recompense. Now, John uses this seventh scene to reiterate the call to each community to conquer. He provides an image of those who exercise victory by refusing to yield to the sociopolitical pressures of their governmental systems. While his original recipients face a powerful world empire, John draws on the exodus motif to emphasize the deliverance of the faithful and the results of divine judgment on those aligned with ungodly kingdoms of the world.

John's use of the exodus motif demonstrates that God can address worldly empires and those who align with them. In his depiction of the people standing beside the sea, John references the song of Moses. He also mentions fire, recalling the story of the Hebrew people and their deliverance from the hands of the Egyptians at the Red Sea (Rev 15:2-3; cf. Ex 14–15). The exodus recounts the Hebrew people at the Red Sea with the mighty Egyptian army behind them and the sea before them. The Lord manifested himself as a cloudy, fiery pillar and fought the Egyptians on behalf of the people of Israel (Ex 14:24-25). In the same way, John explains to the churches that the Lord will fight their worldly governments on their behalf if they remain faithful and conquer. While the new song of Revelation 15 does not parallel the song's words in Exodus 15, both praise God for his activity. Following this song, seven angels dressed like Christ in the opening vision (Rev 15:6; cf. Rev 1:13) receive the seven bowls to pour out and complete the execution of God's wrath on those who align with the injustice of the world's empires.

The seven bowls (Revelation 16:1-21). Following the presentations of universal experiences in the seven scenes, John continues his vision with the seven bowls. These bowls of wrath parallel the seven trumpets but continue John's universal expansion of what must take place. While the blowing of the trumpets generally has a partial impact, the pouring out of the bowls results in universal consequences.[79] The bowls highlight divine activity in judgment

[78]John Strazicich, *Joel's Use of Scripture and the Scripture's Use of Joel* (Leiden: Brill, 2007), 367-70.

[79]Pieter G. R. De Villiers, "The Septet of Bowls in Revelation 15:1–16:21 in the Light of Its Composition," *Acta Patristica et Byzantina* 16, no. 1 (2005), 202-3.

while demonstrating how alignment with oppressive kingdoms and their leaders impacts people as they conform to the same behaviors. Ultimately, the responses of those who espouse the deceptive allure of the earth's systems result in them experiencing destruction and death by divine judgment.

The first three bowls recall the message of the angel who proclaims "an eternal gospel" (Rev 14:6) and instructs the earth dwellers to worship the maker of heaven and earth, the sea, and springs of water (Rev 14:7). In this portion of the vision, a voice "from the temple" (in heaven, Rev 16:1; cf. Rev 11:19; 14:17) instructs the angels who have received these bowls of wrath to pour them out (Rev 16:1). The first three angels pour their bowls onto the earth, the sea, and the springs.

When the first angel pours his bowl on the earth, people—not nature—directly experience the impact. All who affiliated with the beast and received his mark had sores break out on them (Rev 16:2). While the wealthy congregation in Laodicea receives a picture of what could happen to them if they do not give up their economic power, John reveals that the reception of the mark is about more than economic opportunity or fiscal injustice. It is about loyalty to the kingdom of God versus dedication to unjust governmental systems and commitment to their leaders.

The second and third bowls maintain significant parallels. Both are poured directly onto bodies of water. The effects of these judgments indirectly affect people in different ways. When the second angel pours his bowl into the sea, these waters become blood, and everything in the sea dies. While the death of sea creatures does not directly affect the people, it impacts their diet and ability to sell seafood and engage in economic exchange. So, even if someone has received the mark of the beast, they cannot buy or sell if they have no goods to exchange. Such restrictions negatively impact their economic power. The third bowl has a different impact. This time, the angel pours the bowl onto the rivers and springs—sources for drinking. These waters, like the seas, become blood. After this, audiences discover that this judgment results from these people's alignment with an oppressive government that killed those committed to God's kingdom (Rev 16:6). These two judgments have directly addressed the economic and legal injustice of the empire and serve as a warning to those in the church regarding how they align with ungodly governments.

The fourth and fifth bowls reveal more than God's wrath; they expose the attitudes and behaviors of those aligned with the empire. Those who adopt Babylon's culture emulate the behaviors of Jezebel and the beast. When the fourth angel pours his bowl on the sun, it scorches people with fire (Rev 16:8-9). In response, these people behave like the beast. Just as the beast blasphemed God's name (Rev 13:6), these people engage in the same activity (Rev 16:9). Even as Jezebel, a collaborator with the empire, received an opportunity to repent but refused, these people do not "repent of their deeds" (Rev 16:11) nor do they comply with the call of the angel who tells them to glorify God (Rev 14:7). After this, the fifth angel pours his bowl on the beast's throne—the one Satan gave him (Rev 13:2). As a result, the beast's kingdom became dark. In response to this, the people "gnawed their tongues in agony" (Rev 16:10). They move beyond cursing God's name like those mentioned in the fourth bowl. They behave like the beast and blaspheme God for the painful sores (Rev 16:11; cf. Rev 16:2; 13:5-6). They refuse to repent.

The sixth bowl addresses the deception many have already experienced. With the pouring of this bowl onto the Euphrates, no harm comes to people. Instead, the river dries, making it possible for political leaders to come from the east and gather for battle. This gathering results from when the dragon, the beast, and the false prophet all have demonic spirits come out of their mouths and go out performing signs and going to the kings of the entire world (Rev 16:14). The performance of signs has previously appeared in association with the second beast who deceives the earth dwellers (Rev 13:14). Therefore, these spirits performing signs (Rev 16:14) should be recognized as a diabolically inspired deception of the world's kings to gather them for battle on the Almighty God's great day (Rev 16:14). While these kings are deceived and likely convene to garner more worldly power, the assembling of these people functions as a day of divine punishment for those who have opposed God and given themselves over to the empire and the leadership of the beast. Ultimately, John explains that their punishment results from following the deceptive message of the empire and aligning themselves against the Lamb.

The pouring out of the seventh bowl onto the air parallels the blowing of the seventh trumpet. It also fulfills God's promise regarding the judgment of those who have opposed him. The events of the seventh bowl follow a pattern of declaration and destruction, warning the audiences of the Apocalypse of what could await them if they are unfaithful. The pronouncement notes the completion of God's wrath on these people. The great city—Babylon[80]—suffers damage. Multiple cities fall, but God is not through with Babylon. He will act in reciprocity and give "the wine-cup of the fury of his wrath" (Rev 16:19) to the one who "made all nations drink of the wine of the wrath of her prostitution" (Rev 14:8). With this, John guides his readers to his third vision.

THE THIRD AND FOURTH VISION AND THE CHOICE OF THE CHURCHES (REVELATION 17:1–22:5)

While the first two visions of Revelation point out the things that are (Rev 1:9–3:22) and "what must take place" (Rev. 4:1–16:21), John frames his third and fourth visions to provide his audiences with a choice. He draws on his tradition to portray these choices as women. The writer of Proverbs does this when presenting Wisdom and Folly as two women between which the reader will have to choose (Prov 9). Paul appears to do something very similar when he contrasts Sarah and Hagar, challenging those in Galatia to decide which woman they desire as their mother (Gal 4:21-31). John engages in this practice and challenges his audiences to choose the kingdom they will align with—Babylon or the kingdom of God. They must choose either the harlot or the bride.[81]

When considering the last two visions of Revelation, it becomes necessary to remember that the text does not provide a chronological series of events.[82] Instead, John provides the outcomes of two paths. In the fourth vision, the nations walk by the light of the holy city. The kings of the earth bring their glory into it (Rev 21:24). In the third vision, the birds gorge

---

[80]Arthur William Wainwright, *Mysterious Apocalypse: Interpreting the Book of Revelation* (Nashville: Abingdon Press, 1993), 17. Wainwright explains that early interpreters of the Apocalypse understood the book to address Rome's persecution of faithful Christians in the empire. John adds further support for this view in Rev 17:9.

[81]Barbara R. Rossing, *The Choice Between Two Cities: Whore, Bride, and Empire in the Apocalypse* (Harrisburg, PA: Trinity Press International, 1999), 16.

[82]Koester, *Revelation*, 121.

themselves with the flesh of the kings of the earth, the nations, all of whom were slain by the sword (Rev 19:21). If these are the same groups, which the text suggests,[83] the third and fourth visions must introduce different scenarios based on the outcomes of people's decisions. Like the writer of Proverbs and Paul, John provides his audiences with the results of associating with each woman.

Vision 3: Judgment of the empire that enacts injustice (Revelation 17:1–21:8). John's third vision exposes the corrupt city, personified as the harlot, who sits on the backs of her citizens and is upheld by people in power. While this vision depicts the judgment of the harlot, John also notes the judgment and destruction of the beasts—political figures who have partnered with her, the devil who has empowered the political figures who support her, and those who have been unfaithful to Christ and aligned with her. The city and these entities have similar outcomes. While the city is destroyed by fire, the beasts, the devil, and the unfaithful all experience judgment and are cast into the lake of fire.

Corrupt governments do not exist in and of themselves. In many situations, they are carried by evil, corrupt leaders who actively oppress certain people while empowering others. Ultimately, all people living under an oppressive government function as part of that government—some as victims of injustice and others as beneficiaries. Each of John's readers—past and present—must identify themselves in their context.

Description of the harlot (Revelation 17:1-6). The vision begins with the angel promising to show John the judgment of the great harlot sitting on many waters (Rev 17:1). Even as God has established governments (Rom 13), John reveals that sometimes those who have the responsibility of exercising God's rule in a just and righteous manner do not always do so. Rather than submitting to the one identified as their ruler at the beginning of the text (Rev 1:5), these kings commit sexual immorality with the harlot (Rev 17:2). This harlot serves as John's parody of the goddess Roma, "a stunning personification of the civilization of Rome."[84] He shows her true nature as a seductress and explains that those who dwell on the earth have consumed the wine of her sexual immorality and become drunk (Rev 17:2). Though John holds these people responsible for their involvement with the harlot, he has already noted that she has exercised her power over them and made them drink (Rev 14:8).

John's visionary experience begins with connecting the harlot with the first beast of his second vision (Rev 17:3; cf. Rev 13:1-10). The beast on which the woman rides has seven heads and ten horns (Rev 17:3; cf. Rev 13:1). It also has blasphemous names (Rev 17:3; cf. Rev 13:1). In addition to the woman riding the beast, John highlights their shared descriptions, further noting the relationship between the two. The beast is scarlet—a color the woman also wears (Rev 17:3-4).

Her possession of gold, jewels, pearls, and a golden cup highlights her wealth. The uncleanness of her sexual immorality filling the cup suggests that her wealth comes via the exercise of injustice in conjunction with the kings of the earth who commit sexual immorality with her.[85] The name of mystery on her forehead demonstrates the extent to which her

---

[83]Koester, *Revelation*, 833. Koester mentions the new Jerusalem offering "the prospect of a different future" than that presented in the judgment of the Harlot for the kings, suggesting the same group of people in each vision, with alternative outcomes presented in these two sections of the Apocalypse.

[84]Bauckham, *Theology of the Book of Revelation*, 17-18.

[85]Bauckham, *Climax of Prophecy*, 369.

injustice reaches. She is the mother of harlots, meaning that she is possibly the supreme example of corruption or the source of corruption for others.[86] Names written on people throughout the book have highlighted their associations in Revelation (Rev 3:12; 13:16-17; 14:1). The same applies to the harlot. This name reveals her as the unjust empire that persecuted God's people. This explains why she is drunk with the blood of the saints (Rev 17:6). The imperial city has shed and consumed many people's blood, which she now consumes.

The mystery explained (Revelation 17:7-18). When explaining the mystery, the angel begins with the beast. He appears as the same one mentioned in Revelation 11:7 that receives additional attention in Revelation 13:1. In that parody, John reveals that the satanically-empowered beast who has brought death to many of the faithful, along with unjust destruction to others, will be destroyed (Rev 17:8). John's twofold explanation of the beast's seven heads identifies them as the seven mountains on which the woman sits—an apparent reference to Rome.[87] It also identifies them as seven kings—people with political power. The beast is also a political figure—an eighth king—who will be destroyed (Rev 17:11). As for the beast's ten horns, they are kings who will receive royal power for a limited time with the beast. These individuals with political power will war against the Lamb and experience defeat.

John notes how corrupt cities and governments ultimately end in self-destruction. The angel explains that the kings and the beast will come to hate the harlot. As a result, they strip her of her jewels and clothes. They will then devour her flesh and burn her with fire. While these individuals are actively involved, God puts these things into their hearts. These individuals who were already engaged in the destructive use of their political power now find themselves engaging in the same behavior that brings about self-destruction.

Weeping and Rejoicing over Babylon (Revelation 18:1-19:10). In Revelation 18, John highlights for his audiences the biblical reality of corporate sin by people participating in and benefiting from the unjust systems at work around them. This portion of the vision begins by declaring Babylon's fall. Following this declaration, John uses his writing to urge those in the churches to cease participation in Babylon's culture and practices, as such engagement results in them financially benefiting from her injustice. He presents three groups of people who financially profited from their relationship with her. They reflect on and mourn the city's destruction and the swiftness with which it occurred. In response to the city's destruction, others who were victims of Babylon rejoice over her decimation.

While governments maintain a divine mandate to honor God by serving the people who dwell under their authority (Rom 13), this city has failed. In response, an angel declares Babylon's fall. The unjust city has become a place for demons, unclean spirits, birds, and beasts. The nations, the earth's kings, and merchants all participate in and economically benefit from her. While Revelation 14:8 highlights Babylon's activity of making the nations drink, Revelation 18:3 notes the complicity of many in the exercise of Babylon's power.

God does not desire his people to participate in this empire. As a result, they hear a

[86]Paul, *Revelation*, 282. It seems plausible that both possibilities may be a reality in this context.
[87]Bauckham, *Climax of Prophecy*, 395; J. Nelson Kraybill, *Apocalypse and Allegiance: Worship, Politics, and Devotion in the Book of Revelation* (Grand Rapids, MI: Brazos, 2010), 126.

warning to "come out" of Babylon (Rev 18:4). The call admonishes them against participating in this city's sins because participation in them will result in sharing in plagues that come on the city. They need to exit because the cry from heaven is one of justice for God to avenge those who have suffered as victims of her injustice. This government did not serve the people in it; it served itself. As a result, Babylon now sees herself as invincible. Now, she will swiftly suffer the same fate she caused for others.

As the text continues, three groups of people who have benefited from their participation in Babylon weep over her destruction and give cries of "woe" over her. The kings of the earth "lived in luxury with her" (Rev 18:9), but she has been brought down, and they no longer attain wealth because of her. The merchants of the earth who grew rich from the power of her luxury (Rev 18:3) weep because, after her destruction, no one purchased their cargo. John notes that engagements in these economic exchanges came at the cost of others. For the sake of financial profit, the merchants commoditized people through the commercial trade of enslaved people—humans made in the image of God (Rev 18:13). The shipmasters and those on the sea cried over her because they would no longer grow rich by her wealth (Rev 18:19). In response to the weeping of those who had benefited from the economic injustices, a cry comes for those participating in the kingdom of God to rejoice since God brought just judgment on her for those who had suffered at her hands (Rev 18:20).

Following the call to rejoice, an angel provides details regarding the effects of Babylon's fall. Revelation 18:23-24 uses language that parallels the text of Jeremiah 25:10, which occurs in a context where Babylon serves as the instrument of judgment on God's unfaithful people.[88] The angel throwing the millstone into the sea communicates that Babylon will not just fall; it will be thrown down. As a result, for those who refuse to come out of Babylon, the city will serve as the instrument of their divine judgment. In Revelation 18:24, Christian audiences must recognize that even as Revelation focuses on the situations of those in the churches and the church at large, John highlights God's concern for justice for those beyond the church. As the angel concludes his comments, he notes the city's oppressive, destructive behavior. She has killed prophets, saints, and many others outside the church (Rev 18:24).[89] This statement alerts Christian audiences to God's concern for justice not only for those in the church but those beyond it.

Many comply with the call to rejoice over Babylon. Even as three distinct groups gave cries of "woe" over Babylon, three cries of "Hallelujah" over her came from a great multitude.[90] A great multitude gives honor to God for judging the harlot, noting that she had destroyed the earth (Rev 19:2). The multitude gives another shout of praise proclaiming the eternal state of Babylon's destruction (Rev 19:3). Following their praise, the twenty-four elders say, "Amen. Hallelujah." While the first cry of praise mentions God's justice regarding her who "corrupted the earth with her prostitution," it recalls the language of the twenty-four elders who noted the time for God "destroying those who destroy the earth" (Rev 11:18). This may account for the praise from the twenty-four elders and the four living creatures in this

[88]J. A. Thompson, *The Book of Jeremiah* (Grand Rapids, MI: Eerdmans, 1980), 512.
[89]David A. deSilva, *Unholy Allegiances: Heeding Revelation's Warning* (Peabody, MA: Hendrickson, 2013), 48.
[90]Fee, *Revelation*, 263-64.

passage (Rev 19:4). Following this, John seems to hear a multitude give another shout of praise. The corrupt, unjust harlot is gone, and "the marriage of the Lamb has come" (Rev 19:7). This leads to the declaration of blessing on those invited to the marriage supper of the Lamb (Rev 19:9). This invitation likely draws on the Behemoth-Leviathan myth, pointing forward to the destruction of the beast and false prophet.[91]

Waging war against the beast and false prophet (Revelation 19:11-21). After the harlot's destruction, those who refuse to heed the call to come out of her also experience God's wrath. John turns his attention to the judgment and destruction of nations and kings that have committed adultery with her, along with the beasts of the empire. Here, people finally discover the answer to the question of Revelation 13:4, where people ask who is comparable to the beast. For the second time in Revelation, audiences encounter a rider on a white horse (Rev 19:11; cf. Rev 6:2). Unlike the first, this rider, called Faithful and True, judges and makes war righteously. Not only does this individual ride a white horse, but the armies of heaven follow him on white horses, identifying them with him as conquerors. A sharp two-edged sword comes from his mouth. With it, he will strike down the nations (Rev 19:15).

An angel then invites the birds to a supper where they will eat the flesh of kings, captains, mighty men, horses, their riders, and a host of people from a wide variety of social locations, demonstrating that people do not have a specific status with Christ because of their social context. They can have a positive or negative standing with him no matter their social situation. As mentioned in Revelation 17, the beast and the kings of the earth gather to wage war against Christ and his army. Christ does not initiate war; he responds to the rebellion against him (cf. Ps 2). As a result, the representatives of governmental power—the beast and the false prophet—are thrown into the lake of fire (Rev 19:20).[92] The rest are slain with the sword from Christ's mouth. Though an entire army is with him, and they share in the victory, they take no actions against the beast, the kings of the earth, or the nations. They conquer through Christ and his actions. After those who rebel against Christ and his kingdom are slain, the birds feast and have their supper.

Divine reciprocity in Satan's imprisonment (Revelation 20:1-10). Many commentators and authors discussing this passage focus on eschatological views regarding the millennium. Though John mentions "a thousand years" multiple times in the text (Rev 20:2, 3, 4, 5, 6, 7), he does not appear to propose a particular millennial view or specific order of eschatological events. Instead, the repetition of "a thousand years" ties together a series of events that speak directly to issues of divine reciprocity related to acts of legal and economic injustice. John notes Satan's imprisonment for a thousand years (Rev 20:2, 3, 7), as well as the reign of the faithful who experienced economic despair and death at the hands of the empire (Rev 20:4-6).

The message to the church in Smyrna associates the devil with the unjust imprisonment of the faithful who experience poverty (Rev 2:10). Now, he is imprisoned (Rev 20:2-3). John's identification of the dragon as *the devil* and Satan leaves no doubt regarding the connection between the texts. The language of Revelation 20:7 identifies the

---

[91]Bauckham, *Climax of Prophecy*, 190.

[92]Koester, *Revelation*, 532. Admittedly, the text strays away from the Behemoth-Leviathan myth in that both beasts experience the lake of fire, while in Ps 74:14, the creature was to be distributed as food.

abyss (Rev 20:3) as the devil's prison, further recalling the foretold imprisonment of some in Smyrna (Rev 2:10). The devil, who unduly exercised power through the legal and political systems of the empire, finds himself experiencing the very thing he used to persecute others—imprisonment.

The promise to the overcomer in Laodicea also finds fulfillment here. To a wealthy congregation that could later face the challenge of poverty for exhibiting faithfulness to Jesus, John shows the eschatological outcome of such fidelity to the kingdom of God and Christ. Those who died had been beheaded—a further explanation of the deaths of those killed by the second beast (Rev 13:15). Their refusal to worship the beast or its image or to receive the beast's mark prohibited them from engaging effectively in their society's economic systems. It also led to them functioning as victims of the sword—a legal means of execution at the hands of the government.

Though these groups experienced poverty and suffered legal injustice, they "came to life" (Rev 20:4). This language identifies them with Christ (Rev 2:8), who suffered legal injustice at the hands of the empire. The depiction of these people rising from the dead serves as an image of anti-Roman imperial resistance that reveals the impotence of the government's exercise of power—even the power of death—when compared with God's kingdom.[93]

The economic and legal dimensions of Revelation 20:1-10 call audiences to maintain their faithfulness to Christ and to resist the allure of economic prosperity through religious compromise. This faithfulness demands giving up power acquired through affiliation with world financial systems, as would be the temptation for those in Laodicea. It also demands that people demonstrate faithfulness to Christ through nonconformity to culture like those in Smyrna. Both practices could result in death. At the same time, such death comes with the promise of resurrection.

Judgment before the great white throne (Revelation 20:11-15). After the reign of the saints with Christ for a thousand years, others come to life to receive judgment. The subjects of judgment are those who aligned with the empire of the beast, worshiped him, and took his mark (Rev 20:15; cf. Rev 13:8). The opportunities for repentance that appeared throughout the book have ceased. They now receive judgment according to their works (Rev 20:13). Just as the message to Thyatira noted that God judges each one according to their deeds (Rev 2:23), this latter portion of the book challenges all of Revelation's audiences to consider whether their works reflect an alignment with the kingdom of God and Christ or the world empire in which they live. For example, the people in the congregation at Thyatira must reflect on whether they have been doing the works of Jezebel and need to repent. Additionally, this portion of the vision challenges those in Sardis who had incomplete works (Rev 3:2) to consider if they operate as citizens of God's kingdom. Unlike those who resisted the empire, all who aligned with the world's governments by either word or deed maintain that alignment for eternity. Just as Babylon was burned with fire, the people affiliated with her are cast into the lake of fire, where they remain with Satan, the beast, and the false prophet (Rev 20:15; cf. Rev 20:10).

Preview of the new heaven and new earth (Revelation 21:1-8). The vision of the harlot's judgment concludes with the arrival of the holy city. After the annihilation of Babylon and

[93]Jeremy Punt, "Paul, Body, and Resurrection in an Imperial Setting: Considering Hermeneutics and Power," *Neotestamentica* 45, no. 2 (2011): 324.

the destruction of all associated with her, this vision ends with an image of the alternative. Here, John communicates the certainty of the city's arrival, no matter one's desire to function as part of her. As John prepares his audiences for his vision of the bride (Rev 21:9–22:5), he describes this city in terms that contrast with the harlot. He uses nuptial language, noting that the city was "prepared as a bride" (Rev 21:2). The coming of this city brings about the fulfillment of a long-awaited promise of God dwelling among his people (Rev 21:3).

Since humanity's rebellion against God in Genesis 3, the human experience has been filled with the misuse and abuse of power. Through such experiences, people have suffered pain. With the holy city comes the promise that God will respond to the pain of his people. He will remove their tears; death, mourning, crying, and pain will cease (Rev 21:4). With the holy city comes a new order because the one on the throne is "making all things new" (Rev 21:5). In this new era, God continues to do what he has always done—provide for his creation. While the Lamb "will guide them to the springs of the water of life" (Rev 7:17), God will give the water without payment (Rev 21:6; cf. Is 55:1). From those who lacked economic power and could not buy or sell (Rev 13:17), God requires no payment (Rev 21:6). Those who have refused the provision of the Lord in this life and aligned with the worldly empire will not be forced to receive God's provision in the age to come. They will spend eternity with Satan and his imperial representatives "in the lake that burns with fire and sulfur" (Rev 21:8). John provides no other alternatives. His audiences must choose between the unjust imperial city or the kingdom that includes justice for all.

Vision 4: Presentation of a just and righteous city (Revelation 21:9–22:5). After using his third vision to dissuade audiences from finding a home in the harlot, John's fourth vision introduces the Bride as the true essence of what the harlot pretends to be—a place of peace and justice. John presents a just and righteous city that serves as a means of healing and restoration from the harmful effects of the beast's ungodly rule and the oppression of the harlot. Those in the churches receive a glimpse of the eschatological outcome of faithfulness to Jesus. They also see what they will miss if they maintain their associations with Babylon.

Just as Babylon is a present reality, the holy city is a present reality into which God calls his people to live.[94] For those in the seven churches, the promises to the overcomers are present realities they have not yet attained. Christ's followers hold their citizenship in the heavenly city and have a call to live as a countercultural society amid the empires of the world. As John contrasts the new Jerusalem with Babylon, he challenges all who identify with Christ to participate in the new Jerusalem. The second vision shows that affiliation with worldly powers results in assimilation into the practices and cultures of those powers. The third vision highlights the outcome of embracing world systems. This final vision reveals the consequences for those who forsake ungodly, worldly associations and make their home in the holy city.

[94]Jan Fekkes, *Isaiah and Prophetic Traditions in the Book of Revelation: Visionary Antecedents and Their Development* (Sheffield, UK: JSOT Press, 1994), 92. Fekkes explains, "The manifestation of divine renewal and reward outlined in Rev. 21.1–22.5 was already presupposed in the promises of chs. 2–3, projected in the eschatological index of 11.15–18, and anticipated in the hymnic pericopes of 7.9–17, 15.2–4 and 19.5–10." In other words, the lack of experience of the holy city, as presented in Rev 21:1–22:5 in no way detracts from the reality of the holy city in the present age. For example, the presence of the tree of life in the paradise of God is not simply a future reality—it is a present one.

Description of the bride (Revelation 21:9-27). As with the third vision, one of the angels who had one of the bowls of wrath inaugurates this fourth experience. While this angel participates in the outpouring of God's wrath on Babylon, he presents a city that provides life, healing, and hope.[95] From there, John sees the holy city Jerusalem "coming down out of heaven from God" (Rev 21:10). The repetition of the language regarding the new Jerusalem "coming down" connects the beginning of this vision to the end of the third one and reveals that the holy city serves as the ultimate future reality no matter who decides to participate in it.

John contrasts the two cities, describing this one as the bride and the former as the harlot. Moreover, he portrays the bride as the reality of that which the harlot pretended to be. The bride has the glory of God (Rev 21:11). The harlot glorified herself (Rev 18:7). The bride possesses a "radiance like a very rare jewel" (Rev 21:11). To the harlot, a mighty angel declared, "the light of a lamp will shine in you no more" (Rev 18:23). The bride was pure gold with each gate made of an individual pearl (Rev 21:18, 21). Still, the harlot was only adorned with gold and pearls (Rev 17:4). Both the harlot and the bride have names on them. While the harlot had a name written on her, "Babylon the great, mother of whores and of earth's abominations," the bride has inscribed on her gates "the names of the twelve tribes of the Israelites" (Rev 21:12); the names of the twelve apostles are on the foundations of the city wall (Rev 21:14). Though the harlot becomes a haunt for every unclean spirit, bird, and abominable beast (Rev 18:2), "nothing unclean will enter" the bride (Rev 21:27).

Not only does the new Jerusalem look different from Babylon, but the cities also operate on incompatible frameworks. Ultimately, Babylon brings despair for those aligned with her, but the bride brings hope for the kings of the earth and the nations. Though the third vision shows the earth's kings engaging in sexual immorality with the harlot (Rev 18:3), in the fourth vision, they will bring their glory into the bride (Rev 21:24). The kings were not the only ones in the third vision who had a negative relationship with the harlot, the nations consumed the wine of the passion of her sexual immorality (Rev 18:3) which she had given to them, but the nations will walk by the light of the bride (Rev 21:24)—not the darkness of Babylon.

A city of life (Revelation 22:1-5). The abuse of the unjust harlot who deceived the nations (Rev 17:15; 18:23) results in pain and death for many. The city of the bride, however, offers life and healing to those who have suffered the horrors and abuses of the harlot. Though many will experience death, this final part of John's description of the new Jerusalem directs audiences to a city teeming with life. All the audiences of Revelation, no matter their social location, come to see that even if they suffer at the hands of the empire for the sake of Christ, they will have eternal life. They hear that "the river of the water of life" flows "from the throne of God and of the Lamb" (Rev 22:1). "The tree of life with its twelve kinds of fruit" provides healing for those who have suffered the abusive power of Babylon (Rev 22:2). It also reveals restored access to that which humanity lost in the Garden of Eden (Gen 1–3). The provision of healing from the leaves shows that the devastating and abusive work of the harlot and those associated with her has such a negative impact that the nations need the healing the new Jerusalem provides.

While the thrones of God and Satan receive attention in the first and second visions of the

---

[95]Koester, *Revelation*, 811.

book (Rev 2:13; 13:2, 16:10), Revelation's final vision mentions only the throne of God, as Satan's throne fades into oblivion with him. In this vision, no alternative thrones exist; the holy city has no rival kingdoms. Ultimately, John reveals that those kingdoms that oppose the kingdom of God and Christ have no chance of success. The people in the holy city have a permanent place in God's presence. Just as those in Philadelphia were promised, these people in the holy city will have God's name "on their foreheads" (Rev 22:4), signifying his ownership of them.[96] These people in the holy city now righteously fulfill humanity's job of reigning in righteousness with God over his creation throughout eternity (Rev 22:5; cf. Gen 1:28).

EPILOGUE (REVELATION 22:6-21)

As the book of Revelation closes, John shifts away from his visionary experiences and turns his attention to the words he has written to the congregations. He urges his recipients to obey what they have read and heard by noting that his writing is "trustworthy and true" (Rev 22:6), words he used to describe Jesus in Revelation 2:14. Not only does he connect the words with the person of Christ; he concludes the section warning against modifying what he has written.

John uses the book's conclusion to remind those in the churches of their call to follow Jesus faithfully. He does this by drawing on the concepts appearing in the messages to the churches and urges them all to conquer. While the promise to reward each person according to their works speaks prominently to the congregations in Thyatira and Sardis, all the communities should maintain an awareness that Christ knows their works. The pronouncement of blessing on those who wash their robes calls the congregations in Sardis and Laodicea to endure tribulation. The mention of the tree of life challenges the Ephesian congregation to operate in love. Discussion of entering the city recalls Jesus' promise to the Philadelphian community to write the name of the new Jerusalem on the overcomer. John's use of outsider language informs the unfaithful people in Thyatira and Pergamum that if they continue in sexual immorality and idolatry, they will be outside the city. John tells the victims of economic injustice in Smyrna and those who benefit from it, like those in Laodicea, that they need no money to obtain the water of life. Considering Christ's coming, John explains to all the recipients how they are to live. Today's readers should be able to apply the book's principles to their situations and live as the conquering people of God whose citizenship is already in the heavenly city—not the respective earthly empires in which they live.

CONCLUSION

The instruction John receives to write and send Revelation to the seven churches encourages those who participate in the church's life to consider their lives and loyalties. Christianity in the United States has for many years focused on mental assent, articulated through the concepts of "confess and believe." This biblically deficient form of faith that stops with confession and belief has led many to profess and relieve themselves of the responsibility to live according to the Scriptures. John challenges today's readers, as he did in his time, to overcome through obedience to God's word.

The multiple audiences of the Apocalypse bring the beauty of a virtually unlimited application regarding what it means to overcome. The details of overcoming differ for each of the

[96]Paul, *Revelation*, 361; Kraybill, *Apocalypse and Allegiance*, 109-11.

original congregations, much like they would be for most Christian communities today. For John, overcoming directly connects to nonconformity with the world's systems, even when those systems may appear to align with one's desires and outcomes. While many Christians in the contemporary era would oppose some of the world's standards that don't seem to align with their beliefs, those same people will often justify their ungodly actions by asserting that they are aiming for righteous results. Sadly, both are forms of conformity that the Scriptures condemn. As a result, when people read Revelation, they must consider what the Spirit says to the churches and ask in what ways they have overcome by following the practices of an earthly empire and failed to overcome like Christ.

BIBLIOGRAPHY

Aune, David E. "The Form and Function of the Proclamations to the Seven Churches (Revelation 2–3)." *New Testament Studies* 36, no. 2 (1990): 182-204.

———. *Revelation 1–5*. Dallas: Word Books, 1997.

Bandy, Alan S. "Patterns of Prophetic Lawsuits in the Oracles to the Seven Churches." *Neotestamentica* 45, no. 2 (2011): 178-205.

Bauckham, Richard. *The Climax of Prophecy: Studies on the Book of Revelation*. Edinburgh: T&T Clark, 1993.

———. *The Theology of the Book of Revelation*. Cambridge: Cambridge University, 1993.

Beale, G. K. "The Various Ways John Uses the Old Testament." In *John's Use of the Old Testament in Revelation*, edited by Stanley E. Porter, 60-128. Sheffield, UK: Sheffield Academic, 1998.

Betsworth, Sharon. "The Child Snatched Away: Reading Revelation Through a Childist Lens." *Biblical Interpretation* 28, no. 5 (2020): 658-76.

Biguzzi, Giancarlo. "Ephesus, Its Artemision, Its Temple to the Flavian Emperors, and Idolatry in Revelation." *Novum Testamentum* 40, no. 3 (1998): 276-90.

Blount, Brian K. *Revelation: A Commentary*. Louisville, KY: Westminster John Knox, 2009.

Boda, Mark J. *The Book of Zechariah*. Grand Rapids, MI: Eerdmans, 2016.

Boxall, Ian. *The Revelation of Saint John*. Peabody, MA: Hendrickson, 2006.

Bredin, Mark R. J. "The Synagogue of Satan Accusation in Revelation 2:9." *Biblical Theology Bulletin* 28, no. 4 (1998): 160-64.

Collins, Adela Yarbro. *Crisis and Catharsis: The Power of the Apocalypse*. Philadelphia: Westminster, 1984.

Davis, R. Dean. *The Heavenly Court Judgment of Revelation 4–5*. Lanham, MD: University Press of America, 1992.

deSilva, David A. *Unholy Allegiances: Heeding Revelation's Warning*. Peabody, MA: Hendrickson, 2013.

De Villiers, Pieter G.R. "The Septet of Bowls in Revelation 15:1–16:21 in the Light of Its Composition." *Acta Patristica et Byzantina* 16, no. 1 (2005): 196-222.

Fee, Gordon D. *Revelation*. Eugene, OR: Cascade Books, 2011.

Fekkes, Jan. *Isaiah and Prophetic Traditions in the Book of Revelation: Visionary Antecedents and Their Development*. Sheffield, UK: JSOT Press, 1994.

Ford, J. Massyngberde. "The Christological Function of the Hymns in the Apocalypse of John." *Andrews University Seminary Studies* 36, no. 2 (1998): 207-29.

———. *Revelation: Introduction, Translation, and Commentary*. Garden City, NY: Doubleday & Company, 1975.

Friesen, Steven J. *Imperial Cults and the Apocalypse of John: Reading Revelation in the Ruins*. Oxford: Oxford University, 2001.

Gallusz, Laszlo. *The Throne Motif in the Book of Revelation*. London: Bloomsbury T&T Clark, 2014.

Gorman, Michael J. *Reading Revelation Responsibly: Uncivil Worship and Witness: Following the Lamb into the New Creation*. Eugene, OR: Cascade, 2011.

Graves, David Elton. *The Seven Messages of Revelation and Vassal Treaties: Literary Genre, Structure, and Function*. Piscataway, NJ: Gorgias, 2009.

Harris, Murray J. *Slave of Christ: A New Testament Metaphor for Total Devotion to Christ*. Downers Grove, IL: InterVarsity Press, 2001.

Keener, Craig. *Revelation*. Grand Rapids, MI: Zondervan, 2000.

King, Martin Luther, Jr. "Letter from a Birmingham Jail." In *Liberating Faith: Religious Voices for Justice, Peace, and Ecological Wisdom*, edited by Roger S. Gottlieb, 177-87. Lanham, MD: Rowman & Littlefield, 2003.

———. "The Other America." Video recording. Stanford University, 1967. www.youtube.com/watch?v=dOWDtDUKz-U.

Koester, Craig R. *Revelation: A New Translation with Introduction and Commentary*. New Haven, CT: Yale University Press, 2014.

Kraybill, J. Nelson. *Apocalypse and Allegiance: Worship, Politics, and Devotion in the Book of Revelation*. Grand Rapids, MI: Brazos, 2010.

Mathewson, David L. "Social Justice in the Book of Revelation: Reading Revelation from Above." In *The Bible and Social Justice: Old Testament and New Testament Foundations for the Church's Urgent Call*, edited by Cynthia Long Westfall and Bryan R. Dyer, 176-97. Eugene, OR: Wipf and Stock, 2016.

———. *Verbal Aspect in the Book of Revelation: The Function of Greek Verb Tenses in John's Apocalypse*. Leiden: Brill, 2010.

Morris, Leon. *Revelation: An Introduction and Commentary*. Downers Grove, IL: InterVarsity Press, 1987.

Mounce, Robert H. *The Book of Revelation*. Grand Rapids, MI: Eerdmans, 1977.

Nolland, John. *The Gospel of Matthew: A Commentary on the Greek Text*. Grand Rapids, MI: Eerdmans, 2005.

Osborne, Grant R. *Revelation*. Grand Rapids, MI: Baker Academic, 2002.

Paul, Ian. *Revelation: An Introduction and Commentary*. Downers Grove, IL: IVP Academic, 2018.

Perry, Peter S. *The Rhetoric of Digressions: Revelation 7:1-17 and 10:1–11:13 and Ancient Communication*. Tübingen: Mohr Siebeck, 2009.

Punt, Jeremy. "Paul, Body, and Resurrection in an Imperial Setting: Considering Hermeneutics and Power." *Neotestamentica* 45, no. 2 (2011): 311-30.

Rossing, Barbara R. *The Choice Between Two Cities: Whore, Bride, and Empire in the Apocalypse*. Harrisburg, PA: Trinity Press International, 1999.

Rowland, Christopher. *Revelation*. London: Epworth Press, 1993.

Schüssler Fiorenza, Elisabeth. *The Book of Revelation: Justice and Judgment*. Minneapolis: Augsburg Fortress, 1998.

———. "The Followers of the Lamb: Visionary Rhetoric and Socio-political Situation." In *Early Christian Apocalypticism: Genre and Social Setting*, edited by Adela Yarbro Collins, 122-46. Decatur, GA: Society of Biblical Literature, 1986.

———. *Revelation: Vision of a Just World*. Minneapolis: Fortress Press, 1991.

Sheets, Dwight. "Something Old, Something New: Revelation and Empire." In *Jesus Is Lord, Caesar Is Not: Evaluating Empire in New Testament Studies Today*, edited by Scot McKnight and Joseph B. Modica, 197-210. Downers Grove, IL: InterVarsity Press, 2013.

Smith, Gary V. *Isaiah 1-39*. Nashville: Broadman & Holman, 2007.

Stanbridge, Karen, and Howard Ramos. *Seeing Politics Differently: A Brief Introduction to Political Sociology*. New York: Oxford University Press, 2012.

Strazicich, John. *Joel's Use of Scripture and the Scripture's Use of Joel*. Leiden: Brill, 2007.

Tellbe, Mikael. "The Sociological Factors Behind Philippians 3.1-11 and the Conflict at Philippi." *Journal for the Study of the New Testament* 17, no. 55 (1995): 97-121.

Thompson, J. A. *The Book of Jeremiah*. Grand Rapids, MI: Eerdmans, 1980.

Wainwright, Arthur William. *Mysterious Apocalypse: Interpreting the Book of Revelation*. Nashville: Abingdon, 1993.

Wall, Robert W. *Revelation*. Peabody, MA: Hendrickson, 1991.

Winters, Clifford T. *Argument Is War: Relevance-Theoretic Comprehension of the Conceptual Metaphor of War in the Apocalypse*. Leiden: Brill, 2020.

Wright, N. T. *Revelation for Everyone*. London: SPCK, 2011.

Zimmerli, Walther. *Ezekiel 1: A Commentary on the Book of the Prophet Ezekiel, Chapters 1–24*. Translated by Ronald E. Clements. Minneapolis: Fortress Press, 1979.

LIST OF CONTRIBUTORS

Lisa Marie Bowens (PhD, Princeton Theological Seminary) is associate professor of New Testament at Princeton Theological Seminary and the author of two books, *An Apostle in Battle: Paul and Spiritual Warfare in 2 Corinthians 12:1-10* (Mohr Siebeck) and *African American Readings of Paul: Reception, Resistance, and Transformation* (Eerdmans).

Mateus F. de Campos (PhD, Cambridge University) is an associate professor of New Testament and academic dean at Gordon-Conwell Theological Seminary in South Hamilton, MA. He has served as a pastor for ten years in his hometown of Americana, Brazil, and has lived in Canada, England, and the United States. He is the author of *Resisting Jesus: A Narrative and Intertextual Analysis of Mark's Portrayal of the Disciples of Jesus* (Brill, 2021), among other writings.

Diane G. Chen (PhD, Fuller Theological Seminary) is professor of New Testament at Palmer Theological Seminary of Eastern University. She is the author of several books: *God as Father in Luke–Acts* (Peter Lang, 2006), *Let Me More of Their Beauty See: Reading Familiar Verses in Context* (Smyth & Helwys, 2011), and *The Gospel of Luke* in the New Covenant Commentary Series (Wipf and Stock/Cascade, 2017).

Miguel G. Echevarría (PhD, The Southern Baptist Theological Seminary) is associate professor of New Testament and Greek at Southeastern Baptist Theological Seminary. He is the author of *The Future Inheritance of Land in the Pauline Epistles*, *40 Questions about the Apostle Paul*, and *Engaging the New Testament: A Short Introduction for Students and Ministers*. He has taught and ministered in the United States and Latin America.

Dennis R. Edwards (PhD, Catholic University of America) is associate professor of New Testament as well as vice president for church relations and dean of North Park Seminary, Chicago. He has worked in urban ministry for over three decades, including serving as a church planter in Brooklyn and Washington, DC. His books include *Might from the Margins*, the Story of God Bible Commentary on 1 Peter, and *Humility Illuminated: The Biblical Path Back to Christian Character* (IVP Academic).

Daniel K. Eng (DMin, Talbot School of Theology; PhD, University of Cambridge) is assistant professor of New Testament at Western Seminary in Portland, Oregon. His doctoral work was in Asian American Ministry (DMin) and biblical studies (PhD). He is the author or editor of several books, including *Eschatological Approval: The Structure and Unifying Motif of James* and *Faithful Ministry Through Chinese Churches in America.*

Rodolfo Galvan Estrada III (PhD, Regent University) is assistant professor of New Testament at Vanguard University. His doctoral work is in biblical studies, he holds two master's degrees from Duke University, and a bachelor's from Vanguard University.

Christin J. Fort (PhD, Fuller Theological Seminary) is an assistant professor of clinical psychology at Fuller Theological Seminary where she specializes in the integration of clinical psychology and biblical theology. As an

African American woman of enslaved descent, Dr. Fort's scholarship, research, teaching, preaching, and clinical practice lie at the intersections of faith, race, gender, emotional health, systemic sustainability and relational well-being. Her work in these areas is regularly highlighted in a range of academic articles published in journals such as *Journal of Psychology and Theology*, *Journal of Psychology and Christianity*, and *Pastoral Psychology*.

Michael J. Gorman (PhD, Princeton Theological Seminary) holds the Raymond E. Brown Chair in Biblical Studies and Theology at St. Mary's Seminary & University in Baltimore. His publications include books and articles on Paul, the Gospel of John, Revelation, and other subjects. He has also edited *Scripture and Its Interpretation: A Global, Ecumenical Introduction to the Bible*.

Gene L. Green (PhD, University of Aberdeen) is professor emeritus of New Testament at Wheaton College and Graduate School. Previously he served as professor of New Testament, dean, and rector of the Seminario ESEPA in Costa Rica and is currently a board member and professor for the Native American Course of Studies of the United Methodist Church. His publications include two commentaries in Spanish, English commentaries *The Letters to the Thessalonians* (Eerdmans) and *Jude and 2 Peter* (Baker Academic), and *Vox Petri: A Theology of Peter* (Cascade). Green is also the coauthor of *The New Testament in Antiquity* (Zondervan) and coeditor of *Majority World Theology* (IVP Academic) and the "Crosscurrents in Majority World and Minority Theology" series (Cascade).

T. Christopher Hoklotubbe (ThD Harvard University) is an assistant professor of classics at Cornell College (Mount Vernon, Iowa) and Director of Graduate Studies for NAIITS: An Indigenous Learning Community. He is the author of *Civilized Piety: The Rhetoric of Pietas in the Pastoral Epistles and the Roman Empire* (Baylor University Press, 2017) and has written articles on Early Christianity and Indigenous interpretations of the Bible.

Marcus Jerkins (PhD, Baylor University) is a native of Atlanta, GA. He is the pastor of New Pilgrim Missionary Baptist Church in Birmingham, AL and an adjunct professor of New Testament studies in the Ecumenical Institute of St. Mary's Seminary in Baltimore, MD. He is the husband of Courtney and the father of three wonderful children.

Esau McCaulley (PhD, University of St Andrews) is an associate professor of New Testament at Wheaton College. He is the author of many works including *Sharing in the Son's Inheritance* and *Reading While Black: African American Biblical Interpretation as an Exercise in Hope*. He is a contributing opinion writer for the *New York Times*. His writings have also appeared in places such as *The Atlantic* and *Washington Post*.

Daniel I. Morrison (PhD, McMaster Divinity College) is a Lieutenant Commander in the United States Navy. As an active duty chaplain and adjunct faculty member, his research focuses on the practical application of the biblical text to contemporary culture.

Julie Newberry (PhD, Duke University) is assistant professor of Scripture Studies at Sacred Heart Seminary and School of Theology (WI), having previously taught at Wheaton College (IL). A revised version of her dissertation has been published as *Lukan Joy and the Life of Discipleship: A Narrative Analysis of the Conditions that Lead to Joy According to Luke* (Mohr Siebeck, 2022), and her current book project combines intertextual and intersectional analysis in hopes of gaining fresh practical theological insights in the exegesis of New Testament narratives.

Janette H. Ok (PhD, Princeton Theological Seminary) serves as associate professor of New Testament at Fuller Theological Seminary. She is the author of *Constructing Ethnic Identity in 1 Peter: Who You Are No Longer* (T&T Clark, 2021). Currently, she is writing a commentary on the *Letters of John* (NICNT, Eerdmans) and the book *To Be and Be Seen: Reading the New Testament as Asian Americans*, coauthored with Jordan J. Cruz Ryan (Baker Academic). She cochairs the Society of Biblical Literature's Asian and Asian American Hermeneutics unit and is a member of the Underrepresented Racial and Ethnic Minorities in the Profession Committee.

Osvaldo Padilla (PhD, Kings College, University of Aberdeen) is professor of New Testament and Theology at Beeson Divinity School of Samford University, where he has taught for the last fifteen years. He has published on the Acts of the Apostles and Paul. He is a member of the Studiorum Novi Testamenti Societas.

M. Sydney Park (PhD, University of Aberdeen) teaches Biblical Interpretation, New Testament Theology, and Greek at Beeson Divinity School. Her research interests include racial reconciliation and the Gospel of Mark. Park previously taught New Testament at Crown College in St. Bonifacius, MN (2004–2006), and also served as a minister to children, youth and young adults in Korean American churches in Illinois, Texas, and Washington for 11 years. She is the author of *Submission within the Godhead and the Church in the Epistle to the Philippians: An Exegetical and Theological Examination of the Concept of Submission in Philippians 2 and 3* and coeditor of *Honoring the Generations: Learning with Asian North American Congregations*.

Amy Peeler (PhD, Princeton Theological Seminary) is Kenneth T. Wessner Chair of Biblical Studies at Wheaton College and an ordained priest in the Episcopal Church (USA). Author of *Women and the Gender of God* (Eerdmans, 2022) and *Hebrews* (Commentaries for Christian Formation, Eerdmans, 2024), studying Scripture with others is her greatest professional joy.

Madison N. Pierce (PhD, Durham University) is associate professor of New Testament at Western Theological Seminary and the New Testament editor for *Reviews of Biblical and Early Christian Studies*. She is the author of *Divine Discourse in the Epistle to the Hebrews* (CUP, 2020) and the coeditor of *Gospel Reading and Reception in Early Christian Literature* (CUP, 2022) and *Muted Voices of the New Testament* (T&T Clark, 2017).

Eric C. Redmond (PhD, Capital Seminary and Graduate School) is Professor of Bible at Moody Bible Institute in Chicago, IL and Associate Pastor of Preaching and Teaching at Calvary Memorial Church in Oak Park, IL. He is the general editor of *Say It! Celebrating Expository Preaching in the African American Tradition*, the Preaching Magazine 2020 Book of the Year. Eric is a fellow of the St. Augustine Cohort of the Center for Pastor Theologians and a Teaching Fellow for the C. S. Lewis Institute-Chicago.

Jordan J. Cruz Ryan (PhD, McMaster University) is a half-Filipino American scholar. His work centers on the Jewish and Roman archaeological background of the New Testament and he is currently working on a book that presents a Filipino American reading of Jesus for IVP Academic. Dr. Ryan serves as associate professor of New Testament at Wheaton College.

Kay Higuera Smith (PhD, Claremont Graduate University) is professor of Biblical and Religious Studies and program director of the Religious Studies Minor program at Azusa Pacific University. As a bicultural White Latina, she writes about social justice issues as they relate to Gender, Ethnicity, and Decoloniality. Her publications include editor-in-chief of *Postcolonial Evangelical Conversations: Global Awakenings in Theology and Praxis* (Downers Grove: InterVarsity Press, 2014) and contributor to *Reading the Bible Around the World: A Student's Guide to Global Approaches*, edited by Justin M. Smith and Federico A. Roth (InterVarsity Press, 2022). She currently has two books under contract, one on the historical figure of Mary of Nazareth, and another on Latinx Biblical Interpretation.

Ekaputra Tupamahu (PhD, Vanderbilt University) is assistant professor of New Testament and director of Master's programs at Portland Seminary of George Fox University. He is the author of *Contesting Languages* (OUP, 2022)

Jarvis J. Williams (PhD, The Southern Baptist Theological Seminary) is professor of New Testament Interpretation at the Southern Baptist Theological Seminary in Louisville, KY. He is the author of numerous books, including *The Spirit, Ethics, and Eternal Life: Paul's Vision for the Christian Life in Galatians* with IVP Academic.

H. Daniel Zacharias (PhD, University of Aberdeen/Highland Theological College) is a Cree-Anishinaabe and Austrian man originally from Winnipeg, MB (Treaty One territory), with ancestors also residing in Treaty Two, Treaty Three, and Treaty Five territories. He lives in Mi'kma'ki (Nova Scotia) with his wife and four children in Wolfville, and is associate dean and professor of New Testament Studies at Acadia Divinity College. He also serves as an adjunct faculty for NAIITS: An Indigenous Learning Community.